Family Law

Family Law

Ninth edition

N V Lowe
LLB (Sheffield)
of the Inner Temple, Barrister;
Professor of Law at Cardiff Law School, University of Wales

G Douglas
LLB (Manchester), LLM (London)
Professor of Law at Cardiff Law School, University of Wales

Butterworths
London, Edinburgh, Dublin
1998

United Kingdom	Butterworths, a Division of Reed Elsevier (UK) Ltd, Halsbury House, 35 Chancery Lane, LONDON WC2A 1EL and 4 Hill Street, EDINBURGH EH2 3JZ
Australia	Butterworths, a Division of Reed International Books Australia Pty Ltd, CHATSWOOD, New South Wales
Canada	Butterworths Canada Ltd, MARKHAM, Ontario
Hong Kong	Butterworths Asia (Hong Kong), HONG KONG
India	Butterworths India, NEW DELHI
Ireland	Butterworth (Ireland) Ltd, DUBLIN
Malaysia	Malayan Law Journal Sdn Bhd, KUALA LUMPUR
New Zealand	Butterworths of New Zealand Ltd, WELLINGTON
Singapore	Butterworths Asia, SINGAPORE
South Africa	Butterworths Publishers (Pty) Ltd, DURBAN
USA	Lexis Law Publishing, CHARLOTTESVILLE, Virginia

© Reed Elsevier (UK) Ltd 1998

A CIP Catalogue record for this book is available from the British Library.

ISBN 0 406 06330 3

KN
170
B76
1998

Typeset by B & J Whitcombe, Nr Diss, Norfolk, IP22 2LP
Printed and bound in Great Britain by Clays Ltd, St Ives plc

Visit us at our website: http://www.butterworths.co.uk

Preface

This is the first edition with which Peter Bromley himself has not been directly involved, though he has continued his role in a consultative capacity. Happily, the Manchester connection has been maintained by the addition of Gillian Douglas, who is a former student of Peter. We should also like to acknowledge the contribution of our colleague Michael Jones, who wrote the first draft of Chapter 18 on Financial Relief for Family Members on Divorce, Nullity and in Relation to Separation Orders.

In this, the last edition of the twentieth century, we have tried to reflect the general trends in the development of the subject, in particular the increasing emphasis upon the parent–child relationship and the diminishing significance of marriage. We have therefore taken the opportunity to make substantial changes both to the overall structure and to the content of the work. Some changes were inevitable. For example, the chapters on Divorce (Chapter 7) and Family Protection (Chapter 6) have had to be entirely rewritten in the light of the Family Law Act 1996. At the time of writing, it remains uncertain when the divorce reform will actually be implemented, and we have tried to take account of both the present law and the future changes in the text.

What we see as the increasing internationalisation of family law, with the growing number of international conventions affecting the family and the increasing readiness of the domestic courts to consider them – particularly the European Convention on Human Rights (a practice which will undoubtedly accelerate once the Human Rights Act 1998 is implemented), is reflected in a rewritten introductory chapter and by appropriate references and discussion throughout the book. The opportunity has also been taken substantially to rewrite the chapters on Marriage (Chapter 2) and on Financial Support (Chapter 17).

The book has been restructured so as to bring issues of ownership and occupation closer together. Accordingly Chapter 4 now deals with Spouses' and Cohabitants' Rights in Property and Chapter 5 with Ownership of the Family Home while Chapter 6 deals with Family Protection.

So far as children are concerned there has been some restructuring and reordering of the chapters, but the major concern here has been to take account of the explosion of case law that has followed in wake of the Children Act 1989. Indeed, such has been the flood of developments that a number of chapters have been largely rewritten.

As we have neared completion of the text a series of reform proposals has begun to emanate from the government, including those for reforming allocation of parental responsibility and procedures for establishing paternity, ancillary relief, child support and the social security system, to which we have been able to refer in the text. However, publication of the Consultative Paper on 'Support Services in Family Proceedings – Future Organisation of Court Welfare Services' came too late for detailed treatment. Another major development that is anticipated is the publication of the Law Commission proposals for reforming the law relating to the property rights of home sharers.

We should like to record our gratitude and thanks to a number of our colleagues who gave their help and support in the preparation of this edition, in particular Cathy Cobley, Mervyn Murch, Alison Perry, Elspeth Reid, Paul Todd, Philip Wylie and James Young. We should also like to acknowledge the help of our research assistants, Amanda Bell, Jennifer Owusu-Akyuw and Amita Bhardway, generously financed by Cardiff Law School. The final production of this book would, however, not have been possible without the services of those engaged in typing the numerous drafts, and in this respect we are especially indebted to Elizabeth Caddy, Awen Edwards, Usha Siret and in particular to Ann Bladen who undertook most of the Herculean task.

We are also pleased to record our thanks to the staff of Butterworths, both for their unfailing patience and support, and also for their reassuring understanding and encouragement.

We have sought to take account of developments in the law up to 30 June 1998.

Finally, this ninth edition is dedicated to our parents, Marshall and Beryl Lowe and Jack and Doris Douglas.

Nigel Lowe
Gillian Douglas

August 1998

Contents

Table of statutes

List of cases

G

T

Chapter 1

Introduction

A.   The nature and scope of family law

1.   THE MEANING OF 'FAMILY'

The word 'family' is one which it is difficult, if not impossible to define.[1] In one sense it means all persons related by blood or marriage; in another it means all the members of a household, including parents and children with perhaps other relations, lodgers and even servants. But both these definitions are far too wide for our purposes. The fact that two persons can claim descent from a common ancestor may not, of itself, affect their legal relations at all. Similarly, the legal relationship between the head of a household and lodgers and servants is contractual and therefore lies outside the scope of this book.

We regard the family as a basic social unit constituted by at least two people, whose relationship may fall into one of three categories. Most families will consist of three or more members falling into at least two different categories.

First, the relationship may be that of husband and wife or two persons living together in a manner similar to spouses. The large number of people now cohabiting outside marriage has forced the law to adapt to this change in social behaviour. If an extra-marital union comes to an end by separation or death, the parties and their children may need the same protection as spouses and their children, and consequently the legal position of cohabitants has to a certain extent been assimilated to that of married persons. This will be considered further in the next section, but it must be stressed immediately that rights have primarily been accorded only to those living in a heterosexual relationship; homosexual couples are generally in no different legal position from two persons (of either sex) who share accommodation out of friendship or convenience.[2] Secondly, a family may be constituted by a parent living with one or more children. Thirdly, brothers and sisters or other persons related by blood or marriage may be regarded as forming a family. The relationship, however, has only very limited effects on their legal position, and these arise principally on the death of another member of the family.[3]

---

1 See further Hoggett, Pearl, Cooke and Bates *The Family, Law and Society* (1996, 4th edn) ch 1; Parker, Parkinson and Behrens *Australian Family Law in Context* (1994) ch 1; Finlay, Bailey-Harris and Otlowski *Family Law in Australia* (1997, 5th edn).
2 See *Harrogate Borough Council v Simpson* [1986] 2 FLR 91, CA; *Fitzpatrick v Sterling Housing Association* [1997] 4 All ER 991, CA, on which, see Wikeley 'Same-sex partners and succession to Rent Act tenancies' (1998) 10 CFLQ 191. But it may be possible for a homosexual partner to claim provision from the deceased's estate, and immigrant homosexual couples are now treated more favourably than in the past. See post, p 888 and p 72 n 3.
3 For example, claims to a tenancy under the Rent Act 1977 or the Housing Act 1985, succession rights, and claims under the Fatal Accidents Act 1976: see Chapter 19.

2.   THE FUNCTIONS OF FAMILY LAW

In this context the law has two distinct but related functions.

Definition and alteration of status

Historically this was the law's main role because it was primarily concerned with
the rights which one member of the family could claim over another or over the
latter's property. In the case of a man and woman living together, these arose only
if they were married, and their legal relationship still depends largely on their
status. Similarly, there were virtually no rights and duties with respect to children
unless they were legitimate (which in turn depended on whether their parents were
married). A child's status is now of less importance, but a fundamental question –
who prima facie has parental responsibility for a child – still depends on whether
his parents were married to each other when he was born.[4] Questions of status are
also important in public law, for on them may turn such matters as a person's
nationality and right to live in the United Kingdom and claims to contributory
social security benefits.

Akin to the courts' power to define status is their power to alter it. Among the
most important aspects of this is their jurisdiction to grant divorces and make
adoption orders, because a marriage can be dissolved and a child can be legally
adopted only by judicial process.

Remedial role

The courts may be required to resolve disputes between members of the family, to
provide protection for weaker members, and to manage the consequences of the
termination of the family unit, for example, on a divorce.

The protection of the weaker members of the family has two aspects: physical
and economic. The former usually raises the more urgent problems and the courts
can give protection to the victims of domestic violence by making non-molestation
orders and orders excluding a party from the matrimonial home. As a last resort
they may order a child to be taken into the care of a local authority. The economic
protection of a member of the family usually assumes importance when the family
unit ceases to exist, either through separation or death, and the courts have
extensive powers to make orders for financial provision on both these events.

Even though the termination of the family unit may leave the members adequately
provided for, justice may nonetheless require the redistribution of their capital assets,
and the courts have power to make orders for this purpose on the breakdown of a
marriage and, to a more limited extent, on the death of a member of the family.
Similarly, if a person dies intestate, his property will have to be distributed, and the
law of intestate succession is essentially a part of family law because it provides for
the division of a deceased person's property amongst members of his family.

During the past century English family law has shown a steady movement away
from the former of these functions to the latter, and today its remedial role is of
much greater importance than that of conferring rights. The result has been to give
individual judges much greater discretion, for while Parliament and appellate
courts can lay down general principles for, say, the resolution of disputes relating
to children or the award of financial relief, their application will vary enormously
according to the circumstances of each family.

4 For the full meaning of this, see Family Law Reform Act 1987 s 1(3) and (4), discussed post, p 299.

B.   Trends in family law

1.   EQUALISATION OF MEN AND WOMEN

As family law developed during the nineteenth and especially the twentieth centuries, certain major trends became apparent. The first of these was an equalisation in the positions of men and women. The abolition of the position of the husband as possessor of his wife (and owner of her property) was addressed in the nineteenth century as a major element in the move to women's emancipation which culminated in their obtaining the franchise.[5] (Although the last vestige of this common law favouring of men was removed only in 1991 by the House of Lords when they held that a husband may be convicted for rape of his wife).[6] Accompanying the recognition of the position of the woman as *wife* was a corresponding move to give the woman as *mother* the same rights over her legitimate[7] children as the father had traditionally possessed. One of the most significant steps in this development was the enactment of s 1 of the Guardianship of Infants Act 1925, which provided that in proceedings before a court, neither the father nor the mother should be regarded as having a claim superior to the other in respect of the custody or upbringing of the child.[8] But again, the process has been a lengthy one; it was not until 1973 that parents were given equal rights to determine their children's upbringing, by s 1 of the Guardianship Act 1973; and only under the Children Act 1989 was the rule that a father was sole guardian of his legitimate children during his lifetime abolished.

This recognition of equality has had further consequences for women which they may not have found so palatable. There has been an increasing view that women, who, after all, now expect to work in paid employment throughout most of their lives rather than remain at home as housewives and child-carers, should be financially independent of their former partners. A 'clean break' between ex-spouses, whereby the man is no longer expected to support his former wife, has become the favoured disposition of finance and property on a divorce, justified further by a view that those who no longer share married status with each other should not be 'shackled' together by economic bonds either.[9]

2.   SHIFT IN EMPHASIS FROM PAST FAULT TO FUTURE NEEDS

Another crucial trend has been the extent to which the law has withdrawn from seeking to pass judgment on the misconduct of family members towards each

5 Holcombe *Wives and Property* (1983); Stetson *A Woman's Issue: the Politics of Family Law Reform in England* (1982).
6 *R v R* [1992] 1 AC 599, [1991] 4 All ER 481, HL.
7 The mother of a child born outside marriage was, and remains, solely entitled automatically to exercise parental responsibility for that child; the father may now acquire shared parental responsibility with her by agreement or court order under s 4 of the Children Act 1989.
8 See Cretney '"What Will the Women Want Next?" The Struggle for Power Within the Family 1925–1975' (1996) 112 LQR 110, for a description of the political lobbying and history which lay behind its enactment.
9 *Ashley v Blackman* [1988] Fam 85, [1988] 3 WLR 222; *C v C (Financial Provision: Personal Damages)* [1995] 2 FLR 171.

other, as a justification for making an order to settle their future legal positions and relationships.[10] Instead, increasing attention has been focused upon the likely needs of the parties in the aftermath of the breakdown of their relationship. This trend has been fostered by a recognition of the difficulty for a court in ascribing blame for this when it is dependent upon the evidence which a party chooses to place before it. The whole story may never be brought out which would, in theory at least, enable the court to form a valid judgment as to fault. This has been particularly true of divorces, where virtually all suits are undefended. Facts may be highlighted in a party's case in order to fit the constraints of the law, but may bear little relation to their true significance in leading to the breakdown as far as the parties themselves are concerned.[11]

The futility of ascribing blame has also been recognised. A decision that a spouse is responsible for the failure of the marriage does not contribute positively to arriving at a settlement of the financial position where, for example, that 'guilty' spouse is going to continue to care for the couple's children, and hence will need to remain in the former matrimonial home, with the former husband correspondingly being kept out of his share of this capital asset.

3.   SHIFT OF ATTENTION FROM ADULTS TO CHILDREN

There has been a significant shift in the attention of law makers and the courts away from the adults to the children in the family. This seems to be a counterpart to the other trends we have discussed. Adults are presumed capable of looking after themselves and therefore of not requiring the same degree of protection from the law and the courts that those who are vulnerable may need. The most vulnerable family members are, of course, the children. As divorce has become more common, the economic, psychological, health and educational consequences of the marriage break up for the children have been more closely researched and the findings, although not clear-cut, have been sufficiently worrying to prompt greater concern that the law and legal processes at least should not add to any deficit which might be suffered. Changes in the thinking about how children develop psychologically have also fed through into legal proceedings, so that adoption and child care proceedings, as well as disputes between parents when their relationship breaks up, have become informed and infused by the desire to ensure that legal outcomes are the best available for the child. At the same time, a growing willingness to recognise children's developing rights to autonomy has resulted in a concern to provide mechanisms to enable them to express their wishes and feelings about what should happen to them, both within legal proceedings and more generally when decisions about their future are being taken. The desire to place children at the centre of legal attention has not been confined to this country, but is a worldwide phenomenon, culminating in the drafting and opening for signature of the United Nations Convention on the Rights of the Child in 1989.

---

10 O' Donovan 'Love's Law: Moral Reasoning in Family Law' in Morgan and Douglas (eds) *Constituting Families: A Study in Governance* (1994) 40.
11 Stone has shown how, even in the days of Parliamentary divorce, evidence was concocted and colluded in: see *Road to Divorce: England 1530–1987* (1990) Part X .

4. GROWING RECOGNITION OF COHABITATION OUTSIDE MARRIAGE

The large increase in the number of couples living together outside marriage has already been noted: 22 per cent of adults aged 16 to 59 were cohabiting in 1996.[12] There are various reasons for this. Some cannot marry because one of them is in the process of obtaining a divorce (or, occasionally, is unable to do so). Some wish to avoid the financial responsibilities attached to marriage. Others wish to postpone the assumption of the legal incidents of marriage and regard cohabitation as a form of trial marriage or merely 'a pre-marital experience'. Some drift into cohabitation as their relationship becomes more intimate. Some regard marriage as irrelevant and may cohabit because they reject 'the traditional marriage contract and the assumption of the roles which necessarily seem to go with it'.[13]

Until recently cohabitation outside marriage gave the parties no rights over and above those possessed by, say, a brother and sister living together. Indeed, they might have found themselves, legally speaking, in a worse position because their relationship, involving, as it did, 'fornication', might deprive them of rights which they might otherwise have. If, for example, a woman contributed a sum towards the purchase of a house in which she was to live with her brother in consideration of his undertaking to have it conveyed into their joint names, she could enforce the contract; if, however, she entered into a similar agreement with a man with whom she was going to cohabit, the illicit purpose of the transaction probably made it unenforceable. Extra-marital sexual intercourse was regarded as immoral, and consequently any agreement entered into with this object in view was liable to be struck down as contrary to public policy. In *Upfill v Wright*[14] the plaintiff let a flat to the defendant who was to his knowledge the mistress of a man who intended to visit her there. Holding that the plaintiff could not recover the rent, Darling J said:[15]

> 'The flat was let to the defendant for the purpose of enabling her to receive the visits of the man whose mistress she was and to commit fornication with him there. I do not think that it makes any difference whether the defendant is a common prostitute or whether she is merely the mistress of one man . . .'

In *Diwell v Farnes*[16] the Court of Appeal expressed the view that any attempt by a woman to claim an interest in a house bought by the man with whom she had been living by spelling out an agreement that they should buy it as a joint venture was doomed to failure, because such a contract would be unenforceable as founded on an immoral consideration.

A complete change in the courts' attitude came a decade or so later. In 1972 the Court of Appeal held that the property rights of cohabitants who intended to marry as soon as they were free to do so should be determined in the same way as the

---

12 ONS, *Living in Britain 1996* (1998) p 199.

13 Freeman and Lyon *Cohabitation without Marriage* (1983) p 51. For a much fuller discussion of the question see ibid ch 3; Hoggett et al , op cit ch 2. See also Oliver 'Why do People live together?' [1982] JSWL 209.

14 [1911] 1 KB 506.

15 At 510. Later effectively overruled by *Heglibiston Establishment v Heyman* (1977)36 P & CR 351, CA, which decision seems to have limited the rule that a contract to promote illicit sexual relationships is contrary to public policy to transactions involving sexual intercourse for a money consideration.

16 [1959] 2 All ER 379 at 384 (per Ormerod LJ) and 388 (per Willmer LJ) CA: cf *Gammans v Ekins* [1950] 2 KB 328, [1950] 2 All ER 140, CA.

rights of spouses.[17] Three years later they held that a cohabitant could rely on a contractual licence to give her a right to occupy a house bought by her former partner.[18] In the same year they reached the more controversial decision that a cohabitant could claim the transmission of a statutory tenancy under the Rent Act as a member of the deceased tenant's family.[19]

At the same time Parliament started to give claims to cohabitants which could scarcely have been imagined even 25 years before. By enabling a de facto dependant to apply for an order under the Inheritance (Provision for Family and Dependants) Act 1975, it gave a cohabitant the right to claim provision after her (or his) partner's death which she did not have during his lifetime.[20] The Administration of Justice Act 1982, which amended the Fatal Accidents Act 1976 so as to enable a cohabitant to maintain an action under that Act for the death of her (or his) partner, applies to 'a man and a woman living with each other in the same household as husband and wife'. The Housing Acts include 'a man or woman who lived with the tenant as husband or wife' among those who can claim a tenancy on the tenant's death. Part IV of the Family Law Act 1996 enables a court to grant an occupation or non-molestation order to cohabitants who are defined as 'a man and a woman who, although not married to each other, are living together as husband and wife'. Similarly, the Social Security Contributions and Benefits Act 1992 uses this phrase for the purpose of establishing entitlement to certain social security benefits.

The judicial and parliamentary attitude towards extra-marital cohabitation merely reflects the attitude of society generally. But it is not without its critics.[1] Convincing arguments can be put forward on both sides.[2] The strongest reason for giving rights to cohabitants is that, as many unmarried couples are virtually indistinguishable from married ones, the parties (or the survivor) and their children may be as much in need of legal protection as spouses if the union breaks down as a result of separation or is brought to an end by death. This argument is particularly strong if the parties were unable to marry each other for some reason. Against this can be raised a number of counter-arguments. The first is a purely moral one and reflects the old common law position: extra-marital cohabitation is wrong and consequently no legal rights should be granted to those who engage in it. Whilst this view is undoubtedly held by only a minority of people today, its force should not on that account be underestimated, particularly in the light of a possible 'moral backlash'. The second reason for not according rights to cohabitants rests on the indisputable premise that it is in the interests of society generally that the relationship that a couple enter into should be as stable as possible, particularly if they have children. As marriage implies an emotional and legal commitment, marital relationships, it is argued, should be more stable than extra-marital ones. Consequently, by giving to the unmarried rights previously possessed only by the married, the law is weakening the institution of marriage

---

17 *Cooke v Head* [1972] 2 All ER 38, CA.
18 *Tanner v Tanner* [1975] 3 All ER 776, CA; post, p 163.
19 *Dyson Holdings Ltd v Fox* [1976] QB 503, [1975] 3 All ER 1030, CA; post, p 881 n 17.
20 Express recognition of cohabitation was made by the Law Reform (Succession) Act 1995 s 2: see post, p 887.
 1 See Freeman and Lyon *Cohabitation with Marriage* ch 7 and the judgments and writers cited at pp 187–90, particularly Deech 'The Case against Legal Recognition of Cohabitation' in Eekelaar and Katz (eds) *Marriage and Cohabitation in Contemporary Societies: Areas of Legal, Social and Ethical Change* (1980).
 2 See Barton *Cohabitation Contracts:Extra Marital Partnerships and Law Reform* (1985) pp 73–5.

and thus undermining the family. The force of this argument depends on whether the assumption about the comparative stability of marriage is correct, and evidence is beginning to be produced which does lend it some support.[3] Finally, it is argued that the law should not force the parties to accept the obligations of marriage they have consciously chosen to reject, or confer on them the attendant rights, particularly when it is possible for them, in part at least, to regulate their own legal relationship by contract.[4]

In any case, the extension of rights and obligations to persons living together outside marriage raises the difficult question of defining the class to whom they should be extended. The obvious answer is to limit it to those living with each other as husband and wife, but there seems little justification for imposing a minimum period of cohabitation (eg two years, as the Fatal Accidents Act 1976 and the Inheritance (Provision for Family and Dependants) Act 1975 do). The period is bound to be arbitrary and the principle can work injustice: a woman who has been living with a man for 18 months may be as much in need of compensation if he is killed as if she had been living with him for two years. An alternative solution would be to include within the class all who can show financial dependence. This is the solution adopted as an alternative qualification criterion by the Inheritance (Provision for Family and Dependants) Act. Its implications are extensive. If a couple parted, one would be able to claim financial provision from the other (including possibly the transfer of capital assets), and a relationship based on financial dependence may include homosexual couples and other family relations (for example, a brother and sister living together). Whatever test is applied, it could also give rise to a multiplicity of claims, for example by the wife to whom a man is still married and the woman with whom he is living.

English law has adopted a typical compromise and has assimilated the legal position of cohabitants to that of spouses only in isolated fields. This inconsistency no doubt reflects the ambivalence of society generally to the question of cohabitation as well as the number of different reasons that couples have for living together outside marriage. As the number of cohabiting couples increases, the problems resulting from the breakdown of their relationship and the attendant loss of home and support will become more common and more acute. Whatever the difficulties, the introduction of a uniform policy is essential.[5]

5.   PRIVATE ORDERING

Alongside the withdrawal of the law from attempting to pass judgment on the moral failings of those in family relationships, there has been an equally strong drive to discourage the use of legal proceedings to 'resolve' family disputes, by promoting a 'settlement culture'.[6] There are several reasons for this. Historically, couples and their families may have sought to avoid legal proceedings because of the scandal and stigma attached to them, and to seek to arrive at compromises

3 See the discussion by Robertson Elliot *Gender, Family and Society* (1996) pp 13–19 and 25–7; Maclean and Eekelaar *The Parental Obligation* (1997) pp 19–21.
4 But if cohabitants can so regulate their legal position, why should not spouses be able to do so as well (eg by contracting out of their mutual duty of support)?
5 The Law Commission has apparently been reluctant to undertake the task. See the Foreword to Barton , op cit (which was written as a consequence of Law Com No 97). It did, however, decide in 1993 to undertake a study of the *property* rights of *all* home-sharers.
6 Davis et al *Simple Quarrels* (1994) p 211.

satisfactory to all concerned without attracting the attention of the hoi polloi in open court hearings. The extent to which this could be done depended upon the outcome sought: clearly, a quiet separation, with financial support for the wife privately agreed between two families, was more easily achieved than a divorce, which could not be obtained without the glare of publicity, until the 1970s. Yet private negotiations ran the risk that, if discovered, any change in legal status being sought would be denied, on the basis that the parties had acted 'collusively' to conceal relevant matters from the court, and it remains the case that the parties cannot 'oust the jurisdiction of the court' by striking a financial bargain which prohibits them from later asking a court to produce a different outcome.[7] The purpose of retaining this state scrutiny over family relationships is probably twofold: first, to protect weaker parties from exploitation, and secondly, to uphold public order and public policy.[8]

Nonetheless, the desirability of arriving, in private, at a solution agreeable to both sides came to be recognised by courts, lawyers and finally the government. Legal costs can be reduced by avoiding trial (since it is the actual hearing which is the most expensive part of litigation), and this may in turn reduce public expenditure on courts and legal aid and save court time.[9] The 'win–lose' essence of adversarial legal proceedings may antagonise and add to the general unhappiness and bitterness associated with the breakdown of a relationship, and this may be emotionally and psychologically damaging to any children affected.[10] Court orders and legal rules are blunt instruments for dealing with complex human problems, and the legal process is ill-equipped to provide the full range of support needed by family members going through crises and change. They may be particularly inappropriate where there is a need to preserve and foster a relationship notwithstanding a change in legal status. For example, a court may be able to determine the legal parentage of a child, or who should inherit under a will or intestacy, but may be less competent to assess whether children will benefit from continued contact with their absent parent after a divorce, and still less be able to ensure that such contact takes place. Recognition of this legal impotence has coincided with a political preference for less state intervention in the privacy of the family, manifested in an emphasis, in the Children Act 1989, upon parents having responsibility for their children, and consequently being trusted to take decisions for and about them without undue scrutiny by a court. Finally, the breadth of discretion, which, of necessity, is entrusted to courts to determine issues which turn on a myriad individual facts, makes it hard to predict the outcome of litigation, and acts as an incentive to parties to try to minimise uncertainty by arriving at their own agreement. Ironically, at the same time this broad discretion forces legal advisers to attempt to second-guess what courts may do, by relying on either reported precedents, or practice within their local area, and to use such knowledge to persuade clients that a particular outcome is the most

---

7   Matrimonial Causes Act 1973 s 34 post, p 753; Child Support Act 1991 s 9(4) post, p 754.
8   The extent to which such state involvement is compatible with Article 8 of the European Convention on Human Rights, which guarantees the right to respect for private life, is so far largely unexplored. See post, p 20.
9   For a definitive analysis of the problems of the civil justice process, see Rt Hon Lord Woolf MR *Access to Justice, Interim Report* (1995) and *Final Report* (1996).
10 Law Com No 192, *The Ground for Divorce* (1990) paras 2.16, 2.19–2.20; Lord Chancellor's Department, *Looking to the Future: Mediation and the Ground for Divorce* Cm 2424 (1993) paras 5.11–5.15 and Cm 2799 (1995) paras 2.22–2.25.

likely to be obtained, and hence may as well be agreed without waiting for the court to produce a ruling.[11]

For all these reasons, the law now offers forceful encouragement to families in dispute to resort to means other than the courts to arrive at settlements. While lawyer-led negotiations have been the prevailing device for achieving these in the past, 'alternative dispute resolution' is increasingly being called into play. In the family context, the development of mediation services, which can offer a less confrontational approach than traditional legal representation, began to develop in a major way[12] in the 1970s in response to recommendations of the Finer Committee,[13] and focused initially on disputes between parents concerning their children. Such services, operating both within the legal process, usually at a first hearing between the parties and conducted by a welfare officer, and outside for couples who may not yet have begun any legal proceedings, received a major impetus in the Family Law Act 1996, under which divorcing couples will be strongly encouraged to seek to achieve settlements of all the issues involved in their divorce, preferably by recourse to mediation, for which those eligible will be enabled to receive legal aid.[14]

6.   MULTI-DISCIPLINARY AND SPECIALIST APPROACHES TO FAMILY PROBLEMS

As the law and legal process have become increasingly regarded as inappropriate to respond to and deal with family problems, attention has turned to other disciplines and other mechanisms outside or alongside law to fill the gap. A key feature of family law today is the extent to which non-legal professionals are involved in its practice and administration. This operates in several different ways. It is perhaps traditional for accountants and tax advisers to be involved in the provision of financial advice and assistance to wealthy divorcees. A more recent development has been the removal, in most instances, of the calculation, collection and enforcement of child maintenance from the jurisdiction of the courts, which, as noted above, are generally given wide discretion in their handling of family matters, to a governmental agency, the Child Support Agency, staffed by civil servants applying a strict formula to the calculation of the maintenance obligation upon absent parents.[15] Social work professionals, working both within the courts and in local authority social services departments, are largely responsible for the handling of child protection, albeit with some court control. The growth of social work as a response to family problems, and especially children's welfare needs, was one of the most striking developments of the twentieth century, and its interaction with the legal process is a complex and

---

11 Mnookin and Kornhauser 'Bargaining in the Shadow of the Law: The Case of Divorce' (1979) 88 Yale LJ 950.
12 Attempts to resolve family disputes by conciliation, as mediation was originally known, in fact date back to the inter-war years, through initiatives in the magistrates' courts which were then the main jurisdiction dealing with family problems of the working and lower-middle classes. See Dingwall and Eekelaar *Divorce Mediation and the Legal Process* (1988) ch 1; Cretney 'Marriage saving and the early days of conciliation – the role of Claud Mullins' (1998) 10 CFLQ 161.
13 *Report of the Committee on One Parent Families* Cmnd 5629 (1974).
14 Family Law Act 1996 s 13, s 29 and Legal Aid Act 1988 Part IIIA, and see post, pp 245 and 255–7.
15 Child Support Act 1991. Whether this has been a successful innovation is explored post, pp 727–50.

sometimes difficult one.[16] Paediatricians, psychologists, psychoanalysts and psychiatrists play an important role in the diagnosis and treatment of child abuse and neglect, and in the provision of support for children facing trauma during and after family breakdown. The legal process makes use of their expertise as expert witnesses to help determine both the occurrence or likelihood of abusive acts and the best mode of dealing with their aftermath for the child.[17] The rise of mediation and attempts to revive the relevance of marriage counselling[18] to provide support for adults undergoing relationship breakdown are further instances of non-legal approaches to what was once regarded as a strictly legal subject. Mediation is of particular interest, because it is the one 'non-legal specialism' in which lawyers may relatively easily become proficient through training and experience and which they may offer as an additional service to keep clients who might otherwise begin to move away from them. Family lawyers developed a more 'conciliatory' non-adversarial approach to their clients' problems in the 1970s and 1980s, to a great extent through the establishment of the Solicitors Family Law Association, which has a code of conduct for its members which emphasises the need to minimise conflict between family members during legal processes. The shift toward offering mediation as a further refinement of this approach is a relatively easy one for them to make. This possible colonisation of mediation by lawyers raises and illustrates the important question of whether, as has been argued,[19] the law in fact captures these other disciplines and subtly (or not) subverts their discourses to fit its own requirements.

C.   The development of the family court system

Sometimes a question of family law arises in a case of contract or tort or in a criminal prosecution. For example, it may be necessary to determine whether a woman can claim damages in respect of her husband's death or whether the accused's spouse is a compellable witness. Each of these cases will, of course, be tried in the ordinary civil or criminal courts and no special problem arises. What we are concerned with here are the courts which hear and determine cases raising issues solely of family law, for example the annulment or dissolution of marriage, settling with whom a child is to live, and the making of financial provision. As we explain, there has been a gradual grafting onto the basic court hierarchy of a system of linked courts, exercising the same or similar jurisdiction, staffed by judges and magistrates specially trained to deal with family matters. Thus, it can be suggested that family law in England and Wales is now administered by a family court 'system', if not yet a discrete 'family court', the arguments for which we consider after explaining the current arrangements.

---

16   Packman *The Child's Generation: Child Care Policy in Britain* (1981, 2nd edn); Fox Harding *Perspectives in Child Care Policy* (1991); Parton *Governing the Family: Child Care, Child Protection and the State* (1991).

17   Mr Justice Wall (ed) *Rooted Sorrows: Psychoanalytic Perspectives on Child Protection, Assessment, Therapy and Treatment* (1997).

18   Family Law Act 1996 s 22, s 23; see post, pp 242 and 245.

19   King and Piper *How the Law Thinks About Children* (2nd edn, 1995), King and Trowell *Children's Welfare and the Law: The Limits of Legal Intervention* (1992), drawing upon Teubner's theory of 'autopoeisis'; cf Murch and Hooper *The Family Justice System* (1992); Murch 'The cross-disciplinary approach to family law – are we trying to mix oil with water? in Pearl (ed) *Frontiers of Family Law* (1995).

1. HISTORICAL BACKGROUND

Before the nineteenth century, family matters were dealt with by:

(a) the ecclesiastical courts, which had control over marriages (including the power to annul, but not to grant divorces);

(b) the Court of Chancery, which, exercising the prerogative power of the Crown as parens patriae, had a general supervisory jurisdiction over minors, including the power to make orders concerning their custody, education and guardianship and which could, by making them wards of court, exercise a continuing control and supervision of them; and

(c) the justices of the peace, whose Poor Law responsibilities gave them power to enforce maintenance liabilities.

The High Court

The powers of the ecclesiastical courts were removed by the advent of a judicial power vested in a new Divorce Court to grant divorces in 1857. This jurisdiction was transferred in 1875 to the High Court and assigned to the Probate, Divorce and Admiralty Division.[20] The jurisdiction of the Court of Chancery over children was vested in the Chancery Division when the High Court was created in 1875, to which was added the power to make adoption orders when this became possible in 1926.

The fact that two divisions of the High Court possessed the power to make orders with respect to children was anomalous and could be a positive embarrassment when the two jurisdictions came into conflict, as they could, for example, if an order was sought in divorce proceedings with respect to a child who was already a ward of court. The position was made even more complicated by the fact that custody of a minor could also be claimed in the Queen's Bench Division by habeas corpus. A similar confusion arose in appeals from magistrates' courts, which could lie to each of the three divisions of the High Court depending on the nature of the proceedings. It is obviously desirable to concentrate in one division jurisdiction to deal with all matters likely to arise when a marriage breaks down. With this object in view, the Administration of Justice Act 1970 s 1 renamed the Probate, Divorce and Admiralty Division as the Family Division of the High Court. All the matters mentioned above, both at first instance and appellate, were transferred to the Family Division, together with a number of other aspects of family law.[1]

County courts

An expanding jurisdiction for the lower courts was created as the needs of an increasingly urban, industrialised and complex society imposed new demands for legal solutions on the court system. The county courts were given power to make orders with respect to property[2] under the Guardianship of Infants Act 1886 and to make adoption orders in 1926. Further powers followed under the

---

20 Supreme Court of Judicature Act 1873 s 34.

1 See now the Supreme Court Act 1981 Sch 1, as amended. Of the other matters formerly assigned to the Probate, Divorce and Admiralty Division, probate business (other than non-contentious and common form business) is now assigned to the Chancery Division, and admiralty and prize cases are assigned to the Queen's Bench Division.

2 For example, under s 17 of the Married Women's Property Act 1882 (post, p 115).

Inheritance (Provision for Family and Dependants) Act 1975. Most importantly, jurisdiction to grant divorces was extended to the county courts by the Matrimonial Causes Act 1967, which empowered the Lord Chancellor to designate any county court as a divorce court to hear any undefended matrimonial cause. Experience over the next few years indicated that there was no justification for declining to give county courts jurisdiction in most defended cases, and in practice many cases were being released to county court judges or heard by them sitting as deputy High Court judges. Consequently the Matrimonial and Family Proceedings Act 1984 gave divorce county courts jurisdiction to hear all matrimonial causes, both defended and undefended, and all other applications under the Matrimonial Causes Act 1973.[3] All matrimonial causes (that is, actions for divorce, nullity of marriage and separation) must currently be commenced in a divorce county court or in the Principal Registry in London (which is a divorce county court for this purpose). Matrimonial causes tried in a county court must be tried in a divorce county court specially designated as a court of trial.[4]

Magistrates' courts

Extension of the magistrates' jurisdiction stems from the administration of the criminal law. Section 4 of the Matrimonial Causes Act 1878 gave a criminal court, before which a married man had been convicted of an aggravated assault upon his wife, power to make an order that she should no longer be bound to cohabit with him if it felt that her future safety was in peril. The court could also order a husband to pay maintenance to a wife in whose favour such a separation order was made and vest in her the legal custody of any children of the marriage under the age of ten years.

Magistrates' domestic jurisdiction was further increased by a number of Acts over the next century, which extended the grounds on which the wife – and eventually the husband – might apply for an order. The Domestic Proceedings and Magistrates' Courts Act 1978 eventually overhauled the law relating to maintenance, and abolished the magistrates' power to make an order that the complainant should no longer be bound to cohabit with the defendant, replacing it by a power to make an order forbidding one spouse to use violence against the other or against a child and, if necessary, excluding him from the matrimonial home.[5]

Magistrates also had important jurisdiction over both child offenders and children at risk of abuse or neglect, through the creation of the juvenile court in 1908. Views on the causes and appropriate treatment of juvenile offenders have vacillated over the years, at one time considering that such children should be regarded no differently from those whose behavioural problems manifest themselves in non-criminal ways.[6] Thus, the Children and Young Persons Act 1969 gave magistrates the option of dealing with young offenders through care proceedings, alongside child victims of abuse. The pendulum had swung away from this approach by the time of the Children Act 1989, which abolished this option, and the juvenile court was renamed as the 'youth court' in 1991.[7]

3 Matrimonial and Family Proceedings Act 1984 s 33 and s 34.
4 Ibid, s 33.
5 Repealed and replaced by the Family Law Act 1996 Part IV.
6 See Douglas 'The Child's Right to Make Mistakes: Criminal Responsibility and the Immature Minor' in Douglas and Sebba (eds) *Children's Rights and Traditional Values* (1998) p 264 at pp 270–6.
7 Criminal Justice Act 1991 s 70.

2. INCREASING SPECIALISATION IN FAMILY MATTERS

The consequential differences in courts' powers which these piecemeal accretions of jurisdiction had brought about presented a significant obstacle to the efficiency and efficacy of the courts to handle family problems. The successful creation of the Family Division of the High Court, together with the emerging specialisms in the lower courts, demonstrated that a more coherent system staffed by experts in the field could provide a better service to those involved in proceedings. When the law relating to children was fundamentally reformed by the Children Act 1989, the opportunity was taken to develop a more coherent, and flexible, system which at the same time would create a judiciary specially trained to handle family problems. The primary aim was to ensure that any court, regardless of its level in the court hierarchy, would be able to offer the same remedies in respect of a family problem. This would enable litigants to choose which court to utilise, and would facilitate the efficient disposal of cases by permitting transfer of proceedings to other courts where this is desirable on grounds of speed or convenience to the parties. A similar approach was taken when the law on domestic violence was reformed.[8]

County courts

Under the Children (Allocation of Proceedings) Order 1991 there are, for the purpose of hearing cases involving children, the following classes of county court: divorce county courts, family hearing centres and care centres.[9] These classes are in addition to non-designated county courts which have jurisdiction to hear domestic violence proceedings even when these involve children.

Family hearing centres and care centres are in effect specialist courts with exclusive jurisdiction to hear certain types of children cases.[10] Only 'designated family judges' and 'nominated care judges', that is, circuit judges specified by the Lord Chancellor[11] who have undertaken specialist training, have jurisdiction to hear cases at these centres. The thinking behind this development is that the concentration of family work in the centres ensures that specialist judges can be effectively employed to deal with cases expeditiously and that continuous hearings can be assured, thus avoiding the need for lengthy adjournments.[12]

Magistrates' courts

Magistrates' courts were reorganised with the creation of 'family proceedings courts'.[13] These are staffed by magistrates drawn from the 'family panel'[14] and have sole jurisdiction to hear civil proceedings concerning children at this level. 'Family proceedings' are not limited to children cases, however. They include proceedings under the Domestic Proceedings and Magistrates' Courts Act 1978,

8 See Chapter 6.
9 Many courts combine all these functions, including the Principal Registry in London: see Art 19 of the Children (Allocation of Proceedings) Order 1991.
10 Contested s 8 cases and public law cases involving local authorities: see post, Chapters 12 and 14.
11 Under Courts and Legal Services Act 1990 s 9 and *Practice Direction (Family Proceedings: Allocation to Judiciary)* [1991] 4 All ER 764.
12 See Harris and Scanlan *The Children Act 1989, A Procedural Handbook* (1995, 2nd edn) para 10.10.
13 Children Act 1989 s 92(1).
14 See Family Proceedings (Constitution) Rules 1991 and Family Proceedings Courts (Constitution) (Metropolitan Area) Rules 1991.

the Children Act 1989, the Adoption Act 1976 and Part IV of the Family Law Act 1996.[15] A magistrates' court sitting as a 'family proceedings court' must consist of not more than three magistrates (including, so far as is practicable, both a man and a woman) drawn from a special 'family panel'.[16] No one may be present in the court except the officers of the court, the parties, their legal representatives, witnesses, other persons directly concerned in the case (such as welfare officers), representatives of the press, and any other person whom the court may in its discretion permit to be present.[17] The powers of newspapers and sound and television broadcasting services to report family proceedings are also considerably curtailed.[18]

3.   FLEXIBILITY IN HANDLING PROCEEDINGS

To ensure efficiency, the Matrimonial and Family Proceedings Act,1984 provides that certain proceedings may be transferred from the High Court to a county court and vice versa. Thus, while some family proceedings[19] may only be heard in the High Court, others must be dealt with in that court *unless* the nature of the issues of fact or law raised makes them more suitable for trial in a county court (for example, because these issues are not complex, difficult or grave, or the residence of witnesses makes trial there more convenient).[20] The High Court may accordingly order family proceedings in that court (other than those under the Children Act or Adoption Act) to be transferred to a county court if, applying these criteria, they should be dealt with there.[1] Conversely, a county court may order any family proceedings pending before it (other than those under the Children Act or Adoption Act) to be transferred to the High Court if the complexity, difficulty or gravity of the issues justifies such action.[2]

The transfer of cases dealing with children is subject to different rules. Certain 'specified proceedings'[3] must be commenced in the magistrates' court, while others are 'self-regulating' in the sense that, if other proceedings, such as divorce, are already pending in a particular court, actions concerning the children of the

---

15 For the full definition of 'family proceedings', see the Magistrates' Courts Act 1980 s 65, as amended. Until the commencement of the Children Act 1989 such proceedings were known as 'domestic proceedings'. Proceedings for the enforcement of orders and for the variation of periodical payments do not generally come within the definition of family proceedings unless the court otherwise orders.

16 Magistrates' Courts Act 1980 ss 66–68, as amended by the Children Act 1989 Sch 11.

17 Ibid, s 69. Representatives of the press and 'other persons' may not be present during adoption proceedings: s 69(3). See Lowe 'Publicity in Court Proceedings concerning Children' (1981) 145 JPN 256.

18 See ibid, s 71, as amended by the Broadcasting Act 1990 Sch 20.

19 Proceedings which in the High Court are assigned exclusively to the Family Division: Matrimonial and Family Proceedings Act 1984 s 32.

20 Matrimonial and Family Proceedings Act 1984 s 37; *Practice Direction (Family Division: Distribution of Business)* [1992] 3 All ER 151, qv for details.

 1 Matrimonial and Family Proceedings Act 1984 s 39; Children (Allocation of Proceedings) Order 1991 art 5.

 2 Matrimonial and Family Proceedings Act 1984 s 39; Children (Allocation of Proceedings) Order 1991 art 5; *Practice Direction* (supra). In particular the court must have regard to the capital value of assets involved, substantial allegations of fraud, deception or non-disclosure, and substantial contested allegations of conduct.

 3 Those concerning care proceedings, principally care and related proceedings: see Children (Allocation of Proceedings) Order 1991 art 3 and post, p 534.

family must be dealt with in the same court. Apart from these, applications under the Act may be brought at High Court, county court, or magistrates' court level. To speed up the hearing of cases and to match the appropriate degree of judicial expertise to the complexity of the case, there is provision for proceedings to be transferred from one court level to another, and also between courts of the same level.[4]

The Children Act also promoted increased liaison between court administrators and the judiciary at all levels, facilitated by the creation of two committees[5] in each court area. The first, the Family Court Business Committee, is concerned with availability of resources, priorities in relation to other litigation, and sound practice in transferring cases between courts. The second, the Family Court Forum,[6] provides for the exchange of concerns and information between the various agencies and professions involved in administering the Children Act. Both bodies are chaired by the designated family judge and serviced by the court administrator for the particular area. The Business Committee's membership comprises a district judge, a representative of justices' clerks from courts operating family panels, a representative from a local authority's social services and legal departments, a manager of a local guardian ad litem panel and a local representative from the Legal Aid Board. The Forums have a wider membership (reflecting the multi-disciplinary nature of child law especially) comprising inter alia a barrister, a solicitor in private practice, a solicitor from the local authority legal department, a probation officer, an area health authority representative, a member of the medical profession, a police representative, a social worker, a guardian ad litem, a justices' clerk and a district judge.

4.   INCREASED PROFESSIONALISM

The implementation of the Children Act 1989 coincided with the general development of training for the judiciary through the expansion of the activities of the Judicial Studies Board.[7] All judges and magistrates who were to have functions under the Act were given specialist training as to both the terms and procedures of the legislation and the wider context in which children cases should be understood. This innovation heralded a much more professional approach to the acquisition of expertise by the judiciary, and all new circuit judges, district judges and magistrates now undergo training, in family as well as civil and criminal matters, before taking up appointments to the Bench. Training to cope with other new initiatives, such as the implementation of the Family Law Act 1996, and refresher training at periodic intervals, is compulsory.

Alongside a requirement to undergo training, new obligations and ways of working were imposed on the magistrates' courts in particular, in order to bring them into conformity with the higher courts, so that they could exercise the common jurisdiction introduced by the Children Act. For the first time, a requirement of advance disclosure of written evidence was imposed, with an expectation that magistrates will have read the papers in advance of the hearing.

4 See generally the Children (Allocation of Proceedings) Order 1991.
5 See generally Harris and Scanlan, op cit, paras 10.11–10.12.
6 Originally called the Family Court Services Committee.
7 See *Judicial Studies Board Report 1995–97* (1997).

Magistrates, as well as judges, must give reasons for their decisions, and a failure to provide adequate reasons is a ground for appeal.[8]

5.   A MORE MANAGERIAL APPROACH

The Children Act also introduced elements of greater 'court control' over the process of family litigation, by requiring courts to set timetables for the determination of the litigation, and emphasising the importance of judicial directions to the parties in the collection and sharing of written evidence and instruction of expert witnesses.[9] The aims were to speed up litigation and to control costs. The experience gained has influenced similar initiatives both in the family sphere and in civil litigation generally. For example, in determining financial and property issues in divorce cases, certain county courts were selected to test the 'Ancillary Relief Pilot Scheme' under which parties are encouraged, with the rigorous encouragement of the district judge giving directions, to clarify and explore the scope for early settlement of the issues in dispute.[10] The more 'managerial' role entailed in this approach reflects the continuing emphasis, noted above, upon the settlement rather than the adjudication of disputes.

6.   TOWARDS A FAMILY COURT?

What has been put in place as a result of these developments is not yet a family court, but rather a system of family courts operating as distinct divisions within the civil court structure, exercising a common, or very similar, jurisdiction in certain areas of family law. This perhaps typically British approach to reform took the heat out of a long-standing debate concerning the desirability of establishing a discrete Family Court to deal with all aspects of family litigation. Family Courts have existed in the United States for some time and have been introduced in Australia and New Zealand.[11] Impetus for their introduction in this country was given by the Report of the Committee on One-parent Families (the Finer Report) in 1974.[12] In 1983 the Lord Chancellor's Department issued a consultation paper, which was in turn overtaken by the establishment of a review committee which published its own consultation paper in 1986.[13] The issues involved in the creation of a family court may be outlined as follows.

A unified court?

It can be seen that, even with the reforms already introduced, proceedings relating to members of the same family may take place in a number of courts simultaneously. For example, a wife, having taken proceedings for maintenance in a

---

8 Family Proceedings Courts (Children Act 1989) Rules 1991 r 21(5)–(6); *W v Hertfordshire County Council* [1993] 1 FLR 118.
9 See eg Children Act 1989 s 11 and post, pp 339 and 558.
10 Family Proceedings Rules 1991 rr 2.71–2.77 as amended by Family Proceedings (Amendment No 2) Rules 1997. See Burrows *Ancillary Relief Pilot Scheme* (1997).
11 See Brown *The Legal Background to the Family Court* [1966] BJ Crim 139 (USA); the Family Law Act 1975 s 21 (Australia); the Family Courts Act 1980 s 4 (New Zealand).
12 Cmnd 5629 Pt 4, s 13 and s 14.
13 A useful summary of the contents of the paper is to be found in [1986] Fam Law 247.

magistrates' court, may then seek a divorce in a divorce county court; at the same time a child of the family may have been made a ward in the High Court.[14] This fragmented and overlapping jurisdiction causes confusion, complicates proceedings, and leads to inconvenience, unnecessary cost and unreasonable delay.[15] Creating a unified court would obviate these difficulties.

A non-adversarial, multi-disciplinary body?

A fundamental question is what the function of a Family Court should be. In the United States it is frequently seen as fulfilling a therapeutic role, whilst the models put forward by authoritative bodies in this country give it solely adjudicative powers. As we have seen, one of the criticisms levelled against the current family justice system is that the adversarial procedure which may be adopted within it exacerbates the parties' relationship. The Finer Committee emphasised the importance of mediation (or, as they called it then, conciliation) in all family disputes, but they also stressed that the normal safeguards of the judicial process must not be weakened by the court's regarding litigants coming before it as 'clients' or 'patients'. They therefore concluded that, if the parties were unable to reach an agreed solution, 'the Family Court must be an impartial judicial institution, regulating the rights of citizens and settling their disputes according to law'.[16] The court, would be able, as now, to call on the services of welfare officers to make the necessary investigations and reports. This underlines another advantage of a unified Family Court: the integration of welfare and other ancillary services. This would get rid of the present confusing involvement of two different welfare officers with the same family if proceedings in a magistrates' court are followed by further proceedings in a county court, or if public law and private law proceedings take place concerning the same child.[17]

One court?

To be effective, a Family Court must have sole jurisdiction in all family matters and apply a uniform law: the court's powers must not depend on the tribunal before which proceedings are brought. This raises another major issue: should there be an entirely new court or could a Family Court be created out of the High Court and county courts?[18] Further, does the lay magistracy have a part to play in a Family Court? The Finer Committee believed that they had, 'not only as a source of manpower, but as an equally indispensable source of lay experience and

14 As occurred in *Re C (Wardship and Adoption)* (1979) 2 FLR 177, CA. See also Hoggett 'Family Courts or Family Law Reform?' (1986) 6 Legal Studies 1, 3–5.
15 See the Lord Chancellor's Department's Consultation Paper (1986). Hoggett, loc cit p 5; Murch et al *The Overlapping Family Jurisdictions of Magistrates Courts and County Courts – Research Report* (1987).
16 Cmnd 5629, paras 4.285 and 4.283. See generally paras 4.278 et seq. Adherents of the theory of autopoeisis would presumably argue that a court can only take 'legal' decisions in any event.
17 Ibid, paras 4.315–4.336. See, for example, *Re S (A Minor) (Guardian ad Litem/Welfare Officer)* [1993] 1 FLR 110; *Devon County Council v S and L* [1993] 1 FLR 842 (post, p 553). In 1998 the government issued a consultation paper, *Support Services in Family Proceedings – Future Organisation of Court Welfare Services*. The Finer Committee also recommended much closer cooperation between the court and the Department of Social Security: see ibid, Pt 4 s 12, and para 4.337, but the Child Support Act 1991 has, if anything, created a greater gulf between the two.
18 See the three options put forward by the Review Committee. (The third contemplates the retention of the existing courts with a revised jurisdiction to eliminate overlapping.)

outlook which is a traditional feature in the administration of family law in England and Wales'.[19] A further advantage of including magistrates amongst the members of the tribunal is that they, like circuit judges, sit locally, and it is essential that litigants should have ready access to a local court and that most cases should be dealt with expeditiously and cheaply.

A family court 'system'?

It will be seen that, in several respects, we already have in place a family court 'system' which fulfils these criteria in England and Wales.[20] Courts exercising powers under the Children Act apply a uniform code of rules. Proceedings for an order under that Act or the Adoption Act may be brought in the High Court, a designated county court or a magistrates' court sitting as a family proceedings court. The role of the court is primarily to adjudicate, although it can take some steps on its own initiative, and the substantive law is comprehensive and administered uniformly. There is no separate court, but existing courts of all tiers, including magistrates' courts, are involved. When dealing with matters relating to children the tribunal is composed of specialists – judges of the Family Division, specified county court judges and magistrates drawn from the family panel – all of whom have undergone specialist training.

Unfortunately, however, this approach has not been integrated into the rest of the court system. While Part IV of the Family Law Act 1996 enables magistrates, as well as county courts and the High Court, to apply the same criteria in respect of domestic violence remedies, their powers are more limited than those of the higher courts.[1] They have no divorce jurisdiction, and restricted powers when dealing with applications for lump sums and maintenance.[2] Renewed calls for a completely new and fully integrated Family Court may thus continue be heard as further reforms to family law are made.[3]

D.   The international dimension to family law

One of the most important developments in family law in recent years has been the growing significance of international law to the shaping of new thinking about families, and to new legislation regulating them. Beginning with the Universal Declaration of Human Rights (1948), which, in Article 16(3), provides that the family 'is the natural and fundamental group unit of society and is entitled to protection by society and the State,' and culminating in the United Nations International Year of the Family in 1994, there has been increasing attention paid

---

19 Report para 4.348. But their role has undoubtedly diminished since 1974. See also the proposals of the Association of Magisterial Officers [1986] Fam Law 250.

20 The process is helped by the fact that the Lord Chancellor's Department (which has responsibility for administering the High Court and county courts) has responsibility for the administration of magistrates' courts: see the Transfer of Functions (Magistrates' Courts and Family Law) Order 1992. See further Hoggett et al *The Family, Law and Society* (4th edn, 1996) 269–74.

1 See eg s 59(1) – no power to hear application involving disputed question as to party's entitlement to occupy any property; Sch 7 para 1 – no power to transfer tenancy.

2 Children Act 1989 Sch 1 paras 1(1)(b) and 5(2) – no power to make secured periodical payments order, or property adjustment order; no power to order lump sum over £1000.

3 See HH Judge Fricker 'A Unified Family Court and Family Courts Support Services, Part I' [1998] Fam Law 462.

to mechanisms for enhancing the position of the family.[4] In some ways this might be regarded as strange given that the difficulty of defining the family, alluded to above, is even greater in a global context where many different family forms are to be found. There is also a tension, increasingly recognised, between laying down norms for 'family' rights, and providing rights for individual members of families. There may be conflicts of interest between the two. For example, how far should the importance of recognising the family as an entity entitled to protection take priority over the potential need to protect individuals from abuse or exploitation by other family members? The American Convention on Human Rights (1969) attempts, perhaps not wholly successfully, to deal with this problem by heading its Article 17 'Rights of the Family' and then including within that Article the rights of individuals within the family. Nonetheless, international efforts to support families, and to protect family members, have grown apace. These have manifested themselves in a variety of international instruments.

1.   UNITED NATIONS CONVENTION ON THE RIGHTS OF THE CHILD[5]

At the global level, the most important of these may be seen as the United Nations Convention on the Rights of the Child of 1989, now signed by over 190 states. This Convention sets out a variety of rights which must be safeguarded by signatory states through their internal laws. While focusing upon the rights of the child, both within the family, and in relation to the state, it marks an important stage in the international recognition of the family as a distinct unit. Its preamble, for example, states that signatories are:

> '*Convinced* that the family . . . [is] the fundamental group of society and the natural environment for the growth and well-being of all its members and particularly children . . . [and] should be afforded the necessary protection and assistance so that it can fully assume its responsibilities within the community . . .'

Signatories are required to submit reports to a Committee on the Rights of the Child on their progress in implementing the terms of the Convention, and are thus subject to some degree of scrutiny by the international community. Signing the Convention also leaves governments open to both internal and international criticism should they be seen to be failing in fulfilling their international obligations.[6]

Obtaining worldwide agreement to a set of wide-ranging norms which can be implemented nationally is obviously a difficult task, and runs the risk that such norms will be pitched at a fairly minimal or very general level to attract maximum adherence. It may be more fruitful to develop agreed standards at a regional level where there is greater cultural, economic and political similarity between states. There are several Conventions operating at this level,[7] and the one

---

4   Sokalski 'The International Year of the Family: New Frontiers for Families' in Lowe and Douglas (eds) *Families across Frontiers* (1996) 1; Douglas 'The Significance of International Law for the Development of Family Law in England and Wales' in Bridge (ed) *Towards the Millennium: Essays for P M Bromley* (1997) 85.
5   For a definitive study of the international rights of the child, see Van Bueren *The International Law on the Rights of the Child* (1995).
6   Compare Department of Health, *The UK's First Report to the UN Committee on the Rights of the Child* (1994) with Children's Rights Development Unit, *UK Agenda for Children* (1994).
7   See, for example, the American Convention on Human Rights referred to above (although one might query how far the two American continents can be regarded as sharing cultural and economic standards) and the African Charter on Human and People's Rights (1981).

of greatest significance to the United Kingdom is the European Convention on Human Rights.

2.   EUROPEAN CONVENTION ON HUMAN RIGHTS

Although the European Convention for the Protection of Human Rights and Fundamental Freedoms[8] has not hitherto been a part of English domestic law, it has nevertheless had an increasingly significant influence on its development. With incorporation into English law through the Human Rights Act 1998, its importance can be expected to increase. Two Articles are of particular importance in family law: Article 8, which provides that everyone has the right to respect for his private and family life, his home and his correspondence; and Article 12, which provides that men and women of marriageable age have the right to marry and to found a family according to the national laws governing the exercise of this right. Anyone alleging a violation of the Convention may apply to Strasbourg after exhausting local remedies. [9] A range of applications has been made by persons in this country, and these will be referred to in subsequent chapters.

Signatories are bound to change their domestic law if it is found to be in breach of the Convention. Its provisions have been taken into account by the House of Lords in determining a mother's contact with a ward of court,[10] and by the drafters of the Children Act 1989, particularly in dealing with contact with a child in the care of a local authority. It is clear that the future shape of English family law is likely to be determined to an increasing extent by the possibility that a litigant will either successfully plead a breach of the Convention in the domestic legal forum, or, if unsuccessful, will obtain access to the European Court of Human Rights as a tribunal of last resort.

3.   CONVENTIONS FOR HARMONISATION AND CO-OPERATION

The Conventions so far discussed may be seen as operating primarily at a political level, the intention being to educate states to improve their human rights records. Other Conventions have a different function – to provide a mechanism for handling of inter-state family problems. The most notable of these are the two Conventions concerned with international child abduction,[11] and the Hague Convention on Inter-Country Adoption.[12] The aim of these instruments is to promote a uniform international approach to the problem, in the first case, of wrongful removal or retention of the child outside the state of his or her habitual residence, and in the second, of adoption of a child from one country by adopters

---

8 See Douglas 'The Family and the State under the European Convention on Human Rights' (1988) 2 Int J Law and Fam 76.
9 Section II of the Convention (as amended; provision for cases to be dealt with by the Court and not by the Commission first, to come into force when ratified by member states).
10 *Re KD (A Minor) (Ward: Termination of Access)* [1988] AC 806, [1988] 1 All ER 577, HL.
11 The Hague Convention on Civil Aspects of International Child Abduction (1980) and the European Convention on Recognition and Enforcement of Decisions Concerning Custody of Children (1980). See Van Bueren *The Best Interests of the Child – International Co-operation on Child Abduction* (1993).
12 The Hague Convention on Protection of Children and Co-operation in Respect of Inter-Country Adoption (1993).

from another, sometimes with minimal protection for the child and with scope for financial exploitation. The Conventions seek to ensure common procedures and criteria by which courts in the relevant jurisdictions can determine the outcome of the case.[13]

Increasing political and economic co-operation between states and an accompanying encouragement of international commerce and of mobility of workers in Europe has made the consequential problems of 'international' families much more apparent than they once were. A desire for harmonisation of laws and practices at the European level operates not only through the European Union, but also through the much larger Council of Europe.[14] That body, through its Parliamentary Assembly, Committee of Ministers and Conferences, has produced a number of Recommendations and some Conventions intended to promote common policy among its member states, including the European Convention on the Legal Status of Children Born out of Wedlock (1975), which aimed to reduce discrimination against children whose parents are not married. More recently, the Council has produced a Convention on the Exercise of Children's Rights, intended to complement the UN Convention by providing more detailed provisions concerning procedures for enabling children to exercise the rights guaranteed in the UN Convention. We discuss such instruments in greater detail in later chapters.

---

13 See pp 486 and 680 post.
14 See Killerby 'The Council of Europe's Contribution to Family Law (Past, Present and Future)' in Lowe and Douglas (eds) *Families Across Frontiers* (1996) 13.

Chapter 2

Marriage

A. The nature of marriage

Marriage is declining in popularity, although it is still likely that most people will marry at some point in their lives. In 1995, there were 322,000 marriages in the United Kingdom, the lowest recorded figure since 1926. Of these, 192,000 were first marriages (half the number of 1970), while 40 per cent of the total were remarriages. The reduction in marriage rates is not unique to the United Kingdom but is a common phenomenon across Europe. Indeed, the United Kingdom's marriage rate, of about 5 per 1000 population, is in the middle of the scale, compared with Denmark and Portugal (where the rate is over 6 per 1000; the highest in the European Union) and Sweden (the country where marriage is least popular, with a rate of under 4 per 1000). Meanwhile, the age at which people marry is rising. In 1975, the European average age at first marriage was 25.7 for men and 23.0 for women. By 1994, this had risen to 28.7 for men, and 26.3 for women.[1] While these changes mean that the law will increasingly have to cater for relationships which do not fit neatly within the traditional model of family building within marriage, the law of marriage will remain important for the majority of people for some time to come.

Quite apart from its abstract meaning as the social institution of marriage, 'marriage' has two distinct meanings: the ceremony by which a man and woman become husband and wife, or the *act of marrying*; and the relationship existing between a husband and his wife, or the *state of being married*.[2] This distinction largely corresponds with its dual aspect of contract and status.

1. MARRIAGE AS A CONTRACT

In English law, marriage is an agreement by which a man and a woman enter into a certain legal relationship with each other and which creates and imposes mutual rights and duties. Looked at from this point of view, marriage is clearly a contract. It presents similar problems to other contracts – for example, of form and capacity; and like other contracts it may be void or voidable. But it is, of course, quite unlike any commercial contract, and consequently it is sui generis in many respects. In particular we may note the following marked dissimilarities:

(1) The law relating to the capacity to marry is different from that of any other contract.

(2) A marriage may only be contracted if special formalities are observed.

---

1 Data taken from *Social Trends 1998* (1998) p 41 and Charts 2.17, 2.18.
2 Graveson *Status in the Common Law* (1982) pp 80–1.

(3) The grounds on which a marriage may be void or voidable are for the most part completely different from those on which other contracts may be void or voidable.

(4) Unlike other voidable contracts, a voidable marriage cannot be declared void ab initio by rescission by one of the parties, but may be set aside only by a decree of nullity pronounced by a court of competent jurisdiction.

(5) A contract of marriage cannot be discharged by agreement, frustration or breach. Apart from death, it can be terminated only by a formal legal act, pronounced by a court of competent jurisdiction.

2. MARRIAGE AS CREATING STATUS

This second aspect of marriage is much more important than the first. It creates a status, that is, 'the condition of belonging to a particular class of persons [ie married persons] to whom the law assigns certain peculiar legal capacities or incapacities.'[3]

In the first place, whereas the parties to a commercial agreement may make such terms as they think fit (provided that they do not offend against rules of public policy or statutory prohibition), the spouses' mutual rights and duties[4] are very largely fixed by law and not by agreement. An increasing number of these may be varied by consent: for example, the spouses may release each other from the duty to cohabit. But many may still not be altered: thus neither may contract out of his or her power to apply to the court for financial relief in the event of divorce.

Secondly, unlike a commercial contract, which cannot affect the legal position of anyone who is not a party to it, marriage may also affect the rights and duties of third persons and the relationship of the individual with government bodies. So, for example, private or state pensions may be payable to a person by virtue of their status as a surviving spouse.

3. DEFINITION OF MARRIAGE

The classic definition of marriage in English law is that of Lord Penzance in *Hyde v Hyde*:[5]

'I conceive that marriage, as understood in Christendom, may . . . be defined as the voluntary union for life of one man and one woman to the exclusion of all others.'

It will be seen that this definition involves four conditions.

First, the marriage must be *voluntary*. Thus, as we shall see,[6] it can be annulled if there was no true consent on the part of one of the parties.

Secondly, it must be *for life*. If by marriage 'as understood in Christendom' Lord Penzance was referring to the view traditionally taken in Western Europe by the Roman Catholic Church and some other denominations, his statement is of

---

3 Allen 'Status and Capacity' (1930) 46 LQR 277, 288. In this article the author critically discusses a number of other definitions of status and analyses this elusive legal concept. See also Graveson, op cit.

4 For the view that there are virtually no duties attached to marriage any more, see Deech 'Divorce Law and Empirical Studies' (1990) 106 LQR 229 at pp 243–4.

5 (1866) LR 1 P & D 130, 133.

6 Post, pp 91 et seq.

course unexceptional. But it does not mean that by English law marriage is indissoluble: divorce by judicial process had been possible in England for over eight years when *Hyde v Hyde* was decided. The gloss put on the dictum by the Court of Appeal in *Nachimson v Nachimson* [7] – that it must be the parties' intention when they enter into the marriage that it should last for life – is unsatisfactory. This may well be the intention of the vast majority, but, if, say, two people enter into a marriage for the sole purpose of enabling a child to be born within marriage, intending never to live together but to obtain a divorce by consent at the earliest opportunity, it cannot be doubted that their union is a marriage by English law. [8] The only interpretation that can be put on Lord Penzance's statement is that the marriage must last for life unless it is previously determined by a decree or some other act of dissolution. [9]

Thirdly, the union must be *heterosexual*.

Fourthly, it must be *monogamous*. Neither spouse may contract another marriage so long as the original union subsists.

B.   Agreements to marry

A marriage is commonly preceded by an agreement to marry or 'engagement'. At common law such agreements amounted to contracts provided that there was an intention to enter into legal relations (as there probably would not be in the case of an 'unofficial engagement'). Their highly personal and non-commercial nature gave them certain peculiar characteristics, but as a general rule they were governed by the general principles of the law of contract. Consequently, if either party withdrew from the engagement without lawful justification, the other could sue for breach of contract. Such actions became rare after the Second World War (and were seldom, if ever, brought by men), partly no doubt because of the difficulty of proving damage, but probably largely as a result of a change in social views. [10]

The fact that actions for breach of promise of marriage were still occasionally brought raised the question of their utility. If either party to an engagement was convinced that he (or she) ought not to marry the other, it was highly doubtful whether public policy was served by letting the threat of an action push him into a potentially unstable marriage or by penalising him in damages if he resiled. The Law Commission therefore recommended the abolition of these actions [11] and this recommendation was implemented by the Law Reform (Miscellaneous Provisions) Act 1970 s 1. This provides that no agreement to marry shall take effect as a legally enforceable contract and that no action shall lie in this country for breach of such an agreement, wherever it was made.

---

7   [1930] P 217, CA.

8   See post, p 96. The updated definition of marriage proposed at a symposium held in 1994 and reported in [1994] Fam Law 341, has a similar flaw: 'marriage is the voluntary union of a man and a woman, solemnised in public according to law, and is based upon mutual commitment and intended to last for life, to the exclusion of all others'.

9   *Nachimson v Nachimson* (supra) at 225, 227 (per Lord Hanworth MR), 235 (per Lawrence LJ), 243–4 (per Romer LJ).

10   The civil judicial statistics do not disclose how many actions were brought. Nor do we know how far the existence of the action led to settlements out of court.

11   Law Com No 26 *Breach of Promise of Marriage* (1969).

1. CONTINUING SIGNIFICANCE OF ENGAGEMENTS

However, the fact that a couple have agreed to marry each other is not without all legal significance. There may still be advantages to being able to show an engagement having taken place, in relation to certain types of property disputes. Problems can therefore arise in establishing what constitutes a legally recognisable agreement to marry, and in proving that it was ever made.

The meaning of an agreement to marry

It could be argued that an engagement should only be recognised if it would have amounted to a legally enforceable contract at common law. In *Shaw v Fitzgerald*,[12] however, Scott Baker J held that an agreement to marry was capable of recognition under the Law Reform (Miscellaneous Provisions) Act 1970 s 2 (discussed below) even though at common law the contract would have been regarded as contrary to public policy because one of the parties was married to a third person. If this decision is correct, the test must be whether there was an unconditional agreement to marry.

Proof of an engagement

The difficulty of proving an engagement actually took place has been recognised in the Family Law Act 1996 s 44. This provides that where an engagement is relied upon as the basis for seeking orders under Part IV of that Act,[13] there must be produced to the court evidence in writing of the existence of the agreement to marry, or evidence by the gift of an engagement ring by one party to the agreement to the other, in contemplation of their marriage, or evidence of a 'ceremony entered into by the parties in the presence of one or more other persons assembled for the purpose of witnessing the ceremony'.[14] The aim of these requirements is to avoid lengthy enquiries into whether an engagement had, or had not been entered into.[15] But the section seems to leave room for dispute as to its interpretation. For example, does an engagement party constitute a 'ceremony', since the choice of this word might more naturally imply some kind of formal betrothal procedure?

In other contexts, no statutory test is laid down for proving that an engagement existed, but the court is likely to seek evidence of a similar kind as is required under s 44.

Property of engaged couples

Engaged couples acquiring property for use in their married life together are in a position little different from that of a newly married couple, and consequently the Law Reform (Miscellaneous Provisions) Act 1970 s 2(1) seeks to give them some protection, should their engagement be terminated, by enacting:

'Where an agreement to marry is terminated, any rule of law relating to the rights of husbands and wives in relation to property in which either or both has or have a beneficial interest . . . shall apply, in relation to any property in which either or both of the parties to the agreement had a beneficial interest while the agreement was in force, as it applies in relation to property in which a husband or wife has a beneficial interest.'

12 [1992] 1 FLR 357.
13 Non-molestation or occupation orders, discussed post, at pp 194–221.
14 Section 44(2)(b).
15 Law Com No 207 *Domestic Violence and Occupation of the Family Home* (1992) para 3.24.

In order to bring this subsection into play there must have been an agreement to marry and at least one of the parties to it must have had an interest in the property whilst the agreement was in force. It therefore follows, for example, that if the man purchases a house in his own name partly with money provided by his fiancée and they enhance its value by doing work on it, the use of her money and her contribution to the improvement of the house will give her the same interest in it as she would have acquired had the parties been married at the time.[16]

It is possible to interpret this provision in such a way as to give very extensive rights to the parties to an engagement. In one sense of the word, for example, an intestate man's widow could be said to have *rights* in relation to his estate: it could then be argued that the Act gives similar rights to the fiancée of a man who dies intestate. This was clearly not its intention[17] and it is highly doubtful whether any court would construe it so as to give a party rights in anything but specific items of property.[18] Indeed it is doubtful whether the subsection gives the engaged person much advantage that he or she would not otherwise possess. At common law a man who bought property with his own money and had it conveyed into his fiancée's name was presumed to intend to make a gift like a husband who had property conveyed into his wife's name.[19] Similarly, the legal position of a fiancée can scarcely be weaker than that of an unmarried cohabitant, and the courts have held that the latter, like a wife, may take a beneficial interest in property to the purchase of which she has contributed.[20] What is more important is that, in the case of engaged couples, as distinct from cohabitants, there is nothing comparable to the power to adjust rights in property that the court has on divorce.[1]

To enable parties to an agreement that has been terminated to settle disputes over property more expeditiously, either of them may bring summary proceedings under s 17 of the Married Women's Property Act 1882 within three years of the termination of the agreement.[2]

2.   GIFTS BETWEEN ENGAGED COUPLES

At common law a gift made by one party to an engagement to the other in contemplation of marriage could not be recovered by the donor if he was in breach of contract. This meant, for example, that if the man broke off the engagement

---

16 For the interests taken by spouses in each other's property, see post, Chapter 4.

17 See Law Com No 26, paras 35–42.

18 See *Mossop v Mossop* [1989] Fam 77, 82, [1988] 2 All ER 202, CA at 204.

19 *Moate v Moate* [1948] 2 All ER 486. See further post, p 124.

20 See post, pp 139–45. One significant difference is that an engaged person (unlike a mere cohabitant), who spends money on improving property in which the other party to the engagement has a beneficial interest may claim a share or enlarged share in the interest by virtue of s 37 of the Matrimonial Proceedings and Property Act 1970 (see post, p 128).

 1 *Mossop v Mossop* (supra). See also Law Com No 26, paras 35–42; Cretney (1970) 33 MLR 584. The Family Law Act 1996 s 53 and Sch 7 permits the court to transfer a tenancy of a dwelling-house from one cohabitant to the other when they have ceased to live together as husband and wife: see post, p 181.

 2 Law Reform (Miscellaneous Provisions) Act 1970 s 2(2). See further, post, p 118. The Law Commission recommended that this procedure be made open to cohabitants or former cohabitants (Law Com No 207 para 6.14), but this was rejected by Parliament. But note the impact of the Trusts of Land and Appointment of Trustees Act 1996 s 14 discussed post, p 117–18. Where a person relies upon a past engagement as the basis for seeking an order under Part IV of the Family Law Act 1996, he or she must seek the order within three years of the termination of the engagement: s 33(2) and s 42(4). See post, p 197 n 15.

without legal justification, he could not recover the engagement ring, but he could do so if the woman was in breach of contract.[3]

In conformity with the principle that the parties' rights with respect to property should not depend upon their responsibility for the termination of the agreement, s 3(1) of the Law Reform (Miscellaneous Provisions) Act 1970 provides:

'A party to an agreement to marry who makes a gift of property to the other party on the condition (express or implied) that it shall be returned if the agreement is terminated shall not be prevented from recovering the property by reason only of his having terminated the agreement.'[4]

Whether a particular gift was made subject to an implied condition that it should be returned if the marriage did not take place must necessarily be a question of fact to be decided in each case. Normally birthday and Christmas presents will vest in the donee absolutely, whilst property intended to become a part of the matrimonial home (for example, furniture) will be conditional. It is suggested that the general test to be applied should be: was the gift made to the donee as an individual or solely as the donor's future spouse? If it is in the latter class, it will be regarded as conditional, whereas if it is in the former, it will be regarded as absolute and recoverable only in the same circumstances as any other gift – for example, on the ground that it was induced by fraud or undue influence.

The engagement ring is specifically dealt with by the statute. The gift is presumed to be absolute, but this presumption may be rebutted by proving that the ring was given on the condition (express or implied) that it should be returned if the marriage did not take place for any reason.[5] One would have thought that by current social convention an engagement ring was still regarded as a pledge and that the presumption ought to have been the other way. As it is, the ring is likely to be recoverable only in the most exceptional circumstances, for example if it can be shown that it was an heirloom in the man's family.

If a gift in contemplation of marriage is made to one or both of the engaged couple by a third person (as in the case of wedding presents), it is, in the absence of any contrary intention, conditional upon the celebration of the marriage and must therefore be returned if the marriage does not take place for any reason at all.[6] A contrary intention will clearly be shown if the gift is for immediate use before the marriage.

It was formerly believed that the fact that an engaged woman would probably place the greatest confidence in her fiancé raised a presumption in equity that he had exercised undue influence over her with respect to any gift that she made to him or any contract or other transaction that she entered into at his request; consequently if she later sought to set the gift or transaction aside on this ground, the burden immediately shifted to the man to prove that there was in fact no such influence. But there is no presumption of undue influence between spouses: 'society's recognition

---

3 *Cohen v Sellar* [1926] 1 KB 536; *Jacobs v Davis* [1917] 2 KB 532. There is no direct authority for the position if the agreement was terminated otherwise than by breach, eg by agreement or death. It was generally assumed that the donor (or his personal representatives) could recover conditional gifts: see *Cohen v Sellar*.

4 This is an unfortunately worded provision. If the man behaved in such a way as to justify the woman in breaking off the engagement, he could not recover conditional gifts at common law. But as it is she who has strictly terminated the agreement, it is arguable that the statute has no application and he still cannot recover the gift: see Cretney, loc cit.

5 Law Reform (Miscellaneous Provisions) Act 1970 s 3(2). See further Cretney, loc cit.

6 See *Jeffreys v Luck* (1922) 153 LT Jo 139.

of the equality of the sexes has led to a rejection of the concept that the wife is subservient to the husband in the management of the family's finances'[7] and a similar approach is taken to engaged couples.[8]

C.   The contract of marriage

In order that a man and woman may become husband and wife, two conditions must be satisfied: first, they must both possess the capacity to contract a marriage, and secondly, they must observe the necessary formalities.[9]

1.   CAPACITY TO MARRY

In order that a person domiciled in England and Wales should have capacity to contract a valid marriage, the following conditions must be satisfied:

(a)   one party must be male and the other female;
(b)   neither party must be already married;
(c)   both parties must be over the age of 16; and
(d)   the parties must not be related within the prohibited degrees of consanguinity or affinity.[10]

Sex

(a)   Transsexuals [11]

The problem of gender-reassignment surgery – operations to effect a 'sex-change' – had to be considered in *Corbett v Corbett*.[12] The petitioner in this case was a

---

7 *Barclays Bank plc v O'Brien* [1994] 1 AC 180, [1993] 4 All ER 417, HL at 188E and 422f respectively per Lord Browne-Wilkinson. See post, p 125.
8 *Zamet v Hyman* [1961] 3 All ER 933, CA.
9 Where a couple come from different countries, or are married abroad, the question may arise as to which law is to be applied to determining these two matters. As regards the formalities for marriage, these are determined by the law of the place where the marriage is celebrated (the lex loci celebrationis). The position regarding capacity is more difficult, but is broadly based on the law of the parties' domicile (lex domicilii), though whether this depends exclusively upon each party's ante-nuptial domicile, or upon the intended matrimonial domicile, is problematic. For discussion, see the 8th edition of this work at pp 26–33.
10 A further prohibition is to be found in the Royal Marriages Act 1772, which was passed to prevent the contracting of highly undesirable marriages by the younger brothers of King George III. It provides that no descendant of King George II (other than the issue of princesses who have married into foreign families) may marry without the previous consent of the Sovereign formally granted under the great seal and declared in Council. Any marriage coming within the Act, consent to which has not been obtained, will be void; but if the descendant in question is over the age of 25 and gives twelve months' notice of the intended marriage to the Privy Council, it may be validly contracted unless both Houses of Parliament have in the meantime expressly declared their disapprobation of it. For a criticism of the Act and a discussion of how far (if at all) it has any force today, see Farran 'The Royal Marriages Act 1772' (1951) 14 MLR 53. See also Cretney 'The Royal Marriages Act 1772: A Footnote' (1995) 16 Statute Law Review 195.
11 See Edwards *Sex and Gender in the Legal Process* (1996) ch 1.
12 [1971] P 83, [1970] 2 All ER 33; applied in *R v Tan* [1983] QB 1053, [1983] 2 All ER 12, CA (person born male remains a man for the purposes of the Sexual Offences Acts notwithstanding a

man; before the marriage the respondent had undergone a surgical operation for the removal of 'her' male genital organs and the provision of artificial female organs. After dealing at length with the medical evidence Ormrod J (who was also a qualified medical practitioner) concluded that a person's biological sex is fixed at birth (at the latest) and cannot subsequently be changed by artificial means. That being so, the respondent, who was male at birth, was not a woman and the marriage was therefore void.

In this case the respondent was to be regarded as male by three independent biological criteria: chromosomal, gonadal and genital. There are persons, however, who are male by one test and female by another. Ormrod J deliberately left open the question of capacity to marry in such cases, but he was inclined to give greater weight to the appearance of the genital organs.

It has been suggested that from a social and domestic point of view the psychological gender of a transsexual (that is the sex to which the individual feels that he or she belongs) is of greater importance than biological sex.[13] Accordingly, as the parties to such a union regard themselves as belonging to opposite sexes (a view presumably shared by others), a marriage between them should be valid, at least provided that the transsexual party has undergone surgery of the type described. It has also been suggested that s 11(c) of the Matrimonial Causes Act 1973, which requires the parties to be respectively male and female, would now permit a court to take gender, rather than biological sex, into account.[14] It is very doubtful, however, whether this result could or should be achieved in this oblique way. The law relating to consummation emphasises that English law still regards marriage as a normal heterosexual relationship[15] and it is not certain that public opinion would yet support the change advocated.[16] The European Court of Human Rights has held that applying the approach taken in *Corbett v Corbett* does not constitute a breach of Articles 8 or 12 of the European Convention on Human Rights, although the court has recognised the hardship which transsexuals might

---

similar 'sex change operation'); and *Re P and G (Transsexuals)* [1996] 2 FLR 90 (Births and Deaths Registrar entitled to refuse to 'correct' birth entry of two male to female transsexuals to show them as being born 'female', on basis of the *Corbett* test). Also followed in *Lim Ying v Hiok Kian Ming Eric* (Singapore High Court), discussed by Tan 'Transsexuals and the Law of Marriage in Singapore' [1991] Singapore Journal of Legal Studies 509; but not followed by the New Zealand Family Court in *M v M (Marriage: Transsexuals)* [1991] NZFLR 377. For a comparison of the position in England and Wales with Australia, see Sharpe ' Anglo-Australian Judicial Approaches to Transsexuality: Discontinuities, Continuities and Wider Issues at Stake' (1997) 6 Social & Legal Studies 23.

13 See Kennedy 'Transsexual and Single Sex Marriage' 2 (1973) Anglo-American Law Review 112; Taitz 'A Transsexual's Nightmare: The Determination of Sexual Identity in English Law' (1988) 2 Int J of Law and Fam 139. But for the view that this, while providing a solution for individual transsexuals, ignores an underlying problem of social construction of stereotyped gender roles, see O'Donovan 'Transsexual Troubles: The Discrepancy between Legal and Social Categories' in Edwards (ed) *Gender, Sex and the Law*.

14 See Poulter 'The Definition of Marriage in English Law' (1979) 42 MLR 409 at 421–5. Section 11 of the Matrimonial Causes Act 1973 re-enacts s 1 of the Nullity of Marriage Act 1971, which received the royal assent 17 months after judgment was delivered in *Corbett v Corbett*. See further post, p 84.

15 See post, pp 87–91 and cf the judgment of Ormrod J in *Corbett v Corbett* [1971] P 83 at 106, [1970] 2 All ER 33 at 48.

16 An attempt to introduce a private member's bill (the Gender Identity (Registration and Civil Status) Bill) to permit transsexuals to obtain a 'recognition certificate' which would enable them to be re-registered in their chosen gender was not supported by the government in 1995 and did not progress.

suffer from an inflexible law and that social attitudes in Europe are changing, and has stressed the need to keep the law under review.[17]

(b)   Homosexuals

Transsexuals can obviously be distinguished from homosexuals; as Eekelaar argues:

'. . . the essence of the claim of the former is that they should be recognised in their new sexual identity and may wish to form domestic relationships with people holding the opposite identity. Homosexuals, however, may seek domestic relationships with people of the same sexual identity'.[18]

Attempts to allow homosexuals to enter into legally-recognised 'marriages' have been made in several jurisdictions. One approach is to change the law of marriage so as to remove the requirement that the parties be of the opposite sex.[19] Another is to create a new form of legal relationship, the 'registered partnership'. This enables a homosexual couple to register their union and achieve legal recognition thereby, although there may still be some distinctions drawn between their relationship and a full marriage, such as denying them permission to adopt a child together.[20] The recognition of any form of homosexual union would mark such a profound departure from the traditional approach of English law that it could be brought about only by an unambiguously worded statute.[1]

Monogamy

As a result of the English view of marriage as a monogamous union, neither party may contract a valid marriage whilst he or she is already married to someone else. If a person has already contracted one marriage, he cannot contract another until the first spouse dies or the first marriage is annulled or dissolved.[2] It follows that a mistaken belief that the first marriage has been terminated, for example, by the

---

17 *Rees v United Kingdom* (1986) 9 EHRR 56; *Cossey v United Kingdom* [1991] 2 FLR 492. See also *X, Y and Z v United Kingdom* [1997] 2 FLR 892 which concerned whether the refusal to register a female to male transsexual as the father of a child born to the transsexual and 'his' female partner by donor insemination, was a breach of Art 8. The European Court of Human Rights reiterated its view, expressed in *Rees* and *Cossey*, that while there is still a wide variation of views among member states on how far to give legal recognition to transsexuals, the UK's position, which stems from the *Corbett* reasoning, is not open to challenge.

18 Eekelaar 'Families and Children: From Welfarism to Rights' in McCrudden and Chambers (eds) *Individual Rights and the Law in Britain* (1994) at p 315.

19 This may come about by legislation, or by case law re-interpreting marriage statutes, as has occurred in the State of Hawaii, for example. See the discussion of *Baehr v Lewin, Baehr v Miike* 852 P 2d 44 (Haw 1993) by Katz 'State Regulation and Personal Autonomy in Marriage: How Can I Marry and Whom Can I Marry?' in Bainham (ed) *The International Survey of Family Law 1996* (1998) pp 494–504. For a failed attempt to reinterpret the law in New Zealand, see *Quilter v Attorney-General* [1998] 1 NZLR 523, discussed by Butler 'Same-sex marriage and freedom from discrimination in New Zealand' [1998] PL 396.

20 For consideration of legal approaches to the recognition of homosexual relationships, see Nielsen 'Family Rights and the "Registered Partnership" in Denmark' (1990) 4 Int J of Law and the Family 297; Dupuis 'The Impact of Culture, Society and History on the Legal Process: An Analysis of the Legal Status of Same-Sex Relationships in the United States and Denmark' (1995) 9 Int J of Law and the Family 86.

1 See *Fitzpatrick v Sterling Housing Association* [1997] 4 All ER 991, CA, where the majority of the Court of Appeal, while deprecating the courts' inability to permit a homosexual to succeed to his partner's tenancy under the Rent Act 1977 because of the wording of the legislation, and considering the law to be discriminatory and arbitrary, ruled that only Parliament could make the political judgment to change it.

2 But this does not apply if the first marriage was *void*: post, p 78.

death of the spouse,[3] is immaterial: what is relevant is whether it has in fact been terminated. Consequently, the second marriage may be void even though no prosecution for bigamy will lie in respect of it.

Age

Both by canon law and at common law a valid marriage could be contracted only if both parties had reached the legal age of puberty, viz 14 in the case of a boy and 12 in the case of a girl. If either party was under this age when the marriage was contracted, it could be avoided by either of them when that party reached the age of puberty; but if the marriage was ratified (as it would impliedly be by continued cohabitation), it became irrevocably binding.[4]

It is perhaps surprising that this remained the law until well into the present century. In the words of Pearce J:[5]

'According to modern thought it is considered socially and morally wrong that persons of an age, at which we now believe them to be immature and provide for their education, should have the stresses, responsibilities and sexual freedom of marriage and the physical strain of childbirth. Child marriages by common consent are believed to be bad for the participants and bad for the institution of marriage.'

This change of thought led to the passing of the Age of Marriage Act in 1929. Section 1 (now re-enacted in the Marriage Act 1949 s 2) effected two changes in the law. First, it was enacted that a valid marriage could not be contracted unless both parties had reached the age of 16, and secondly any marriage in which either party was under this age was made *void* and not voidable as before.[6] However, the problems identified by Pearce J do not seem to be affected by marriage age – the proportion of people marrying at a young age has steeply declined, while sexual experience among young people has increased in recent years.[7]

Prohibited degrees

Most, if not all, states prohibit certain marriages as incestuous. The prohibited relationship may arise from consanguinity (ie blood relationship) or from affinity (ie relationship by marriage). Before the Reformation, English law adopted the canon law of consanguinity and affinity,[8] but one of the results of the break with the Roman Catholic Church was the adoption of a modified table of prohibited

3 Or by the grant of a divorce decree or order which is void, eg *Butler v Butler (Queen's Proctor Intervening)* [1990]1 FLR 114; *Manchanda v Manchanda* [1995] 2 FLR 590, CA.
4 Co Litt 79; Blackstone *Commentaries*, i, 436.
5 *Pugh v Pugh* [1951] P 482 at 492, [1951] 2 All ER 680 at 687. See further Law Com No 33 *Nullity of Marriage* (1970), paras 16–20; Report of the Latey Committee on the Age of Majority 1967, Cmnd 3342, paras 166–177.
6 In Australia, a court may authorise the marriage of a person aged up to two years under the minimum age (18) in 'exceptional and unusual' circumstances: Marriage Act 1961 s 12 (as amended). For discussion of this provision meeting the needs of ethnic minorities, see Parkinson 'Multiculturalism and the Regulation of Marital Status in Australia' in Lowe and Douglas (eds) *Families across Frontiers* (1996) 309.
7 The proportion of women aged 16 to 24 who were married declined from 33% in 1976 to 8% in 1996: *General Household Survey 1976* Table 4.10 and *Living in Britain* (1996) Table 12.2(b). 'Almost all' women and men in this age group have their first sexual intercourse outside marriage: Wellings et al *Sexual Behaviour in Britain* (1994) pp 74–5.
8 See Pollock and Maitland *History of English Law*, ii, 383–7. The rules that emerged lacked theological or sociological justification and 'are the idle ingenuities of men who are amusing themselves by inventing a game of skill which is to be played with neatly drawn tables of affinity and doggerel hexameters': ibid, 387.

degrees. Since 1949 the prohibitions have been statutory and are contained in the First Schedule to the Marriage Act, as amended:

PART I

Mother	Father
Adoptive mother or former adoptive mother	Adoptive father or former adoptive father
Daughter	Son
Adoptive daughter or former adoptive daughter	Adoptive son or former adoptive son
Father's mother	Father's father
Mother's mother	Mother's father
Son's daughter	Son's son
Daughter's daughter	Daughter's son
Sister	Brother
Father's sister	Father's brother
Mother's sister	Mother's brother
Brother's daughter	Brother's son
Sister's daughter	Sister's son

PART II

Daughter of former wife	Son of former husband
Former wife of father	Former husband of mother
Former wife of father's father	Former husband of father's mother
Former wife of mother's father	Former husband of mother's mother
Daughter of son of former wife	Son of son of former husband
Daughter of daughter of former wife	Son of daughter of former husband

PART III

Mother of former wife	Father of former husband
Former wife of son	Former husband of daughter

(a)   Consanguinity

In the case of consanguinity, prohibition is based on moral and eugenic grounds. Most people view the idea of sexual intercourse (and therefore marriage) between, say, father and daughter or brother and sister with abhorrence; furthermore, the more closely the parties are related, the greater will be the risk of their children inheriting undesirable genetic characteristics. The degrees of relationship based on consanguinity are set out in Part I of the Schedule to the Marriage Act; marriage within these degrees is completely prohibited.[9] Because of the eugenic basis of the prohibition it includes not only relationships traced through the whole blood but also those traced through the half blood,[10] and it is immaterial that the parents of either of the parties (or of any person through whom the relationship is traced) have not been married to each other.[11]

Interestingly, the number of persons between whom marriage is forbidden is greater than those between whom sexual intercourse is a criminal offence under the Sexual Offences Act 1956,[12] although of course all the relationships set out in the latter Act come within the prohibited degrees.

---

9   Marriage Act 1949 s 1(1).
10   See the definitions of 'brother' and 'sister' in the Marriage Act 1949 s 78(1).
11   *Hains v Jeffell* (1696) 1 Ld Raym 68; *R v Brighton Inhabitants* (1861) 1 B & S 447.
12   Sections 10 and 11.

(b) Affinity

In the case of affinity, prohibition was originally based on the theological concept that husband and wife were one flesh, so that marriage with one's sister-in-law was as incestuous as marriage with one's own sister.[13] Today, the justification must be sought on social and moral grounds. (Some will also have religious objections to certain marriages,[14] but in a pluralist society this must be a matter for the individual's conscience.) Marriage with a near relation of a former spouse is always liable to create tensions within the family, particularly if the spouse is still alive, and the possibility of marriage to a stepchild could in some cases lead to sexual exploitation. Even if this were not so, difficulties could well arise if, say, a man were to become the brother-in-law of his other stepchildren and the stepbrother-in-law of his own children. There is a stronger reason for forbidding marriage with a stepchild to whom the other party has been in loco parentis, for this can readily be seen as an abuse of the relationship. In circumstances of this sort prohibition could be justified on the ground that the function of the marriage laws is to support the family and the relationships that uphold it. On the other hand, it must be remembered that degrees of affinity can be created only by marriage: there is nothing to prevent a man from cohabiting with his stepdaughter outside marriage or marrying the daughter (by another man) of a woman with whom he has himself been living.[15]

Wide dissatisfaction with the rules relating to affinity has been expressed for a century, and the restrictions have been gradually relaxed, most recently in 1986 by the Marriage (Prohibited Degrees of Relationship) Act, passed after the publication of *No Just Cause*, the report of a group set up by the Archbishop of Canterbury to consider the problem following four private Acts to permit marriage within the prohibited degrees.[16]

The present law represents a compromise between the conflicting principles mentioned above. The remaining prohibited degrees of affinity are divided into two groups, but in neither case is the prohibition absolute. The first group (set out in Part II of the Schedule to the Marriage Act) is retained in order to protect stepchildren against possible exploitation. A person may not marry his or her stepchild or stepgrandchild unless both parties have attained the age of 21 and the latter was not at any time before reaching the age of 18 a 'child of the family' in relation to the other.[17] 'Child of the family' is defined as a child who has lived in the same household as the other and been treated by the latter as a child of his or her family.[18] It will thus be seen that there is nothing to prevent a man from marrying his stepdaughter if, say, she was brought up by her grandparents so that he was never in loco parentis to her. The inclusion of the second group (set out in

---

13 For the same reason in the Middle Ages extra-marital sexual intercourse created prohibited degrees.
14 See Archbishop of Canterbury's Group, *No Just Cause, The Law of Affinity in England and Wales* (1984) pp 30–2.
15 For an example, see *Smith v Clerical Medical and General Life Assurance Society* [1993] 1 FLR 47.
16 See also Chester and Parry 'Reform of the Prohibition on Marriage of Related Persons' [1984] Fam Law 237.
17 Marriage (Prohibited Degrees of Relationship) Act 1986 s 1(1); Marriage Act 1949 s 1(2), (3) and Sch 1, Pt II, as amended by Sch 1 to the Act of 1986.
18 Marriage (Prohibited Degrees of Relationship) Act 1986 s 1(5); Marriage Act 1949 s 78 (as amended). The phrase 'treated as a child of the family' also appears in the definition of 'child of the family' in the Matrimonial Causes Act 1973 and is presumably intended to be interpreted in the same way: see post, pp 288–90.

Part III of the Schedule) is the result of a compromise between those who, like the majority of the Archbishop's group, saw no reason for prohibiting marriage with a son-in-law or daughter-in-law and those who feared that the possibility of such a union might give rise to sexual rivalry between parent and child and thus undermine family relationships. Consequently, a man may not marry his son's wife unless both his son and the son's mother are dead; similarly a woman may not marry her daughter's husband unless both the daughter and the daughter's father are dead. In addition, in either case both parties must be over the age of 21.[19]

2.   FORMALITIES OF MARRIAGE

Historical introduction

The history of the English law relating to the formalities of marriage – even the state of the law immediately before the passing of Lord Hardwicke's Act in 1753 – is still a matter of considerable doubt.[20] Canon law emphasised the consensual aspect of the contract and before the Council of Trent in 1563 no religious ceremony had to be performed: all that was necessary was a declaration by the parties that they took each other as husband and wife, either by a promise expressed in the present tense – 'per verba de praesenti' – (eg 'I take you as my wife [or husband]'), in which case the marriage was binding immediately, or by a promise for the future – 'per verba de futuro' – (eg 'I shall take you as my wife [or husband]'), in which case it became binding as soon as it was consummated. But it became customary for the marriage to be solemnised in church after the publishing of banns (unless this was dispensed with by papal or episcopal licence) and with the consent of the parents of either party who was under the age of 21. The marriage would then be contracted at the church door in the presence of the priest, after which the parties would go into the church itself for the celebration of the nuptial mass.[1]

The common law favoured such open ceremony, for upon the existence of the union might depend many property rights and the identity of the heir at law. But in the course of time the reason for the common law's preference for such a marriage was forgotten, and neither the publishing of banns nor the presence of any other witness was any longer considered necessary; the emphasis shifted to the presence of the priest (or, after the Reformation, a clerk in holy orders), so that eventually the rule was laid down that a valid marriage at common law could be contracted only per verba de praesenti exchanged in his presence.[2]

---

19 Marriage (Prohibited Degrees of Relationship) Act 1986 s 1(3), (4); Marriage Act 1949 s 1(4), (5) and Sch 1, Pt III (as amended).
20 See the conflicting opinions expressed in *R v Millis* (1844) 10 Cl & Fin 534, HL. See Swinburne *Spousals*; Pollock and Maitland *History of English Law* ii 362 et seq; the judgment of Sir W Scott in *Dalrymple v Dalrymple* (1811) 2 Hag Con 54; the opinion of the judges in *Beamish v Beamish* (1861) 9 HL Cas 274, HL.
 1 The marriage service of the Church of England still preserves this ancient form. The first part of the service takes place in the body of the church and consists of the espousals (in which each party replies 'I will') followed by the contracting of the marriage. This concludes the civil aspect of the marriage: the remainder of the service is purely religious in character.
 2 *R v Millis* (1844) 10 Cl & Fin 534, HL. There is little doubt that the decision was based on a misunderstanding of the medieval law: Pollock and Maitland, loc cit. See further Hall 'Common Law Marriage' [1987] CLJ 106 at pp 112 et seq; Lucas 'Common Law Marriage' [1990] CLJ 117. During the Commonwealth, marriages could be celebrated before Justices of the Peace.

But the old marriage per verba de praesenti was not wholly ineffective. Until the middle of the eighteenth century a marriage could be contracted in one of three ways:

(a) In church, after the publishing of banns or upon a licence, before witnesses, and with the consent of the parent or guardian of a party who was a minor. Such a marriage was obviously valid for all purposes.
(b) Clandestinely, per verba de praesenti before a clerk in holy orders, but not in church. This, as we have seen, was as valid as if it had been solemnised in church.
(c) Per verba de praesenti or per verba de futuro with subsequent sexual intercourse, but where the words were not spoken in the presence of an ordained priest or deacon. Whilst this would no longer produce all the legal effects of marriage at common law, it was nevertheless valid for many purposes. Such a union was indissoluble, so that, if either party to it subsequently married another, the later marriage could be annulled.[3]

Lord Hardwicke's Act

It needs little imagination to picture the problems which resulted from such a state of law. A person who had for years believed himself to be validly married would suddenly find that his marriage was a nullity because of a previous clandestine or irregular union, the existence of which he had never before suspected. Children could marry without their parents' consent, and if the minor was a girl with a large fortune, the old common law rule that a wife's property vested in her husband on marriage made her a particularly attractive catch. The 'Fleet' parsons thrived – profligate clergy who traded in clandestine marriages. By the middle of the eighteenth century matters had come to such a pass that there was a danger in certain sections of society that such marriages would become the rule rather than the exception.[4]

It was to stop these abuses that Lord Hardwicke's Act was passed in 1753.[5] The principle underlying this Act was to secure publicity by enacting that no marriage[6] should be valid unless it was solemnised according to the rites of the Church of England in the parish church of the parish in which one of the parties resided, in the presence of a clergyman and two other witnesses. Unless a licence had been obtained, banns had to be published in the parish church of the parish in which each party resided for three Sundays. If either party was under the age of 21, parental consent had to be obtained as well, unless this was impossible to obtain or was unreasonably withheld, in which case the consent of the Lord Chancellor had to be obtained. If these stringent provisions were not observed, the marriage would in the vast majority of cases be void.

Marriage Act 1823

Whilst Lord Hardwicke's Act effectively put a stop to clandestine marriages in England, it caused an almost greater social evil. For the new law was so stringent

3 *Bunting v Lepingwell* (1585) 4 Co Rep 29a. This rule was abrogated by 32 Hen 8, c 38, in 1540 but revived in 1548 by 2 & 3 Ed 6, c 23.
4 Stone *Uncertain Unions: Marriage in England 1660–1753* (1992).
5 Parker 'The Marriage Act 1753: A Case Study of Family Law-Making' (1987) 1 Int J Law and Fam 133.
6 Marriages according to the usages of the Society of Friends (Quakers) and according to Jewish rites were exempt from the provisions of the Act.

and the consequence of failing to observe it – the avoidance of the marriage – so harsh, that many couples deliberately evaded it by getting married in Scotland. This was particularly the case when one of the parties was a minor and parental consent was withheld; so that the 70 years following the passing of the Act saw an increasing number of 'Gretna Green' marriages. It was in an attempt to prevent this that the Marriage Act 1823 was passed to replace Lord Hardwicke's Act. A marriage was now to be void only if both parties *knowingly and wilfully* intermarried in any other place than the church wherein the banns might be published, or without the due publication of banns or the obtaining of a licence, or if they *knowingly and wilfully* consented to the solemnisation of the marriage by a person not in holy orders. In all other cases the marriage was to be valid notwithstanding any breach in the prescribed formalities. But if the marriage of a minor, whose parent or guardian had not given his consent, had been procured by fraud, the Attorney-General, on the relation of the parent or guardian, might sue for the forfeiture of any property acquired as a result of the marriage by the party who had perpetrated the fraud.

This Act remained the principal Act governing the formalities of marriage in England for over 125 years, although it was substantially amended during that time.[7] Two Acts in particular introduced principles which were so radically different from those of the Acts of 1753 and 1823 that they must be mentioned separately.

Marriage Acts 1836 and 1898

The principal criticism raised against the two earlier Acts was that they forced Roman Catholics and Protestant dissenters to go through a religious form of marriage which might well be repugnant to them. The growth of religious toleration generally during the early years of the nineteenth century eventually led to the removal of this grievance by the Marriage Act 1836.

This Act, together with the Births and Deaths Registration Act 1836, brought into existence the superintendent registrars of births, deaths and marriages, who were empowered to issue certificates to marry as an alternative to the publication of banns or the obtaining of a licence. But the real importance of the Act lay in the fact that it permitted marriages to be solemnised on the authority of a superintendent registrar's certificate (with or without a licence) in other ways than according to the rites of the Church of England. For the first time since the Middle Ages, English law recognised the validity of a marriage, which was purely civil in character and completely divorced from any religious element, by permitting the parties to marry in the presence of a superintendent registrar and a registrar of marriages and two other witnesses. The Act went even further by permitting places of worship of members of denominations other than the Church of England to be registered for the solemnisation of marriages; and it now became lawful for marriages to be celebrated in these 'registered buildings' in accordance with whatever religious ceremony the members wished to adopt, provided that at some stage the parties took each other as husband and wife per verba de praesenti in the presence of a registrar of marriages and at least two other witnesses. The Marriage Act 1898 permitted such marriages to be celebrated in the presence of a person

---

7 For example, jurisdiction to make an order dispensing with parental consent was extended to county courts and magistrates' courts by the Guardianship of Infants Act 1925 s 9, and it became possible to marry in a church which was the regular place of worship of one of the spouses, even though it was the parish church of neither: Marriage Measure 1930.

authorised by the trustees or governing body of the registered building, rather than a registrar, and such 'authorised person' was usually the minister of the particular denomination. The combined effect of the two Acts was therefore to permit ministers of all religions to solemnise marriages.

Marriage Acts 1949–1994

By 1949 the law relating to the formalities of marriage could be found only by reference to more than 40 statutes, quite apart from the case law which had grown up as the result of their judicial interpretation. The purpose of the Marriage Act 1949 was to consolidate these enactments in one Act.

The 1949 Act has since been amended by a series of Acts.[8] First, restrictions governing the place in which the marriage ceremony may be performed have been liberalised,[9] and secondly, the reduction of the age of majority to 18 by the Family Law Reform Act 1969 meant that anyone aged 18 or over may now marry without the consent of any other person.[10]

In addition to laying down the legal requirements relating to the preliminaries to marriage and the place and method of solemnisation, the Marriage Acts also regulate the registration of marriages.[11] Proper registration is of extreme importance not only to the parties themselves but also to others (including government departments) who may wish to have evidence of the marriage.

Marriages of persons under the age of 18

If either party to the marriage is over the age of 16 but under the age of 18, certain persons are normally required to give their express consent to the marriage or are given a power to dissent from it. The purpose of this provision is, of course, to prevent children contracting unwise marriages. Doubtless in 1753 Parliament was primarily concerned to see that property did not get into the hands of undesirable suitors; today the object is to cut down the number of potentially unstable unions.[12] Should the marriage be solemnised without consent, the damage will have been done; consequently lack of consent will normally not make the marriage void.[13]

---

8 The Marriage Act 1949 (Amendment) Act 1954; Marriage Acts Amendment Act 1958; Marriage (Enabling) Act 1960; Marriage (Wales and Monmouthshire) Act 1962; Marriage (Registrar General's Licence) Act 1970; Marriage Act 1983; Marriage (Wales) Act 1986; Marriage (Prohibited Degrees of Relationship) Act 1986; Marriage Act 1994.

9 The Marriage (Registrar General's Licence) Act 1970 permits a licence to be issued to authorise a marriage anywhere when one of the parties is suffering from a serious illness and cannot be moved; the Marriage Act 1983 permits a certificate to be issued to authorise a marriage of a house-bound or detained person in the place where he or she is confined or detained; and the Marriage Act 1994 permits the solemnisation of civil marriages in premises approved by local authorities: see post, pp 45, 44, 43.

10 Section 2(1) implementing the recommendations of the Latey Committee on the Age of Majority 1967, Cmnd 3342.

11 See Pt IV of the Marriage Act 1949 (as amended) and the Marriage (Registrar General's Licence) Act 1970 s 15. See Law Com No 53 *Report on Solemnisation of Marriage* (1973), Annex, para 104–118 for a critical review of the present law and for suggestions for reform.

12 Report of the Latey Committee (supra) paras 135–177; Priest 'Buttressing Marriage' [1982] Fam Law 40 pp 43–5. Such marriages are indeed more unstable than those entered into at a later age: 19% of marriages entered into by women aged under 20 between 1985 and 1989 ended within three years, and 32% within five years, compared with 7% and 11% of all marriages: *Living in Britain* (1998).

13 Law Com No 53, Annex, para 49. See post, pp 91–6. But this is not the case if the parent or other person publicly dissents on the publication of banns, which will then be void: post, p 86.

The law relating to those whose consent is required was extensively changed by the Children Act 1989. Normally it will be that of each parent with parental responsibility and each guardian (if any). Hence an unmarried father cannot withhold consent unless he has acquired parental responsibility by means of a parental responsibility agreement or order.[14] But if a residence order is in force with respect to the child, the consent required is that of the person or persons with whom the child is living or is to live under the order and not that of parents or guardians.[15] If a care order is in force, the local authority designated in the order must consent *in addition to* parents and guardians.[16]

If it is impossible to obtain the necessary consent or, more particularly, if the consent is withheld, the consent of the court may be obtained instead. The 'court' for this purpose is the High Court, a county court or a magistrates' court sitting as a 'family proceedings court'.[17]

The Law Commission recommended that the consent requirement be repealed, considering it 'illogical, easily circumvented or surmounted, and of doubtful benefit to the very children whom it is trying to help.'[18] It noted that there has never been a consent requirement in Scotland, yet the divorce rate for teenage marriages there was better than in England and Wales. Given the declining number of teenage marriages, this issue is likely to wither away eventually.

3.   CELEBRATION OF MARRIAGES

The rules governing celebration of marriage differentiate first between marriages to be performed according to the rites of the Church of England and the rest. For non-Anglican marriages, the rules then distinguish between whether the ceremony is to be according to another religion (in turn providing different requirements for religions such as Roman Catholic, Muslim, Hindu or Sikh on the one hand, and Jewish or Quaker on the other), or not. Finally, if the wedding is to be a civil one, the rules vary according to the place of celebration of the marriage. Civil weddings made up the majority (58.7 per cent) of weddings in 1996/97.[19]

Marriages according to the rites of the Church of England

A marriage may be solemnised according to the rites of the Church of England (which includes the Church in Wales)[20] only after the publication of banns or on the authority of a common licence, a special licence or a superintendent registrar's certificate.[1]

---

14 See post, pp 378–87.
15 If a residence order was in force immediately before the child reached the age of 16 but is no longer in force, the consent required is that of the person or persons with whom he lived or was to live.
16 Marriage Act 1949 s 3(1), (1A), and (1B), as amended and added by the Children Act 1989, Schs 12 and 15. If the child is a ward of court, the court's consent must be obtained: ibid, s 3(6). No consent is required at all if the child is a widow or widower: s 3(1), (3).
17 Ibid, s 3(5), as amended. For the meaning of 'family proceedings court', see ante, p 13. There is no statutory right of appeal from an order of the court giving or withholding consent: *Re Queskey* [1946] Ch 250, [1946] 1 All ER 717.
18 *Review of Child Law: Guardianship and Custody* (Law Com No 172 (1988) para 7.11).
19 ONS, *First data for marriages at 'approved premises'* ONS (98) 62 (1998).
20 Marriage Act 1949 s 78(2), s 80(3). A few technical provisions of the Act do not apply in Wales: see ibid, Sch 6, as amended by the Marriage (Wales and Monmouthshire) Act 1962 and the Marriage (Wales) Act 1986.
 1 Marriage Act 1949 s 5.

(a) Publication of banns

Publishing banns is intended to publicise the proposed marriage (so that, for example, a parent of a person under 18 could declare his dissent and thus render publication of the banns void). They must normally be published in the parish church of the parish in which the parties reside, or if they reside in different parishes, in the parish church of each of the two parishes.[2] If the parties wish to be married in another church or authorised chapel which is the normal place of worship of either of them, banns must be published there as well as in their parish churches.[3]

(I) MANNER OF PUBLICATION

Banns must be published on three Sundays normally during morning service by a clergyman of the Church of England.[4] The form of words is prescribed by the rubric in the Book of Common Prayer.[5]

(II) NAMES IN WHICH BANNS SHOULD BE PUBLISHED

Since the purpose of publishing banns would be defeated if the parties could not be identified, they must be referred to by the names by which they are generally known. This will usually be their original Christian names and surname, or in the case of a woman who has been previously married, her married surname;[6] but if a person has assumed some other name by which he is generally known, the banns should be published in that name.[7]

(b) Common licences

Licences dispensing with the necessity of the publication of banns have been granted since the fourteenth century. They are now known as common licences (to distinguish them from special licences granted only by the Archbishop of Canterbury) and may be granted by the bishop of a diocese acting through his chancellor or one of the latter's surrogates.

Unlike the publication of banns, for which no statutory declaration need be made, before a licence may be granted, one of the parties must swear:

(i) that he or she believes that there is no impediment to the marriage;

(ii) that either party has resided for 15 days in the parish or district, or that the

---

2 Marriage Act 1949 s 6(1). For details of exceptions, see the previous edition of this work at pp 45–6.
3 Marriage Act 1949 s 6(4), s 72.
4 Ibid, s 7 and s 9. A clergyman is entitled to a week's notice in writing before he publishes banns: s 8.
5 Ibid, s 7(2). 'I publish the banns of marriage between M of   and N of   . If any of you know cause or just impediment why these two persons should not be joined together in holy matrimony, ye are to declare it. This is the first [second, *or* third] time of asking.'
6 Per Sir R Phillimore in *Fendall v Goldsmid* (1877) 2 PD 263, 264. But see *Chipchase v Chipchase* [1942] P 37, [1941] 2 All ER 560 for an example of a long-deserted wife going by a name other than her married surname, with a consequent holding that there had been undue publication.
7 For an example of due publication under an assumed name, see *Dancer v Dancer* [1949] P 147, [1948] 2 All ER 731. See also *R v Billinghurst Inhabitants* (1814) 3 M & S 250. For the converse case of an undue publication under the original surname, see *Tooth v Barrow* (1854) 1 Ecc & Ad 371. For undue publication where a false name has been used to conceal a party's identity, see *Small v Small* (1923) 67 Sol Jo 277; *Gompertz v Kensit* (1872) LR 13 Eq 369. But if banns are published in a name by which the party is not known at all, there cannot be a due publication even though there is no intention to deceive.

church in which the marriage is to take place is the regular place of worship of one of them; and

(iii) if either of them is a minor, that all consents required by the Act have been obtained or dispensed with, or that the court has consented to the marriage, or that there is no person whose consent is required.[8]

Any person seeking to prevent the granting of a licence may enter a caveat stating the ground of his objection. In such a case the licence may not be granted until the caveat is withdrawn or the ecclesiastical judge with jurisdiction has decided that it ought not to obstruct the grant.[9] Although a caveat is rarely entered, the power to do so might be exercised, for example, by a parent who fears that his minor child may obtain a licence by falsely swearing that his consent to the marriage had been given.

(c)   Special licences

A special licence may be granted only by the Archbishop of Canterbury acting through the Master of the Faculties.[10] A special licence differs from any other authorisation to marry according to the rites of the Church of England in that it may permit the parties to marry at any time and in any place;[11] it is, therefore, the only way in which they may marry in a church or chapel in which their banns could not be published or for which a common licence or a superintendent registrar's certificate could not be issued.[12] In practice, special licences are granted only in exceptional circumstances.

(d)   Superintendent registrar's certificates

As an alternative to banns, or where a person is house-bound or detained, a marriage may be solemnised on the authority of a superintendent registrar's certificate, but not a certificate *by licence*.[13]

(e)   The solemnisation of the marriage

All marriages according to the rites of the Church of England must be solemnised by a clerk in holy orders of that Church in the presence of at least two other witnesses.[14] Except where the marriage is solemnised on the authority of a special licence, it must also be solemnised between 8 am and 6 pm.[15] The marriage must be solemnised within three months of the completion of the publication of the banns, the grant of the licence or the entry of notice in the superintendent registrar's marriage notice book, as the case may be.[16]

No clergyman is obliged to solemnise the marriage of a divorced person whose

---

8 Marriage Act 1949 s 16(1).
9 Marriage Act 1949 s 16(2).
10 The office of the Master of the Faculties is performed by the Dean of the Arches.
11 Marriage Act 1949 s 79(6).
12 But the marriage ceremony may be celebrated there after a marriage in a register office: see post, p 43.
13 Marriage Act 1949 s 17, s 26(2). See further post, p 41.
14 Ibid, s 22, s 25. The precise words of the ceremony need not be spoken by the parties and consent may be given by signs, eg in the case of a mute person: *Harrod v Harrod* (1854) 1 K & J 4. The marriage is probably contracted as soon as the parties have taken each other as husband and wife: *Quick v Quick* [1953] VLR 224 (Australia).
15 Ibid, s 4, s 75(1)(a). The wedding may take place only in one of the churches or chapels in which banns were published, or in the church or chapel specified in the common licence or certificate: s 12(1), s 15 and s 25(a), (d).
16 Ibid, s 12(2), s 16(3), s 33.

former spouse is still alive or to solemnise a marriage which would have been void before the passing of the Marriage (Prohibited Degrees of Relationship) Act 1986 because of the relationship of the parties. Nor can he be forced to permit such a marriage to be solemnised in the church or chapel of which he is the minister.[17]

Marriages solemnised otherwise than according to the rites of the Church of England

All marriages other than those celebrated according to the rites of the Church of England may be solemnised only on the authority of a superintendent registrar's certificate, either without a licence or by licence, or on the authority of the Registrar General's licence.[18] The difference between a certificate simpliciter and a certificate with a licence corresponds roughly to that between banns and a common licence, in that in the latter case the superintendent registrar is concerned with the residence qualification of one party only and the authorisation to marry may be obtained much more quickly. The Registrar General's licence corresponds to a special licence in that it enables the parties to marry elsewhere than in a register office, registered building or approved premises.

(a)   Issue of a superintendent registrar's certificate without a licence

Written notice of the proposed marriage must be given to the superintendent registrar of the registration district in which the parties have resided for at least seven days immediately beforehand, or, if they have resided in different districts, then to the superintendent registrar of each district.[19] The party giving the notice must at the same time make a solemn declaration in similar terms to that required for a common licence.[20] The superintendent registrar must then enter the details of the notice in his marriage notice book and display the notice or a copy of it in a conspicuous place in his office for 21 successive days.[1]

As with the granting of a common licence, anyone may enter a caveat against the issue of a certificate. The certificate may not then be issued until either the caveat has been withdrawn or the superintendent registrar or the Registrar General has satisfied himself that it ought not to obstruct the issue of the certificate.[2] If no

---

17 Matrimonial Causes Act 1965 s 8(2); Marriage Act 1949 s 5A (added by the Marriage (Prohibited Degrees of Relationship) Act 1986 s 3).

18 The Marriage Act 1949 does not expressly so enact, but this is its obvious intention and must be its effect. For arguments to the contrary, see Barton 'Irregular Marriages' (1973) 89 LQR 181 and Hall 'Common Law Marriage' [1987] CLJ 106. See also Thompson 'Irregular Marriages' (1974) 90 LQR 28.

19 Marriage Act 1949 s 27(1). For the matters which the notice must contain, see s 27(3), s 27A, s 27B, and s 27C (as amended). The marriage need not be solemnised in that district, however: Marriage Act 1949 ss 35–36 (as amended by the Marriage Act 1994 s 2).

20 Ibid, s 28. The superintendent registrar is entitled to demand written evidence that the consents required have been given if either party is a minor: Family Law Reform Act 1969 s 2(3).

1 Ibid, s 27(4), s 31(1).

2 Ibid, s 29. Where the objection is that a consent to the marriage of a child has not been obtained, any person whose consent is required may effectively prevent the marriage by the much simpler means of writing 'forbidden' against the entry in the marriage notice book, in which case the certificate may not be issued unless the consent of the court has been obtained: s 30. An objection that one of the parties is the other's stepdaughter, stepgranddaughter, stepson or stepgrandson and that the conditions permitting them to intermarry are not satisfied may be made by written statement to the superintendent registrar; he may not then issue the certificate until the parties have obtained a declaration from the High Court that the conditions are satisfied and that there is no impediment to the marriage on this ground: s 27B(4), (5). Either party may apply for a declaration even though no formal objection has been made.

impediment has been shown and the issue of the certificate has not been forbidden, the superintendent registrar must issue it at the end of the 21 days.[3]

(b)   *Issue of a superintendent registrar's certificate with a licence*

The law relating to the issue of a certificate with a licence is the same as that relating to the issue of a certificate simpliciter except in two important respects. First, notice is to be given to only one superintendent registrar – that of the registration district in which either party has resided for a period of *fifteen* days immediately beforehand.[4] The residence of the other party is irrelevant provided that it is in England or Wales.[5] Secondly, the superintendent registrar is not required to display the notice or a copy of it in his office, and, unless an impediment to the marriage has been shown or the issue of the certificate has been forbidden, he must issue the certificate and licence at any time after the expiration of one whole day after the giving of the notice.[6] Clearly, there is no effective way of challenging a proposed marriage in advance under this procedure.

(c)   *Solemnisation of the marriage*

A marriage on the authority of a superintendent registrar's certificate (whether by licence or without a licence) may be solemnised in a registered building; according to the usages of the Society of Friends or of the Jews; in a superintendent registrar's office; in approved premises; or the place where a house-bound or detained person is.[7] In any case the marriage must be solemnised within three months of the entry being made in the marriage notice book; and, unless it is a Quaker or Jewish marriage, it must also be solemnised between 8 am and 6 pm, with open doors and in the presence of at least two witnesses in addition to the superintendent registrar and registrar or, alternatively, the registrar or authorised person.[8]

(d)   *Religious marriages*

(I)   MARRIAGE IN A REGISTERED BUILDING

Any building which is certified as a place of religious worship[9] may be registered by the Registrar General for the solemnisation of marriages.[10] Bradney has suggested that relatively few buildings used by non-Christian faiths are registered, owing, in his view, to the stringent requirements for such registration.[11]

---

3 Ibid, s 31(2). Quaere whether he can revoke the certificate before the marriage is solemnised if he discovers some impediment (eg that one party is a minor and parental consent has not been given).
4 Ibid, s 27(2).
5 The Act specifically states 'whether the persons to be married reside in the same or in different districts' and thus implies that one of these two conditions must be satisfied.
6 Ibid, s 32. Hence, if notice is given on Monday, the certificate and licence may be issued on Wednesday.
7 Ibid, s 26(1) (as amended by the Marriage Act 1983 Sch 1 and the Marriage Act 1994 s 1(1)). The marriage of a house-bound or detained person may not be solemnised on a certificate by licence. For marriages in the Church of England on a certificate without licence, see ante, p 40.
8 Ibid, s 4, s 22, s 33, s 44(2), s 45(1), s 45A(2), (3) and s 75(1)(a) (as amended and added by the Marriage Act 1983 Sch 1). The requirement that the marriage must be solemnised with open doors does not apply to the marriage of a house-bound or detained person.
9 Under the Places of Worship Registration Act 1855.
10 See the Marriage Act 1949 s 41 and s 42, as amended by the Marriage Acts Amendment Act 1958 s 1(1), and the Marriage (Registration of Buildings) Act 1990 s 1(1). The marriage must normally be solemnised in the registration district in which one of the parties resides: s 34, s 36; but see s 35 for exceptions
11 Bradney 'How not to marry people' [1989] Fam Law 408.

A marriage in a registered building may take place only if there is present a registrar of marriages or an 'authorised person'[12] who will normally be a minister of the particular faith or denomination. The functions of the registrar (or authorised person) are to ensure that certificates (and, if necessary, a licence) have been issued, that the provisions of the Marriage Act relating to the solemnisation are complied with, and to register the marriage. The marriage may be in any form provided that, at some stage in the ceremony, a declaration is made similar to that required when the marriage is in a register office, and the parties contract the union per verba de praesenti.[13]

(II) QUAKER AND JEWISH MARRIAGES

The 1949 Act preserves the right of the Society of Friends to solemnise marriages according to their own usages. Provided that the rules of the Society permit it, a marriage may be contracted in this way even though one or both parties are not members of the Society.[14] The privilege of the Jewish community to celebrate marriages according to their own rites is also preserved. In this case, however, both parties must profess the Jewish religion.[15]

(e) Civil marriages

(I) MARRIAGE IN A REGISTER OFFICE

The parties may marry in a register office[16] in the presence of the superintendent registrar and also of a registrar of marriages. They must declare that they know of no impediment why they should not be joined in matrimony and then contract the marriage per verba de praesenti.[17] No religious service may be used in a superintendent registrar's office, but, if the parties so wish, the marriage there may be followed by a religious ceremony in a church or chapel. In this case the marriage which is *legally* binding for all purposes is that in the register office.[18] This provision is useful if the parties wish to be married in a private chapel in which banns may not be published (eg the chapel of an Oxford or Cambridge college) without being put to the expense of obtaining a special licence, or in a non-conformist place of worship which is not a registered building.[19]

(II) MARRIAGE IN APPROVED PREMISES

The Marriage Act 1994[20] gives effect to some of the proposals the government put forward in a White Paper in 1990, *Registration: proposals for change*.[1] The main

12 Ibid, s 44(2). A marriage conducted in breach of these requirements is void: *Gereis v Yagoub* [1997] 1 FLR 854; see post, p 82.
13 Marriage Act 1949 s 44(1), (3).
14 Ibid, s 47. This privilege was first granted by the Marriage (Society of Friends) Act 1860.
15 Marriage Act 1949 s 26(1)(d).
16 Which may be in a district other than that where the certificate or licence was issued: s 35, s 36 (as amended by Marriage Act 1994 s 2(2)), s 45(1).
17 Marriage Act 1949, s 45(1), s 44(3). The form of words to be used is: 'I call upon these persons here present to witness that I, *AB*, do take thee, *CD*, to be my lawful wedded wife [or husband].' A Welsh form may be used: s 52. As to marriages of mute persons, see *Harrod v Harrod*, p 40 n 14 ante.
18 Ibid, s 45(2), s 46.
19 The addition of 'approved premises' for the performance of weddings does not render this redundant, since such premises may not be used for religious services: Marriage Act 1949 s 46A(4).
20 See Barton 'Weddings to Go – the Marriage Act 1994' [1995] Fam Law 153.
1 Cm 939, following a Green Paper, Cm 531 (1988). On the latter, see Bradney, loc cit.

reform was to permit local authorities to give approval for certain premises to be used for weddings,[2] so that couples who do not want a religious ceremony may marry in more pleasant surroundings than those at many register offices. Guidance from the Registrar General explains that the Act is intended:

> '. . . to allow civil marriages to take place regularly in hotels, stately homes, civil halls and similar premises without compromising the fundamental principle of English marriage law and Parliament's intention to maintain the solemnity of the occasion.'[3]

'Premises' is defined in r 2(1) of the Marriages (Approved Premises) Regulations 1995 as 'a permanently immovable structure comprising at least a room, or any boat or other vessel which is permanently moored.' Marriages may not take place in the open air or on a moving vehicle, nor in a building with a recent or continuing religious connection. Thus, while a wedding could take place in the Brighton Pavilion, it could not be celebrated under the posts at Cardiff Arms Park; 'an old ironclad battleship'[4] would be suitable, but the Mersey ferry would not. Perhaps disappointingly, a marriage could not take place in a chapel in a stately home, even if the room is no longer used as such. Weddings at home are not permitted, and the provision of Las Vegas-style wedding chapels is unlikely to satisfy the requirement that the solemnity of the occasion be maintained. Over 2,000 premises have been approved, and weddings in them accounted for 5.6 per cent of all weddings in 1996/97.[5]

Only civil weddings may be performed in approved premises; the marriage must be solemnised in the presence of two witnesses and the superintendent registrar and a registrar of the registration district in which the premises are situated. There must be access to the general public, and each of the parties must make the same declaration and use the same form of words as are used in weddings in registered buildings in the presence of a registrar.[6]

(III)   MARRIAGES OF HOUSE-BOUND AND DETAINED PERSONS

The requirement that the marriage must be solemnised in a register office or a registered building (or now on approved premises) meant that a person could not marry on a superintendent registrar's certificate at all if he was incapable of leaving home or any other building (for example, a hospital or prison) where he happened to be.[7] As we shall see, the position was partly ameliorated by the provisions of the Marriage (Registrar General's Licence) Act 1970, but these apply only to those who are fatally ill. A complaint to the European Commission of Human Rights was made by a prisoner that Article 12 of the European Convention on Human Rights – the right to marry – had been infringed when he was refused permission to leave the prison to get married, and there was no mechanism to enable him to marry inside the prison.[8] As part of a friendly settlement of the case, the government introduced a wider relaxation in the Marriage Act 1983, which enables a house-bound or detained person to be married in the place where he is for the time being.

---

2 Inserting s 46A into the Marriage Act 1949.
3 *Guidance in pursuance of s 26(1)(bb) of the Marriage Act 1949* para 3.
4 ONS *First data for marriages at 'approved premises'* ONS (98) 62 (1998).
5 Ibid.
6 Marriage Act 1949 s 46B inserted by the 1994 Act.
7 Although it was not uncommon for a prisoner to be released for a short period to enable him to marry.
8 *Hamer v UK* (1982) 24 D & R 5; see also *Draper v UK* (1980) 24 D & R 72 (European Commission on Human Rights).

A house-bound person is defined as one who, owing to illness or disability, ought not to be moved from the place where he is and who is likely to remain in this condition for three months. A detained person is one who is detained in a mental hospital (otherwise than for short periods of assessment) or prison.[9] The marriage may take place only in the building where the house-bound or detained person is. It may take the form of a civil ceremony or a religious ceremony (including a ceremony according to the rites of the Church of England) but Quaker and Jewish marriages are unaffected by the Act. Unless the marriage is solemnised according to the rites of the Church of England (when the service must be taken by a clerk in holy orders), a registrar must be present and, if the ceremony is a purely civil one, the superintendent registrar must be present as well.[10]

(f) Marriages solemnised on the authority of the Registrar General's licence

Until 1970 the only way in which a person could be married elsewhere than in a church or authorised chapel, a registered building or a register office was on the authority of a special licence. Consequently, if he was unable to attend such a building and wished to marry (for example on his deathbed), he had to do so according to the rites of the Church of England, with a special licence. To overcome this difficulty the Marriage (Registrar General's Licence) Act 1970 was passed to enable the Registrar General to issue a licence authorising the solemnisation of a marriage elsewhere than in a register office, registered building or now, approved premises. But whereas a special licence can serve one of two purposes – to enable a person to marry even though he is too ill or infirm to be moved and to permit a wedding to take place for purely social reasons in a church or private chapel where the parties' banns could not be published – the Registrar General's licence is intended to serve only the first. Consequently, its issue is subject to two important limitations. First, the Registrar General must be satisfied that one of the parties is seriously ill and not expected to recover and that he cannot be moved to a place where the marriage could be solemnised under the provisions of the 1949 Act. Secondly, no such marriage may be solemnised according to the rites of the Church of England, for which a special licence may be obtained.[11]

These provisions were made largely redundant by the Marriage Act 1983 which enables a house-bound person to be married at home or in hospital, but there may still be occasions when the Registrar General's licence will be required: for example, Quaker and Jewish marriages cannot be solemnised under the 1983 Act, but they can be on the Registrar General's licence. Secondly, as the marriage of a house-bound person cannot take place on the authority of a superintendent registrar's certificate by licence, the Registrar General's licence will have to be sought if there is a danger that the party will die within the 21 days before the certificate could be issued. Thirdly, the wording of the statement under the 1983 Act, which the house-bound person's medical practitioner is required to sign before a certificate can be issued, implies that the house-bound person is likely to survive for three months.[12] If this strict interpretation is correct, a person cannot be

---

9 Marriage Act 1983 s 1 and Sch 1 (amending the Marriage Act 1949 s 78). If a doctor in charge of a mental patient believes that the patient could not give a valid consent to marry (see post, p 92), he may enter a caveat with the Superintendent Registrar: LAC (84) 9, para 9.
10 Marriage Act 1949 s 17 and s 45A (as amended and added); Marriage Act 1983 s 1(6).
11 Marriage (Registrar General's Licence) Act 1970 s 1.
12 'It is likely that it will be the case for at least . . . three months . . . that . . . he ought not to move or be moved from [the place where he is].'

'house-bound' if he is expected to die within that period. It seems unfortunate that the 1983 Act was not drafted so as to cover these cases and thus eliminate the need for the Registrar General's licence.

(g)   Marriages in naval, military and air force chapels

Part V of the Marriage Act enables certain persons to marry in naval, military and air force chapels certified as such by the Secretary of State for Defence. The purpose of this is to enable members of the Forces and their daughters to marry in garrison churches etc. Consequently, before a marriage may be solemnised in such a chapel, at least one of the parties must be a serving or former member of one of the regular armed forces or a daughter[13] of such a person.[14]

4.   PROPOSALS FOR REFORM

The present law relating to the formalities of marriage is still in principle based upon the provisions of Lord Hardwicke's Act and the Marriage Act 1836. It thus reflects the desire to prevent the clandestine marriages which were the disgrace of eighteenth-century England. In this respect the law is now hopelessly out of date. Clandestine marriages are no longer the social evil that they were at that time; nor does the modern law effectively prevent them. Provided that both parties are over the age of 18, a marriage can usually be solemnised on a common licence or a superintendent registrar's certificate and licence without the knowledge of the parties' friends or relations. The ease with which people can travel round the country and acquire a new residence makes it virtually impossible for the parents of a determined minor to forbid his marriage before it takes place. Another problem is presented by the speed with which the parties can rush into marriage without giving due thought to the implications of their act. A superintendent registrar's licence may be obtained in 48 hours and a common licence in as many minutes.

The law was reviewed by a Working Party set up by the Law Commission and the Registrar General in 1973[15] and again in the White Paper of 1990.[16] The earlier review (which was the more extensive) began by saying:[17]

'We have assumed that the purpose of a sound marriage law is to ensure that marriages are solemnised only in respect of those who are free to marry and have freely agreed to do so and that the status of those who marry shall be established with certainty so that doubts do not arise, either in the minds of the parties or in the community, about who is married and who is not. To this end it appears to us to be necessary that there should be proper opportunity for the investigation of capacity (and, in the case of minors, parental consent) before the marriage and that the investigation should be carried out, uniformly for parties to all marriages, by persons trained to perform this function. We suggest that the law should guard against clandestine marriages, that there should be proper opportunity for legal impediments to be declared or discovered, that all marriages should be publicly solemnised and that the marriage should be duly recorded in official registers. At the same time we recognise that a marriage ceremony is an important family and social occasion and we feel that unnecessary and irksome restrictions on its celebration should be avoided.

---

13 But not a son.

14 Marriage Act 1949 s 68, as amended by the Armed Forces Act 1981 Schs 3 and 5.

15 See Law Com No 53 (*Solemnisation of Marriage*), 1973.

16 *Registration: proposals for change*, Cm 939, following a green paper *Registration: a modern service*, Cm 531 (1988).

17 Law Com No 53, Annex, paras 4–5.

Moreover, since nearly every person who attains maturity marries at least once and attends numerous marriages of friends and relations and since the marriage creates a status which vitally concerns the public, the law of marriage should be as simple and easily understood as possible.'

They concluded that these aims could be achieved only if the superintendent registrar's certificate became the standard legal authorisation to marry.[18] This would ensure that any necessary investigations would be made by an officer trained to conduct them. Furthermore, the abolition of both common licences and superintendent registrar's licences would achieve some measure of publicity of the parties' intention to marry: the number of cases in which a licence is sought because of genuine urgency is apparently very small.

In the White Paper the government rejected the proposal to introduce a registrar's certificate as a universal preliminary largely because a working party set up by the General Synod of the Church of England had opposed it, but they agreed that the certificate and licence should be abolished. To meet the few cases of real urgency they recommended that the registrar to whom notice is given should be permitted to reduce the period before the certificate is issued.[19] The reports were at one in recommending that *both* parties should be required to give notice. This would mean that each would have to make a declaration about his or her own age, status etc, and might reduce the chance of marriage by a person who did not understand the nature of the ceremony or who was under some improper pressure. Both the Working Party and the government proposed that the person celebrating the marriage should be under a duty to ensure that both parties understand that they are entering into a monogamous marriage and, if their native tongue is not English (or Welsh, where a Welsh form is permitted), that they understand the words used. The government also made two proposals enacted in the 1994 Act: to permit couples to marry in districts other than where they currently are living, and to allow civil weddings in approved premises. They also recommended that the civil ceremony could be made less bleak by permitting additions 'such as poetry readings . . . provided that they do not detract from the dignity of the occasion'.[20] But the combination of complicated yet ineffective requirements remains the prevailing feature of the present system, and it is regrettable that the opportunity has not been taken to carry out a thorough overhaul.

D.   The recognition of foreign marriages[1]

1.   MONOGAMOUS MARRIAGES

An increasingly pluralistic society, comprising several communities with different ethnic and cultural heritages, and the growing mobility of people seeking work abroad means that it is likely that many marriages will be contracted abroad

---

18 But the Church of England could still retain the publication of banns (or the issue of a licence) as an additional ecclesiastical formality if it wished.

19 The Working Party recommended that only the Registrar General should have power to reduce the period in order to insulate the person exercising the discretion from pressure and to ensure a uniform exercise.

20 Readings would have to be approved by the registrar and no religious service should be used. See now s 46B(3) of the 1949 Act.

1 See Hartley 'The Policy Basis of the English Conflict of Laws of Marriage' (1972) 35 MLR 571.

by people who live, or later come to live, in this country. Such marriages may be contracted according to notions quite different from the definition of marriage formulated by Lord Penzance in *Hyde v Hyde*,[2] and the question arises whether such marriages will be recognised in this country.

It is clear that they will be where they do satisfy that definition. Although Lord Penzance referred to 'marriage as it is understood in Christendom', it must not be supposed that this is synonymous with 'a Christian marriage'. If the marriage satisfies the four conditions he laid down, it will be recognised by English courts even though neither party professes the Christian faith, provided that each had capacity by the law of the relevant domicile and they complied with the formalities laid down by the law of the place where the marriage was celebrated.[3]

Most cases dealing with the recognition of foreign marriages have been concerned with polygamous unions. It is still an open question how far English courts will recognise monogamous unions which fail to satisfy the other requirements laid down by Lord Penzance or which would have been void for some other reason if they had been contracted in England. It is submitted that the proper test to apply is that formulated by Simon P in *Cheni v Cheni*,[4] where he said:

> 'I believe the true rule to be that the courts of this country will exceptionally refuse to give effect to a capacity or incapacity to marry by the law of the domicile on the ground that to give it recognition and effect would be unconscionable . . . What I believe to be the true test [is] whether the marriage is so offensive to the conscience of the English court that it should refuse to recognise and give effect to the proper foreign law. In deciding that question the court will seek to exercise common sense, good manners and a reasonable tolerance.'

In that case the court recognised a marriage between an uncle and niece which was valid by the law of the parties' domicile (Egypt) even though it would have been void by English law because they were related within the prohibited degrees.[5] On the other hand, it seems unlikely that English courts would recognise a union between two persons of the same sex; and it is doubtful whether they would recognise a child marriage, at least unless the parties had ratified it when they were old enough to understand the nature and significance of marriage.[6]

2.   POLYGAMOUS MARRIAGES[7]

After *Hyde v Hyde*, the courts refused to recognise the validity of any marriage which did not satisfy Lord Penzance's definition,[8] which in practice meant the

2 (1866) LR 1 P & D 130. See further ante, pp 23–4.
3 *McCabe v McCabe* [1994] 1 FLR 410 (marriage according to Ghanaian customary law).
4 [1965] P 85 at 98–9, [1962] 3 All ER 873 at 882–3.
5 But would the court recognise a marriage if the relationship is regarded as criminally incestuous (eg between brother and sister)?
6 See Poulter 'Ethnic Minority Customs, English Law and Human Rights' (1987) 36 ICLQ 589, 610–11. The issue regarding same sex unions may arise sooner rather than later in the light of European developments concerning registered partnerships and the moves to permit homosexuals to marry in Hawaii (see ante, p 30).
7 See Law Com No 146; House of Lords, *Private International Law (Miscellaneous Provisions) Bill, Proceedings of Special Public Bill Committee* HL Paper 36, Session 1994–95, pp 30–5.
8 See *Re Bethell* (1888) 38 Ch D 220, and the remarks of Avory J in *R v Naguib* [1917] 1 KB 359, CCA at 360.

refusal to recognise polygamous unions. More recently, however, the attitude of Parliament and the judges towards polygamous marriages has become more liberal. Change has been hastened by the need to do justice to people who have immigrated to this country whose marriages are contracted in countries where polygamy is permitted. By 1968 Lord Parker CJ was able to say that a polygamous marriage is now 'recognised in this country unless there is some strong reason to the contrary'.[9]

Which marriages are polygamous?

Whether the marriage is to be regarded as monogamous or polygamous must initially be determined by the law of the place it was celebrated (lex loci celebrationis).[10] If that law prohibits polygamy (as English law does), all marriages celebrated under it must be monogamous.[11] Conversely, if it permits polygamy, any marriage contracted in that country by a person who is permitted by the law of his domicile (lex domicilii) to enter into a polygamous union will be polygamous.[12]

It was at one time believed that if a person whose lex domicilii forbids polygamy went through a polygamous form of marriage abroad, the marriage would be void by English law.[13] At first sight s 11(d) of the Matrimonial Causes Act 1973 appeared to give statutory effect to this principle by providing that, if a person domiciled in England entered into a polygamous marriage outside this country after 31 July 1971, the marriage was void. In *Hussain v Hussain*,[14] however, the Court of Appeal reached the opposite conclusion. The husband, who was unmarried and domiciled in England (and therefore was unable to contract a valid polygamous marriage), married in Pakistan a woman domiciled in that country. By Pakistani law a man may take a second wife but a woman may not take a second husband. The court held that, as neither party had the capacity to enter into a second marriage whilst that contracted in Pakistan subsisted, the latter was monogamous and therefore valid.

Hussain v Hussain went part way to removing an anomaly. It is not uncommon for members of ethnic minorities to return to their family's homeland to marry, and it would be unjust to recognise the marriage if the husband retained a domicile in, say, Pakistan but not if he had acquired one in England. On the other hand, if a woman domiciled in England marries in Pakistan a man domiciled there, the marriage would still be polygamous (because the husband may take further wives) and therefore void. This is clearly discriminatory, and the complexity of the law meant that parties could assume they were validly married and subsequently discover that under the recognition rules, they were not. The Law Commission therefore recommended that every man and woman domiciled in this country should have capacity to enter into any marriage which is de facto monogamous, even though it is celebrated in a form appropriate to polygamous marriages.[15] The

9 *Mohamed v Knott* [1969] 1 QB 1 at 13–14, [1968] 2 All ER 563 at 567.
10 *Hussain v Hussain* [1983] Fam 26, [1982] 3 All ER 369, CA.
11 See *R v Hammersmith Superintendent Registrar of Marriages, ex p Mir-Anwaruddin* [1917] 1 KB 634, CA; *Maher v Maher* [1951] P 342 at 346, [1951] 2 All ER 37 at 39.
12 *Risk v Risk* [1951] P 50, [1950] 2 All ER 973.
13 See *Re Bethell* (1888) 38 Ch D 220.
14 [1983] Fam 26, [1982] 3 All ER 369, CA.
15 Law Com No 146 *Polygamous Marriages: Capacity to Contract a Polygamous Marriage and Related Issues* (1985), paras 2.17–2.31.

Private International Law (Miscellaneous Provisions) Act 1995 accordingly amends s 11(d) of the 1973 Act,[16] and provides that:

'A marriage entered into outside England and Wales between parties neither of whom is already married is not void under the law of England and Wales on the ground that it is entered into under a law which permits polygamy and that either party is domiciled in England and Wales.'[17]

This provision applies to marriages contracted *before* the commencement of the Act, unless a party to such a marriage entered into a second marriage relying on the old s 11(d) rendering the first marriage void – an unlikely but possible event.[18] Another potential problem may arise where a husband whose marriage is valid by virtue of the 1995 Act later acquires a foreign lex domicilii in a country which permits polygamy, and contracts a valid second marriage under that law. For example, a Pakistani man, having lived in this country, returns to Pakistan and acquires a domicile there. Under Pakistani law, he could marry without divorcing his first wife, and his second marriage would be recognised in this country under the criteria set out above. His first wife would therefore find herself validly married to a man who has contracted a second marriage, perhaps against her wishes. The solution for such a wife, in the view of the Law Commission (and of Parliament) lies in divorce law, and not in further change to the recognition rules.[19]

Problems created by polygamous marriages

Although polygamous marriages are now generally recognised in this country, we must consider cases in which difficulty may still arise.[20]

(a)   Matrimonial causes

Hyde v Hyde established that matrimonial relief was not open to the parties to a polygamous marriage in this country. This was rigidly enforced for over a century, with the result that English courts would not entertain proceedings for divorce,[1] nullity,[2] or matrimonial relief in a magistrates' court.[3] This bar operated even if the marriage was de facto monogamous; consequently in recent years a large number of immigrants resident in this country but domiciled in, say, Pakistan or Nigeria found themselves unable to obtain any form of matrimonial relief here. Thus a wife, deserted by her husband, could obtain maintenance only by applying for social security benefits. Such a situation was clearly intolerable and the position

---

16 By the Schedule, para 2.
17 Section 5(1).
18 Section 6(2).
19 See House of Lords, *Private International Law (Miscellaneous Provisions) Bill, Proceedings of Special Public Bill Committee* HL Paper 36, Session 1994–95 pp 31–2.
20 Another point that has been left open in the past is whether parties to a polygamous marriage can be together guilty of conspiracy: *Mawji v R* [1957] AC 126 at 135–6, [1957] 1 All ER 385, PC at 387. There seems to be no reason why they should not be in the same position as parties to a monogamous marriage. For the position in relation to personal relief as a married man under the Income and Corporation Taxes Act when the taxpayer has more than one wife, see *Nabi v Heaton* [1983] 1 WLR 626, CA, where the Crown consented to an appeal from the decision of Vinelott J, [1981] 1 WLR 1052, and conceded that the taxpayer was entitled to relief with respect to his second wife. For the defence of marital coercion, see post, p 65.
1 *Hyde v Hyde* (1866) LR 1 P & D 130.
2 *Risk v Risk* [1951] P 50, [1950] 2 All ER 973.
3 *Sowa v Sowa* [1961] P 70, [1961] 1 All ER 687, CA.

was reversed by the Matrimonial Causes Act 1973 s 47,[4] which permits a court to grant matrimonial relief or a declaration concerning the validity of the marriage notwithstanding that it is polygamous.[5]

(b)   Rights in property

Problems with respect to rights in property are likely to arise only if the marriage is de facto polygamous. It has been held that one of two widows may apply for an order under the Inheritance (Provision for Family and Dependants) Act 1975:[6] obviously both could apply if necessary. The Family Law Act 1996 Part IV applies if the marriage is polygamous, whether de jure or de facto.[7] Although the Rent Act and the Housing Acts are silent on the point, it is submitted that two widows who have been living together require the same protection against eviction from the former matrimonial home as one does and that the husband's tenancy should vest in them as joint tenants after his death. Intestate succession[8] presents a more complicated problem: do both widows take the full statutory legacy each or as joint tenants or tenants in common? In fairness to other beneficiaries, they should not take more than the statutory sum in total, and it seems more just to divide this between them equally as tenants in common.[9]

(c)   Social welfare legislation

Refusal to allow benefit to a woman who had been married under a system allowing polygamy resulted in legislation to define the position of spouses in such cases. Entitlement to contributory or non-contributory benefits will usually depend upon the marriage being de facto monogamous,[10] but for income-related benefits, a reduced allowance is made for the additional wife (or wives).[11] The polygamously married husband is liable to support all his wives, thus reducing the burden on the Exchequer, but a balance is struck, when calculating entitlement, between keeping benefits fixed at a level set for the usual marriage form – a monogamous one – and preventing undue hardship to the actually polygamous household.

The truth is that English law, designed for monogamous relationships, cannot easily be adapted to deal with polygamous ones.[12] This is hardly surprising, for, as

4 Re-enacting Matrimonial Proceedings (Polygamous Marriages) Act 1972 s 1.
5 The Act implemented the recommendations of the Law Commission: Law Com No 42 (*Report on Polygamous Marriages*), 1971. 'Matrimonial relief' includes divorce, nullity, separation, and presumption of death and dissolution of marriage, orders on the ground of failure to provide reasonable maintenance, and for the alteration of maintenance agreements, ancillary orders in all such proceedings, and orders under the Domestic Proceedings and Magistrates' Courts Act 1978 and Pt III of the Matrimonial and Family Proceedings Act 1984 (maintenance after foreign divorce etc): Matrimonial Causes Act 1973 s 47(2), as amended by the two Acts mentioned and by the Private International Law (Miscellaneous Provisions) Act 1995 Sch, para 2. See also the Family Law Act 1986 Sch 1, para 14.
6 *Re Sehota* [1978] 3 All ER 385.
7 Section 63(5).
8 Discussed post, pp 875–81.
9 The personal chattels would have to be divided equally between them too.
10 See eg *Bibi v Chief Adjudication Officer* [1998] 1 FLR 375, CA (widowed mother's allowance).
11 See s 121 and s 147(5) Social Security Contributions and Benefits Act 1992 (as amended by the Private International Law (Miscellaneous Provisions) Act 1995 Sch, para 4); Income Support (General) Regulations 1987 reg 18; Family Credit (General) Regulations 1987 reg 46; *Din v National Assistance Board* [1967] 2 QB 213, [1967] 1 All ER 750.
12 See, for example, the problem of prosecution for bigamy, discussed in the previous edition at pp 65–6.

was indicated in Chapter 1, there is a continuing debate as to whether family policy should seek to lay down uniform rules, and privilege some, rather than other, relationships, on the one hand, or establish basic minimum norms, or countenance a variety of family forms, on the other. The issue of polygamy is merely an example of this tension.

E.   Presumption of marriage and declarations of status

It has long been established that, if a man and woman cohabit and hold themselves out as husband and wife, this in itself raises a presumption that they are legally married. Consequently, if the marriage is challenged, the burden lies upon those challenging it to prove that there was in fact no marriage and not upon those alleging it to prove that it has been solemnised. This may be important, for example, if the parties have been married abroad and have no written or other evidence of the solemnisation, or if the validity of the marriage is called into question indirectly when the parties can no longer give evidence, as it may be if the legitimacy of their children is put in issue after their deaths.[13]

1.   DECLARATIONS OF STATUS

With increasing international migration, many people living in this country have been married or divorced abroad. Occasionally the question of the marital status of a person in this position may be raised – for example, to determine whether he or she is free to marry here or can claim a pension or other benefit as the spouse or widow or widower of another – and legal machinery must be provided to resolve it. This is now done by s 55 of the Family Law Act 1986, which confers a power to make a declaratory order regarding marital status on the High Court and county courts.[14]

An application may be made for one or more of the following declarations:

(a) that a marriage was at its inception a valid marriage;
(b) that a marriage subsisted, or did not subsist, on a given date;
(c) that a divorce, annulment or legal separation obtained outside England and Wales is, or is not, entitled to recognition in this country.

It will be observed that there is no power to apply for a declaration that a marriage was void ab initio: in this case the correct procedure is to petition for a decree of nullity, when the court may make ancillary orders relating to children and financial relief.[15]

Although a declaration will normally be sought by one of the parties to the marriage, others may be legitimately interested in its validity. For example, the trustees of a pension fund may wish to establish whether a woman is the widow of a

---

13 For examples, see *Mahadervan v Mahadervan* [1964] P 233; *Re Spence* [1990] 2 FLR 278. For a full discussion, see the 8th edition of this work, pp 67–70.
14 See also s 63 (meaning of 'court'). These provisions implemented the Law Commission's recommendations in Law Com No 132 (*Report on Declarations in Family Matters*). Previously the power had derived partly from statute (going back to the Legitimacy Declaration Act 1858) and partly from the inherent jurisdiction of the High Court (which was abolished in this respect by s 58(4)). There was also a decree of jactitation of marriage which restrained the respondent from wrongfully boasting or asserting that he or she was married to the petitioner. Proceedings for jactitation (which were virtually obsolete) were abolished by s 61 of the 1986 Act.
15 Ibid, s 58(5)(a), (b). See post, pp 78–80 and Chapter 18.

former employee. Applications for a declaration may therefore be brought by anyone, but the court must refuse to hear a case if it considers that the applicant does not have a sufficient interest in the outcome of the proceedings.[16] In any event it may refuse to make a declaration if to do so would be manifestly contrary to public policy.[17]

A declaration is a judgment in rem and binds everyone including the Crown (which may be important if, for example, the applicant is seeking British citizenship or claiming the right to live in this country).[18] Consequently, the Attorney-General is to be given notice of an application and may intervene in any proceedings.[19]

2. JURISDICTION

The court has jurisdiction only if one of the parties to the marriage is domiciled in England and Wales at the time of the application or has been habitually resident in this country for one year before that date or, alternatively, if one of them is dead and he or she satisfied either of these conditions at the time of his or her death.[20]

F.   The effects of marriage

1. INTRODUCTION

When considering the legal effects produced by marriage, two issues arise. First, how does it affect the spouses' legal relationship vis-à-vis each other? Here, the common law doctrine of unity of the spouses, explained below, is important historically, but now has little continuing significance in the wake of the political and social movement towards sexual equality between men and women. Secondly, how far is the marriage relationship legally privileged over other domestic relationships, such as cohabitation? Here, one can see, in the face of a declining marriage rate and an increase in cohabitation and other family forms, a trend towards providing uniform rules to deal with people's relationships, regardless of their legal form, but, as will be seen, it is premature to argue that marital status is irrelevant to determining a person's legal rights and obligations.

2. THE DOCTRINE OF UNITY

The principal effect of marriage at common law was that for many purposes it fused the legal personalities of husband and wife into one. According to Blackstone:[1]

'By marriage, the husband and wife are one person in law; that is, the very being or legal existence of the woman is suspended during the marriage, or at least is incorporated and

---

16 Ibid, s 55(3).
17 Ibid, s 58(1).
18 Family Law Act 1986 s 58(2). But no declaration is to affect any judgment or decree already made: s 60(3).
19 Ibid, s 59 and s 60(2)(c); Family Proceedings Rules 1991 r 3.16(4). Other interested persons may also be required to be made parties: s 60(2)(b).
20 Ibid, s 55(2). This brings jurisdiction into line with that in nullity: see post, p 81.
 1 *Commentaries*, i, 442.

consolidated into that of the husband; under whose wing, protection, and *cover*, she performs everything; and is therefore called in our law-French a *feme-covert* . . . Upon this principle of a union of person in husband and wife, depend almost all the legal rights, duties, and disabilities, that either of them acquire by the marriage.'

The principle was enunciated in the *Dialogus de Scaccario* in the twelfth century and repeated by every leading common law writer since.[2] But it may be doubted whether this doctrine was ever a firmly established rule of the common law. For example, while it operated to prevent any action at common law between the spouses, if a tort was committed either by or against a married woman, both she and her husband were joined as co-defendants or co-plaintiffs to the action, and, if the husband predeceased the wife, she could still be sued or sue in person. In another context, a woman on marriage ipso facto acquired her husband's domicile but not his nationality.

Neither equity nor the ecclesiastical law accepted the doctrine of unity of personality, and both gave married women access to their courts and even permitted actions between spouses. But it was not until the Married Women's Property Act 1870 that a wife was given an extremely limited right to maintain an action in her own name in the courts of common law. Whilst a series of statutes culminating in the Law Reform (Married Women and Tortfeasors) Act 1935 substantially put a married woman in the same legal position as a single woman, they were typical of so much English legislative reform in that they created extensive exceptions to the old rules without abolishing outright the fundamental principle on which the anomalies were based.

The doctrine of unity was doubtless biblical in origin[3] but in time, it became the legal justification for subordinating the wife's will and acts to those of her husband, and the embodiment of patriarchy. It is doubtful whether the view that marriage as such creates a legal unity of personalities, irrespective of the social implications, survived the decision of the Court of Appeal in *Midland Bank Trust Co Ltd v Green (No 3)*.[4] A husband and wife were sued for conspiracy; it was argued that they could not be liable on the ground that they were one person in law and therefore could not conspire with each other. This defence failed. At first instance Oliver J concluded:[5]

'Unless I am compelled by authority to do so – and I do not conceive that I am – I decline to apply, as a policy of law, a mediaeval axiom which was never wholly accurate and which appears to me now to be as ill-adapted to the society in which we live as it is repugnant to common sense.'

The same sentiments were expressed in the Court of Appeal, where Oliver J's judgment was affirmed. Lord Denning MR expressed himself in these words:[6]

'Nowadays, both in law and in fact, husband and wife are two persons, not one . . . The severance in all respects is so complete that I would say that the doctrine of unity and its ramifications should be discarded altogether, except in so far as it is retained by judicial decision or by Act of Parliament.'

2 See Williams 'The Legal Unity of Husband and Wife' (1947) 10 MLR 16 at pp 16–18, and the exhaustive judgment of Oliver J in *Midland Bank Trust Co Ltd v Green (No 3)* [1979] Ch 496, [1979] 2 All ER 193.

3 Genesis 2, 24; Genesis 3, 16. See Fortescue *De Laudibus Legum Angliae* c XLII.

4 [1982] Ch 529, [1981] 3 All ER 744, CA.

5 [1979] Ch 496 at 527, [1979] 2 All ER 193 at 220.

6 At 538–9 and 748, respectively.

In more picturesque language Sir George Baker P said that to hold that a husband and wife could not be liable in the tort of conspiracy because they were one person:

> '... would ... be akin to basing a judgment on the proposition that the Earth is flat, because many believed that centuries ago. We now know that the Earth is not flat. We now know that husband and wife in the eyes of the law and in fact are equal.'[7]

Notwithstanding such statements, a residual notion of married couples as forming one unit can still be seen in the taxation system. Until 1990, the general rule was that husbands were responsible for dealing with the Inland Revenue and paying the tax owed by the married couple. Only in that year did it become the general rule that each spouse is responsible for making his or her own tax return and paying the tax assessed on it.[8] A married couple continue to be given an additional tax allowance, by virtue of their married state, which is not available to cohabitants. This replaced the 'married man's allowance', and may be payable to either spouse, or apportioned between them, although in the first instance it is still paid to the husband. While this might once have been justified as reflecting the economic reality that in many instances the husband was the main breadwinner in the family and the head of the household, it is nowadays endorsed by those arguing that marriage must be supported and encouraged for the stability of society.

3.   CONSORTIUM

The slow movement toward equality of the spouses was reflected by changes in the common law concept of consortium, an abstract notion which appears to mean living together as husband and wife with all the incidents (insofar as these can be defined) that flow from that relationship.[9] At one time it would have been said that the husband had the right to his wife's consortium whilst the latter had not so much a reciprocal right to her husband's consortium as a correlative duty to give him her society and her services – a view which was not entirely obsolete in the middle of the nineteenth century. A clear illustration of the wife's legal subjection to her husband can be seen in the old common law rule that a woman who murdered her husband was guilty of petit treason, like the vassal who slew his lord or the servant who slew his master.[10] The husband was also accepted at one time as having the right physically to restrain or confine his wife to the house,[11] and it was only in 1891 that this view was finally rejected. In *R v Jackson*[12] the wife had gone to live with relations whilst her husband was absent in New Zealand. After his return she refused to live with him again. Consequently he arranged with two men that they should seize her as she came out of church one Sunday afternoon. She was then put into a carriage and taken to her husband's residence, where she was allowed complete freedom of the house but was not permitted to leave the building. She then applied for a writ of habeas corpus and it was unanimously held by the Court of Appeal that it was no defence that the husband was merely confining her in order to enforce his right to her consortium. This principle was

---

7 At 542 and 751, respectively.
8 Finance Act 1988 s 32.
9 Per Lord Campbell in *Lynch v Knight* (1861) 9 HL Cas 577 at 589: 'conjugal society'.
10 The distinction between petit treason and murder was abolished in 1828 by 9 Geo 4, c 31 s 2.
11 And thus also physically to punish her. See *R v Lister* (1721) 1 Stra 478, *Re Cochrane* (1840) 8 Dowl 630.
12 [1891] 1 QB 671, CA.

reinforced subsequently by the Court of Appeal in *R v Reid*,[13] where it was held that a husband who steals, carries away or secretes his wife against her will is guilty of the common law offence of kidnapping her. As Cairns LJ said:[14]

'The notion that a husband can, without incurring punishment, treat his wife, whether she be a separated wife or otherwise, with any kind of hostile force is obsolete.'

The movement for the equality of the rights of the sexes gradually extended into the field of private law. In 1923 Parliament equated the rights of the spouses to petition for divorce;[15] in 1925 it established the principle that they have equal rights with respect to their children;[16] in 1967 it gave each of them the power to apply for an order regulating their rights to occupy the matrimonial home;[17] and in 1978 it gave them reciprocal rights to seek maintenance from each other.[18] All these changes reflect the modern view that the wife is no longer the weaker partner subservient to the stronger, but that both spouses are the joint, co-equal heads of the family. It seems to be clear that, insofar as consortium still exists, 'a husband has a right to the consortium of his wife, and the wife to the consortium of her husband',[19] and these rights must now be regarded as exactly reciprocal.

The incidents of consortium

Consortium connotes as far as possible the sharing of a common home and a common domestic life, but it is difficult to go beyond this and to define with more precision the duties which the spouses owe to each other. Nevertheless it is worthwhile to examine in more detail some aspects which have been directly or indirectly the subject of judicial decision.

(a)   Use of surname

Adults may use any surname they choose provided that there is no intention to perpetrate a fraud.[20] Most wives still take their husband's surnames on marriage, although they may continue to be known by their former names for professional or business purposes.[1] Likewise a woman usually retains her former husband's name after the marriage has been terminated either by death or by divorce, and a man has no such property in his name as to entitle him to sue for an injunction to prevent his divorced wife from using it unless, at any rate, she is doing so for the purpose of defrauding him or some other right of his is being invaded.[2] Similarly, an

---

13 [1973] QB 299, [1972] 2 All ER 1350, CA.
14 At 303 and 1353, respectively.
15 Matrimonial Causes Act 1923.
16 Guardianship of Infants Act 1925; see Cretney '"What will the women want next?"' (1996) 112 LQR 110. In point of fact, their position was not exactly equal until implementation of the Children Act 1989. See post, p 305.
17 Matrimonial Homes Act 1967.
18 Domestic Proceedings and Magistrates' Courts Act 1978.
19 Per Scrutton LJ in *Place v Searle* [1932] 2 KB 497, CA at 512.
20 The execution and enrolment of a deed poll merely provide evidence of the executant's intention to be known by a different name and have no other legal significance.
 1 Other countries take a much stricter approach and lay down firm rules to determine whose surname may be used, but this may amount to a breach of Arts 8 and 14 of the European Convention on Human Rights: see *Burghardz v Switzerland* [1995] Fam Law 71 (European Court of Human Rights).
 2 *Cowley v Cowley* [1900] P 305, CA; affd [1901] AC 450, HL; cf *Du Boulay v Du Boulay* (1869) LR 2 PC 430, PC at 441. Thus, if she holds herself out as his wife after he has remarried, she may be guilty of libel or slander if the reasonable inference is that he is not legally married to his second wife.

unmarried woman may use the surname of the man with whom she is living if she wishes, although she may be civilly or criminally liable if she does so for the purpose of defrauding another.

(b) The matrimonial home

It was at one time accepted as the duty of the spouses to live together as far as their circumstances would permit, and remedies were available to a spouse who found him or herself deserted.[3] In accordance with the view that the husband was the head of the household, the earlier opinion was that he had the right to determine where the matrimonial home was to be, and a judicial dictum to this effect is to be found as late as 1940.[4] Today, however, this, like other domestic matters of common concern, is something in which both spouses have a right to be heard and which they must settle by agreement,[5] or, failing that, ultimately by separation and divorce. We discuss later the avenues open to spouses seeking to control each other's occupation of the family home.[6]

(c) Sexual intercourse

As we shall see, each spouse owes the other a duty to consummate the marriage and (with certain exceptions) the incapacity of either or the wilful refusal of the respondent to do so will entitle the petitioner to a decree of nullity.[7] As regards sexual intercourse *after* consummation, Hale wrote in the eighteenth century:[8]

> 'But the husband cannot be guilty of a rape committed by himself upon his lawful wife, for by their mutual matrimonial consent and contract the wife hath given up herself in this kind unto her husband which she cannot retract.'

Although Hale cited no authority for this view, it was generally regarded as a correct statement of the common law.[9] But the change in attitude towards the relationship of the spouses during the present century led the courts to seek ways of limiting the scope of the husband's immunity,[10] and the issue was ultimately reviewed by the House of Lords in *R v R*[11] in 1991.

---

3 See the discussion in the 8th edition of this work at pp 118–20. Such remedies were largely ineffective with regard to bringing about a reconciliation of the spouses, and were used primarily as pegs on which to hang applications for financial relief.

4 *Mansey v Mansey* [1940] P 139 at 140, [1940] 2 All ER 424 at 426. See also *King v King* [1942] P 1 at 8, [1941] 2 All ER 103 at 110.

5 *Dunn v Dunn* [1949] P 98 at 103, [1948] 2 All ER 822, CA at 823. See also *McGowan v McGowan* [1948] 2 All ER 1032 at 1035; *Walter v Walter* (1949) 65 TLR 680; *Hosegood v Hosegood* (1950) 66 (pt 1) TLR 735, CA at 739.

6 See pp 65–9 and 199–211.

7 Post, pp 87–91.

8 1 Hale PC 629. But he could be guilty of aiding and abetting another to rape her: *Lord Audley's Case* (1631) 3 State Tr 401, HL; *R v Leak* [1976] QB 217, [1975] 2 All ER 1059, CA.

9 It was not until *R v Clarence* (1888) 22 QBD 23 that judicial doubts were expressed about its correctness.

10 A number of cases held that consent could be retracted following a court order or by the parties' agreement: *R v Clarke* [1949] 2 All ER 448 (consent withdrawn after decree of judicial separation); *R v O'Brien* [1974] 3 All ER 663 (decree nisi of divorce); *R v Steele* (1976) 65 Cr App Rep 22, CA (non-molestation injunction); *R v Roberts* [1986] Crim LR 188, CA (separation deed). In *R v Miller* [1954] 2 QB 282, [1954] 2 All ER 529 it was also held that a husband could not insist on his right to have intercourse by force, and thus would be guilty of assault on his wife. See also *R v Kowalski* [1988] 1 FLR 447, CA (husband guilty of indecent assault by forcing wife to submit to fellatio before sexual intercourse).

11 [1992] 1 AC 599, [1991] 4 All ER 481, HL.

The wife left the husband and told him that she intended to petition for divorce. Some three weeks later he broke into her parents' house, where she was living, and attempted to have sexual intercourse with her against her will. The trial judge ruled that the husband's immunity had been lost, whereupon he pleaded guilty to attempted rape. He then appealed to the Court of Appeal and, when his appeal was dismissed, to the House of Lords. Lord Keith, with whose speech the other members of the House agreed, maintained that the common law is capable of evolving in the light of changing social, economic and cultural developments. Marriage, he pointed out, 'is in modern times regarded as a partnership of equals and no longer one in which the wife must be the subservient chattel of the husband'. Consequently any reasonable person must now regard Hale's proposition as unacceptable.[12] The only obstacle to declaring that a husband had no immunity was the Sexual Offences (Amendment) Act 1976 s 1 which, for the first time, laid down a statutory definition of rape including the words '*unlawful* sexual intercourse'. This phrase usually connotes extra-marital intercourse[13] and consequently it could be argued that the Act had reintroduced the old common law rule by making it impossible for a husband to rape his wife in any circumstances. Lord Keith rejected this argument on the grounds that it was inconceivable that Parliament had this intention and that 'unlawful' in this context could not reasonably import the existing common law exceptions. The House therefore concluded that the word was mere surplusage and that 'in modern times the supposed marital exception in rape forms no part of the law of England'.[14]

The European Court of Human Rights subsequently rejected a complaint by R that the House of Lords' ruling was in breach of Article 7 of the European Convention because it had retrospectively criminalised his act, the court holding that the line of cases which had already eroded the marital immunity had rendered their Lordships' ultimate ruling reasonably foreseeable, and further that:

> '. . . the abandonment of the unacceptable idea of a husband being immune against prosecution for rape of his wife was in conformity not only with a civilised concept of marriage but also, and above all, with the fundamental objectives of the Convention, the very essence of which is respect for human dignity and human freedom.'[15]

Until the Family Law Act 1996, it could be argued that there remained a mutual right to, or perhaps legitimate expectation of, sexual intercourse after the marriage had been consummated, and that a refusal to have intercourse, or perhaps an unreasonable rationing of its frequency, might ground a petition for divorce based upon behaviour such that one spouse could not reasonably be expected to live with the other.[16] However, with the abolition by the 1996 Act of all forms of

---

12 At 483–4.

13 See *R v Chapman* [1959] 1 QB 100, [1958] 3 All ER 143, CCA.

14 At p 489. Section 1 was subsequently amended by the Criminal Justice and Public Order Act 1994 s 142 to delete the reference to 'unlawful' sexual intercourse. See also Law Com Report No 205 (*Rape within Marriage*).

15 *CR v United Kingdom; SW v United Kingdom* [1996] 1 FLR 434 para 42 (at 448–9). See Palmer 'Rape in Marriage and the European Convention on Human Rights' (1997) 5 Fem LS 91; Ghandhi and James 'Marital rape and retrospectivity – the human rights dimensions at Strasbourg' (1997) 9 CFLQ 17; Osborne 'Does the end justify the means? Retrospectivity, Article 7 and the marital rape exemption' (1996) 4 EHRLR 406.

16 *P(D) v P(J)* [1965] 2 All ER 456 (wife guilty of cruelty in refusing intercourse, although due to invincible fear of conception and childbirth) but cf *Mason v Mason* (1980) 11 Fam Law 143 (wife's refusal to have intercourse more than once a week was not behaviour such that the husband could not be expected to live with her).

matrimonial misconduct (which might include sexual behaviour) as grounds for founding a divorce or application for maintenance, it is difficult to argue that such a *right* or expectation still exists.

(d) Marital confidences

If a marriage breaks down, bitterness and vindictiveness may lead one spouse to break marital confidences and to broadcast information imparted and received on the shared understanding that it would go no further. Does the law offer the other any remedy in such circumstances?

As a general principle it now seems settled that, in the absence of a contract, three elements are required if an action for breach of confidence is to succeed:

(1) the information must have 'the necessary quality of confidence about it';
(2) it must have been imparted in circumstances importing an obligation of confidence; and
(3) there must be an unauthorised use of that information to the detriment of the party communicating it.[17]

It is clear that the relationship of husband and wife will satisfy the second condition. As Ungoed-Thomas J said in *Argyll v Argyll*:[18]

'There could hardly be anything more intimate or confidential than is involved in that relationship, or than in the mutual trust and confidences which are shared between husband and wife. The confidential nature of the relationship is of its very essence and so obviously and necessarily implicit in it that there is no need for it to be expressed.'

It is more difficult to predict whether the information in question will have 'the necessary quality of confidence' to satisfy the first condition. Information about the parties' sexual conduct will be protected;[19] to this might be added information about their health, financial matters or any other matter publication of which was not contemplated at the time it was imparted.

It is also probable that equity will assist the plaintiff only if he or she comes to the court with clean hands. An attempt to raise this defence was made in the *Argyll* case. Some two years after divorcing the plaintiff on the ground of her adultery, the defendant wrote a series of articles for a newspaper, some of which contained information relating to the plaintiff's 'private life, personal affairs and private conduct communicated to the defendant in confidence during the subsistence of the marriage'. The defendant argued that an injunction should be refused on the grounds that the plaintiff had herself published articles disclosing matrimonial secrets and that her own view of marriage, as exemplified by her adultery, could only be described as immoral. Ungoed-Thomas J rejected this defence, first because the defendant proposed to disclose much more intimate confidences so that his breaches would have been 'of an altogether different order of perfidy', and secondly because, however reprehensible the plaintiff's own adultery may have been, her subsequent conduct could only undermine confidence for the future and not retrospectively release the defendant from his duty to keep confidences already disclosed. An injunction was therefore granted

17 See *Coco v A N Clark (Engineers) Ltd* [1969] RPC 41 at 47, applying *Saltman Engineering Co, Ltd v Campbell Engineering Co Ltd* (1948) [1963] 3 All ER 413n, CA, and followed in *Stephens v Avery* [1988] Ch 449, [1988] 2 All ER 477.
18 [1967] Ch 302 at 322, [1965] 1 All ER 611 at 619.
19 *Stephens v Avery* (supra).

to prevent the defendant from divulging the confidences in question and the newspaper from publishing them.

However, it appears that it is no longer the fact of marriage which is the important factor in such cases. The courts may adopt a similar stance in relation to unmarried couples. In *Stephens v Avery*[20] Sir Nicholas Browne-Wilkinson V-C held that an injunction could be granted to prevent the defendant from disclosing to a newspaper details of the plaintiff's lesbian relationship with a third person which had been communicated and received expressly in confidence. He left open the question whether the relationship of unmarried sexual partners in itself creates a duty of confidentiality (so as to satisfy the second element necessary for a successful action for breach of confidence without an express undertaking)[1] or whether an earlier case, in which it had been held that a homosexual relationship did not raise such a duty,[2] was correctly decided. As the relationship of a man and woman cohabiting outside marriage can be as intimate and confidential as that of a married couple, it is submitted that confidences exchanged between them should be entitled to the same protection as similar confidences between spouses.

(e)   Evidence in legal proceedings

When one considers the question of testimony in legal proceedings, two principles of public policy may come into conflict. The first is the need to protect marital confidences and, more generally, to protect a person from having to give evidence against his or her spouse. The second is that in any proceedings, civil or criminal, no evidence should be excluded if it will help the court or the jury to arrive at the truth.

(I)   COMPETENCE

At common law neither the parties nor their spouses were competent witnesses in civil proceedings or (with very few exceptions) in criminal proceedings. A spouse's evidence was excluded for a number of reasons: the fact that it might be untrustworthy, the wish to preserve marital harmony and to protect marital confidences, and the undesirability of having a witness giving evidence against his or her spouse and the consequent unfairness of permitting evidence to be given for the spouse. In civil proceedings this rule was abolished by the Evidence Amendment Act 1853 and spouses became competent to give evidence for any party. In criminal proceedings, the Criminal Evidence Act 1898, which also for the first time made the accused generally competent to give evidence on his or her own behalf, enabled a spouse to give evidence for the defence subject to some qualifications. Various statutes also made the spouse a competent witness for the prosecution in the case of certain crimes, mainly of a sexual nature or against children.

The Police and Criminal Evidence Act 1984 s 80 made the accused's spouse a competent witness for the prosecution, the accused and any co-accused in all cases unless the husband and wife are charged jointly, in which case neither is competent to give evidence *for the prosecution* so long as he or she is liable to be convicted. Consequently, if one of them pleads guilty, he can do so because he cannot then be jeopardised by his own evidence.

20 Ibid.
 1 At 454 and 481 respectively.
 2 *M and N v Kelvin MacKenzie and News Groups Newspapers Ltd* (1988) (unreported) cited in *Stephens v Avery* (supra) at 456 and 482–3 respectively.

(II) COMPELLABILITY

Once spouses became competent in civil proceedings, the main reason for their not being compelled to give evidence disappeared. The Evidence Amendment Act 1853 accordingly made them compellable as well as competent.

The arguments against forcing a person to give evidence against his or her spouse in *criminal* proceedings are, however, more cogent.[3] The Police and Criminal Evidence Act struck a compromise.[4] For the first time the spouse was made a compellable witness for the *accused* in all cases unless the spouses are charged jointly. But he or she may be compelled to give evidence for the *prosecution* or a person jointly charged with the accused in only three cases. These are:

(a) if the offence charged involves an assault on, or injury or a threat of injury to, the spouse or a person under the age of 16;
(b) if the offence charged is a sexual offence[5] against a person under the age of 16; and
(c) if the offence charged consists of attempting or conspiring to commit any of the above offences or of aiding, abetting, counselling, procuring or inciting their commission.

However repugnant it may seem to force a person to give evidence against his or her spouse facing a criminal charge, in these cases the principle is outweighed by the need to enable the prosecution to produce evidence without which it would often be impossible to prove the offence. This will be effective, however, only if the witness is prepared to give evidence, and there is no doubt that a number of prosecutions, particularly of offences involving assault, are not brought because of the victim's unwillingness to testify, whether from fear or some other cause.[6]

The arguments for and against the compellability of spouses apply equally to unmarried couples and to other family relationships. In view of the current trend to bring spouses more into line with other witnesses, however, it is highly unlikely that the remaining exceptional rules would be extended to these other relationships.

(f) Interference with the right to consortium

At common law, because the husband was regarded as having a quasi-proprietary interest in the wife and her services, he could obtain damages against anyone who interfered with his right. This could take the form of enticement (a tort also available to a wife),[7] harbouring the wife,[8] or adultery. The last began as the common law action for criminal conversation[9] by which the husband could obtain compensation for the loss of his wife's comfort and society as the result of the adulterer's wrongful act. This action was abolished by the Matrimonial Causes Act 1857 and replaced by a statutory claim for damages in the divorce court which was almost always made on a petition for divorce. In addition, if the husband lost

3 See *Hoskyn v Metropolitan Police Comr* [1979] AC 474, [1978] 2 All ER 136, HL, and the critique by Edwards *Sex and Gender in the Legal Process* pp 202–5.
4 Section 80. See Creighton 'Spouse Competence and Compellability' [1990] Crim LR 34.
5 As defined in s 80(7).
6 See Edwards, loc cit.
7 *Gray v Gee* (1923) 39 TLR 429. This replaced an earlier writ of ravishment or trespass vi et armis de uxore rapta et abducta available only to the husband.
8 This was probably obsolete before it was formally abolished: see the judgment of Devlin J in *Winchester v Fleming* [1958] 1 QB 259, [1957] 3 All ER 711.
9 See Stone *Road to Divorce* Part IX.

his wife's services as the result of a tort committed against *her*, he could maintain a separate and independent action against the tortfeasor. This served a useful purpose: if, for example, the wife was seriously injured as the result of the defendant's negligence, it provided a means by which the husband could recover the expenses to which he had been put, such as for medical and nursing care, the provision of help to look after himself and the children, and visiting her whilst she was in hospital. But although a wife might be put to similar expenses if her husband was injured, the action was not available to her.[10] Actions of this kind came to be regarded as out-moded and patriarchal, and by 1982, had all been abolished.[11] However, more general provisions to compensate family members where a relative is *killed* as a result of wrongdoing were introduced by statute as early as 1846 by the Fatal Accidents Act (commonly called Lord Campbell's Act). This permitted certain dependants of a person killed as the result of the dependant's wrongful act, neglect or default to recover the financial loss suffered as a result of the death. The Act was extensively amended by further legislation in the course of the next 100 years, and eventually consolidated in the Fatal Accidents Act 1976.[12]

(g)   Contract

(I)   CONTRACTS WITH THIRD PARTIES

At common law a married woman had no contractual capacity and neither she nor her husband could sue or be sued on any contract made by her except as his agent. Equity did not take the same strict view, and if a wife had separate property, she could bind this by contract although she could not render herself *personally* liable on any agreement. To enable wives to carry on dealings with tradesmen for household goods, clothes etc, the law recognised them as agents for their husbands, and would enforce, against the husband, the pledging of his credit for the purchase of such articles. The agency device was particularly important for deserted wives with no means of support, who had what was called an 'agency of necessity', finally abolished only in 1970, which permitted them to incur debts against the husband's liability.[13]

Legislation gradually recognised the contractual capacity of married women. The Married Women's Property Act 1882 (which provided that all property acquired by a wife after 1882 should remain her separate property) gave a wife full contractual capacity and enacted that every contract entered into by her otherwise than as an agent should be deemed to be a contract with respect to her separate property and should bind it. Section 1 of the Law Reform (Married Women and Tortfeasors) Act 1935 provided that a married woman is capable of rendering herself and being rendered liable in respect of any contract, debt or obligation, and

10 *Best v Samuel Fox & Co Ltd* [1952] AC 716, [1952] 2 All ER 394, HL.
11 It is, however, possible to obtain compensation in tort for losses incurred where a relative gives up work or incurs expenses to care for a family member injured by the defendant's negligence, but in such a situation the nature of the relationship is immaterial, and damages would be payable whether it is a cohabitant, spouse, parents or other who gives up work to look after the injured plaintiff: *Cunningham v Harrison* [1973] QB 942, [1973] 3 All ER 463, CA; *Donnelly v Joyce* [1974] QB 454, [1973] 3 All ER 475, CA.
12 This in turn was amended by s 3 of the Administration of Justice Act 1982. These provisions are discussed post, at pp 902–5.
13 This agency was distinct from that pertaining while the spouses lived together, and was lost if the wife were herself guilty of a matrimonial offence. See further, post, p 715.

of suing and being sued in contract, and also that she is subject to the law relating to bankruptcy and the enforcement of judgments and orders as if she were a feme sole.

(II) CONTRACTS BETWEEN THE SPOUSES

An agreement between the spouses will clearly be enforceable if it represents a business arrangement, but the courts are not prepared to interfere in the running of the home by giving legal effect to the sort of arrangements that spouses living together make every day in order to regularise their domestic affairs. The leading case is still *Balfour v Balfour*[14] where the Court of Appeal held that an agreement, under which the husband, who was about to go abroad, promised to pay the wife £30 a month in consideration of her not looking to him for further maintenance, was unenforceable because there was no intention to enter into legal relations. If the spouses are cohabiting when they enter into the agreement, there is a presumption that they do not intend to be legally bound.[15]

Although public policy obviously demands that the courts should not be compelled to adjudicate on matters of domestic convenience, this principle can work injustice where the spouses subsequently separate and the wife takes no steps to obtain a maintenance order in reliance on her husband's promise to make her periodical payments. Consequently, its application should be strictly limited. The presumption does not operate if the parties have separated or are at arm's length and about to separate: in these circumstances their intention becomes a question of fact to be inferred from all the evidence. In most cases of this kind, where the agreement relates to financial arrangements, it will be almost impossible to conclude that they did not intend to be legally bound by the terms.[16]

(h) Torts

The fiction of legal unity produced two separate rules in tort:

(1) If a tort was committed by or against a married woman, her husband had to be joined as a party to the action and failure to do so could be pleaded in abatement.
(2) No liability in tort could arise between spouses and no action in tort could be brought by either of them against the other.

We must now consider how far these rules still apply.

A married woman was given the power to maintain an action in her own name to recover her separate property by the Married Women's Property Act 1870[17] and a full power to sue in respect of any tort committed against her by the Married Women's Property Act 1882.[18] But it was not until the Law Reform (Married Women and Tortfeasors) Act 1935 that husbands *qua husbands* finally ceased to be liable for their wives' torts in all circumstances. And it was only by the Law

---

14 [1919] 2 KB 571, CA. See also *Spellman v Spellman* [1961] 2 All ER 498, CA (agreement as to ownership of car unenforceable).
15 This appears to be the view of the majority of the Court of Appeal in *Gould v Gould* [1970] 1 QB 275, [1969] 3 All ER 728.
16 For further discussion of this issue, and for the separate question of pre-nuptial agreements, see post, pp 750 and 805.
17 Section 11.
18 See now the Law Reform (Married Women and Tortfeasors) Act 1935 s 1(c).

Reform (Husband and Wife) Act 1962 s 1 that each spouse was given the same right of action against the other in tort as though they were not married. This applies equally to an action brought after the marriage has been dissolved (or presumably annulled) in respect of a tort committed during matrimony,[19] but in one respect the law here is different, for if the action is brought during the subsistence of the marriage, the court has a discretion to stay the action in two cases. First, it may do so if it appears that no substantial benefit would accrue to either party from the continuation of the proceedings. This is designed to prevent trivial actions brought to air matrimonial grievances;[20] consequently, it is not contemplated that the power would be exercised if the parties were no longer living together as an economic unit and the damage was real, or if the spouse was a purely nominal defendant and the real purpose of the action was to recover damages from a source outside the family. Such would be the case, for example, if the driver of a car wished to claim an indemnity from his insurance company. Secondly, the court may stay the action if it relates to property and the questions in issue could more conveniently be disposed of by an application under s 17 of the Married Women's Property Act 1882.

(i)   Criminal law

The doctrine of unity never applied generally in the criminal law so as to make a husband vicariously liable for his wife's crimes or to prevent either of them from being liable in most cases for a crime committed against the other, but it does still have certain consequences which should be considered.

(1)   MARITAL COERCION[1]

There was a rule of common law that if a married woman committed certain offences in the presence of her husband, this raised a rebuttable presumption[2] that she had committed the crime under his coercion and consequently he and not she was prima facie liable to be convicted. Both the origin and the extent of this rule are uncertain, and it had become anomalous by the twentieth century. It was abolished by the Criminal Justice Act 1925 s 47 which replaced it with the following statutory defence:

'On a charge against a wife for any offence other than treason or murder it shall be a good defence to prove that the offence was committed in the presence of, and under the coercion of, the husband.'

In other words, this section changed the law by placing the burden of proof upon the wife to prove the coercion.[3] Coercion means something other than a threat of physical violence, which is a defence available to anyone charged with a criminal offence except murder and, perhaps, treason. It is apparently sufficient for the wife to show that her will was overborne by the wishes of her husband so that she is forced against her will to commit the offence.[4]

This defence must be strictly construed. Hence it is not available to a woman

19 Section 3(3).
20 See Ninth Report of the Law Reform Committee 1961, Cmnd 1268, paras 10–13.
 1 See Smith and Hogan *Criminal Law* (8th edn, 1998) pp 249–51.
 2 *R v Smith* (1916) 12 Cr App Rep 42, CCA; *R v Torpey* (1871) 12 Cox CC 45.
 3 On the balance of probabilities: *R v Shortland* [1995] Crim LR 893.
 4 Ibid.

cohabiting with a man outside marriage[5] or to a woman who mistakenly believes that she is married to the man applying coercion.[6]

(II)   CONSPIRACY

It is now provided by statute that a husband and wife may not be convicted of conspiring together, and it is generally believed that this was the position at common law.[7] But this does not prevent them from being convicted of conspiring with the other and a third person.[8]

(III)   THEFT

Under the doctrine of unity husband and wife were deemed to have unity of possession, so that neither could be guilty of stealing the other's property. But once the concept of separate property had been extended by the Married Women's Property Act 1882, it was obvious that the fiction once more worked an anomaly. Under the current law, for the purposes of the Theft Acts, a husband and wife are to be regarded as separate persons and each can now be convicted of theft of the other's property, obtaining it by deception and so forth.[9] But neither the spouse nor a third person may usually institute proceedings against anyone for any offence of stealing or doing unlawful damage to property which at the time belongs to the accused's spouse, or for any attempt, incitement or conspiracy to commit such an offence, without the consent of the Director of Public Prosecutions. The purpose of this provision is to reduce the risk of a prosecution which might prejudice a continuation of married life.

(j)   'Matrimonial home rights'[10]

(I)   BACKGROUND

If the spouses are joint tenants in law or if both of them have a beneficial interest in the matrimonial home, each will prima facie be entitled to occupy it as owner, and have equal rights to stay in the property or seek to dispose of it. If the legal and equitable title is vested in the husband alone, the wife can claim a common law right of occupation by virtue of her right to her husband's consortium and her right to be maintained by him, which right is primarily discharged by his providing her with a home.[11] However, in *National Provincial Bank Ltd v Ainsworth*[12] the House of Lords rejected a series of cases decided between 1952 and 1965 which had created the so-called 'deserted wives' equity' under which it had been held that a

---

5 *R v Court* (1912) 7 Cr App Rep 127, CCA.
6 *R v Ditta, Hussain and Kara* [1988] Crim LR 42, CA. The court also queried, obiter, whether a wife could raise the defence if the marriage were polygamous.
7 Criminal Law Act 1977 s 2(2)(a). Either spouse may be convicted of inciting the other to commit a crime.
8 *R v Chrastny* [1992] 1 All ER 189, CA.
9 Theft Act 1968 s 30(1); Theft Act 1978 s 5(2). Either of them may also be guilty of the theft of property belonging to them both jointly.
10 See Horton *Family Homes and Domestic Violence: The New Legislation* (1996) ch 5; La Follette and Purdie *A Guide to the Family Law Act 1996* (1996) ch 7.
11 See *Price v Price* [1951] P 413 at 420–1, CA; *W v W (No 2)* [1954] P 486 at 515–16, [1954] 2 All ER 829, CA at 840. Husbands had the same right where the wife was sole legal and equitable owner, arising from the wife's duty to cohabit with the husband: *Shipman v Shipman* [1924] 2 Ch 140, CA.
12 [1965] AC 1175, [1965] 2 All ER 472, HL.

deserted wife could assert her common law right to remain in the matrimonial home not only against her husband, but also against third parties. They ruled that, where the husband had left the wife and children in the matrimonial home, and then conveyed it to a company in which he had a controlling interest, which in turn charged the home to the appellant bank as security for a loan, the wife's interest in remaining in the home could not prevail against the creditors' interest in realising their security in the property.[13]

The Matrimonial Homes Act 1967 was enacted to improve the position of such 'deserted wives' by clarifying what rights to occupy the home arise on marriage, and by providing a mechanism whereby third parties could be bound by spousal rights. The legislation, which laid down 'rights of occupation' was amended and consolidated,[14] and is now contained in Part IV of the Family Law Act 1996, which adopts slightly different terminology, now referring to 'matrimonial home rights'.

(II)   THE DEFINITION OF 'MATRIMONIAL HOME RIGHTS'

By s 30(1) and (2) of the 1996 Act, if

'(a) one spouse is entitled to occupy a dwelling-house by virtue of –
   (i) a beneficial estate or interest or contract; or
   (ii) any enactment giving that spouse the right to remain in occupation; and
(b) the other spouse is not so entitled,
...
the spouse not so entitled has the following rights ("matrimonial home rights") –
(a) if in occupation, a right not to be evicted or excluded from the dwelling-house or any part of it by the other spouse except with the leave of the court given by an order under s 33;[15]
(b) if not in occupation, a right with the leave of the court so given to enter into and occupy the dwelling-house.'

One spouse entitled to occupy   Matrimonial home rights only arise where one of the spouses is entitled to occupy the dwelling-house. Such entitlement may be by virtue of a beneficial estate or interest, contractual right or a statutory right. Where entitlement depends upon an estate or interest, any right to possession conferred on a mortgagee under or by virtue of the mortgage, is disregarded.[16] A spouse who lives in a house because he is a lodger or domestic servant will have a contractual right to occupy, while a statutory tenant under the Rent Acts[17] will have a statutory right.

Other spouse not entitled   Where the other spouse in fact has an equitable interest in the dwelling-house, she is to be treated as *not* having such an interest for the purpose of establishing her matrimonial home rights.[18] This enables her to take advantage of the protection offered by s 30 and s 31 in the event of a sale of the property by the husband.

13 In many cases, the wife could have the sale set aside as a transaction intended to defeat her claim for financial relief in divorce proceedings (see post, p 861) but the argument failed in *Ainsworth* as against the Bank, because the Bank was a bona fide purchaser for value without notice of the husband's intention.
14 Matrimonial Homes Act 1983.
15 See post, pp 199–202.
16 Section 54(1)(2).
17 See post, pp 172–4.
18 Section 30(9).

Dwelling-house   Section 63 provides that 'dwelling-house' includes

'(a) any building, or part of a building which is occupied as a dwelling,[19]
(b) any caravan, house-boat or structure occupied as a dwelling,
and any yard, garden, garage or outhouse belonging to it and occupied with it.'[20]

The dwelling-house must have been, or been intended by the spouses to be, a matrimonial home of theirs.[1] This means that where, for example, a property has been bought by one spouse, with the intention that it will be the matrimonial home, but the parties separate before they move into it, the non-entitled spouse may claim matrimonial home rights in respect of it. Similarly, if the spouses live in a town house and have a country cottage, each property may be a dwelling-house in respect of which matrimonial home rights may arise.[2] On the other hand, if the spouses live in one home, and rent out another, never intending to live in it, matrimonial home rights do not exist in respect of the rented-out property,[3] nor do they arise in respect of property acquired by one spouse for him- or herself to live in subsequent to their separation.

(III)   THE EFFECT OF HAVING MATRIMONIAL HOME RIGHTS

Where a spouse has rights under s 30, he or she cannot be excluded from the dwelling-house by the other spouse except by a court order[4] and, where not currently in occupation, may be given the right to enter by order. In either case, the order to be sought is an occupation order under s 33 of the Act, and the spouse is an 'entitled applicant' for the purposes of that section.[5]

Where the entitled spouse leaves home and stops paying the mortgage, rent or other outgoings, the spouse with matrimonial home rights has the right to keep up the payments in order to preserve his or her occupation and prevent the mortgagee or landlord from seeking possession.[6] Should possession proceedings be instituted by a mortgagee, the latter spouse has the right to be joined as a party to the proceedings, provided the court is satisfied that he or she can meet the payments and liabilities under the mortgage, the application to be joined as a party is made before the action is finally disposed of, and the court sees no special reason against joining the spouse in the action.[7] A similar right to resist possession proceedings is given where the dwelling-house is held under a secure or assured tenancy.[8]

---

19 In *Kinzler v Kinzler* [1985] Fam Law 26, CA, it was held that the whole of a hotel owned by the parties, and not just their living quarters, was the matrimonial home, because there was only one front door and one kitchen.
20 Para (b) does not apply where matrimonial home rights are being asserted against third parties under s 31: s 63(4).
1 Section 30(7).
2 But a spouse may only register rights against one home at a time: see post, p 68.
3 See *Collins v Collins* (1973) 4 Fam Law 133, CA, for an example.
4 '[T]he right is in essence a personal and non-assignable statutory right not to be evicted from the matrimonial home in question during marriage or until the court otherwise orders' per Megarry J in *Wroth v Tyler* [1974] Ch 30 at 46G.
5 See post, p 199.
6 Section 30(3)–(6).
7 Section 55(2), (3). Note that a former spouse, cohabitant or former cohabitant who is granted an occupation order under Part IV has the same right: s 55(3)(a).
8 Housing Act 1985 s 85(5); Housing Act 1988 s 9(5). The right extends to those other than spouses, who have an occupation order in their favour: Family Law Act 1996 Sch 8, paras 53, 59.

(IV)   REGISTRATION OF MATRIMONIAL HOME RIGHTS

The main aim in enacting the original Matrimonial Homes Act 1967 was to strike a balance between protecting a non-entitled spouse from eviction and ensuring that those who *bona fide* acquired rights in the dwelling-house from her husband should not be prevented from enjoying those rights. The mechanism chosen to achieve this balance was by enabling, and requiring, the non-entitled spouse to register her rights as a charge on the dwelling-house where that was held by virtue of an estate or interest.

Section 31 of the 1996 Act provides that a spouse's matrimonial home rights are a charge on the estate or interest, with the same priority as if it were an equitable interest created at whichever is the latest of the following dates – the date on which the entitled spouse acquired the estate or interest, the date of the marriage, or 1 January 1968.[9] To bind a third party, the charge *must* be registered.[10] In the case of registered land, this is done by means of a notice under the Land Registration Act 1925.[11] Where the title is unregistered, registration is achieved by means of a Class F land charge under the Land Charges Act 1972.[12] The charge will bind any person deriving title under the other spouse, except that it will be void against any purchaser of the land or any interest in it for value if it is not registered before completion.[13] As a spouse out of occupation may need even greater protection than one physically in the house, her charge may be registered even though she has not yet been given leave by the court to enter and occupy.[14]

A spouse is entitled to have only one charge registered at a time. Consequently, if the spouses have two homes, she must decide against which one she will register her charge. If, after registering one, she registers another, the first registration must be cancelled.[15]

(V)   DURATION OF MATRIMONIAL HOME RIGHTS

Matrimonial home rights will usually come to an end on the other spouse's death or on the dissolution or annulment of the marriage, unless the court has ordered that they should continue after the termination of the marriage (whether by death or a court order).[16] Rights will also come to an end if the owning spouse disposes of his estate or interest in the home, unless they have been registered and hence are binding upon the purchaser.[17] It may be advisable to seek an order extending rights beyond the termination of the marriage, as this may be the only way of protecting

---

9   Section 31(2), (3). The last of these is the date the Matrimonial Homes Act 1967 came into force. Where the matrimonial home rights are a charge on the interest of the other spouse under a trust, and there is or could be no other beneficiary under the trust, they are a charge also on the estate or interests of the trustees: s 31(5).

10   But for discussion of the development of the doctrine of undue influence as a mechanism to protect a spouse's continuing occupation of the matrimonial home against attempts by purchasers and creditors to obtain possession, see post, p 125.

11   Section 31(10). Matrimonial home rights are not capable of amounting to an overriding interest within s 70(1) of that Act: s 31(10)(b).

12   Section 2(7).

13   Land Charges Act 1972 s 4(8); 'purchaser' includes a mortgagee, but in the usual situation where a property is purchased with the aid of a mortgage, the matrimonial home rights charge is not protected by registration until after the mortgage is created, and hence the mortgagee takes priority.

14   *Watts v Waller* [1973] QB 153, [1972] 3 All ER 257, CA. If the spouse subsequently makes an unsuccessful application for such leave, the registration will be cancelled.

15   Sch 4, para 2.

16   Section 33(5).

17   See above.

the spouse if the home cannot be made the subject of a property adjustment order.[18] However, where the object of registration is purely to freeze assets with a view to an ancillary relief claim, the court may set the registration aside.[19] A court has also awarded damages to a purchaser where a spouse registered her charge without informing her husband before he could complete a sale, thus preventing him from giving the purchaser vacant possession.[20]

A prospective purchaser will not usually remain ignorant of a charge having been registered before completion of the purchase, and a failure to detect such registration may well give rise to an action against the purchaser's solicitor for negligence. However, should a purchaser be placed in such circumstances, the easiest remedy will be to seek an occupation order to terminate the spouse's matrimonial home rights.[1] This was done, under the former law, in *Kashmir Kaur v Gill*.[2] There, the wife left home because of the husband's violence and registered her charge. The husband sold the property to a blind respondent, whose solicitors failed to discover the registration. The Court of Appeal, by a majority, upheld the trial judge's rejection of the wife's claim for an order declaring her right to occupy the house and prohibiting the respondent from entering, because the respondent's need to occupy outweighed that of the wife. Under s 34(2) of the 1996 Act, the court may make an occupation order in proceedings between a spouse with matrimonial home rights and a person deriving title from the other spouse 'if it considers that in all the circumstances it is just and reasonable to do so.' While Sir Denys Buckley dissented in *Kashmir Kaur v Gill* on the basis that the respondent could have no better claim to occupy than the husband from whom he had derived title, and that the court should therefore have considered the *husband's* circumstances when weighed against the wife's rather than the respondent's, the broad test set out in s 34(2) would appear to leave it open to a court to find in the purchaser's favour in a similar case in the future.

If the owning spouse becomes bankrupt, the other's matrimonial home rights do not terminate, but bind the trustee in bankruptcy.[3] However, the trustee in bankruptcy may seek an occupation order under s 33 of the Family Law Act 1996, and the Insolvency Act 1986 provides that, where application is made more than one year after the bankruptcy, the court is required to assume that the creditors' interests outweigh all other considerations, unless the circumstances of the case are exceptional,[4] so that the spouses will almost always be required to leave the home at that point.

(k) Citizenship and the right to live in the United Kingdom [5]

Although at first sight the question of citizenship appears to have little to do with family law, in fact it has close connections with it for a number of reasons. In the first place, a person's right of abode in the United Kingdom may be valueless to him if other members of his family do not share it. In turn the acquisition of British citizenship depends in most cases upon the possession of such citizenship by at

---

18 See post, p 797.
19 *Barnett v Hassett* [1981] 1 WLR 1385.
20 *Wroth v Tyler* ante.
1 Family Law Act 1996 s 33(3)(e) and s 34.
2 [1988] Fam 110, [1988] 2 All ER 288, CA.
3 Insolvency Act 1986 s 336(1) as amended by Family Law Act 1996 Sch 8, para 57(2).
4 Insolvency Act 1986 s 336(4), (5).
5 See Dummett and Nicol *Subjects, Citizens, Aliens and Others* (1990), Supperstone and O'Dempsey *Immigration:The Law and Practice* 3rd edn (1994).

least one parent. Finally, the rules relating to the naturalisation of the spouse of a British citizen are less stringent than those relating to the naturalisation of other persons.

(I)   BRITISH CITIZENSHIP

Since the Second World War the concept of British nationality has radically changed. At one time, citizens of independent Commonwealth countries and United Kingdom Colonies had an automatic right to enter and stay in this country. However, immigration controls imposed by the Immigration Act 1971, in its original form, provided that this 'right of abode' was to be confined to those citizens of the United Kingdom and Colonies who satisfied certain conditions, together with women who were Commonwealth citizens and were or had been married to men with a right of abode.

The British Nationality Act of 1981 substantially amended the law. It created three new categories of citizens: British citizens, British Dependent Territories citizens and British Overseas citizens.[6] In addition, a person may have the status of 'British subject under the Act' or 'British Protected Person', but this does not entail citizenship.[7] Generally, only the first of these has the right of abode in the United Kingdom.[8]

There are five ways in which a person can acquire British citizenship: by birth, descent, adoption, registration and naturalisation. We discuss the first three of these in Chapters 8 and 15 below. It is important to note, regarding the last two, that whereas registration is in most cases a matter of *right*, naturalisation is *discretionary*.

Registration   Any British Dependent Territories citizen, British Overseas citizen, British subject under the Act, or British protected person, who has been in the United Kingdom for five years, is entitled to be registered as a British citizen provided that he was not in breach of the immigration laws during any part of that period and that during the last 12 months he was not subject at any time under those laws to any restriction on the period for which he might remain in this country.[9]

Naturalisation: British citizens' spouses   The doctrine of unity had no application at common law with respect to nationality. A foreign woman did not acquire British nationality by marrying a British subject, and a woman who was a British subject did not lose her status by marrying a foreigner. This rule was reversed by legislation during the nineteenth century,[10] but a series of statutes

---

6 British Nationality Act 1981 Parts I–III. Note that persons connected with Hong Kong may acquire the status of British National (Overseas) (Hong Kong) but this does not give the right of abode and is not recognised by China: Hong Kong (British Nationality) Order 1986 SI 1986/948.

7 British Nationality Act 1981 s 30, s 31 and s 37.

8 There are numerous exceptions; see Supperstone and O'Dempsey, op cit, ch 3 for details.

9 Section 4(1)–(4), as amended by the Hong Kong (British Nationality) Order 1986. Absences totalling not more that 450 days in all and not more than 90 days in the last 12 months are to be disregarded. The Secretary of State has power to waive any of the conditions. For British subjects without citizenship, see Pt IV of the Act. There is a discretionary power to register any British Dependent Territories citizen etc as a British citizen if he has been in Crown or similar service: see s 4(5), (6).

10 Aliens Act 1844 s 16; Naturalization Act 1870 s 10(1).

passed since 1914 reflected the change in status of married women by reverting to the common law principles.[11]

Whilst this meant that a woman who was not a citizen of the United Kingdom and Colonies did not become such a citizen by marrying a man who possessed citizenship, she was nevertheless entitled to acquire it by registration. One of the more radical changes made by the British Nationality Act of 1981 was the removal of this entitlement. At the same time both husbands and wives of citizens were placed on the same footing. Now, if a woman (or man), who is not a British citizen, marries a citizen and wishes to acquire citizenship herself, she must apply for naturalisation unless she qualifies to be registered as a citizen in one of the ways already mentioned. The conditions for naturalisation that have to be fulfilled by the spouse of a British citizen, however, are less stringent than those imposed on others: in particular she (or he) need have been in the United Kingdom for only three years (and not five years) and does not have to have any knowledge of English, Welsh or Scottish Gaelic. She must be of good character and not subject to any restriction under the immigration laws on the period for which she may remain here.[12]

A woman who is a British citizen no longer loses her citizenship on marrying an alien although, if she acquires her husband's nationality, she may divest herself of British citizenship by registering a declaration of renunciation like anyone else possessing dual nationality.[13]

(II)   RIGHT OF ABODE AND FREEDOM OF MOVEMENT

'All those who . . . have the right of abode in the United Kingdom shall be free to live in, and to come and go into and from, the United Kingdom without let or hindrance' except for the need to establish their right.[14] It is possessed by all British citizens and those Commonwealth citizens who had the right before 1 January 1983, when the British Nationality Act 1981 came into force. Persons coming from the Channel Islands, the Isle of Man and the Republic of Ireland are generally exempt from immigration control.[15] Nationals of countries within the European Economic Area Agreement[16] are entitled to enter and reside in a territory in order to exercise a Community right (ie to take up employment or self-employment). Except for these and one or two other special cases,[17] all other

---

11 Status of Aliens Act 1914 s 10; British Nationality and Status of Aliens Act 1918 s 2(5); British Nationality and Status of Aliens Act 1933 s 1(1). These Acts provided that a British woman marrying a foreigner should not lose her British nationality if she did not acquire that of her husband, that the status of the wife of a man who acquired or lost British nationality after the marriage should not automatically follow that of her husband but that she should be given the option of doing likewise, and that a woman who was a British subject at birth should be entitled to resume British nationality if the state of which her husband was a subject was at war with this country. The same principles were applied to citizenship of the United Kingdom and Colonies under the British Nationality Act 1948.
12 Section 6(2) and Sch 1, paras 3 and 4. Absences may be disregarded if they total no more than 270 days of which no more than 90 days may have been in the last twelve months. The applicant must not have been in breach of the immigration laws at any time during the three years.
13 British Nationality Act 1981 s 12.
14 Immigration Act 1971 s 1(1).
15 Ibid s 1(3), s 9 and Sch 4, as amended.
16 Immigration Act 1988 s 7. European Economic Area Agreement, signed at Oporto, 1993 and amended by Protocol at Brussels, 1993, incorporated into English law by the European Economic Area Act 1993 and Immigration (European Economic Area) Order 1994 SI 1994/1895.
17 Immigration Act 1971 s 8.

persons, whatever their citizenship or nationality, may enter this country and stay here only if they are permitted to do so under the Immigration Rules made by the Home Secretary.[18] Permission may be unconditional or, if the individual is here for a particular purpose (for example, as a student or to take up employment), it may be given for a limited period of time and made subject to other conditions such as registration with the police.[19]

A person with the right of abode has no right to be accompanied by members of his family: they must obtain entry clearance or leave to enter or remain.[20] Anyone refused such leave may seek to complain under Article 8 of the European Convention on Human Rights,[1] which protects a person's right to respect for his family life, but the proviso, Article 8(2), which permits a state to interfere with the right where this is in accordance with the law and necessary 'in the interests of national security, public safety or the economic well-being of the country . . .' must be borne in mind. The European Commission and Court have been wary of allowing complainants to circumvent immigration controls by reliance upon the Convention, but are more likely to support the argument where the person is liable to deportation which would mean separation from a family he has established in the country from which he is to be deported, than where a person is complaining that a family member is being refused entry so that a family life can be developed.[2] The Immigration Rules and guidance to immigration officers have been amended in the light of Convention jurisprudence to try to ensure that decisions taken are not in breach of its terms.

Spouses[3]   Under the Immigration Rules no one is to be regarded as the husband or wife of another if he or she is under the age of 16.[4] Secondly, because problems were apparently being caused by men entering the country with two or more wives, a woman, W, will not be given permission to enter or stay here as the wife of a man, H, if (a) her marriage is de facto polygamous (even though the husband had no other wife when she married him) and (b) another wife of H has been in the United Kingdom since her marriage or has been granted entry clearance to enter

---

18 The current rules are to be found in the Statement of Changes in Immigration Rules HC 395 (1994) as amended. 'They are not to be construed with all the strictness applicable to the construction of a statute or statutory instrument. They must be construed sensibly according to the natural meaning of the language which is employed': per Lord Roskill in *Alexander v Immigration Appeal Tribunal* [1982] 2 All ER 766, HL at 770. See Supperstone and O'Dempsey, op cit, ch 5.

19 Immigration Act 1971 s 1(2), (4) and s 3, as amended.

20 *R v Secretary of State for the Home Department, ex p Rofathullah* [1989] QB 219, [1988] 3 All ER 1, CA. Rules which made it harder for husbands to join their wives in this country were ruled contrary to Arts 8, 13 and 14 of the European Convention on Human Rights in *Abdulaziz, Cabales and Balkandali v UK* (1985) 7 EHRR 471. The rules were accordingly amended (HC 503) to make it equally hard for wives to join their husbands.

 1 Note that Protocol 4 to the Convention guarantees the right to freedom of movement, but has not been ratified by the United Kingdom. For discussion of Art 8 and its application to immigration issues, see Douglas 'The Family and the State under the European Convention on Human Rights' (1988) 2 Int J Law & Fam 76 at 80–4; Storey 'The Right to Family Life and Immigration Case Law at Strasbourg' (1990) 39 ICLQ 328.

 2 Douglas, Storey, op cit.

 3 Cohabitants may be granted entry on the same basis as spouses, by exercise of the immigration officer's discretion: see [1986] 1 INL & P 89–90. This concession was extended to unmarried partners who are legally unable to marry under United Kingdom law (other than by reason of consanguinity or age) – ie to homosexual partners – who have been living together for four years or more in a 'relationship akin to marriage', from 13 October 1997: Statement by Minister of State, 10 October 1997.

 4 HC 395 para 277.

this country as H's wife, unless W has been lawfully in this country otherwise than as a visitor at a time when there was no such wife satisfying condition (b).[5]

The spouse of a person who has been given permission to enter the country for a limited period as a student will usually be given leave to enter for the same period if they can be maintained and accommodated without recourse to public funds.[6] Similar rules apply to the spouse of a person admitted to seek or take up employment or as a businessman, self-employed person or a person of independent means.[7]

If a person of either sex is present and settled[8] in the United Kingdom or is admitted for settlement, his or her spouse will be granted entry clearance provided that they show that their marriage is genuine, ie that the parties have met and intend to live together permanently as husband and wife. They must also demonstrate that they can maintain and accommodate themselves and any dependants without recourse to public funds.[9] Before 1997, there was an additional requirement to show that the 'primary purpose' of the marriage was *not* to obtain entry into the United Kingdom. The restriction was imposed because of the belief that in the past some men (particularly from the Indian subcontinent) were obtaining entry into this country by contracting arranged marriages, sometimes by proxy, to women (or possibly young girls) whom they had never met. The rule was abolished because, in the words of the Home Secretary, it was 'arbitrary, unfair and ineffective and has penalised genuine marriages, divided families and unnecessarily increased the administrative burden on the immigration system'.[10] He added that it also treated British citizens worse than EEA nationals resident in Britain, but this would still seem to be the case since, as noted below, the spouse of an EEA national must prima facie be admitted if the other is exercising a Community right, and the burden of proof is on the government to justify their exclusion. He could also have added that the rule was racially discriminatory and placed the applicants in the frequently hopeless position of having to prove a negative.

The spouse will be admitted initially for no more than 12 months: this provides a probationary period at the end of which the time limit may be removed provided that the marriage has not been terminated and each party still has the intention of living permanently with the other as his or her spouse.[11]

If an EEA national exercises a Community right to enter and remain in the United Kingdom, permission to enter must be given to his spouse (regardless of the nationality of the spouse).[12] Thus, a non-EEA national who marries a British

5 Ibid, paras 278–280. This restriction does not apply if W has been in the United Kingdom before 1 August 1988 and she came for settlement as H's wife. See also the Immigration Act 1988 s 2, which applies to women who had the right of abode under s 2(2) of the Immigration Act 1971 as originally enacted.

6 HC 395 para 76.

7 Ibid paras 194, 240, 271.

8 If he is here lawfully, is ordinarily resident here and is free from any restriction on the period for which he may remain: ibid, para 6.

9 HC 395 para 281, as amended.

10 HC, Hansard Written Answers, 5 June 1997 col 219. The rule was abolished with effect from that date in respect of both pending and future applications.

11 HC 395 para 287.

12 Regulation EEC 1612/68 Art 10, extended to EEA nationals by the EEA Agreement (supra, p 71 n 16). Cohabitants of EEA nationals are not within Art 10: *Reed v Staatsecretariat van Justitie* [1987] 2 CMLR 164, but must be considered for entry subject to the same exercise of discretion as would apply to any others.

citizen with the right of abode may avoid the requirements for entry set out above if the British citizen exercises a Community right abroad and the couple then return to this country again to exercise a Community right. For example, suppose W, a British citizen, goes to work in France, where she meets and marries H, a non-EEA citizen. If they then come to the United Kingdom so that W can take up a job here, H must be permitted to enter and remain by virtue of European law.[13]

Engaged couples   A man or woman seeking admission to the United Kingdom to marry a person who is present and settled in this country or who is admitted for settlement on the same occasion must hold entry clearance granted for this purpose. This will be issued only if conditions are satisfied similar to those applicable to spouses.[14] The applicant will be admitted for six months in the first instance, and if the marriage does not take place within this time, an extension will be granted only if good cause is shown for the delay, there is satisfactory evidence that the marriage will take place at an early date, and the other requirements, eg as to provision of accommodation and maintenance, will continue to be met.[15] If the marriage takes place within the initial or extended period, permission to stay in this country will be extended for a further 12 months; the time limit will then be removed in the same circumstances as apply to other spouses seeking permission to stay here.

(III)   DEPORTATION

Where a person who is not a British citizen is liable to deportation (eg because he has overstayed the limit on his permission to remain in the country, or has been convicted of a criminal offence and the court has recommended his deportation), the immigration officer must consider all the known relevant factors before making a decision and, in particular, the length of residence in this country, the strength of connections with this country, domestic or compassionate circum-stances and any representations made on their behalf.[16] Where the person has married a spouse who is settled in the United Kingdom, deportation action will not generally be taken where he or she has a –

> '. . . genuine and subsisting marriage with someone settled here and the couple have lived together in this country continuously since their marriage for at least two years before the commencement of enforcement action; and . . . it is unreasonable to expect the settled spouse to accompany his or her spouse on removal.'[17]

The onus is on the settled spouse to establish why it would be unreasonable for him or her to move abroad with the deportee. Factors relevant to this deter-mination include the strength and closeness of family ties in the United Kingdom, whether the spouse has been settled and living here for at least the past 10 years,

---

13 *R v Immigration Appeal Tribunal and Surinder Singh, ex p Secretary of State for the Home Department*: C- 370/90 [1992] Imm AR 565. However, such a person may be refused entry on grounds of public policy, public security or public health: EC Directive 64/221; see *Van Duyn v Home Office*: 41/74 [1975] Ch 358, [1975] 3 All ER 190 (action can only be taken based upon the personal conduct of the individual, and criminal convictions are relevant only so far as they provide evidence of a present threat to public policy or security).

14 HC 395 para 290.

15 Ibid para 293.

16 Ibid para 364.

17 Home Office Circular on Deportation, DP/3/96 para 5. (This applies to cases coming to the notice of the Immigration and Nationality Department after 13 March 1996. For cases before that date, DP 2/93 applies.)

and whether the spouse suffers from ill health and can present medical evidence which conclusively shows that his or her life would be significantly impaired or endangered if he or she were to accompany the deportee.[18]

Deportation may be ordered against the spouse of a deportee where he or she has no right of abode.[19] The Home Secretary will not normally order the deportation of a spouse who has qualified for settlement in his or her own right or who has been living apart from the other spouse.[20]

18 Compare decisions of the European Court of Human Rights focusing upon similar factors: *Gul v Switzerland* (1996) 22 EHRR 93 – no breach of Art 8 to refuse entry to Turkish couple's two sons when mother too ill to leave Switzerland to go back to Turkey, because the boys had never lived in Switzerland and the father had kept up contact with them in Turkey; *Boughaneni v France* (1996) 22 EHRR 228 – no breach of Art 8 to deport a Tunisian national from France where he had cohabited with a woman and formally acknowledged their child, because he had sufficient links with Tunisia and the criminal offences which had resulted in his deportation were serious. (Note that a parent may seek leave to enter the United Kingdom to have 'access' (contact) with his child: Immigration Rules paras 246–248, see post, p 287 n 8.)
19 Immigration Act 1971 s 3(5) and s 5, as amended by the British Nationality Act 1981 Sch 4, and Immigration Act 1988 Sch. See HC 395 Part 13.
20 HC 395 para 365. A deported spouse may seek re-admission if the marriage comes to an end: para 389.

Chapter 3

Void and voidable marriages

A. Introduction

1. HISTORICAL BACKGROUND

The view of the Roman Catholic church that marriage is a sacrament inevitably meant that the law relating to marriage would become a part of the canon law, over which the ecclesiastical courts successfully claimed exclusive jurisdiction.[1] This had a profound effect on subsequent legal developments. Not only were these courts the only tribunals competent to declare whether the parties were validly married, but the Roman Catholic doctrine of the indissolubility of marriage became a tenet of English law.

Whilst this doctrine precluded the courts from granting decrees of divorce, it did not stop them from declaring that, although the parties had gone through a ceremony of marriage, some impediment prevented their acquiring the status of husband and wife. Clearly there was no valid marriage if either of the spouses was already married to somebody else, if they were related within the prohibited degrees, or if one of them did not fully consent to the solemnisation. Furthermore, since a marriage was not regarded as consummated until the parties had become one flesh by sexual intercourse, if either was impotent, he or she was regarded as lacking capacity to contract the union, which could therefore be annulled. The same principles were applied by the English ecclesiastical courts after the breach with Rome in the sixteenth century. Such marriages were said to be void for, although the parties by going through a ceremony had apparently contracted a marriage, the result of the impediment was that there was never a marriage either in fact or in law. Consequently the marriage could be formally annulled by a decree of an ecclesiastical court and, even without such a decree, either party was free to contract another union (unless he or she was already married to somebody else). As the marriage was a complete nullity, its validity could also be put in issue by any other person with an interest in so doing, even after the death of one or both of the parties to it. So, for example, after the death of a tenant in fee simple his brother might claim his estate on the ground that the tenant's marriage was void, with the result that his children, being illegitimate, could not inherit and his 'widow', never having been married, could not claim dower.

By the beginning of the seventeenth century, however, the royal courts were becoming concerned at the ease with which marriages could be set aside and the issue bastardised. This was more likely to work injustice after the parties' death, when relevant evidence might no longer be available. Accordingly, using the writ of prohibition, they cut down the ecclesiastical courts' jurisdiction by forbidding

---

1 Pollock and Maitland *History of English Law*, ii, 364–6.

them to annul marriages in certain cases after the death of either party.[2] This had the result of dividing impediments into two kinds: civil and canonical. If the impediment was civil – for example, the fact that one of the parties was married to a third person at the time of the ceremony – the marriage was still void ab initio and its validity could be put in issue by anyone at any time, whether or not the parties were still alive. If the impediment was canonical – for example, the fact that one of the parties was impotent – the validity of the marriage could not be questioned after either party had died. The rule thus developed that such a marriage must be regarded as valid unless it is annulled during the lifetime of both parties. Until that time it has the capacity to be turned into a void marriage: in other words, it is voidable. Once a decree of nullity had been pronounced, however, it acted retrospectively and the marriage was then regarded as having been void from the beginning. Consequently, the parties reverted to their pre-marital status and their children were automatically bastardised. The distinction between void and voidable marriages was thus described by Lord Greene MR:[3]

> 'A void marriage is one that will be regarded by every court in any case in which the existence of the marriage is in issue as never having taken place and can be so treated by both parties to it without the necessity of any decree annulling it: a voidable marriage is one that will be regarded by every court as a valid subsisting marriage until a decree annulling it has been pronounced by a court of competent jurisdiction.'

After the introduction of judicial divorce in 1857, the voidable marriage came to occupy a position midway between the void marriage and the valid marriage. The annulment of a voidable marriage, like divorce, changes the parties' status by a judicial act, and whatever the theoretical differences between them are, both are means of terminating a marriage that has broken down. Divorce, however, does not act retrospectively; the parties are still regarded as having been husband and wife up to the time when the decree was made absolute. Some of the inconveniences of the retrospective operation of the decree of nullity of a voidable marriage were removed by statute or avoided by the courts: for example, children of the marriage remain legitimate[4] and it has never been possible to set aside transactions carried out on the assumption (valid at the time) that the parties to a voidable marriage were husband and wife.[5] Nevertheless, many anomalies remained and the retrospective effect of the decree was artificial and confusing and 'in truth perpetuated a canonical fiction'.[6]

The law of nullity was reviewed by the Law Commission in 1970.[7] In view of the criticisms that had been levelled against the anomalous nature of the voidable marriage, the Law Commission examined the question whether the concept should be abolished altogether and the grounds for annulling a voidable marriage included amongst the facts from which irretrievable breakdown of the marriage might be inferred as the ground for divorce. They rejected the proposal for three reasons. First, certain Christian denominations and their members draw a clear

---

2 See Jackson *Formation and Annulment of Marriage* (2nd edn, 1969) pp 54–5.
3 *De Reneville v De Reneville* [1948] P 100 at 111, [1948] 1 All ER 56, CA at 60. Newark considered that historically this distinction is incorrect: 'The Operation of Nullity Decrees' (1945) 8 MLR 203.
4 Originally, Law Reform (Miscellaneous Provisions) Act 1949 s 4 (1), but see now the Matrimonial Causes Act 1973 s 16, discussed post, p 102.
5 See *Re Eaves* [1940] Ch 109, [1939] 4 All ER 260, CA.
6 Per Lord Goddard CJ in *R v Algar* [1954] 1 QB 279 at 288, [1953] 2 All ER 1381, CCA at 1384.
7 Law Com No 33, *Nullity of Marriage*, 1970.

distinction between the annulment and the dissolution of marriage and would be offended if the distinction were blurred. Secondly, some people, associating divorce with stigma, preferred to keep matters involving no moral blame such as impotence and mental disorder as grounds for nullity.[8] Thirdly, the bar which then applied to divorce within the first three years of marriage was clearly inappropriate to the grounds for nullity.[9] The Law Commission, however, made extensive recommendations with the object of resolving uncertainties and removing anomalies. Effect was given to these by the Nullity of Marriage Act 1971, which to a large extent codified the law of nullity.[10] This Act was in turn repealed and its provisions re-enacted in the Matrimonial Causes Act 1973.

2.   THE CURRENT DISTINCTION BETWEEN VOID AND VOIDABLE MARRIAGES

Grounds for annulment

Essentially, a marriage will be void if either party lacks capacity to contract it or if the ceremony is formally defective.[11] Formerly it was doubtful whether lack of consent made a marriage void or voidable but now, in the case of marriages contracted after 31 July 1971, the 1973 Act specifically provides that this will make them voidable.

With the doubtful exception of lack of consent, the only ground on which a marriage could be voidable after 1929[12] was that one of the parties was impotent. The Matrimonial Causes Act 1937 added four new grounds: the respondent's wilful refusal to consummate the marriage, either party's mental disorder, the respondent's venereal disease, and the respondent wife's pregnancy per alium. Now, under the 1973 Act, impotence, the four statutory grounds (with some modifications) and lack of consent are the grounds on which a marriage is voidable.

Necessity for decree

The vital distinction between a void and a voidable marriage is that the former, being void ab initio, needs no decree to annul it, whilst the latter is in all respects a valid marriage until a decree absolute of nullity is pronounced. Hence, if either party dies before a decree is granted, a voidable marriage must be treated as valid for all purposes and for all time.[13] On the other hand either party to a *void* marriage may lawfully contract a valid marriage with someone else without having the first marriage formally annulled.

---

8 But this overlooks the fact that moral blame attaches to some of the grounds for nullity (eg pregnancy per alium).

9 During the ten years 1976–84 there were on average just over 1,000 petitions a year. In the years 1985–90 the average was 567 and in the years 1991–96 the average was 699. It is significant that the large drop in 1985 occurred in the first full year in which it became possible to petition for divorce after the first year of marriage. About 85% of all petitions are based on impotence or wilful refusal to consummate.

10 See generally Hall 'The Nullity of Marriage Act 1971' [1971] CLJ 208; Cretney 'The Nullity of Marriage Act 1971' (1972) 35 MLR 57.

11 See ante, pp 34–7.

12 When the Age of Marriage Act 1929 rendered a marriage void if either party was under the age of 16: see ante, p 31.

13 *Re Roberts* [1978] 3 All ER 225, CA (revocation of will executed before marriage).

Even though, in respect of a void marriage, a decree of nullity can only be declaratory and cannot effect any change in the parties' status, there may be good reason for obtaining such a decree. First, there may be some doubt whether on the facts or the law applicable the marriage is void: whether, for example, one party was already married or there was a due publication of banns. Secondly, a decree of nullity is a judgment in rem, so that no one may subsequently allege that the marriage is in fact valid. But the most important reason for bringing proceedings is that the court has power on granting a decree to make certain ancillary orders, and a party may therefore present a petition in order, for example, to obtain a property adjustment order or financial provision for herself[14] and any children of the family.[15] As the parties are not married, this is in fact the only way in which the 'wife' may obtain maintenance purely for herself.

Third parties' rights

From what has been said, it follows that third parties must treat a voidable marriage as valid unless a decree has been pronounced. On the other hand, if it is alleged that a marriage is void, any person with an interest in so doing may prove as a question of fact that there has never been a marriage at all. Suppose that property is settled on trust for A for life with remainder to his widow or, if he leaves no widow, to B absolutely. A goes through a ceremony of marriage with W who survives him. Even though the marriage between W and A was voidable, B cannot dispute its validity to prove that W is not A's widow: but he can show, even after A's death, that the marriage between them was void and that consequently the remainder over to him takes effect, for W, never having been A's wife, cannot now be his widow. But if a decree of nullity had been pronounced before A's death, then, whether the marriage was void or voidable, everyone is bound by it and W may not now assert that she is A's widow. It is easy to imagine other cases in which the validity of a marriage might be impeached: for example, others interested in property might wish to prove that the alleged marriage had not revoked the will of one of the parties to it.[16]

Conversely, it might be in the interest of one of the parties to prove that the marriage was void. Suppose that a testator devises property to W so long as she remains his widow and, if she remarry, to X. W subsequently goes through a ceremony of marriage with K. In the event of a dispute between W and X over the beneficial interest in the property after the ceremony, W clearly succeeds if she can show that the marriage between herself and K is void.[17]

Effect of the decree

If the marriage is void ab initio, the decree does not affect the parties' status at all. In the case of a voidable marriage, effect has been given to the Law Commission's recommendation that to remove the difficulties caused by the retrospective effect

---

14 See eg *J v S-T (Formerly J) (Transsexual: Ancillary Relief)* [1997] 1 FLR 402, CA, explaining *Whiston v Whiston* [1995] Fam 198, [1995] 3 WLR 405, CA, discussed post, pp 828–9.

15 The powers to order financial provision for children are subject to the restrictions under the Child Support Act 1991, discussed post, pp 746ff. The meaning of 'children of the family' is discussed post, pp 288–90.

16 See *Harrod v Harrod* (1854) 1 K & J 4; *Re Peete* [1952] 2 All ER 599; *Re Park's Estate* [1954] P 89, [1953] 2 All ER 408, and *Re Spence* [1990] Ch 652, [1990] 2 All ER 827, CA.

17 *Allen v Wood* (1834) 1 Bing NC 8.

of the decree, it should operate to annul the marriage only as respects any time after it had been made absolute and that the marriage should continue to be treated as having existed up to that time.[18]

3. PETITIONS

Jurisdiction to grant decrees of nullity (whether the marriage was alleged to be void or voidable) was transferred from the ecclesiastical courts to the new Divorce Court set up by the Matrimonial Causes Act 1857, and was vested in the High Court by the Judicature Act 1873. Divorce county courts now have jurisdiction to hear all petitions.[19]

It was an established practice in the ecclesiastical courts to permit a petition to be presented not only by one of the parties to the marriage but also, in certain circumstances, by third persons as well. If the parties were related within the prohibited degrees (and presumably if the marriage was bigamous) any member of the public could invoke the so-called criminal jurisdiction of the court to abate a scandal, and if the allegation were found to be true, the court would pronounce a decree of nullity.[20] In other cases a third person could bring proceedings if he had a proprietary or financial interest[1] in the validity of the marriage. Proceedings based on the criminal jurisdiction were no longer possible once the ecclesiastical courts ceased to have jurisdiction in matrimonial causes, but the rule that a person with an interest could bring nullity proceedings apparently survived and there are dicta indicating that it is still good law.[2]

In *A v B*[3] it was held that impotence is a matter of personal complaint and consequently could be raised only by the parties to the marriage themselves. This principle applies with equal force to some of the other grounds for nullity, for example the respondent's pregnancy or venereal disease. It is submitted that a third person can no longer petition if the marriage is voidable.[4] So far as void marriages are concerned, there seems to be a confusion between two principles: first, that anyone can show that a marriage is (or was) void in any proceedings in which this is

---

18 Matrimonial Causes Act 1973 s 16, discussed post, p 102.

19 Matrimonial and Family Proceedings Act 1984 s 33. See further, ante, pp 12ff.

20 *Turner v Meyers* (1808) 1 Hag Con 414; *Blackmore v Brider* (1816) 2 Phillim 359; *Chick v Ramsdale* (1835) 1 Curt 34.

 1 The relationship of parent and child did not per se entitle the parent to petition unless, perhaps, the child was a minor: *Sherwood v Ray* (1837) 1 Moo PC 353, 397, PCC; *Turner v Meyers* (supra). On the other hand a 'slight interest' was enough: see eg *Faremouth v Watson* (1811) 1 Phillim 355, where proceedings were successfully brought by husband's statutory next of kin, who had an interest under the mother's will contingent on his dying with legitimate issue; and *Sherwood v Ray* (supra), in which the wife's father had a potential liability under the Poor Law to maintain any children she might have if they were indigent and their father could not support them.

 2 See the Matrimonial Causes Act 1857 s 22, which provided that the Divorce Court should apply the same principles as the ecclesiastical courts had applied. The rule was regarded as good law by Collingwood J in *J v J* [1953] P 186, [1952] 2 All ER 1129, by Ormrod J in *Kassim v Kassim* [1962] P 224 at 234, [1962] 3 All ER 426 at 432, and by the Law Commission in Law Com No 33 para 87, and Law Com No 48 (*Jurisdiction in Matrimonial Causes,* 1972), para 50. Its existence is confirmed by implication by the Domicile and Matrimonial Proceedings Act 1973 s 5(3)(c), dealing with the court's jurisdiction after the death of one or both parties: see post, p 81.

 3 (1868) LR 1 P & D 559.

 4 See *Re Roberts* [1978] 3 All ER 225 at 227 (per Walton J). This view is supported by the fact that it is now expressly provided by statute that the respondent may raise the petitioner's own conduct as a bar in all such cases: see post, pp 98–9. This scarcely makes sense if the petitioner is not the other spouse.

relevant and, secondly, that it is open to the parties to obtain a decree of nullity which, as a judgment in rem, binds all the world. There is, however, a fundamental difference between, on the one hand, permitting a third person to prove that a marriage was void in order to establish a claim to one party's estate after his death and, on the other, permitting him to seek a judgment in rem to this effect before or after the death of the two persons involved. Petitions are now rarely, if ever, brought by strangers and it is urged that the power to do so should be abolished.[5]

4. JURISDICTION OF ENGLISH COURTS

Following the Law Commission's recommendations,[6] aimed at removing the anomalies of the former law[7] and harmonising the jurisdictional rules governing nullity and divorce, s 5(3) of the Domicile and Matrimonial Proceedings Act 1973 provides that the court has jurisdiction in nullity proceedings if (and only if) either of the parties to the marriage:

'(a) is domiciled in England and Wales on the date when the proceedings are begun; or
(b) was habitually resident in England and Wales throughout the period of one year ending with that date; or
(c) died before that date and either –
    (i) was at death domiciled in England and Wales, or
    (ii) had been habitually resident in England and Wales throughout the period of one year ending with the date of death.'[8]

It will be seen that the same rules apply whether the marriage is alleged to be void or voidable and that it is immaterial whether the party domiciled or resident here is the petitioner or the respondent.

The court also has jurisdiction if proceedings for divorce, nullity or separation, over which it has jurisdiction, have already begun, even though it would not have jurisdiction when the nullity petition is presented.[9] Accordingly, if, for example, a wife petitions for divorce and the sole ground on which the court could assume jurisdiction is that she is habitually resident in this country, then notwithstanding that she ceases to be resident here, the husband can still cross-petition for nullity whilst the divorce proceedings are pending even though he could not have brought proceedings if the wife had not previously petitioned herself.

Although there are no obligatory stays in nullity proceedings as there are in divorce,[10] the court has a discretionary power to stay nullity proceedings here if before the beginning of the trial it appears that any proceedings in respect of the marriage or capable of affecting its validity or subsistence are continuing in any country outside England or Wales.[11]

---

5 See the Law Commission's view, Law Com No 132 (*Declarations in Family Matters*, 1984), paras 3.29–3.32.
6 Law Com No 48 (*Report on Jurisdiction in Matrimonial Causes*, 1972).
7 Discussed at pp 77–8 of the 8th edition of this work.
8 Para (c) presupposes that the court has jurisdiction to pronounce a decree of nullity after the death of one or both parties and will therefore apply only if the marriage is void: see ante, p 80.
9 Domicile and Matrimonial Proceedings Act 1973 s 5(5), as prospectively substituted by Sch 8, para 26 of the Family Law Act 1996.
10 The reason is that, although a conflict has always been possible between different jurisdictions in the United Kingdom, in practice this did not give rise to any problems.
11 If the other proceedings are for divorce or separation, the nullity suit should always be disposed of first. See Law Com No 48 para 88.

5.   DECREES

A decree of nullity is made in two stages: the decree nisi followed by the decree absolute.[12] The rules relating to the application for a decree nisi to be made absolute (including the restrictions imposed where children of the family are involved) are exactly the same as they were in divorce before implementation of the Family Law Act 1996.[13] The marriage is finally annulled when the decree is made absolute and a party to a voidable marriage may not remarry until then.

B.   Void marriages

1.   INTRODUCTION

We have seen that a void marriage is strictly speaking a contradiction in terms: to speak of a void marriage is merely a compendious way of saying that, although the parties have been through a ceremony of marriage, they have never acquired the status of husband and wife owing to the presence of some impediment. If they have never been through a ceremony at all, however, their union cannot even be termed a void marriage. However, this in turn raises the difficult problem of what form of ceremony will be sufficient to enable the court to grant a decree of nullity. The matter may be of considerable practical importance, because in certain circumstances the issue of a void marriage can be legitimate, and only if the court pronounces a decree does it have power to make orders relating to financial provision for the spouses and the adjustment of their rights in property.[14]

This first reported case where this precise issue was raised is *Gereis v Yagoub*.[15] In that case the parties went through a purported ceremony of marriage at a Coptic Orthodox Church not licensed for marriages,[16] the ceremony being conducted by a priest who was not licensed to conduct marriages and without notice of the marriage having been given to the superintendent registrar. In fact the parties had been advised by the priest to go through a civil ceremony of marriage first, but no civil ceremony was performed. After the church ceremony the parties lived together for nearly a year, but after the breakdown of their relationship the petitioner sought a decree of nullity which the respondent opposed on the basis that there had not even been a void marriage.

In granting the decree Judge Aglionby, relying on earlier statements[17] that the ceremony 'must be at least one which will prima facie confer the status of husband and wife', considered that the ceremony in this case 'bore the hallmarks of an ordinary Christian marriage and . . . both parties treated it as such, at least to the

---

12 Matrimonial Causes Act 1973 s 15, the prospective amendments to which by the Family Law Act 1996 (see post, p 254) will confine this two stage process to nullity proceedings and decrees of death and dissolution of marriage.

13 See post, p 231.

14 Though it by no means follows that the court will grant ancillary relief following the granting of a nullity decree: see *J v S-T (Formerly J) (Transsexual: Ancillary Relief)* [1997] 1 FLR 402, CA and *Whiston v Whiston* [1995] Fam 198, [1995] 3 WLR 405, CA, discussed post, pp 828–9.

15 [1997] 1 FLR 854.

16 See ante, p 42.

17 Such as that of Humphreys J in *R v Mohamed (Ali)* (1943) [1964] 2 QB 350n, cited by Thompson J in *R v Bham* [1966] 1 QB 159 at 169B, [1965] 3 All ER 124, CCA at 129.

extent that they cohabited after it, whereas they had not before, that they had sexual intercourse, which they had not before, and that the respondent had claimed married man's tax allowance, which he had not before'.[18] Moreover, he was satisfied that those who attended the ceremony clearly assumed that they were attending an ordinary Christian marriage. Having found as a fact that both parties were aware of the need to go through some form of ceremony at the civil Register Office, the judge held that the marriage was void in that both had knowingly and wilfully intermarried in disregard of the formalities required by the Marriage Act 1949.[19]

In reaching this decision the judge accepted that proceedings which were a sham or a charade, such as where the ceremony takes place in a play, could not be regarded as creating any marriage at all, not even a void marriage. Similarly, in these cases where what had happened could not possibly amount to a marriage as, for example, a ceremony of engagement, there could be no marriage at all. The judge also referred to the decision in *R v Bham*[20] in which a prosecution had been brought against the accused for performing a ceremony of marriage contrary to s 75(2)(a) of the Marriage Act 1949. In that case a ceremony of Nishan (a potentially polygamous marriage in accordance with Islamic form) was performed in a private house in England between a Muslim man and a 16-year-old English girl who had adopted the Muslim faith. Quashing a conviction for knowingly and wilfully solemnising a marriage, the Court of Criminal Appeal said:[1]

'What, in our judgment, was contemplated by [the Marriage Act] . . . in dealing with marriage and its solemnisation, and that to which alone it applies, was the performing in England of a ceremony in a form known to and recognised by our law as capable of producing, when there performed, a void marriage.'

If this is the correct test, then, as has been pointed out elsewhere,[2] a union between two homosexuals would not qualify even as a void marriage, notwithstanding that s 11(d) of the 1973 makes a marriage void on the grounds that the parties are not respectively male and female.[3] Presumably, that provision should be regarded as operating only where there is some genuine doubt as to the gender identity of a party.[4]

Another problem with this approach is that it could lead to injustice in the case of those, particularly members of ethnic minorities, who may go through religious ceremonies even in private houses[5] under the misapprehension that they are thereby contracting a legally recognised marriage. It is submitted that in deciding whether to grant a decree some regard should be paid to the parties' belief that they were contracting a legally valid marriage: only if both knew that the ceremony could not make them husband and wife by English law should they be in the same position as a couple who cohabit without going through any ceremony at all.[6]

---

18 Ibid, at 858.
19 And therefore within the Matrimonial Causes Act 1973 s 11(a)(iii): see below at pp 85–7.
20 Supra.
 1 At 169 and 129, respectively. See (1965) 81 LQR 474.
 2 See Bailey-Harris [1997] Fam Law at 476.
 3 Discussed post, p 84.
 4 In the classic case of transsexuals: see eg *Corbett v Corbett* [1971] P 83, [1970] 2 All ER 33, discussed ante, p 28. Note also *J v S-T (Formerly J) (Transsexual: Ancillary Relief)* [1997] 1 FLR 402, CA, discussed at pp 828–9.
 5 Particularly now that licences can be granted to marry outside churches or Register Offices – see ante, p 43.
 6 Though even then a distinction may have to be drawn between knowing of defects, as in *Gereis v Yagoub*, and believing that the ceremony will not make them husband and wife.

2.   GROUNDS ON WHICH A MARRIAGE WILL BE VOID

Section 11 of the Matrimonial Causes Act 1973 expressly provides that a marriage celebrated after 31 July 1971 (when the Nullity of Marriage Act 1971 came into force) shall be void only on the grounds there set out.[7]

The present grounds can be divided into two: those relating to capacity and those relating to formal requirements.

Lack of capacity

Obviously lack of capacity to marry will ipso facto make the marriage void. If the relevant law is English, the marriage will be void on the following grounds:

(a)   That the parties are related within the prohibited degrees of consanguinity or, if the conditions set out in the Marriage Act 1949 are not observed, within the prohibited degrees of affinity.[8]

(b)   That either of them is under the age of 16.

(c)   That either of them is already married.[9]

(d)   That they are not respectively male and female. This provision is designed to cover the case of a party who has previously undergone an operation to achieve an alleged change of sex or about whose sex there is genuine doubt.[10] It is a matter of debate as to whether the wording of the Act is sufficiently wide to enable a petition for nullity to be brought where each party knows that both are of the same sex but leads all concerned with the solemnisation of the marriage to believe that one of them is of the opposite sex.

(e)   That either party to a polygamous marriage celebrated abroad was at the time of the ceremony domiciled in England. This is subject to the overriding principle that a foreign rule of law must be applied instead of the English rule when the conflict of laws so requires.[11] Consequently, if the proper law to apply is that of the proposed matrimonial home, the marriage may still be valid notwithstanding that one of the parties is domiciled in this country.[12]

Formal defects

Whether failure to comply with the formal requirements relating to the marriage ceremony will make the marriage void must be determined by reference to the lex loci celebrationis.[13]

If the marriage is solemnised in England and Wales, not every defect in the formalities set out in the Marriage Act 1949 will render the ceremony a nullity. Whilst public policy requires that these formalities should be strictly observed, the consequences of avoiding any marriage where there was some technical defect,

---

7   These are all grounds on which a marriage celebrated before that date would be void. In addition, it is probable that lack of consent on the part of one of the parties formerly made a marriage void, in which case a marriage celebrated before 1 August 1971, affected by lack of consent, will remain void. See further post, pp 91ff. It is also possible that a marriage celebrated before 1 August 1971 was void if one of the parties was divorced and the time for appealing against the decree absolute had not expired: see *Dryden v Dryden* [1973] Fam 217 at 239, [1973] 3 All ER 526 at 542.

8   See ante, pp 32ff.

9   See, for example, *Whiston v Whiston* [1995] Fam 198, [1995] 3 WLR 405, CA.

10   See ante, pp 28–30.

11   Matrimonial Causes Act 1973 s 14 (1).

12   See *Radwan v Radwan (No 2)* [1973] Fam 35, [1972] 3 All ER 1026.

13   See ante, p 28 n 9.

however slight, would be socially even more undesirable. English law has reached a compromise between these conflicting demands of public policy in that some formal defects will not render the marriage void at all, whilst in the case of the rest the marriage will be void only if *both* parties contracted it with knowledge of the defect. In other words, it is impossible for a person in England and Wales innocently to contract a marriage which is void because of a formal defect. The real sanction is afforded by the criminal law, for if a party knowingly fails to comply with the Marriage Act, he will frequently have to make a false oath or declaration and thus commit perjury.[14] This should adequately safeguard the marriage law without prejudicing the position of the innocent spouse.

(a) Defects which will never invalidate a marriage

The Marriage Act 1949 specifically enacts that a marriage shall not be rendered void on any of the following grounds:[15]

(a) that any of the statutory residence requirements was not fulfilled (whether for the purpose of the publication of banns or of obtaining a common licence or superintendent registrar's certificate);

(b) that the necessary consents had not been given in the case of the marriage of a minor by common licence or a superintendent registrar's certificate;[16]

(c) that the registered building in which the parties were married had not been certified as a place of religious worship or was not the usual place or worship of either of them; or

(d) that an incorrect declaration had been made in order to obtain permission to marry in a registered building in a registration district in which neither party resided on the ground that there was not there a building in which marriages were solemnised according to the rites of the religious belief which one of them professed.

Although these are the only formal defects specifically stated not to invalidate a marriage, it is a general rule that, if the irregularity is not one which the Act expressly states may invalidate it, the defect will never make the ceremony a nullity.[17] Hence, for example, even though the parties are aware that two witnesses are not present at the ceremony, the marriage will still be perfectly valid.[18]

(b) Defects which may invalidate a marriage

In the following cases only will a failure to comply with the provisions of the Marriage Act make the marriage void, and then only if *both* parties were aware of

---

14 See the Perjury Act 1911 s 3, and the discussion in *J v S-T (Formerly J) (Transsexual: Ancillary Relief)* [1997] 1 FLR 402 at 425–6, per Ward LJ. If a material alteration is made to any document (eg the date on a superintendent registrar's certificate), this will be punishable under the Forgery Act 1913. See also the Marriage Act 1949 s 75, and the Marriage (Registrar General's Licence) Act 1970 s 16 (punishment of offences relating to the solemnisation of marriages).

15 Section 24 and s 48. See also s 47(3) (authorisation of marriage according to the usages of the Society of Friends), s 71 (evidence of marriages in naval, military and air force chapels) and s 72 (usual place of worship), and the Marriage (Registrar General's Licence) Act 1970 s 12 (marriages solemnised on the Registrar General's licence).

16 The Act refers to consents only where the parties are married on the authority of a superintendent registrar's certificate, but the same is true where they are married by common licence: *R v Birmingham Inhabitants* (1828) 8 B & C 29.

17 *Campbell v Corley* (1856) 28 LTOS 109.

18 *Campbell v Corley* (supra); *Wing v Taylor* (1861) 2 Sw & Tr 278.

the irregularity at the time of the ceremony.[19]

In the case of a marriage according to the rites of the Church of England (otherwise than by special licence), the following come within the rule:[20]

(a)   That (except in the case of the marriage of a house-bound or detained person) the marriage was solemnised in a place other than a church or chapel in which banns may be published.

(b)   That banns had not been duly published, a common licence obtained or a superintendent registrar's certificate duly issued. Since failure to comply with the residence qualification will never invalidate a marriage, an undue publication of banns will usually occur when one or both of the parties have been wrongly named or where there has been no publication at all.[1] But the object of giving publicity to the intended union (which is the purpose of the publication of banns) does not apply to a licence or, apparently, to a certificate; so that provided that either of these was issued for the marriage of the parties which in fact took place, the marriage will not be void even though one of the parties was designated by a wholly false name.[2]

(c)   That, in the case of the marriage of a child by banns, a person entitled to do so had publicly dissented from the marriage at the time of the publication of the banns.[3]

(d)   That more than three months had elapsed from the completion of the publication of the banns, the grant of a common licence or the entry of the notice of marriage in the superintendent registrar's marriage notice book, as the case may be.

(e)   That, in the case of a marriage by superintendent registrar's certificate, the ceremony was performed in a place other than the church, chapel or other building specified in the notice of marriage and certificate.

(f)   That the marriage was solemnised by a person who was not in Holy Orders.

In the case of other marriages, the following come within the rule:[4]

(a)   That due notice of marriage had not been given to the superintendent registrar.[5]

---

19   The Act speaks of 'knowingly and wilfully' intermarrying, and it is not clear whether it is sufficient that both parties should know as a question of fact that the formality is not complied with or whether in addition they must know as a question of law that the defect will invalidate the marriage. The point was left open by Lord Penzance in *Greaves v Greaves* (1872) LR 2 P & D 423 at 424–5. The former construction seems the more natural, even though its adoption would have the effect of invalidating more marriages. The issue was not adverted to in *Gereis v Yagoub* [1997] 1 FLR 854, discussed ante, p 82.

20   Marriage Act 1949 s 25 (as amended by the Marriage Act 1983 Sch 1).

 1   But there would presumably be an undue publication, eg if the banns were not published at a service specified in the Act or by a clergyman or authorised lay reader.

 2   *Bevan v M'Mahon* (1861) 2 Sw & Tr 230; *Plummer v Plummer* [1917] P 163, CA; *R v Lamb* (1934) 50 TLR 310, CCA; *Puttick v A-G* [1980] Fam 1, [1979] 3 All ER 463 (where the petitioner, better known as Astrid Proll, had entered this country on another woman's passport and was married in the name of an identifiable third person). The application of this principle to the issue of a certificate without licence is surprising because it defeats the purpose of giving publicity to the intended marriage by displaying the notice for 21 days.

 3   Contrast the position where the marriage of a child is by common licence or a superintendent registrar's certificate: see supra.

 4   Marriage Act 1949 s 49 (as amended by the Marriage Act 1983, Sch 1 and the Marriage Act 1994 s 1(3). The same rules apply mutatis mutandis if the marriage is solemnised on the authority of the Registrar General's licence: Marriage (Registrar General's Licence) Act 1970 s 13. In particular, such a marriage will be void if the parties knowingly and wilfully intermarry more than one month after the entry of notice.

 5   In the due form. Lack of notice to the superintendent register was relied upon in *Gereis v Yagoub*, supra. Notice in a false name does not invalidate the notice or the marriage: see supra.

(b) That a certificate and, where it is necessary, a licence had not been duly issued.

(c) That more than three months had elapsed since the entry of the notice in the superintendent registrar's marriage notice book.

(d) That the marriage was not solemnised in the building specified in the notice and certificate.

(e) That in the case of a marriage on approved premises the marriage was solemnised on premises that were not approved.

(f) That the marriage was solemnised in the absence of a superintendent registrar or registrar or (if it was solemnised in a registered building or on approved premises) in the absence of a registrar or authorised person or (in the case of the marriage of a house-bound or detained person) in the absence of a superintendent registrar or registrar whose presence was required.

(c) Proposals for reform

The present rule that a marriage will not be void on the ground of a formal defect unless both parties were aware of it has the advantage that it is impossible for a party mistakenly to contract such a marriage. It also produces uncertainty, however. If there has been some irregularity which could invalidate the marriage, dishonest parties may have the option of deciding whether it is to be regarded as valid or void, for it may be extremely difficult to disprove whatever evidence they give about their knowledge or lack of knowledge of the defect at the time of the ceremony. Similar uncertainty could surround the validity of the marriage of the scrupulous 'for most people have no difficulty in sincerely convincing themselves that what they would like to have occurred is what in fact occurred'.[6] Consequently the Law Commission concluded that the test of whether a marriage is void on the ground of formal irregularity should be objective and not depend on the parties' knowledge or complicity.[7]

C.   Voidable marriages

1.   GROUNDS ON WHICH A MARRIAGE WILL BE VOIDABLE

The six grounds on which a marriage celebrated after 31 July 1971 will be voidable are set out in s 12 of the Matrimonial Causes Act 1973.[8] Five of these grounds are, with two slight modifications, the same as those which existed before 1 August 1971. The remaining ground – lack of consent – probably made the marriage void before that date, although this is a matter of some doubt.[9] If this was the effect of lack of consent, marriages affected by it and celebrated before 1 August 1971 will, of course, still be void.

The unconsummated marriage

Even in canon law a marriage was not always finally and irrevocably indissoluble if it had not been consummated by the sexual act. If at the time of the ceremony

---

6 Law Com No 53 (*Report on Solemnisation of Marriage in England and Wales*) 1973, Annex, para 121.

7 See further, ibid, paras 121–133. For their proposals relating to formalities of marriage, see ante, pp 46ff.

8 Re-enacting the Nullity of Marriage Act 1971 s 2, which came into force on 1 August 1971.

9 For a full discussion of the problem, see the 4th edition of this book, at pp 79–83.

either spouse was incapable of consummating it, he or she was regarded as lacking the physical capacity (as distinct from the legal capacity) to contract a valid marriage and the union could therefore be annulled. If, on the other hand, the marriage remained unconsummated because of one party's refusal to have sexual intercourse, canon law offered no relief because the ground of complaint was conduct following the ceremony.[10] Despite this, decrees were probably in fact given in some cases in reliance on the presumption that, if the marriage had not been consummated after three years' cohabitation through no fault of the petitioner, the respondent must be impotent.[11] The law was put on a more rational footing by the Matrimonial Causes Act 1937, which enacted that a marriage should be voidable if it had not been consummated owing to the respondent's wilful refusal to do so. This was frequently criticised because it offended against the principle that an impediment avoiding a marriage should exist at the time of the ceremony. The Law Commission, however, recommended that it should remain a ground for nullity; the most cogent reason they advanced was that the petitioner is often uncertain whether failure to consummate is due to the respondent's impotence or wilful refusal, and in practice will then plead both grounds in the alternative.[12] Notwithstanding this practical justification, the whole concept seems artificial. The petitioner's real complaint is that he (or she) is being deprived of normal sexual relations because of the respondent's impotence or conduct. If intercourse takes place once (perhaps after great delay and difficulty), the petitioner's power to petition for nullity disappears and his sole remedy lies in divorce if the respondent is unable or unwilling to have further sexual relations.

It must be emphasised that non-consummation as such does not make a marriage voidable. There are two separate grounds on which a party may petition: that the marriage has not been consummated owing to the incapacity of either party to consummate it, or that it has not been consummated owing to the respondent's wilful refusal to do so.[13] Clearly, it would be wholly unjust to permit the petitioner to rely on his own wilful refusal, but that is no reason to deny a petitioner the right to plead his own impotence.[14]

(a)   Meaning of consummation

A marriage is said to be consummated as soon as the parties have sexual intercourse after the solemnisation.[15] The distinction between the act of intercourse and the possibility of that act resulting in the birth of a child must be kept clear: once the parties have had intercourse the marriage is consummated even though one or both are infertile.[16] If this were not so, the marriage could never be consummated if, for example, the wife were beyond the age of child bearing.

---

10 *Napier v Napier* [1915] P 184, CA.
11 *G v M* (1885) 10 App Cas 171, HL, at 189–90; cf *S v S (otherwise W)* [1963] P 162 at 171, [1962] 2 All ER 816, CA at 818–19. The petitioner did not have to rely on this presumption and could always allege impotence during the first three years of marriage.
12 Thus in the five years 1973–77 of all petitions alleging impotence and wilful refusal 23% alleged impotence alone, 55% alleged wilful refusal alone, and 22% alleged both in the alternative. No separate figures for the last category have been published since 1977.
13 Matrimonial Causes Act 1973 s 12(a), (b).
14 See post, p 89.
15 Not before the solemnisation. Hence the marriage is not consummated by reason of the fact that the parties have had pre-marital intercourse: see *Dredge v Dredge* [1947] 1 All ER 29.
16 *D-E v A-G* (1845) 1 Rob Eccl 279; *Baxter v Baxter* [1948] AC 274, [1947] 2 All ER 886, HL.

Conversely, if the spouses have not had intercourse, the birth of a child as the result of fecundation ab extra or artificial insemination or other methods of assisted reproduction will not amount to consummation.[17]

To amount to consummation, the intercourse must, in the words of Dr Lushington in *D-E v A-G*[18] be 'ordinary and complete, and not partial and imperfect'. Hence, as in *D-E v A-G*, there will be no consummation if the husband does not achieve full penetration in the normal sense. The necessity of complete intercourse has raised difficulties where the spouses use some form of contraception. In *Baxter v Baxter*,[19] however, the House of Lords held that the marriage had been consummated notwithstanding the husband's use of a condom. As Lord Jowitt LC pointed out, the possibility of conception is irrelevant to the question of consummation, and when Parliament passed the Matrimonial Causes Act in 1937 (the statute on which the petition was based) it was common knowledge that many people, especially young married couples, used contra-ceptives and that in common parlance this would amount to consummation.[20] The House of Lords deliberately left open the question whether coitus interruptus would amount to consummation,[1] but it has since been held at first instance that it does.[2] It has also been held that a marriage is consummated even though the husband is physically incapable of ejaculation after penetration,[3] but not if he is incapable of sustaining an erection for more than a very short period of time after penetration.[4]

(b) Inability to consummate

A marriage is voidable if it has not been consummated owing to the incapacity of either party to consummate it.[5]

Inability to consummate may be due to physiological or psychological causes and may be either general or merely as regards the particular spouse.[6] As s 12 (a) enacts the common law rule that a petitioner may show that the marriage has not been consummated because of *either* spouse's incapacity, petitions can be based on the petitioner's own impotence.[7] This follows from the premise that one of the objects in giving relief when the marriage cannot be consummated is to prevent the formation of an adulterous union[8] and the recognition of the fact that a spouse

---

17 See *Clarke v Clarke* [1943] 2 All ER 540; *L v L* [1949] P 211, [1949] 1 All ER 141.
18 Supra at 298.
19 [1948] AC 274, [1947] 2 All ER 886, HL, overruling in this respect *Cowen v Cowen* [1946] P 36, [1945] 2 All ER 197, CA.
20 At 286 and 290, 890 and 892, respectively.
1 At 283 and 888, respectively.
2 *White v White* [1948] P 330, [1948] 2 All ER 151; *Cackett v Cackett* [1950] P 253, [1950] 1 All ER 677. But the contrary was held in *Grimes v Grimes* [1948] P 323, [1948] 2 All ER 147.
3 *R v R* [1952] 1 All ER 1194.
4 *W (otherwise K) v W* [1967] 3 All ER 178n. Note also that there can be consummation even though the wife's vagina has been artificially extended (or, perhaps, wholly constructed): *SY v SY (otherwise W)* [1963] P 37, [1962] 3 All ER 55, CA. But she must be biologically female to begin with: *Corbett v Corbett* [1971] P 83, [1970] 2 All ER 33. See, however, Taitz 'The Law Relating to the Consummation of Marriage where one of the spouses is a Post-Operative Transsexual' (1986) 15 Anglo-American LR 141.
5 Matrimonial Causes Act 1973 s 12(a).
6 Impotence from psychological causes must amount to invincible repugnance and not merely unwillingness or reluctance: *Singh v Singh* [1971] P 226, [1971] 2 All ER 828, CA.
7 This rule was finally established in *Harthan v Harthan* [1949] P 115, [1948] 2 All ER 639, CA.
8 See *D-E v A-G*, supra at 299.

may be impotent quoad the other but be perfectly capable of having normal sexual intercourse with others.[9]

At common law it was said that relief would be granted only if the impotence was incurable and the term 'incapacity' presumably still imports this element. In this context, however, 'incurable' has received an extended meaning and impotence will be considered incurable not only if it is wholly incapable of any remedy, but also if it can be cured only by an operation attended by danger or, in any event, if it is improbable that the operation will be successful or the party refuses to undergo it.[10] But where petitioners rely upon their own impotence, it is submitted that the court might well take the view that they should not be allowed to complain of the situation if the impediment could be removed without danger.[11]

The petitioner's knowledge of the respondent's impotence before marriage is not necessarily a bar to the petition,[12] although if he knew that impotence was a ground for nullity, his marrying the respondent in the circumstances might amount to such conduct as would entitle the latter to invoke the statutory bar under s 13 of the 1973 Act.[13] But if the petitioner relied upon his *own* impotence, he failed at common law if he was aware of it beforehand and deceived the respondent, if at the time of the marriage he knew that the respondent was also impotent.[14] It is not clear whether these restrictions survive under the Act. If they are regarded as bars, they appear to have been swept away along with all the other common law bars;[15] it is possible to argue, however, that the absence of these conditions was a prerequisite to the petitioner's being able to bring proceedings at common law,[16] in which case they will have survived. The balance of authorities indicates that the latter view is correct.

At common law impotence was a ground for avoiding the marriage only if it existed at the time of the solemnisation and there was still no practical possibility of the marriage being consummated at the date of the hearing.[17] Consequently, if a party was capable of having sexual intercourse at the time of the ceremony but became impotent before the marriage was consummated (for example, as the result of an injury), it is doubtful whether a petition for nullity could have succeeded. The Act, however, makes no reference to incapacity at the time of the marriage, and it therefore seems that a petition could succeed in these circumstances.

---

9   See *C v C* [1921] P 399. Hence, if each is impotent quoad the other, either may petition: *G v G* [1912] P 173.

10   *S v S (otherwise C)* [1956] P 1 at 11, [1954] 3 All ER 736 at 741; *M v M* [1957] P 139, [1956] 3 All ER 769; cf *L v L* (1882) 7 PD 16; *G v G* (1908) 25 TLR 328.

11   A wilful refusal to take treatment in such a case might amount to wilful refusal to consummate the marriage: *S v S (otherwise C)* supra at 15–16, and 743–4 respectively.

12   *Nash v Nash* [1940] P 60 at 64–5, [1940] 1 All ER 206 at 209; *J v J* [1947] P 158 at 163, [1947] 2 All ER 43, CA at 44 (overruled on another point by *Baxter v Baxter*, supra).

13   See post, p 98.

14   *Harthan v Harthan* [1949] P 115 at 129, [1948] 2 All ER 639, CA at 644. In the latter case, therefore, he should petition on the ground of the respondent's impotence, for the knowledge will not necessarily bar him. See Bevan 'Limitations on the Right of an Impotent Spouse to Petition for Nullity' (1960) 76 LQR 267.

15   By the Nullity of Marriage Act 1971 s 3(4). See post, p 97.

16   See the cases cited in Jackson, op cit, pp 352–4; Bevan, loc cit.

17   *Napier v Napier* [1915] P 184, CA; *S v S (otherwise W)* [1963] P 162, [1962] 2 All ER 816, CA, approving *S v S (otherwise C)* [1956] P 1, [1954] 3 All ER 736. For if the party is cured or curable at the time of the hearing, he or she could not have been incurably incapable at the time of the solemnisation. In Scotland, it has been held that the party must have been incurable at all times since the solemnisation: *M v W* 1966 SLT 25. This is a logical extension of the rule.

(c) Wilful refusal to consummate

A marriage will be voidable if it has not been consummated owing to the *respondent's* wilful refusal to do so.[18] (As the petitioner is complaining of marital misconduct, he may not of course rely on his own refusal.) Wilful refusal connotes 'a settled and definite decision come to without just excuse', and the whole history of the marriage must be looked at.[19] In *Kaur v Singh*[20] where the parties, who were both Sikhs, married in a register office on the understanding that they should not cohabit until they had gone through a religious ceremony of marriage in a Sikh temple, it was held that in the circumstances the husband's refusal without excuse to make arrangements for such a ceremony amounted to wilful refusal to consummate the marriage.

Refusal to have intercourse in any form will clearly come within the statute, and so may wilful refusal to take treatment (attended by no danger) to remove a physical or psychological impediment to consummation.[1] If there has been no opportunity to consummate the marriage (for example, because one party is in prison), an indication by one of them that he will not consummate it at any time in the future has been held to entitle the other to petition forthwith: the latter is not bound to wait to see whether the respondent changes his mind when the opportunity arises.[2] There will not be a wilful refusal to consummate if one spouse insists upon the use of contraceptives or, probably, of coitus interruptus.

Once the marriage has been consummated, it will not be voidable if one spouse subsequently refuses to continue to have intercourse. In such a case, as in the case of the use of contraceptives or the practice of coitus interruptus against the other spouse's will, the latter's only remedy lies in divorce.

Lack of consent

Section 12(c) of the Matrimonial Causes Act 1973 provides that a marriage shall be voidable if either party did not validly consent to it, whether in consequence of duress, mistake, unsoundness of mind or otherwise. As has already been pointed out,[3] lack of consent probably made the marriage void at common law. The reason for making such a marriage voidable is that the parties themselves may wish to ratify it when true consent can be given and consequently third parties should not be able to impeach it.[4]

It will be seen that the petitioner may rely on the fact that the respondent did not consent to the marriage even though the petitioner himself was responsible for this

---

18 Matrimonial Causes Act 1973 s 12(b).
19 Per Lord Jowitt LC in *Horton v Horton* [1947] 2 All ER 871, HL at 874. He left open the question whether the petitioner could succeed if he had originally refused to consummate but then changed his mind, by which time the respondent had changed her mind and refused to let the petitioner have intercourse; cf *Potter v Potter* (1975) 5 Fam Law 161, CA (husband's refusal due to loss of sexual ardour for wife in similar circumstances not wilful).
20 [1972] 1 All ER 292, CA, following *Jodla v Jodla* [1960] 1 All ER 625. See also *A v J* [1989] 1 FLR 110 (wife's decision to postpone indefinitely a religious ceremony was found to be 'adamant and uncompromising'), and cf *Boggins v Boggins* [1966] CLY 4041 (husband who deserted wife before consummating marriage held to have wilfully refused to do so).
1 *S v S (otherwise C)* [1956] P 1 at 15–16, [1954] 3 All ER 736 at 743–4.
2 *Ford v Ford* [1987] Fam Law 232. The result is socially desirable, but it is difficult to see how the respondent's conduct comes within the wording of the Act (the marriage *has not been* consummated, not *will not* be consummated).
3 See ante, p 87.
4 See Law Com No 33, paras 11–15.

state of affairs, for example by inducing a mistake or uttering threats. Whilst this logically followed when lack of consent made the marriage void, it may leave a respondent who wishes to adopt the marriage with a legitimate sense of grievance in such circumstances. Nevertheless, he will have no defence to the petition unless he can plead one of the statutory bars.[5]

We must now consider what facts will be regarded in law as vitiating consent.[6]

(a)   Unsoundness of mind

This will affect a marriage only if, as a consequence, *at the time of the ceremony* either party was unable to understand the nature of the contract he was entering into. There is a presumption that he was capable of doing so, and the burden of proof therefore lies upon the party impeaching the validity of the marriage.[7] The test to be applied was formulated by Singleton LJ in *In the Estate of Park*:[8]

> 'Was the [person] . . . capable of understanding the nature of the contract into which he was entering, or was his mental condition such that he was incapable of understanding it? To ascertain the nature of the contract of marriage a man must be mentally capable of appreciating that it involves the responsibilities normally attaching to marriage. Without that degree of mentality, it cannot be said that he understands the nature of the contract.'

(b)   Drunkenness and the effect of drugs

In the absence of any binding English authority, it is submitted that the effect of drunkenness and drugs will be the same as that of unsoundness of mind. Consequently, the marriage will be voidable if, as a result of either, one of the parties was incapable of understanding the nature of the contract into which he was entering.[9]

(c)   Mistake

A mistake will affect the marriage in two cases only. First, a mistake as to the identity (but not as to the attributes) of the other contracting party will make the marriage voidable if this results in one party's failing to marry the individual whom he or she intends to marry. In the New Zealand case *C v C*,[10] the woman

---

5   See post, pp 98ff.

6   The following discussion may not be exhaustive. To take a further example, if one of the parties to a marriage contracted abroad was so young at the time of the ceremony that he (or she) could not be said to have given full and free consent, the marriage may be voidable by English law, unless he ratified it after attaining an age when he was capable of understanding the nature of the contract. See Poulter 'Ethnic Minority Customs, English Law and Human Rights', (1987) 36 ICLQ 589 at 610–11.

7   *Harrod v Harrod* (1854) 1 K & J 4, 9. But if the person is proved to have been generally insane, there will be a presumption that he was insane at the time of the marriage, and the burden of proof will consequently shift onto the party seeking to uphold its validity: *Turner v Meyers* (1808) 1 Hag Con 414 at 417.

8   [1954] P 112 at 127, [1953] 2 All ER 1411, CA at 1430; cf Karminski J (in the Div Court) [1954] P 89 at 99, [1953] 2 All ER 408 at 414; Birkett LJ at 134–5 and 1434; Hodson LJ at 137 and 1436–7 respectively; *Hunter v Edney* (1881) 10 PD 93 at 95; *Durham v Durham* (1885) 10 PD 80 at 82.

9   See *Legey v O'Brien* (1834) Milw 325; *Sullivan v Sullivan* (1818) 2 Hag Con 238 at 246 (per Sir W Scott).

10   [1942] NZLR 356. But if A becomes engaged to B, whom she has never seen before, by correspondence, and C successfully personates B at the wedding, the marriage would be voidable because A intends to marry B and nobody else: ibid, p 359. It would be void if the personation invalidated the publication of banns: see ante, p 39.

married the man in the erroneous belief that he was a well-known boxer called Miller. It was held that the marriage was not invalidated by the mistake because she married the very individual she meant to marry. Secondly, the marriage will be voidable if one of the parties is mistaken as to the nature of the ceremony and does not appreciate that he is contracting a marriage. In *Valier v Valier*[11] the husband, who was an Italian and whose knowledge of the English language was poor, was taken to a register office by the wife and there went through the usual form of marriage. He did not understand what was happening at the time, the parties never cohabited and the marriage was never consummated. It was held that he was entitled to a decree of nullity.

But if each party appreciates that he is going through a form of marriage with the other, no other type of mistake apparently can affect the contract.[12] Thus, it has been held that the marriage will not be invalidated by a mistake as to the monogamous or polygamous nature of the union,[13] the other party's fortune,[14] the woman's chastity,[15] or the recognition of the union by the religious denomination of the parties.[16]

(d) Fraud and misrepresentation

Unlike the case of a commercial contract, neither a fraudulent nor an innocent misrepresentation will of itself affect the validity of a marriage.[17] But if the misrepresentation induces an operative mistake (eg as to the nature of the ceremony), the marriage will be made voidable by the latter.[18]

(e) Fear and duress

If, owing to fear or threats, one of the parties is induced to enter into a marriage which, in the absence of compulsion, he would never have contracted, the marriage will be voidable.

The fear may be due to a number of causes. In *Buckland v Buckland*,[19] for example, the petitioner, a youth aged 20 resident in Malta, was groundlessly charged with defiling the respondent, a girl of 15. Although he protested his innocence, he was twice advised that he stood no chance of an acquittal but would probably be sent to prison for a period of up to two years unless he married her. He did so and it was held that he was entitled to a decree of nullity. Nor is it necessary that the fear should have been inspired by any acts on the other party's part. A striking example of duress imposed ab extra is to be seen in *Szechter v*

11 (1925) 133 LT 830. See also *Ford v Stier* [1896] P 1, and *Kelly v Kelly* (1932) 49 TLR 99 (mistaken belief that ceremony was formal betrothal); *Mehta v Mehta* [1945] 2 All ER 690 (mistaken belief that Hindu marriage ceremony was ceremony of religious conversion).
12 *Moss v Moss* [1897] P 263 at 271–3; *Kenward v Kenward* [1950] P 71 at 79, [1949] 2 All ER 959 at 963 (per Hodson J); revsd [1951] P 124 at 133–4, [1950] 2 All ER 297, CA at 302 (per Evershed MR).
13 *Kassim v Kassim* [1962] P 224, [1962] 3 All ER 426.
14 *Wakefield v Mackay* (1807) 1 Hag Con 394 at 398.
15 Even though she is pregnant per alium: *Moss v Moss* (supra).
16 *Ussher v Ussher* [1912] 2 IR 445.
17 *Swift v Kelly* (1835) 3 Knapp 257 at 293; *Moss v Moss* (supra) at 266.
18 *Moss v Moss* (supra), at 268–9.
19 [1968] P 296, [1967] 2 All ER 300. See also *Scott v Sebright* (1886) 12 PD 21 (threats to make petitioner bankrupt, to denounce her and finally to shoot her); *Griffith v Griffith* [1944] IR 35 (fear of prosecution for unlawful carnal knowledge); Poulter 'The Definition of Marriage in English Law' (1979) 42 MLR 409 at 410–18. All the earlier cases are collected and exhaustively discussed by Manchester 'Marriage or Prison: the Case of the Reluctant Bridegroom' (1966) 29 MLR 622.

Szechter.[20] The petitioner was a Polish national who had been arrested by the security police in Warsaw. After 14 months' interrogation and detention in appalling conditions she was sentenced to three years' imprisonment for 'anti-state activities'. Her health, which had always been poor, deteriorated rapidly and she came to the conclusion that she would not survive the sentence; if she did come out of prison alive, she believed that she was likely to be re-arrested and in any case would be unable to get any job other than one of a menial nature. The respondent was a distinguished Polish historian of Jewish origin whose presence in Poland was something of an embarrassment to the authorities and whom they were prepared to allow to emigrate. In order to effect the petitioner's release he divorced his wife and went through a ceremony of marriage with the petitioner in prison. The scheme was successful, and eventually all the parties reached England, where the petitioner brought proceedings for nullity so that the respondent and his first wife could remarry. A decree was granted. In so doing Simon P applied the following test:[1]

> 'It is, in my view, insufficient to invalidate an otherwise good marriage that a party has entered into it in order to escape from a disagreeable situation, such as penury or social degradation. In order for the impediment of duress to vitiate an otherwise valid marriage, it must, in my judgment, be proved that the will of one of the parties thereto has been overborne by genuine and reasonably held fear caused by threat of immediate danger (for which the party is not himself responsible), to life, limb or liberty, so that the constraint destroys the reality of consent to ordinary wedlock.'

There may be rare cases where the party is so terrified that he (or she) does not know what he is doing at all: a marriage contracted in such circumstances must be voidable as there is no consent whatever. In other cases the reference to the party's will being overborne has been criticised on the ground that he does in fact consciously choose to enter into marriage rather than accept the alternative presented to him.[2] The court must then decide whether the circumstances were such that it would be socially more objectionable to tie the party to the union than to permit him to repudiate it: the need to uphold the institution of marriage must be balanced against the need to do justice to the individual. This must depend on what he perceived to be the probable consequences of refusing to enter into the marriage and his capacity to resist the pressure brought to bear on him. If he is more susceptible to this pressure than another might be, the marriage should still be annulled even though a person of ordinary courage and resilience would not have yielded to it.[3]

Applying this test, it may be doubted whether the three limitations which Simon P placed upon the operation of duress as a ground for nullity are desirable or supported by earlier authorities. First, if the condition that the fear must be reasonably held means that the marriage will be voidable only if a reasonable person, placed in the position of the petitioner, would have concluded that the threats would have been implemented if the marriage had not taken place, it is

---

20 [1971] P 286, [1970] 3 All ER 905. See also *H v H* [1954] P 258, [1953] 2 All ER 1229 (marriage contracted in Budapest to enable woman to escape from Hungary where she was likely to be sent to prison or concentration camp); *Parojcic v Parojcic* [1959] 1 All ER 1 (fear imposed by petitioner's father).

1 At 297–8 and 915, respectively.

2 Ingman and Grant 'Duress in the Law of Nullity' [1984] Fam Law 92, citing Atiyah (1982) 98 LQR 197 and *DPP for Northern Ireland v Lynch* [1975] AC 653, [1975] 1 All ER 913, HL.

3 *Scott v Sebright* (1886) 12 PD 21 at 24; *Cooper v Crane* [1891] P 369 at 376.

directly contrary to the view stated earlier by Butt J in *Scott v Sebright*[4] and it is submitted that the latter is to be preferred. If a person is in a mental state in which he is no longer capable of offering resistance to threats, it seems immaterial that it would be obvious to a reasonable person, similarly placed, that the other has no intention of carrying them out at all.[5] Secondly, although Scarman J's decision in *Buckland v Buckland* is clear authority for the proposition that the fear must arise from some external circumstances for which the party is not himself responsible, it is doubtful whether this rule is correctly expressed. In that case the petitioner succeeded because his fear arose from the false charge preferred against him; presumably he would have failed had he actually been guilty of defiling the respondent. Originally it was said that the fear must be unjustly imposed;[6] and whilst it could not be justly imposed if the party was not responsible for the events which had given rise to the threat; it does not follow that it will be justly imposed if he was responsible. If a man is threatened with being pursued for child support unless he marries the woman allegedly carrying his child, it seems proper that he should be able to petition for nullity if he is not the father but that he should not be able to do so if the child is his. If, however, the woman's father threatens to shoot him if he does not marry her or, to take a different situation, if an employer threatens to prosecute a clerk for theft if he does not marry his daughter, one feels that the marriage should be voidable in both cases whether or not the man in question is responsible for the pregnancy or has committed the theft. The distinction is that it is reasonable to face a man with the choice between marriage and maintenance proceedings but not to face him with the choice between marriage and death or prosecution for theft.

More problematical is whether Simon P's third condition can be regarded as correct, namely that the fear must be caused by 'threat of immediate danger to life, limb or liberty'. The Court of Appeal applied it in *Singh v Singh*[7] and *Singh v Kaur*,[8] but only a year after the latter case Ormrod LJ, delivering the leading judgment of the court in *Hirani v Hirani*,[9] denied the need for such threats and stated that the question is 'whether the pressure . . . is such as to destroy the reality of consent and overbears the will of the individual'. The Court of Appeal is now free to apply either test[10] and it is strongly urged that it should apply the less stringent one.[11] The threat of financial or social ruin may work as strongly as the

---

4   (1886) 12 PD 21 at 24. But Simon P's views are supported by *Buckland v Buckland* [1968] P 296 at 301, [1967] 2 All ER 300 at 302 (per Scarman J) and *H v H* [1954] P 258 at 269, [1953] 2 All ER 1229 at 1234 (per Karminski J).

5   This is the view of the Law Commission in Law Com No 33, at p 27. Davies 'Duress and Nullity of Marriage' (1972) 88 LQR 549 suggests that the rule that the fear must be reasonably entertained applies only when it is imposed by someone other than the respondent or his agent. This is ingenious but it is not the basis of any reported case and could work injustice. In *Parojcic v Parojcic* (supra), for example, the petitioner entered into the marriage because her father threatened to send her back to Yugoslavia if she did not do so; why should she be tied to the marriage if a reasonable woman in her position would have realised that he had no intention of implementing his threat?

6   *Griffith v Griffith* [1944] IR 35 at 43–4.

7   [1971] P 226, [1971] 2 All ER 828, CA.

8   (1981) 11 Fam Law 152, CA.

9   (1982) 4 FLR 232, CA. Ormrod LJ had also given the leading judgment in *Singh v Kaur*.

10   *Young v Bristol Aeroplane Co Ltd* [1944] KB 718, [1944] 2 All ER 293, CA.

11   In Scotland the '*Hirani* test' rather than the '*Szechter* test' has been followed in two cases in which the petitioning Pakistani woman was forced to go through with an arranged marriage due to family pressure: see *Mahmood v Mahmood* 1993 SLT 589 and *Mahmud v Mahmud* 1994 SLT 599. For an interesting analysis of these cases see Bradney 'Duress, Family Law and the Coherent Legal System' (1994) 57 MLR 963.

threat of physical violence on some minds,[12] and in some ethnic communities failure to comply with parental wishes in this regard may lead to ostracism and a complete break with the family.[13] If any of these facts have deprived a person of the effective power of refusing to enter into a marriage, he or she should be able to resile from it.[14]

It is therefore submitted that the only limitation on duress or fear as a ground for nullity is that a marriage will not be voidable if the fear is justly imposed in the sense that the party is responsible for the state of affairs which has given rise to the threat and it is reasonable to face him with the choice between marriage and the implementation of the threat.[15]

(f)   'Sham marriages'

Cases like *Szechter v Szechter* raise a further question: is a 'sham marriage' – that is, where the parties go through the form of marriage purely for the purpose of representing themselves as married to the outside world with no intention of cohabiting – to be regarded in law as a nullity? This problem is more likely to arise with restrictive immigration laws: for example, a woman who is a citizen of state X may go through a form of marriage with a citizen of state Y merely in order to enter or remain in Y on the strength of her husband's nationality or passport.

Since the House of Lords' decision in *Vervaeke v Smith*[16] there can be no doubt that such marriages are perfectly valid provided the parties freely consented to contracting them. In that case a Belgian prostitute went through a ceremony of marriage with a British subject so that she could apply for British citizenship and thus escape deportation. The parties had no intention of living together and saw each other again on only one or two occasions. The majority of the House considered it indisputable that the marriage was valid.

Mental disorder

A marriage is voidable if, at the time of the ceremony, *either party*, though capable of giving a valid consent, was suffering (whether continuously or intermittently) from mental disorder within the meaning of the Mental Health Act 1983 of such a kind or to such an extent as to be unfitted for marriage.[17] 'Unfitted for marriage' in

---

12 See *Scott v Sebright* (1886) 12 PD 21, where the respondent's threats to see that bankruptcy proceedings were taken against the petitioner and to 'accuse her to her mother and in every drawing-room in London of having been seduced by him' were apparently regarded as grounds (along with a threat to shoot her) for annulling the marriage.

13 This was the threat in *Hirani v Hirani*.

14 See further Davies, loc cit at p 552; Ingman and Grant, loc cit; Poulter *English Law and Ethnic Minority Customs*, 2.19–2.24; Bradney 'Arranged Marriages and Duress' [1984] JSWL 278; Pearl 'Arranged Marriages' [1971] CLJ 206; Bates 'Duress as Grounds for Nullity: A New Perspective' (1980) 130 New LJ 1035 and the Australian cases there cited; Bradley 'Duress and Arranged Marriages (1983) 46 MLR 499 and Bradney (1994), loc cit.

15 See also Law Com No 33, paras 63–66 (to which Scarman J, as chairman, was a party): Davies, loc cit.

16 [1983] 1 AC 145, [1982] 2 All ER 144, per Lord Hailsham LC at 151–2 and 148, and Lord Simon at 162 and 156. Lord Brandon agreed with both speeches. See also *Silver v Silver* [1955] 2 All ER 614; *Puttick v A-G* [1980] Fam 1, [1979] 3 All ER 463; Rogers 'Sham Marriages' (1974) 4 Fam Law 4; Wade 'Limited Purpose Marriages' (1982) 45 MLR 159, particularly at 169–70.

17 Matrimonial Causes Act 1973 s 12 (d). For the meaning of 'mental disorder', see the Mental Health Act 1983 s 1 (2).

this context has been defined as 'incapable of carrying out the ordinary duties and obligations of marriage'.[18]

This ground must be distinguished from that already considered, namely, mental illness producing lack of consent. In the case of mental disorder it is presumed that the party was capable of giving a valid consent to the marriage but that the general state of his mental health at the time of the ceremony was such that it is right that the marriage should be annulled. It will be observed that the petitioner does not have to rely on the respondent's mental disorder, but may rely on his own. This is necessary to enable a party to withdraw from a marriage if he entered into it in ignorance of the existence or extent of his illness or the effect which it would have upon his married life.

Venereal disease and pregnancy by another

A marriage is voidable if at the time of the ceremony *the respondent* was suffering from venereal disease in a communicable form.[19] 'Venereal disease' is not defined in the Act.[20]

A husband may petition for nullity if at the time of the marriage *the respondent wife* was pregnant by someone other than himself.[1]

Both these grounds, which were introduced by the Matrimonial Causes Act 1937, were thought necessary because there was otherwise no matrimonial relief for fraud or misrepresentation, and it was thought unjust to bind a person to marriage in these circumstances.[2]

2.   BARS TO RELIEF

Like any other voidable contract, at common law a party to a voidable marriage might effectively put it out of his own power to obtain a decree of nullity by his own conduct. In addition to specific limitations attached to the statutory grounds for nullity, there were two bars of general application: approbation (which we discuss shortly) and collusion. The essence of collusion was that the initiation or conduct of the suit had been in some measure procured or determined by an agreement or bargain between the parties, and the reason that it was a bar was that the existence of such an agreement raised doubts whether the decree would be granted on the merits at all. This did not prevent the presentation of a false case in an undefended suit, however, and withholding a decree for collusion was open to the objection that it implied that 'the sanctity of marriage is maintained by insisting that people should remain married as a punishment for their misbehaviour'.[3] Consequently, on the Law Commission's recommendation, collusion was abolished as a bar by the Nullity of Marriage Act 1971 and all the others were replaced by three statutory bars which are now the only ones applicable.[4]

---

18 *Bennett v Bennett* [1969] 1 All ER 539.
19 Matrimonial Causes Act 1973 s 12 (e).
20 In the 8th edition of this work (at p 96) we discussed whether venereal disease includes AIDS, but on reflection we do not think that that point is arguable given the various ways in which the HIV infection can be transmitted.
 1 Ibid, s 12 (f).
 2 Quaere whether the case for their continued retention as grounds for nullity is now so compelling?
 3 Law Com No 33 para 37.
 4 See Law Com No 33, paras 36–45 and 76–86.

Petitioner's conduct

Section 13(1) of the Matrimonial Causes Act 1973 provides:

'The court shall not . . . grant a decree of nullity on the ground that the marriage is voidable if the respondent satisfies the court –

(a) that the petitioner, with knowledge that it was open to him to have the marriage avoided, so conducted himself in relation to the respondent as to lead the respondent reasonably to believe that he would not seek to do so; and

(b) that it would be unjust to the respondent to grant the decree.'

This replaces the former bar of approbation (or lack of sincerity, as it was called in the other cases). The principle underlying this bar was summarised by Lord Watson:[5]

'In a suit for nullity of marriage there may be facts and circumstances proved which so plainly imply, on the part of the complaining spouse, a recognition of the existence and validity of the marriage, as to render it most inequitable and contrary to public policy that he or she should be permitted to go on to challenge it with effect.'

The same principle underlies the statutory bar, and consequently much of the old law remains unaltered, although there have been some changes in detail and some doubts have been resolved. Before we examine the question of the petitioner's conduct in more detail, however, three preliminary points must be made. First, the court will be bound to apply the bar only if the respondent satisfies it that the statutory conditions are fulfilled. Not only does this mean that the burden of proof is on the respondent, but if he chooses not to raise the bar at all, the court must grant a decree if a ground has been made out even if it is clear from the facts that these conditions are satisfied:[6] the bar no longer rests on public policy.[7] Secondly, no conduct on the petitioner's part can raise the bar unless he knew at the time that it was open to him to have the marriage avoided. This means that he must have been aware not only of the facts upon which the petition is based (for example, that he is not the father of the child that the respondent was carrying at the time of the marriage), but also that these facts would entitle him to petition for a decree of nullity.[8] Any act or omission when he was ignorant of either of these matters must be disregarded.[9] Thirdly, only conduct in relation to the petitioner can act as a bar.

(a)   Positive acts

Any positive act by the petitioner may raise the bar if a reasonable person in the respondent's position would have concluded that the petitioner intended to treat the marriage as valid and the respondent in fact drew this conclusion. In *D v D*[10] the parties adopted two children at a time when the husband knew that he could have the marriage annulled because of his wife's refusal to consummate it. He later brought nullity proceedings. It was held that by agreeing to the adoption he

---

5 *G v M* (1885) 10 App Cas 171, HL at 197–8.

6 This point was not taken in *D v D* [1979] Fam 70, [1979] 3 All ER 337, where the wife, having raised the defence, then elected not to pursue it. Dunn J, however, held that in such circumstances it could not be said to be unjust to grant the decree.

7 *D v D* (supra).

8 The respondent is presumed to know the law and the burden is on him to prove that he did not: *W v W* [1952] P 152 at 162, [1952] 1 All ER 858, CA at 863.

9 This re-enacts the common law rule: see *G v M* (supra), at 186.

10 [1979] Fam 70, [1979] 3 All ER 337.

had so conducted himself in relation to the wife as to lead her to believe that he would not seek to do so.

In some cases spouses may well resort to adoption, artificial insemination or some other form of assisted reproduction if one of them is infertile so that a child cannot be conceived in the normal way, and the same principle will apply. If by consenting to the act the petitioner admits that the marriage is never likely to be consummated and also implies that any child which may be conceived will be born into a normal family where the husband and wife are validly married, the respondent may well infer that he will not thereafter petition for nullity. Nor can it make any difference if the petitioner gives consent in the hope that the adoption or birth of the child will remove a psychological impediment. If, however, he has made the position clear to the respondent, he can still petition if his purpose fails and the marriage remains unconsummated, because nothing he has done will have led the respondent to believe that he will not seek to have the marriage annulled. But he may not later rely on a mental reservation 'locked in his bosom and not declared' to the respondent if the reasonable conclusion from his acts and declared intentions is that he is waiving his power to bring proceedings.[11]

In some circumstances the mere fact that the petitioner has married the respondent at all may reasonably lead the latter to believe that the former will not subsequently petition for nullity. If a man marries a woman knowing that one of them is impotent or suffering from mental disorder and knowing also that this is a ground for nullity, she may reasonably conclude that he intends to treat the marriage as valid and thus raise the marriage itself as a bar if he does petition. For the same reason a party who has deprived the other of the power of consenting freely to the marriage by inducing a mistake or uttering threats may not be able to petition. A similar case arises if the parties entered into an agreement before marriage that they would not have sexual intercourse. Although this is regarded as contrary to public policy and is therefore not binding on them,[12] it may preclude either of them from obtaining a decree of nullity if the marriage is in fact never consummated and the agreement led the respondent to believe that the petitioner would not bring proceedings.[13] If one of the parties is old, infirm or seriously crippled, the marriage may well have been on this understanding, express or implied. A fortiori an agreement between the spouses that the petitioner will not institute proceedings for nullity will be a good defence to a petition.[14]

Although estoppel in the strict sense of the term cannot apply if the marriage is voidable, a party who brings other matrimonial proceedings with the knowledge that it is open to him to have the marriage annulled may thereby bar himself from petitioning for nullity later if the other spouse draws the conclusion that he does not intend to do so. Thus a wife who knows that her marriage is voidable because of her husband's impotence may lose her power to petition for nullity if she brings court proceedings for maintenance.[15] Her husband might likewise lose his power to petition if he took part in the proceedings without indicating that he reserved the right to have the marriage avoided later.

---

11 See *W v W* [1952] P 152 at 168, [1952] 1 All ER 858, CA at 866.
12 See *Brodie v Brodie* [1917] P 271.
13 See *Morgan v Morgan* [1959] P 92, [1959] 1 All ER 539; *Scott v Scott* [1959] P 103n, [1959] 1 All ER 531.
14 See *Aldridge v Aldridge* (1888) 13 PD 210.
15 See *Tindall v Tindall* [1953] P 63, [1953] 1 All ER 139, CA. Similarly, a wife might bar herself if she continued to accept income from a trust in her favour in a marriage settlement.

(b)   Delay

Just as some active step on the petitioner's part may bar him from bringing proceedings for nullity, delay in bringing them may equally bar him if he knows that it is open to him to have the marriage avoided and the delay has led the respondent reasonably to believe that he does not intend to do so. The question must be one of fact: did the petitioner's delay lull the respondent into a false sense of security or a false belief that he would not petition?

(c)   Injustice of decree

In addition to proving that the petitioner has led the respondent to believe that he will not seek to have the marriage avoided, the latter must also show that it would be unjust to him (or her) to grant the decree. As in the case of divorce, justice will rarely be served by refusing to set aside a marriage that is already dead, but there will undoubtedly be some cases when it would be manifestly unjust to grant a decree against an unwilling respondent. For example, a respondent in a position of the wife in *D v D* [16] might satisfy the court that it would be unjust to her to annul the marriage because she would be left with two adopted children. The defence is perhaps most likely to succeed if the petitioner relies on his own impotence (or mental disorder), for consideration must necessarily be given to the respondent's attitude and reaction to a situation for which he is in no way responsible. [17] Among the matters which the court should take into account in deciding whether to grant a decree are the length of time the marriage has lasted, the existence of any children of the family, any religious or other personal objections that the respondent has to the decree, and the financial loss that he (or she) might suffer as a result of nullity (for example, the loss of pension rights or Social Security benefits).

Lapse of time

In all cases, except those based on impotence or wilful refusal to consummate (see below), a decree of nullity must normally be refused if the proceedings were not instituted within three years of the date of the marriage. [18]

The reason for this bar is to ensure that the parties' status is not left in doubt for too long: consequently there is no power to extend the period, even though the petitioner was unaware of the facts or that they made the marriage voidable. This may well work injustice, however. The Law Commission concluded that hardship was most likely to arise if the complaining party was mentally disordered. They had in mind two problems in particular: old and lonely people not fully in possession of their faculties may well become the object of attention of fortune

---

16 For the facts see ante, p 98. In this case it was held not to be unjust to grant the decree because the respondent did not pursue the defence.

17 See *Pettit v Pettit* [1963] P 177, [1962] 3 All ER 37, CA. The husband did not discover that he could petition on the ground of his own impotence for more than 20 years after the marriage and after the birth of a child as the result of fecundatio ab extra. Under the old law of approbation the court refused to grant the decree because it would have been inequitable to do so. If the husband had known all along that he could petition, it is submitted that the decision would be the same today.

18 Matrimonial Causes Act 1973 s 13(2). This is independent of the bar last considered, and even if the petition is brought within three years, the respondent may still raise the petitioner's delay or other conduct as a bar if it reasonably led him to conclude that the petitioner would not seek to have the marriage annulled.

hunters, and a petition may have to be presented by the party's next friend who may not become aware of all the facts during the first three years of the marriage.[19] Following the Commission's recommendation, the court is now empowered[20] to grant leave for the presentation of a petition based on any ground, notwithstanding that more than three years have elapsed since the date of the marriage, provided that the petitioner has suffered from mental disorder within the meaning of the Mental Health Act 1983 at any time during the first three years of the marriage and that the court considers that it would be just to do so.

Lapse of time is not a bar in the case of inability or wilful refusal to consummate the marriage, because the petitioner may properly try to overcome the impediment or aversion for a longer period than three years.[1]

Petitioner's knowledge

If the petition is based on the respondent's venereal disease or pregnancy per alium, the decree must be refused unless the court was satisfied that the petitioner was ignorant of the facts alleged at the time of the marriage.[2]

3. EFFECT OF DECREE

Although a decree has always been necessary to annul a voidable marriage, at common law (as in the case of a void marriage) it pronounced the marriage 'to have been and to be absolutely null and void to all intents and purposes in the law whatsoever'. Consequently, before the decree the parties were regarded as husband and wife both in law and in fact but after the decree absolute they were deemed in law never to have been married at all. The logical application of this anomalous doctrine produced some startling results. Children of a voidable marriage were automatically bastardised by the decree; the trusts under a marriage settlement all failed and the interest of the person entitled before the solemnisation of the marriage revived; and if a widow remarried and the second marriage was annulled, she reverted to the status of her first husband's widow and could therefore claim an annuity payable to her dum vidua.[3] Some of these anomalies were swept away by statute – for example, children of a voidable marriage retained their legitimacy – and after the Second World War there was an increasing tendency for the judges to regard decrees of nullity in respect of voidable marriages more like decrees of divorce.[4] This doctrine was never consistently applied, however, and by 1971 it was becoming increasingly difficult to predict in any given case what approach the court would adopt.

---

19 See Law Com No 116 (*Time Restrictions on Presentation of Divorce and Nullity Petitions*, 1982), Pt III.
20 Matrimonial Causes Act 1973 s 13(2) and (4) as amended by the Matrimonial and Family Proceedings Act 1984 s 2. Note that the petition does not have to be based on the petitioner's mental disorder.
1 See Law Com No 33, paras 79–85.
2 Matrimonial Causes Act 1973 s 13(3).
3 *Re Wombwell's Settlement* [1922] 2 Ch 298 (marriage settlement); *Re d'Altroy's Will Trusts* [1968] 1 All ER 181 (widow's annuity). See also *Newbould v A-G* [1931] P 75, and *Re Rodwell* [1970] Ch 726, [1969] 3 All ER 1363 (parties regarded as never having been married).
4 *R v Algar* [1954] 1 QB 279, [1953] 2 All ER 1381, CCA (wife remained incompetent to give evidence against husband); *Wiggins v Wiggins* [1958] 2 All ER 555 (second marriage contracted during subsistence of voidable marriage remained void notwithstanding annulment of the first).

With the purpose of sweeping away the remaining anomalies and clarifying the law it is now provided: [5]

> 'A decree of nullity granted after 31st July 1971 in respect of a voidable marriage shall operate to annul the marriage only as respects any time after the decree has been made absolute, and the marriage shall, notwithstanding the decree, be treated as if it had existed up to that time.'

Unfortunately the effect of this obscurely worded section is far from clear. It leaves no doubt that the parties must now be regarded as having been married throughout the whole period between the celebration of a voidable marriage and the decree absolute. Two examples will illustrate the operation of this part of the provision:

(1) If H marries W, then marries X, and then obtains a decree of nullity of the first marriage on the ground of W's impotence, the marriage to X will still be void because H was married to W when he contracted it.

(2) If a pension is payable to W, the widow of A, until she remarries and she then contracts a voidable marriage with H which is later annulled, she cannot reclaim her pension because she is still regarded as having remarried. [6]

What is not clear is the effect of the decree on the parties' status after it has been made absolute. The Act expressly states that it shall operate to annul the marriage, not to terminate it. This implies that the effect is different from that of a decree of dissolution, and it is arguable that the parties revert to their previous status. Thus, in the second example given above W would once more be regarded as the widow of A even though she is also regarded as having been married to H; consequently, although she could not claim a pension payable until remarriage, she could claim it if it were payable during her widowhood. It is difficult to believe that Parliament really intended such a Gilbertian situation and, despite the infelicitous wording of the Act, it is submitted that the consequences of the annulment of a voidable marriage must be the same as those of the dissolution of a valid one.

The section has effect only if the decree absolute was granted on or after 1 August 1971 (when the Nullity of Marriage Act came into operation). In the case of a decree pronounced before this date it may still be necessary to consider the law as it was before the Act was passed. [7]

D.   Estoppel

If it is alleged that a marriage is void, the court is usually bound to find in favour of the party making the allegation if one of the grounds considered above is established, whether he is petitioning for nullity or the question of the validity of the marriage has arisen in some other proceedings. The question arises, however, whether a party can ever be estopped from asserting the invalidity of the marriage

---

5 Matrimonial Causes Act 1973 s 16, re-enacting the Nullity of Marriage Act 1971 s 5, and implementing the recommendations of the Law Commission: Law Com No 33, paras 21–22 and 25.
6 *Ward v Secretary of State for Social Services* [1990] 1 FLR 119.
7 See the 4th edition of this book, pp 69–71.

even though he could prove that it is void. Two illustrations will indicate the sort of problem that can arise:

(1) If a married man goes through a form of marriage with a woman after representing to her that he is a bachelor or a widower and then leaves her unsupported, may he raise the nullity of this marriage as a defence to any action brought by her for maintenance?

(2) Alternatively, if previous matrimonial proceedings have been brought between the same parties on the assumption that the marriage is valid, may either subsequently petition for nullity or put the validity of the marriage in issue in later proceedings?

It is submitted that a distinction must be drawn between estoppel by conduct and estoppel per rem judicatam for this purpose. In the former case the better view seems to be that the parties by their own conduct cannot prevent the court from enquiring into the real state of affairs and declaring what their true status is. In *Miles v Chilton*,[8] where the husband petitioned for nullity on the ground that the wife was already married at the time of the ceremony in question, it was held that the wife's averment that the husband had deceived her into believing that she had already been divorced by her first husband was no answer to the petition.

The position with respect to estoppel per rem judicatam is more complicated. Decrees of nullity, and orders for divorce or separation are all judgments in rem and bind not only the parties but the whole world. Hence nobody can assert the validity of a marriage after a decree of nullity has been pronounced.[9] If a petition for nullity is dismissed, this will create an estoppel inter partes only. If, for example, H unsuccessfully petitions for a decree of nullity on the ground that the other party to the marriage, W, was married to another man at the time of the ceremony, neither H nor W can now assert that the marriage is void for this reason, although a third person who was not a party to the proceedings or privy to them could still do so.[10] If the outcome of any other proceedings between the parties in the High Court rests on the validity of their marriage, this will presumably also create an estoppel inter partes, so that neither of them could assert that the marriage was void if, for example, successful proceedings for maintenance had been previously brought under s 27 of the Matrimonial Causes Act 1973.[11] It has been held that proceedings before magistrates cannot create an estoppel in the High Court[12] or, presumably, in a county court. Although non-matrimonial proceedings in a county court have been held to create an estoppel in a magistrates' court, it has been stated obiter that they

---

8 (1849) 1 Rob Eccl 684. The contrary view, stated obiter by the Divisional Court in *Bullock v Bullock* [1960] 2 All ER 307 at 309 and 313, does not seem to be supported by the authorities there cited.

9 See Tolstoy 'Marriage by Estoppel, or an Excursion into Res Judicata' (1968) 84 LQR 245, and the authorities there cited, particularly *Woodland v Woodland* [1928] P 169.

10 The problem arose in an acute form in *Wilkins v Wilkins* [1896] P 108, CA. On the wife's petition for divorce the respondent husband's answer had been that the marriage was void because the wife's first husband was alive at the time of his marriage to the petitioner. This fact was expressly found against him. The first husband later returned to England and the second husband then petitioned for nullity. It was held that the first judgment estopped him from doing so, but the Court of Appeal solved the problem by giving him leave to apply for a new trial on that issue.

11 See post, p 763.

12 *Hayward v Hayward* [1961] P 152 at 161, [1961] 1 All ER 236 at 243. But note Ward J's reluctance to follow this in respect of proceedings under the Children Act 1989 in *K v P (Children Act Proceedings: Estoppel)* [1995] 1 FLR 248 at 253.

cannot bind the High Court in matrimonial proceedings.[13]

When questions of status are involved, estoppel inevitably creates difficulties. There may be little justification for permitting either party to assert the invalidity of a marriage when he or she has already had an opportunity of doing so but, as Phillimore J said in *Hayward v Hayward*,[14] public policy demands that, when status is in issue, the courts should declare the truth unencumbered by technical rules. If the statement of law above is correct, a man may be validly married to one woman but estopped from denying that he is also married to a second: a result no less absurd than the fact that a stranger may be able to show that a marriage is void whilst, as between themselves, the parties are prevented from doing so. For this reason the doctrine of estoppel should be applied as narrowly as possible in matrimonial causes. It is submitted that it should be limited to cases where the issue has already been expressly litigated: hence earlier proceedings for maintenance should not prevent either party from alleging that the marriage is void if that question was never before the court. It may also be possible for a party to reopen an issue which has been the subject of a finding in previous proceedings if further relevant evidence, which he could not have adduced with reasonable diligence in those proceedings, has since become available to him.[15]

In any event, estoppel should be confined to cases where the marriage in question is alleged to be void and not extended to those where it is voidable. Now that a voidable marriage is to be treated as having existed up to the decree absolute, there is nothing inconsistent in an earlier decision based on the assumption that the marriage is valid and a later decree declaring the marriage to be voidable.

E.   Is there a continuing need for nullity?

In practical terms the law of nullity has little current relevance. The number of orders is small[16] (though there are those that argue[17] that, because of the length of time it will take to obtain a divorce under the Family Law Act 1996,[18] the number of nullity petitions might rise again when that Act is implemented) and for the

---

13 *Whittaker v Whittaker* [1939] 3 All ER 833 at 837. Presumably matrimonial proceedings in a county court will raise an estoppel in all courts; they have been held to create an estoppel in non-matrimonial proceedings in the High Court: *Razelos v Razelos* [1969] 3 All ER 929.

14 [1961] P 152 at 158–9, [1961] 1 All ER 236 at 241–2; approved obiter in *Rowe v Rowe* [1980] Fam 47 at 53 and 58, [1979] 2 All ER 1123, CA at 1127 and 1131, and by Lord Hailsham LC in *Vervaeke v Smith* [1983] 1 AC 145 at 157, [1982] 2 All ER 144, HL at 152. It is submitted, however, that Phillimore J did not sufficiently differentiate between estoppels per rem judicatam and estoppels in pais. In *Taylor v Taylor* [1967] P 25 at 29, [1965] 1 All ER 872 at 875, it was conceded that no estoppel of any kind would bind the court, but the point was not argued. It may be noted that there is marked reluctance to apply estoppel in children cases: see *K v P*, supra, *Re S, S and A (Care Proceedings: Issue Estoppel)* [1995] 2 FLR 244 and *Re B (Children Act Proceedings) (Issue Estoppel)* [1997] 1 FLR 285.

15 See *Mills v Cooper* [1967] 2 QB 459 at 468–9, [1967] 2 All ER 100, CA at 104, per Diplock LJ.

16 In 1996, for example, only 702 petitions were filed and only 332 decrees nisi and 669 decrees absolute were granted.

17 See eg Bird and Cretney *Divorce The New Law. The Family Law Act 1996* (1996) para 9.1.

18 Through the requirements of having to attend an information meeting, filing a statement of marital breakdown and waiting during the period for reflection and consideration (see Chapter 7) the minimum period is 54 weeks, nor in any event can divorce proceedings be started in the first year of marriage.

most part those that want to end the marriage tie can do so by divorcing. More-over, since annulments only affect voidable marriages after the decree,[19] it has now become conceptually hard to distinguish voidable marriages ended by an annulment and marriages ended by divorce. However, in contrast, following the implementation of the Family Law Act 1996, there will be *marked* difference in the procedure to obtain annulments and divorces. Whether this difference can be justified and indeed whether the law of nullity in its current form should be retained, and if not, how it should relate to the new law of divorce, are questions that need to be addressed.

Although the inevitable corollary of having criteria governing the validity of marriage is to have a concept of a void marriage, it does seems questionable to retain the concept of a voidable marriage. It seems particularly hard to justify having wilful refusal to consummate as a ground of voidability since that arises purely from a post-marital decision and is surely properly regarded as a reason for divorce.[20] The concept of the voidable marriage has been abolished in Australia,[1] and it is submitted that this example should be followed. Whether in consequence the law of divorce should further be amended so as to provide a 'fast track' for the current s 12 grounds (other than wilful refusal to consummate) is debatable. There may be a case for not operating the 12 month time bar on starting proceedings, but this could equally be argued for in other cases, for example, domestic violence, where no such abridgement has been deemed suitable.[2]

19 Under s 16 of the Matrimonial Causes Act 1973, discussed ante, p 102.
20 Compare the Law Commission's view (Law Com No 33, *Nullity of Marriage*, 1970), discussed ante, p 88. The government's White Paper on Divorce *Looking to the Future* (1995) Cm 2799, para 4.52 stated that 'consultees did not view the law of nullity as relevant to a revision of the divorce law' and that the 'possibility that the ground for nullity of wilful refusal to consummate the marriage should be removed because of the need to prove fault was not supported'.
1 By reason of the Family Law Act 1975 (Cth).
2 See post, p 244.

Chapter 4

Rights in property: spouses and cohabitants

A. Introduction

In this chapter we are concerned to discuss the law of property as it is affected both by the relationship of husband and wife and that of unmarried cohabitants. Reflecting the previous pre-eminent importance that society attached to marriage, the law of 'family' property had, until the 1970s and 1980s, virtually been exclusively concerned with the effects of marriage. In this regard, however, the development of the law clearly reflects the development of the status of the wife from being a subservient member of the family to becoming its co-equal head. In contrast, the impact of cohabitation outside marriage upon the concept and development of property ownership has been negligible. This is so even though, as we have seen,[1] the incidence of cohabitation has steadily increased and can certainly no longer be regarded as being unusual. Time will tell whether the law of property ownership will be adapted to meet the particular needs of cohabitants.[2] In the meantime it is to be observed that one of the key contemporary roles of so-called strict property law is the determination of disputes between cohabitants although that law was essentially conceived and developed for married couples.

We begin our discussion of ownership with a brief historical résumé of the effects of marriage upon rights in property.[3]

B. Effects of marriage: historical introduction

1. COMMON LAW

Interests in freehold

Medieval law looked to the husband rather than to the wife for the performance of feudal dues which arose from feudal tenure. Consequently, upon marriage the husband gained seisin of all freehold lands which his wife held at the time of marriage or which she subsequently acquired during marriage. He was also entitled to the rents and profits of them.[4] The wife had no power to dispose of her

---

1 See ante, p 5.
2 The Law Commission is currently working on proposals to deal with the rights of 'home sharers' including cohabitants: see its Sixth Programme of Law Reform (1995) Law Com No 234, Item 8.
3 For further details and authorities reference must be made to the editions of standard works on real and personal property and equity published during the nineteenth and early twentieth centuries. The classic exposition of the common law position is to be found in Blackstone's *Commentaries*, vol ii. See also Dicey *Law and Opinion* (2nd edn) pp 371–95.
4 A similar rule applied to copyhold tenure.

realty during marriage,[5] nor could the husband alone dispose of it for more than his own interest.[6] They could, however, dispose of the whole estate together by each of them levying a fine. In such cases the court would examine the wife separately to ensure that her consent had been freely given.[7]

If the husband died before the wife, she immediately resumed the right to all her freeholds; if she predeceased him, her estates of inheritance descended to her heir subject to the husband's right to retain seisin as tenant by the courtesy of England (ie where the husband had issue born alive by the wife which was *capable* of inheriting her freeholds,[8] he was entitled as tenant by the courtesy to an estate for his life in all her freeholds of inheritance to which on her death she was entitled in possession otherwise than as a joint tenant).[9]

Not surprisingly, during marriage the wife took no interest in her husband's realty but, if she survived him, she became entitled by virtue of her dower to an estate for life in a third of all her husband's freeholds of inheritance of which he had been seized in possession (otherwise than as a joint tenant) *at any time during marriage* provided that she *could* have borne a child capable of inheriting,[10] whether such a child was ever born or not.[11] Since dower created a legal estate, it attached even though the husband alienated the land and, originally, it could be barred only by the wife levying a fine. Under the Statute of Uses 1535, however, dower could be barred by making a jointure in favour of the wife. Subsequently, the Dower Act 1833 provided that dower should not attach to any land which the husband disposed of during his lifetime or by will, and that the wife's right of dower out of his estates of inheritance in respect of which he died intestate should be barred if he made a declaration to this effect by deed or will. As a quid pro quo the Act gave the wife dower in her husband's equitable freeholds in respect of which he died intestate, if he had not barred her right by declaration.

If land were granted to a husband and wife, they were said to take by entireties and received an interest which could not be turned into a tenancy in common by severance. Hence, unless they disposed of the estate during marriage, the survivor was bound to take the whole. Similarly, if land were granted to a husband, his wife and a third person, the spouses were regarded as one person and consequently they were entitled to only one-half of the rent and profits and the third person was entitled to the other half.

5　But even at common law she could exercise a power of appointment given to her without her husband's concurrence.

6　Contrast the position with regard to the wife's leaseholds, which did belong to the husband during marriage and over which he had absolute power of disposal.

7　After the Fines and Recoveries Act 1833 the disposition was effected by deed, which had to be separately acknowledged by the wife before a judge or commissioner, who still had to examine her. This necessity of acknowledgment was abolished by the Law of Property Act 1925 s 167.

8　Hence, if the wife were tenant in tail female, the birth of a son would not give the husband courtesy. Once the child was born alive, it was immaterial that it did not survive. See further Farrer 'Tenant by the Courtesy of England' (1927) 43 LQR 87.

9　So far as copyhold was concerned the husband did not take as tenant by courtesy unless there was a custom of the manor to that effect.

10　Hence, if land were limited to H and the heirs of his body by his wife, W, and after W's death H married X, X could not claim dower in the land, since no child of hers could ever succeed to the tail special.

11　The widow's interest in her deceased husband's copyhold was known as her freebench. Although its exact nature varied from place to place, usually it only attached to land that her husband had neither devised nor alienated in his lifetime.

Interests in pure personalty

All choses in possession belonging to the wife at the time of the marriage or acquired by her during coverture vested absolutely in the husband, who therefore had the power to dispose of them inter vivos or by will. Even if he died intestate during the wife's life, they did not revert to her. The only exception to this rule applied to those articles of apparel and personal ornament (known as the wife's paraphernalia) which were suitable to her rank and degree. Whilst the husband could dispose of these during his lifetime, the wife having no such powers, he could not deprive her of them by bequest, and on his death they became her property and did not form a part of his estate.[12]

The wife's choses in action belonged to the husband if he reduced them into possession or obtained judgment in respect of them during marriage. If he died before this was done, the right of action survived to the wife; if she predeceased him, he could sue by taking out letters of administration.[13] If the chose in action was reversionary, the husband would not be entitled to it if he died before it fell into possession leaving his wife surviving him.[14]

2.   EQUITY

Equity generally followed the law. In only one case was there a marked difference: whilst the husband was entitled to a life interest in his deceased wife's equitable freeholds as a tenant by the courtesy, the wife was not entitled to dower in her deceased husband's equitable freeholds until the passing of the Dower Act in 1833.[15]

The husband's right to his wife's equitable interests in property was indefeasible once he had got possession of it, as would be the case, for example, if a trustee paid over the trust fund or an executor paid over a legacy. But if the husband was obliged to invoke the aid of Chancery to obtain the property, the court gave the wife an 'equity to a settlement'. It applied the maxim 'He who seeks equity must do equity' and, if the property was such that the husband would have an absolute power to dispose of it, it would lend him its assistance only on condition that he settled an adequate part of it on his wife and children for their maintenance.[16]

The wife's separate estate

The most important contribution of equity to the law relating to a married woman's property was the development of the concept of the separate estate. By the end of the sixteenth century[17] it was established that if property was conveyed to trustees *to the separate use* of a married woman, she retained in

---

12 Unless the husband's estate was insolvent, in which case his creditors could take the wife's paraphernalia in satisfaction but not her necessary clothing.
13 See ante, p 62.
14 Hence, it was impossible for them even jointly to make an absolute assignment of a reversionary interest before the passing of the Married Women's Reversionary Interests Act 1857 (Malin's Act).
15 But then only if he died intestate with respect to them and had not barred her dower: see ante, p 107.
16 The wife could compromise her claim. Usually the husband would be ordered to settle half his interest, but this would clearly depend upon the wife's financial circumstances and on occasion he was ordered to settle the whole fund. The husband took the reversionary interest.
17 See Holdsworth *History of English Law*, v, pp 310–15.

equity the same right of holding and disposing of it as if she were a feme sole.[18] This applied whether the interest was in realty or personalty and whether it was in possession or reversion. She could therefore dispose of it inter vivos or by will and, like any other beneficiary of full age who was absolutely entitled, she could call upon her trustees to convey the legal estate. Only if she died intestate in respect of her separate estate did the husband obtain the same interest that he would have had in her equitable property had it not been settled to her separate use. Moreover, it was finally held that not even the interposition of trustees was necessary, and if property were conveyed, devised or bequeathed to a married woman to her separate use so that the legal estate vested in the husband jure mariti, he was deemed in equity to hold it on trust for her and he acquired no greater interest in it than he would have done if it had been conveyed to trustees on similar terms.

The restraint upon anticipation

Whilst the separate estate in equity did much to mitigate the harshness of the common law rule, there remained one situation which it did not meet. There was nothing to prevent a married woman from assigning her beneficial interest to her husband, thereby vesting in him the interest which the separate use had sought to keep out of his hands. To circumvent this, equity developed about 1800 the concept known as the restraint upon anticipation.[19] This could be imposed only if property was conveyed, devised or bequeathed to a woman's separate use, and, once it attached, it prevented her from anticipating and dealing with any income until it actually fell due.

A restraint on anticipation could even be attached to the separate property of an unmarried woman. In this case she could deal with the property as if there were no restraint and could also totally remove the restraint by executing a deed poll to this effect. A woman to whose separate property a restraint had been attached before or during marriage could do the same after the marriage was terminated by her husband's death or by divorce. But, in the absence of any such deed, as soon as she married or remarried, the restraint became operative as regards any property not alienated whilst she was a feme sole.

The restraint on anticipation was designed to protect not only the wife but also the members of her family who would be entitled to the property on her death.[20] Whilst it effectively kept the property out of the hands of her husband and his creditors, it had one obvious drawback in that even where it was in the wife's interest to deal with property subject to a restraint, nothing short of a private Act of Parliament could remove it. To overcome this difficulty the Conveyancing Act 1881 gave the court power to bind her interest in such property provided that this was for her benefit.[1] But the court could only render a specific disposition binding. It had no general power to remove the restraint altogether.

18 In other words, an unmarried woman. If property were settled on an unmarried woman to her separate use, it also remained her separate estate after marriage. Hence, if an engaged woman settled her property on herself to her separate use without her fiancé's concurrence, he could have the settlement set aside as a fraud on his marital rights.
19 See Hart 'The Origin of the Restraint upon Anticipation' (1924) 40 LQR 221.
20 Kahn-Freund in *Matrimonial Property Law* (ed Friedmann) p 274. For the position in equity generally, see Dicey *Law and Opinion* (2nd edn) pp 375–82.
 1 Section 39, subsequently replaced by the Conveyancing Act 1911 s 7, and the Law of Property Act 1925 s 169.

3.   STATUTORY REFORM[2]

By the middle of the nineteenth century it was clear that the old rules would have to be reformed. More women were earning incomes of their own, either in trade, or on the stage or by writing, and there were a number of scandalous cases of husbands impounding their wives' earnings for the benefit of their own creditors, or even mistresses. No relief could be obtained by the woman whose husband deserted her and took all her property with him. The separate use and restraint upon anticipation were clumsy creatures which in practice only affected the property of the daughters of the rich, who would have carefully drawn marriage settlements and would be the beneficiaries under complicated wills. Agitation for reform eventually produced a series of Acts of ever wider scope.[3]

The Matrimonial Causes Act 1857

This Act sought to remedy two defects in the law relating to married women's property. First, while a judicial separation was in force the wife was deemed to be a feme sole with respect to any property which she should acquire. Hence, for the first time under English law she had the sole power to dispose of a legal interest inter vivos or by will.[4] If the parties resumed cohabitation, all property so acquired was to be held for her separate use. Secondly, if a wife were deserted, she could obtain a protection order to prevent her husband and his creditors seizing any property and earnings to which she became entitled after the desertion and to vest them in her as if she were a feme sole.[5]

The Married Women's Property Act 1882

Historically this Act is the most important of the nineteenth century reforms.[6] It provided that any woman marrying after 1882 should be entitled to retain all property owned by her at the time of the marriage as her separate property and that, whenever she was married, any property acquired by a married woman after 1882 should be held by her in the same way.[7] Section 1(1) stated:

> 'A married woman shall . . . be capable of acquiring, holding and disposing, by will or otherwise, of any real or personal property as her separate property, in the same manner as if she were a feme sole, without the intervention of any trustee.'

It further provided that the law relating to restraint upon anticipation should remain unaffected.[8]

The sweeping nature of these changes should be appreciated. It became impossible for a married man to acquire any further interest in his wife's property jure mariti by operation of law. No further tenancies by entireties could be created. A widower could claim an interest in his deceased's wife's property acquired after 1882 only if she died intestate with respect to it. The necessity of both spouses joining in a conveyance of the wife's realty became obsolescent. But in one sense

---

2 See Stetson *A Woman's Issue: the politics of family law reform in England* (1982).
3 See Dicey, op cit, pp 382–95.
4 Section 25.
5 Section 21.
6 In fact many of the 1882 Act's wider provisions had been anticipated in an earlier Bill which, in its cut down form, became the Married Women's Property Act 1870. That Act, which was repealed by the 1882 Act, remains of historical importance in that it gave a statutory extension to the existing equitable concept of the separate estate, the device that was later to be used in the Act of 1882.
7 Section 2 and s 5.
8 Section 19.

the changes were even more fundamental than these, for whilst the statute adopted the equitable concept of separate property,[9] it went further by vesting in the wife the *legal* interest in her property. Indeed, subject to the restraint on anticipation, a married woman's capacity to hold and dispose of property was very nearly the same as that of a feme sole.

The property legislation of 1925

This legislation only incidentally affected rights in property of spouses as such. Its most important effect in this field lay in the changed rules of succession on an intestacy;[10] in particular dower and freebench[11] were abolished. Any remaining tenancies by entireties were abolished, and a grant to a husband, his wife and a third person will now give each of them a third interest in the property.[12]

The Law Reform (Married Women and Tortfeasors) Act 1935

By 1935 to speak of 'separate property' was becoming something of an anomaly, since married women in almost all cases had the same capacity to hold and dispose of it as a man or a feme sole. This was eventually recognised in the Law Reform (Married Women and Tortfeasors) Act 1935, which abolished the concept of the separate estate and gave to the wife the same rights and powers as were already possessed by other adults of full capacity.

Although the Act did not affect any existing restraint on anticipation, it rendered void any attempted imposition of a restraint in any instrument executed after 1935 and in the will of any person dying after 1945.

The Married Women (Restraint upon Anticipation) Act 1949

Although after 1945 restraint upon anticipation was bound to disappear in the course of time, the 1935 Act did not affect the validity of restraints already imposed. Although the court could sanction individual dispositions if these were for the wife's benefit,[13] the only way in which a restraint could be wholly removed was by a private Act of Parliament. It was the presentation of a bill for this purpose that ultimately led to the passing of the Married Women (Restraint upon Anticipation) Act 1949, which removed all restraints whenever imposed, and thus rendered the property to which they were attached freely alienable.

C.   The modern law[14]

1.   GENERAL PRINCIPLES

The effect of the Married Women's Property Acts

By extending the equitable principle of the separate estate, the Married Women's Property Acts replaced the total incapacity of a married woman to hold property at

9 Hence, for example, a married woman still could not be made bankrupt unless she came within the express provisions of s 1(5) by carrying on a trade separately from her husband.
10 See post, pp 875ff.
11 Copyhold tenure was emancipated and converted into freehold tenure by the Law of Property Act 1922.
12 Law of Property Act 1925 s 37, After 1882 the spouses could sever their half share because *between themselves* they took as ordinary joint tenants.
13 See ante, p 109. If the restraint were attached to land, the woman could sell the land under the provisions of the Settled Land Act 1925, but the restraint continued to attach to the capital.
14 See generally Miller *Family Property and Financial Provision* (3rd edn, 1993); Lesser 'The Acquisition of Inter Vivos Matrimonial Property Rights in English Law' (1973) 23 University of Toronto LJ 148.

common law with a rigid doctrine of separate property. In Dicey's words,[15] 'the rules of equity, framed for the daughters of the rich, have at last been extended to the daughters of the poor'. But, as Kahn-Freund pointed out,[16] the effects of the Acts were much wider than this. Spouses' property may be broadly divided into that intended for common use and consumption in the matrimonial home and that intended for personal use and enjoyment. The latter is often in the form of investments or derived from the interest on investments, and it is obvious that, whilst in a poor family almost the whole of the property will fall into the first category, the richer the spouses the greater the fraction of their property which will fall into the second. Before 1883 the matrimonial home and its contents would almost invariably be vested in the husband to the exclusion of the wife, and the latter's separate property did little more than protect her investments. But, impelled by a movement which was ultimately to secure the almost complete legal equality of the sexes, Parliament extended the doctrine of separation to property forming the matrimonial home as well – a situation which the equitable concept was never intended to cover and with which it was ill adapted to deal.

This was inevitably bound to produce difficulties. During the Second World War many married women were wage earners as well, and what before then had been something of an exception has now become the usual situation in most families. To apply the strict doctrine of separate property to matrimonial assets in such circumstances is manifestly absurd. As a result, judges sought to adapt the principle by regarding both spouses as having an interest in the matrimonial home in many cases, even though the legal estate is vested solely in the husband,[17] and a similar approach was later employed in relation to unmarried cohabitants.[18]

Impact of the legislative reform of the 1970s

Although property ownership can be in issue both during and after the spouses' cohabitation, in practice most problems arise following marital breakdown. Until the 1970 reforms spouses, like anyone else, had to resolve their disputes under the strict law, and for the most part they would do so by applying under s 17 of the Married Woman's Property Act 1882.[19] Towards the end of the 1960s there were numerous such applications. In 1968–69, for example, there were 900 applications in the High Court alone.[20] In the early 1970s, however, this picture changed dramatically, for under what was originally s 4 of the Matrimonial Proceedings and Property Act 1970 and later re-enacted as s 24 of the Matrimonial Causes Act 1973, the court was given wide powers for the transfer and settlement of property on divorce, nullity and judicial separation.[1] In *Williams v Williams*[2] the Court of Appeal made it clear that whenever possible spouses should rely on the court's wide powers to adjust property rights. Consequently, the need to make an enquiry into the precise interest that each spouse has in the matrimonial home or other assets has in this context been largely removed.

15 *Law and Opinion* (2nd edn) p 395.
16 In Friedmann (ed) *Matrimonial Property Law*, pp 267 et seq. See also his article, 'Recent Legislation on Matrimonial Property' (1970) 33 MLR 601.
17 See post, Chapter 5.
18 See post, Chapter 5.
19 Discussed below at p 115–17.
20 See *Pettitt v Pettitt* [1970] AC 777 at 806, [1969] 2 All ER 385 at 399, per Lord Hodson. In 1969 there were also 1,220 applications to the county court.
 1 Discussed post, pp 777ff.
 2 [1976] Ch 278, [1977] 1 All ER 28, CA.

It should not be thought, however, that even between spouses the question of ownership is now merely academic.[3] Strict property rights are still of the greatest importance on the death or insolvency of one spouse, because they alone will have to be applied to resolve any dispute between the other spouse and the personal representatives or creditors. Furthermore, a spouse may not wish to take matrimonial proceedings, or may not be able to apply for a property adjustment order because she (or he) has remarried.

In any event, since the court's adjustive powers are confined to divorce, nullity and separation proceedings, the strict law remains the governing law to determine property rights between cohabitants.[4]

Reform proposals

The real trouble is that, except for family provision on death, such legislation as there has been during the twentieth century has sought to deal with isolated problems. There needs, however, to be a complete overhaul of the whole field of matrimonial property law. Solutions adopted by other legal systems include community of property (under which the property belonging to both spouses is administered by the husband or both spouses and divided between them or their personal representatives when the marriage comes to an end), community of gains (which limits community to property acquired during the marriage otherwise than by gift or inheritance), and deferred community (under which each spouse remains free to acquire and dispose of his or her own property, but at the end of the marriage any net gain or surplus is divided equally between them). English courts already have a wide discretion to adjust rights by ordering the transfer and settlement of property following divorce, nullity and separation. There are also extensive powers to order provision for members of the family and other dependants out of the estate of a deceased person. Bearing these points in mind, the Law Commission concluded in 1978 that it was not necessary to introduce any form of community of property in this country: most remaining hardship would be avoided if the spouses were co-owners of the matrimonial home, which is the most substantial asset in the majority of families. Even at that time well over a half of all married couples who owned their homes did so jointly,[5] and the Commission recommended that the principle of co-ownership should be extended by statute to all spouses.[6]

What they envisaged was that spouses should be statutory co-owners of any property, freehold or leasehold, used as their matrimonial home unless they otherwise agreed or, in the case of a gift, the donor, settlor or testator otherwise stipulated.[7] Once the statutory trust attached to the land, neither would be able to dispose of it unless the other consented or the court dispensed with his or her consent.[8] The Commission rejected the possibility of introducing compulsory

---

3 See *Kowalczuk v Kowalczuk* [1973] 2 All ER 1042, CA at 1045; *Griffiths v Griffiths* [1974] 1 All ER 932, CA at 941.

4 See Chapter 5.

5 See Todd and Jones *Matrimonial Property* (HMSO). Joint ownership is becoming much more popular than this figure suggests, because the proportion of spouses buying a house in the decade 1962–71 and having it conveyed into joint names rose from 47% to 74%.

6 Law Com No 86 (Third Report on *Family Property*). See also Law Commission Working Paper No 42 and Law Com No 52 (First Report on *Family Property*); report of the Morton Commission, Cmd 9678, Pt IX.

7 The Commission contemplated other exceptions. The most important was the ability of a spouse to exclude the house from co-ownership if he owned it at the time of the marriage.

8 If one spouse's name did not appear on the title, she (or he) would be able to protect her interest by registering it as a land charge.

co-ownership of goods, partly because the value of used goods is so much less than half that of new goods that compensation in the form of half their actual value would not enable the loser to replace them. Instead they proposed that either spouse should be able to apply for an order concerning the use and enjoyment of 'household goods'.[9] In deciding whether to make such an order, the court should be guided particularly by the extent to which the applicant needed them to meet the normal requirements of his or her daily life and family responsibilities. If the other spouse contravened an order, the court could order him to pay the applicant such sum (which could be the replacement value) as it thought fair and reasonable by way of compensation.[10]

These proposals represented a compromise between the present English system of separate property and a comprehensive adoption of a system of community. They did not, however, command universal support and were not implemented. Ten years later the Commission considered the problem again insofar as it concerns pure personalty.[11] They highlighted a number of anomalies and inequalities in the law, including the rules relating to the acquisition of property out of a housekeeping allowance and the operation of the presumption of advancement.[12] They also pointed out that the law can work arbitrarily: for example, if the wife pays all the housekeeping bills out of her own earnings and the husband uses his to buy a car for the parties' joint use, the car will belong to him, whilst if they pool their earnings in a joint account, it will belong to them both.[13] The Commission went back on their earlier recommendation and proposed that, if one spouse acquires property intended wholly or mainly for the use or benefit of both, beneficial ownership should vest in both jointly. This would be subject to a contrary intention on the part of the purchaser or transferor, provided that it was made known to the other at the time, and would not apply to property acquired by way of gift or inheritance or purchased or transferred wholly or mainly for the purpose of business.[14] The reason for proposing that the property should be held jointly and not in equal shares was the belief that this is what the parties themselves would wish and intend.

The implementation of this proposal would obviously lead to a considerable increase in the number of chattels jointly owned and there is the risk that a purchaser from one party only would not acquire a good title. This risk, however, exists already: the buyer of a family car assumes that the seller is the absolute owner and does not enquire about the source of the funds with which it was originally bought. The Commission believed that the proposed change would introduce a fair rule and provide much greater certainty in this area of the law. It is certainly less complex than their earlier recommendations, but at present it seems no more likely to be implemented.

9   That is, 'any goods, including a vehicle, which are or were available for use and enjoyment in or in connection with any home which the parties to the marriage have at any time during the marriage occupied as their matrimonial home'. Goods would be excepted if third parties had an interest in them, eg goods subject to hire, hire-purchase and conditional sale agreements.

10 This would be in addition to the usual penalties for disobeying an order of the court. A person receiving the goods could also be ordered to pay compensation if he was aware of the order. In appropriate cases the party disposing of the goods could be ordered to pay compensation even though no order was in force.

11 Law Com No 175 (*Matrimonial Property*, 1985). Land was excluded from the Commission's recommendations because of its peculiar nature.

12 See Law Com Working Paper No 90 (Transfer of Money between Spouses). See post, pp 122–3 (housekeeping allowances) and p 124 (presumption of advancement).

13 See post, p 120.

14 The Commission would also exclude policies of life assurance, which could mature many years after the termination of the parties' relationship.

Disputes between the spouses

Two questions arise here: in whom are the legal and equitable interests in the property vested and what rights short of ownership may one spouse have in the property of the other? So long as they are living amicably together, these questions rarely have to be answered, but they become vital if the marriage breaks down. This adds considerably to the difficulty, for the parties rarely contemplate the collapse of the marriage when they acquire property, and their respective rights in it are never discussed, let alone defined. Hence the courts are faced with the problem of having to infer an intention which the spouses never formulated at all.[15]

There are four different ways of solving disputes open to them.

(a) Action for damages in tort

Either spouse may protect his or her interests in property by suing the other in tort, for example in trespass or conversion.[16] Either may also bring an action against the other for the recovery of land. In this connection it should be remembered that, if the spouses are jointly in possession of property or are jointly entitled to possession, one may be liable in trespass if he or she completely ousts the other, or in conversion if he or she destroys the property or disposes of it.[17]

(b) Proceedings for an injunction

Either spouse may obtain an injunction to prevent the other from committing a continuing or threatened wrong against the plaintiff's property.[18] In practice this remedy is most frequently sought when the wife is trying to exclude the husband from entering the matrimonial home, and the particular problems that arise here are dealt with in Chapter 6.[19]

(c) Proceedings under s 17 of the Married Women's Property Act 1882

Section 17[20] provides that 'in any question between husband and wife as to the title to or possession of property'[1] either of them may apply for an order to the High

15 See *Re Rogers' Question* [1948] 1 All ER 328, CA; *Cobb v Cobb* [1955] 2 All ER 696, CA at 699.
16 Ante, p 64.
17 Torts (Interference with Goods) Act 1977 s 10; Salmond and Heuston *Law of Torts* (21st edn by Heuston and Buckley, 1996) pp 50–2, 110–11. The court may stay the action if the questions in issue could be disposed of more conveniently by an application under s 17 of the Married Women's Property Act 1882: see ante, p 64. For proceedings under s 17, see infra.
18 This may be done by bringing an action in tort under the Law Reform (Husband and Wife) Act 1962, in proceedings under the Family Law Act 1996, or by way of ancillary relief in other matrimonial proceedings.
19 Post, pp 199ff.
20 Replacing and extending the Married Women's Property Act 1870 s 9. The section was amended by the Law Reform (Husband and Wife) Act 1962 Sch (repealing s 23 of the Act of 1882) and the Statute Law (Repeals) Act 1969 Sch, Pt III, which took away the power of a deceased wife's personal representatives and of banks, companies and other bodies to take proceedings under s 17, and by the Matrimonial and Family Proceedings Act 1984 s 43, which now governs court jurisdiction over the proceedings.
1 Including choses in action (*Spellman v Spellman* [1961] 2 All ER 498, CA at 501) and property of which the claimant is a bare trustee and in which he has no beneficial interest at all (*Re Knight's Question* [1959] Ch 381, [1958] 1 All ER 812). The court may make an order with respect to property (including immovable property) situated abroad, but will not do so if the order is likely to be ineffective (eg because a foreign court would disregard it) and the court has no means of enforcing it against the defendant in personam: *Razelos v Razelos (No 2)* [1970] 1 All ER 386n, approved in *Hamlin v Hamlin* [1986] Fam 11, [1985] 2 All ER 1037, CA. If there is no question as to title or possession but one spouse is, eg, seeking to enforce what is now a trust for land (formerly a trust for sale: see below) against the other, proceedings under s 17 are inappropriate and the same proceedings should be taken as would be taken between strangers: *Rawlings v Rawlings* [1964] P 398, [1964] 2 All ER 804, CA.

Court or a county court and the judge 'may make such order with respect to the property in dispute . . . as he thinks fit'.[2] These proceedings are of course usually invoked when the marriage has broken down. Disputes over rights in property may still be going on after the marriage has been legally terminated, and consequently s 17 was extended to enable former spouses to make an application for a period of three years after a decree absolute of divorce or nullity.[3]

It will be seen that under s 17 the court has jurisdiction to determine questions of title and possession. In order that it may do this, it had been held that there must be in existence specific property or a specific fund with respect to which the order might be made and that, if the property or fund had ceased to exist, there was no power to make what would be in effect an order for damages for trespass, conversion or debt.[4] This clearly worked injustice if the defendant had already disposed of the property or fund in question: this was remedied by s 7 of the Matrimonial Causes (Property and Maintenance) Act 1958, which gives the court power in such a case either to order the defendant to pay to the plaintiff such sum of money as represents the latter's interest in the property or fund, or to make an order with respect to any other property which now represents the whole or part of the original.[5]

For some years there was considerable judicial controversy over the width of the powers which the wording of the section gave to the judges.[6] It was, however, finally settled by the House of Lords in *Pettitt v Pettitt*[7] that the court has no jurisdiction under this section to vary existing titles and no wider power to transfer or create interests in property than it would have in any other type of proceedings. At the most it has, in the words of Lord Diplock, 'a wide discretion as to the enforcement of the proprietary or possessory rights of one spouse in any property against the other'.[8] Furthermore, the fact that the marriage has broken down, the circumstances of the breakdown and the conduct of the parties cannot affect title in the absence of an agreement between the spouses, and are therefore all irrelevant to the outcome of proceedings brought under s 17.[9] But by using its powers to make different types of orders, the court may effectively control the way in which the property is used without departing from the principle that it cannot alter the title. Thus it may order a spouse to give up possession of a house, to deliver up chattels, to transfer shares and other choses in action, or to pay over a specific fund, and it may even forbid him to dispossess the other spouse or to deal with the property in any way inconsistent with the other's rights.[10] Similarly, the

2 Proceedings in the High Court are now assigned to the Family Division.
3 Matrimonial Proceedings and Property Act 1970 s 39. The summary procedure under s 17 has also been made available to parties to an agreement to marry that has been terminated: see post, p 118.
4 *Tunstall v Tunstall* [1953] 2 All ER 310, CA.
5 But a specific property or fund must have been in existence originally and proceedings cannot be brought under s 17 for the recovery of a debt: *Crystall v Crystall* [1963] 2 All ER 330, CA. The Limitation Act has been held not to apply to such proceedings, and consequently an order may be made even though the property was disposed of more than six years earlier: *Spoor v Spoor* [1966] 3 All ER 120.
6 See further post, pp 135–6.
7 [1970] AC 777, [1969] 2 All ER 385, HL.
8 At 820 and 411, respectively.
9 *Pettitt v Pettitt* (supra).
10 As in *Lee v Lee* [1952] 2 QB 489n, [1952] 1 All ER 1299, CA. In *Re Bettinson's Question* [1956] Ch 67, [1955] 3 All ER 296, it was held that an order could be made with respect to property which was subject to the doctrine of community of property under the law of the parties' domicile (California).

court may order the property to be sold and direct how the proceeds of sale are to be divided[11] or, if both spouses have an interest, it may order one of them to transfer his or her share to the other on the latter's paying the value of the property transferred.[12]

On the breakdown of a marriage one of the spouses will normally seek a divorce, nullity or separation and invoke the court's wider powers to make a property adjustment order under s 24 of the Matrimonial Causes Act 1973. Consequently proceedings under s 17 are now likely to be invoked in respect of land[13] only if the spouse seeking relief is unable or unwilling to take matrimonial proceedings, or has remarried before applying for a property adjustment order.[14]

(d) Proceedings under s 14 of the Trusts of Land and Appointment of Trustees Act 1996 [15]

Before implementation of the 1996 Act, a trust for sale arose whenever land was conveyed to two or more people either as beneficial joint tenants or as tenants in common. As its name implied, the creation of such trusts imposed an ultimate obligation upon the trustees to sell the property,[16] and, if the trustees refused to sell the trust property, s 30 of the Law of Property Act 1925 enabled any person interested to apply to the court for an order directing them to give effect to the trust, whereupon the court could make such order as it thought fit. Section 30 could be used to force the sale of a matrimonial home, because, if both spouses had a beneficial interest in it either as joint tenants or as tenants in common, a trust for sale was automatically created. In practice, however, for the reasons stated in the last paragraph the future of a married couple's home was usually settled by property adjustment under the Matrimonial Causes Act 1973.

Following the Law Commission's recommendations,[17] trusts for sale have been replaced by trusts of land. Under the Trusts of Land and Appointment of Trustees Act 1996[18] all existing trusts for sale, whether express or implied, became trusts of land, and in situations where formerly an implied trust for sale would have arisen there now arises a trust of land. One of the crucial differences between trusts of land and trusts for sale is that *implied* trusts of land no longer carry an obligation to sell, and even in *express* trusts there is an implied power to postpone sale indefinitely.[19] The former power under s 30 of the 1925 Act has been replaced by a new power

11 Matrimonial Causes (Property and Maintenance) Act 1958 s 7(7).
12 *Bothe v Amos* [1976] Fam 46, [1975] 2 All ER 321, CA.
13 Especially in view of the new powers under s 14 of the Trusts of Land and Appointment of Trustees Act 1996, discussed below. But note s 14 has no application in respect of pure personalty.
14 See post, pp 136–7 and p 783. Even so, proceedings are sometimes still taken by spouses involved in marital breakdown: see eg *A v A (Costs Appeal)* [1996] 1 FLR 14.
15 See generally Baughen 'Trusts of Land and Family Practice' [1996] Fam Law 736; Harwood 'A Home for Life – The New Trusts of Land Act' [1997] Fam Law 182; Hopkins 'The Trusts of Land and Appointment of Trustees Act 1996' (1996) 60 Conv 411 and Pettitt *Equity and the Law of Trusts* (8th edn, 1997) 64–5 and 377–8.
16 Though the Law Commission have said (Law Com No 181, *Transfer of Land, Trusts of Land*) para [3.4]) even under the old definition set out by the LPA 1925 s 205 (1)(xxix) (this section has now been amended) the courts considered that it meant something other than the trustees being under a duty to sell: see eg *Re Parker's Settled Estates* [1928] 1 Ch 247; *Re Ryder and Steadman's Contract* [1927] 2 Ch 62; *Re Norton* [1929] 1 Ch 84; *Re Beaumont Settled Estates* [1937] 2 All ER 353; and *Re Sharpe's Deed of Release* [1939] Ch 51.
17 See Law Com No 181, *Transfer of Land, Trusts of Land* (1989).
18 This Act came into force in January 1997.
19 See s 5 and s 4 respectively.

under s 14 of the 1996 Act. This provision enables any person who is a trustee of land or who has interest in property subject to a trust of land[20] to seek a court order either relating to the exercise by the trustees of any of their functions or to 'declare the nature or extent of a person's interest in property subject to the trust'. In each case the court may make such order as it thinks fit.[1] Although s 14 will still allow a court to order a sale, its powers are not limited to this. It will be noticed in particular that it includes the power to declare the nature and extent of a person's interest in the land in question, which is the same power as under s 17 of the Married Women's Property Act 1882. Whether spouses will be disposed to use this new power rather than s 17 remains to be seen but, as we have said, most disputes between spouses will continue to be decided under the Matrimonial Causes Act 1973.

Disputes between engaged couples and between unmarried cohabitants

The main distinction between the property rights of unmarried cohabitants and spouses is that property adjustment orders are not available to the former. Similarly, property adjustment orders are not available to engaged couples.[2] Consequently, disputes between cohabitants or former cohabitants and engaged or formerly engaged couples over the ownership, occupation or use of property must be resolved, generally speaking, by applying the ordinary legal rules applicable to strangers. There is, however, one distinction between former engaged couples and cohabitants in that the former can apply for an order under the Married Women's Property Act 1882 s 17. Engaged couples could well start to buy a house in contemplation of their marriage, and this may give them rights in property which are virtually indistinguishable from those acquired by married couples. However, it was the abolition of actions for damages for breach of promise of marriage, which deprived them of the means of recovering the expenses they had lost if the marriage did not take place, that prompted[3] making the summary procedure of s 17 available to the parties to an agreement to marry which has been terminated.[4] How far applying under s 17 will be considered more advantageous than applying for an order with respect to land under s 14 of the Trusts of Land and Appointment of Trustees Act 1996 is debatable, for while the powers under the latter are at least as extensive,[5] they are not fettered, as are those under s 17, by having to relate to property in which either or both had an interest while the agreement was in force or by the requirement to bring the action within three years of the termination of the agreement.[6] Furthermore, an action under s 14 avoids any problems of deciding whether there was an agreement to marry in the first place.[7]

If a couple (whether engaged or not) have a child or children for whom one of them applies for financial provision, the court has power inter alia to order the

---

20 This is narrower than that recommended by the Law Commission, in that it does not permit *any* interested person to apply. See also *Re NG (A Bankrupt), Trustee of the Estate of NG v NG* [1998] 2 FLR 386.

1 Section 15 sets out matters to which the court must have regard when exercising these powers: see post, p 154.

2 See *Mossop v Mossop* [1989] Fam 77, [1988] 2 All ER 202, CA.

3 See Law Com No 26, *Breach of Promise of Marriage*, paras 35–42. For the abolition of actions for breach of promise, see ante, p 24.

4 By the Law Reform (Miscellaneous Provisions) Act 1970 s 2(2).

5 See above. But note s 14 has no application in respect of pure personalty.

6 These requirements for an application under s 17 are set out in s 2(2) of the Law Reform (Miscellaneous Provisions) Act 1970.

7 See, for example, *Shaw v Fitzgerald* [1992] 1 FLR 357, discussed ante at p 25.

other to transfer property to the applicant and to order the settlement of property to which either of them is entitled, in each case for the benefit of the child.[8] As the Court of Appeal held in *K v K (Minors: Property Transfer),*[9] 'benefit' in this context is not limited to a purely financial benefit. Consequently, one of the ways in which this power can be exercised is by ordering the parties' former home to be transferred to whichever of them has the day-to-day care of the child. This comes within the statute because it gives the child the benefit of a home even though it also confers a benefit on the parent looking after the child.[10] However, in practice this power is limited by the court's acceptance that, save in exceptional circumstances (for example where the child has a physical or mental disability), capital provision should not be made to provide benefits for the child after he or she has attained independence.[11]

Disputes between one of the partners[12] and a stranger

The question to be considered here is how far rights in property created or affected by marriage, engagement or cohabitation can be enforced by one of the partners against a third person. The latter may claim in one of a number of capacities, for example, as a purchaser for value from the other partner, as the other's creditor or trustee in bankruptcy, or as a beneficiary entitled to a deceased partner's estate. It is essential to decide first what rights the claiming partner has against the other partner and then how far these rights are enforceable against the third person. This will depend upon the application of general principles of the law of property, and in particular the nature of the latter's title. If he is, say, the man's donee, the woman may enforce against him all those rights (other than purely personal rights) which she would have against her partner; if he is a purchaser of a legal estate or interest for value, he will take the property subject to the woman's legal rights, but will not be bound by her equitable interests if he purchased in good faith and without notice of them.

2.   PROPERTY ACQUIRED BY THE PARTNERS

Property owned by the partners at the time of the marriage, engagement or cohabitation

Presumptively marriage and a fortiori engagement or cohabitation will not affect the ownership of property vested in either of the partners at the time. This will also be true of property which is used by them jointly in the matrimonial or family home (for example, furniture) in the absence of an express gift of a joint interest in law or in equity.

---

8 Children Act 1989 s 15(1) and Sch 1, paras 1 and 2. See further post, pp 767ff.
9 [1992] 2 All ER 727, CA. Note also *Pearson v Franklin* [1994] 2 All ER 137, CA, in which it was suggested that an appropriate remedy for an unmarried mother seeking to reside with her two young children at the family home (held on a joint tenancy from a housing association) without their father was to apply for an order under the Children Act 1989 Sch 1, para 1(2)(e)(i) requiring the father to transfer to her, for the benefit of the children, his interest in the joint tenancy.
10 The Law Commission observed that few commentators considered this a valid objection: Law Com No 118 (*Illegitimacy*) para 6.6.
11 See *A v A (A Minor: Financial Provision)* [1994] 1 FLR 657 and *T v S (Financial Provision for Children)* [1994] 2 FLR 883.
12 The term 'partner' is used here as a generic term to refer to spouses, engaged couples and cohabitants.

Income

So far as income is concerned spouses, cohabitants and former engaged couples are in the same legal position. Case law, however, tends only to relate to spouses.

The income of either partner, whether from earnings or from investments, will prima facie remain his or her own property.[13] But where the partners pool their incomes and place them into a common fund, it seems that they both acquire a joint interest in the whole fund. Further, it seems clear that the principle of a joint interest in a common fund rests not upon the relationship between the contributors, but upon the purpose for which the fund was founded and the use to which it is put.[14]

(a)   Common fund

In *Jones v Maynard*[15] the husband, who was about to go abroad with the RAF, authorised his wife to draw on his bank account, which was thereafter treated as a joint account. Into this account were paid dividends on both the husband's and the wife's investments, the husband's pay and allowances, and rent from the matrimonial home which was their joint property and which had been let during the War. The husband's contributions were greater than the wife's; the spouses had never agreed on what their rights in this fund were to be, but they regarded it as their joint savings to be invested from time to time. The husband withdrew money on a number of occasions and invested it in his own name, and finally, after the spouses had separated, he closed the account altogether. The marriage was later dissolved and the plaintiff sued her former husband for a half share in the account as it stood on the day it was closed and in the investments which he had previously purchased out of it. Vaisey J held that the claim must succeed. He said:[16]

> 'In my judgment, when there is a joint account between husband and wife, a common pool into which they put all their resources, it is not consistent with that conception that the account should thereafter . . . be picked apart, and divided up proportionately to the respective contributions of husband and wife, the husband being credited with the whole of his earnings and the wife with the whole of her dividends . . . In my view a husband's earnings or salary, when the spouses have a common purse and pool their resources, are earnings made on behalf of both; and the idea that years afterwards the contents of the pool can be dissected by taking an elaborate account as to how much was paid in by the husband or the wife is quite inconsistent with the original fundamental idea of a joint purse or common pool.
>
> In my view the money which goes into the pool becomes joint property. The husband, if he wants a suit of clothes, draws a cheque to pay for it. The wife, if she wants any housekeeping money, draws a cheque, and there is no disagreement about it.'

What, then, constitutes a 'common purse'? It would seem on principle to be essential that there must be a fund intended for the use of both partners from which either may withdraw money, and this will normally take the form of a joint bank account. Where they both contribute to this fund, as in *Jones v Maynard*, it is submitted that this intention will be imputed to the parties in the absence of any other agreement; where, however, the fund is derived from the income of one

---

13 See *Dixon v Dixon* (1878) 9 Ch D 587 (stock settled to the wife's separate use); *Barrack v M'Culloch* (1856) 3 K & J 110 (rents from houses settled to the wife's separate use); *Heseltine v Heseltine* [1971] 1 All ER 952 (income from wife's investments).
14 *Paul v Constance* [1977] 1 All ER 195, CA.
15 [1951] Ch 572, [1951] 1 All ER 802.
16 At 575 and 803, respectively.

partner alone, it is a question of fact whether this is to remain his or her exclusive property, or whether there is an intention to establish a common fund. In this instance, however, as between spouses and, possibly, engaged couples, the presumption of advancement may come into play. Hence, whereas if the wife (or fiancée) is the sole contributor to the joint account she may take the whole beneficial interest,[17] if the husband (or fiancé) is the sole contributor, the presumption may operate so as prima facie to give her an interest;[18] but this will be rebutted if, for example, it can be shown that the power to draw on the account was given for the husband's convenience by enabling the wife to draw cheques for the payment of housekeeping expenses.[19] Even though the beneficial interest in a joint account is initially vested in one spouse alone, his or her intention may change, and it may be converted into a joint interest.[1] The courts will probably tend to find a joint beneficial interest today much more readily than they did in the past.

If either spouse withdraws money from the common purse, property bought with it prima facie belongs solely to that spouse if it is for his or her personal use (for example, clothes), but to both jointly if it is for their joint use (for example, a car). Investments purchased by means of the common purse will similarly belong to the purchaser unless it is clear that they are intended to represent the original fund. In *Re Bishop*[2] large sums had been withdrawn by both spouses to purchase investments in their separate names. In many cases blocks of shares were bought and half put in one name and half in the other; other money was spent in taking up shares offered to the husband by virtue of rights which he possessed as an existing shareholder in the companies concerned. In these circumstances Stamp J held that the presumption could not be rebutted, so that the spouse in whose name the shares had been purchased was entitled to the whole beneficial interest in them. He distinguished *Jones v Maynard*, where Vaisey J held that the husband was to be regarded as trustee for them both of investments which he had purchased; for in that case the spouses had agreed that when there had been a sufficient accumulation the money should be invested and that that was to be their savings.

Like any other joint interest the balance of the fund will accrue to the survivor on the death of either spouse, as it did in *Re Bishop*. It can of course be severed by agreement or assignment in the lifetime of both; in such a case or where, as in *Jones v Maynard*, the marriage breaks down and the court is asked to effect a partition, then, as we have seen from the passage of Vaisey J's judgment quoted above, the spouses will hold the balance of the fund as tenants in common in equal shares.[3]

17 *Heseltine v Heseltine* (supra) (houses purchased by husband out of joint account provided by wife's money held to belong to her absolutely). Contrast *Boydell v Gillespie* (1970) 216 Estates Gazette 1505 (wife's directing that property bought with her money should be conveyed into names of both spouses jointly held to give both an interest in it).
18 *Re Figgis* [1969] 1 Ch 123, [1968] 1 All ER 999. Although the effect of these presumptions is considerably weaker today than it used to be (see post, p 124), they could still operate in a case like *Re Figgis*, where both parties are dead and there is virtually no direct evidence of the parties' intentions at all, although, as Nourse LJ observed in *McGrath v Wallis* [1995] 2 FLR 114 at 115, even in these circumstances he was unable to recollect a case in which the presumption was applied in the last 30 years.
19 *Marshal v Crutwell* (1875) LR 20 Eq 328; *Hoddinott v Hoddinott* [1949] 2 KB 406, CA at 413; *Harrods Ltd v Tester* [1937] 2 All ER 236, CA (where the whole of the balance of a bank account opened by the husband in the wife's name was held to belong to the husband); *Simpson v Simpson* [1992] 1 FLR 601 at 617 (transfer of money by husband into joint account intended only to ensure that wife could pay expenses during his final illness).
1 *Re Figgis* (supra) at 145 and 1011, respectively.
2 [1965] Ch 450, [1965] 1 All ER 249.
3 But see post, p 138.

Allowances for housekeeping and maintenance

This question is obviously closely allied to the last, and originally the same principles were applied. Hence, it was consistently held that if a husband supplied his wife with a housekeeping allowance out of his own income, any balance and any property bought with the allowance prima facie remained his property.[4] This could work an injustice, for it took no account of the fact that any savings from the housekeeping money were as much due to the wife's skill and economy as to her husband's earning capacity.[5] It was to remedy this that the Married Women's Property Act 1964 was passed. Section 1 provides:

> 'If any question arises as to the right of a husband or wife to money derived from any allowance made by the husband for the expenses of the matrimonial home or for similar purposes, or to any property acquired out of such money, the money or property shall, in the absence of any agreement between them to the contrary, be treated as belonging to the husband and wife in equal shares.'

The Act applies only if the allowance is provided by the husband; it does not apply to the case where the wife goes out to work to support a husband who does the housekeeping. In such a case the allowance and any property bought with it presumably remain the wife's.[6] The Act does not apply at all to cohabitants,[7] nor to engaged couples; consequently the common law rules are still relevant and any unspent balance or property or investments purchased with it will belong to the provider of the housekeeping allowance. It is nevertheless open to the courts to infer an intention that the unspent allowance should belong to the partners jointly: it remains to be seen whether they will do so.

So far as the application of the 1964 Act is concerned, it is not clear what the phrase 'expenses of the matrimonial home or similar purposes' covers. If, for example, a husband gives his wife money to pay off instalments of the mortgage on the matrimonial home, she may well be regarded as no more than his agent and thus acquire no interest in the house; but if he gives her a housekeeping allowance out of which it is intended that she should pay the instalments, it has been suggested that the effect of the section is to give her a half share in the fraction represented by each payment.[8] In the absence of any binding authority the words 'expenses of the matrimonial home' seem more apt to describe money spent in running it than in acquiring it.

If the allowance is made for this purpose, the rule applies not only to the money but also to any property bought with it. Hence, if the wife were to buy furniture

---

4 *Blackwell v Blackwell* [1943] 2 All ER 579, CA; *Hoddinott v Hoddinott* [1949] 2 KB 406, CA, in which the husband was held entitled to winnings from the football pools, the stake for which had been paid by the wife out of the housekeeping allowance.

5 See the judgments of Denning LJ in *Hoddinott v Hoddinott*, supra, at 416, and *Rimmer v Rimmer* [1953] 1 QB 63 at 74, [1952] 2 All ER 863, CA at 868–9.

6 Earlier cases indicate that if the wife gives money to her husband for use in the home, she is deemed to give it to him as head of the family and the money therefore becomes his: see eg *Edward v Cheyne (No 2)* (1888) 13 App Cas 385, HL; *Re Young* (1913) 29 TLR 319 (where the presumption was rebutted on the facts). But it is very doubtful whether the courts would take such a view today. The Morton Commission recommended that the allowance should belong to both spouses equally, whichever of them provided it: Cmd 9678, para 701. See further Law Com Working Paper No 90 (*Transfer of Money between Spouses*) and Law Com No 175, *Matrimonial Property Law* (1989).

7 The Scottish Law Commission (see Scot Law Com No 135, 1992, paras 16.12–16.13) did recommend extending the equivalent provision in Scotland to cohabitants.

8 See the conflicting views in *Tymoszczuk v Tymoszczuk* (1964) 108 Sol Jo 676, and *Re Johns' Assignment Trusts* [1970] 2 All ER 210n at 213.

with the housekeeping savings, it would presumptively belong to her and her husband equally. This can be rebutted by proof of an express agreement between the spouses. Presumably, though this has yet to be established, such agreements may be express or implied. It would be absurd, for example, where the wife uses part of the allowance to buy clothes for herself, that a half share of them should belong to the husband.[9]

The Act has two further weaknesses. First, the money or property is to be treated as belonging to the spouses in equal shares. Consequently, on the death of one, the whole beneficial interest will *not* automatically pass to the survivor (as it does in the case of the 'common purse'),[10] but half will go to the personal representatives of the other. It is highly doubtful whether this is what the spouses will want or expect.[11] Neither this rule nor its consequences will be known to the vast majority of spouses and it is not inconceivable that a half-share of furniture will inadvertently pass under a residuary bequest. Secondly, it is unclear whether the Act has retrospective effect. As there is no clear intention to affect vested rights, it is submitted that money and property belonging to the husband when the Act came into force[12] should remain his.

Given these difficulties, it is hardly surprising that little use seems to have been made of the Act. The Law Commission[13] has recommended its repeal and that instead there should be a statutory presumption that property bought for the joint use or benefit of spouses should belong to them jointly.

Property purchased by one partner

Any property purchased by one partner with his or her own money will presumptively belong exclusively to the purchaser. Property bought out of money coming from the 'common purse' will also presumptively belong to the purchaser if it is for his or her own use.[14]

But this presumption is obviously rebuttable. Thus, property bought by one partner as a gift for the other will become the donee's. Hence, if a man buys clothes for his partner or gives her money to buy them for herself, they become her property,[15] and the same rule will prima facie apply in any other case where goods are bought for the other's personal use.[16]

9 Perhaps a more difficult case would arise if the wife bought herself an expensive piece of jewellery. In the case of a 'common purse' contributed to by both, the property would belong to the wife exclusively: see ante, p 121.
10 See ante, p 121.
11 In their desire to remedy the injustice caused by earlier cases where the marriage had broken down, the promoters of the Bill apparently overlooked the obvious fact that most marriages survive and that, whilst a joint interest can always be severed by the unilateral act of one party, it requires the conscious act of both to turn a tenancy in common into a joint tenancy.
12 25 March 1964. This view seems to have recommended itself to Goff J in *Re Johns' Assignment Trusts* (supra) on the ground that the Act creates a presumption and therefore changes adjective law. For further difficulties that may arise, see Stone (1964) 27 MLR 576.
13 Law Com No 175 (*Matrimonial Property*, 1985). Note that the Government considers the Act to be incompatible with Protocol 7 of the European Convention on Human Rights and has undertaken to reform it so that the UK can ratify this Protocol: Hansard, HL Written Answers, col 197, 21 April 1998.
14 See ante, p 121.
15 *Masson, Templier & Co v De Fries* [1909] 2 KB 831, CA. Contrast *Rondeau, Le Grand & Co v Marks* [1918] 1 KB 75, CA, where it had been agreed that they should remain the husband's property.
16 *Re Whittaker* (1882) 21 Ch D 657 (piano). But cf *Windeler v Whitehall* [1990] 2 FLR 505 at 517 (dressing table bought for unmarried cohabitant remained purchaser's property).

Difficulties can arise if one partner's money is used to buy property which is conveyed into the other's name or into joint names or, alternatively, if both partners' money is used to buy property which is conveyed into the name of only one of them. In this respect a distinction needs to be drawn between spouses (and possibly engaged couples) and unmarried cohabitants. So far as the latter are concerned, property bought by one partner and put into the name of the other is presumptively held on a resulting trust by the latter for the purchaser. So far as spouses are concerned, the classic way of solving the problem is by applying two maxims of equity. If the wife alone provides the purchase money, there is a resulting trust in her favour, and the husband (or the spouses jointly if the legal estate is vested in both) is presumed to hold the property on trust for her absolutely. On the other hand, if the husband provides the purchase money and has the property put into his wife's name or into joint names, he is presumed to intend a gift to his wife, and the presumption of advancement operates to give her prima facie the sole or a joint beneficial interest.[17] Precisely the same rules operate if both provide the money. If the property is conveyed into the husband's name alone, he will hold it on trust for them both and each will be entitled to a share proportionate to the contribution.[18] If the property is conveyed into the wife's name alone, the husband will be presumed to have made a gift of the whole of the property to her. These presumptions have always been rebuttable by evidence that the wife intended a gift in the first case or that the husband intended to keep the beneficial interest in the second.[19] But, as the members of the House of Lords agreed in *Pettitt v Pettitt*,[20] they are much less strong today because some explanation of the parties' conduct will usually be available unless they are both dead. Lord Diplock went so far as to question whether they were still valid at all. As he observed, they are no more than a judicial inference of what the spouses' intention most probably was, drawn in cases relating to the propertied classes of the nineteenth and early twentieth century among whom marriage settlements were common and where the wife rarely contributed to the family income by her earnings. Even Lord Upjohn, who, as Nourse LJ later commented,[1] was 'more loyal to the presumption

---

17 *Mercier v Mercier* [1903] 2 Ch 98, CA (presumption of resulting trust for wife); *Silver v Silver* [1958] 1 All ER 523, CA (presumption of advancement). Hence, if the husband had property conveyed to both spouses and a stranger, all three would hold on trust for the husband and wife jointly: *Re Eykyn's Trusts* (1877) 6 Ch D 115. There is a presumption of advancement even though the marriage is voidable: *Dunbar v Dunbar* [1909] 2 Ch 639; but not if the husband knows it to be void, for then there is to his knowledge no duty to maintain: *Soar v Foster* (1858) 4 K & J 152. Quaere if he does not know it is void. The presumption of advancement is also raised if a man has property conveyed into his fiancée's name: *Moate v Moate* [1948] 2 All ER 486, but the correctness of this decision is not beyond doubt: see Lowe 'The Advancement of an Intended Wife: A Reply' (1976) 120 Sol Jo 141.

18 This could be relevant, eg, if furniture or a car were bought by the husband on hire purchase and both spouses contributed to the payment of the instalments. See Law Com Working Paper No 42, pp 131–4.

19 The husband may not rebut the presumption by adducing evidence of his own fraudulent or unlawful intention: *Re Emery's Investments' Trusts* [1959] Ch 410, [1959] 1 All ER 577 (evasion of tax in the USA); *Tinker v Tinker* [1970] P 136, [1970] 1 All ER 540, CA (defrauding creditors). The current tendency is to apply this principle only if not to do so would affront the public conscience: see *Tinsley v Milligan* [1994] 1 AC 340, [1993] 3 All ER 65, HL, and *Tribe v Tribe* [1995] 2 FLR 966, CA. Contrast *Griffiths v Griffiths* [1973] 3 All ER 1155 (fraudulent statements made after acquisition of interest held not to prevent husband's claiming it).

20 [1970] AC 777, [1969] 2 All ER 385, HL; at 793 and 389, per Lord Reid; at 811 and 404, per Lord Hodson; at 814–15 and 406–7, per Lord Upjohn; at 824 and 414, per Lord Diplock.

1   In *McGrath v Wallis* [1995] 2 FLR 114 at 122.

of advancement' than the other Law Lords, accepted[2] that it was readily rebutted by comparatively slight evidence. Accordingly, it has little significance today when the parties may be legally aided, the wife is working, and their biggest asset, the matrimonial home, is being purchased by means of a mortgage.[3]

Gifts to partners from third parties

Whether a gift made by third parties belongs to one partner alone or to both of them is a question of the donor's intention. In the case of wedding presents it is reasonable to assume in the absence of any evidence to the contrary that the husband's friends and relations intended to make the gift to him and the wife's to her.[4] There is no rule of law to this effect, however, and the court, exercising its discretion under s 17 of the Married Women's Property Act 1882, may order the presents to be divided equally between them both.

3. TRANSACTIONS BETWEEN PARTNERS

Gifts between partners

(a) Undue influence

With the exceptions discussed below in the case of chattels, gifts between partners are subject to the general law. Indeed, it should be noted that even the relationship of marriage does not ipso facto give rise to a presumption (now known, following *Barclays Bank plc v O'Brien*,[5] as a 'Class 2A presumption') that either has exercised undue influence over the other.[6] This is somewhat surprising when one bears in mind the special treatment that equity accorded to married women in the past and the fact that spouses rarely take independent legal advice unless they are already at arm's length.

However, as Lord Browne-Wilkinson said in *Barclays Bank plc v O'Brien*:[7]

'Although there is no Class 2A presumption of undue influence as between husband and wife, it should be emphasised that in any particular case a wife may well be able to demonstrate

---

2 At 823–4 and 414, respectively. See also Lord Denning MR in *Falconer v Falconer* [1970] 3 All ER 449, CA at 452. Nonetheless, the government considers that the presumption would need to be abolished before the UK could ratify Protocol 7 to the European Convention on Human Rights: see Hansard, HL Written Answers, col 197, 21 April 1998.

3 See further Chapter 5.

4 *Samson v Samson* [1960] 1 All ER 653, CA. Contrast *Midland Bank plc v Cooke* [1995] 4 All ER 562, CA, discussed post, p 148 (a wedding cash present provided by the groom's parents held to be intended to be a gift to both spouses equally) and *Kelner v Kelner* [1939] P 411, [1939] 3 All ER 957 (£1,000 deposited by the wife's father at the time of the marriage in a joint bank account in both spouses' names ordered to be divided equally between them). Spouses' subsequent conduct may turn a gift to one of them into joint property: *Samson v Samson*. Presumably, a similar approach is applicable to engagement presents, assuming that they are intended as an unconditional gift (ie they are not returnable if the marriage does not take place).

5 [1994] 1 AC 180, [1993] 4 All ER 417, HL per Lord Browne-Wilkinson. 'Class 2A presumptions' comprise certain relationships (eg solicitor and client, medical adviser and patient) which as a matter of law raise the presumption that undue influence has been exercised. In contrast, under 'Class 2B', notwithstanding the absence of a Class 2A relationship, if the complainant can prove the de facto existence of a relationship under which the complainant generally reposed trust and confidence in the wrongdoer, the existence of such a relationship raises the *presumption* of undue influence. See eg *Royal Bank of Scotland v Etridge (No 2)* [1998] NLJR 1390, CA.

6 *Howes v Bishop* [1909] 2 KB 390, CA; *Mackenzie v Royal Bank of Canada* [1934] AC 468, PC; *Bank of Credit and Commerce International SA v Aboody* [1990] 1 QB 923, CA at 953 and *Dunbar Bank plc v Nadeem* [1998] 2 FLR 457, CA. Contrast *Bank of Montreal v Stuart* [1911] AC 120, PC, where undue influence was in fact exercised.

7 Ibid at 190 and 424 respectively.

that de facto she did leave decisions on financial affairs to her husband thereby bringing herself within Class 2B, ie that the relationship between husband and wife in the particular case was such that the wife reposed confidence and trust in her husband in relation to their financial affairs and therefore undue influence is to be presumed.'

Although Lord Browne-Wilkinson had in mind undue influence over a wife, it is clear that 'Class 2B presumptions' are not so confined. In *Simpson v Simpson*,[8] for example, where the husband's mental capacity had been reduced by a cerebral tumour and the effect of the transfer (which was out of character) was to defeat bequests to his children by a former marriage, undue influence by the wife was presumed. It is also probably fair to say that the courts will look with particular care at any transaction entered into at the time of the breakdown of the marriage when both spouses are likely to be in an emotional state.[9] If its effect is to give one of them a considerable advantage with no counterbalancing advantage to the other, it will be set aside if the transferor is relatively poor and ignorant of the effects of property transactions in general and of the transaction in question in particular, and has neither received independent advice nor been urged to seek it.[10]

Since it is dependent upon the 'de facto existence of a relationship under which the complainant generally repose[s] trust and confidence in the wrongdoer',[11] there seems no reason to suppose that 'Class 2B presumptions' cannot also be established between cohabitants and, a fortiori, engaged couples.

(b)   Chattels

To perfect a gift of a chattel there must be an intention on the part of the donor to pass property to the donee and, in addition, either a deed executed by the former or a delivery of the chattel to the latter. Gifts by deed will be rare between partners but, when they do occur, will present no difficulties since the intention can be inferred from the execution of the deed. But a partner who alleges that the other has effected a gift by delivery has to surmount two obstacles.[12] First, since partners frequently use each other's property, an intention to make a gift cannot readily be inferred from permission to use the chattel in question, and consequently the burden of proof upon a partner alleging a gift will probably be higher than upon a stranger.[13] Secondly, it may be well-nigh impossible in many cases to prove delivery. Where the goods are intended for the exclusive use of the donee (for example, clothes or jewellery), delivery will normally take place at the time the gift is made by a physical handing over and taking; but if the goods in question have already been used by both partners in the family home and will continue to be used in this way (for example, articles of furniture), there is not likely to be any apparent change of possession. There may indeed be an effective symbolic

---

8   [1992] 1 FLR 601. See also *Goode Durrant Administration v Biddulph* [1994] 2 FLR 551 and *Bank of Scotland v Bennett* [1997] 1 FLR 801. But note that such presumptions may be rebutted on the facts: see eg *Allied Irish Bank plc v Byrne* [1995] 2 FLR 325.

9   *Backhouse v Backhouse* [1978] 1 All ER 1158 at 1166.

10   *Backhouse v Backhouse* (supra), following *Creswell v Potter* [1978] 1 WLR 255n. See Smith (1979) 123 Sol Jo 193. It is submitted that *Heseltine v Heseltine* [1971] 1 All ER 952, CA, must be incorrectly decided. The court imputed to the spouses an intention to create a trust 'for the benefit of the family'. The court was obviously anxious to protect the wife after the marriage had broken down and took into account the husband's conduct, which cannot affect title. The wife's proper remedy now would be to apply for a property adjustment order in matrimonial proceedings.

11   Per Lord Browne-Wilkinson in *Barclays Bank plc v O'Brien*, supra, at 190 and 424 respectively.

12   See Thornely 'Transfer of Choses in Possession between Members of a Common Household' (1953) 11 CLJ 355; Diamond 'When is a Gift . . . ?' (1964) 27 MLR 357.

13   See *Bashall v Bashall* (1894) 11 TLR 152, CA.

delivery of one chattel as representing the whole, but partners are hardly likely to carry out such an artificial act, the significance of which will not occur to them.[14] Where the possession of goods could be in one of two people (as will happen in the case of furniture used by both partners in the family home), it is presumed to be in the owner, so that if ownership is changed by deed of gift, the buyer or donee will be presumed to have taken possession as soon as the transaction is complete;[15] but this presumption cannot apply in the case of a gift by delivery, since the delivery must be proved before a change in ownership can be established.[16]

English courts have been slow to infer a delivery of a chattel from one spouse to the other,[17] doubtless because of the danger that they may fraudulently allege a prior gift of the husband's goods to the wife in order to keep them out of the hands of the former's creditors. A good example of this reluctance is *Re Cole*,[18] in which the husband completely furnished a new house before his wife set foot in it. When she arrived, he put his hands over her eyes, took her into the first room, uncovered her eyes and said, 'Look'. She then went into all the other rooms and handled various articles; at the end the husband said to her, 'It's all yours'. The furniture nevertheless remained insured in his name. He subsequently became bankrupt and the question arose whether the trustee or wife was entitled to the goods in question. It was held that she had failed to establish an effective delivery, and consequently the gift to her was never perfected. In the circumstances it would always seem wisest for a gift of goods used by both spouses to be made by means of a deed.[19]

Two statutory provisions should also be noticed. Under s 10 of the Married Women's Property Act 1882, a gift made by a husband to his wife may be avoided by his creditors if the property continues to be 'in the order and disposition or reputed ownership of the husband'. The Court of Appeal in *French v Gething*[20] in effect rendered this section inapplicable to goods in the matrimonial home by holding that the maxim 'possession follows title' puts the goods outside the order and disposition or reputed ownership of the husband once the property has changed hands by the execution of a deed or by delivery;[1] but it will presumably apply to goods on, say, the husband's business premises of which the wife is never in apparent possession at all.[2] Secondly, a bill of sale will be void against the transferor's creditors with respect to goods in his possession or apparent possession seven days after the bill is executed, unless the bill is registered or the

---

14 *Lock v Heath* (1892) 8 TLR 295 (husband held to have given all his furniture to wife by symbolic delivery of chair); Thornely, loc cit, pp 357–8. For an effective constructive delivery by a father to his daughter, see *Kilpin v Ratley* [1892] 1 QB 582.
15 *Ramsey v Margrett* [1894] 2 QB 18, CA; *French v Gething* [1922] 1 KB 236, CA.
16 *Hislop v Hislop* [1950] WN 124, CA.
17 Nor is there any reason to think that any different attitude would be taken in the case of alleged gifts between unmarried partners.
18 [1964] Ch 175, [1963] 3 All ER 433, CA. Would the court have arrived at the same decision if, say, after the husband's death the question had arisen whether the goods belonged to the wife or to his personal representatives? See also *Bashall v Bashall* (supra); *Valier v Wright & Bull Ltd* (1917) 33 TLR 366.
19 A similar difficulty would arise if one spouse pledged goods with the other. A mortgage would not create this problem, but it would have to comply with the Bills of Sale Acts: see Thornely, loc cit, pp 373–4.
20 [1922] 1 KB 236, CA.
1 This assumes, of course, that the delivery can be proved.
2 Bankes LJ suggested in *French v Gething* at 244 that the operation of the Act might be limited to cases where the spouses were living on premises where the husband was carrying on business.

transferee obtains possession of the goods before the transferor becomes bankrupt, or assigns his property for the benefit of his creditors generally, or before an execution creditor levies execution.[3] A bill of sale is defined to include a number of documents by which property is transferred in goods capable of transfer by delivery.[4] But with respect to furniture and other goods used by both spouses in the matrimonial home and transferred by one of them to the other, *French v Gething* has made the provisions of the Bills of Sale Act as inapplicable as those of s 10 of the Married Women's Property Act, since the goods will be in the actual possession of the transferee and not in the apparent possession of the transferor.[5]

Improvements to property

By s 37 of the Matrimonial Proceedings and Property Act 1970, if one spouse or former fiancé(e),[6] but not an unmarried cohabitant[7] makes a substantial contribution to the improvement of any property in which the other has a beneficial interest, he or she is to be regarded as having thereby acquired an interest or a greater interest, as the case may be, in the property in question. This provision is of particular importance in relation to the matrimonial home, and will be considered in detail later.[8]

Voidable transactions

It is easy to see how transactions between husband and wife or cohabitants might be used as a means of defrauding creditors. To a man who is on the verge of bankruptcy or who is about to engage in a hazardous business operation, there is a great temptation to settle the bulk of his property on trust for his partner and children and thus keep it out of the hands of his creditors and at the same time ensure that his family will be provided for. Parliament has sought to protect the creditors of the rogue who incidentally benefits his family, whilst not prejudicing the members of the family of a man who settles property in good faith and then runs into financial difficulties. If, for example, a husband, fearing insolvency, transfers the matrimonial home or other property to his wife or children, his creditors or trustee in bankruptcy could seek to have the transfer set aside in the following circumstances.

(a)   Transactions defrauding creditors

Section 423 of the Insolvency Act 1986[9] is designed to protect the creditors of a person who has entered into a transaction at an undervalue with the intention of defeating their claims. This could take the form, for example, of disposing of

---

3   Bills of Sale Act 1878 s 8, which applies to unmarried partners as well as to spouses.

4   Ibid, s 4.

5   For the Act to apply, the goods must in effect remain in the transferor's sole possession, or apparent sole possession, or be in premises solely occupied by him, or be solely used or enjoyed by him: *Koppel v Koppel* [1966] 2 All ER 187, CA. See also *Ramsay v Margrett* (ante),and contrast *Hislop v Hislop* (ante). But the Act would apply in the case of a sale of goods if the property was not to pass immediately and the buyer's title depended on a written contract: Thornely, loc cit, p 371.

6   To whom s 37 was extended by the Law Reform (Miscellaneous Provisions) Act 1970 s 2(1).

7   Such cohabitants would have to rely on equity, the application of which is not entirely certain: see *Pettitt v Pettitt* [1970] AC 777, [1969] 2 All ER 385, HL.

8   See post, pp 150–1.

9   Replacing s 172 of the Law of Property Act 1925, which in turn replaced (with amendments) 13 Eliz 1, c 5.

property which would otherwise be available to satisfy a judgment debt, or of dealing with property that has been charged in such a way as to deprive the creditor of the value of his security. Unlike s 339 (discussed below), s 423 is neither time-limited nor confined to insolvencies.

A 'transaction' for this purpose includes any gift, agreement or arrangement.[10] A transaction is deemed to be at an undervalue if the party entering into it (whom we will call the debtor) received no consideration,[11] or the value he received was significantly less than the value he gave,[12] or if he entered into it in consideration of marriage.[13] The court must be satisfied that the debtor's purpose in entering into the transaction which is being attacked was to put assets beyond the reach of a person who is making (or may at some time make) a claim against him or, alternatively, to prejudice the interests of such a person in some other way.[14] This may be inferred from the circumstances in which the transaction was entered into, for example from his being about to engage in a hazardous business undertaking,[15] or from the fact that defrauding his creditors would be the natural and probable consequence of the transaction,[16] but any inference may be rebutted by other evidence.[17] Once the court is satisfied that the transaction was entered into to put the debtor's interest in property out of the reach of his creditors, it is irrelevant whether or not the transferor was about to enter into business involving a high degree of risk.[18]

Proceedings may be brought by anyone prejudiced by the transaction or capable of being prejudiced by it (who is referred to as a 'victim of the transaction'). Presumably in the latter case he must establish that there is a very strong probability that he will be prejudiced in the future; it cannot have been Parliament's intention to permit anyone to apply to have a transaction set aside on the ground that he might possibly be prejudiced by it. Proceedings may also be brought by the debtor's trustee in bankruptcy or by the supervisor of a voluntary arrangement approved by his creditors.[19]

If the conditions set out above are satisfied, the court may make such order as it thinks fit to restore the position to what it would have been if the transaction had not been entered into and to protect victims' interests.[20] Its powers are extensive.

---

10 Insolvency Act 1986 s 436. Thus a tenancy for a farm or a lease may be set aside if a husband granted it to his wife with the intention of depriving the mortgagees of the land in question of the right to take vacant possession of it; see respectively *Agricultural Mortgage plc v Woodward* [1996] 1 FLR 226, CA and *Lloyd's Bank Ltd v Marcan* [1973] 3 All ER 754, CA.

11 See eg *Midland Bank plc v Wyatt* [1995] 1 FLR 697 (transfer of interest to daughters).

12 See *Re Kumar (A Bankrupt), ex p Lewis v Kumar* [1993] 2 FLR 382, where a transfer of the house to the wife was held to be at an 'undervalue' because, notwithstanding that she undertook sole liability for the mortgage, the equity in the home was substantial, viz £110,000 on a home valued at £140,000.

13 Insolvency Act 1986 s 423(1).

14 Ibid, s 423(3).

15 *Mackay v Douglas* (1872) LR 14 Eq 106; *Re Butterworth* (1882) 19 Ch D 588, CA. But the enterprise does *not* have to be hazardous: *Midland Bank plc v Wyatt*, supra.

16 *Freeman v Pope* (1870) 5 Ch App 538.

17 See *Re Wise* (1886) 17 QBD 290, CA.

18 *Midland Bank plc v Wyatt*, supra.

19 Insolvency Act 1986 s 423(5) (definition of 'victim') and s 424. Any application is to be treated as made on behalf of every victim of the transaction.

20 Ibid, s 423(2). In *Re Maddever* (1884) 27 Ch D 523, CA, it was held (under earlier legislation) that a speciality creditor could have a conveyance set aside 10 years after it had been executed and that the doctrine of laches had no application.

In particular it may order a person (whether or not he was a party to the transaction) to transfer to another (either absolutely or for the benefit of all victims) any property in his hands transferred as part of the transaction (or any other property, including money,[1] representing the proceeds of sales of such property) and to account for any benefits received. It may also release or discharge the whole or part of any security given by the debtor.[2]

The transaction is voidable and not void: consequently no order can be made against anyone who was not a party to it if he acquired an interest in it in good faith, for value and without notice of the circumstances by virtue of which an order could be made under s 423.[3] Hence if, say, the debtor gave property to his wife with intent to defraud a creditor and she then sold it to X, she could be made to account for the value of the benefit she had received, but X could not if he was a bona fide purchaser without notice of the fraud.

(b)   Transactions at an undervalue entered into by a bankrupt

Section 339 of the Insolvency Act 1986[4] gives even wider protection to creditors. It is not necessary to prove any intent to defraud a creditor, but the debtor must have been made bankrupt. The trustee of his estate may apply to the court for an order if the bankrupt entered into a transaction at an undervalue. The trustee may attack any transaction effected up to five years before the presentation of the petition on which the debtor was adjudged bankrupt, but if it was entered into more than two years before that date, no order may be made unless at the time of the transaction the bankrupt was insolvent or became insolvent in consequence of entering into it. There is a rebuttable presumption that this condition is satisfied if the transaction was entered into with 'an associate', including, among others, the bankrupt's spouse, former spouse, reputed spouse, or relative.[5] The phrase 'reputed husband or wife' is unusual. It looks at first sight as though it is intended to apply to transactions between parties living together as husband and wife but, if this is so, the draftsman may largely have failed in his purpose, because the word 'reputed' implies that they must also be regarded as married.[6]

The terms 'transaction' and 'at an undervalue' bear the same meaning as they do under s 423.[7] In the absence of consideration, a benefit is not protected merely because it was conferred in pursuance of an order for financial provision made

---

1 See the definition of 'property' in s 436 of the Insolvency Act 1986.
2 Ibid, s 425(1).
3 Ibid, s 425(2)–(3). Presumably constructive notice will deprive the transferee of protection: see (under s 172 of the Law of Property Act 1925) *Lloyds Bank Ltd v Marcan* [1973] 2 All ER 359 at 369.
4 Replacing s 42 of the Bankruptcy Act 1914.
5 Insolvency Act 1986 s 339, s 341(1)(a), (2) and s 435. There is a special period in the case of a criminal bankruptcy: s 341(4)–(5). A person is insolvent if he is unable to pay his debts or his assets are less than his liabilities (including contingent and prospective liabilities): s 341(3). 'Relative' means brother, sister, uncle, aunt, nephew, niece, lineal ancestor or lineal descendant, including relations of the half blood, and treating a person's illegitimate child, stepchild and adopted child as his own child. 'Associate' also includes the spouse, former spouse and reputed spouse of a relative, and a relative of the bankrupt's spouse, former spouse or reputed spouse: s 435(1), (2) and (8).
6 This also begs the question: by whom must they have been regarded as husband and wife? In the Scots law of presumption of marriage by cohabitation with habit and repute, the parties must be generally regarded as married amongst the circle in which they move: see Clive *Law of Husband and Wife in Scotland* (2nd edn) pp 64–5.
7 Ibid, s 339(3) and s 436. See (under the Bankruptcy Act 1914) *Re Windle* [1975] 3 All ER 987 at 994; *Re A Debtor* [1965] 3 All ER 453; *Re Vansittart* [1893] 1 QB 181; *Re Ashcroft* (1887) 19 QBD 186, CA.

under s 24 of the Matrimonial Causes Act 1973 on divorce, nullity or separation.[8] On the other hand, settling a compromise to a provision in matrimonial proceedings is capable of being consideration in money or money's worth: consequently, if a consent order is made in pursuance of a genuine compromise, the agreement may provide adequate consideration such that the property comprised in the order cannot be touched, provided that the parties acted in good faith.[9]

The court may make such order as it thinks fit to restore the position to what it would have been had the bankrupt not entered into the transaction. It has much the same powers as it has under s 423, except that property has to be transferred to the trustee in bankruptcy. Similarly property may be recovered from a third person into whose hands it has come unless he is, or acquired it through, a bona fide purchaser for value and without notice of the circumstances entitling the court to make an order.[10] In addition, the court may permit anyone adversely affected by the order to prove in the bankruptcy for the loss he has suffered.[11]

Money lent by one partner to the other

A loan by one partner to the other usually raises no presumption of a gift by way of advancement, so that the lender will be able to recover the sum lent in the absence of evidence that a gift was intended.[12] This same principle has been applied to other transactions of a similar nature, for example the guarantee of the other's credit,[13] and the fulfilling of the other's legal obligations;[14] in each case the spouse making the payment is prima facie entitled to recover it from the other.

If the borrower becomes bankrupt, his or her spouse is not entitled to any payment out of his estate until all other creditors have been paid in full.[15]

4.   CONTRACTS OF INSURANCE

Insurable interests

(a)   As between spouses

Because of the relationship of husband and wife and their mutual rights and duties, each has an insurable interest in the life of the other. This means that if, say, a husband insures his wife's life up to any amount, he may recover the sum due on

---

8 Matrimonial Causes Act 1973 s 39, as amended by the Insolvency Act 1985 Sch 8, and the Insolvency Act 1986 Sch 14; cf *Re Kumar (A Bankrupt)*, supra, in which, on the strength of a transfer of their matrimonial home by the husband to the wife some six months earlier, a consent order was made in divorce proceedings by which the wife agreed not to make any further claims on her husband. This transfer, however, was subsequently set aside pursuant to s 339 because it had been made at an undervalue (see n 12 above).

9 *Re Abbott* [1983] Ch 45, [1982] 3 All ER 181, as explained by Ferris J in *Re Kumar*, supra at 393.

10 Insolvency Act 1986 s 342(2), (4).

11 Ibid, s 342(1), (3).

12 *Hall v Hall* [1911] 1 Ch 487 (mortgage of the wife's property to secure a loan to the husband). Contrast *Paget v Paget* [1898] 1 Ch 470, CA, where the facts indicated that a gift was intended. See further George 'Disputes over the Matrimonial Home' (1952) 16 Conv 27 at 31–3.

13 *Re Salisbury-Jones* [1938] 3 All ER 459; *Anson v Anson* [1953] 1 QB 636, [1953] 1 All ER 867.

14 *Outram v Hyde* (1875) 24 WR 268 (husband's discharging encumbrance on wife's realty); *Re McKerrell* [1912] 2 Ch 648 (wife's paying money due from husband on insurance policy). But if the husband purchases realty in the wife's name (thus raising a presumption of advancement) and raises the purchase money by a mortgage, sums paid on the mortgage will likewise be construed as a gift: *Moate v Moate* [1948] 2 All ER 486; cf *Silver v Silver* [1958] 1 All ER 523, CA.

15 Insolvency Act 1986 s 329. This applies if the lender was the bankrupt's spouse at the commencement of the bankruptcy, whether or not they were married when the loan was made.

her death without proving any financial loss at all.[16] Each may also apparently insure any of the other's property which forms a part of the matrimonial home, as the use which he or she enjoys is sufficient to create an insurable interest.[17]

(b)   As between cohabitants

It remains an unresolved point as to whether a cohabitant has an insurable interest in the other's life so as to be able to recover the sum payable on the latter's death without proof of financial loss. In *Griffiths v Fleming*[18] the reason given by the majority of the Court of Appeal for the rule that a husband has an insurable interest in his wife's life was that he was not likely to indulge in 'mischievous gaming' on it, which brought the policy outside the mischief of the Life Assurance Act 1774. This argument applies with equal force to cohabitants. Nevertheless, there must be some doubt as to whether they are in the same position as spouses, because the courts may regard their relationship as less permanent and therefore not entitled to the protection given to married couples. If this is so, the survivor could recover on the policy only if he or she could establish an actual financial loss (for example, the loss of financial support or the value of housekeeping services).

Life assurance policies in favour of the spouse[19] or children of the assured

By s 11 of the Married Women's Property Act 1882, if either spouse effects a policy of assurance on his or her own life[20] expressed to be for the benefit of the assured's spouse or any or all of his or her children[1] (or for the benefit of both the spouse and children), this creates a trust in favour of those persons. This has two important results. First, as objects of the trust they can enforce the policy even though there is no privity of contract between them and the insurance company.[2] Secondly, as beneficiaries under a trust they are entitled to the whole of the sum assured notwithstanding the bankruptcy of the assured or the insolvency of his estate. In only one case will his or her creditors have any claim on the policy, for the Act specifically provides that if the policy was effected to defraud them, they shall be entitled to receive out of the money payable under the policy a sum equal to the premiums paid.[3]

---

16 *Reed v Royal Exchange Assurance Co* (1795) Peake Add Cas 70; *Griffiths v Fleming* [1909] 1 KB 805, CA; Married Women's Property Act 1882 s 11. Otherwise the policy would be void under the Life Assurance Act 1774. For joint policies taken out on both lives to be paid to the survivor on the death of either, see *Griffiths v Fleming*.

17 *Goulstone v Royal Insurance Co* (1858) 1 F & F 276.

18 Supra.

19 No special rules apply to cohabitants – who may, therefore, have difficulty in enforcing any such policy.

20 This includes a policy providing for payment on death or disablement as the result of an accident, provided that the sum is in fact paid on death: *Re Gladitz* [1937] Ch 588, [1937] 3 All ER 173; and an endowment policy payable on the earlier death of the assured: *Re Ioakimidis' Policy Trusts* [1925] Ch 403. In this latter case it was held that the fact that the secured would also be a possible beneficiary did not take the policy outside s 11. This analysis was accepted by Rattee J in *Re S (Forfeiture Rule)* [1996] 1 FLR 910 at 915.

1 This includes adopted children and, in the case of policies effected after 1969, children whose parents are not married to each other: Adoption Act 1976 s 39(1); Family Law Reform Act 1969 s 19(1), (3).

2 See *Lort-Williams v Lort-Williams* [1951] P 395, [1951] 2 All ER 241, CA in which a policy taken out by the husband was held to be a post-nuptial settlement and, as such, could be varied on the application of the divorcing wife.

3 Section 11. This is particularly important in the case of a single premium policy. But note that the benefit of a policy can be forfeited by the beneficiary under the Forfeiture Act 1982, if for example he or she kills the assured – cf *Re S (Forfeiture Rule)*, supra.

If the policy is taken out in favour of a named spouse or children, they take an immediate vested interest in equity. Thus, in *Cousins v Sun Life Assurance Society*,[4] where the policy was issued for the benefit of Lilian Cousins, the assured's wife, who predeceased the life assured, it was held that the husband held the policy on trust for her personal representatives. But where the beneficiaries are merely designated as the husband, wife or children of the assured without being specifically named, this is construed as referring to those who fall into this category at the moment when the trust falls in, ie at the assured's death, and before that time the spouse and existing children have only a contingent interest dependent upon their surviving the assured. In *Re Browne's Policy*[5] H, who was then married to W, took out a policy on his own life for the benefit of his wife and children. W predeceased H, who then married X. He was survived by X, five children of his first marriage and one child of his second. It was held that X and the six surviving children took a joint interest in the insurance money. If all the objects fail, there will be a resulting trust in favour of the assured's estate.[6]

Unless other trustees are appointed, the assured holds the policy as trustee, and as such must exercise options and otherwise deal with it in the way most favourable to the beneficiaries.[7] Similarly, after the death of a named object with a vested interest, the assured is presumed to continue to pay premiums to preserve the property for those entitled to the deceased beneficiary's estate and consequently may recover premiums paid after the death from the deceased's personal representatives.[8]

4 [1933] Ch 126, CA. See also *Re Smith's Estate* [1937] Ch 636, [1937] 3 All ER 472. If there are more beneficiaries than one, they take a joint interest: *Re Seyton* (1887) 34 Ch D 511. But the interest may of course be made expressly conditional upon the beneficiary's surviving the assured, in which case the former will have only a contingent interest during the assured's life: *Re Fleetwood's Policy* [1926] Ch 48.
5 [1903] 1 Ch 188. See also *Re Parker's Policies* [1906] 1 Ch 526; *Re Seyton* (supra).
6 *Re Collier* [1930] 2 Ch 37; cf *Cleaver v Mutual Reserve Fund Life Association* [1892] 1 QB 147, CA.
7 *Re Equitable Life Assurance Society of the United States Policy and Mitchell* (1911) 27 TLR 213.
8 *Re Smith's Estate* (supra). For a fuller discussion of the operation of the section and criticisms of the existing law, see Finlay 'Family Life Insurance Problems under the Married Women's Property Act, 1882' (1939) 2 MLR 266.

Chapter 5

The family home

A. Introduction

The critical importance of the family home (whether the parties are married or not) requires that it be given separate treatment. Difficulty arises because it may have two functions. Its primary purpose is to provide shelter for the parties and their family. At the same time, if it is held in freehold or on a long lease, it will constitute the most significant asset that most couples own and is thus an extremely valuable investment. If the relationship breaks down, these two aspects may come into conflict. Both parties may wish to continue in exclusive occupation (with or without children); alternatively, one may wish to do so while the other may wish to realise his or her investment. A party deprived of both the value of the home and the right to occupy it will often find it impossible to purchase other accommodation, and if the house is sold and the proceeds divided between them, both may face the same predicament. The problem may also arise if one party is insolvent, for a mortgagee may wish to realise his security or a trustee in bankruptcy may wish to sell the home to enlarge the assets available to the creditors. It will therefore be seen that the interests of the creditors may come into direct conflict with those of the rest of the family who still need a roof over their heads.

There are thus two distinct but interrelated problems: ownership and occupation. The first is concerned with the question, in whom are the legal and beneficial interests in the property vested? The second is concerned with the question, what rights of occupation does each party have in the home irrespective of ownership? After discussing these, we consider the problems that arise if one of the parties is insolvent. Finally, we examine the additional security a party may enjoy if the property is leasehold and subject to statutory control.

B. Ownership

1. THE BACKGROUND TO THE CURRENT LAW

Unlike continental systems, English law has never developed a special regime for dealing with matrimonial or family property. Consequently, whenever ownership of family assets is in issue recourse must be had to the ordinary rules governing property law.[1]

---

1 See post, pp 136–7 for the circumstances in which issues of ownership will need to be settled in the family context.

Before the Second World War the potential injustice of applying ordinary property rules to the ownership of family assets was barely an issue. At that stage few working class families owned their own homes and cohabitation outside marriage was almost non-existent. In the vast majority of middle class families the husband was the sole earner and, if the home was purchased, it was conveyed into his name with the result that the whole beneficial interest would vest in the husband to the exclusion of the wife.[2] With low divorce rates and stable home prices, litigation was uncommon.

After the War the social and economic climate changed. It became common for wives to work during marriage. Property ownership increased,[3] with purchases being made with the aid of mortgages. Property prices began to rise and divorce rates spiralled upwards. The combination of these factors resulted in much more litigation being brought in respect of what for most was the key asset, the family home.[4] This in turn brought into sharp relief the starkness of the application of strict rules of property ownership and the doctrine of separation of ownership as between the spouses. It thus became crucial to determine which spouse paid what bills and expenses, since only payments related to the purchase of the property could give rise to ownership. The iniquities of this approach were only too plain to see for, as Lord Denning MR pointed out, it may be purely a matter of convenience which spouse pays off the mortgage and which pays the other household expenses: they give no thought to the legal consequences of their acts (of which they are probably ignorant) and it is unjust to give the wife an interest in the house if she happens to pay the mortgage but not if she pays the household bills instead.[5]

True to form Lord Denning MR was not content to allow what he considered to be an injustice. Seizing on the wording of s 17 of the Married Women's Property Act 1882:

'In any question between husband and wife as to the title to or possession of property, either party . . . may apply by summons or otherwise in a summary way to any judge of the High Court of Justice . . . and the judge . . . may make such order with respect to the property in dispute . . . as he thinks fit',

he held that the court had a discretionary power over family assets. As he put it in *Hine v Hine*:[6]

'. . . the jurisdiction of the court over family assets under section 17 is entirely discretionary. Its discretion transcends all rights, legal or equitable, and enables the court to make such order as it thinks fit. This means, as I understand it, that the court is entitled to make such order as appears to be fair and just in all the circumstances of the case'.

In his view, therefore, provided the spouse (normally the wife at that time) had made a substantial contribution to the overall household expenses she would be

---

2 *Re Sims* [1946] 2 All ER 138. Hence rent received from a lodger was held to belong exclusively to the husband: *Montgomery v Blows* [1916] 1 KB 899, CA.
3 Just under half of all households were in owner-occupied property in 1971, increasing to 67 per cent by 1996 (ONS, *Living in Britain 1996* Table 3.1).
4 In *Pettitt v Pettitt* [1970] AC 777, [1969] 2 All ER 385, HL, Lord Hodson said that, in 1968–69, 900 applications were made to the High Court alone, in connection with disputes between husbands and wives as to ownership of property.
5 See eg *Fribance v Fribance* [1957] 1 All ER 357, CA at 360, and *Falconer v Falconer* [1970] 3 All ER 449, CA at 452.
6 [1962] 3 All ER 345 at 347 E–F, [1962] 1 WLR 1124, CA at 1127–8.

held to have a beneficial share of the property regardless of whether the money was put towards the deposit or mortgage, even though the property was in the husband's name alone.

Lord Denning MR's approach was controversial, and eventually the issue came before the House of Lords, first in *Pettitt v Pettitt*[7] and then in *Gissing v Gissing*,[8] where it was delivered a death blow. It was held that properly interpreted, s 17 is purely a procedural provision designed to facilitate the speedy disposal of property disputes between the spouses, whereby the court could make a declaration of ownership. As Lord Morris put it in *Pettitt v Pettitt*,[9] under s 17 the question for the court was '"Whose is this" and not – "To whom shall this be given"'. Following this unanimous ruling two fundamental rules emerged. First, it is clear from *Pettitt v Pettitt* that English law knows of no doctrine of community of property or any separate rules of law applicable to family assets.[10] Consequently, if one spouse buys property intended for common use with the other – whether it is a house, furniture or a car – this cannot per se give the latter any proprietary interest. From this follows the second principle, stated in *Gissing v Gissing*,[11] that if either of them seeks to establish a beneficial interest in property, the legal title to which is vested in the other, he or she can do so only by establishing that the legal owner holds the property on trust for the claimant. This latter principle, however, masks considerable difficulties which, as we discuss shortly, continue to arise today.

The injustice which Lord Denning in particular sought to avoid was largely removed by the Matrimonial Proceedings and Property Act 1970, which gave the court a power to make property adjustment orders on pronouncing a decree of divorce, nullity or judicial separation and expressly required it to take into account inter alia 'the contributions which each of the parties has made . . . to the welfare of the family'.[12] This makes it unnecessary to resort to other means to compensate the wife, and the power that the court has to take all relevant matters into account in making the fairest adjustment possible on the breakdown of the marriage has led the Court of Appeal to deprecate a spouse's taking other proceedings to establish property rights when an application could be made for an order in matrimonial proceedings.[13] Important though the court's post-divorce adjustive powers are, however, they have not rendered otiose the need to determine ownership in all disputes involving the family. Indeed, there are at least four cases in which it will still be necessary to determine what interest in property a *spouse* has, ie where:

(1) she (or he) is unable or unwilling to take matrimonial proceedings;
(2) she has remarried without applying for a property adjustment order in

---

7 Supra.
8 [1971] AC 886, [1970] 2 All ER 780, HL.
9 [1970] AC 777 at 798E–F and [1969] 2 All ER 385 at 393B.
10 At 800–1 and 395 (per Lord Morris), 810 and 403 (per Lord Hodson), and 817 and 409 (per Lord Upjohn).
11 At 896 and 782 (per Lord Reid), 900 and 785 (per Lord Dilhorne), and 904–5 and 789 (per Lord Diplock).
12 See now the Matrimonial Causes Act 1973 s 24 and s 25(2)(f) and post, pp 778 and 839.
13 *Williams v Williams* [1976] Ch 278, [1977] 1 All ER 28, CA; *Fielding v Fielding* [1978] 1 All ER 267, CA. It is evident, however, that practitioners were slow to appreciate the significance of the new post-divorce adjustive powers and the number of applications under s 17 made in the county court did not immediately decline, and indeed rose significantly in 1975 to 2,166 as opposed to 1,511 in 1970 and 1,610 in 1971.

proceedings for divorce or nullity (when her power to do so will be barred);[14]
(3) it has to be decided, on the death of one of the spouses, whether an interest forms part of his or her estate or vests in the survivor;
(4) it has to be decided, on the insolvency of one of the spouses, what property is available for his or her creditors.

Furthermore, as unmarried cohabitants are unable to petition for divorce or other matrimonial relief, neither can apply for a property adjustment order in matrimonial proceedings. Hence, unless they have children (when a property adjustment order can be made under the Children Act 1989),[15] any claims they may have must be resolved solely by reference to the law of property. With the growing incidence of cohabitation this particular use of property law has become of major concern (and is currently under review by the Law Commission). It is perhaps ironic that the law evolved to settle the property claims of spouses now derives much of its contemporary significance in relation to unmarried couples.[16]

Former engaged couples are, like unmarried cohabitants, barred from using the court's adjustive powers under the Matrimonial Causes Act 1973.[17] However, in two other respects they are treated in the same way as spouses in that they can use s 17 of the Married Women's Property Act 1882 to seek judicial resolution of property disputes between them, and s 37 of the Matrimonial Proceedings and Property Act 1970 to claim a beneficial interest by means of improvements they have made to each other's property.[18] Although the former right is hardly significant now that it is broadly settled that the ordinary principles of the law of trusts apply to the property of married and unmarried couples alike, and anyway summary relief in respect of land may be sought under s 14 of the Trusts of Land and Appointment of Trustees Act 1996, the latter right can be useful.[19]

2.   THE CURRENT LAW

The primary importance of the documents of title

As we have said, *Pettitt v Pettitt* and *Gissing v Gissing* established that no special rules apply to the ownership of family assets and that instead one must apply

---

14 See post, p 783.
15 See post, p 768.
16 Though whether exactly the same principles apply to cohabitants as to spouses has been questioned: see for example Griffiths LJ who said in *Bernard v Josephs* [1982] Ch 391 at 402, [1982] 3 All ER 162, CA: 'The legal principles to be applied are the same whether the dispute is between married or unmarried couples, but the nature of the relationship between the parties is a very important factor when considering what inferences should be drawn from the way they have conducted their affairs. There are many reasons why a man and a woman may decide to live together without marrying, and one of them is that each values his independence and does not wish to make the commitment of marriage; in such a case it will be misleading to make the assumptions and to draw the same inferences from their behaviour as in the case of a married couple. The judge must look most carefully at the nature of the relationship, and only if satisfied that it was intended to involve the same degree of commitment as marriage will it be legitimate to regard them as no different from a married couple.'
17 *Mossop v Mossop* [1989] Fam 77, [1988] 2 All ER 202, CA.
18 Section 17 and s 37 respectively were extended to former engaged couples by the Law Reform (Miscellaneous Provisions) Act 1970 s 2(1)–(2). It may also be that the presumption of advancement applies to engaged couples: see *Moate v Moate* [1948] 2 All ER 486, but note ante, p 124 n 17.
19 For a discussion of the application of s 37, see post, p 150.

ordinary property principles. The application of these principles requires first having to establish legal ownership and then to determine equitable or beneficial ownership. To determine these issues one should first have recourse to the documents of title, for as Lord Upjohn said in *Pettitt v Pettitt*:[20]

> ' If the property in question is land there must be some lease or conveyance which shows how it was acquired.
>
> . . .
>
> If that document declares not merely in whom the legal title is to vest but in whom the beneficial title is to vest that necessarily concludes the question of title as between the spouses for all time, and in the absence of fraud or mistake at the time of the transaction the parties cannot go behind it any time thereafter even on death or break-up of the marriage.'

Although this dictum went further than the ratio of any previous decision, it is evident that this is now the accepted position. Hence, as the Court of Appeal held in *Goodman v Gallant*,[1] if the document of title expressly declares in whom not only the legal title but also the beneficial interests are to vest, it will be conclusive in the absence of fraud or mistake.[2] Accordingly, if, as is common in the case of spouses, the family home is conveyed to both partners on express trust for themselves as joint tenants in equity, this must give them a joint interest in the proceeds of sale, and if either of them severs the joint interest, they will become equitable tenants in common in equal shares.[3] If the conveyance declares they are to hold as tenants in common in equal shares or in some other proportion, they will be similarly bound by the wording. For this reason solicitors acting for parties buying their home should enquire what their intentions are and spell them out in the conveyance to prevent dispute in the future.[4]

If the document is silent as to the beneficial ownership, then it is open to the non-legal owner and even joint legal owners[5] to claim entitlement to a share of the property under a trust. To substantiate such a claim the claimant must establish that the legal owner holds the property in trust inter alia for the claimant. The establishment of such a trust is dependent upon the parties' common intention.

---

20 [1970] AC 777 at 813 E and [1969] 2 All ER 385 at 405I.
 1 [1986] Fam 106, [1986] 1 All ER 311, CA. Contrast *Re Gorman* [1990] 1 All ER 717, where the parties were not bound by the declaration because they had not signed the transfer. The transfer was nevertheless evidence (in the circumstances conclusive) of their common intention at the time the property was acquired.
 2 As in *Thames Guaranty Ltd v Campbell* [1985] QB 210, [1984] 2 All ER 585, CA. The spouses had agreed that the property should belong beneficially to the wife but that it should be conveyed into their joint names. The solicitor, assuming that they wished to take a joint beneficial interest, drafted the transfer to them as joint tenants in law *and equity*. It was held that the transfer could be rectified by deleting the words italicised, thus leaving both spouses as trustees for the wife alone.
 3 *Goodman v Gallant* (supra). The presentation of a divorce petition including a prayer for a property adjustment order does not effect a severance, so that if one spouse dies before the order is made, the whole interest will vest in the other by survivorship: *Harris v Goddard* [1983] 3 All ER 242, CA.
 4 Per Bagnall J in *Cowcher v Cowcher* [1972] 1 All ER 943 at 959. As Dillon LJ repeated in *Springette v Defoe* [1992] 2 FLR 388 at 390, 'it is very much to be deplored that solicitors should fail to take steps to find out and declare what the beneficial interests are to be, when the legal estate in a house is acquired by two persons in their joint names. See also *Bernard v Josephs* [1982] Ch 391 at 403, [1982] 3 All ER 162, CA at 170; *Walker v Hall* [1984] FLR 126, CA at 129; *Marsh v von Sternberg* [1986] 1 FLR 526 at 528.
 5 See eg *Springette v Defoe*, CA, supra and *Huntingford v Hobbs* [1993] 1 FLR 736, CA.

Establishing a beneficial interest

Although, as we have said, the creation of a beneficial interest depends upon the common intention of the legal owner and the claimant to share the property in question, precisely how that intention can be established has proved problematic. It should be appreciated at the outset that the concept of 'intention' in this context is a notional one.[6] It does not necessarily reflect both parties' intentions, for, as Lord Diplock pointed out in *Gissing v Gissing*,[7] a party's intention in this context must mean that which his words and conduct led the other to believe that he holds. It is therefore no objection that the party making the representation actually intended to hold the property for himself.[8] Further, it was held in *Midland Bank plc v Cooke*[9] that even if both parties admit that neither had discussed or intended any agreement as to the proportion of their interests, this did not preclude the court from inferring one. Another complicating factor is the requirement under the Law of Property Act 1925 s 53(1)(b) that a valid declaration of trust of a beneficial interest in land[10] needs to be in writing. This means that if, for example, one partner purchases the home entirely out of his own money and has it conveyed into his own name, an oral agreement between the partners that the other is to take a beneficial share will not per se give her an interest. It will amount to no more than an imperfect gift, which equity will not perfect, or to a declaration of trust, which is required to be evidenced in writing.

Section 53(2) of the 1925 Act, however, does not require 'the creation or operation of resulting, implied or constructive trusts' to be in writing. Accordingly, as Lord Diplock said in *Gissing v Gissing*,[11] in the absence of writing the claimant to a beneficial interest will need to establish an interest under a resulting, implied or constructive trust. Although his Lordship went on to say[12] that from this point of view it does not matter what type of trust it is, such a classification is important when it comes to assessing the quantum of any interest established.[13] As we shall see, however, this classification issue is not without its problems.

Another complicating factor is that, while the creation of a beneficial interest depends upon the parties' common intention, all too frequently the parties themselves have given no thought to the question of ownership. According to the majority in *Pettitt v Pettitt* it was not open to the court to impute an agreement to the parties where the evidence adduced showed there was none. As Lord Morris put it:[14] 'The court does not devise or invent a legal result.' The minority, Lords Reid and Diplock, however, thought that in the absence of evidence of a common intention it was open to the court to impute to them a constructive intention which, in the court's opinion, would have been formed by reasonable partners had they

---

6 See the analyses of Glover and Todd 'The myth of common intention' (1996) 16 Legal Studies 325 and Gardner 'Rethinking Family Property' (1993) 109 LQR 263 at 264–5.

7 *Gissing v Gissing*, supra at 906 and 791 respectively.

8 As in *Eves v Eves* [1975] 3 All ER 768, CA and *Grant v Edwards* [1986] Ch 638, [1986] 2 All ER 426, CA, discussed post, p 141.

9 [1995] 4 All ER 562, CA at 574–5.

10 Note, however, there is no requirement for writing to create express trusts in respect of chattels. Hence an oral assurance that furniture is a joint asset is good enough to create a beneficial interest: *Paul v Constance* [1977] 1 All ER 195, CA.

11 Supra, at 905 and 789.

12 Ibid.

13 See post, p 147.

14 Ibid at 804 and 398.

thought about it. In *Gissing v Gissing* Lord Diplock (but not Lord Reid) accepted that it was not open to the court to impute an agreement to the parties but held that it could nevertheless *infer* an intention from their conduct or words insofar as they would be reasonably understood by the other party. Hence, if one partner led the other to believe that she would share a joint beneficial interest in the house, such an intention will be imputed to him whatever his inward intention. In other words, the court may have to infer an intention the parties never articulated, but it cannot impute to them an agreement they clearly did not make.

Although *Pettitt* and *Gissing* were important decisions, settling once and for all that there was no power under s 17 of the Married Women's Property Act 1882 to vary property interests and that non-economic contributions to the purchase of the family home could never give rise to a beneficial interest, they nevertheless left a number of uncertainties. In particular, it was unclear precisely what type of conduct could properly be considered to give rise to an inference that the parties intended to share the property. There was also uncertainty as to whether their Lordships, particularly in *Gissing v Gissing*, were really considering the creation of resulting or constructive trusts.

Although there was considerable litigation in the 20 years following the decisions in *Pettitt* and *Gissing*, the next House of Lords' decision was not given until 1990 in *Lloyds Bank plc v Rosset*.[15] In that case Lord Bridge set out, albeit obiter, what he considered to be the proper approach in ownership cases, which, as Waite J said in *Hammond v Mitchell*,[16] now provides the template for current analysis.

The *Rosset* tests

According to Lord Bridge a distinction needs to be made in cases where there has been an agreement between the parties to share the property and those where there has not. For convenience we will label these situations respectively *Rosset 1* and *Rosset 2*.

Rosset 1

According to Lord Bridge:[17]

> 'The first and fundamental question *which must always be resolved* is whether independently of any inference to be drawn from the conduct of the parties in the course of sharing the house as their home and managing their joint affairs, there has at any time prior to acquisition, or exceptionally at some later date, been any agreement, arrangement or understanding reached between them that the property is to be shared beneficially.'

Such a finding must be based upon evidence of express discussions between the parties 'however imperfectly remembered and however imprecise their terms must be have been'.

As Waite J subsequently observed in *Hammond v Mitchell*,[18] this first requirement means –

> '... that the tenderest exchanges of a common law courtship may assume an unforeseen significance many years later when they are brought under equity's microscope and

---

15 [1991] 1 AC 107, [1990] 1 All ER 1111, HL.
16 [1992] 2 All ER 109.
17 Ibid at 132 and 1118 respectively.
18 [1992] 2 All ER 109 at 121.

subjected to an analysis under which many thousands of pounds of value may be liable to turn on this fine question as to whether the relevant words were spoken in earnest or in dalliance and with or without representational intent.'

Yet it is clear that such discussions must be pleaded in the greatest detail both as to the language and to the circumstance. In *Hammond* itself it was held sufficient that the man had said to the woman soon after completion:

> 'Don't worry about the future because when we are married [the house] will be half yours anyway and I'll always look after you and [their child]'.

In contrast, in *Springette v Defoe* [19] it was held insufficient that the parties had a mutual but uncommunicated belief or intention to share the property for, as Steyn LJ said, [20] 'Our trust law does not allow property rights to be affected by telepathy.'
Provided such an agreement can be proved then, according to Lord Bridge:

> '. . . *it will only be necessary for the partner asserting a claim to a beneficial interest against the partner entitled to the legal estate to show that he or she has acted to his or her detriment or significantly altered his or her position in reliance on the agreement in order to give rise to a constructive trust or proprietary estoppel.*' [1]

Lord Bridge himself instanced two 'outstanding examples' of cases falling into this first category, namely *Eves v Eves* [2] and *Grant v Edwards*. [3] Both cases involved cohabiting couples, and in both the female partner had clearly been led by the male partner to believe that when they set up home together the property would belong to them jointly. In *Eves* the man told his female partner that the only reason the home was to be in his name alone was because she was under 21 and that but for her age he would have had the house put in joint names. [4] Subsequently the woman did a great deal of manual work including breaking up concrete, demolishing and rebuilding a shed, stripping wallpaper and painting the woodwork, to renovate the dirty and dilapidated house that the man had bought.

In *Grant v Edwards* the defendant told the plaintiff that her name was not going on the title because that would prejudice her in matrimonial proceedings between her and her husband. The plaintiff made no contributions to the initial purchase price but, despite having four children, went out to work and applied her earnings to the household expenses without which, the Court of Appeal accepted, the mortgage could not have been paid whilst at the same time leaving the family enough money to live on.

What seemed to characterise the contributions in these two cases is that it comprised conduct on which, in Nourse LJ's words, [5] 'the woman could not reasonably have been expected to embark unless she was to have an interest in the house.' In other words, even where there has been a prior agreement to share, detrimental reliance requires more than living with the man, having a baby by him and looking after the family and home, for as Nourse LJ again put it, [6] ' the law is

---

19 [1992] 2 FLR 388, CA.
20 Ibid at 394.
1 For detrimental reliance see generally Lawson 'The things we do for love – detrimental reliance in the family home' (1996) 16 Legal Studies 215.
2 [1975] 3 All ER 768, CA.
3 [1986] Ch 638, [1986] 2 All ER 426, CA; Sufrin (1987) 50 MLR 94, and Warburton [1986] Conv 291.
4 He admitted in evidence that this was just an excuse.
5 [1986] Ch 638 at 648, [1986] 2 All ER 426 at 639.
6 Ibid at 648 and 439 respectively. But note the comment by Sufrin (1987) 50 MLR 94 at 99: 'One can argue that the law should not be so sentimental as to infer that she will live with him and have his children without understanding that her interest in the house to which she is thereby unable to contribute financially is secure.'

not so cynical as to infer that a woman will only go to live with a man . . . if she understands that she is to have an interest in the home.'

A common intention to share is not of itself sufficient to establish a beneficial interest. The claimant must also prove detrimental reliance.[7] In *Midland Bank plc v Dobson*[8] the wife's claim, as against her husband's creditors, to a beneficial interest in the matrimonial home, which was in her husband's name alone, failed even though the spouses said that they had both thought of marriage as a partnership and did not consider putting the wife's name on the title because, accepting the principle of sharing everything, they had commonly understood that the house was jointly owned. In that case it was held that the wife's using part of her income for household expenses, including the purchase of domestic equipment, and doing some ordinary decorating, did not amount to detrimental reliance.

Whether detrimental reliance can be established otherwise than by contributions of money or money's worth seems doubtful.[9] There are some hints, however, in *Hammond v Mitchell*[10] that non-financial contributions can be relevant. In that case the main evidence of detrimental reliance lay in the claimant agreeing to postponing her interest in the property to that of the bank's charge (executed to secure a loan for the defendant's business ventures, which, had they had been unsuccessful, might have involved the whole property having to be sold), but Waite J also took account, at any rate when considering the quantum of the claimant's interest,[11] of the claimant's contribution as 'mother/helper/unpaid assistant and at times financial supporter to the family prosperity.' As one commentator has observed:[12] 'Although this does not amount to an explicit recognition of domestic labour or child care as a detriment in itself, it does show a willingness to take it into account as part of the overall picture,' and in particular into determining the quantum of any interest acquired.

Hammond v Mitchell is important for another point, namely, that where there is more than one property involved it is essential to establish whether the agreement to share applies to all properties or just one. In *Hammond* itself the arrangement was only held to extend to the matrimonial home in England and not to another property in Spain.

Notwithstanding that conduct considered sufficient to establish detrimental reliance may be limited to contributions in money or money's worth, it is clear that the test of such reliance is less onerous than having to establish an interest where there is no prior agreement to share. As Lord Bridge observed in *Lloyds Bank plc v Rosset*,[13] the contributions made in both *Eves v Eves* and *Grant v Edwards*, 'fell far short of such conduct as would by itself have supported the claim in the absence of an express representation by the male partner that she was to have such an interest.'

---

7 Though note *Wayling v Jones* [1995] 2 FLR 1029, CA, in which it was held that once conduct had been proved from which detrimental reliance could be inferred, the burden switches to the defendant to show that the claimant had not acted in reliance upon the promise.
8 [1986] 1 FLR 171, CA at 177.
9 See the discussion in Moffat *Trusts Law Text and Materials* (2nd edn, 1994) pp 455ff.
10 [1992] 2 All ER 109.
11 Discussed further, post, pp 147–50.
12 Moffat, op cit, at 456.
13 [1991] 1 AC 107 at 133, [1990] 1 All ER 1111 at 1119.

Rosset 2

According to Lord Bridge in *Rosset*: [14]

'In sharp contrast with this situation [ie *Rosset 1*] is the very different one where there is no evidence to support a finding of an agreement or arrangement to share, however reasonable it might have been for the parties to reach such an arrangement if they had applied their minds to the question, and where the court must rely entirely on the conduct of the parties both as the basis from which to infer a common intention to share the property beneficially and as the conduct relied on to give rise to a constructive trust. In this situation direct contributions to the purchase price by the partner who is not the legal owner, whether initially or by payment of mortgage instalments, will readily justify the inference necessary to the creation of a constructive trust. But, as I read the authorities, it is at least extremely doubtful whether anything less will do'.

In *Rosset* itself, where there was found to be no prior agreement or arrangement to share the property, it was held that neither a common intention that the house was to be renovated as a joint venture nor a common intention that it is to be shared as the family home was sufficient to indicate that both parties were to take an interest; nor could such an inference be drawn from the wife's own renovations to the property and her supervision of the building works over a period of some six weeks before completion and for another six weeks after that. Echoing earlier sentiments as to what type of work a woman could normally be expected to do, Lord Bridge commented: [15]

'. . . it would seem the most natural thing in the world for any wife, in the absence of her husband abroad, to spend all the time she could spare and to employ any skills she might have, such as the ability to decorate a room, in doing all she could to accelerate progress of the work quite irrespective of any expectation she might have of enjoying a beneficial interest in the property.'

Lord Bridge instanced both *Pettitt v Pettitt* [16] and *Gissing v Gissing* [17] as falling into this second category and in neither did the claim for a beneficial interest succeed. In the former, where the house was bought in the wife's name, the husband failed to establish an interest by reason of the 'ephemeral' improvements he effected to the property by his internal decoration, the laying of a lawn and his construction of a well and a garden side wall. [18] Similarly, Mrs Gissing failed since, rather than paying for the deposit or mortgage on the home, she paid for her own and the son's clothes and supplemented the housekeeping allowance.

But perhaps the most infamous example of a second category case where the claim failed is *Burns v Burns*. [19] In that case Mrs Burns (as she was known), who had lived with her partner for 19 years, failed to establish a beneficial interest in the family home, having given up her job to have the couple's two children and then, when she did begin to earn money, had spent it on the household's expenses,

14 Ibid at 132–3 and 1119 respectively.
15 Ibid at 131 and 1118 respectively.
16 [1970] AC 777, [1969] 2 All ER 385, HL. But note that substantial improvements can now be sufficient for a spouse to obtain an interest under s 37 of the Matrimonial Proceedings and Property Act 1970, discussed post, p 150.
17 [1971] AC 886, [1970] 2 All ER 780, HL.
18 See also *Midland Bank plc v Cooke* [1995] 4 All ER 562, CA, in which it was held that the wife's contribution to the maintenance and improvement of the property was not itself sufficient to raise an inference that the property was to be shared. See further below.
19 [1984] Ch 317, [1984] 1 All ER 244, CA; Lowe and Smith (1984) 47 MLR 341 and Dewar (1984) 47 MLR 735.

fixtures and fittings in the house and the family's clothing.

In none of these cases was there a contribution either to the initial deposit or legal charges or to subsequent mortgage repayments. Where there is such a direct financial contribution, then even if it is relatively small (see below), it seems that the court will readily infer a common intention to share the property. This is implicit in all the speeches in *Gissing v Gissing* and was spelled out by Viscount Dilhorne and Lord Diplock,[20] as well as by Lord Bridge in *Rosset*. This contribution may come directly out of the claimant's own earnings or resources, or out of a common fund to which both parties contributed.[1]

A most extreme example of a finding of a direct contribution of this nature is *Midland Bank plc v Cooke*,[2] in which it was held that a wedding cash present of just over £1,000 provided by the groom's parents was intended to be a gift to both spouses equally, so that the wife could be credited with half of it. Since it was used towards the payment of the initial deposit on the house, it was held there could properly be inferred a common intention to share the property.

Whether anything less than direct contributions to the deposit, legal charges or mortgage will now give rise to an inference that the parties intended to share the property is uncertain. Lord Bridge was clearly of the view that indirect contributions by way of payments to the household expenses could never give rise to such an inference, even if it could be shown that without these contributions the legal owner could not have paid the mortgage instalments. This is evident from his Lordship's comment that the woman's contribution in *Grant v Edwards*, without which, as the Court of Appeal accepted, the payments could not have been paid and the household expenses met, would not have been sufficient in the absence of an express agreement to share. However, Lord Bridge's comments are obiter and seem at variance with those of Lord Diplock in particular in *Gissing v Gissing*. In that case Lord Diplock pointed out that if the wife had made an initial contribution to the deposit or legal charges which indicated that she was to take some interest in the property, the court should also take account of her contribution to the mortgage instalments, even though these were indirect, because this would be consistent with a common intention that the payment of other household expenses would release the husband's money to pay off the mortgage and would thus be her contribution to the purchase of the home. But, he added, if the wife had made no initial contribution to the purchase, no direct contribution to the repayment of the mortgage, and 'no adjustment to her contribution to other expenses of the household which it can be inferred was referable to the acquisition of the house', she cannot claim an interest in it 'merely because she continued to contribute out of her own earnings or private income to other expenses of the household'.[3] Lord Pearson similarly considered that there could be a contribution 'if by arrangement between the spouses one of them by payment of the household expenses enables the other to pay the mortgage instalments'.[4]

---

20 [1971] AC 886 at 900 and 907, [1970] 2 All ER 780 at 786 and 790–2.

1 See eg *Gordon v Douce* [1983] 2 All ER 228 (woman contributed through past savings of the deposit and then contributed towards the housekeeping expenses and repairs and improvements, and outgoings); *Risch v McFee* [1991] 1 FLR 105, CA (woman initially made a loan to her partner so as to buy out his wife's interest in the house in divorce proceedings and later paid a sum to the man to pay off some of the outstanding mortgage; no interest was paid on the loan nor was repayment sought: it was held that the plaintiff succeeded in establishing a beneficial interest). See also *Drake v Whipp* [1996] 1 FLR 826, CA in which the woman provided 40 per cent of the purchase price.

2 [1995] 4 All ER 562, CA, discussed further below.

3 [1971] AC 886 at 907–10, [1970] 2 All ER 780, HL at 792–3.

4 At 903 and 788 respectively.

Griffiths LJ indicated the way the court should approach the problem in *Bernard v Josephs*:[5]

'. . . the fact that one party paid the mortgage may indicate that it was recognised by the couple that that party was solely responsible for providing the purchase price and therefore to be regarded as the sole beneficial owner. But often where a couple are living together and both are working and pooling their resources, which one of them pays the mortgage may be no more than a matter of internal accounting between them. In such a case the judge must look at the contributions of each to the "family" finances and determine as best he may what contribution each was making towards the purchase of the house. This is not to be carried out as a strictly mathematical exercise; for instance, if the man was ill for a time and out of work so that the woman temporarily contributed more, that temporary state of affairs should not increase her share, nor should her share be decreased if she was temporarily unable to work whilst having a baby. The contributions must be viewed broadly by the judge to guide him to the parties' unexpressed and probably unconsidered intentions as to the beneficial ownership of the house.'

It is submitted that, notwithstanding Lord Bridge's comment to the contrary, an inference that the property is to be shared can be drawn if the claimant can show that the financial contributions freed the legal owner's own money and thus enabled him to pay the deposit, legal charges or mortgage instalments.[6]

Proprietary estoppel

According to Lord Bridge in *Lloyds Bank plc v Rosset*,[7] once an agreement to share property has been found the claimant must show –

'. . . that he or she has acted to his or her detriment or significantly altered his or her position in reliance on the agreement in order to give rise to a constructive trust or proprietary estoppel.'

In so commenting his Lordship seemed therefore to equate constructive trusts with proprietary estoppel. This in turn has led to much academic speculation[8] as to whether the two concepts have been assimilated. There can be little doubt that the two have been increasingly drawn together. This is evident from Browne-Wilkinson V-C's comments in *Grant v Edwards* that:[9]

'. . . useful guidance may in the future be obtained from the principles underlying the law of proprietary estoppel which in my judgment are closely akin to those laid down in *Gissing v Gissing*. In both, the claimant must to the knowledge of the legal owner have acted in the belief that the claimant has or will obtain an interest in the property. In both, the claimant must have acted to his or her detriment in reliance on such belief. In both, equity acts on the conscience of the legal owner to prevent him from acting in an unconscionable manner by defeating the common intention. The two principles have been developed separately without cross-fertilisation between them: but they rest on the same foundation and have on all other matters reached the same conclusions.'

---

5 [1982] Ch 391 at 403–4, [1982] 3 All ER 162, CA at 170.
6 *Gissing v Gissing* (supra) at 903 and 788 (per Lord Pearson) and 980 and 792 (per Lord Diplock); *Burns v Burns* [1984] Ch 317 at 329, [1984] 1 All ER 244 at 252 (per Fox LJ) and 344 and 265 (per May LJ).
7 [1991] 1 AC 107 at 132, [1990] 1 All ER 1111 at 1119.
8 See Moffat *Trusts Law*, op cit, 458–62; Hayton 'Equitable Rights of Cohabitees' (1990) 54 Conv 370; and Gardner 'Rethinking Family Property' (1993) 109 LQR 263.
9 [1986] Ch 638 at 656.

However, it is premature to say that the two are one and the same. As Nourse LJ subsequently observed in *Stokes v Anderson*,[10] while it is possible that the House of Lords will, at some future point, assimilate the two, 'they have not yet been assimilated'. One plausible distinction is that recourse to constructive trusts needs to be had in cases where the claim is that the property in issue has been jointly acquired, whereas estoppel becomes relevant where the property has unquestionably already been acquired by one person who, by his or her *subsequent* conduct, has led the claimant to think that he or she will share it. It remains now to consider those cases where recourse has been had to proprietary estoppel.

The essence of proprietary estoppel was described by Edward Nugee QC (sitting as a deputy High Court judge) in *Re Basham*:[11]

> 'Where one person, A, has acted to his detriment on the faith of a belief, which was known to and encouraged by another person, B, that he either has [been] or is going to be given a right in or over B's property, B cannot insist on his strict legal rights if to do so would be inconsistent with A's belief.'

To this should be added the requirement that B must know of the existence of his own right which is inconsistent with that claimed by A, for otherwise he is in the same position as A, who will therefore acquire no prior equity.[12] If these conditions are established, B is bound to make good, as far as he can, the expectation he has encouraged.

The similarity to a constructive trust is immediately apparent in that in each case the person claiming the interest in property must have acted to his or her detriment, but one distinction is that the claimant under a constructive trust must prove that she (or he) acted in reliance on a common intention that she should take an interest in the property, whereas an estoppel will arise if her acts result from her being misled by the other's conduct. A further distinction lies in the fact that, if the claimant adopts a detrimental course of conduct, there is a rebuttable presumption that she has done so in reliance on the assurances given to her.[13]

As with constructive trusts, the claimant may have acted to her detriment either by incurring expenditure or by prejudicing herself in some way. In either case, however, her acts must have been induced by her mistaken belief.[14] So in *Coombes v Smith*[15] it was held that the plaintiff's leaving her husband, moving into a house provided by the defendant, having his child and looking after it could not found a proprietary estoppel, because the reason for her conduct was that she preferred to live with the defendant and have his child rather than live with her husband. The

---

10 [1991] 1 FLR 391, CA at 399.
11 [1987] 1 All ER 405 at 410, cited with approval by Balcombe LJ in *Wayling v Jones* [1995] 2 FLR 1029 at 1031. But note the criticism in *Taylor v Dickens* [1998] 1 FLR 806 at 831E–G, per Weeks J.
12 *Coombes v Smith* [1986] 1 WLR 808. Estoppel can give the claimant an interest only in a specific piece of property and not in the other's assets generally: *Layton v Martin* [1986] 2 FLR 227 at 239.
13 *Greasley v Cooke* [1980] 3 All ER 710, CA; *Coombes v Smith* supra at 821. It is also to be noted that, according to *Wayling v Jones*, supra, the promises relied upon do not have to be the *sole* inducement for the conduct.
14 Hence there can be no estoppel if the claimant knew that the other reserved his right to change his mind or to revert to the original position: see *A-G of Hong Kong v Humphreys Estate (Queen's Gardens) Ltd* [1987] AC 114, [1987] 2 All ER 387, PC.
15 [1986] 1 WLR 808; cf the same principle applied to constructive trusts: ante, pp 141–2. The plaintiff also failed in *Coombes v Smith* because the defendant's statement that he would never see her without a roof over her head could not be construed as a promise that she could stay in the house against his wishes if their relationship broke down.

owner of the property must also know of the claimant's mistake: he cannot encourage a belief of which he was ignorant.[16] On the other hand, as the Court of Appeal held in *Wayling v Jones*,[17] once it is established that the promise has been made and that there has been conduct by the claimant of such a nature that an inducement could be inferred, the burden of proof shifts to the defendant to establish that the plaintiff had not relied on the promise.

A good example of the operation of proprietary estoppel is *Pascoe v Turner*,[18] in which the plaintiff and defendant, who was his housekeeper, began to live together as husband and wife. After the relationship broke down, the plaintiff, who had moved out, told the defendant, 'The house is yours and everything in it'. Relying on his statement, she spent money on redecoration, improvements and repairs. On his claim to possession of the house, the Court of Appeal held that, by encouraging or acquiescing in the defendant's belief that the house was hers, he was estopped from denying this and that the only way in which the equity thus arising could be satisfied was by compelling him to transfer the house to her.

The remedy granted in *Pascoe v Turner*, namely the complete transfer of the property, was an extreme one[19] and it by no means follows that the court will always be so generous. In *Greasley v Cooke*,[20] for instance, the claimant was only granted a right of occupation.

Quantification of shares

Up to now we have been discussing the circumstances in which a spouse or cohabitant may take a beneficial interest in the matrimonial home. We must now consider the further question: what is the size of the interest that each acquires? This in turn will depend upon the nature of interest established. So far as trusts are concerned the interest may be created by means of an express trust (if in writing), a resulting trust, or a constructive trust.[1] In the first two instances there is little difficulty in quantifying the parties' shares. Thus, if the conveyance spells out the beneficial interests, the court must give effect to it.[2] If the property is vested in the parties jointly on an express trust for themselves as joint tenants, they will become equitable tenants in common in equal shares if either of them severs the joint interest.[3] Similarly, if they take as tenants in common, the court must give effect to the trust thereby created and divide the proceeds in the proportions stated. If the circumstances in which the property was bought are held to give rise to a resulting trust, the beneficial interests will be proportionate to the parties' contributions.[4] It

16 *Brinnand v Ewens* (1987) 19 HLR 415, CA.
17 Supra.
18 [1979] 2 All ER 945, CA. See Sufrin (1979) 42 MLR 574.
19 See also *Wayling v Jones*, where the plaintiff was awarded the proceeds of sale of the deceased's hotel that he had promised the plaintiff.
20 Supra.
 1 For a detailed discussion of the nature of each type of trust readers should consult the standard works on trusts, but broadly a resulting trust is based on the presumed intention of the parties that where the person puts money into someone else's property the latter holds it in trust for the contributor. A constructive trust, on the other hand, is imposed on the parties where equity considers it unconscionable for the legal owner to hold the whole property for his or her own benefit.
 2 Unless the conveyance can be rectified as a result of fraud or mistake: see ante, p 138.
 3 *Goodman v Gallant* [1986] Fam 106, [1986] 1 All ER 311, CA.
 4 This is not to say that it is always easy to quantify the contributions. For some examples of the application of resulting trusts see eg *Huntingford v Hobbs* [1993] 1 FLR 736, CA; *Springette v Defoe* [1992] 2 FLR 388, CA; *Cowcher v Cowcher* [1972] 1 All ER 943; and *Marsh v Von Sternberg* [1986] 1 FLR 526.

is evident, however, that the courts are reluctant to rely on resulting trusts, at any rate in cases involving family homes. Certainly Lord Bridge's analysis in *Lloyds Bank plc v Rosset* seemed to contemplate that in both types of cases, ie where there is detrimental reliance following a promise or agreement to share, and where there is conduct from which an agreement to share can be inferred, a constructive trust is created. This approach is very much evident in the subsequent Court of Appeal decisions in *Midland Bank plc v Cooke*[5] and *Drake v Whipp*.[6] Indeed, in the latter case counsel for the claimant was rebuked for conceding, notwithstanding the claimant's substantial direct contribution to the purchase price, that this was a case where there was no common intention to share so that the share should be assessed on the basis of a resulting trust.

Just occasionally however, it is proper to rely on a resulting trust where, for example, a constructive trust would be held void under the insolvency rules.[7] Thus in *Re Densham*,[8] although the Court of Appeal was prepared to accept that the parties' pooling of resources was clear evidence of an intention to share the property equally, since such an interest would have been void as against the trustee in bankruptcy on the basis that it was a 'voluntary' gift by the legal owner, reliance had instead to be placed on a resulting trust based upon the claimant's financial contribution to the initial deposit.

Quantifying the interests held under a constructive trust is not straightforward,[9] since the court is entitled to approach the matter broadly taking into account the parties' entire course of conduct together.

In principle, the parties' interests must reflect their common intention when the property was acquired; in practice, as we have seen, an express agreement is rare and the court will have to infer their intention from their actions.[10] All the available evidence must be considered. As Waite LJ put it in *Midland Bank plc v Cooke*:[11]

> '. . . to determine (in the absence of express evidence of intention) what proportions the parties must be assumed to have intended for their beneficial ownership, the duty of the judge is to undertake a survey of the whole course of dealing between the parties relevant to their ownership and occupation of the property and their sharing of its burdens and advantages. *That scrutiny will not confine itself to the limited range of acts of direct contribution of the sort that are needed to found a beneficial interest in the first place.* It will take into consideration all conduct which throws light on the question what shares were intended. Only if that search proves inconclusive does the court fall back on the maxim that "*equality is equity*"' [emphasis added].

In *Cooke* itself, Mrs Cooke worked throughout the marriage, notwithstanding that she had three children. Although she was credited with a contribution towards the initial deposit (by means of a wedding gift from the husband's parents), she made no direct contributions to the mortgage repayments but instead used her earnings to pay for the other household outgoings including paying contractors' bills in

---

5 [1995] 4 All ER 562, CA. See Battersby ' How not to judge the quantum (and priority) of a share in the family home' (1996) 8 CFLQ 261; Wylie 'Computing Shares in the Family Home' [1995] Fam 633; Pawlowski '*Midland Bank v Cooke* – A New Heresy?' [1996] Fam Law 484.
6 [1996] 1 FLR 826, CA.
7 Discussed further, post, pp 166ff.
8 [1975] 3 All ER 726, CA, which is therefore authority for saying that a resulting trust can lie alongside a constructive trust. See also *McHardy & Sons (A Firm) v Warren and Hutton* [1994] 2 FLR 338, CA (resulting trust relied upon because of a third party claim).
9 The same problems could equally well arise if the claimant establishes an estoppel.
10 See Lord Diplock in *Gissing v Gissing* [1971] AC 886 at 908, [1970] 2 All ER 780, HL at 793.
11 Supra at 574.

connection with improvements to the house and garden. She also undertook joint and several liability for certain legal charges taken out by her husband. The Court of Appeal concluded that the 'inescapable' inference from the parties' joint conduct was their presumed intention to share the property equally. Accordingly, they awarded Mrs Cooke a half interest in the house.

Similarly, in *Grant v Edwards*,[12] both parties had made substantial contributions to the purchase of their home, the legal title to which was vested in the defendant and his brother (who was a purely nominal party with no beneficial interest). Following a fire at the house, the balance of the insurance money after the payment of repairs was put into a building society account in the joint names of the plaintiff and defendant. The Court of Appeal held that this was the best evidence of how they intended that the property should be shared and that each was entitled to a half interest.

It by no means follows, however, that because the contributions are substantial the appropriate division is half and half. In *Drake v Whipp*,[13] for instance, where the woman claimant provided 40 per cent of the total initial purchase price and paid for food and other household expenses and contributed a further £13,000 (about 10 per cent of the total costs of improvements carried out on the property), the appropriate division was held to be one-third of the total value of the property. It is not entirely easy to see why if Mrs Cooke should get a half share, Mrs Drake should only have been awarded one-third.

It will be noted that by looking at the whole history of the parties' conduct the courts are effectively recognising that the proportions are not fixed at the outset of the purchase. Although this principle can be criticised as creating a 'wavering equity',[14] Lord Diplock in *Gissing v Gissing*[15] saw –

'... nothing inherently improbable in [the spouses] acting on the understanding that the wife should be entitled to a share which was not to be quantified immediately upon the acquisition of the home but should be left to be determined when the mortgage was repaid or the property disposed of, on the basis of what would be fair having regard to the total contributions, direct or indirect, which each spouse had made by that date.'

In practice it may be well-nigh impossible to determine what proportion each party's contribution bore to the whole. In these circumstances it is understandable that 'an equitable knife must be used to sever the Gordian Knot' when the spouses' financial affairs have become so inextricably entangled that an equal division presents the only possible solution.[16] But at times the courts seem to go much further and fall back on the principle of dividing the property in such proportions as seem fair in the circumstances, despite the criticisms against such a wide use of judicial discretion voiced by the House of Lords in *Pettitt v Pettitt*[17] and *Gissing v Gissing*.[18] In *Eves v Eves*,[19] where there was a clear understanding that the parties should take a joint interest, the Court of Appeal nevertheless awarded the plaintiff

12 [1986] Ch 638, [1986] 2 All ER 426, CA.
13 Supra.
14 See *Marsh v Von Sternberg* [1986] 1 FLR 526 at 533.
15 [1971] AC 886 at 909, [1970] 2 All ER 780, HL at 793.
16 See Lord Upjohn in *National Provincial Bank Ltd v Ainsworth* [1965] AC 1175 at 1236, [1965] 2 All ER 472, HL at 487.
17 [1970] AC 777, [1969] 2 All ER 385, HL.
18 [1971] AC 886 at 896, [1970] 2 All ER 780, HL at 782.
19 [1975] 3 All ER 768, CA. Brightman J would apparently have preferred an equal division and concurred in the result 'without great confidence' (at 775).

only a quarter share because, in the words of Lord Denning MR, 'one half would be too much'. Conversely, in *Stokes v Anderson*,[20] where the house was worth over £100,000 and the defendant had provided at the most £14,500 towards buying out the half share owned by the plaintiff's former wife, the court made 'a broad approach' and took 'the fair view' that she was entitled to a quarter of the whole. Whether this approach produced a just solution is debatable; in any case it is to be deprecated as making it more difficult for the parties' advisers to negotiate a settlement.

Agreement to vary beneficial interests

It is possible for the parties to agree to vary the size of their beneficial interests after the property has been bought. The variation is required to be in writing;[1] if it is not, it will be enforceable as a parole agreement of which equity will grant specific performance only if it is supported by valuable consideration.[2] Even if the parties did not enter into an express agreement, it might be possible to infer one from their conduct, for example by the use of a legacy to pay off the mortgage or by a permanent or substantial change in the contributions which they originally agreed or intended to make.[3]

Improvements to the matrimonial home

It may be argued that the parties' interests in the matrimonial home have been varied if, after purchase, one of them has been solely responsible for enhancing its value by extension or improvement (either by cash payments or by doing the work himself). Unlike a contribution to the purchase price, the mere fact that A does work on B's property does not of itself give A any interest in it. To establish such an interest, A must show that the expenditure was incurred or the work done in pursuance of an agreement or common intention that it should do so or, alternatively, that B has led A to believe that the improvement would confer an interest on him so as to give rise to a proprietary estoppel.[4]

(a)   The position of spouses and former engaged couples

So far as spouses and former engaged couples are concerned, the injustice that this could cause led to the passing of s 37 of the Matrimonial Proceedings and Property Act 1970.[5] This provides:

> '. . . where a husband or wife contributes in money or money's worth to the improvement of real or personal property in which or in the proceeds of sale of which either or both of them has or have a beneficial interest, the husband or wife so contributing shall, if the contribution is of a substantial nature and subject to any agreement to the contrary express or implied, be treated as having then acquired by virtue of his or her contribution a share or an enlarged share, as the case may be, in that beneficial interest . . .'

---

20 [1991] 1 FLR 391, CA at 401.
1 Law of Property Act 1925 s 53.
2 *Cowcher v Cowcher* [1972] 1 All ER 943 at 950.
3 See *Gissing v Gissing*, supra, at 908 and 792 respectively; *Burns v Burns*, supra, at 344–5 and 265 respectively.
4 *Pettitt v Pettitt* (supra), particularly at 818 and 409–10 respectively (per Lord Upjohn). See also *Thomas v Fuller-Brown* [1988] 1 FLR 237, CA; *Harwood v Harwood* [1991] 2 FLR 274, CA at 294.
5 Enacted on the recommendation of the Law Commission: see Law Com No 25, paras 56–58 and pp 102–5. For difficulties arising under the section, see Oerton (1970) 120 NLJ 1008. It applies to engaged couples by virtue of s 2(1) of the Law Reform (Miscellaneous Provisions) Act 1970.

Section 37 (which refers to the improvement of any property and not merely to that of the matrimonial home) applies whether the contribution is in money or money's worth: in other words, it does not matter whether the spouse does the job himself or pays a contractor to do it. In the latter case, however, he must show that his contribution is identifiable with the improvement in question: a general contribution to the family's finances (like an indirect contribution to the price) will give him an interest in the home only if it is referable to the improvement.[6]

There are two limitations on the operation of the section. First, it will apply only if the contribution is of a substantial nature. Whether any particular improvement is sufficiently substantial to bring it within the ambit of the section is a question of fact: in *Re Nicholson*[7] the installation of central heating for £189 in premises worth £6,000 was regarded as a substantial contribution, but the purchase of a gas fire worth less than £23 was not. Secondly, the section applies 'subject to any agreement between the spouses to the contrary express or implied', so that if they agreed that the improvements should confer no interest on the party making them, this will be conclusive.

Section 37 applies in any proceedings including, for example, litigation between one spouse and a stranger claiming through the other. If the parties agreed on the size of the interest which the improvements were to confer on the spouse making them, the court must give effect to the agreement; in other cases it has power to make such order as appears just in all the circumstances. Normally this should reflect the amount by which the value of the property was increased at the time: if, for example, the wife puts the value of the husband's house up from £80,000 to £100,000, she should obtain one-fifth of the price when it is sold. The section also applies if both spouses have a beneficial interest in the property before the improvements are made: hence, if in the above example the spouses were tenants in common of the house in equal shares when the wife made the improvements, she should now obtain three-fifths of the price.[8]

(b) The position of cohabitants

As s 37 does not apply to unmarried couples unless they are engaged to be married, one of them may claim an interest or enhanced interest in the matrimonial home as a consequence of improvement only by reference to the general law. The claimant may be able to prove or spell out an agreement between the parties that the work should have this effect; alternatively, it may be possible to infer from their conduct that this was their common intention. As in other cases of constructive trusts, however, the court will not be justified in drawing this conclusion unless the work is such that the party in question could be expected to carry it out only if he or she were to acquire an interest in the property as a result. In *Pettitt v Pettitt*[9] (where the parties were married) the husband alleged that as the result of doing work on the matrimonial home (which had been purchased by the wife out of her own money) he had increased its value by over £1,000. Most of the work consisted of redecorating the bungalow in question, but he had also made a garden, built a wall and patio, and done other jobs outside. The House of Lords

6 *Harnett v Harnett* [1973] Fam 156 at 167, [1973] 2 All ER 593 at 603, per Bagnall J. (The question did not arise on appeal: [1974] 1 All ER 764, CA.)
7 [1974] 2 All ER 386.
8 *Re Nicholson* (supra).
9 [1970] AC 777, [1969] 2 All ER 385, HL. The husband had to rely on the general law because the case was decided before the passing of the Matrimonial Proceedings and Property Act 1970.

unanimously held that he could claim nothing on the ground that, in the absence of an express agreement, he could acquire no interest by doing work of an ephemeral nature or 'do-it-yourself' jobs which any husband could be expected to do in his leisure hours.

The size of the interest so created will depend on the parties' common intention. In the absence of an express agreement it will presumably be calculated in the same way as an interest acquired by virtue of s 37 of the Matrimonial Proceedings and Property Act.[10]

Accounting for profits

The principle that a trustee must not take advantage of his position to make a personal profit for himself[11] applies when one spouse holds the matrimonial home or other property on trust for the other. In *Protheroe v Protheroe*[12] the husband owned the leasehold of the matrimonial home which he held for himself and his wife in equal shares. He later purchased the freehold reversion and it was held that he held this on the same trusts subject to his right to be repaid the price and legal costs incurred.

Reform [13]

The current law is under review.[14] Such a review is clearly timely, for, as the Law Commission has said:[15]

'The present legal rules are uncertain and difficult to apply and can lead to serious injustice.'

It is indeed difficult to defend the current law, since it is based on ascribed intentions which commonly the parties never had or thought of, which can have significant yet almost arbitrary consequences. It takes no account of the very real non-financial contributions that partners make to family prosperity and, being exclusively retrospective, it takes no account of the parties' present or future needs.

However, although it would be quixotic to defend the current law, it is much more difficult to decide how to reform it. Should the court, for example, be given a general adjustive power akin to that under the Matrimonial Causes Act 1973? Should any distinction be made between spouses and those who have chosen to live together without marrying?[16] Should the presence of children make any

---

10 By analogy with the cases concerned with the acquisition of a beneficial interest by contribution to the purchase price.
11 See the rule in *Keech v Sandford* (1726) 2 Eq Cas Abr 741.
12 [1968] 1 All ER 1111, CA. For a criticism of the case, see Cretney 'The Rationale of *Keech v Sandford*' (1969) 33 Conv 161.
13 See eg Browne-Wilkinson 'Constructive Trusts and Unjust Enrichment' (1991 Holdsworth Club Lecture); Gardner 'Rethinking Family Property' (1993) 109 LQR 263; Bailey-Harris 'Financial rights in Relationships Outside Marriage: A Decade of Reform in Australia' (1995) 9 Int J of Law and Family 233 and 'Dividing the Assets on Breakdown of Relationships Outside Marriage: Challenges for Reformers' (1998) SPTL Address.
14 At the time of writing the Law Commission's report on the property rights of home sharers, which review was announced in the Law Commission's Sixth Programme of Law Reform (Law Com No 234, 1995) Item 8, is still awaited.
15 Law Com No 234 at p 34.
16 On which see Bailey-Harris 'Law and the Unmarried Couple: Oppression or Liberation?' (1996) 8 CFLQ 137.

difference? Should only special consideration be given to marriage-like relationships and, if not, where should the line be drawn? How are third party interests to be fairly balanced? Each of these issues is fraught with difficulties and admits of no simple solution, which is no doubt why the Law Commission has spent so long in their deliberations. The report is therefore awaited with eager expectation.

3.   ENFORCING THE TRUST

The court's powers under s 14 of the Trusts of Land and Appointment of Trustees Act 1996

If both spouses or cohabitants have a beneficial interest in the family home, their equitable joint tenancy or tenancy in common must take effect behind a trust of land.[17] Unlike trusts for sale, which trusts of land now replace, there is no general duty to sell.[18] Instead, the Act confers upon the trustees all the powers of an existing owner,[19] including, therefore, the power either to sell or retain the land. However, as one commentator has observed,[20] the Act is nevertheless biased against sale, since s 14(1) empowers trustees in all cases to postpone the sale for an indefinite period. Of course, while the parties are living together, they are likely to agree on the disposal of their home, but if their relationship breaks down and they separate, one may well wish to remain in the former home and the other to have it sold so as to realise the capital. If the parties are married, the courts prefer to use their wide powers to make property adjustment orders under the Matrimonial Causes Act 1973, because they can then make a fair order after taking all relevant facts into account.[1] This can be done only if one of them seeks a divorce, a decree of nullity, or separation order; consequently, if no such proceedings are taken and, a fortiori, if they are unmarried, this course is not open to them, and they will be compelled to invoke the court's powers under s 14 of the Act 1996.[2]

Section 14 (1) permits any trustee or beneficiary under a trust of land or any secured creditor of a beneficiary to apply to the court, which by s 14(2) is empowered to make, as it sees fit, any order relating to the exercise by the trustees of any of their functions or to declare the nature and extent of a beneficiary's interest. The provisions are sufficiently wide, it is thought,[3] to enable the court both to order the trustees not to exercise their powers and to make intermediate orders, such as ordering an occupying beneficiary to pay an occupation rent to another beneficiary not in occupation.

One innovation of the 1996 Act is the set of guidelines provided by s 15 on matters to be taken into account when exercising the powers under s 14. The aim of the guidelines is, in the Law Commission's words,[4] to 'consolidate and rationalise'

---

17 Trusts of Land and Appointment of Trustees Act 1996 s 1(2), Sch 2. See generally Baughen 'Trusts of Land and Family Practice' [1996] Fam Law 736 and Hopkins 'Trusts of Land and Appointment of Trustees Act 1996' (1996) 60 Conv 411.
18 Section 1(2)(b). In the case of a post-1996 Act express trust, a duty to sell can be created, but even then the trustee will incur no liability for postponing sale: see s 4(1).
19 Section 6.
20 Hopkins, op cit, at 414.
 1 See ante, p 136. For property adjustment orders, see post, pp 796–8 and 844ff.
 2 Which replaces the former power under s 30 of the Law of Property Act 1925.
 3 See Baughen, op cit, at 737.
 4 Law Com No 181 (*Transfer of Land, Trusts of Land*, 1989) para 12.9.

the former approach adopted by the courts under s 30 of the Law of Property Act 1925. They are not, however, designed to restrict the exercise of judicial discretion[5] and the Commission envisaged that case law on s 30 will continue to be of value, notwithstanding that those cases assumed that there was a duty to sell.[6]

Under s 15(1) the guidelines are:

'(a) the intentions of the person or persons (if any) who created the trust,
(b) the purpose for which the property subject to the trust is held,
(c) the welfare of any minor who occupies or might reasonably be expected to occupy any land subject to the trust as his home, and
(d) the interests of any secured creditor or any beneficiary.'

It should be noted that these guidelines do not apply where a trustee in bankruptcy is seeking an order,[7] in which case different guidelines apply.[8]

Although in general terms these guidelines may be said[9] to 'mirror' the factors formerly considered by the court when determining the 'collateral purpose' of a trust under the 1925 Act, an important change is the guideline relating to children's welfare. By making such welfare an independent consideration, the Act has implemented the Law Commission's recommendations[10] aimed at ensuring that a case such as *Re Evers' Trust*,[11] in which the mother's need for a home with her three children was fully taken into account, is likely to be preferred to those such as *Re Holliday (a bankrupt)*,[12] in which the court dismissed the notion that it was a collateral object of the trust to preserve the house as a home for the children. This will be especially likely now that the court can clearly order the occupying beneficiaries to pay an occupation rent.[13]

On the other hand, there is no reason to suppose that the new powers will have altered the court's basic stance, that if two people (whether married or not) buy property as a home for themselves (together with any children they may have), the underlying purpose of the trust is to provide a home and not an investment. Consequently, so long as that purpose subsists, the trust should not be executed and the property should not be sold.[14] But once that purpose is discharged, the court will order a sale.[15] Sales are more likely to be ordered where there are no children. In *Jones v Challenger*[16] the Court of Appeal ordered a sale when the marriage had broken down and the husband was living alone in the house, as it was no longer required as the matrimonial home. Nevertheless, even this is not an invariable rule. In *Bedson v Bedson*,[17] for example, where the wife had deserted her husband, and

---

5 Ibid at 12.10. See also *TSB Bank plc v Marshall, Marshall and Rodgers* [1998] 2 FLR 769.
6 Ibid at 12.9, n 141.
7 Section 15(4).
8 Viz those under the Insolvency Act 1996 s 335A, discussed post, p 170.
9 Baughen, op cit, 737.
10 Law Com No 181 at para 12.9.
11 [1980] 3 All ER 399, CA.
12 [1980] 3 All ER 385, CA. See also *Chhokar v Chhokar* [1984] FLR 313 and *Dennis v McDonald* [1982] Fam 63, [1982] 1 All ER 590, CA.
13 Compare *Bernard v Josephs* [1982] Ch 391, [1982] 3 All ER 162, CA, in which the court ordered the property to be sold, but attached a condition that the order should not be enforced if the one paid the other the value of his share within a stated period.
14 *Re Buchanan-Wollaston's Conveyance* [1939] Ch 738, [1939] 2 All ER 302, CA; *Williams v Williams* [1976] Ch 278, [1977] 1 All ER 28, CA; *Re Evers' Trust* [1980] 3 All ER 399, CA; *Bernard v Josephs*, CA, supra; *Chhokar v Chhokar*, supra.
15 *Jones v Challenger* [1961] 1 QB 176, [1960] 1 All ER 785, CA.
16 [1961] 1 QB 176, [1960] 1 All ER 785, CA. See also *Bernard v Josephs* (supra).
17 [1965] 2 QB 666, [1965] 3 All ER 307, CA.

the property in question (a draper's shop with a flat over it) had been bought out of the husband's savings and was his sole livelihood, the sale was refused.

Two particular points should be noted. First, on the death of one of the parties the other's share will become a part of his estate (unless the parties were joint tenants) and may not pass to the survivor. In this situation the court should take the same facts into account as it does when the parties separate during their joint lives and should not order a sale unless the property no longer serves the purpose of providing a family home for the survivor.[18] Secondly, if one party becomes insolvent, there may be a dispute between his creditors and the other party. The particular problems that this gives rise to will be considered later in this chapter.[19]

Distribution of assets after sale: equitable accounting

Even though the primary purpose of the trust may have come to an end on the separation of the parties, the trust for land nevertheless remains and the property in effect becomes an investment. This cannot affect the size of the beneficial interests, however: hence, as the Court of Appeal held in *Turton v Turton*,[20] if the parties hold as tenants in common in equal shares, each will be entitled to half the proceeds when the property is sold or, if one of them buys the other out, to half the value at the time of the transfer.[1]

Further accounting between the parties, however, may be necessary. If one of them spends money on the property after they have separated, he will usually be entitled to call on the other to contribute to the expenditure if this preserves or enhances the value of the asset, because both will derive the benefit of the increased value when the investment is realised. In *Bernard v Josephs*,[2] for example, the proceeds of sale were divided between the parties only after the plaintiff had paid to the defendant the sum of £2,650 which the latter had spent on decorating the house and so increased the price obtained. The position regarding the payment of mortgage instalments is less clear. In *Cracknell v Cracknell*,[3] where the matrimonial home was owned jointly, the wife left to live with another man. The husband continued to pay the instalments and the Court of Appeal held that she should compensate him for half the total payments he had made after their separation. In *Suttill v Graham*,[4] on the other hand, on virtually identical facts the

---

18 *Stott v Ratcliffe* (1982) 126 Sol Jo 310, CA.
19 Post, pp 166ff.
20 [1988] Ch 542, [1987] 2 All ER 641, CA, following *Walker v Hall* [1984] FLR 126, CA, and disapproving *Hall v Hall* (1981) 3 FLR 379, CA, where it had been held that in the case of unmarried cohabitants the home should be valued at the time of separation.
1 If the property is subject to a mortgage which, as between the parties, one alone is responsible for repaying, the unpaid debt should be debited to his share. Suppose that H and W buy a house for £50,000, of which W provides £25,000 in cash and H provides £25,000 borrowed from X. Each will get half the proceeds of sale, but H will have to repay the loan out of his half. The same result should follow if the lender is a building society which takes a mortgage on the property. This principle was applied in *Cowcher v Cowcher* [1972] 1 All ER 943 at 959, and *Re Densham* [1975] 3 All ER 726. See Sparkes 'The Quantification of Beneficial Interests' (1991) 11 OJLS 39 at 46–52.
2 Supra. Quaere whether the plaintiff should have had to pay only half of the expenditure, which is the extent to which the value of her half share had been increased. It was accepted that the wife should recover only half her expenditure in similar circumstances in *Re Gorman* [1990] 1 All ER 717.
3 [1971] P 356, [1971] 3 All ER 552, CA. See also *Wilson v Wilson* [1963] 2 All ER 447, CA; *Davis v Vale* [1971] 2 All ER 1021, CA.
4 [1977] 3 All ER 1117, CA. The Court of Appeal purported to follow *Leake v Bruzzi* [1974] 2 All ER 1196, CA, but see infra.

Court of Appeal concluded that the wife should be required to compensate the husband only for the capital sum he had repaid, apparently on the ground that that alone increased the value of the equity. As we shall see below, the position may be complicated by the need to pay an occupation rent. Leaving this question aside, in the face of conflicting decisions of the Court of Appeal, *Cracknell v Cracknell* is to be preferred because, as was pointed out in *Re Gorman*,[5] the mortgagee will have a charge on the property for both unpaid interest and capital, so that the value of the equity is increased by the payment of both.

A similar question that arises after separation is whether the party who has left the home is entitled to an occupation rent from the other. The answer can be given with more certainty following the decision of the Court of Appeal in *Dennis v McDonald*.[6] If the parties are co-owners, whether in law or equity, each is entitled to possession: consequently, if one leaves voluntarily, he or she is not entitled to any rent. If, however, one forces the other to leave, justice demands that he should pay rent to compensate the latter for the right she has lost and the need to pay for accommodation elsewhere: in *Dennis v McDonald* the sum ordered to be paid was one-half of what would be a fair rent under the Rent Act.[7] What is not settled is what amounts to an 'ouster' in this context. *Dennis v McDonald* was a clear case, because the plaintiff had left as the result of the defendant's violence: it is suggested that it is probably sufficient that one party's behaviour has been such that the other could have obtained an occupation order against him.[8]

If the party in occupation is bound to pay rent and is also paying mortgage instalments, it may be simpler to regard the payment of interest as equivalent to the payment of rent and thus avoid a double computation. In such circumstances it would be proper to order the party who has left to account for his or her proportionate part of the repayment of capital only. This occurred in *Leake v Bruzzi*,[9] where the wife left the husband and obtained a divorce based on the fact that her husband's behaviour had been such that she could not reasonably be expected to live with him.

4.   PROTECTION OF BENEFICIAL INTERESTS

Although the Trusts of Land and Appointment of Trustees Act 1996 in some ways strengthens the beneficiary's right to be consulted before trustees can exercise any of their powers,[10] it does not obviate the problem that if the house is sold or mortgaged, the beneficiaries' equitable interests are overreached and a purchaser of a legal estate (including a legal mortgagee or chargee) is not bound by them even though he has notice of them, provided that he pays the proceeds of sale or other capital money to two or more trustees (or a trust corporation).[11] Hence, once

5 [1990]1 All ER 717. The court followed *Bernard v Josephs* (supra) where, however, *Suttill v Graham* was not cited.
6 [1982] Fam 63, [1982] 1 All ER 590, CA. See Martin (1982) 46 Conv 305; Webb (1982) 98 LQR 519; Schuz [1982] Fam Law 108; Thompson (1984) 48 Conv 103.
7 Rent Act 1977 s 70(1)–(2), and disregarding s 70(3).
8 Compare *Leake v Bruzzi*, supra. For the facts, see below.
9 [1974] 2 All ER 1196, CA. The wife was urged to adopt this solution in *Re Gorman*, supra. But this may not be the proper approach if little remains to be paid on the mortgage so that the interest element is low.
10 Viz by s 11 of the 1996 Act.
11 Law of Property Act 1925 s 27(1) as amended by the Trusts of Land and Appointment of Trustees Act 1996 Sch 3, para 4(8).

the property is sold and the beneficial interests overreached, the beneficiaries are no longer entitled to enjoy the rents and profits either in cash or in specie and cannot enforce any right of occupation or possession even though they were not parties to the conveyance. Similarly, if the property is mortgaged by two or more trustees, the beneficiaries' interest shifts onto the equity of redemption, and whilst they will be able to remain in possession so long as the mortgage remains in existence, they cannot enforce any right to do so if the mortgagee exercises his statutory right of sale. In *City of London Building Society v Flegg*[12] a husband, wife and the wife's parents agreed to buy a house in which all four could live. The property was conveyed to the husband and wife alone but the wife's parents, who had provided part of the purchase money, also had a beneficial interest. The husband and wife later mortgaged the property to the plaintiffs, who sought possession of the premises when the spouses became insolvent. It was held that, although the wife's parents had a right to occupy the premises against their son-in-law and daughter, they had none whatever against the building society who were protected by having paid the sum borrowed to the two trustees.

The same conclusion would be reached if the husband and another were joint legal tenants of the matrimonial home in which the wife had a beneficial interest either under an express trust or by virtue of a resulting or constructive trust. If the owners of the legal estate sold or mortgaged it, the wife's interest would be overreached and so unenforceable against the purchaser or mortgagee.[13] A similar result would obtain in the case of cohabitants. In practice difficulty arises if the legal estate is vested in one partner only (say, the man) and the woman has a beneficial interest under a resulting or constructive trust. The man should appoint another trustee (who would normally be his partner) but in many cases this will not be done, and if the man sells or mortgages the house, the purchaser or mortgagee will deal with him alone. If the man acts without the knowledge or consent of the wife, can she enforce her rights against the new legal owner if he seeks possession of the premises or takes steps to realise his security?

If the legal title is registered under the Land Registration Act 1925, any interest arising under a trust for sale is a minor interest which may be protected by lodging a caution.[14] In practice this may be of little use because the wife or cohabitant is unlikely to know the relevant law, although a caution might be lodged before the man dealt with the land if she sought legal advice on the breakdown of her relationship. The woman is much more likely to be helped by the fact that her undivided share gives her an overriding interest. In *Williams and Glyn's Bank Ltd v Boland*[15] the husband was registered as the sole proprietor of the legal estate of

12 [1988] AC 54, [1987] 3 All ER 435, HL. Some caution must be exercised when reading Lord Oliver's judgment, since some of his reasoning is based on the doctrine of conversion, which has since been abolished by the Trusts of Land and Appointment of Trustees Act 1996. Nevertheless, it seems clear that the decision survives the 1996 Act. For contemporary comments on the decision see Smith (1987) 103 LQR 520; Swadling (1987) 51 Conv 451; Gardner (1988) 51 MLR 365; Harpum [1987] CLJ 392 and [1990] CLJ 277; Thompson 'Dispositions by Trustees for Sale' (1988) 52 Conv 108; Sparkes (1988) 52 Conv 141; Evans 'Land Law: An Overview after *Flegg*' (1990) Lit 13.
13 If the wife could raise a proprietary estoppel against the husband, it is not clear whether this would still be good against the purchaser or mortgagee: see Thompson (1988) 52 Conv 108 at 120. It would be anomalous if an estoppel gave her greater protection than an express trust. A similar result would be obtained in the case of cohabitants.
14 Land Registration Act 1925 s 3(xv) and ss 54–55; *Elias v Mitchell* [1972] Ch 652. The interest could also be protected by restriction if the husband deposited the land certificate at the registry.
15 [1981] AC 487, [1980] 2 All ER 408, HL; Freeman (1980) 43 MLR 692 and [1981] Fam Law 37; Smith (1981) 97 LQR 12; Murphy and Clark *The Family Home* (1983) ch 6.

the matrimonial home, but the wife had contributed a substantial sum towards the purchase and was admittedly an equitable tenant in common to the extent of her contribution. The husband later executed a legal mortgage to the appellant bank, which made no enquiries of the wife. When the husband failed to pay the sum secured, the bank started proceedings for possession of the house with a view to selling it under their powers as mortgagees. The wife resisted the action on the ground that her interest took priority over the bank's by virtue of s 20(1) of the Land Registration Act 1925. This provides that a disposition of registered land shall, when registered, confer on the transferee the estate expressed to be created subject to any overriding interests affecting it, and by s 70(1) of the Act:

'All registered land shall . . . be deemed to be subject to such of the following overriding interests as may be for the time being subsisting in reference thereto . . .

(g) The rights of every person in actual occupation of the land or in receipt of the rents and profits thereof, save where the enquiry is made of such person and the rights are not disclosed.'

The House of Lords held that the wife's physical presence in the house coupled with the right to exclude others without a right to occupy clearly gave her actual occupation, and the fact that the husband (the owner of the legal estate) was also in actual occupation could not affect this. Furthermore, although the land was held on (what was then a) trust for sale, pending sale the wife had an interest subsisting in reference to the land itself.[16] Her claim must therefore succeed.

Williams and Glyn's Bank Ltd v Boland created a number of difficulties for prospective purchasers (and particularly prospective mortgagees),[17] some of which were considered by the House of Lords in *Abbey National Building Society v Cann*.[18] The respondent bought a house as a home for his mother and stepfather. It was conveyed into his sole name and was paid for in part by the proceeds of sale of another house and in part (as his mother knew) by a mortgage, which the respondent negotiated with the appellant building society. He told the appellant that the property was being purchased for his sole occupation. The respondent and his stepfather arrived on the premises about an hour before the transfer was completed and the charge created, and workmen began to lay the mother's carpets and bring in her furniture. The transfer and charge were not registered for another month, by which time the mother had moved into the premises herself. The appellant claimed possession of the property when the son fell behind with the payment of the mortgage; he did not resist the claim but his mother, relying on *Boland*'s case, did so on the ground that she had an overriding interest by reason of her contribution to the purchase of the first home.

The House of Lords was primarily concerned with the effect of the mother's moving into actual occupation between the creation of the charge and its registration. There will inevitably be a delay between these two events; any inspection must obviously be made before the first but, as we have seen, s 20(1) of the Land Registration Act provides that the transferee or chargee will take subject to overriding interests subsisting at registration. Taken literally, this produces the 'conveyancing absurdity'[19] that the purchaser, having made all possible enquiries

16 The right to enjoy the rents and profits in specie: see ante, p 157.
17 See Law Com No 115 (*Implications of Williams and Glyn's Bank Ltd v Boland*) 1982; Law Com 188 (*Overreaching: Beneficiaries in Occupation*) 1989.
18 [1991] 1 AC 56, [1990] 1 All ER 1085, HL.
19 Per Lord Oliver in *Abbey National Building Society v Cann* (supra) at 88 and 1097 respectively, citing Nicholls LJ in *Lloyds Bank plc v Rosset* [1989] Ch 350 at 373, [1988] 3 All ER 915, CA at 922.

and parted with his money, will be bound by an interest claimed by an occupant coming onto the land between completion and registration. To avoid this conclusion, the House held that, in order to assert an overriding interest against the purchaser, the claimant must be in occupation at the date of completion (and, presumably, also at the date of registration).[20] This reduces one of the hazards likely to arise following *Boland*'s case, but there is clearly still a risk that the claimant will come into occupation during the delay between inspection and completion. If, as in *Cann*'s case, the purchase of the property depends on the execution of a charge, the chargee would still appear to have priority because, as the House of Lords held, the two transactions are to be regarded as indivisible, so that the purchaser acquires nothing but an equity of redemption to which the claimant's beneficial interest can attach. But if the owner of the legal estate mortgages it later, the owner of an overriding interest coming into occupation after the mortgagee has made enquiries but before the charge is created will be able to assert it against the mortgagee.

Another question that arose in *Abbey National Building Society v Cann* is the meaning of 'actual occupation'. It should be given its ordinary meaning of possession or presence on the land: 'actual' indicates physical possession as distinct from legal possession by receipt of rents and profits.[1] The term is apparently not synonymous with 'reside':[2] a person can obviously occupy one property and reside in another, and he can occupy premises by an agent, eg a caretaker.[3] The facts of *Lloyds Bank plc v Rosset*[4] illustrate the difficulties that can arise. The husband purchased a semi-derelict house, partly with the aid of a charge in favour of the appellant bank. The vendor let the husband and his wife into possession some six weeks before completion and the creation of the charge, and during this time the wife spent almost every day on the premises directing building work and doing some decorating herself, and she occasionally slept there. The majority of the Court of Appeal held that the presence of the builders (who were agents of both parties) coupled with that of the wife amounted to actual occupation by her because 'there was . . . physical presence on the property by the wife and her agent of the nature that one would expect of an occupier having regard to the then state of the property'.[5] Mustill LJ, dissenting on this point, thought that the tradesmen's presence would not indicate to an enquirer that a person with a claim adverse to the owner's was in occupation: they were working on the site rather than in occupation of it, and the wife's activities were more in keeping with preparing the house for occupation than with occupation itself.[6] Bearing in mind that the statutory scheme

---

20 Because, if he goes out of occupation before registration, his interest will cease to be an overriding interest. The beneficial interest must exist before completion; if it arises between completion and registration, the purchaser's equitable interest which arises by the payment or advance of money on completion will in any case take priority over it: see *Abbey National Building Society v Cann* (supra) at 87 and 1096 respectively.

1 Per Lord Wilberforce in *Williams and Glyn's Bank Ltd v Boland* [1981] AC 487 at 505, [1980] 2 All ER 408, HL at 413. For a detailed discussion of the difficulties this interpretation creates, see Sparkes 'The Discoverability of Occupiers of Registered Land' (1980) 44 Conv 342.

2 See *Lloyds Bank plc v Rosset* [1989] Ch 350, [1988] 3 All ER 915, CA.

3 *Lloyds Bank plc v Rosset*, supra; *Abbey National Building Society v Cann*, supra, at 93 and 1101 respectively (per Lord Oliver).

4 [1989] Ch 350, [1988] 3 All ER 915, CA. Having held that the wife acquired no beneficial interest (see ante, p 143), the House of Lords found it unnecessary to consider whether she was in actual occupation when the charge was created: [1991] 1 AC 107, [1990] 1 All ER 1111, HL.

5 Per Nicholls LJ at 379 and 927 respectively.

6 At 398–9 and 941–2 respectively.

replaces constructive notice in equity, this view is to be preferred. It certainly accords with that of the House of Lords in *Abbey National Building Society v Cann*,[7] where they held that the activities of the workmen laying carpets and carrying in furniture were no more than preparatory steps leading to the assumption of actual residential occupation later, and that consequently the respondent's mother could not be said to be in actual occupation of the house when the charge was created. Like possession, 'occupation' connotes some form of continuity rather than periodic visits and, it is submitted, should be unambiguous.

Temporary absence cannot bring occupation to an end, and the fact that a spouse's or cohabitant's occupation may be intermittent presents a further hazard to the prospective purchaser. In *Kingsnorth Finance Ltd v Tizard*[8] the husband slept in the matrimonial home with the two children of the marriage; because the marriage was in difficulty, the wife slept elsewhere but came to the house each day to feed the children. When the husband was away (as happened frequently), she slept there. The husband then applied for a loan from the plaintiffs to be secured by a mortgage on the house. It was held that the wife was in occupation, even though she was not there when the plaintiff's agent made his enquiries, and the husband had temporarily removed all signs of her periodic visits.

If the land is unregistered, the position is more complex. The wife cannot register her interest under the Land Charges Act 1972.[9] The basic principle was thus summarised by Lord Oliver in *City of London Building Society v Flegg*:[10]

'The reason why a purchaser of the legal estate (whether by way of outright sale or by way of mortgage) from a single proprietor takes subject to the rights of the occupying spouse is . . . because, having constructive notice of the trust as a result of the beneficiary's occupation, he steps into the shoes of the vendor or mortgagor and takes the estate subject to the same equities as those to which it was subject in the latter's hands, those equities and their accompanying incidents not having been overreached by the sale . . .'

This implies that anyone dealing with the land will be protected only by the general equitable doctrine that a bona fide purchaser of a legal estate for value will take it free of any equitable interest of which he does not have actual or constructive notice.[11] Hence, if he takes an equitable interest (for example, if a bank takes an equitable charge from the husband), the wife must have priority. A purchaser of a legal estate will normally have constructive notice of the rights of any person in occupation of the land: this raises the question whether the fact that the spouse or cohabitant is residing in the house will itself be sufficient notice of their interest to give priority over the purchaser. In *Caunce v Caunce*[12] Stamp J held that it will not do so, because her presence is not inconsistent with the husband's being the sole beneficial owner, but this case was doubted, although not expressly overruled, in *Williams and Glyn's Bank Ltd v Boland*.[13] One of the

7 [1991] 1 AC 56, [1990] 1 All ER 1085, HL. For the facts, see ante, p 158.
8 [1986] 2 All ER 54; Thompson (1986) 50 Conv 283. The case dealt with unregistered land, but this can make no difference to this point.
9 Interests arising under a trust of land are expressly excluded from the definition of a general equitable charge: Land Charges Act 1972 s 2(4) (as amended).
10 [1988] AC 54 at 83, [1987] 3 All ER 435, HL at 448.
11 See Megarry and Wade *Real Property* (5th edn) pp 404–5; Rudden 'The Wife, the Husband and the Conveyancer' (1963) 27 Conv 51; Garner 'A Single Trustee for Sale' (1969) 33 Conv 240.
12 [1969] 1 All ER 722.
13 [1981] AC 487 at 505, [1980] 2 All ER 408 at 413 (per Lord Wilberforce, with whom three other members of the House agreed); ibid at 511 and 418 respectively (per Lord Scarman).

principal objections to holding that the wife's occupation (and a fortiori a female cohabitant's) gives the purchaser constructive notice of her rights is that this compels him to make distasteful and embarrassing enquiries. In an earlier case dealing with the so-called 'deserted wife's equity', Upjohn J, refusing to cast upon a prospective purchaser or mortgagee the duty to enquire whether the owner of the property in question had deserted his wife, said: [14]

'If the law were otherwise it would mean that every intending purchaser or lender must inquire into the relationship of husband and wife and inquire into matters which are no concern of his and will bring thousands of business transactions into the area of domestic life and ties. That cannot be right.'

This applies with equal force to the problem we are considering here. It is doubtful, however, whether these cases can still be regarded as good law since the decisions in *Williams and Glyn's Bank Ltd v Boland* and *Abbey National Building Society v Cann*. Clearly nothing said in either case is binding in this context because both were concerned with registered land. But in *Boland*'s case the House of Lords was obviously more concerned to protect the wife than the purchaser. In the words of Lord Wilberforce: [15]

'The extension of the risk area follows necessarily from the extension, beyond the paterfamilias, of rights of ownership, itself following from the diffusion of property and earning capacity. What is involved is a departure from an easy-going practice of dispensing with enquiries as to occupation beyond that of the vendor and accepting the risks of doing so. To substitute for this a practice of more careful enquiry as to the fact of occupation and, if necessary, as to the rights of occupiers cannot, in my view of the matter, be considered as unacceptable except at the price of overlooking the widespread development of shared interests in ownership.'

Although he was speaking only of conveyancing practice when the land is registered, precisely the same principles apply to unregistered land, as was pointed out in *Cann*'s case; [16] and in *Kingsnorth Finance Co Ltd v Tizard* [17] the court declined to follow *Caunce v Caunce*. It is possible, however, that there is a difference between registered and unregistered land as regards the type of notice that binds a purchaser. In *City of London Building Society v Flegg* Lord Oliver expressly approved an earlier dictum of Lord Wilberforce to this effect. [18] Under the Land Registration Act it is the fact of occupation that creates an overriding interest, whereas if the land is unregistered the intending purchaser probably has constructive notice only of matters that would have come to light had he made such enquiries or carried out such inspection as is reasonable in the circumstances. If he acts in this prudent fashion and does not find the wife in occupation or evidence which will give him notice of her occupation, he is protected; but if he does find such evidence and fails to make proper enquiries, the interest he acquires will be subject to hers. [19] A fortiori this must be so if the spouses have separated and the wife is living in the house alone.

---

14 *Westminster Bank Ltd v Lee* [1956] Ch 7 at 22, [1955] 2 All ER 883 at 889.
15 *Williams and Glyn's Bank Ltd v Boland*, supra, at 508–9 and 415–16 respectively.
16 [1991] 1 AC 56 at 87, [1990] 1 All ER 1085, HL at 1096.
17 [1986] 2 All ER 54. See also *Hodgson v Marks* [1971] Ch 892 at 934–5, [1971] 2 All ER 684, CA at 690 (per Russell LJ).
18 [1988] AC 54 at 88, [1987] 3 All ER 435 at 451, citing *National Provincial Bank Ltd v Ainsworth* [1965] AC 1175 at 1261, [1965] 2 All E 472, HL at 503.
19 *Kingsnorth Finance Co Ltd v Tizard*, supra, at 63–4.

If the wife consents to the transaction – and a fortiori if she is a party to the conveyance of mortgage – she cannot argue that any interest she may have in the property takes priority over the purchaser's or mortgagee's. Furthermore, if she knows that the house can be bought only with the help of a loan and supports the husband's proposal that this would be secured by a mortgage, then, as the Court of Appeal held in *Bristol and West Building Society v Henning*,[20] it must have been the spouses' common intention that the charge should take priority over both parties' beneficial interests. To secure his position the mortgagee may insist on the wife's being party to the charge, and this will in any event be necessary if the legal estate is vested in both spouses jointly. He runs an obvious risk, however, if he leaves the husband to procure the wife's signature to the instrument. In practice, this is most likely to occur if the husband seeks a secured loan or overdraft to finance a business venture and the only security he can offer is that of the matrimonial home.[1] If he knows that the wife may be unwilling to agree, he may resort to undue influence or misrepresentation to obtain her consent. This will not of itself affect the mortgagee, but will do so in two cases. First, he will be in no better position than the husband and therefore cannot enforce the security against the wife, if the husband was acting as his agent in procuring her signature. As Dillon LJ put it in the leading judgment in the Court of Appeal in *Kingsnorth Trust Ltd v Bell*,[2] in this context the husband will be the mortgagee's agent 'if the creditor entrusts to the husband himself the task of obtaining the execution of the legal document'. Hence the bank will take subject to the wife's interest if, as in that case, the husband was given the necessary documents to take home for the wife to sign, but not if he was merely left to tell her that the bank would grant a loan on the security of the house or, even, to obtain her agreement in principle.[3] Secondly, as the Court of Appeal held in *Bank of Credit and Commerce International SA v Aboody*,[4] the mortgage will not be enforceable against the wife if the creditor or his agent (for example, his solicitor) has notice of any misrepresentation made by the husband, or of the circumstances which are alleged to constitute undue influence, or from which any presumption of undue influence is alleged to arise.[5]

---

20 [1985] 2 All ER 606, CA (unregistered land). See also *Paddington Building Society v Mendelsohn* (1985) 50 P & CR 244, CA (registered land); *Equity and Law Home Loans Ltd v Prestidge* [1992] 1 All ER 909, CA (replacement mortgage). Had the House of Lords found in *Abbey National Building Society v Cann*, supra, that the respondent's mother had an overriding interest, they would have held that it would not have prevailed over the appellant's interest for the same reason. See also Thompson (1986) 49 MLR 245 and (1986) 50 Conv 57.

1 For an empirical study of this phenomenon, see Fehlberg 'Money and Marriage: Sexually Transmitted Debt in England' (1997) 11 Int Jo of Law and Family 320.

2 [1986] 1 All ER 423, CA at 427. In *Barclays Bank plc v Kennedy* [1989] 1 FLR 356, CA at 364, Purchas LJ referred to the bank's 'being content to leave it to the husband to obtain the wife's consent', but it is apparent from his judgment as a whole that he was applying the test laid down by Dillon LJ in *Kingsnorth Trust Ltd v Bell*.

3 As in *Midland Bank plc v Perry* [1988] 1 FLR 161, CA.

4 [1990] 1 QB 923, CA at 973. Although the bank had notice through its solicitor that the husband had exercised undue influence over the wife, the action failed because the transaction was not to her manifest disadvantage. Contrast *Lloyds Bank plc v Egremont* [1990] 2 FLR 351, CA, where there was a misrepresentation but no agency or notice. Agency and notice are two separate grounds on which the creditor may be affected by the husband's conduct, and if he was acting as the creditor's agent, it is not necessary that the latter should also have notice of the misrepresentation or undue influence: *Bank of Credit and Commerce International SA v Aboody* at 972.

5 The relationship of husband and wife does not of itself give rise to any presumption of undue influence: see eg *Barclays Bank plc v O'Brien* [1994] 1 AC 180, [1993] 4 All ER 417, HL, and *Royal Bank of Scotland v Etridge (No 2)* [1998] NLJR 1390, CA, discussed ante, p 125.

If the purchaser or mortgagee takes a legal estate subject to the wife's beneficial interest, the transaction will still have the effect of granting him whatever beneficial interest the husband has.[6] But even if he finds himself saddled with the wife's interest, it does not follow that she will be able to stay in occupation indefinitely. The purchaser will be entitled to take proceedings for an order for sale: in deciding whether to order the property to be sold, the court must take into account the same facts as it would if the proceedings had been brought by the husband, in whose shoes the purchaser now stands. If the husband is insolvent, the court may enforce a sale in bankruptcy proceedings and leave the wife to claim her share of the proceeds.[7]

C.   Occupation

Legal and beneficial ownership of land carries with it a prima facie right of occupation. Furthermore, at common law a wife had a right to occupy the matrimonial home by virtue of her right to her husband's consortium. This latter right has now become a statutory right as provided for by the Family Law Act 1996. We discuss these rights and the power to regulate occupation rights in Chapters 2 and 6. What we are now concerned to discuss are other means by which rights of occupation may be acquired. This issue is of principal relevance to unmarried couples, since if ownership is vested in one of them alone the other's right of occupation must be found by reference to the general law of property. In the following discussion we assume for the purpose of illustration that the property is vested in the man.[8]

1.   CONTRACTUAL LICENCE

If the woman has given up some existing right or suffered some other detriment to go and live with the man, it may be possible to regard this as consideration and thus give the woman a contractual licence. In *Tanner v Tanner*,[9] for example, the plaintiff bought a house for the defendant and their twin daughters and the defendant surrendered a rent-controlled tenancy to move into it. When the plaintiff later claimed possession of the house, it was held that, as the defendant had furnished consideration by giving up the security of her flat, the licence was a contractual one.

The facts of *Tanner* were unusual in that the parties never lived in the house together. The problem more likely to arise is that facing a woman who, having set

---

6 *Ahmed v Kendrick* [1988] 2 FLR 22, CA. In this case the husband and wife were joint tenants in law and equity. The husband sold the house to the defendant and forged the wife's signature on the transfer. It was held that, whilst this could not convey the legal estate, it severed the husband's joint tenancy in equity so that the spouses now held the property on trust for the wife and the defendant in equal shares. The court held that the decision to the contrary in *Cedar Holdings Ltd v Green* [1981] Ch 129, [1979] 3 All ER 117, CA, could not be regarded as authority since *Williams and Glyn's Bank Ltd v Boland* (supra).
7 See post, pp 169ff.
8 See generally Murphy and Clark, op cit, pp 102–23 and ch 7.
9 [1975] 3 All ER 776, CA. Contrast *Horrocks v Forray* [1976] 1 All ER 737, CA.

up home with a man in property belonging to him, is ordered to leave when their relationship breaks down. Even if she suffered a detriment, for example by giving up a secure tenancy like the defendant in *Tanner*, it would usually be impossible to spell out any promise by the man that she could continue to reside in the house if he no longer wished to live with her. Any such undertaking is more likely to be given at the point of breakdown if the man leaves, but unless the woman suffers some fresh detriment (such as a reciprocal undertaking to pay rent or other outgoings), any consideration would be past and therefore ineffective to establish a contract.

Even if it is possible to spell out a contractual licence, it may well be difficult to infer the period for which the parties intended that the woman should be entitled to stay in the premises for, like spouses, cohabitants are apt not to contemplate the breakdown of their relationship. In *Tanner v Tanner* the Court of Appeal took the view that the defendant had a licence to remain in the house so long as the parties' children were of school age and it was reasonably required as a home for them and their mother. There is necessarily something arbitrary about terminating the licence when the children reached the age of 16 because they might continue in full-time education after that, but it was reasonable to imply that it should cease, say, if their mother married. The woman is likely to be less favourably treated if the children of the owner of the property are not living with her. In *Chandler v Kerley* [10] the defendant and her husband had sold their former matrimonial home to the plaintiff on the understanding that the defendant (who proposed to marry the plaintiff after her divorce) would continue to live there with him and the two children of her marriage. The relationship between the parties broke down very shortly afterwards and the plaintiff sought possession of the house. The Court of Appeal held that he could not have intended to assume the burden of housing the defendant and another man's children indefinitely, and that the licence was terminable on her being given 12 months' notice, which would enable her to find other accommodation.

2.   LICENCE BY ESTOPPEL

By analogy with proprietary estoppel, one party may claim a licence if the other has led her to believe (or has acquiesced in her belief) that she has, or will be given, permission to remain in the house and she acts to her detriment in reliance on this belief. A classic example is *Greasley v Cook*.[11] The defendant had entered the service of a family as a maid. Later she and one of the sons cohabited in the family house for nearly 30 years; she looked after the family as a whole and in particular cared for the daughter who was mentally ill. She received no payment and asked for none because the members of the family had led her to believe that she would be entitled to remain in the house as long as she wished. In those circumstances, it was held that she should be able to do so and the plaintiffs' action for possession failed. As in other cases of proprietary estoppel, it must be shown that the woman acted in reliance on the belief that she was to have a licence; the

---

10 [1978] 2 All ER 942, CA. It is not clear what the consideration for the licence was: presumably it was the defendant's taking less than half the proceeds of sale because she was to continue to live in the house.
11 [1980] 3 All ER 710, CA. See also *Maharaj v Chand* [1986] AC 898, [1986] 3 All ER 107, PC.

fact that she goes to live with the owner of the property and permits herself to become pregnant will not of itself give her any right to remain there.[12]

As the cases cited above show, the extent of the resulting equity is to make good the expectations which the owner has encouraged, insofar as fairness between the parties permits this to be done.[13]

3. CONSTRUCTIVE TRUST

In one case, *Ungurian v Lesnoff*,[14] it was held that the facts established a trust rather than a licence. The defendant had left Poland and abandoned her career there in reliance on the parties' common intention that the plaintiff would buy a house where she could live with her children. In these circumstances Vinelott J held that full effect would not be given to this intention by inferring an irrevocable licence to occupy the house, but that the plaintiff held it on trust to permit her to live there for the rest of her life.[15] While this must turn on the inference that the court drew from the parties' conduct, it is not immediately obvious why the judge reached this conclusion, for which he gave no reason.[16]

4. BARE LICENCE

In other cases the woman will find herself no more than a bare licensee and the owner may recover possession of the premises after giving her reasonable notice to quit. The period given must be sufficient to enable her to find accommodation for herself and any children living with her.

5. RIGHTS AGAINST THIRD PERSONS

Even though the owner of the parties' home or former home cannot evict the other party, the latter's position may become precarious if the former dies or disposes of the property.

If the occupant holds under a trust, a purchaser will be bound by her right of occupation in the same circumstances as he would be bound by a beneficial interest in the property itself, and her presence there will necessarily give him constructive notice of her rights.[17] In particular, a volunteer (for example, a devisee of the home) will take subject to them. A contractual licence, on the other hand, confers only a personal right on the licensee.[18] Consequently, a cohabitant who has such a licence could enforce it against the other party's personal

---

12 *Coombes v Smith* [1986] 1 WLR 808.
13 See *Re Basham* [1987] 1 All ER 405 at 417; Moriarty 'Licences and Land Law' (1984) 100 LQR 376.
14 [1990] Ch 206, [1989] 3 WLR 840.
15 Unless and until the plaintiff sold the property with the defendant's consent and bought another residence for her in substitution for it.
16 It can have important consequences if the owner sells the property without the occupant's consent. But note the analysis in *Ungurian v Lesnoff* has now been superseded by the Trusts of Land and Appointment of Trustees Act 1996.
17 See ante, pp 157ff.
18 *Ashburn Anstalt v Arnold* [1989] Ch 1, [1988] 2 All ER 147, CA.

representatives, who are bound by his contractual obligations,[19] but not against a purchaser (even though he took with notice of it) unless the circumstances of the purchase make him a constructive trustee. A constructive trust will not be imposed in reliance on slender material:[20] the purchaser must have behaved in such a way as to make it unconscionable to permit him to deny the occupant's rights, for example by giving an express assurance that they would be respected,[1] or paying a lower price because the land was subject to them.[2] The threat of litigation may be sufficient to deter a prospective purchaser, but a vendor anxious to dispose of the property at the highest price is unlikely to impose terms which would create a trust.

A licence by estoppel may put the occupant in a stronger position, because there is authority for the proposition that an estoppel binds the licensor's successors in title.[3] The position, however, is not clear. At the most, it is submitted, the requirement that the owner should satisfy the expectations raised by his conduct makes him in effect a constructive trustee; on the other hand, the same facts could give rise to a contractual obligation or an estoppel, and it would be anomalous if a person relying on the latter were in a stronger position than one given an express promise that she would remain in occupation.

D.   Insolvency and the matrimonial home

1.   MORTGAGES AND CHARGES

If a spouse or unmarried cohabitant who is the sole legal owner of the matrimonial or quasi-matrimonial home mortgages it and later fails to pay the mortgage instalments, the mortgagee may wish to obtain vacant possession in order to realise his security. Even though the mortgagor has no defence to the claim, his or her spouse or partner may be protected if she or he did not concur in the mortgage, in which case of course the mortgagor will be able to remain in occupation as well. Again for the purpose of illustration it will be assumed that legal ownership is vested in the husband or male cohabitant.

We have already considered the circumstances in which a mortgagee will take subject to any beneficial interest which the wife or cohabitant has in the property.[4] Even if she has no such interest, a wife will be able to enforce her rights of occupation under the Family Law Act 1996 provided that she registered them before the mortgage was taken.[5] In most cases this will be valueless, because she will not have registered her rights if the home was mortgaged before the spouses

---

19 This was apparently assumed in *Horrocks v Forray* [1976] 1 All ER 737, CA, supra, although the executor's claim for possession succeeded because it was held that the defendant did not have a contractual licence.

20 *Ashburn Anstalt v Arnold*, supra, at 26 and 167 respectively.

 1 As in *Lyus v Prowsa Developments Ltd* [1982] 2 All ER 953. The fact that the land is transferred expressly subject to the occupant's rights does not of itself create a constructive trust, because this merely gives the transferee notice of their existence.

 2 As in *Binions v Evans* [1972] Ch 359, [1972] 2 All ER 70, CA.

 3 See Megarry and Wade *Real Property* (5th edn) 806–8; Martin (1980) 44 Conv 207; Hill (1988) 51 MLR 226.

 4 See ante, pp 156ff.

 5 See ante, p 68.

went into possession, and in practice she is unlikely to have done so even if she was in occupation when the husband charged the property. An unmarried cohabitant's position will similarly depend on whether a purchaser is bound by such right of occupation as she has.[6]

If a wife's or cohabitant's beneficial interest takes priority over a mortgage, the mortgagee, as a person interested, may bring proceedings to enforce the trust of land under the Trusts of Land and Appointment of Trustees Act 1996 s 14. On principle, the mortgagee should have no greater right than the husband. Hence, if the wife and children are occupying the house as the family home, the primary object of the trust will still be in existence and the court should not order a sale. Conversely, it will normally do so if the spouses have separated and the wife is living in the house alone.[7] A more difficult problem arises if the spouses are living there together without children. Although the house will still be the family home, the right of the mortgagee to enforce his security cannot be entirely ignored, and there seems little justification for permitting the wife to remain when the husband has no defence against a claim for possession, particularly if the mortgagee could take bankruptcy proceedings, when the court would almost certainly order the house to be sold.[8] Similar considerations would apply if the mortgagee brought proceedings to terminate the wife's or cohabitant's right of occupation.[9]

If the mortgagee is aware of the wife's or cohabitant's rights, he will insist on her agreeing that the charge should take priority over them, and it would be prudent for him to give himself the maximum protection by insisting on her concurring in the mortgage in any event. Even if she does so, a wife (as distinct from an unmarried cohabitant) is still given a degree of protection by the Family Law Act 1996. This provides that, if a spouse entitled under the Act to occupy the whole or part of the matrimonial home makes any payment or tender in respect of rent, mortgage payments or other outgoings affecting the home, this shall be as effective as though it were made by the owner.[10] If the mortgagee brings proceedings to enforce his security, the court may stay or suspend the execution of any order made, if the mortgagor is likely to be able to pay all sums due within a reasonable time.[11] The wife is given further protection by the requirement that the mortgagee must serve her with notice of proceedings if her right of occupation is registered; in any event she is generally entitled to be made a party if the court is satisfied that she may be expected to make such payments (or do anything else in satisfaction of the mortgagor's obligations) as might affect the outcome of the proceedings.[12] The difficulty is that the mortgagee is not bound to give her notice of the husband's default. As a result, such massive arrears may have accumulated before she gets to hear of them that she will find it impossible to pay them off within a reasonable time, even though she might have been able to pay each instalment as it fell due.

The provisions mentioned in the last paragraph do not apply to an unmarried cohabitant, whose only hope of preserving her right would be to seek an agreement with the mortgagee that she should pay off the arrears.

6 See ante, pp 165–6.
7 See ante, pp 154–5.
8 See post, pp 169–71.
9 See ante, pp 65–9 and 165–6.
10 Section 30(3).
11 Administration of Justice Act 1973 s 8; *Halifax Building Society v Clark* [1973] 2 All ER 33, CA; *Governor & Co of the Bank of Scotland v Grimes* [1985] 2 All ER 254, CA.
12 Family Law Act 1996 ss 55–56.

Charging orders

If a judgment creditor obtains a charging order, this will have the same effect as an equitable charge created by the judgment debtor.[13] If it is imposed on the matrimonial home in which the wife has a beneficial interest, the judgment creditor will have to bring proceedings under s 14 like any other chargee, and the court must apply the same criteria when deciding whether to order a sale. But the court's power to make a charging order is discretionary, and if the marriage has broken down and the wife is bringing divorce or other matrimonial proceedings, she may try to frustrate the judgment creditor by seeking to have the home transferred to her free of the charge by means of a property adjustment order under the Matrimonial Causes Act 1973.[14] If the charging order has been made absolute before she commences matrimonial proceedings, the creditor's right to the order will prevail and any protection the wife has will be in s 14 proceedings. If she has already petitioned, the court should make the charging order absolute if it appears that after a sale enough money would be left to provide the wife and children with adequate alternative accommodation; if this is not so, the application should be transferred to the Family Division so that the same court can consider the position of both the wife and the judgment creditor. Normally the latter's right should not be extinguished completely: the most the court should do is impose a condition that the order should not be enforced so long as the wife is living in the house with children in full-time education.[15]

2.   BANKRUPTCY

If the family home forms part of the assets of a bankrupt, his interest in it will vest in the trustee in bankruptcy immediately his appointment takes effect.[16] Hence, if the bankrupt and his (or her) spouse or cohabitant are tenants in common,[17] the latter will retain her equitable share which will not be available for the other's creditors. Consequently, in bankruptcy the parties' interest in property will be of paramount importance.

The law relating to bankruptcy underwent extensive changes following the report of the Cork Committee and is now governed by the Insolvency Act 1986.[18]

Voidable transactions

The trustee may wish to have the spouse's or cohabitant's interest set aside under s 339 or s 423 of the Insolvency Act, the details of which have already been

13 Charging Orders Act 1979 s 3(4).
14 See post, pp 796–8 and 844ff.
15 Despite the court's reluctance to make a *Mesher* order: see post, pp 847ff. See *Harman v Glencross* [1986] Fam 81, [1986] 1 All ER 545, CA, and contrast *First National Securities Ltd v Hegerty* [1985] QB 850, [1984] 3 All ER 641, CA, where the court upheld a charging order absolute. See also Brown (1992) 55 MLR 284.
16 Some tenancies protected by statute will not vest in the trustee unless he serves a notice on the bankrupt (as he might do, for example, if the tenancy had a saleable value): Insolvency Act 1986 s 283(3A) and s 308A (added by the Housing Act 1988 s 117).
17 If they are equitable joint tenants, the joint tenancy will be severed when the property vests in the trustee, and the trustee and the other party will become equitable tenants in common in equal shares.
18 See the Report of the Review Committee on Insolvency Law and Practice (the Cork Committee), 1982, Cmnd 8558; Miller 'The Family Home and the Insolvency Act 1985' (1986) 50 Conv 391.

discussed.[19] Homes recently purchased may well be caught by s 339. If within the period of two years preceding the presentation of the bankruptcy petition the man had bought the family home with his own money and had it conveyed into the partners' joint names as equitable beneficial owners, the trustee may claim the spouse's or cohabitant's beneficial interest as one obtained in a transaction at an undervalue. The same result would follow if the partner had contributed significantly less than the value of her equitable share or, in similar circumstances, if the house had been purchased more than two years but less than five years before the petition and the purchaser was then insolvent.

Protection of members of the bankrupt's family [20]

Whether the bankrupt (who, for the sake of example, will be assumed to be the husband) is the sole beneficial owner of the matrimonial home or has a limited beneficial interest, the trustee in bankruptcy will normally wish to sell it to increase the assets available for the creditors. This will bring their interests into direct conflict with those of the members of the bankrupt's family who wish to retain the property as a family home.

Section 336 of the Insolvency Act protects the occupation rights of the bankrupt's spouse. No matrimonial home right under Part IV of the Family Law Act 1996 may be acquired in the period between the presentation of the petition and vesting of the bankrupt's property in the trustee, so that if the bankrupt marries during that period his wife will have no statutory rights. But existing rights of occupation under the Act will continue in force and bind the trustee, whether or not they are registered. The trustee has the same power to apply to the court to have these rights terminated, suspended or restricted as the husband would have had.[1] It will be observed that these provisions do not apply to an unmarried cohabitant.

Children are given protection by s 337, which applies when the bankrupt is entitled to occupy a dwelling house[2] by virtue of any estate or interest. If any person under the age of 18, who had his home with the bankrupt when the bankruptcy petition was presented and when the bankruptcy order was made, had at any time occupied that house with the bankrupt, the latter has the same right of occupation against the trustee as a spouse under the Family Law Act 1996 and cannot be evicted from the house without the leave of the court.[3] This protection is additional to that given by s 336 and is of importance if the children are living with the bankrupt but not with his wife (eg because she is dead or the spouses are divorced), or if the mother is living with the bankrupt but is not married to him.

If the bankrupt and his spouse or former spouse are trustees of land or the beneficial owners of a dwelling house, the trustee in bankruptcy may apply to the court for an order to sell the property under s 14 of the Trusts of Land and Appointment of Trustees Act 1996. Alternatively, he may apply to have the occupation rights of the bankrupt's spouse or former spouse terminated. In either case the court must make such order as it thinks just and reasonable 'having regard to the interests of the creditors, to the conduct of the spouse or former spouse so far as

---

19 See ante, pp 128ff.
20 See generally Davey 'Creditors and the family home' in Bridge (ed) *Family Law Towards the Millennium: Essays for P M Bromley* (1997) 331 at 347–52.
1 Insolvency Act 1986 s 336(1)–(2), as amended by the Family Law Act 1996 Sch 8, para 57.
2 This is defined as in the Family Law Act 1996: see ante, p 67; ibid, s 385(1).
3 Ibid, s 337(1)–(4). Note that the children need not be the bankrupt's own children.

contributing to the bankruptcy,[4] to the needs and financial resources of [that person], to the needs of any children and to all the circumstances of the case other than the needs of the bankrupt'.[5] If the application is made to terminate the bankrupt's own rights of occupation given by s 337, regard must be had to 'the interests of the creditors, the bankrupt's financial resources, the needs of the children and all the circumstances of the case other than the needs of the bankrupt'.[6] The court may make any order that it could make under Part IV of the Family Law Act 1996 and so could permit the bankrupt to remain in occupation if he paid an occupation rent or other outgoing.[7] In either case, if the application is made more than a year after the property vested in the trustee, it is to be assumed that the creditors' interests outweigh all other considerations, unless the circumstances are exceptional.[8]

In the absence of any reported cases it is difficult to predict how the courts will exercise their discretion if an application is made during the first year of the bankruptcy. The prime need of the wife and children is the provision of a home, and the different approach the court is required to make before and after this period implies that during the first year it should give much greater weight to the interests of the bankrupt's family than was the practice in the past. Insolvency practitioners will generally delay making any application under either section for a year so as to be able to take advantage of the more favourable provisions. This will effectively give the bankrupt and his spouse or partner a year in which to find other accommodation. After this period the Act gives statutory effect to the position under the old law, when the creditors would always prevail unless the circumstances were exceptional.[9] The fact that the family will be rendered homeless is an inevitable consequence of the sale and is not exceptional;[10] and, whilst the bankrupt or his wife would not be ordered to surrender possession until they had had reasonable time to make other arrangements,[11] there are few reported cases in which a sale was deferred for a longer period. One rare example of a sale being refused is *Judd v Brown*,[12] in which the bankrupt's wife had had recent major surgery for cancer and was about to undergo extensive chemotherapy treatment.

A sale was also refused in *Abbey National plc v Moss*,[13] in which Mrs Moss transferred the family home into the joint names of herself and her daughter on the express understanding that the property was to be the mother's home for life. The

4 Such as her irresponsible prodigality, having regard to the bankrupt's financial position.
5 Insolvency Act 1986 s 335A (added by the Trusts of Land and Appointment of Trustees Act 1996 Sch 3, para 23); s 336(4). The addition of s 335A implements the Law Commission's recommendation (Law Com No 181), supra, at para 12.12 to provide similar guidelines even where the bankrupt spouse is a beneficial owner.
6 Ibid, s 337(5).
7 The payment of outgoings will not give him any proprietary interest in the property: ibid, s 338.
8 Ibid, s 336(5) and s 337(6).
9 *Zandfarid v Bank of Credit and Commerce International SA (in liquidation)* [1997] 1 FLR 274; *Barclays Bank plc v Hendricks* [1996] 1 FLR 259; *Lloyds Bank plc v Byrne and Byrne* [1993] 1 FLR 369, CA; *Re Lowrie* [1981] 3 All ER 353, CA; *Re Citro* [1991] Ch 142, [1990] 3 All ER 952, CA; *Re Gorman* [1990] 1 All ER 717.
10 *Re Lowrie* (supra) at 356.
11 *Barclays Bank plc v Hendricks*, supra; *Re Turner* [1975] 1 All ER 5; *Re McCarthy* [1975] 2 All ER 857. But immediate possession might be given to the trustee eg if the spouse was being obstructive: *Re McCarthy* at 859.
12 [1997] BPIR 470, sub nom *Re Judd v Brown (Bankrupts) (Nos 9587 and 9588 of 1994)* [1998] 2 FLR 360, cited by Davey, op cit, at 349.
13 [1994] 1 FLR 307, CA; see Clarke 'A Bankrupt Principle?' (1994) Conv 331; Hopkins 'Creditors and Collateral Purposes' (1995) 111 LQR 73 and 'Trusts of Land and Appointment of Trustees Act 1996' (1996) 60 Conv 411 at 423 and 426; and Davey, op cit, at 350–2. See also *Re Raval (A Bankrupt)* [1998] 2 FLR 718.

daughter purportedly mortgaged the house (having forged her mother's signature) and defaulted on the mortgage repayments. The mortgagee, who was treated as being analogous to a trustee in bankruptcy, sought an order for sale under what was then s 30 of the Law of Property Act 1925. In refusing the application the Court of Appeal held that, since the purpose of the trust was to provide a home for Mrs Moss only, that purpose could not be affected by the daughter's bankruptcy. In *Re Holliday*[14] the husband and wife were beneficial joint tenants of the matrimonial home. The husband presented a petition in his own bankruptcy to frustrate the wife's application for a property transfer order in divorce proceedings, and there was no evidence that any of his creditors would have petitioned. If an immediate sale had been ordered, the wife was unlikely to have been able to find alternative accommodation for herself and her three children in the neighbourhood, so that their education would have been upset, and in the particular circumstances of the case a postponement would not have worked undue hardship on the creditors. The Court of Appeal held that in these exceptional circumstances 'the voice of the wife seeking to preserve a home for herself and the children ought in equity to prevail' and ordered that the house should not be sold for five years.

It remains to be seen whether the courts will be as generous to innocent family members in the future. Subsequent case law suggests that they may not be.[15] On the other side of the coin, it must remain true that there can be few cases in which creditors will not be prejudiced by a delay of more than a few months; consequently, if the trustee applies for an order after the first year, the court is likely to order an immediate sale unless the welfare of the children makes it imperative that they should stay in the matrimonial home, eg because they have reached a critical stage in their education.[16]

E. Statutory protection of leasehold property[17]

The owners of many homes hold them on a lease and we must now consider their position in the light of the relevant statutory provisions.

1. THE PRIVATE SECTOR

Rent control is the outcome of a chronic shortage of rented property and began in this country in 1915 as the result of the shortage in the First World War. Until 1988 it was coupled with security of tenure, on the ground that limiting the rent a landlord could charge gave no protection if he could evict the tenant, and security of tenure was valueless if the landlord could charge a rent which the tenant could not afford to pay. Rent control, however, itself produces a shortage of accommodation since

14 [1981] Ch 405, [1980] 3 All ER 385, CA.
15 Viz *Zandfarid v BCCI*, supra, and *Barclays Bank plc v Hendricks*, supra.
16 See *Re Lowrie*, supra, at 356.
17 See Furber et al *Redman's Law of Landlord and Tenant* (18th edn, 1998); Arden and Partington *Arden and Partington on Housing Law* (2nd edn, 1994); Arden and Hunter *Manual of Housing Law* (6th edn, 1997); Smith, Evans and Smith *The Law of Landlord and Tenant* (5th edn, 1996). Agricultural tenancies are not dealt with in the text and the reader should consult the works noted for details of these.

landlords may be prevented from charging the market rent. Consequently, when houses became vacant, many landlords preferred to sell rather than re-let and there was no incentive for developers to build new property for letting. During the 1980s the Conservative Government introduced legislation in an attempt to bring more rented accommodation onto the market. The result was to leave a bewildering array of types of tenancy offering differing levels of protection to the tenant.

Regulated tenancies under the Rent Act 1977

These are a diminishing proportion of private tenants, since it has not been possible to create a new tenancy according to the Rent Act's terms since 15 January 1989 when the Housing Act 1988 Part I came into force. However, tenants still falling within the 1977 Act have significant protection both as regards the rent they can be charged, and their security of tenure.

A tenancy governed by the Rent Act is known as a regulated tenancy. A tenant in occupation under a contractual lease is known as a 'protected tenant' and is protected from arbitrary eviction by the terms of the contract. The Act also gives the tenant a wide measure of protection *after* the lease ends. If he remains in possession after his contractual lease has been determined – for example, if his term has expired or he has been given notice to quit in accordance with the provisions of the lease – his tenancy becomes a 'statutory tenancy'.[18] In certain circumstances a deceased tenant's spouse or cohabitant also becomes a statutory tenant.[19] A statutory tenant is generally speaking bound by all the terms and conditions in the original lease and entitled to the benefit of them.[20]

(a)   Fair rent

In the absence of agreement between them, either the landlord or the protected tenant may apply, during the contractual period of the tenancy, for a 'fair rent' to be determined and registered by a Rent Officer. Once this is registered, it becomes the maximum rent that the landlord can charge under that, or any subsequent regulated tenancy, for the next two years.[1]

(b)   Protection from eviction

In order to claim the protection given by the Act against eviction, the statutory tenant must occupy the premises as his residence, for the policy of the Act is to protect the home and not to give the tenant any wider privileges.[2] A person may be in occupation of more than one home for this purpose simultaneously, as where he

---

18 Rent Act 1977 ss 1–2; if there were two or more joint contractual tenants, but not all are in possession at the end of the contractual tenancy, those remaining become statutory tenants: *Lloyd v Sadler* [1978] QB 774, [1978] 2 All ER 529, CA. A husband's permitting his wife to remain in possession of the matrimonial home as a condition of paying a reduced sum under a maintenance order does not create the relationship of landlord and tenant so as to give the wife the protection of the Rent Act: *Bramwell v Bramwell* [1942] 1 KB 370, [1942] 1 All ER 137, CA; cf *Marcroft Wagons Ltd v Smith* [1951] 2 KB 496, [1951] 2 All ER 271, CA (daughter permitted to remain in possession after her mother's death for a short time not protected by the Act).
19 See post, pp 881–2.
20 Rent Act 1977 s 3.
 1 Section 67.
 2 *Kavanagh v Lyroudias* [1985] 1 All ER 560, CA (tenant sleeping in one house but spending rest of time in another not in occupation of first house as his residence). See Brierley 'The Rent Act 1977 and the Absent Tenant' (1991) 54 Conv 345.

works in two places and has a home in each of them which he occupies when he is at that particular place: whether he can be said to occupy one as his second home is a question of fact and degree.[3] Likewise, a temporary absence will not suffice to bring his statutory tenancy to an end. But he must retain both the corpus of possession and an intention to return. Thus it was held that a wife who had gone away because of illness, leaving her furniture in the house in which her husband occasionally slept and to which she hoped to return as soon as her health improved, was still in occupation and was entitled to the protection of the Act.[4] But a mere intention without the corpus will not be sufficient, and consequently it was held that a man who left his house deserted whilst serving a sentence of imprisonment ceased to be a statutory tenant.[5] He could have averted this result only 'by coupling and clothing his inward intention with some formal, outward, and visible sign of it', for example by installing a caretaker or relative to preserve the premises for his homecoming.[6] Conversely, if the tenant leaves the premises with no intention of ever returning, he loses the status of a statutory tenant, even though he leaves his furniture there with a caretaker or relative.[7]

But there is one important exception to this rule, designed to protect the tenant's spouse – particularly the deserted wife. If one spouse is a protected or statutory tenant but the other is in occupation of the premises by virtue of his or her matrimonial home rights under the Family Law Act 1996, s 30(4)(a) of that Act provides that this is to be regarded as occupation by the tenant himself.[8] This is so even though the spouse in occupation is there against the tenant's will. This exception was originally grafted onto earlier Acts by the Court of Appeal and was based on the husband's common law obligation to maintain his wife and to provide her with accommodation.[9] So long as the tenant's spouse is occupying the premises as her (or his) residence, the protected or statutory tenancy will continue notwithstanding that the tenant is residing elsewhere.[10] No such protection exists for a cohabitant.

---

3 See *Hampstead Way Investments Ltd v Lewis-Weare* [1985] 1 All ER 564, HL.
4 *Wigley v Leigh* [1950] 2 KB 305, [1950] 1 All ER 73, CA. See also *Camden London Borough Council v Goldenberg* [1997] 1 FLR 556, CA (McCowan LJ dissenting) – a grandson who moved out of his grandmother's flat on marriage, but failed to find permanent alternative accommodation with his wife and moved back in after a few months, retained continuity of residence for purpose of being assigned a *secure* tenancy (see post, p 175) because the flat remained his postal address and he left his possessions there.
5 *Brown v Brash* [1948] 2 KB 247, [1948] 1 All ER 922, CA.
6 Per Asquith LJ, ibid, at 254–5 and 926, respectively.
7 *Skinner v Geary* [1931] 2 KB 546, CA (sister); *Robson v Headland* (1948) 64 TLR 596, CA (divorced wife and son); *Beck v Scholz* [1953] 1 QB 570, [1953] 1 All ER 814, CA (caretakers); *Colin Smith Music Ltd v Ridge* [1975] 1 All ER 290, CA (deserted cohabitant and their children); *Duke v Porter* (1986) 19 HLR 1, CA (nobody resident).
8 Hence the tenancy will not have the protection of the Rent Act if it has never been the matrimonial home, because neither the Family Law Act 1996 (see ante, p 66) nor the case law carried forward from the earlier Acts will apply: *Hall v King* [1988] 1 FLR 376, CA. No order need have been made under the Act. A spouse (like a tenant) who is temporarily absent will remain in occupation for the purpose of the Act if he retains the corpus of possession and the intention to return: *Hoggett v Hoggett* (1979) 39 P & CR 121, CA.
9 *Brown v Draper* [1944] KB 309, [1944] 1 All ER 246, CA.
10 See *Hall v King* (supra) and the judgment of Kerr LJ (with which Ewbank J agreed) in *Griffiths v Renfree* [1989] 2 FLR 167 at 172–3. Once the landlord has obtained an order for possession and this has taken effect, the tenant is no longer entitled to remain in possession by virtue of the Rent Act, and consequently the spouse loses his or her matrimonial home rights and becomes a trespasser, but she (or he) can still apply for the order to be suspended: Rent Act 1977 s 100, as amended by the Housing Act 1980 s 75(3).

(c)   Recovery of possession

If a statutory tenant and his or her spouse both leave the premises, this automatically brings the tenancy to an end, and the landlord may retake possession or, if necessary, recover it by suing any trespasser on the property.[11] But so long as a protected or statutory tenancy is in existence, the landlord may obtain an order for possession only if the conditions laid down by the Rent Act are fulfilled. These are of two kinds. First, where suitable alternative accommodation is available to the tenant or one or more of the 'discretionary grounds' for possession (such as non-payment of rent) exist,[12] the court may make an order unless it thinks this unreasonable. Secondly, if the landlord establishes one or more 'mandatory grounds' (for example, the landlord is an 'owner-occupier', ie had previously himself occupied the property, and requires it again for his own residence), then the court must make the order and has no overriding discretion to refuse.[13]

Tenancies under the Housing Act 1988

The Housing Act 1988 Part I created two new forms of tenancy for the private rented sector: 'assured' and 'assured shorthold' tenancies.

(a)   Assured tenancies

An assured tenancy enables the landlord to charge the market rent for the property,[14] although the tenant may still only be evicted if the landlord can prove one or more of a (wider range of) statutory grounds for possession against him, not including the expiry of the contractual period. An assured tenancy becomes a 'statutory' periodic assured tenancy at the end of that period.

(b)   Assured shorthold tenancies

An assured shorthold tenancy, in addition to enabling the landlord to charge the market rent,[15] also provides for possession to be obtained simply by virtue of the tenancy coming to the end of the contractual period, by proceedings following the serving of a possession notice.[16] As originally enacted, the shorthold had to be granted for a term certain of not less than six months. This is no longer a requirement, although the landlord cannot ask for an order for possession until six months after the beginning of the tenancy.[17] The shorthold tenant, unlike an assured tenant, may not terminate a fixed-term shorthold before the expiry of the term.[18]

Because it became clear that there was little advantage to landlords in granting assured, as opposed to shorthold, tenancies, and that accordingly most tenancies being granted were of the latter type, the Housing Act 1996 s 96 provides that,

---

11 *Brown v Draper* [1944] KB 309, [1944] 1 All ER 246, CA; *Middleton v Baldock* [1950] 1 KB 657 at 661–2, [1950] 1 All ER 708, CA at 710.
12 Rent Act 1977 s 98(1) and Sch 15 Part I.
13 Sch 15 Part II.
14 Although, if the landlord proposes an increase in the rent, the tenant may refer the increase to a rent assessment committee, which must determine the appropriate market rent: Housing Act 1988 ss 13–14.
15 Again, subject to the possibility of a review of any increase.
16 Ibid, s 21.
17 Section 21, as amended by Housing Act 1996 s 99.
18 See Smith, Evans and Smith *The Law of Landlord and Tenant* (5th edn, 1996) p 340 and n 18.

from 28 February 1997, a tenancy satisfying the criteria is presumed to be an assured shorthold tenancy, subject to certain exceptions.[19]

Like a regulated tenancy, either type of assured tenancy must be of a dwelling house let as a separate dwelling. The tenant (or each of joint tenants) must be an individual (and not a corporation) and the tenant, or at least one of joint tenants, must occupy the dwelling house as his only or principal home.[20] A tenant who leaves the premises temporarily will presumably continue to occupy them so long as he retains the corpus of possession and the intention of returning, but if during his absence his principal residence is elsewhere, the tenancy will cease to be assured even though he leaves someone else (other than his spouse) in occupation. During his absence neither he nor the occupant can claim the benefit of security of tenure given by the Act (although if the tenancy is a contractual one, the landlord will be able to determine it only in accordance with the terms of the lease). Occupation by a spouse with matrimonial home rights is to be treated as that of the other.[1] The tenancy presumably remains assured if a sole tenant moves out leaving his or her spouse in occupation, at least so long as the dwelling house remains the latter's only or principal home.

2. PUBLIC SECTOR TENANCIES

Tenants of premises let by various public authorities formerly lacked security from eviction, but the gap was largely closed by the provisions of the Housing Act 1980, now consolidated in the Housing Act 1985, which created a new concept, that of the 'secure tenancy', under which the landlord may only gain possession by order of the court on proof of various statutory grounds.

Secure tenancies under the Housing Act 1988

A secure tenancy arises (subject to the grant of an introductory tenancy, discussed below) whenever the landlord is a local authority or one of certain other public bodies[2] and the tenant is an individual occupying the dwelling house as his only or principal home (or, in the case of joint tenants, each of them is an individual and at least one of them satisfies this condition).[3] Where the secure tenancy is for a fixed-term, on expiry of the term a 'periodic secure tenancy' will automatically arise unless the landlord grants a fresh fixed term or other periodic tenancy.[4] Thus, the tenant has the same kind of protection from eviction as a protected or assured tenant in the private sector.

Since public authority housing policies could be frustrated if the tenant could assign the tenancy to anyone he chose, there are restrictions on such assignment.

---

19 Housing Act 1988 s 19A and Sch 2A. The most notable are where there is express provision in the tenancy to the contrary, and where local authority tenancies (which had 'secure tenancy' status, discussed infra) have been transferred to the private sector, in which case the tenants are assured tenants of the new landlord.

20 Housing Act 1988 s 1 and Sch 1. For accommodation partly shared with persons other than the landlord and the effect of subletting part of the premises, see ss 3–4.

1 Family Law Act 1996 s 30(4)(b).

2 But not, as originally enacted, housing associations, which may only grant assured tenancies: Housing Act 1985 s 80(1) as amended.

3 Ibid, s 81 as amended.

4 Ibid, s 86(1).

Any purported assignment of a secure tenancy will be ineffective unless it is made:

(a) by way of exchange with another secure or an assured tenant;[5]
(b) in pursuance of a property adjustment order made under s 23A or s 24 of the Matrimonial Causes Act 1973;[6] or
(c) to a person who could have been a qualified successor had the tenant died immediately before the assignment.[7]

The tenancy will cease to be a secure tenancy if the tenant parts with possession of the dwelling house or sublets the whole of it or if it is vested or disposed of in the course of the administration of a deceased tenant's estate. Unless the tenancy passes to a qualified successor, once it has ceased to be a secure tenancy, it cannot become one again.[8] The provisions of the Act apply equally to a person occupying a dwelling house as a licensee if he would have had a secure tenancy had his licence been a lease.[9]

(a)   Recovery of possession

The landlord can bring a secure tenancy to an end only by obtaining an order for possession, and the court cannot make such an order unless certain conditions are fulfilled. There are 16 grounds on which an order can be made. The first eight of these, including non-payment of rent or other breach of covenant, and domestic violence by the tenant or the tenant's partner,[10] are 'discretionary' grounds, in that the court must find it reasonable to make the order for possession in addition to being satisfied that the ground has been proved. Grounds 9 to 11, which include overcrowding and the need of the landlord to redevelop the property, are 'mandatory' grounds where, if the landlord also proves that suitable alternative accommodation will be available to the tenant and his family, possession must be ordered once the ground has been established. Grounds 12 to 16, which apply, for example, where the property was let to the tenant in consequence of his employment, require the court to be satisfied as to *both* the reasonableness of making the order, *and* the availability of alternative accommodation.[11]

As with a protected or assured tenant, the secure tenant may terminate the tenancy by notice to quit or surrender.[12]

(b)   Right to buy

As valuable as his security of tenure is the secure tenant's 'right to buy' his property from the landlord. This right was granted to 'council tenants' by the Thatcher government of the 1980s as one of its most significant pieces of social engineering, with the aim of bringing about a full 'property-owning democracy'.

---

5 Ibid, s 91(3)(a).
6 Section 91(3)(b). The court may consider the authority's housing policy when deciding whether to make the order: *Jones v Jones* [1997] 1 FLR 27, CA. It is unclear why no reference is made to the possibility of transfer being ordered under the Family Law Act 1996 Sch 7.
7 Section 91(3)(c); *Camden London Borough Council v Goldenberg* [1997] 1 FLR 556, CA; see post, p 884.
8 Housing Act 1985 ss 90–93 as amended. For the meaning of 'qualified successor' see post, p 181.
9 Section 79(3).
10 Added (as Ground 2A) by the Housing Act 1996 s 147(1). See further post, p 217.
11 Housing Act 1985 s 84(2) and Sch 2.
12 Section 79 and s 81.

Not only can the tenant buy the property and thus deplete the local authority's housing stock, but he may do so at a highly preferential price. The Housing Act 1985 Part V provides that the right is to buy the freehold in the case of a house, and a long lease in respect of a flat. The secure tenant (or his or her spouse) must have resided in the property for two years.[13] The price at which the property is bought is fixed according to the open market value (not including inter alia the fact that the tenant is in occupation, and the value of any improvements he may have made), subject to a discount ranging, according to the length of time the tenant has resided in the property, from 32 to 60 per cent (in the case of a house) or from 44 to 70 per cent (in the case of a flat).[14]

If the tenant sells the property within three years, he is required to repay a proportion or all of the discount, depending upon the period elapsed since he acquired the property.[15] This caused problems in the past in the event of a divorce. In *R v Rushmoor Borough Council, ex p Barrett*,[16] it was held that an order for sale made under s 24A of the Matrimonial Causes Act 1973[17] attracted the operation of this penalty, whereas a property adjustment order made under s 24 was exempt within s 160 of the Housing Act. This was obviously anomalous, and s 24A was added to the list of exempt disposals by the Housing Act 1996.[18]

(c)   Introductory tenancies

To enable local authorities to deal more easily with antisocial tenants, Part V of the Housing Act 1996 also permits such authorities to grant new tenants (or licensees) a special introductory tenancy to operate as a 'trial run' for one year. The landlord may seek possession within the year without proof of grounds (although a court order is still necessary), although notice of the reasons for such possession must be given to the tenant, who may seek a review.[19] If the tenant survives the trial period, the tenancy is automatically converted into a secure tenancy.

3.   THE POSITION OF THE SEPARATED SPOUSE

If the wife (or husband) of a tenant remains in the matrimonial home after the spouses separate and continues to pay the rent herself, a number of legal consequences follow. The payment of rent by the spouse in occupation who has matrimonial home rights under the Family Law Act 1996 is as good as if made by the tenant.[20] If the landlord is unaware of the separation and assumes that the husband is still in personal occupation of the premises, he will regard the wife as the husband's agent and the lease will still be vested in the husband. If the landlord is aware that the husband has left but continues to take the rent from the wife, it is a question of fact whether he treats the wife as her husband's agent (in which case the husband will remain the legal tenant) or whether he has accepted her as a new tenant (in which case she will become a new contractual tenant). The fact that the

13 Section 119.
14 Sections 126–129.
15 Section 155.
16 [1988] 2 All ER 268, CA.
17 See post, pp 800–1.
18 Section 222, Sch 18 para 15(3).
19 Housing Act 1996 s 129.
20 Family Law Act 1996 s 30(3).

landlord accepts rent from the wife with full knowledge of the facts is not per se evidence of his having granted her a new lease, for he cannot automatically evict her and consequently has no alternative to taking the rent from her.[1] But if no new tenancy is brought into existence, the original tenant, and not the spouse, continues to hold under the old tenancy.

Where the property is held on a joint tenancy, any one of the tenants may serve a notice to quit to bring the contractual tenancy to an end before the term expires, but the consent of all is required to continue a periodic tenancy. Consequently if, say, husband and wife are joint tenants and one of them indicates to the landlord that he or she does not intend to renew the tenancy at the end of the current period, the other will lose her or his protection as well.[2]

A spouse who is *not* a joint tenant, but has matrimonial home rights,[3] is in a stronger position. By enacting that the occupation of a spouse with rights of occupation is to be treated as occupation by the other spouse for the purpose of the Rent Act 1977 or Housing Acts 1985 or 1988, the Family Law Act 1996 gives the separated spouse the same protection from eviction as the tenant himself (albeit that, in the case of assured shortholds, as we have seen, such protection is much reduced). Unless the landlord can establish one of the statutory grounds, the wife cannot be evicted even though her husband wishes to terminate the tenancy. In *Middleton v Baldock*[4] the husband had deserted his wife and left her in the matrimonial home. The landlord served a notice to quit on the husband who acknowledged the landlord's right to the premises and offered to give him immediate possession. The landlord then brought separate actions against the spouses for possession, which the wife alone defended. The Court of Appeal held that, as the landlord's claim was based on none of the statutory grounds for obtaining possession, he could succeed only if the premises were vacated; and as the husband could not lawfully evict his wife, his acknowledgement of the landlord's right to enter could have no legal effect whatever.

The landlord can obtain possession only if the husband obtains an order under the Family Law Act 1996 s 33(3)(e) terminating the wife's matrimonial home rights. The husband remains liable for the rent,[5] but as non-payment of rent is one of the grounds on which the landlord may obtain possession, the wife may clearly have to pay it herself to secure her own occupation.[6] It seems strange that a spouse

---

1 See *Morrison v Jacobs* [1945] KB 577, [1945] 2 All ER 430, CA. See also the alternative ground for the decision in *Wabe v Taylor* [1952] 2 QB 735, [1952] 2 All ER 420, CA, as explained in *SL Dando Ltd v Hitchcock* [1954] 2 QB 317 at 324, [1954] 2 All ER 335, CA at 337–8, and *Cove v Flick* [1954] 2 QB 326n at 327, [1954] 2 All ER 441n, CA at 442.

2 *Hammersmith and Fulham London Borough Council v Monk* [1992] 1 AC 478, [1992] 1 All ER 1, HL. An alternative device may be to convert the tenancy into a sole one via a deed of release: *Burton v Camden London Borough Council* [1998] 1 FLR 681, CA.

3 See ante, p 65.

4 [1950] 1 KB 657, [1950] 1 All ER 708, CA. See also *Brown v Draper* [1944] KB 309, [1944] 1 All ER 246, CA; *Old Gate Estates Ltd v Alexander* [1950] 1 KB 311, [1949] 2 All ER 822, CA.

5 *Griffiths v Renfree* [1989] 2 FLR 167, CA (where the husband gave notice to the landlord).

6 See *Church Comrs for England v Al-Emarah* [1997] Fam 34, where the wife's inability to pay off arrears meant that she could not resist a suspended possession order and hence could not have the tenancy transferred to her: see further post, p 179. The possibility of the husband and landlord seeking to defeat the wife's right by collusively agreeing that the landlord shall falsely allege a ground for obtaining possession which the husband will not deny is averted only if the wife is joined as a party, when she can challenge the landlord herself. She should be joined as the person actually in possession: see Miller 'Expenses of the Matrimonial Home' (1971) 35 Conv 332 at 347–50. The husband must be joined, as he is the statutory tenant: *Brown v Draper*, supra. See also Crane 'After the Deserted Wife's Licence' (1965) 29 Conv 254 at 264–5.

who is not a tenant of the landlord can obtain greater protection from eviction, by virtue of matrimonial home rights, than a spouse who is a joint tenant (and hence does not have such rights).[7]

4. TRANSFER OF TENANCIES ON DIVORCE, NULLITY AND SEPARATION[8]

If the marriage is dissolved or annulled, the tenant's spouse will lose his or her matrimonial home rights given by the Family Law Act 1996 and consequently could be evicted.[9] To meet this difficulty, the court granting a divorce or decree of nullity (or a separation order)[10] may make an order transferring the tenancy to the tenant's spouse.[11] In the case of a divorce, an order may not be made while the period for reflection and consideration is interrupted under s 7(8) of the 1996 Act, or when the process has lapsed.[12] Nor may it be made after the divorce order has been made or while a separation order is in force, unless the application was made before the order was made or the court gives leave.[13] The transfer order may not take effect before a decree of nullity is made absolute,[14] or before a divorce or separation order is made, except where the court is satisfied that the circumstances of the case are exceptional and it would be just and reasonable for the order to be so made.[15] A spouse may not make an application if he or she has remarried.[16]

The tenancy must still be in existence when the application for a transfer is made. Consequently, if the tenant (who we will assume is the husband) leaves the premises and gives notice to quit after a divorce order has been made absolute, the wife cannot apply for a transfer, since her occupation is no longer attributed to her former husband and he has effectively terminated the tenancy.[17]

The Family Law Act 1996 sets out, for the first time, guidelines to which the

7 Family Law Act 1996 s 30(1); see Mendes Da Costa 'Keeping Alive the Tenancy in the Matrimonial Home' [1995] Fam Law 622, but note that it has since been held that a protected tenancy under the Rent Act 1977 *may* be surrendered by the tenant (*Bolnore Properties v Cobb* (1996) 29 HLR 202, CA), so there would seem no obstacle to a joint tenant surrendering the protected tenancy, in line with the position in respect of assured (and secure) tenancies.

8 See Horton *Family Homes and Domestic Violence: The New Legislation* (1996) ch 11; La Follette and Purdie *A Guide to the Family Law Act 1996* (1996) ch 13.

9 While an occupation order under s 33(5)(b) or s 33(10) may provide for these rights to continue after termination of the marriage, it would seem, by analogy with *Harrow v London Borough Council v Johnstone* [1997] 1 All ER 929, [1997] 1 FLR 887, HL (discussed post, p 217) that this does not prevent the tenant from giving a lawful and effective notice to quit, thus bringing the tenancy to an end.

10 Or, until the Family Law Act 1996 s 2 comes into force, a decree of judicial separation.

11 Family Law Act s 53 and Sch 7. The landlord must be given an opportunity of being heard: 1996 Act Sch 7, para 14(1). Orders for transfer of tenancies other than *statutory* tenancies may be made under s 24 (or when the 1996 Act is implemented, s 23A and s 24) of the Matrimonial Causes Act 1973 (see eg *Jones v Jones* [1997] 1 FLR 27, CA and the discussion post, p 796) and under Sch 1 to the Children Act 1989, discussed post, p 768; for the advantages of using Sch 7 rather than these alternatives, see Horton, op cit, pp 219–20.

12 See post, p 245.

13 Matrimonial Causes Act 1973 s 23B(2)–(4).

14 Family Law Act 1996 Sch 7 para 12(1).

15 Family Law Act 1996 Sch 7, para 12(2); Matrimonial Causes Act 1973 s 23B(1).

16 Sch 7, para 113.

17 *Lewis v Lewis* [1985] AC 828, [1985] 2 All ER 449, HL.

court must have regard when deciding whether to order a transfer.[18] The court must consider the circumstances in which the tenancy was granted to either or both spouses, or the circumstances in which either or both became a tenant under the tenancy. It must also take into account the respective housing needs and resources of the parties and any relevant child,[19] the parties' financial resources, the likely effect of transferring or not transferring the tenancy on the health, safety or well-being of the parties and any relevant child, and the suitability of the parties as tenants.[20] The Law Commission, on whose recommendations these provisions are based,[1] drew an analogy with the case law governing orders for sale of property under s 30 of the Law of Property Act 1925[2] and Horton suggests that where the purpose of acquiring the tenancy was to provide a home for the parties and their children, the court might be disposed to transfer the tenancy to the spouse looking after the children.[3]

A transfer takes effect as a compulsory assignment, and the transferee takes subject to all the benefits and burdens of the covenants and the transferor ceases to be liable on them,[4] in the absence of a court order directing otherwise.[5] In the case of a statutory tenancy the transferee becomes the statutory tenant in place of the transferor. If the spouses are joint tenants, the court has a similar power to extinguish the interest of one of them and vest the tenancy exclusively in the other.[6]

The Family Law Act gave an additional power to the court to order the applicant to pay either immediate, or deferred, compensation to the transferor of the tenancy, by lump sum or instalments. This is a potentially far-reaching provision, although the Law Commission did not consider such orders to be very likely.[7] In deciding whether to exercise the power to make an order for compensation, the court must have regard to all the circumstances, including the financial loss that would otherwise be suffered by the transferor, the financial needs and resources of the parties, and their present and future financial obligations to each other and any relevant child.[8] The matters which might be relevant could range from the payment of removal expenses, to the transferor's loss of his right to buy in respect of a secure tenancy.

5.   UNMARRIED COHABITANTS

Until the enactment of Sch 7 to the Family Law Act 1996, discussed above and further below, the special position of the spouse under the legislation we have been considering was not shared by the tenant's unmarried partner. If unmarried cohabitants are joint tenants, obviously each will be able to claim the benefits of

18 Sch 7, para 5.
19 Defined by s 63(2) as a child who is living with, or who might reasonably be expected to live with either party to the proceedings; or whose welfare is in question in Children Act or Adoption Act proceedings, or whose interests the court considers relevant.
20 Section 33(6)(a)–(c) and Sch 7, para 5(3).
 1 Law Com No 207, *Domestic Violence and Occupation of the Family Home* (1992) paras 6.3–6.9.
 2 Now see Trusts of Land and Appointment of Trustees Act 1996 ss 14–15, discussed ante, p 153.
 3 Op cit, p 221.
 4 Family Law Act 1996 Sch 7, para 7(1)–(2).
 5 Family Law Act 1996 Sch 7, para 11.
 6 Family Law Act 1996 Sch 7, para 8(1)–(2).
 7 Law Com, op cit, paras 6.10–6.11.
 8 Sch 7, para 10(4).

security afforded to the tenant, but, as we have seen, if the tenancy is a periodic one, a notice to quit by one tenant determines the tenancy of both at the end of the current period,[9] although a deed of release may convert the tenancy into a sole one.[10] If one of them (say, the man) is sole tenant and he temporarily leaves the premises with the intention of returning, the occupation of the other will enable the tenant to continue to enjoy the protection given by the various Acts (just as the occupation of a relative would) provided that, if he is an assured or secure tenant, he does not in the meantime establish his principal home elsewhere. If, on the other hand, he leaves permanently, his partner's occupation will not be attributed to him, so she will not have security of tenure: the landlord can terminate the lease, as the premises will no longer be the tenant's home.

If the tenancy is secure, a *heterosexual* cohabitant's position is stronger in one respect than if it were in the private sector: as she could be a qualified successor on the tenant's death, the latter can assign his tenancy to her so as to make her a secure tenant, provided that he does so while they are still living together as husband and wife.[11] Otherwise, if she wishes to remain on the premises, she must try to persuade the landlord to terminate the lease and grant her a fresh tenancy, or, if a joint tenant, obtain a deed of release to convert the tenancy into a sole one. Alternatively, she can try to take advantage of the provisions of Sch 7 to the Family Law Act 1996.

Transfer of tenancies under Family Law Act 1996 Sch 7

Notwithstanding concerns in Parliament that the extension of protection to cohabitants under Part IV of the Family Law Act 1996[12] might undermine the institution of marriage, it appears to have been happy with, or to have failed to take notice of, a highly significant step on the way towards equalising the position of married and unmarried couples. The power under Sch 7 to transfer tenancies, which we discussed above, applies to cohabitants (and former cohabitants)[13] as well as to spouses and former spouses.

Cohabitants are defined, by s 62(1), as 'a man and a woman who, although not married to each other, are living together as husband and wife'. As with the definition of those entitled to succeed to a tenancy, therefore, only heterosexual partners are included. The court may make an order to transfer the tenancy of the dwelling-house in which the couple lived together as husband and wife, when they have ceased living together.[14] When deciding whether to make an order, the court must have regard, in addition to the matters noted in respect of spouses,[15] the following factors:

- the nature of the parties' relationship, including the fact that they have not given each other the commitment involved in marriage;
- the length of time they cohabited;

---

9 *Hammersmith and Fulham London Borough Council v Monk* [1992] 1 AC 478, [1992] 1 All ER 1, HL.
10 *Burton v Camden London Borough Council* [1998] 1 FLR 681, CA.
11 Section 91(3)(c) and s 113(1). But homosexual cohabitants are not within the definition of a member of the tenant's family: *Fitzpatrick v Sterling Housing Association* [1997] 4 All ER 991, CA, discussed post, p 882.
12 See post, pp 194–211.
13 Sch 7, para 1.
14 Sch 7, paras 3(2), 4(b).
15 Ante, p 180.

- whether they have had any children together, or have had parental responsibility for any children; and
- the length of time since they ceased to cohabit.[16]

The court may also exercise its powers, noted above, to adjust the parties' liabilities in respect of the tenancy and to order the transferee to compensate the transferring tenant. Unlike former spouses, a former cohabitant may apply even after he or she has married or begun to cohabit with someone else, although this will clearly be a factor the court will take into account when determining whether to make the order.

How far courts will be prepared to make these orders in respect of cohabitants remains to be seen. If they demonstrate a willingness to do so in appropriate cases (presumably where the couple lived together for a long time, and perhaps more likely where they were joint tenants), it may well be asked why there is no equivalent power to make a transfer order in respect of owner-occupied property.[17] Of course, as the discussion throughout this chapter will have demonstrated, should that development be enacted, the whole law of family property will have been fundamentally realigned.

---

16 Section 33(6)(e)–(h), discussed post, p 205.
17 See the comment by Hayes in her written evidence to the House of Lords Special Public Bill Committee, Session 1994–95 HL 55, p 37.

Chapter 6

Family protection

A.   Introduction

This chapter deals with the legal responses to a variety of forms of personal behaviour within the domestic sphere which may amount to physical or emotional abuse. At one time, one might have limited discussion to the vague, but perhaps readily understandable term 'domestic violence',[1] or to the more graphic 'battered wives'. The former expression appears to signify a concern purely with violent behaviour, and the latter with conduct within the recognised legal relationship of marriage. However, the law has gradually widened its recognition of the range of personal relationships which might require protection, and of the range of behaviour which ought to be controlled. A useful definition which embraces this broad understanding is as follows:

> '... any form of physical, sexual or emotional abuse which takes place within the context of a close relationship.'[2]

It is now understood that infliction of violence is not restricted to spousal relationships but may involve cohabitants and others;[3] while unacceptable behaviour may include not just acts of violence but also acts of harassment, or pestering and unwanted attentions (now sometimes referred to, in extreme cases, as 'stalking'), or sometimes even simply the unpleasantness associated with the breakdown of a close relationship.[4] At the same time, there has also been a growing recognition that violence is not to be excused, just because it takes place between family members, and that it may amount to criminal offences ranging from the minor to the most serious.

Domestic violence is a global phenomenon, with countries as diverse as China and Barbados having laws specifically designed to tackle it. Violence against women is now viewed as an aspect of human rights violations to be tackled by the United Nations, and it has been suggested that an optional protocol specifically dealing with the issue be attached to the Convention on the Elimination of All

---

1   For discussion of the difficulties with this terminology, see Smith *Domestic Violence: an overview of the literature* Home Office Research Study No 107 (1989) ch 1.
2   Taken from the House of Commons Home Affairs Committee Third Report, *Domestic Violence* HC 245-1 (1992–93) para 5.
3   Children may also be the victims, and indeed, there is a strong correlation between abuse of an adult and abuse of the child (see Davidson 'Child Abuse and Domestic Violence: Legal Connections and Controversies' (1995) 29 Fam LQ 357), but this chapter is confined to consideration of adult relationships. Mechanisms expressly designed to deal with violence against children are discussed in Chapter 14.
4   Although in one study of 299 cases, none was found which did not involve some element of physical violence or the threat of such violence: Jones, Lockton, Ward and Kashefi 'Domestic violence applications: an empirical study of one court' (1995) 17 JSWFL 67.

Forms of Discrimination Against Women.[5]

It remains impossible, however, to estimate the scale of domestic violence or abuse with any confidence. All that can be said is that it is accepted that the phenomenon is common and widespread.[6] The range of legal mechanisms used to control the perpetrator's behaviour and provide effective protection for the victim may go well beyond the traditional criminal responses normally associated with the terms 'violence' or 'abuse'. In particular, the solution may lie in controlling the occupation of the family home, or in the provision of alternative accommodation for the family or individual family members, rather than in penal sanctions. In this chapter, we begin with a brief summary of the legal history, then consider the remedies offered by the criminal law, the civil law, and housing law.

1.   HISTORICAL DEVELOPMENTS

Violence in the home is a phenomenon long recognised by legal commentators. Although Hale had denied that a husband had a legal power to administer corporal punishment to his wife,[7] it was stated in Bacon's *Abridgment* in 1736 that a husband might beat his wife (but not in a violent or cruel manner) and confine her.[8] Blackstone, writing some 30 years later, maintained that, whilst the practice had become obsolete in polite society, 'the lower rank of people, who were always fond of the old common law, still claim and exert their ancient privilege'.[9] Little was heard of the problem for another century until Parliament intervened in 1878 following a campaign drawing attention to the brutal treatment of many working-class women.[10] The Matrimonial Causes Act 1878 gave a criminal court, before which a man was convicted of aggravated assault on his wife, the power to make a separation and maintenance order in her favour and to vest in her the legal custody of the children of the marriage under the age of 10 years if it felt that her future safety was in peril.[11]

Almost another 100 years passed before the question again became one of public concern. Publicity was generated by the setting up of women's aid refuges[12]

---

5 See the discussion by Van Bueren 'Annual Review of International Family Law' in Bainham (ed) *The International Survey of Family Law 1995*.
6 See Smith, op cit, p 14 and Home Affairs Committee, op cit, paras 7–11.
7 *Lord Leigh's Case* (1674) 3 Keb 433, where he said that *castigatio* meant no more than admonition and confinement.
8 Tit Baron and Feme (B).
9 *Commentaries* i 455.
10 See Frances Power Cobbe *Wife Torture in England* (1878); and for modern examinations of the Victorian response, see Hammerton *Cruelty and Companionship: Conflict in Nineteenth-Century Married Life* (1992) and Doggett *Marriage, Wife-Beating and the Law in Victorian England* (1992).
11 Section 4.
12 Particularly by Erin Pizzey in Chiswick. See her *Scream Quietly or the Neighbours will Hear* (1974), and also *Violence in the Family* (ed Borland), and Borkowski, Murch and Walker *Marital Violence* (1983). It has been argued that from 1948 to 1966, 'an unrecognised and hidden refuge for women and children from violent men' was provided by the power of local authorities to provide emergency accommodation to homeless families under Part III of the National Assistance Act 1948. When government policy was widened in 1966 (after the famous 'Cathy Come Home' television drama had highlighted the breakup of families due to the lack of accommodation) to include husbands within the category of those eligible for assistance, this refuge was lost: Morley and Pascall 'Women and homelessness: proposals from the Department of the Environment Part II, Domestic Violence' (1996) 18 JSWFL 327 at 328.

to which women and their children could flee from violence, and the feminist movement lobbied for action. A Select Committee of the House of Commons was established which heavily criticised the effectiveness of the existing remedies open to women who were the victims of violence at the hands of their husbands or the men with whom they were cohabiting.[13] At that time, remedies were limited to taking criminal proceedings or to pursuing civil actions (eg for damages in tort for a battery, or to assert a property right in the home), and seeking to have an injunction attached, under which the respondent was enjoined from 'molesting, assaulting or otherwise interfering with' the applicant and/or any children. It was also possible during the course of divorce or other matrimonial or family proceedings between the parties, to apply for an injunction to require a party to leave the matrimonial home or let the applicant back in.[14] However, it was considered that it was unduly burdensome to require an applicant to take substantive proceedings when she really only wanted the injunction, and accordingly it was provided in the Domestic Violence and Matrimonial Proceedings Act 1976 that a spouse or cohabitant could seek a non-molestation or ouster injunction from the county court without having to take any other proceedings. Magistrates were subsequently given similar powers by the Domestic Proceedings and Magistrates' Courts Act 1978 to make 'personal protection' and 'exclusion orders', although only in respect of physical violence inflicted by a spouse.[15]

Notwithstanding these express statutory provisions, it continued to be common for a party to seek an injunction, especially to exclude the other party from the home, during divorce or other proceedings relating to the children. However, in 1983, Lord Brandon, delivering the leading speech in the House of Lords in *Richards v Richards*,[16] pointed out that a spouse with statutory rights of occupation of the matrimonial home given under the Matrimonial Homes Act 1967 (later consolidated in the 1983 Act of the same name)[17] could not be evicted or excluded from the matrimonial home except with the leave of the court *given by an order under that section*. He added that it must follow that the owner of the property could be evicted only under a like order, and presumably the same argument would apply if both had a legal estate in the land. Consequently, if the parties were married, an ouster injunction could be granted only in proceedings taken under that Act or under the Domestic Violence and Matrimonial Proceedings Act 1976. After this decision, it could be said that the civil law relating to protection and control of occupation of the home was contained in three statutory jurisdictions, each governed by different rules and criteria – the Domestic Violence and Matrimonial Proceedings Act 1976 which applied to both married and cohabiting couples, the Domestic Proceedings and Magistrates' Courts Act 1978 and the Matrimonial Homes Act 1983, which each applied only to spouses – and a residual jurisdiction, through the Supreme Court Act 1981 s 37 and the County Courts Act 1984 s 38 or under the court's inherent powers, to grant an injunction to any applicant as an adjunct to substantive proceedings.

---

13 See the *Report of the Select Committee on Violence in Marriage* HC 553 (1974–75) and on *Violence in the Family* HC 329 (1976–77).
14 See the discussion in the last edition of this work at pp 161–3, and for the continuing relevance of these powers, see post, p 212.
15 Sections 16–18, following the recommendations of the Law Commission in Law Com No 77, *Report on Matrimonial Proceedings in Magistrates' Courts*.
16 [1984] AC 174, [1983] 2 All ER 807, HL.
17 See ante, p 66.

2.   PROPOSALS FOR REFORM

In *Richards v Richards* Lord Scarman observed: [18]

'The statutory provision is a hotchpotch of enactments of limited scope passed into law to meet specific situations or to strengthen the powers of specified courts. The sooner the range, scope and effect of these powers are rationalised into a coherent and comprehensive body of statute law, the better.'

The invitation to review the law was taken up by a number of bodies, who also took the opportunity to review services and policy. 'Victim Support' convened an inter-agency working party to review the type and extent of service provision available to the victims of domestic violence. It reported in 1992, and regarded the provision of refuges, and a greater emphasis upon tackling violence through the criminal justice system as the keys to improved protection. [19] The Home Affairs Committee of the House of Commons also conducted an inquiry into the scale of the problem of domestic violence, and the responses to it. They produced no radically new proposals, concentrating upon the promotion of greater public awareness of the problem, and, as had Victim Support, upon heightening official commitment to existing remedies such as the provision of refuges and initiatives in the criminal justice system. [20]

The Law Commission proposals

The Law Commission examined the civil law. [1] They identified a number of inconsistencies and anomalies: the scope of the remedies offered by the various courts differed; the criteria they applied in exercising their discretion when deciding whether to make an ouster order were outdated and failed to take account of the different situations with which the courts have to deal; no protection was given to former cohabitants and others falling outside specific categories of applicant, except for the often inadequate remedies offered by the law of torts; and the courts had no means of adjusting cohabitants' rights of occupation apart from their limited powers under the Domestic Violence and Matrimonial Proceedings Act. The aim of the Law Commission's proposals for reform was threefold. First, to remove these gaps, anomalies and inconsistencies from the law; secondly, to provide at least as much protection to victims as was currently available; and thirdly, to seek to minimise hostilities between the adults. [2] The Commission proposed revising the existing law to give all courts the same powers to make orders, and in respect of a wider range of applicants who could be broadly described as associated with the respondent by virtue of a family or similar relationship. They also proposed altering the criteria upon which orders were to be granted. There was a particular problem concerning the grant of ouster injunctions, because, since *Richards v Richards*, courts considering whether to issue such an injunction had been required to apply the

18 [1984] AC 174 at 206–7, [1983] 2 All ER 807, HL at 818.
19 Victim Support, *Domestic Violence: Report of a National Inter-Agency Working Party* (1992).
20 Home Affairs Committee, *Third Report Domestic Violence* HC 245 (1993).
 1 *Report on Domestic Violence and Occupation of the Family Home*, Law Com No 207, 1992, following Law Com Working Paper No 113 *Domestic Violence and Occupation of the Matrimonial Home*.
 2 Ibid para 1.2.

criteria laid down in s 1(3) of the Matrimonial Homes Act 1983, under which the court had to have regard to:

'. . . the conduct of the spouses in relation to each other and otherwise, to their respective needs and financial resources, to the needs of any children and to all the circumstances of the case.'

This focused the court's attention as much upon the reasonableness of the respondent's conduct as upon the needs of the applicant and children, and led courts to regard ousters as 'Draconian' orders,[3] not to be made lightly. The effect was to place the dominant emphasis upon the parties' conduct, and to reduce the significance of the effects felt by the victims.[4] The Commission considered that courts should be encouraged to make ouster orders more readily.

The Family Homes and Domestic Violence Bill

In 1995, the Conservative Government, intending to implement most of the Law Commission's proposals, duly introduced these, in the Family Homes and Domestic Violence Bill, into the House of Lords, under a procedure intended to speed up the legislative process in respect of 'uncontroversial' law reform measures based on the recommendations of the Law Commission.[5] However, although the Bill proceeded successfully through the upper Chamber, when it moved to the House of Commons, it was lost when a number of Conservative MPs opposed it, fearing that its provisions would undermine marriage by offering protection from violence and the ability to remain in the family home to unmarried couples.[6] With shortage of Parliamentary time, and a wish to avoid trouble with his own back benches, the Lord Chancellor withdrew the Bill 'to look again at the details'. The following session, it emerged as part of the Family Law Bill, and, with some changes, now forms Part IV of the 1996 Act, which is discussed below.

Stalking and harassment

Alongside these careful reviews of the existing law and practice, a concern to produce speedy legislation to deal with an apparently new problem, that of 'stalking', also produced more hurried reforms. 'Stalking' has been defined as:

'. . . a campaign of harassment or molestation of another, usually with an undertone of sexual attraction or infatuation.'[7]

During 1995 and 1996, a number of cases appeared in the media, from which it seemed that the criminal law[8] could not be used successfully to cope with such conduct, and calls were made to introduce new legislation to plug the gap. Eventually, after an unsuccessful attempt by a private member to introduce

---

3 *Summers v Summers* [1986] 1 FLR 343, CA; *Wiseman v Simpson* [1988] 1 All ER 245, CA.
4 Some courts, however, were prepared to grant an order even though violence could not be proved: *Scott v Scott* [1992] 1 FLR 529, CA, *Khan v Khan* [1995] 2 FLR 221, CA.
5 See *Family Homes and Domestic Violence Bill Proceedings of the Special Public Committee* (1994–95) HL Paper 55.
6 While one might not be surprised at the ignorance of the editor and columnists of the Daily Mail who appear to have been unaware that cohabitants had been protected by the law for nearly twenty years under the Domestic Violence and Matrimonial Proceedings Act 1976, the equal ignorance of this fact by MPs might appear to be less excusable.
7 Wells 'Stalking: The Criminal Law Response' [1997] Crim LR 463. See also Lawson-Cruttenden 'Is there a law against stalking?' (1996) 146 NLJ 418.
8 The civil law was also inadequate, due to the limitations noted at p 185 above.

legislation, proposals were brought forward by the government,[9] resulting in the Protection from Harassment Act 1997, containing both civil and criminal powers.[10] The breadth of the provisions in this Act, and the vagueness of its language, are a stark contrast to the careful and detailed, not to say complex, provisions in Part IV of the Family Law Act 1996.

B.   Protection afforded by the criminal law[11]

1.   PROBLEMS WITH THE CRIMINAL JUSTICE SYSTEM

A family member is in a similar legal position to any other person who may be prosecuted for assaulting another (whether for common assault or an assault occasioning actual bodily harm) or for committing one of the more serious offences of wounding, causing grievous bodily harm, rape (within or outside marriage)[12] or even attempted murder. In practice, however, the criminal law has been little used by victims of domestic violence. The reasons are numerous. First, there was a traditional reluctance by the police to become involved in a 'domestic' incident, partly because of a perception that the complainant would decline to press charges and so waste police time, and partly because of the strongly male, and sexist, 'canteen culture' which pervades the police service.[13] Recognition of the seriousness of violence within the family led to an attempt by government to change this attitude by issuing a Home Office Circular in 1990 reminding police officers 'of their responsibility to respond as law enforcement officers to requests from victims for help, and of their powers to take action in cases of violence.'[14] A number of police services revised their policies in respect of domestic violence as a result of this circular, and several established Domestic Violence Units to provide a specialist service offering liaison between police and victims, advice to investigating officers, training in how to handle domestic violence incidents, and co-operation with other agencies in tackling the problem.[15] However, the problems of police sometimes failing to arrest an attacker at the scene of the crime, or of failing to record a domestic incident as a crime, apparently still continue.[16]

Where police action is taken, the criminal justice system may still operate to deter or discourage victims from making a complaint. The Crown Prosecution Service, which must decide on whether to proceed with a charge, and on what offence to prosecute, has been accused of frequently discontinuing, or 'down criming' a charge,[17] thus reinforcing the perception that 'domestic' violence is regarded as less

9 *Stalking – The Solutions*, July 1996.
10 See Lawson-Cruttenden and Addison *Guide to the Protection from Harassment Act 1997* (1997).
11 See Edwards *Policing 'Domestic' Violence* (1989) ch 2 and *Sex and Gender in the Legal Process* (1996) ch 5; Victim Support, op cit ch 2.
12 See ante, p 57, and for consideration of the legality of the retrospective declaration that rape within marriage is a criminal offence, see Gandhi and James 'Marital rape and retrospectivity – the human rights dimensions at Strasbourg' (1997) 9 CFLQ 17.
13 See Edwards *Sex and Gender in the Legal Process* pp 196–8.
14 Home Office Circular 60/1990, quoted in Home Affairs Committee Third Report, *Domestic Violence* HC 245 para 14.
15 Ibid, paras 23–32, and see Edwards *Sex and Gender in the Legal Process* pp 193–5.
16 Home Affairs Committee, op cit, paras 15–22, Edwards *Sex and Gender in the Legal Process* pp 195–7, Victim Support, op cit, paras 2.3–2.19.
17 Edwards, ibid, p 200–1; Cretney and Davis 'Prosecuting "Domestic" Assault' [1996] Crim LR 162.

serious than other crime, and deterring victims from making complaints. Where a prosecution is brought, the complainant may be placed under considerable emotional strain and may have good reason to fear reprisals if the accused is released on bail pending his trial or, in any case, after his ultimate release. Although an accused's spouse is now a compellable witness for the prosecution in cases of assault and unmarried partners have always been compellable,[18] there have been instances of insensitive handling of victims who are too scared to testify. In one notorious case, where the victim refused to give evidence, thus forcing the prosecution to drop charges against her boyfriend who had allegedly attacked her, the trial judge committed her to prison for contempt of court.[19] While one might applaud the judge's wish to bring home to the victim, and to others, the importance that should be attached to dealing seriously with domestic violence, the method of doing so was hardly calculated to appear as if a 'justice' system was operating. In fact, complainants may not always have to give oral testimony, since under s 23 of the Criminal Justice Act 1988 a statement made in a document by a person to a police officer may be admissible as evidence of any fact of which direct oral evidence by that person would be admissible, where the witness does not give oral evidence through fear. The court has a discretion whether to admit the statement, and must take account of the risk of unfairness to the accused in the lack of an opportunity to cross-examine the witness. This could provide a means of protecting a victim from some of the stress of giving evidence, but appears to have been rarely invoked by the prosecution in domestic violence cases.[20]

Even where a prosecution is successful, there remains the question of the appropriate sentence. In the past, it appeared that leniency was frequently shown to 'domestic' violence perpetrators, and although the Court of Appeal held in *R v Cutts* that:

> '. . . the fact that a serious assault occurs in a domestic scene is no mitigation whatsoever and no reason for proceedings not being taken and condign punishment following in a proper case',[1]

there is a concern that too often a perpetrator is fined, or sentenced to a community penalty, which obviously runs the risk of leaving the victim vulnerable to further abuse. Yet imprisonment may be equally damaging, curtailing the perpetrator's income which may have supported the family, and, unless some form of treatment is available during his sentence, leaving him no better able to manage his behaviour than before.

2.   PROTECTION FROM HARASSMENT [2]

Notwithstanding these problems, public recognition of 'harassment' as behaviour deserving of criminal sanction has led to a number of initiatives to widen the ambit

---

18 Police and Criminal Evidence Act 1984 s 80, see ante, p 61.

19 *R v Renshaw* [1989] Crim LR 811.

20 See Home Affairs Committee, op cit paras 60–61.

1 [1987] Fam Law 311 per Michael Davies J.

2 Before the enactment of the 1997 Act, one means of obtaining protection from harassment was to apply to the magistrates for an order binding over the other party to be of good behaviour. Failure to comply is punishable by committal to prison for a period of six months or until compliance: Magistrates' Courts Act 1980 s 115. The defendant may also be required to find sureties. See Parker 'The Taking of Recognizances as a Matrimonial Remedy' (1997) 9 Fam Law 76.

of existing offences,[3] and to create new offences designed expressly to deal with the problem.

Extending the ambit of existing offences

A series of unwanted telephone calls during which the caller simply remained silent, but which put the recipients in immediate fear for their safety and caused them psychological injury, was held capable of amounting to assault occasioning actual bodily harm in *R v Ireland, R v Burstow*.[4] Such pestering by phone-calling is well-documented in the law reports as a form of harassment when a relationship has broken down,[5] and the precedent could therefore be used in an appropriate 'domestic' case. However, it should be noted that the appellant had pleaded guilty, and it may be difficult to establish the apprehension of immediate personal violence required for the offence of assault.[6]

There are other, statutory, offences which might be relevant.[7] Section 4A of the Public Order Act 1986[8] makes it an offence if a person, with intent to cause harassment, alarm or distress, uses threatening, abusive or insulting words or behaviour thereby causing the victim harassment, alarm or distress. Section 1 of the Malicious Communications Act 1988 provides that it is an offence to send a letter which conveys, inter alia, a threat, with the purpose of causing distress or anxiety to the recipient.[9] Section 43 of the Telecommunications Act 1984 provides that a person who sends, by means of a public telecommunications system, a message or other matter which is, inter alia, of a menacing character, or persistently makes use of the system for the purpose of causing annoyance, inconvenience or needless anxiety to another, commits an offence.[10] The difficulty of convicting under these provisions lies primarily in proving the appropriate mens rea on the part of the accused.

New offences – the Protection from Harassment Act 1997

The Protection from Harassment Act 1997 is intended to overcome these problems. It is intended to apply primarily to 'stalkers',[11] who may often be strangers to the victim, but it is drafted in broad terms, and could well be invoked by a spouse or partner, or by someone who falls outside the range of those covered by the Family Law Act 1996 Part IV, discussed below. The Act contains both criminal and civil law provisions. The former are dealt with here, and the latter below.[12]

---

3 See the discussion by Wells, op cit pp 465–9; Lawson-Cruttenden 'Psychological assault and harassment' (1996) 146 NLJ 1326.
4 [1998] AC 147, [1997] 4 All ER 225, HL. See Gardner 'Stalking' (1998) 114 LQR 33.
5 See, for example, *Khorasandjian v Bush* [1993] QB 727, [1993] 3 All ER 669, CA (overruled as to the law by *Hunter and Others v Canary Wharf Ltd* [1997] 2 All ER 426, HL), *Johnson v Walton* [1990] 1 FLR 350, CA, *Smith v Smith* [1988] 1 FLR 179, CA.
6 Where psychiatric illness is the injury complained of as a result of an assault, psychiatric evidence must be produced to establish the causal link: *R v Morris* [1998] 1 Cr App Rep 386, CA.
7 For a full survey of 'threats' offences, some of which would be applicable to the domestic sphere, see Alldridge 'Threats Offences – A Case for Reform' [1994] Crim LR 176.
8 Inserted by Criminal Justice and Public Order Act 1994 s 154. The offence is punishable by up to six months' imprisonment and/or a fine not exceeding level 5 of the standard scale.
9 The penalty is a fine not exceeding level 4 on the standard scale.
10 Punishable by up to six months' imprisonment and/or a fine not exceeding level 5 on the standard scale.
11 The term probably derives from the United States, where the first 'anti-stalking' law was enacted by California; see Morville 'Stalking Laws: Are They Solutions for More Problems?' (1993) 71 Wash ULQ 921.
12 At p 211.

(a) Harassment

Section 1 of the Act provides that:

'(1) A person must not pursue a course of conduct –
    (a) which amounts to harassment of another; and
    (b) which he knows or ought to know amounts to harassment of the other.
(2) For the purposes of this section, the person whose course of conduct is in question ought to know that it amounts to harassment of another if a reasonable person in possession of the same information would think the course of conduct amounted to harassment of the other.'

Although the Act does not define harassment, s 7(2) provides that 'references to harassing a person include alarming the person or causing the person distress'.[13] It also provides that a '"course of conduct" must involve conduct on at least two occasions'.[14] A person who pursues a course of conduct in breach of s 1 is guilty of the offence of harassment, and liable on summary conviction to imprisonment for up to six months or a fine not exceeding level 5 on the standard scale or both.[15] It is clear that the objective test of mens rea utilised in s 1(1)(a) is designed to overcome the problems of the other statutory offences discussed above. The provision that harassment includes causing alarm or distress should obviate the need to prove psychological injury as is required for a charge of assault. It is necessary, however, to show that the conduct complained of has occurred on at least two occasions, so that a single incident (for example, bursting in on the estranged spouse while he or she is at work, and shouting and swearing at her in front of colleagues, or sending photographs of the victim in a semi-nude state to a national newspaper[16]) would not be an offence under this Act, though the former activity might be under the Public Order Act 1986 s 4A, and the latter might be covered by the 1997 Act if, as appears to occur frequently, the perpetrator gave the 'exclusive' prints to a number of different tabloid newspapers.[17] The requirement to show a course of conduct appears to differentiate the kind of harassment intended to be covered from eg sexual harassment in the workplace, where a single incident would suffice.[18]

(b) Putting in fear of violence

The Act also creates a more serious offence under s 4, which provides that:

'A person whose course of conduct causes another to fear, on at least two occasions, that violence will be used against him is guilty of an offence if he knows or ought to know that his course of conduct will cause the other so to fear on each of those occasions.'

13 It has been said that the courts should interpret these words narrowly: *Huntingdon Life Sciences Ltd v Curtin* (1997) Times, 11 December (political protests and demonstrations are outside the ambit of the Act).
14 Section 7(3).
15 Section 2.
16 *Johnson v Walton* [1990] 1 FLR 350, CA.
17 But cf *C v C (Non-Molestation Order: Jurisdiction)* [1998] Fam 70, [1998] 1 FLR 554, where a former husband was refused a non-molestation order under Part IV of the Family Law Act 1996 to restrain his ex-wife making revelations to a tabloid newspaper, because, inter alia, the aim was to seek to impose a gagging order which would threaten the freedom of the press. It is arguable that a court would apply similar reasoning to refuse to find the offence under s 1 made out.
18 *Porcelli v Strathclyde Regional Council* [1986] ICR 564, Court of Session; *Scott v Combined Property Services Ltd* (1996) EAT/757/96.

It has been suggested, by Lord Steyn in *R v Ireland*, that it will be difficult to prove that a victim has cause to fear that violence *will*, rather than *may* be used against her, and that therefore this provision is not well-suited to dealing with the problem of menacing phone calls.[19] However, the mens rea is to be judged objectively, which should make the burden of proof somewhat easier for the prosecution. For this offence, the maximum sentence, if the accused is convicted on indictment, is five years' imprisonment, a fine, or both, or, on summary conviction, to imprisonment for six months, the statutory maximum fine, or both.[20] Where a person is tried on indictment, the jury may return a verdict under s 2 where they find him not guilty under s 4.[1]

(c)   Restraining orders

A novel and important feature of the 1997 Act is the power, contained in s 5, to enable a court sentencing a person under s 2 or s 4[2] to make an order, similar to a civil injunction, called a 'restraining order', which prohibits the defendant from doing anything which would amount to further harassment or would cause a fear of violence on the part of the victim of the offence or any other person mentioned in the order. Thus, a criminal court, sentencing the defendant for an offence of harassment of his wife, could make a restraining order against him in respect of their children as well. The order may be of fixed or indefinite duration,[3] and breach of its terms without reasonable excuse is itself an offence punishable by imprisonment of up to five years and/or a fine.[4] Such an order is intended to deal with the problem, noted above, that criminal penalties may be inadequate to protect the victim from further offences.

The extent to which these provisions might be used is difficult to estimate.[5] It may be that prosecuting authorities may welcome the opportunity to use provisions clearly geared to tackling the difficult problem of pestering, rather than having to strain the definition of existing offences to fit the circumstances, and they may see some deterrent value in using the Act vigorously. Victims too may see sufficient value in the restraining order to overcome their prior well-founded reluctance to engage with the criminal law. On the other hand, the underlying problems of using the criminal law, discussed above, are likely to affect the 1997 Act as well, in which case, the civil law will remain the preferred avenue of redress.

3.   CRIMINAL INJURIES COMPENSATION

While it is likely that a domestic violence victim's main concern will be to obtain protection from the abuser, either in the form of penal measures which remove him from the scene or deter him from repetition, or in the form of the provision of

---

19 [1997] 4 All ER 225 at 228g.
20 Section 4(4).
 1 Section 4(5).
 2 The power is not, therefore, available where the person has been acquitted of the charge.
 3 Section 5(3)(b). The prosecutor, defendant or any person mentioned in the order may apply to the court for it to be varied or discharged: s 5(4).
 4 Where convicted on indictment; on summary conviction, the penalty is imprisonment for up to six months and/or the maximum statutory fine: s 5(5).
 5 It has been suggested, without explanation, that there may be as many as 5,000 cases of harassment each year, of which 2,000 could be prosecuted, although the government put the likely number of prosecutions at only 200: Lawson-Cruttenden and Addison 'The Protection from Harassment Act' (1997) 147 NLJ 983.

safe housing (discussed below), the winning of compensation may also be valuable, both in the financial redress it may give, and also as public recognition that the victim was not to blame for the violence.[6] In many instances, the perpetrator may not have sufficient assets to make him worth suing in tort, but the Criminal Injuries Compensation Scheme[7] provides a state-funded avenue of redress. Under the scheme, compensation may be paid to an applicant who has sustained a criminal injury directly attributable to a crime of violence (including arson or an act of poisoning). It seems that a threat of violence, such as an assault without physical contact, or possibly a threat amounting to harassment under the 1997 Act, would suffice.[8] Mental injury, in the form of a medically recognised psychiatric or psychological illness, is included within the scheme. An application must normally be brought within two years of the incident giving rise to the injury.[9] It is not necessary for the perpetrator to have been convicted for an award to be made. Any award will be made up of a standard amount of compensation according to a tariff of amounts for differing injuries (ranging from £1,000 for a simple broken nose, to £250,000 for permanent severe brain damage[10]) together with a sum for loss of earnings.

Originally, the scheme excluded virtually all cases of domestic violence. There were a number of reasons for this: it was feared that it would be difficult to establish the facts; there would be a large number of claims, many of them trivial; if the parties were subsequently reconciled, any compensation awarded would increase the family assets as a whole and consequently the offender would benefit from his own wrong.[11] It was obvious, however, that many seriously injured women were being prevented from making genuine claims. Consequently the scheme was modified in 1979 to permit domestic violence claims,[12] although some account is still taken of these fears.

Under the scheme, a claims officer employed by the Criminal Injuries Compensation Authority must be satisfied that there is no likelihood that an assailant would benefit if an award were made, or, if the victim is a minor, that it would not be against his interest to make an award. If, at the time of the injury, the victim and assailant were living in the same household as members of the same family, compensation can be claimed only if the following conditions are satisfied:[13]

(a) The assailant must have been prosecuted for the offence, except where a claims officer considers that there are practical, technical or other good reasons for there having been no prosecution.
(b) In the case of violence between adults in the family, the victim and the assailant must have stopped living in the same household before the application for compensation was made and it must seem unlikely that they will share the same household again.

---

6 Cobley 'Financial Compensation for Victims of Child Abuse' (1998) 20 JSWFL 221.
7 The scheme, which had been a non-statutory ex gratia scheme since its inception in 1964, was placed on a statutory footing by the Criminal Injuries Compensation Act 1995, and the current rules came into force on 1 April 1996.
8 Criminal Injuries Compensation Authority, *Victims of Crimes of Violence: A Guide to the Criminal Injuries Compensation Scheme* TS2 4/96 paras 7.7, 7.9.
9 Home Office, *The Criminal Injuries Compensation Scheme* TS1 (1996) para 17.
10 Home Office, op cit, pp 19, 21.
11 Freeman *Violence in the Family* p 182.
12 Claims based on domestic violence before that date cannot be brought: *R v CICB, ex p P* [1993] 2 FLR 600.
13 Home Office, *The Criminal Injuries Compensation Scheme* para 16.

The claims officer may withhold or reduce compensation if all reasonable steps have not been taken promptly to inform the police; the applicant has failed to co-operate with the police or other authority in attempting to bring the assailant to justice, or has failed to co-operate with the authority in connection with the compensation application; the applicant's conduct before, during or after the incident giving rise to the application makes it inappropriate to make a full, or any award at all; or the applicant's character, as shown by his criminal convictions, makes it inappropriate to make a full (or any) award.[14]

It will be seen that these requirements impose some burdens upon the victims of domestic violence. We have seen that victims may be reluctant to prosecute, for a variety of reasons, which are not usually 'practical' or 'technical' but have more to do with fear of the repercussions of taking action. Are such reasons 'good' ones in the eyes of claims officers? If the victim, having initiated police action, then withdraws her complaint, will her conduct make it inappropriate to make an award? And, most importantly, only where the parties' relationship has broken down and appears to be over, will an award be made. Clearly, relationships where, despite violence or other abusive behaviour having occurred, there is still some scope for reconciliation, are outside the scope of this scheme, a fact already underlined by the £1,000 minimum award in the tariff.

It is not surprising, with all the shortcomings surrounding the criminal justice system, that victims may prefer to turn to the civil law for a remedy.

C.   Civil law remedies

As noted above, the law relating to the grant of orders intended to enjoin the respondent from attacking or pestering the victim, or to exclude him from the family home, had become a confused and complicated jumble of jurisdictions. Part IV of the Family Law Act 1996 is intended to simplify and improve the protection given by the civil courts, largely by bringing jurisdictions together, but there remains a residual power in the courts to issue injunctions ancillary to substantive proceedings, and there is a new power to bring a claim in civil proceedings for breach of s 1 of the Protection from Harassment Act 1997, backed up by an injunction. There is also power, available to courts dealing with both spouses and cohabitants whose home is held on a tenancy, to provide a long-term solution to their problem by transferring the home between them, and these are dealt with in the next sections. Here, we consider the remedies provided by the 1996 Act.

1.   THE FAMILY LAW ACT 1996 PART IV [15]

The scheme of Part IV

Part IV sets out the rights of spouses to occupy the matrimonial home where they lack a proprietary right to do so.[16] It provides for two categories of orders to be

---

14 Ibid, para 13.
15 Horton *Family Homes and Domestic Violence: The New Legislation*; Bird *Domestic Violence and Protection from Harassment*; La Follette and Purdie *A Guide to the Family Law Act 1996*.
16 These are called 'matrimonial home rights' and are discussed in detail in Chapter 2.

made, occupation orders[17] and non-molestation orders.[18] The High Court, county courts and magistrates' courts all have jurisdiction to make such orders, subject to the Lord Chancellor's power to specify that certain types of proceedings be commenced in, or transferred to, a specified level of court,[19] and to a restriction in s 59(1) preventing magistrates from hearing cases where there is a disputed question as to a party's entitlement to occupy any property, unless it is unnecessary to determine that question in order to deal with the case. The Law Commission's aim of creating a unified jurisdiction has therefore not quite been achieved, although all courts will at least be applying the same rules in the same types of case. Part IV also continues, and enhances, former powers to grant orders ex parte,[20] to accept undertakings in lieu of making orders,[1] to enforce orders,[2] and to deal with abuse against children.[3] These are discussed in turn.

(a) Non-molestation orders

Although the Act deals with non-molestation orders after occupation orders, we discuss them first, because they are the more likely and common order to be granted. Under the Domestic Violence and Matrimonial Proceedings Act 1976, nearly seven times as many non-molestation injunctions as ouster injunctions were granted by county courts,[4] and although the number of occupation orders will probably increase under the new law, they are likely to remain only a small proportion of the overall total.

Section 42(1) provides that a non-molestation order:

> '. . . means an order containing either or both of the following provisions –
> (a) provision prohibiting . . . the respondent from molesting another person who is associated with the respondent;
> (b) provision prohibiting the respondent from molesting a relevant child.'[5]

(b) What is molestation?

Reflecting the response to the Law Commission's proposals that any attempt at a definition might reduce the level of protection afforded by the former law, 'molestation' is deliberately not defined in the Act.[6] Instead, its meaning is left to case law under the previous legislation, where it had been regarded as meaning 'deliberate conduct which substantially interferes with the applicant or child, whether by violence, intimidation, harassment, pestering or interference sufficiently

---

17 Sections 33–41.
18 Section 42.
19 Section 57. The Family Law Act 1996 (Part IV) (Allocation of Proceedings) Order 1997 SI 1997/1896 provides that proceedings will generally be commenced in either the family proceedings court or county court. Applications by children must be made to the High Court.
20 Section 45.
 1 Section 46.
 2 Section 47, ss 50–51.
 3 Section 52 and Sch 6, discussed in Chapter 14 at pp 577 and 594.
 4 In 1996, 19,707 non-molestation injunctions and 2,945 ouster injunctions were granted: *Judicial Statistics 1996* Table 5.9, Cm 3716.
 5 A 'relevant child' is defined by s 62(2) as any child who is living with, or might reasonably be expected to live with either party to the proceedings, any child in relation to whom an order under the Adoption Act 1976 or the Children Act 1989 is in question in the proceedings, or any other child whose interests the court considers relevant.
 6 Law Com No 207 at para 3.1.

serious to warrant intervention by a court.'[7] This clearly overlaps with, though is wider in terms than, the concept of harassment under the Protection from Harassment Act 1997, since there is no requirement to prove a 'course of conduct', meaning conduct on at least two occasions. On the other hand, the 1997 provision may be broader in scope, since it provides that harassment includes causing alarm or distress, whereas molestation must pass a 'seriousness' hurdle, and it is open to a court to consider that the conduct complained of is not sufficiently serious to warrant its intervention.[8]

(c)   Who may apply for an order?

Under the former law, problems arose because only spouses or cohabitants could seek an injunction or order without also having to take civil proceedings, usually in tort. The Law Commission were concerned to extend the range of applicants for non-molestation orders, but were against providing a remedy open to anyone, regardless of their relationship with the respondent.[9] They reasoned that a domestic or family relationship justifies special remedies and procedures because the proximity of the parties gives rise to heightened emotions in situations of stress, and because of the likelihood that the relationship will continue. They considered that extending equal protection to neighbours, tenants and victims of sexual harassment would be going too far.[10] However, the Protection from Harassment Act 1997, as we shall see, opens up the possibility of obtaining an injunction to restrain harassment to any person who can prove that the respondent has acted in breach of s 1.

Instead, the Law Commission proposed basing eligibility upon a person's 'association' with another, and suggested a range of such associations. Not all of these were accepted by the government, but the list which emerged as s 62(3) is as follows:

'a person is "associated with" another person if –
(a) they are, or have been married to each other;[11]
(b) they are cohabitants[12] or former cohabitants;[13]
(c) they live or have lived in the same household, otherwise than merely by reason of one of them being the other's employee, tenant, lodger or boarder;

---

7 His Honour Judge Fricker 'Molestation and Harassment after *Patel v Patel*' [1988] Fam Law 395 at 399.
8 In *C v C (Non-Molestation Order: Jurisdiction)* [1998] Fam 70, [1998] 1 FLR 554, Sir Stephen Brown P held that a non-molestation order should only be granted where there was some conduct which clearly harassed and affected the applicant to such a degree that the court's intervention was called for, and refused an order to prevent a former wife passing details about her ex-husband and their marriage to a tabloid newspaper. See also *Spindlow v Spindlow* [1979] Fam 52, [1979] 1 All ER 169, CA, where, although the respondent father was excluded from the home (on grounds which were later disapproved by the House of Lords in *Richards v Richards* [1984] AC 174, [1983] 2 All ER 807), a non-molestation order was lifted because the only conduct complained of was one incident where he pushed the mother onto a settee, shouting at her, and threatening to smack her daughter.
9 As is possible in New South Wales, South Australia, Western Australia and Tasmania: see the discussion by the Law Commission in Report No 207 para 3.9. Similar concern at the problems of opening up the jurisdiction too far were expressed, in a related context, by Lord Goff of Chievely in *Hunter v Canary Wharf Ltd* [1997] 2 All ER 426 at 439h, discussed further below at p 212.
10 Ibid paras 3.17, 3.19.
11 The provisions of Part IV apply to polygamous as well as monogamous marriages: s 63(5).
12 Defined by s 62(1)(a) as meaning a man and a woman who, although not married to each other, are living together as husband and wife.
13 This phrase does not include a couple who subsequently marry: s 62(1)(b).

(d) they are relatives; [14]
(e) they have agreed to marry one another (whether or not that agreement has been terminated); [15]
(f) in relation to any child, they are both persons falling within subsection (4); or
(g) they are parties to the same family proceedings'. [16]

Section 62(4) provides that:

'a person falls within this subsection in relation to a child if –
(a) he is a parent of the child; or
(b) he has or has had parental responsibility for the child.' [17]

Under s 43, a child under the age of 16 may seek an order, with leave of the court, which may be granted if the court is satisfied that the child has sufficient understanding to make the application. The test is the same as applies in relation to a child seeking leave to seek a s 8 order under the Children Act 1989, and the case law relating to that test is equally applicable. [18]

This list covers the main groups who were regarded as needing protection by virtue of an order. Couples whose marriage or cohabitation relationship has ended were excluded from the ambit of the former law, yet it appears that a significant number of cases of domestic violence may involve such couples, [19] and hence they are now included. Once it is accepted that those in a relationship which does not *presently* involve cohabitation ought to be able to seek an order, yet not to open up the jurisdiction to all-comers, it then becomes necessary to determine where to draw the boundaries and thereby define what apparently amounts to a domestic or family relationship. This list gives us a picture of modern thinking on this issue, although it is not unproblematic. For example, it does not expressly include homosexual couples, although it is clear that if they live, or have lived together, they will come within category (c). The Law Commission proposed a broader definition which would have included both hetero- and homo-sexual relationships without cohabitation, defined, rather cunningly, as those who 'have or have had a sexual relationship with each other (whether or not including sexual intercourse)' [20] but this was rejected. It may be pondered, however, why it is felt appropriate to permit an applicant to obtain an order against a former cohabitant's stepmother, for

14 Defined in s 63(1) as '(a) the father, mother, stepfather, stepmother, son, daughter, stepson, stepdaughter, grandmother, grandfather, grandson or granddaughter of that person or that person's spouse or former spouse, or (b) the brother, sister, uncle, aunt, niece or nephew (whether of the full blood or the half blood or by affinity) of that person or of that person's spouse or former spouse, and includes, in relation to a person who is living or has lived with another person as husband and wife, any person who would fall within paragraph (a) or (b) if the parties were married to each other'.
15 Section 44 provides that such an agreement must be evidenced in writing, or by the gift of an engagement ring, or by a ceremony entered into by the parties in the presence of witnesses – which looks like the definition for an old-fashioned betrothal ceremony, but quaere whether it would be satisfied by an engagement party? See ante, p 25. No application for a non-molestation order may be brought in reliance on a former engagement more than three years after the date on which it was terminated: s 42(4).
16 These are defined in s 63(1) and (2).
17 Additionally, s 62(5) provides that, if a child has been adopted or freed for adoption, two persons are also associated with each other if one is the natural parent, or parent of such a natural parent, and the other is the child, or any person who is an adoptive parent of the child, or has had the child placed with him for adoption. The aim of this provision is presumably to enable adopters to utilise the Act to obtain orders to prevent birth relatives from 'pestering' the adoptive family.
18 Children Act 1989 s 10(8), discussed below at pp 437–8.
19 See Law Com No 207 para 3.18.
20 Ibid, para 3.26.

example, but not against the 'boyfriend' from whom they have split up after a lengthy period of non-cohabitational courtship, or their former 'mistress'.

(d)   When may an order be made?

The court may make an order on a free-standing application, or where an application is made in other family proceedings.[1] It may also make an order of its own motion in any family proceedings to which the respondent is a party, if it considers that the order should be made for the benefit of any other party, or of any relevant child.[2] These provisions give flexibility both to parties and the court. Clearly, an applicant should be able to obtain an order without having to take other proceedings, as was recognised by the Domestic Violence and Matrimonial Proceedings Act 1976, but it is equally useful to enable an application to be attached to proceedings already under way, and to give the court a reserve power to make an order even where no application has been made. Indeed, such a power might prove helpful where a party is reluctant to be seen to be seeking an order for fear of antagonising the respondent.

(e)   Criteria for the grant of an order

In deciding whether to make the order, and if so, in what manner:

> '. . . the court shall have regard to all the circumstances, including the need to secure the health, safety and well-being –
> (a) of the applicant, or . . . the person for whose benefit the order is being made; and
> (b) of any relevant child.'[3]

The purpose of this test is to focus the court's attention upon the victim's need for protection, rather than to scrutinise the nature and quality of the perpetrator's conduct, and to give guidance, especially to magistrates, in exercising the powers under the section. Courts operating the old law apparently experienced little difficulty in determining when it would be appropriate to grant non-molestation injunctions, and the new test is not expected to cause problems.[4]

(f)   Terms of a non-molestation order

Formerly, a non-molestation injunction generally ordered the respondent not to use violence, threaten, harass or pester the applicant or a named child. Under s 42(6), a non-molestation order may be expressed so as to refer to molestation in general, to particular acts of molestation, or to both, which gives the court flexibility to outline certain kinds of prohibited conduct or to leave the prohibition in general terms.[5] For example, a court could prohibit the respondent from telephoning the victim, or from loitering outside her place of work, or from coming within a certain distance of her home.[6]

---

1   Section 42(2)(a). Family proceedings are defined in s 63(1), (2) and include proceedings where the court has made an emergency protection order under s 44 of the Children Act 1989 which includes an exclusion requirement: see post, p 594.
2   Section 42(2)(b). A relevant child is any child who is living with or might reasonably be expected to live with either party to the proceedings; any child in relation to whom an order under the Adoption Act 1976 or the Children Act 1989 is in question in the proceedings; and any other child whose interests the court considers relevant: s 62(2).
3   Section 42(5).
4   See Law Com No 207 para 3.6.
5   Ibid para 3.2.
6   As in *Burris v Azadani* [1995] 4 All ER 802, CA, discussed post, p 200.

The order may be for a fixed period or until further order, and one made in other family proceedings will cease to have effect if those proceedings are withdrawn or dismissed.[7] This is regrettable: the withdrawal or dismissal of a party's application for, say, a contact order in children proceedings does not necessarily mean that a non-molestation order, which the court considered appropriate in the light of those proceedings, is no longer required. Presumably, the onus would be on the victim to apply for a free-standing order in such circumstances.

The order may be varied or discharged on application by the respondent or applicant, and, where it was made on the court's own motion, may be varied or discharged by the court, even though no application has been made.[8]

Occupation orders

The second type of order which can be made under the 1996 Act is far more complicated. An occupation order may declare or regulate the right to occupy the family home, but the detailed terms of the order will vary according to the eligibility of the applicant, as will the criteria determining whether the order should be granted. Declaratory orders may 'declare, confer or extend occupation rights', while regulatory orders 'just control the exercise of existing rights'.[9]

(a) Who may apply?

Applications may be free-standing or made in other family proceedings, but the court has no power to make an order of its own motion.[10] The range of permitted applicants is much narrower than in the case of non-molestation orders, because the Law Commission were concerned that the interference with the enjoyment of property rights when requiring a respondent to leave his own home or let the applicant into it is harder to justify where the applicant has no such property rights herself.[11] They also considered that, for non-entitled applicants, the purpose of seeking an order is to obtain short-term protection until they can find an alternative home, whereas entitled applicants might be seeking medium- or long-term regulation of the property.[12] The Act accordingly does not employ the concept of the 'associated person' used in relation to non-molestation orders, but instead distinguishes between two categories of applicant: those deemed 'entitled', and those who are 'non-entitled' applicants, in property law terms. We deal with the position of entitled applicants first, and then with non-entitled applicants.

(b) Entitled applicants

Under s 33(1)(a), an entitled applicant is a person who:

'(i) is entitled to occupy a dwelling-house by virtue of a beneficial estate or interest or contract or by virtue of any enactment giving him the right to remain in occupation, or
(ii) has matrimonial home rights[13] in relation to a dwelling-house'.

---

7 Section 42(7) and (8).
8 Section 49(1) and (2).
9 Law Com No 207 para 4.1.
10 Section 39(2).
11 Law Com No 207 para 4.7.
12 Ibid.
13 Matrimonial home rights are granted by s 30(2) and discussed in Chapter 2, ante.

Such an applicant may seek an order where the dwelling-house[14] is or at any time has been the home of the applicant and a person with whom he is associated,[15] or was intended by them to be their home.[16]

(c)   Types of occupation orders in favour of entitled applicants

Under s 33, the applicant may seek an order containing any of a list of provisions specified. Declaratory orders may simply declare that the applicant is entitled to occupy the home by virtue of property law or matrimonial home rights,[17] or may provide that the applicant's matrimonial home rights are to continue beyond the death of the other spouse or the termination of the marriage.[18] Such orders per se seem to have limited utility, except in situations where, perhaps, the spouse is contesting a property claim by a third party with whom he or she is associated, such as, for example, her brother-in-law who is a joint owner of the family home,[19] or where there is a need to safeguard the applicant's position after divorce or death of the other party, perhaps pending resolution of any ancillary relief or family provision claim which might be made.

Of greater utility are regulatory orders. These may:

'(a)   enforce the applicant's entitlement to remain in occupation as against the . . . respondent . . . ;

(b)   require the respondent to permit the applicant to enter and remain in the dwelling-house or part of the dwelling-house;

(c)   regulate the occupation of the dwelling-house by either or both parties;

(d)   if the respondent is entitled [as mentioned in s 33(1)(a)(i)], prohibit, suspend or restrict the exercise by him of his right to occupy the dwelling-house;

(e)   if the respondent has matrimonial home rights in relation to the dwelling-house and the applicant is the other spouse, restrict or terminate those rights;

(f)   require the respondent to leave the dwelling-house or part of the dwelling-house; or

(g)   exclude the respondent from a defined area in which the dwelling-house is included.'[20]

These provisions can be used flexibly to meet the circumstances of the particular case. For example, an order could prevent the respondent from changing the locks of the home to keep the applicant out, or require him to let her back in; require either party to quit the home at certain times, for example, at weekends; require the respondent to leave the home, or prohibit him from entering certain parts of it, eg a bedroom; or, as in *Burris v Azadani*,[1] prohibit him from entering within a certain distance of the home.

---

14   Section 62(1) defines a dwelling house, for the purposes of an occupation order, as including (a) any building, or part of a building which is occupied as a dwelling, and (b) any caravan, house-boat or structure which is occupied as a dwelling.

15   As defined by s 62(3). No application may be brought based on a former agreement to marry after the period of three years beginning with the date the engagement was terminated: s 33(2).

16   Section 33(1)(b).

17   Section 33(4).

18   Section 33(5), but an order may not be made after the death of either of the parties: s 33(9)(a). The Matrimonial Homes Act 1983 s 2(4) contained a similar provision.

19   But cf *Kalsi v Kalsi* [1992] 1 FLR 511, CA: a wife was not entitled to declaration of her rights of occupation in the matrimonial home as against her husband's three brothers who were legal owners, with her husband, of the property.

20   Section 33(3).

1   [1995] 4 All ER 802, CA; 250 yards from the home.

(d)   Criteria for an order in favour of entitled applicants

No test is laid down for the court to apply when deciding whether to make a simple declaratory order that the applicant is a person entitled, since the issue will depend purely on whether the court finds that the applicant has the property or matrimonial home rights contended for. Where the court is considering whether to extend matrimonial home rights, it may do so whenever it considers that, in all the circumstances, it is just and reasonable.[2]

(e)   The balance of harm test

In relation to making a regulatory order, the Law Commission were concerned to provide a test which would meet the varied circumstances which might arise in individual cases, such as the degree of danger being faced by the applicant, the ability to find alternative accommodation at short notice, and any need for a longer-term solution to the problem. They were also keen to deal with the perceived shortcomings of the test under the Matrimonial Homes Act 1983 which, as we have seen, placed emphasis upon the misconduct of the respondent rather than upon the needs of the applicant and any children, effectively reintroducing the concept of fault into the law when the trend has been to promote settlement of problems without recrimination.[3] Accordingly, they proposed a 'balance of harm' test, which would enable the court to strike a balance between being fair to respondents on the one hand, and ensuring the protection of the victims on the other, and which would elevate the court's *power* to make an order into a *duty* to do so, where the effects upon the victims are sufficiently grave.

Under s 33(6), the court is required to have regard to all the circumstances, including:

'(a) the housing needs and resources of each of the parties and of any relevant child;
(b) the financial resources of each of the parties;
(c) the likely effect of any order, or of any decision by the court not to exercise its powers under subsection (3), on the health, safety or well-being of the parties and of any relevant child; and
(d) the conduct of the parties in relation to each other and otherwise.'

This test largely[4] reproduces the former test under the Matrimonial Homes Act 1983 s 1(3), but paragraph (c) helps to emphasise the importance of considering the effect of the court's decision, rather than the conduct which triggered the application.

(f)   Presumption of harm test

If it appears to the court that the applicant or a relevant child is likely to suffer significant harm attributable to conduct of the respondent if an order is not made, the court *must* make an order unless it appears that the respondent or a relevant child is likely to suffer greater harm in consequence of the order being made. 'Significant harm' is a term taken from the Children Act 1989.[5] 'Harm' is defined in s 63(3) to mean, in relation to a person aged 18 or over, ill-treatment or the impairment of health, and, in relation to a *child*, ill-treatment or the impairment of

2 Section 33(8).
3 Law Com No 207 paras 4.20, 4.23.
4 Conduct was not included in the test proposed by the Law Commission: see ibid para 4.33.
5 See s 31, discussed post, p 539.

health or development. Interestingly, the section provides that ill-treatment includes sexual abuse only in relation to a child. The reason for this limitation is unclear.

There is thus a *presumption* that an order will be made where there is evidence that the applicant or a child might otherwise suffer significant harm from the respondent's conduct, and this ought to make courts more willing to make an order against the respondent than was the case under the former law. However, it should be noted that the Law Commission's formulation of this presumption did not require a causal connection between the harm and the respondent's conduct.[6] It will be for the courts to determine whether, for example, the harm suffered by a mother and her children having to stay in an overcrowded refuge because of fear of the father's violence is attributable to his conduct, or to the inadequate provision of refuges. If the latter, the court would not be bound to make an order, although it still has the discretion to do so. More problematically, the mother may seek to exclude the father from the home because the marriage has broken down and the atmosphere is very tense and the children are consequentially distressed. Even though it is well-documented that children may suffer harm as a result of conflict between the parents,[7] it would be difficult to argue that such harm is attributable to the *father's*, as distinct from the *mother's* conduct so as to bring the presumption into operation. Again, the court would have to exercise its discretion.

(g)   Duration of orders in favour of entitled applicants

By s 33(10), orders may be made for a specified period, until the occurrence of a specified event, or until further order. Under the former law, orders were generally limited to three months' duration with the possibility of renewal,[8] but this was felt to be inadequate in many instances to achieve a resolution of the parties' problems, and 'not obviously appropriate to the regulation of occupation between those who have equal rights to occupy'.[9] As with non-molestation orders, either party may apply for a variation or discharge of the order.[10]

Non-entitled applicants

The Law Commission considered that, where a person has no property right in the home, the possibility of obtaining an occupation order should be limited to cohabitants (who were protected under the Domestic Violence and Matrimonial Proceedings Act 1976 anyway), former cohabitants, and former spouses, as these were the classes of relationship most in need of protection.[11] Accordingly, the Act provides that they may seek an occupation order where the respondent is entitled under property law to occupy the dwelling-house but the applicant is not, as 'non-

---

6   Ibid.
7   Cockett and Tripp *The Exeter Family Study* (1994), Richards and Dyson *Separation, Divorce and the Development of Children: A Review* (1982).
8   *Practice Note* [1978] 1 WLR 1123. Orders were also made of indefinite duration in some cases: see *Spencer v Camacho* (1983) 4 FLR 662, CA and *Galan v Galan* [1985] FLR 905, CA.
9   Law Com No 207 para 4.35, 4.36.
10   Section 49. Where a spouse's matrimonial home rights are a charge on the estate or interest of the other spouse or of trustees for the other spouse, an order under s 33 against the other spouse may be varied or discharged on the application of any person deriving title under the other spouse or trustees and affected by the charge: s 49(3).
11   See Law Com No 207 para 4.8.

entitled applicants'.[12] The order must be in respect of a dwelling-house which is the home they are living in, or have at any time lived in or intended to live in together (if formerly married, as their matrimonial home).[13] Additionally, spouses, former spouses, cohabitants and former cohabitants may seek an order where *neither* party is entitled to occupy the dwelling-house, in respect of the home they are currently living in.[14] This category is intended to deal with the, perhaps relatively uncommon, situation where the couple are occupying a property either as squatters or, more likely, as bare licensees.

(a) Non-entitled applicants where the respondent has property rights

In respect of applications brought by non-entitled applicants where the respondent has property rights, it is necessary to consider three separate issues. First, what provisions may be included in an order? Secondly, what criteria apply to the grant of an order, and to the provisions included within it? Thirdly, how long may an order last? On these last two issues the Act distinguishes, more sharply than the Law Commission had proposed, between former spouses, and current or former cohabitants.

(I) PROVISIONS IN THE ORDER

Declaratory provisions If the applicant is currently in occupation in the dwelling-house an order must contain the following provisions:

'(a) giving the applicant the right not to be evicted or excluded from the dwelling-house or any part of it by the respondent for the period specified in the order; and
(b) prohibiting the respondent from evicting or excluding the applicant during that period.'[15]

Where the applicant is not in occupation, the order must include provision:

'(a) giving the applicant the right to enter into and occupy the dwelling-house for the period specified in the order; and
(b) requiring the respondent to permit the exercise of that right.'[16]

These provisions were termed by the Law Commission as 'occupation rights orders', granting a right to occupy the home to applicants who do not already possess such a right.[17]

Regulatory provisions Additionally, it is provided that a court may also include provisions in the order to:

'(a) regulate the occupation of the dwelling-house by either or both of the parties;
(b) prohibit, suspend or restrict the exercise by the respondent of his right to occupy the dwelling-house;

---

12 Under the former law, it was clearly established by the House of Lords in *Davis v Johnson* [1979] AC 264, [1978] 1 All ER 1132, HL that non-entitled cohabitants could obtain ouster injunctions under the Domestic Violence and Matrimonial Proceedings Act 1976, but the jurisdiction did not extend to those whose cohabitation had ceased a significant time before proceedings were brought: *Harrison v Lewis* [1988] 2 FLR 339, CA, *McLean v Nugent* (1980) 1 FLR 26, CA. Former spouses were outside the ambit of the 1976 Act.
13 Section 35(1) – former spouses; s 36 – cohabitants or former cohabitants.
14 Section 37(1) – spouses and former spouses; and s 38(1) – cohabitants and former cohabitants.
15 Section 35(3) – former spouses; and s 36(3) – cohabitants and former cohabitants.
16 Section 35(4) – former spouses; and s 36(4) – cohabitants and former cohabitants.
17 Law Com No 207 para 4.3.

(c) require the respondent to leave the dwelling-house or part of the dwelling-house; or
(d) exclude the respondent from a defined area in which the dwelling-house is included.

Taken together, these two types of provisions provide the same protection in practice to a non-entitled applicant as to an entitled applicant.[18]

(II)   CRITERIA FOR AN ORDER

Former spouses   In respect of the declaratory provisions in an order, s 35(6) provides that the court must have regard to all the circumstances, including:

'(a) the housing needs and housing resources of each of the parties and of any relevant child;
(b) the financial resources of each of the parties;
(c) the likely effect of any order, or of any decision by the court not to [grant an order], on the health, safety or well-being of the parties and of any relevant child;
(d) the conduct of the parties in relation to each other and otherwise;
(e) the length of time that has elapsed since the parties ceased to live together;
(f) the length of time that has elapsed since the marriage was dissolved or annulled; and
(g) the existence of any pending proceedings between them [relating to property].'[19]

The first four of these factors are the same as apply to applications by entitled applicants. The last three factors are intended to focus attention upon the 'qualification' of the applicant for an order. By this, the Law Commission appear to have meant that, where an applicant is not on an equal footing in property rights terms with the respondent, she needs to show some justification for obtaining a declaratory order giving rights she would not otherwise have, separate from the basic need for protection which is catered for in the regulatory parts of the order.[20]

As far as determining which regulatory provisions might be included, the court is directed to consider the factors in paragraphs (a) to (e) – which may perhaps be viewed as the 'practical' issues, as distinct from ones concerning legal status and proceedings – and then apply the same 'balance of harm' presumption as applies to entitled applicants.[1]

Cohabitants and former cohabitants   Clearly, some of the factors relevant to former spouses, such as the length of time which has elapsed since their marriage ended, cannot be applicable to cohabitants. Equally, the length and nature of a cohabitational relationship can vary enormously, and may be highly relevant to the question whether it would be just to make an order against a respondent. Accordingly, the Law Commission recommended that courts consider certain specific factors pertaining to the cohabitants' relationship when determining whether to make a declaratory order.[2] Parliament chose to emphasise the distinction in the 'quality' of the relationship of married (or formerly married) couples as compared with cohabitants, and added to the relevant criteria. Thus, the

18 But the permitted duration of an order is different: see post, p 205.
19 The proceedings specified are those for a property adjustment order under the Matrimonial Causes Act 1973, for a property order against a parent under the Children Act 1989 Sch 1, or relating to the legal or beneficial ownership of the dwelling-house: s 35(6)(g).
20 See Law Com No 207 para 4.10.
1 Section 35(7)–(8); see the discussion ante, p 201.
2 Law Com No 207 paras 4.10–4.13.

court is obliged to consider, in addition to the factors common to entitled applicants and former spouses:[3]

- the nature of the parties' relationship;
- the length of time they have lived together as husband and wife;
- whether they have, or had, any children together, or whether they share or shared parental responsibility for any child;
- the length of time since they ceased to live together; and
- the existence of any pending proceedings between them over property.[4]

In assessing the nature of the parties' relationship, s 41 requires the court 'to have regard to the fact that they have not given each other the commitment involved in marriage.' This provision was included by Parliament to stress the symbolic significance of marriage and to penalise cohabitation, but it is doubtful whether it adds very much to the other factors which are specified. It is unlikely that a court, hearing an application by a woman who has lived with her partner for twenty years, raised their children and run a business together, is going to reject her application because they 'did not get round to the paperwork'. By the same token, a court is perhaps unlikely to show much sympathy to a financially independent applicant with no children who moves into her boyfriend's house for a month and then, having given up her own rented property, attempts to exclude him from his home.

When determining whether to include any regulatory provisions in the order, the court is required to consider the same common factors as before, and the balance of harm test.[5] However, for cohabitants and former cohabitants, this test does not operate as a *presumption* but only as a further consideration. This differentiation was inserted by Parliament as a further attempt to differentiate marriage from cohabitation, and out of concern that courts should not be constrained to make orders where the applicant could point neither to property entitlement nor to recognised marital status as a qualification for an order.

(III)   DURATION OF AN ORDER

The Law Commission considered that the purpose of occupation orders for non-entitled applicants is to provide relatively short-term protection to enable the applicant to find alternative accommodation, await the outcome of any legal proceedings over the property, or, one might add, to reconcile with the respondent.[6] Whereas entitled applicants are able to obtain orders of unlimited duration, the Act restricts this for non-entitled applicants, once again distinguishing between those who have been married and those who have not.[7]

Former spouses   Section 35(10) limits the length of an order in favour of a non-entitled former spouse to a specified period not exceeding six months, although the order may be extended on one or more occasions.

Cohabitants and former cohabitants   Section 36(10) similarly limits the duration of an order to a *maximum* period of six months, but, in line with Parliament's

3 Sections 33(6) and 35(6)(a)–(d).
4 Section 36(6). The proceedings specified are those for a property order under the Children Act 1989 Sch 1 or those relating to the legal or beneficial ownership of the dwelling-house.
5 Section 36(7)–(8).
6 Law Com No 207 paras 4.7 and 4.19.
7 The order may be varied or discharged on the application of either party: s 49.

concern to restrict protection for non-marital applicants, additionally provides that only one extension may be given, for a further maximum period of six months.

The consequence of these provisions, especially for cohabitants, is to provide a clear advantage, not simply to those who are married as opposed to those who cohabit, but to those who can establish property rights compared with those who cannot. If Parliament had really wished to stress the value it attached to marriage, it could have discriminated against even those cohabitants who have property rights, for example, by requiring the court to consider the nature of their relationship with the respondent, or by imposing a limit on the duration of any order, but it chose to do so only against those applicants who are the most vulnerable – those who have not acquired a proprietary right or interest in their home.

Applicants, whether former spouses or cohabitants, are likely wherever possible to attempt to bring themselves within the entitled category by seeking to establish a property right. However, this is not straightforward. It is open to a person to apply for an order as a non-entitled applicant, whilst preserving the right to claim a legal or equitable interest in any property in other proceedings,[8] but the crucial question under s 33, where no *legal* title can be established, is not whether a person has a beneficial interest, but whether such an interest gives him the right to occupy the dwelling-house. Sections 35(11) and 36(11) provide that a person who has an equitable interest in the house, or in the proceeds of sale of the house, but no legal title, is to be treated as a non-entitled applicant, so that the application is governed by s 35 or s 36, whilst still having the option of establishing such right to occupy and hence the right to apply under s 33.[9] Bearing in mind that most applicants are likely to be seeking an order as a matter of some urgency, and considering that magistrates' courts may not determine disputed questions of entitlement to occupy,[10] it seems likely that, in cases of doubt, applicants may have to cut their losses by relying on the non-entitled provisions, in the hope that they will satisfy the criteria for the grant of an order. There is, at least, a back-stop provision, since a court may grant an order under the appropriate qualifying section, even though the application has been brought under another.[11]

(b)   Neither party entitled to remain in occupation of the home

Where neither spouse has a property right in respect of the family home, then neither can have matrimonial home rights, and therefore cannot be classed as an entitled applicant.[12] Similarly, former spouses or cohabitants may be living in property in which neither has the right to remain, for example, as bare licensees or squatters. Since the former law permitted spouses and cohabitants to obtain ouster injunctions in such circumstances, the Law Commission recommended that the protection continue, and be extended to the other classes of non-entitled applicants – *former* spouses and *former* cohabitants.[13] Sections 37 and 38 duly permit applicants to obtain regulatory orders [14] to control occupation of the property by the applicant and respondent. In respect of spouses and former spouses, the criteria for making such an order are the same as apply to entitled applicants,

---

8 Section 39(4).
9 Sections 35(12) and 36(12).
10 Section 59, discussed ante, p 195.
11 Section 39(3).
12 See s 30(1)(a).
13 See Law Com No 207 para 4.8.
14 Declaratory orders cannot be made, since, by definition, the parties have no right to occupy the property. The provisions which may be included in the order are set out in s 37(3) – spouses and former spouses – and s 38(3) – cohabitants and former cohabitants.

including the balance of harm presumption.[15] No consideration of the applicant's qualification to seek an order is required, since she has no lesser entitlement to occupy the property than the respondent. However, any order made is subject to a maximum duration of six months, although it may be extended on more than one occasion.[16] A court considering whether to make an order in favour of a cohabitant or former cohabitant must have regard to the factors common to all applications,[17] and then consider the balance of harm test, although not as a presumption.[18] The order may have effect for up to six months, and may be renewed once.[19]

Additional provisions

Where the court makes an order under s 33, s 35 or s 36, it may, at the same time, or at any time afterwards, include additional provisions.[20] It may impose on either party an obligation as to the repair and maintenance of the property or the payment of rent, mortgage or other outgoings. This may be important to preserve the long-term security of the property. For example, it would clearly be regrettable to control the parties' occupation but leave it open to the occupant to neglect the property, or fall behind with payments, resulting in repossession. It may also require the occupying party to make periodical payments to the other where that person would otherwise be entitled to occupy, as compensation for that person's loss of occupation.[1] Further, it may grant either party the possession or use of furniture or other contents of the home; order either party to take reasonable care of these, and order either party to take reasonable steps to keep the dwelling-house and contents secure. Such provisions may be important, as it is not unknown for a party, before letting an applicant back into the property, to strip the home of its contents, or to damage it.[2] Equally, where a respondent is kept out of his home, it is right to require the applicant to take proper care of it and its contents. But, although it is obviously inappropriate to impose obligations to repair, or pay rent, for example, where neither party is entitled to occupy the property, it is unclear why the obligations to take care of the home and its contents should not be imposed when an order is made under s 37 or s 38.

Enforcing orders

Breach of the terms of a court order is a civil contempt of court, but contempt procedures normally take a number of days and in the meantime the victim may be at risk. Consequently, the Domestic Violence and Matrimonial Proceedings Act 1976 and the Domestic Proceedings and Magistrates' Courts Act 1978 both empowered the court, on making an order restraining the respondent from using violence (but not just molestation), or excluding a respondent from the home, to attach a power of arrest to the order. This enabled the police to arrest a respondent without a warrant, and to detain him for up to 24 hours before bringing him before a judge. Such a power could only be included where there was proof that the respondent had caused physical (or in the case of the 1976 Act, psychological) harm to the applicant or a child, and was likely to do so again. Coupled with this

---

15 Section 37(4).
16 Section 37(5).
17 Section 38(4). Viz: housing needs, financial resources, likely effect of any order on the health, safety or well-being of the parties or a relevant child and the parties' conduct.
18 Section 38(5).
19 Section 38(6).
20 Section 40.
 1 Both of these powers were contained in the Matrimonial Homes Act 1983 s 1(3)(b)–(c).
 2 See *Davis v Johnson* [1979] AC 264, [1978] 1 All ER 1132, HL.

limitation, courts also considered that the civil liberties implications of empowering summary arrest and detention for breach of a civil order were such that the power should only be used 'where men or women persistently disobey injunctions and make a nuisance of themselves to the other party and to others concerned'.[3] Thus, the power was attached in only a minority of cases.[4]

The Law Commission were impressed by the weight of opinion supporting a presumption in favour of attaching a power of arrest in any case where there had been violence or threatened violence, viewing the power as 'a simple, immediate and inexpensive means of enforcement which underlines the seriousness of the breach to the offending party',[5] and they recommended accordingly. Section 47 of the Family Law Act 1996 therefore provides that if a court makes an occupation or non-molestation order and it appears to the court that the respondent has used or threatened violence against the applicant or a relevant child:

> '. . . it shall attach a power of arrest to one or more provisions of the order unless satisfied that in all the circumstances of the case the applicant or child will be adequately protected without such a power of arrest.'[6]

Although there is still a need to show violence, rather than 'mere' pestering etc, before a power may be attached, the addition of evidence of the threat of violence makes the provision much wider than under the former law, and the incorporation of a presumption in favour of attachment should tilt the balance towards a focus upon protection of the victim from further harm rather than, as in *Lewis v Lewis*,[7] concentration upon the extent and seriousness of past breaches. Where the power is attached, it is important that the police are aware of it, and therefore rules provide that a copy of the relevant provisions of the order must be sent to the police station for the applicant's address.[8]

Where a power of arrest is *not* attached, or has been attached only to certain provisions in the order, it will still be open to an applicant to apply to the court for the issue of a warrant for the respondent's arrest where there are reasonable grounds for believing that there has been a breach of the order,[9] thus obviating the need to invoke the more cumbersome committal powers of the courts.

Upon arrest without warrant, the respondent must be brought before the relevant judicial authority within 24 hours,[10] and may be remanded, on bail or in custody,[11] or dealt with for the breach.[12]

---

3   Per Ormrod LJ in *Lewis v Lewis* [1978] Fam 60 at 63, [1978] 1 All ER 729, CA at 731. A similar approach was taken under the magistrates' jurisdiction: *Widdowson v Widdowson* (1982) 4 FLR 121.
4   In 1996, of 22,652 injunctions granted under the 1976 Act, 10,049 had powers of arrest attached: *Judicial Statistics 1996* Table 5.9.
5   Law Com No 207 para 5.13.
6   Section 47(2).
7   Supra, n 3.
8   Family Proceedings Rules 1991 (as amended) r 3.9A(1) – High Court and county court; Family Proceedings Courts (Matrimonial Proceedings Etc) Rules 1991 (as amended) r 20(1) – magistrates' courts.
9   The application must be substantiated on oath: s 47(8), (9).
10 Excluding Christmas Day, Good Friday or any Sunday: s 47(7). Where the arrest is pursuant to a warrant, the respondent must be brought before the court immediately. For 'relevant judicial authority' see s 63(1).
11 The remand may be for the purpose of enabling a medical examination of the respondent to be carried out. Should it be suspected that the respondent is suffering from mental illness or mental impairment, he may be remanded under the Mental Health Act 1983 s 35 for a report: s 48.
12 The possible sanctions range from making no order but warning the respondent as to his future conduct, to sequestration of assets, (immediate or suspended) committal to prison or committal to a hospital under the Mental Health Act 1983: s 51; see Horton, op cit para 9.5.2. A serious breach should be met by immediate imprisonment: *N v R (Non-molestation Order: Breach)* (1998) Times 1 September, CA.

Ex parte orders

It was possible under the former legislation to obtain an order ex parte, although this was rare, especially in respect of ouster orders. The courts considered that orders should only be made where it was necessary to act quickly to avert a real and immediate danger of serious injury or irreparable damage,[13] and that, where possible, substituted service or abridgement of the period of notice should be used instead. The Law Commission recognised the drawbacks of ex parte orders: they might be based on misconceived or malicious allegations with no opportunity for the court to test these out. There is, moreover, no opportunity to try to resolve the parties' differences by agreed undertakings,[14] nor is there scope for bringing home to the respondent the seriousness of the situation and the importance of compliance with the order.[15] However, the need to provide a protective remedy as a matter of urgency, or to provide a breathing-space to enable an applicant to pursue her remedy, led them to recommend a test which would balance these competing considerations.

Section 45 now provides that a court may make either a non-molestation or occupation order ex parte where 'it considers it just and convenient to do so', but must have regard to all the circumstances, including

'(a) any risk of significant harm to the applicant or a relevant child, attributable to conduct of the respondent, if the order is not made immediately;
(b) whether it is likely that the applicant will be deterred or prevented from pursuing the application if an order is not made immediately; and
(c) whether there is reason to believe that the respondent is aware of the proceedings but is deliberately evading service and that an applicant or a relevant child will be seriously prejudiced by the delay involved [in effecting service].'[16]

The court making an order must afford the respondent the opportunity of a full hearing as soon as is just and convenient, and the duration of any occupation order made at the full hearing must be calculated taking into account the date when the ex parte order was made.[17] The court may attach a power of arrest to an ex parte order if it appears that the respondent has used or threatened violence against the applicant or a relevant child, and there is a risk of significant harm to them, attributable to the respondent's conduct, if the power of arrest is not attached to the order immediately. In such a case, the court may provide that the power of arrest is to last for a shorter period than the other provisions in the order, which reflects the concern that the respondent's civil liberties are doubly jeopardised in a case where, first, he is at risk of arrest for a civil matter, and secondly, he has had no opportunity to contest the making of the order.[18]

Undertakings

An undertaking whereby the respondent gives a promise to the court in the terms of the proposed order, for example, that he will not molest the applicant, and will

---

13 *Ansah v Ansah* [1977] Fam 138, [1977] 2 All ER 638, CA; *G v G (Ouster: Ex Parte Application)* [1990] 1 FLR 395, CA; *Practice Note* [1978] 2 All ER 919.
14 Discussed below.
15 Law Com No 207, para 5.6.
16 Section 45(2).
17 Section 45(3)–(4).
18 See *President's Direction: Family Law Act 1996 Part IV* [1998] 1 FLR 496.

leave the home within seven days, became a common[19] and popular alternative mechanism to the making of an order under the former law. It was to the respondent's advantage, since no finding of fact would be made on the applicant's allegations against him. It was to the court's advantage, because it obviated the need for a full hearing and thus saved time. And it was to the applicant's advantage, inter alia because she did not need to give evidence against the respondent in court, and because an undertaking has the effect of an order of the court and is therefore enforceable through contempt proceedings. It was also said to reduce confrontation and defuse explosive situations.[20] The Association of District Judges submitted to the House of Lords Special Public Bill Committee that the practice of giving undertakings should be covered by legislation and not simply by rule,[1] and s 46 now deals with the issue by empowering courts to accept an undertaking from any party to the proceedings.

Although an undertaking 'is enforceable as if it were an order of the court',[2] it was formerly well-established[3] that a police power of arrest could not be attached to it, and this has now been put into statutory form under s 46(2). The applicant who agrees to an undertaking rather than proceeding with her application therefore runs the risk of facing difficulty if she needs practical enforcement measures to be taken in the future.[4] However, s 46(3) provides that 'the court shall not accept an undertaking . . . in any case where apart from this section a power of arrest would be attached to the order.'[5] Accordingly, a court ought not to accept an undertaking where it would otherwise make an order to which a power of arrest would be added – and it will be recalled that there is a presumption that such a power will be attached to any order where there is past evidence against the respondent of the threat or use of violence. The provision has therefore been criticised on the basis that it will prevent courts, and deter applicants, from accepting undertakings, even though these may otherwise be appropriate solutions to the family crisis.[6] However, given the policy underlying the arrest 'presumption' in cases of violence, and a concern that applicants may feel pressurised into accepting an undertaking,[7] it may be right that courts should be constrained from continuing their former practice. In any case, faced with the offer of an undertaking, a court may well conclude that a power of arrest is unnecessary to protect the applicant or child, and therefore need not be attached to any order, so that s 46(3) does not apply.

---

19 Jones et al, op cit Tables 15 and 16 found nearly half of non-molestation applications were resolved by means of an undertaking in the court they studied, and District Judge Bird put the proportion at 80% in his memorandum to the House of Lords Special Public Committee, *Written Evidence* p 7. Magistrates did not have the power to accept undertakings.

20 District Judge Gerlis 'The Family Homes and Domestic Violence Bill – Undermining the Undertaking' [1994] Fam Law 700. The problems of utilising mediation to deal with domestic violence are discussed by Kaganas and Piper 'Domestic Violence and Divorce Mediation' (1994) 16 JSWFL 265 and Raitt 'Domestic Violence and divorce mediation: A rejoinder' (1996) 18 JSWFL 11.

1 House of Lords Special Public Committee, *Written Evidence* p 6.

2 Section 46(4).

3 *Carpenter v Carpenter* [1988] 1 FLR 121, CA.

4 See the concerns expressed by Kewley 'Pragmatism before principle: the limitations of civil law remedies for the victims of domestic violence' [1996] JSWFL 1.

5 There is uncertainty as to whether a warrant for arrest may be issued for breach of an undertaking; see Gerlis 'Undertakings Redeemed' [1996] Fam Law 233.

6 Gerlis, op cit.

7 Kewley, op cit p 5.

Actions brought by representatives of the victim

While the procedure of giving undertakings implies a bargaining or negotiating process between applicant and respondent, perhaps aided by mediation, there may be cases where the victim is so disempowered by the abuser that she is unable to take action of any kind to protect herself and her family. The Law Commission were impressed by the power, in certain Australian states, given to the police to seek civil remedies on the victim's behalf. This was said to remove the burden of stress upon the victim to take action, to reduce the workload of the police in the long term by lowering the level of repeat violence, to emphasise to the respondent the seriousness of the action being taken against him, and to raise the significance of 'domestic' violence. The Law Commission therefore recommended that this power be given to the police in England and Wales.[8] This recommendation was not supported by the House of Commons Home Affairs Select Committee,[9] or accepted by the government, on the basis that introducing a power to seek a civil remedy would represent too radical a departure from the core criminal justice functions of the police. However, the opposition pressed an amendment to the Family Law Bill to introduce a paving provision, which became s 60 of the Act, to enable some form of representative action to be introduced through rules of court. Section 62 [10] will enable rules to be drafted to provide for a prescribed person, or category of persons, to act on behalf of another in seeking a non-molestation or occupation order, and may prescribe the conditions to be satisfied before such an application may be made, and the criteria to be considered when a court is determining whether to make an order. These provisions enable rules to specify, for example, that the police, or possibly other organisations, are within the prescribed category of representatives; that a victim's consent to the action be obtained first; and that it is appropriate for the proceedings to be brought by someone other than the victim.

2. PROTECTION FROM HARASSMENT ACT 1997

Before the Protection from Harassment Act 1997, considerable attempts were made to extend the existing law of tort to cover harassment. It was held in *Patel v Patel*[11] that harassment does not amount to a distinct tort. However, relying upon old cases,[12] where it had been held that conduct calculated to impair the plaintiff's health, and having that effect, was a tort, the Court of Appeal in *Burnett v George*[13] was able to hold that pestering having the like consequence could be restrained by injunction. An attempt to broaden tort law further by classifying harassment as a form of private nuisance was made in *Khorasandjian v Bush*.[14] There, it was held, in addition to applying *Burnett v George*, that persistent telephone calls made to the plaintiff at the home she shared with her parents, constituted an actionable interference with her ordinary and reasonable use and

---

8 Law Com No 207 paras 5.18, 5.20.
9 *Third Report: Domestic Violence* HC 245-I (1992–93) para 118.
10 Which was not implemented at the same time as the remainder of Part IV.
11 [1988] 2 FLR 179, CA.
12 *Wilkinson v Downton* [1897] 2 QB 57; *Janvier v Sweeney* [1919] 2 KB 316, CA.
13 [1992] 1 FLR 525, CA.
14 [1993] QB 727, [1993] 3 All ER 669, CA.

enjoyment of the property which amounted to nuisance, even though she was not the legal occupier of the property. However, in *Hunter v Canary Wharf Ltd* [15] the House of Lords overruled the decision on this point, although not on the view that there is a tort of carrying out conduct calculated to harm, and resulting in harm to, the victim.

The civil law has now been tidied up by the 1997 Act, which, as well as creating the new criminal offences of harassment and putting a person in fear of violence, [16] also creates a statutory tort of harassment, based on a claim brought 'by the person who is or may be the victim of the course of conduct in question'. [17]

Section 3(2) provides for damages to be awarded for, inter alia, any anxiety caused by the harassment, and any financial loss which results. The High Court or county court may also issue an injunction to prohibit further harassment, and the plaintiff may apply for a warrant for arrest to be issued where he or she considers that the defendant has broken the terms of such an injunction. [18] Breach of the injunction may be punishable either as a contempt of court or, where the defendant has no reasonable excuse, as an offence. [19]

The potentially broad scope of the 1997 Act and its sometimes loose drafting, resulting from its hasty enactment, sit uncomfortably alongside the immensely detailed, but circumscribed, terms of Part IV of the 1996 Act. It remains to be seen how the two will operate together.

3.   INJUNCTIONS IN OTHER CIVIL PROCEEDINGS

The 1996 Act is intended to cater for a wide range of family relationships where some form of protective order is required, and the Protection from Harassment Act 1997 provides a jurisdiction dealing with harassment as statutorily defined, but there may remain a need to consider the general jurisdiction of the courts to provide injunctions, ancillary to substantive proceedings, in situations which might fall outside these two statutes.

There is considerable uncertainty in the case law regarding the basis of a general jurisdiction to grant injunctions. It is proposed to discuss first, the *statutory* basis to do so. The Supreme Court Act 1981 s 37 and the County Courts Act 1984 s 38 provide that the High Court and county courts may grant an interlocutory or final injunction 'in all cases in which it appears to the court to be just and convenient to do so.' In *Richards v Richards*, [20] the House of Lords held that an injunction may be granted under this jurisdiction only to support an existing legal or equitable right. Secondly, we discuss the existence of an

15 [1997] 2 All ER 426, HL.
16 See the discussion ante at p 191.
17 Section 3(1).
18 But the court cannot attach a power of arrest at the time of issuing the injunction. As with an application for an arrest warrant under s 47(8) of the Family Law Act 1996, the application must be substantiated on oath, and the court must have reasonable grounds for believing that the defendant has broken the injunction: s 3(5).
19 Section 3(6)–(8). The offence is punishable on indictment by imprisonment for a term not exceeding five years and/or a fine; or, on summary conviction, to imprisonment for a term not exceeding six months, and/or a fine: s 3(9).
20 [1984] AC 174, [1983] 2 All ER 807, HL per Lord Hailsham LC at 200 and 813, Lord Scarman at 212 and 822 and Lord Brandon at 218 and 827. Lord Diplock and Lord Bridge concurred.

'*inherent jurisdiction*',[1] to grant injunctions. This has been relied upon to protect litigants in pending proceedings, and also, so far as the High Court is concerned, to protect children.

Injunctions under the statutory jurisdiction

(a) Injunctions to restrain a tort

The usual means of demonstrating interference with a right of the plaintiff is to establish that the defendant has committed a tort or other actionable wrong. An owner or tenant of property may rely upon the torts of trespass[2] or nuisance, although the former will not lie against a defendant who is also entitled to occupy the property.[3] A battery or assault by the defendant upon the plaintiff will clearly give rise to an action in damages and the possibility of an injunction to restrain repetition of the behaviour, and we have seen that harassment which is intended to cause, and results in, harm to the victim, may be actionable. However, this is narrower in scope than the statutory tort of harassment and there would appear to be little point in seeking to rely upon it. Furthermore, Lord Hailsham, in *Richards v Richards* considered that, where Parliament had laid down a statutory regime to govern a particular issue – ouster from the family home – it was not open to the courts to determine the matter without applying that regime.[4] The same reasoning may be held to apply to attempts to invoke the common law torts where statute, either under the Family Law Act or the Protection from Harassment Act, has laid down alternative criteria.[5]

(b) Injunctions to support rights in relation to children

There appears to be no difficulty in granting a *non-molestation* order under the jurisdiction conferred by the Supreme Court Act or County Courts Act, ancillary to a s 8 order under the Children Act 1989 to protect a person's exercise of parental responsibility,[6] but there are conflicting decisions as to whether an *ouster* can be ordered.[7] In *Ainsbury v Millington*[8] the Court of Appeal held that such an order could not be granted against a father who was the joint tenant of the home in which he and the mother had formerly cohabited, allied to a claim for custody, care and control by the mother.[9] The mother could not assert a

1 In *Richards v Richards* [1984] AC 174, [1983] 2 All ER 807, HL, it was asserted that the 'inherent jurisdiction' to grant injunctions is either absorbed by statute (Lord Hailsham at 199G, 812j), or its exercise is governed by statute (Lord Scarman at 212E, 822e, Lord Brandon at 218F, 827a). However, the 'inherent jurisdiction' has continued to be referred to and relied upon, as is discussed below at p 215.
2 *Lucas v Lucas* [1992] 2 FLR 53, CA.
3 *Ainsbury v Millington* [1986] 1 All ER 73, CA.
4 [1984] AC 174 at 199–200, [1983] 2 All ER 807 at 813a. Concurred in by Lord Diplock.
5 On this basis, old cases suggesting that a non-molestation injunction may be granted to a spouse simply qua spouse may be open to doubt: *Robinson v Robinson* [1965] P 39, [1963] 3 All ER 813; *Montgomery v Montgomery* [1965] P 46, [1964] 2 All ER 22, although these decisions may be explicable as examples of protecting a litigant during pending proceedings, see below, p 214.
6 *M v M (Residence Order: Ancillary Injunction)* [1994] Fam Law 441. See also *C v K (Inherent Powers; Exclusion Order)* [1996] 2 FLR 506.
7 See the discussion by HH Judge Fricker 'Inherent Jurisdiction, Ouster and Exclusion' [1994] Fam Law 629, and by HH Judge Barnett, 'Inherent Jurisdiction, Ouster Orders and Children' [1997] Fam Law 96.
8 [1986] 1 All ER 73, CA.
9 An order may be granted in favour of a *sole* tenant allied to such proceedings: *Re W (a minor)* [1981] 3 All ER 401, CA.

superior property right to his, and there was no power to grant the order ancillary to the child proceedings, as this would run counter to the House of Lords' reasoning in *Richards v Richards* to the effect that an ouster application was not a proceeding in which the custody or upbringing of a minor was in question. The decision was followed in *M v M*,[10] a case involving former spouses, where the father was the sole owner of the property. However, in *Wilde v Wilde*,[11] again involving former spouses, the court, considering itself bound by an earlier decision,[12] but without referring to *Ainsbury v Millington*, held that there was either an inherent jurisdiction to make an ouster order where this was desirable in the interests of the child, or a power under the statutory jurisdiction to grant injunctions to enforce the mother's right of care and control.[13] The main thrust of the court's reasoning in *Wilde v Wilde* related to the existence of an inherent jurisdiction, which is discussed further below, but the court's view that an injunction could be used to enforce a parental right was adopted by Wall J in *C v K (Inherent Powers: Exclusion Order)*,[14] where he held, preferring *Wilde v Wilde* to *Ainsbury v Millington*, that a joint tenant could be excluded from the former cohabitational home in order to ensure the free exercise by the other tenant of a residence order in respect of her granddaughter. The factual situations arising in all of these cases would now be within the ambit of the Family Law Act 1996, but the question of their impact on the surviving jurisdiction to issue injunctions remains unclear.

(c)   Injunctions to support right to pursue litigation free from intimidation

It has long been established that a court may grant an injunction to protect a litigant from intimidation from another party to pending proceedings,[15] and it has been argued that such cases are explicable as supporting a right to pursue remedies before the courts free from any pressure or influence from another party to the litigation.[16] However, they may also be viewed as illustrations of the exercise of the court's inherent jurisdiction, discussed below.

LINK BETWEEN CAUSE OF ACTION AND INJUNCTION

Even where the plaintiff can point to an actionable wrong, an injunction may only be granted to protect the right being asserted. Thus, it must 'bear some sensible relationship to the cause of action'.[17] An injunction ordering a person out of the house is clearly related to an action based on trespass to the property, but would not be if allied to a claim for financial provision, for example.[18] Defining an

---

10 [1988] 1 FLR 225, CA.
11 [1988] 2 FLR 83, CA.
12 *Quinn v Quinn* (1983) 4 FLR 394, CA.
13 An attempt to rationalise these cases was made by Thorpe J in *Pearson v Franklin (Parental Home: Ouster)* [1994] 2 All ER 137, CA on the basis that they must be distinguished according to the marital status of the parties. However, given that the Family Law Act 1996 now caters for both married and formerly married, and cohabiting and formerly cohabiting couples, his explanation has been superseded and no longer helps in determining the continuing rationale for the exercise of the jurisdiction.
14 [1996] 2 FLR 506.
15 *Silverstone v Silverstone* [1953] 1 All ER 556; *Montgomery v Montgomery* [1965] P 46, [1964] 2 All ER 22.
16 See Barnett, op cit.
17 Per Finer J in *McGibbon v McGibbon* [1973] Fam 170 at 173, [1973] 2 All ER 836 at 838.
18 *Des Salles d'Epinoix v Des Salles d'Epinoix* [1967] 2 All ER 539, CA (non-molestation order).

'exclusion zone' around a property within which the defendant must not go may be permitted where it is necessary to protect the plaintiff.[19]

A remaining inherent jurisdiction?

Notwithstanding the views of Lord Hailsham and Lord Scarman in the House of Lords in *Richards v Richards* to the effect that the 'inherent jurisdiction' is contained within the statutory power in the Supreme Court Act 1981 and County Courts Act, courts have continued to assert the existence of such a jurisdiction not subsumed within the statute.[20]

It is clear that the High Court exercising its parens patriae jurisdiction may make orders to protect children where necessary, and the old decisions asserting an 'inherent jurisdiction' may be examples of the exercise of that power. For example, in *Stewart v Stewart*[1] Sir George Baker P held that he had power to grant an ouster injunction 'because there are two young children who have to have a roof over their heads', and in *Wilde v Wilde*[2] Purchas LJ traced the origins of this view back to the exercise of the wardship jurisdiction, in *Re Spence*.[3] What is unclear is whether more recent decisions are similarly explicable. The difficulty is that they appear to assert that this inherent jurisdiction exists in the county court, yet such a view is in clear conflict with decisions of the Court of Appeal that the county court has no inherent power to grant injunctions to protect children at all.[4]

It is also unclear whether there is a further 'inherent' jurisdiction to protect litigants during proceedings, or whether this has been subsumed within the statutory provisions. It is submitted that it should be so regarded, as more in keeping with the thrust of the reasoning in *Richards v Richards*, and compatible with the view that the county court is a statutory jurisdiction which enjoys no inherent powers at all.

As far as the High Court's parens patriae jurisdiction is concerned, it is now understood that wardship is an aspect of this jurisdiction.[5] On this basis, it has been held that the inherent jurisdiction may be invoked by a local authority to obtain an injunction preventing a suspected sexual abuser from visiting the home and children of his woman friend.[6] More controversially, in *Re S (Minors)(Inherent Jurisdiction: Ouster)*,[7] the same approach was taken by Connell J in response to a local authority's application to have the children's father excluded from the home. The father conceded that the court had power to make the order, but his Lordship's view that the inherent jurisdiction was applicable and appropriate took no account of the statutory regime governing exclusion from the matrimonial home, and on that account appears to be in conflict with the House of Lords' approach in *Richards v Richards*.[8]

19 *Burris v Azadani* [1995] 4 All ER 802, CA (but note that the injunction was interlocutory in that case).
20 *Wilde v Wilde* [1988] 2 FLR 83,CA; *Re S (Minors) (Inherent Jurisdiction: Ouster)* [1994] 1 FLR 623; *C v K (Inherent Powers; Exclusion Order)* [1996] 2 FLR 506 (obiter).
1 [1973] Fam 21.
2 [1988] 2 FLR 83, CA.
3 (1847) 2 Ph 247.
4 *D v D (County Court Jurisdiction: Injunctions)* [1993] 2 FLR 802, CA; *Devon County Council v B* [1997] 1 FLR 591, CA.
5 See post, p 684.
6 *Devon County Council v S* [1994] Fam 169, [1995] 1 All ER 243.
7 [1994] 1 FLR 623.
8 It would probably now be regarded as also conflicting with the power of a court to include an exclusion requirement in the terms of an emergency protection or interim care order, under Sch 6 to the Family Law Act 1996, discussed at pp 594 and 577.

It is regrettable that, as Wall J put it, there remains 'a substantial degree of confusion, both about the nature of the inherent jurisdiction and the extent of the powers exercisable under it.'[9] Indeed, there appears to be confusion as to whether there is one inherent jurisdiction, or two, and whether, assuming there are two, that one at least of these extends to the county court. It is also discomfiting to find that there is so much uncertainty surrounding the question of when a party can be ousted from property. It must be hoped that the statutory jurisdictions providing civil remedies will prove sufficient, in most cases, to render these questions academic.

D.   Remedies through housing law

1.   ACTIONS IN RELATION TO TENANCIES[10]

Transfer of tenancy

One long-term solution to the housing dilemma of a victim of violence, which is available to a spouse or cohabitant whose home is rented, is to seek a transfer of the tenancy by court order. We note this option here and discuss it in detail elsewhere.[11] The courts have the power to effect such a transfer in respect of couples whose marriage has been terminated, under the Matrimonial Causes Act 1973 s 23A or s 24,[12] and in s 53 of, and Sch 7 to the Family Law Act 1996. There is also power to make such a disposition for the benefit of children, under Sch 1 to the Children Act 1989.[13] Sch 7 extends the court's power to apply to cohabitants who have ceased to live together as husband and wife.[14] The Law Commission recommended this extension (which already existed in Scotland), to ensure that a tenancy, probably granted by a local authority or housing association on the assumption that it would provide a home for the cohabiting couple and their children, should continue to provide a secure home for the children even though

---

9   In *C v K (Inherent Powers; Exclusion Order)* [1996] 2 FLR 506 at 511.
10 It may be noted that a local authority is empowered under the Housing Act 1996 s 152 to seek an injunction from the High Court or county court against a person to prohibit him from conduct causing or likely to cause a nuisance or annoyance to a person residing in premises provided by the authority, or from entering premises or being found in the locality of the premises. The injunction may be granted where the court is of the opinion that the respondent has used or threatened to use violence against the victim, and that there is a significant risk of harm to that person, or to a similar person, if the injunction is not granted. The injunction may be made ex parte; and a power of arrest may be attached. There seems nothing to prevent a local authority from taking action under these provisions on behalf of a victim of domestic violence too frightened to act herself. Such a course side-steps the concern expressed during the passage of Part IV of the Family Law Act 1996 at the idea of the police doing so. The objection of involving a criminal justice agency in civil proceedings does not apply to a housing authority. Whether such an authority would be prepared to act in this way is another matter. The object of the provisions is to deal with 'anti-social behaviour', epitomised by gangs of youths terrorising estates, and the authority will naturally be reluctant to spend its money on obtaining a remedy for a victim which she could obtain for herself.
11 At pp 179 and 796.
12 See post, p 796.
13 Post, p 768.
14 Defined, as under Part IV of the Act, in s 62(1). See Bridge 'Transferring Tenancies of the Family Home' [1998] Fam Law 26.

their parents' relationship has broken down,[15] and also to do justice between the couple.

If the victim could therefore obtain some short- to medium-term protection, possibly under Part IV of the 1996 Act, she might then be able to seek an order under Sch 7 for a permanent solution to her housing problem.

Eviction

The Housing Act 1996 provides that where a dwelling-house held on a secure or assured tenancy was occupied by a married or cohabiting couple, and one partner has left because of violence or threats of violence against him or her or a member of his or her family,[16] the landlord may seek an order for possession. It might be thought that this could be a useful device to justify the landlord terminating the violent partner's right to occupy, and then granting the victim a new tenancy for herself. However, the court must be satisfied that the partner who has left is unlikely to return.[17] Moreover, as these provisions only enable the landlord to oust a violent tenant, and do not help the victim return to the property, they will not be of assistance in the common case where the violent partner refuses to quit and has already driven the victim out.

Victim terminating tenancy

A more effective device is for a victim who is herself a joint tenant of the property to give notice of termination to the landlord, on the understanding that the landlord will then grant her a fresh tenancy in her sole name. It was held by the House of Lords in *Hammersmith and Fulham London Borough Council v Monk*[18] that the appropriate notice, as required under the tenancy, given unilaterally by one joint tenant is effective to bring the tenancy to an end, notwithstanding the other tenant's lack of agreement, or even knowledge.[19] Since such a device avoids the usual requirement of notice before eviction, and enables the victim effectively to obtain a transfer of the tenancy which could normally only be done by order under Sch 7 to the Family Law Act 1996,[20] it is perhaps not surprising that in *Hounslow London Borough Council v Pilling*[1] the Court of Appeal attempted to curtail the ambit of the decision, by holding that the notice given to the landlord must be 'appropriate', ie given at the end of the tenancy period, and not in the middle of it. Nor must the notice be in breach of the Protection from Eviction Act 1977, under which at least four weeks' notice in writing must be given.[2]

However, in *Harrow London Borough Council v Johnstone*,[3] the House of Lords continued its robust approach, holding that where a husband had obtained an injunction prohibiting his wife from excluding him from the matrimonial home, it was still open to the wife to give notice to the landlord terminating the tenancy on the understanding that they would grant her a new tenancy once her

15 Law Com No 207 para 6.3.
16 Section 145 (secure tenancy) and s 149 (assured tenancy).
17 Ibid.
18 [1992] 1 AC 478, [1992] 1 All ER 1, HL.
19 A joint tenant who gives notice without the other's knowledge does not act in breach of trust: *Crawley Borough Council v Ure* [1996] QB 13, [1996] 1 All ER 724, CA.
20 Above.
 1 [1994] 1 All ER 432, CA.
 2 Section 5(1) as amended.
 3 [1997] 1 All ER 929, HL.

husband was evicted. The House considered that the narrow terms of the injunction did not extend to prohibiting the wife from giving notice to quit, and hence the wife and landlord had not acted in contempt of the court's order in seeking to bring the husband's right to occupy the house to an end, but were entitled to do what they had. Their Lordships also accepted that the local authority's action was in accordance with their housing allocation policy, whereby they would not grant a new tenancy to a family already in possession of another, unless that were surrendered first.[4] It remains for decision whether the terms of s 33(3) and (4) of the Family Law Act 1996 are broad enough to encompass a prohibition on a respondent giving a notice to quit.[5] It might be argued that an order under s 33(4), declaring that the applicant is entitled to occupy the house, is sufficient to bring the respondent and landlord into contempt if they act so as to defeat that order, or that an order under s 33(3)(a), enforcing the applicant's right to remain in occupation as against the respondent, is sufficient to bar the respondent from taking steps to terminate that right by surrendering the tenancy. On the other hand, the tenor of the two House of Lords decisions, and the detailed provisions governing obligations as to rent and repairs in s 40, may suggest that express statutory provision would need to be directed to the issue.

2.   SEEKING HELP UNDER THE HOMELESSNESS LEGISLATION

A victim of domestic violence or other intolerable behaviour may decide that it is preferable – and safer – to move out of the family home rather than attempt to continue to live there, with or without having taken criminal or civil action against the other party. Short-term accommodation may be available in a refuge, but these are intended to provide a shelter for no more than about three months. Long-term, but slow, solutions lie in taking matrimonial proceedings if the couple are married, with the aim of acquiring a share of capital which will permit the establishment of a new home. If the couple are not married, the victim may have a property entitlement which could be enforced and the property sold to release capital again to rehouse her, or, in the case of rented property, may seek a transfer of the tenancy. A further course of action is to seek help from the local authority in finding alternative accommodation, on the basis that she is homeless, as defined by statute. Around 15 per cent of those accepted as statutorily homeless have been victims of domestic violence leading to the breakdown of their relationship, and this group consists overwhelmingly of lone female parents with children.[6]

Part VII of the Housing Act 1996,[7] which updates and amends provisions previously contained in the Housing (Homeless Persons) Act 1977 and Housing Act 1985, imposes a duty on all local housing authorities[8] to secure that advice and

4 Nor is a notice to quit a 'disposition' of property which may be set aside under the Matrimonial Causes Act 1973 s 37 in divorce proceedings: *Newlon Housing Trust v Al-Sulaimen* (29 July 1998, unreported), HL. See post, p 862.
5 But an undertaking could be given.
6 Morley and Pascall 'Women and homelessness: proposals from the Department of the Environment Part II, Domestic Violence' [1996] JSWFL 327 at 328.
7 For a full review, see Arden and Hunter *Homelessness and Allocations* 5th edn (1997).
8 Viz, district councils, borough councils in London or the Common Council of the City of London, county or county borough councils in Wales, and unitary authorities: s 230.

information about homelessness and its prevention, are available free of charge to any person in their district;[9] where they have reason to believe that a person may be homeless or threatened with homelessness, to enquire into the circumstances to determine whether he is eligible for assistance, and if so, what duties they owe to him;[10] and in certain circumstances, to secure accommodation for a homeless person.[11]

An applicant for assistance must satisfy a number of tests before the housing authority will owe him the full range of duties imposed under the legislation. He must be homeless, or threatened with homelessness; in priority need; and not intentionally homeless or threatened with such homelessness.[12]

Definition of homeless

A person is homeless for the purpose of the Act if he has no accommodation available for his occupation in the United Kingdom or elsewhere, which he (together with any other person who normally resides with him as a member of his family or any other person who might reasonably be expected to reside with him):[13]

'(a) is entitled to occupy by virtue of an interest in it or by virtue of an order of a court, or
(b) has an express or implied licence to occupy, or
(c) occupies as a residence by virtue of any enactment or rule of law giving him the right to remain in occupation or restricting the right of another person to recover possession.'[14]

He is also homeless if he has such accommodation but he cannot secure entry to it.[15]

Section 175(3) provides that a person shall not be treated as having accommodation unless it is accommodation which it would be reasonable for him to continue to occupy, and in so determining, domestic violence is expressly to be taken into account:

'It is not reasonable for a person to continue to occupy accommodation if it is probable that this will lead to domestic violence against him, or against –
(a) a person who normally resides with him as a member of his family, or
(b) any other person who might reasonably be expected to reside with him.
For this purpose "domestic violence", in relation to a person, means violence from a person with whom he is associated, or threats of violence from such a person which are likely to be carried out.'[16]

The definition of domestic violence is a relatively narrow one; clearly, pestering and harassment are not included. But it does not follow that the victim of such behaviour could not seek assistance under the Act, albeit that she could not rely on

9 Section 179.
10 Section 184.
11 Sections 188, 190.
12 An applicant must also be eligible for assistance. This means that he must not be subject to immigration control, or be an asylum seeker: s 185, s 186.
13 Section 176; an unborn child is not such a person – *R v London Borough of Newham, ex p Dada* [1996] QB 507, [1995] 2 All ER 522, CA.
14 Section 175(1). Paragraph (c) covers a spouse with matrimonial home rights.
15 Section 175(2)(a). Thus, a spouse who cannot gain entry because the locks have been changed may be regarded as homeless.
16 Section 177(1). Authorities vary in the extent of proof they require to be satisfied that a person is at risk of violence. Malos and Hague found that while some accept the victim's own word, others require corroboration from doctors, police, solicitors etc: Malos and Hague *Domestic Violence and Housing: Local authority responses to women and children escaping from violence in the home* (1993).

this particular provision to demonstrate that it is not reasonable for her to continue to occupy the property.

Interestingly, while the Act incorporates the same definition of 'associated person' in relation to the person who is inflicting the violence as is to be found in Part IV of the Family Law Act 1996, it does not define what is meant by 'family'. Although the term 'associated person' is intended to convey some form of domestic relationship, it is wider than what is conveyed by the word 'family'. The Code of Guidance, to which housing authorities are to have regard in discharging their functions under the Act, suggests that it would include cohabiting couples, foster children, housekeepers and companions, and carers of the elderly or disabled.[17]

A person is to be regarded as threatened with homelessness if it is likely that he will become homeless within 28 days.[18]

'Accommodation' means a place which can fairly be described as accommodation and which it would be reasonable, having regard to the general housing conditions in the district, for the person to continue to occupy, and in *R v Brent London Borough Council, ex p Awua*[19] the House of Lords held, contrary to earlier case law, that there is no requirement that it be settled or permanent. The question arises whether a woman who has fled with her children to a refuge may be regarded as homeless notwithstanding that she has a roof over her head. In *R v Ealing London Borough Council, ex p Sidhu*[20] it was held that she should be so regarded, otherwise she could not call on the housing authority for assistance unless the refuge gave her 28 days' notice to leave, in which case she would be 'threatened with homelessness': a procedure which would merely pile stress on stress unnecessarily. Lord Hoffmann in *Awua* agreed that a person whose only accommodation was a night shelter or hostel which he had to leave during each day and could only return to at night would not be regarded as 'having accommodation',[1] but it is unclear whether a refuge would be treated in the same way.[2]

The housing authority must make appropriate inquiries in all cases where they have reason to believe that a person may be homeless or threatened with homelessness and determine whether the applicant has a priority need. In such a case, a duty may arise to provide, not just advice, but accommodation itself.

Priority need

Persons with a priority need include inter alia:

'(a) a pregnant woman or a person with whom she resides or might reasonably be expected to reside;

17 Department of Environment/Department of Health, *Code of Guidance* para 13.2. Query whether homosexual couples are included? The Code is not binding upon housing authorities, although they are obliged to have regard to it under s 182: *De Falco v Crawley Borough Council* [1980] QB 460, [1980] 1 All ER 913, CA.
18 Section 175(4).
19 [1996] AC 55, [1995] 3 All ER 493, HL. It was held that temporary accommodation is not, ipso facto, unsuitable, although accommodation likely to be available for under 28 days would not be sufficient, as the applicant would then be threatened with homelessness within the statutory definition.
20 (1982) 3 FLR 438; cf *R v Purbeck District Council, ex p Cadney* [1986] 2 FLR 158 (wife who had left home voluntarily and was then required to leave temporary accommodation was not homeless).
1 At 67A, 497b.
2 The Code of Guidance states that it should not be regarded as reasonable to expect a person to continue to stay in a refuge in the longer term (para 13.8).

(b) a person with whom dependent children reside or might reasonably be expected to reside;[3]

(c) a person who is vulnerable as a result of old age, mental illness or handicap or physical disability or other special reason,[4] or with whom such a person resides or might reasonably be expected to reside . . .'[5]

A dependent child may not apply for accommodation in his own right as being in priority need, as his accommodation is provided for him by his family, and the housing authority owes no separate duty to the child. Thus, it was held not to be open to parents to put forward an application for help in the name of their four-year-old son, because they had become homeless intentionally and were hence not eligible for assistance.[6]

Intentional homelessness

The extent of the authority's duty to a homeless person in priority need depends upon whether or not they are satisfied that he became homeless (or threatened with homelessness) intentionally. If they are not so satisfied, they must secure that accommodation is available for his occupation, and will remain under this duty for a minimum period of two years.[7] In the case of a person threatened with homelessness, they must take reasonable steps to secure that his accommodation

---

3 The child need not be wholly and exclusively dependent on the applicant or reside solely with him: *R v London Borough of Lambeth, ex p Vagliviello* (1990) 22 HLR 392, CA (applicant could have priority need although child residing with him only 3½ days a week). It is not necessary to have a residence order in the applicant's favour to demonstrate that she has a child residing, or reasonably expected to reside, with her: *R v Ealing London Borough Council, ex p Sidhu* (above n 20), but see Yell 'Point of Order' (1992) LS Gaz 26 August p 20, who found in her survey that many authorities still insisted upon this.

4 This could include a young person or an adult with no children who has left home to escape abuse or violence: *Kelly v Monklands District Council* 1986 SLT 169, Ct of Sess (young person); *R v Kensington and Chelsea London Borough Council, ex p Kihara* (1996) 29 HLR 147, CA.

5 Section 189(1).

6 *R v Oldham Metropolitan Borough Council, ex p Garlick* [1993] AC 509, [1993] 2 All ER 65, HL; it was also held in that case that an application may not be made in the name of an adult dependent who is mentally incapacitated, since any offer of accommodation must be considered and evaluated by the applicant. Where the applicant is intentionally homeless, a housing authority is not obliged to comply with a request under s 27 of the Children Act 1989 from the social services department, seeking to fulfil its duties under Part III of that Act, to help find accommodation in order to keep a family together: *R v Northavon District Council, ex p Smith* [1994] 2 AC 402, [1994] 3 All ER 313, HL. See post, p 522.

7 Section 193. There was no time limit under the legislation before the 1996 Act, so that authorities assumed (until *Awua*, above n 19) that they had to provide permanent housing for those satisfying all the statutory requirements. It was the assumption that the result was to enable the homeless to jump over others, already on the local authority's list for rehousing (see DoE, *Access to Local Authority and Housing Association Tenancies*; DoE Housing Research Summary No 16, *Routes into Local Authority Housing*) that led the government to propose setting a time limit to the duty to provide accommodation under the homelessness provisions (although it is open to the authority to continue to provide housing, and to the applicant to re-apply under these). The government was keen to eradicate this apparent unfairness, and hence legislated to ensure that even those who are homeless must take their turn on the list for permanent housing: *Our Future Homes* Cm 2901; DoE *Allocation of Housing Accommodation by Local Authorities*. The applicant's acquisition of permanent re-housing from the public sector will depend upon the length of the authority's waiting list and her qualifications under the allocation rules: see Part VI of the Housing Act 1996. (But note that a consultation paper issued by the new Labour Government in 1997 suggested the re-introduction of a degree of priority to the homeless in determining allocation of permanent housing: DoE, *Restoring Hope to Homeless People*.)

does not cease to be available.[8] If they are so satisfied, they are bound only to secure accommodation for his occupation for such period as they consider will give him a reasonable opportunity of securing accommodation for himself, and provide him with advice and appropriate assistance to help him find accommodation.[9] The question of whether a person is or is not intentionally homeless is therefore a crucial one.

A person is to be regarded as becoming homeless intentionally if he deliberately does or fails to do something as a result of which he ceases to occupy accommodation which is available for his occupation and which it would have been reasonable for him to continue to occupy.[10] Thus a tenant will become homeless intentionally if he loses possession of premises as a result of *wilfully* failing to pay rent or breaking some other covenant in his lease: there is no need to prove that he intended to become homeless. If another member of the family encourages or acquiesces in conduct which results in the tenant's becoming homeless intentionally (for example, a wife who turns a blind eye or does nothing to prevent her husband from dissipating his earnings instead of paying the rent), that person will be regarded as intentionally homeless as well. The housing authority are entitled to assume acquiescence unless the evidence indicates the contrary;[11] but they are bound to give separate consideration to the position of each resident and in the absence of acquiescence they will be obliged to secure accommodation for the person at fault if he resides with one who has not become homeless intentionally.[12]

It will be observed that the question is whether the tenant became homeless intentionally, not whether he is now homeless intentionally. Consequently if, as in *Din v Wandsworth London Borough Council*[13] the applicant deliberately left available accommodation, he will be considered to have become homeless intentionally even though he would probably have been evicted later and thus have become homeless unintentionally. Conversely, if, as in *Gloucester City Council v Miles*,[14] the applicant became homeless because her husband had vandalised her home to such an extent that it became uninhabitable, she will not be homeless intentionally even though, had she stayed there, she would probably have become so through non-payment of rent.

The same test is to be applied mutatis mutandis to determine whether a person is *threatened* with becoming homeless intentionally.

If a wife or cohabitant has been forced to leave home because of her husband's or partner's violent behaviour towards her or their children, she should obviously not be regarded as having become homeless intentionally. Consequently, if she has a priority need, the housing authority are under a duty to secure accommodation for her. If she has been locked out, it is submitted that the authority should look at the reason for the husband's act and if this has been caused by her conduct – for example, by her own violent behaviour – it should be attributed to her, in which case she would be regarded as intentionally homeless.[15]

---

8 Section 195.
9 Section 190.
10 Section 191(1).
11 *Lewis v North Devon District Council* [1981] 1 All ER 27. If the spouse acts in good faith in ignorance of a relevant fact, she will not be regarded as having acquiesced and therefore will not be intentionally homeless: *R v Mole Valley District Council, ex p Burton* (1988) 20 HLR 479.
12 *R v Mole Valley District Council, ex p Burton* (supra); *R v London Borough of Ealing, ex p Salmons* (1990) 23 HLR 272.
13 [1983] 1 AC 657, [1981] 3 All ER 881, HL.
14 [1985] FLR 1043, CA.
15 But cf *R v Wandsworth London Borough Council, ex p Nimako-Boateng* [1984] FLR 192.

The duty to house homeless persons has placed an almost intolerable burden on many authorities. Some have taken the view that, if the need to provide accommodation for a married woman arises from her husband's behaviour, it is not unreasonable to expect her to ease the strain by obtaining what is now an occupation order and thus solving the problem herself.[16] There is nothing in the Act justifying the authority's putting pressure on the wife in this way and their doing so was roundly condemned by the Court of Appeal in *Warwick v Warwick*.[17] Ormrod LJ said:[18]

'I think it would be an abuse of the process of the court to use the court's very extensive powers in dealing with the occupation of matrimonial homes during the stress of divorce proceedings to allow those powers to be used in order to play the obscure housing policy games of local authorities.'

These words scarcely do justice to the authorities' attempts to deal with an often insoluble problem and were admittedly spoken in the course of a judgment allowing an appeal from an order requiring the husband to leave a house in an area to which the wife had no intention of returning because she feared interference from him. Nevertheless, whilst it might be proper to encourage the wife to take proceedings in an appropriate case, it cannot be right to put pressure on her if she is reluctant to do so.

Local connection

Where a victim of violence leaves not simply her home, but also the area where it is situated, the housing authority to whom she applies for help may argue that she has no close connection with their area, and should be housed by the authority for the area from which she came. They may seek to refer her case to that other authority under s 198 of the Act. However, they cannot do this where the applicant or any person who might reasonably be expected to reside with the applicant will run the risk of domestic violence from a person with whom they are associated, or of threats of violence from such a person which are likely to be carried out.[19]

Working of the provisions

These provisions clearly have the potential to offer a victim of violence and her children a safe, alternative and relatively secure new home, away from the violent partner. Unfortunately, research into the working of the legislation before its amendment in the Housing Act 1996 did not suggest that it was an easy route for a victim to take. One early study found that almost half of applications from women victims of violence were refused, because a lack of visible injuries led the authority to doubt the seriousness of the victim's plight, or, notwithstanding the guidance offered in the Code, or in case law, because a place in a refuge was deemed to be sufficient accommodation so as to render her not homeless, or

---

16 See the research by Thornton 'Homelessness through Relationship Breakdown' [1989] JSWL 67.
17 (1981) 3 FLR 393, CA.
18 At 395.
19 Section 198(2), (3). The housing authority have a duty to ascertain if an applicant would suffer violence if she returned or stayed at home: *R v Greenwich London Borough Council, ex p Patterson* [1993] 2 FLR 886, CA. However, if the applicant has previously been secured accommodation by another authority within the previous five years, that authority retains the duty to assist, even where domestic violence is proved: s 198(4). This hardly addresses the problem found by Malos and Hague that women may often be pressured to return to the authority for the area they have left to seek help there: Malos and Hague, op cit.

because leaving the family home was deemed intentional homelessness. Women were frequently given conditions to satisfy before help would be offered, including taking matrimonial proceedings and paying off rent arrears.[20] A more recent study found that it could take anything from one month to 18 months for an applicant to obtain a decision, and from four months to two years to obtain secure rehousing.[1] It is doubtful, with a continued dearth of available housing in the public sector, and a lack of suitable and affordable properties in the private sector, that the experience of victims seeking to use these provisions will improve significantly.

---

20 Binney et al *Leaving Violent Men: A Study of Refuges and Housing for Battered Women* (1981).
 1 Malos and Hague, op cit.

Chapter 7

Divorce

A.   Introduction[1]

The history of divorce law and its reform is marked by two features. First, there has always been a gap, sometimes wide, sometimes narrower, between the letter of the law and the means by which spouses and their legal advisers use or sidestep its terms to achieve their objective of ending the marriage tie. A bar on divorce did not, of itself, prevent marriage breakdown (although it is a continuing matter of debate as to how far a restrictive divorce law would restrain breakdowns or encourage couples to reconcile).[2] The second, and related, feature of divorce law is the extent to which it is the procedures, rather than the substance, of the law which determine the grant of the divorce. Indeed, it could be argued that the most recent reform, in the Family Law Act 1996, has now replaced all pretence that substantive law is involved, by overtly introducing a purely procedural set of hurdles which must be jumped in order to achieve the desired divorce order.

1.   DIVORCE BEFORE 1857

The doctrine of the indissolubility of marriage was accepted by the English ecclesiastical courts after the Reformation, so that these courts had no power to pronounce a decree of divorce (as opposed to nullity) which would permit the parties to remarry.[3] The only way in which an aggrieved party could obtain a full divorce ('divorce a vinculo matrimonii') was by Act of Parliament, the expense of which was beyond the reach of most. Adultery alone would not suffice in the case of a bill presented on behalf of the wife, who had to show that the adultery was aggravated (for example, bigamous or incestuous) or that her husband had committed an unnatural offence.[4]

2.   THE MATRIMONIAL CAUSES ACT 1857

The possibility of obtaining a divorce without having to petition Parliament was eventually introduced by this Act. In addition to vesting the existing jurisdiction of

---

1 See the *Finer Report on One-Parent Families* (1974) Cmnd 5629, Pt 4, s 2 and s 3; Stone *Road to Divorce: England 1530–1987* (1990) and *Broken Lives: Separation and Divorce in England 1660–1857* (1993).
2 Compare Deech 'Divorce Law and Empirical Studies' (1990) 106 LQR 229 with Eekelaar and Maclean 'Divorce Law and Empirical Studies – A Reply' (1990) 106 LQR 621.
3 Although they could pronounce decrees of restitution of conjugal rights (which called upon a deserting spouse to resume cohabitation), and of divorce 'a mensa et thoro', which was a decree of separation relieving the petitioner from the duty of cohabiting with the respondent.
4 There were on average fewer than two divorces by statute a year on the husband's petition, while in total only four were granted on the wife's petition. See Stone, op cit.

the ecclesiastical courts in a new statutory Divorce Court (from which it was transferred to the High Court in 1875)[5] the Act for the first time in English law permitted full divorce by judicial process. But the distinction between the position of the husband and that of the wife was retained, for a husband could petition for divorce on the ground of adultery alone, whilst a wife had to prove either adultery coupled with incest, bigamy, cruelty or two years' desertion, or, alternatively, rape or an unnatural offence.[6]

The purpose of the Act was primarily to change the process by which divorce was obtained from a legislative one to a judicial one: adultery remained the one matrimonial offence which would justify the dissolution of the marriage bond. Here one sees reflected the mid-Victorian attitude to sexual morality: whilst one act of adultery by a wife was considered unforgivable and gave the husband the power to petition for divorce without more, she could not even rely on a series of associations by him unless the adultery was 'aggravated'. The principle that divorce was a remedy for a matrimonial wrong was further applied in provisions absolutely precluding the court from pronouncing a decree if there were evidence of connivance or collusion between the parties.

3.   EXTENSION OF THE GROUNDS FOR DIVORCE

The law remained in this state until the Matrimonial Causes Act 1923 put the husband and wife in the same position by permitting the latter to petition on the ground of adultery simpliciter.[7] A P Herbert's Matrimonial Causes Act 1937 further extended the grounds for divorce by permitting either spouse to base a petition on the other's cruelty, desertion for three years, or (subject to certain other conditions) supervening incurable insanity.[8] This last provision introduced, for the first time, the possibility of obtaining a divorce even though the respondent was in no way at fault.

4.   THE DIVORCE REFORM ACT 1969

In the decades following the Second World War there was a vast increase in the number of divorces, and although this must in some measure reflect an increase in the number of marriages that had broken down, other factors came into play. Legal aid enabled many to obtain a divorce who could not previously have afforded it; the attitude of society towards divorced spouses (particularly 'guilty' spouses) had changed; and many religious bodies were taking a far less rigid attitude. More than 90 per cent of all petitions were undefended, and some of these undoubtedly amounted to divorce by consent.

---

5 By the Judicature Acts 1873–75.
6 Matrimonial Causes Act 1857 s 27.
7 Matrimonial Causes Act 1923 s 1. It did not strictly equate the spouses' rights, for the wife could still petition on the grounds of the husband's rape or unnatural offence, while there was no corresponding basis for the husband's petition.
8 The Act largely gave effect to the recommendations of the majority of members of a Royal Commission appointed in 1909 (the Gorrell Commission, Cd 6478). For a lively account of the history of the passage of this bill through Parliament, see Sir Alan Herbert's *The Ayes have it* (1937), and for a more recent discussion of it, see S Redmayne 'The Matrimonial Causes Act 1937: A Lesson in the Art of Compromise' (1993) 13 OJLS 183.

Consequently, the idea that the purpose of divorce was to provide a remedy available only to the 'innocent' spouse for a matrimonial wrong committed by the other seemed to many to be an outdated concept. It was argued that divorce should be available to either spouse when the marriage has irretrievably broken down: to insist on the commission of a matrimonial offence lays stress upon the symptoms of breakdown rather than on the breakdown itself. The introduction of this principle would, it was argued, reduce the number of stable illicit unions where there was no foreseeable chance of the parties being able to marry or of their children being legitimated because the spouse of one of them refused to release his or her partner on account of religious or moral scruple, financial advantage or vindictiveness. On the other hand, some regarded the idea as fundamentally unjust in that it would enable a party to take advantage of his own wrong and obtain a divorce against the will of an innocent spouse, who might have a conscientious objection to divorce, and because an 'innocent' wife in particular might suffer serious financial hardship as a consequence of the decree.

Against this background, a Royal Commission (the Morton Commission) was appointed to enquire into the law of England and Scotland concerning marriage and divorce, and published its report in 1956.[9] The Commission were divided on how far the concept of the matrimonial offence should remain the exclusive basis for divorce, and could not reach a clear consensus on reform. Consequently nothing significant happened until two major publications appeared in 1966. In the first, *Putting Asunder*, a group appointed by the Archbishop of Canterbury to consider the law of divorce in contemporary society came down in favour of the breakdown theory. Logically they argued that this must be the sole ground of divorce and that possible abuse must be guarded against by a judicial inquest in each case. *Putting Asunder* was referred to the Law Commission, who in turn reported in *Reform of the Grounds of Divorce: the Field of Choice*.[10] They concluded that the Archbishop's group's proposals for a full judicial enquiry in every case were impracticable, and put forward a number of possible alternatives based on the fundamental assumption that the aims of a good divorce law are:

'. . . to buttress, rather than undermine, the stability of marriage, and when, regrettably, a marriage has irretrievably broken down, to enable the empty legal shell to be destroyed with the maximum fairness and the minimum bitterness, distress and humiliation.'

Their own preference was for introducing as an additional ground for divorce the breakdown of the marriage as evidenced by a period of separation, which should be shorter if the respondent consented than if he did not.

The consequence was the passing of the Divorce Reform Act 1969. It represented a compromise between the views put forward by the Archbishop's group and the Law Commission. All the old grounds for divorce were abolished and replaced by one ground, that the marriage had irretrievably broken down. This, however, could only be established by proof of one or more of five facts set out in the Act. The old bars to divorce, such as collusion, were abolished, but various safeguards for the financial protection of the respondent, who was now potentially at risk of being divorced against his or her will, and after having committed no matrimonial wrong, were given instead.

9 Cmd 9678.
10 Cmnd 3123.

B.   The Matrimonial Causes Act 1973

This Act consolidated the Divorce Reform Act together with reforms relating to the financial and property consequences of divorce.[11]

1.   THE SUBSTANTIVE LAW

Irretrievable breakdown the sole ground for divorce

By s 1(1) of the Matrimonial Causes Act 1973 there is only one ground for divorce, that the marriage has broken down irretrievably. Irretrievable breakdown, however, may be established only by proving one or more of the five facts set out in s 1(2).[12] If none of these is established, the court may not pronounce a decree even though it is satisfied that the marriage is at an end.[13] Although it is the duty of the court 'to inquire, so far as it reasonably can, into the facts alleged' by both parties,[14] in practical terms the burden on the petitioner is solely to establish one of the facts and it is for the respondent in a defended suit to show, if he wishes, that the marriage has not broken down irretrievably.

The five facts for proving irretrievable breakdown

(a)   The respondent's adultery

The first fact on which the petitioner may rely is that the respondent has committed adultery and that the petitioner finds it intolerable to live with him.[15] It will be seen that there are two limbs. Adultery by itself is not sufficient: Parliament accepted that infidelity may be a symptom of breakdown rather than a cause of it and that an isolated act of adultery may not even be a symptom.

(b)   The respondent's behaviour

The petitioner may establish that the marriage has irretrievably broken down by showing that the respondent has behaved in such a way that the petitioner cannot reasonably be expected to live with him.[16] This provision is frequently, but erroneously, abbreviated to 'unreasonable behaviour',[17] thereby suggesting that all one has to look at is the quality of the respondent's behaviour, whereas in fact what is important is the effect of that conduct upon the petitioner.[18]

---

11 Matrimonial Proceedings and Property Act 1970.
12 No petition may be brought during the first year of the marriage: Matrimonial Causes Act 1973 s 3 as amended by the Matrimonial and Family Proceedings Act 1984. This bar will remain in the law: see post, p 242.
13 As in *Richards v Richards* [1972] 3 All ER 695.
14 Matrimonial Causes Act 1973 s 1(3).
15 Ibid, s 1(2)(a).
16 Ibid, s 1(2)(b).
17 Described as a 'linguistic trap' by Ormrod LJ in *Bannister v Bannister* (1980) 10 Fam Law 240, CA.
18 *Ash v Ash* [1972] Fam 135; *Pheasant v Pheasant* [1972] Fam 202, [1972] 1 All ER 587; *Livingstone-Stallard v Livingstone-Stallard* [1974] Fam 47, [1974] 2 All ER 766; *O'Neill v O'Neill* [1975] 3 All ER 289, CA.

(c) The respondent's desertion

The petitioner may show that the marriage has irretrievably broken down by proving that the respondent has deserted the petitioner for a continuous period of at least two years immediately preceding the presentation of the petition.[19] Desertion is defined as the unjustifiable withdrawal from cohabitation without the consent of the other spouse and with the intention of remaining separated permanently.

This fact has come to be relied upon only rarely, because the petition will usually be based on two years' separation if the respondent consents. A petitioner might wish to use it, however, if the respondent is in desertion and refuses to consent to a decree; and even after five years' separation (when the respondent's consent was not required) it avoids the possibility that the respondent will use s 5 or s 10 of the Matrimonial Causes Act to oppose or delay the granting of the decree absolute.[20]

(d) Two years' separation and the respondent's consent to the decree

The petitioner may establish that the marriage has broken down irretrievably by showing that the spouses have lived apart[1] for a continuous period of at least two years immediately preceding the presentation of the petition and that the respondent consents to the decree being granted.[2] This was one of the most controversial provisions of the Divorce Reform Act, because it introduced, albeit to a limited extent, divorce by consent.

(e) Five years' separation

The fifth fact on which a petitioner may rely is that the spouses have lived apart for a continuous period of at least five years immediately preceding the presentation of the petition.[3] This provision was even more controversial than the last, because it enabled the marriage to be dissolved against the will of a spouse who has committed no matrimonial offence and who has not been responsible for the breakdown of the marriage. On the one hand it was hailed as a measure that would bring relief to hundreds of couples who would otherwise live in stable illicit unions unable to marry because one or both of them could not secure release from another union; on the other hand it was castigated as a 'Casanova's charter'.

Protection of the respondent and children

(a) Protection of the respondent

Two provisions of the Matrimonial Causes Act are designed to give protection to the respondent when the petitioner relies on two or five years' separation – in other words, when the petition does not disclose any fault or breach of matrimonial obligation on the respondent's part. If the petitioner relies on *five years' separation*, s 5 of the Act permits the respondent to oppose the grant of a decree nisi on the ground that the dissolution of the marriage would result in grave

---

19 Matrimonial Causes Act 1973 s 1(2)(c).
20 See below.
 1 Matrimonial Causes Act 1973 s 2(6), See *Mouncer v Mouncer* [1972] 1 All ER 289; *Santos v Santos* [1972] Fam 247, [1972] 2 All ER 246, CA.
 2 Section 1(2)(d).
 3 Matrimonial Causes Act 1973 s 1(2)(e).

financial or other hardship to him and that it would be wrong in all the circumstances to dissolve the marriage. If a decree nisi is granted on the basis of *two or five years' separation*, the respondent may apply for it not to be made absolute unless the court is satisfied: (a) that the petitioner should not be required to make financial provision for the respondent; or (b) that the financial provision made by the petitioner for the respondent is reasonable and fair or the best that can be made in the circumstances.[4]

(b)   Protection of children

In every case where there are children of the family under the age of 16, or whom the court expressly directs should be included,[5] it has to consider the arrangements proposed for the children's future after their parents' divorce, and whether it should exercise any of its powers under the Children Act 1989 with respect to them. In exceptional circumstances the court may direct that the decree is not to be made absolute until further order, if it is of the opinion that it is likely to have to exercise its powers under the Children Act with respect to certain children of the family and it needs to give further consideration to the case.[6] The district judge may, if not satisfied, direct that further evidence be filed, that a welfare report be ordered, or that the parties attend before him.

2.   RECONCILIATION

The emphasis of the law is on *irretrievable* breakdown and certain provisions in the Matrimonial Causes Act are designed to promote a reconciliation between the parties. For example, if the petitioner instructs a solicitor to act for him, the latter is required to certify whether or not he has discussed with the petitioner the possibility of a reconciliation and given him the names and addresses of persons qualified to help effect a reconciliation between estranged spouses.[7] However, many applicants for a divorce do not instruct a solicitor, and the provision is generally regarded as serving little purpose.[8]

3.   THE PROCEDURE FOR OBTAINING THE DIVORCE[9]

The special procedure

Before 1973 in almost every undefended case a decree was granted following the uncontested evidence in open court of the petitioner and any other witness necessary to support his case. Appearance in court often led to considerable anxiety for the petitioner and to costs which, whether borne by the parties or the legal aid fund, were significant and growing rapidly. It also involved a great deal

4   Matrimonial Causes Act 1973 s 10(2),(3).
5   For example, because a child is disabled.
6   Matrimonial Causes Act 1973 s 41 (as amended). For an assessment of this provision before the Children Act amendments, see Davis, Macleod and Murch 'Undefended divorces: should section 41 of the Matrimonial Causes Act 1973 be repealed?' (1983) 46 MLR 121.
7   Ibid, s 6(1); Family Proceedings Rules 1991 r 2.6(3) and Form M3.
8   *Report of the Matrimonial Causes Procedure Committee* (the Booth Committee) (1985) paras 4.42–4.43. For further provisions aimed at facilitating reconciliation, see the Matrimonial Causes Act 1973 s 2 and s 6.
9   Family Proceedings Rules 1991 r 2.

of judicial time.[10] Consequently, in 1973 a 'special procedure' was introduced to dispense with the need to give evidence in court if the case was not defended. Originally it applied only to petitions based on two years' separation, but from 1977 all undefended petitions for divorce were dealt with under this procedure. At the same time, legal aid for the divorce itself was withdrawn.[11] This change in procedure may in some ways be seen as the most fundamental, yet relatively unremarked-upon change in divorce since the introduction of judicial divorce in 1857, since it seems to have marked the end of attempts to provide any effective scrutiny of a party's case for obtaining a divorce.

Under the special procedure, the petitioner commences proceedings by issuing a petition to the divorce county court, accompanied by a statement of the arrangements proposed for the minor children of the family and an affidavit verifying the contents of these, together with certain other information and any corroborative evidence on which the petitioner intends to rely. The district judge then enters the cause in the special procedure list. If he is satisfied that the petitioner has proved his case and is entitled to a decree, he makes and files a certificate to this effect and a day is fixed on which a judge or district judge pronounces the decree nisi in open court. Neither party needs to be present when this is done. While scrutiny of the documentation might reveal technical errors, it is unlikely to reveal defects of substance.[12]

The effect of the introduction of this procedure was inevitably to ensure that there can be no real investigation of the truth of the allegations made in the divorce petition if the respondent chooses not to challenge them.[13] Parties seeking a quick divorce have little to lose by bringing the petition on the basis of one of the fault facts – adultery or behaviour – rather than waiting the two years for a no fault decree. About three-quarters of petitions are based on the first two facts, with two years' separation only the third most often relied upon fact.[14]

Decrees

The divorce decree is made in two stages: the decree nisi, followed by the decree absolute.[15] The petitioner may apply for the decree to be made absolute at any time after the expiration of six weeks from the granting of the decree nisi unless the court fixes a shorter time in the particular case;[16] if the petitioner fails to apply for a decree absolute, the respondent may apply at any time after the expiration of three months from the earliest date on which the petitioner could have applied.[17] The delay is intended to provide an opportunity for an unsuccessful respondent to

10 Elston, Fuller and Murch 'Judicial Hearings of Undefended Divorce Petitions' (1975) 38 MLR 609.
11 Although it may still be obtained to make or oppose an application for an order for non-molestation or occupation, financial relief or in relation to children, but not to make an application in relation to children if there is no reason to believe that it would be opposed. Many petitioners find themselves having to draft their own divorce petition, the pitfalls of which exercise were demonstrated in *Young v Purdy* [1996] 2 FLR 795, CA.
12 Law Com No 192 *The Ground for Divorce* (1990) para 2.2.
13 See *Callaghan v Hanson-Fox* [1992] Fam 1, [1992] 1 All ER 56; *Moynihan v Moynihan (Nos 1 and 2)* [1997] 1 FLR 59.
14 See Law Com No 192 Appendix C, Tables 2–4.
15 Subject to the provisions of s 10 and s 41 of the 1973 Act: ante, p 230.
16 Matrimonial Causes Act 1973 s 1(5) and *Practice Direction* [1977] 2 All ER 714.
17 Matrimonial Causes Act 1973 s 9(2). But there is a discretion whether to permit the respondent's application, and it may be refused where financial matters are outstanding and the petitioner will be prejudiced if the respondent is permitted to obtain the freedom to remarry before these are resolved: *Smith v Smith* [1990] 1 FLR 438; *Manchanda v Manchanda* [1995] 2 FLR 590, CA; *Wickler v Wickler* [1998] 2 FLR 326.

appeal against the granting of the decree nisi, or for the Queen's Proctor or any other person to intervene to show cause why the decree should not be made absolute. The marriage ceases as soon as the decree is made absolute, and either spouse is then free to remarry. The decree nisi does not have this effect, and if either party remarries before it has been made absolute, the second marriage is void.

C.   Mediation[18]

Dissatisfaction with the procedural aspects of the law and the ineffectiveness of the provisions intended to encourage reconciliation led individual courts and practitioners to introduce an alternative mechanism for helping couples to deal with the consequences of their divorce – mediation, or, as it was originally known, conciliation.[19] A clear lead was given by the *Finer Report on One-Parent Families*, which defined conciliation as:

> '. . . assisting the parties to deal with the consequences of the established breakdown of their marriage, whether resulting in a divorce or a separation, by reaching agreements or giving assents or reducing the area of conflict upon custody, support, access to and education of the children, financial provision, disposition of the matrimonial home, lawyers' fees, and every other matter arising from the breakdown which calls for a decision on future arrangements'.[20]

Mediation has two main objects: to define the matters on which the parties are in dispute, and to encourage them to come to an agreed solution. The mediator must be – and must be seen to be – neutral: he may clarify issues and propose possible solutions, but he must not seek to impose any of them on the parties.[1]

The growth of interest in mediation reflects the changed attitude towards divorce generally, and the shift of emphasis from the fact of dissolution to its financial consequences and especially its effect on the children of the marriage. Research suggests that the children find emotional adjustment more difficult if the parents' relationship is hostile and conflict between them continues after divorce or separation, particularly if contact with one parent is not maintained.[2] One of the strongest arguments in favour of mediation is that the possibility of bitterness will be reduced and the prospects of both spouses continuing to play an active role as parents will be enhanced if they can reach agreement. The adversarial procedure of the courts, on the other hand, may well exacerbate antagonism.[3] Mediation also,

---

18   There is a vast literature. See, in particular, Davis *Partisans and Mediators* (1988); Parkinson *Conciliation in Separation and Divorce* (1986); Haynes *Alternative Dispute Resolution: The Fundamentals of Family Mediation* (1993); Walker et al *Mediation: The Making and Re-Making of Co-operative Relationships* (1994).

19   Mediation has become the preferred term in recent years.

20   Cmnd 5629, para 4.288 (1974).

1   This distinguishes a mediator from an adjudicator (who has the power to impose a solution), an arbitrator (by whose decision the parties have agreed to be bound), and a negotiator (who acts on behalf of one party only).

2   Wallerstein and Kelly *Surviving the Break-Up: How Children and Parents Cope with Divorce* (1980), Wallerstein and Blakeslee *Second Chances: Men, Women and Children a Decade after Divorce* (1990).

3   See eg the *Report of the Inter-departmental Committee on Conciliation* (1983), para 1.13; Parkinson, op cit p 69; Murch *Justice and Welfare in Divorce* (1980) 210; the Family Law Sub-committee of the Law Society *A Better Way Out* (1979) para 15.

it is argued, enables the parties to retain control of their own affairs rather than have a solution imposed on them.

Two types of mediation developed alongside the statutory divorce procedure: 'in-court' and 'out-of-court'.

1.   IN-COURT MEDIATION

In 1971, courts were encouraged to refer a case to the court welfare officer when it was considered that conciliation might be helpful.[4] In 1977, a scheme to incorporate this approach into the normal divorce process was launched in the Bristol county court, and similar schemes were subsequently introduced in many others.[5] The parties and their solicitors attend an appointment for directions before the district judge; if the issues are essentially issues of law or fact, the district judge can assist by pointing the way towards a possible resolution, but if they are 'emotional or involve children, the parties withdraw . . . with a welfare officer who adopts a combination of conciliatory and investigatory techniques'.[6] If agreement is reached, the district judge can make the necessary consent orders. In such schemes, both parties and their legal advisers are required to attend a mediation appointment; and they may be accompanied by any of their children, usually over the age of about nine, where it is thought appropriate for them to be seen by the district judge or welfare officer. Parties may retire to a private room with a welfare officer, and if mediation is successful, the district judge will make such orders as are appropriate.[7] If the parties cannot reach an agreement, the welfare officer acting as mediator may subsequently be asked to make a report to the court, but it is accepted that these two roles cannot be combined and that the same officer should not carry out both functions.[8] Similar schemes relating to financial and property issues in the divorce were introduced in 1996 in a pilot project in various parts of the country, under the auspices of the Lord Chancellor's Advisory Group on Ancillary Relief, and with the support of the Solicitors' Family Law Association and the Family Law Bar Association.[9]

There is some evidence that parties may feel under pressure to reach a decision in as short a time as possible in these kinds of appointment, and some complain of crude arm-twisting and a search for a compromise regardless of the justice of the case.[10] District judges and welfare officers may try to impose their own solutions on the parties, and so far from leading them to reach their own agreement, the procedure may come to resemble that of a contested court appearance. Research by Davis et al[11] into an ancillary relief mediation appointments scheme begun in 1986 in Bristol found a similar picture, but considered that, since the parties understood the pressure upon them to settle and that authority lay with the judge, these appointments were open to less criticism than those centring upon children's

---

4 *Practice Direction* [1971] 1 All ER 894.
5 For a brief summary of what has developed since in Bristol, see Davis, Cretney and Collins *Simple Quarrels* (1994) pp 172–7.
6 Parmiter, 78 LS Gaz 196.
7 *Practice Directions* [1982] 3 All ER 988, [1984] 3 All ER 800, [1992] 1 All ER 421.
8 *Scott v Scott* [1986] 2 FLR 320, CA; *Re H (Conciliation: Welfare Reports)* [1986] 1 FLR 476; *Practice Direction* [1986] 2 FLR 171. See also Booth Committee Report supra paras 4.61–4.63.
9 *Ancillary Relief Pilot Scheme: Practitioners' Guide* (1996); Family Proceedings (Amendment No 2) Rules 1997, SI 1997/1056.
10 Davis and Bader [1985] Fam Law 42, 82; Piper *The Responsible Parent* (1993).
11 *Simple Quarrels* ch 8.

issues. Such findings will have significance for the increased emphasis upon mediation which is to be found in the Family Law Act 1996.[12]

2. OUT-OF-COURT MEDIATION

Out-of-court mediation is independent of the court in the sense that parties are not referred to it by the court, and a mediator's services are available to them before they embark on litigation. The chances of success of out-of-court mediation are said to be greater because the parties are more likely to resort to it before they take up entrenched positions. It began in 1978, also in Bristol, as a result of the initiative of a group committed to taking action following the publication of the *Report of the Committee on One-Parent Families*. Most couples are referred by solicitors or refer themselves. A number of other independent schemes have since been set up in other parts of the country.[13]

3. MEDIATION AT THE HEART OF THE DIVORCE PROCESS

Initially, the potential costs of introducing mediation throughout the country, either as a part of divorce procedure, or outside of proceedings, appeared to deter the government from support for the process. In 1982 an inter-departmental governmental committee was set up to report on the nature, scope and effects of existing mediation services. The committee considered that, while there was a role for mediation, out-of-court schemes do not save money and appear to be more expensive than in-court schemes. They therefore concluded that government funding of out-of-court schemes was not justified and that mediation should be provided by in-court schemes.

Their report met with considerable criticism,[14] but they had recommended that a research unit should be established to monitor different types of in-court mediation. As a result a Conciliation Project Unit, based at the University of Newcastle-upon-Tyne, was set up with wider terms of reference to include an examination of the costs and effectiveness of out-of-court schemes as well. The Unit recommended the establishment of a national service, which would be part of a network of local services covering both mediation and counselling and would be independent of the courts and the probation service. The Unit's report appears to have revitalised the pressure to widen the availability of mediation, and when the government introduced its own plans for reform,[15] mediation had become the cornerstone of its proposed divorce procedure. This new faith in mediation has been reflected in other aspects of the civil justice system[16] and is also a growing international trend, with mediation schemes well established in many countries, and the subject of attention in the Council of Europe.[17]

---

12 See post, pp 255–7.
13 See the *UK College of Family Mediators Directory and Handbook* (1998, 2nd edn) for a list of those offering family mediation.
14 Davis and Westcott 'Report of the Inter-Departmental Committee on Conciliation' (1984) 47 MLR 215.
15 See post, pp 238–40.
16 The Woolf Report *Access to Justice:Final Report to the Lord Chancellor on the Civil Justice in England and Wales* (1996) places considerable emphasis upon mediation and other forms of alternative dispute resolution in civil cases.
17 See Dingwall and Eekelaar (eds) *Divorce Mediation and the Legal Process* (1988); Council of Europe, 4th European Conference on Family Law, Strasbourg 1998; Recommendation No R(98)1 on Family Mediation (provisional), DIR/JVR (98)4.

D. Proposals for reform

1. THE BOOTH COMMITTEE ON MATRIMONIAL CAUSES PROCEDURE

In 1982 a committee chaired by Booth J was established to examine the whole question of matrimonial procedure. The main thrust of their Report, published in 1985, was that bitterness between the parties might be reduced if unnecessary acrimonious allegations were eliminated and defended suits kept to a minimum; furthermore, parties should be encouraged and helped to settle financial matters and questions relating to children themselves with the benefit of legal advice and, if necessary, the assistance of mediators.

They also proposed that there should be an initial hearing within about 10 weeks of filing the application in every case involving children to whom s 41 of the 1973 Act applied[18] and also in cases where the respondent had stated an intention to oppose the grant of the decree. The purpose of the hearing would be to make orders in respect of agreed matters, to refer the parties to mediation where appropriate, to define the issues remaining between them, and to give directions.[19]

The Committee recommended that the terms 'decree nisi' and 'decree absolute' be replaced by 'provisional decree' and 'final decree', and that the latter should normally issue automatically four weeks after the grant of the former. To protect a party where this would work hardship (for example, because no order had been made for financial relief) the court would be given a power to delay the final decree in appropriate cases.

Although no action was taken on most of their recommendations, a number were later developed by the Law Commission in their own proposals for more thorough-going reform of the law.

2. THE LAW COMMISSION'S PROPOSALS

Research showed that the objectives of the law, as laid down by the Law Commission in their 1966 Report, were not being met,[20] and the Law Commission looked again at the problem, issuing a Discussion Paper in 1988[1] and a report in 1990.[2]

The Law Commission's criticisms of the 1973 Act

(a)   'It is confusing and misleading'

The sole ground for divorce is stated to be the irretrievable breakdown of the marriage, suggesting that fault is not the basis for granting a divorce, but such breakdown, no matter how profound, will not lead to a divorce decree unless a spouse can point to one of the five facts, three of which do involve fault. Further, the real reason for the breakdown might have nothing to do with the fact presented in the petition, the allegations becoming a peg on which to hang the petition,

---

18 See ante, p 230.
19 Report para 3.5.
20 See, in particular, Davis and Murch *Grounds for Divorce* (1988).
 1 *Facing the Future – A Discussion Paper on the Ground for Divorce* Law Com No 170.
 2 *The Ground for Divorce* Law Com No 192.

regardless of their significance (or insignificance) for the parties. No real scrutiny can be conducted into the truth of the allegations, and a petitioner might be encouraged to bolster the petition with trivial or exaggerated allegations.[3]

(b)   'It is discriminatory and unjust'

The two years' separation with consent fact is relied upon more often by those in the higher socio-economic groups, while the poorer have to rely on the less satisfactory fault facts in order to obtain a speedier divorce and hence resolution of their financial and property problems.[4] It is discriminatory and unjust to provide a civilised no fault basis for divorce which is, in practice, unavailable to a large part of the population because many couples cannot afford to part and establish separate households before the divorce. The fault facts themselves do not result in a clear allocation of 'blame' for the breakdown of the marriage, since the petitioner might have been equally to blame although his conduct is not raised because the respondent does not defend the case. Even where respondents wish to dispute the allegations made in the petition by defending the suit, they are usually told that it would be a waste of time and money because the divorce will be granted anyway.

(c)   'It distorts parties' bargaining positions'

Given the difficulty facing a spouse in challenging allegations in the divorce suit itself, the scope for dispute is usually displaced from the divorce petition itself to the ancillary matters. One party who is more anxious or reluctant for the divorce to occur might be placed in a correspondingly weaker or stronger position in bargaining over matters relating to money and the children.

(d)   'It provokes unnecessary hostility and bitterness'

A fundamental objective of the Divorce Reform Act was to minimise the bitterness, distress and humiliation experienced by the parties in obtaining their divorce. But the system encourages each to make allegations against the other and to portray the other in as bad a light as possible to support the petition. This provokes resentment, hostility and distress in the other spouse at a time when the couple are experiencing severe stress and unhappiness in coming to terms with the ending of their marriage. Their emotional misery is simply compounded by the legal process.

(e)   'It does nothing to save the marriage'

Despite the provisions intended to promote reconciliation which, as we saw,[5] have had little effect, the law in fact thrusts the parties further apart by encouraging the making of allegations of misconduct against each other or by requiring them to separate. Attention is placed upon how to prove irretrievable breakdown rather than on how to try to mend the marriage.

---

3 Law Com No 192 paras 2.8–2.12.
4 Examination of 477 cases begun in the years 1980 to 1984 revealed that 36% of those in social group I relied upon the two years' separation fact, compared with 17% in social group V: Law Com No 192 Appendix C, Table 2.
5 See ante, p 230.

(f) *'It can make things worse for the children'*

Children whose parents divorce may suffer more subsequently if the parents remain in conflict.[6] The law does nothing to reduce such conflict: indeed, it frequently exacerbates it.

The options for reform

These criticisms convinced the Law Commission that the law required further reform. In deciding how to achieve this, the Law Commission drew up a new set of objectives for the law, which show interesting differences from their 1966 formulation.[7] It was 'generally agreed' that the law should:

> '. . . try to support those marriages which are capable of being saved . . . enable those which cannot be saved to be dissolved with the minimum of avoidable distress, bitterness and hostility . . . encourage, so far as possible, the amicable resolution of practical issues relating to the couple's home, finances and children and the proper discharge of their responsibilities to one another and to their children . . .'

and

> '. . . seek to minimise the harm that the children of the family may suffer, both at the time and in the future, and to promote so far as possible the continued sharing of parental responsibility for them.'[8]

These objectives reflect both the new emphasis on mediation, and also the shift of attention towards the children of the marriage and the fundamental ideology of parental responsibility which underpins the Children Act 1989 (enacted shortly before this report was published).

With these objectives in mind, the Commission rejected a return to a fault-based system on the basis that, first, the law is capable of assessing fault only in the crudest way, and secondly, that denying divorce except on grounds of fault is an illogical and ineffective way of promoting good marital conduct. Equally, divorce by immediate unilateral demand was rejected as providing no means of protecting the respondent, and divorce by mutual consent would not cater for cases where one spouse steadfastly refuses to consent. In many other jurisdictions which reformed their law after the Divorce Reform Act, the preferred model was a simple period of separation, but the Law Commission criticised it for its discriminatory effects against those who are poor. Instead, they recommended that divorce should no longer be seen as a single event but should be granted only after a process continuing for a period of time. This would demonstrate that the breakdown is irretrievable, give the parties the opportunity of facing up to the consequences of divorce and enable the practical problems to be resolved.

The Law Commission's proposed scheme

The process they contemplated would begin by either (or preferably both) of the parties lodging at a court a sworn statement that he or she (or both) believes that the marriage has broken down. Each party would then be given a comprehensive information pack explaining inter alia the purpose of the period of consideration and reflection, the effects of divorce and separation, the powers of the court, and

---

6 Richards and Dyson *Separation, Divorce and the Development of Children: A review* (1982).
7 Ante, p 227.
8 Law Com No 192 para 3.1.

the nature and purpose of counselling, reconciliation and mediation. No later than 12 weeks after the making of the statement, the court would hold a preliminary assessment to review progress, make directions and consider whether mediation might be appropriate in helping the parties reach agreements.[9] After 11 months either or both of them would be able to apply for an order for divorce on making a declaration that the maker (or makers) believe that the breakdown of their marriage is irretrievable. In the intervening period the parties could be offered counselling or mediation, and the court could make orders relating to children, financial provision and property adjustment. This would reflect the principle that the practical consequences of divorce should ideally be settled before the marriage is dissolved. The court would normally make an order for divorce a month after the application (giving a minimum period of 12 months from the lodging of the initial statement). As under the 1973 Act, however, it should be able to postpone the order in exceptional circumstances, if this were necessary to enable it to consider whether it should exercise any of its powers under the Children Act in respect of any children of the family or to make any proper financial arrangements. The court would also be able to refuse an order for divorce if this would result in grave financial or other hardship to one of the parties and it would be wrong in the circumstances to dissolve the marriage.

3.   THE GOVERNMENT'S RESPONSE[10]

Notwithstanding the government's unhappy experience in enacting the Child Support Act 1991, and the fact that hitherto divorce legislation had been regarded as too controversial to be handled as a government measure, the Lord Chancellor decided to introduce plans to reform the divorce law, issuing a consultation paper in 1993,[11] followed by a White Paper in 1995.[12] The key to this insistence on taking control of divorce reform would appear to lie, at least in part, in the government's further refinement of the objectives of divorce law. Now, these were stated as being:

 – to support the institution of marriage;
 – to provide practicable steps to prevent the irretrievable breakdown of marriages;
 – to ensure that couples understand the practical consequences of divorce before making any irreversible decision;
 – where divorce is unavoidable, to minimise the bitterness and hostility between the parties and to reduce the trauma for the children; and
 – to keep costs to the minimum.[13]

---

9   The assessment would be roughly equivalent to the initial hearing recommended earlier by the Booth Committee: ante, p 235.
10 For assessments of the government's proposals, see Bainham 'Divorce and the Lord Chancellor: Looking to the Future or Getting Back to Basics?' (1994) 35 Cambridge LJ 253; Cretney 'Divorce Reform in England: Humbug and Hypocrisy or a Smooth Transition?' in Freeman (ed) *Divorce, Where Next?* (1996).
11 *Looking to the Future: Mediation and the Ground for Divorce* Cm 2424 (hereafter, 'Green Paper').
12 Cm 2799 (hereafter, 'White Paper'). The White Paper had the same title as the earlier Consultation Paper.
13 Ibid, para 3.5. For a sceptical view of the feasibility of realising these objectives, see Davis 'Divorce Reform – Peering Anxiously into the Future' [1995] Fam Law 564.

The government accepted the Law Commission's recommended scheme of a period of consideration and reflection having to elapse as evidence of the irretrievable breakdown of the marriage. It also seized upon mediation as a mechanism which would, it was said, be better able than the legal process to identify marriages capable of being saved, and would thus enhance the opportunities for reconciliation. Where reconciliation was not achievable, the couple would be encouraged to resolve their differences and co-operate in sorting out the arrangements necessary for their, and their children's future lives more amicably. Finally, the government considered that, contrary to earlier research,[14] mediation is cheaper than litigation and hence will save money for both the parties and the taxpayer. The government estimated that the average cost of comprehensive mediation (in which both financial and child issues are dealt with) was about £550 per case, while the average cost of a matrimonial bill paid by the Legal Aid Fund in 1992/93 was £1,565.[15] Faced with such potential savings, the government proposed that legal aid would be channelled to pay for mediation as well as legal assistance and representation, and indeed, a party would have to make out a case to the Legal Aid Board as to why he or she should have legal assistance as opposed to mediation.[16]

The government's proposals differed from those of the Law Commission in significant respects. First, they placed much greater emphasis upon the role of mediation. Secondly, instead of having a preliminary assessment during the period for consideration and reflection, they proposed that a dual information and assessment function could be fulfilled by an initial interview where essential information could be given about the law, legal procedures, marriage guidance and mediation. This interview could help identify saveable marriages, point couples towards mediation and also determine their eligibility for legal aid. The idea that a welfare officer or possibly some other official should have such a wide-ranging role was not well received, and the White Paper instead proposed that the initial appointment become a purely information-giving service (albeit a compulsory one for anyone initiating the divorce process).[17]

A third important change related to the settling of ancillary arrangements *before* the divorce would be granted. The Law Commission argued that, while one of the strengths of the period for consideration and reflection would be that it would enable the parties to decide upon the financial and other arrangements consequent upon the divorce, and while there should be power for the courts to make final orders relating to these before the dissolution of the marriage, it would be wrong to *require* the parties to have resolved all issues concerning children, property and finance before a divorce order could be made. They reasoned that this would 'create a formidable bargaining chip for the more powerful or determined party', who could thereby delay the grant of the divorce.[18] Instead, they proposed that the court should have the power to postpone the divorce where granting it without any delay would cause hardship to the spouse or children.[19] The government, however, reversed this position. They were influenced by the argument that 'people who marry should discharge their obligations undertaken when they contracted their

---

14 Ante, p 234.
15 Green Paper paras 9.28, 9.30.
16 *Legal Aid – Targeting Need* Cm 2854 (1995).
17 Green Paper para 8.12; White Paper para 6.15.
18 Law Com No 192 para 5.56.
19 Ibid, para 5.58.

earlier marriage, and also their responsibilities which they undertook when they became parents, before they became free to remarry.'[20] Accordingly, there should be no divorce until arrangements have been finalised, *unless* delay would cause hardship to a spouse or child.

The government's Family Law Bill had a difficult passage through Parliament, and several further changes were made to the legislation before it received the Royal Assent in 1996. Many aspects of the working of the law remain to be determined by statutory instruments and guidance, and pilot schemes have been launched to test these out before the new law is brought into force.

E.   Divorce under the Family Law Act 1996[1]

1.   THE 'GENERAL PRINCIPLES'

Section 1 of the Act requires the court, and any person exercising functions under Parts II and III of the Act (which relate to divorce and mediation), to have regard to the following general principles:

'(a)   that the institution of marriage is to be supported;
(b)   that the parties to a marriage which may have broken down are to be encouraged to take all practicable steps, whether by marriage counselling or otherwise, to save the marriage;
(c)   that a marriage which has irretrievably broken down and is being brought to an end should be brought to an end –
  (i)   with minimum distress to the parties and to the children affected;
  (ii)   with questions dealt with in a manner designed to promote as good a continuing relationship between the parties and any children affected as is possible in the circumstances; and
  (iii)   without costs being unreasonably incurred in connection with the procedures to be followed in bringing the marriage to an end; and
(d)   that any risk to one of the parties to a marriage, and to any children, of violence from the other party should, so far as reasonably practicable, be removed or diminished.'

These principles are intended to guide courts and others in their application of the Act's provisions. These others could include the Lord Chancellor, in drawing up the detailed regulations underpinning the Act, lawyers acting for divorcing couples, mediators, marriage counsellors and Legal Aid Board officials. The parties themselves do not exercise functions under the Act and hence are not required to take these principles into account, but part of the task of those who do will be to bring home to spouses their significance.

2.   JURISDICTION UNDER THE FAMILY LAW ACT

The court's jurisdiction to entertain 'marital proceedings'[2] is set out in s 19 of the Act. At least one of the parties to the proceedings must have been domiciled in

20   White Paper para 4.26 and Hansard HL Debs, 30 November 1995, col 703.
  1   See Bird and Cretney *Divorce: The New Law* (1996), La Follette and Purdie *A Guide to the Family Law Act 1996* (1996), Bishop et al *Divorce Reform: A Guide for Lawyers and Mediators* (1996).
  2   Defined, by s 20 of the Family Law Act 1996, as covering both divorce and separation (but not nullity) proceedings.

England and Wales on the date the statement of marital breakdown[3] was received by the court,[4] or habitually resident in England and Wales throughout the period of one year ending with that date, or nullity proceedings are pending in relation to the marriage when the marital proceedings commence.[5] In addition, where a separation order is in force or an order preventing divorce has been cancelled,[6] the court continues to have jurisdiction to deal with a divorce sought on the basis of that order.[7] These rules and the way they are exercised are the same as under the former law.[8]

3. DIVORCE PROCEDURE UNDER THE FAMILY LAW ACT

The information meeting

Section 8 provides that a party who initiates the divorce must (except in prescribed circumstances) have attended an information meeting first.[9] Where both spouses jointly seek the divorce, both must attend a meeting, but need not do so together.[10] Where one spouse initiates the process, the other need not attend a meeting unless he or she wishes to make an application to the court with respect to a child of the family,[11] or to prescribed types of property or finance, or wishes to contest any such application.[12]

The purpose of the meeting is to communicate a range of information relating to divorce, the process and its consequences, and also to 'mark the seriousness of the step being taken'.[13] It will also provide an opportunity to meet a marriage counsellor, and parties will be encouraged to attend such a meeting.[14] The person conducting the meeting must not have any financial or other interest in any marital proceedings between the parties.[15] The meeting will be a private one for the party or parties concerned, rather than, as had been envisaged in the White Paper, a group session for a batch of intending divorcees.[16]

The information to be given in the meeting must, pursuant to s 8(9), include that relating to:

'(a) marriage counselling and other marriage support services;
 (b) the importance to be attached to the welfare, wishes and feelings of children;

---

3 Discussed post, p 242.
4 Family Law Act 1996 s 19(7).
5 Ibid, s 19(2).
6 See post, p 253.
7 Section 19(3)(a) and (4). Separation orders and their conversion to divorce orders are discussed post at pp 257–60.
8 See 8th edition pp 230–3.
9 Family Law Act 1996 s 8(2). No circumstances had been prescribed at the time of writing.
10 Ibid, s 8(4).
11 Section 24(1) applies the same definition as under the Matrimonial Causes Act 1973 s 52, see post, pp 288–90.
12 Ibid, s 8(5). No property had been prescribed at the time of writing.
13 Hansard HL Debs, 30 November 1995, col 702 (Lord Mackay LC).
14 Ibid, s 8(6)(b).
15 Ibid, s 8(7).
16 Group meetings are used in Australia and parts of the United States of America and were strongly favoured by the government in the White Paper: Cm 2799, paras 7.14–7.16. For withering criticism of such an innovation, see Cretney 'Divorce Reform in England: Humbug and Hypocrisy or a Smooth Transition?' in Freeman (ed) *Divorce, Where Next?* p 48, Davis 'Divorce Reform – Peering Anxiously into the Future' [1995] Fam Law 564. Group meetings may be offered additionally on a voluntary basis, however.

(c) how the parties may acquire a better understanding of the ways in which children can be helped to cope with the breakdown of a marriage;
(d) the nature of the financial questions that may arise on divorce or separation, and services which are available to help the parties;
(e) protection available against violence, and how to obtain support and assistance;
(f) mediation;
(g) the availability to each of the parties of independent legal advice and representation;
(h) the principle of legal aid and where the parties can get advice about obtaining legal aid;
(i) the divorce and separation process.'

Paragraphs (b) and (c) reflect the greater attention now paid to the needs of the children of divorced couples. The aim is also to ensure that couples understand the implications of starting the divorce process.[17]

Statement of marital breakdown

(a) Commencement of divorce proceedings

Divorce proceedings commence on receipt by the court of a statement of marital breakdown.[18] Such a statement may not (except in prescribed circumstances) be made within three months of the party making it having attended an information meeting.[19] The object of this delay is to provide a 'cooling-off period' during which parties may explore the scope for reconciliation, and hence, the information meeting will have given details of marriage counselling services available to the parties.[20] The statement may be made by one, or both parties to the marriage,[1] and states that the maker or makers believe that the marriage has broken down,[2] that they are aware of the purpose of the period for reflection and consideration and wish to make arrangements for the future.[3]

Once a statement has been made, or a divorce or separation order has been applied for, or a separation order is in force, any further statement will be ineffective.[4] Thus, once one spouse has issued a statement, the other cannot do so as a form of 'cross-petition', as was common under the former law. The statement may be withdrawn by both spouses by giving notice to the court, but a statement made by one spouse cannot be withdrawn by that spouse alone.[5]

(b) One-year time bar on making a statement

A statement made before the first anniversary of the marriage is ineffective for the purposes of any application for a divorce order (although not for a separation

17 Compare the findings of Davis and Murch *Grounds for Divorce* (1988) pp 57–67 and the government's findings that there is widespread ignorance of the possibilities open to couples whose marriage is in difficulty but who have not yet decided on a divorce: See White Paper para 7.1.
18 Ibid, s 20(1).
19 Ibid, s 8(2).
20 A person who would receive free legal aid for mediation is not required to pay towards the cost of any meeting arranged under s 8 with a marriage counsellor: s 8(12).
1 Ibid, s 5(1)(a).
2 Not that they believe it has broken down irretrievably, since it is the purpose of the period for reflection and consideration to test this.
3 Ibid, s 6(2), (3). Rules will prescribe information to accompany the statement, including whether the party has made any attempt at reconciliation during the cooling off period, and will also set out how the statement is to be given to the court and served on the other spouse.
4 Section 6(7). For separation orders see post, pp 258–60.
5 Section 5(3)(a).

order).[6] This preserves the bar on early divorce introduced originally in 1937 (when a discretionary bar on divorce within three years of the marriage was first enacted) and revised to a one-year complete bar in 1984.[7]

Period for reflection and consideration

(a)   Duration of the period

The irretrievable breakdown of the marriage will be established by the passing of the due period for reflection and consideration. This period commences on the 14th day after the day on which the statement of marital breakdown is received by the court,[8] and the basic period is nine months. However, this minimum duration before a divorce order can be made may, or must be, extended according to various circumstances. These are as follows.

(I)   EXTENSION FOR DELAY IN SERVING NOTICE OF STATEMENT

Under s 7(4), where a copy of the statement should have been served on the other party and failure to comply with the rules has caused inordinate delay in service, then, on that party's application, the court may extend the period to cover that delay.Thus, if there were a delay of two months in effecting service, the court could extend the usual period by up to two months (but it could choose a lesser extension, or order none at all).[9]

(II)   EXTENSION TO ALLOW FOR ATTEMPTED RECONCILIATION

Both spouses may jointly give notice to the court that they are attempting a reconciliation but require additional time. Where this is done, the period is suspended on the day the court receives the notice, but resumes when *either* spouse gives notice that the attempted reconciliation has been unsuccessful. Once the suspension of the period has lasted 18 months, a new statement of marital breakdown will have to be made and the process started all over again.[10]

(III)   AUTOMATIC EXTENSION WHERE A PARTY SEEKS FURTHER TIME FOR REFLECTION

Section 7(10) enables one spouse to seek an extension of time, after the other has applied for a divorce order (not after the other has filed the statement of marital breakdown). This means that the extension is sought, not during the main period of reflection, but at almost the final hurdle, for the other spouse will have applied for the order on the basis that all the requisite conditions, including the making of financial arrangements, have been met.[11] The spouse seeking an extension must do so within a prescribed period, which will presumably be fairly short. The effect of the application is automatically to extend the period by six months.[12]

---

6 Ibid, s 7(6). Separation orders are discussed post at p 257.
7 Matrimonial and Family Proceedings Act 1984 s 1, amending s 3 of the Matrimonial Causes Act 1973. For detailed discussion of the policy objectives of the bar, see the 8th edition of this work, pp 186–7.
8 Section 7(3).
9 Section 7(5).
10 Section 7(7)–(9).
11 See post, p 246 for the application under s 3 of the Act.
12 Section 7(13).

(IV)   AUTOMATIC EXTENSION WHERE A CHILD OF THE FAMILY IS UNDER SIXTEEN

The argument that divorce should be harder – or, at least, take longer – where children are involved had previously been resisted because it could cause the parties to feel bitter and resentful towards their children.[13] However, consequent upon an amendment inserted into the Bill, the Act provides that where there is a 'child of the family'[14] under the age of 16, then, on an application for a divorce order, the period is extended automatically by six months.[15]

(V)   EXCEPTIONS TO AUTOMATIC EXTENSIONS

When the Law Commission proposed that the lapse of an appropriate period of time should be the only means of proving irretrievable breakdown of the marriage, it was argued that this would be an unnecessary burden to those who could sort out their post-divorce arrangements more quickly, and unfair to a spouse who might be the victim of domestic violence. Why should she have to wait a lengthy period before being able to divorce her husband? The response was that only by lapse of the appropriate period of time could the *irretrievable* breakdown of the marriage be established with certainty, and that it was important to symbolise the significance attached to marriage by not allowing for an abridgement of the period. Remedies to tackle violence would be in place to solve immediate problems anyway, and there was a danger that a power to abridge the period would recreate a 'fast track' procedure based on allegations of fault, and encourage litigation.[16] However, Parliament decided that, where the period would otherwise be extended under the two provisions discussed immediately above, it would be right to reinstate the basic nine month period if the applicant for the divorce order has an occupation or non-molestation order in force in her favour (or such an order is in force in favour of a child of the family) against the other spouse. In such a case, the period will not be extended.[17]

Secondly, the extension will not apply if the court is satisfied that delaying the making of the divorce order would be significantly detrimental to the welfare of any child of the family. It will be for the party seeking to lift the extension to satisfy the court of this.[18]

(b)   Counselling and mediation during the period for reflection and consideration

Parties are expected to use the period for consideration and reflection to explore the scope for reconciliation, or to seek to come to terms with the ending of the marriage and settle their post-divorce arrangements. The main mechanisms to assist them to do these will be non-legal. Both marriage counselling and mediation are seen as providing the basic and major services for divorcing couples. Legal assistance is seen by the government as consequential and subsidiary.[19]

---

13 Law Com No 192 para 5.28; White Paper para 4.18.
14 See post, pp 288–90.
15 Section 7(11). The aim of the amendment was to provide further protection for the children by giving parents more time to attempt a reconciliation: see Hansard HL Debs, 11 March 1996, col 622 (Baroness Young) and HC Debs, 24 April 1996, col 523 (Dame Jill Knight MP). The extension comes to an end on there ceasing to be any children of the family under 16: s 7(14).
16 Law Com No 192 para 5.64; White Paper paras 4.19–4.23.
17 Section 7(12)(a).
18 Section 7(12)(b). Lord Irvine of Lairg considered that there would be 'very many cases' where concern that delaying the divorce would be detrimental to a child's interests would be justified: Hansard HL Debs, 27 June 1996, col 1071.
19 White Paper paras 6.17–6.21.

(I)   COUNSELLING

We have seen that an opportunity to seek marriage counselling will be given at the information meeting. A further chance may be given during the period for reflection and consideration (or during its suspension for attempted reconciliation) but, rather oddly, the provision of marriage counselling under the Act is limited to those eligible for free mediation and legal aid.[20] Presumably, the better off are expected to explore the possibility for themselves.

(II)   MEDIATION

The provision of mediation is intended to lie at the heart of the new divorce procedure. After the court has received a statement, it may give a direction, on the application of either spouse or on its own initiative,[1] requiring each party to attend a meeting for the purpose of having an explanation given to them of the facilities available for mediation, and of giving them the opportunity to take advantage of those facilities.[2] The parties must attend the same meeting unless one or both asks for separate meetings or the court considers these to be more appropriate.[3] The court's direction will specify who is to arrange and conduct the meeting, and require that person to report to the court stating whether the parties have complied with the direction and, if so, whether they have agreed to take part in any mediation.[4] The court may adjourn proceedings connected with the breakdown of the marriage[5] to enable the parties to comply with a direction, having regard in particular to the need to protect the 'interests' of any child of the family.[6]

Anyone financially eligible for legal aid will be eligible for financial assistance for mediation, and will not be granted legal representation unless he or she:

'has attended a meeting with a mediator –
(a) to determine –
    (i) whether mediation appears suitable to the dispute and the parties and all the circumstances, and
    (ii) in particular, whether mediation could take place without either party being influenced by fear of violence or other harm; and
(b) if mediation does appear suitable, to help the person applying for representation to decide whether instead to apply for mediation.'[7]

The corollary of this must be that where mediation does not appear suitable, or could not take place without a party being influenced by fear of violence, legal aid for legal representation ought to be available.

(c)   Ending of the period

Where a period of one year (the 'specified period') has passed since the end of the appropriate period for reflection and consideration,[8] the statement which had been

---

20 Section 23(3).
 1 Section 13(3).
 2 Section 13(1).
 3 Section 13(4).
 4 Section 13(5).
 5 Defined by s 25 as meaning proceedings under the Children Act 1989 Parts I to V with respect to a child of the family, or any proceedings resulting from an application under s 10 or Part IV of the Family Law Act 1996, or for financial provision or property adjustment orders under Part II of the Matrimonial Causes Act 1973, or any other proceedings connected with the breakdown of the marriage.
 6 It is unclear what the term 'interests', as distinct from 'welfare', is intended to mean.
 7 Section 29, inserting s 15(3F) into the Legal Aid Act 1988.
 8 See ante, pp 243–4.

made to commence the period running can no longer be relied upon in making an application for a divorce order.[9]

Application for the divorce order

Either or both of the parties may apply for the divorce order under s 3.[10] Where one party does so, this need not be the party who made the initial statement of marital breakdown.[11] The applicant must show that the following requirements are satisfied:[12]

(1) The marriage has broken down irretrievably. This requirement will be satisfied where –
   (a) the statement of marital breakdown has been made in accordance with s 6;
   (b) the period for reflection and consideration has ended; and
   (c) the application is accompanied by a declaration by the applicant that, having reflected on the breakdown, and having considered the statutory requirements as to the parties' future arrangements, he or she believes that the marriage cannot be saved.[13]
(2) The requirements as to information meetings have been satisfied.[14]
(3) The requirements as to the parties' arrangements for the future are satisfied.

It will be recalled that the government decided that no divorce order should usually be made unless the parties' future arrangements had been finalised. Where a reconciliation proves impossible, the parties are expected to use the period for reflection and consideration in reaching settlements, ideally through mediation, on these arrangements. There are three kinds of arrangements specified under s 9 of the Act relating to the parties' finances and property, any religious usages concerning divorce, and arrangements for the welfare of their children. These are discussed in turn.

Financial arrangements

Financial arrangements for the purposes of s 9 of, and Sch 1 to the Family Law Act[15] are defined under s 34(2) of the Matrimonial Causes Act 1973 as:

'. . . provisions governing the rights and liabilities towards one another when living separately of the parties to a marriage . . . in respect of the making or securing of payments or the disposition or use of any property, including such rights and liabilities with respect to the maintenance or education of any child, whether or not a child of the family.'

(a)   Form of arrangements

Section 9(2) of the Family Law Act provides that there must be produced to the court one of the following documents.

---

9 Section 5(3)(b). The specified period may be interrupted for a continuous period of up to 18 months where the parties jointly give notice to the court that they are attempting reconciliation but require additional time, but thereafter a fresh statement must be made and the period for reflection and consideration must start again: s 5(5)–(7).
10 Section 3(1).
11 Section 5(2). We noted, ante at p 242, that the party making a statement cannot withdraw it unilaterally.
12 Section 3(1).
13 Section 5(1).
14 These have been discussed ante, p 241.
15 Sch 1 para 6.

(I) COURT ORDER, MADE BY CONSENT OR OTHERWISE

Sch 1, para 5 provides that the order need not have been carried into effect at the time when the court is considering whether the appropriate arrangements have been made: indeed, the order will not usually have taken effect at that time.[16]

(II) NEGOTIATED AGREEMENT

This is defined by Sch 1, para 7, as a *written* agreement between the parties 'which has been reached as the result of mediation or any other form of negotiation involving a third party' and which satisfies any requirements imposed by rules of court. This provision clearly envisages agreements reached with the aid of a mediator, and presumably also includes those negotiated by (or through) solicitors, although whether the involvement of a solicitor acting for one party only would suffice is not certain. The government contemplated the possibility of one solicitor acting as an advisor to both parties,[17] and it may be that this is what is intended to be included within this provision.

(III) DECLARATION BY BOTH PARTIES THAT THEY HAVE MADE THEIR FINANCIAL ARRANGEMENTS

Sch 1, para 8, provides that the declaration must be in prescribed form and conform with any other prescribed requirements, for example, as to accompanying documents. This provision gives the parties the opportunity to work out their financial arrangements with no third party assistance, but there must be scope in such cases for exploitation of the weaker party, and the status of the arrangements reached would be likely to carry less weight than a consent order, or even a private agreement.[18] The possibility that the parties will have to attach documentation to the declaration suggests that the court is expected to check whether the parties have actually made the arrangements, but there is no power to *approve* them (or reject them as inadequate or unfair).

(IV) DECLARATION BY ONE PARTY THAT NO FINANCIAL ARRANGEMENTS ARE TO BE MADE

A declaration by one party, to which the other does not object, that he has no significant assets and does not intend to apply for financial provision, that he believes the other party is in the same position, and that there are therefore no financial arrangements to be made, will suffice under s 9. This provision is intended to cover those couples who have no assets to divide and who are not seeking any support from each other or for their children (whose maintenance may be dealt with under the Child Support Act).

Any inaccuracy in declarations of either type will not invalidate the divorce order made.[19] As with the special procedure under the Matrimonial Causes Act 1973, there would appear to be very little scope for a court to determine whether a declaration was in fact appropriately made.

16 Section 22B and s 23A, Matrimonial Causes Act 1973, inserted by Sch 2 paras 3 and 5 to the Family Law Act 1996. See Chapter 18 post, p 782. The fact that an appeal is pending against the order is to be disregarded: Sch 1 para 5(2).
17 White Paper paras 6.22–6.23.
18 Bird and Cretney, op cit para 4.15. See *Edgar v Edgar* [1980] 3 All ER 887, CA and discussion of agreements post, pp 750–3.
19 Where the parties' arrangements include a division of pension assets or rights under s 25B of the Matrimonial Causes Act (post, p 795), the declaration must be a statutory declaration: s 9(8).

(b)   Exceptions to requirements under s 9(2)

There will be occasions, either within, or beyond a party's control, where the period for reflection and consideration has ended, but financial arrangements have not been finalised. In requiring that such arrangements normally be a pre-condition of the divorce order, the government recognised that this might 'play into the hands of an unreasonable, spiteful or malicious spouse or provide a formidable bargaining chip for the more powerful or determined party'.[20] Section 9(7) and Sch 1 accordingly enable a party to apply to the court, in certain circumstances, to make the divorce order notwithstanding that arrangements have not been settled. There are four such 'exemptions'. In all of them, the requirements as to future arrangements for children must have been satisfied.

(I)   OBSTRUCTION BY OTHER PARTY, OR LACK OF INFORMATION REQUIRED BY COURT TO MAKE FINANCIAL ORDER

Under the first exemption, the applicant must satisfy the court that he or she has, during the period for reflection and consideration, taken such steps as are reasonably practicable to try to reach agreement as to finances, has applied to the court for financial relief and complied with all requirements pertaining to that application, but the other party has delayed in complying with these requirements or has otherwise been obstructive, or for reasons beyond the control of the applicant, or of the other party, the court has been prevented from obtaining information needed to enable it to determine the parties' financial position.

This exemption therefore contemplates two types of case. In the first, the other spouse has deliberately delayed or obstructed resolution of the financial arrangements, and it would therefore be unfair to the applicant to withhold the divorce. This is clearly intended to forestall a spouse attempting to protract the proceedings in order to improve his or her position in the financial negotiations.

In the second type of case, the delay may be beyond the spouses' control. Examples might be where a final valuation of the parties' assets cannot yet be made, perhaps because the ownership of an asset is the subject of separate litigation, a will has not yet cleared probate, or damages for personal injury have not been settled.[1] Again, there is no good reason to hold up the divorce order simply because of this delay.

(II)   ILL HEALTH, DISABILITY OR INJURY PREVENTING AGREEMENT BEING REACHED

Under this exemption the applicant must satisfy the court that he or she has taken reasonable steps to try to reach agreement, but that, because of the ill health or disability (whether physical or mental) of the applicant, the other party, or a child of the family, the applicant has not been able to reach agreement with the other party and is unlikely to be able to do so in the foreseeable future. The applicant must then satisfy the court that delay in making the divorce order would either be significantly detrimental to the welfare of any child of the family, or would be seriously prejudicial to the applicant. It is unclear why this second hurdle is necessary. One would have thought that passing the first hurdle would be sufficient justification for not delaying the divorce. It is also unclear when this provision would need to be relied upon, since, presumably, if a party cannot reach agreement, he or she could seek a financial relief *order* instead. Thirdly, it is

20 White Paper para 4.29.
 1 Hansard HL Debs, 30 January 1996, col 1414 (Lord Mackay LC).

unclear what significant detriment and serious prejudice mean. Significant detriment to a child's welfare may be similar to, but clearly not identical with, the test of significant harm under Part IV of the 1996 Act[2] or s 31 of the Children Act 1989.[3] Serious prejudice is presumably different from the substantial hardship test which applies where an order preventing divorce is sought.[4]

(III)   IMPOSSIBILITY OF CONTACTING THE OTHER PARTY

Where the applicant has found it impossible to contact the other party and it has therefore been impossible to reach agreement about their financial arrangements, it would clearly be wrong to deprive the applicant of the divorce order, and the third exemption accordingly enables the court to make the order in such circumstances.

(IV)   ORDER IN FORCE AGAINST THE OTHER PARTY UNDER PART IV OF THE ACT

The final exemption applies where there is an occupation or non-molestation order in force against the other party and in favour of the applicant or a child of the family, the applicant has taken reasonable steps to reach agreement regarding financial arrangements, but has not been able and is unlikely in the foreseeable future to be able to do so, and delay in making the divorce order would be significantly detrimental to the welfare of any child of the family, or would be seriously prejudicial to the applicant.

It will be recalled that mediation during the period of reflection and con- sideration may be rejected as inappropriate where a party fears violence, and it is likely in such a case that agreement as to finances will not have been reached. This exemption therefore enables a divorce order to be made in favour of a victim of violence or molestation even though finances have not been settled. But since a party in such a situation could seek a court *order* instead, it is unclear when this exemption would have to be relied upon.

Religious arrangements

In recent years, Orthodox Jewish women seeking a divorce have publicised the problem of the 'agunah', or 'anchored woman'.[5] Under Jewish law, only the husband can divorce his wife. Where he refuses to do so, then, although she may have obtained a divorce under English law, she remains married in the eyes of her religion and is unable to remarry according to Jewish rites. A husband could exploit this rule by only agreeing to divorce the wife under Jewish law (referred to as giving her a *get*) upon her acceptance of a smaller financial settlement. Section 9(3) seeks to redress this unfairness. It provides that if the parties were married to each other in accordance with usages of a kind mentioned in the Marriage Act 1949 s 26(1) (which relates to Jewish or Quaker marriages),[6] and are required to co-operate if the marriage is to be dissolved in accordance with those usages,[7] the court may, on the application of either party, direct that there must be

2 See ante, pp 201–2.
3 See post, pp 538–9.
4 Section 10. See post, p 252.
5 See Freeman 'Law, Religion and the State: The Get Revisited' in Lowe and Douglas (eds) *Families Across Frontiers* (1996) 361–83.
6 See ante, p 43.
7 Quakers do not have their own divorce laws, so this provision in fact applies only to Jews.

produced to the court a declaration by both parties that they have taken such steps as are required to dissolve the marriage in accordance with those usages. The direction may only be given if the court is satisfied that in all the circumstances of the case it is just and reasonable to give it, and it may be revoked (presumably on the application of either party) by the court at any time.[8] Thus, if a Jewish husband sought a civil divorce from his wife, she could apply to the court for a direction, in effect, that he give her a *get*.[9] However, where the *wife* seeks the divorce and the husband either opposes or does not care if the marriage is terminated, it would seem that he could still frustrate her, since he could simply ignore the direction or delay his compliance, again potentially exploiting the wife's financial vulnerability by forcing her to agree to an inferior settlement.

Arrangements for the children

The third arrangement for the future which must be settled before the divorce order is made concerns the children of the family. It was noted[10] that s 41 of the 1973 Act provides that the court has to consider the arrangements proposed for the children's future after their parents' divorce, and whether it should exercise any of its Children Act 1989 powers with respect to them. In exceptional circumstances the court may delay the grant of the divorce if it considers that it is likely to have to exercise its powers under the Children Act with respect to certain children of the family and it needs to give further consideration to the case.[11] Section 11 of the 1996 Act repeats this provision, but emphasises that the court is to treat the welfare of the child as paramount when scrutinising the proposed arrangements,[12] and sets out a 'checklist' of factors to which the court must have particular regard:

'(a) the wishes and feelings of the child considered in the light of his age and understanding and the circumstances in which those wishes were expressed;
(b) the conduct of the parties in relation to the upbringing of the child;
(c) the general principle that in the absence of evidence to the contrary, the welfare of the child will be best served by –
  (i) his having regular contact with those who have parental responsibility for him and with other members of his family; and
  (ii) the maintenance of as good a continuing relationship with his parents as is possible; and
(d) any risk to the child attributable to –
  (i) where the person with whom the child will reside is living or proposes to live;
  (ii) any person with whom that person is living or with whom he proposes to live; or
  (iii) any other arrangements for his care and upbringing.'

The aim behind this checklist is to ensure that the court addresses the issues considered by Parliament to be most relevant to the child's welfare at the point of the parents' divorce. At present, the district judge carries out the requirements of s 41 by scrutinising a detailed 'Statement of Arrangements Form' filed by the petitioner. The checklist requirements will presumably be incorporated into the revised Form, but this may cause problems. It is unclear, for example, how the child's wishes and

---

8 Section 9(4).
9 See Conway 'New Provisions for Jewish Divorces' [1996] Fam Law 638.
10 *Ante*, p 230.
11 See Douglas, Murch and Perry 'Supporting children when parents separate – a neglected family justice or mental health issue?' (1996) 8 CFLQ 121.
12 Section 11(3).

feelings are to be recorded, so that they can be taken into account. Requiring a welfare officer to interview each child in every case would be costly, but if the applicant could merely report the child's apparent views to the court on paper, the scope for distortion or plain invention could be considerable.[13] Similarly, where both spouses are in agreement, one is unlikely to reveal any 'conduct' by the other in relation to the upbringing of the child which might result in delay of the divorce order and investigation by the court.

Orders preventing divorce

(a) Background

As already discussed,[14] the Matrimonial Causes Act 1973 s 5 provides that a divorce based on five years' separation may be refused where the respondent can show that dissolution of the marriage would result in grave financial or other hardship to him or her, and that it would, in all the circumstances, be wrong to dissolve the marriage. The aim of this provision is to safeguard the position of an 'innocent' spouse who does not wish to be divorced. It is rarely invoked and very rarely succeeds in preventing the divorce.[15] This is due mainly to the fact that the hardship alleged has to result from the *dissolution* of the marriage: not from the marriage breakdown and separation itself.[16] If the spouse seeking the divorce (usually the husband) can compensate for any financial loss (such as the loss of a pension dependent upon marital status) through the payment of maintenance, the purchase of annuities, or the payment of a lump sum or transfer of some asset, the divorce will be granted.[17] The courts have also declined to uphold any claims of 'other grave hardship' (based on social ostracism or religious objection).[18] Even if the respondent does prove that the decree would cause her grave hardship, the court has still to pronounce a decree, unless also of the opinion that it would be wrong to do so.

The Law Commission considered that s 5 offers 'an important protection for a small group of people who may still face serious hardship which the law is unable at present to redress in other ways'[19] and recommended its retention (making it applicable to all divorces, since there would no longer be a five year separation

---

13 There is provision, in s 64 of the Act, for the Lord Chancellor by regulations to provide for the separate representation of children in the proceedings, but this could hardly be done in every case, given the stance on discouraging representation for the *parents*. See further post p 255.
14 Ante, p 229.
15 See Law Com No 192 para 5.72.
16 *Talbot v Talbot* (1971) 115 Sol Jo 870.
17 See, for example, *Le Marchant v Le Marchant* [1977] 3 All ER 610, CA. In *K v K (Financial Provision)* [1996] 3 FCR 158, the husband's petition for divorce was adjourned until the spouses could agree a settlement which would protect the wife's pension needs. But cf *Julian v Julian* (1972) 116 Sol Jo 763, where the difference between a pension of £790 per annum (which the respondent could claim as the petitioner's widow) and an annuity of £215 (which was all the petitioner could afford to purchase) was sufficient to establish grave financial hardship.
18 *Banik v Banik* [1973] 3 All ER 45, CA at 48, where the court remitted the case for rehearing and a decree was later pronounced because the wife's statement that she would become a social outcast could be discounted and it would not be wrong to dissolve the marriage: (1973) 117 Sol Jo 874. *Parghi v Parghi* (1973) 117 Sol Jo 582 (Hindu wife resident in Bombay); *Rukat v Rukat* [1975] Fam 63, [1975] 1 All ER 343, CA (Roman Catholic wife with family in Sicily); *Balraj v Balraj* (1980) 11 Fam Law 110, CA (wife resident in Kshatriya community in India; divorce would also reduce daughter's marriage prospects).
19 Law Com No 190 para 5.75.

fact). The government agreed, noting that, although the bar hardly ever succeeds in preventing a divorce, it might well provide a useful 'bargaining chip' to a weaker spouse during negotiations.[20] The government intended to keep the same wording as s 5, and presumed that the law would continue to be applied as in the past.[1] Previous case law will therefore remain relevant, but the provision which eventually emerged as s 10 of the Family Law Act 1996 is somewhat different to s 5, and may well lead to a different interpretation.

(b) Hardship under the 1996 Act

Section 10 provides that where a party has applied for a divorce order, the other may apply for an order that the marriage is not to be dissolved. Thus, the bar on the divorce can only be imposed once the time for reflection and consideration has expired. The court must be satisfied –

'(a) that dissolution of the marriage would result in substantial financial or other hardship to the other party or to a child of the family; and
(b) that it would be wrong, in all the circumstances (including the conduct of the parties and the interests of any child of the family), for the marriage to be dissolved.'

The hardship experienced must be due to the divorce, not the breakdown of the marriage, as under the former law, but the degree of hardship must now be 'substantial' rather than 'grave'. The intention behind the change is to introduce a less onerous test than before.[2] However, since the Act also gives extended powers to deal with occupational and private pension arrangements after a divorce,[3] more women than was previously possible should be able to receive compensation for ceasing to be eligible for a pension based on marital status, thus reducing the likelihood of their seeking a s 10 order. As far as the *state* pension is concerned, it was held, in *Reiterbund v Reiterbund*[4] that recourse to income-related benefits, such as income support, was a sufficient remedy for any shortfall caused by its loss, since no stigma attached to their receipt, and it could make no difference to the respondent which public fund the money came from.

The second change in the wording of the bar is that the hardship may be suffered by the other spouse, *or by a child of the family*, whereas under s 5 hardship to the respondent was the criterion. The intention appears to have been to ensure that a case such as *Lee v Lee*[5] would clearly come within the section. There, the wife needed accommodation to look after her son, who needed constant nursing and caring. The husband's proposal to sell the matrimonial home and give the wife half the proceeds of sale would not have enabled her to buy a flat for this purpose, and his petition was dismissed.[6] It has also been speculated[7] that research suggesting that emotional distress is caused to a child by parental divorce might be relied upon, but the difficulty of determining that distress would flow for

---

20 Green Paper para 6.62; White Paper para 4.47; cf *Wickler v Wickler* [1998] 2 FLR 326, where the husband's application for a decree absolute was refused because there was a risk that he would wash his hands of any further involvement in the financial proceedings if it were granted.
1 Ibid.
2 Hansard HL Debs, 4 March 1996, cols 25–33.
3 See post, p 795.
4 [1975] Fam 99, [1975] 1 All ER 280, CA.
5 (1973) 117 Sol Jo 616.
6 On appeal, the divorce was granted because the son had died in the meantime: (1975) 5 Fam Law 48.
7 Bird and Cretney, op cit para 5.12.

the particular child from the *divorce*, as distinct from the breakup of the parents' *relationship*, would surely render this hard to establish.

As under s 5, 'other' hardship may be pleaded, but it is uncertain if the reduction to a test of 'substantial' hardship will persuade more courts that cultural or religious factors would suffice. A party's religious or conscientious objection to divorce per se would probably not be adequate. It is possible that, where a Jewish husband is refusing to give his wife a *get*, she could, as an alternative or in addition to seeking a direction under s 9(3), obtain an order preventing the divorce, especially since such an order may include conditions which must be satisfied before an application to cancel the order may be made.[8]

Having been satisfied as to the requisite hardship, the court has then to determine whether it would be 'wrong' for the marriage to be dissolved. The use of 'wrong' in this context is unusual and its meaning is ambiguous and obscure; in *Brickell v Brickell*[9] Davies LJ thought that it meant 'unjust or not right in all the circumstances of the case'. Under s 5 the court has also to take into account specifically the conduct and interests of the parties and the interests of any children[10] and other persons concerned (for example, the person whom the petitioner wished to marry). Section 10 is slightly different. The parties' conduct, yet not their interests, is expressly mentioned, while the interests of children of the family only are included. The interests of a child born to one spouse and his or her new partner would not fall within this category. However, since the court must consider all the circumstances, these minor variations are probably insignificant. Ultimately, the court, taking into consideration the general principles set out in s 1 of the Act, will have to balance the parties' conflicting interests in recognising that the marriage has irretrievably broken down *and* that its termination will cause substantial hardship. The resisting spouse's age, earning capacity and intention to remarry and the length of time that the parties have cohabited will be relevant, and in practice the courts are unlikely to refuse a divorce if the wife is young, healthy and capable of earning her own living, or if the marriage has lasted for only a short time, or has been effectively over for many years.[11]

(c)   Effects of the order

Under s 3(2) a s 10 order prevents a divorce order being made. It also stops the clock running during the one year 'specified period' at the end of the period for reflection and consideration.[12]

(d)   Cancellation of the order

Both the Law Commission and the government considered that it would be unjust to permit an order preventing divorce to remain in force indefinitely, even though the circumstances of the parties had changed and the divorce would no longer cause hardship. Under the 1973 Act, a spouse seeking a divorce in such circumstances would have to commence divorce proceedings all over again, but under

---

8 Section 10(5).
9 [1974] Fam 31, [1973] 3 All ER 508, CA.
10 Who include children over the age of 18: *Allan v Allan* (1973) 4 Fam Law 83.
11 *Mathias v Mathias* [1972] Fam 287 at 301–2, [1972] 3 All ER 1, CA at 8; *Rukat v Rukat* (supra) at 76 and 353, respectively.
12 Section 5(4). It also affects the conversion of a separation order into a divorce order, dealt with post at pp 259–60.

s 10(3) it is possible for either, or both parties, to apply for the cancellation of the order. On such application, the court must cancel the order, unless still satisfied that the grounds for its making continue to exist. One would envisage cancellation being sought once a financial package has been satisfactorily agreed, or once any conditions imposed have been fulfilled (which might be of a financial nature or, as suggested above, might relate to the obtaining of a religious divorce). When the order is cancelled, the court continues to have jurisdiction to deal with applications in relation to the divorce, even where neither party would otherwise satisfy the jurisdictional requirements.[13]

The divorce order

Provided that the requirements under s 3 of the 1996 Act have been fulfilled: ie that the marriage has broken down irretrievably, the requirements as to information meetings have been satisfied, the arrangements for the parties' future have been settled, the application for the divorce order has not been withdrawn, and there is no order under s 10 in force, the court shall make the divorce order. Under s 2, a divorce order dissolves the marriage, and comes into force on its being made. Thus, there will no longer be a two-stage process of decree nisi and absolute. The parties' marital status will end on the making of the order, and they will regain their freedom to remarry at that moment.

4.   THE ROLE OF LAWYERS IN THE NEW DIVORCE SYSTEM[14]

As we have seen, a key aim of the government's proposals for reform was to encourage couples to explore the value of mediation as the main means of achieving a settlement of their arrangements at the end of the marriage.[15] Where does this leave lawyers? The government, in drawing up its proposals, postulated two basic models of the divorce process. In the traditional model, the parties would, at the instigation of their lawyers, take up opposing stances and exploit, at considerable financial cost to themselves and the Legal Aid Fund, the adversarial nature of the legal system to battle to a standstill, either through prolonged negotiation or, at last, through resort to the court, and emerge at the end, embittered and hostile, to the detriment, most significantly, of their children's emotional well-being.[16] As the White Paper put it:

> 'Marriage breakdown and divorce are . . . intimate processes, and negotiating at arm's length through lawyers can result in misunderstandings and reduction in communication between the spouses. Lawyers have to translate what their clients say and pass it on to the other side. The other side's lawyer then translates again and passes information on to his or her client. There can thus be a good deal of misunderstanding and a good deal of anger about what is said and how it is said.'[17]

By contrast, in their alternative model, couples would engage constructively, through mediation, to arrive at an agreement worked out by themselves, face to

---

13 Section 19(3)(b) and (4).
14 See Walker 'Is there a future for lawyers in divorce?' (1996) 10 Int J of Law, Policy and the Family 52.
15 Ante, p 239.
16 For research findings which illuminate, to some extent, the validity of this model, see Davis and Murch *Grounds for Divorce* (1988); Davis, Cretney and Collins *Simple Quarrels* (1994).
17 White Paper, para 5.19.

face, with an enhanced ability to communicate with each other, in an atmosphere of greater co-operation:

> '. . . bitterness and hostility are reduced through the mediation process and couples are helped to manage conflict to the benefit of their children and themselves. Communication is improved, making it more likely that arrangements for the children will last, or if they need to be changed by force of circumstances, making it more likely that the couple can negotiate new arrangements in a constructive manner, and in the best interests of each child.'[18]

Predictably, the government proposed that lawyers should be utilised as an adjunct to mediation services, rather than, under the present system, the other way round. In the government's thinking, lawyers will still have a role to play, but a diminished one, mainly at the beginning and end of the divorce process. Parties might still wish to consult a lawyer for initial advice, and the Green Form scheme will remain available for this purpose for those financially eligible.[19] The Lord Chancellor is given powers, under s 12(2) of the 1996 Act, to require a lawyer acting for a divorcing party to provide, or to certify whether he or she has provided, a variety of information to the client, boosting the former requirement under s 6 of the Matrimonial Causes Act to certify whether reconciliation has been discussed. Now, rules may require the lawyer to inform the client about the availability of marriage support services and of mediation, and 'where there are children of the family, that in relation to the arrangements to be made for any child the parties should consider the child's welfare, wishes and feelings'.[20] In addition, lawyers may be required to give clients the names and addresses of persons qualified to help to effect a reconciliation, or in connection with mediation. They may also be required to certify whether they have discussed with the client the possibility of reconciliation.[1] The aim is to encourage parties away from reliance upon lawyers as the main source of help during their divorce. The lawyer might, the government recognised, be a useful resource if legal advice is needed during the mediation process, and at the end to translate the parties' agreement into a legal arrangement, usually perhaps a draft consent order to be laid before the court (or, as is now envisaged under s 9(2), a declaration in prescribed terms). But beyond this, the intention is to limit assistance to the Green Form except where it is clear that mediation is unsuitable because of the parties' particular circumstances.[2]

Where couples are in agreement as to their future arrangements, and simply need help to draft the terms, or to maximise tax and benefit advantages, the government sees scope in their instructing the same solicitor to act for them. Many solicitors are training as mediators, and are bringing in counsellors and other family support services, in the hope of being able to provide clients with the broad range of help they will seek under the new system.[3]

5.   MEDIATION SERVICES UNDER THE NEW SYSTEM

While resort to lawyers is to be downgraded in importance in the new divorce system, clearly mediation is going to be the main mechanism for assistance. The

---

18 Ibid, para 5.24.
19 Ibid, para 6.18. The Green Form provides initial advice and assistance to those eligible for free legal aid.
20 Section 12(2)(a).
 1 Section 12(2)(b)(c).
 2 Legal Aid Act 1988 s 15(3F), (3G), (3H).
 3 See Bishop et al *Divorce Reform: A Guide for Lawyers and Mediators* (1996).

Legal Aid Board is empowered[4] to secure the provision of mediation in disputes relating to family matters.[5] The Board may make franchise agreements with appropriate mediation schemes, which, by s 13B(6), may be required to comply with a code of practice laying down arrangements designed to ensure:

'(a) that parties participate in mediation only if willing and not influenced by fear of violence or other harm;

(b) that cases where either party may be influenced by fear of violence or other harm are identified as soon as possible;

(c) that the possibility of reconciliation is kept under review throughout mediation; and

(d) that each party is informed about the availability of independent legal advice.'

Where there are one or more children of the family, the code:

'... must also require the mediator to have arrangements designed to ensure that the parties are encouraged to consider –

(a) the welfare, wishes and feelings of each child; and

(b) whether and to what extent each child should be given the opportunity to express his or her wishes and feelings in the mediation.'

Whether mediation is appropriate in situations where one party may have subjected the other to domestic violence, or has threatened such violence, is debatable.[6] It may be that, where the threatened party feels protected by the mediator, she (usually) can then feel able to participate. However, the legislation itself recognises that this will not always be so (it will be recalled that the extension of the period for reflection and consideration may be lifted where an order relating to non-molestation or occupation is in force against the other spouse). It will be important that the Legal Aid Board does not put undue pressure upon a person who feels intimidated and in potential or actual danger to 'try' mediation before legal representation is offered.

It is questionable how far mediators will wish to see their role as one where reconciliation must be kept under review throughout the process. Generally, mediation is distinguished from reconciliation, because its focus is upon coming to practical terms with the ending of the marriage, rather than upon preserving it.[7] It is also unclear how the mediator can legitimately 'inform' parties about the 'availability' of independent legal advice if, as we have seen, the provision of such advice will be heavily circumscribed under the Legal Aid scheme. Finally, while mediators would no doubt regard the children's interests as central to most mediation work, the question of how far they should be involved in the mediation process itself is an open one, and it is unclear what the mediators' code would be expected to lay down in relation to this.

4 By s 13B of the Legal Aid Act 1988, as amended by s 27 of the Family Law Act 1996.

5 'Family matters' are defined in s 13A of the Legal Aid Act (inserted by s 26 of the Family Law Act 1996) as 'matters which are governed by English law and in relation to which any question has arisen, or may arise – (a) under any provision of the Matrimonial Causes Act 1973, the Domestic Proceedings and Magistrates' Courts Act 1978, Parts I to V of the Children Act 1989, Parts II and IV of the Family Law Act 1996, or any other prescribed enactment, jurisdiction or rule of law'.

6 Compare Roberts 'Family Mediation and the Interests of Women – Facts and Fears' [1996] Fam Law 239, who suggests that domestic violence may make mediation inappropriate (although she also argues that research evidence finds few other situations where women are disadvantaged by mediation), and Black and Price 'Mediation and the Shadow of the Past' [1996] Fam Law 693, who report positively on the use of mediation in cases of violence.

7 The Finer Committee on One Parent Families (1974) Cmnd 5629 para 4.313 drew this distinction, and the government in its White Paper Cm 2799 also focused upon mediation as a process to assist couples to deal with their future arrangements: para 5.4.

Where a spouse is granted legal aid for mediation, then, as with legally-aided representation, he or she may be required to make a contribution to the costs, and a statutory charge will be attached to any property recovered or preserved as a result of the mediation.[8]

Communications made in the course of mediation

Mediation is unlikely to be successful if there is a danger that a statement made by one party in the course of negotiations may later be put in evidence by the other if they fail to arrive at an agreement. In *Re D (Minors) (Conciliation: Disclosure of Information)*[9] the Court of Appeal held that evidence of statements or communications made in conciliation relating to proceedings under the Children Act is inadmissible in the proceedings except where it clearly indicates that the maker has caused, or is likely to cause, serious harm to the well-being of the child. In relation to financial matters, this privilege does not appear to apply.[10] However, the Practice Direction relating to the ancillary relief pilot scheme, which incorporates mediation appointments, suggests that statements or admissions made in the dispute resolution appointment are similarly inadmissible in court.[11] In its White Paper the government proposed introducing a statutory privilege for mediation except where the material relates to abuse of children[12] but it has not done so as yet.

Binding nature of agreements

No agreement between the parties can oust the jurisdiction of the court,[13] so that any terms on which they agree in the course of mediation will be binding only when approved by the court. The court may take the view that it should give effect to a clause in an agreement relating to financial provision freely entered into between the parties, even though it would have made a more generous award.[14] Although a party could resile from an agreement if he or she had been misled, it would obviously be imprudent to accept an offer in ignorance of the other's income and assets. Mediators therefore advise clients that they should consult lawyers before they seek to have their agreement formalised, but it is unclear how flexible the legal aid authorities will be in permitting legal assistance or further mediation sessions to be used to renegotiate a mediated settlement where the party's solicitor cautions that it should not be accepted.

F. Separation orders

1. HISTORY

The principal effect of a decree of judicial separation was to relieve the petitioner of the duty to cohabit with the respondent, so that neither spouse could be held in

---

8 Legal Aid Act 1988 s 13c, inserted by s 28 of the Family Law Act 1996.
9 [1993] Fam 231, [1993] 2 All ER 693, CA.
10 Singer 'FDR and the Holy Grail' [1996] Fam Law 751 at 752.
11 *Practice Direction (Ancillary Relief Procedure: Pilot Scheme)* [1997] 2 FLR 304, but see the criticism by Burrows 'Ancillary Relief Review' [1997] Fam Law 673.
12 White Paper, para 7.36.
13 See post, p 753.
14 *Edgar v Edgar* [1980] 3 All ER 887, CA: see post, p 805.

desertion while it was in force.[15] But the parties remained husband and wife, so that neither of them was free to remarry.

The advantage of the decree lay mainly in the fact that it gave the court jurisdiction to order financial provision for the wife; consequently, as long as the grounds for divorce were limited, she could obtain a degree of both financial and physical protection. But alternative ways of obtaining maintenance, the relative ease with which divorce can now be obtained, and the possibility of obtaining remedies for domestic violence, have long tended to provide more appropriate mechanisms for spouses than judicial separation per se. Nonetheless, an order denoting a legal separation rather than a divorce may still be useful. First, a spouse may have a conscientious or religious objection to divorce (although the religion itself may not recognise the civil divorce anyway); secondly, an elderly spouse whose marriage has broken down will remain entitled to a widow's or widower's pension on the death of the other, which may be of substantial financial importance.

Research in the early 1980s found that many petitions for separation were at that time brought within the first three years of marriage, when, until the law was changed by the Matrimonial and Family Proceedings Act 1984, no petition for divorce could be presented unless the petitioner established that he or she would suffer exceptional hardship or that the respondent had behaved with exceptional depravity.[16] The separation would be converted into a divorce once the three year time bar was passed. The Law Commission noted[17] a decline in the number of petitions and decrees granted for judicial separation after the 1984 change, no doubt reflecting the ability to obtain an earlier divorce. The annual number has remained roughly steady since then, with 2,795 petitions and 1,199 decrees in 1996.[18]

When divorce law was reformed by the Divorce Reform Act 1969, the basis for obtaining a judicial separation was also amended to keep the law in line, and the same approach was taken in the Family Law Act 1996.

2.   UNDER THE FAMILY LAW ACT 1996

When it came to examine divorce reform, the Law Commission recommended retaining the possibility of an order which would provide an alternative to divorce,[19] and the government agreed.[20] The new law relating to what will be called separation orders[1] requires proof that the requirements as to attendance at information meetings and as to the parties' future arrangements have been satisfied,[2] and proof of the irretrievable breakdown of the marriage,[3] which will be

---

15 Matrimonial Causes Act 1973 s 18(1).
16 See Law Com No 116 (Time Restrictions on Presentation of Divorce and Nullity Petitions); Garlick 'Judicial Separation: A Research Study' (1983) 46 MLR 719; Maidment *Judicial Separation – A Research Study* (1982).
17 Law Com No 192 para 4.8.
18 *Judicial Statistics 1996* Cm 3716 (1997) Table 5.5.
19 Law Com No 192 para 4.11.
20 White Paper paras 4.48–4.50.
 1 Family Law Act 1996 s 2(1)(b).
 2 Ibid, s 3(1).
 3 Under the existing law, the five facts for proving irretrievable breakdown in divorce are treated as grounds for a judicial separation, and irretrievable breakdown as such does not have to be alleged: Matrimonial Causes Act 1973 s 17(1).

evidenced, as with divorce, by showing compliance with the requirements of s 5 of the 1996 Act.[4]

Particular features relating to separation orders

There are certain differences between the detailed requirements for divorce and for separation. First, just as it was always possible to seek a decree of judicial separation despite the time bar on petitioning for divorce, it is possible to file a statement of marital breakdown during the first year of marriage.[5] However, a separation *order* cannot be made during the first year, since the requirements as to waiting three months after attendance at an information meeting before filing the statement, and waiting for the period of reflection and consideration to elapse must be complied with.[6] Secondly, the period for reflection and consideration may not be extended automatically where a spouse requests further time for reflection, nor where there is a child of the family, since those provisions apply only where an application for a divorce order has been made.[7] Thirdly, a separation order may be made notwithstanding that an order under s 10 preventing divorce is in force.[8]

There is no longer any statutory reference to the effect that a separation order removes the duty of the spouses to cohabit, although s 21 provides that, as under the old law, where one spouse dies intestate, the property shall devolve as if the other spouse had died before the intestacy occurred. There is now an express power, under s 2(3), to cancel a separation order on the joint application of the spouses.

Concurrent divorce and separation proceedings

Where a court is considering concurrent applications for a divorce order and for a separation order in respect of the same marriage, then, unless there is an order under s 10 in force, or it makes such an order, or s 7(6) or (13)[9] applies, it must proceed to consider only the application for divorce.[10]

Conversion of separation orders into divorce orders

We have seen that, under the old law, the majority of judicial separation decrees were followed by divorce. However, there was no means of converting a decree into a divorce. The Law Commission proposed that there should be a mechanism for converting a separation order into a divorce, without the need to fulfil the requirements for a divorce which have already been satisfied for the separation.[11] Accordingly, s 4 of the Family Law Act 1996 provides that a separation order may be converted into a divorce order on the application of one or both parties,[12] provided the following requirements are satisfied.[13] First, the second anniversary of the marriage must have passed. Secondly, the extended period for reflection and

---

4 See ante, p 242.
5 Family Law Act 1996 s 7(6).
6 Ibid, s 3(1) and s 5(1).
7 Ibid, s 7(10) and (11).
8 See s 3(2).
9 See pp 242–3.
10 Section 3(3).
11 Law Com No 192, paras 5.86–5.87.
12 This is the only way the parties can proceed to divorce unless the separation order is first cancelled (which can only be done on their joint application), since a statement made while a separation order is in force is ineffective: s 6(7).
13 Which are mainly concerned with ensuring that conversion does not enable a couple to obtain a divorce sooner than would otherwise be possible.

consideration where one spouse has sought time for further reflection or there is a child of the family must have elapsed (unless this extension does not apply because there is an occupation or non-molestation order in force against the other spouse, or delay would be significantly detrimental to the welfare of any child of the family).[14] Thirdly, there must be no s 10 order in force.

Where a separation order is in force, the court continues to have jurisdiction to entertain an application (such as an application to convert the order into a divorce order) made by reference to it.[15]

---

14 Family Law Act 1996 s 4(5).
15 Ibid, s 19(3)(a) and (4).

Chapter 8

Parents and children

A. Introduction

The parent–child relationship is obviously one of the key relationships in family law and, as we shall see, the nature and focus of that legal relationship has undergone profound change. However, before we discuss this relationship we must first consider the equally fundamental questions of who in law is a parent and who a child.

With regard to parentage it will be seen that the acquisition of the legal status can be achieved in three ways: it can be assigned automatically, or it can be acquired through the making of a parental order under the Human Fertilisation and Embryology Act 1990 or through adoption. It has been observed[1] that this multiplicity of mechanisms operates on a continuum of state regulation, from minimal, if any, control in the case of the mother who happens to be unmarried, to lengthy state investigation with the applicant's suitability to be a parent in the case of adoption.

We begin this chapter by discussing the first two of these mechanisms of ascribing parenthood. We discuss adoption in Chapter 15.

B. Who are the parents of a child?

1. INTRODUCTION

At one time it would have gone without saying that the person who gave birth to the child was the mother and the person by whom she conceived was the father. Indeed, traditionally the law has taken the blood tie or genetic link as the test of parenthood.[2] However, with the advance of medical science, and in particular with the advent of human assisted reproduction, the position has now become more complicated.

Reflecting these advances and following detailed inquiry into the whole subject by the Warnock Committee on Human Fertilisation and Embryology,[3] there is now comprehensive legislation in the form of the Human Fertilisation and Embryology Act 1990 governing issues arising from assisted reproduction, including, inter alia, the question of who is to be regarded as a parent.

---

1 Douglas and Lowe 'Becoming a Parent in English Law' (1992) 108 LQR 414.
2 Hence the use of blood tests to determine parentage: see post, p 276. For the legal significance of being a parent see post, p 284.
3 Report on the Committee of Inquiry into Human Fertilisation and Embryology (1984) Cmnd 9314 whose recommendations were essentially accepted in the government's White Paper *Human Fertilisation and Embryology: A Framework for Legislation* (1987) Cm 259.

Before discussing who in law are regarded as parents of a child it is helpful to say a little about the different techniques of assisted reproduction.

2.   TECHNIQUES OF HUMAN ASSISTED REPRODUCTION[4]

Artificial insemination

Artificial insemination refers to the placing of semen into a woman's vagina, cervix or uterus (ie womb) by means other than sexual intercourse. If the woman's husband's sperm is used, the process is referred to as artificial insemination by husband or AIH. If someone else's sperm is used, it is known as artificial insemination by donor, or AID (or, these days, DI – donor insemination).

In vitro fertilisation (IVF)

The technique of in vitro fertilisation is to take a ripe egg from the woman's ovary just before ovulation (ie when the egg would have been released naturally). It is then mixed with sperm in a dish (in vitro) so that fertilisation can occur. If the egg is fertilised, it is returned to the uterus, where it may implant, and then develop as normal.

Egg and embryo donation

Egg collection technology coupled with IVF makes it possible to obtain an egg from a donor for transfer to another woman having been fertilised with either the husband's or a donor's sperm in vitro. It will be appreciated that IVF treatment has therefore created the possibility that the woman who gives birth to a child may not be the genetic mother. In the case of embryo transfer neither the woman nor her partner (unless his sperm is used) will be genetically related to the child.

Surrogacy

Surrogacy[5] involves one woman carrying a child for another with the intention that the child be handed over. It is not to be confused with the techniques for human assisted reproduction just described, though the surrogate may well have conceived by one of those methods. We discuss the effect and regulation of surrogacy agreements later in this chapter.[6]

3.   WHO IS THE LEGAL MOTHER?

Until the advent of in vitro fertilisation, provided the fact of the birth could be proved, there could be no doubt that the woman giving birth must in law be the child's mother. As Lord Simon was able to say as late as 1976 in *The Ampthill*

---

4   See generally Douglas *Law, Fertility and Reproduction* (1991) ch 6 and the Warnock Report, op cit, chs 3–7. New techniques are being continually developed and refined, and the text refers only to the main types used, which have particular significance for family law.

5   See the definition in the Surrogacy Arrangements Act 1985 s 1(2).

6   Post, p 270.

Peerage case,[7] 'Motherhood, although also a legal relationship, is based on a fact, being proved demonstrably by parturition.'

There is no doubt that, where the woman has conceived by artificial insemination or by in vitro fertilisation of her ovum, she is the legal mother. The difficulty arises where the person giving birth is not the child's genetic mother but is the carrying mother as a result of egg or embryo donation. As Scott Baker J said in *Re W (Minors) (Surrogacy)*,[8] 'The advent of IVF presented the law with a dilemma: whom should the law regard as the mother?' Arguments can be led either way. On the one hand, given the biological connection, it could be argued that the genetic mother should be regarded as the child's legal mother. On the other hand, because of the bizarre consequences that would follow if the genetic mother is unknown (for example, the child's birth would have to be registered with the name of the mother unknown), there would seem a strong case for considering the carrying mother the legal mother.[9] An alternative approach altogether is to hold the *intending* parent the legal parent.

This approach was adopted in the Californian decision *Johnson v Calvert*.[10] In that case, in pursuance of a surrogacy agreement, one of the commissioning mother's eggs was fertilised in vitro with her husband's sperm and transferred to the surrogate, who successfully carried it to term. During the pregnancy the surrogate and the commissioning couple fell out, and each sought a declaration of parentage of the child. It was accepted that blood tests showed the commissioning parents to be the genetic parents of the child. In holding that it was the commissioning parents who were the child's legal parents, Panelli J commented that it was they who 'affirmatively intended the birth of the child, and took the steps necessary to effect in vitro fertilisation. But for their acted-on intention the child would not exist' and the commissioning mother, 'who intended to procreate the child – that is she who intended to bring about the birth of a child that she intended to raise as her own – is the natural mother under California law'.

Although the application of this notion of intending to be a parent is a rational way of solving the so-called 'womb leasing' problems as in *Johnson v Calvert*, one important problem in using it as a *general* test of determining parenthood is that it would involve accepting the corollary that lack of intention is a means of avoiding parenthood. As one commentator[11] has pointed out:

'Hitherto, the law in the United Kingdom has generally refused to permit someone to avoid liability (if not responsibility) for a child on the ground that he or she had not *intended* the child's conception or birth. It is no answer to the Child Support Agency for the absent parent to say that he thought the child's mother was on the pill, or even that his condom split during intercourse'

But she adds:

'. . . it is possible for a sperm or egg donor to waive their parental status and responsibility in respect of any resulting child under the terms of the Human

---

7 [1977] AC 547 at 577, [1976] 2 All ER 411, HL at 424.
8 [1991] 1 FLR 385 at 386.
9 See Bromley 'Aided Conception – the Alternative to Adoption' in Bean (ed) *Adoption, Essays in Social Policy, Law and Sociology* ch 11 at pp 189–90.
10 5 Cal 4th 84 (1993), noted by Douglas (1994) 57 MLR 636. For the view that a person's intention or desire to be regarded as a parent and to fulfil the functions of parent is in fact the primary test of legal parentage in English law, see Barton and Douglas *Law and Parenthood* (1995) 50ff.
11 Douglas, op cit, at 640.

Fertilisation and Embryology Act 1990. Parents may also give their child up for adoption. So our law does recognise the intention *not* to be a social parent in certain circumstances.'

So far as English law is concerned, the position at common law has still to be determined. The matter was raised in *Re W (Minors) (Surrogacy)* [12] (which, like *Johnson v Calvert*, was a womb leasing case), but left open upon an undertaking by the commissioning genetic parents that [13] they would apply for a 'parental order' under s 30 of the Human Fertilisation and Embryology Act 1990 [14] as soon as the provision was implemented. However, adopting the Warnock Committee's recommendation, [15] s 27(1) of the Human Fertilisation and Embryology Act 1990 provides:

'The woman who is carrying or has carried a child as a result of the placing in her of an embryo or of sperm and eggs, and no other woman, is to be treated as the mother of the child.'

Where this provision applies, then in all cases the woman giving birth and no other woman will, unless the child is subsequently adopted [16] or a parental order [17] is subsequently made, be treated as the legal mother regardless of genetic connection. Section 27, however, does *not* have retrospective effect [18] and only applies in relation to children carried by women as a result of the placing in them of embryos or of sperm and eggs, or of their artificial insemination on or after 1 August 1991. [19] For this reason it may still be necessary to resolve the position at common law. On the other hand, the section applies regardless of whether the woman was in the United Kingdom or elsewhere at the time of the placing in her of the embryo or the sperm and eggs. [20]

4.   WHO IS THE LEGAL FATHER?

The position regarding who is the legal father is more complicated than that of the mother, for while in general the genetic father (ie the man whose sperm fertilised the egg) [1] is regarded as the legal father, this is subject to two exceptions. Conversely, there are occasions when, notwithstanding the absence of any genetic link, a man will be treated as the legal father.

---

12 Supra.
13 The genetic mother had no womb but was able to produce the eggs, which were taken from her medically and fertilised in vitro by her husband's sperm. Two resultant embryos were implanted in the surrogate host mother, who gave birth to the twins who, having been handed over by the surrogate, had lived with the 'commissioning couple' ever since. The local authority argued that the couple should register themselves as private foster parents, which prompted them to seek a declaration of parentage.
14 Discussed post, pp 267ff.
15 Op cit, at para 6.8.
16 Section 28 (2).
17 Parental orders are discussed post, pp 267ff.
18 Section 49 (3) See also *Re M (Child Support Act: Parentage)* [1997] 2 FLR 90, discussed further below at p 266 n 13.
19 The date on which s 27 came into force, by SI 1991/1400.
20 Section 27(3). But there is no domicile requirement, nor is there a requirement that the child be born in England and Wales, but the provisions can only apply where, by the conflict of law rules, English law is held to be the applicable law.
 1 As Bracewell J pointed out in *Re B (Parentage)* [1996] 2 FLR 15 at 21, it is irrelevant *how* the sperm fertilises the egg; sexual intercourse is *not* a prerequisite to fatherhood.

When genetic fathers are not legal fathers

Two exceptions to the general rule that the genetic father is the legal father are provided by s 28(6) of the Human Fertilisation and Embryology Act 1990.[2] These are:

(a) where he is a donor whose sperm is used for 'licensed treatment'[3] and whose consent to the use of his sperm has been obtained in accordance with the requirements of Sch 3 to the 1990 Act (ie sperm donors whose sperm is used for assisted reproduction treatment); and

(b) where his sperm is used after his death.[4]

One incidental but important effect of these exceptions is that there will be occasions when a child has no legal father.[5]

Where non-genetic 'fathers' are treated as legal fathers

At common law only genetic fathers could be regarded as legal fathers. The strictness of this position, however, made no allowance for the use of the various techniques of assisted reproduction, the object of which is for childless couples to have children that they can regard as their own. A good example is the DI child conceived by a wife because her husband was infertile or because he was the possible carrier of an inheritable disease, but whom (as usually will be the case) the couple wished to treat as though he or she were the husband's child.[6] The absence of legal fatherhood made little difference to the legal relationship between him and the child, because his treating the child as his own made the latter a child of the family[7] and, since the sperm donor's identity would not normally be divulged, there was virtually no risk of legal claims arising between the donor and the child.[8] Nevertheless, there were potentially a number of longer-term problems. For example, the child had no entitlement to the husband's estate, if the latter died intestate,[9] nor any claim if any of his mother's relatives died intestate, nor if property was held on trust for the husband's children or the wife's legitimate children. If the child made such a claim and the spouses knew that the husband was not the father, they had either to connive at the deception or be forced to disclose facts which they had wished to keep secret.

---

2 Which only applies to children carried by women as a result of the placing in them of embryos or of sperm and eggs, or of their artificial insemination on or after 1 August 1991: s 49(3).

3 Treatment requiring those who offer it to be licensed under the 1990 Act Sch 2. See generally Douglas *Law, Fertility and Reproduction*, op cit, p 110ff.

4 In any event, before sperm can be used or stored the donor must have consented in writing: 1990 Act Sch 3 para 1; cf *R v Human Fertilisation and Embryology Authority, ex p Blood* [1997] 2 All ER 687, CA, in which, following the Court of Appeal ruling that the Human Fertilisation and Embryology Authority had failed to pay sufficient regard to the effect of the EC Treaty whereby a citizen was entitled to receive services in another member state, the applicant was allowed to take her dead husband's sperm to Belgium for treatment, notwithstanding that written consent to the obtaining of his sperm had not been given by the husband before his death.

5 Such as in those cases where such children are born to a woman who has no husband or partner deemed to be the legal father under s 28(2) and (3), discussed below.

6 They might even register the husband as the father. If the husband is known not to be the father, the person registering the birth will commit an offence under the Perjury Act 1911 s 4.

7 Unless the spouses separated before the child's birth. See post, pp 289–90.

8 Before the 1990 Act good clinical practice required the doctor carrying out the insemination not to divulge the donor's identity.

9 Although he would have a claim to provision under the Inheritance (Provision for Family and Dependants) Act 1975 as a 'child of the family': see post, p 887.

Following pressure to change the law[10] the Family Law Reform Act 1987 s 27 provided that a child born in England and Wales after implementation of its provisions (viz 4 April 1988) as the result of the artificial insemination of a woman who at the time of the insemination was a party to a marriage,[11] and who was artificially inseminated with the semen of someone other than the other party to the marriage, 'shall not be treated as the child of any person other than the parties to that marriage', unless it is proved to the court's satisfaction that the other party to the marriage did not consent to the insemination. In other words, under this provision, a DI child born to a married couple is presumptively the child of both parties, and the presumption can be rebutted only by showing[12] that the husband did not consent to the artificial insemination of his wife.

Section 27 only applied to DI children and not to those born as a result of using other forms of assisted reproduction. Section 28 of the Human Fertilisation and Embryology Act 1990, however, makes provision for other forms of assisted reproduction, as well as artificial insemination.[13] Specifically, s 28(2) provides that where a married woman[14] is carrying or has carried a child as the result of the placing in her of an embryo, or sperm and eggs, or of her insemination, then notwithstanding that the sperm was not that of her husband, he and no other person[15] is treated as the father of the child,[16] unless it is shown that he did not consent to his wife's treatment. This provision is, however, subject to s 28(5)(a), by which the common law presumption of legitimacy based on marriage[17] takes priority over the requirement of the husband's consent. What this seems to mean[18] is that the husband will be regarded as the father unless the issue is raised, when, if he did not consent, the presumption will have to be rebutted, usually by means of blood tests.

The 1990 Act goes further by enacting in s 28(3) that, where donated sperm is used for a woman in the course of licensed 'treatment services'[19] provided for her and a man together, then that man, and no other person, shall be treated as the father of the child if s 28(2) does not apply (for example, where the woman is not married or where there is a separation order in force). Although in practice such a man is likely to be the male cohabitant of the treated woman, there is no necessity to prove cohabitation, nor, conversely, does it follow that 'simply because a man is living with a treated woman he is being provided with treatment services'.[20]

Precisely what is meant by 'treatment together' is unclear. According to Johnson J

---

10 Both the Law Commission (Law Com No 118 paras 12.9 and 12.11) and the Warnock Committee (ibid at para 4.17) had recommended change.

11 Being a marriage not at the time annulled or dissolved, but including a void marriage if, at the time of the insemination, both or either of the parties reasonably believed that the marriage was valid. It is presumed, unless the contrary is shown, that one of the parties did so believe: s 27(2). It will be noted that the problem about whether a mistake of law can support a reasonable belief (discussed post at p 293) would appear to be relevant in this context.

12 Presumably, upon the balance of probabilities.

13 Note that this provision is not retrospective: s 49(3). This means that s 27 of the Family Law Reform Act 1987 will continue to apply to DI children born on or after 4 April 1988 but before the commencement of s 28 (viz 1 August 1991): s 49(4). Neither Act applies to children born *before* 4 April 1988: see *Re M (Child Support Act: Parentage)* [1997] 2 FLR 90.

14 For these purposes, marriage includes a void marriage if, as is presumed until the contrary is shown, at the time of the treatment resulting in the child's birth, one of the parties reasonably believed that the marriage was valid: s 28(7)(b); but it does not include the case where a judicial separation was in force: s 28(7)(a).

15 Section 28(4).

16 See, for example, *Re CH (Contact: Parentage)* [1996] 1 FLR 569.

17 See post, pp 272ff.

18 See Douglas, op cit, at p 129.

19 See s 2(1).

20 Per Johnson J in *Re Q (Parental Orders)* [1996] 1 FLR 369 at 372.

in *Re Q (Parental Order)*,[1] the provision envisages a situation in which the man involved himself receives medical treatment. This interpretation, however, seems unnecessarily restrictive and the preferable approach, it is submitted, is that of Bracewell J in *Re B (Parentage)*,[2] namely to consider on all the facts whether the man and woman could be said to have embarked on a joint enterprise the object of which is for the woman to conceive and give birth, rather than to concentrate on what happens to the individual partner. In *Re B* it was held to be such a joint enterprise where the couple attended the hospital together and, knowing that the sperm which the man donated[3] was not to be used for impregnation that day, had waited a short time to ensure that the donation was satisfactory. It did not matter that the man had not been counselled,[4] nor that at the time of insemination the couple had since separated. Bracewell J's approach was later approved by the Court of Appeal in *R v Human Fertilisation and Embryology Authority, ex p Blood*,[5] though in that case itself it was held that the posthumous use of sperm taken from the husband while in a coma was not capable of constituting 'treatment . . . together'. Finally, in *U v W (A-G Intervening)*,[6] it was held that an unmarried couple's voluntary joint attendance at a fertility clinic even after they knew that donor sperm as well as the man's own sperm was to be used constituted 'treatment . . . together'.

There is no requirement that the resulting child be born in England and Wales, but s 28 can only apply where, by the conflict of laws rules, English law is the applicable law, which means that at least one of the parties must either be domiciled or habitually resident here at the time of the treatment or insemination. On the other hand, s 28(8) expressly states that the provisions apply 'whether the woman was in the United Kingdom or elsewhere at the time of placing in her of the embryo or the sperm and eggs or her artificial insemination.' However, this provision is effectively limited to children born to married women since, as Wilson J pointed out in *U v W*,[7] in the case of an unmarried mother, for the man to be regarded as the father under s 28(3), the 'treatment services' must be provided by a 'licensed person'. Accordingly, treatment abroad will fall outside the provision, even though that could be said to be restrictive of the freedom to provide services for all nationals of member states within the European Union.[8]

5.   PARENTAL ORDERS[9]

Under s 30(1) of the Human Fertilisation and Embryology Act 1990 the court[10] is empowered to make what is known as a 'parental order' providing for a child to be

---

1 Supra.
2 [1996] 2 FLR 15.
3 Bracewell J rejected the man's argument that his donation of sperm had been a casual favour and there had been no joint enterprise to conceive a child.
4 As Bracewell J (ibid at 21) pointed out, s 2(1) which defines treatment services as 'medical, surgical or obstetric services', makes no mention of counselling.
5 [1997] 2 All ER 687 at 697, per Lord Woolf MR.
6 [1998] Fam 29, [1997] 2 FLR 282, per Wilson J.
7 Supra at 37 and 292 respectively.
8 Viz under Art 59 of the Treaty of Rome: see the division on *U v W*, supra at 40ff and 295ff respectively.
9 See generally Douglas *Law Fertility and Reproduction* pp 158–61; Barton and Douglas *Law and Parenthood* pp 69–72; Morgan and Lee *Human Fertilisation and Embryology Act 1990* pp 153–4. This section was a late addition to the legislation prompted by the much publicised 'Cumbria' case, subsequently reported as *Re W (Minors) (Surrogacy)* [1991] 1 FLR 385 (discussed ante at p 264). It was brought into force on 1 November 1994: SI 1994/1776.
10 The High Court, county court or magistrates' court: HFEA 1990 s 30(8)(a).

treated in law as the child of the parties to a marriage in circumstances where the child has been carried by a woman other than the wife, as a result of the placing in her of an embryo or sperm and eggs, or her artificial insemination following the use of gametes of one or both of the spouses.[11] This power is subject to a number of conditions.

Applications can only be made by a husband and wife, both of whom must be at least 18 and at least one of whom must be domiciled in part of the United Kingdom or the Channel Islands or Isle of Man.[12] The application must be made within six months of the child's birth.[13] At the time of the application the child's home must be with the husband and wife.[14] Before any order can be made, the court must be satisfied that the carrying woman and the father (including a person who is a father by virtue of s 28(2) or s 28(3))[15] have freely and with full understanding of what is involved, agreed unconditionally to the making of an *order* (ie not to the application).[16] In this regard the surrogate mother's agreement is ineffective if given less than six weeks after the child's birth.[17] No agreement is required if a person cannot be found or is incapable of giving an agreement.[18]

The wisdom of requiring the surrogate's (and, where appropriate, the father's) consent to the making of the order rather than to the making of the application is surely questionable, since a late withdrawal of consent after the child has been placed with the applicants will bar the court from making a s 30 order (though not an adoption order[19] nor a s 8 order under the Children Act 1989)[20] regardless of the child's welfare.

The court must also be satisfied that no money or other benefit has been given, paid or received by the spouses in connection with the making of the order, the giving of agreement, the handing over of the child, or the making of any arrangements with a view to the making of the order.[1] This prohibition does not apply to payment of reasonable expenses, which presumably will cover such things as the surrogate's expenses for maternity clothes, travel for the assisted reproduction treatment and for ante-natal check ups, and possibly for her loss of earnings consequent on giving up work to have the baby. Further payments or benefits may be authorised by the court. Although the point had been made[2] that, since the court will only become apprised of the matter when the application is made, to be

---

11 Section 30 does not apply if the child was conceived as the result of normal intercourse between the husband and the surrogate mother, as occurred in *Re Adoption Application (Payment for Adoption)* [1987] Fam 81, [1987] 2 All ER 826.

12 HFEA 1990 s 30(2), (3)(a) and (4).

13 Section 30(2). Special retrospective provision was made for children born before the Act, permitting application to be made within six months of the coming into force of the Act.

14 Section 30(3)(a).

15 See *Re Q (Parental Order)* [1996] 1 FLR 369. But cf in Scotland *C and C (Petitioners and Respondents to Adopt X)* [1997] Fam Law 9 and 226.

16 Section 30(5). Evidence of the agreement is governed by the Adoption Act 1976 s 61 as applied to parental orders by the Parental Orders (Human Fertilisation and Embryology) Regulations 1994.

17 Section 30(6). A similar provision is made in adoption: see post, p 635.

18 Section 30(6). 'Cannot be found' and 'incapable of giving agreement' presumably have the same meaning as in adoption: see post, pp 637–8.

19 See eg in Scotland *C v C (Petitioners and Respondents to Adopt X)*, supra.

20 Discussed post, pp 412ff.

 1 Section 30(7). Nor can the court hear the application if a previous application in respect of the same child by the same applicants has been dismissed, unless the court dismissing the application directed that the provision was not to apply, or there has been a significant change of circumstances: Adoption Act 1976 s 24 as applied to the parental orders by the 1994 Regulations.

 2 By Douglas, op cit, at pp 159–60.

effective, authorisation will have to be retrospective, it has been held that the court does indeed have such a power.[3]

While an application is pending, no parent or guardian can remove the child from the applicant's home against the applicant's will without leave of the court.[4]

In deciding whether or not to make a parental order the court is bound by s 6 of the Adoption Act 1976, rather than s 1(1) of the Children Act 1989, and must therefore give first (but not paramount) consideration 'to the need to safeguard and promote the welfare of the child throughout his childhood'.[5]

As s 30(8) makes clear, parental order proceedings are to be regarded as 'family proceedings' for the purpose of the Children Act 1989, which means that, as well as making or refusing a parental order, the court is also empowered to make a s 8 order',[6] or to give a s 37 direction inviting the local authority to investigate the circumstances of the case,[7] whether or not such an application is made.[8]

The effect of parental orders is governed not by the primary legislation but instead by the Parental Orders (Human Fertilisation and Embryology) Regulations 1994,[9] which specifically apply (suitably amended) certain provisions of the Adoption Act 1976.[10] It is thus clear that, like an adoption order, a parental order vests parental responsibility for the child *exclusively* in the applicants, and extinguishes the parental responsibility any person had before the order. It also extinguishes any prior order under the Children Act 1989 and any previous duty to make maintenance payments.[11] The child who is the subject of a parental order shall be treated in law 'as if he had been born as the child of the marriage of the husband and wife (whether or not he was in fact born after the marriage was solemnised).[12] Such a child shall be treated in law as if he were not the child of any other person.[13] The status prevents the child being illegitimate.[14] Notwithstanding the making of a parental order, the child stays within the prohibited degrees with his birth family for the purpose of marriage and incest.[15] For the purpose of disposition of property, while the 's 30 child' is not to be treated as the child of any person other than the new parents, this does not prejudice any interest or expectant interest vested in possession before the making of the parental order.[16]

All parental orders are registered in a Parental Order Register maintained by the Registrar General in the General Register Officer.[17] Provision is made for the person who is the subject of a parental order and who has attained the age of 18 to be supplied with information enabling him to obtain a copy of his birth certificate, having first been advised of the counselling services available to him.[18]

---

3 Per Johnson J in *Re Q (Parental Orders)*, supra at 373.
4 Adoption Act 1976 s 27(1) as applied to parental orders by the 1994 Regulations.
5 Adoption Act 1976 s 6 as applied to parental orders by the 1994 Regulations. The application of s 6 is discussed post, pp 625ff.
6 Discussed post, pp 445ff.
7 Section 37 is discussed post, p 455.
8 See s 10(1)(b) of the 1989 Act, discussed post, pp 446–7.
9 SI 1994/2767.
10 The power to do this is provided by s 30(9)(a) of the 1990 Act.
11 Adoption Act 1976 s 12(1)–(3) as applied by the 1994 Regulations.
12 Adoption Act 1976 s 39(1) as applied by the 1994 Regulations.
13 Adoption Act 1976 s 39(2) as applied by the 1994 Regulations.
14 Adoption Act 1976 s 39(4) as applied by the 1994 Regulations.
15 Adoption Act 1976 s 47(1) as applied by the 1994 Regulations.
16 Adoption Act 1976 s 42, ss 44–46 as applied by the 1994 Regulations.
17 Adoption Act 1976 s 50 as applied by the 1994 Regulations: see also the Forms of Entry to Parental Orders Regulations 1994, SI 1994/2981.
18 Adoption Act 1976 s 51 as applied by the 1994 Regulations.

6.   SURROGACY AGREEMENTS [19]

Although the precise arrangements may differ, a surrogacy agreement is basically one by which a woman ('the carrying mother') agrees to bear a child for someone else ('the commissioning parents'). For the purposes of the Surrogacy Arrangements Act 1985, a 'surrogacy arrangement' is one made before the woman began to carry the child 'with a view to any child carried in pursuance of it being handed over to, and parental responsibility being met (so far as practicable) by another person or persons'.[20] It is the essence of such agreements that the carrying mother agrees to hand over the baby at birth to the commissioning parents and not to exercise any parental responsibility that she may have in respect of the child. Such agreements came into prominence as a result of the much publicised 'Baby Cotton' case,[1] which is believed to be the first case in the United Kingdom of a commercially arranged surrogacy agreement.[2]

The 'Baby Cotton' case aroused public debate about the desirability of such agreements in general and of commercial surrogacy in particular. Notwithstanding that the weight of public opinion seemed to be against the practice of surrogacy,[3] the Warnock Committee nevertheless did not recommend imposing a complete ban. Instead they recommended that it be a criminal offence for a person to be involved in negotiating or making a surrogacy arrangement on a commercial basis.[4] Adopting this recommendation, s 2(1) of the Surrogacy Arrangements Act 1985 provides:

'No person shall on a commercial basis do any of the following acts in the United Kingdom, that is –
(a) initiate or take part in any negotiations with a view to the making of a surrogacy arrangement,
(b) offer or agree to negotiate the making of a surrogacy arrangement, or
(c) compile any information with a view to its use in making, or negotiating the making, of surrogacy arrangements,
and no person shall in the United Kingdom knowingly cause another to do any of those acts on a commercial basis.'

Section 3 also makes it an offence for *anyone* to advertise that a woman is willing to enter into or to facilitate the making of a surrogacy arrangement or that any person is looking for a woman to become a surrogate mother.[5]

To constitute an offence the arrangement must be made before the surrogate mother begins to carry the child, and it must be made with a view to the child being handed over to, and the parental responsibility being exercised (so far as practicable) by another person or persons. It is to be noted that the surrogate

---

19 See generally Douglas *Law, Fertility and Reproduction* ch 7; Bromley 'The Legal Aspects of Surrogacy Agreements' in *Children and The Law* (ed Freestone) p 1; and the Report of the Committee of Inquiry into Human Fertilisation and Embryology (the Warnock Report) Cmnd 9314, ch 8. See also Hibbs 'Surrogacy Legislation – Time for Change' [1997] Fam Law 564 and Harding 'The Debate on Surrogate Motherhood' [1987] JSWL 37.
20 Section 1(2) as amended by the Children Act 1989 Sch 13 para 56.
1 Reported as *Re C (A Minor) (Wardship: Surrogacy)* [1985] FLR 846.
2 But it was not the first surrogacy agreement to come before the court: see *A v C* [1985] FLR 445, CA (decided in 1978).
3 Cmnd 9314 at para 8.10.
4 Ibid at para 8.18.
5 The penalty for involvement in a surrogacy arrangement is imprisonment for up to three months and a fine not exceeding level five, and for unlawful advertising, a fine not exceeding that level. The consent of the Director of Prosecutions is necessary for prosecution. The offences are triable summarily and an information can be laid up to two years after the commission of the offence instead of the usual period of six months.

mother and the 'commissioning' parents are excluded from liability for their participation in the arrangements (though they can be liable for the advertising offence). It is also to be noted that it is only an offence knowingly to assist in the negotiations for a commercial surrogacy arrangement.[6]

Although the participating individuals might not commit an offence under the 1985 Act, in cases where the arrangement was expressly made with a view to the child's adoption by the commissioning parents, where money is paid or agreed to be paid, the contracting parties prima facie commit an offence under the adoption legislation.[7] Now, however, as we have seen, s 30 of the Human Fertilisation and Embryology Act 1990 permits a court to order that a child born as a result of a surrogacy arrangement be treated as that of the commissioning parents, if a number of conditions are met. Hence, provided arrangements do not infringe the Surrogacy Arrangements Act 1985, those made in contemplation of a parental order cannot be held illegal.

The availability of a parental order does not however solve all problems about enforceability. What, for example, is the position if the surrogate mother refuses to hand over the child, or if the commissioning parents refuse to accept the child? In its original form, notwithstanding the recommendation of the Warnock Committee,[8] the 1985 Act was silent on whether surrogacy arrangements were enforceable, although the generally accepted view was that they were not. The matter has now been put beyond doubt by s 1A of the Surrogacy Arrangements Act 1985,[9] which unequivocally states that 'No surrogacy arrangement is enforceable by or against any of the persons making it'.

Given that such arrangements are unenforceable, what then happens to the child? If there is no dispute between the parties, there is no compulsion to go to court. However, given that the surrogate mother will be treated as the child's legal mother even if she is not the genetic mother,[10] it would seem advisable for the commissioning parents to seek a parental order. If they are unable to do this because, for example, the surrogate mother has withdrawn her consent or has refused to hand over the child, the commissioning parents can still seek a s 8 order[11] under the Children Act 1989. In this event it is clear that in resolving any disputes the court is bound to treat the child's welfare as its paramount consideration and is not bound by the terms of the agreement.[12] Another possibility,

---

6 It is not an offence to help in carrying out the arrangement after it has been made. An unsuccessful attempt was made to change this in the Surrogacy Arrangements (Amendment) Bill 1986.

7 Viz Adoption Act 1976 s 57, though the court could subsequently authorise payment: see eg *Re An Adoption Application* [1992] 1 FLR 341; and *Re Adoption Application (Payment for Adoption)* [1987] Fam 81, [1987] 2 All ER 826 (discussed post, p 667); and in Scotland see *C and C (Petitioners and Respondents to Adopt X)* [1997] Fam Law 9 and 226. See also, in relation to parental orders, *Re Q (Parental Order)*, supra.

8 Cmnd 9314 at para 8.19.

9 Introduced by s 36(1) of the Human Fertilisation and Embryology Act 1990.

10 Under s 27 of the Human Fertilisation and Embryology Act 1990, discussed ante at p 264. Furthermore, if she is married and conception has resulted from assisted reproduction methods (commonly surrogacy agreements take the form of the woman agreeing to be artificially inseminated with the commissioning man's semen), her husband may be treated as the legal father pursuant to s 28 of the 1990 Act (discussed ante, p 266).

11 Discussed in Chapter 12.

12 Section 1(1) of the Children Act 1989. Nevertheless, it seems likely that if the carrying mother wishes to keep the child and is in a position to give the child a loving and caring home, she will be allowed to do so – cf *A v C* [1985] FLR 445, CA and *Re P (Minors) (Wardship: Surrogacy)* [1987] 2 FLR 421; cf in the USA the notorious decision *Re Baby M* 537 A 2d 1227 (1988) in which the terms of the agreement were applied.

provided the child is handed over, is for the commissioning parents to apply to adopt the child.[13]

Whether the current law adequately balances all the relevant interests can be debated. Some additional protection is afforded to the child, or potential child, in that local authorities have been reminded of their responsibilities to ensure that the child is not at risk as a result of a surrogacy agreement, whether or not it is for money.[14] However, the difficulty of the English position of not banning such arrangements even where money changes hands,[15] yet not allowing such arrangements to be enforceable, was highlighted in the much publicised Karen Roche case. It seems[16] that this woman, having made an arrangement with a Dutch couple, falsely claimed that she had terminated the pregnancy, and then entered into a second arrangement. Following the disquiet raised by this case, the government announced a review of the law.[17]

C.   Proof of parentage

1.   MOTHERS

Normally, proving who the mother is presents no difficulties, because the fact of birth and identity can be established by the evidence of the doctor or other persons present at the birth and, as Lord Simon said in the *Ampthill Peerage* case,[18] motherhood is proved demonstrably by parturition: mater est quam gestatio demonstrat. However, it is not unknown for mothers to be given the wrong children in maternity hospitals and there have been cases where parents have attempted to pass off a suppositious child as their own, usually in order to defraud others who would be entitled to property in default of children of the marriage.[19] Difficult problems of proof may also arise in the context of immigration where first-hand evidence of the birth may be absent.[20]

2.   FATHERS

Use of presumptions

(a)   Presumption that the mother's husband is the father[1]

Before the advent of blood tests and more recently DNA testing, paternity could normally be inferred only from the fact that the alleged father had sexual

---

13 As happened in *C and C (Petitioners and Respondents to Adopt X)*, supra.
14 See DHSS Circular LAC 85 (12).
15 Under British Medical Association guidelines, surrogate mothers can be paid 'reasonable expenses' of up to £10,000. See Hibbs, op cit, at 565.
16 See Hibbs, op cit.
17 At the time of writing the outcome of this review is not known.
18 [1977] AC 547, [1976] 2 All ER 411, HL at 424.
19 See eg *Slingsby v A-G* (1916) 33 TLR 120, HL, where the wife deceived her own husband; cf the popular belief, current at the time, that the son born to James II's consort was smuggled into the queen's room in a warming pan in order to prevent the descent of the Crown to James's Protestant daughters.
20 See eg the case of Mrs Sabah referred to in [1986] Fam Law 66.
 1 See Barton and Douglas, op cit, 54ff.

intercourse with the mother about the time when the child must have been conceived. Consequently, if two men had intercourse with her during the relevant period, it would be impossible to prove affirmatively which is the father. Moreover, the fact that intercourse took place can in most cases be proved only by the evidence of the parties themselves or circumstantially from their conduct and the opportunities which were presented to them.

The impossibility of proving affirmatively the paternity of the child led at least as early as the twelfth century to the adoption of the civil law maxim: Pater est quem nuptiae demonstrant – that is, if a child is born to a married woman, her husband is presumed to be his father until the contrary is proved.[2] This means that, if it is alleged that the husband is not the father, the burden of rebutting the presumption is cast on the asserter. This presumption applies even though the child is born so soon after the marriage that he must have been conceived beforehand[3] and, in the case of a posthumous child, if he was born within the normal period of gestation after the husband's death.[4] Difficulty arises, however, if the birth takes place an abnormally long time afterwards. In *Preston-Jones v Preston-Jones*[5] the House of Lords agreed that judicial notice could be taken of the fact that there is a normal period of gestation (although the period is variously given as 270 to 280 days or as nine months),[6] but Lord MacDermott added that judicial notice must also be taken of the fact that the normal period is not always followed. It would seem, however, that the longer the period deviates from the normal, the more easily will the presumption be rebutted, until there comes a time when it is not raised at all, although it is difficult to say where the line is to be drawn.[7]

The presumption applies equally in the case of a child born after a decree of divorce. In *Knowles v Knowles*[8] the child could have been conceived before or after the decree absolute. Wrangham J held that the presumption of legitimacy operated in favour of presuming that conception took place whilst the marriage was still subsisting and that the husband was the father, although, as he pointed out, in such circumstances the presumption may be rebutted much more easily.

Conflicting presumptions arise if the child must have been conceived during the subsistence of a marriage since terminated by the husband's death or divorce and the mother has remarried before the birth. It is submitted, however, that in the absence of evidence to the contrary the first husband should be presumed to be the father, since it ought to be presumed that the mother had not committed adultery.[9] If, however, the child must have been conceived when the husband and wife were living apart under a decree of judicial separation, there is no presumption that the

---

2 Glanvil, book 7, ch 12. See also Bracton, fol 6, Co Litt 373; Blackstone's *Commentaries* i, 457; Nicolas *Adulterine Bastardy*; and Lord Simon who said in the *Ampthill Peerage* case [1977] AC 547 at 577, [1976] 2 All ER at 424: "'Fatherhood' . . . is a presumption'.
3 See *Gardner v Gardner* (1877) 2 App Cas 723, HL; *R v Luffe* (1807) 8 East 193; *Anon v Anon* (1856) 23 Beav 273; *Turnock v Turnock* (1867) 36 LJP & M 85.
4 *Re Heath* [1945] Ch 417 at 421–2 per Cohen J.
5 [1951] AC 391, [1951] 1 All ER 124, HL. See further, post, p 276 n 9.
6 Per Lord Simonds at 401 and 127, Lord Morton at 413 and 136, Lord MacDermott at 419 and 139–40 respectively.
7 See ibid, at 402, 403, 407, 413–14 and 128, 130, 132, 135–6 respectively.
8 [1962] P 161, [1962] 1 All ER 659; cf *Re Leman's Will Trusts* (1945) 115 LJ Ch 89. It is submitted that the dictum to the contrary in *Re Bromage* [1935] Ch 605 at 609 cannot be supported.
9 See *Re Overbury* [1955] Ch 122, [1954] 3 All ER 308, where Harman J found in favour of the first husband's paternity on the facts.

husband is the father, since it is presumed that the spouses observed the decree and did not have intercourse.[10]

A Lord Chancellor's Consultation Paper[11] raises the question whether the presumption of paternity should be put on a statutory footing in line with Scotland.[12]

Former proceedings may also raise an estoppel as to paternity. For example, if the issue of the child's parentage has been determined in divorce proceedings, the finding will bind the spouses as between themselves, but it cannot bind either of them as against a third person, nor can it bind the child or any other person who was not a party to the proceedings.[13] On the other hand, under the Civil Evidence Act 1968,[14] where a person has been found to be the father in any relevant proceedings[15] before any court in the United Kingdom, that is prima facie evidence[16] of paternity in any subsequent proceedings.

(b)   No presumption where child is born to an unmarried mother

Where a child is born to an unmarried mother there is no presumption of paternity, even where the child is born to a cohabiting couple. However, entry of a man's name as that of the father on the registration of the child's birth is prima facie evidence of paternity.[17] It is a nice point whether the making of a parental responsibility agreement[18] will be regarded as prima facie evidence of paternity. In other cases the burden for establishing paternity will lie on the asserter, though no doubt strong inferences may be drawn from the fact of cohabitation.

Whether there should be a presumption of paternity in the case of cohabiting

---

10 *Hetherington v Hetherington* (1887) 12 PD 112; *Ettenfield v Ettenfield* [1940] P 96 at 110, [1940] 1 All ER 293, CA at 301. The reason is hardly satisfactory, because the decree relieves the petitioner from the duty of cohabiting with the respondent: it does not forbid cohabitation, let alone sexual intercourse. The same rule applied to magistrates' separation orders when they had power to make them, but the presumption would not be displaced if there was in force a maintenance order but no separation order: *Bowen v Norman* [1938] 1 KB 689, [1938] 2 All ER 776. In any event, the reasoning has no application to voluntary separation; cf *Ettenfield v Ettenfield* (supra), but the presumption may be rebutted more easily: *Knowles v Knowles* [1962] P 161 at 168, [1962] 1 All ER 659 at 661.

11 *1. Court Procedures for the Determination of Paternity* (1998) paras 31ff.

12 Viz Law Reform (Parent and Child) (Scotland) Act 1986 s 5, which also includes a man registered as the father.

13 *B v A-G* [1965] P 278, [1965] 1 All ER 62. But the husband's failure to deny that a child is a child of the family in undefended proceedings will not raise an estoppel, because to permit it to do so might invite unnecessary litigation: *Rowe v Rowe* [1980] Fam 47, [1979] 2 All ER 1123, CA.

14 Section 12, as amended by the Family Law Reform Act 1987 s 29 and SI 1995/756.

15 Defined to mean National Assistance Act 1948 s 42, Social Security Act 1986 s 26, proceedings under the Children Act 1989, and proceedings which would have been relevant proceedings for the purposes of s 12 of the Civil Evidence Act 1968 in the form in which it was in force before the passing of the Children Act 1989 (viz Family Law Reform Act 1969 s 6, Guardianship of Minors Act 1971, Children Act 1975 s 34(1)(a), (b) or (c), Child Care Act 1980 s 47, Family Law Reform Act 1987 s 4, and proceedings for revocation of a custodianship order under the Children Act 1975 s 35) and the Child Support Act 1991 s 27: Civil Evidence Act 1968 s 12(5), as amended by the Courts and Legal Services Act 1990 s 116, Sch 16, para 2, Child Support Act 1991 s 27(5) and SI 1995/756, art 6.

16 It is not, however, binding. As to whether declarations of parentage under the Child Support Act should be binding, see post, p 282.

17 *Brierley v Brierley* [1918] P 257. It has been mooted whether a man who is registered as the father should have *automatic* parental responsibility: see post, p 390. Presumably, if he were, registration would have to raise a *presumption* of paternity.

18 Discussed post, p 384. The Lord Chancellor's Consultation Paper, supra at para 28, thought it does.

couples, as there is in some Commonwealth jurisdictions,[19] was considered but rejected by the Law Commission[20] on the basis that, unlike marriage, which requires no further evidence, cohabitation is not so easy to prove. It is submitted, however, that there is no reason why there should not be a *presumption* of paternity in cases where a couple have made a parental responsibility agreement.

(c) Rebutting the presumption

STANDARD OF PROOF

At common law the generally accepted view was that the presumption could only be rebutted by evidence establishing beyond reasonable doubt that the husband could not be the father. However, the Family Law Reform Act 1969 s 26 states that the presumption may be rebutted upon the balance of probabilities.[1] The effect of this change is not altogether clear.[2] In *S v S, W v Official Solicitor (or W)*[3] Lord Reid thought that it meant that even weak evidence must prevail if there is no other evidence to counterbalance it. On the other hand, in *Serio v Serio*[4] it was held that the standard of proof required was not simply that needed in an ordinary civil action but that commensurate with the seriousness of the matter at issue. However, this latter decision has since been discredited for, as Lord Lloyd pointed out in *Re H (Minors) (Sexual Abuse: Standard of Proof)*,[5] requiring that the standard of proof should be 'commensurate with the seriousness of the issue involved' implies that it might be more than a mere balance of probabilities, which 'seems to read words into the statute which are not there'. *Re H* establishes that there is but one civil standard of proof, namely the balance of probabilities.[6] However, in Lord Nicholls' view,[7] in applying this test one should have in mind that 'the more serious the allegation the less likely it is that the event occurred and, hence, the stronger should be the evidence before the court concludes that the allegation is established on the balance of probabilities'.

WHAT HAS TO BE REBUTTED

The husband's paternity is based on the twofold presumption that the husband and wife had sexual intercourse and that the child is the issue of the intercourse. Before the advent of blood tests it was by rebutting the former presumption (for example, by showing that, at the time when the child must have been conceived, the husband was either permanently impotent, at least quoad the wife, or temporarily impotent, whether from illness or any other cause)[8] that the husband was most likely to prove

---

19 Such as Tasmania, New South Wales and Ontario; see Law Com No 118 at para 10.53, n 120.
20 Ibid, at para 10.54.
 1 This implements the recommendations of the Law Commission: see Law Com No 16, *Blood Tests and the Proof of Paternity in Civil Proceedings* (1968), para 15. In criminal proceedings apparently the presumption must still be rebutted by evidence placing the matter beyond reasonable doubt.
 2 See Bradney 'Blood Tests, Paternity and the Double Helix' [1986] Fam Law 378.
 3 [1972] AC 24 at 41, [1970] 3 All ER 107, HL at 109.
 4 (1983) 4 FLR 756 at 763, CA per Sir David Cairns. See also *Re JS (A Minor) (Declaration of Paternity)* [1981] Fam 22, [1980] 1 All ER 1061, CA and *W v K (Proof of Paternity)* [1988] 1 FLR 86.
 5 [1996] AC 563 at 577, [1996] 1 All ER 1, HL at 8: Lord Lloyd dissented, but not specifically on this issue.
 6 *Re H* was concerned with the application of s 31 of the Children Act: see post, pp 544ff.
 7 Ibid at 586 and 16 respectively.
 8 The *Banbury Peerage Case* (1811) 1 Sim & St 153, HL, for a full account of which see Nicolas, op cit, 291 et seq. While impotence would generally suffice to show that he is not the father, it must be remembered that the wife could have been pregnant as a result of AIH (as in *REL v EL* [1949] P 211, [1949] 1 All ER 141) or of fecundatio ab extra (as in *Clarke v Clarke* [1943] 2 All ER 540).

that he was not the father. However, the presumption could also be rebutted by showing that the husband could not have had intercourse with his wife because of his absence at the relevant time[9] or even by showing that intercourse was so unlikely that it can be concluded on the balance of probability that it did not take place.[10]

Once it is established that the spouses had intercourse at the relevant time, the husband must show that the child is not the issue of that intercourse to rebut the presumption of paternity. This normally implies that the wife has committed adultery. It is established, however, that the fact that the wife has committed adultery does not per se[11] rebut the presumption, because this merely shows that the husband or the adulterer could be the father.[12] Although, as we shall see,[13] the most common way to rebut the presumption is by the use of blood tests, it is possible to do so in other ways, for example, by reference to common physical characteristics. In the past the courts were slow to admit evidence suggesting that the child had inherited some physical characteristics from a particular man and must therefore be his child and on a number of occasions excluded evidence of facial resemblance on the ground that it was too vague.[14] This is obviously a matter of degree, however; it would clearly be wrong to exclude such evidence in all cases (particularly in view of the changed standard of proof) and it was admitted in *C v C and C (legitimacy: photographic evidence)*.[15] In many cases little weight should be attached to it, but in others it should put the matter well beyond the balance of probabilities. Other evidence – for example, that of race[16] or genetic characteristics[17] – is much more cogent. If both spouses are white but the child and the alleged adulterer are black, it will be hard to resist the conclusion that the adulterer is the father.

The use of blood and DNA tests to establish parentage[18]

(a)   The nature of the tests

In cases where parentage (usually paternity) is in issue the most cogent evidence is likely to be obtained by blood tests in general and DNA tests in particular. Such

---

9 This would be difficult to prove in cases where the husband had been absent for a relatively short time and it is sought to show that the child must have been conceived during that period. In that situation regard is to be had to *Preston-Jones v Preston-Jones* [1951] AC 391, [1951] 1 All ER 124, HL, where the husband did not have access to his wife for a period of 360 days to 186 days before the child's birth, and it was held that the evidence adduced was sufficient to rebut the presumption that he was the father.

10 See eg the *Aylesford Peerage* case (1885) 11 App Cas 1, HL; *Morris v Davies* (1837) 5 Cl & Fin 163, HL. In *Smith v May* (1969) 113 Sol Jo 1000 the presumption was rebutted even though the parties admitted sharing the same bed.

11 Aliter if the husband can be shown to be infertile.

12 It was formerly held that this was so even though the husband invariably used a contraceptive (*Francis v Francis* [1960] P 17, [1959] 3 All ER 206) but this might now rebut the presumption on the balance of probability if the other man did not use one. Similarly, if the presumption is raised by the wife's pregnancy at the time of the marriage, it cannot be rebutted merely by showing that she had intercourse with another man before her marriage: *Gardner v Gardner* (1877) 2 App Cas 723, HL.

13 Below.

14 *Slingsby v A-G* (1916) 33 TLR 120, HL at 122–3, *Plowes v Bossey* (1862) 31 LJ Ch 681 at 683.

15 [1972] 3 All ER 577.

16 Such evidence was apparently admissible even before the standard of proof was changed: *Slingsby v A-G* (supra), at 122.

17 Such as webbed toes. In some countries 'anthropological tests', as they are known, can be ordered by the courts in cases where blood tests are inconclusive. The Law Commission (Law Com No 16 *Blood Tests and the Proof of Paternity in Civil Proceedings*, para 16), however, did not recommend the introduction of such tests in England because of the then doubts about their medical validity.

18 See generally Grubb and Pearl *Blood Testing, Aids and DNA Profiling* (1990) ch 6.

tests may be used either to rebut the presumption or allegation of paternity or to establish parentage.

Until DNA tests became publicly available[19] reliance was placed on blood tests. Based on the fact that certain characteristics of a person's blood are inherited and that if the mother's blood does not possess a characteristic possessed by the child, he must have inherited it from the father, blood tests could go some way in resolving issues of paternity. The great drawback of such tests, however, is that, although they can definitely show that a man *cannot* be the father, they can only show with varying degrees of probability that he *is* the father.[20] In contrast, DNA tests (or genetic fingerprinting as it is sometimes known) can, by matching the alleged father's DNA bands with that of the child's (having excluded those bands that match the mother's) make positive findings of paternity with virtual certainty.[1]

Although DNA tests can be made from a variety of bodily samples, because courts are currently only permitted to direct blood tests, they are commonly made from blood samples. Indeed, it is for the very reason that DNA profiling can be used in court-directed tests and thus can be accommodated under the existing scheme, that it has not been felt necessary to implement s 23 of the Family Law Reform Act 1987 which does provide for scientific tests.[2] It might be noted that under the Child Support Act 1991 there is a 'voluntary system' of DNA testing carried out on behalf of the Child Support Agency, the costs of which are now recoverable if the alleged father is found *not* to be the father.[3] However, the Lord Chancellor's Consultation Paper on Court Procedures for the Determination of Paternity[4] has signalled the intent, 'subject to the views of consultees', to implement s 23 of the 1987 Act.

(b) The power to give directions for the use of blood tests

The power to give directions for the use of blood tests is governed by s 20 of the Family Law Reform Act 1969.[5] This provides that any court may direct blood tests to be used in any *civil* proceedings[6] in which the paternity of any person is to be determined. The power under s 20 is sometimes loosely referred to as a power to *order* blood tests, but as Ward LJ pointed out in *Re H (A Minor) (Blood Tests: Parental Rights)*:[7]

> '. . . section 20 does not empower the court to order blood tests, still less to take blood from an unwilling party: all it does is permit a direction for the use of blood tests to ascertain paternity'.[8]

19 1 June 1987 – cf *Re J (A Minor) (Wardship)* [1988] 1 FLR 65.
20 Though, as these tests were being perfected, the degree of probability could be very high, in some cases over 99.8 per cent: see the scales referred to in *Armitage v Nanchen* (1983) 4 FLR 293. See also *Serio v Serio* (1983) 4 FLR 756, CA.
1 See Barton and Douglas, op cit at 59–60. See Yaxley 'Genetic Fingerprinting' [1988] Fam Law 403; Grubb and Pearl, op cit, p 161 et seq; and Bradney 'Blood Tests, Paternity and the Double Helix' [1986] Fam Law 378.
2 See Wall J's comments in *Re CB (A Minor) (Blood Tests)* [1994] 2 FLR 762 at 768 referring to Home Office Circular 91/1989 para 10, discussed by Grubb and Pearl, op cit at p 173.
3 Child Support Act 1991 s 27A, discussed further post, p 733.
4 1998, para 38.
5 For the common law position see *S v S; W v Official Solicitor* [1972] AC 24, [1970] 3 All ER 107, HL discussed in the 7th edition of this work at p 248 and Law Com No 16, *Blood Tests and the Proof of Paternity in Civil Proceedings* (1968).
6 'Civil proceedings' includes proceedings under the Child Support Act 1991,s 27 (discussed post, p 733): *Re E (A Minor) (Child Support Act: Blood Test)* [1994] 2 FLR 548.
7 [1996] 4 All ER 28, CA at 36.
8 Accordingly orders should not state that the various parties 'do provide blood samples' but should take the form of a direction, pursuant to s 20, that 'blood tests be used to ascertain whether the applicant is or is not excluded from being the father of the child'.

Notwithstanding Ward LJ's clear statement, it seems that a distinction should be drawn between adults and children, since, according to Hale J in *Re R (A Minor) (Blood Tests: Constraint)*,[9] while there is an absolute embargo against forcing an adult to supply blood against his will, there is no such bar against ordering a supply of blood from a child even to the extent of ordering physical restraint against him or her.

The purpose of the tests must be to show whether a party to proceedings is or is not the child's father. In the absence of such proceedings there is no jurisdiction to make a free-standing order directing blood tests.[10] Consequently, no order may be made, for example, in administration proceedings if the question is whether a claimant is the child of a deceased parent, information about whose blood happens to be available. Similarly, there is no power to make a blood test direction if paternity is not in issue.[11]

It is important to appreciate that s 20 does not inhibit the giving of evidence. If all the parties agree, they do not have to obtain the court's consent before having a test carried out.[12] What the Act does is to give the court a discretion to direct a test if they do not agree. Section 20 is silent as to when such a direction should be made, but in *S v S, W v Official Solicitor (or W)*[13] Lord Reid expressed the view that the provision could not have possibly been intended to confer an unfettered discretion on county courts and magistrates' courts and that instead it must be left to the superior courts to settle the principles.

S v S established the important point that, when considering whether to make a direction, the court was not exercising its so-called custodial jurisdiction, but was instead exercising its protective jurisdiction.[14] This meant that the correct test was not to make a direction where it is in the child's best interests to do so, but only to refuse to make a direction where it would be against the child's interests to do otherwise,[15] for example, where, 'having regard to the facts and circumstances of a particular case, his interests are such that their protection necessitates the withholding from a court of evidence which may be very material',[16] or if 'it would be unjust to order a test for a collateral reason to assist a litigant in his or her claim'.[17] The House of Lords refused to accept that the mere fact that a test could establish conclusively that the child was illegitimate was sufficiently against his interest to withhold consent, even though, as in *W v Official Solicitor*, this would leave him with no known father at all. This danger is far outweighed by the demands of public policy that all relevant evidence should be made available. Furthermore, the suppression of evidence would not encourage the mother's husband, whose suspicions would be unallayed, to accept the child as his, whereas he might be prepared to do so if a test did not exclude his paternity; and the child

9 [1998] Fam 66, [1998] 1 FLR 745.
10 Per Balcombe L J in *Re E (Parental Responsibility: Blood Tests)* [1995] 1 FLR 392 at 400–1, CA.
11 See *Hodgkiss v Hodgkiss* [1985] Fam Law 87, where it was held in divorce proceedings that there was no power to direct a test to satisfy the husband's curiosity, since no issue as to paternity had been raised in the proceedings and the husband had conceded that the children were 'children of the family'. But see the comment at [1985] Fam Law 87.
12 See for example the practice under the Child Support Act, discussed post, p 733.
13 [1972] AC 24, [1970] 3 All ER 107, HL. See Hayes 'The Use of Blood Tests in the Pursuit of Truth' (1971) 87 LQR 86.
14 The distinction between the two jurisdictions is explored further post at pp 327–8.
15 Per Lord Reid at 45 and 113 respectively.
16 Per Lord Morris at 53 and 120 respectively.
17 Per Lord Hodson at 58 and 124 respectively.

himself in later life might resent the fact that a full investigation was not conducted at the time. It will usually be in the child's interest – as well as in the public interest – that the truth should out,[18] and a direction is usually given.[19]

As Balcombe LJ later put it in *Re F (A Minor) (Blood Tests: Parental Rights),*[20] *S v S* established inter alia that:

> 'Public policy no longer requires that special protection should be given by the law to the status of legitimacy . . . The interests of justice will normally require that available evidence be not suppressed and that the truth be ascertained whenever possible . . . In many cases the interests of the child are also best served if the truth is ascertained . . . However, the interests of justice may conflict with the interests of the child. In general the court ought to permit a blood test of a young child to be taken unless satisfied that that would be against the child's interests; it does not first need to be satisfied that the outcome of the test will be for the benefit of the child . . . It is not really protecting the child to ban a blood test on some vague or shadowy conjecture that it may turn out to be for its advantage or at least to do it no harm.'

Notwithstanding general agreement as to what the test is, there has been some difficulty and inconsistency in applying it.[1] In *Re F* itself, the Court of Appeal upheld a refusal to direct a blood test to be taken upon the application of a man claiming to be the father (and who had never seen the child) and opposed by the mother, in a case where the child had been conceived and brought up in an existing marriage, albeit that at the time of conception the mother had been having sexual relations with her husband and the applicant. The court held that the child's welfare depended upon her relationship with the mother and on the stability of the family unit, which included the mother's husband. Anything which might disturb that stability was likely to be detrimental to the child's welfare and therefore, unless this could be counter-balanced by other advantages to her of ordering a test, it would be wrong to do it.

In *Re F* the Court of Appeal seemed to be saying that, if the child is being brought up in an intact family and the test is opposed by the parent, then it is likely to be thought contrary to the child's interests for a direction to be made. However, this decision should be contrasted with *Re H (a minor) (blood tests parental rights).*[2] In that case, soon after a married woman began a sexual relationship with another man she became pregnant. However, notwithstanding this affair she continued to have sexual relations with her husband, who five years previously had had a vasectomy (though he had never checked on the success of that operation). At first the mother intended to leave her husband and set up home with her lover, but she ended the affair before the child was born. When the child was born, his birth was registered in her husband's name. As in *Re F*, the mother opposed the making of a blood test direction upon an application by the lover, who was seeking contact. She argued that pursuing contact would destabilise her own marriage which had only recently been put together again, and that that would be to the child's disadvantage.

---

18 *S v S* (supra), at 45 and 113 (per Lord Reid) 55–6 and 122 (per Lord Morris), 59 and 124 respectively (per Lord Hodson).

19 *Practice Direction (Paternity: Guardian ad litem)* [1975] 1 All ER 223, qv for the circumstances in which a guardian ad litem should be appointed for the child.

20 [1993] Fam 314 at 318, [1993] 3 All ER 596, CA at 599, on which see Fortin 'Re F: The Gooseberry Bush Approach' (1996) 57 MLR 296 and Barton and Douglas, op cit, at 61.

1 See generally Fortin *Children's Rights and the Developing Law* (1998) 323–6.

2 [1996] 4 All ER 28, CA.

In making the direction the Court of Appeal emphasised that the mother's refusal to undergo a test herself was *not* determinative of whether the court should direct such a test,[3] though it remained a factor to be taken into account.[4] But a more important factor was, according to Ward LJ, the right of every child to know the truth about their parentage unless their welfare clearly justifies the 'cover up'. As he pointed out, this right to know is underlined by Article 7 of the UN Convention on the Rights of the Child. Among other factors to be considered, his Lordship considered that[5] any gain to the child from preventing any disturbance to his security had to be balanced against the loss to him of the certainty of knowing who he was. Accordingly, while the risk of disruption to the child's life both by the continuance of the paternity issue as well as the pursuit of the s 8 order were obviously factors which impinged on the child's welfare, they were not, in his judgment, determinative of the blood testing in question. Although Ward LJ himself did not accept that the two cases were indistinguishable,[6] it is hard to reconcile *Re F* and *Re H*, though the latter seems more in tune with the House of Lords' approach in *S v S*. It remains to be seen whether in the future the destabilising of the family argument will be successful, though it is to be observed that on that score neither case was particularly strong in the sense that the alleged father brought his action within weeks of the child's birth. It might conceivably be different if an action is brought many years after the child's birth.[7]

Notwithstanding *Re H* it must not be supposed that directions will always be made. Indeed, one profitable line of argument has been to persuade the court that there is no need to determine paternity to settle an issue at all. As the Court of Appeal stressed in *Re JS (A Minor)*,[8] a paternity issue should be pursued only if it has a material bearing on some other issue which has to be tried, and a blood test should be directed only when this condition is satisfied.

Re JS was followed in *K v M (Paternity: Contact)*,[9] in which it was held unnecessary to consider the paternity of the child to determine the only live issue, namely contact. Similarly, in *O v L (Blood Tests)*,[10] in which the mother asserted that the husband was not the father of the child after they separated nearly three years after the child's birth and, in response to her husband's application for contact, only sought a blood test in an effort to forestall this, it was held unnecessary to define the precise nature of the relationship between the husband and the child in order for contact between them to be fostered.

(c)   The need for consent

As we have said, in the case of adults (and those aged 16 or 17) there is no compulsion attached to the direction. This is made clear by s 21 which expressly provides that, except in the case of a person suffering from mental disorder,[11] samples may not be taken without his consent if he is over 16. Section 21(3) also

---

3 Wall J's conclusion to the contrary in *Re CB (A Minor) (Blood Tests)* [1994] 2 FLR 762 at 773H was therefore disapproved.
4 In the case of a haemophiliac father, for example, it may be a very powerful argument: per Ward LJ, ibid at 38b.
5 Ibid at 41d.
6 Ibid at 42a.
7 See eg *O v L (Blood Tests)* [1995] 2 FLR 930, CA, discussed below, and *McC (RD) v McC (JA)* [1971] 2 All ER 1097, CA.
8 [1981] Fam 22, [1980] 1 All ER 1061, CA.
9 [1996] 1 FLR 312.
10 Supra.
11 For persons suffering from mental disorder: s 21(4).

provides that a blood sample may be taken from a person under the age of 16 years 'if the person who has the care and control of him consents'. Although at first sight this would seem to prevent the court ordering a test on a child against the parent's will, Hale J in *Re R (A Minor) (Blood Tests: Constraint)* [12] felt able to overcome this possible objection by the simple expedient of ordering the delivery of the child into the care and control of the Official Solicitor at a particular time and place for the purpose of taking a blood sample, and made it plain that the Official Solicitor was permitted to consent on the child's behalf.

Although there is a power of refusal under s 21, s 23(1) permits the court to draw such inferences as appear proper from a person's failure to give consent or to take steps to give effect to the direction.

It has been held that these powers of inference are wholly at large and are wide enough to extend to an inference drawn as to the child's actual paternity. Indeed, in *Re A (A Minor) (Paternity: Refusal of Blood Test)* [13] Waite LJ went so far as to say that given the background of scientific advance:

'... if a mother makes a claim against one of the possible fathers,[14] and he chooses his right not to submit to be tested, the inference that he is the father of the child should be virtually inescapable. He would certainly have to advance very clear and cogent reasons for his refusal to be tested – reasons which it would be just and fair and reasonable for him to be allowed to maintain.'

Following this, in *Re G (Parentage: Blood Sample)* [15] Ward LJ said:

'... the forensic process is advanced by presenting the truth to the court. He who obstructs the truth will have the inference drawn against him.'

In that case the trial judge was held to have misdirected himself when failing to make an inference against the man's paternity (a husband seeking contact) following his refusal to submit to a test.[16] Under s 23(2), if a party claims relief in reliance on the presumption of legitimacy, the court may dismiss the claim even though there is no evidence to rebut the presumption. The last provision would apply, for example, to a wife claiming maintenance for a child whom she alleges is that of her husband and who refuses to have herself and the child tested.[17] To bar the claimant from relief in such circumstances appears on the face of it to be reasonable: the difficulty is that an adverse inference drawn against an adult party might also be adverse to the child. It is questionable whether the Act was right to give a court power to refuse to make an order for maintenance because the mother declines to submit to a blood test, when it could have made submission compulsory; what one must guard against is drawing the wholly illogical conclusion that the child cannot be that of the husband.

(d)   Procedure [18]

Under s 20(1A) of the 1969 Act [19] a person applying for a direction for blood tests must specify who is to carry out the tests. This allows the applicant to choose the

---

12 [1998] Fam 66, [1998] 1 FLR 745.
13 [1994] 2 FLR 463, CA at 473. For an earlier example of a husband reasonably refusing to submit to a blood test, see *B v B and E (B intervening)* [1969] 3 All ER 1106, CA.
14 At the time of conception the mother was having sexual relationships with three different men.
15 [1997] 1 FLR 360, CA at 366.
16 Though in fact in the appeal he was given a further opportunity to change his mind.
17 See *Re H (a minor) (blood tests: parental rights)*, supra.
18 See generally the Blood Tests (Evidence of Paternity) Regulations 1971.
19 Added by the Children Act 1989 s 89, substituted by the Courts and Legal Services Act 1990 s 116, Sch 16, para 3.

tester and therefore effectively the type of test.[20] This matter, however, is not entirely left in the applicant's hands, because the court may decline to make the direction if it considers that it would be inappropriate to specify the person named in the application.[1]

The person responsible for carrying out the tests must make a report of the results to the court.[2] Such a report is received as evidence[3] and must be in prescribed form stating inter alia whether or not any party is excluded by the tests from being the father.[4]

3.   LEGAL PROCEDURES FOR ESTABLISHING PARENTAGE

As the Lord Chancellor's Consultation Paper says,[5] there are a variety of reasons why a determination of paternity may be needed: the child may require it in order for example to amend his birth certificate, or to establish a right to inherit property, or to acquire nationality or citizenship; the father may require it to seek a parental responsibility order, or a s 8 order under the Children Act 1989; and the mother or Child Support Agency may need it to establish paternity, so that the father can be required to contribute to the child's maintenance. There is, however, no single procedure applicable to all the foregoing circumstances to establish parentage. Instead there are three different ways in which the issue of parentage may be determined by the court.

First, as we have just discussed, a direction for blood tests under s 20 of the Family Law Reform Act 1969 may be made in cases where the court is called upon to resolve a dispute about paternity in the course of existing civil proceedings. Secondly, a declaration may be made under the Child Support Act 1991 s 27, but this declaration is only effective for child support and maintenance purposes.[6] The third procedure for establishing parentage is by means of a declaration under s 56 of the Family Law Act 1986, but, as we discuss later in this chapter,[7] though such declarations are binding for all purposes, they can only be sought by the 'child' in question and hence not by a 'parent' seeking to establish his legal ties to the child.

The Lord Chancellor's Consultation Paper[8] raises the question of whether a single procedure could be introduced for obtaining a declaration of parentage which would be valid in all circumstances. While it remains to be seen whether a single procedure can be devised, some rationalisation and simplification seems desirable.

20 That is, since DNA tests are more expensive, whether they are prepared to pay the higher price.
 1 Section 20 (1B)(b), added by the Children Act 1989 s 89, substituted by the Courts and Legal Services Act 1990 s 116, Sch 16, para 3. The chosen tester must be on the Home Secretary's approved list: Home Office Circular 91/1989. Note the proposal set out in the Lord Chancellor's consultation paper, op cit, at para 38, that, instead of approving individual testers, there should be a new system of accreditation of laboratories, which would in turn be responsible for determining which of its staff is qualified to conduct paternity tests.
 2 Section 20(2).
 3 Section 20(3). It should rarely be necessary to call persons conducting tests to give oral evidence.
 4 Section 20(4).
 5 Op cit at paras 6 and 7.
 6 See s 27(5). Section 27 declarations are discussed further post, pp 773–4. An unsuccessful attempt was made during the passage of the Child Support Act 1995 to amend s 27 so as to make a declaration of paternity binding for *all* purposes.
 7 Post, p 295.
 8 Op cit at para 25.

4. REGISTRATION OF BIRTHS

As we have seen,[9] inclusion of the father's name in the register of births is prima facie evidence of his paternity. Under the Births and Deaths Registration Act 1953 s 2 the child's married parents are obliged to register the birth within 42 days. In contrast, the unmarried father has no obligation to register himself as the father and indeed has no general right to do so. The unmarried father's name may, however, be entered on the register in the following circumstances:[10]

   (i) at the joint request of the mother and the father, in which case both must sign the register;
  (ii) at the mother's request upon production of a declaration[11] by her and the father to the effect that he is the father;
 (iii) at the father's request upon production of a declaration by him and the mother to the effect that he is the father; or
  (iv) at the written request of either the mother or the father upon the production of a copy of a parental responsibility agreement, a parental responsibility order or a court order requiring him to make financial provision for the child.

It will be noted, however, that a declaration under s 27 of the Child Support Act 1991 is *not* acceptable for birth registration purposes.[12] This omission seems hard to defend.[13]

If the child's birth has been registered with no father named, it may be re-registered showing the father's name if one of the above conditions is satisfied.[14]

5. DISCOVERING GENETIC PARENTAGE[15]

Children may of course consult the birth register to discover who their registered parents are. Moreover, as we discuss in Chapter 15, when they reach 18, adopted children are generally entitled to see their original birth certificate, thus enabling them to trace their birth parents. In addition, following the recommendations of the Warnock Committee[16] that a child should have a right, when 18, to basic information about his ethnic and genetic origins, s 31(4) of the Human Fertilisation and

---

9 Ante, p 274.
10 Births and Deaths Registration Act 1953 s 10 as substituted by the Family Law Reform Act 1987 s 24 and amended by the Children Act 1989 Sch 12, para 6.
11 Namely a duly signed and witnessed declaration on a prescribed from – viz Form 2 under Sch 1 to the Registration of Births and Deaths Regulations 1987.
12 See Lord Chancellor's Consultation Paper, op cit, at para 30.
13 The Consultation Paper, ibid at para 31, specifically asks whether a s 27 declaration should at least be acceptable proof of paternity for the purpose of registering a birth outside marriage.
14 Births and Deaths Registration Act 1953 s 10A, as substituted by the Family Law Reform Act 1987 s 25 and amended by the Children Act 1980 Sch 12, para 6. Re-registration can also be made following a declaration of parentage: s 14(a) of the 1953 Act, added by the Family Law Reform Act 1987 s 26. Special arrangements are made for the registration of parental orders under s 30 of the Human Fertilisation and Embryology Act 1990 by Sch 1 to the Parental Orders (Human Fertilisation and Embryology) Regulations 1994 and for adoptions under the Adoption Act 1976 Sch 1.
15 See generally Masson and Harrison 'Identity: Mapping the Frontiers' in Lowe and Douglas (eds) *Families Across Frontiers* (1996) 277–94, and Barton and Douglas, op cit, 83–9.
16 Report of the Committee of Inquiry into Human Fertilisation and Embryology (1984) Cmnd 9314, para 4.21.

Embryology Act 1990 provides that an adult,[17] having been given a suitable opportunity to receive proper counselling,[18] may apply to the Human Fertilisation and Embryology Authority to give him notice stating whether or not the information contained in the Authority's register shows that, but for ss 27–29 of the 1990 Act, some other person would or might be his parent. If it does, the Authority must give the applicant such information as is permitted by the regulations about the person concerned or about whether a person specified in the request as a person whom the applicant proposes to marry would or might be related. However, in many cases such information can only be of a non-identifying nature, since s 31(5) specifically prohibits identifying the licensed donor of eggs or sperm. It was thought that permitting children to discover the donor's identity would deter people from acting as donors, and there was a sharp division of opinion as to whether it would be in the child's interest to learn of the fact of donation.[19]

D.   The legal significance of parentage

Like a number of other legal systems, English common law refused to accept that the mere fact of parenthood gave rise to a legally recognised relationship between parent and child. Instead it chose to recognise only the legal relationship between parent and legitimate child. We discuss the concept and significance of legitimacy when considering the child's position (see below). Suffice to say here that, although the significance of status has declined, English law continues to distinguish parents, and in particular fathers, whose children have been born in lawful wedlock from those whose children have not. Hence, while all mothers automatically have parental responsibility, only fathers whose children are legitimate automatically have such responsibility.[20]

That, however, is not to say that parenthood per se has no legal significance. For example, each parent is liable to maintain his child, and an application for child support may be brought under the Child Support Act 1991 against absent parents. Rights of succession automatically flow from the parent–child relationship,[1] as do the rules on prohibited degrees of marriage[2] and incest. All parents have a right to apply without leave for a s 8 order under the Children Act 1989[3] and there is a presumption that a child in local authority care should have reasonable contact with each parent.[4] We consider these issues elsewhere, but another issue which we will now discuss is that of citizenship and the right to remain and settle in the United Kingdom.

---

17 A person under the age of 18 has a more limited right to request information about a person he proposes to marry: ibid, s 31(6)(b) and (7).
18 Section 31(3) of the Human Fertilisation and Embryology Act 1990.
19 See Douglas *Law Fertility and Reproduction* op cit, 132–6. But see the criticisms of Maclean and Maclean 'Keeping secrets in assisted reproduction: the tension between donor anonymity and the need of the child for information' (1996) 8 CFLQ 243; and O'Donovan 'What shall we tell the children?' in Lee and Morgan (eds) *Birthrights* (1994) 105–8.
20 Children Act 1989 s 2(1) and (2), discussed post, p 376.
 1 See Chapter 19.
 2 See ante, p 31.
 3 See post, p 432.
 4 Children Act 1989 s 34, discussed post, pp 581ff.

1. ACQUISITION OF BRITISH CITIZENSHIP

By birth

At common law, birth in this country automatically conferred British nationality. However, under the British Nationality Act 1981 a child will be a British citizen by virtue of birth here only if one of his parents (or, if he was born outside marriage, his mother)[5] is at the time a British citizen or settled in this country (ie ordinarily resident in the United Kingdom without being in breach of the immigration laws or subject to any restriction on the period for which he or she may remain).[6] If a child is born here outside marriage to a non-British mother and a British father, and his parents subsequently marry, he will acquire British citizenship from the date of the marriage.[7]

Where a child born here is not a British citizen at birth, he is entitled to be registered as one during his minority if either of his parents (or his mother if he was born outside marriage) becomes a British citizen or settles in this country.[8]

A child born in this country is also entitled to be registered as a British citizen if, during each of the first ten years of his life he was not absent from the United Kingdom for more than 90 days.[9] This provision is aimed at enabling children who can be said to have a real link with this country and who have not spent a substantial part of their early childhood in, for example, their parents' homeland, to acquire citizenship.

By descent

At common law, children not born within British territory acquired British nationality only in very limited circumstances (for example, if they were the children of a British ambassador). Legislation later widened the rules, but the British Nationality Act 1948 reimposed limitations and these were extended by the 1981 Act. Under this Act a person born outside the United Kingdom is a British citizen only if, at the time of his birth, either of his parents (or his mother, if he was born outside marriage) is a British citizen otherwise than by descent, or is a British citizen in service under the Crown or a European Community institution or in some similar designated service.[10] This has had the effect of considerably reducing the number of children to whom citizenship by descent can be transmitted.

The severity of the Act is partly mitigated by two provisions granting an *entitlement*[11] to be registered as a British citizen, which are designed to protect a child of a citizen by descent with a substantial connection with this country. First,

---

5 Section 50(9).
6 Section 1(1) and s 50(2)–(5). The parent will not be regarded as settled, however, if he has been specially exempt from the immigration laws or his exemption flows from being a member of a Commonwealth or foreign force or, generally speaking, of a diplomatic mission. A newly born infant found abandoned in this country will be presumed to be a British citizen unless the contrary is shown: s 1(2). A posthumous child's nationality will depend upon the citizenship status of the parent in question at the time of the parent's death: s 48.
7 Section 47.
8 Section 1(3).
9 Section 1(4). In special circumstances the Secretary of State may permit registration even though the applicant has been absent for more than 90 days in any one or more years: s 1(7).
10 Section 2.
11 The Secretary of State also has a *discretion* to register a minor on application, if he thinks fit: s 3(1).

if the parent was in the United Kingdom during some period of three years preceding the child's birth and one of that parent's own parents was a British citizen otherwise than by descent, the child is entitled to be registered as a British citizen within twelve months of his birth, even though this event occurred abroad[12] (it will be seen that this limits transmission by this means to the second generation). Secondly, if either parent is a citizen by descent and the child and both his parents have been in the United Kingdom for three years since his birth, he may be registered as a British citizen provided that he is still a minor and both his parents consent.[13]

2.   LEAVE TO REMAIN AND SETTLE IN THE UNITED KINGDOM[14]

Where indefinite leave[15] to enter the United Kingdom is sought for a child, entry clearance from abroad will first be required, unless he or she was born here.[16] The child must be under 18 years of age, unmarried, not leading an independent life nor having formed an independent family unit, and must be able to be maintained without recourse to public funds in suitable accommodation.[17] The child must be seeking to enter in order to accompany or join either or both parents[18] who are settled, or entering to settle, here, or a relative who is settled here if there are serious and compelling family or other considerations making exclusion of the child undesirable and suitable arrangements have been made for the child's care.

Where the child is seeking to live with only one parent when the other is still alive, it must be shown that the parent has sole responsibility for the child's upbringing.[19] The fact that other relatives have had day-to-day care of the child will not prevent such sole responsibility being established[20] (indeed, how could it, since by definition in many cases the child will be seeking to *join* a parent from whom he or she has been separated), but sharing responsibility between parents

---

12 Section 3(2)–(3). Absences totalling no more than 270 days during the period of three years are to be disregarded. In special circumstances the Secretary of State may accept an application for registration up to six years after the child's birth: s 3(4).

13 Section 3(5)–(6). Absences totalling not more than 270 days are to be disregarded in each case. Only one parent need satisfy these conditions if the other has died or their marriage has been terminated or they are legally separated. If the child was born outside marriage, his mother must satisfy them.

14 See Rosenblatt and Lewis *Children and Immigration* (1997).

15 Similar requirements apply where limited leave is sought, but the child must be accompanying or joining a parent: HC 395 paras 301 and 302. For children of students or other special categories, see Rosenblatt and Lewis, op cit, ch 3. Children who are EEA nationals are admitted to accompany or join the EEA national exercising their right to freedom of movement: paras 255–262. Where the child is not himself an EEA national, an EEA family permit can be issued: paras 258–261.

16 Ibid, para 299 as amended.

17 Para 297, as amended.

18 Defined to include a step-parent where the birth parent is dead, adoptive parent provided the adoption order is recognised by the United Kingdom, and an unmarried father whose paternity has been proved: para 6. There is a government scheme for DNA testing to prove blood relationships: see Supperstone and O'Dempsey *Immigration: The Law and Practice* (3rd edn, 1994) pp 222–3 for details.

19 Para 297(i)(e). The Home Office does not apply this test where the child is aged under 12, provided there is adequate accommodation and maintenance and, if the parent is the father, there is a female relative in the household willing and able to look after the child: Supperstone and O'Dempsey, op cit, p 226.

20 *R v Immigration Appeal Tribunal, ex p Uddin* [1986] Imm AR 203.

will prevent leave being given.[1] Such an approach is hardly compatible with the emphasis upon shared parental responsibility under the Children Act 1989. However, it is clear that 'responsibility' in this context is not intended to convey any legal significance, and the role of all relevant members of the child's family must be taken into account.[2]

Where the child was born in the United Kingdom, but does not have British citizenship, no prior entry clearance is required, provided that the child has not been absent from the United Kingdom for more than two years. The same requirements as above must be satisfied, except those concerning maintenance and accommodation.[3] The definition of 'parent' is also widened to include 'a person to whom there has been a genuine transfer of parental responsibility on the ground of the original parent(s)' inability to care for the child'.[4]

A child of a polygamous marriage cannot be given leave to enter or remain, where the mother would not be granted such leave.[5]

3. DEPORTATION

At one time it was considered that no account need be taken of the provisions of the European Convention on Human Rights in determining whether to deport a child (or his parents) from the United Kingdom.[6] However, since 1993, immigration officers have been instructed to do so, in the light of European Court of Human Rights case law stressing the importance of enabling parents and children to preserve their family ties.[7]

A child will not normally be deported if he and his mother are living apart from the deportee, he has spent some years in the United Kingdom and is nearly 18, he has left home and is financially independent, or he married before deportation came into prospect.[8] If a child is still at school, the Home Secretary will take into account the effect deportation would have on his education as well as plans for his care and maintenance if he stays here.[9]

Where family proceedings are taken in order to enable either a parent or the child to evade immigration control, the Treasury Solicitor may be instructed to intervene in the proceedings as a respondent, filing an affidavit setting out the child's immigration history and the Secretary of State's objections.[10] Where a

---

1 *Williams v ECO Bridgetown Barbados* [1975] Imm AR 111.
2 *Martin v Secretary of State for the Home Department* [1972] Imm AR 71.
3 Para 305.
4 Para 6.
5 Para 296.
6 *R v Immigration Appeal Tribunal, ex p Chundawadra* [1987] Imm AR 227.
7 *Berrehab v Netherlands* (1988) 11 EHRR 322. See Storey 'The Right to Family Life and Immigration Case Law at Strasbourg' (1990) 30 ICLQ 328; O'Donnell 'Parent-Child Relationships within the European Convention' in Lowe and Douglas (eds) *Families Across Frontiers* (1996) 135–50.
8 Para 366. O'Donnell (op cit, p 143) notes that, where *the absent parent* is at risk of deportation, he may paradoxically be in a stronger position to resist than if the family were intact, when the court is more predisposed to expect the other family members to follow him abroad. But note that paras 246–248 of the Immigration Rules make specific provision for absent parents to be given leave to enter the United Kingdom to exercise 'rights of access' to a child, and DP 4/96 accordingly advises immigration officers that enforcement action 'should not necessarily be conceded' in such cases.
9 Para 367: see *R v Immigration Appeal Tribunal, ex p Bakhtaur Singh* [1986] Imm AR 352.
10 *Home Office Circular on Deportation* DP/4/96 paras 10 and 11.

parent is to be deported, and his child was born here and is now aged 10 or over, or has lived in the United Kingdom for 10 years or more from an early age, the authorities will consider, in particular, whether return to the parents' country of origin will cause extreme hardship to the child or put his health seriously at risk.

E.   The meaning of 'child'

At common law a child attained his majority at the age of 21 but, following the Latey Committee's recommendation,[11] the age of majority, as enacted by s 1(1) of the Family Law Reform Act 1969, is now 18. A 'child' (which term is now preferred to 'minor' and 'infant') may therefore be said to be a person under the age of 18.[12] This definition is also in line with Article 1 of the UN Convention on the Rights of the Child 1989 which states:

> 'For the purposes of the present Convention a child means every human being below the age of 18 years unless, under the law applicable to the child, majority is attained earlier.'

Although for some purposes an unborn child may be regarded as a 'child', whenever the term is used in a statute it is presumed, unless the contrary intention can be shown, that it only refers to a live child, ie after the child has been born.[13]

F.   The meaning of 'child of the family'

It is convenient to discuss here a recurring concept employed in family legislation, namely that of 'child of the family'. Broadly speaking, this concept is intended to embrace those children who have been brought up as if they were members of the spouses' family, it being felt reasonable to fix on those spouses duties of maintenance and protection whether or not they are the biological parents. At one stage, the definition differed according to which legislation was involved but, although the concept is employed in a number of different statutes,[14] happily the definition is now the same. It is to be noted that a child may only be a 'child of the family' where he has been brought up by parties to a marriage, and not therefore by cohabitants. The common definition is that in relation to the parties to a marriage, a child of the family is:

> '(a)   a child of both of those parties; and
> (b)   any other child, not being a child who is placed with those parties as foster parents

---

11 Committee on the Age of Majority 1967, Cmnd 3342, para 134.
12 This is the definition of 'child' under s 105(1) of the Children Act 1989. It is to be noted that not all laws relating to children are linked to the age of majority. In fact there is little consistency in the age below which legislation concerning children applies. For a helpful summary see eg the Consumers Association's *Children, Parents and the Law* pp 156–61.
13 See *Elliot v Joicey* [1935] AC 209, HL; *D (A Minor) v Berkshire County Council* [1987] AC 317, [1987] 1 All ER 20, HL; and *R v Newham London Borough Council, ex p Dada* [1996] QB 507, [1995] 2 All ER 522, CA.
14 See Matrimonial Causes Act 1973 s 52, as amended by the Children Act 1989 Sch 12, para 33; Domestic Proceedings and Magistrates Court Act 1978 s 38, as amended by the Children Act 1989 Sch 12, para 43; and the Children Act 1989 s 105(1).

by a local authority or voluntary organisation,[15] who has been treated by both of those parties as a child of the family.'

Category (a) refers to any child, including an adopted child, who is treated in law as being a child of the spouses. Subject to the exceptions mentioned above, category (b) includes any child whom both parties to a marriage have treated as a member of the family. There is no requirement that either spouse be the natural parent of the child. Hence, relatives (or even foster parents, provided the child is not in the care of a local authority or voluntary organisation) caring for the child on a 'long' term basis may be held to be treating the child as one of the family. In the case of grandparents it has been said[16] that the court should always give due weight to the pre-existing relationship between the grandparent and the child and in particular investigate whether the grandparents were simply providing everyday or secondary cover, or whether the parents had left them to assume primary responsibility for their child in the foreseeable future. Whether a child has been so treated is a question of fact. Common sense excludes some children, for example, young lodgers, and relatives who are being looked after during their parents' temporary absence. In all cases, however, the test is an objective one, namely to consider as an independent outside observer whether the evidence shows that the child was treated as a member of the family.[17] It has been held, for instance, that a child can be a 'child of the family' even though a maintenance order against the natural father in respect of the child remains in force,[18] and the fact that the husband mistakenly believed the child to be his will not prevent the child from being a child of the family if the husband treated him as such.[19]

There are two sets of circumstances in which it may be legally impossible for a child to be treated as a child of the family. First, there must be a family of which the child may be treated as a member: consequently a child may not become a child of the family if the unit never existed in the first place,[20] or if it has ceased to exist. In the latter regard, if, for instance, the wife has a child by another man after her husband has left her, but the husband agrees to treat the child as his own even though they continue to live apart, such a child cannot be a child of the family.[1] Once a family has been shown to exist, however, a child can be a child of the family even if the spouses have lived together for an extremely short period.[2] Secondly, there is authority for the proposition that a child cannot be treated as a child of the

15 This is in line with the general policy of limiting the right of foster parents to apply for orders vesting some control over the child so as not to discourage parents from allowing their child to be fostered.
16 Per Thorpe LJ in *Re A (Child of the Family)* [1998] 1 FLR 347 at 350.
17 See *Teeling v Teeling* [1984] FLR 808, CA at 809, per Ormrod LJ, and *D v D (Child of the Family)* (1981) 2 FLR 93, CA.
18 See *Carron v Carron* [1984] FLR 805, CA, where, following their marriage, the mother and stepfather took the mother's two children into their household and lived together for four years. That, according to Ormrod LJ, made it inevitable that there should be a finding that the two children were children of the family. In the case of private foster parents, the fact that a child is still being maintained by the natural parents could well indicate that the child was not a child of the foster parents' family, but it will not be decisive: see Law Com No 25, *Report on Financial Provision in Matrimonial Proceedings*, paras 23–32.
19 See *W (RJ) v W(SJ)* [1972] Fam 152, [1971] 3 All ER 303.
20 See *W v W (Child of the Family)* [1984] FLR 796, CA.
 1 *M v M (Child of the Family)* (1980) 2 FLR 39, CA. Aliter if the parties resume living together: see *Teeling v Teeling*, supra.
 2 See *W v W (Child of the Family)*, supra, where the man spent barely a fortnight with his wife and the child.

family before he is born. In *A v A (Family: Unborn Child)*[3] the husband had married the wife knowing her to be pregnant and believing himself to be the father. Six days after the marriage the wife left him. When the child was born five months later, she was obviously not the husband's child but the daughter of a Pakistani with whom the mother had also had intercourse before the marriage. The only evidence that the husband had treated the child as his own was the fact that he had married the mother, but Bagnall J held that 'treatment' involved behaviour towards a child who must be in existence. This seems a narrow and technical interpretation which is capable of working injustice[4] and it is urged that it ought not to be followed.[5]

It is submitted that a child of the parties who has subsequently been adopted by someone else or has been freed for adoption cannot normally be a 'child of the family'. An adopted child ceases in law to be a child of the parties and therefore falls outside the first part of the definition, and the provisions about treating a child cannot refer to conduct before the adoption. The position with regard to a freeing order is less clear since its effect is confined to extinguishing parental responsibility,[6] but it is submitted that while the order is in force the child will not be regarded as a child of his natural parents' family.[7] A husband's failure to deny that a child is a child of the family in undefended divorce proceedings does not estop him from asserting otherwise in subsequent proceedings.[8]

G.   The child's status

1.   INTRODUCTION

Most systems of jurisprudence have drawn a distinction between the legal position of a child born of a legally recognised union and that of a child born of an illicit union or as a result of a casual act of intercourse. Children born in the latter circumstances are commonly accorded an inferior legal status and have markedly fewer rights than those born to formal unions. This was certainly true of the common law, which, like Roman law and the modern systems based on it,[9] adhered rigidly to the rule that no child could be legitimate unless he was born or conceived in wedlock.[10] At common law an illegitimate child had no legal

---

3 [1974] Fam 6, [1974] 1 All ER 755.
4 This may be particularly harsh with regard to family provision after death, where the same definition is used under the Inheritance (Provision for Family and Dependants) Act 1975 s 1(1)(d). See post, p 887.
5 However, the decision has since been approved by Sheldon J, sitting in the Court of Appeal, in *W v W (Child of the Family)*, supra. See also *Re Leach* [1986] Ch 226 at 223, [1985] 2 All ER 754, CA at 758, per Slade LJ.
6 For the effect of adoption orders and freeing orders, see Chapter 15.
7 The Law Commission Working Paper No 96, *Custody*, at para 2.15, draws attention to the fact that once a child has been treated as a child of the family, jurisdiction appears to exist whether or not the treatment continues.
8 *Rowe v Rowe* [1980] Fam 47, [1979] 2 All ER 1123, CA. See also *Healey v Healey* [1984] Fam 111, [1984] 3 All ER 1040.
9 But this was not the only criterion accepted in Western Europe. See, further, Woolf *Private International Law* (2nd edn) p 385, and the *American Restatement of the Conflict of Laws* s 137 and *Comment*, where it is pointed out that in some legal systems a person may be the legitimate child of one parent but not of the other.
10 Though it has always been possible for the legislature to legitimate a person illegitimate at common law.

relationship with his father or, initially, with his mother. However, as a result of successive Acts of Parliament, the harshness of this position has been significantly mitigated and the concept of legitimacy has been widened: children born illegitimate may now be legitimated if their parents subsequently intermarry and, most importantly, the legal disadvantages attached to illegitimacy have nearly all been removed.[11] As a result of these changes the question whether a child is legitimate or illegitimate has become markedly less important. Nevertheless, unlike some systems such as that in New Zealand,[12] and despite a suggestion by the Law Commission that the concept should be abolished here,[13] the basic status of legitimacy and illegitimacy remains and is to some extent still relevant in determining the legal relationship between a child and his parents.

2. THE CONCEPT OF LEGITIMACY

The position at common law

At common law a child is legitimate if his parents were married at the time of his conception or at the time of his birth.[14] Commonly, legitimate children are both conceived and born in wedlock, but a similar status is accorded to other classes of children:

(a) those whose parents were married when they were born even though they must have been conceived before the marriage;[15] and
(b) those whose parents were married at the time of their conception, even though the marriage was terminated before their birth.

Consequently, a posthumous child may be legitimate, as will be the child whose parents' marriage was terminated by divorce between the time of his conception and his birth.[16]

In the absence of authority, it is thought that a child conceived as a result of pre-marital intercourse, whose parents then marry but whose father dies before his

---

11 For the drawing of an interesting parallel between the decline in importance of legitimacy and the decline of the great landed families for whom the protection of patrilineal descent was crucial, see Eekelaar *Family Security and Family Breakdown* 13–15.

12 Where as a result of the Status of Children Act 1969 s 3(1) no distinction is drawn between the status of children born to married parents and those born to unmarried parents: see *Butterworth's (NZ) Family Law Guide* (2nd edn) 6.71, and Bromley and Webb *Family Law* pp 429–39. The New Zealand enactment has served as a model for other legislation in parts of Australia and Canada: see Eekelaar *Family Law and Social Policy* (2nd edn) p 139. Soviet law, which in 1918 abolished the distinction between legitimate and illegitimate children, nevertheless found it necessary for certain purposes in 1944 to draw a distinction between those born to parents who had registered their marriage and others: see the comments of Gsovski *Soviet Civil Law* Vol 1 p 111 and pp 121–2. See also Butler *Soviet Law* p 192 et seq, and Lapenna 'The Illegitimate Child in Soviet Law' (1976) 25 ICLQ, 156.

13 Law Com Working Paper No 74, *Illegitimacy*; see further post, pp 297ff. But note the Lord Chancellor's Consultation Paper (1998) on *The Law on Parental Responsibility for Unmarried Fathers* (discussed post, p 390) canvasses views on whether all fathers should have parental responsibility. If that view prevailed, there would be little point in maintaining the distinction between legitimate and illegitimate children.

14 Blackstone's *Commentaries* i 446 and 454–7. For a full account of the common law relating to legitimacy and a detailed examination of the cases before 1836, see Nicolas *Adulterine Bastardy*.

15 Co Litt 244 a; Blackstone's *Commentaries* i 454. See also Nicolas, op cit, and the cases cited ante, p 273 n 3.

16 *Knowles v Knowles* [1962] P 161, [1962] 1 All ER 659.

birth, is legitimate. Had the father survived, the child would certainly have been legitimate[17] and, as we have seen, the common law does not bastardise a child merely because he is born posthumously.

It seems beyond argument that a child conceived during the marriage as a result of artificial insemination with the husband's own semen (AIH) is legitimate and, conversely, at common law, the child conceived as a result of artificial insemination by the semen of a donor other than the husband (DI) is illegitimate. What, however, is the child's status if the wife conceives by AIH after her husband's death? At common law,[18] such a child must surely be illegitimate, for were the position otherwise children *conceived* by the parties *after* their divorce would also have to be regarded as legitimate.[19] The common law has still to determine the status of a child born to a host mother but genetically of commissioning parents.[20]

Statutory changes

(a)   Legitimacy of children of void marriages

Since a void marriage is a marriage neither in fact nor in law, children of such a marriage were necessarily illegitimate at common law. However, following the recommendation of the Morton Commission on Marriage and Divorce,[1] the law was changed by the Legitimacy Act 1959, now replaced by the Legitimacy Act 1976. Section 1(1) provides:[2]

> 'The child of a void marriage, whenever born, shall . . . be treated as the legitimate child of his parents if at the time of the insemination resulting in the birth or, where there is no such insemination, the child's conception (or the time of the celebration of marriage if later) both or either of the parties reasonably believed that the marriage was valid.'

In common with other provisions relating to status, s 1(2) provides that the section applies only if the child's father was domiciled in England and Wales at the time of the child's birth or, if he died before the birth, immediately before his death.[3]

It has been held by the Court of Appeal in *Re Spence*[4] that s 1(1) does not apply to a child *born*[5] before his parents entered into a void marriage.

As originally worded, the Act seemed to lay the burden of proof upon the person asserting the legitimacy, a burden which might be difficult to discharge, particularly

---

17   Similarly, if the child was born to a mother who is 'brain dead' but kept alive on a life support machine until the child's birth.

18   The common law is still relevant where the artificial insemination took place before 1 August 1991. After that the position is governed by the Human Fertilisation and Embryology Act 1990, discussed on this point, ante at p 266.

19   See Bromley 'Aided Conception: The Alternative to Adoption' in Bean (ed) *Adoption, Essays in Social Policy, Law and Sociology* (1984) 174 at 175.

20   Again the common law remains relevant in cases where in vitro fertilisation took place before 1 August 1991. After that the position is governed by the Human Fertilisation and Embryology Act 1990, discussed ante, p 264.

1   Cmnd 9768, paras 1184–1186. This recommendation was intended to reflect the position in Scottish common law and many other jurisdictions which recognised the harshness of declaring as illegitimate children of parents whose marriage turned out to be void, at least where one, if not both, of the parents was ignorant of the invalidity.

2   As amended by the Family Law Reform Act 1987 s 28(1).

3   See the provisions relating to legitimatio per subsequens matrimonium, post, p 294.

4   [1990] Ch 652, [1990] 2 All ER 827, CA. Douglas (1990) 2 Journal of Child Law 56 (comment on the first instance decision subsequently upheld by the Court of Appeal).

5   Aliter if conceived before but born after the putative ceremony.

if the issue is raised many years after 'the marriage'. However, s 1(4) now provides[6] that, in relation to any child born on or after 4 April 1988,[7] it is to be presumed, unless the contrary is shown, that one of the parties reasonably believed, at the relevant time, that the marriage was valid. Another problem with the provision is the meaning of 'reasonably believed'. It seems to be established that this imports an objective test, ie the belief must be one that a reasonable person would have held in the circumstances.[8] This test led to doubt whether a mistake of law would support a reasonable belief. However, following the Law Commission's recommendations,[9] s 1(3)[10] now provides that such a mistake can support a reasonable belief.

(b) Legitimacy of children of voidable marriages

At common law a decree of nullity, where the marriage was voidable, had retrospective effect and automatically bastardised the issue of the marriage.[11] When the grounds for nullity were extended by the Matrimonial Causes Act 1937, it was appreciated that this rule might work hardship in those cases where the marriage was annulled because the respondent was of unsound mind, or epileptic, or was suffering from a venereal disease in a communicable form, since the wife might conceive before the petitioner discovered the existence of the impediment. Consequently the 1937 Act provided that in these two cases any child born of the marriage should be legitimate notwithstanding the annulment of the marriage.[12] Where the respondent was pregnant by a man other than the petitioner, the question of the legitimacy of the child did not arise, and apparently the legislature did not foresee that any child would be born if the marriage had not been consummated. Since then, however, cases concerning children born as a result of pre-marital intercourse,[13] or fecundatio ab extra,[14] and of artificial insemination have come before the courts.[15]

This anomaly was first removed by the Law Reform (Miscellaneous Provisions) Act 1949 s 4(1) which provided that any child who would have been the legitimate child of the parties to a voidable marriage had it not been annulled should be deemed to be their legitimate child.[16] The same result is now reached by s 16 of the Matrimonial Causes Act 1973 which, by enacting that a voidable marriage shall be treated as if it had existed up to the date of the decree absolute, must necessarily preserve the legitimacy of any child born or conceived between the date of the marriage and the date of the decree, as well as that of any child legitimated by the marriage.[17]

---

6 Added by s 28(2) of the Family Law Reform Act 1987 following the Law Commission's recommendation in Law Com No 118 *Illegitimacy* at para 10.51.
7 The date on which the amendment came into force.
8 *Hawkins v A-G* [1966] 1 All ER 392 at 397. Note the criticisms of this test by Bevan *Child Law* (1989) 247.
9 Law Com No 118, para 10.52.
10 Added by the Family Law Reform Act 1987 s 28(2).
11 See ante at p 101.
12 Section 7(2).
13 As in *Dredge v Dredge* [1947] 1 All ER 29.
14 As in *Clarke v Clarke* [1943] 2 All ER 540.
15 As in *REL v EL* [1949] P 211, [1949] 1 All ER 141.
16 This provision, however, did not have retrospective effect. Consequently, except in those cases provided for in s 7(2) of the Matrimonial Causes Act 1937, the children of voidable marriages annulled before 16 December 1949 remain illegitimate: *Re Adams* [1951] Ch 716, [1951] 1 All ER 1037.
17 For s 16, see ante, p 102. The section will not legitimate a child who never was legitimate (eg because the husband was not the father): *Re Adams*, supra.

(c)   Legitimation

Canon law adopted the Roman law rule that a bastard would become legitimate if his parents subsequently intermarried, provided that they had been free to marry each other at the time of the child's birth. But the importance of establishing the identity of the heir at law, to whom descended the valuable private rights and important public duties of the ownership of an inheritable estate of freehold land in the Middle Ages, led the common law to reject this doctrine of legitimatio per subsequens matrimonium, and an attempt to introduce it by the Statute of Merton in 1235 was successfully resisted by the temporal peers. Consequently, no form of legitimation was recognised by English law until the passing of the Legitimacy Act 1926, by which time the property legislation of 1925 had rendered it almost wholly unnecessary to establish the identity of the heir save in the case of the descent of an unbarred entailed interest.

The Legitimacy Act 1926 provided that a child should be legitimated by the subsequent marriage of his parents. But it also adopted the canon law rule that legitimation was impossible if either parent was married to any other person at the time of the child's birth.[18] However, a child conceived whilst one of his parents was married could still be legitimated if this marriage was terminated before his birth, and in many cases decrees of divorce were expedited for this reason. The Legitimacy Act 1959 extended those provisions to children born when either or both of their parents were married.[19] These Acts have now been repealed and their provisions re-enacted in the Legitimacy Act 1976. Section 2 provides:

'. . . where the parents of an illegitimate person marry one another, the marriage shall, if the father of the illegitimate person is at the date of the marriage domiciled in England and Wales, render that person, if living, legitimate from the date of the marriage.'

A person will be legitimated by this section only if his father was domiciled in England and Wales at the time of the marriage. Legitimation does not have retrospective effect, so that no one can be legitimated unless he is still alive when his parents marry.[20] The fact that an adopted child is to be regarded as the child of the adoptive parent and of no other person does not prevent an illegitimate child from being legitimated if he has been adopted solely by one of his parents who then marries the other parent.[1]

3.   DECLARATIONS OF PARENTAGE AND STATUS[2]

As we have seen,[3] the question of a child's status may be put in issue in a number of ways. Normally, however, any judicial decision will be a judgment in personam and consequently will bind only the parties to it and their privies, ie persons claiming

---

18 Section 1(2).

19 Section 1.

20 Or, if they were married before the date on which the Act by virtue of which he was legitimated came into force, on that date. Legitimacy Act 1926 s 1(1); Legitimacy Act 1959 s 1(2); Legitimacy Act 1976 Sch 1 para 1. But if the parents had married before the relevant Act came into force, the children could be legitimated on that date, even though one or both parents had already died: *Re Lowe* [1929] 2 Ch 210.

1 Legitimacy Act 1976 s 4. For the effect of adoption, see post, pp 676ff.

2 For declarations in other family matters, see ante, pp 52ff.

3 Ante, p 282.

through them. The desirability of a procedure to enable a disputed question of legitimacy to be settled once and for all led to the passing of the Legitimacy Declaration Act 1858, which was repealed and substantially re-enacted in the Matrimonial Causes Act 1973 s 45. Under s 45 any person could petition for a decree that he was legitimate or that he or his parents or grandparents were validly married. But a petitioner could not obtain a declaration of legitimacy of anyone other than himself,[4] nor was there any power to declare anyone illegitimate,[5] or to make a declaration of paternity of any illegitimate child.[6]

Following a review by the Law Commission,[7] s 45 was repealed and replaced by s 56 of the Family Law Act 1986 and rewritten by the Family Law Reform Act 1987.[8] Under s 56 the 'child' but no one else can seek the following declarations:

(1) that the person named in the application is the father or the mother, or that particular persons are the parents of the applicant;
(2) that the applicant is the legitimate child of his parents; and
(3) that the applicant has become or has not become a legitimated person.

Such applications may be made either in the High Court or county court.[9]

It will be noted that, unlike under the old law, an unmarried person can be declared to be a parent, but it remains the case that it is not possible to obtain a declaration of illegitimacy.[10] Furthermore, as before, an applicant may only seek a declaration about his own status and not that of anyone else (though in determining his own status, the marital status of the alleged parents may also be put in issue).[11]

These provisions are subject to a number of safeguards, reflecting the Law Commission's concern that bare declarations could be abused. Hence, as before, no application can be made unless the applicant is domiciled or has been habitually resident for one year in England and Wales at the date of the application.[12] There is power, at any stage of the proceedings, to send the papers to the Attorney General and, whether or not such papers are sent, the Attorney General can intervene in the proceedings.[13]

Where the truth of the proposition to be declared has been proved to the court's satisfaction, the court shall make that declaration 'unless to do so would be manifestly contrary to public policy'.[14] If a declaration is made, it is binding upon the Crown and all other persons,[15] and the Registrar General will be informed.[16] If the declaration is refused, the court cannot grant a declaration for which an application has not been made.[17]

---

4 *Aldrich v A-G* [1968] P 281, [1968] 1 All ER 345.
5 *B v A-G* [1966] 2 All ER 145n.
6 *Re JS (A Minor) (Declaration of Paternity)* [1981] Fam 22, [1980] 1 All ER 1061, CA.
7 See Law Com No 118, paras 10.1–10.27 and Law Com No 132, *Declarations in Family Matters*, paras 3.9–3.14.
8 Section 22.
9 Family Law Act 1986 s 63. The procedure is governed by Family Proceedings Rules 1991 r 3.13 for declarations of parentage and r 3.14 for declarations of legitimacy and legitimation.
10 Ibid, s 58 (5)(b).
11 But not grandparents, as previously.
12 Family Law Act 1986 s 56(4).
13 Ibid, s 59.
14 Section 58(1). This proviso seems to put into statutory form the power exercised in *Puttick v A-G* [1980] Fam 1, [1979] 3 All ER 463: see also ante, pp 52–3.
15 Section 58(2).
16 Section 56(5) as added by the Family Law Reform Act 1987.
17 Section 58(3).

The Lord Chancellor's Consultation Paper[18] raises a number of questions about the ambit of s 56. In particular it queries the need for possible intervention by the Attorney General, particularly where there is apparently conclusive DNA evidence available. It also canvasses views as to whether s 56 should be:

(a) confined to 'children' (but, if not, who else should be permitted to seek a declaration?); and

(b) extended to making declarations that a named person is *not* the parent of a particular child.

4.   THE SIGNIFICANCE OF THE CHILD'S STATUS

At common law the illegitimate child, being filius nullius, had no legal relationship with either of his parents and consequently had no rights, for example, to receive maintenance,[19] to succeed to their property, or to other benefits normally accruing from the relationship of parent and child. Many of these disabilities subsisted until well after the Second World War, but have since been whittled away. For example, following the reforms of the Family Law Reform Acts of 1969 and 1987, children whose parents are not married now have full rights of intestate succession.[20] They can also succeed as an heir to an entailed estate.[1] Such children can now make claims as dependants both under the Inheritance (Provision for Family and Dependants) Act 1975 and the Fatal Accidents legislation.[2] Substantial improvements have been made to the right of support. Indeed, under the Children Act 1989 Sch 1 either parent can be ordered to pay to the other or to the child secured or unsecured periodic payments, lump sum payments, or make property transfers.[3]

Despite these important changes it cannot yet be said that children whose parents are unmarried are in exactly the same legal position as those whose parents are married.

One important difference is that, whereas parties seeking a divorce must necessarily have their plans for their child's future scrutinised by the court,[4] there is no similar compulsion in cases where unmarried parents separate.

There are two further areas of major discrimination, namely with regard to citizenship and succession to a title of honour.

Citizenship

For the purposes of claiming citizenship an illegitimate child is regarded as the child of his mother and not his father.[5] Although the Law Commission could see no reason in principle why this rule should not be changed, they felt unable to make definite proposals since, being a United Kingdom matter, it was outside their terms of

---

18 *Court Procedures for the Determination of Paternity* (1998), pp 4–7.
19 But see Cretney *Principles of Family Law* (4th edn) 1984, p 594.
20 Post, pp 887 and 903.
 1 Family Law Reform Act 1987 s 19(2).
 2 Fatal Accidents Act 1976 as substituted by the Administration of Justice Act 1982: discussed post, pp 902ff.
 3 Discussed post at pp 767ff.
 4 Under s 41 of the Matrimonial Causes Act 1973, discussed ante, pp 230 and 250ff.
 5 British Nationality Act 1981 s 50(9). See further ante, p 285.

reference.[6] It is, however, surely a matter of regret that the government felt unable to change the rule. As one commentator has pointed out,[7] with the advent of DNA fingerprinting, by which it has become significantly easier to establish parentage, it is now particularly hard to justify the retention of this discriminatory rule.

Titles of honour

With regard to titles of honour, s 19(4) of the 1987 Act makes it clear that, despite the new construction of the term 'heir', children of unmarried parents will not be able to succeed to property which is limited to devolve along with a dignity or title of honour. However, this should not be read as meaning that such children will never be able to succeed, since that will depend upon the terms of the letters patent issued under the Great Seal. At the moment they are in a form[8] which limits succession to the 'heirs . . . of his body lawfully begotten', which is enough to show a contrary intention against devolvement to children whose parents are unmarried. However, if in the future the form 'to X and the heirs of his body' were used, then any child could succeed under the terms of s 19(2).

The position of legitimated children

With regard to a *legitimated* child, it is expressly provided that such a person shall have the same rights and obligations in respect of the maintenance and support of himself and other persons as if he had been born legitimate, and any legal claim for damages, compensation, allowances etc, by or in respect of a legitimate child shall apply in the case of one legitimated.[9] Similarly, for the purpose of determining whether he is a British citizen he is to be treated as being born legitimate as from the date of his parents' marriage, and is able to claim through his father or his mother.[10] Subject to what is said later with respect to rights in property,[11] a legitimated person is in the same position as if he had been born legitimate. On the other hand, a legitimated person is not entitled to succeed to a title of honour.[12]

5.   SHOULD REFERENCE NOW BE MADE TO LEGITIMACY AND ILLEGITIMACY?

Background to the Family Law Reform Act 1987

At one time the Law Commission favoured what at the time was thought to be the radical plan that the status of illegitimacy should be abolished altogether.[13] They

6 See Law Com No 118, para 11.9. The Scottish Law Commission came to a similar conclusion: see Scot Law Com No 82, paras 8.3–8.5.
7 Cretney [1987] Fam Law 404.
8 See the discussion in Law Com No 118 at para 8.26.
9 Legitimacy Act 1976 s 8.
10 British Nationality Act 1981 s 47(1).
11 See post, pp 879–80.
12 Legitimacy Act 1976 Sch 1, para 4(2). A similar disability attaches to children who are treated in law as the child of the mother and her husband in cases where the child has been carried by a woman as a result of her artificial insemination, or the placing in her of an embryo or of sperm and eggs.
13 For an influential argument against giving all fathers automatic rights, see Hayes (1980) 43 MLR 299, though Eekelaar 'Second Thoughts on Illegitimacy Reform' [1985] Fam Law 261 argued that the status could have been abolished without giving all fathers equal rights. But for the current debate as to whether all fathers should have automatic parental responsibility see post, pp 388ff.

argued that since the label was itself discriminatory, true equality demanded not simply the removal of the remaining areas of legal discrimination but the abolition of the very status. Indeed, so strongly were they committed to this view that they were prepared to countenance the necessary corollary of their recommendations: that all fathers should be treated equally. The overwhelming response, however, was against giving all fathers automatic rights,[14] and accordingly, in their full report on *Illegitimacy*,[15] the Law Commission did not advocate abolition of that status, but recommended instead a change in terminology, with the terms 'marital' and 'non marital' replacing so far as possible 'legitimate' and 'illegitimate'.

Before these recommendations were acted upon, the issue was examined by the Scottish Law Commission.[16] They observed[17] that:

> '. . . so long as marriage exists and children are born there will be children born out of marriage. In some cases of children born out of marriage, the parents will marry each other after the birth: in others they will not. These are facts and, short of abolishing marriage, there is nothing the law can do about them.'

Like the English Law Commission they did not recommend abolishing the status of illegitimacy, but unlike that body the Scots could see no merit in introducing the new terms 'marital' and 'non marital'. As they said,[18] that 'was just another way of labelling children, and experience in other areas, such as mental illness, suggests that new labels can rapidly take on old connotations'. They concluded that they did not wish to see 'a discriminatory concept of "non-marital" gradually replace a discriminatory concept of "illegitimacy"'. Accordingly, they recommended that the terms 'legitimate' and 'illegitimate' as applied to people, should wherever possible cease to be used in legislation. To achieve this they recommended that, where distinctions based on marriage were necessary, future legislation should distinguish between fathers rather than children. Where it was thought necessary to distinguish people on the basis of whether or not their parents were married to each other at any relevant time (which they hoped would be a 'very rare exception') it should be done expressly in those terms. The Scottish Law Commission's proposals were enacted in the Law Reform (Parent and Child) (Scotland) Act 1986.

Following these developments, the English Law Commission reconsidered its proposals and in a second report, published in October 1986,[19] advocated reform along the Scottish lines. Their recommendations were enacted by the Family Law Reform Act 1987.

The Family Law Reform Act 1987

Apart from making important changes to the status of some children born as a result of donor insemination and amending the provision dealing with children of void marriages, the 1987 Act has left untouched the basic concept of legitimacy. However, implementing the strategy of reducing the need to refer to the concept, in cases where it is still necessary to distinguish between children born within

---

14 See their Working Party No 74 on *Illegitimacy* (1979).
15 Law Com No 118 (1982), particularly at Part IV.
16 Scot Law Com No 82 (1984). It was also examined by the Irish Law Reform Commission: see Duncan 'Abolishing Illegitimacy – A Discussion of the Law Reform Commission's Proposals' (1983) 5 Dublin University Law Journal 29–41.
17 Ibid, at para 9.1.
18 Ibid, at para 9.2.
19 Law Com No 157.

marriage and those born without, the Act introduced the important change that reference be made to the parents, rather than to the children, and whether or not they are married to each other. This general approach is set out by s 1 of the 1987 Act.

Section 1(1) provides that references in the 1987 Act and any succeeding Act or statutory instrument to 'mothers' or 'fathers' or 'parents' refers, unless the contrary intention appears, to all such persons regardless of whether they have or had been married to each other at any time. The clarity of this opening provision is immediately obscured by definitional provisions designed to distinguish (in simple terms) parents (primarily fathers) of legitimate from those of illegitimate children. To avoid using the words 'legitimate' or 'illegitimate', s 1(2) refers instead to a person whose parents were not married to each other at the time of the child's birth. However, it was recognised that this shorthand definition was insufficient by itself, because a child can be legitimate even though his parents were not married at the time of his birth. Accordingly s 1(2) is made subject to s 1(3), so that references to 'a person whose father and mother were not married to each other at the time of the child's birth'[20] do not include (and correspondingly, references to a person whose parents were married to each other at the time of his birth *do* include) cases where the child is:

(a) rendered legitimate by s 1 of the Legitimacy Act 1976 even though his parents' marriage is void;
(b) legitimated by reason of his parents' subsequent marriage;
(c) adopted; and
(d) 'otherwise treated in law as legitimate'.[1]

The resulting law can be confusing. For example, as will be seen,[2] s 2(1) of the Children Act 1989 states that: 'where a child's father and mother were married to each other at the time of his birth, they shall each have parental responsibility for the child', whereas according to s 2(2) if they were not so married then only the mother has such responsibility. The unsuspecting reader might think that these provisions mean what they say and conclude that parental responsibility is only automatically vested in a father if he is married to the mother at the time of the child's birth. In fact, however, he will also have responsibility if he had divorced his wife at the time of the child's birth, and he will acquire it automatically if he subsequently marries the mother.

Whether the law needed to have been so complex is debatable.[3] It might have been less confusing, for example, simply to have referred to the *parents* being legitimate or illegitimate. Despite its resulting complexity, in deference to the clear spirit of the 1987 Act, we shall avoid where possible labelling children and, as a matter of shorthand convenience, will refer to mothers or fathers as 'unmarried' when referring to parents of a child whose mother and father are not and have not been married to each other.

---

20 By s 1(4) a child's birth is to be taken to include the period beginning with insemination resulting in his birth or, where there was no such insemination, his conception, and ends with his birth.

1 This covers the case, for example, where the child is conceived through the placing in the woman of an embryo or sperm and eggs or of her artificial insemination and is born to a married woman and who therefore, by virtue of ss 27–29 of the Human Fertilisation and Embryology Act 1990, is treated as being the child of the woman and her husband.

2 Post, p 376.

3 See eg Lowe 'The Family Reform Act 1987 – Useful Reform but an Unhappy Compromise ?' (1988) Denning LJ 77.

H.   The changing nature of the parent–child relationship[4]

1.   INTRODUCTION

Like society's views about the role of the family and of the individual members within the unit, the legal attitude towards the parent–child relationship has not remained static. The principal catalyst for legal change in the past has been the rise of individualism, first with respect to women and then, perhaps even more important, with respect to children.[5] With regard to the former, the growing calls for women's rights during the nineteenth century led in the end to the fundamental change that, whereas formerly parental rights were vested in the father (at any rate in respect of legitimate children), they are now shared between the father and the mother. The growing acceptance that a child is a person in his own right[6] led first to concern about his welfare and protection and, more recently, to the recognition that in certain circumstances at least he might have rights of his own. This in turn has led to a fundamental change in the nature of parental authority. In the past it was accurate to think of the parental position in terms of rights and duties, for at common law fathers had almost complete autonomy over their legitimate children, and their interest was akin to a proprietorial one;[7] by the 1980s, however, the emphasis had clearly shifted towards parental responsibility,[8] which position is now firmly entrenched in the Children Act 1989.

Although the overall effect of these developments has been to weaken the parents' position, it would be a mistake to infer that the issue of parental responsibility is no longer important. On the contrary, the position of parents remains of key importance in English law. Indeed, it is through the medium of parental responsibility that the law in effect recognises the general *right* of parents both to bring up their own children and to a large extent to do so in their own way. We discuss in detail the concept of parental responsibility in Chapter 10, but we conclude this chapter by examining the changing nature of the parent–child relationship, particularly over the past two centuries.

2.   THE INITIAL STRENGTH OF THE FATHER'S POSITION

Legitimate children

(a)   The position at common law

Common law recognised the natural duties of protecting and maintaining one's legitimate minor children, and although the machinery for enforcing these duties

---

4 See generally Lowe 'The Legal Position of Parents and Children in English Law' [1994] Singapore Journal of Legal Studies 332.

5 The legal and social background to these developments is well summarised by Maidment *Child Custody and Divorce* (1985) chs 4 and 5.

6 There are those who maintain that until the seventeenth century the concept of childhood did not exist: see eg Aries *Centuries of Childhood*, though this view has not escaped criticism. See the references in Maidment, op cit, at 91–2.

7 See further below. Ironically, the common law has not been entirely immutable: see, for instance, *R v D* [1984] AC 778, [1984] 2 All ER 449, HL, where in holding that even a father could be guilty of the common law offence of kidnapping his own child, Lord Brandon said (at 805 and 456 respectively), 'The common law, however, while generally immutable in its principles . . . is not immutable in the way it adapts those principles in a radically changing world and against the background of radically changed social conventions and conditions.'

8 See eg Woolf J in *Gillick v West Norfolk and Wisbech Area Health Authority* [1984] QB 581 at 596, [1984] 1 All ER 365 at 373, who said that the interests of parents are more accurately described as responsibilities and duties.

was almost wholly ineffective, nevertheless they could properly be regarded as unenforceable legal obligations.[9] Moreover, it is obvious that, at any rate in early law, these duties could be performed only if the parent actually had the custody of the child, and in many cases the father would be the only member of the family who would be physically capable of carrying them out. Consequently, it is not surprising to discover that his duty to protect carried with it the correlative right to the custody of all minor children and that this right was absolute even against the mother, except in the rare cases where the father's conduct was such as gravely to imperil the children's life, health or morals. Custody carried with it many rights and powers in addition to care and control. A father was entitled to the services of his children in his custody and to correct them by administering reasonable corporal punishment. He alone might determine the form of their religious and secular education. Whilst his powers were never as wide as those of the paterfamilias in Roman law, the same fundamental approach is apparent. Physical control represented the kernel of this right; without it the others could not be enforced, and the procedural machinery of the common law was such that only his right could be specifically enforced by the writ of habeas corpus.

At common law, therefore, the father was entitled to the legal custody of his legitimate children until they reached the age of 21,[10] but his rights could be lost if to enforce them would probably lead to the physical or moral harm of the child,[11] or if his claim was not made bona fide.[12] After his death, the mother was entitled to the legal custody of her minor children for nurture,[13] but even this right was superseded after 1660 if the father appointed a testamentary guardian under the provisions of the Tenures Abolition Act.[14] Common law accorded no other right to the mother as such, and so absolute against her were the father's rights that he could lawfully claim from her possession even a child at the breast.[15]

(b)   The intervention of equity

The common law position was tempered by the intervention of equity. The jurisdiction of equity to intervene between parent and child is derived from the prerogative power of the Crown as parens patriae to interfere to protect any person within the jurisdiction not fully sui juris. This power was naturally exercised by the Lord Chancellor, and although it fell into abeyance when the Court of Wards was set up in 1540, successive Chancellors began to use their powers more and more extensively when this court was abolished in 1660.[16] From the Court of

---

9   For a more detailed account see Pettit 'Parental Control and Guardianship' in Graveson and Crane (eds) *A Century of Family Law* (1957) ch 4.
10   *Thomasset v Thomasset* [1894] P 295, CA; *Re Agar-Ellis* (1883) 24 Ch D 317, CA.
11   Such as apprehension of cruelty or grossly immoral or profligate conduct: *Re Andrews* (1873) LR 8 QB 153 at 158.
12   If his purpose was to hand the child over to another, for example: *Re Turner* (1872) 41 LJQB 142.
13   *R v Clarke* (1857) 7 E & B 186 at 200.
14   See the 7th edition of this work at p 350.
15   *R v De Manneville* (1804) 5 East 221 – a father who had separated from his wife forcibly removed an eight-month child while it was actually at the breast and carried it away almost naked in an open carriage in inclement weather. The court, in upholding his right to custody, said it would draw no inferences to the disadvantage of the father. See also *R v Greenhill* (1836) 4 Ad & El 624 – a father's right to custody of his three daughters aged five and under was upheld notwithstanding he was living with an adulteress and nothing could be said against the mother. The children went to live with their paternal grandmother.
16   Holdsworth *History of English Law*, vi 648. The Court of Wards was set up by the 32 Hen 8, c 45, and abolished by the Tenures Abolition Act 1660.

Chancery the jurisdiction passed to the High Court under the Judicature Acts of 1873 and 1875.

One advantage that equity had over the common law was that its procedure was much better adapted to deal with disputes concerning children. Common law, limited as it was to the issue of a writ of habeas corpus, could only enforce the right to physical control; equity, on the other hand, acts in personam, so that it could not only make orders concerning, for example, the child's education, but also effectively ensure that they were carried out. A further step that could be taken was to have the child made a ward of court.[17] This procedure had a number of advantages. Not only could the person to whom care and control was given always turn to the court for advice, but the ward remained under the permanent control of the court during minority, so that any dereliction of duty on the part of the carer and any interference with the ward were punishable as a contempt of court. Furthermore, the court could give care and control of the child to his own parent, which meant that the child would remain in the latter's possession whilst the court could ensure that the parental powers were exercised in the child's best interests.

(c)   The increasing influence of equity [18]

At first the intervention of equity scarcely had any impact upon the father's position. It left untouched the common law duties of a parent and indeed gave prima facie effect to the father's right to custody of his legitimate children, unless he had forfeited it by his immoral or cruel conduct, or was seeking to enforce it capriciously or arbitrarily. As Cotton LJ said in *Re Agar-Ellis*:[19]

'This court holds this principle – that when, by birth, a child is subject to a father, it is for the general interest of families, and for the general interest of children, and really for the interest of the particular infant, that the Court should not, except in very extreme cases, interfere with the discretion of the father, but leave to him the responsibility of exercising that power which nature has given him by the birth of the child.'

On the other hand there was a growing view,[20] which ultimately prevailed, that the welfare of the child was the first consideration and equity would not hesitate to deprive a father of his rights if it would clearly be contrary to the child's interests to give effect to them. In the words of Lord Esher MR in *R v Gyngall*:[1]

'The court is placed in a position by reason of the prerogative of the Crown to act as supreme parent of the child, and must exercise that jurisdiction in the manner in which a wise, affectionate, and careful parent would act for the welfare of the child. The natural parent in the particular case may be affectionate, and may be intending to act for the child's good, but may be unwise, and may not be doing what a wise, affectionate, and careful parent would do. The Court may say in such a case that, although they can find no misconduct on the part of the parent, they will not permit that to be done with the child

17   For the history and development of wardship see Lowe and White *Wards of Court* (2nd edn, 1986), ch 1 and Seymour 'Parens Patriae and Wardship Powers: Their Nature and Origins' (1994) 14 Ox J of Legal Studies 159. Wardship is discussed further in Chapter 16.

18   See Lowe 'The House of Lords and the Welfare Principle' in Bridge (ed) *Family Law Towards the Millennium – Essays for P M Bromley* (1997) 125 and 127–34.

19   (1883) 24 Ch D 317, CA at 334, in which the father's right to custody was upheld and communication with her mother prevented on the grounds that his daughter's affection for him might thereby be alienated.

20   Arguably the 'germ' of the welfare principle was sown in two early House of Lords' decisions, *Johnstone v Beattie* (1843) 10 Cl & Fin 42 and *Stuart v Marquis of Bute* (1861) 9 HL Cas 440, both of which concerned guardians rather than parents.

1   [1893] 2 QB 232, CA at 241–2. See also *Re O'Hara* [1900] 2 IR 232, CA; *Official Solicitor v K* [1965] AC 201, [1963] 3 All ER 191, HL.

which a wise, affectionate, and careful parent would not do. The court must, of course, be very cautious in regard to the circumstances under which they will interfere with the parental right . . . The court must exercise this jurisdiction with great care, and can only act when it is shown that either the conduct of the parent, or the description of the person he is, or the position in which he is placed, is such as to render it not merely better, but – I will not say "essential", but – clearly right for the welfare of the child in some very serious and important respect that the parent's rights should be suspended or superseded; but . . . where it is so shown, the Court will exercise its jurisdiction accordingly.'

Hence, although originally equity interfered with the father's rights hardly less readily than the common law, by the end of the nineteenth century it would do so if there was any threat of physical or moral harm to the child; and if a father once abandoned or abdicated his right, he would not be allowed to reassert it arbitrarily if this would be contrary to the child's interests.[2]

As in other fields, equity ensured that, where its own rules were in conflict with those of common law, the former should prevail. It would not only grant an injunction to restrain a person from applying for a writ of habeas corpus to obtain the custody of a child,[3] but would also prevent a person who had already obtained the writ from interfering with the child if this was not in his interests.[4] As in the case of other conflicts between law and equity, the Judicature Act 1873 expressly provided that the rules of equity relating to the custody and education of minors should prevail over those of common law.[5] Notwithstanding this enjoinder, it seems evident that on occasion at least the courts continued to apply common law principles at the expense of equity even into this century.[6] Moreover, it seems fair to say that at the end of the nineteenth century, notwithstanding the growing influence of equity, the courts remained essentially 'parent focused', though undoubtedly the seeds had been sown for the development of the welfare principle which would eventually take precedence over parents' rights.

The position with regard to illegitimate children

At common law a bastard was *filius nullius* and consequently none of the legal powers or duties which flowed from the relationship of parent and legitimate child was accorded him or his parents.[7] This meant, inter alia, that the father could not claim custody.[8] Eventually it became accepted that the right of control vested in the mother,[9] who indeed as against third parties was in as strong a position as the father in respect of his legitimate children.[10]

---

2 See *Re O'Hara*, supra, at 240–1; *Re Fynn* (1848) 2 De G & Sm 457 at 474–5.
3 Per Lindley LJ in *R v Barnardo, Jones's Case* [1891] 1 QB 194, CA at 210.
4 *Andrews v Salt* (1873) 8 Ch App 622.
5 Section 25(10) (now the Supreme Court Act 1981 s 49). But even before this the common law courts recognised the superiority of the jurisdiction of the Court of Chancery to the extent that, if proceedings were pending in the latter court, an application for habeas corpus would be stayed until the decision of Chancery was known: *Wellesley v Duke of Beaufort* (1827) 2 Russ 1 at 25–6, *R v Isley* (1836) 5 Ad & El 441.
6 See eg *Re Agar-Ellis*, supra, and *R v New* (1904) 20 TLR 583; see further, n 10 below.
7 Blackstone *Commentaries* i, 458–9.
8 See eg *R v Soper* (1793) 5 Term Rep 278.
9 See eg *Barnardo v McHugh* [1891] AC 388, HL, in which an unmarried mother successfully invoked habeas corpus proceedings following Dr Barnardo's failure to deliver her illegitimate son to a person named by her.
10 See eg *R v New*, supra, in which the Court of Appeal upheld a mother's right of custody to her illegitimate daughter, as against foster parents with whom the child had been living for 10 years, to the extent of removing the child and placing her in a Church of England Home where no one would be allowed to visit her until she had been there for two years.

Although, as we have seen,[11] most of the legal disabilities attached to illegitimacy have now been removed by statute, it remains the case that unless he subsequently acquires it by order or by agreement, parental responsibility is vested in the mother to the exclusion of the father, even though the latter's paternity is not in doubt.[12]

3.   THE STRENGTHENING OF THE MOTHER'S POSITION

The inevitable corollary of the strength of the father's position was the weakness of the mother's in respect of legitimate children. However, during the nineteenth century Parliament intervened in a series of statutes, the effect of which was to whittle down the father's rights further and also to give the mother positive rights to custody which even equity did not accord to her. The history of this change in attitude can best be seen by a brief examination of the principal provisions of each statute.

Talfourd's Act 1839

This Act marks a decisive point in the history of family law, for it empowered the Court of Chancery to give the mother custody of her children until they reached the age of seven and access to them until they came of age. But the Act specifically provided that no order was to be made if the mother had been guilty of adultery.

Custody of Infants Act 1873

This extended the principle of Talfourd's Act by empowering the court to give the mother custody until the child reached the age of 16. It did not, however, repeat the proviso relating to her adultery. The Act provided that arrangements as to custody or control in separation deeds (which had formerly been void as contrary to public policy) were to be enforceable so long as they were for the child's interests.

Guardianship of Infants Act 1886

Neither of these two earlier Acts gave mothers rights as such, but were concerned to extend the court's discretion to grant orders in the mother's favour. However, a third Act, the Guardianship of Infants Act 1886, not only extended judicial discretion by empowering the court to give the mother custody of her children until they reached the age of 21, but also stopped the father from defeating the mother's right after his death by appointing a testamentary guardian and enacted that the mother was to act jointly with any guardian so appointed. Furthermore, for the first time it gave limited powers to a mother to appoint testamentary guardians.

Twentieth century developments

Although, as we shall see, the move to establish maternal rights proved to be of passing significance, with attention becoming more focused on the child's welfare, the process of equalising parental rights continued in the twentieth century. The Guardianship of Infants Act 1925 provided that in any proceedings before any court[13] neither the father nor the mother should be regarded as having a claim

11   Ante, p 296.
12   See now the Children Act 1989 s 2 (1)–(2), discussed post, p 376.
13   Jurisdiction to make orders relating to custody etc, which had formerly been exercisable only by the High Court and (since 1886) by county courts, was extended (subject to certain exceptions) to magistrates' courts.

superior to the other in respect of the custody or upbringing of the child. It also gave the mother the same right to appoint testamentary guardians as the father. The Guardianship Act 1973 gave each parent (of a legitimate child) equal and separately exercisable rights. Finally, with the abolition of the archaic rule that during his lifetime the father was the sole guardian of his legitimate child by s 2(4) of the Children Act 1989, it can now be said that the legal position of married parents with respect to their children is equal.[14]

4. THE INCREASING RECOGNITION OF THE CHILD'S POSITION

The evolution and development of the welfare principle[15]

(a) The position before 1925

A striking feature of the early law was its apparent lack of concern for the child. By the end of the last century, however, there seemed to be a growing awareness of the child's welfare, possibly triggered by the movement in the mid-nineteenth century that children should have a right to basic education and the general rise of individualism.[16] For example, under the Custody of Infants Act 1873 a parental agreement about custody could not be enforced if the court did not think that it was for the child's benefit. Further, the Guardianship of Infants Act 1886 directed the court to have regard to the child's welfare as well as to the conduct and wishes of the parents when deciding custody applications. The most obviously child-centred statute was the Custody of Children Act 1891, which was passed as the direct result of a number of cases in which parents had succeeded in recovering from Dr Barnardo children whom they had placed in his now famous 'homes', or whom they had abandoned and he had taken in. It provided that if a parent had abandoned or deserted his child or allowed him to be brought up by, and at the expense of, another person, school, institution or local authority, in such circumstances as to show that he was unmindful of his parental duties, he had to prove that he was fit to have custody of the child claimed.

The more enduring development, however, was judicially inspired. We have already noted[17] equity's changing attitude during the last century, beginning with a marked reluctance to interfere with a father's right to custody and ending with its increasing readiness to interfere if it was in the child's interests to do so.[18] It is evident that during the early part of this century still more weight was being placed upon the child's welfare.[19]

A key case in this respect is *Ward v Laverty*,[20] in which a paternal great-aunt of three orphaned children applied for a writ of habeas corpus with a view to the

14 Note, however, that in relation to unborn children fathers seem to have no rights: see *Paton v British Pregnancy Advisory Service Trustees* [1979] QB 276, [1978] 2 All ER 987 and *C v S* [1988] QB 135, [1987] 1 All ER 1230, CA, discussed post, p 392.

15 See generally Lowe 'The House of Lords and the Welfare Principle', op cit, 127ff; Maidment *Child Custody and Divorce* ch 4. See also Hall 'The Waning of Parental Rights' [1972B] CLJ 248.

16 See further Pinchbeck and Hewitt *Children in English Society* Vol 1 (1969) and Vol 2 (1973).

17 Ante, p 302.

18 Maidment, op cit, at pp 99–100 argues that this readiness was promoted by the provisions of the Guardianship of Infants Act 1886.

19 In fact the first recorded judicial use of the word 'paramount' in this context seems to be in *Re A and B (Infants)* [1897] 1 Ch 786 at 792, per Lopes LJ; see Lord Upjohn in *J v C* [1970] AC 668 at 722C, [1969] 1 All ER 788 at 830F. Note also the reference to the paramountcy of the child's welfare in *Scott v Scott* [1913] AC 417, HL at 437 per Viscount Haldane.

20 [1925] AC 101.

children being placed in the custody of their paternal relatives and being brought up, according to their deceased father's wishes as set out in his will, as Roman Catholics. At the time of the application the children were living with their maternal grandparents and being brought up as Presbyterians. They had been brought there nearly four years previously by their mother when she left their father before his death. Immediately after leaving her husband she removed her eldest daughter from the Catholic school she had been attending and sent her instead to a Protestant school. After his death the mother herself reverted to being a Presbyterian and died a member of that church nearly three years later. Viscount Cave LC, with whom the other Law Lords agreed, considered the law to be well settled:[1]

> 'On the question of religion in which a young child is to be brought up, the wishes of the father of the child are to be considered; and if there is no other matter to be taken into account, then according to the practice of our Courts, the wishes of the father prevail. But that rule is subject to the condition, that the wishes of the father only prevail if they are not displaced by considerations relating to the welfare of the children themselves. *It is the welfare of the children, which according to rules which are now well accepted, forms the paramount consideration in these cases.* Some of the earlier judgments contain sentences in which perhaps greater stress is laid upon the father's wishes than would be placed upon them now, but in the more recent decisions and especially since the passing of the Guardianship of Infants Act, 1886, s 5 of which Act shows the modern feeling in these matters, the greater stress is laid upon the welfare and happiness of the children' (emphasis added).

Viscount Cave observed that before the mother's death the father's family had shown little interest in the children and even in their evidence before the courts did not profess any affection for them. In contrast, the children were happy where they were and the grandparents were fond of them and ready and willing to care for them. The eldest child was found to be bright and intelligent and had strong convictions in favour of the Presbyterian faith. Moreover, she was happy where she was. The court had no doubt that her welfare was best served by leaving her with her maternal grandparents. With regard to the two younger children the court considered that they were too young to have religious convictions, but it was accepted that it was not for their welfare to be separated from their elder sister nor from their loving grandparents. Accordingly, these considerations were held to 'prevail over the wishes of the father'.

Ward v Laverty has generally been overlooked by academic writers,[2] yet by applying a child-centred approach to a habeas corpus application, what it seemed to establish was that, no matter what jurisdiction was being invoked, the court was bound to apply the paramountcy of the child's welfare test to resolving the dispute. Whether Viscount Cave was right to say that it was 'settled law' that the child's welfare was 'paramount' is debatable[3] but, given that this was a House of Lords decision, it was surely authoritative in its own right.

Perhaps one reason why *Ward v Laverty* has never really been regarded as a leading decision was that it was an appeal from Northern Ireland.[4] Alternatively, it

1   At 108.
2   See the analysis by Lowe, op cit, at 132.
3   See Pettit 'Parental Control and Guardianship' in Graveson and Crane (eds) *A Century of Family Law* ch 4 at 76.
4   Though this should surely have been irrelevant, as a decision of the House of Lords from Northern Ireland is as binding as an appeal from England.

may have been thought to have been limited to the resolution of disputes concerning the religious upbringing of children. More likely, however, it may have been thought to have been overtaken by a s 1 of the Guardianship of Infants Act 1925,[5] which provided that in –

'. . . *any proceedings* before *any* court [in which] . . . the custody or upbringing of an infant or the administration of any property belonging to or held on trust for an infant, or the application of the income thereof, is in question, the court, in deciding that question, shall regard the welfare of the infant as the first and paramount consideration.'

Whatever the true position was before 1925, the striking difference between this Act and that of 1886 with regard to the weight to be placed on the child's welfare is evidence of quite a remarkable change of thought within a short period. Whether the 1925 Act was intended to do anything more than further the process of equalising parental rights, whilst at the same time extending the courts' discretionary power to override the absolute rights of the father in custody cases, seems debatable.[6] Furthermore, it now seems clear that at that time Parliament was certainly not intending the child's welfare to be the court's sole consideration.[7] However, as we shall see, that is how the provisions were subsequently interpreted by the House of Lords in their landmark decision of *J v C*.[8]

(b)   *J v C*

Notwithstanding *Ward v Laverty*, the courts began to interpret s 1 of the 1925 Act narrowly and indeed, immediately before *J v C*, there remained Court of Appeal authority[9] for saying that the Act only applied to disputes between fathers and mothers over their legitimate children, and apparent authority[10] for saying that the wishes of an unimpeachable parent were to be preferred to the welfare of the child. Both propositions, however, were firmly laid to rest by the House of Lords in *J v C*. In that case a Spanish couple came to England looking for work. Whilst here the mother gave birth to a boy, but because she was ill the baby went to live with English foster parents. When the couple later returned to Spain they took the boy with them, but whilst they were in Spain the boy's health deteriorated and at the parents' request he was returned to the foster parents in England. The parents meanwhile went to West Germany to look for work and, having successfully improved their economic position, returned to Spain some two years later. Whilst in West Germany the parents made no attempt to contact their son and were only prompted to seek his return after receiving a somewhat tactless letter from the foster parents explaining how 'English' the boy had become. The ensuing

---

5 Which ironically, as Lord Upjohn observed in *J v C* [1970] AC 668 at 723, [1969] 1 All ER 788 at 831, was destined never to apply to Northern Ireland.

6 See post, p 308 n 12.

7 See the scholarly analysis of the history of the 1925 legislation by Cretney ' "What will the Women Want Next?" The Struggle for Power within the Family 1925–1975' (1996) 112 LQR 110 at 129–31, who convincingly shows that it was definitely intended not to be the sole consideration, since, ironically, it was Viscount Cave who had the word 'sole' removed from the Bill and replaced by the words 'first and paramount'.

8 Ibid.

9 *Re Carroll* [1931] 1 KB 317 in which the Court of Appeal upheld the mother's wish to remove her illegitimate daughter from a Protestant Adoption Society so as to place her with another Society where she would be brought up as a Catholic, notwithstanding the lower court's finding that the child's welfare would be best served by leaving her where she was.

10 *Re Thain* [1926] Ch 676, although in *J v C* [1970] AC 668 at 711, [1969] 1 All ER 788 at 821 Lord MacDermott considered the headnote misleading.

proceedings proved protracted and in any event the parents were poorly advised and only belatedly formally applied for care and control. Consequently, it took a further five years before the case was heard by the House of Lords. By that time the boy, who had spent all but 18 months of his 10½ years with the foster parents in England, had become well integrated into the family. Moreover, he had been brought up as an English boy, spoke little Spanish and scarcely knew his parents. On the other hand, the Spanish parents now lived in 'an entirely suitable' modern three-bedroomed flat in Madrid. The father had a good steady job and the mother's health was completely restored.[11]

At first instance Ungoed-Thomas J awarded care and control to the English foster parents, and this decision was unanimously upheld by the Court of Appeal. On appeal to the Lords it was accepted that the decision was only challengeable if it could be shown that the trial judge had exercised his discretion upon some wrong principle. Accordingly, it was submitted that united parents were prima facie entitled to the custody of their infant children and the court should only deprive them of care and control if they were unfitted by character, conduct or position in life to have this control. Thus in the case of unimpeachable parents (which for the purposes of argument the appellants were assumed to be) the court should, save in very exceptional cases, give care and control to those parents. It was consequentially argued that, notwithstanding s 1 of the Guardianship of Infants Act 1925 which, it was contended, only applied to disputes between parents and not between parents and non-parents, the child's welfare was not the first and paramount consideration. The House of Lords unanimously rejected these submissions.

All their Lordships were agreed that s 1 of the 1925 Act was not confined, as the preamble seemed to imply,[12] to disputes between parents, but was of 'universal application', and insofar as *Re Carroll*[13] held otherwise, it was overruled. As Lord MacDermott (with whom Lord Pearson expressly agreed) pointed out, the wording of s 1 seemed to be deliberately wide and general, relating to *any* proceedings before any court and, so worded,[14] 'would apply to cases, such as the present, between parents and strangers'.

With regard to the meaning of 'first and paramount' Lord MacDermott said:[15]

'Reading these words in their ordinary significance and relating them to the various classes of proceedings which the section has already mentioned, it seems to me that

11 All this was in stark contrast to the position when the parents first returned to Spain after leaving England, when the father was a lowly paid worker and the family lived in what were virtually slum conditions.

12 The preamble stated: 'Whereas Parliament by the Sex Disqualification (Removal) Act 1919, and various other enactments has sought to establish equality in law between the sexes, and it is expedient that this principle should obtain with respect to the guardianship of infants and the rights and responsibilities conferred thereby'. However, as their Lordships pointed out, relying on *A-G v Prince Ernest Augustus of Hanover* [1957] AC 436, [1957] 1 All ER 49, preambles cannot control the ambit of sections of an Act. Interestingly, notwithstanding this unanimous view, in the later House of Lords decision, *A v Liverpool City Council* [1982] AC 363 at 371, [1981] 2 All ER 385 at 387, Lord Wilberforce described the provision as a 'sex equality' enactment. See also in similar vein *Richards v Richards* [1984] AC 174 at 203, [1983] 2 All ER 807 at 815, per Lord Hailsham LC. See also Cretney ' "What will the Women Want Next?" The Struggle for Power within the Family 1925–1975', op cit, 128–33 who examines the Parliamentary history of s 1 and concludes 'It seems inconceivable that legislation which would have resulted in a child being kept from his family by an outsider able to offer a better upbringing would have been well received in 1925; and this outcome was certainly unforeseen by anyone involved in drafting the 1925 Act'.

13 Supra.

14 [1970] AC 668 at 710, [1969] 1 All ER 788 at 820.

15 At 710–11 and 820–1 respectively.

they must mean more than that the child's welfare is to be treated as the top item in a list of items relevant to the matter in question. I think they connote a process whereby when all the relevant facts, relationships, claims and wishes of parents, risks, choices and other circumstances are taken into account and weighed, the course to be followed will be that which is most in the interests of the child's welfare as that term has now to be understood. That is the first consideration because it is of first importance and the paramount consideration because it rules on or determines the course to be followed.'

Although none of the other Law Lords expressed themselves quite as forcibly on this issue, as we shall see, it was the MacDermott view that subsequently carried the day.

The significance of *J v C* cannot be over-emphasised. First, it established that s 1 of the 1925 Act applied as much to disputes over a child's upbringing between parents and third parties as it did to disputes between parents. Indeed, it is clear that the decision was meant to have a general application to proceedings concerning the upbringing of children.[16] As Lord Guest put it, s 1 had 'universal application'. Secondly, it unequivocally established that the child's welfare is so overwhelmingly important that it can outweigh the interests of even so-called unimpeachable parents in seeking to look after their own child against a third party. A fortiori it is the dominant consideration in disputes between parents. Thirdly, and perhaps even more significantly, is the fact that in their first detailed assessment of the application of the welfare principle under s 1 the Law Lords, particularly Lord Guest and especially Lord MacDermott were so committed to and appreciative of the child's welfare. *J v C* set the pattern of the development for succeeding decades and must still be regarded as the locus classicus on the application of the welfare principle.

(c) Subsequent applications of *J v C*

Shortly after the decision in *J v C*, s 1 of the 1925 Act was repealed and re-enacted in s 1 of the Guardianship of Minors Act 1971. The influence of *J v C* became more apparent. For example, the Court of Appeal in *S (BD) v S(DJ) (Children: Care and Control)*[17] finally quashed the notion that the so-called 'unimpeachable parent' stood in a more favourable position as against the other who was guilty of matrimonial misconduct, and established in effect that the interests of justice as between the parents do not outweigh the welfare principle. In other words, if the welfare of the child so demands, he or she should be looked after by the so-called 'guilty' parent, however unjust the other will believe the decision to be. Hence, matrimonial misconduct is relevant only insofar as it reflects on that person as a parent. Furthermore, in *S (BD) v S (DJ)* Ormrod LJ (who was a great champion of

---

16 In this respect it should be noted that the Law Lords dismissed the argument that in the interests of comity the court ought not to exercise its jurisdiction in the face of the united *foreign* parents' request for the child's return. Lord Guest (ibid at 701 and 812 respectively) considered the argument wholly misconceived and said that, even if there had been a foreign court order (which in this case there was not), an English court would still not have been prevented from making a custody order according to the child's welfare. In other words, even in international abduction cases the court remains bound to apply the paramountcy of the child's welfare. In this respect the House of Lords were taking the same position as that of the Privy Council in *McKee v McKee* [1951] AC 352, [1951] 1 All ER 942, discussed further post at p 484.

17 [1977] Fam 109, [1977] 1 All ER 656. See also *Re K (Minors) (Children Care and Control)* [1977] Fam 179, [1977] 1 All ER 647, CA. See Hall [1977] CLJ 252.

children's welfare) deprecated the use of the term 'unimpeachable' parent in this context. As he said: [18]

> 'I have never known and still do not know what it means. It cannot mean a parent who is above criticism because there is no such thing. It might mean a parent against whom no matrimonial offence has been proved. If so it adds nothing to the record which is before the court and in any event is now outmoded. I think in truth it is really an advocate's phrase.'

In *Re B (A Minor) (Wardship: Sterilisation)* [19] the application of the welfare principle can be seen in another context. In that case an application was made to sanction the sterilisation of a 17-year-old girl who inter alia had a severely limited intellectual capability. Evidence was adduced that, while she had already been shown to be vulnerable to sexual approaches, she could not be placed on any contraceptive regime and was incapable of knowing the causal connection between intercourse and childbirth. It was further shown that she could not understand the nature of pregnancy nor what was involved in delivery. In sanctioning the operation notwithstanding its irreversible nature, the Law Lords unanimously rejected the argument based on the Canadian Supreme Court decision in *Re Eve* [20] and an earlier English High Court decision in *Re D (A Minor) (Wardship: Sterilisation)* [1] that, because what was in issue was 'non-therapeutic' treatment, the court had no power to act. As Lord Bridge put it: [2]

> 'To say that the court can never authorise sterilisation of a ward as being in her best interests would be patently wrong. To say that it can only do so if the operation is "therapeutic" as opposed to "non therapeutic" is to divert attention from the true issue, which is whether the operation is in the ward's best interest, and remove it to an area of arid semantic debate as to where the line is to be drawn between "therapeutic" and "non therapeutic" treatment.'

Similarly, Lord Oliver observed [3] that if –

> '. . . the expression 'non therapeutic' was intended to exclude measures taken for the necessary protection from future harm of the person over whom the jurisdiction is exercisable, then I respectfully dissent from it for it seems to me to contradict what is the sole and paramount criterion for the exercise of the jurisdiction, viz the welfare and benefit of the ward.'

In short, the Law Lords saw themselves as being *solely* concerned with the child's welfare and interpreted 'welfare' in its widest sense to embrace the child's whole future well-being even in adulthood.

Further important reaffirmation of *J v C* was made by the House of Lords in *Re KD (A Minor) (Ward: Termination of Access)*,[4] in which a local authority sought the termination of a mother's already limited contact with her son, who for the previous four of his four-and-three-quarter years of life had been living with foster parents. It was argued for the mother that the right to see her son was a

---

18 At 115–16 and 661 respectively. In *Re R (Minors) (Wardship: Jurisdiction)* (1981) 2 FLR 416 at 425, Ormrod LJ referred to the 'unimpeachable parent' as being in 'forensic limbo'.
19 [1988] AC 199, [1987] 2 All ER 206, HL.
20 (1986) 31 DLR (4th) 1.
 1 [1976] Fam 185, [1976] 1 All ER 326. See also Lowe and White *Wards of Court* (2nd edn) paras 7-6, note 6, and 7-11.
 2 [1988] AC at 205, [1987] 2 All ER at 214.
 3 At 212 and 219 respectively.
 4 [1988] AC 806, [1988] 1 All ER 577, HL.

parental right which would only be displaced where the court was satisfied that the exercise of the right would be positively inimical to the interest of the child. It was further contended that this right had been affirmed as a fundamental human right under the European Convention on Human Rights. Both contentions were rejected. As Lord Oliver put it:[5]

> '. . . the contention that a parent has a right of access was out of line with an approach which has been universally acted upon ever since the decision of your Lordships' House in *J v C*.'

In Lord Oliver's view, adopting Lord MacDermott's analysis in *J v C* which, as we have seen,[6] was the most child welfare orientated of the judgments in that case, the law recognised the parent's position by taking it to be a normal assumption that a child benefits from having continued contact with both parents. Nevertheless that position must always be qualified by considerations of what is best for the welfare of the particular child in question. So understood, his Lordship could find nothing in the European Court of Human Rights' decision *R v UK*[7] which 'contradicts or casts any doubt upon that decision [ie in *J v C*] or which calls now for any re-appraisal of it by your Lordships'.

Re KD provided important authority for saying that in resolving disputes over a child's upbringing, including access, the court's sole consideration was to promote the child's welfare. Whilst no doubt being predisposed to consider that children were better off being brought up with their own parents rather than with third parties and benefited by having continued contact with each parent, this was not because parents had 'rights' as such but because such a position was prima facie in children's interests.

By the end of the 1980s it seemed clear that when called upon to determine a child's upbringing the courts were effectively treating the child's welfare as the sole consideration in the sense that all the circumstances of the case were weighed in the balance to determine what was in the best interests of the child concerned. Nevertheless the fact remained that under the 1971 Act the child's welfare was still expressed to be '*the first* and paramount interest'.

However, reflecting the fact that the words 'first and' had become redundant, the Children Act 1989 s 1(1) now simply states that:

> 'When a court determines any question with respect to –
> (a) the upbringing of a child; or
> (b) the administration of a child's property or the application of any income arising from it,
> the child's welfare shall be the court's paramount consideration.'

We shall consider in more detail the history and application of s 1 in the next chapter. Suffice to say here that the new formulation was neither intended nor has it in fact altered the pre-1989 Act position, though that is not to say that there have been no problems concerning the application of the paramountcy principle.

---

5 Ibid at 827 and 590 respectively.
6 Ante, pp 308–9.
7 (1988) 10 EHRR 74, [1988] 2 FLR 445 in which the United Kingdom was found to be in breach of Article 8 of the Convention (right of respect for family life) because under the then law parents had no means of challenging access decisions in relation to a child in local authority care. In fact, this and other European Court of Human Rights' decisions did cause the government to provide under s 34 of the Children Act 1989 a presumption of reasonable contact between a child in care and his family. See White, Carr and Lowe *The Children Act in Practice* (2nd edn) para 1.6.

Children's ability to make decisions for themselves[8]

As we have seen, the application of the welfare principle effectively overrides any other person's rights in respect of the child once the issue comes before the court. This obviously dilutes parental authority but it does not in itself give a child rights as such. Indeed, until the issue comes before the court, parents still generally have considerable authority over their children. There has, however, been a discernible trend towards the greater empowerment of children, though, as will be seen, English law has (so far) generally stopped short of giving children what are sometimes referred to as autonomy rights.

(a)   *R v D*[9]

In *R v D* the question was raised as to whether at common law a father could be guilty of kidnapping his own child. In his defence the father had sought to rely on the alleged paramountcy of his position at common law. In rejecting this defence the House of Lords, whilst acknowledging that it might well have succeeded in the nineteenth century, were not prepared to apply it in the case before them. As Lord Brandon put it:[10]

'The common law ... while generally immutable in its principles, unless different principles are laid down by Statute, is not immutable in the way in which it adapts, develops and applies those principles in a radically changing world and against the background of radically changed social conventions.'

As his Lordship pointed out:

'... the paramountcy of a father's position in the family home [has] been progressively whittled away, until now, in the second half of the 20th century, [it] can be regarded as having disappeared altogether.'

Having rejected this defence, the House of Lords further considered whether the child's consent to removal would be a defence. In ruling that it could, Lord Brandon said:[11]

'I see no good reason why, in relation to the kidnapping of a child, it should not in all cases be the absence of the child's consent which is material, whatever its age may be. In the case of a very young child, it would not have the understanding or intelligence to give its consent, so that absence of consent would be a necessary inference from its age. In the case of an older child, however, it must, I think be a question of fact for a jury whether the child concerned has sufficient understanding and intelligence to give its consent ... While the matter will always be for the jury alone to decide, I should not expect a jury to find at all frequently that a child under 14 had sufficient understanding and intelligence to give its consent.'

The significance of *R v D* is twofold. First, it puts the final nail in the coffin of the father's supremacy within the family even under the common law. Secondly, it accepts the proposition that children even as young as 14 might be competent to make some decisions for themselves. It is this latter point that became developed further in the next House of Lords decision, *Gillick v West Norfolk and Wisbech Area Health Authority*.

---

8 See generally Freeman *The Rights and Wrongs of Children* (1983), particularly ch 2; and Fortin *Children's Rights and the Developing Law* (1998), particularly 13–59.
9 [1984] AC 778, [1984] 2 All ER 449, HL, on which see Lowe (1984) 134 NLJ 995.
10 Ibid at 805 and 456 respectively.
11 Ibid at 806 and 457 respectively.

(b)   *Gillick v West Norfolk and Wisbech Area Health Authority* [12]

Gillick concerned a government circular in which doctors were advised that in 'most unusual circumstances' it would be proper for them to give contraceptive advice and treatment to a girl under the age of 16 without her parents' knowledge or consent. The applicant, a mother of four daughters under the age of 16, sought a declaration that this was unlawful, because it infringed her parental right to be informed and to veto any medical treatment of her children, at any rate until they were 16. [13] The action failed and her contention about parental rights was rejected, because it was held that the law does not recognise any rule of absolute parental authority until a fixed age and that even with regard to contraceptive treatment a girl of sufficient maturity and understanding could give a valid consent. On this basis the circular could not be said to be unlawful, since girls of sufficient maturity, even if under the age of 16, could themselves consent to the contraceptive treatment. Indeed, the majority view seemed to be that as parental authority exists for the benefit of the child and not for the parent, it lasts only as long as a child needs protection, and will consequently end when the child is sufficiently mature to make the decision for himself. As Lord Scarman put it: [14]

'The underlying principle of the law . . . is that parental right yields to the child's right to make his own decisions when he reaches a sufficient understanding and intelligence to be capable of making up his own mind on the matter requiring decisions.'

Of course, even under this analysis a crucial question is, when will a child be considered to have sufficient understanding to be considered what has since become known as '*Gillick* competent'? In part this will depend upon the nature of the issue involved. In the context of consenting to medical treatment, for example, it would not require much intelligence to appreciate that a broken leg needs mending whereas, as *Gillick* itself shows, considerable understanding is required in the case of consenting to the prescription of contraceptive treatment. In that context Lord Scarman said: [15]

'It is not enough that she should understand the advice which is being given: she must also have sufficient maturity to understand what is involved. There are moral and family questions, especially her relationship with her parents, long-term problems associated with the emotional impact of pregnancy and its termination; and there are risks to health of sexual intercourse at her age, risks which contraception may diminish but cannot eliminate.'

With respect to Lord Scarman this looks suspiciously like importing into this area of law the doctrine of informed consent, which in the context of the tort of negligence at least the House of Lords has rejected. [16] It may indeed be doubted whether many adults – let alone a child under the age of 16 – could validly consent to contraceptive treatment under Lord Scarman's test. In practice it seems likely

---

12 [1986] AC 112, [1985] 3 All ER 402, HL, for an extended analysis of which see Barton and Douglas, op cit, 118ff; Fortin *Children's Rights and the Developing Law*, op cit, chs 3 and 5; Eekelaar (1986) 102 LQR 4; Bainham 'The Balance of Power in Family Decisions' [1986] CLJ 262; and also Eekelaar 'The Emergence of Children's Rights' [1986] 6 OJLS 161.
13 When by reason of s 8 of the Family Law Reform Act 1969 children can give a valid consent.
14 [1986] AC 112 at 184A, [1985] 3 All ER 402 at 420d.
15 Ibid at 189 and 424 respectively.
16 In *Sidaway v Board of Governors of the Bethlem Royal Hospital and the Maudsley Hospital* [1985] AC 871, [1985] 1 All ER 643, HL. See also Cretney *All ER Annual Review 1985* at 175.

that consideration will only be give to whether the child has sufficient maturity to understand the advice.[17] Even this, however, will not be easy for a practitioner to judge.

It might have been supposed that once it is established that a *Gillick* competent child has consented to the proposed treatment, no further inquiry need be made and the continued involvement of the parent may be ignored. In fact, however, the *Gillick* decision does not go that far. It does not give doctors a carte blanche to prescribe contraceptives to girls under the age of 16. According to Lord Fraser,[18] as well as being satisfied that the girl understands his advice, the doctor must also be satisfied that he cannot persuade her to allow him to inform her parents, that she is very likely to begin or continue to have sexual intercourse with or without contraceptive treatment, that without the advice or treatment her health is likely to suffer and that her best interests require him to give the advice, treatment or both without parental consent. Even with respect to simpler treatment Lord Fraser seemed to contemplate some parental involvement. Hence, while he did not doubt the capacity of a 15-year-old to consent to having a broken arm set, he added that 'of course the consent of the parents should normally be asked.'[19]

(c)   Gillick – a false dawn?

Although *Gillick* may simply be seen as a further (albeit important) example of the diminution of parental authority in the eyes of English law, potentially it was of much greater significance, for it seemed to acknowledge that children themselves have the power to make their own decisions. Had this been how the decision was interpreted, then it might fairly have been described as a landmark of children's rights. However, as we shall now see, it has been subsequently restrictively interpreted, and for those who saw *Gillick* as establishing autonomy rights for mature children it has so far proved a false dawn. The two leading cases are *Re R (A Minor) (Wardship: Medical Treatment)*[20] and *Re W (A Minor) (Medical Treatment: Court's Jurisdiction)*,[1] both decided by the Court of Appeal.

Re R concerned a 15-year-old girl who had suffered emotional abuse and had become suicidal. Fears for her mental state led the local authority to intervene and a place was found for her at an adolescent psychiatric unit. Her condition was felt to warrant the use of sedatives and drugs. However, during a lucid period the girl indicated that she would refuse any such treatment. Despite the unit's insistence on the necessity of the treatment the local authority declined to consent and instead took the issue to court. Perhaps controversially, the court unanimously held that R lacked the necessary maturity to decide whether to take the medication on the basis that '*Gillick* competence' could not fluctuate on a day-to-day basis, so that the child is one day regarded as competent, while on another day she is not.

---

17 Which is all Lord Fraser seemed to require: see *Gillick v West Norfolk and Wisbech Area Health Authority*, supra, at 174 and 413 respectively.

18 Ibid at 174 and 413 respectively. It must be a matter of doubt whether in practice a medical practitioner will always be so thorough as Lord Fraser's test demands.

19 Ibid at 169 and 409 respectively.

20 [1992] Fam 11, [1991] 4 All ER 177, CA; Douglas 'The Retreat from *Gillick*' (1992) 55 MLR 569.

1 [1993] Fam 64, [1992] 4 All ER 627, CA; Lowe and Juss 'Medical Treatment – Pragmatism and the Search for Principle' (1993) 56 MLR 865; Eekelaar 'White Coats and Flak Jackets – Doctors, Children and the Courts Again' (1993) 109 LQR 182; and Masson 'Re W: Appealing from a golden cage' (1993) 5 Jo of Child Law 37; see also *Re C (Detention: Medical Treatment)* [1997] 2 FLR 180 and *Re L (Medical Treatment: Gillick Competence)* [1998] Fam Law 567.

Accordingly, they all agreed to sanction the treatment. Lord Donaldson MR, however, went further. He held (obiter) that all *Gillick* had decided was that a competent child could consent to medical treatment but that it did not decide that such a child could veto medical treatment. In his view, both parents (and presumably anyone with parental responsibility) and the court retain the power to consent to treatment even of a '*Gillick* competent child', notwithstanding that the child has refused treatment. He considered that there are concurrent powers to consent (which he described as being 'keys which unlock the door') and only if *all* the 'key holders' fail or refuse to consent will a veto be treated as binding.

This important limitation on the effect of *Gillick* has since been confirmed in the second Court of Appeal case, *Re W*. This concerned a 16-year-old girl who suffered anorexia and who refused treatment. Her condition was such that without treatment she would shortly die. Because the child was 16 she had a statutory right (under Family Law Reform Act 1969 s 8)[2] to give a valid consent to treatment. The question was, however, did s 8 or *Gillick* give her an absolute power of veto? Again the Court of Appeal, though this time unanimously, held that neither s 8 nor *Gillick* could be considered to vest in the child a power of veto. Instead they held that the High Court could (and in this case, should) overrule the child's wishes. They rejected the argument that implicit in a right to consent must also be a power of veto. In so concluding, Lord Donaldson MR and Balcombe LJ acknowledged that Lord Scarman's reference to the termination of parental authority upon the child's reaching competence could be taken to suggest that the refusal of a child below the age of 16 to accept medical treatment was determinative. Both, however, doubted whether Lord Scarman meant anything more than that the child's parents lose their exclusive rights to consent upon the child becoming '*Gillick* competent.' Even if he had meant that such children have a right of veto, then both their Lordships thought he was wrong. Rejecting the notion that the child's views were determinative did not mean that the court would pay no regard to the child's wishes. On the contrary, as Lord Donaldson MR said, 'good parenting involves giving minors as much rope as they can handle without an unacceptable risk that they will hang themselves'. Yet, as Balcombe LJ said, 'if the court's powers are to be meaningful there must come a point at which the courts, whilst not disregarding the child's wishes, can override them in the child's own best interest, objectively considered'. In his view, such a point comes when the child, in refusing treatment, is threatened with death or severe permanent injury. He cited in support Ward J's trenchant comment in *Re E (A Minor)*[3] that the court, 'in exercising its prerogative of protection, should be very slow to allow an infant to martyr himself'.

Not surprisingly, these decisions have generated considerable comment, for they bring into sharp relief the issue of allowing competent children to make decisions for themselves (ie whether they have autonomy rights) as against the paternalistic approach of protecting them from doing (at any rate, irreparable) harm to themselves. As can be seen, the Court of Appeal favour the latter approach, though one of the intrinsic difficulties of doing so is being able to accept that a child can be competent to give a valid consent yet not be competent to exercise a power of veto.[4] One suggestion, however,[5] is that based on the premise

2   Discussed in detail at p 306 of the 8th edition of this work.
3   (1990) 9 BMLR 1.
4   With respect to Lord Donaldson MR, it is difficult to follow his distinction between consenting to and determining treatment.
5   See Lowe and Juss, op cit, 871–2.

that, since a doctor will act in the best interests of his patient, it is perfectly rational for the law to facilitate this and hence allow a '*Gillick* competent' child to give a valid consent, and also to protect the child against parents opposed to what is professionally considered to be in his or her best medical interests. In contrast, it is surely right for the law to be reluctant to allow a *child* to be able to veto treatment designed for his or her benefit, particularly if a refusal would lead to the child's death or permanent damage. In other words, the clear and consistent policy of the law is to protect children against wrong-headed parents and against themselves with the final safeguard, as *Re W* unequivocally establishes, of giving the court the last word in cases of dispute.

The international dimension [6]

Discussion of the legal relationship between parent and child can no longer focus solely on the domestic position. Regard must also be had to international instruments and in particular to the UN Convention on the Rights of the Child 1989, to which the UK is a party, and to the initiative of the Council of Europe, which are beginning to have increasing influence.

So far as the UN Convention is concerned, two Articles in particular may be noted. First, Article 3(1) provides:

> 'In all actions concerning children, whether undertaken by public or private social welfare institutions, courts of law, administrative authorities or legislative bodies, the best interests of the child shall be a primary consideration.'

As can be seen, this Article provides an international obligation to apply the best interests of the child test and as such is clearly similar to the paramountcy test under s 1(1) of the Children Act 1989. It may be observed, however, that in one sense Art 3 is narrower than the domestic provision, in that the enjoinder to regard the best interests as *a primary* consideration is not as strong as to regard the child's welfare as the *paramount* consideration. On the other hand, Art 3, by applying to administrative authorities and legislative bodies, is wider than s 1(1) which only applies to court proceedings.[7]

The second important Article is Art 12 which provides:

> '1. States parties should assure to the child who is capable of forming his or her own views the right to express those view freely in all matters affecting the child, *the view of the child being given due weight in accordance with the age and maturity of the child* [emphasis added].
> 2. For this purpose the child shall in particular be provided the opportunity to be heard in any judicial and administrative proceedings affecting the child, either directly, or through a representative or an appropriate body, in a manner consistent with the procedural rules of national law.'

It will be seen that Art 12(1) stops short of giving even mature children autonomy rights. Although the precise meaning of the phrase 'the views of the child being

---

6 See inter alia Barton and Douglas, op cit, 34–43; Fortin, op cit, ch 2; Van Bueren *The International Law on the Rights of the Child* (1993); Detrich 'Family Rights Under the United Nations Convention on the Rights of the Child' and O'Donnell 'Parent-Child Relationships Within the European Convention', both in Lowe and Douglas (eds) *Families Across Frontiers* (1996) at 95–114, and 135–50 respectively.

7 Though local authorities have a general duty to safeguard and promote the welfare of children in need in their area and of those they are 'looking after' under s 17 and s 22 of the Children Act 1989 (discussed post at pp 520 and 529). Adoption agencies have a similar duty under s 6 of the Adoption Act 1976, discussed post, p 625.

given due weight in accordance with the age and maturity of the child' is unclear, it is submitted that the English position of reserving the power of the court to override the wishes of a *Gillick* competent child does not breach Art 12(1). Neither *Re R* nor *Re W* establishes that the views of such competent children are ignored; far from it: considerable stress was placed on the need to have the greatest regard to such views. Further, as we shall see,[8] s 1(3)(a) of the Children Act 1989 specifically directs the court, at any rate in contested private law proceedings for s 8 orders, to have regard to the ascertainable wishes and feelings of the child. The Act also provides a mechanism for children of sufficient understanding to initiate proceedings in their own right.[9] Although these provisions go a long way to satisfying the requirements of Art 12, it can be argued[10] that a possible breach could be occasioned in cases where the parents are agreed and the views of children are consequently overlooked.[11]

As Fortin has commented,[12] the European Convention on Human Rights has not proved a particularly effective vehicle for the promotion of children's rights as such. Nevertheless, there have been some important initiatives by the Council of Europe, as for example, through its 1990 Recommendation[13] inter alia to appoint a special ombudsman for children and its 1996 Recommendation[14] to encourage governments to adopt co-ordinated and child-focused policies at national and local levels. One result of these initiatives has been the drafting of the European Convention on the Exercise of Children's Rights 1996, which is aimed at supplementing the UN Convention by assisting children to exercise their substantive rights set out in the Convention. At the time of writing, however, the UK has not signed that Convention, nor has it followed all the Recommendations.

8 Post, p 337.
9 Children Act 1989 s 10(2)(b), discussed post, pp 433 and 437–8.
10 See Lowe 'The Legal Position of Parents and Children in English Law' [1994] Singapore Journal of Legal Studies 332 and 346.
11 See further post, p 343.
12 Op cit at 56.
13 Recommendation No 1121 on the *Rights of Children*.
14 Recommendation No 1286 on a *European Strategy for Children*.

Chapter 9

The Children Act 1989 and the application of the welfare principle

A.   Introduction and background to the Act

1991 was a landmark year for child law for it was on 14 October 1991 that the Children Act 1989 was fully implemented.[1] The 1989 Act brought about the most fundamental change in our child law and has been fairly described by Lord Mackay LC as: 'the most comprehensive and far reaching reform of child law which has come before Parliament in living memory.'[2]

In association with the new legislation new rules (since modified in the light of practice) brought about important changes in procedure and rules of evidence. Fundamental changes were also made to the court structure, creating in effect a specialist division dealing with children at every court level.[3] Even the very function and role of the courts when dealing with children was changed by the 1989 Act and its accompanying rules.[4] In short, the 1991 reform was not simply directed to substantive law changes but radically altered all aspects of legal practice concerning children. What then prompted the wholesale change in this key area of law?

1.   THE GENESIS OF THE ACT

The Child Care Law Review

The Act was the product of a long and thorough consultation process during the course of which virtually the whole of English child law was subjected to detailed review.[5] The process began with the Review of Child Care Law set up in 1984 (in response to a recommendation by the House of Commons Social Services Select Committee)[6] by the then Department of Health and Social Services and assisted by the Family Law team at the Law Commission. That review produced 12 informal consultation papers during 1984 and 1985 and a Report to Ministers in September 1985 which was published as a further consultation paper.[7] The reviews recommendations were essentially accepted by the government in their White Paper: 'The Law on Child Care and Family Services'.[8]

The Review of Child Care Law was concerned with the public law relating to

---

1 Save for s 5(11)–(12) (discussed post, p 401), which was not implemented until 1 February 1992: Children Act 1989 (Commencement No 2 Amendment and Transitional Provisions) Order 1991, art 2. A few provisions had been implemented earlier.
2 502 HL Official Report (5th series) col 488.
3 See ante, p 13.
4 See ante, p 16.
5 The outstanding exception was adoption law, which itself became the subject of review in 1990: see Chapter 15.
6 Second Report 1983–84 on Children in Care HC 360–1 (the Short Report).
7 *Review of Child Care Law* (DHSS, 1985).
8 1987 Cm 62.

children, and in particular the local authority services to be provided for children and their families and the procedures to protect children where families fail.

Review of private law

At the same time as the review was investigating child care law, the Law Commission undertook a full-scale review of the private law relating to children. That process began with a review of the law dealing with the consequences of birth outside marriage[9] and the resulting legislation, the Family Law Reform Act 1987, removed most of the remaining differences between children whose parents were married to each other and those who were not.[10] Against this background the Commission examined most of the remaining aspects of the private law, publishing Working Papers on *Guardianship*,[11] *Custody*,[12] *Care, Supervision and Interim Orders in Custody Proceedings*[13] and *Wards of Court*.[14] The first three of these Working Papers resulted in the Commission's Report on *Guardianship and Custody*, published in 1988.[15] Annexed to that Report was a Bill to give effect not only to the Law Commission's recommendations, but also to show how an integrated scheme of court orders might look. That Bill was taken up by the government and expanded into what eventually became the Children Act 1989.

Other important influences

(a) The Cleveland and other child abuse inquiry reports

Important though the reviews of both the public and private law were, it was the 'Cleveland crisis' that provided the final impetus for reform. As Lord Mackay LC said, it was the coincidence of the two reviews together with the Cleveland Report[16] which provided: 'an historic opportunity to reform English law into a single rationalised system as it applies to the care and upbringing of children'.[17]

The Cleveland Report was concerned with the removal of scores of children from their families because of alleged sexual abuse. In those cases the concern was that the local authority social services department had acted too precipitately but in a number of other inquiries, notably those investigating the deaths of Jasmine Beckford,[18] Heidi Koseda,[19] Tyra Henry,[20] Kimberly Carlile[1] and Doreen

9 Law Com No 118, *Illegitimacy* (1982) and Law Com No 157, *Illegitimacy* (1986).
10 Discussed in Chapter 8.
11 1985, Working Paper No 91.
12 1985, Working Paper No 96.
13 1987, Working Paper No 100.
14 1987, Working Paper No 101.
15 Law Com No 172. It might also be mentioned that various procedural aspects of child law were examined in the *Report of the Matrimonial Causes Procedure Committee* (the 'Booth Committee'), 1985 and further explored in the Lord Chancellor's Department's Consultative Paper: *Improvements in the Arrangements for Care Proceedings*, 1988.
16 *Report of the Inquiry into Child Abuse in Cleveland*, 1987 (The 'Butler-Sloss Report'), 1988 Cm 412.
17 'The Child: A View Across the Tweed' (1988) Denning LJ 89, 93.
18 *A Child in Trust: Report of the Panel of Inquiry Investigating the Circumstances Surrounding the death of Jasmine Beckford*, London Borough of Brent, 1985.
19 1986.
20 *Whose Child: The Report of the Public Inquiry into the death of Tyra Henry*, London Borough of Lambeth, 1987.
1 *A Child in Mind: Protection of Children in a Responsible Society, Report of the Inquiry into the Circumstances surrounding the death of Kimberly Carlile*, London Borough of Greenwich, 1989.

Aston,[2] all of whom either were or had been in local authority care, the concern was that the local authority had not acted quickly enough. However, all these reports were influential in the final shaping of the 1989 Act and, in the words of one commentator,[3] 'contributed much to a balanced view of the procedures needed to protect children, especially in the early stages where abuse is suspected'.

(b)   The European Convention on Human Rights and the UN Convention on the Rights of the Child

An important influence on the final shape of the 1989 Act was the European Convention on Human Rights. There was pressure to reform English law to give effect to the fundamental rights of parents and children, especially in relation to family life as protected by Article 8. In particular, there had been much concern about the then inability of parents to challenge local authority decisions restricting parental access to children in care.[4] As others have pointed out,[5] many of the reforms relating to care proceedings, and in particular those giving parents and others the right to challenge contact decisions made by local authorities,[6] were inspired, if not positively mandated by the UK's obligations under the Convention.

Coincidentally, at the same time that the Children Act was being debated the final touches to the UN Convention on the Rights of the Child were also being made, and no doubt the latter's provisions were borne in mind by those drafting the domestic Act.

(c)   The Gillick decision

Another influence on the 1989 Act was the House of Lords decision in *Gillick v West Norfolk and Wisbech Area Heath Authority*,[7] which was concerned with an older child's capacity to consent to medical treatment in cases where he has sufficient understanding to make up his own mind. The Act recognises in several places the importance of ascertaining and taking into account the child's own wishes to an extent commensurate with his age and understanding. The question of whether the preferences of a mature child should not only be taken into account but be determinative of the matter in question provoked considerable debate during the passage of the Bill.[8] In general, however, save in certain specified instances,[9] the Act does not give mature children the right to act independently of those with parental responsibility. On the other hand, the effect of its promotion of the child's own view, and in particular of provisions allowing the child himself to apply for leave to seek certain orders,[10] should not be underestimated.

---

2 Report to the Area Review Committee for Lambeth, Lewisham and Southwark London Boroughs, 1989.
3 Brenda Hoggett in her introduction to White, Carr and Lowe *A Guide to the Children Act 1989* (1990).
4 See eg *R v United Kingdom* [1988] 2 FLR 445, E Ct HR; (1987) 10 EHRR 82, E Ct HR; *H v United Kingdom* (1987) 10 EHRR 95, E Ct HR; *W v United Kingdom* (1987) 10 EHRR 29, E Ct HR; and *B v United Kingdom* (1987) 10 EHRR 87, E Ct HR.
5 Such as Bainham *Children, The New Law* (1990) at p 5.
6 Under s 34 of the 1989 Act, discussed post, p 581.
7 [1986] AC 112, [1985] 3 All ER 402, HL, discussed ante, pp 313ff.
8 See Bainham, op cit, p 5.
9 Viz under s 38(6), s 43(8) and s 44(7), discussed post, pp 576, 589 and 594.
10 Under s 10(2)(b) and s 10(8), discussed post, p 437.

2. THE NEED TO RATIONALISE AND SIMPLIFY THE PREVIOUS LAW

One of the main architects of the 1989 Act has said[11] that it has two main aims, namely, 'to gather together in one place, and (it is hoped) one coherent whole, all the law relating to the care and upbringing of children and the provision of social services for them, and to provide a consistent set of legal remedies which will be available in all courts in all proceedings'. To appreciate the significance of such apparently simple aims it is necessary to say something of the old law.

Before the Children Act 1989, child law, like so much of English law, had developed upon an ad hoc basis through both statute and case law and predominantly in terms of remedies rather than rights. The resulting law had become complicated and technical and had no underlying general philosophy. Remedies and procedure varied according to the jurisdiction invoked and the court involved. There were, for example, separate statutes conferring different powers on the courts to make orders relating to children in divorce proceedings,[12] in proceedings for financial relief before magistrates,[13] and in so-called free standing proceedings, ie those solely concerned with disputes about children.[14]

Within this complicated framework there were in fact two distinct systems:

(a) that dealing with private law (ie with individuals' disputes over children); and
(b) that governing public law (ie with local authorities' dealings with children).

Each of these systems developed and operated independently of the other, with the anomalous result, for example, that, whereas children could be committed to local authority care in private law proceedings, private law orders were not available in care proceedings.

Furthermore, the interrelationship between the two sets of orders was uncertain: for example, did a custody order override a care order in every case? Another oddity of the pre-1989 Act law was that whereas the higher courts, principally the divorce county court, were generally involved in private law disputes, the predominant court dealing with local authority applications to remove children from their families was the magistrates' juvenile court.[15]

Even in this brief résumé of the position before the Children Act 1989 mention must be made of the High Court's wardship jurisdiction,[16] which straddled the divide between private and public law. Under this ancient jurisdiction the court had wide powers to protect children, including a statutory power to commit children into care.[17] Because of its width and flexibility, wardship was increasingly used to deal with difficult or complex cases. The jurisdiction was chiefly invoked by local authorities, who had been encouraged to use it as a means of obtaining

11 See Hoggett 'Children Bill: The Aim' [1989] Fam Law 217.
12 See the Matrimonial Causes Act 1973, ss 41–44, discussed in the 7th edition of this work at pp 294–8.
13 See the Domestic Proceedings and Magistrates' Court Act 1987 ss 8–11, s 14 and s 34, discussed in the 7th edition of this work at pp 305–6.
14 See the Guardianship of Minors Act 1971 discussed in the 7th edition of this work at pp 307–8. There was also the further jurisdiction under the Children Act 1975 to grant custodianship to those other than parents, discussed in Chapter 11 of the 7th edition.
15 Though the county court and High Court each had powers to commit children to care in matrimonial proceedings. The High Court also had such powers in wardship proceedings: see further below.
16 For a discussion of this jurisdiction, see Chapter 16.
17 Under s 7(2) of the Family Law Reform Act 1969.

committal to care orders in circumstances where the statutory scheme would otherwise have been unavailable, inconvenient or unsuitable. It could even be used in cases where previous applications under the statutory scheme had failed.[18]

The ability of local authorities to use wardship rather than the statutory scheme not only called into question the standing of the latter, but highlighted another anomaly, namely the differing criteria justifying the child's removal from the family into local authority care. For example, whereas in care proceedings under the Children and Young Persons Act 1969 relatively precise child-centred grounds had first to be satisfied, under the Child Care Act 1980 the assumption of parental rights had to be justified by reference to the parents' conduct. In wardship and matrimonial proceedings, on the other hand, although technically committals to care could only be made in exceptional circumstances where it was impracticable or undesirable for the child to be placed in the care of his parents or other individuals,[19] in practice the matter was resolved upon what was considered best for the child.

The not inconsiderable achievement of the Children Act is to have rid the law of most of these complications and anomalies and to draw together both the private and public law under a single statutory scheme. As one commentator has observed of the Act, 'it is remarkable that, at least in terms of volume, so much has been replaced by so little'.[20]

B.   The ambit of the 1989 Act

The 1989 Act has a wide ambit covering both the private and public law relating to the care and upbringing of children, and the provision of services to them and their families. Under the Act there is a unified structure both of law and jurisdiction. In general all courts have the same powers when dealing with children.[1] For the first time, for example, there is concurrent jurisdiction at all levels to hear care proceedings.[2] Similarly, for the first time proceedings can be transferred from a magistrates' court to a county court and vice versa, as well as between county courts and the High Court.

In providing a uniform set of powers the Act replaced much of the previous legislation and amended the Matrimonial Causes Act 1973 and the Domestic Proceedings and Magistrates' Courts Act 1978 to ensure that the powers to make

---

18 See generally Lowe 'The Role of Wardship in Child Care Cases' [1989] Fam Law 38.

19 See eg Family Law Reform Act 1969 s 7(2), Matrimonial Causes Act 1973 s 43(1), Guardianship Act 1973 s 2 and the Domestic Proceedings and Magistrates' Courts Act 1978 s 10.

20 Bainham, op cit, p 6.

1 An important exception, however, is in respect of the powers to make financial orders under Sch 1 to the 1989 Act, discussed in Chapter 17. Note also that only the High Court has jurisdiction to deal with international child abduction cases: see Chapter 13. One unexpected result of this general uniformity of jurisdiction is that it has been held that magistrates' decisions as well as those of the higher courts can create an estoppel per rem judicatam. As Ward J put it in *K v P (Children Act Proceedings: Estoppel)* [1995] 1 FLR 248 at 253: 'one of the fundamental philosophies of [the 1989 Act] was that there should be a common jurisdiction exercised by the magistrates' courts, county courts and High Court. It seems to me to be wholly invidious to say that if a matter is heard and determined by the justices, the High Court shall not take any account of their findings and should act dismissively towards them. That seems to me to undermine the important foundation of this new jurisdiction, namely, that we all exercise it in the same way.'

2 Under the Children (Allocation of Proceedings) Order 1991, however, proceedings must normally be started in the magistrates' court: see post, p 534.

orders relating to children in those proceedings are governed by the Children Act 1989.

Apart from providing the new orders in both the private and public law field, the Act also completely rewrote the law relating to:

(a) the provision of services for children and families by local authorities;[3]
(b) community and voluntary homes;[4] and
(c) private fostering and child minding.[5]

The scope of the Act goes beyond even this. For example, both substantive and consequential amendments were made to adoption law[6] and a number of other statutes, notably those dealing with child abduction, were also substantially amended to bring them into line with the 1989 Act. Also the power to make the new s 8 orders in any 'family proceedings', which for these purposes includes both adoption and domestic violence proceedings,[7] further extended the impact of the Act to areas not primarily governed by it.

C.   Some key changes

In producing what the Department of Health's *Introduction to the Children Act 1989*[8] described as a 'practical and consistent code' the 1989 Act embodies three fundamental changes of concept, parenthood replacing guardianship as the primary concept, 'parental responsibility' replacing the concept of parental rights and duties and new powers to make residence orders rather than custody orders.

With regard to the first, as the Law Commission had observed,[9] before the Children Act the law had no coherent legal concept of parenthood as such. Instead, rights and duties were based upon the concept of guardianship, rather than parenthood, and although its significance had diminished it was still the case immediately before the 1989 Act that the father was, during his lifetime, the sole guardian of his legitimate child. The 1989 Act abolished the concept of parental guardianship[10] and the term 'guardian' is now reserved for those formally appointed to take the place of parents upon their death.[11]

The introduction of the new concept of 'parental responsibility' is of particular importance under the Act. As Professor Hoggett (now Hale J) has said:[12]

'The [Act] assumes that bringing up children is the responsibility of their parents and that the State's principal role is to help rather than to interfere. To emphasise the practical reality that bringing up children is a serious responsibility, rather than a matter of legal rights, the conceptual building block used throughout the [Act] is "parental responsibility". This covers the whole bundle of duties towards the child, with their

---

3 Under Part III and Sch 2 to the 1989 Act.
4 Under Parts VI–VIII.
5 Under Parts IX and X.
6 By Sch 10 to the 1989 Act: see Chapter 15.
7 See s 8(3), discussed post, pp 445–6.
8 HMSO, 1989, Foreword.
9 Law Com No 172, *Guardianship and Custody*, 1988, para 2.2.
10 See s 2(4) of the 1989 Act, discussed further post, p 305.
11 Guardianship is discussed in Chapter 11.
12 'The Children Bill: The Aim' [1989] Fam Law 217.

concomitant powers and authority over him, together with some procedural rights to protection against interference . . . It therefore represents the fundamental status of parents.'

The meaning and scope of this vital concept is discussed in Chapter 10.

The third change was the provision through s 8 of a new set of powers replacing former powers to make custody and access orders. These new powers[13] are more flexible than the former and are intended to be less emotive. To this end they are drafted in clear and simple terms designed to settle practical questions (principally with whom the child is to live and whom the child can see) and not to confer abstract rights. In this way it was hoped that the symbolism of victory[14] that had come to be attached to custody and related orders would not be associated with the new s 8 orders.

Section 8 orders provide the 'basic menu' of the Act in that they can be made, either upon application or by the court acting on its own motion, in any 'family proceedings', including therefore proceedings brought by individuals or by local authorities. Moreover, the Act adopts an 'open door' policy by allowing anyone (not otherwise entitled to seek an order) to seek the court's leave to apply for an order.[15]

D. General principles under the Children Act 1989

1. THE PARAMOUNTCY OF THE CHILD'S WELFARE

Section 1(1) of the Children Act 1989 lays down the cardinal principle that:

'When any court determines any question with respect to:
(a) the upbringing of a child; or
(b) the administration of a child's property or the application of any income arising from it,
the child's welfare shall be the court's paramount consideration.'

As we discussed in Chapter 8,[16] the 1989 Act's paramountcy formulation reflects the previously well established position that effectively the child's welfare is the court's sole concern and other factors are relevant only to the extent that they can assist the court in ascertaining the best solution for the child.

In choosing the paramountcy formulation, the government rejected the Law Commission's recommendation,[17] that 'when determining any question under the Act the welfare of *any child likely to be affected* shall be the court's *only* concern.' The Commission were unhappy with a pure paramountcy formulation, being concerned inter alia[18] that litigants might still be tempted to introduce evidence that had no relevance to the child in the hope of persuading the court to balance one against the other. Even if this fear had been justified,[19] the Law Commission's

---

13 Discussed in detail in Chapter 12.
14 See King 'Playing the Symbols – Custody and the Law Commission' [1987] Fam Law 186.
15 Under s 10 of the 1989 Act, discussed post, p 433.
16 See ante, p 311.
17 Clause 1(2) of the Draft Bill published in Law Com No 172, *Review of Child Law, Guardianship and Custody*, 1988.
18 See ibid, para 3.14.
19 Which was doubtful given that the paramountcy formulation had been well tested before the Act and seemed to produce the right balance both in terms of the evidence submitted and the weight put on it.

own formulation carried the equally undesirable risk of courts refusing to hear evidence unless it directly addressed the question of what is best for the child.

The Law Commission's proposal to consider the welfare of *any* child was also open to the objection that it could lead to wide and speculative enquiries, which ultimately could blur the court's view and duty towards the welfare of the child before it,[20] and force it to compromise between the interests of two or more children.[1] In any event, once the enjoinder to consider the welfare of the particular child before the court is departed from, there seems no reason to stop at the welfare of other children. A plausible case could be made out to include the welfare of others, eg an adult but disabled sibling who is still living with the family or an infirm parent or grandparent, each of whom could be argued to have a claim for equal consideration. However, any such broadening might have had the effect of weakening the protection of children, which the Law Commission itself was not prepared to contemplate.[2]

2. WHEN THE PARAMOUNTCY PRINCIPLE APPLIES[3]

As s 1(1) states, the paramountcy principle applies whenever a court is called upon to determine any question about the child's upbringing or the administration of his property. Section 1(1) is therefore of general application and is not restricted to Children Act proceedings. It is established, for example that the provision is applicable to wardship proceedings,[4] including non-Convention[5] child abduction cases,[6] and is similarly applicable to the exercise of the High Court's inherent jurisdiction.[7]

As we discussed in Chapter 8,[8] *J v C*[9] establishes that the principle applies equally to disputes between parents and other individuals, as well as to disputes between parents.[10] So far as Children Act proceedings are concerned, as the Department of Health's Guidance on the 1989 Act states,[11] it applies *whenever* a court is considering whether to make a s 8 order (ie regardless of who the parties are or in which proceedings the issue is raised). It has been held that it applies when considering whether to make a parental responsibility order under s 4[12] and

---

20 It will be noted, however, that the largely redundant s 2 of the Child Support Act 1991 does enjoin the Secretary of State or any child support officer to 'have regard to the welfare of any child likely to be affected by his decision'. See post, p 730.

1 For the application of s 1(1) to more than one child, see post, p 333.

2 Law Com No 172 at para 3.12.

3 See generally, White Carr and Lowe *The Children Act in Practice* (2nd edn, 1995) paras 2.5ff; and Clarke Hall and Morrison on *Children* 1[25]ff.

4 *J v C* [1970] AC 668, [1969] 1 All ER 788, HL, discussed ante, p 307. Wardship is discussed in Chapter 16.

5 That is, cases not governed by either the European or Hague Conventions on international child abduction: see Chapter 13.

6 See *Re L (Minors) (Wardship: Jurisdiction)* [1974] 1 All ER 913, CA but note the conflict between *Re M (Abduction: Non-Convention Country)* [1977] 1 FLR 89, CA and *Re JA (Child Abduction: Non-Convention Country)* [1998] 1 FLR 231, CA, discussed post, p 485.

7 See *Re W (A Minor) (Medical Treatment: Court's Jurisdiction)* [1993] Fam 64, [1992] 4 All ER 627, CA and *Re T (A Minor) (Wardship: Medical Treatment)* [1997] 1 All ER 906, CA.

8 Ante, p 308.

9 Ibid.

10 Though this is not to say that parents and non-parents stand on exactly the same footing: see post, p 470.

11 *Guidance and Regulations*, Vol 1, *Court Orders*, para 2.57.

12 Per Butler Sloss LJ in *Re H (Parental Responsibility)* [1998] 1 FLR 855 at 659. This issue, however, may not be beyond argument: see Balcombe LJ in *Re G (A Minor) (Parental Responsibility Order)* [1994] 1 FLR 504 at 507–8 and *Re E (Parental Responsibility)* [1994] 2 FLR 709 at 715 who pointed out that it was arguable that such applications do not concern the upbringing of the child.

when considering whether to give leave under s 13 to change a child's surname.[13]

With regard to public law proceedings under the Children Act, it is clear that the paramountcy principle applies at the welfare stage of care proceedings,[14] ie after deciding whether or not the statutory threshold under s 31[15] has been crossed. It also applies to deciding whether to make contact orders under s 34[16] and to applications to discharge care orders under s 39.[17] It has also been held[18] that the paramountcy principle applies to deciding whether leave should be given to a local authority to withdraw their application for a care order.

3.   WHEN THE PARAMOUNTCY PRINCIPLE DOES NOT APPLY[19]

The paramountcy principle is not of unlimited application. It does not directly apply outside the context of court litigation, and even where an issue is before a court it will only apply provided the child's upbringing or the administration of his property is *directly* in question, and even then only if the principle has not been expressly or impliedly excluded either by the 1989 Act itself or by some other statute.

The paramountcy principle does not apply outside the context of litigation

The paramountcy principle only applies, if at all, in the course of litigation. It does not therefore apply to parents or other individuals with respect to their day-to-day or even long-term decisions affecting the child. As one commentator has put it:[20]

> 'It can hardly be argued that parents, in taking family decisions affecting a child, are bound to ignore completely their own interests, the interests of other members of the family and, possibly, outsiders. This would be a wholly undesirable, as well as an unrealistic objective.'

Accordingly, parents are not bound to consider their children's welfare in deciding whether to make a career move, to move house or whether to separate or divorce.[1]

It is also established that the paramountcy principle does not govern the application of Part III of the 1989 Act.[2] As Butler-Sloss LJ said in *Re M (A Minor) (Secure Accommodation Order):*[3]

> 'The framework of Part III of the Act is structured to cast upon the local authority duties and responsibilities for children in its area and being looked after. The general duty[4] of a

---

13 Per Wilson J in *Re B (Change of Surname)* [1996] 1 FLR 791, CA at 793.
14 *Humberside County Council v B* [1993] 1 FLR 257 per Booth J, cited with approval in *F v Leeds City Council* [1994] 2 FLR 60, CA. See further post, pp 550–1.
15 Discussed post, pp 536ff.
16 *Re T (Minors) (Termination of Contact: discharge of order)* [1997] 1 All ER 65, CA and *Re B (Minors) (Termination of Care: Paramount Consideration)* [1993] Fam 301, [1993] 3 All ER 524, CA.
17 See eg *Re T and E (Proceedings: Conflicting Interests)* [1995] 1 FLR 581.
18 *Southwark London Borough v B* [1993] 2 FLR 559, CA.
19 See Lowe 'The House of Lords and the welfare principle' in Bridge (ed) *Family Law towards the Millennium – Essays for P M Bromley* (1997) 125 at 150ff.
20 Bainham *Children: The Modern Law* (1993) 46.
 1 See Dickens 'The Modern Function and Limits of Parental Rights' (1981) 97 LQR 462 at 471, who asserts (correctly, it is submitted) that parental responsibility is not to do positive good but to avoid harm.
 2 Discussed post, pp 520ff.
 3 [1995] Fam 108 at 115, [1995] 3 All ER 407, CA at 412.
 4 Pursuant to the Children Act 1989 s 17(1) and s 22(3).

local authority to safeguard and promote the child's welfare is not the same as that imposed upon the court in s 1 (1) placing welfare as the paramount consideration.'

In Butler-Sloss LJ's view[5] s 1 was not designed to be applied to Part III of the Act. Accordingly, in deciding pursuant to s 17(1) what level of services to provide for children in need in their area, local authorities are not obliged to treat the welfare of individual children as their paramount consideration,[6] nor, similarly, when deciding pursuant to s 22 how best to discharge their duties in relation to children looked after by them.[7]

The paramountcy principle does not apply to issues only indirectly concerning the child's upbringing

An important limitation on the application of the paramountcy principle established by the House of Lords in *S v S, W v Official Solicitor*[8] is that it only applies where the child's upbringing or the administration of his property etc is *directly* in issue. In *S v S* the court was asked to direct the taking of a blood test on a child for the purpose of determining paternity. It had been submitted that no blood test should be sanctioned unless it could be shown to be in the child's interest that there should be such a test. In other words, the court was bound to apply the paramountcy principle. Rejecting that submission, the House of Lords unanimously held that the correct approach was for the court to make a blood test direction unless it could be shown to be against the child's interests to do so. In Lord MacDermott's view what the court was being asked to do was to exercise its protective rather than its custodial jurisdiction, because the question raised:[9]

'. . . is quite distinct from the question of custody and other questions mentioned in s 1 of the Guardianship of Infants Act. It is true that in deciding as to the custody of a child its welfare may depend on the weighing and assessment of various factors including the rights and wishes of the parents and that the question of paternity may therefore not only arise but be very relevant. But that is not to make the question of paternity a question of custody. It is only part of the process in deciding the ultimate and paramount question, namely, what is best for the welfare of the child.'

This distinction between issues directly and indirectly concerning the child's upbringing was later adopted by the majority in *Richards v Richards*,[10] in which an application made in divorce proceedings by a mother to exclude her husband from the matrimonial home was held not to be governed by the paramountcy principle. Lord Hailsham LC said:[11]

'In my view the Guardianship of Minors Act criterion is to be applied only in proceedings of the type specified in the section, ie proceedings in which custody, upbringing, or the proprietary jurisdiction implied by s 1(b) fall to be decided as a matter *directly* in issue . . .' (Emphasis added.)

---

5 Ibid, expressly disagreeing with comments to the contrary in Vols 1 and 4 of the Department of Health, *Guidance and Regulations* on the 1989 Act.
6 It is generally thought that s 17 is so phrased as to avoid the duty being applied to individual children: see post, p 520 n 4.
7 Section 22(6) expressly states that the need to protect members of the public from serious injury overrides any duty even to promote and safeguard the interests of any individual child, let alone treating that child's welfare as the paramount consideration.
8 [1972] AC 24, [1976] 3 All ER 107. See also ante, p 278.
9 At 50g and 117h respectively. See also Lord Hodson at 58C–D and G–H, and 123g and 124c–d respectively.
10 [1984] AC 174, [1983] 2 All ER 807, HL, discussed ante, p 185.
11 Ibid at 203H, and 815. See also Lord Brandon at 223F and 830j respectively.

Richards can also be taken to vindicate Sir John Pennycuick's view in *Re X (A Minor) (Wardship): Jurisdiction)*[12] that an application to restrain the publication of a book containing salacious details of a child's dead father, on the grounds that it would be harmful to the child, was not governed by the paramountcy principle because the subject-matter only indirectly concerned the child's upbringing.

In summary, what *S v S* established and *Richards v Richards* confirmed was that:

(i) the paramountcy principle only applies when the child's upbringing etc is directly in issue;

(ii) even where the paramountcy principle does not apply, the court retains a protective jurisdiction to prevent a child from suffering harm; but

(iii) in exercising the latter jurisdiction, the child's welfare is not the only or necessarily the most important consideration to be taken into account.

Not surprisingly, given the weight of judicial authority, it is clear that s 1(1) of the 1989 Act only applies where the child's upbringing is directly in issue. For example, it was partly on this basis that the Court of Appeal held in *Re A (Minors) (Residence Orders: Leave to Apply)*[13] that s 1(1) does not apply when determining whether to grant adults[14] leave to apply for a s 8 order, since, in Balcombe LJ's words, 'in granting or refusing an application for leave to apply for a section 8 order the court is not determining a question with respect to the upbringing of the child concerned'. That question only arises when the court hears the substantive application. It has been confirmed by the Court of Appeal in *Re H (a minor) (blood tests: parental rights)*[15] that the child's welfare is not the paramount consideration when determining whether to give directions for blood testing in paternity issues. It has been held that the paramountcy principle does not apply to determining whether an unmarried father should be served with notice of care proceedings,[16] nor to resolving a mother's application that the father cease to be party to the discharge of care proceedings.[17] It is similarly established that the paramountcy principle does not apply when considering whether a parent be committed to prison for a flagrant breach of a court order concerning a child,[18] nor to determining whether to issue a witness summons against a child,[19] nor to the issue of making directions for interim assessments under s 38(6) of the Children Act 1989.[20]

Notwithstanding that this basic distinction is firmly established, it can still be a matter of fine judgment as to what amounts to 'direct' and 'indirect' for these purposes. There are two areas in particular in which the application of the paramountcy principle is problematic, namely with regard to publicity and to procedural issues.

12 [1975] Fam 47, [1975] 1 All ER 697, CA.

13 [1992] Fam 182 at 191G–H, [1992] 3 All ER 872 at 873a–b. It has been similarly held that the paramountcy principle does not apply to applications for leave under s 91(17): *Re T (Minor) (Termination of Contact: discharge of order)* [1997] 1 All ER 65, CA.

14 According to Booth J in *Re SC (A Minor) (Leave to Seek Residence Order)* [1994] 1 FLR 96 and Stuart-White J in *Re C (Residence: Child's Application for Leave)* [1995] 1 FLR 927, a similar position obtains in respect of children seeking leave; cf *Re C (A Minor) (Leave to Seek Section 8 Orders)* [1994] 1 FLR 26, per Johnson J.

15 [1996] 4 All ER 28, CA.

16 *Re X (Care: Notice of Proceedings)* [1996] 1 FLR 186, per Stuart-White J.

17 *Re W (Discharge of Party to Proceedings)* [1997] 1 FLR 128.

18 *A v N (Committal: Refusal of Contact)* [1997] 1 FLR 533, CA.

19 *Re P (Witness Summons)* [1997] 2 FLR 447, CA.

20 Per Holman J in *Re M (Residential Assessment Directions)* [1998] 2 FLR 371 at 381–2. See further post, p 575.

Publicity

With regard to publicity the Court of Appeal held in *R v Central Independent Television plc* [21] that, if the allegedly harmful publication does not relate to the care and upbringing of children over whose welfare the court is exercising a supervisory role, then not only is the child's welfare not paramount but it is not relevant at all. Even where the publicity does directly concern the child and the court's supervisory jurisdiction, the line generally taken is that, since the curbing of publicity only indirectly concerns the child's upbringing, the child's welfare is not paramount but must instead be weighed in the balance with freedom of the press.[1] In *Re Z (A Minor) (Identity: Restrictions on Publication)*,[2] however, in a case where the mother wanted her child, as Ward LJ put it, 'to perform for the making of the film' about her treatment at the unit dealing with special educational needs, it was held, restraining its publication, that the child's welfare was paramount. This was because, unlike the other cases, the issue was concerned with a parent's exercise of parental responsibility in waiving the child's right to confidentiality with respect to her education.

Procedural issues

With regard to procedural issues, it is certainly arguable that, in deciding that a parent did not have a right to see the Official Solicitor's report compiled in connection with an application to look after the child, and that the court had the power to withhold it from the parties, the House of Lords in *Official Solicitor v K* [3] was applying the paramountcy principle. It has been argued,[4] however, that notwithstanding the numerous references in the judgments to the court's *paramount* duty towards its wards,[5] the better explanation of the decision is that, whilst the court was motivated to relax the rules of natural justice so as not to disable itself from being able to safeguard and promote the interests of its ward, nevertheless, in deciding whether to withhold disclosure the court was in fact exercising its protective rather than its custodial jurisdiction. In other words, their Lordships did not hold that the withholding of the report depended on the child's best interests, but rather that disclosure would be ordered unless to do so would be harmful to the child.[6]

Such an analysis can be justified by saying that disclosure only indirectly concerned the child's upbringing and is arguably supported by another House of Lords decision, *Re L (A Minor) (Police Investigation: Privilege)*.[7] In that case, to assist an investigation as to whether a criminal offence had been committed, the

---

21 [1994] Fam 192, [1994] 3 All ER 641, CA. See also *Re R (Wardship: Restrictions on Publications)* [1994] Fam 254, [1994] 3 All ER 658, CA, but note Hobhouse LJ's dissenting judgment, discussed post, p 372.

1 See eg *Re H (Minors) (Injunction: Public Interest)* [1994] 1 FLR 519, CA.

2 [1997] Fam 1, sub nom *Re Z (A Minor) (Freedom of Publication)* [1995] 4 All ER 961, CA, discussed post, p 371.

3 [1965] AC 201, [1963] 3 All ER 191, HL.

4 See Lowe, op cit at 153–8.

5 Reflected in the headnote statement at [1965] AC 202, 'that the paramount consideration of the Chancery Division in exercising its jurisdiction over wards of court was the welfare of the infants'. The headnote to the All England report is in similar terms: see [1963] 3 All ER 191.

6 See also *Re D (Minors) (Adoption Reports: Confidentiality)* [1996] AC 593, [1995] 4 All ER 385, HL, which establishes that non-disclosure of reports should be the exception not the norm and should be ordered only when the case for doing so is compelling.

7 [1997] AC 16, [1996] 2 All ER 78.

police sought leave to have sight of a medical report written by an expert engaged by the mother in the course of care proceedings and filed with the court. It was argued for the mother that, because legal professional privilege attached to the report, the court had no power to disclose it, or if it had, that the trial judge (Bracewell J) had balanced the competing interests erroneously.

It was held by a majority that disclosure should be ordered. Lord Jauncey (giving the majority judgment) drew a distinction between privilege attaching to communications between solicitor and client and that attaching to reports by third parties prepared on the instructions of a client for the purposes of litigation. Whilst the former, perhaps properly referred to as legal professional privilege, was absolute,[8] the latter, better described as 'litigation privilege', was a creature of adversarial procedure and as such had no place in proceedings under the Children Act 1989. In drawing this conclusion Lord Jauncey had in mind the approach of *Official Solicitor v K*, namely that the court should not disable itself from being able to safeguard and promote the interests of children involved in Children Act proceedings by rigidly applying procedural rules. As he put it:[9]

> '. . . if litigation privilege were to apply . . . it would have the effect of subordinating the welfare of the child to the interests of the mother in preserving its confidentiality. This would appear to frustrate the primary object of the Act.'

Having ruled that the court had a discretion to order disclosure even to non-parties, the majority could not fault the trial judge's exercise of discretion. In this respect it should be noted that Bracewell J expressly said:[10]

> 'The application before me does not relate to the upbringing of the child and, therefore, is not governed by s 1 of the Children Act 1989. Welfare must be weighed, but it can be displaced in some circumstances. The interests of the child or children must always be very important factors, since it is the essence of the proceedings to protect those interests and the reason why the courts have imposed the curtains of privacy. There is the competing claim of public interest in the due administration of justice which requires police forces to make informed decisions before deciding whether to prosecute. The potential charge of administering a noxious substance to a child is a very serious criminal offence with life threatening implications, not only for E [the child in question], but for any other child which the mother may have.'

Balancing these interests, Bracewell J came down in favour of disclosure and her approach, endorsed by the House of Lords, is a classic exposition of the exercise of the protective jurisdiction which, as the learned judge pointed out, was relevant here because disclosure did not directly concern the child's upbringing.

The minority (Lords Nicholls and Mustill) did not accept the separate distinction of litigation privilege nor that there was no element of an adversarial character in Children Act proceedings. Lord Nicholls considered that parents and other parties should be entitled to a fair hearing notwithstanding any special role of judges in family proceedings. As he strikingly put it,[11] 'The paramountcy principle must not be permitted to become a loose cannon destroying all else around it.' With respect, this seems to be going too far: the reason for relaxing the procedural rule was not because of the paramountcy principle but rather so as not

---

8 Following the House of Lords ruling in *R v Derby Magistrates' Court, ex p B* [1996] AC 487, [1995] 4 All ER 526.
9 [1997] AC at 27F and [1996] 2 All ER at 85j–86a respectively.
10 [1995] 1 FLR 999 at 1007.
11 [1997] AC at 13B, [1996] All ER at 91a.

to prevent courts in general from being able to safeguard and promote children's interests as set out in the Children Act. Actual disclosure, as we have seen, is not based on the paramountcy principle but on preventing the child (or possibly others) from being harmed, and the child's interests have to be weighed against other interests. Such a process can hardly be described as a loose cannon.

It is implicit in *Re L* that not all procedural rules can be changed even to protect children – so for example, legal professional privilege attaching to solicitor–client communications is absolute. The same is true for the rules of appeal, as was established in *G v G*,[12] in which the House of Lords rejected the argument based on the paramountcy principle that special rules of appeal apply in custody cases. Instead the Lords specifically endorsed the principles set out by Lord Scarman in *B v W (wardship: appeal)*,[13] that an appellate court cannot intervene:

> '. . . unless it is satisfied either that the judge exercised his discretion on a wrong principle or that, the judge's decision being so plainly wrong, he must have exercised his discretion wrongly.'

Perhaps the most convincing reason for reaching this conclusion, which after all in practice still leaves a wide area of discretion to the appellate court,[14] is the point made by Lord Fraser that:[15]

> '. . . the desirability of putting an end to litigation, which applies to all classes of cases, is particularly strong because the longer legal proceedings last, the more are the children, whose welfare is at stake, likely to be disturbed by the uncertainty.'

Put in theoretical terms, the issue of when an appellate court should intervene does not directly concern a child's upbringing and hence the paramountcy principle does not apply. Furthermore, as the normal rules of appeal do not inhibit the courts from performing their proper role of safeguarding the child's interests, there is no need to provide special rules.

The paramountcy principle does not apply if excluded by other statutory provisions

Even where a child's upbringing is directly in issue the court is not always bound by the paramountcy principle. It clearly will not be if statute expressly provides an alternative test or expressly excludes its operation. Adoption applications, for example, directly concern the child's upbringing, but in deciding these matters[16] the court is expressly bound by s 6 of the Adoption Act 1976 to treat the child's welfare as its first (but not paramount) consideration.[17] The child's welfare is similarly expressed to be the first consideration in proceedings relating to the adjustment of property and financial matters on divorce,[18] while s 105(1) of the

---

12 [1985] 2 All ER 225, HL.
13 [1979] 3 All ER 83 at 96.
14 Perhaps the use of the phrase 'plainly wrong' is too inhibiting, at any rate where the trial judge is a High Court judge, since erstwhile colleagues in the Court of Appeal might be reluctant to arrive at such an apparently damning conclusion.
15 [1985] 2 All ER at 228j. But for an excellent critique of this case see Eekelaar (1985) 48 MLR 704.
16 Aliter if, in the adoption proceedings the court is considering whether to make an order under s 8 of the Children Act 1989.
17 See for example *Re B (Adoption: Child's Welfare)* [1995] 1 FLR 895, discussed post, pp 625–6.
18 By the Matrimonial Causes Act 1973 s 25(1), for the application of which see *N v N (Consent Orders: Variation)* [1993] 2 FLR 868, CA and *Suter v Suter and Jones* [1987] Fam 111, [1987] 2 All ER 336, CA, discussed post, p 818.

Children Act 1989 expressly excludes maintenance from the definition of child's upbringing and so disapplies the paramountcy principle.[19]

It is also well established that the paramountcy principle can be *impliedly* excluded by statute. This could occur, for example, where the guidelines that are laid down are incompatible with the paramountcy principle. This was another reason why the House of Lords held in *Richards v Richards*[20] that the child's welfare was not paramount in deciding whether to make an ouster order against the father, since the guidelines set out under what was then the Matrimonial Homes Act 1967 s 1(3),[1] which were held to govern the case, were inconsistent with the child's welfare overriding other factors there mentioned. It has since been held that the paramountcy principle is inconsistent with the duties of local authorities under s 25(1)(b) of the Children Act 1989 and therefore has no application to the question of making secure accommodation orders.[2] Similarly, the criteria set out in s 10(9) for determining whether to grant adults leave to apply for s 8 orders have been held to be inconsistent with the application of the paramountcy principle.[3] It is also clear that while the paramountcy principle applies in proceedings under Parts IV and V of the 1989 Act, it will only come into play provided the applicant can satisfy the court that the preconditions for a care order or for an emergency protection order have been made out.[4] As Bainham has pointed out:[5]

> '. . . the more limited application of the welfare principle in care proceedings reflects the need to set limits to the power of the state to intervene in the family by defining more specifically the circumstances in which this is permissible while in other areas the differing weighting of the child's welfare is the mechanism whereby Parliament stipulates the relative importance to be attached to the often conflicting interests of children and adults.'

In other cases, it may not be a specific provision that impliedly excludes the paramountcy principle but rather the whole scheme of legislation. The courts have refused, for example, to apply the paramountcy principle so as to interfere with discretionary powers clearly vested by Parliament in another body or court. Hence it is clearly established that the principle cannot be invoked to interfere with the discretionary powers vouchsafed to local authorities to look after and manage

---

19 This means that s 1(1) has no application to court applications for maintenance (insofar as they are still permitted under the Child Support Act 1991: see post, p 746) and probably has no application to proceedings for lump sums or property orders for the child under Sch 1 to the 1989 Act; cf *K v H (Child Maintenance)* [1993] 2 FLR 61.

20 [1984] AC 174 at 202D (per Lord Hailsham LC) and 223G (per Lord Brandon), [1983] 2 All ER 807 at 814j and 830j–831a respectively. The Court of Appeal have since held that *Richards* has not been overruled by the Children Act 1989: see *Gibson v Austin* [1992] 2 FLR 437 and *Re M (Minors) (Disclosure of Evidence)* [1994] 1 FLR 760.

 1 Which subsequently became s 1(3) of the Matrimonial Homes Act 1983. It remains to be seen what the courts will make of the provisions under the Family Law Act 1996, particularly s 33(6)–(7), though in each case it seems implicit that the child's welfare will not be paramount when making an occupation order: see ante, p 201.

 2 *Re M (A Minor) (Secure Accommodation Order)* [1995] Fam 108, [1995] 3 All ER 407, CA. In that case Butler-Sloss LJ also thought that the paramountcy principle does not govern the application of Part III of the 1989 Act. See Clarke, Hall & Morrison on *Children* at 1[28].

 3 *Re A (Minors) (Residence Orders: Leave to Apply)* [1992] Fam 182, [1992] 3 All ER 872, CA.

 4 See *Humberside County Council v B* [1993] 1 FLR 257.

 5 *Children, The New Law*, op cit, p 11.

children in their care,[6] nor to interfere with the discretionary power vested in the immigration service.[7]

4. APPLYING THE PARAMOUNTCY PRINCIPLE TO MORE THAN ONE CHILD

One of the inherent difficulties in applying the paramountcy principle is with respect to cases involving two or more children with conflicting interests. This issue can arise either where the applicant is a child or where the application concerns siblings.

Child-parents and babies

The leading case on the application of the paramountcy principle as between parents who are also children and their babies is *Birmingham City Council v H (A Minor)*.[8] This concerned a 15-year-old child and her baby who had both been made the subjects of interim care orders. The mother was disturbed and aggressive and made attempts to harm herself, as a result of which the baby was removed to foster parents. At the subsequent full care hearing the mother sought contact with her child. The evidence suggested that it was not in the baby's interests for contact to continue but it was in the mother's interests that it should. The question was, therefore, squarely raised as to whose welfare was paramount, the baby's or the mother's?

The House of Lords ruled that the baby's welfare was paramount. In reaching that decision, notwithstanding the wider arguments that had been addressed on the application of other sections, judgment was confined to the application of s 34 (which governs contact with a child in care). According to Lord Slynn (who gave the main judgment) s 34 made it clear that the subject-matter of the application is the child in care in respect of whom an order is sought (ie in this case, the baby) and that, accordingly, the –[9]

'. . . question to be determined relates to that child's upbringing and it is that child's welfare which must be the court's paramount consideration. The fact that the parent is also a child does not mean that both parent's and child's welfare is paramount and that each has to be balanced against the other.'

Lord Slynn said that the same analysis would be applicable if the child was the applicant, because it would still be –

'. . . that child's welfare which is directly involved and which is paramount even if the other named person is also a child. The welfare of any other named person, even if a child, is not also paramount so as to require a balancing exercise to be carried out.'

---

6 *A v Liverpool City Council* [1982] AC 363, [1981] 2 All ER 385, HL, which remains good law. See also *Re B (Minors) (Termination of Contact: Paramount Consideration)* [1993] Fam 301 at 309, [1993] 3 All ER 524 at 529–30, per Butler-Sloss LJ. See further post, pp 602–3.

7 *Re Mohamed Arif (An Infant)* [1968] Ch 643, [1968] 2 All ER 145, CA. Note also *R v Secretary of State for the Home Department, ex p Gangadeen, R v Secretary of State for the Home Department, ex p Khan* [1998] 1 FLR 762, CA in which it was held that the treating of the child's welfare as an important but not paramount consideration was not contrary to Article 8 of the European Convention on Human Rights, having regard to such decisions as *Abdulaziz v UK* (1985) 7 EHRR 471.

8 [1994] 2 AC 212, [1994] 1 All ER 12, HL (discussed further post, p 584) and see Douglas 'In Whose Best Interests?' (1994) 110 LQR 379.

9 At 222 and 18 respectively.

The *Birmingham* decision has been criticised[10] both for being confined to s 34 and for its application of the 'subject-matter-of-the-application' approach even when interpreting s 34. However, with regard to the former point it now seems evident from the subsequent Court of Appeal decision in *F v Leeds City Council*[11] that such an approach is of broad application. In that case the court rejected a 17-year-old mother's argument that in deciding whether to make a care order in respect of her baby (who had been removed from her within hours of the birth) the baby's welfare alone should not be treated as the paramount consideration since she herself was a child whose upbringing was in question. The Court of Appeal held, following *Birmingham*, that, since the baby and not the mother was the subject matter of the application and the only child to be named in the order, no question relating to the mother's upbringing arose and hence there was no requirement to treat her welfare as paramount.

With regard to the legal analysis adopted by the House of Lords, it has been pointed out that, while it 'breaks the tie' as between a parent who is a child and her baby, it will not do so where one sibling in care applies for contact with another sibling in care, for it will not be possible to say which child is the subject-matter of the application unless this is to be determined simply by the accident of who brought the application.[12] As against this, however, it seem right to treat a baby's welfare as superior to the mother's for, as was argued in the *Birmingham* case,[13] 'vulnerable infants ought not to be deprived of the protection of the welfare principle because they have a teenage mother'. Accordingly it is submitted that, instead of leaving it open,[14] the Lords should have adopted the wider argument that an application by a parent (who is still a child) for contact with his or her own child falls outside the scope of s 1(1), since it only relates to the child's position as a parent and not to the child parent's own upbringing. Such an approach would have been well in line with the well developed jurisprudence of confining the paramountcy principle to issues *directly* concerning the child's upbringing and would have provided a simpler test.

Balancing the interests of siblings

As has been suggested, the *Birmingham* decision is not easy to apply, if at all, in cases involving siblings. In *Re F (Contact: Child in Care)*,[15] in which a child in care wanted contact with his four siblings who were not in care, Wilson J observed that where an application was properly made under s 34 (viz where the parents or siblings were content to have contact but the resistance emanated from the local authority) the child in care's welfare would be the paramount consideration, since that child would be the 'named person'. On the other hand, if that child were to apply for a s 8 contact order with his siblings, it would be the latter's welfare that would be paramount. Whether it is sensible for the issue of paramountcy to depend on which application is brought can be surely questioned,[16] but even accepting this

---

10 By Douglas, op cit.
11 [1994] 2 FLR 60, CA.
12 See the detailed analysis by Douglas, ibid at 382, and see *Re F (Contact: Child in Care)* [1995] 1 FLR 510, discussed below.
13 [1994] 2 AC at 215G.
14 [1994] 2 AC at 223H and [1994] 1 All ER at 19f.
15 Ibid.
16 Nor does it seem satisfactory that the problem should be 'solved' because the sibling children happen to be involved in different proceedings in which the statutory weight placed on the child's welfare is different, as in *Re T and E (Proceedings: Conflicting Interests)* [1995] 1 FLR 581, where the welfare of a child subject to discharge of care proceedings took precedence over a child involved in freeing for adoption proceedings because, in the former, welfare was the paramount consideration but only the first consideration in the latter. See the comments of Cromach and Parry 'Welfare of the Child – conflicting interests and conflicting principles *Re T and E (Proceedings: Conflicting Interests)*' (1996) 8 CFLQ 72.

analysis it will still not solve the problem of competing interests between sibling children each of whom is in care, in the case of applications by each of them for contact with the other.

In such a situation the Court of Appeal's approach in the *Birmingham* case seems more apposite, ie to balance the children's interests and find a preponderance in favour of one or the other.[17] A similar approach also seems inevitable in resolving private law applications concerning sibling children where their interests conflict. This was Wall J's view in *Re T and E (Proceedings: Conflicting Interests)*,[18] in which he commented, obiter:

> '. . . where a number of children are all the subject of an application or cross-application to the court in the same set of proceedings, and where it was impossible to achieve what was in the paramount interests of each child, the balancing exercise described in the Court of Appeal (in the *Birmingham* case) had to be undertaken and the situation of least detriment to all the children achieved.'

A good example is the pre-Children Act decision in *Clarke-Hunt v Newcombe*,[19] in which the Court of Appeal, having commented that there was not really a right solution but which of two 'bad solutions was the least dangerous' to the children's long-term interest, upheld a decision not to separate two brothers but to place them together with their mother even though it was against the elder boy's wishes and possibly slightly detrimental to his interests.

5. THE MEANING OF WELFARE

The term 'welfare' as such is not defined in the 1989 Act and, although the welfare principle had been the cornerstone of child law for some considerable time before the new legislation, it is surprisingly difficult to find judicial articulation of its meaning. One of the few statements is that of Lindley LJ who in 1893 said:[20]

> '. . . the welfare of the child is not to be measured by money alone nor by physical comfort only. The word welfare must be taken in its widest sense. The moral and religious welfare must be considered as well as its physical well-being. Nor can the ties of affection be disregarded.'

Perhaps the best modern statement of the meaning of 'welfare' is that made in a New Zealand case by Hardy Boys J who said:[1]

> '"Welfare" is an all-encompassing word. It includes material welfare, both in the sense of an adequacy of resources to provide a pleasant home and a comfortable standard of living and in the sense of an adequacy of care to ensure that good health and due personal pride are maintained. However, while material considerations have their place, they are secondary matters. More important are the stability and the security, the loving and understanding care and guidance, the warm and compassionate relationships, that are essential for the full development of the child's own character, personality and talents.'

---

17 See Douglas, op cit, at 382.
18 [1995] 1 FLR 581 at 587.
19 (1982) 4 FLR 482, CA.
20 *Re McGrath (Infants)* [1893] 1 Ch 143 at 148.
1 In *Walker v Walker and Harrison*, noted in [1981] NZ Recent Law 257 and cited by the Law Commission Working Paper No 96, *Custody* (1985), para 6 10.

Ideally, the court should be concerned to promote the child's long-term future.[2] However, while there are cases where the court has clearly anticipated future contingencies such as parental acquisition of employment and remarriage,[3] or where regard has been had to furthering the child's education and general prospects,[4] inevitably the court will tend to concentrate on the immediate ties and environment of the child.

It is sometimes said that in applying the welfare principle the court must act in the child's best interests and, indeed, that is the phrase used by Article 3(1) of the UN Convention on the Rights of the Child.[5] However, this may put an unduly sanguine gloss on the court's functions: it should be appreciated that a judge is not dealing with what is ideal for the child but simply with what is the best that can be done in the circumstances. Perhaps not untypical of the dilemmas faced by the court is that described by Cumming-Bruce LJ as being before the trial judge in *Clarke-Hunt v Newcombe*:[6]

> 'There was not really a right solution; there were two alternative wrong solutions. The problem for the judge was to appreciate the factors in each direction and to decide which of the two bad solutions was the least dangerous, having regard to the long-term interests of the children . . .'

(a) The check list

Although the 1989 Act does not define 'welfare', it has introduced a check list of relevant factors to which in certain circumstances (discussed below) the court must have regard when deciding what, if any, order to make. The introduction of a check list had been recommended by the Law Commission,[7] both as 'a means of providing greater consistency and clarity in the law' and 'as a major step towards a more systematic approach to decisions concerning children'.

In other words, the object is not to redefine what is meant by 'welfare' but to provide a means by which greater homogeneity can be achieved in exercising the court's undoubtedly wide discretion in determining what is best for the child. The inestimable advantage of a list is that it enables everyone from the judge to the litigant, the advocate to the welfare officer, to focus on the same issues at the same time.

(b) The contents of the 'list'

The check list, which is contained in s 1(3) is as follows:

> '(a) the ascertainable wishes and feelings of the child concerned (considered in the light of his age and understanding);
> (b) his physical, emotional and educational needs;
> (c) the likely effect on him of any change in his circumstances;

---

2 Unless perhaps where the short-term disadvantages are so overwhelming as to rule out the long-term option: see eg *Thompson v Thompson* [1987] Fam Law 89, CA.
3 See respectively *Re DW (A Minor) (Custody)* [1984] Fam Law 17, CA and *S (BD) v S(DJ)* [1977] Fam 109, [1977] 1 All ER 656, CA.
4 See *May v May* [1986] 1 FLR 325, CA (order made in favour of father who was more academic than the mother); and cf *Re DW*, supra, and *Re O (Infants)* [1962] 2 All ER 10, CA (boy's long-term future better in Sudan, girl's in England).
5 Discussed ante, p 316.
6 (1982) 4 FLR 482, CA.
7 Law Com No 172, paras 3.17 et seq.

(d) his age, sex, background and any characteristics of his which the court considers relevant;

(e) any harm which he has suffered or is at risk of suffering;

(f) how capable each of his parents, and any other person in relation to whom the court considers the question to be relevant, is of meeting his needs;

(g) the range of powers available to the court under this Act in the proceedings in question.'

We shall consider later[8] in more detail how the check list applies in particular cases, but at this stage it is relevant to make the following observations.

First, the check list is not exhaustive and indeed might properly be regarded as the minimum that will be considered by the court. It has been held, for instance, that it is quite proper to take into account financial considerations as well.[9] It is always open to the court to specify other matters which it would like to see included in the welfare officer's report.[10]

Secondly, the content of the check list follows that recommended by the Law Commission save for the addition of that under s 1(3)(g), the purpose of which is to emphasise the court's duty to consider not only whether the order being sought is the best for the child but also the alternatives that the Act makes available. This, as we shall see,[11] has particular application in care proceedings, in which it is incumbent upon the court to consider not just whether or not to make the care order but whether, for example, a residence order under s 8 would better serve the child's interests. This duty also reflects the general policy of vesting in the courts at all levels greater responsibility for the management and conduct of children cases.

Thirdly, although the statutory check list was new to the Children Act, with the exception of s 1(3)(g), the factors themselves were drawn from previous practice. Nevertheless, it is to be noted that s 1(3)(a) provided the first mandatory direction to the courts to have regard[12] to the child's own wishes both in the context of private disputes over children following their parents' separation or divorce and in care proceedings.[13] Whether the child's wishes should have been part of the check list can be debated. It could be argued that such wishes are independent of their welfare.[14] Moreover, making it a separate requirement to listen to children would have given greater recognition to children being treated as individuals in their own right.

(c) When the check list applies

Section 1(4) directs the courts to have regard to the check list in contested s 8 applications and in *all* proceedings under Part IV of the 1989 Act including therefore all applications for care and supervision orders. There is, however, nothing to prevent the courts from considering the factors in other proceedings if they so choose,[15] and indeed, particularly in contested applications under s 4 and

---

8 See post, pp 465 et seq.

9 *Re R (Residence Order: Finance)* [1995] 2 FLR 612, CA.

10 See post, p 458.

11 Post, p 551.

12 Though note: the child's wishes are *not* expressed to be determinative. See further post, p 466.

13 Compare adoption, where it has long been a statutory requirement: Adoption Act 1976 s 6, discussed post at pp 625–6.

14 See Eekelaar, op cit.

15 *Southwark London Borough v B* [1993] 2 FLR 559, CA; *Re W (A Minor) (Medical Treatment: Court's Jurisdiction)* [1993] Fam 64, CA, per Thorpe J.

s 5,[16] it would seem prudent to do so. In *Re B (Change of Surname)*,[17] Wilson J commented that, notwithstanding that he did not have to apply the check list to determine an application for leave to change a child's surname, the list remained 'a most useful aide memoire of the factors that may impinge on the child's welfare'.

The reason for restricting the application of s 1(3) to contested s 8 cases is that in many family proceedings such as divorce there is often no choice as to where and with whom the child should live. If s 1(3) applied to all s 8 cases, courts might feel compelled to investigate even these cases in depth.[18] Such an investigation would not only be a waste of resources but also, arguably, an unwarranted intrusion into family autonomy.

Although s 1(3) specifically directs *the court* to have regard to the check list, it is clearly useful to legal advisers and their clients both in preparing and in arguing their case. The Law Commission envisaged[19] that the list would enable parties to prepare relevant evidence and that focusing clients' minds on the real issues might help to promote settlements.

6.   DELAY PRIMA FACIE PREJUDICIAL TO CHILD'S WELFARE[20]

Section 1(2) enjoins the court, in any proceedings in which any question with respect to a child's upbringing arises, 'to have regard to the general principle that any delay in determining the question is likely to prejudice the welfare of the child'. It will be noted that this principle applies to all proceedings concerning a child's upbringing[1] and is not therefore confined to proceedings under the 1989 Act, but applies equally, for example, to adoption proceedings and to proceedings under the High Court's inherent jurisdiction.[2]

The case for making some provision about the deleterious effect of delay was cogently argued by the Law Commission.[3] They pointed out that 'prolonged litigation about their future is deeply damaging to children, not only because of the uncertainty it brings for them, but also because of the harm it does to the relationship between the parents and their capacity to co-operate with one another in the future'. Despite its importance, however, neither the Law Commission's draft Bill nor the Bill originally presented to Parliament made the avoidance of delay a general principle. Indeed, it was only at the final House of Lords stages that this provision was promoted to the opening section.[4] Notwithstanding s 1(2) it should not be thought that delay[5] is always detrimental to the child's welfare.

16 Discussed post at pp 380 and 404 respectively.
17 [1996] 1 FLR 791, CA at 793.
18 See Law Com No 172 at para 3.19.
19 Law Com 172 at para 3.18.
20 See generally Booth *Avoiding Delay in Children Act Cases* (1996), summarised at [1996] Fam Law 598–601, 643–5.
 1 Note, however, the exclusion of maintenance from the definition of 'upbringing' under s 105(1).
 2 However, the timetabling provisions do not apply to proceedings other than those under the Children Act. According to Wall J in *B v B (Interviews and Listing Arrangements)* [1994] 2 FLR 489, CA at 497, s 1(2) applies to proceedings governed by the pre-1989 Act Law.
 3 Law Com No 172, para 4.55.
 4 See 512 HL Official Report (5th Series) Vol 720.
 5 See Butler et al 'The Children Act and the Issue of Delay' [1993] Fam Law 412, who point out that 'delay is a relative phenomenon and needs to be distinguished from "duration". A complex case may, quite appropriately and expeditiously, remain in the courts for several weeks while a relatively simple matter that ought to be dealt with within days might take three weeks and hence be subject to significant delay, yet still be of moderate duration.'

As Ward J observed in *C v Solihull Metropolitan Borough Council*,[6] while delay is ordinarily inimical to the welfare of the child, planned and purposeful delay may well be beneficial. Hence, the delay of a final decision for the purpose of ascertaining the result of an assessment is obviously for rather than against the child's interests. In *Re B (A Minor) (Contact) (Interim Order)*,[7] for example, magistrates were held to be 'plainly wrong' in refusing to make an interim contact order during which arrangements for the reintroduction of contact were to be assessed, because it infringed the principle of the avoidance of delay as set out in s 1(2). It may be similarly beneficial to a child to make a temporary order to allow 'a volatile family situation' involving children to settle down.[8] On the other hand, what s 1 (2) aims to prevent is unnecessary and unplanned delay for reasons that have nothing to do with the child's welfare.[9] It has been said, for example, that to delay a harsh decision is to delay for 'no purpose'.[10]

The principal effect of s 1(2) is to place the onus upon the courts[11] to ensure that all proceedings concerning children are conducted as expeditiously as possible. As Wall J put it:[12]

'The non-adversarial approach in children's litigation means . . . that whatever the forensic stance of the litigant, delay in the prosecution of applications relating to children should not be permitted even where it is perceived to be in the interests of one of the adult parties. Furthermore . . . the courts have a duty to be proactive in ensuring that applications once launched are not allowed to moulder.'

To this end the courts are directed[13] both in applications for s 8 orders and for orders under Part IV to draw up a timetable and to give appropriate directions for adhering to that timetable. The procedure for the timetabling of proceedings is governed by the Rules,[14] the general strategy of which is that, until the application is finally disposed of, a definite return date must be fixed before the end of any directions appointment or other hearing of the case.[15] Once the time has been fixed, it cannot be extended save by leave of the court.[16] Among the possible sanctions against practitioners for failing to comply with the timetable are being personally penalised in costs, being held guilty of professional misconduct,[17] or ultimately being held guilty of contempt of court.

---

6 [1993] 1 FLR 290 at 304.

7 [1994] 2 FLR 269.

8 As in the pre-Children Act decision *Re S (Minors) (Custody)* [1992] 1 FCR 158, [1992] Fam Law 148, CA.

9 For examples of cases in which delay was thought to have prejudiced the children's welfare, see *B v B (Minors) (Interviews and Listing Arrangements)* [1994] 2 FLR 489, CA and, most strikingly, *Re A and B (Minors) (No 2)* [1995] 1 FLR 351.

10 Per Ward LJ in *Re M (Child's Upbringing)* [1996] 2 FLR 441, CA at 460.

11 But note that, according to Wall J in *B v B (Child Abuse: Contact)* [1994] 2 FLR 713 at 736, practitioners too have a duty to ensure that cases do not drift.

12 In *B v B (Minor) (Interviews and Listing Arrangements)* [1994] 2 FLR 489, CA at 492. See also *Re A and B (No 2)*, supra.

13 By s 11(1) and s 32(1).

14 The Family Proceedings Rules 1991 (FPR), which govern proceedings in the High Court and county court, and the Family Proceedings Courts (Children Act 1989) Rules 1991 (FPCA), which govern proceedings in the magistrates' courts.

15 FPR 1991 r 4.4(2), FPCA 1991 r 4(2), for details of which see eg Clarke Hall and Morrison on *Children* 1[53].

16 FPR 1991 r 4.15(1), FPCA 1991 r 15(4).

17 See *Re M* (1989) Times, 29 December, CA.

7.   ORDERS TO BE MADE ONLY WHERE BETTER THAN NO ORDER

Introduction and background

One of the most innovative and potentially influential directives of the Act is that laid down by s 1(5), ie that whenever a court is considering whether to make one or more orders under the 1989 Act with respect to a child, it 'shall not make the order or any of the orders unless it considers that doing so would be better for the child than making no order at all'. Section 1(5) is intended to focus attention as to whether any court order is necessary. It can also be seen as part of the underlying philosophy of the 1989 Act to respect the integrity and independence of the family save where court orders have some positive contribution to make towards the child's welfare.

According to the Department of Health's *Guidance and Regulations*,[18] s 1(5) has two main aims:

> '. . . the first is to discourage unnecessary court orders being made, for example as part of a standard package of orders. If orders are restricted to those cases where they are necessary to resolve a specific problem this should reduce conflict and promote parental agreement and co-operation. The second aim is to ensure that the order is granted only where it will positively improve the child's welfare and not simply because the grounds for making the order are made out as, for example, in care proceedings where the court may decide that it would be better for a particular child not to be in local authority care.'

In the last edition we said[19] that this provision reflects a basic philosophy of the 1989 Act, memorably described as 'privatising the family',[20] though perhaps more accurately by others as a policy of deregulation[1] or non-intervention, which in turn rests 'on the belief that children are generally best looked after within the family with both parents playing a full part and without resort to legal proceedings'.[2] We further pointed out that respect for family autonomy, which in any event is encouraged by Article 8 of the European Convention on Human Rights,[3] was not new to English law. Indeed, historically, the family was largely left unregulated[4] and has generally remained so where the family unit is healthy. During the past century, however, English law had become increasingly interventionist over the protection of children, but where the 1989 Act marked a new turning point was that, even where the family unit has broken down, the non-interventionist principle still applies.

Bainham, however,[5] has taken issue with these and other like comments. He points out that neither the Law Commission nor the statute says that court orders are presumed to be unnecessary and 'most certainly' neither suggested that in public care proceedings there was a legal presumption against the making of care or supervision orders. He therefore strongly disagrees with saying that s 1(5) establishes a 'non-intervention principle' or a 'no order principle', but if epithets

---

18 Vol 1, *Court Orders*, para 1.12.
19 At 345.
20 Inter alia by Cretney 'Privatising the Family: The Reform of Child Law', (1989), Denning LJ 15 and Bainham 'The Privatisation of the Public Interest in Children' (1990) 53 MLR 206.
1   See eg Douglas 'Family Law under the Thatcher Government' (1990) 17 JLS 411 at 425, n 17.
2   *Introduction to the Children Act 1989* (HMSO 1989) para 1.3.
3   Which provides for 'respect for family life': see ante, p 20.
4   See, for example, Eekelaar 'What is Critical Family Law' (1989) 105 LQR 244.
5   'Changing families and changing concepts – reforming the language of family law' (1998) 10 CFLQ 1 at 2–4.

are required he suggests a more accurate one could be the 'no *unnecessary* order principle'.

Although it was not intended to suggest that orders are presumed to be unnecessary (and for this reason we agree that the epithet 'non-intervention principle' is too strong), it is nevertheless to be borne in mind that s 1(5) certainly demands that the court be satisfied that it is for the child's welfare that an order to be made. Accordingly, arguments may need to be led, particularly where there is no dispute between the parties, as to why it is for the particular child's welfare that an order be made. It might also be pointed out that further evidence of a less interventionist standpoint was the profound change made to the court's duty under s 41 of the Matrimonial Causes Act 1973[6] to investigate the child's circumstances in divorce proceedings in that, as we have seen,[7] instead of having to be satisfied that the arrangements were satisfactory or the best that could be made in the circumstances or that it was impracticable for the party or parties to make any such arrangements, the court only has to *consider* the proposed arrangements and then only in exceptional circumstances should it delay the granting of the divorce.[8]

We will consider in later chapters[9] what impact s 1(5) has had in particular proceedings, but we conclude discussion of the provision with consideration first of the technical question of when it applies and then its interrelationship with the paramountcy principle.

When s 1(5) applies

As s 1(5) itself states, it applies where a court is considering whether or not to make one or more orders under the 1989 Act. Accordingly, it has no direct application in proceedings in which courts are considering whether or not to make orders relating to children outside the Act.[10] In this respect, s 1(5) has a narrower ambit than either s 1(1) or s 1(2).

In *K v H (Child Maintenance)*[11] Sir Stephen Brown P held that s 1(5) does not apply to applications for financial provision[12] for a child under Sch 1 to the Act. The principal reason for so holding was that like s 1(1), which his Lordship took to be the general controlling provision for the overall application of s 1, s 1(5) 'is principally directed to orders relating to the upbringing of a child, the administration of a child's property or the application of any income arising from it'. Accordingly, since an application for financial provision neither concerns the child's upbringing nor the administration of his property, s 1(5) does not apply. The alternative reason for holding s 1(5) inapplicable was that, given it is clearly in a child's interests that proper provision be made for his financial needs, a court

---

6 To be replaced by Family Law Act 1996 s 11.
7 Ante, pp 230 and 250.
8 Matrimonial Causes Act 1973 s 41 as amended by Sch 12, para 31 to the 1989 Act. Accompanying this substantive change was the equally important procedural change that, instead of conducting this inquiry by means of a formal hearing, the duty is now discharged essentially by reading the papers: FPR 1991, r 2.2(2). See inter alia Douglas, Murch and Perry 'Supporting children when parents separate – a neglected family justice or mental health issue?' (1996) 8 CFLQ at 127–8.
9 Viz Chapter 12 (private law proceedings, pp 462ff) and Chapter 14 (public law proceedings, pp 551–2).
10 Such as orders under the Adoption Act 1976 or under the wardship or inherent jurisdiction. Presumably, however, there is nothing to prevent the court from taking a similar approach, if they so choose.
11 [1993] 2 FLR 61.
12 That is, periodical payments, which was what *K v H* concerned, or lump sums or property orders.

order is preferable to relying on the parties' oral agreement,[13] since that proves a better means of safeguarding the future both in the sense of providing for future variations and of being able to deal with any subsequent enforcement issues.

Whether his Lordship was right to say that s 1(1) was intended to provide the overall criteria for the operation of s 1 may be debated, but in practice it is likely to be the case that s 1(5) will not apply if s 1(1) does not. For example, in *Re M (Secure Accommodation Order)*,[14] which established that s 1(1) does not apply to the question of whether to make a secure accommodation order under s 25, Butler-Sloss LJ expressly held that, because of the need to protect the public as well as the child, s 1(5) does not apply either. Again, in deciding whether to grant leave to apply for a s 8 order where it is established that the paramountcy principle does not apply,[15] it seems right to say that s 1(5) is also subsumed by the criteria set out in s 10(9).[16]

Form of order

If the court decides to make no order because it feels that it is in the best interests of the child that no order be made, then a formal order to that effect must be made.[17] A decision not to make an order still ranks as a 'decision', and reasons for making it should therefore be given.[18]

8.   THE INTERRELATIONSHIP OF THE PARAMOUNTCY PRINCIPLE AND SECTION 1(5)

Although s 1(5) can be seen as complementing the welfare principle, since it cannot be in the best interest of a child to be the subject of unnecessary court orders, it has been argued[19] that in reality the welfare principle has been 'hijacked by non-interventionism' on the basis that the non-interventionist stance taken in the 1989 Act means that parental wishes, especially where both are in agreement, will determine an increasing number of issues affecting children.

That there is some tension between s 1(1) and 1(5) cannot be denied, but it is surely going too far to suggest that the paramountcy principle has been 'hijacked' by the operation of s 1(5). In fact, as will be seen,[20] even in the private law context, the proportion of 'no orders' made under s 1(5) is relatively small (though of course it is unknown how many applications are simply not being pursued).[1]

---

13 Aliter for *written* agreements which can, subject to the Child Support Act 1991, be varied by the court, eg under Sch 1, paras 10 and 11 to the 1989 Act.
14 [1995] 1 FLR 418, CA.
15 See *Re A (Minors) (Residence Orders: Leave to Apply)* [1992] Fam 182, [1992] 3 All ER 872, CA, discussed ante, p 328.
16 In particular s 10(9)(c), which directs the court to consider the risk of harm to the child that the proposed application might cause. See further paras 5.83 et seq.
17 FPR 1991 r 4.21(4), FPCA 1991 r 21(6).
18 *S v R (Parental Responsibility)* [1993] 1 FCR 331.
19 Bainham 'The Privatisation of the Public Interest in Children' (1990) 53 MLR 206 at 221. See also Bainham 'The Children Act 1989, Welfare and Non-Interventionism' [1990] Fam Law 143 at 145.
20 Post, p 464.
 1 Nor should the number of withdrawn applications be overlooked, since a proportion of these withdrawals may have been motivated by a desire to avoid a 'no order'. The number of withdrawals greatly exceeds that of 'no orders'. For example, in 1993, 379 care order applications were withdrawn compared with 123 'no orders'; 168 contact applications were withdrawn compared with 104 'no orders': *Judicial Statistics*, Annual Report 1993, Table 5.2.

Furthermore, most agreements are likely to provide the best arrangements that can be made for the children in the circumstances. In any case it may be questioned whether the pre-1989 Act law was so very different.[2] Under the former law the courts were generally reluctant to interfere with arrangements agreed between the parents. Under the 1989 Act the difference may simply be that the court may make no order at all rather than make an order reflecting the parents' agreement. Nevertheless there is a danger that by making no order in the light of parental agreement the court could overlook the child's wishes. If they do so in the case of older children, there could be a breach of Article 12 of the UN Convention on the Rights of the Child.[3] Accordingly, courts should be alive to this possibility and seek some assurance that the child in question does not object to the arrangements agreed between the parents.

2 In any event, it may be questioned whether the welfare principle itself is truly child-centred. See eg Maidment *Child Custody and Divorce*, op cit, p 149, who argues that decisions in the past were 'made for adults by adults about adults'.
3 Under which there is an international obligation for courts to give due weight to a child's views: see post, p 461.

Chapter 10

Parental responsibility

A. Introduction

1. THE LAW COMMISSION'S PROPOSALS

Before the Children Act 1989 statutes still referred to 'parental rights and duties' or 'parental powers and duties' or the 'rights and authority' of a parent. Not only were these terms inconsistent with one another but, as the Law Commission had earlier commented:[1] 'It can be cogently argued that to talk of 'parental rights' is not only inaccurate as a matter of juristic analysis but also a misleading use of ordinary language'. In their Report on Guardianship and Custody[2] the Commission were concerned that because of the continued use of such terms the law did not adequately promote the view that parenthood is a matter of responsibility rather than of rights. Accordingly they recommended the introduction of the concept of 'parental responsibility' to replace all the ambiguous and misleading terms previously employed in statutes. In the Commission's view, this concept 'would reflect the everyday reality of being a parent and emphasise the responsibility of all who are in that position'.[3] They also noted that such a change would bring English Law into line with the Recommendation on Parental Responsibilities adopted in 1984 by the Committee of Ministers of the Council of Europe.[4]

The government accepted the Commission's recommendation, and 'parental responsibility' has now become a pivotal concept of the 1989 Act.

2. INTERNATIONAL ACCEPTANCE OF THE CONCEPT OF PARENTAL RESPONSIBILITY

The shift away from parental power as reflected by such expressions as 'parental rights and duties' or 'parental power and duties' to that of parental care as encapsulated by the concept of 'parental responsibility' was by no means peculiar to English law. Such a change was effected, for instance, in what was then West Germany, when the term 'parental power' (elter Gewalt) was replaced by 'parental care' (elterliche Sorge) in 1970.[5] In Norway, the term 'parental responsibility' was introduced in their Children Act 1981, replacing such terms as 'parental authority' and 'parental power'.[6] More recently the term has been adopted in the domestic

---

1 Law Com No 118 *Illegitimacy* (1982) para 4.18.
2 Law Com No 172 (1988).
3 Ibid at para 2.4.
4 Recommendation No R(84)4, for further details of which see below.
5 See Frank 'Family Law and the Federal Republic of Germany's Basic Law' (1990) 4 Int Jo of Law, Policy and the Family 214.
6 See Smith and Lodrup *Children and Parents – The relationship between children and parents according to Norwegian Law*, ch 5.

legislation of Australia,[7] the Isle of Man,[8] Northern Ireland[9] and Scotland.[10]

International impetus for change was first given by the already mentioned Council of Europe's 1984 Recommendation on Parental Responsibilities, the Council agreeing that:[11]

> 'The term "parental responsibilities" described better the modern concept according to which parents are, on a . . . basis of equality between parents and in consultation with their children, given the task to educate, legally represent, maintain, etc their children. In order to do so they exercise powers to carry out duties in the interests of the child and not because of an authority which is conferred on them in their own interests.'

World wide recognition of the concept of parental responsibility has been given by its use in the UN Convention on the Rights of the Child[12] and the term is now regularly used in international instruments concerning children.[13]

3. CONTEXTS IN WHICH PARENTAL RESPONSIBILITY IS RELEVANT

To have a better understanding of the concept of parental responsibility it is important to appreciate that it is concerned with a number of different relationships. In his leading analysis, Eekelaar[14] argues that the concept can represent two ideas: one, that parents must behave dutifully towards their children; the other, that responsibility for bringing up a child belongs to parents, not the State. Both these ideas are important and both are embodied in the Act. The former idea is well summed up by Lord Mackay LC, who said[15] when introducing the Bill, the concept of 'parental responsibility':

> '. . . emphasises that the days when a child should be regarded as a possession of his parents, indeed when in the past they had a right to his services and to sue on their loss, are now buried forever. The overwhelming purpose of parenthood is the responsibility for caring and raising the child to be a properly developed adult both physically and morally.'

This comment is echoed by the Department of Health's introductory guide to the Children Act[16] which states that parental responsibility:

> '. . . emphasises that the duty to care for the child and to raise him to moral, physical and emotional health is the fundamental task of parenthood and the only justification for the authority that it confers.'

---

7 Under the Family Law Reform Act 1995 (Cth), which came into force in June 1996.
8 Under the Manx Family Law Act 1991.
9 Under the Children (Northern Ireland) Order 1995, which came into force in November 1996.
10 Under the Children (Scotland) Act 1995, which came into force in November 1996.
11 See para 6 of the Explanatory Memorandum to the Recommendation.
12 See in particular Art 18(1) which states: 'States Parties shall use their best efforts to ensure recognition of the principle that both parents have common responsibilities for the upbringing and development of the child. Parents or, as the case may be, legal guardians, have the primary responsibility for the upbringing and development of the child. The best interests of the child will be their basic concern.' See also Arts 5 and 9.
13 See, for example, the 1993 Hague Convention on the Protection of Children and Co-operation in Respect of Intercountry Adoption, Art 21(1)(b) and the 1996 Hague Convention on Jurisdiction, Applicable Law, Recognition, Enforcement and Co-operation in respect of Parental Responsibility and Measures for the Protection of Children, Art 16(1).
14 'Parental responsibility: State of Nature or Nature of the State?' [1991] JSWFL 37.
15 502 HL Official Report (5th series) col 490.
16 *Introduction to the Children Act 1989* (HMSO, 1989) para 1.4.

Both these comments reflect in turn the earlier landmark decision of *Gillick v West Norfolk and Wisbech Area Health Authority*,[17] in which Lords Fraser and Scarman emphasised that parental power to control a child exists not for the benefit of the parent but for the benefit of the child.

Although the Law Commission themselves considered[18] that the change of terminology from rights and duties to responsibility would make little change in substance to the law, symbolically saying a parent has responsibilities rather than rights in itself conveys a quite different message.

It is the enduring nature of responsibility, particularly when allied with the so-called presumption of non-intervention under s 1(5),[19] that embodies the second idea referred to by Eekelaar, namely that responsibility for child care belongs to parents rather than the State. As another commentator has put it,[20] by providing that responsibility should continue despite, for example, a court order that the child should live with one of them, parents 'are to understand that the state will not relieve them of their responsibilities'. This is further underscored by the fact that responsibility cannot be voluntarily surrendered to a public body[1] and that, even where a care order is made compulsorily placing the child in local authority care, the parents still retain their responsibility.[2] In short, the 1989 Act through the concept of parental responsibility emphasises the idea that 'once a parent always a parent', and that prima facie the primary responsibility for deciding what should happen to their children even upon their separation should rest with the parents themselves.

Important though the parent-child and the parent-state relationships are, there are other relationships in which the concept of parental responsibility is relevant, for example, as between parents and other individuals. It can be as important to parents that they can look after their children without interference by other individuals as by the State. On the other hand, de facto carers (whether short-term or long-term) need some authority to take normal 'day-to-day' decisions whilst looking after the child. These potentially conflicting standpoints are accommodated by the 1989 Act since, although in the first instance only those with parental responsibility are entitled to make decisions in relation to the child, such persons are nevertheless permitted to 'arrange for some or all [of their responsibility] to be met by one or more persons acting on his behalf.'[3] Furthermore, those without parental responsibility but who have care of the child can 'do what is reasonable in all the circumstances of the case for the propose of safeguarding or promoting the child's welfare.'[4] In other words, while those with parental responsibility are, as against other individuals, primarily in control of the child's upbringing, other persons can take decisions about the child either on the basis of parental delegation or, in the case of de facto carers, on the basis of (short-term) necessity.

---

17 [1986] AC 112, [1985] 3 All ER 402, HL, discussed ante at pp 313ff.
18 Law Com No 172 at para 2.4.
19 Discussed post at pp 340ff.
20 S M Cretney 'Defining the Limits of State Intervention: The Child and the Courts' in *Children and the Law* (ed Freestone, 1990) 58 at p 67.
 1 When the child is 'accommodated' by a local authority under s 20, discussed in Chapter 14, parental responsibility is not acquired by the authority: see the discussion by Eekelaar, op cit at pp 40–2.
 2 The effect of care orders is discussed post, pp 563ff.
 3 Section 2(9), discussed post, p 396.
 4 Section 3(5)(b), discussed post, p 397.

It is important to appreciate that, as s 2 makes clear, not only can more than one person have parental responsibility at the same time but, perhaps more importantly, a person does not cease to have responsibility just because someone else acquires it.[5] Furthermore, each holder of responsibility can in theory[6] continue to exercise it by himself or herself without the need to consult any other holder, subject only to the overriding condition that he or she must not act incompatibly with any existing court order.[7]

It remains now to consider the meaning and scope of parental responsibility; who has parental responsibility; in respect of whom there is responsibility; the duration of responsibility; the position of those sharing responsibility; and the position of those caring for children without parental responsibility.

B. The meaning and scope of 'parental responsibility' [8]

1. THE NEED TO DEFINE PARENTAL RESPONSIBILITY

It is obviously necessary that parental responsibility be definable by one means or another, for how else will parents know what they can or cannot do in relation to their child and, as importantly, how can others know what the parents' position is? Do they need to obtain parental permission to take a child on an educational outing? Do doctors need parental consent before medically treating the child and is that consent binding on the child?

Quite apart from the individual's point of view, the courts' powers can sometimes be dependent upon the scope of parental responsibility. They can only make a 'prohibited steps order' to prevent any 'step which could be taken by a parent in meeting his parental responsibility for a child' and a 'specific issue order' to determine 'a specific question which has arisen, or which may arise in connection with any aspect of parental responsibility for a child.' [9]

Notwithstanding the demonstrable need to be able to define what parental responsibility comprises, the question remains as to whether this should be done by means of a general statutory provision or simply left to case law and statutory provisions dealing with specific points. The Scottish Law Commission considered that there are advantages in having a general statutory statement of parental responsibilities, namely: [10]

'(a) that it would make explicit what is already implicit in the law;
 (b) that it would counteract any impression that a parent has rights but no responsibilities; and
 (c) that it would enable the law to make it clear that parental rights are not absolute or unqualified, but are conferred in order to enable parents to meet their responsibilities.'

5 Section 2(5) and (6) discussed post at pp 394ff.
6 But note *Re G (Parental Responsibility: Education)* [1994] 2 FLR 964, CA and *Re PC (Change of Surname)* [1997] 2 FLR 730, discussed post at p 395.
7 Section 2(7) and (8) discussed post at p 395.
8 See Lowe 'The Meaning and Allocation of Parental Responsibility – A Common Lawyer's Perspective' (1997) 11 Int Jo of Law, Policy and the Family 192 at 193–7.
9 Under s 8(1) of the Children Act, discussed post, pp 421ff.
10 See Scot Law Com, Discussion Paper No 88 *Parental Responsibilities and Rights, Guardianship and the Administration of Children's Property* (1990) para 2.3.

These arguments seem convincing. It is surely right that as a matter of principle some attempt be made to give general statutory guidance on the meaning of what is after all a pivotal concept of child law.

2.   CAN THERE BE A MEANINGFUL GENERAL DEFINITION?

In contrast to the Scottish Law Commission, the earlier inquiry of the English Law Commission concentrated on whether there could be a comprehensive definition of parental responsibility. They concluded[11] that although there was a superficial attraction in providing a comprehensive list of the incidents of responsibility, it was impracticable to do so. They pointed out that such a list would have to change from time to time to meet differing needs and circumstances, and would have to vary with the age and maturity of the child and circumstances of the case.

While there is some validity in this view, particularly if it is sought to provide a comprehensive definition, it by no means follows that *some* useful guidance cannot be given, but this more limited approach was not apparently considered by the Commission. In the event the Children Act implements the strategy recommended by the Law Commission, and s 3(1) simply provides that:

> '... "parental responsibility" means all the rights, duties, powers, responsibility and authority which by law a parent of a child has in relation to the child and his property.'

This provision seems a poor one, for not only might it rightly be said to be 'a non-definition',[12] but it also immediately throws one back to the rights and duties model which 'responsibility' was supposed to replace.[13]

In contrast to the English position, the Children (Scotland) Act 1995, implementing the recommendation of the Scottish Law Commission[14] provides first by s 1(1):

> 'A parent has in relation to his child the responsibility –
> (a) to safeguard and promote the child's health, development and welfare;
> (b) to provide, in a manner appropriate to the stage of development of the child –
>   (i)   direction;
>   (ii) guidance,
>   to the child;
> (c) if the child is not living with the parent, to maintain personal relations and direct contact with the child on a regular basis; and
> (d) to act as the child's legal representative,
> but only in so far as compliance with this section is practicable and in the interests of the child.'

To enable a parent to fulfil those parental responsibilities, s 2(1) provides that a parent:

> 'has the right –
> (a) to have the child living with him or otherwise to regulate the child's residence;
> (b) to control, direct or guide, in a manner appropriate to the stage of development of the child, the child's upbringing;

---

11 Law Com No 172 para 2.6.
12 So described by Lord Meston in the debate on the Bill: HL Debs Vol 502, col 1172.
13 Note Ward LJ's criticisms in *Re S (Parental Responsibility)* [1995] 2 FLR 648 at 657. A not dissimilar 'definition' is provided in the Australian legislation: see Family Law Act 1975 (Cth) s 61B, save that there is no mention of 'rights'.
14 Scot Law Com No 125 *Report on Family Law* (1992) paras 2.1 ff.

(c) if the child is not living with him, to maintain personal relations and contact with the child on a regular basis; and

(d) to act as the child's legal representative.'

The Scottish legislation shows that it is possible to provide helpful general guidance as to the meaning of parental responsibility. It neatly handles the problem of dealing with children of different ages and maturity by the simple expedient of stating that the responsibility to give direction and guidance should be 'in a manner appropriate to the stage of development of the child.' By making separate provisions for responsibilities and rights, it grapples with the problem of having to deal not only with the parent-child relationship (in which context the expression 'responsibility' seems absolutely right, because parents ought to act on their children's behalf rather than on their own)[15] but also with the relationship both between the parents themselves and between parents and third parties (in which context the expression 'rights' still seems appropriate, since, as against others, parents can still be regarded as having the power and authority to bring up their children as they see fit).[16] It also avoids the problem of being too specific and instead leaves the courts free to determine particular issues on a case by case basis.

However, although the Scottish approach seems preferable to the English on this point, English law seems to have worked reasonably well so far and it is probably not now worth amending the 1989 Act.[17]

3. FURTHER PRELIMINARY OBSERVATIONS

Before examining some of the more important aspects of parental responsibility, some preliminary observations may be made. First, although the broad definition under s 3(1) necessarily refers to the pre-1989 Act position,[18] it must do so subject to the change of emphasis from rights to responsibilities. One problem in particular is deciding whether a former 'right' attaches only to a parent or guardian or to anyone with parental responsibility.[19] As the Law Commission commented,[20] the incidents of parenthood with which they were concerned were those that related to the care and upbringing of a child and not specifically incidents that attached to parents qua parents.

Secondly, the exercise of parental responsibility may be qualified by agreement of the parties (for example, the father agreeing that the child is to live with the mother) or by order of the court. In the latter instance the extent to which

---

15 See Barton and Douglas *Law and Parent*, op cit, 18–28.

16 Using Hohfeld's analysis (Hohfeld *Fundamental Legal Conceptions as Applied in Judicial Reasoning*, 1919), it might be more accurate to say that, at any rate as against third parties, parents have a 'privilege' to bring up children as they see fit in the sense that others have a 'no right' to interfere. As against the State, however, this privilege is more limited since the State can interfere with parental upbringing once it falls below the accepted threshold as set out in s 31 of the Children Act 1989, discussed post, pp 536ff.

17 But note the call for reform along the Scottish lines in *People Like Us* (Report of the Review of the Standards for Children Living Away from Home – the Utting Report) (Department of Health and Welsh Office, 1997) para 6.2 and recommendation 9.

18 For which see Eekelaar 'What are Parental Rights?' (1973) 89 LQR 210; Hall 'The Waning of Parental Rights' [1972B] CLJ 248; Maidment 'The Fragmentation of Parental Rights' [1981] CLJ 135 and Law Com Working Paper No 91 *Guardianship* paras 2.25 et seq.

19 For example, the right to confer a child's name (discussed post at p 362) or to dispose of a child's corpse (discussed post at p 363).

20 Law Com No 172 para 2.7.

responsibility can be asserted is effectively limited by the paramountcy of the child's welfare, which principle the court is bound to apply in any proceedings concerning his upbringing or the administration of his property.[1]

Thirdly, the older the child the less extensive and important parental responsibility may become. As Lord Denning MR eloquently put it in respect of custody:[2]

> '. . . it is a dwindling right which the court will hesitate to enforce against the wishes of the child, the older he is. It starts with the right of control and ends with little more than advice.'

Fourthly, the ambit of responsibility varies. It is widest when enjoyed by parents or guardians, but less extensive when vested in others by means of a residence order, or in local authorities by reason of a care order.[3] It is narrowest when vested in those who have obtained an emergency protection order.[4]

Fifthly, the absence of responsibility does not necessarily mean that a person has no obligation towards the child. For example, unmarried fathers have a statutory duty to maintain their children regardless of whether they also have parental responsibility.[5] Conversely, as the Department of Health's *Introduction to the Children Act 1989* observes:[6]

> '. . . the effect of having parental responsibility is to empower a person to take most decisions in the child's life.'

4.   WHAT PARENTAL RESPONSIBILITY COMPRISES[7]

In the absence of an agreed list it is suggested that parental responsibility comprises at least the following:[8]

- Providing a home for the child.
- Having contact with the child.
- Determining and providing for the child's education.
- Determining the child's religion.
- Disciplining the child.
- Consenting to the child's medical treatment.
- Consenting to the child's marriage.
- Agreeing to the child's adoption.
- Vetoing the issue of a child's passport.
- Taking the child outside the United Kingdom and consenting to the child's emigration.
- Administering the child's property.
- Protecting and maintaining the child.

1 Discussed ante, Chapter 9.
2 *Hewer v Bryant* [1970] 1 QB 357 at 369, [1969] 3 All ER 578, CA at 582. Even so, parents do not lose all their responsibility even where their child is '*Gillick* competent': see ante, pp 315ff.
3 See post at pp 387 and 565 respectively.
4 See post, p 593.
5 See post, pp 724 and 730.
6 Para 2.4.
7 See also Barton and Douglas, op cit, 114 ff; Clarke Hall and Morrison on *Children* (10th edn) 1 [61]ff; Butterworths *Family Law Service* Div E, ch 2; and Hershman and McFarlane *Children Law and Practice*, Division A.
8 Some commentaries include children's services, but as will be seen (see post, p 364) parental responsibility cannot now be said to include a right to domestic services.

- Naming the child.
- Representing the child in legal proceedings.
- Disposing of the child's corpse.
- Appointing a guardian for the child.

Whether parental responsibility can also be said to comprise the right to receive information about the child and the power to control publicity about the child can be debated and will be discussed later in this chapter.[9]

Consenting to a child's marriage was considered in Chapter 2. Appointment of a testamentary guardian, agreeing to a child being adopted or freed for adoption and maintenance are discussed respectively in Chapters 11, 15 and 17.

Providing a home for the child

A key aspect of parental responsibility is that of looking after and bringing up the child. Based upon the common law right of a person to possession of his child, it now seems better to say that those with responsibility have a prima facie right to provide a home for the child and the power to determine where the child should live. This is protected by the criminal law to the extent that persons without responsibility commit the crime of child abduction if they remove the child without lawful authority.[10] As between individuals with parental responsibility the right is qualified to the extent that removal of a child outside the United Kingdom without the consent of other individuals with parental responsibility can amount to a crime.[11]

Associated with providing a home is the power physically to control a child's movements, at any rate until the years of discretion.[12] It is also established that responsibility includes the power to control the child's movements whilst in someone else's care.[13] On the other hand, it is also established that a parent, and therefore presumably any other person with parental responsibility, can commit the common law crime of kidnapping[14] or unlawful imprisonment[15] if a child (old enough to make up his own mind) is forcibly taken or detained against his will.

Associated with the prima facie responsibility to provide a home for the child are questions about the child's domicile and habitual residence. Under the Domicile and Matrimonial Proceedings Act 1973 s 3 a child cannot have an independent domicile until he attains the age of 16. Until then the legitimate child takes the father's domicile, unless he has his home with his mother and has no home with his father.[16] The illegitimate child takes the mother's domicile.

Normally, while the parents live together the child is regarded as having the same habitual residence as the parents.[17] Although in cases where the parents separate the child's habitual residence will in due course follow that of the

---

9 See post, pp 369ff
10 Child Abduction Act 1984 s 2: discussed post, p 374.
11 Under the Child Abduction Act 1984 s 1 (as amended by the Children Act 1989). Note the defences, however, under s 1(5).
12 *R v Rahman* (1985) 81 Cr App Rep 349, CA at 353, per Lord Lane CJ. See also *Hewer v Bryant* [1970] 1 QB 357 at 373, [1969] 3 All ER 578, CA at 585, per Sachs LJ.
13 *Fleming v Pratt* (1823) 1 LJOS 194.
14 *R v D* [1984] AC 778, [1984] 2 All ER 449, HL: See Lowe (1984) 134 NLJ 995.
15 *R v Rahman* (supra). See Khan [1986] Fam Law 69.
16 Domicile and Matrimonial Proceedings Act 1973 s 4.
17 See eg *Re M (Minors) (Residence Order: Jurisdiction)* [1993] 1 FLR 495 at 500, per Balcombe LJ. NB it is not, however, a proposition of law that a child's habitual residence is that of the parents: *Re M (Abduction: Habitual Residence)* [1996] 1 FLR 887 at 895, per Sir John Balcombe.

principal carer, neither parent with parental responsibility has a unilateral right to change their child's residence without the other's consent.[18] In principle there seems no reason why a child of sufficient maturity cannot establish his own residence.[19]

Contact with the child

Prima facie parental responsibility encompasses seeing or otherwise having contact with the child (though it is commonly said that contact is a right of the child rather a right of the parent).[20] While not an absolute right, since in any litigation it will be contingent upon the child's welfare, nevertheless as Lord Oliver said in *Re KD (A Minor) (Ward: Termination of Access)*:[1]

> 'As a general proposition a natural parent has a claim to [contact with] his or her child to which the court will pay regard and it would not I think, be inappropriate to describe such a claim as a "right".'

This 'right' is protected to the extent that there is a statutory presumption of reasonable contact between a child in local authority care or under emergency protection and, amongst others, those with parental responsibility.[2] These latter provisions were enacted following the European Court of Human Rights ruling[3] that the absence of any right to challenge a termination of contact by a local authority amounted to a breach of Articles 8 and 13 of the Convention. It should also be noted that Article 9(3) of the UN Convention on the Rights of the Child 1989 provides:

> 'States Parties shall respect the right of the child who is separated from one or both parents to maintain personal relations and direct contact with both parents on a regular basis, except if it is contrary to the child's best interests.'

It has been argued[4] that since it is a normal assumption that a child will benefit from continued contact with both parents,[5] it may be that parental responsibility properly encompasses the prima facie duty to allow the child to have contact with either or both parents. Whether such responsibility extends to a parent having an obligation him or herself to maintain contact with the child can be debated.[6]

If parental responsibility encompasses the power to control the child's movements, it would seem to follow that it includes the power to restrict those

---

18 See eg *Re S (Minors) (Abduction: Wrongful Retention)* [1994] Fam 70, [1994] 1 All ER 237.

19 See *Re A (Wardship: Jurisdiction)* [1995] 1 FLR 767 per Hale J.

20 See eg *M v M (Child: Access)* [1973] 2 All ER 81, per Wrangham J, and see Art 9(3) of the UN Convention on the Rights of the Child 1989, set out below.

1 [1988] AC 806 at 827, [1988] 1 All ER 577, HL at 590.

2 Children Act 1989, s 34(1) and s 44(13) discussed at pp 582 and 593 respectively. As Cretney and Masson observe in *Principles of Family Law* (6th edn, 1997) at 622: 'although parental responsi-bility does not give an absolute right to contact with a child those with such power . . . do have a right to a court adjudication of restriction of contact'.

3 See *R v UK, O v UK, W v UK* [1988] 2 FLR 445. In *Hokkanen v Finland* (1995) 14 EHRR 139, [1996] 1 FLR 289, the failure by the State to enforce a parent's right of access was held to be breach of Art 8.

4 See Clarke Hall and Morrison, op cit, at para 1[63].

5 See eg Lord Oliver in *Re KD*, supra, at 827 and 590 respectively and *M v M (Child: Access)* [1973] 2 All ER 81, per Wrangham J at 85 and per Latey J at p 88.

6 In Scotland the Children (Scotland) Act 1995 s 1(1)(d) (set out at p 348 above) clearly states that a parent has a responsibility to maintain personal relations and direct contact with the child. But even supposing that there is a theoretical duty to see the child, it would be difficult to enforce this order on an unwilling parent. See further post, pp 447–50.

with whom the child may have contact. In *Nottingham County Council v P*,[7] in which it was sought to exclude the father from the matrimonial home and to restrict his contact with his children (on the basis of his sexual abuse), Ward J saw 'the force of the submission' that steps taken by a parent in meeting his parental responsibility are necessarily wide steps and could extend to controlling contact with the other parent. In *Re M (Care: Leave to Interview Child)*[8] Hale J was more forthright, commenting: 'Until the child is old enough to decide for himself, a parent undoubtedly has some control over whom he may see and who may see him'. Accordingly, it seems that parental responsibility embraces controlling those with whom the child may have contact.[9]

Education[10]

As Ward LJ observed in *Re Z (A Minor) (Identification: Restrictions on Publication)*[11] 'arranging for education commensurate with the child's intellectual needs and abilities is [an] . . . incident of the parental responsibility which arises from the duty of the parent to secure the child's education'. This responsibility is long established and derives from the common law right of a parent to determine what education the child should receive.[12] Parents' rights to determine their children's education are also protected by the European Convention on Human Rights to the extent of respecting their religious and philosophical convictions.[13]

At common law, because the duty was unenforceable,[14] parents could formerly choose not to have their children educated. This right, however, has long since been overturned: since the Education Act 1944 (now consolidated by the Education Act 1996) parents of every child between the ages of five and 16 have had to ensure that the child receives 'efficient full-time education suitable (a) to his age, ability and aptitude and (b) to any special educational needs he may have, either by regular attendance at school or otherwise'.[15]

'Parent' for these purposes includes any person who is not a parent but who has parental responsibility for the child or who has care of the child.[16]

Those with parental responsibility or who have care of children can discharge their duty by ensuring that they attend independent[17] rather than state schools or

---

7 [1994] Fam 18, 23.
8 [1995] 1 FLR 825. See also *Re F (Specific Issue: Child Interview)* [1995] 1 FLR 819, CA.
9 This point is not without significance when determining the ambit of specific issue and prohibited steps orders under s 8: see post, pp 421ff.
10 See generally Harris *Law and Education, Regulation, Consumerism and the Education System* (1993); Piper 'Parental Responsibility and the Education Act' [1994] Fam Law 146 (but note both publications pre-date the 1996 Education Act).
11 [1997] Fam 1 at 26, sub nom *Re Z (a minor) (freedom of publication)* [1995] 4 All ER 961 at 980.
12 For a striking example see *Tremain's Case* (1719) 1 Stra 167, discussed by Cretney and Masson, op cit at p 615–16. See also *Andrews v Salt* (1873) 8 Ch App 622 – father's wishes to be respected after his death.
13 Protocol No 1, Art 2.
14 See *Hodges v Hodges* (1796) Peake Add Cas 79.
15 Education Act 1996 ss 7–8. If the child is living with both parents, the statutory duty is cast on both of them: *Plunkett v Alker* [1954] 1 QB 420, [1954] 1 All ER 396. For a useful discussion of the 1996 Act see Clarke Hall and Morrison, Division A.
16 Education Act 1996 s 576(1). This definition can cover a local authority foster parent: *Fairpo v Humberside County Council* [1997] 1 FLR 339.
17 Disputes between the parents about appropriate schooling may be resolved by means of a specific issue or prohibited steps order under s 8 of the Children Act 1989: see eg *Re P (A Minor) (Education)* [1992] 1 FLR 316, CA.

even by educating them at home, provided in this latter instance that the local education authority is satisfied that the child is receiving efficient and full-time education suitable to his age etc. Where state education is relied upon, education authorities are required to comply with 'parental' wishes as to choice of school, so far as is compatible with the provision of efficient instruction and training and the avoidance of unreasonable public expenditure.[18] To enable a reasoned choice to be made 'parents' must be given information about the primary and secondary education available[19] and inter alia the curriculum and subject choice.[20]

The obligation to ensure that a child is receiving education suitable to his or her needs is enforceable in different ways. For example, it remains possible for a local authority social services department to institute care proceedings in cases of persistent non school attendance.[1] However, action is more likely to be taken by the local education authority. If it appears to an education authority that a child is not receiving suitable education, they may serve a notice requiring a parent to satisfy the authority that the child is receiving such education.[2] If a parent on whom a notice has been served fails to satisfy the authority that the child is receiving suitable education or in the authority's opinion it is expedient for the child to attend school, the authority must then serve on the parent a school attendance order.[3] Failure to comply with the order is an offence.[4] However, before instituting proceedings for the offence, the education authority must consider whether it would be appropriate to apply instead, or in addition, for an education supervision order under s 36 of the Children Act 1989.[5]

Before instituting proceedings for an education supervision order, the education authority must consult the appropriate social services authority.[6] The latter may decide to provide support for the child and family under Part III[7] or to institute care proceedings.[8]

An education authority may apply for an education supervision order on the ground that the child concerned is of compulsory school age and is not receiving full-time education suitable to his age, ability and aptitude and any special education needs he may have.[9] Unless proved to the contrary, the ground is deemed to be satisfied if a school attendance order is not complied with or the

---

18 Education Act 1996 s 9 and s 411; it will be noted therefore that education authorities are not under an absolute duty to comply with parental wishes.
19 Ibid, s 414.
20 Ibid, s 408.
1 Formerly truancy was a specific ground for making a care order, but now under the Children Act application has to be made under s 31 (discussed post at pp 536ff). But for a case where such an application succeeded see *Re O (a minor) (care: order: education: procedure)* [1992] 4 All ER 905, discussed post at p 539.
2 Education Act 1996 s 437(1).
3 Section 437(3).
4 Section 443. There is also a separate offence under s 444 if a child of compulsory school age and who is a registered pupil fails to attend school regularly. For either offence the parent can be fined but not imprisoned: see s 443(4) and s 444(8).
5 Section 447. Where prosecutions are brought, the court trying the case may direct the education authority to apply for an education supervision order, but the latter has a discretion not to apply if, after consulting the local authority, it is thought that the child's welfare will be satisfactorily safeguarded without an order: s 447(2).
6 Children Act 1989 s 36(8)–(9).
7 Discussed post, p 520.
8 See note 1 above
9 Section 36(3)–(4).

child is not regularly attending the school at which he is a registered pupil.[10]

Under an education supervision order, the supervisor has the duty to advise, assist and befriend and give directions to the child and the parents so as to secure that the child is properly educated.[11]

The supervisor must also consider what further steps to take if his directions are not complied with.[12] He may seek new directions or apply for a discharge of the order. A parent who persistently fails to comply with a direction is guilty of an offence.[13] Where a child persistently fails to comply with a direction, the education authority must notify the social services authority, which is obliged to investigate the child's circumstances.[14]

An education supervision order may last up to one year but may be extended for up to a further three years at a time.[15] It ceases to have effect when the child reaches the compulsory school leaving age or when he becomes subject to a care order.[16] The order may be discharged upon the application of the child, parent or education authority.[17]

Religious upbringing[18]

A person with parental responsibility has a right to determine the child's religious education, though there is no duty to give a child a religious upbringing. Based on the common law,[19] this right to determine the child's religious education is protected to the extent that a local authority cannot cause a child in their care 'to be brought up in any religious persuasion other than that in which he would have been brought up if the order had not been made'.[20] Adoption agencies are also required, when placing a child for adoption, to have regard, so far as practicable, to any wishes of the child's parent or guardian as to the child's religious upbringing.[1] Parents with parental responsibility and those caring for the child can require a child's exclusion from religious studies lessons and school assembly.[2] Although the courts will seek to pay 'serious heed to the religious wishes of a parent'[3] (and indeed to prevent a parent bringing up his child *simply* on the basis of his religious belief is contrary to the European Convention on Human Rights),[4] in the event of a dispute the court must treat the child's welfare as the paramount consideration.[5]

---

10 Section 36(5).
11 Sch 3, para 12(1)(a).
12 Sch 3, para 12(1)(b).
13 Sch 3, para 18.
14 Sch 3, para 19.
15 Sch 3, para 15(1)–(5).
16 Sch 3, para 15(6).
17 Sch 3, para 17.
18 See generally Hamilton *Family Law and Religion* (1995) and Mumford 'The Judicial Resolution of Disputes Involving Children and Religion' (1998) 47 ICLQ 117.
19 See *Andrews v Salt* (1873) 8 Ch App 622 and Bevan *Child Law* (1989) paras 11.02–11.16.
20 Children Act 1989 s 33(6)(a).
 1 Adoption Act 1976 s 7 (discussed post, p 635). See also cl 27(7) of the draft Adoption Bill which would prevent prospective adopters changing the child's religion following the making of a placement order.
 2 Education Act 1996 s 389.
 3 *J v C* [1969] 1 All ER 788 at 801, per Ungoed-Thomas J.
 4 See *Hoffmann v Austria* (1993) 17 EHRR 293, [1994] 1 FCR 193, E Ct HR. Note the comment at [1994] Fam Law 673.
 5 See eg *Re S (Minors) (Access: Religious Upbringing)* [1992] 2 FLR 313, CA.

Discipline[6]

A person with parental responsibility may lawfully chastise and inflict moderate and reasonable corporal punishment for the purpose of correcting a child or punishing an offence.[7] Such powers may be delegated either expressly[8] or impliedly,[9] but it seems they can only be exercised by those in loco parentis to the child.[10] Whether or not the punishment is reasonable must depend upon all the facts of the case, and in particular the age and strength of the child and the nature and degree of the punishment. If it goes beyond what is reasonable, it is unlawful and renders the individual criminally liable for assault or, depending on the gravity, for more serious offences[11] and, if it amounts to degrading punishment[12] or is inflicted without parental consent, is in breach of the European Convention on Human Rights.[13]

Reflecting the growing concern about the propriety of corporal punishment, notwithstanding parental approval, it is no longer permissible for such punishment to be exercised in schools,[14] community homes,[15] or in local authority foster placements.[16] These embargoes do not outlaw forms of discipline falling short of corporal punishment.[17]

Whether or not parents should continue to have the right to hit their children has frequently been debated, but unlike some other countries where it is banned[18] and

---

6 See generally Fortin *Children's Rights and the Developing Law* (1998) 228–38.

7 *R v Hopley* (1860) 2 F & F 202; *R v Woods* (1921) 85 JP 272; Children and Young Persons Act 1933 s 1(7). It has also been held that restraint of a child's movement is usually well within the realms of reasonable parental discipline: per Lord Lane CJ in *R v Rahman* (1985) 81 Cr App Rep 349, CA at 353.

8 See *Sutton London Borough Council v Davis* [1994] 1 FLR 737 in which a local authority's decision to refuse to register a child minder who would not comply with their 'no smacking policy' (the child minder had had the parent's permission to smack her daughter) was overturned by the court. See now LAC (94) 23 in which the Department of Health has issued new guidance permitting smacking by child minders if the parent consents. Note the comments on this decision by Dewar at [1994] Fam Law 493–4.

9 As in the case of schools, for example.

10 See eg *R v Woods*, supra, in which it was held to be unlawful for an elder brother to administer corporal punishment where both sons were living with their father, and consequently the older could not be considered as being in loco parentis to the younger.

11 Children and Young Person Act 1933 s 1; *R v Derriviere* (1969) 53 Cr App Rep 637, CA – West Indian father convicted of occasioning actual bodily harm to his 13-year-old son. If the child dies, the parent could be guilty of manslaughter or even murder: see post, p 366. An unreasonable restraint of a child's movement can render a parent guilty of unlawful imprisonment: *R v Rahman*, supra.

12 See *Costello-Roberts v UK* [1994] ELR 1, in which slippering a 7-year-old was held not to be degrading.

13 Corporal punishment without parental consent was held to be in breach of the European Convention on Human Rights: see *Campbell and Cosans v UK* (1982) 4 EHRR 293, E Ct HR (albeit in the context of a parent's right to determine the child's education), discussed by Douglas (1988) 2 Int J Law and Fam 76. Note also Art 37 of the UN Convention on the Rights of the Child, which inter alia states that no child shall be subject to degrading treatment.

14 Education Act 1996 s 448.

15 Reg 8(2)(a) of the Children Homes Regulations 1991 (SI 1991/1506).

16 Sch 2, para 5 to the Foster Placement (Children) Regulations 1991 (SI 1991/901).

17 It should also be noted that under the Education Act 1996 s 550A, school staff are empowered to use 'such force as is reasonable in the circumstances' to prevent a pupil committing an offence. The distinction between this so-called restraining power and corporal punishment can be a fine one. See the discussion by Hamilton 'Rights of the child – a right to and a right in education' in Bridge (ed) *Family Law Towards the Millennium, Essays for P M Bromley* ch 6.

18 In Sweden (1979), Finland (1984), Denmark (1986), Norway (1987) and Austria (1989), for example.

notwithstanding a Council of Europe Recommendation that legislation on corporal punishment of children be reviewed,[19] all attempts to curb the power in the UK have so far failed.[20]

Medical treatment[1]

Any person over the age of 16 who has responsibility (in the sense of having de facto control) for a child under the age of 16 has a duty to obtain essential medical assistance for that child.[2] However, in most cases, before any treatment can be given, medical practitioners need a valid consent, for without it they may be open to a prosecution for battery upon the child or for one of the graver forms of assault, or be subject to a claim in tort for trespass for which the practitioner may be liable regardless of fault.[3] Such consent is not always required: practitioners have long been advised that in an emergency treatment may be given if the well-being of the child could suffer by delay caused in obtaining consent.[4] There is also some authority[5] for saying that consent is not required if those with parental responsibility have abandoned or, possibly, neglected the child. In cases of doubt, however, a ruling can be sought from the court because it is well established (see below) that the High Court can override either the giving or the refusal to give consent. Conversely, consent might not always exonerate a medical practitioner, as for example where the treatment is clearly against the child's interests, though even then there might be some situations where leave can properly be given. For example, the transplant of a child's kidney to a twin may not be in the donor's medical interests, but if, having been properly guided by medical advice, a reasonable person with parental responsibility, weighing the risks to the donor against the advantage to the other, would give his consent, all concerned should be

19 Recommendation No R85(4) on Violence in the Family (1985), para 12. As the explanatory memorandum notes: 'It is the very assumption that corporal punishment of children is legitimate that opens the way to all kinds of excesses and makes the traces or symptoms of such punishment acceptable to third parties.' Note also Art 19 of the UN Convention on the Rights of the Child which enjoins States to take appropriate measures to protect children from violence whilst inter alia in the care of their parents.
20 For an extensive marshalling of the arguments for and against abolishing the right see Scot Law Com Discussion Paper No 88 *Parental Responsibilities and Rights, Guardianship and the Administration of Children's Property* (1980) paras 2.44ff and Scot Law Com No 135 *Report on Family Law* (1992) paras 2.67ff. Notwithstanding public support for their recommendations that striking a child with an implement should be banned, no such provision was included in what became the Children (Scotland) Act 1995. In England see also Law Com Consultation Paper No 139 *Consent in Criminal Law* (1995) para 11.5 and for wider discussion see Newell *Children are people too* (1989).
1 For consent to medical treatment see generally Kennedy and Grubb *Medical Law: Text and Materials* (2nd edn, 1994) chs 3 and 4, and Mason and McCall Smith *Law and Medical Ethics* (4th edn, 1994) 222–9.
2 Children and Young Persons Act 1933 s 1. Note especially s 1(2)(a) under which parents, guardians and other persons legally liable to maintain the child are deemed to have neglected the child in a manner likely to cause injury to the child's health by failing to provide, or to take steps to procure the provision of, inter alia, medical aid.
3 See eg *Re R (A Minor) (Wardship: Medical Treatment)* [1992] Fam 11 at 22, [1991] 4 All ER 177 at 184, per Lord Donaldson MR.
4 Upon the basis of the common law defence of necessity: cf Ministry of Health Circular F/19/113 1967 and Home Office Circular 63/1968. See also *Re F (Mental Patient: Sterilisation)* [1990] 2 AC 1 at 52, sub nom *F v West Berkshire Health Authority (Mental Health Act Commission intervening)* [1989] 2 All ER 545 at 548, per Lord Bridge.
5 *Gillick v West Norfolk and Wisbech Area Health Authority* [1986] AC 112, [1985] 3 All ER 402, HL per Lord Scarman at 189 and 424 and Lord Templeman at 204 and 435.

given legal protection.[6] Although this absence of any consent may lay the practitioner open to an action *by or on behalf of the child*, apart from seeking an injunction to prevent the proposed treatment, it is difficult to see what other legal action a person with parental responsibility could bring in his own right.[7]

Prima facie anyone with parental responsibility (including a local authority)[8] can give a valid consent to the child's surgical, medical or dental treatment. This prima facie position, however, is subject to some limitations and uncertainty. For example, it seems that this power of consent does not necessarily extend to all forms of treatment and, furthermore, is without prejudice to the ability of a 16-to-17-year-old or a '*Gillick* competent' child under the age of 16 to give a valid consent;[9] nor does it preclude the court from subsequently overriding an otherwise valid consent or from sanctioning treatment otherwise opposed. In any event, no practitioner can be forced to give treatment contrary to his clinical judgment.[10] Hence, as Lord Donaldson MR observed in *Re W (A Minor) (Medical Treatment: Court's Jurisdiction)*,[11] no question of consenting or refusing consent arises unless and until a medical or dental practitioner advises such treatment and is willing to undertake it.

(a)   The position of those with parental responsibility

Although, as we have said, as a general rule anyone with parental responsibility can give a valid consent to the child's medical treatment, the power is subject to a number of qualifications. First, not all those with parental responsibility are in the same position. In particular, those having responsibility by virtue of an emergency protection order only have authority to take such action 'as is reasonably required to safeguard or promote the welfare of the child'.[12] Hence, while such persons may be able to give a valid consent to day-to-day treatment, they could not do so with respect to major elective surgery.

Secondly, even parents with parental responsibility are not empowered to consent to all forms of treatment. According to Lord Templeman in *Re B (A Minor) (Wardship: Sterilisation)*[13] sterilisation of a girl under the age of 18 can only be lawfully carried out with leave of a High Court judge. Notwithstanding that Lord Templeman was the only Law Lord to say this and that the precise legal basis for his assertion remains uncertain, it has since been accepted as the basic position,[14] though whether a similar requirement extends to other forms of treatment has yet to be decided.[15] However, it has also been held[16] that High Court

---

6 For a discussion of this problem see Kennedy and Grubb *Medical Law: Text and Materials* op cit at 256ff.

7 Parents no longer have the right to sue for the loss of their child's services: see post, p 364. However, practitioners could be subject to disciplinary action by their professional body.

8 See *R v Kirklees Metropolitan Borough Council, ex p C (A Minor)* [1992] 2 FLR 117 and *A Metropolitan Borough Council v DB* [1997] 1 FLR 767.

9 See the discussion ante at pp 313ff.

10 *Re J (A Minor) (Child In Care: Medical Treatment)* [1993] Fam 15, [1992] 4 All ER 614, CA.

11 [1993] Fam 64 at 83, [1992] 4 All ER 627, CA at 639.

12 Children Act 1989 s 44(5)(b).

13 [1988] AC 199 at 205, [1987] 2 All ER 206, HL at 214, discussed by Grubb and Pearl 'Sterilisation and the Courts' [1987] CLJ 439. A similar conclusion was reached by the Australian High Court in *Department of Health v JWB and SMB* (1992) 66 ALJR 300.

14 At any rate, as Lord Donaldson MR put it in *Re W (A Minor) (Medical Treatment)* [1993] Fam 64 at 79, [1992] 4 All ER 627 at 635: 'parties might well be advised to apply to the court for assistance'.

15 It might conceivably cover all irreversible treatment for non-therapeutic reasons.

16 *Re E (A Minor) (Medical Treatment)* [1991] 2 FLR 585 per Sir Stephen Brown P.

leave is not required for an operation the inevitable effect of which is to sterilise the child, provided its object is for therapeutic reasons[17] to relieve the child of a medical condition. Furthermore, it has been held that notwithstanding that a decision as to sterilisation is a matter for the judge, not all responsibility is thus removed from parents (or others with parental responsibility), since they retain the responsibility to bring the issue before the High Court.[18]

Apart from these qualifications, the power of consent vested in those with parental responsibility extends to most forms of surgical, medical or dental treatment and would include treatment by drugs or for drug abuse and, by analogy with s 8(2) of the Family Law Reform Act 1969, diagnostic procedures such as HIV testing and, by reason of s 21(3) of the 1969 Act, the taking of blood samples from the child to be used in tests to determine paternity.[19]

The third important qualification on the power of consent vested in those with parental responsibility is the age of the child. Although the matter is not entirely free from doubt, following *Re W (A Minor) (Medical Treatment: Court's Jurisdiction)*,[20] it seems that those with parental responsibility retain their power to give a valid consent throughout the child's minority.[1] This, however, is subject to three important qualifications namely:

(1) that a child aged 16 or 17 or who is '*Gillick* competent' if under the age of 16 can give a valid consent – which cannot be countermanded by an adult;[2]

(2) although in theory a valid consent may be given by an adult with parental responsibility notwithstanding the opposition of the '*Gillick* competent' or 16- or 17-year-old child, in practice no treatment should be given without prior court sanction;[3] and

(3) any decision by a parent can subsequently be overridden by the High Court.[4]

(b) The court's powers

It has long been established that the High Court can override a decision by a parent to consent or refuse consent to the child's medical treatment. For example, in *Re D (A Minor) (Wardship: Sterilisation)*[5] a gynaecologist intended to sterilise a mentally handicapped girl aged 11 (with her parent's consent) to prevent the possibility of her having children in the future. An educational psychologist concerned with the case then made the child a ward of court. Heilbron J concluded

---

17 It should be noted, however, that in *Re B*, supra, the Law Lords considered the notion of a non-therapeutic sterilisation unhelpful.

18 *Re HG (Specific Issue Order: Sterilisation)* [1993] 1 FLR 587. See also *Practice Note* [1993] 3 All ER 222. Discussed further post at p 420.

19 Though in this case the power can be overridden by the court: see *Re R (A Minor) (Blood Tests: Constraint)* [1998] Fam 66, [1998] 1 FLR 745, discussed ante, p 278.

20 [1993] Fam 64, [1992] 4 All ER 627, CA, discussed further below.

1 This view was most clearly expressed by Lord Donaldson MR, but it seemed also to be accepted by Balcombe LJ, both of whom expressly rejected the contention that Lord Scarman should have been taken to be saying in *Gillick v West Norfolk and Wisbech Area Health Authority* [1986] AC 112, [1985] 3 All ER 402, HL that parents of a '*Gillick* competent' child had no right at all to consent to medical treatment of the child.

2 See Lord Donaldson MR in *Re W* ibid [1993] Fam at 83–4, [1992] All ER at 639. The child's consent can, however, be overridden by the court: see ante, p 314.

3 This, at any rate, was Nolan LJ's view in *Re W* [1993] Fam at 94, [1992] 4 All ER at 648–9. Even Lord Donaldson MR, ibid at 84 and 640 respectively, thought that a child's refusal was a very important consideration for parents deciding whether themselves to give consent.

4 See below.

5 [1976] Fam 185, [1976] 1 All ER 326.

that there was no foreseeable risk of an unwanted pregnancy and that, as the girl would have sufficient understanding to be able to make up her own mind on the matter when she was older, the operation should not take place. Conversely, in *Re B (A Minor) (Wardship: Medical Treatment)*[6] the court sanctioned, contrary to the parents' wishes, a life-saving operation for a newly born Down's Syndrome child, and in *Re B (Wardship: Abortion)*[7] overruling the mother's objections, gave permission for a 12-year-old to have an abortion.

It is also accepted that the High Court's powers of consent are wider than those of a parent and thus can extend to sanctioning a child's sterilisation.[8] It has been held in relation to a terminally ill child that a court can authorise treatment to relieve the child's suffering even if this means shortening the child's life.[9]

In deciding what order to make it is established that the court's paramount duty is to decide what is in the best interests of the child,[10] not the reasonableness of the parents' refusal of consent.[11] This approach does not, however, mean that the parents' standpoint can be ignored. A good, if controversial, example is *Re T (a minor) (wardship: medical treatment)*.[12] In that case a child aged 18 months was suffering from a life-threatening liver defect. The medical advice was that the child should have a liver transplant as the prospects of success were good, whereas without the transplant the child's life expectancy was just over two years. The parents refused to consent. The child had already undergone surgery which had caused much pain and distress, and the mother, who had a deep-seated concern as to the benefits of major invasive surgery and post-operative treatment and about the dangers of failure long-term as well as short-term, refused to consent, taking the view that it was better for her child to spend the rest of his short life without the pain, stress and upset of intrusive surgery. No one doubted the sincerity of the mother's views and both parents were described as caring and devoted to the child. An added complication of the case was that at the time of the action the family were living abroad, so that it was not certain that an order authorising the treatment would be implemented.

The court was acutely aware of the difficulties that the case presented – was it in

---

6 [1981] 1 WLR 1421, CA.
7 [1991] 2 FLR 426.
8 See *Re B (A Minor) (Wardship: Sterilisation)* [1988] AC 199 at 205, [1987] 2 All ER 206 at 214, per Lord Templeman. See also *Re R (A Minor) (Wardship: Consent To Medical Treatment)* [1992] Fam 11 at 25B and 28C–F, [1991] 4 All ER 177, CA at 186g and 189c–d.
9 *Re C (A Minor) (Wardship: Medical Treatment)* [1990] Fam 26, [1989] 2 All ER 782, CA. Note also *Re C (A Baby)* [1996] 2 FLR 43 in which the court authorised the discontinuation of artificial ventilation of a brain-damaged child. See also *Re C (Medical Treatment)* [1998] 1 FLR 384 in which the court approved a hospital's proposal – opposed by the child's parents who, being Orthodox Jews, could not contemplate a course of action which would indirectly shorten life – to withdraw ventilation and thereafter not to reinstate it in the case of a 16-month-child suffering from a fatal disease, since life-sustaining treatment would simply delay death without significantly alleviating suffering.
10 For a discussion of whether the test is different when considering whether to overrule a competent child's decision, see Lowe 'The House of Lords and the welfare principle' in Bridge (ed) *Family Law Towards the Millennium, Essays for P M Bromley* (1997) 125 at 170.
11 Per Butler-Sloss LJ in *Re T (a minor) (wardship: medical treatment)* [1997] 1 All ER 906 at 913, applying inter alia *Re B (A Minor) (Wardship: Sterilisation)* [1988] AC 199, [1987] 2 All ER 206, HL.
12 Ibid. For a criticism of this decision see Bridge 'Parental power and the medical treatment of children' in *Family Law Towards the Millennium, Essays for P M Bromley* , op cit, 295 at 325–8, who considers the decision to be too parent-centred. It is instructive to compare this decision with that of Heilbron J in *Re D (A Minor) (Wardship: Sterilisation)*, supra, discussed above.

the best interests of the child to have a peaceful if short life with devoted parents, or should the court give its consent to the liver transplant and order the child's return to this country with all the distress and uncertainties that that would entail? In the exceptional circumstances of the case it was held that the child's best interests required that his future treatment should be left in the hands of his devoted parents.

Vetoing the issue of a passport

Until October 1998 children under the age of 16 could be included on their parent's passport or issued with their own, but after that date only the latter facility is available.[13] As the guidance issued by the UK Passport Agency explains,[14] in the absence of any objection being lodged at the Agency's passport office, standard passport facilities are normally granted to children with the consent of either parent or a person acting in loco parentis. Where the child's parents are not married to each other, the mother's consent is required if the father does not have parental responsibility.[15] Where it is known that the child is a ward of court,[16] the court's consent is required.

In the absence of any court order, objections to the issue of a passport will usually only be considered in limited circumstances, namely from an unmarried mother, or from the police where they have notified the Agency of an intention to exercise their power of arrest under the Child Abduction Act 1984.[17] However, objections will also be considered inter alia where the court has ordered that the child is not to be removed from the jurisdiction and, as is expressly stated on the face of a contact or residence order: '*Any* person with parental responsibility may ask the United Kingdom Passport Agency . . . not to issue a passport allowing the child to go abroad without the knowledge of that person'.[18]

Taking the child abroad and arranging for the child's emigration

Subject to the obtaining of the necessary passports, parents with parental responsibility acting in unison have the power to take their child outside the United Kingdom and can therefore arrange for his emigration. Neither parent has the *unilateral* right, if the other parent has parental responsibility, to take or remove the child, under the age of 16 from the United Kingdom without the other's consent,[19] since to do so is an offence under the Child Abduction Act 1984 s 1(1). Guardians are empowered to remove the child from the United Kingdom

---

13 Home Office News Release 142/98.
14 Reproduced at [1994] Fam Law 651. See also *Practice Direction* [1986] 1 All ER 983.
15 For the position of unmarried fathers with respect to parental responsibility see post, pp 377ff.
16 Wardship is discussed in Chapter 16.
17 Discussed further post, p 480.
18 Form C43. Emphasis added.
19 'United Kingdom' means England and Wales, Scotland and Northern Ireland: Interpretation Act 1978 Sch 1. It is a defence under s 1(5) of the Child Abduction Act 1984 if the child is removed: (a) in the belief that the other person has consented or would have done had he been aware of all the relevant circumstances; (b) after taking all reasonable steps to communicate with the other person the accused had been unable to do so; or (c) the other person has unreasonably refused to consent. Section 1(5)(c) does not apply if the person who refused consent had a residence order or custody order in his favour: s 1(5A), added by the Children Act 1989 Sch 12, para 37(3). In cases where there is sufficient evidence to raise the application of s 1(5) the burden is on the prosecution to show that s 1(5) does not apply: s 1(6).

unless there are other persons with parental responsibility, in which case their consent is also required.

The powers of removal are further fettered in the event of the making of a residence or care order. A person in whose favour a residence order is made is thereby entitled to remove the child from the United Kingdom for a period of less than one month without anyone's permission,[1] but can only remove the child for a period in excess of one month with the *written* consent of every person having parental responsibility or with leave of the court.[2] The making of a care order prevents any person from removing the child from the United Kingdom without the written consent of every person with parental responsibility[3] or leave of the court, though the local authority themselves can arrange for the child's removal for a period of less than one month without anyone's permission[4] and, with approval of the court, may make arrangements for the child in their care to live outside England and Wales.[5]

The net result of these provisions is that where the child is to be removed from the United Kingdom for more than one month the consent all those who have parental responsibility or leave of the court must be obtained.

Naming the child[6]

By convention a child born to married parents takes his father's surname, though it would seem that the father cannot insist upon this.[7] A child whose parents are not married normally takes his mother's surname, but he may be known by his father's,[8] although the father has no right to insist upon this.[9] As was held in *Re PC (Change of Surname)*,[10] once the child's name has been registered, neither married parent may change it without the other's consent save where that other parent is dead.

In *Re PC* Holman J rejected the argument, based on s 2(7) of the Children Act 1989 (which allows any one holder of parental responsibility to act alone without the other),[11] that one spouse can now unilaterally change a child's surname. In his Lordship's view, in the absence of a residence order being made, the 1989 Act cannot be taken to have altered the former law[12] under which it was clear that one parent could not change his child's name without his spouse's consent.[13]

Where only one person has parental responsibility (as, for example, where a married parent survives the other, or where the child's parents are not married to

1 Children Act 1989 s 13(2).
2 Ibid, s 13(1).
3 Ibid, s 33(7)(b).
4 Ibid, s 33(8)(a).
5 Ibid, s 33(8)(b) and Sch 2, para 19.
6 See generally Bond 'Reconstructing families – changing children's surnames' (1998) 10 CFLQ 17.
7 There is nothing in the Registration of Births, Deaths and Marriages Regulations 1987 requiring the father's name to be given priority and it seems that the mother is entitled to register the child in her name: *D v B (Surname: Birth Registration)* [1979] Fam 38, sub nom *D v B (Otherwise D) (Child: Surname)* [1979] 1 All ER 92, CA.
8 See eg *Re P (Parental Responsibility)* [1997] 2 FLR 722, CA.
9 See eg *Dawson v Wearmouth* [1998] 1 All ER 271, CA.
10 [1997] 2 FLR 730.
11 See post, p 395.
12 His Lordship relied upon *Y v Y (Child: Surname)* [1973] Fam 147, [1973] 2 All ER 574, but for an earlier authority to the same effect see *Re T (otherwise H) (An Infant)* [1963] Ch 238, [1962] 3 All ER 970.
13 *Practice Direction* [1995] 1 All ER 832.

each other and no parental responsibility order or agreement has been made), then in Holman J's words 'that person has the right and power lawfully to cause a change of surname without any other permission or consent.'[14]

A person in whose favour a residence order has been made is not entitled to change the child's surname unless he has the *written* consent of every person who has parental responsibility for the child or the leave of the court.[15] Similarly the making of a care order does not entitle a local authority to cause the child to be known by a new surname without the *written* consent of every person with parental responsibility or the leave of the court.[16]

There is no requirement to execute a formal deed for change of surname, since a person may call himself what he likes. However, the execution and enrolment of a deed may be useful for evidential purposes.[17] There is no formal provision for changing a child's forename.

Representation

In general a child can only bring legal proceedings, at any rate in the High Court and county court, by his 'next friend'.[18] Similarly, if civil proceedings are brought against him he must be represented by a guardian ad litem.[19] Parents have long been regarded as having the prima facie[20] entitlement to act in each of those capacities, and presumably anyone with parental responsibility is in the same position.[1] It should be noted that with respect to proceedings under the Children Act 1989 and under the High Court's inherent jurisdiction special rules apply, so that children may not need to act through a next friend or guardian ad litem.[2]

Disposing of the child's corpse

It is established that a parent who has the means to do so is bound to provide for the burial of his deceased child.[3] Such a duty, which presumably may also be discharged by cremating the child, may therefore properly be considered to be an aspect of parental responsibility. However, in *R v Gwynedd County Council*[4] it

---

14 In *Re PC*, ibid at 739.
15 Children Act 1989 s 13(1), discussed post, p 439. Note that in the case of older children, particularly those over the age of 16, the child's consent may also be required – see Holman J in *Re PC*, ibid, at 739.
16 Ibid, s 33(7), discussed post, p 566.
17 See the Enrolment of Deeds (Change of Name) Regulations 1983, SI 1983/680.
18 RSC Ord 80 r 2(1); CCR Ord 10 r 1(1).
19 RSC Ord 80 r 2(2); CCR Ord 10 r 1(2). It should be noted that RSC Ord 80 and CCR Ord 10 only apply to proceedings before the High Court and county court. The better view is that in the absence of any express restrictions children are entitled to conduct their own proceedings before magistrates' courts.
20 *Woolf v Pemberton* (1877) 6 Ch D 19. Note there is a power of removal if a proper case is made out: *Re Taylor's Application* [1972] 2 QB 369, [1972] 2 All ER 873 (successful application to remove a parent who refused to accept compromise of thalidomide application, though decision to remove the particular parent was reversed on appeal).
1 In Scotland the matter is put beyond doubt by s 2(1)(d) of the Children (Scotland) Act 1995: see ante, p 349.
2 Family Proceedings Rules 1991 r 9.2A, added by the Family Proceedings (Amendment) Rules 1992 r 6, for the operation of which see Sawyer 'The competence of children to participate in family proceedings' (1995) 7 CFLQ 180.
3 *R v Vann* (1851) 2 Den 325, 15 JP 802, approved by Lord Alverstone LJ in *Clark v London General Omnibus Co Ltd* [1906] 2 KB 648, CA at 659 and followed in *R v Gwynedd County Council, ex p B* [1992] 3 All ER 317, CA.
4 Supra.

was held that, as the local authority's responsibility towards a child in care ceased upon the child's death, the right to bury the child vested in the parent rather than the foster parent. Put into the language of the 1989 Act it can be said that, as the local authority's responsibility ended upon the child's death, the right to bury the child vested exclusively in the parents with parental responsibility.[5] Similarly, those who have parental responsibility by means of a residence order will lose it upon the child's death. Accordingly, the right to dispose of a child's corpse seems exclusively to be vested in parents with parental responsibility and guardians.

Arguably, this aspect of parental responsibility falls outside the scope of the Children Act 1989, since that Act might properly be considered to be confined to dealing with live children.[6] In *F v W*,[7] which concerned a dispute as to the disposal of a dead child's ashes, it was accepted that the 1989 Act was not the appropriate statutory vehicle to decide the matter, but neither did the judge think it was, properly considered, a matter of administering the child's estate.[8] In the judge's view the issue was more in the nature of a dispute between two equally entitled trustees (ie the mother and father) and decided the issue on the basis of an evaluation of the arguments advanced by each parent. Whether this approach will be accepted by the appellate courts remains to be seen, but it is submitted that the appropriate procedure for resolving disputes of this kind is to invoke the High Court's inherent jurisdiction.[9]

Child's services

Formerly, at common law, persons with parental rights were entitled to the domestic services of their unmarried children under the age of 18 actually living with them as part of the family. The significance of this lay in the fact that it provided the parent with his only common law remedy against a stranger for interference with parental rights.[10] However, insofar as the loss of service is due to a tort committed against the child, the parents' cause of action has been abolished by the Administration of Justice Act 1982 s 2(b). Furthermore, it has been held[11] that there is no cause of action against a stranger for interference with parental rights in respect of the relationship with their children. For practical purposes, therefore, parental responsibility cannot be said to include a right to domestic services.[12]

---

5   It should be noted, however, that local authorities have permissive powers to arrange for the child's burial or cremation should the parents not wish or be able to exercise their rights: Children Act 1989 Sch 2, para 20.

6   Section 105(1) defines child as 'a person under the age of eighteen' and following the normal rules of construction 'person' presumptively refers to a live person: see eg *Elliot v Joicey* [1935] AC 209, HL, and *R v Newham London Borough Council, ex p Dada* [1996] QB 507, [1995] 2 All ER 522, CA. For a similar interpretation of 'child' under the Children and Young Persons Act 1969 s 70(1) see *Re D (A Minor)* [1987] AC 317, [1987] 1 All ER 20, HL.

7   Unreported, per His Honour Judge Boggis QC sitting as a High Court judge.

8   Hence RSC Ord 85 r 2(3)(c) under which a court can direct one parent to do or to abstain from doing a particular act, and which applies where there is a 'question arising in the administration of the estate', had no application to this dispute.

9   The inherent jurisdiction is discussed post at pp 701ff.

10   Discussed in extenso in the 6th edition of this work at pp 329 et seq.

11   *F v Wirral Metropolitan Borough Council* [1991] Fam 69, [1991] 2 All ER 648, CA and *Re S (A Minor) (Parental Rights)* [1993] Fam Law 572, discussed further post, pp 375–6.

12   See post, p 375 n 15.

Administration of property

Parental responsibility includes the rights, powers and duties which a guardian of the estate (appointed before the Children Act 1989 came into force)[13] would have had in relation to the child and his property.[14] Such rights include the right 'to receive or recover in his own name, for the benefit of the child, property of whatever description and wherever situated which the child is entitled to receive or recover.'[15]

Parental responsibility does *not* include rights of succession to the child's property.[16] Indeed, it seems that a parent has no rights as such in the property of a child of any age and therefore, in the absence of any agreement, has no claim, for instance, on the child's wages.[17] The ownership of gifts to a child is more problematic and would in the first place depend on the value of the gift and the age of child. In the case of gifts to young children the legal interest probably vests in the parents (or other persons having parental responsibility for the child), but as a result of s 3(3) of the 1989 Act such goods would then be held on trust for the child. In the case of gifts to older children,[18] it is thought that the property belongs to the child. In practice, if a minor is entitled to property of any value, he will normally derive it under a settlement or will or on an intestacy, and the legal ownership will therefore usually vest in trustees.[19]

Notwithstanding that parental responsibility does not include a right of succession, since children cannot generally[20] make a valid will, in practice parents (but not others with parental responsibility) have a right to inherit their children's property.[1]

Protection

(a) Physical and moral protection

Although it is undoubtedly an aspect of parental responsibility to afford physical protection to the child, at common law a duty is owed by anyone who willingly undertakes to look after another who is incapable of looking after himself. Hence this duty can be owed to a step-child or foster child[2] and can continue after the child reaches his majority, if he is unable to look after himself owing to some physical or mental disability.[3] Whether the duty exists in any given case depends inter alia upon the necessity of protection. A crippled mother, for example, would

---

13 Before 14 October 1991.
14 Children Act 1989 s 3(2).
15 Ibid, s 3(3).
16 Ibid, s 3(4)(b).
17 See *Williams v Doulton* [1948] 1 All ER 603.
18 At what stage a child makes the transition from younger to older for these purposes is uncertain and will be a question of fact to be determined in each case.
19 If a child is absolutely entitled to property under a will or on an intestacy, the personal representatives may appoint trustees of the gift for the beneficiary and vest the property in them: Administration of Estates Act 1925 s 42(1). Depending upon the terms of the instrument creating the interest, parents (or others with parental responsibility) may be able to make a claim on the fund for the child's maintenance and education.
20 Aliter if they are on actual military service: Wills (Soldiers and Sailors) Act 1918 s 1 (as amended by the Family Law Reform Act 1969 s 3(1)(b)).
1 Administration of Estates Act 1925 Pt IV and the Family Law Reform Act 1987 s 18(2).
2 *R v Bubb* (1850) 4 Cox CC 455; *R v Gibbins and Proctor* (1918) 13 Cr App Rep 134, CCA.
3 *R v Chattaway* (1922) 17 Cr App Rep 7, CCA (starvation of a helpless daughter aged 25).

not be under any duty to protect a healthy son aged 17. In *R v Shepherd*,[4] where a girl aged 18, who normally lived away in service but returned home from time to time, died there in childbirth, it was held that her mother was under no duty to send for a midwife because the girl was beyond the age of childhood and was entirely emancipated.

As will be seen, breach of the duty can lead both to criminal and civil liability.

(b)   Criminal liability

A person will be criminally liable for assault if he inflicts physical injury on a child or puts him in fear that he will do so. However, where breach of the duty to protect the child takes the form of neglect, abandonment or some other omission, the common law criminal sanctions are wholly inadequate to ensure the child's protection, not least because no offence is committed unless the child's health actually suffers as a result. In practice, so far as the criminal law is concerned, the common law duty has been superseded by the statutory duty contained in the Children and Young Persons Acts 1933 to 1969.[5]

Section 1(1) of the 1933 Act provides:

> 'If any person[6] who has attained the age of sixteen years and has responsibility for any child or young person under that age, wilfully assaults, ill-treats, neglects, abandons, or exposes him, or causes or procures him to be assaulted, ill-treated, neglected, abandoned, or exposed, in a manner likely[7] to cause him unnecessary suffering or injury to health (including injury to or loss of sight, or hearing, or limb, or organ of the body, and any mental derangement), that person shall be guilty of [an offence] . . .'[8]

This is subject to s 1(7) under which 'the right of any parent, teacher, or any other person having lawful charge of the child or young person to administer punishment' is preserved.[9] By s 17 of the Act the following are liable under s 1:[10]

> '(a)   any person who –
>   (i)   has parental responsibility for him (within the meaning of the Children Act 1989); or
>   (ii)   is otherwise legally liable to maintain him; and
> (b)   any person who has care of him.'

This wording is extremely wide and would cover, for example, a schoolteacher and anyone over the age of 16 acting as a baby-sitter.

The object of the Act is to make criminal any wilful course of conduct likely to cause physical or mental injury to the child. The Act itself specifies that neglect

---

4   (1862) Le & Ca 147. (The age of majority was then 21.)
5   Viz the Children and Young Persons Act 1933; Children and Young Persons (Amendment) Act 1952; Children and Young Persons Act 1963; Children and Young Persons Act 1969 as amended by the Children Act 1989 Schs 12 and 13.
6   There can be joint liability: see *R v Gibson and Gibson* [1984] Crim LR 615, CA.
7   It has been held that 'likely' should be understood as excluding only what would fairly be described as highly unlikely: *R v Willis* [1990] Crim LR 714, applying remarks of Lord Diplock in *R v Sheppard* [1981] AC 394 at 405, [1980] 3 All ER 899 at 904.
8   The phrase 'in a manner likely to cause . . . injury to health' governs the whole of the preceding phrase 'wilfully assaults . . . abandoned, or exposed': *R v Hatton* [1925] 2 KB 322, CCA. The section has virtually superseded the Offences against the Person Act 1861 s 27, which relates to the abandonment and exposure of children under two years of age.
9   Discussed ante at p 356.
10   The Act says 'presumed to be liable', but the presumption is apparently irrefutable: *Brooks v Blount* [1923] 1 KB 257.

shall include failure to provide adequate food, clothing, medical aid[11] or lodging or, if the parent or guardian is unable to provide any of these, failing to take steps to procure them through the Department of Social Security.[12] But clearly many other types of cruelty and neglect are covered, such as beating a child, locking him up alone, leaving him in an otherwise deserted house or shutting him out in inclement weather, if such acts are likely to cause the child concerned suffering or ill-health. A person will be liable, however, only if his act is wilful: hence he must either know that his conduct might cause suffering or injury to health, or not care whether this results or not.[13] A parent who does not know that the child's health is at risk will not be guilty of an offence if he fails to summon medical aid even though a reasonable person would be aware of this fact: if he does know this, however, he will presumably be guilty even though he has some religious or other reason for refusing to provide assistance.[14]

Parents (and others having responsibility for children) may also be criminally liable for causing the death of a child under the age of three by overlying it in bed whilst drunk,[15] for allowing a child under the age of 12 to be in a room containing an unguarded fire or other heating appliance with the result that the child is killed or seriously injured,[16] or for permitting children under the age of 16 (subject to certain exceptions) to take part in or train for dangerous performances.[17]

Although there was no positive method either at common law or in equity of ensuring that parents took adequate steps to secure their child's *moral* welfare, as a result of statutory intervention there is at least a partial obligation to afford moral protection. An attempt has been made to prevent the acquisition of sexually depraved habits by making it an offence inter alia for anyone with parental responsibility to cause or encourage the seduction or prostitution of his daughter under the age of 16, or to permit a child between the ages of four and 16 to be in a brothel.[18] Similarly it is an offence to allow a child under the age of 16 to beg,[19] and penalties are imposed upon parents who permit children to take part in entertainments or to go abroad for the purpose of performing for profit except under stringent conditions.[20]

(c)   Civil liability

It seems clear that there are two possible civil actions arising from a breach of the duty to protect, namely an action for assault and a common law action for damages in negligence. So far as the former is concerned, parents or others having responsibility or care of the child stand in no special position. Like anyone else they can be liable in damages for such assaults and, though such actions are rare,

11 Unreasonable refusal to permit a surgical operation may amount to wilful neglect: *Oakey v Jackson* [1914] 1 KB 216.
12 Children and Young Persons Act 1933 s 1(2)(a).
13 *R v Sheppard* [1981] AC 394, [1980] 3 All ER 899, HL.
14 As in *R v Senior* [1899] 1 QB 283 (religious objection to calling in medical aid), which appears to have been approved on its facts in *R v Sheppard* (supra).
15 Children and Young Persons Act 1933 s 1(2)(b).
16 Ibid, s 11 as amended by the Children and Young Persons (Amendment) Act 1952 s 8.
17 Ibid, ss 23–24; Children and Young Persons Act 1963 s 41 and Schs 3 and 5.
18 Sexual Offences Act 1956 s 28 (as amended by the Children Act 1989); Children and Young Persons Act 1933 s 3 (as amended by the Children Act 1989). These provisions also apply to anyone having the care of the child.
19 Children and Young Persons Act 1933 s 4.
20 Ibid, s 25; Children and Young Persons Act 1963 ss 37–40 and 42.

an example can be found in *Pereira v Keleman* [1] in which a father was held liable in damages to each of his three daughters in respect of his physical and indecent assaults.

So far as negligence claims are concerned, the child must prove that he has been injured as a result of the other's breach of duty to take care to avoid such acts or omissions as are foreseeably likely to injure him. Where a duty of care exists independently so that, had the injured person been a stranger, he could have recovered from the tortfeasor, the relationship of parent and child should not ipso facto bar the action. An obvious example would occur if a child, who is a passenger in his father's car, is injured as a result of the latter's negligent driving. The father's duty of care similarly extends to an unborn child, whereas the mother's duty to an unborn child arises only when she is driving a motor vehicle. [2]

Where there is no independent duty, so that the child has to rely solely on the common law duty to protect owed to him by his parent or other person having parental responsibility or of those simply looking after him, the position is less clear. The leading case is *Surtees v Kingston-upon-Thames Borough Council* [3] in which the plaintiff, then aged two, had, whilst in foster care, an accident in which she sustained serious injuries to her foot. The injuries were caused by immersion in water hot enough to cause third degree burns. Although the precise circumstances were disputed, the court accepted the foster parents' explanation that whilst the foster mother was out of the bathroom the plaintiff somehow placed her foot in the wash basin and switched on the hot water tap. The foster mother took the plaintiff immediately to a doctor, who treated her daily. It was held that on these facts the action for negligence should fail. [4] With respect to the foster parents it was held that, in the domestic circumstances in which the foster mother was performing her normal household duties, the kind of injury sustained by the plaintiff was not foreseeable. In reaching this decision both Stocker LJ and Browne-Wilkinson V-C were mindful of the danger of imposing an impossibly high standard of care in domestic situations. It was expressly accepted that for this purpose the duty owed by foster parents was exactly the same as that owed by a parent. Browne-Wilkinson V-C further observed: [5]

'There are very real public policy considerations to be taken into account if the conflicts inherent in legal proceedings are to be brought into family relationships . . . The studied realm of the Royal Courts of Justice . . . is light years away from the circumstances prevailing in the average home. The mother is looking after a fast-moving toddler at the same time as cooking the meal, doing the housework, answering the telephone, looking after the other children and doing all the other things that the average mother has to cope with simultaneously, or in quick succession, in the normal household. We should be slow to characterise as negligent the care which ordinary loving and careful mothers are able to give to individual children, given the rough-and-tumble of home life.'

1 [1995] 1 FLR 428.
2 The Congenital Disabilities (Civil Liability) Act 1976 s 2. Liability can only accrue provided the child is born alive: s 4(2)(a).
3 [1991] 2 FLR 559, CA. But note also *X (Minors) v Bedfordshire County Council* [1995] 2 AC 633, [1995] 3 All ER 353, HL and *W v Essex County Council* [1998] 3 All ER 111, CA, on the possible liability of local authorities, discussed post, p 608.
4 It was conceded that the authority could not be liable if the foster parents were exonerated from blame, though in any event Stocker LJ considered obiter that as a matter of causation the claim against the authority was bound to fail unless the injuries were deliberately inflicted. For a criticism of this observation see Douglas [1991] Fam Law 426–7. It is established that foster parents are not agents of the local authority: *S v Walsall Metropolitan Borough Council* [1986] 1 FLR 397, CA.
5 [1991] 2 FLR at 583–4; but cf Beldam LJ, who dissented.

The reluctance to impose too high a standard of care upon those looking after children should not be taken to imply that such carers will never be held to be negligent. An instructive decision is that of the New Zealand Court of Appeal in *McCallion v Dodd*.[6] In that case parents alighted from a bus at night with their two children and started to walk along the road in the dark. The mother, who was deaf and, as the father knew, was not wearing her hearing aid, took the plaintiff, aged four, by the hand and the father carried the baby in his arms. A car driven by the defendant hit the mother and the plaintiff, killing the mother and severely injuring the boy. The plaintiff sued the defendant in negligence, and the defendant claimed contribution from the father on the ground that he had also broken a duty of care owed to the plaintiff. The jury found that the defendant had been negligent and that the father had been negligent in permitting the boy to walk in the road on the wrong side and in the path of oncoming traffic. On appeal it was unanimously held that, even though the boy was under the immediate control of his mother, the father continued to be under a special duty because of her deafness. Turner and McCarthy JJ thought that no duty of care was created purely by the relationship of parent and child, but that it arose from the fact that the father had taken the boy onto the road,[7] although admittedly the relationship is evidence of the fact that the parent has undertaken the duty to supervise and control the child's conduct.[8] North P, however, thought that, although a stranger would be liable in negligence only if he had assumed or accepted the care of the child, parents 'at all times while present are under a legal duty to exercise reasonable care to protect their children from foreseeable dangers' and that duty cannot be shed by a parent who is present.[9] In most cases it will make little difference which view is correct, but the wider rule formulated by North P is to be preferred. Indeed, it is submitted that it should be even more broadly based. If a parent leaves a child in the care of one known to be unreliable and the child comes to harm as the result of the latter's irresponsibility, the parent should be civilly liable.

It was unanimously held that there was no question of the plaintiff's damages being reduced as the result of the father's negligence. The court followed *Oliver v Birmingham and Midland Omnibus Co Ltd*.[10] in which the plaintiff, aged four, was crossing a road with his grandfather, who was holding his hand, when an omnibus bore down on them. The grandfather let go of the plaintiff's hand and jumped to safety; the plaintiff was struck by the omnibus owing to the driver's negligence and was injured. It was held that his action for damages against the omnibus company was not affected by his grandfather's contributory negligence.

Information about the child

There is a growing jurisprudence both as to the right to obtain information about a child and as to whether parental responsibility carries with it the power to control publicity about a child. Nevertheless, as will be seen, it remains unclear both as to whether parental responsibility confers a right per se to the obtaining of information about the child and, insofar as it confers the power to control publicity, whether this

---

6 [1966] NZLR 710. See Mathieson (1967) 30 MLR 96. See also *S v Walsall Metropolitan Borough Council*, supra, where damages were awarded against foster parents in respect of injuries suffered by a child whilst in their care.

7 At 725 and 728.

8 Per McCarthy J at 729.

9 At 721.

10 [1933] 1 KB 35.

can be said be a separate incident of responsibility or simply another aspect of the power to protect the child. It is for these reasons that rights in respect of information about a child were not included in the 'list' of what parental responsibility comprises.[11] Nevertheless it is convenient to discuss the foregoing issues under the one umbrella heading. We begin by considering the power to obtain information about the child.

(a)   Obtaining information about the child

The common law is largely silent on a parent's position with regard to having access to information about the child. Case law has been concerned with the issue of disclosure of evidence in court proceedings, but in those cases the parents claimed a right to see the evidence on the basis of their alleged rights as parties to the litigation rather than as parents per se.[12] In *Re C (Disclosure)*,[13] however, a guardian ad litem successfully sought leave to withhold information gained in care proceedings and which the 16-year-old child concerned did not want to be revealed, from the mother who was party to the proceedings Johnson J commented[14] that quite apart from her entitlement as a party to the proceedings to know all the evidence 'her very status as . . . mother must give her some strong entitlement to information about her daughter.' On the facts, however, Johnson J held that, because he was satisfied that there was a high degree of probability that disclosure would be harmful to the child, the information should be withheld. This observation has led one commentary to say[15] that 'the status of parents gives some strong entitlement to information about the child but this does not override the right of a mature child to confidentiality'. Even if *Re C* can be relied upon to support the first part of this statement (and it remains to be seen whether it will be followed), it does not support the second part (though this may well be how the law might develop), for what it decided was that the *court* can override any such entitlement.

There is a specific statutory right under the Access to Health Records Act 1990 s 3(1)(cc)[16] for any person with parental responsibility for a child to apply to the holder of such records for access to them. However, although the general scheme of the Act[17] is to provide access in what might best be described as '*Gillick* type provisions',[18] s 4(2) provides that in the case of applications for access to children's records, the holder must first be satisfied either:

'(a)   that the patient has consented to the making of the application; or
(b)   that the patient is incapable of understanding the nature of the application and the giving of access would be in his best interests.'

Although neither the Access to Personal Files Act 1987 nor the Access to Personal Files (Social Services) Regulations 1989 specifically mention the parent's right of access to personal information about his child held by local authority social

---

11 See ante, pp 350–1.
12 See, for example, *Official Solicitor v K* [1965] AC 201, [1963] 3 All ER 191, HL, discussed ante at p 312.
13 [1996] 1 FLR 797.
14 Ibid at 803.
15 Cretney and Masson, op cit, at 622.
16 As added by the Children (Scotland) Act 1995 Sch 4, para 50(2).
17 See s 3(2), but note the exceptions under s 4 and s 5.
18 See ante, pp 313ff.

services, the Guidance[19] clearly states that, subject to a parental declaration that the child has authorised the applications or does not understand the nature of the request, information about the child can be sought by the parent. Parents[20] also have a right to receive, free of charge, school reports about their children.[1]

(b) Controlling publicity about the child

Until recently it was generally thought that questions concerning publicity about a child fell outside the ambit of parental responsibility.[2] It has become evident through case law, however, that the position is not so straightforward. There is, as Ward LJ pointed out in the leading case, *Re Z (A Minor) (Identification: Restrictions of Publicity)*,[3] a number of different situations in which the issue of publicity can be involved. At one end of the spectrum is the situation where some third party, such as the media, publishes without parental involvement information about the child and/or his family. It seems clear that in this type of instance the issue of publicity cannot be regarded as an aspect of parental responsibility.[4] At the other end of the spectrum is the publication of information that is properly regarded as being confidential to the child. That, as *Re Z* establishes, clearly involves an aspect of parental responsibility. In *Re Z* a mother sought the discharge of an injunction restraining publicity about her child so that a film could be broadcast publicising treatment of the child (who would have been clearly identified in the film) at a unit specialising in the treatment of children with special educational needs. In holding that the restraint of publicity in these circumstances was an aspect of parental responsibility, Ward LJ held that:[5]

'Placing this particular child at this institute is a proper discharge by this mother of her responsibility to secure her [ie the child's] medical and educational advancement. It then becomes her duty to respect the confidence of her treatment and/or education at the institute. *It is an incident of her parental responsibility to decide whether to preserve or to publish matters relating thereto which are confidential to the child.*' [Emphasis added.]

In between these two extremes is the type of situation that arose in *Re W (Wardship: Publicity)*[6] in which a father stood by and acquiesced in his teenage sons taking their story to the press.[7] The majority view[8] in that case was that it was at least 'arguable' that publishing information about a child was a 'non-parental

---

19 See LAC 89(2), Appendix, paras 40–45.
20 Including those with legal authority to act on the child's behalf, which presumably would include anyone with parental responsibility.
1 See the Education Act 1996 s 408 and the Education (Schools Records) Regulations 1989 (SI 1989/1261) reg 6.
2 See, for example, the comment in White, Carr and Lowe *The Children Act in Practice* (2nd edn, 1995), para 5.49.
3 [1997] Fam 1, sub nom *Re Z (a minor) (freedom of publication)* [1995] 4 All ER 961, CA, discussed also ante at p 329.
4 See eg *Re M and N (Minors) (Wardship: Publication of Information)* [1990] Fam 211, sub nom *Re M (Minors) (Wardship: Freedom of Speech)* [1990] 1 All ER 205, CA and *R v Central Independent Television plc* [1994] Fam 192, [1994] 3 All ER 641, CA, discussed ante, p 329.
5 Ibid at 26 and 980 respectively.
6 [1995] 2 FLR 466, CA.
7 An article was published in the *Independent* newspaper entitled 'Our fight to stay with Dad', together with a picture of the boys in silhouette from which they could nevertheless be identified.
8 Per Balcombe LJ, ibid at 472, with whom Waite LJ agreed.

activity' and, as such, was not an aspect of parental responsibility. However, Hobhouse LJ disagreed, commenting:[9]

> 'Whether or not an immature child should become involved with the media is something which clearly can affect the welfare of the child and falls within the scope of the proper discharge of parental duties . . . An immature child will often be unable to judge when it is truly to his advantage to invite the media into his life; he may not appreciate the distress and harm it may cause him and not be able to cope with it when it occurs. There is a risk of harm to the child which requires the exercise of parental responsibility in the interests of the child's welfare. A parent has the responsibility and the authority and power as part of his upbringing of the child to control, if needs be, his child's contact with the media.'

Although it must be stressed that it was a dissenting judgment, Hobhouse LJ's view seems a powerful one, and moreover is in line with the cases that establish[10] that giving leave to interview a child by solicitors acting for the father in criminal proceedings is an aspect of parental responsibility. It remains to be seen whether the law will be developed along these lines.

Even if the above-mentioned distinctions are more clearly established, it is by no means easy to predict into which category a particular situation might fall. What information, for example, will be thought to be confidential to the child and what freedom does the parent or those with parental responsibility have to publicise their own story?[11]

5.   LIABILITY FOR CHILDREN'S ACTS

Hitherto we have been concerned with what responsibility comprises, but another related issue is the potential liability of those having parental responsibility.

Contracts

It is established that a parent (and therefore any person with parental responsibility) will never be liable as such for any contract made by the child.[12] Such persons may, however, be liable on the ordinary principles of agency if they have authorised the child to make the contract or, in the case of unauthorised contracts, by estoppel or ratification.[13]

Torts

As in the case of contracts, neither parents nor others with parental responsibility will be liable as such for a child's tort unless they have authorised its commission.

---

9 Ibid at 476–7.
10 See *Re M (Care: Leave to Interview Child)* [1995] 1 FLR 825 and *Re F (Specific Issue: Child Interview)* [1995] 1 FLR 819, CA, discussed ante, p 353. It also seems to be favoured by Ward LJ in *Re Z*, ibid at 27 and 981 respectively, who also pointed out that in any case the majority's views were obiter.
11 In *Re H-S (Minors) (Protection of Identity)* [1994] 3 All ER 390 in which a transsexual father, with whom the children were now living, wanted to publicise the family story, Ward J seemed to think that the issue of publicity did not involve an aspect of parental responsibility, yet might not the children's care and upbringing be thought to be confidential? See also Moriarty 'Parents and Performing Children' [1996] CLJ 212–14.
12 *Mortimore v Wright* (1840) 6 M & W 482.
13 See generally works on the law of contract and agency.

A parent or someone with parental responsibility[14] may also be personally liable if he himself has been negligent by affording the child an opportunity of injuring another. This is a particular application of the tort of negligence, and the test is therefore: did the parent by his act or omission cause or permit his child to do an act which was foreseeably likely to harm the person injured and against which a reasonably prudent parent would have guarded? If so, he will be liable. In *Newton v Edgerley*[15] the defendant permitted his son aged 12 to have possession of a shotgun but did not instruct him how to handle it when others were present. Although the defendant had forbidden his son to use the gun when other children were near, he was nonetheless held personally liable in negligence for the injury to a child who was accidentally shot by his son, because he ought to have foreseen that his son would succumb to temptation and consequently should either have forbidden him to use the gun at all or have instructed him how to handle it in the presence of others. On the other hand, in *Donaldson v McNiven*[16] the defendant had let his son aged 13 buy an airgun. He forbade him to fire it outside the house (he was only permitted to fire it in the cellar) and the boy gave his word that he would not do so. One day, however, he took it outside, fired it and put out the plaintiff's eye. The father was held not to be liable, for he had taken all reasonable precautions to ensure that the gun was fired in a safe place and no damage would have resulted but for the son's disobedience and folly, which the defendant could not reasonably have foreseen.

Although these cases both deal with liability for permitting a child to have a dangerous toy or weapon, there is no reason why it should be restricted to this field. Thus, if an adult in charge of a young child on a busy road negligently lets him run into the traffic with the result that the driver of a car, in swerving to avoid the child, injures himself or another, that adult must on principle be liable for the damage.[17]

Crimes

At common law a parent was not liable for his child's crimes unless he himself was guilty of aiding and abetting. But the fact that a child's criminal propensities may be due to bad home influence or a lack of parental supervision has now been recognised by statute. If a court imposes a fine or costs or makes a compensation order for the commission of an offence by a child under the age of 17, it may order that these be paid by the child's parent or guardian (but not other persons even if they have parental responsibility) unless the latter cannot be found or the court is satisfied that he has not conduced to the commission of the offence by neglecting to exercise due care or control of the child.[18] Under the Crime and Disorder Act 1998, where a child under the age of 16 has been convicted of an offence and the court is satisfied that a

---

14 Note the difficulty of ever establishing negligence by a local authority in respect of a child in their care in the light of *X (Minors) v Bedfordshire County Council* [1995] 2 AC 633, [1995] 3 All 353, HL; but cf *W v Essex County Council* [1998] 3 All ER 111, CA, discussed post, p 608.

15 [1959] 3 All ER 337. See also *Bebee v Sales* (1916) 32 TLR 413.

16 [1952] 2 All ER 691, CA. See also *Jauffir v Akhbar* (1984) Times, 10 February; *Gorely v Codd* [1966] 3 All ER 891.

17 See *Carmarthenshire County Council v Lewis* [1955] AC 549, [1955] 1 All ER 565, HL, where a school authority was liable in similar circumstances for negligently letting a child run out of the school premises onto a road with the result that a lorry driver was killed. See further Waller 'Visiting the Sins of the Children' (1963–65) 4 Melbourne ULR 17.

18 Children and Young Persons Act 1933 s 55; Children and Young Persons Act 1969 s 3(6) and Schs 5 and 6; Administration of Justice Act 1970 Sch 11; Criminal Justice 1972 Sch 5. The court must exercise this power if the child is under 14. A local authority having parental responsibility for a child or young person who is in their care or who is being provided with accommodation by them is regarded as a parent or guardian for these purposes: Children and Young Persons Act 1933 s 55(5)

'parenting order' would help prevent a re-occurrence of the offending behaviour, it is obliged to make such a parenting order. A parent can subsequently be fined up to a maximum of £1,000 for failing to comply with the parenting order.

6.   LIABILITY FOR INTERFERENCE WITH PARENTS' AND CHILDREN'S RIGHTS

Criminal liability

Although the contrary view was once held,[19] there is apparently no common law offence of taking a child against his parents' will.[20] A number of statutory offences has been created, however. They are now principally contained in s 2 of the Child Abduction Act 1984 and ss 19–21 of the Sexual Offences Act 1956. Three distinct cases must be considered.

(a)   Children under the age of 16 years

Under the Child Abduction Act 1984 s 2, it is an offence for a person 'unconnected'[1] with the child to take or detain, without lawful authority or reasonable excuse, a child under the age of 16 so as to remove him from or to keep him out of the lawful control[2] of any person having or entitled to lawful control of him.[3] The offence may be committed in respect of a child of either sex, and regardless of whether the interference is permanent or temporary.[4] There is no need to prove force or fraud, so it can be an offence to persuade a child to leave his parents. Under this Act a person

---

(added by the Criminal Justice Act 1991 s 57(2)), reversing *Leeds City Council v West Yorkshire Metropolitan Police* [1983] 1 AC 29, [1982] 1 All ER 274, HL. See also *D (a minor)v DPP* [1995] 2 FLR 502 in which it was held to be a defence for the local authority (as for a parent) that they have done everything that could reasonably and properly be done to protect the public from the offender. Where a local authority allows a child to be under the charge or control of a parent or guardian, that person can be liable, though it is a question of fact whether the arrangements made between the parties constitute a transfer of control: *Leeds City Council v West Yorkshire Metropolitan Police*, supra. See Samuel (1982) 98 LQR 358. See also the Criminal Law Act 1977 s 36 (liability of parent or guardian for unpaid fine).

19   East *Pleas of the Crown*, 429–30.
20   The removal must be against the *child's* will: *R v Hale* [1974] QB 819, [1974] 1 All ER 1107. It is now established that a parent can be guilty of the common law offence of kidnapping his own child: *R v D* [1984] AC 778, [1984] 2 All ER 449, HL, and see Lowe 134 NLJ 995; and of unlawfully imprisoning his own child: *R v Rahman* (1985) 81 Cr App Rep 349; CA; see Khan [1986] Fam Law 69. For a discussion of the statutory offence under s 1 of the Child Abduction Act 1984, see post, p 480.
1   One who is not a parent or guardian and has no residence or custody order in his favour: s 1(2) of the Child Abduction Act 1984.
2   Lawful control is a question of fact and the concept of control may vary according to the person having the control, whether it be a parent, a schoolmaster or a nanny: *R v Mousir* [1987] Crim LR 561, CA. 'Control' does not have a spatial element and 'taking' does not involve detaining: *R v Leather* [1993] 2 FLR 770, [1993] Crim LR 516, CA – the accused was held rightly convicted for asking two children to help him look for a stolen bicycle since the children were deflected from what they would have otherwise been doing.
3   This provision implements with some modification the recommendations of the Criminal Law Revision Committee in their 14th Report, *Offences Against the Person*, 1980 Cmnd 7844, paras 239–49. The offence carries a maximum penalty of seven years' imprisonment: Child Abduction Act 1984 s 4.
4   There is no requirement of substantial interference, which ought to obviate the problems created by *R v Jones* [1973] Crim LR 621, infra n 8.

is regarded as 'taking' a child if he causes or induces the child to accompany him or any other person or causes the child to be taken.[5] It is a defence if the accused can show that he reasonably believed that the child was 16[6] or, in the case of an unmarried father, that he was or reasonably believed himself to be the child's father.[7]

(b) Girls under the age of 16 years

It is an offence for a person acting without lawful authority or excuse to take an unmarried girl (but not a boy) under the age of 16 out of the possession[8] of her parent or other person having the parental responsibility for or care of her against the latter's will.[9]

The age of the girl is a strict matter of fact and it is no defence that the accused believed her to be over 16.[10] Prosecutions are rare under this Act[11] since it is more likely that an accused will be charged with the offence of having unlawful sexual intercourse with a girl under the age of 16, contrary to s 6 of the 1956 Act.

(c) Girls under the age of 18 years

It is an offence to abduct any unmarried girl under the age of 18 with the intention that she should have unlawful sexual intercourse.[12] The offence is the same as the case of a girl under the age of 16 except that the prosecution must also prove the accused's intent,[13] and it is a defence that the accused had reasonable cause to believe that the girl was over the age of 18.[14]

Civil liability

(a) Damages for loss of services

The former tort of wrongfully depriving a parent of his child's services was abolished by the Administration of Justice Act 1982.[15]

(b) Damages for interference with parental responsibility

There is no known tort of interference with parental rights nor therefore with parental responsibility.[16] The leading case is *F v Wirral Metropolitan Borough*

5 Child Abduction Act 1984 s 3(a). There is a similar definition of 'detain' under s 3(c).
6 Ibid, s 2(3)(b).
7 Ibid, s 2(3)(a). But note there can be no such defence where a man abducts the wrong child by mistake: *R v Berry* [1996] 2 Cr App R 226, CA.
8 Therefore taking a girl for a walk will not constitute an offence under this section: *R v Jones*, supra.
9 Sexual Offences Act 1956 s 20 as amended by the Children Act 1989 Sch 12, para 12.
10 *R v Prince* (1875) LR 2 CCR 154.
11 For a more detailed discussion of this Act see the 8th edition of this work at pp 320–1.
12 Sexual Offences Act 1956 s19 as amended by the Children Act 1989 Sch 12, para 11. 'Unlawful' sexual intercourse means intercourse outside the marriage bond: *R v Chapman* [1959] 1 QB 100, [1958] 3 All ER 143, CCA. Hence no offence will be committed if the accused takes the girl away from her parents with the honest and bona fide intention of marrying her first.
13 *R v Henkers* (1886) 16 Cox CC 257.
14 Section 19(2).
15 Section 2(b). But cf *Donnelly v Joyce* [1974] QB 454, [1973] 3 All ER 475, CA on the question of damages in an action brought by the child. See also *Hunt v Severs* [1994] 2 AC 350, [1994] 2 All ER 385, HL.
16 Note, however, *C v K (Inherent Powers: Exclusion Order)* [1996] 2 FLR 506, in which Wall J pointed out that persons can be restrained from interfering with the exercise of parental responsibility and that the courts could use their powers to exclude a third party from the family home to protect the exercise of parental responsibility. For the court's power generally to exclude persons from the family home, see Chapter 6.

Council,[17] which involved a complaint by the parents that what was originally understood by them to be a short-term placement with foster parents, to which arrangement they had agreed, became a long-term arrangement, to which they had not agreed, and that this therefore constituted a wrongful interference with their rights. In support of this argument they prayed in aid Art 8 of the European Convention of Human Rights and the European Court's decision in *R v United Kingdom*[18] as recognising a right of consortium between parent and child as one of the 'fundamental elements of family life'. After an exhaustive review of the law the Court of Appeal unanimously concluded, in Purchas LJ's words that 'neither under the old common law, apart from the action per quod servitium amisit, nor under modern authority is there a parental right necessary to found a cause of action against a stranger upon which the common law would grant a remedy in damages.'

(c)   The Fatal Accidents Act 1976

Parents and children come within the category of dependants for the purposes of the Fatal Accidents Act 1976,[19] so that either may sue any person who has unlawfully caused the death of the other for compensation for pecuniary loss resulting from the death.[20]

C.   Who has parental responsibility[1]

1.   THE POSITION AT THE CHILD'S BIRTH

Married parents

Section 2(1) of the 1989 Act provides that where the father and mother of the child were married to each other at the time of the child's birth, they each have parental responsibility. The phrase 'married to each other at the time of the child's birth' has to be interpreted in accordance with s 1 of the Family Law Reform Act 1987.[2] Read with s 1(2)–(4) of the 1987 Act,[3] s 2(1) refers to a child whose parents were married to each other at any time during the period beginning with insemination or (where there was no insemination) conception and ending with birth, but also includes a child who:

(a)   is treated as legitimate by virtue of the Legitimacy Act 1976, s 1;[4]
(b)   is a legitimated person within the meaning of s 10 of the 1976 Act;[5]

---

17   [1991] Fam 69, [1991] 2 All ER 648, on which see Bainham 'Interfering with Parental Responsibility. A New Challenge for the Law of Torts?' (1990) 3 Jo of Child Law 3. See also *Re S (A Minor) (Parental Rights)* [1993] Fam Law 572.
18   [1988] 2 FLR 445, E Ct HR.
19   Section 1, as substituted by the Administration of Justice Act 1982 s 3(1).
20   See Chapter 19.
 1   See generally Lowe 'The Meaning and Allocation of Parental Responsibility – A Common Lawyer's Perspective' (1996) 11 Int Jo of Law, Policy and the Family 192 at 197ff.
 2   Section 2(3) of the Children Act 1989.
 3   Discussed ante, p 299. For a discussion of the legal position of the man whose wife makes a parental responsibility agreement with another man, see post, p 384.
 4   See ante, p 292.
 5   See ante, p 294.

(c) is an adopted child;[6] or

(d) is otherwise treated in law as legitimate.[7]

Stated simply, this means that both the father and the mother automatically each have parental responsibility in respect of their legitimate children.[8]

Unmarried parents

Where the father and mother of the child were not married to each other at the time of the child's birth (effectively meaning where the child is illegitimate) then s 2(2) of the Children Act 1989 provides that the mother but not the father has parental responsibility for the child.

Non-parents

Since only parents have automatic parental responsibility for a child, then normally no other person has such responsibility at the time of the child's birth.

2. ACQUISITION OF PARENTAL RESPONSIBILITY SUBSEQUENT TO THE CHILD'S BIRTH

Although parental responsibility is automatically assigned either to each of the married parents or to the unmarried mother at the time of the child's birth, the Act makes clear provision for others to acquire responsibility after the child's birth. In this respect a distinction needs to be made between unmarried fathers and others, the former having more extensive means than the latter to acquire parental responsibility.

Acquisition of parental responsibility by the unmarried father[9]

Although the unmarried father does not automatically have parental responsibility, as s 2(2)(b) states, he can subsequently acquire it in accordance with the provisions of the 1989 Act. He can acquire responsibility in the following ways:

(1) by subsequently marrying the child's mother;

(2) upon taking office as a formally appointed guardian of the child;

(3) by making a parental responsibility agreement with the mother;

(4) by obtaining a parental responsibility order;

(5) by obtaining a residence order, in which case a separate parental responsibility order *must* be made.

(a) Subsequent marriage

By subsequently marrying the mother, the father brings himself within s 2(1) of the 1989 Act and, provided the child is under the age of 18 at the time,[10] will

---

6 See post, p 675.

7 See ante, pp 291ff.

8 Which expression should also be taken to include children in respect of whom a parental order has been obtained under the Human Fertilisation and Embryology Act 1990 s 30, discussed ante at p 269.

9 See generally Doggett 'Unmarried fathers and section 4 before and after the Children Act 1989' (1992) 4 JCL 39.

10 It is therefore possible for a child to be legitimated by his parents' subsequent marriage, yet for the father not to have or to have had parental responsibility.

therefore automatically have parental responsibility. Because conferment of responsibility is an automatic consequence, although the Act does not expressly say so, the parents' subsequent marriage must be regarded as overriding any prior parental responsibility order or agreement. Furthermore, in such cases responsibility cannot then be ended by a court order other than adoption or a parental order.[11]

(b)   Guardianship

To become a guardian, the father must formally have been appointed as such by the child's mother, or by the court in accordance with the terms set out in s 5 of the 1989 Act (discussed in Chapter 11). Such an appointment can only take effect after the mother's death.

(c)   Parental responsibility agreements

Pursuant to s 4(1)(b) the father and mother may by a parental responsibility agreement provide for the father to have parental responsibility for the child. Such agreements, however, only have effect if they are made in prescribed form and recorded in the prescribed manner.[12] Both the prescribed form and manner of recording are provided for by the Parental Responsibility Agreement Regulations 1991.[13]

There are no prescribed age limits on those making agreements and there is no reason to suppose that valid agreements cannot be made by parents under the age of 18.[14] On the other hand, it seems unlikely that valid agreements can be made with respect to an unborn child.[15] By analogy with *Re S (Parental Responsibility: Jurisdiction)*[16] it would appear that the child concerned has neither to be habitually resident nor present in England and Wales.

This power to make parental responsibility agreements implements the recommendation of the Law Commission. As the Commission pointed out,[17] although the father could apply for what was then a parental rights and duties order under s 4 of the Family Law Reform Act 1987, the need to resort to judicial proceedings to obtain parental responsibility seemed 'unduly elaborate, expensive and unnecessary unless the child's mother object[ed]'. On the other hand, in recommending this new power, the Commission was also aware of the dangers of undue pressure being exerted upon mothers to make such agreements.[18]

---

11 Viz under s 30 of the Human Fertilisation and Embryology Act 1990. For the court's power to end agreements see post, p 386.
12 Section 4(2). However, as Masson and Morris *Children Act Manual* point out at 24, an informal agreement could still operate as a delegation of responsibility under s 2(9): discussed post at p 396.
13 SI 1991/1478, as amended by SI 1994/3157, discussed below.
14 An analogy should *not* be drawn with capacity to make contracts: parental responsibility agreements are probably best regarded as being agreements sui generis and not strict contracts, since it is difficult to see what consideration is given by the father when making the agreement.
15 Agreements may only be made in respect of a 'child' as defined by s 105(1). There is a presumption against interpreting such definitions as including children en ventre sa mere: see *Elliot v Joicey* [1935] AC 209, HL, and *R v Newham London Borough Council, ex p Dada* [1996] QB 507, [1995] 2 All ER 522, CA.
16 [1998] Fam Law 528, CA, discussed post, p 380. The rules set out in the Family Law Act 1986, discussed post, p 443, do not apply to s 4 orders or agreements.
17 Law Com No 172 para 2.18.
18 Indeed, it was because of the potential pressure, that the Law Commission did not originally recommend the power to make binding agreements – see Law Com No 118 *Illegitimacy* (1982) para 4.39.

Accordingly, they recommended a relatively formal procedure whereby, in order to be binding, the agreement would have to be in a prescribed form and checked by the county court, to ensure that the parents were fully aware of the importance and effect of what they were doing.[19] However, this recommendation was not initially implemented. Instead, all that was formally required was that the agreement in prescribed form should be signed by both parents and witnesses and subsequently filed in the Principal Registry of the Family Division. However, as the Children Act Advisory Committee observed,[20] this highly informal scheme had not been without its difficulties. In some cases agreements had apparently been filed with the mother's signature forged. Accordingly, a new procedure was introduced in 1995[1] under which applicants must take their completed form to a local family proceedings court or county court or to the Principal Registry, where a justice of the peace, a justices' clerk or court officer authorised by a judge to administer oaths will witness the parents' signature and sign the certificate of the witness. As before, the duly completed form, together with two copies, should then be taken or posted to the Principal Registry.[2] Sealed copies will be returned to the mother and father,[3] while the record is open to public inspection. No fee is charged to the parents for the formal recording of their agreement, though a charge is payable by those wishing to inspect the record.[4]

Notwithstanding the recent changes, the formalities for making binding parental responsibility agreements remain perfunctory. In particular, there is no investigation of whether the agreement is in the child's best interests nor of why the parents are entering into it. Indeed there is no effective check on whether, for example, the man is the father of the child concerned. Notes attached to the Agreement Form explain that the agreement will not take effect until the form has been received and recorded at the Principal Registry but that, once it has, it can only be brought to an end by a court order or upon the child reaching 18. It also warns: 'The making of this agreement will affect the legal position of mother and father. You should both seek legal advice before you make the Agreement.'

Whether such warnings, together with the need to take the agreement to court, are sufficient to allay the fears, expressed both by the Law Commission and during the passage of the Bill,[5] that mothers may be bullied into conferring rights upon the fathers at a time when they are particularly vulnerable to pressure, remains to be seen.[6] Perhaps not surprisingly, given the new requirement of having to have the agreement witnessed in the courts, following a steady rise in the number of agreements from 1992 to 1994, the number fell in 1995.[7]

---

19 Which was argued to be unworkable anyway by Cretney: see 'Defining the Limits of State Intervention: The Child and the Courts' in *Children and the Law* (ed Freestone) at pp 65–6.
20 In their Report 1992/93, p 13.
1 See the Parental Responsibility Agreement Regulations 1991 SI 1994/3157.
2 Art 3(1).
3 Art 3(2).
4 Art 3(3).
5 See particularly Lord Banks, 502 HL Official Report (5th series) cols 1180–82 and 503 HL Official Report col 1319.
6 In *Re W (A Minor) (Residence Order)* [1992] 2 FLR 332, CA, a mother did assert that she had signed an agreement under pressure, though this was under the old procedure.
7 According to the CAAC Report 1993–94 (Appendix 1) 2941 agreements were registered in 1992, 4,411 in 1993 and 'around' 5,280 in 1994. In 1995, the numbers fell 36% to an 'estimated' 3,455 (CAAC Report 1994/1995 Appendix 1). In 1996, however, the number of agreements rose 4% to an estimated 3,590 (CAAC Final Report 1997, Appendix 2).

(d)   Parental responsibility orders

Under s 4(1)(a) of the 1989 Act the court may, upon the application of an unmarried father (ie not upon its own motion), order that he shall have parental responsibility for the child. Applications may be made to the High Court, county court or the family proceedings court.[8] If the applicant's paternity is in doubt and a fortiori if it is disputed, it will have to be proved before the action may proceed.[9] An application may be made only in respect of a 'child', that is a person under the age of 18.[10] Applications under s 4 are sometimes referred to as free-standing applications to distinguish them from residence order applications by unmarried fathers, in which s 4 orders are made as an ancillary but automatic consequence of making the residence order.[11] It has been held by the Court of Appeal that the child need not be habitually resident nor present in England and Wales before a s 4 order can be made,[12] though presumably the applicant must have some appropriate connection with the jurisdiction.

It is accepted that in deciding whether or not to make a parental responsibility order the court must, in line with the general principles of the Act, treat the child's welfare as its paramount consideration[13] and be satisfied that making the order would be better for the child than making no order at all.[14]

The restriction under s 9(6) which prevents the court from making a s 8 order in respect of a child aged 16 or over save in 'exceptional circumstances'[15] does not apply to the making of s 4 orders. Similarly, there is no enjoinder to have regard to the check-list set out by s 1(3),[16] though there is nothing to prevent the court from considering them if it so wishes. This means that the court is not obliged to have regard to older children's wishes: yet, as has been pointed out,[17] given that, if the

---

8   Section 92(7). In practice the majority of applications are made to the family proceedings courts; nearly 70% of the 3,332 orders made in 1992/93 were made by magistrates – CAAC Report 1992/93, Appendix 1, p 93.

9   See *Re F (A Minor) (Blood Tests: Parental Rights)* [1993] Fam 314, [1993] 3 All ER 596, CA.

10   Section 105(1). For the reasons discussed above at p 378 n 15 it is not thought orders can be made in respect of unborn children.

11   Section 12(1). As Waite J commented in *Re CB (A Minor) (Parental Responsibility Order)* [1993] 1 FLR 920 at 929, '. . . there is an unusual duality in the character of a parental responsibility order: it is on the one hand sufficiently ancillary by nature to pass automatically to a natural father without inquiry of any kind when a residence order is made in his favour; and, on the other hand, sufficiently independent, when severed from the context of a residence order, to require detailed consideration upon its merits as a free-standing remedy in its own right.'

12   *Re S (Parental responsibility: Jurisdiction)* [1998] Fam Law 528, relying on the fact that the jurisdictional rules set out under the Family Law Act 1986 do not expressly apply to s 4 orders. In fact the court ruled that before jurisdiction should be exercised the child's existence needed to be proved.

13   Pursuant to s 1(1), discussed ante at pp 324ff; *Re H (Parental Responsibility)* [1998] 1 FLR 855, CA at 859 per Butler-Sloss LJ. But note *Re G (A Minor) (Parental Responsibility Order)* [1994] 1 FLR 504 at 508 in which Balcombe LJ seemed not to have regarded as beyond argument that an application for a parental responsibility order is not a question relating to the child's upbringing and is therefore not governed by s 1(1). But for convincing arguments that such an order does relate to the child's upbringing, see Hershman at [1994] Fam Law 650.

14   Pursuant to s 1(5), discussed post at p 340. However, in White, Carr and Lowe *The Children Act in Practice* (2nd edn) at para 3.43, n 2 it is pointed out that it could be argued that s 1(5) does not apply, since a parental responsibility order relates to the parent and not the child. The authors considered, however, that such an argument was likely to be rejected.

15   Discussed post, p 429.

16   Discussed ante, pp 336ff.

17   By Doggett, op cit at p 41. See also White, Carr and Lowe, op cit at para 3.43 and Clarke Hall and Morrison on *Children* Vol 1, para 1[103].

father applies instead for a residence order which is opposed by the mother, the court must have regard to the child's wishes, it is difficult to see why the check list should not apply at the very least to contested s 4 applications. Furthermore, since a child with sufficient understanding may, with leave, apply to have the order ended[18] it is logical to assume that such a child's view may be relevant to deciding whether to make the order in the first place.[19]

According to *Re H (Minors) (Local Authority: Parental Rights) (No 3)*[20] in deciding whether or not to make an order the following factors will undoubtedly be material, namely:

> '(1) the degree of commitment which the father has shown towards the child; (2) the degree of attachment which exists between the father and the child; (3) the reasons of the father for applying for the order.'[1]

In *Re C (Minors)*[2] Mustill LJ stated the basic test to be:

> '. . . was the association between the parties sufficiently enduring; and has the father by his conduct during and since the application shown sufficient commitment to the children, to justify giving the father a legal status equivalent to that which he would have enjoyed if the parties had married?'

For some time *Re H* was considered to be the leading case and it became established, for instance, that the so-called '*Re H*' considerations should be expressly considered in all free-standing s 4 applications[3] and furthermore, provided a concerned though absent father fulfils the '*Re H* test', then 'prima facie it would be for the welfare of the child that such an order is made.[4] However, in *Re H (Parental Responsibility)*[5] the Court of Appeal signalled an important shift of view. Butler-Sloss LJ, in particular, disapproved of the notion that case law had created a presumption that a devoted father will ordinarily be granted an order. As she put it, the '*Re H* requirements' are an important starting point in the making of a responsibility order, but they are not the only factors, and even if they are satisfied the court has an overarching duty to apply the paramountcy test and determine whether the making of an order is for the child's welfare. Notwithstanding this shift it is evident that the courts are still disposed to grant orders to deserving fathers. As Ward LJ put it in *Re C and V (minors) (contact and parental responsibility)*,[6] because it is desirable for the sake of a child's self-esteem to grow up, wherever possible, having a favourable and positive image of an absent parent, then applying the paramountcy test: 'wherever possible, the law should confer on a concerned father that stamp of approval because he has shown himself willing and anxious to pick up the responsibility of fatherhood and not to deny or avoid it'.

Ward LJ made a similar comment in his earlier decision in *Re S (Parental*

18 Section 4(3)(b) and (4), discussed post, p 387.
19 In practice it is not unusual to ask for a welfare report, when no doubt the child's view can be brought to the court's notice.
20 [1991] Fam 151 at 158, sub nom *Re H (minors) (adoption: putative father's rights) (No 3)* [1991] 2 All ER 185, CA at 189.
 1 The basic application form for a parental responsibility order specifically asks the applicant to state his reasons for making the application: Family Proceedings Rules 1991, Form C 1.
 2 [1992] 2 All ER 86 at 93.
 3 *S v R (Parental Responsibility)* [1993] 1 FCR 331, per Thorpe J.
 4 Per Balcombe LJ in *Re G (A Minor) (Parental Responsibility Order)* [1994] 1 FLR 504 at 508. See also his similar comments in *Re E (Parental Responsibility: Blood Tests)* [1995] 1 FLR 392 at 398.
 5 [1998] 1 FLR 855, CA.
 6 [1998] 1 FCR 52 at 57.

Responsibility).[7] In that case, after the breakdown of his relationship with the mother, an unmarried father was convicted of possession of obscene literature (comprising indecent photographs of children). Because of this the mother severed contact between the father and his daughter but resumed it when the child's resulting distress and deterioration of her behaviour became apparent. That contact later developed into unsupervised staying contact. Notwithstanding these developments the father applied for a parental responsibility order, which the mother vigorously opposed upon the basis of the father's conviction and his unreliability about money. At first instance the father's application was rejected primarily because it would 'give him scope to interfere in many different ways with the present arrangements for the child'. This decision was, however, reversed on appeal, Ward J stressing[8] that objecting to the order because of the rights and power that it would confer demonstrated 'a most unfortunate failure to appreciate the significant change that the Act has brought about where the emphasis is to move away from rights and to concentrate on responsibilities' His Lordship continued:

> 'It is wrong to place undue and therefore false emphasis on the rights and duties and the powers comprised in "parental responsibility" and not to concentrate on the fact that what is at issue is conferring upon a committed father the status of parenthood for which nature has already ordained that he must bear responsibility.'

He added that it seemed to him to be important to ensure that wherever possible:

> '. . . the law confers upon a committed father that stamp of approval, lest the child grow up with some belief that he is in some way disqualified from fulfilling his role and that the reason for the disqualification is something inherent which will be inherited by the child, making her struggle to find her own identity all the more fraught.'

In the subsequent decision, *Re S (Parental Responsibility)*[9] Sir Stephen Brown P again emphasised that a s 4 order does not affect the day-to-day care of children,[10] but does provide status for the father.

Consistent with the emphasis upon the consequent status conferred by a s 4 order it has been held that orders can be made notwithstanding that the child is in local authority care or is about to be freed for adoption,[11] nor is the question of enforcement necessarily decisive.[12] In *Re H (A Minor) (Contact and Parental Responsibility)*,[13] an order was made even though the father had been denied a contact order, and indeed in *Re C and V (minors) (contact and parental responsibility)*[14] the Court of Appeal stressed that applications for contact and parental responsibility were to be treated as wholly separate applications, so that

---

7   [1995] 2 FLR 648, CA, on which see Eekelaar 'Parental Responsibility – A New Legal Status?' (1996) 112 LQR 233.

8   Ibid at 657.

9   [1995] 2 FLR 648, CA.

10 For the effects of a s 4 order see below at p 384.

11 See respectively *D v Hereford and Worcester County Council* [1991] Fam 14, [1991] 2 All ER 177 and *Re H (Minors) (Local Authority: Parental Rights) (No 3)* supra; freeing for adoption is discussed post at p 650. But cf *W v Ealing London Borough Council* [1993] 2 FLR 788, CA, in which the application was dismissed because the children were being prepared for a termination of contact with their parents pending their introduction to prospective adopters, and to change that would have left them in limbo and confused.

12 *Re C (Minors)*, supra.

13 [1993] 1 FLR 484, CA.

14 Supra.

the dismissal of the former did not necessarily mean that the latter should also be dismissed. It has also been held[15] that the court should not use its power to make a parental responsibility order as a weapon to force a father to make maintenance payments for the upkeep of his child.

In all cases, however, the test remains whether it is for the child's welfare that an order be made. Lack of insight into a daughter's needs and an inability to get on with social workers is not reason in itself to refuse an order,[16] nor similarly is it justifiable to base a refusal solely on the acrimony between the parents,[17] nor because of transsexuality.[18]

Notwithstanding that in the majority of reported cases parental responsibility orders have been granted, it is important to stress, particularly in the light of the caution signalled by the Court of Appeal in *Re H (Parental Responsibility)*,[19] that not all applications succeed. In *Re H* itself the order was refused because the father had been found to have injured his son in circumstances indicating deliberate cruelty and possibly sadism. In *Re P (Parental Responsibility)*[20] the application was refused because of the father's inappropriate motives, namely, to undermine the mother's care for the child. In *Re T (A Minor) (Parental Responsibility)*[1] an order was refused where the father had treated the mother with hatred and violence, showing no regard for the child's welfare. In *Re P (Parental Responsibility)*[2] the Court of Appeal declined to interfere with a refusal to make an order based in part on the father's criminal conduct, holding that a court was entitled to take into account, as relevant but not conclusive, factors such as that the father was in prison and the circumstances of the criminal conduct for which the sentence was imposed. Notwithstanding the relative paucity of reported cases of orders being refused, the statistics show that in practice refusals are perhaps a little less unusual than might be supposed.[3]

One type of case still to be tested is the position of the unmarried father who has never seen his child but who nevertheless wishes to establish a relationship. On the face of it such an applicant cannot even fulfil the so-called '*Re H* test' since he will not be able to demonstrate any degree of attachment between himself and the child. On the other hand, it may well be that the fact that the father is concerned enough to apply, when coupled with the court's recognition of the child's right to know his or her father's identity and to have some convincing relationship with him,[4] would be enough to persuade the court to grant the order, provided at any rate that the applicant is not violent. Once it is found to be in the child's interests

---

15 *Re H (Parental Responsibility: Maintenance)* [1996] 1 FLR 867, CA.
16 *Re G (A Minor) Parental Responsibility Order)*, supra.
17 *Re P (A Minor) (Parental Responsibility Order)* [1994] 1 FLR 578.
18 *Re L (Contact: Transsexual Application)* [1995] 2 FLR 438, in which a 'father' who to outward appearances was a woman was granted a s 4 order.
19 [1998] 1 FLR 855, CA.
20 [1998] 2 FLR 96, CA.
 1 [1993] 2 FLR 450, CA. See also *Re P (Terminating Parental Responsibility)* [1995] 1 FLR 1048 where an agreement was terminated on the grounds of the father's violence and Ward J's comment in *D v Hereford and Worcester County Council* [1991] Fam 14 at 22, [1991] 2 All ER 177 at 183.
 2 [1997] 2 FLR 722, CA. But cf *Re S (Parental Responsibility)* [1995] 2 FLR 648, discussed above at p 382.
 3 In 1996, for example, out of 8,653 disposals, 559 (6%) were refused: *Judicial Statistics 1996*, Table 5.3.
 4 See eg *Re H (Paternity: Blood Test)* [1996] 2 FLR 65, CA, and *Re R (A Minor) (Contact)* [1993] 2 FLR 762, CA which respectively prayed in aid Arts 7(1) and 9(1) of the UN Convention on the Rights of the Child.

that both parents should have parental responsibility, this should be reflected by the making of a s 4 order and not by making 'no order' pursuant to s 1(5).[5]

(e)   Residence orders

If a court grants an unmarried father who does not otherwise have parental responsibility[6] a residence order (but not any other s 8 order),[7] then by s 12(1) the court is also bound to make a *separate* s 4 order. The importance of the s 4 order being made separately is that it will not automatically come to an end if the residence order is ended, but will require an express order ending it, if the child is still a minor.

(f)   The effect of parental responsibility orders and agreements

The effect of a court order or a properly recorded agreement is the same, namely it confers parental responsibility upon the unmarried father. In most cases he will share responsibility jointly with the mother or, if the mother is dead, with any formally appointed guardian. He could also share responsibility with some other person in whose favour a residence order has been made. The legal position of a husband whose wife makes a parental responsibility agreement with another man is not clear. Prima facie that agreement confers responsibility on that other man, yet because of the presumption of paternity[8] the woman's husband could also be regarded as having responsibility. Of course, once the issue is before the court the conundrum can be solved by a finding of paternity, but what is the position before that? Although there is no objection in principle to two men having parental responsibility in relation to a child, because in this situation only one man can actually be the child's father, only one of them can be regarded as having responsibility. Although the making of an agreement is some evidence that the husband might not be the father, it seems unlikely that the court would regard an agreement alone as sufficient to rebut the presumption of the husband's paternity. One cannot shut one's eyes to the possibility that both the mother and the other man might know that the husband is or could be the father, but want to exclude him if the other man is prepared to accept the child is his. In many cases, however, there is likely to be other evidence, for example that before the birth the woman had left her husband to live with the other man.[9]

Although in general terms it is correct to say[10] that an unmarried father with parental responsibility is in the same legal position with regard to the child as if he had married the mother, the effect should be neither overestimated nor underestimated. Even without responsibility the father is regarded as a 'parent' for the purposes of the Children Act 1989.[11] He therefore has, for example, the right to apply to the court for a s 8 order[12] and is entitled to reasonable contact with a child in local authority care.[13] Furthermore, the lack of parental responsibility, does not

---

5 Per Wilson J in *Re P (A Minor) (Parental Responsibility Order)* [1994] 1 FLR 578. In 1996 according to the *Judicial Statistics*, Table 5.3, 313 applications (or just under 4% of all disposals) ended in a 'no order'. For discussion of the application of s 1(5), see ante, p 340.
6 Where he has previously made a parental responsibility agreement, for example.
7 Section 8 orders are discussed in Chapter 12.
8 Discussed ante, pp 272ff.
9 It is also relevant to know who is registered as the father.
10 See eg Department of Health's *Guidance and Regulations*, Vol 1, 'Court Orders', para 2.5.
11 See ante, p 299.
12 Under s 10(4), discussed post, p 432.
13 Under s 34, discussed post, p 581.

mean that such fathers have no statutory duty to maintain their children.[14] On the other hand, conferring parental responsibility upon unmarried fathers does not alter the status of the child. Hence the child will still not take British citizenship through the father, nor will he be able to succeed to a title of honour through his parents.[15] Furthermore, as the courts have stressed,[16] the granting of a s 4 order does not per se entitle the father to interfere with the day-to-day running of affairs affecting the child, at any rate whilst the child is living with another carer.[17]

Notwithstanding the courts' entreaties not to concentrate on the rights conferred by a s 4 order, it is nevertheless instructive to enquire how the legal position of an unmarried father changes upon being vested with parental responsibility. The principal effects are:

(1) he becomes a 'parent' for the purposes of the adoption legislation and can therefore withhold his agreement to a proposed adoption or an order freeing the child for adoption;[18]
(2) he becomes entitled to remove his child (under the age of 16) from local authority accommodation,[19] and, if he is willing and able to provide accommodation or to arrange for accommodation to be provided for his child, may object to his child being accommodated in the first place;[20]
(3) he can appoint a guardian;[1]
(4) he can give a valid consent to his child's medical treatment[2] and require full medical details from the child's medical practitioner;[3]
(5) he has the power to consent to his child's marriage;[4]
(6) he is empowered to express a preference as to the school at which he wishes his child's education to be provided; to initiate and be involved in the procedure for statementing of a child with special needs; to withdraw his child from sex education in local education authority or grant maintained schools and to receive full comprehensive reports from his child's school;[5]
(7) the mother will need to obtain his consent to take the child (under the age of 16) outside the United Kingdom;[6]
(8) he will be entitled to sign passport applications and to oppose the granting of a passport for his child;[7]

---

14 On the contrary, unmarried fathers can be 'absent parents' for the purposes of the Child Support Act 1991: see post, p 730. For this reason Waite J must be regarded as being mistaken when he commented in *Re C (Minors) (Parental Rights)* [1992] 1 FLR 1 at 9 that *upon* being vested with parental responsibility the father assumes 'an immediately enforceable burden' to maintain the child.
15 Ante at p 297.
16 *Re S (A Minor) (Parental Responsibility)* [1995] 3 FCR 564; *Re A (A Minor) (Parental Responsibility)* [1996] 1 FCR 562; *Re P (A Minor) (Parental Responsibility Order)* [1994] 1 FLR 578.
17 And note *Re P (Parental Responsibility)* [1998] 2 FLR 96, CA, where the motivation to undermine the mother's care was held to justify refusing to make an order in favour of a devoted father.
18 Adoption Act 1976 s 72(1): see post, p 633.
19 Children Act 1989 s 20(8), discussed post at p 526.
20 Ibid, s 20(7); discussed post at p 526.
1 Section 5(3).
2 See ante, p 357.
3 For instance, under the Access to Health Records Act 1990: see ante, p 370. See also *Re H (A Minor) (Shared Residence)* [1994] 1 FLR 717, CA.
4 Marriage Act 1949 s 3(1A)(a)(i): see ante, p 37.
5 Under the Education Act 1996: see ante, p 353.
6 Child Abduction Act 1984 s 1(3)(a)(ii): see ante, pp 361–2.
7 See the Guidance issued by the UK Passport Agency reproduced at [1994] Fam Law 651, discussed ante at p 361.

(9) he will be considered to have 'rights of custody' for the purposes of the Hague convention on international child abduction.[8]

Notwithstanding that a s 4 order undoubtedly strengthens the unmarried father's legal position in relation to his child, it is important to stress that the mother loses relatively little by the making of the order. She is under no general obligation (but see below) to consult the father about the child's upbringing[9] and, so long as the child is living with her, the father has no right to interfere with the day-to-day management of the child's life, and indeed any attempt or threat to do so can be controlled by a s 8 order.[10] What the mother undoubtedly loses is the *unilateral* right to remove the child from the UK[11] and, more controversially, it may be that she needs to consult the father about a change of school,[12] or surname.[13] She also loses the ability to appoint a guardian to take effect upon her death, unless she has a residence order in her favour.[14]

The fact that a s 4 order does not entitle an unmarried father to intermeddle in the day-to-day management of the child prompts the question as to why applications are made. Indeed the judiciary themselves have sometimes commented that the growing number of applications is based on a fundamental misunderstanding of the nature of the order.[15] For some, however, the judicial recognition of what has been described[16] as the exercise of their 'social parenthood' will undoubtedly be important. Whatever the reasons, the numbers of such orders have steadily increased, from 2,762 in 1992 to 5,587 in 1996,[17] though, as has also been pointed out,[18] such figures only represent a tiny proportion of the overall number of unmarried fathers.

(g)   Ending parental responsibility orders or agreements

Parental responsibility orders and agreements remain effective notwithstanding that the couple live together or subsequently separate. They will, however, automatically end once the child attains his majority[19] and, as we have discussed,[20] if the father subsequently marries the mother during the child's minority. Apart from these instances parental responsibility may be brought to an end only upon a

---

8 He will have locus standi to seek the child's return under the Hague Convention: see the discussion post, pp 493ff.
9 By reason of s 2(7), discussed further post at p 395.
10 See eg Ward LJ's comments in *Re S (Parental Responsibility)* [1995] 2 FLR 648 at 657.
11 Under s 1 of the Child Abduction Act 1984 she will require the father's consent to leave the country.
12 See *Re G (A Minor) (Parental Responsibility: Education)* [1994] 2 FLR 964, CA, discussed post at pp 395–6.
13 See *Re PC (Change of Surname)* [1997] 2 FLR 730, discussed ante, p 362.
14 Children Act 1989 s 5(7), discussed post, p 403.
15 See eg *Re S (Parental Responsibility)*, supra, per Ward LJ who said that s 4 applications 'have become one of those little growth areas born of misunderstanding', and *Re S (A Minor) (Parental Responsibility)* [1995] 3 FCR 564, in which Sir Stephen Brown P said that was 'a fundamental misunderstanding of the nature of a parental responsibility order.'
16 Eekelaar 'Parental Responsibility – A New Legal Status' (1996) 112 LQR 233 at 235.
17 See *Judicial Statistics 1996*, Table 5.3.
18 Butler, Douglas, Lowe, Noakes and Pithouse 'The Children Act 1989 and the unmarried father' (1993) 5 *Journal of Child Law* 157. The authors also questioned whether parents were being advised about making parental responsibility *agreements*. See also the Lord Chancellor's Consultation Paper on *The Law of Parental Responsibility for Unmarried Fathers*, at para 52.
19 Children Act 1989 s 91(7) and (8).
20 Ante at p 378.

court order to that effect. Such an order may be made upon the application (ie not of the court's own motion) of:

(1) any person who has parental responsibility for the child (this will include the father himself) or,
(2) with leave of the court, the child himself.[1]

In the latter case, the court may grant leave only if it is satisfied that the child has sufficient understanding to make the proposed application.[2] The court may not end a s 4 order while a residence order in favour of the unmarried father remains in force.[3]

In deciding whether to end a s 4 order or agreement, the court must regard the child's welfare as its paramount consideration and be satisfied that discharging the order is better than making no order at all.[4] Nevertheless, it is submitted that the court should be slow to make such an order, particularly when it made a s 4 order in the first place. The position might be different following an agreement where, for example, it could be shown that the mother had been subjected to undue pressure to sign. It should be borne in mind that parental responsibility vested in the married father may be ended only upon the child's adoption, so that the ending of a residence order in the father's favour should not automatically mean that parental responsibility should also come to an end. In any event, a separate order expressly ending the s 4 order will be required to end the father's parental responsibility. In *Re P (Terminating Parental Responsibility)*,[5] Singer J emphasised that the ability to apply to terminate parental responsibility should not be used as a weapon by the dissatisfied mother of a non-marital child. Nevertheless, on the facts responsibility was terminated, the father having been responsible for inflicting appalling injuries on the child.

3.   ACQUISITION OF PARENTAL RESPONSIBILITY BY NON-PARENTS

Those who are not parents do not have parental responsibility automatically, but they can acquire it. For example, any person taking office as a guardian has parental responsibility for the child concerned.[6] Similarly any person (who is not a parent or guardian) in whose favour a residence order has been made has parental responsibility for the duration of the order,[7] though this will not entitle him to consent to an order freeing the child for adoption, or an adoption order, nor may he appoint a guardian.[8] An individual also acquires parental responsibility upon being granted an emergency protection order, though this will only entitle him to take 'such action in meeting his responsibility for the child as is reasonably

---

1 Section 4(3).
2 Section 4(4). For a similar requirement when seeking leave to apply for a s 8 order, see s 10(8), discussed below at p 437.
3 Section 11(4). Read literally, this would allow a court to end a s 4 agreement even though a residence order in favour of the father is still in force, but it seems inconceivable that a court would do so.
4 Pursuant to s 1(1) and (5); and see *Re P (Terminating Parental Responsibility)* [1995] 1 FLR 1048.
5 Supra; cf *Re G (Child Case: Parental Involvement)* [1996] 1 FLR 857, CA in which an appeal against a revocation of a parental responsibility agreement was successful.
6 Section 5(6).
7 Section 12(2).
8 Section 12(3).

required to safeguard or promote the welfare of the child (having regard in particular to the duration of the order)'.[9]

Local authorities can also acquire parental responsibility. They will do so on the making of a care order,[10] when they will share responsibility with any parent or guardian. If they are satisfied that it is necessary to do so to safeguard or promote the child's welfare, however, they may determine the extent to which a parent or guardian of the child may meet his parental responsibility for him.[11] In no event, however, will a local authority be empowered to change the child's religion, to consent to an order freeing him for adoption, to agree to his adoption, or to appoint a guardian.[12] Local authorities also acquire parental responsibility to the same limited extent as individuals upon being granted an emergency protection order.

4.   SHOULD THE ALLOCATION OF PARENTAL RESPONSIBILITY BE MODIFIED?

Unmarried fathers[13]

Parental responsibility is not automatically vested in any person other than each married parent and the unmarried mother. Should it be? One candidate is the unmarried father, particularly if he is living with the mother in a stable union and is sharing the upbringing of the child. As we have seen,[14] the Law Commission at one stage proposed abolishing the concept of illegitimacy altogether, with the consequence that all fathers would be in the same legal position with regard to their child.[15] That suggestion, however, met with little favour[16] and it was not recommended. The Law Commission also rejected any compromise solution by which automatic responsibility could be vested in so-called 'meritorious' fathers, principally because no adequate definition of such men could be found. The system operating in New Zealand,[17] under which parental rights are vested jointly in both parents provided that they are living together as man and wife at the time of the child's birth, was rejected inter alia because it was both arbitrary and difficult to operate and it was thought it would not necessarily promote the welfare of children.[18] Instead the Law Commission favoured the proposal first implemented in the Family Law Reform Act 1987 and now enacted in the Children Act 1989 that unmarried fathers should be able to apply to a court to obtain full parental status.

---

9   Children Act 1989 s 44(4)(c) and s 44(5)(b). Emergency protection orders are discussed post at pp 590ff.

10   Section 33(3)(a). The effect of care orders is discussed post, pp 563ff.

11   Section 33(3)(b) and (4).

12   Section 33(6).

13   See generally Lowe 'The Meaning and Allocation of Parental Responsibility – A Common Lawyer's Perspective' (1997) 11 Int Jo of Law, Policy and the Family 192 at 198ff and the Lord Chancellor's Consultation Paper (1998) on *The Law on Parental Responsibility for Unmarried Fathers.*

14   Ante, pp 297–8.

15   Working Paper No 74 *Illegitimacy.*

16   For a summary of the criticisms see Law Commission No 118 (1st Report on *Illegitimacy*) para 4.26; Hayes (1980) 43 MLR 299 and Scot Law Com Discussion Paper No 88 *Parental Responsibilities and Rights, Guardianship and Administration of Children's Property* (1990) para 2.23.

17   Under the Guardianship Act 1968 (as amended) s 6.

18   See Law Com No 118 paras 4.23–4.36. Other suggestions, eg that parental rights should be based on voluntary acknowledgement of paternity, were also rejected: see paras 4.37–4.40.

In their later review of the law the Commission considered[19] that the issue of giving unmarried fathers automatic parental status had been fully canvassed and rejected though, as we have seen, their new recommendation, since implemented by the 1989 Act, was that unmarried fathers and mothers should be able to make binding agreements conferring parental responsibility on fathers.

Initially, the Scottish Law Commission similarly rejected the idea of conferring an automatic status on the unmarried father,[20] but unlike its English counterpart it decided to examine the issue afresh when considering further reform of child law. Addressing the common arguments against giving automatic parental responsibility to unmarried fathers, the Commission observed:[1]

1. It was not self evident that where a child is born as a result of a casual liaison the unmarried father should not have parental responsibility. As they put it: 'some fathers . . . will be uninterested but that is no reason for the law to encourage and reinforce an irresponsible attitude'.

2. The argument that conferring automatic parental responsibility on the unmarried father would cause offence to mothers struggling to bring up their children without support from the fathers was not thought to be a weighty argument for denying responsibility to all unmarried fathers for, as they observed: 'the important point in all these cases is that it is not the feelings of one parent in a certain type of situation that should determine the content of the law but the general interests of children and responsible parents.'

3. The Commission dismissed the argument that there might be a risk of interference and harassment by the father if he had automatic responsibility,[2] essentially because this was a parent-centred rather than a child-centred argument. In the Commission's view it 'seems unjustifiable to have what is in effect a presumption that any involvement by an unmarried father is going to be contrary to the child's best interests.' In any event the Commission did not believe that the risk of harassment would be increased by the proposed change of law.

4. The argument that it is undesirable to involve all unmarried fathers in care and adoption proceedings was countered by pointing out that it could equally be said to be a grave defect that a man who has been the social father to the child should have no legal position in such matters merely because he and the child's mother have not married each other.

The Commission additionally observed that, provided each holder of parental responsibility can exercise that responsibility independently of the other,[3] the completely absent parent (whether married or not) is not a problem, since the care-giving parent can make any decision about the child's upbringing without consulting the other. Finally, the Commission considered that under the UN Convention on the Rights of the Child 1989 there is an obligation to treat all fathers equally. Specifically, the Commission pointed[4] to Art 9(3), under which

19 Law Com No 172 para 2.17.
20 Scot Law Com No 82 (1984) paras 2.2–2.5.
1 See Discussion Paper No 88 paras 2.4ff and Scot Law Com No 135 *Report on Family Law* (1992) paras 2.38ff and discussed inter alia by Bainham 'Reforming Scottish Children Law – sense from North of the border' (1993) 5 Jo of Child Law 3 at 5–7.
2 This was an argument which weighed heavily with the English Law Commission: see above.
3 As they generally can under English law under s 2(7): discussed post 395. For the equivalent provision in Scotland, see the Children (Scotland) Act 1995 s 2(2).
4 Scot Law Com No 135 para 2.49.

States Parties are obliged to respect the child's right to contact with both parents, and Art 18(1), which obliges States Parties to: 'Use their best efforts to ensure recognition of the principle that both parents have common responsibilities for the upbringing and development of the child.'[5]

Having set out the arguments, the question of giving unmarried fathers automatic responsibility was put out for public consultation.[6] In contrast to the earlier English experience, more agreed than disagreed with the idea. Furthermore, support came from a wide variety of sources including, significantly, several women's groups. The Commission accordingly recommended that:[7] 'In the absence of any court order regulating the position, both parents of the child should have parental responsibilities and rights whether or not they are or have been married to each other.' As the Commission powerfully observed:[8]

> *'The question is whether the starting position should be that the father has, or has not, the normal parental responsibilities and rights. Given that about 25% of all children born in Scotland in recent years have been born out of wedlock,[9] and that the number of couples cohabiting outside marriage is now substantial, it seems to us that the balance has now swung in favour of the view that parents are parents, whether married to each other or not. If in any particular case it is in the best interest of a child that a parent should be deprived of some or all of his or her parental responsibilities and rights, that can be achieved by means of a court order.'*

Despite what would appear to be a carefully argued case, the government rejected the Commission's recommendation, so that under the Children (Scotland) Act 1995, as under the English Children Act 1989, the unmarried father does not automatically have parental responsibility. At that stage it seemed unlikely that the government would reconsider the position of the unmarried father, but in 1998 the Lord Chancellor issued a Consultation Paper[10] inviting views on the current position. The Paper asks, for example, whether it would be right in principle to make it easier for unmarried fathers to acquire parental responsibility. It canvasses views as to whether automatic parental responsibility should be limited to certain categories of fathers such as those living with the mother at the time of the child's birth or, more interestingly, to fathers who register the child's birth jointly with the mother. In this latter regard the Paper queries whether such a change in the law might have the perverse effect of discouraging unmarried fathers from identifying

---

5 This interpretation of Art 18 has not gone unchallenged, for it has been suggested that the provision was simply intended 'to focus upon responsibility in the strict sense of duty, rather than the expanded English and Scottish definitions which embrace rights as well.' In other words, imposing a duty to support a child on *all* parents regardless of marital status could be said to satisfy any obligation under the Article: Douglas 'The significance of international law for the development of family law in England and Wales' in Bridge (ed) *Family Law Towards the Millennium – Essays for P M Bromley* 85 at 106, n 19. Although some (see eg Norrie in his commentary on the Children (Scotland) Act 1995 in *Current Law Statutes* 1995, Vol 3 at 36-13) have argued that there is an obligation under the European Convention on Human Rights to treat all fathers equally, the better view would seem to be that case law does not yet go this far: see *Re W; Re B (Child Abduction: Unmarried Father)* [1998] 2 FLR 146 at 164–8, per Hale J. See also Lowe (1997) 11 Int Jo of Law, Policy and the Family 192 at pp 202–5. The Lord Chancellor's Consultation Paper, infra, at para 67 also takes the view that the current law complies with Articles 8 and 14.

6 By the Scottish Law Commission's Discussion Paper No 88: see para 2.31.

7 Scot Law Com No 135 *Report on Family Law* (1992) para 2.50.

8 Ibid at para 2.48.

9 The percentage of such children is even higher, almost 34% in England and Wales in 1995, according to the figures from the Office of National Statistics.

10 *1. Court Proceedings for the Determination of Paternity; 2. The Law on Parental Responsibility for Unmarried Fathers*, paras 39 ff.

themselves at registration or even lead to a general reduction of the rate of birth registrations. The Paper also seeks views on whether parental responsibility should be conferred automatically on all unmarried fathers and, if so, whether it should be revocable or whether there should be any circumstances in which the mother can override the assumption that the father had parental responsibility.

Some of these questions, for example whether automatic parental responsibility should be limited to certain categories of fathers, represent a reprise on the earlier enquiry by the Law Commission. What is striking about the Consultation Paper is its neutral stance and the general absence of arguments either way. This is in distinct contrast to the Scottish Law Commission document which, as has been said, presented a powerful argument for vesting in all fathers automatic parental responsibility. It remains to be seen what response this latest consultation draws.

Step-parents

Another person in whom a case for vesting automatic responsibility can be made is the step-parent who marries one of the child's parents and shares in day-to-day care.[11] Indeed, now that it is clear[12] that even the absent parent will not lose parental responsibility if a step-parent subsequently acquires it by obtaining a residence order, there would seem less objection in principle to vesting it automatically in the latter. However, pleas for any automatic parental responsibility for step-parents have not yet attracted significant support,[13] although in the proposed Adoption Bill provision is made for the step-parent who is married to the child's parent to acquire responsibility either by agreement or by a court order.[14] In effect, under this proposal such step-parents would be put in the same position as the unmarried father. This seems a reasonable compromise, though the question might well be asked as to why non-marital step-parents should not be similarly treated?

Giving the courts a general power to make parental responsibility orders

Unlike both Scottish and Australian law,[15] English law does not vest in the courts a *general* power to make parental responsibility orders. Experience suggests that such a power would be useful in this jurisdiction. A good example is *Re WB (Residence Orders)*[16] where a man, who thought he was the child's father and only discovered he was not as a result of a paternity test, found that because the child was to live with the mother there was no means by which he could be given parental responsibility.[17] The power could also be useful in the case of orphans.[18]

---

11 One advocate for this change is Masson: see her arguments inter alia in 'Old families into new: a status for step-parents' in Freeman (ed) *State, Law and the Family* (1984) ch 14 pp 237 et seq.
12 See post, p 394.
13 See Law Com Working Paper No 91 *Guardianship* paras 4.15 to 4.19 which canvassed views about the possibility of step-parents acquiring responsibility by administrative rather than judicial means, but did not pursue the point because it attracted little support at the time: Law Com No 172 *Guardianship and Custody* para 2.22.
14 See cl 85 of the Draft Adoption Bill attached to 'Adoption – A Service for Children' (Department of Health and Welsh Office, 1996).
15 The powers to make respectively a parental responsibility or a parenting order are conferred by s 11(2) of the Children (Scotland) Act 1995 and s 61D of the Australian Family Law Act 1975.
16 [1995] 2 FLR 1023. For a different type of example see *Re W (Arrangements to Place for Adoption)* [1995] 1 FLR 163
17 The court refused to grant him a shared residence order for the 'artificial' purpose of allocation of responsibility; cf *Re H (Shared Responsibility: Parental Responsibility)* [1995] 2 FLR 883, where such an order was made to alleviate confusion in the child's mind.
18 For the position of taking orphans into local authority care, see post, p 547.

D.   In respect of whom is there responsibility?

Parental responsibility exists in respect of a 'child', that is, a person under the age of 18.[19] It is a moot point as to whether responsibility exists for a married child.[20]

1.   THE POSITION WITH REGARD TO UNBORN CHILDREN[1]

The 1989 Act is silent on when parental responsibility begins but, in the absence of any indication to the contrary, it is suggested that references to 'child' in the Act mean a live child.[2] Accordingly, it is submitted that no one has parental responsibility until the child is born, and that therefore the parents' position with regard to their unborn child is unaffected by the 1989 Act.[3]

It would appear that fathers have no rights over foetuses. At any rate, this was the reasoning of Sir George Baker P in *Paton v British Pregnancy Advisory Service Trustees*[4] when he refused a husband's application for an injunction to prevent his wife from having an abortion. An unmarried father was similarly refused an injunction in *C v S*.[5] In *Paton*'s case strong obiter doubts were also expressed as to whether the court should interfere even if the medical practitioners involved had not acted in good faith in issuing the certificate required by the Abortion Act 1967 and there was an obvious attempt to commit a crime: it is not for the civil courts to interfere with the exercise of doctors' discretion under the Act. This view may appear to have been weakened by the fact that both Heilbron J and the Court of Appeal in *C v S* were prepared to hear argument that the proposed abortion was contrary to the provisions of the Infant Life (Preservation) Act 1929 s 1. However, Sir John Donaldson MR commented that even if a breach of the 1929 Act could have been proved, 'strong consideration' would still have been paid to Sir George Baker P's comment that the matter would be better left to the Director of Public Prosecutions, who could then consider whether prosecutions should be brought. It is submitted that even if the abortion were ex facie illegal the father still could not obtain an injunction to prevent the commission of the proposed criminal act once it is accepted that he has no right which would be affected.[6]

Re F (In Utero)[7] unequivocally establishes that there is no power to ward an

---

19 Children Act 1989 s 105 (1).
20 See post, p 393.
 1 See generally Douglas *Law, Fertility and Reproduction* pp 82–3 and 187–9.
 2 See *Elliot v Joicey* [1935] AC 209, HL. For a similar interpretation of the meaning of 'child' under the Children and Young Persons Act 1969 s 70(1) see Re *D (A Minor)* [1987] AC 317, [1987] 1 All ER 20, HL. Note also *R v Newham London Borough Council, ex p Dada* [1996] QB 507, [1995] 2 All ER 522, CA interpreting the Housing Act 1985 s 75.
 3 If Parliament had intended to make a change it would surely have expressly done so.
 4 [1979] QB 276, [1978] 2 All ER 987. See further Kennedy (1979) 42 MLR 324; Phillips (1979) 95 LQR 332; Lowe (1980) 96 LQR 29 and Lowe and White *Wards of Court* (2nd edn, 1986) paras 2–3. The husband also failed before the European Commission of Human Rights, which ruled that although he had locus standi to bring the complaint, there had been no breach of the Convention since the abortion was certified as being necessary for the wife's health: (1980) 3 EHRR 408.
 5 [1988] QB 135, [1987] 1 All ER 1230, CA.
 6 See *Gouriet v Union of Post Office Workers* [1978] AC 435, [1977] 3 All ER 70, HL. But see Kennedy, loc cit.
 7 [1988] Fam 122, [1988] 2 All ER 193, CA. Lowe 'The Limits of Wardship Jurisdiction' (1988) 1 Journal of Child Law 6 and Fortin 'Can You Ward a Foetus?' (1988) 51 MLR 768. For a further discussion of this case see Chapter 16.

unborn child, though interestingly the principal reason for so holding was the unacceptable clash between the unborn child's interests and those of the mother that the exercise of wardship would inevitably entail, rather than the foetus's having no rights of its own to protect.

2. THE POSITION WITH REGARD TO EMBRYOS [8]

As one commentator has said: [9] 'The advent of assisted reproduction and the ability to fertilise an ovum in vitro and to maintain the resulting embryo for a number of days has required the law to work out whether, and how, to protect such an embryo'. The legal framework is now provided for by the Human Fertilisation and Embryology Act 1990, which in turn is based upon the recommendations of the Warnock Report. [10] Detailed consideration of this Act lies outside the scope of this work; [11] nevertheless, it is worth noting that in contradistinction to his position with regard to a foetus, the father (as well as the mother) does have rights with respect to an embryo in vitro whilst outside the womb. Whilst stopping short of providing for ownership, the 1990 Act nevertheless provides that embryos can only be used, stored or disposed of with the consent of the persons whose gametes were used to create the embryo in vitro. [12]

E. Duration of parental responsibility

An important aspect of parental responsibility under the Children Act 1989 is its enduring nature, and in particular that it is not lost merely because someone else acquires it. Nevertheless, responsibility does not have an unlimited duration. As it can only exist in respect of a 'child', parental responsibility ends upon the child attaining his majority. It will clearly end upon the child's death. [13] Non-parents who have responsibility by reason of a residence order, local authorities which have responsibility by reason of a care order, and anyone who has responsibility by reason of an emergency protection order, only have responsibility for the duration of the order. [14]

Apart from the above-mentioned circumstances there is uncertainty as to whether other events can end parental responsibility. Before the Children Act 1989 there was authority for saying that the right of custody ended upon the child's marriage [15] and that it was suspended whilst the child was serving in the

---

8 See Douglas, op cit, ch 3 and Kennedy and Grubb *Medical Law: Text and Materials* (2nd edn) 793ff.

9 Douglas, op cit at p 33.

10 Report of the Committee of Inquiry into Human Fertilisation and Embryology (1984) Cmnd 9314.

11 For more detailed reading, see eg Morgan and Lee *The Human Fertilisation and Embryology Act 1990* and Douglas 'The Human Fertilisation and Embryology Act 1990' [1991] Fam Law 110.

12 Sch 3.

13 It is established, however, that even if the child had been in care the parent retains the right to bury (or, presumably, cremate) the child: *R v Gwynedd County Council, ex p B* [1992] 3 All ER 317, CA, discussed ante, pp 363–4.

14 See respectively s 12(2), s 33(3) and s 44(4)(c).

15 See eg *Hewer v Bryant* [1970] 1 QB 357 at 373, [1969] 3 All ER 578, CA at 585 per Sachs LJ; *R v Wilmington Inhabitants* (1822) 5 B & Ald 525 at 526 and *Lough v Ward* [1945] 2 All ER 338 at 348.

armed forces,[16] but it remains to be seen whether a similar position will be taken with regard to parental responsibility. There is also conflicting opinion as to whether responsibility ceases in respect of any aspect of a child's upbringing about which the child himself is sufficiently mature to make his own decisions.[17] Perhaps the better view in each of these situations is that parental responsibility does not end, but that the scope for its exercise is limited.

Unlike under Scottish Law[18] there is no general power under English law to divest a parent[19] of parental responsibility. Whether there should be a general divesting power can be debated. On the one hand, such a possibility would deal with the point made by others[20] that, just as it may be wrong to deny automatic parental responsibility to 'meritorious' unmarried fathers, so it is questionable to vest it in 'unmeritorious' *married* fathers, as for example where conception took place as a result of rape within marriage. Furthermore, there are certainly cases where a parent has behaved so appallingly, either towards the child or other members of the family, that one could argue that that person should no longer have responsibility. On the other hand, a general divesting power cuts across the principle that responsibility should be enduring.[1] On balance, however, provided any divesting power is subject to the overarching principle of the paramountcy of the child's welfare, there does seem a case for amending English Law.

F.   Sharing parental responsibility for a child

Although self-evident, given the position of married parents under s 2(1) of the Children Act 1989, s 2(5) nevertheless expressly provides that more than one person may have parental responsibility for the same child at the same time. Section 2(6) further provides that a person with parental responsibility does not cease to have it solely because some other person subsequently acquires it. This latter provision which, in the words of one commentator,[2] 'encapsulates the ethos of continuing parental responsibility' means, for example, that a parent will not lose responsibility because someone else such as a step-parent, grandparent, foster parent or, even, a local authority acquires it. Section 2(6) should not, however, be

---

16 *R v Rotherfield Greys Inhabitants* (1823) 1 B & C 345 at 349–50.
17 See the comment of Lord Scarman in *Gillick v West Norfolk and Wisbech Area Health Authority* [1986] AC 112 at 186, [1985] 3 All ER 402 at 421–2, which suggests it does, but which was specifically rejected by Lord Donaldson MR in *Re R (A Minor) (Wardship: Medical Treatment)* [1992] Fam 11 at 23, [1991] 4 All ER 177 at 185; and both by Lord Donaldson MR and Balcombe LJ in *Re W (A Minor) (Medical Treatment) (Court's Jurisdiction)* [1993] Fam 64 at 75–6 and 87, [1992] 4 All ER 627 at 633 and 642–3, discussed ante at pp 314–6.
18 See s 11(2)(a) of the Children (Scotland) Act 1995.
19 A mother or married father. Parental responsibility orders and agreements can be ended by the court under s 4(3): see above. Those who acquire responsibility via a residence order only have it for the duration of the order.
20 Such as the Scottish Law Commission: see Scot Law Com No 88 para 2.47 and Barton and Douglas *Law and Parenthood* 93–4.
 1 The enduring nature of responsibility is emphasised, in the case of an unmarried father acquiring responsibility by virtue of a residence order made in his favour, by the requirement under s 12(1) to make a separate parental responsibility order, so that the subsequent ending of the residence order will not ipso facto end the responsibility.
 2 Bainham *Children, The New Law, The Children Act 1989* para 2.18.

read as meaning that a court order can never end a parent's responsibility. An adoption order clearly does, because the statute expressly says so.[3]

Where parental responsibility is shared, then, as s 2(7) provides, each person in whom it is vested 'may act alone and without the other (or others) in meeting that responsibility' except where a statute expressly requires the consent of more than one person in a matter affecting the child.[4] This power to act independently, however, is subject to the important limitation under s 2(8), namely, that a person with parental responsibility is not entitled to act in any way that could be incompatible with a court order.[5]

The ability to act independently was intended to mean, not simply that neither parent has a right of veto, but also that there is no legal duty upon parents to consult each other[6] since, in the Law Commission's view,[7] such a duty was both unworkable and undesirable. It was expressly contemplated that even where a residence order had been granted in one parent's favour, subject to not acting incompatibly with a court order, each parent could still exercise that responsibility without having to consult the other and with neither having a right of veto over the other's action. By way of illustration the Law Commission cited[8] the example of a child living with one parent and going to a school nearby. In the Commission's view it would be incompatible for the other parent to arrange for the child to have his hair done in a way which would exclude him from the school, but it would be perfectly permissible for that parent to take the child to a sporting occasion over the weekend, no matter how much the parent with whom the child lived might disapprove. According to the Commission the intended independence of each parent was to be seen as part of the general aim of encouraging both parents to feel concerned and responsible for the welfare of the children.[9]

The intended scheme of the Act had been criticised on the basis that it was difficult to see how failing to provide for consultation, at any rate with respect to serious or long-term decisions affecting the child, could promote joint parenting following breakdown.[10] Evidently the courts have sympathy for that point of view for, despite the apparently clear wording of s 2(7), the Court of Appeal in *Re G (A Minor) (Parental Responsibility: Education)*[11] seemed to have assumed that there

---

3   Adoption Act 1976 s 12(3)(a), discussed post, p 675. As Lord Mackay LC said, during the Debates on the Children Bill (588 HL Official Report (5th series) col 1175), the word 'solely' is used advisedly in s 2(6), ie an adoption order deprives a parent of responsibility not solely because adoptive parents acquire it but because the 1976 Act expressly extinguishes it.

4   This latter qualification preserves, for example, the embargo imposed by the Child Abduction Act 1984 s 1 against one parent taking the child (under the age of 16) outside the United Kingdom without the other's consent (in this regard it will be noted that neither parent can unilaterally change the child's habitual residence: *Re S (Minors) (Child Abduction: Wrongful Retention)* [1994] 1 FLR 82 per Wall J and *Re A (Wardship: Jurisdiction)* [1995] 1 FLR 767 per Hale J) and maintains the need to obtain *each* parent's agreement to an adoption order as laid down by s 16 of the Adoption Act 1976.

5   The absence of a court order does not necessarily mean that parental responsibility may be exercised without qualification. For example, since ultimate responsibility for a ward of court rests with the court (see post, p 686), the warding of a child must immediately operate at least to limit freedom of action.

6   This resolved the uncertainty of the former law, which seemed to impose no duty to consult but did confer a power of veto: see Law Com Working Paper No 96 *Custody* para 2.34 et seq.

7   Law Com No 172 para 2.07.

8   Ibid at para 2.11.

9   Ibid at para 2.10.

10 See Bainham [1990] Fam Law 192 at 193, discussed below.

11 [1994] 2 FLR 964, CA.

remains[12] a duty to consult, at any rate over long-term decisions. In that case a father who had custody, care and control under a court order arranged for his son to attend a local education authority boarding school without informing the mother. In Glidewell LJ's view the '. . . mother, having parental responsibility, was entitled to and indeed ought to have been consulted about the important step of taking her child away from day school that he had been attending and sending him to boarding school. It is an important step in any child's life and she ought to have been consulted.'[13]

The full ramifications of these decisions have still to be explored. For example, it remains to be established whether the duty to consult extends to other 'important steps' and, if so, what constitute such steps. In one sense, it makes no difference whether or not there is a duty to consult, for in either case in the event of a disagreement the burden will be on the complaining parent to take the issue to court. However, once the issue is before the court, the existence of a duty to consult may be important, since a parent who has failed to discharge it could be penalised in costs.

G.   Effect of third parties acquiring parental responsibility

As s 2(6) makes clear, neither parent loses parental responsibility solely because someone else has acquired it through a court order. This means, for example, that upon divorce a father does not lose responsibility even if a step-father also acquires it under a residence order made in his favour.[14] In this situation the mother, step-father and father all share responsibility for the child and, subject to not acting incompatibly with a court order, and subject to the ruling in *Re G*, each can exercise their responsibility independently of the others. A similar situation arises if grandparents or other relations or foster parents have residence orders made in their favour. Another effect of s 2(6) is that parents do not lose parental responsibility when a local authority obtains a care order, nor where an emergency protection order is made.[15]

H.   Delegation of parental responsibility

Section 2(9) preserves the common law position that a person with parental responsibility cannot surrender or transfer any part of his responsibility to another. Section 2(9), however, recognises for the first time the power of a person with responsibility to 'arrange for some or all of it to be met by one or more persons acting on his behalf'. Such delegation can be made to another person who already

---

12 This seems a throw-back to the pre-1989 Act law and in particular to *Dipper v Dipper* [1981] Fam 31, [1980] 2 All ER 722, CA, discussed in the 7th edition of this work at pp 295 and 302.

13 It has also been held that s 2(7) does not entitle one spouse to change the child's surname without the consent of the other: see *Re PC (Change of Surname)* [1997] 2 FLR 730 per Holman J.

14 It will be noted that step-parents may acquire parental responsibility only through a residence order or upon being appointed a guardian. They do not acquire responsibility simply by marrying the child's parent.

15 Discussed post at pp 563 and 593 respectively.

has parental responsibility[16] or to those who have not, such as schools or holiday camps. The aim of this provision is to encourage parents (regardless of whether or not they are separated) to agree among themselves on what they believe to be the best arrangements for their children. Section 2(9) does not, however, make such arrangements legally binding. Consequently, they can be revoked or changed at will. Furthermore, as s 2(11) provides, delegations will not absolve a person with parental responsibility from any liability for failure on his part to discharge his responsibilities to the child.[17]

I.   Caring for a child without having parental responsibility

Resolving the confusion of the pre-1989 Act law[18] the Children Act clarifies the legal position of those who are caring for a child but who do not have parental responsibility, by providing that they 'may (subject to the provisions of this Act) do what is reasonable in all the circumstances for the purpose of safeguarding or promoting the child's welfare'. As is observed in the Department of Health's *Guidance and Regulations*,[19] what is reasonable 'will depend upon the urgency and gravity of what is required and the extent to which it is practicable to consult a person with parental responsibility'. Prima facie, while a carer may be able to consent to the child's medical treatment in the event of an accident, he will not be able to consent to major elective surgery. Indeed, it may be difficult for the carer to convince a doctor that he has sufficient authority to consent to medical treatment which may be desirable but not essential.[20] Whether a significantly greater latitude for action should be given to those caring for orphans remains an interesting point.

It is on the basis of s 3(5) that it is thought that a foster parent of a child being accommodated by a local authority could properly refuse immediately to hand over the child to a parent who is drunk or who turns up in the middle of the night. On the other hand, it is clear that s 3(5) does not empower a de facto carer to change a child's habitual residence merely by taking the child out of the jurisdiction.[1] Anyone who cares for a child is obliged not to assault, ill-treat, neglect, abandon or expose the child in a manner likely to cause unnecessary suffering or injury to health.[2]

---

16 Section 2(10).
17 For example, not to neglect, abandon, expose or cause or procure a child under the age of 16 to be assaulted or ill-treated etc under s 1 and s 17 of the Children and Young Persons Act 1933: see ante, pp 366–7.
18 See Law Com No 172 para 2.16.
19 Vol 1, *Court Orders*, para 2.11.
20 See, for example, Johnson J's comments in *B v B (A Minor) (Residence Order)* [1992] 2 FLR 327 at 330. His Lordship also observed that notwithstanding s 3(5) a maternal grandmother, who was the de facto carer, found in practice that the education authorities were reluctant to accept her authority to give consent, for example, to the child going on a school trip, and insisted upon having the mother's written authority.
1   See *Re S (A Minor) (Custody: Habitual Residence)* [1997] 4 All ER 251, HL at 257 per Lord Slynn.
2   Children and Young Persons Act 1933 s 1.

Chapter 11

Guardianship

A. Introduction

The term 'guardian' has a variety of meanings,[1] but the specific concern of this chapter is the institution of legal guardianship over children during their minority. Formerly, the concept of guardianship was a complex one and it was well described[2] as a formula used to attribute powers over a child's upbringing to a particular individual or individuals. However, following its reform by the Children Act 1989 guardianship can now be said to be the legal status under which a person has parental responsibility for a child following the death of one or both of the child's parents. In short, a 'guardian' is someone who has been formally appointed to take the place of the child's deceased parent.

1. THE POSITION OF GUARDIANS BEFORE THE CHILDREN ACT 1989

Before its reform by the Children Act 1989, guardianship had become a complicated product of common law, equity and statute.[3] Its early history was succinctly described by the Law Commission as follows:[4]

> 'The institution of guardianship was originally of concern only to those who had property. It began as a lucrative incident of feudal tenure and developed as a means of safe-guarding a family's property and securing its transmission from one generation to another. Subsequently it became the instrument for maintaining the authority of the father over the upbringing of his children.'

Before the 1989 Act the law recognised both parental and non-parental guardianship. With regard to the former, notwithstanding the general equalisation of spouses' rights,[5] it remained the case that during his lifetime the father was the sole guardian of his legitimate children. It was only upon his death that the mother became a guardian either alone or jointly with any other guardians appointed by the father. The common law made no provision for guardianship of illegitimate children and, even though the mother was eventually recognised[6] as having

---

1 See, for example, the use of 'guardianship' under the Mental Health Act 1983 s 10(1), under which a guardian may be appointed for a person who has attained the age of 16 and who is, or appears to be, suffering from a mental disorder. The term 'guardian' is not to be confused with 'guardian ad litem', who is a person appointed to represent a child in legal proceedings: see post, pp 552ff.
2 Cretney *Principles of Family Law* (4th edn, 1984) p 296.
3 For an excellent summary of the history see the Law Commission Working Paper No 91 on *Guardianship* (1985), Part 11. For a detailed history see eg Holdsworth *History of English Law* (7th edn, 1966) Vol 111. See also Bevan *Child Law* (1989) ch 4, and ch 10 of the 7th edition of this work.
4 In their Working Paper No 91 at para 3.1.
5 See ante, pp 303ff.
6 Children Act 1975 s 85(1).

exclusive parental rights and duties, she was not formally regarded as a guardian.[7] With regard to non-parental guardianship, statute eventually conferred[8] equal rights on mothers and fathers to appoint a testamentary guardian in respect of legitimate children, with the mother having the exclusive right to do so with respect to her illegitimate children. Testamentary appointments took effect upon the death of the appointing parent even if the other parent was still alive. However, if the latter objected, he or she could apply to the court to prevent the appointee from acting. A guardian could also apply to court if he considered the parent unfit to have custody, and the court had various powers to resolve such disputes.[9]

The courts also had power to appoint guardians. Under the Guardianship of Minors Acts 1971 and 1973 a magistrates' court, county court or High Court each had power to make appointments following the death of either or both parents. In addition it was generally thought that the High Court retained an inherent jurisdiction to appoint guardians.[10]

Historically, the law recognised two separate functions of guardians: the protection of the person and the protection of the property of the ward. These functions could be vested in two entirely different sets of people: guardians of the person, with no right to control the ward's property, and guardians of the estate, with no right to control the ward's person.[11] Although the 1925 property legislation virtually rendered the latter type of guardianship obsolete, it remained useful to appoint the Official Solicitor, for example, to administer an award made to the child by the Criminal Injuries Compensation Board in respect of injuries caused by the parents.[12]

Guardians (unless of the estate only) had broadly similar rights and duties with respect to the child as a parent,[13] but they were not in exactly the same position.[14] For example, unlike parents, guardians could not be made liable to maintain their wards, nor could they appoint a guardian themselves. On the other hand, they probably had wider powers than parents in respect of the child's property.[15] There was uncertainty as to whether a guardian had a right of access to the child and, indeed, as to who had the right to care and control of the child where the parent was still alive. As the Law Commission concluded,[16] the interrelationship between the legal status of parent and guardian was obscure, particularly where the parent was also described as a guardian.

7 Though in *Re A* (1940) 164 LT 230 it was held that the Guardianship of Infants Act 1925 had given the mother the right to appoint a testamentary guardian for her illegitimate child.
8 Restricted rights were first conferred by the Guardianship of Infants Act 1886 and equal rights by the Guardianship of Infants Act 1925, which was then consolidated by the Guardianship of Minors Act 1971.
9 See pp 352–3 of the 7th edition of this work.
10 Though this had been doubted by *Re C (Minors) (Adoption by Relatives)* [1989] 1 All ER 395, CA. In fact the Guardianship Act 1973 s 7(2) expressly preserved the High Court's inherent power to appoint a guardian of the estate.
11 If there was no separate guardian of a minor's estate, a guardian appointed by a deceased parent or by the court under the Guardianship of Minors Act 1971 had all the rights, powers and duties of a guardian of the estate in addition to being guardian of the person: Guardianship Act 1973 s 7.
12 See Law Commission Working Paper No 91, note 95.
13 For example, both had a statutory right to consent to the marriage of a child under the age of 18 and to agree to the child's adoption.
14 For a detailed analysis of the former position see Law Commission Working Paper No 91, paras 2.24–2.35, and pp 355–60 of the 7th edition of this work.
15 For example, a guardian but not a parent could give a valid receipt on the child's behalf for a legacy: see Law Com Working Paper No 91, para 2.33.
16 Working Paper No 91, para 2.35.

2.   THE NEED FOR REFORM

The notion of parental guardianship confused the separate legal concepts of parenthood and guardianship and in the Law Commission's view it was both sensible and practical to regard parenthood as the primary concept and to distinguish it from the role of a guardian who acts in loco parentis.[17] Accordingly they recommended abolishing the rule under which parents, who for all practical purposes had the same rights and authority, were sometimes guardians and sometimes not.[18] On the other hand, although little was known about the frequency of guardianship appointments,[19] the Commission considered[20] that the law should provide some means of supplying a person or persons who could step into the shoes of a parent or parents who have died. Following consultation the Commission found unanimous support for the power both of the parents and courts to appoint guardians.[1] The Commission also canvassed opinion as to whether there should be some form of public control of guardians appointed by parents, for example, by subjecting non-related guardians to the same provisions as private foster parents.[2] In the event, however, these suggestions were not pursued,[3] nor were the suggestions for extending guardianship to permit inter vivos appointments.[4] A number of other suggestions for reform[5] were, however, recommended, namely vesting full parental responsibility in guardians, simplifying the method by which parents can appoint a guardian, providing in general that parental appointments come into force only upon the death of the surviving parent, and changing and clarifying the courts' powers both to appoint and remove guardians. Save for the abolition of guardians of the estate,[6] the Law Commission's recommendations on guardianship were enacted by the Children Act 1989.

B.   The current law

The law of guardianship is now exclusively controlled by s 5 and s 6 of the Children Act 1989. The concept of parental guardianship has been abolished[7] and, save for the exceptional case where the unmarried father becomes a guardian,[8] the status is now confined to those formally appointed to take the place of a deceased parent or parents.

---

17   Ibid, para 3.2.

18   Law Com Report No 172 on *Guardianship and Custody* (1988) para 2.2.

19   Though they did commission a small study undertaken by Priest in the North East of England – see Appendix B of Working Paper No 91.

20   Working Paper No 91 para 3.17.

1   Law Com No 172 para 2.2.

2   Law Com Working Paper No 91, paras 3.23 et seq.

3   Law Com No 172 para 2.32.

4   Discussed in Working Paper No 91 paras 4.19 et seq. Note, however, the subsequent proposal (in the Consultative Document on Adoption Law, para 6.5) that courts be empowered to appoint so-called 'inter vivos' guardians.

5   See Law Com No 172 paras 2.23–2.31.

6   Law Com No 172 para 2.24 – see further below at p 401.

7   Following the express abolition of the rule of law that a father is the natural guardian of his legitimate children by s 2(4) of the Children Act 1989, and the repeal (by Sch 15) of s 3 of the Guardianship of Minors Act 1971 which provided that upon the death of one parent the other became the guardian of any legitimate child.

8   Such as upon the mother's death following an appointment by her or the court.

With one exception it is no longer possible to appoint different types of guardians. This one exception is the High Court's inherent power to appoint a guardian of a child's estate, which has been preserved by s 5(11) and (12).⁹ This power, however, is limited in that only the Official Solicitor can be so appointed, and even then only when the consent of the persons with parental responsibility has been signified to the court or when, in the court's opinion, such consent cannot be obtained or may be dispensed with.¹⁰ In practice such appointments are likely to be confined to cases where the parents are dead or where it is unsuitable for them to be involved (for example, where they had caused injuries to the child in respect of which compensation has been paid).

Guardians of the estate apart, all guardians have parental responsibility for the child,¹¹ which effectively places them in the same legal position as parents, at least so far as the care and upbringing of the child is concerned. The conferment of full parental responsibility was central to the role of guardians as envisaged by the Law Commission. As they put it:¹²

'The power to control a child's upbringing should go hand in hand with the responsibility to look after him or at least to see that he is properly looked after. Consultation confirmed our impression that it is now generally expected that guardians will take over any responsibility for the care and upbringing of a child if the parents die. If so, it is right that full legal responsibility should also be placed upon them.'

One consequence of having parental responsibility is that guardians can themselves appoint guardians.

1. APPOINTMENT OF GUARDIANS

Private appointment of guardians

Any parent with parental responsibility (ie not an unmarried father without such responsibility) and any guardian may appoint an individual to be the child's guardian.¹³ Although reference is made to 'an individual', more than one person may be appointed as a guardian.¹⁴ Furthermore, an additional guardian or guardians can be appointed at a later date.¹⁵ There is nothing to prevent an appointment being made by two or more persons jointly.¹⁶

There is no restriction or control upon who may be appointed (even another

---

9 Implemented 1 February 1992: SI 1991/828. The Law Commission (see Law Com No 172 para 2.24) recommended the abolition of this power, arguing that trusteeship would adequately and more appropriately fill any gap.
10 See RSC Ord 80 r 13(1). Appointments may be made only in certain defined circumstances, for example, when the Criminal Injuries Compensation Board has made or intends to make an award to the child, when payment to the child has been ordered by a foreign court or tribunal, or when the child is entitled to the proceeds of a pension fund, and in each case only where, in the court's view, such an appointment seems desirable: Ord 80 r 13(2).
11 Children Act 1989 s 5(6).
12 Law Com No 172 para 2.23.
13 Section 5(3)–(4).
14 This is implicit in s 6(1) which refers to 'an additional guardian'. In any event, under the Interpretation Act 1978 s 6(c), unless there is a contrary intention, words in the singular in a statute presumptively include the plural. But 'individual' does not include a 'body': see post, pp 404–5.
15 Section 6(1).
16 Section 5(10). Such an appointment only takes effect on the death of all the appointers: see further below at p 403.

child, it seems, could be appointed),[17] nor are there any means of scrutinising an appointment unless a dispute or issue is subsequently brought before the court.[18] Appointments can be made only in respect of children under the age of 18.[19]

Whereas formerly the appointment had to be by deed or will, under s 5(5) it is now sufficient that the appointment is made in writing, dated and signed by the person making it. This simpler method of appointment is intended to encourage parents (particularly young parents who are notoriously reluctant to make wills) to appoint guardians.[20] Section 5(5) does not preclude appointments being made in a will since such means will satisfy the minimum requirements.[1] An appointment made by will but not signed by the testator will be valid if it is signed at the direction of the testator in accordance with the Wills Act 1837 s 9.[2] An appointment will also be valid in any other case provided it is signed at the direction of the person making the appointment, in his presence and in the presence of two witnesses who each attest the signature.[3] These latter provisions cater for the blind or physically disabled persons who cannot write.[4]

(a)   Revoking an appointment

Section 6 of the Children Act 1989 deals with the formerly complex question of revocation of appointments. Under s 6(1) a later appointment revokes an earlier appointment (including one made in an unrevoked will or codicil) made by the same person in respect of the same child, unless it is clear that the purpose of the later appointment is to appoint an additional guardian. Under s 6(2) the person who made the appointment (including one made in an unrevoked will or codicil) can expressly revoke it in a signed written and dated instrument. Under s 6(3A) a dissolution or annulment of marriage on or after 1 January 1996 revokes an appointment of the former spouse as a guardian unless a contrary intention appears from the appointment.[5] Section 6(4) further provides that an appointment made in a will or codicil is revoked if the will or codicil is revoked. An appointment, *other than* one made by will or codicil, will also be revoked if the person making it destroys the document with the intention of revoking the appointment.[6]

---

17 Though, as Hershman and McFarlane *Children – Law and Practice* at G [9] comment, it seems highly questionable that one child should have parental responsibility over another. Nevertheless, the power can occasionally be useful: see *Re A, J and J (minors) (Residence and Guardianship Orders)* [1993] Fam Law 568; and see post, p 405 n 8.
18 See post, p 409 for discussion of the courts' powers to remove a guardian. The complete absence of regulation is commented upon by Douglas and Lowe 'Becoming a Parent in English Law' (1992) 108 LQR 414 at 428. See further, post at p 410.
19 Section 105(1). Quaere whether (a) an appointment would take effect once the child is married, or (b) a valid appointment may be made before the child is born: see post, p 406.
20 See Law Com No 172 para 2.29.
 1 See Lord Mackay LC's comments at 502 HL Official Report (5th Series), col 1199.
 2 Section 5(5)(a).
 3 Section 5(5)(b).
 4 But not those who are mentally incapacitated: cf Department of Health's *Children Act 1989: Guidance and Regulations*, Vol 1 *Court Orders*, para 2.18.
 5 This provision was added by the Law Reform (Succession) Act 1995 (on which see Barton and Wells 'A Matter of Life and Death – The Law Reform (Succession) Act 1995' [1996] Fam Law 172 at 174, who make the point that an appointment of a cohabitant would *not* be revoked by the couple's subsequent estrangement). For the purposes of this provision the dissolution or annulment includes both those made by a court of civil jurisdiction in England and Wales and those recognised in England and Wales by virtue of Part II of the Family Law Act 1986.
 6 Section 6(3).

(b) When the appointment takes effect

Unlike under the previous law, an appointment no longer automatically takes effect upon the death of the appointing parent. Instead, the appointment normally takes effect upon the death of the sole remaining parent with parental responsibility.[7] If the appointing person is already the sole parent with parental responsibility, then the appointment will take effect immediately upon his death.[8] Under s 5(7)(b), however, an appointment takes effect immediately upon the death of the appointing person if there was a sole[9] residence order in his favour at the time of his death. In this latter instance, the surviving parent has no right to object, but he can apply to the court for an order ending the appointment.[10] The rationale for delaying the operation of a guardianship appointment is to avoid unnecessary conflict between a surviving parent and a guardian appointed by the deceased parent. As the Law Commission said,[11] there seems little reason why the surviving parent should have to share parental responsibility with a guardian who almost invariably will not be living in the same household. In effect the law protects the surviving parent from interference by an outsider; though, of course, if that parent wishes informally to seek the help of the appointee, he can do so without jeopardising his parental status. In such circumstances, however, the surviving parent cannot object to the appointment, although under s 6(7) he can seek a court order to end it. On the other hand, if the *appointee* wishes to challenge this position, he will need to seek the court's leave to obtain a s 8 order.

While this basic stand-point seems right (and furthermore, brings our law into line with the Council of Europe recommendation on guardianship)[12] where the child was living with both parents in a united family before the death of one of them, different considerations apply where the parents are divorced or separated. Endorsing the Law Commission's view,[13] the law takes the position that, if there was a court order that the child should live with the parent who had died, that parent should be able to provide for the child's upbringing in the event of his death. However, this standpoint has been called into question by one commentator, who said:[14]

'The survivor will, of course, have joint parental responsibility with the guardian but will have the onus of bringing the child's position before the court in the event of a disagreement between them.[15] This is not very easy to reconcile with the ethos of continuing parental responsibility following divorce. It casts the non-residential parent in the role of an outsider who is liable to interfere with the child rather than that of a concerned parent who is anxious to step into the breach left by the deceased'.

---

7 Section 5(8).
8 Section 5(7)(a).
9 Aliter, if a residence order had also been made in favour of a surviving parent: s 5(9). Quaere the position where a joint appointment has been made? Hershman and McFarlane, op cit at G [41] consider that the appointment will not take effect until the death of the surviving parent, relying on s 5(10), but the position is perhaps not beyond doubt.
10 Section 6(7), discussed further post at p 409.
11 Law Com No 172 para 2.28.
12 Recommendation R84(4) *Parental Responsibilities*, Principle 9. Indeed, as the Law Commission pointed out (ibid at para 2.27), before the Children Act amendments the UK was the only member country of the Council of Europe that permitted guardianship to operate during the lifetime of a surviving parent.
13 Ibid at para 2.28.
14 Bainham *Children: The New Law* (1990), para 2.40. See also Bainham *Children: The Modern Law* (1993) 192.
15 Under s 6(7), for example, he can seek a court order to end the appointment: see further below.

In any event, this new position creates uncertainty about who is entitled to take over the physical care of the child, since prima facie both the guardian and the surviving parent have equal claims.[16] This new standpoint has also been criticised for *not* making provision for cases where the spouses are separated, or even divorced, but where there is no residence order.[17] The father, for example, may simply have abandoned his family. As the Scottish Law Commission said:[18]

> 'In many of these cases it might well be desirable for an appointment of a guardian to be capable of coming into operation, even though there is a surviving parent somewhere.'

(c)   Disclaiming the appointment

Section 6(5) of the Children Act 1989 provides, for the first time, a formal right for a guardian to disclaim an appointment. This right, which applies only to appointments made by a parent or a guardian (ie not to court appointments), must be exercised 'within a reasonable time of his first knowing that the appointment has taken effect'.[19] Furthermore, it must be disclaimed by an instrument in writing, signed by the appointee. There is provision to make regulations for the recording of such disclaimers (which would then be ineffective unless recorded)[20] but at the time of writing no regulations have been made.

As White, Carr and Lowe comment:[1]

> 'Welcome as this new power is, it does make it all the more important for parents to discuss their proposed appointment with the person concerned. It seems desirable for some official guidance to be published reminding parents of the desirability of prior consultation.'

The court's power to appoint guardians

(a)   When the power may be exercised

Under s 5(1) of the 1989 Act the High Court, a county court or a magistrates' court[2] may appoint an 'individual' to be a child's guardian if:

> '(a) the child has no parent with parental responsibility for him; or
> (b) a residence order has been made with respect to the child in favour of a parent or guardian of his who has died while the order was in force.'

Although by reason of the Interpretation Act 1978 s 6(c),[3] the court is not prevented from appointing more than one guardian, nevertheless by confining the

---

16 In *Children: The Modern Law*, Bainham concludes, at 192 'The rather unsatisfactory outcome . . . is that the onus to commence proceedings will be on the person wishing to change the existing arrangements'.

17 Such a scenario is now more likely to arise, since it will be by no means uncommon, because of the so-called non-intervention principle under s 1(5), for no orders to have been made.

18 Scot Law Com No 135 *Report on Family Law* (1992), para 3-11, repeating what was said in Discussion Paper No 88 *Parental Responsibilities and Rights, Guardianship and the Administration of Children's Property* (1990) para 3.11. Accordingly, no change was recommended, so that in Scotland (see the Children (Scotland) Act 1995 s 7) it remains the case that a guardianship appointment made by the deceased parent comes into effect notwithstanding the survival of the other parent. For an example of where the Scottish position could be advantageous see *Re A, J and J (Minors) (Residence and Guardianship Orders)* [1993] Fam Law 568: see post, p 405 n 8.

19 See by way of example *Re SH (Care Order; Orphan)* [1995] 1 FLR 746 in which it was said that local authority foster parents intended to revoke a guardianship appointment by the mother.

20 Under s 6(6).

1 *The Children Act in Practice* (2nd edn, 1995) para 3.91.

2 See s 92(7).

3 See ante, p 401 n 14.

power to the appointment of an 'individual', a court cannot appoint a *body* such as a local authority to be a guardian.[4] This latter restriction is contrary to the recommendations made in the Government White Paper, *The Law on Child Care and Family Services*,[5] and has already proved inconvenient.[6] It is suggested that this restriction could profitably be removed.

In line with the general restriction against appointing guardians during the lifetime of a parent with parental responsibility, the court's power arises only:

(1) where the child has no parent with parental responsibility; or
(2) upon the death of a parent or guardian in whose favour a residence order was in force.[7]

Although the former embargo is strict,[8] it nevertheless only applies where the child has no *parent* with parental responsibility. The court can therefore appoint a guardian even though the child already has a guardian (other than the child's unmarried father)[9] and it can also make an appointment notwithstanding that the child's unmarried father is still alive, provided he has not obtained parental responsibility.[10]

(b)   Who may apply?

The Act is silent as to who can apply to become a guardian, but it is generally thought that *any* individual[11] (including, in theory, a child) may apply to be appointed. There is no requirement that leave of the court must first be obtained. On the other hand, an application can only be made under s 5 by an individual himself wishing to be a guardian. However, since under s 5(2) the court has power in any family proceedings to make an appointment of its own motion, once proceedings are in train there would seem to be nothing to stop any other interested person, including the child himself, from seeking the appointment of another individual to be a guardian.[12]

(c)   In respect of whom may applications be made?

An application may be made only in respect of a 'child', that is, a person under the age of 18.[13] There is no express embargo against making an appointment in respect

---

4 Nor can this embargo be overcome by seeking the appointment of what was described as an 'artificial individual', namely the director of social services: per Hollis J in *Re SH (Care Order: Orphan)* [1995] 1 FLR 746 at 749.

5 Cm 62, 1987.

6 See *Birmingham City Council v D, Birmingham City Council v M* [1994] 2 FLR 502, in which the local authority unsuccessfully sought care orders in respect of orphans accommodated by them, essentially in order to obtain parental responsibility; cf *Re SH (Care Order: Orphans)* [1995] 1 FLR 746 and *Re M (Care Order: Parental Responsibility)* [1996] 2 FLR 84, in which, in rather different circumstances, care orders *were* made in respect of orphans. See further post, p 547.

7 Except where a residence order was also made in favour of the surviving parent: s 5(9).

8 See eg *Re A, J and J (Minors) (Residence and Guardianship Orders)* [1993] Fam Law 568 – no power to appoint an elder sibling to be a guardian because father was still alive, notwithstanding that he was living out of the jurisdiction and was believed to be suffering from mental illness.

9 Since a guardian has parental responsibility (s 5(6)), presumably an unmarried father who is a guardian will be regarded as a 'parent' with parental responsibility for these purposes.

10 By agreement with the mother or by a court order in accordance with s 4, discussed ante at pp 378ff.

11 But not a 'body' such as a local authority.

12 Such a possibility was canvassed by the Law Commission in their Working Paper No 91 at para 3.49.

13 Section 105(1).

of a married child, although it remains to be seen whether in practice the courts would be prepared to make an appointment in such a case.[14] On normal principles of construction there would appear to be no power to appoint a guardian of a child until it is born.[15]

(d)   Exercising the power

In accordance with the general principles under s 1, when deciding whether to make an appointment, the court is enjoined to regard the child's welfare as the paramount consideration and to be satisfied that making an order is better than making no order at all. It is not, however, obliged to have specific regard to the circumstances set out in s 1(3), though the court is free to do so if it so wishes. There is no restriction comparable to that under s 9(6) appertaining to s 8 orders that appointments with respect to 16- or 17-year-olds should only be made in 'exceptional circumstances'.

Since s 5 proceedings rank as 'family proceedings' the court can make, either upon application or upon its own motion, any s 8 order in addition to or instead of appointing a guardian.[16]

As we have said, the court is empowered to appoint more than one guardian at one time or indeed on different occasions. However, as one commentary has pointed out,[17] it seems unlikely that a court would appoint a subsequent guardian knowing that the two or more guardians would be in conflict. It has also been said[18] that it would be unusual, though not an absolute bar, to appoint persons as guardians who have never actually seen the children.

2.   EFFECT OF BEING APPOINTED A GUARDIAN

Apart from where the Official Solicitor is appointed guardian for a child's estate,[19] all persons appointed as guardians, whether by private appointment or by the court, have parental responsibility for the child.[20]

Distinguishing guardians from parents

Following the Children Act 1989 reforms, the *concepts* of parenthood and guardianship are now legally distinct: parents are no longer regarded as guardians and, apart from exceptional cases in which an unmarried father is appointed a guardian, no guardians will be parents. Guardians are nevertheless in a similar legal position to parents with parental responsibility. The key difference is that, unlike a parent, a guardian cannot be a 'liable relative' under the Social Security Administration Act 1992,[1] nor an 'absent parent' under the Child Support Act 1991,[2] and no court may

---

14   A similar problem obtained in respect of the former law, but the Law Commission (see Working Paper No 91 para 3.64) was inclined to leave the question open.
15   See *Elliot v Joicey* [1935] AC 209, HL and *R v Newham London Borough Council, ex p Dada* [1996] QB 507, [1995] 2 All ER 522, CA.
16   Section 10(1).
17   Hershman and McFarlane, op cit, at G [30] relying on *Re H (an infant)* [1959] 3 All ER 746, [1959] 1 WLR 1163.
18   Per Purchas LJ in *Re C (Minors) (adoption by relatives)* [1989] 1 All ER 395, CA.
19   For an account of the legal position of a guardian of the estate, see Law Com Working Paper No 91 para 2.23.
20   Section 5(6).
 1   Section 78(6) and s 105(3), discussed post at p 724.
 2   Section 3, discussed post at p 730.

order a guardian to make financial provision for, or a transfer of property to a child, under the Children Act 1989.[3] This means that, although guardians are under a duty to see that the child is provided with adequate food, clothing, medical aid and lodging[4] and to educate the child properly,[5] no financial orders can be made against them. The absence of any general legal liability on guardians to maintain children might seem at odds with the general policy of awarding them full parental responsibility. The Law Commission, however, considered[6] that, apart from representing a major change of policy, the imposition of financial liability upon guardians might 'act as a serious deterrent to appointments being made or accepted'. It should also be added that guardians have no rights of succession upon the child's death, nor can a child take British citizenship from his guardian.

Distinguishing guardians from 'non-parents' with residence orders in their favour

Guardianship, like a residence order made in favour of a non-parent, vests parental responsibility for the duration of the order but, unlike the latter,[7] it also gives a guardian the right to consent to or withhold consent to an application being made to free a child for adoption, to agree to or withhold agreement from the child's adoption and to appoint a guardian. Furthermore, although the process of granting residence orders to third parties bears some resemblance to the court process of appointing guardians, the resulting orders are conceptually different, in that the guardian replaces the deceased parent or parents, whereas a person will normally be granted a residence order whilst the child's parents are alive and will therefore share parental responsibility with them.

Distinguishing guardians from de facto carers

The key difference between guardians and de facto carers is that the latter, even though they have the de facto control, have no parental responsibility for the child. If a parent is dead or is unfit to exercise his responsibilities, it is clearly essential for someone to stand in loco parentis to a child; but by English law parental responsibility will not vest in a person unless he has been formally appointed as a guardian either by a deceased parent or by a court order. In a large number of cases, of course, this never happens; and if both parents die, a child's grandparents or other near relations will assume de facto control of the child without taking steps to have themselves appointed legal guardians. Although such persons do not have parental responsibility, nevertheless, as we have seen,[8] under s 3(5) of the 1989 Act they 'may (subject to the provisions of this Act) do what is reasonable in all the circumstances for the purpose of safeguarding or promoting the children's welfare'. There is also, both at common law and under the Children and Young Persons Act 1933, a duty to afford protection.[9] Furthermore, anyone who cares for a child will be

---

3 Viz s 15 and Sch 1, discussed post at p 767. However, in divorce, nullity and separation proceedings between a guardian and his or her spouse, there is power under the Matrimonial
   Causes Act 1973 to make financial provision for the child, provided he or she is a 'child of the
   family'.
4 Pursuant to the Children and Young Persons Act 1933 s 1(2)(a): see ante, p 357.
5 Pursuant to the Education Act 1996 s 7, s 8 and s 576(1): see ante, p 353.
6 Law Com No 172 at para 2.25.
7 See s 12(3), discussed ante, p 387.
8 Ante at p 397.
9 See ante at pp 365ff.

criminally liable under the 1933 Act[10] if they wilfully fail to provide the child with adequate food, clothing, medical aid or lodging. Similarly, the Education Act 1996 places such persons under a duty to see that the child receives full-time education.[11]

Distinguishing guardians from private foster parents

An important difference between a privately appointed guardian and a private foster parent is that, unlike the former, the latter, despite the absence of any formal legal status, is nevertheless still subject to public scrutiny and regulation. If a child is deemed to be privately fostered, then the carers will be subject to the provisions of Part IX of the Children Act 1989, the purpose of which is to ensure that the child is visited periodically by local authority officers, who must satisfy themselves that the child's welfare is being satisfactorily safeguarded and who must give any necessary advice to the foster parents.[12]

A privately fostered child is a child, under the age of 16, who is cared for and accommodated (whether for reward or not) by someone *other than* his parent,[13] a person having parental responsibility for the child or a relative[14] for a period or intended period of 28 days or more.[15] However, to ensure that normal domestic arrangements are not within the scope of these provisions, they do not apply if the child lives in the same premises as a parent or a person having parental responsibility for the child, or a relative who has assumed responsibility for him. The provisions are also excluded where the child is being looked after by a local authority,[16] or lives in accommodation provided by a voluntary organisation, or in a school in which he is receiving full-time education,[17] a hospital, a nursing or mental nursing home, or is subject to a supervision order.[18]

3.   TERMINATION OF GUARDIANSHIP

Automatic termination

The guardian's duties clearly cease if the child dies,[19] and automatically end when he attains the age of 18.[20] Whether the guardian's powers cease upon the child's

---

10 Section 1 and s 17.

11 Sections 7–8 and s 576(1).

12 Children Act 1989 s 67(1) and the Children (Private Arrangements for Fostering) Regulations 1991 (SI 1991/2050). For a discussion of private fostering under the Children Act see Vol 8 of the Department of Health's *Guidance and Regulations* and Clarke Hall and Morrison on *Children* 1 [1451]ff.

13 Including the unmarried father.

14 Defined by s 105(1) of the 1989 Act as 'grandparent, brother, sister, uncle or aunt (whether of the full blood or half blood or by affinity) or a step-parent'.

15 Children Act 1989 s 66. An intention to look after a child for more than 28 days may be inferred from the facts: cf *Surrey County Council v Battersby* [1965] 2 QB 194, [1965] 1 All ER 273.

16 The selection and supervision of *local authority* foster parents is highly regulated under the Foster Placement (Children) Regulations 1991 (SI 1991/910).

17 Note that children under 16 who are pupils at a school which is not maintained by a local education authority are treated as privately fostered if they live at the school during school holidays for more than two weeks: Sch 8, para 9.

18 As these provisions are complementary to those relating to protected children under the Adoption Act 1976, they do not apply to such children either: Sch 8, para 5. For 'protected children' see post, p 662.

19 Though quaere whether a guardian has a duty to bury or cremate the child? – cf *R v Gwynedd County Council, ex p B* [1992] 3 All ER 317, CA, discussed ante at pp 363–4.

20 Section 91(7)–(8).

marriage is perhaps debatable for, while s 5 imposes no such express limitation, it may well be held that there is no scope for the operation of guardianship, save perhaps in respect of the child's property. In any event, it seems unlikely that a guardian would be permitted to interfere with the activities of a married child even if the guardianship continues. Guardianship also ends upon the death of a sole guardian, unless, pursuant to the powers vested by s 5(4), the guardian has appointed another individual to be the child's guardian in his place. If a guardian dies leaving others in office, the survivors continue to be guardians.

Removal by the court

Under s 6(7) of the Children Act 1989 a court[1] can make an order bringing any appointment made under s 5 to an end. Such an order can be made at any time upon the application of:

(1) any person who has parental responsibility including the guardian; or
(2) the child himself, with leave of the court; or
(3) upon the court's own motion in any family proceedings, if the court considers that the appointment should be brought to an end.

In deciding whether to end the guardianship, the court must be guided by the welfare principle, pursuant to s 1(1) of the 1989 Act.[2] If, for example, the guardian expresses an unwillingness to continue, the court is unlikely to consider it to be for the child's welfare that the appointment should continue. But the power to end the appointment is not confined to cases where the guardian wishes to be released. In the past appointments have been brought to an end because of actual or threatened misconduct of the guardian (for the court will attempt to avert a possible danger to the ward rather than wait for it to happen),[3] the abandonment of his rights for such a length of time that it would not be in the child's interests to permit him to reassert them,[4] or merely because of a change of circumstances which rendered it for some reason better for the child to have a new guardian.[5] If it decides to end the guardianship, the court may appoint another individual to take the former guardian's place. It is also open to the court to make a s 8 order. Indeed, as one commentator has pointed out,[6] where the court orders a guardian's removal it may have to consider the appointment of a new guardian to prevent a hiatus in parental responsibility for the child.

4. EVALUATING THE CURRENT LAW

Following the reforms of the Children Act 1989 guardianship now has the clearly defined role of facilitating the replacement of a deceased parent by another person in whom is vested parental responsibility. Furthermore, by simplifying the procedure for making private appointments, the law has arguably done all that it

---

1 The High Court, county court or a magistrates' court: s 92(7).
2 It is not, however, *bound* to apply the checklist in s 1(3) – see s 1(4) – but it should only, pursuant to s 1(5), make an order upon being satisfied that to do so is better than making no order at all.
3 *Beaufort v Berty* (1721) 1 P Wms 703 at 704–5; *Re X* [1899] 1 Ch 526, CA at 531.
4 *Andrews v Salt* (1873) 8 Ch App 622.
5 *Re X* (supra) at 535–6; *F v F* [1902] 1 Ch 688, where a guardian who had become a Roman Catholic was removed although she had made no attempt to influence her ward, a Protestant.
6 Bainham *Children – The Modern Law* 194.

can to encourage the making of such appointments. However, as has been commented on elsewhere,[7] the complete absence of control on private appointments is striking and is in marked contrast, for example, to the plethora of controls on adoption and even private fostering. The closest analogy is with making parental responsibility agreements, but such agreements can only be made between unmarried parents, and even these have to be witnessed in court and centrally recorded.[8]

This absence of control could be justified on the basis that parents are in a better position than either the courts or local authorities to decide who is best able to care for their children after their death. In any event, there remains the safeguard of the local authority's investigative powers to protect children in need or at risk. In practice, little is known about the operation of private guardianship.[9] Research is needed, for example, to discover how common such appointments are; how many are made without even the appointee's knowledge or consent; how many such appointments are disclaimed; and most important, whether there is any evidence to suggest that children may be at risk of abuse by guardians. Similarly, little is known about the use made of the court's powers to make guardianship appointments. There are, for example, no national statistics of the numbers of applications and orders made under s 5. However, judging from the paucity of case law, little use seems to be made of the courts' powers. Again, further research is needed.

7 Douglas and Lowe 'Becoming a Parent in English Law' (1992) 108 LQR 414, at 428 and 432.
8 See ante, pp 378ff.
9 Apart from the valuable but small scale study by Priest appended to Law Com Working Paper No 91. See also Scot Law Com, Discussion Paper No 88 para 3.2.

Chapter 12

The court's powers to make orders under Part II of the Children Act 1989

A. Introduction

This chapter considers the courts' powers under Part II of the Children Act 1989 to make orders in what are termed 'family proceedings'.

Part II is based on the Law Commission's recommendations contained in its *Report on Guardianship and Custody*.[1] The Commission commented[2] that, while the main principles of the pre-1989 Act law were reasonably clear and well accepted, the details were complicated and confusing, with the result that it was 'undoubtedly unintelligible to ordinary people, including the families involved' and on occasion may have prevented families or the courts from 'finding' the best solution for their children.

The Commission were also concerned that the former law made the stakes too high. As they pointed out,[3] all the research evidence[4] shows that children who fare best after their parents' separation are those who are able to maintain a good relationship with both parents. While recognising the obvious limitation that law cannot make people co-operate, the Commission argued that at least it should not stand in their way. Hence, if the parties can co-operate with each other, the law should intervene as little as possible, but if they cannot, the law should at least try to 'lower the stakes' and avoid the impression that the 'loser loses all'.

With the above considerations in mind and with the general aim of making the law 'clear, simple and, we hope, fairer for families and children alike' the Law Commission recommended that the differing powers of the various courts should be replaced by a new set of powers common to all courts and which are designed to be less emotive and more flexible.

Replacing the previous statutory powers[5] to make custody, care and control, custodianship and access orders, the courts are empowered to make a range of orders, collectively known as 's 8 orders', ie residence orders, contact orders, prohibited steps orders and specific issue orders. As well as providing a new range

---

1 Law Com No 172, 1988.
2 Ibid at para 1.1. See also the supplemental study by Priest and Whybrow *Custody Law And Practice in Divorce and Domestic Courts* (1986) (Supplement to Law Com Working Paper No 96).
3 Law Com No 172, para 4.5.
4 Notably that of Wallerstein and Kelly *Surviving the Breakup* (1980). See also Wallerstein and Blakeslee *Second Chances: Men, Women and Children a Decade After Divorce* (1990); Cockett and Tripp *The Exeter Study: Family Breakdown and its impact on Children* (1994); Richards and Dyson *Separation, Divorce and the Development of Children: A Review* (1982); and Rodgers and Pryor *The Development of Children from Separated Families: A Review of Research from the United Kingdom* (1998).
5 Viz under the Matrimonial Causes Act 1973 s 42(1)–(2); the Domestic Proceedings and Magistrates' Courts Act 1978 s 8(2) and s 14; the Guardianship of Minors Act 1971 ss 9–11 and s 14A; the Children Act 1975 s 33(1) and s 34(1); and the Adoption Act 1976 s 25 – all of which were repealed by Sch 15 to the 1989 Act.

of powers, Part II also makes clear provision for determining who can apply for an order. The basic scheme (under s 10) is that some people, for example parents or guardians, are entitled to apply for any s 8 order, while others, eg relatives, are required to seek the court's leave either to intervene in existing family proceedings or to initiate their own proceedings to seek a s 8 order.

Another important change under the 1989 Act is the removal of the court's power in matrimonial and other private law proceedings concerning children to make committal to care or supervision orders.[6] Instead, under s 37 the courts are empowered only to invite the local authority to investigate the circumstances and to decide whether to apply for a care or supervision order. However, in place of these former powers is the power under s 16 to make 'family assistance' orders, the object of which is to provide short-term help for the family.

B.   Section 8 orders

1.   THE POWERS

The expression 'a section 8 order' means any of the orders mentioned in s 8(1), ie a contact order, a prohibited steps order, a residence order and a specific issue order. It also includes any order varying or discharging a s 8 order.[7] In making any s 8 order the court has further supplemental powers (designed to ensure maximum flexibility) under s 11(7) to:

(a) include directions as to how the order is to be carried out;
(b) impose conditions to be complied with by any person in whose favour the order has been made or any parent or other person who has parental responsibility, or any parent with whom the child is living;
(c) specify the period for which the order or any provision in it is to have effect; and
(d) make such incidental, supplemental or consequential provision as the court thinks fit.

Residence orders

A residence order –

> '. . . means an order settling the arrangements to be made as to the person with whom the child is to live'.

As the provision clearly states, residence orders determine with whom the child is to live, and indeed, in its simplest form the order need do no more than name the person *with whom* the child is to live. Although by determining with whom the child will live the order effectively determines *where* the child will live, unless the court adds a direction or condition,[8] the person in whose favour the residence order has been made is free to live in or subsequently move to any

6 For details see pp 297–8, 306, 308 and 369 of the 7th edition of this work.
7 Section 8(2).
8 Viz under s 11(7) (discussed post, pp 423ff), or as a prohibited steps order: see post, p 419. In practice the courts are reluctant to restrain the residence holder's freedom of movement: see post, pp 427–8.

location within the UK.[9]

It is important that residence orders should be seen for what they are, namely orders determining with whom the child is to live. In particular they should not be regarded primarily as a means of reallocating parental responsibility. This is more obviously so as between married parents since, based on the fundamental principle that 'changes in the child's residence should interfere as little as possible in his relationship with both his parents',[10] each parent retains full parental responsibility and with it the power to act independently, unless this is incompatible with a court order, regardless of who has a residence order.[11] But even where the making of a residence order does have the effect of conferring parental responsibility, as it does when made in favour of those who do not already have it,[12] as was held in *Re WB (Residence Orders)*,[13] it is inappropriate to make such an order *solely* for that purpose. In that case a cohabitant, having discovered just before the hearing that he was not the child's father, failed in his attempt to obtain a shared residence order.[14] Although it was acknowledged that this was the only means by which he could acquire parental responsibility, Thorpe J nevertheless refused to interfere with the justices' decision to grant a residence order to the mother and defined contact to the applicant, holding that it would be inappropriate and 'quite artificial' to make a shared residence order solely for that purpose. *Re WB* was, however, distinguished in *Re H (Shared Residence: Parental Responsibility)*,[15] in which the Court of Appeal upheld the making of a shared residence order so as to vest the stepfather with parental responsibility for his step-son, since on the facts it would alleviate the confusion in the child's mind if he did not have the comfort and security of knowing not only that his stepfather (whom he had only just discovered was not his natural father) wished to treat him as his child but that the law would give some stamp of approval to that de facto position. In Ward LJ's view[16] this was a case where a shared residence order was 'not artificial but of important practical therapeutic importance' and where its making reflected 'the reality of the father's involvement and . . . the need for him to be given some status with the school to continue to play his part as both parties wish to do.'

(a) Joint and shared residence orders

Although residence orders are said to settle the arrangements to be made as to *the person* with whom the child is to live, because of the general presumption under the Interpretation Act 1978 s 6(c) that words appearing in a statute in the singular include the plural, residence orders may be made in favour of more than one person.[17] A court could therefore make an order in favour of a parent and

---

9 But not outside the UK without either court leave or the consent of everyone with parental responsibility: s 13(1)(b), discussed post, p 441.
10 See Law Com No 172, para 4.16.
11 See paras 3.62 et seq. But note *Re G (A Minor) (Parental Responsibility: Education)* [1994] 2 FLR 964, CA, and *Re PC (Change of Surname)* [1997] 2 FLR 730, discussed ante, pp 395–6.
12 Under s 12(2)–(3), discussed post, p 438.
13 [1995] 2 FLR 1023 (decided in 1992).
14 'Shared' residence orders are discussed below.
15 [1995] 2 FLR 883, CA. Note also *Re AB (Adoption: Joint Residence)* [1996] 1 FLR 27 in which an adoption order was made in favour of one partner and a joint residence order was made in favour of the unmarried couple, in part to ensure that both had parental responsibility.
16 Ibid at 889.
17 In theory there is nothing to stop the court making an order in favour of more than two people, although in practice it is rarely likely to do so.

step-parent,[18] a cohabiting couple,[19] grandparents,[20] or foster parents. In these cases, what may be conveniently described as 'joint residence orders' are being made in favour of couples living together, but the power is not so restricted, for under s 11(4) residence orders may also be made in favour of two or more persons who do not live together. These latter type of orders have become known as 'shared residence' orders. In theory it is within the court's powers to make both a joint and shared residence order in favour of both parents and their respective new partners, though as yet there is no reported example of such an order.

'Shared residence orders' can take different forms, ranging from an extreme arrangement of providing for the child to spend alternative weeks with each parent to the more common arrangement, for example, that the child spends weekdays with one parent and weekends with the other, or term time with one parent and school holidays with the other. In each of these latter two examples it is equally open to the court to sanction the arrangement by making a residence order in favour of one parent with staying contact for the other. However, if it can be shown that a shared residence order would reduce the hostility between the parents, it would seem to be in the interests of the child's welfare to make a shared residence order.[1]

The argument that a child needs a single settled home will be a strong one in most cases and will generally militate against making a shared residence order under which the child divides his time between each of his parents. In *A v A (Minors) (Shared Residence Order)*[2] the Court of Appeal expressly approved the following passage contained in the Department of Health's *Guidance and Regulations*:[3]

'. . . it is not expected that it will become a common form of order because most children will still need the stability of a single home, and partly because in the cases where shared care is appropriate there is less likely to be a need for the court to make any order at all. However, a shared care order has the advantage of being more realistic in those cases where the child is to spend considerable amounts of time with both parents, [and] brings with it certain other benefits (including the right to remove the child from accommodation provided by a local authority under section 20), and removes any impression that one parent is good and responsible whereas the other parent is not.'

Nevertheless, in *A v A* the Court of Appeal resiled from previous comments[4] suggesting that shared residence orders should only be made in exceptional circumstances. Instead it preferred the test that there needs to be a positive benefit for the child in making such 'non-conventional' orders.[5] On the facts of *A v A* the

---

18 See *Re H (Shared Residence: Parental Responsibility)*, supra.
19 See eg *Re AB (Adoption: Joint Residence)*, supra at n 15 and *Re C (A Minor) (Residence Order: Lesbian Co-parents)* [1994] Fam Law 468 (joint residence order made to the mother and her female cohabitant).
20 See eg *Re W (A Minor) (Residence Order)* [1993] 2 FLR 625, CA.
 1 This argument commended itself to the first instance judge in *A v A (Minors) (Shared Residence Order)* [1994] 1 FLR 669 at 675.
 2 Supra at 674.
 3 Volume 1, *Court Orders*, para 2.28.
 4 Such as those of Purchas LJ in *Re H (A Minor) (Shared Residence)* [1994] 1 FLR 717 at 728.
 5 But note Butler-Sloss LJ's comments ([1994] 1 FLR 669 at 677) that a shared residence order is unlikely to be made if there are concrete issues still arising between the parties (such as the amount of contact, whether it should be visiting or staying contact); or if any other issue (such as education) is still creating difficulties between the parties.

Court of Appeal upheld an order dividing equally the time the children were to live with each parent outside school term time. In *Re H (Shared Residence: Parental Responsibility)*,[6] in which, as we have seen, the court made a shared residence order in part to allay the child's confusion about his stepfather's status, Ward LJ still referred to such orders as being 'unusual'. Although there are other reported examples,[7] it is clear that the appellate courts at least are not keen to make such orders. As Hale J put it in *Re N (Section 91(14) Order)*:[8]

'... it has always been acknowledged in the Court of Appeal that orders that a child should share his time between two homes are not orders that should become standard and that, in many cases, the child needs the security of knowing where his home is.'

Where a residence order is made in favour of two persons who do not live together, under s 11(4) the order may specify the periods during which the child is to live in the different households concerned. Such directions may be general rather than specific and in some cases may not be needed at all. Since a residence order only settles the arrangements as to the person with whom the child is to live, any other conditions that are needed must be specified separately by the court acting under the powers vested by s 11(7).[9]

Where as a result of a residence order 'the child lives, or is to live, with one of two parents who each have parental responsibility for him', that order will cease to have effect if the parents live together for a continuous period of more than six months.[10]

(b) 'Interim' residence orders

Under s 11(3) the court can make, inter alia, a residence order 'even though it is not in a position to dispose finally of those proceedings'. Furthermore, under s 11(7)(c) such orders can have effect for a specified period. By these provisions the court can make interim provision by way of a residence order for a limited period.[11] It should be noted, however, that the Act makes no distinction between a final residence order and one made as an interim measure. Indeed, as Bracewell J has observed in *S v S (Custody: Jurisdiction)*:[12] 'It has become common parlance to speak of "interim residence orders", but in fact there is no such creature within the Children Act 1989.' Hence *all* such orders, even those expressed to last for a matter of days, have the same effect and will, for example, discharge any existing care order,[13] confer, for the duration of the order, parental responsibility on those

6 [1995] 2 FLR 883 at 883G.
7 See eg *Re R (Residence Order: Finance)* [1995] 2 FLR 612, CA; *M v A (Wardship: Removal From Jurisdiction)* [1993] 2 FLR 715; *G v G (Joint Residence Order)* [1993] Fam Law 615. Note also *Re A, J and J (Minors) (Residence and Guardianship Orders)* [1993] Fam Law 568, in which a shared residence order was made in favour of an elder sister and the deceased mother's friend.
8 [1996] 1 FLR 356, CA at 359. Note also *H v H (A Minor) (No 2) (Forum Conveniens)* [1997] 1 FCR 603, in which Bracewell J refused to make a shared residence order because she thought that in that case it would be 'a recipe for future conflict'.
9 Discussed post, pp 423ff.
10 Section 11(5). For an example of where such an order did come to such an end see *Re P (Abduction: Declaration)* [1995] 1 FLR 831, CA at 834.
11 It is apparently possible to make an interim residence order run alongside the main order: see *Re M (Minors) (Interim Residence Order)* [1997] 2 FCR 28, CA.
12 [1995] 1 FLR 155 at 157.
13 Under s 91(1): see post, pp 566–7. Where an 'interim' order is thought justified, careful thought needs to be given to its length and, mindful of the general enjoinder under s 1(2) to treat 'delay' as prima facie detrimental to the child's interest, courts should ensure that it is no longer than absolutely necessary: see eg *Re O (Minors) (Leave To Seek Residence Order)* [1994] 1 FLR 172, where, on the facts, five weeks' duration was thought too long. See also *Re Y (A Minor) (Ex Parte Interim Orders)* [1993] 2 FCR 422, [1994] Fam Law 127.

who do not already have it,[14] and will empower the residence holder to remove the child from the UK for a period of less than one month.[15]

(c)   Ex parte applications and orders

As originally drafted the Rules only made provision for ex parte applications[16] to be made in respect of specific issue and prohibited steps orders. However, in *Re B (Minors) (Residence Order)*[17] the Court of Appeal refused to accept that applying the maxim, expressio unius exclusio alterius, the Rules should be interpreted as preventing ex parte applications for residence orders being made. Following this ruling the Rules were amended and now[18] expressly provide that applications for *any* s 8 order, including therefore residence and contact orders, can be made ex parte. Notwithstanding the change in the rules it is well established that ex parte residence orders should only be made exceptionally. It is accepted, for instance, that they are appropriate in cases of child abduction,[19] while in *Re Y (A Minor) (Ex Parte Interim Orders)*[20] an ex parte order in favour of a grandmother was thought justified in a case where the mother, who had a history of mental instability, had phoned her threatening to commit suicide. It is evident, however, that the circumstances need to be compelling. In *Re G (Minors) (Ex Parte Interim Residence Order)*,[1] for instance, an allegation that the mother had been taking cannabis was not thought to justify making an ex parte order in favour of the father. In *Re P (A Minor) (Ex Parte Interim Residence Order)*[2] an ex parte order was held to have been wrongly granted where the child was in no immediate danger, since she was already under the scrutiny of the local authority.

Even where it is appropriate to make an ex parte order, that order should normally only be for a short duration.[3] In most cases those wishing to challenge such orders should await the full hearing rather than appeal.[4]

Contact orders

A contact order requires –

> '. . . the person with whom the child lives, or is to live, to allow the child to visit or stay with the person named in the order, or for that person and the child otherwise to have contact with each other'.

---

14 Under s 12(2): see post, p 438.
15 Under s 13(2) (discussed post, p 441). Presumably this power of removal is subject to the length of the order – an order expressed to last only a few days cannot be taken to vest a power of removal in excess of that. 'Interim' orders are recognised and enforceable under the European Convention on Recognition and Enforcement of Decisions Concerning Children 1980: see *Re S (A Minor) (Custody: Habitual Residence)* [1997] 4 All ER 251, HL, discussed post, p 507.
16 That is, where notice is not given to the respondent.
17 [1992] Fam 162, [1992] 3 All ER 867, CA.
18 Family Proceedings Rules 1991 r 4.4(4) as amended by SI 1992/2067, and Family Proceedings Courts (Children Act 1989) Rules 1991 r 4(4) as amended by SI 1992/2068.
19 See *Re B*, supra, per Butler-Sloss LJ.
20 [1993] 2 FCR 422.
 1 [1993] 1 FLR 910, CA.
 2 [1993] 1 FLR 915, CA. See also *Note: Re J (Children: Ex Parte Orders)* [1997] 1 FLR 606 – an ex parte order requiring the handing over of a young child [aged three] to a parent with whom he had not lived for 20 months was only likely to be justified in exceptional circumstances.
 3 See *Re Y*, supra, in which Johnson J held that 12 weeks was too long and that the norm should be seven days.
 4 Per Purchas LJ in *Re P*, supra at 917–18.

By providing for the child to visit or stay with the person named in the order, the emphasis is clearly on the child rather than the parent.[5] As the words 'otherwise to have contact with each other' make clear, contact orders embrace both physical and non-physical contact and may therefore range from long or short visits to contact by letter or telephone.[6] Whether a contact order is *necessarily* directed against the person with whom the child lives or is to live, as the opening part of the definition suggests, or whether the closing words 'or for the person and the child otherwise to have contact with each other' can properly be regarded as empowering a court to make an independent order simply providing for the child to have contact with a person named in the order, has not expressly been addressed by the courts. However, in *Re H (minors) (prohibited steps order)*[7] it seemed to be the underlying assumption that such orders are directed against the person with whom the child is living etc. As will be seen, the distinction is not without importance when determining the court's power to (a) prohibit contact,[8] (b) make provision for contact in a freeing for adoption order,[9] or (c) enforce the order.[10]

Orders may provide for the child to have contact with any person (including, where appropriate, a sibling) and more than one contact order may be made in respect of a child. A contact order can be the sole order made even between parents and is likely to be so where there is no dispute as to the person with whom the child is to live.

It is within a court's power to make an order for 'reasonable contact',[11] but if that is the sole order between parents, then, having regard to s 1(5),[12] one may question the need to make the order at all. On the other hand, such an order might be justified where the applicant is not a parent, eg a grandparent, since without an order such a person has no locus standi in relation to the child.[13] Such an order might also be valuable if the person with whom the child lives is likely to be hostile to the absent parent having contact and might therefore seek to prevent it. Where restricted or supervised contact is thought appropriate the court may attach any directions or conditions under s 11(7).

Like residence orders, contact orders requiring one parent to allow the child to visit the other parent[14] will automatically lapse if the parents subsequently live

5 This is more in keeping with the views expressed by Wrangham J in *M v M (Child: Access)* [1973] 2 All ER 81 that access is properly to be regarded as a right of the child rather than a right of the parent.
6 For examples of contact by post see eg *A v L (Contact)* [1998] 1 FLR 361 and *Re M (A Minor) (Contact: Conditions)* [1994] 1 FLR 272 – both involving letter contact with a father in prison, and *Re L (Contact: Transsexual Applicant)* [1995] 2 FLR 438 (indirect contact with transsexual father). Note also *Re J (A Minor) (Contact)* [1994] 1 FLR 729, CA in which it was held that non-physical contact does not for the purposes of what is now RSC Ord 59 r 1B(f)(ii)–(iii) rank as 'contact', and so leave is not required to appeal to the Court of Appeal.
7 [1995] 4 All ER 110, CA, discussed further below at p 418.
8 See post, p 418.
9 See post, p 670 n 18.
10 See post, p 447.
11 Before the 1989 Act orders for 'reasonable' access were very common and the Department of Health's *Guidance and Regulations*, Vol 1, *Court Orders* at para 2.29 anticipated that orders for reasonable contact would be the 'usual order'. Interestingly a similar comment is made in the Department of Health and Social Services' *Guidance and Regulations to the Children (Northern Ireland) Order 1995*, Vol 1, *Court Orders and Other Issues*, para 5.11 (published in 1996).
12 Discussed ante at p 340 and post, p 462.
13 See post, pp 463–4.
14 Aliter if the order is directed against someone other than a parent or if the child is permitted contact with a third party.

together for a continuous period of more than six months.[15] Under the general provisions of s 11(3) a court can make an 'interim contact order' in cases where it is not in a position finally to dispose of proceedings. However, it has been held[16] that courts should be cautious about making such interim orders where the principle of contact is in dispute and substantial factual issues are unresolved.

While the child is with a parent on a contact visit that parent may exercise parental responsibility, at any rate with respect to short term matters,[17] without consulting the other, provided he does nothing which is incompatible with any existing court order.[18]

Prohibiting contact

When the 1989 Act was first implemented it was thought that orders denying contact required a prohibited steps order. As the Department of Health's *Guidance and Regulations* stated:[19]

'. . . a s 8 order is a positive order in the sense that it requires contact to be allowed between an individual and a child and *cannot be used to deny contact*' [emphasis added].

However, this reasoning was rejected by the Court of Appeal in *Nottingham County Council v P.*[20] Sir Stephen Brown P commented:

'Submissions were made to the court to the effect that a contact order in any event necessarily implied a positive order and that an order which merely provided for "no contact" could not be construed as a contact order. There are certain passages in editorial comment which seem to support that view. We do not share it. We agree with the judge that the sensible and appropriate construction of the term contact order includes a situation where a court is required to consider whether any contact should be provided for. An order that there shall be "no contact" falls within the general concept and common sense requires that it should be considered to fall within the definition of 'contact order' in section 8(1).'

However, in the subsequent decision, *Re H (minors) (prohibited steps order)*,[1] the Court of Appeal made a prohibited steps order against a mother's former cohabitant preventing him from having or seeking contact with her children, to whom it was considered he posed a risk. It was held that it was only by this means that the order could be directed (and thus enforced) against the man. Butler-Sloss LJ commented that had a 'no contact' order been made it would have been directed against the mother, who would thus have been obliged to prevent contact. That would have been inappropriate in this case, since she neither wanted the children to have such contact nor had she the power to control it.[2]

---

15 Section 11(6).
16 Per Wall J in *Re D (Contact: Interim Orders)* [1995] 1 FLR 495. An example of where such an order might be justified is where previously satisfactory contact has been arbitrarily terminated by the 'residential parent'.
17 But, possibly, not to take important steps that have long term consequences for the child: see *Re G (Parental Responsibility: Education)* [1994] 2 FLR 964, CA discussed ante at pp 395–6.
18 See ante, p 395.
19 Vol 1, *Court Orders*, para 2.30.
20 [1994] Fam 18 at 38–9, [1993] 3 All ER 815 at 824, CA, discussed further post at pp 423 and 430–1.
 1 [1995] 4 All ER 110, CA.
 2 The children were of school age and, as Butler-Sloss LJ said, 'With the best will in the world the mother could not protect her children going to and from school or at play . . .'

In the light of these decisions it would now seem that the appropriate order for prohibiting contact is determined by considering against whom it should be directed.[3] If it is against the person with whom the child is living or is to live, then an order for 'no contact' should be made. If, as seems more likely to be the case, it is against some other person, then a prohibited steps order is appropriate.[4] It has to be said that the current position is unnecessarily complicated. The better view is, surely, as was originally envisaged, that a complete denial of contact should be made by a prohibited steps order.[5] Accordingly, it is submitted that in this respect the ruling in *Nottingham* was wrong.

Prohibited steps orders

A prohibited steps order –

'. . . means an order that no step which could be taken by a parent in meeting his parental responsibility for a child, and which is of a kind specified in the order, shall be taken by any person without the consent of the court'.

This is one of two orders under the 1989 Act (the other being a specific issue order), which are modelled on the wardship jurisdiction, and intended to broaden all the courts' powers when dealing with children.

It empowers a court to place a *specific* embargo upon the exercise of any aspect of parental responsibility. This is in contrast to the vague requirement in wardship that 'no important step' in the child's life be taken without the court's prior consent.[6] The Law Commission instanced[7] as an example an embargo that the child should not be removed from the United Kingdom, which they said might be useful in cases where no residence order has been made so that the automatic restriction against removal under s 13 does not apply.[8] But there are many other examples, such as prohibiting contact with a parent or someone else,[9] restraining a particular medical operation, restraining changing the child's surname,[10] preventing the child's schooling from being changed, preventing repeated removal of children outside the United Kingdom for periods of less than one month by the residential parent, and preventing the child's removal from his home before the court has had time to decide what order, if any, should be made.[11]

3 Though, as was observed earlier (ante, p 417), it is not beyond argument that a contact order is not necessarily directed against anyone.
4 Presumably, on this analysis, where it is thought necessary and appropriate to direct an order against both persons, both a 'no contact' and a prohibited steps order should be made.
5 Interestingly, the *Guidance* to the Northern Ireland Order, supra, states at para 5.15 that, although it will be a matter for judicial interpretation whether a contact order can be used to deny contact, in the light of the *Nottingham* and *Re H* decisions 'it would seem appropriate to use a prohibited steps order to deny contact.'
6 Wardship is discussed in Chapter 16. It is assumed that an order as vague as prohibiting any important step could not be made as a prohibited steps order.
7 Law Com No 172, para 4.20. This comment is repeated by the Department of Health's *Guidance and Regulations*, Vol 1, *Court Orders*, at para 2.31.
8 The embargo under s 13(1)(b) and (2) is discussed post, p 441. It should be noted that, in the absence of a residence order, the Child Abduction Act 1984 (see ante, p 361) operates to prevent unilateral removal. However, a prohibited steps order could be made to prevent a child's removal outside England and Wales rather than the United Kingdom as a whole.
9 *Re H (a minor) (prohibited steps order)* [1995] 4 All ER 110, CA, discussed above at p 418.
10 At any rate in the absence of a residence order: see *Dawson v Wearmouth* [1998] 1 All ER 271, CA. Where there is a residence order, applications concerning a change of name should be made under s 13: see *Re B (Change of Surname)* [1996] 1 FLR 791, CA, discussed post, p 439.
11 See *Guidance and Regulations*, Vol 1, *Court Orders* at para 2.31.

Although the order itself must relate to parental responsibility, it is clear that it can be made against anyone regardless of whether he has parental responsibility. Hence orders can be made against an unmarried father whether or not he has responsibility and similarly against a third party, for example to restrain a former cohabitant (notwithstanding that he was not even a party) from contacting or seeking to have contact with the child,[12] or to restrain an individual or group from associating with the child.

Provided the order is of some value to the applicant it can be made even though the child is abroad.[13] Applications for prohibited steps orders can be made ex parte, and an order may be made either in conjunction with another s 8[14] order or on its own.

Specific issue order

A specific issue order –

'. . . means an order giving directions for the purpose of determining a specific question which has arisen, or which may arise, in connection with any aspect of parental responsibility for a child'.

These orders enable a specific question relating to the child to be brought before the court, the aim of which is not to give one parent or the other a general 'right' to make decisions in a particular respect, but to enable a particular dispute to be resolved.[15] It was held in *Re HG (Specific Issue Order: Sterilisation)*[16] that there is no necessity for there to be a dispute between the parties before the power arises to make a specific issue order; it is sufficient that there is a question to be answered. In that case an unopposed application[17] for a specific issue order was granted giving High Court sanction for the sterilisation of a 17-year-old mentally subnormal child. Like prohibited steps orders, applications for specific issue orders may be made ex parte[18] and orders may be made either in conjunction with another s 8 order or on their own. Examples of specific issue orders made since the Act include *Re R (A Minor) (Blood Transfusion)*,[19] in which the court ordered inter alia that, in an imminently life-threatening situation, the child in question be given a blood transfusion without the consent of her parents, who were Jehovah's

---

12 *Re H* supra. In the case of non-parties, orders cannot be enforced until they have been served on the respondent: see Clarke Hall and Morrison on *Children* Vol 1 at 1[274].

13 See *Re D (a minor)* [1992] 1 All ER 892, CA – a mother, in breach of an undertaking given to the English court, failed to return the child from Turkey: an order for the child's return was thought helpful to the father in bringing proceedings in Turkey.

14 FPR 1991 r 4.4(4); FPC (CA 1989) R 1991 r 4.4. Such orders are sometimes made in the context of international child abduction, often at the request of the abducting parent, to prevent removal by the other. See eg *Re AZ (A Minor) (Abduction: Acquiescence)* [1993] 1 FLR 682; *Re B (Minors) (Abduction) (No 2)* [1993] 1 FLR 993; *D v D (Child Abduction: non-Convention Country)* [1994] 1 FLR 137 and *Re S (Minors) (Abduction)* [1994] 1 FLR 297, CA.

15 Department of Health's *Guidance and Regulations*, Vol 1, *Court Orders*, para 2.32.

16 [1993] 1 FLR 587.

17 The application was thought necessary in view of Lord Templeman's lone dictum in *Re B (A Minor) (Wardship: Sterilisation)* [1988] AC 199 at 205, [1987] 2 All ER 206 at 214 (discussed ante at p 358) that High Court sanction is always required for a child's sterilisation. See also *Practice Note* [1993] 3 All ER 222.

18 Family Proceedings Rules 1991 r 4.4(4); Family Proceedings Courts (Children Act 1989) Rules 1991 r 4(4). For an example of an *order* being made ex parte see *Re D (a minor)* [1992] 1 All ER 892, CA.

19 [1993] 2 FLR 757.

Witnesses; *Re F (Specific Issue: Child Interview)*,[20] in which an order was made permitting a defence solicitor to interview children for the purpose of providing evidence in criminal proceedings against their father; and *Re D (a minor)*,[1] in which the court ordered a mother to return the child to the jurisdiction. Another obvious example is in connection with disputes over a child's education in which the court could make a specific issue order specifying which school the child should attend.[2] It is also established[3] that, in the absence of a pre-existing residence order, disputes about a child's surname can be resolved inter alia by means of a specific issue order.

Limits on the courts' powers to make specific issue and prohibited steps orders[4]

(a) Orders must concern 'an aspect of parental responsibility'

An important limitation both on prohibited and specific issue orders is that they must concern an aspect of parental responsibility. The court may not, therefore, make a prohibited steps order forbidding contact between the parents,[5] or protecting one parent from being assaulted by the other,[6] nor may it make a specific issue order compelling a local authority to provide support services,[7] since neither contact between adults nor the provision of support services has anything to do with parental responsibility. At one time it had been widely assumed[8] that neither a prohibited steps order restricting, nor a specific issue order sanctioning publicity about a child could be made, since publicity about a child could not be considered to be an aspect of parental responsibility, and such was the majority view in *Re W (Wardship: Discharge: Publicity)*.[9] However, as we discussed in Chapter 10,[10] this view has not gone unchallenged. In particular, note needs to be taken of Hobhouse LJ's well-reasoned dissenting judgment in *Re W (Wardship: Publicity)*[11] and of the Court of Appeal decision in *Re Z (A Minor) (Identification: Restriction on Publication)*,[12] in which a prohibited steps order restraining publicity was made upon the basis that the mother's waiver of the child's right of confidentiality to the particular information (viz the attendance at a specialist unit dealing with children's

20 [1995] 1 FLR 819, CA. See also *Re M (Care: Leave To Interview Child)* [1995] 1 FLR 825, discussed ante at p 353.
1 Supra.
2 For a pre-Children Act example of a dispute about a child's education that would now be resolved by a specific issue order see *Re P (A Minor) (Education)* [1992] 1 FLR 316, CA.
3 See *Dawson v Wearmouth* [1998] 1 All ER 271, CA.
4 See also post, p 429 for a discussion of the general restrictions on making s 8 orders and, in particular, pp 430–2 in relation to the fetters on local authority use.
5 *Croydon London Borough Council v A* [1992] Fam 169, [1992] 3 All ER 788; cf *F v R (Contact)* [1995] 1 FLR 227 in which Wall J accepted that such an embargo could be incorporated as a condition to a residence or contact order under s 11(7), though this decision is now difficult to square with *D v N (Contact Orders: Conditions)* [1997] 2 FLR 797, CA discussed post, p 426.
6 *M v M (Residence Order: Ancillary Jurisdiction)* [1994] Fam Law 440 in which Johnson J also held that an injunction could nevertheless be sought under the appropriate domestic violence legislation, as an ancillary action to the Children Act application.
7 *Re J (Specific Issue Order: Leave To Apply)* [1995] 1 FLR 669, per Wall J.
8 See Department of Health's *Guidance and Regulations*, Vol, *Court Orders* at para 2.31, and, more recently, the *Guidance* to the Northern Ireland Order, Vol 1, *Court Orders and Other Legal Issues*, para 5.17.
9 [1995] 2 FLR 466.
10 See ante at pp 371–2.
11 [1995] 2 FLR at 476.
12 [1997] Fam 1, sub nom *Re Z (a minor) (freedom of publication)* [1995] 4 All ER 961, CA.

educational needs) was an aspect of parental responsibility. Accordingly, it would now appear that on occasion at least publicity about a child can be restrained by a prohibited steps order.

(b)   No power to make ouster orders

For some time it was uncertain whether a prohibited steps and/or a specific issue order could be made to oust a parent from the matrimonial home. In *Nottingham County Council v P*[13] Sir Stephen Brown P, however, commented that 'it is very doubtful indeed whether a prohibited steps order could in any circumstances be used to "oust" a father from a matrimonial home.' Similarly, in *Pearson v Franklin*[14] Nourse LJ commented that Parliament could not have intended that ouster orders are capable of being made under the guise of specific issue orders. It was therefore held that a specific issue order (and by implication a prohibited steps order) could not be used to interfere with rights of occupation. In *Re M (Minors) (Disclosure of Evidence)*[15] the Court of Appeal took *Nottingham* to have established that there is no jurisdiction under the Children Act to exclude a parent from the home for the protection of the child, and in *Re D (Prohibited Steps Order)*[16] Ward LJ clearly stated that there is no jurisdiction to make an ouster order under the Children Act.[17]

Aside from justifying this position as a matter of policy (ie that because of their drastic effect Parliament should be taken to confer the power to make ouster orders only where a statute clearly so provides) a possible theoretical justification for this lack of power is that ouster orders relate to matters of occupation rather than parental responsibility.[18]

(c)   No power to make disguised residence or contact orders

Section 9(5)(a) prevents the court from making a prohibited steps or a specific issue order 'with a view to achieving a result which could be achieved by a residence or contact order'. This provision was made to guard against the slight risk, particularly in uncontested cases, that the orders might be used to achieve the same practical results as residence or contact orders but without the same legal effects.[19] Section 9(5)(a) can have a surprisingly wide impact. In *Re B*

---

13   [1994] Fam 18 at 39E–F, [1993] 3 All ER 815, CA at 825b.
14   [1994] 2 All ER 137, CA at 141d–e, per Nourse LJ.
15   [1994] 1 FLR 760.
16   [1996] 2 FLR 273. See also *Re D (Residence: Imposition of Conditions)* [1996] 2 FLR 281, CA. Both these cases also establish that the inability to make an ouster order by way of a prohibited steps or specific issue order cannot be overcome by using s 11(7). See also *D v N (Contact Order: Conditions)* [1997] 2 FLR 797, CA, discussed post, p 426.
17   Though probably an application for an occupation order under Part IV of the Family Law Act 1996 (discussed ante at pp 199ff) can be brought as an ancillary action to the Children Act application; cf *M v M (Residence Order: Ancillary Injunction)* [1994] Fam Law 440 in which Johnson J held that a prohibited steps order cannot be used to prevent one parent from assaulting the other, but that an injunction under the appropriate domestic violence legislation can be sought as an ancillary action to the Children Act application. For the court's power to make ouster orders upon making an emergency protection or interim care order, see post, pp 594 and 577 respectively.
18   This line of argument was hinted at by Nourse LJ in *Pearson v Franklin*, supra, but it is not beyond question, since ouster orders are viewed as being primarily about protection and only incidentally about occupation.
19   Law Com No 172, para 4.19. Department of Health's *Guidance and Regulations*, Vol 1, *Court Orders*, para 2.34.

(Minors) (Residence Order),[20] for example, it was held that it operates to prevent the making of a specific issue order to return a child to a parent in the case of a snatch, since such an order could be made by means of a residence order with appropriate conditions attached under s 11(7).[1] In *Nottingham County Council v P*[2] the Court of Appeal upheld Ward J's ruling that it is contrary to s 9(5)(a) to order, upon a local authority application under s 8, that a father vacate the household and that the child should have no further contact with him save under local authority supervision. In the court's view the application patently sought to determine the residence of the children (that is, by regulating who could live in the household) and the degree of contact which the children might have with the father. In reaching this latter conclusion the Court of Appeal, as we discussed earlier,[3] rejected the argument that an order for 'no contact' could not be made as a contact order under s 8. However, in the subsequent Court of Appeal case, *Re H (minors) (prohibited steps orders),*[4] it was held that a prohibited steps order restricting a former cohabitant from contacting or seeking contact with the children did not contravene s 9(5), since unlike an order for no contact under s 8 it could properly be directed and enforced against the man rather than the mother.

(d)   No power to make orders that are denied to the High Court acting under its inherent jurisdiction

Section 9(5)(b) prevents the court from exercising its power to make a specific issue or prohibited steps order 'in any way which is denied to the High Court (by s 100(2)) in the exercise of its inherent jurisdiction.'[5] According to the Department of Health's *Guidance and Regulations,*[6] s 9(5)(b) prevents local authorities applying for a prohibited steps or specific issue order as a way of obtaining (a) the care or supervision of a child; (b) an order that the child be accommodated by them, and (c) any aspect of parental responsibility. In *Re S and D (Children: Powers of Court)*[7] it was held that a court had, by reason of s 9(5)(b) and s 100(2)(b) no power to restrain a parent from removing the child from local authority accommodation[8] pursuant to the rights conferred by s 20(7). It must also follow that there is similarly no power to restrain a parent from objecting to his child being accommodated in the first place pursuant to the right conferred by s 20(7).[9]

Additional directions and conditions

Wide though s 8 orders are, they do not expressly provide the power to make interim orders, to delay implementation of orders, or to attach other special

---

20 [1992] Fam 162, [1992] 3 All ER 867, CA; cf *Re D (a minor)* [1992] 1 All ER 892, CA, in which a specific issue order *was* made ordering a parent abroad to return the child to the jurisdiction.
1 The power to add conditions etc under s 11(7) is discussed below.
2 [1994] Fam 18, [1993] 3 All ER 815, CA.
3 See ante, p 418.
4 [1995] 4 All ER 110, CA.
5 The High Court's inherent jurisdiction is discussed in Chapter 16.
6 Supra, at para 2.33.
7 [1995] 2 FLR 456, CA.
8 Local authority accommodation is discussed post at pp 524ff.
9 Discussed post, p 526. Quaere whether it is possible for a prohibited steps order to be made upon the parent's application to prevent the other parent from objecting to the child's accommodation?

conditions. For these powers one must look to s 11(7).[10] That section provides that a s 8 order may:

(a) contain directions as to how the order is to be carried out;
(b) impose conditions to be complied with by any person in whose favour the order has been made or any parent or any non-parent who has parental responsibility, or any parent with whom the child is living;
(c) specify the period for which the order or any provision in it is to have effect; and
(d) make such incidental, supplemental or consequential provision as the court thinks fit.

These powers are exercisable by *any* court making a s 8 order.

(a)   Directions and limited duration orders

The power under s 11(7)(a) to give directions as to how an order is to be put into effect is designed[11] to enable the court to smooth the transition in cases, for example, where the child's residence is changed or to define more precisely what contact is to take place under a contact order. It also provides a means by which a first instance court can stay an order, for example by directing that any transfer of residence be delayed pending an appeal.[12]

The power under s 11(7)(c) to specify the period for which a s 8 order, or any provision in it, is to have effect is intended[13] to empower the court inter alia to make what are effectively interim orders. Accordingly, the court can make an order for a limited duration coupled with a direction that the matter be brought back to court at a later specific date. This type of order could be useful in cases where more information is required,[14] or to allow time to monitor the effectiveness of, for example, the contact arrangements.[15] Another use of a limited duration order might be to make a holding order pending an appeal.

(b)   Conditions and other supplemental orders

Although on its face the power under s 11(7)(b) and (d) to add conditions and to make 'such incidental, supplemental or consequential provision as the court thinks fit' seems to give the court considerable scope for making a wide range of supporting provisions to s 8 orders, it is clear that it was never intended to expand the courts' armoury to any great extent. In recommending what were described as 'supplemental provisions' the Law Commission specifically said[16] that they did 'not expect these supplemental powers to be used at all frequently, as most cases will not require them and all are subject to the general rule that orders should only

---

10 Occasionally, however, courts accept undertakings rather than imposing conditions. See eg *Re R (A Minor) (Residence; Religion)* [1993] 2 FLR 163, CA (aunt granted contact on the undertaking that she would not speak or communicate with the child in any way in relation to religious or spiritual matters).
11 See Law Com No 172, para 4.22.
12 See *Re J (A Minor) (Residence)* [1994] 1 FLR 369 at 375, per Singer J.
13 Law Com No 172, para 4.24.
14 Under s 11(3) courts can make a s 8 order even though they are not in a position finally to dispose of proceedings.
15 As in *Re B (A Minor) (Contact: Interim Order)* [1994] 2 FLR 269.
16 See Law Com No 172 at para 4.21. All that the *Guidance and Regulations*, Vol 1, *Court Orders* at para 2.22 states is that the supplemental etc powers 'enable the new orders [ie s 8 orders] to be as flexible as possible and so reduce or remove the need to resort to wardship'.

be made where they are the most effective means of safeguarding or promoting the child's welfare'. The Commission instanced[17] three examples of when they could be useful:

(1)   in the case of a dispute about which school the child should attend, making it a condition of a residence order that the child attend a particular school;
(2)   where there is a real fear that on a contact visit the parent will remove the child from the country and not return him, making it a condition of the contact order that any such removal is prohibited;[18] and
(3)   where there is real concern that the person with whom the child will live will not agree to a blood transfusion, making it a condition of the residence order to require the parent to inform the other parent so that the latter can agree to it.[19]

Notwithstanding the intention that they should have a limited role, these provisions have generated considerable case law and even now their full ambit cannot be stated with certainty. Indeed, in *D v N (Contact Order: Conditions)*[20] Sir Stephen Brown P commented (in the context of imposing conditions on a contact order) that he considered 'that it may be necessary for a court in the future to give further consideration to the true nature, meaning and effect of conditions imposed under s 11(7)'.

The general application of the power to add conditions etc

Case law has noticeably shifted in direction. Earlier decisions[1] emphasised the width of the powers, particularly in the private law context, whereas later judgments[2] have become more restrictive in their approach. However, certain points do seem to be established. First, it seems clear that s 11(7) is properly regarded as only vesting ancillary or supportive powers to those under s 8. Accordingly, it cannot be regarded as giving the courts completely novel and independent powers to make, for example, conditions about the parties' finances or property ownership.

Furthermore, it is also well established that s 11(7) cannot be used to interfere with rights of occupation, for, as Ward LJ said in *Re D (Prohibited Steps Order)*:[3]

'Section 11(7), in my judgment, is ancillary to the making of a s 8 order. It is governed by the provisions for the making of a s 8 order and does not allow the importation by the back door of the matters laid down in the Matrimonial Homes Act[4] or proper adjustment of rights of occupation.'

---

17   Ibid at para 4.23.
18   Lord Mackay LC at 505 HL Official Report (5th Series) col 345 envisaged conditions being imposed forbidding a parent from moving the child to another town. But cf *Re E (Residence: Imposition of Conditions)* [1997] 2 FLR 638, CA, discussed post, pp 427–8.
19   See the pre-Children Act decision, *Jane v Jane* (1983) 4 FLR 712, CA, in which effectively the father was given the power to consent to medical treatment but the mother (a Jehovah's Witness) looked after the child.
20   [1997] 2 FLR 797, CA at 802.
 1   Namely *Re B (A Minor) (Residence Order)* [1992] Fam 162, [1992] 3 All ER 867, CA and *Re O (Contact: Imposition of Conditions)* [1995] 2 FLR 124, CA, discussed below.
 2   See eg *Re D (Residence: Imposition of Conditions)* [1996] 2 FLR 281, CA; *D v N (Contact Order: Conditions)*, supra, and *Re E (Residence: Imposition of Conditions)* [1997] 2 FLR 638, CA, discussed below.
 3   [1996] 2 FLR at 279. Note also *D v N (Contact Order: Conditions)*, supra, discussed post, p 426.
 4   Now repealed and replaced by Part IV of the Family Law Act 1996: see Chapter 6.

Similarly, it was held in *D v N (Contact Order: Conditions)*[5] when making an order for defined contact that it was wholly inappropriate to use s 11(7) to make orders (inter alia forbidding the father to molest the mother or her relatives, from entering or damaging certain premises belonging to those relatives, or from corresponding with the mother's employers) which related more to the protection of the mother from perceived harassment than to the management of the contact.

What is properly regarded as supportive or supplemental can be problematic. In *Re M (A Minor) (Contact: Conditions)*[6] Wall J considered that since the powers were only supportive there was no jurisdiction under s 11(7) to direct one parent to write to the other about the child's progress. In *Re O (Contact: Imposition of Conditions)*,[7] however, the Court of Appeal overruled this proposition, holding instead that s 11(7) empowered the courts to compel one parent to send to the other such information about the child's progress as would promote meaningful contact between the child and the non-residential parent. In the subsequent decision, *F v R (Contact: Justices' Reasons)*[8] Wall J approved an agreed condition to an indirect contact order that the father was not to contact or enter a day centre or school at which the child was a pupil without either the mother's or the court's prior permission. It might also be possible to make an order for supervised contact provided the supervisor is one of the persons listed in s 11(7)(b).[9]

Secondly, as s 11(7)(b) itself expressly states, conditions may only be imposed on the persons there listed and, according to Booth J in *Leeds County Council v C*,[10] the power to make incidental etc orders under s 11(7)(d) is similarly confined.[11] This means that, as local authorities are not listed, there is no power under s 11(7) to order contact to be supervised by a local authority.[12] However, notwithstanding the aforementioned inability, it is to be noted that the list itself is quite wide, enabling the court to impose obligations not only upon the person in whose favour the s 8 order is made, but also upon any parent,[13] any other person who has parental responsibility, or any other person with whom the child is living. Furthermore, provided the person is included in the list it is no objection that he is not a party.[14]

Thirdly, it is well established that restraints on making s 8 orders in the public law context apply equally to the exercise of the supplemental powers under s 11(7). As Balcombe LJ observed in *D v D (County Court Jurisdiction: Injunctions)*:[15]

'. . . s 11, just as much as s 8, falls within Part II (the private law part) of the 1989 Act and those words cannot be construed as giving the court a power to interfere with the

---

5 [1997] 2 FLR 797, CA.
6 [1994] 1 FLR 272 at 281.
7 [1995] 1 FLR 124 at 132 –3 per Sir Thomas Bingham MR.
8 [1995] 1 FLR 227.
9 See below.
10 [1993] 1 FLR 269.
11 As Booth J pointed out, ibid at 273, if it were not, then s 11(7)(b) would be unnecessary. See also *Re DH (A Minor) (Child Abuse)* [1994] 1 FLR 679 at 700–1, per Wall J.
12 In Booth J's view the appropriate remedy is a family assistance order, discussed post, pp 453ff.
13 Including, therefore, the unmarried father who does not have parental responsibility for the child.
14 See *Re H and others (minors) (prohibited steps order)* [1995] 4 All ER 110, discussed ante, p 420, in which it was held that when making a prohibited steps order against a non-party there was power under s 11(7)(d) to give that person liberty to apply on notice to vary or discharge the order.
15 [1993] 2 FLR 802, CA at 813.

exercise by other bodies[16] of their statutory or common law power, whether derived from other parts of the 1989 Act or elsewhere.'

Similarly, as *Nottingham County Council v P*[17] shows, courts should not use their s 11(7) powers effectively to allow local authorities to intervene in family life under the Act's private law provisions.

Fourthly, as with all Part II powers, s 11(7) is governed by the paramountcy principle and should only be invoked where the child's welfare requires.[18]

As already indicated, beyond the foregoing four points, the overall application of s 11(7)(b) and (d) is still a little uncertain, but to complete the discussion consideration will now be given to the application of the supplemental powers specifically in relation to residence orders.

With regard to residence orders it seemed at first that the courts were prepared to interpret s 11(7) widely, for in *Re B (A Minor) (Residence Order)*,[19] Butler-Sloss LJ, having referred to the powers under s 11(7)(a) to add directions, commented:

> 'Speaking for myself, I read that very broadly as giving the judge who makes a residence order the jurisdiction to attach conditions or directions which I think are very much the same thing, as to how the children should be cared for and where they should be once the residence order has been made.'

She accordingly held that s 11(7) empowered a court, when making a residence order, to require a child to be returned; to direct the return of the child to the former matrimonial home and to the interim care of one parent; and to direct that the child remain with that parent pending the full inter partes hearing. It has become apparent, however, that a significant restriction on the application of s 11(7) is that the condition must not be incompatible with the residence order itself. This was first established in *Birmingham City Council v H*,[20] in which Ward J refused to make a residence order with the conditions that the mother was to live at a particular unit and that she should comply with all reasonable instructions from the unit's staff, perhaps even to hand over the child to the care of the staff. As his Lordship pointed out, this latter condition was tantamount to saying that some other person could assume parental responsibility, which was clearly inconsistent with the residence order to which the condition would have been attached.

The point has since been developed in two important Court of Appeal decisions, *Re D (Residence: Imposition of Conditions)*[1] and *Re E (Residence: Imposition of Conditions)*.[2] In the former case a consent order was made under which two children were returned to live with their mother (they had previously been living with their paternal grandmother) on condition that she did not in the interim bring the children into contact with a former partner, nor allow him to reside at her current address or such other address as she may reside with the children. Subsequently, the mother applied to the court to allow her former partner to reside

16 In this case, the local authority and the police.
17 [1994] Fam 18, [1993] 3 All ER 815, CA, discussed post at pp 430–1.
18 See Law Com No 172 at para 4.21.
19 [1992] Fam 162 at 165, [1992] 3 All ER 867, CA at 869.
20 [1992] 2 FLR 323; cf *C v Solihull Metropolitan Borough Council* [1993] 1 FLR 290 in which Ward J made a residence order conditional upon the parents undertaking a programme of assessment, and co-operating with all reasonable requests by the local authority to participate in that programme.
 1 [1996] 2 FLR 281.
 2 [1997] 2 FLR 638.

at her home. At first instance, the application was refused, but on appeal the Court of Appeal considered the judge had failed to look at the matter as a contested residence application and remitted the case for a full consideration of the competing claims of the mother and the father and grandmother. In so concluding Ward J commented that the:[3]

'. . . case concerned a mother seeking, as she was entitled to, to allow this man back into her life because that is the way she wished to live it. *The court was not in a position so to override her right to live her life as she chose.* What was before the court was whether, if she chose to have him back, the proper person with whom the children should reside was herself or whether it would be better for the children that they lived with their father or with the grandmother' (emphasis added).

This restrictive view of the application of s 11(7) seems to have been confirmed in the second decision, *Re E*, in which the Court of Appeal held that s 11(7) did not empower a court to impose upon the carer of a child the condition that he or she should reside at a particular address, since such a restriction 'sits uneasily with the general understanding of what is meant by a residence order.' As Butler-Sloss LJ explained:[4]

'A general imposition of conditions on residence orders was clearly not contemplated by Parliament and where the parent is entirely suitable and the court intends to make a residence order in favour of that parent, a condition of residence is in my view an unwarranted imposition upon the right of the parent to choose where he/she will live within the UK or with whom. There may be exceptional cases, for instance, where the court, in the private law context, has concerns about the ability of the parent to be granted a residence order to be a satisfactory carer but there is no better solution than to place the child with that parent. The court might consider it necessary to keep some control over the parent by way of conditions which include a condition of residence. Again, in public law cases involving local authorities, where a residence order may be made by the court in preference to a care order, s 11(7) conditions might be applied in somewhat different circumstances.'

On the strength of these two decisions it seems that, in the private law context particularly, it will be difficult to justify imposing on any residence order conditions restricting the care-giver's movements and choice of where and with whom to live. Instead, the proper approach is to consider whether it is right to make the residence order in the first place. However, as Butler-Sloss LJ indicated in *Re E*, tighter restrictions may be justified in the public law context in which, given the choice between local authority care and a residence order, it might be right to opt for the latter, provided the court is given some degree of control. In this context note might also be taken of *Re T (A Minor) (Care Order: Conditions)*,[5] in which rather than make a care order the court made both a supervision order and a residence order, coupling the latter with a condition that the father was not to share a bed with the child in any circumstances. In adding the latter condition the court was aware of the practicalities of enforcing any such order, but given the rigorous scrutiny which the court was confident that the local authority would exercise, it felt that any breach was likely to come to the authority's attention and as such the condition was 'a useful addition to the child protection measures already in force'. However, there surely does come a point when conditions simply become

---

3 [1996] 2 FLR 281 at 284.
4 [1997] 2 FLR 638 at 642.
5 [1994] 2 FLR 423, CA at 440, per Nourse LJ.

unrealistic, as the court recognised in the pre-Children Act decision in *B v B (Custody: Conditions)*,[6] in which it struck out as impracticable a condition that the custodial parent put the children to bed by 6.30pm.

2. GENERAL RESTRICTIONS ON MAKING SECTION 8 ORDERS

Children aged 16 or over

Implementing the Law Commission's recommendation,[7] s 9(7) and (6) respectively provide that a s 8 order (other than a variation or discharge) should not be made in respect of a child who has attained the age of 16, nor should any order be expressed to have effect beyond a child's sixteenth birthday, unless the court is satisfied that the 'circumstances of the case are exceptional'. Orders not expressed to extend beyond the child's sixteenth birthday automatically end when he reaches 16.[8] Where a direction is made, the order will cease to have effect when the child reaches the age of 18.[9]

There is no definition of what is meant by 'exceptional circumstances' in this context, but the Department of Health's *Guidance and Regulations* gives as an example a case where the child concerned is mentally handicapped.[10] In *Re M (A Minor) (Immigration: Residence Order)*[11] it was held that the requirement of 'exceptional circumstances' was satisfied in the case of a child who had no relatives in this country and who needed protection until adulthood.

Children in local authority care

Section 9(1) prevents the court from making a s 8 order, other than a residence order, with respect to a child who is already the subject of a local authority care order.[12] This embargo is based on the well established principle,[13] endorsed both by the *Review of Child Care Law*[14] and the Law Commission[15] that in general the court's 'private law' powers should not be used to interfere with local authorities' exercise of their statutory parental responsibility.

However, residence orders are different from the other s 8 orders, since their whole purpose is to determine with whom the child is to live. Hence, such orders may be made even though the child is in care. Obviously, if the court thinks the child ought to be living with someone else (who will also have parental responsibility), this is inconsistent with the continuation of the care order. The

---

6 (1979) 1 FLR 385.
7 Law Com No 172, para 3.25.
8 Children Act 1989 s 91(10).
9 Section 91(11).
10 Vol 1, *Court Orders*, para 2.49. The Law Commission, ibid at para 3.25, whilst holding to the view that circumstances where it is right to make an order will be rare, instanced the case in which it is necessary to protect an older child from the consequences of immaturity, citing *Re SW (A Minor) (Wardship: Jurisdiction)* [1986] 1 FLR 24 where a 17-year-old girl was made a ward for the few remaining months of her minority in an attempt to control her behaviour.
11 [1993] 2 FLR 858, per Bracewell J (order expressed to last until child's eighteenth birthday).
12 But there is no embargo against a s 8 contact order being made at the behest of a child in care for contact with siblings who are not in care: see *Re F (Contact: Child in Care)* [1995] 1 FLR 510, discussed post, pp 584–5, and *Re W (Application for Leave: Whether Necessary)* [1996] 3 FCR 337n.
13 See *A v Liverpool City Council* [1982] AC 363, [1981] 2 All ER 385, HL, discussed post at p 602.
14 DHSS, 1985, paras 8.2–8.10.
15 Law Com No 172, para 4.52.

Law Commission[16] thought that, in principle, just as care orders may supersede whatever previous arrangements for the child's upbringing have been made, so should residence orders. Accordingly, s 91(1) provides that the making of a residence order discharges any existing care order.

Applications for residence orders in respect of a child in care operate, therefore, as applications to discharge care orders. For those with parental responsibility this remedy provides an alternative to seeking a discharge under s 39.[17] For others, eg fathers who do not have parental responsibility and relatives, an application for a residence order is the only means open to them to seek a discharge of a care order.

One effect of the embargo under s 9(1) is that the court cannot make a care order *and* a s 8 order.[18] However, because the embargo only applies where a child is subject to a care order there is nothing to prevent a court making a supervision order and a s 8 order,[19] nor will s 9(1) apply where the child is being 'accommodated' by a local authority under s 20.[20] Furthermore, even if the child is initially the subject of a care order, once a residence order has been made, since that discharges the care order, any other s 8 order can *then* be made.[1]

Restrictions in the case of local authorities

Section 9(2) prevents local authorities from applying for and the courts from granting them a residence or contact order.[2] The embargo is intended to prevent local authorities from obtaining parental responsibility other than by a care order under s 31.[3] If local authorities wish to restrict contact to a child accommodated by them, they must seek a care order and have the matter dealt with in those proceedings. The combined effect of s 9(1) and (2) is that where a child is in care, a local authority cannot apply for *any* s 8 order. On the other hand, authorities may seek leave of the court to obtain a prohibited steps or specific issue order in respect of a child *accommodated* by them, though this provision may not be used as a disguised route to seeking a residence or contact order.[4]

Notwithstanding their entitlement to seek leave to apply for a prohibited steps or specific issue order in respect of a child not in their care, it is established by *Nottingham County Council v P*[5] that, where intervention is thought necessary to protect children from significant harm, authorities must take direct action under Part IV of the 1989 Act (ie by initiating care proceedings) rather than seeking to invoke the court's powers under Part II. In that case, following allegations of

---

16 Ibid at 4.53.

17 Discussed post at p 579.

18 But where there are competing care and residence order applications the judge is not bound to make a positive finding on the residence order application before considering whether there is jurisdiction to grant a care order: *Oldham Metropolitan Borough Council v E* [1994] 1 FLR 568, CA. On the other hand, a court should not make a final care order if a parent's residence order application is pending and a final assessment is needed: *Hounslow London Borough Council v A* [1993] 1 WLR 291.

19 See eg *Re T (A Minor) (Care Order: Conditions)* [1994] 2 FLR 423, CA.

20 Discussed post at pp 524ff.

1 At least in favour of the individual. The position with regard to local authorities is more complicated as explained below.

2 The embargo also extends to variations of residence or contact orders: see *Re C (Contact: Jurisdiction)* [1995] 1 FLR 777, CA. Quaere whether an authority could apply for a residence order in favour of someone else? See post, p 438.

3 Discussed post, pp 536ff.

4 Section 9(5), discussed ante at pp 422–3.

5 [1994] Fam 18, [1993] 3 All ER 815, CA.

sexual abuse made against her father by the eldest daughter, the local authority obtained emergency protection orders in respect of two younger children. The father voluntarily left the family home leaving the two girls residing with their mother. The local authority, resisting judicial encouragement to bring care proceedings,[6] persisted in their application for a prohibited steps order[7] requiring the father neither to reside in the same household as the girls nor to have any contact with them unless they wished it. In rejecting their application, Sir Stephen Brown P commented:[8]

'We consider that this court should make it clear that the route chosen by the local authority in this case was wholly inappropriate. In cases where children are found to be at risk of suffering significant harm within the meaning of section 31 of the Children Act 1989 a clear duty arises on the part of local authorities to take steps to protect them. In such circumstances a local authority is required to assume responsibility and to intervene in the family arrangements in order to protect the child. A prohibited steps order would not afford the local authority any authority as to how it might deal with the children. There may be situations, for example, where a child is accommodated by a local authority, where it would be appropriate to seek a prohibited steps order for some particular purpose. However, it could not in any circumstances be regarded as providing a substitute for an order under Part IV of the 1989 Act.'

Nottingham was subsequently applied in *F v Cambridge County Council*[9] to prevent a local authority being granted leave to intervene in private law proceedings. In that case the father, a Schedule 1 offender, sought limited contact with his children who were living with their mother. The local authority were opposed to the father having contact, but did not themselves seek a care order since they accepted that the mother was able to look after the children properly. Stuart-White J held, following *Nottingham*, that unless and until the s 31 threshold had been met, the local authority could not intervene in family life, and hence leave to join as a party to private law proceedings should be refused.

Although these decisions severely limit local authority use of prohibited steps and specific issue orders, they do not mean that the powers can never be used. They could properly be invoked, for example, to protect a child accommodated by a local authority from a threat posed by a non-family member[10] or to resolve specific problems concerning an orphan.[11] It may also be a proper use of s 8 for local authorities to obtain court sanction (or restraint) of medical treatment.[12] In other words, provided the local authority is not seeking to be vested with parental responsibility, nor directly to interfere with the exercise of responsibility by

6 Both Judge Heald, at first instance, and Ward J had made s 37 directions. These directions are discussed post, p 455.
7 For which they had been granted leave to apply.
8 [1994] Fam at 39, [1993] 3 All ER at 824. In any event, it was doubted whether there was any power to make an ouster order under s 8. For a critique of this decision see inter alia Cobley and Lowe 'Ousting Abusers – Public or Private Law Solution?' (1994) 110 LQR 38.
9 [1995] 1 FLR 516. See also *Re K (Contact: Psychiatric Report)* [1995] 2 FLR 432, CA. See also the comments of Wall J 'The courts and child protection – the challenge of hybrid cases' (1997) 9 CFLQ 354 at 355–6.
10 To prevent abduction by a friend, for example, or possibly by a relative.
11 See *Birmingham City Council v D, Birmingham City Council v M* [1994] 2 FLR 502, discussed post, p 547.
12 See *Re R (A Minor) (Blood Transfusion)* [1993] 2 FLR 757 in which Booth J held that the proper remedy for a local authority wishing to obtain sanction for a blood transfusion for a child not being looked after by them, contrary to his parents' (who were Jehovah's Witnesses) wishes was a specific issue order. Quaere whether this discussion can now stand in the light of the *Nottingham* ruling?

others, then it continues to be open to them to seek leave to apply for a prohibited steps or specific issue order.

Other restrictions

It has been said that residence orders cannot be made in favour of a child applicant.[13] However, it is submitted that it cannot be said that a residence order can *never* be made in favour of a child. It must be open to the court to make a residence order in favour of a mother who herself is a child in respect of her own child, and there seems no objection in principle[14] to granting such an order in appropriate cases in favour of a child applicant in respect of a sibling.

According to Wall J in *Re MD and TD (Minors (No 2)*[15] a court has no power to make a residence order on its own motion in favour of local authority foster parents if those persons were themselves barred from applying by reason of s 9(3).[16] With respect to Wall J, it is by no means clear that the court's powers, once family proceedings are on foot, are so limited.

3.   WHO MAY APPLY FOR SECTION 8 ORDERS?

The Act adopts what may be described as an 'open door' policy whereby some persons are entitled to apply, while others can, with leave of the court, apply for s 8 orders either by intervening in existing 'family proceedings' or by initiating their own proceedings.

The detailed scheme, set out by s 10 (which governs both initiating and intervening in family proceedings) is as follows.

Persons entitled to apply without leave

Parents, guardians and those with a residence order in their favour are entitled to apply for any s 8 order.[17] As Bainham points out,[18] this group of people have such a close connection with the child that it would be inappropriate to present them with the additional hurdle of applying for leave to obtain a court hearing.

Following the Family Law Reform Act 1987 the expression 'parent' clearly includes the unmarried father. It does not, however, include 'former parents' whose child has been freed for adoption.[19]

In addition to the above, certain other persons are entitled to apply for a residence order or contact order without leave:[20]

(a)   Any party to a marriage (whether or not subsisting) in relation to whom the child is a 'child of the family'; this provision primarily refers to step-parents

---

13 Per Booth J in *Re SC (A Minor) (Leave To Seek Residence Order)* [1994] 1 FLR 96 at 100.
14 It cannot be objected that because the making of a residence order confers parental responsibility on those who do not already have it an order cannot be made in favour of a child, since of course mothers (and married fathers) have parental responsibility even if they are minors.
15 [1994] Fam Law 489.
16 Discussed post, pp 433–4.
17 Section 10(4).
18 *Children, The New Law*, para 3.36.
19 See *Re C (Minors) (Adoption: Residence Order)* [1994] Fam 1, sub nom *Re C (minors) (parent: residence order)* [1993] 3 All ER 313, CA (sometimes referred to as 'the Calderdale case'). For a discussion of the 1987 Act, see ante, pp 298–9.
20 See s 10(5).

but can include any married person[1] who has treated the child as a 'child of the family'.[2]

(b) Any person with whom the child has lived for a period of at least three years (this period need not be continuous but must not have begun more than five years before, or ended more than three months before the making of the application);[3]

(c) Any person having the consent of:

(i) each of the persons in whose favour a residence order is in force;

(ii) the local authority, if the child is subject to a care order; or

(iii) in any other case, each of the persons who have parental responsibility for the child.

A person not otherwise included in the above mentioned categories will nevertheless be entitled, pursuant to s 10(6), to apply for a variation or discharge of a s 8 order if either the order in question was made on his application or, in the case of a contact order, he is named in that order. This means, for instance, that a child named in a contact order will not need leave to apply to vary it.[4] Section 10(7) reserves the power of rules of court to prescribe additional categories of people who may make applications without prior leave. These powers have not yet been exercised.

Persons entitled to apply with leave

The general scheme is that anyone, including the child himself (which is reflective of the obligation under Art 12(1) of the UN Convention on the Rights of the Child)[5] and any body, authority or organisation professionally concerned with children, who is not otherwise entitled to apply, can seek leave of the court to apply for any s 8 order.[6] The only exception to this scheme is any person 'who is, or was at any time during the last six months, a local authority foster parent' who must have the consent of the local authority to apply for the court's leave, unless he is a relative of the child or the child has been living with him for at least three years preceding the application.[7] This latter period need not be continuous but must not have been more than five years before the making of the application.[8] Because of the different wording of s 9(4) and s 10(10), where foster parents provided a home for the child for three years but not within three months preceding the application, the consent of a local authority is not required but leave of the court is.[9]

The purpose of imposing this additional restriction on local authority foster parent applications is to prevent applications unduly interfering with the local

---

1   Including grandparents: see *Re A (Child of the Family)* [1998] 1 FLR 347, CA.

2   For the meaning of which see ante, pp 288–90.

3   Section 10(10).

4   Per Wilson J in *Re W (Application For Leave: Whether Necessary)* [1996] 3 FCR 337n, [1996] Fam Law 665. For this purpose no distinction is to be made between direct and indirect contact.

5   See further post, p 461.

6   Section 10(1)(a)(ii). Local authorities are subject to the restrictions in s 9, discussed ante, pp 430–2. Note that it is within the court's power to give a person leave to intervene but not to become a party: see *Re S (Care: Residence: Intervener)* [1997] 1 FLR 497, CA.

7   Section 9(3).

8   Section 9(4).

9   Where the three-year period immediately precedes the application or has not ended more than three months before the application, the foster parents can, pursuant to s 10(5)(b), apply as of right for a residence or contact order.

authority's plans for the child and so undermining their efforts to bring stability to the child's life.[10] It is also intended to guard against the risk of deterring parents from voluntarily using the fostering services provided by local authorities which, it is argued, could easily happen if the restrictions were relaxed. However, despite the importance of these objections, the restriction lies at odds with the position in adoption, where foster parents can apply for an order after providing a home for the child for 12 months,[11] and many might agree with the observation that having to obtain local authority consent *and* leave of the court is one hurdle too many.[12]

Ironically, in the one case to consider s 9(3), *C v Salford City Council*,[13] parents sought to challenge the propriety of the consent given by the local authority. In that case a child suffering from Down's Syndrome had been accommodated by the local authority and placed with foster parents. Subsequently, the foster parents expressed their wish to adopt, but as Roman Catholics they were unacceptable as prospective adopters to the parents, who were Jewish. The foster parents accordingly, and with the consent of the local authority, sought leave to apply for a residence order. The parents argued that, because of their dual function as an adoption agency and as an accommodating local social services authority, the local authority should not or could not have consented to the foster parents' application. Rejecting this argument, it was held that for the purposes of s 9(3) it was the consent of the social services authority accommodating the child that was required, and therefore the authority's role as an adoption agency was not part of that consent. It was held that the difficult balance of the welfare factors in the case was justification in itself for having the issues resolved by the court. Accordingly, leave to apply for a residence order was granted.

The leave criteria

In considering the issue of leave a distinction must be drawn between adults seeking leave and children seeking leave. In the former case s 10(9) provides specific guide-lines, but these do not apply to applications by children. Instead the court is simply directed by s 10(8) to grant leave to child applicants provided it is satisfied that the child has sufficient understanding to make the proposed application.[14]

(a)   The position re adults

The criteria for deciding whether to grant adults leave are provided by s 10(9) which directs the court to consider:

> '(a)   the nature of the proposed application for the section 8 order;
> (b)   the applicant's connection with the child;

---

10 See Lord Mackay LC in 502 HL Official Report (5th series), cols 1221–2. This provision had not been recommended by the Law Commission.
11 Adoption Act 1976 s 13(1)–(2), discussed post, p 660. Note also *Re C (A Minor) (Adoption)* [1994] 2 FLR 513 at 515 in which the anomalies of the current position were discussed. In this respect it seems a pity that Lord Meston's move (see 502 HL Official Report (5th series) col 1222) to have the three year period in s 9(3) reduced to 12 months did not attract support.
12 Per Lord Meston, ibid at col 1221.
13 [1994] 2 FLR 926, per Hale J.
14 This interpretation, however, has been fundamentally challenged by Charles J in *Re S (Contact: Application by Sibling)* [1998] 2 FLR, forthcoming, who points out that s 10(8) only applies where the applicant is the child concerned, ie the subject of the application. If he is not, eg where he is seeking contact with a sibling, then in Charles J's view s 10(9) and not s 10(8) applies. Section 10(9) does *not* apply to considering whether to give a party leave following a s 91(14) direction (discussed post, p 478): see *Re A (Application for Leave)* [1998] 1 FLR 1, CA.

(c) any risk there might be of that proposed application disrupting the child's life to such an extent that he would be harmed by it; and
(d) where the child is being looked after by a local authority –
    (i) the authority's plans for the child's future, and
    (ii) the wishes and feelings of the child's parents'.[15]

The Court of Appeal held in *Re A (Minors) (Residence Order: Leave to Apply)*[16] that when deciding whether to grant leave the paramountcy principle under s 1(1) has no application. In Balcombe LJ's view there were three reasons for reaching this conclusion. First, in granting or refusing a leave application the court is not determining a question with respect to the child's upbringing. That question only arises when the court hears the substantive application. Secondly, some of the guidelines, for example s 10(9)(a), (c) and (d)(i), would be otiose if the child's welfare was paramount. Thirdly, in any event there 'would have been little point in Parliament providing that the court was to have particular regard to the wishes and feelings of the child's parents, if the whole decision were to be subject to the overriding (paramount) consideration of the child's welfare'. Notwithstanding this ruling, s 10(9) is not to be regarded as providing the *exclusive* guidelines, nor as preventing the court from considering the check list under s 1(3). It is therefore quite proper to consider the child's own views.[17]

At one time it had been held[18] that in deciding whether or not to grant leave, the court should assess whether the substantive application would have a reasonable prospect of success, but it is now accepted that this test is too rigid and that instead the proper approach should be to enquire whether there is a 'good arguable case'. Summarising the position, Ward LJ said in *Re M (Care: Contact: Grandmother's Application for Leave)*:[19]

'If the application is frivolous or vexatious or otherwise an abuse of the process of the court, of course it will fail. (2) If the application for leave fails to disclose that there is any eventual prospect of success, if those prospects of success are remote so that the application is obviously unsustainable, then it must also be dismissed . . . (3) The applicant must satisfy the court that there is a serious issue to try and must present a good arguable case.'

Where leave has been given there is no consequent presumption that such an order be made.[20]

The requirement of leave is intended to act as a filter to protect the child and his family against unwarranted interference with their comfort and security, whilst ensuring that the child's interests are properly respected.[1] In general terms the

---

15 Though not, as Bainham points out, ibid at para 3.43, the wishes and feelings of the child. But see below.
16 [1992] Fam 182, sub nom *Re A and others (minors) (residence orders)* [1992] 3 All ER 872, CA.
17 *Re A (A Minor) (Residence Order: Leave To Apply)* [1993] 1 FLR 425, per Hollings J.
18 See *G v Kirklees Metropolitan Borough Council* [1993] 1 FLR 805, per Booth J.
19 [1995] 2 FLR 86, CA at 98.
20 See eg *Re A (Section 8 Order: Grandparents' Application)* [1995] 2 FLR 153, CA and *Re W (Contact: Application by Grandparent)* [1997] 1 FLR 793. The refusal to give leave is a serious issue and failure to give reasons for the decision constitutes a fundamental defect: per Connell J in *T v W (Contact: Reasons for Refusing Leave)* [1996] 2 FLR 473.
1 As Lord Mackay LC eloquently put it (502 HL Official Report (5th Series), col 1227): 'There is clearly a danger both in limiting and expanding the categories of person who may apply for orders in respect of children. On the one hand, a too wide and uncontrolled gateway can expose children and families to the stress and harm of unwarranted interference and the harassment of actual or threatened proceedings. If too narrow or overcontrolled the gateway may prevent applications which would benefit or safeguard a child from harm.'

more tenuous the applicant's connection with the child the harder it will be to obtain leave.[2] Conversely, the closer the connection the more readily leave should be given. As the Law Commission put it,[3] the requirement of leave will 'scarcely be a hurdle at all to close relatives such as grandparents . . . who wish to care for or visit the child'. On the other hand, as Lord Mackay LC commented[4] in his response to the many attempts during the passage of the Bill to give grandparents an entitlement to apply for a residence or contact order:

> '. . . [t]here is often a close bond . . . between a grandparent and a grandchild . . . and in such cases leave, if needed, will no doubt be granted. Indeed, in many cases it will be a formality; but we would be naive if we did not accept that not all interest shown by a grandparent in a child's life is necessarily benign, even if well intentioned. Arguably, at least until we have some experience of wider rights of application, the law should provide some protection to children and their parents against unwarranted applications by grandparents when they occur'.

Since implementation, another concern voiced by the court is the consequential delay in having too many parties to the proceedings, and Butler-Sloss LJ has said that it is undesirable that grandparents whose interests are identical with those of the mother should be separately represented.[5] In short, even grandparents are not always granted leave.[6]

Careful consideration also needs to be given to applications for leave by individuals in respect of children in care. In *Re A (Minors) (Residence Order: Leave to Apply)*[7] the Court of Appeal refused an application for leave to apply for a residence order in respect of four children originally placed with the applicant for long-term fostering but who had been removed from her by the local authority nearly six months earlier.[8] Section 10(9)(d)(i) expressly provides that the court is to have particular regard to the authority's plans for the child. Furthermore, in view of the authority's statutory duty under s 22(3) to safeguard and promote the welfare of any child in its care, it was held that the court should approach the application for leave on the basis that ' the authority's plans for the child's future are designed to safeguard and promote the child's welfare and that any departure from those plans might well disrupt the child's life to such an extent that he would

---

2 Any person seeking leave must file a written request setting out the reasons for the application and a draft of the application for making of which leave is sought: Family Proceedings Rules 1991 r 4.3(1); Family Proceedings Courts (Children Act 1989) Rules 1991 r 3(1). Leave can be granted with or without a hearing: ibid, r 4.3(2) and r 3(2) respectively. In practice such applications are 'almost always an application on the papers' and there will rarely be a welfare report available: *Re A (Section 8 Order: Grandparents' Application)* [1995] 2 FLR 153 at 157, per Butler-Sloss LJ.

3 Law Com No 172, para 4.41.

4 503 HL Official Report (5th series), col 1342. For a discussion of the legal position of grandparents under the 1989 Act see generally *The Children Act – What's in it for Grandparents?* (3rd edn, Grandparents' Federation, 1996). For a study of the grandparents' position before the Act see generally: Douglas and Lowe 'Grandparents and the Legal Process' [1990] JSWL 90 and Kaganas and Piper 'Grandparents and the Limits of the Law' (1990) 4 Int J of Law and Family 27.

5 *Re M (Minors) (Sexual Abuse: Evidence)* [1993] 1 FLR 822 at 825. The difficulty in practice is that the parties themselves will not always consider their interests identical.

6 See eg *Re (A Minor) (Contact: Leave to Apply)* [1995] 3 FCR 543 in which Douglas Brown J upheld a magistrate's refusal to give a grandmother leave since, given the total opposition by the parents and the serious disharmony between them, the application had no prospect of success.

7 [1992] Fam 182, [1992] 3 All ER 872.

8 In fact the application was made one week before the expiry of six months from the removal, but it was agreed between the parties that the local authority would not object to the application as they could have done under s 9(3), and that the mother would not pursue her action for judicial review.

be harmed by it'.[9] In short, in these circumstances the court should not allow such applications to become a back door means of reviewing local authority decisions.[10]

(b) The position re children

Applications by children for leave to apply for s 8 orders should be made in the High Court.[11] Under s 10(8) leave can only be granted if the court is satisfied that the child has sufficient age and understanding. As Sir Thomas Bingham MR said in *Re S (A Minor) (Independent Representation)*:[12]

> '. . . the rules eschew any arbitrary line of demarcation based on age and wisely so. Different children have differing levels of understanding at the same age. And understanding is not absolute. It has to be assessed relatively to the issues in the proceedings. Where any sound judgment on these issues calls for insight and imagination which only maturity and experience can bring, both the court and the solicitor will be slow to conclude that the child's understanding is sufficient.'

Apart from requiring the court to be satisfied about the child's understanding, the Act itself gives little further guidance. The guidelines under s 10(9) do not apply where a child is seeking leave.[13] There is, however, a conflict of opinion as to whether the court should apply the paramountcy principle when determining whether to grant leave. According to Johnson J in *Re C (A Minor) (Leave to Seek Section 8 Orders)*[14] the court should do so, but that proposition was rejected by Booth J in *Re SC (A Minor) (Leave to Seek Residence Order)*[15] on the basis of the Court of Appeal ruling in *Re A (Minors) (Residence Orders: Leave to Apply)*[16] that an application for leave (in Booth J's view whether by a child or an adult) did not raise any question regarding the upbringing of a child and therefore fell outside the ambit of s 1(1). It is submitted that this latter view is to be preferred for, quite apart from being in line with the Court of Appeal, it also has the merit of according to a child of sufficient understanding some degree of autonomy, which seems more in keeping with the spirit of the Act.

It has been said that leave should not be granted to children if the proceedings are doomed to failure,[17] but it is submitted that as with adults the correct test now is whether the applicant has a good arguable case.[18]

---

9 Per Balcombe LJ [1992] Fam at 189, [1992] 3 All ER at 879.
10 See also *Re M (Prohibited Steps Order: Application for Leave)* [1993] 1 FLR 275 in which a former guardian sought leave to challenge a local authority's decision not to take care proceedings – application remitted to justices for a re-hearing.
11 *Practice Direction (applications by children: leave)* [1993] 1 All ER 820.
12 [1993] Fam 263 at 276, [1993] 3 All ER 36, CA at 43–4.
13 The wording of s 10(9) itself makes this quite clear, as was accepted both in *Re C (a minor) (leave to seek section 8 orders)* [1994] 1 FLR 26 and *Re SC (a minor) (leave to seek residence order)* [1994] 1 FLR 96.
14 Supra at 28. Leave was refused to a 14-year-old girl seeking a residence and a specific issue order so that she could live with friends and go on holiday to Bulgaria with them.
15 Supra at 99. It was also rejected by Stuart White J in *Re C (Residence: Child's Application for Leave)* [1995] 1 FLR 927, and by Douglas Brown J in *North Yorkshire County Council v G* [1994] 1 FCR 737.
16 [1992] Fam 182, [1992] 3 All ER 872, discussed ante at p 435.
17 Per Booth J in *Re SC*, ibid at 99C, but applying the earlier test she held that the court had 'to have regard to the likelihood of success of the proposed application.' In that case a 14-year-old girl who was in local authority care successfully sought leave to apply for a residence order in favour of a friend who agreed to care for her, notwithstanding that the application was opposed by the mother and that the friend had previously been rejected as the girl's foster mother.
18 See the discussion ante at p 435.

According to *Re HG (Specific Issue Order: Sterilisation)* [19] parents, at any rate when applying for leave that their child be sterilised, can apply for leave on that child's behalf in cases where the child lacks the necessary understanding to apply on his own behalf. The advantage of this ruling is that in these cases legal aid can be sought on behalf of the child rather than the parents.[20]

Applying for orders in favour of someone else

The Act is silent on whether applications may be made for a s 8 order in favour of someone else. However, implicit in the ability of a child to obtain leave for such orders is that they, at least, can seek a residence order in favour of another person.[1] As Booth J said in *Re SC (A Minor) (Leave to Seek Residence Order):*[2]

> 'In my judgment the court should not fetter the statutory ability of the child to seek any s 8 order, including a residence order, if it is appropriate for such an application to be made. Although the court will undoubtedly consider why it is that the person in whose favour a proposed residence order would be made is not applying, it would in my opinion be wrong to import into the Act any requirement that only he or she should make the application.'

Whether the courts would be disposed to permit applications other than by children for residence or contact orders in favour of someone else remains to be seen. However, it seems unlikely that local authorities would be permitted to do so,[3] for, even supposing that s 9(2) (which provides: 'No application may be made by a local authority for a residence order or contact order and no court shall make such an order in favour of a local authority') is interpreted as not barring residence or contact applications in favour of someone else,[4] there is still the objection that, contrary to the ruling in *Nottingham County Council v P,*[5] local authorities would thereby be permitted to intervene in family life via Part II rather than Part IV of the 1989 Act.

4.   EFFECT OF RESIDENCE ORDERS

Parental responsibility

Whilst in force, residence orders confer parental responsibility on those in whose favour they are made such as grandparents or other relatives, or foster parents, who would not otherwise have that responsibility.[6] In the case of 'unmarried fathers' however, upon making a residence order in their favour, the court is *bound* to make a *separate* parental responsibility order under s 4.[7]

---

19 [1993] 1 FLR 587, per Peter Singer QC (as he then was).
20 In *Re HG* the parents did not qualify for legal aid.
1   As Booth J pointed out in *Re SC (A Minor) (Leave to Seek Residence Order)* [1994] 1 FLR 96 at 100, residence orders cannot be made in favour of the child applicant himself, since that would vest parental responsibility in him by reason of s 12(2).
2   Ibid, at 100 E–F.
3   They might plausibly wish to apply, for example, for a residence order in favour of grandparents who, though capable, are reluctant to apply for themselves.
4   If the word 'and' is read conjunctively rather than disjunctively it could be argued that all that s 9(2) prevents is local authorities applying for residence or contact orders on their own behalf.
5   [1994] Fam 18, [1993] 3 All ER 815, CA, discussed ante, pp 430–1.
6   Section 12(2). Note the restrictions on that responsibility under s 12(3), discussed ante at p 387.
7   Section 12(1), discussed ante at p 384.

Change of child's surname

Under s 13(1)(a), it is an automatic condition of residence orders[8] that no person may cause the child to be known by a new surname without either the written consent of every person who has parental responsibility or leave of the court.[9] Although it is not a *statutory* requirement to have the *child's* consent,[10] in *Re PC (Change of Surname)*[11] Holman J expressly left open whether the consent of an older child, particularly if over the age of 16, was both necessary and sufficient. During the debates on the Bill it was suggested that if the child objects he may seek leave to apply for a prohibited steps order to prevent the change.[12] In *Re B (Change of Surname)*[13] Wilson J observed that s 13(1)(a) can only operate as an inhibition on the adult residence holder not to cause the children to be known by a different surname. As he put it:

> 'It does not, because in effect it cannot, proscribe the surname which the children ask teachers, friends and relatives to attribute to them.'

According to *Practice Direction (minor: change of surname: deed poll)*[14] applications for formal change of surname should be made to the Central Office (Filing Department), and must be supported by the production of the consent in writing of every person having parental responsibility. In the absence of such consent the application will be adjourned until court leave is given.

Section 13(1)(a) implements the recommendation of the Law Commission[15] which, like the Court of Appeal in the pre-Children Act decision, *W v A (Minor: Surname)*,[16] considered a child's surname to be an important symbol of his identity and relationship with his parents and that, while it may be in his interests for it to be changed, it was not a matter on which a parent with whom the child lives should be able to take unilateral action.

Case law since the Act very much reflects this attitude. It is established[17] that, wherever there is a pre-existing residence order,[18] applications to change names

---

8 For similar rules where the child is subject to a care order, see s 33(7)–(8) discussed post, pp 565–6.

9 It is perhaps a moot point as to whether leave is necessary to use a hyphenated name: see *P v N (Child: Surname)* [1997] 2 FCR 65 (Dorchester county court) which suggested it is not. Sed quaere?

10 Attempts were in fact made to amend s 13 so as to require the child's consent: see 502 HL Official Reports (5th series) col 1262, by Lord Meston, and 503 HL Official Reports, col 1347 by Lord Elwyn Jones.

11 [1997] 2 FLR 730 at 739. Nonetheless the support inter alia of a 16-year-old for a name change did not inhibit the court from refusing the change in *Re B (Change of Surname)* [1996] 1 FLR 791, CA, discussed below.

12 See Lord Mackay LC, 502 HL Official Report (5th series), col 1264.

13 [1996] 1 FLR 791, CA at 795.

14 [1995] 1 All ER 832.

15 Law Com No 172, para 4.14.

16 [1981] Fam 14, [1981] 1 All ER 100, CA, which in turn decisively rejected such cases as *R (BM) v R (DN)* [1978] 2 All ER 33, CA and *D v B* [1979] Fam 38, [1979] 1 All ER 92, CA, which had held that the issue was relatively unimportant and that fathers were tending to lay too much emphasis on it when the purpose was to avoid embarrassment and there was no intention of destroying their links with their children.

17 By *Re B (Change of Surname)* [1996] 1 FLR 791, CA. See also *Re C (Change of Surname)* [1998] 1 FLR 549, CA.

18 Similarly if there is a pre-existing custody or care and control order made before the 1989 Act, as in *Re B*, supra.

are properly made under s 13(1)(a) rather than as a specific issue order under s 8.[19] Although technically this means that there is no *obligation* to apply the welfare checklist,[20] it is accepted that it remains a useful aide mémoire.[1] A more serious consequence of requiring applications to be made under s 13 is that the consequential directions are probably not enforceable.[2] As with all applications directly concerning children's upbringing, in resolving disputes over children's names, the child's welfare is the court's paramount consideration.

Court leave for a change of name has proved hard to obtain. As Ward LJ has put it in *Re C (Change of Surname):*[3]

'. . . there is a heavy responsibility on those who seek to change a child's surname . . . good and cogent reasons should be shown to allow a change.'

Examples of refusal under s 13(1) include *Re F (Child: Surname),*[4] in which it was held that there was no reason to suppose that a little girl at school was going to be embarrassed or particularly unusual in being registered at a school under a different name from the current surname of her mother. In other words, applying the paramountcy of the child's welfare test under s 1(1), there was no case for saying that it was in the child's interests to change her name.

Similarly, leave was refused in *Re B (Change of Surname),*[5] in which the Court of Appeal rejected the argument that a first instance judge had erred when refusing to give leave for a change of name because he had not taken notice of the children's views. Whilst agreeing that 'orders which ran flatly contrary to the wishes of normal adolescent children were virtually unknown to family law', that principle did not extend to the formal change of surname from that of the father to the stepfather.[6] In Wilson J's view that would only serve to injure the link between the father and the children, which was not in the latter's best interests. In so ruling Wilson J rejected the argument that it was embarrassing for the children to be known by a surname other than that of the adult care givers, commenting that 'there was no opprobrium nowadays for a child to have a different surname from that of adults in the household'.

---

19 This in any event is implicit in r 4.1(2)(a) and (c) of the Family Proceedings Rules 1991 and by the different form for the order under s 13, viz Form C 44 as opposed to C 43, which is required by r 4.21(5). Where there is no pre-existing order, application should be made for a prohibited steps or specific issue order: see *Dawson v Wearmouth* [1998] 1 All ER 271, CA and *Re C (a Minor) (Change of Surname)* (1998) Times, 2 February, CA.
20 Viz that provided by s 1(3), discussed post, pp 465ff.
 1 Per Wilson J in *Re B*, supra at 793. In *Re C*, supra, Ward LJ suggested the check list would apply regardless of whether the application was under s 8 or s 13.
 2 See *Re P (Minors) (Custody order: Penal Notice)* [1990] 1 WLR 613, CA, discussed post, p 448.
 3 [1998] 2 FLR 656, CA.
 4 [1993] 2 FLR 837n. See also *Re T (Change of Name)* [1998] 2 FLR 620, CA and *G v A (Children: Surname)* [1995] 2 FCR 223n, in which an unmarried father obtained a prohibited steps order restraining the mother from changing the children's surnames. For a striking pre-Children Act example, see *W v A (Minor: Surname)* [1981] Fam 14, [1981] 1 All ER 100, in which the Court of Appeal refused to reverse a decision declining to permit a change of name even though the child was emigrating to Australia with his mother and stepfather. Quaere whether it would be sufficient if the father had disappeared from the scene entirely or if his name had notorious associations because of his conduct?
 5 [1996] 1 FLR 791, CA.
 6 This was because the inhibition against a change of name lay against the mother rather than against the child. As Wilson J pointed out, ibid at 795, the child himself is free to ask others to address him in whatever name he chooses regardless of any s 13 directions.

Where the name has already been changed (whether lawfully or not), the issue as to what the child should continue to be called is still governed by the welfare principle. However, it may be too stark to concentrate simply on whether it is in the child's interests for the name to be changed back, since attention also needs to be paid to whether it was in the child's interests to change the name in the first place.[7] Nevertheless, it seems on the case law easier to persuade the court to sanction a change of name that has already occurred than to permit a prospective change. In *Re P (Parental Responsibility)*[8] the court rejected an application by an unmarried father that his name be restored to his two children. The court noted that the names had been changed some time ago, following the father's long term imprisonment, when the mother decided to make a fresh start both for herself and her children. It was not thought to be in their interest for the name to be changed back. Even in *Re C (Change of Surname)*,[9] where it was held that the unmarried mother's original decision to change her child's surname following the breakdown of her relationship with the father was not initially justified, the Court of Appeal resolved nevertheless that a further change now was not in the child's interests.

Removal of child from the United Kingdom

(a) Temporary removals for less than one month

Under s 13(1)(b), where a residence order is in force, no person may remove the child from the United Kingdom (ie England and Wales, Scotland and Northern Ireland), without either the *written* consent of every person who has parental responsibility or leave of the court. Under s 13(2), however, a person in whose favour a residence order has been made can remove the child for a period of less than one month without anyone's permission. This latter provision places those with a residence order in a special position for, as we have seen,[10] it is normally an offence under the Child Abduction Act 1984 to remove a child under the age of 16 without the consent[11] of those having parental responsibility or leave of the court.

These provisions implement the Law Commission's recommendations,[12] and are intended to provide simple and clear rules which can be remembered and observed. Permitting unrestricted temporary removals is intended to allow a person in whose favour a residence order has been made to make arrangements for holidays without having to seek the permission of the 'non-residential' parent or parents, and without even having to give notice. This principle presumably extends to each person in whose favour a joint or shared residence order is made. Although there is no limit on the number of temporary removals permitted, in cases of dispute parents are entitled to seek a prohibited steps order to curtail the

---

7 See eg *Re T (Change of Name)* [1998] 2 FLR 620, CA.
8 [1997] 2 FLR 722, CA.
9 [1998] 2 FLR 656, CA. See also another *Re C (Change of Surname)* [1998] 1 FLR 549, CA where the children concerned were living with their unmarried father and had already assumed his name, the court rejected the mother's application that they should be known by her maiden name since she herself no longer used it as she had married someone else.
10 Ante at pp 361–2.
11 Though, unlike the requirement under the 1989 Act, the consent does not have to be in writing.
12 Law Com No 172, para 4.15.

right or to apply for a restriction of the right to be added to the residence order, pursuant to the court's powers to add conditions under s 11(7).[13]

(b)   Removals for more than one month

Where permission is sought to take the child out of the country for more than one month specific application for leave must be made to the court.[14] Under s 13(3), the court may grant leave either generally or for specified purposes. In deciding whether to grant leave the court must apply the principle of the paramountcy of the child's welfare under s 1(1). The most extreme of the problems likely to come before the court in this context is where the 'residential' parent wishes to emigrate and seeks leave to take the child out of the country, but is opposed by the other parent upon the basis that he will thereby effectively be deprived of further contact. The test generally applied by the courts is that, provided the request is reasonable and bona fide,[15] leave will be granted unless it can be shown to be against the child's interests.[16] In the case of very young children it will be difficult to show harm, but in the case of older children factors such as education and the relationship with the 'non-residential' parent are likely to be of more weight.

In *M v M (Minors) (Jurisdiction)*,[17] for example, leave was refused because the first instance judge had given insufficient weight to the children's (aged 12 and 10) own views. Leave was also refused in *MH v GP (Child: Emigration)*[18] because of the overriding importance of maintaining and developing the relationship between the child (a boy aged four) and his father. In *Tyler v Tyler*[19] the father, who had enjoyed frequent contact with his two boys now aged nine and six, successfully opposed the mother's request for leave to emigrate to Australia to join her family. It was found in that case, however, that the mother's dominant motive was bitterness towards her husband and that furthermore she would be able to cope with the disappointment if permission were refused. In contrast, in *Re H (Application to Remove from Jurisdiction)*,[20] a father, who had played a large part in caring for the child (now aged five), unsuccessfully opposed the granting of a residence order coupled with leave to take the child out of the jurisdiction in favour of the mother who was now married to an American, and who therefore wished to set up home in the USA.

13 See eg Department of Health's *Guidance and Regulations*, Vol 1, *Court Orders*, para 2.27 and Lord Mackay LC, 503 HL Official Report (5th series), col 1354.
14 According to Thorpe J in *MH v GP (Child: Emigration)* [1995] 2 FLR 106 such cases should be heard either in the High Court or county court depending on the complexity of the decision; cf his earlier comment in *Re L (A Minor) (Removal from Jurisdiction)* [1993] 1 FCR 325 that such applications should be made to the High Court.
15 See eg *Tyler v Tyler* [1989] 2 FLR 158, CA, discussed below.
16 See *Re H (Application to Remove from Jurisdiction)* [1998] 1 FLR 848, CA, in which Thorpe LJ cautioned that not a lot was to be gained from detailed analysis of the facts of previous decisions. *M v M (Minors) (Removal from Jurisdiction)* [1992] Fam Law 291, CA; *Re F (A Ward) (Leave to Remove Ward Out of the Jurisdiction)* [1988] 2 FLR 116; *Belton v Belton* [1987] 2 FLR 343, CA; *Lonslow v Hennig (formerly Lonslow)* [1986] 2 FLR 378, CA; *Chamberlain v de la Mare* (1982) 4 FLR 434, CA; and *P (LM) v P (GE)* [1970] 3 All ER 659, CA. This issue is also of great concern in Canada and the USA: see eg *Gordon v Goertz* (1996) 134 DLR (4th) 321, Can Sup Ct, which similarly applied the child's best interests test but was predisposed to favour the primary carer. See Barton 'When did you next see your father' (1997) 9 CFLQ 73.
17 [1993] 1 FCR 5, CA.
18 Supra.
19 Supra. This was the first reported instance of permission to emigrate with the children being refused. But note the criticisms of this case at [1989] Fam Law 316–17. See also *M v M*, supra, where the case was remitted for a re-hearing because the court had not applied the right test.
20 Supra.

In all cases it is important for the persons seeking leave to demonstrate to the court's satisfaction that their plans for removing the child are well prepared and thought out.[1] Against this the courts also seem prepared to give some weight to the unhappiness or bitterness that a refusal of leave might cause.[2]

The question of whether a parent should be given leave to remove a child permanently from the jurisdiction is distinct from that of who should have residence of the child. Accordingly, it by no means automatically follows that because an application for leave to remove has been refused, the applicant should lose residence of the child.[3]

5. WHEN SECTION 8 ORDERS CAN BE MADE

General jurisdictional rules

Part I of the Family Law Act 1986[4] governs jurisdiction to make what are referred to as 'Part 1 orders', which inter alia[5] comprise s 8 orders under the Children Act 1989 (but not the power to vary or discharge them).[6] The general aim of the Act is to avoid conflicts of jurisdiction[7] arising within the United Kingdom[8] and specified dependent territories (that is, at the moment, the Isle of Man).[9] To this end the Act provides for uniform jurisdictional rules when making 'Part I orders', the scheme of which is:

(a) jurisdiction is prima facie vested in the UK court in which divorce, nullity or separation proceedings are continuing; but

(b) if there are no such proceedings, jurisdiction is vested in the UK court of the jurisdiction in which the child is habitually resident; and

(c) where neither (a) or (b) applies, jurisdiction is vested in the UK court of the place where the child is physically present.

---

1 See eg *K (A Minor) (Removal From Jurisdiction)* [1992] 2 FLR 98; *M v A (Wardship: Removal From Jurisdiction* [1993] 2 FLR 715 and *Re T (Removal From Jurisdiction)* [1996] 2 FLR 352, sub nom *Re T (A Minor) (Order as to Residence)* [1996] 3 FCR 97, CA in which leave was refused because the applicant's plans were ill-thought out and little researched; cf *Re W (Minors) (Removal From Jurisdiction)* [1994] 1 FCR 842 where the allegation of ill-thought plans failed on the facts, Thorpe J holding that the applicant was not required to guarantee the precise details of the future life but merely had to establish the interest, capacity and capability to pursue the plans.

2 See eg *Re B (Minor) (Removal From Jurisdiction)* [1994] 2 FCR 309, [1994] Fam Law 11, CA.

3 *Re T (Removal from Jurisdiction)* [1996] 2 FLR 352, CA.

4 This Part implements the recommendations of the English and Scottish Law Commissions in their Report, *Custody of Children – Jurisdiction and Enforcement within the United Kingdom* (Law Com No 138, Scot Law Com No 91, 1985).

5 The Act also governs the High Court's inherent jurisdiction to make certain other orders: post, pp 690–1 and 702.

6 Section 1(1)(a). See *Re S (Residence Order: Forum Conveniens)* [1995] 1 FLR 314 in which jurisdiction to vary a contact order was exercised notwithstanding that the child was living in Holland with his mother.

7 Though this has not prevented all such conflicts: see eg *T v T (Custody: Jurisdiction)* [1992] 1 FLR 43 (in which conflicting orders were made in England and Scotland). See also *Re K (A Minor) (Wardship: Jurisdiction: Interim Order)* [1991] 2 FLR 104 where there were concurrent English and Scottish proceedings, but it was held on the facts that the English wardship proceedings took precedence; cf *D v D (Custody: Jurisdiction)* [1996] 1 FLR 574 – application to English court dismissed as Scottish court already had jurisdiction.

8 Meaning England and Wales, Scotland and Northern Ireland: s 42.

9 Section 43 and the Family Law Act 1986 (Dependent Territories) Order 1991, SI 1991/1723. References to the UK court also include the Isle of Man court.

In more detail the effect of the 1986 Act is as follows: while divorce or nullity proceedings under the Matrimonial Causes Act 1973, or the Family Law Act 1996 when it comes into force,[10] (where jurisdiction is based on a *spouse's* domicile or habitual residence for one year)[11] are continuing, the court can make a s 8 order in relation to children of the family.[12] Proceedings are 'continuing' for this purpose from the time the petition is filed (or from the time a statement of marital breakdown under s 5 of the Family Law Act 1996 with respect to the marriage of the parents of the child concerned has been received by the court)[13] until the child reaches 18 in Northern Ireland or the Isle of Man or 16 in Scotland, unless those proceedings have been dismissed.[14] Even if the proceedings have been dismissed, there is still jurisdiction to make a s 8 order if it is made forthwith or where an application had been made on or before the dismissal.[15] A similar position obtains in respect of judicial separation (and separation order) proceedings save that there is no jurisdiction to make a s 8 order if divorce or nullity proceedings are 'continuing' in Scotland, Northern Ireland or the Isle of Man.[16] Even if the court has jurisdiction, where it considers it more appropriate for matters relating to the child to be determined outside England and Wales, it can direct that no s 8 order be made by any court in or in connection with these matrimonial proceedings.[17]

In the case of 'non-matrimonial proceedings', ie proceedings for financial relief under s 27 of the Matrimonial Causes Act 1973, s 2 and ss 6–7 of the Domestic Proceedings and Magistrates' Courts Act 1978, and Sch 1 to the Children Act 1989[18] and in respect of free-standing applications concerning children under s 10 of the Children Act 1989,[19] jurisdiction to make s 8 orders is confined[20] to children who are, at the date of application, habitually resident in England and Wales or who are present here and not habitually resident in Scotland, Northern Ireland or the Isle of Man. Jurisdiction on either basis, however, is excluded[1] if divorce, nullity or judicial separation (or separation order) proceedings are 'continuing' in Scotland, Northern Ireland or the Isle of Man and the child is a 'child of the family'.[2]

In all cases the court has a discretion to refuse an application if the matter has already been dealt with outside England and Wales, or to stay the application if proceedings are continuing outside England and Wales,[3] or if it feels that the

---

10 See respectively s 2A of the Family Law Act 1986 or, once the Family Law Act 1996 is fully implemented, for divorce, nullity or separation order proceedings, see s 2A of the 1986 Act as amended by Sch 8, para 37(3) to the 1996 Act.
11 See the Domicile and Matrimonial Proceedings Act 1973, which also provides a not dissimilar scheme of priority within the UK, for the application of which see *M v M (Abduction: England and Scotland)* [1997] 2 FLR 263, CA.
12 Defined by s 42(4)(a) in line with the definition in s 105(1) of the Children Act 1989, discussed ante at pp 288–90.
13 Section 2 and s 2A(1), as amended, when the 1996 Act is fully implemented, by the Family Law Act 1996 Sch 8 para 37(3).
14 Section 42(2)–(3). See eg *B v B (Scottish Contact Order: Jurisdiction to Vary)* [1996] 1 WLR 231, [1996] 1 FLR 688.
15 Section 2A(1)(c).
16 Section 2A(2). Note the prospective amendments by the Family Law Act 1996 Sch 8, para 37(4).
17 Section 2A(4).
18 Discussed in Chapter 17.
19 Discussed post at p 446.
20 By s 2(2) and s 3 of the Family Law Act 1986.
 1 By s 3(2).
 2 See s 42(4).
 3 By s 5. See eg *T v T (Custody Jurisdiction)* [1992] 1 FLR 43 and *H v H (Minors) (Forum Conveniens) (Nos 1 and 2)* [1993] 1 FLR 958.

matter is better dealt with outside the jurisdiction.[4]

There is no jurisdiction to make orders under the Children's Act 1989 in relation to children who are members of the household of a parent claiming diplomatic immunity.[5] Save where the person enjoying immunity initiates proceedings, that immunity can only be waived by the sending state and not the individual concerned.[6]

Family proceedings

Under s 10(1) the court[7] is empowered to make a s 8 order 'in any family proceedings in which a question arises with respect to the welfare of any child'. The term 'family proceedings' is defined by s 8(3)[8] as meaning any proceedings 'under the inherent jurisdiction of the High Court in relation to children' or under the enactments listed in s 8(4). With regard to the former, which refers both to wardship and to proceedings under the general inherent jurisdiction of the High Court,[9] s 8(3) states that local authority applications to invoke the High Court's inherent jurisdiction fall outside the definition.

The enactments listed in s 8(4)[10] are as follows:

- Parts I, II and IV of the 1989 Act;
- Matrimonial Causes Act 1973;
- Adoption Act 1976;
- Matrimonial and Family Proceedings Act 1984, Part III;
- Family Law Act 1996.

Applications under s 30 of the Human Fertilisation and Embryology Act 1990 also rank as 'family proceedings'.[11]

Based on the Law Commission's recommendation[12] and intended to rationalise,

---

4 Section 2A(4), as applied by *Re S (Jurisdiction to Stay Application)* [1995] 1 FLR 1093. Note also *Re M (Jurisdiction: Forum Conveniens)* [1995] 2 FLR 224, *Re F (Residence Order: Jurisdiction)* [1995] 2 FLR 518, *Re K (Abduction: Consent: Forum Conveniens)* [1995] 2 FLR 211 and *H v H (A Minor) (No 2) (Forum Conveniens)* [1997] 1 FCR 603.
5 *Re P (Children Act: Diplomatic Immunity)* [1998] 1 FLR 624, per Stuart-White J (on which see Craig (1998) 10 CFLQ 211) applying the Vienna Convention on Diplomatic Relations 1961 as incorporated into English law by the Diplomatic Privileges Act 1964 Sch 1. In so holding Stuart-White J rejected the argument that this Convention was incompatible with the European Convention on Human Rights and the UN Convention on the Rights of the Child, for as his Lordship rightly pointed out, irrespective of the theoretical merits of that argument, since the Vienna Convention was the only one of these Conventions to have been directly incorporated into domestic law, the court was bound to apply it. (Of course, this will be different once the Human Rights Act 1998 is implemented incorporating the European Convention on Human Rights into domestic law.) For a similar position in wardship see *Re C (An Infant)* [1959] Ch 363, [1958] 2 All ER 656, discussed post at p 689.
6 *Re P (Children Act: Diplomatic Immunity)*, supra, applying Art 32 of the Vienna Convention.
7 The High Court, county court or magistrates' court: s 92(7).
8 It may be noted, however, that while s 8(3) provides the exclusive definition of 'family proceedings' for the purpose of making s 8 orders, for other purposes, eg the admission of hearsay evidence, recourse might also be had to the definition in s 92(2): *R v Oxfordshire County Council (Secure Accommodation Order)* [1992] Fam 150, sub nom *R (J) v Oxfordshire County Council* [1992] 3 All ER 660.
9 Discussed in Chapter 16.
10 As amended by the Family Law Act 1996 Sch 8, para 60(1).
11 Human Fertilisation and Embryology Act 1990 s 30(8). For a discussion of s 30, see ante, pp 267ff.
12 Law Com No 172, para 4.37.

harmonise[13] and, in some cases, expand the courts' powers, the wide ambit of the definition of 'family proceedings' should be noted. For example, the inclusion of Part IV of the 1989 Act means that the court can make s 8 orders in care proceedings. Similarly, the court can now make s 8 orders in adoption, in family protection proceedings under the Family Law Act 1996 and in applications for financial relief proceedings. The reason for including these proceedings is that by extending the range of options the court will be better able to meet the child's needs.[14]

The inclusion of wardship proceedings under 'family proceedings' furthers the policy of reducing the need to resort to the jurisdiction,[15] because there will be less incentive to use it if the outcome is likely to be the same as in other proceedings. Furthermore, where an application is made the expectation is that, where appropriate, the court will make a s 8 order and discharge the wardship.[16]

Wide though the definition is, however, it does not include all proceedings concerning children. In particular it does not include those under Part V of the 1989 Act. This means that in applications for emergency protection orders and child assessment orders the court cannot make a s 8 order. There is similarly no power to make s 8 orders in international child abduction proceedings under the Child Abduction and Custody Act 1985,[17] nor in proceedings brought under the Family Law Act 1986.[18]

Any child

Section 10(1) allows an order to be made in respect of 'any child'. In other words, the court's powers are not limited to 'children of the family',[19] or to the biological children of the parties, though, as we have discussed, the powers are restricted when the child reaches the age of 16.[20] By the normal rules of interpretation[1] 'child' only refers to live persons. There is therefore no power to make s 8 orders in respect of unborn or deceased children

Upon application or upon the court's own motion

Section 10(1) provides that s 8 orders can be made either upon application or, once proceedings have begun, by the court itself whenever it 'considers that the order

---

13 It might be noted, however, that, whereas the court is obliged to consider the children in applications for financial relief under the Domestic Proceedings and Magistrates' Courts Act 1978, there is no such duty in an application order under s 27 of the Matrimonial Causes Act 1973.

14 In the case of family protection proceedings, as the Law Commission observed (ibid at para 4.25), the needs of the children are frequently an important factor in determining the relief sought and it was 'highly artificial' for the court to be able to exclude one person from the matrimonial home, at least in part for the children's sake, yet not to be able to order that the child should live with the parent remaining in the home. It might be noted, however, that in these proceedings the court is not *obliged* to consider children and that in many cases the matter will be too urgent for it to do so.

15 Law Com No 172, para 4.25. Wardship is discussed in Chapter 16.

16 As was done in *Re T (Minor) (Child: Representation)* [1994] Fam 49, [1993] 4 All ER 518, CA and *C v Salford City Council* [1994] 2 FLR 926, discussed post, pp 699–700.

17 Discussed in Chapter 13.

18 The 1986 Act deals inter alia with abduction within the UK (see Chapter 13), and declarations of status, discussed ante at pp 52 and 295.

19 The meaning of which is discussed post, pp 288–90.

20 Pursuant to s 9(6): see ante, p 429.

1 See *Elliot v Joicey* [1935] AC 209, HL; *D (A Minor) v Berkshire County Council* [1987] 1 All ER 20, HL; and *R v Newham London Borough Council, ex p Dada* [1996] QB 507, [1995] 2 All ER 522, CA.

should be made *even though no such application has been made*' [emphasis added]. Although the Law Commission expected[2] that orders would normally be made upon application, the significance of the courts' ability to make s 8 orders on their own motion should not be overlooked, since in theory once family proceedings are on foot there is at least a risk that the court might choose to make a s 8 order in respect of the child regardless of the parties' wishes. It is, however, established that if a court is minded to make an order that has not been argued for, it should inform the parties of that intention and give them the opportunity to make submissions on the desirability of the proposed option.[3] Furthermore, it has also been said[4] that it could only be in wholly exceptional circumstances that a residence order should be imposed on unwilling recipients.

6.   ENFORCING SECTION 8 ORDERS[5]

Enforcing s 8 orders can be a difficult and protracted matter which in any event needs to be handled sensitively. The imposition of penal sanctions for breaking court orders (discussed below) should not be thought of as being the norm in children cases. On the contrary, they should be sought only where all other alternatives are seen to be ineffective. Even then, careful thought needs to be given to the provocative and emotional effect that applications for enforcement can have in themselves. Above all it is important not to lose sight of the *child's* welfare in these disputes though, as we shall see, in deciding whether to impose a penal sanction the child's welfare has been held *not* to be the paramount consideration.[6]

Family Law Act 1986 s 34

Under s 34 of the Family Law Act 1986, where a person is required by a s 8 order to give up a child to another person and the court that made the order is satisfied that the child has not been given up, it may make an order authorising an officer of the court or a constable to take charge of the child and deliver him to that other person.[7] Since this power, which is available to *any* court, enables such orders to be enforced without recourse to penal procedures, it should normally be preferred to those latter powers. However, because an order under s 34 cannot be granted unless or until the order to give up the child has been disobeyed,[8] it might be

---

2 Law Com No 172, para 4.38.
3 See eg *Croydon London Borough Council v A* [1992] Fam 169, [1992] 3 All ER 788 and *Devon County Council v S* [1992] Fam 176, [1992] 3 All ER 793. In both these cases the observations were made in respect of magistrates' court decisions, but the principle ought to be of general application. Quaere the position on appeal: see eg *Re F (Minors) (Denial of Contact)* [1993] 2 FLR 677 in which the Court of Appeal refused to make a family assistance order inter alia because the point had not been argued at first instance.
4 Per Stuart-White J in *Re K (Care Order or Residence Order)* [1995] 1 FLR 675 at 683, in which devoted grandparents did not wish to have legal responsibility in respect of two grandsons (who were suffering from a muscle wasting disease) they were looking after.
5 See generally Lowe (1992) 4 Journal of Child Law 26.
6 *A v N (Committal: Refusal of Contact)* [1997] 1 FLR 533, CA, discussed below at p 450.
7 Note also the power under s 33 of the 1986 Act for a court to order any person who it has reason to believe may have relevant information as to the child's whereabouts to disclose it to the court.
8 Though it can be applied to a suitably worded contact order, viz one that formally requires the handing over of the child for contact purposes.

preferable in emergencies to obtain an ex parte order under the High Court's inherent jurisdiction[9] authorising the tipstaff to find and recover the child.[10]

The courts' general enforcement powers

More general powers of enforcement are, in the case of the High Court and county court, provided by the law of contempt of court, and in the case of magistrates' courts, by s 63(3) of the Magistrates' Courts Act 1980.

As far as the two higher courts are concerned, the breaking of a court order or an undertaking incorporated in an order constitutes a contempt of court for which the contemnor may be fined, imprisoned or have his property sequestered.[11] The first remedy is unusual.[12] The latter remedy (under which the contemnor's assets are frozen)[13] is useful in cases where the offender is abroad but has assets in this country.[14] The major sanction for breaking a s 8 order is by committal, by which means the offender can be imprisoned.

Before any committal order may be made the court has to be satisfied beyond reasonable doubt[15] that the defendant knowingly broke the order. Furthermore, it is a requirement[16] that a penal notice (that is, a notice formally warning the person against whom the order is made that failure to obey it constitutes a contempt of court for which the offender may be sent to prison) must have been attached to the order in question. Penal notices, however, can only be attached to orders that are injunctions or injunctive in form.[17] In other words, to be enforceable at all the order must, as the Children Act Advisory Committee states:[18] 'set out in explicit terms precisely what it is that the person in question must do, or must refrain from doing' and in the former case it must also specify the time within which the act is to be done.

The requirement that the order be in injunctive form means that not all s 8 orders and associated directions can be enforced by committal. It is clear, for example, that the embargoes against changing the child's surname and removing him from the UK, as provided for by s 13[19] and clearly stated on the face of a residence order,[20] are not *per se* enforceable by committal orders.[1] If therefore

---

9 Discussed in Chapter 16.
10 See Fricker, Adams, Pearce, Salter, Silver and Whybrow *Emergency Remedies in the Family Courts*, para B6.54 and Fricker 'Injunctive Orders Relating to Children' [1993] Fam Law 226 at 229–30.
11 These powers are briefly referred to in the Children Act Advisory Committee (CAAC) Report 1992/93 ch 5, but for detailed discussion reference should be made to Borrie and Lowe's *The Law of Contempt* (3rd edn, 1996) ch 14.
12 See Miller *Contempt of Court* (2nd edn, 1989) 32 and Borrie and Lowe, op cit, 635–9.
13 There is, however, power both to order the sale of sequestered assets and to direct that money raised by the sequestrators be used to pay for the costs of tracing the child and instituting proceedings abroad: see respectively *Mir v Mir* [1992] Fam 79, [1992] 1 All ER 765 and *Richardson v Richardson* [1989] Fam 95, [1989] 3 All ER 779.
14 It is therefore particularly useful in cases of child abduction – see post, p 483.
15 See eg *Dean v Dean* [1987] 1 FLR 517, CA, and *Re Bramblevale Ltd* [1970] Ch 128, [1969] 3 All ER 1062, CA.
16 RSC Ord 45 r 7(4) and see *Supreme Court Practice* 45/1/7 for forms (High Court); CCR Ord 29 r 1(3) (county court).
17 *Re P (Minors) (Custody Order: Penal Notice)* [1990] 1 WLR 613, CA, and *D v D (Access: Contempt: Committal)* [1991] 2 FLR 34, CA.
18 CAAC Report 1992/93 at 44. For the procedure of adding a penal notice, see Family Proceedings Rules 1991 r 4.21A.
19 Discussed ante, pp 439ff.
20 Viz Form C 43.
 1 See *Re P* supra.

sanctions for contempt are being sought, it will be necessary to obtain a prohibited steps order[2] clearly setting out what action must be refrained from and backed by a penal notice.

Since residence orders are said only to settle 'the arrangements to be made as to the person with whom the child is to live', they are clearly not injunctive in form and are not therefore enforceable in themselves in the two higher courts.[3] To make such orders prima facie enforceable courts must attach precise directions or conditions, for example that the child be returned to a specific place at a specific time,[4] pursuant to their powers under s 11(7).

Although in their statutory form contact orders *are* injunctive in terms and are therefore prima facie enforceable, as *D v D (Access: Contempt: Committal)*[5] shows, an order which is declaratory in terms, eg providing for reasonable contact, cannot have a penal notice attached to it and cannot therefore be enforced by committal. As the Children Act Advisory Committee has said:[6] 'To be enforceable by committal, an order for contact . . . [has] . . . to specify when and probably where, the child [is] to be allowed contact as well as with whom'. It is similarly necessary to spell out in a prohibited steps or specific issue order precisely what is prohibited or required, and in the latter case by when the act in question is required to be completed.

Orders are normally only enforceable against parties to the proceedings, but it can also be a contempt for someone else knowingly to frustrate a court order.[7]

Magistrates' enforcement powers are governed by the Magistrates' Courts Act 1980 s 63(3) which provides:

'Where any person disobeys an order of a magistrates' court . . . to do anything other than the payment of money or to abstain from doing anything the court may –

(a) order him to pay a sum not exceeding £50 for every day during which he is in default or a sum not exceeding £5,000; or

(b) commit him to custody until he has remedied his default for a period not exceeding 2 months;

but a person who is ordered to pay a sum for every day during which he is in default or who is committed to custody until he has remedied his default shall not by virtue of this section be ordered to pay more than [£5,000][8] or be committed for more than 2 months in all for doing or abstaining from doing the same thing contrary to the order (without prejudice to the operation of this section in relation to any subsequent default).'

Section 14 of the 1989 Act makes express provision for the enforcement of residence orders under s 63(3) of the Magistrates' Courts Act 1980. At first sight this special provision might be thought to mean that the other s 8 orders are not

---

2 But note the decision in *Re B (Change in Surname)* [1996] 1 FLR 791, CA (discussed ante at pp 439–40), in which it was held that where there is an existing residence order an application to change name had to be made under s 13 rather than s 8.

3 See the arguments of Lowe, op cit, at p 27. This would seem to be the raison d'être for s 14 in relation to enforcing orders in the magistrates' court. See below.

4 For an example of this type of order see *Re B (Minors) (Residence Order)* [1992] Fam 162, [1992] 3 All ER 867, CA.

5 [1994] 1 FLR 34.

6 CAAC Report 1992/93, p 44.

7 See *Re K (Minors) (Incitement to Breach Contact Order)* [1992] 2 FLR 108 (solicitor held guilty of contempt for advising a client mother to break an access order); *Re S (Abduction: Sequestration)* [1995] 1 FLR 858 (contempt for a friend to assist mother in abducting child).

8 The provision in fact still mentions £1,000, but it clearly should be changed in line with the maximum fine provided by subsection (a).

enforceable in the magistrates' court. However, the reason for making such provision for residence orders is that they might otherwise be thought declaratory only and therefore not enforceable.[9] No such difficulty attends the other s 8 orders (at any rate, in their statutory form), which accordingly are enforceable under s 63(3).

Unlike in the higher courts there is no provision for adding a penal notice to a magistrates' courts order. According to the Family Proceedings Courts (Children Act 1989) Rules 1991 r 24 a person (in whose favour a residence order has been made) wishing to enforce it must:

'. . . file a written statement describing the alleged breach of the arrangements settled by the order, whereupon the justices' clerk shall fix a date, time and place for a hearing of the proceedings and give notice as soon as practicable, to the person whom it is alleged is in breach of the arrangements settled by that order, of the date fixed'.

No specific rule is laid down for the enforcement of s 8 orders other than residence orders, but it seems sensible to assume that a similar procedure is applicable to them. It is at any rate clear that to be enforceable under s 63(3) an order must specify exactly what is to be done. In *Re H (Contact: Enforcement)* [10] it was held that the failure to specify in a contact order where the handover was to take place was fatal to the complaint.

Section 63(3) of the 1980 Act is not happily worded and seems more apt to deal with continuing breaches. Nevertheless the provision can be interpreted[11] as empowering magistrates to punish past breaches, though this point has still to be authoritatively resolved.

Even if the court is satisfied that an order has been knowingly broken by the defendant, it should regard the enforcement powers both for contempt and under the 1980 Act to imprison or fine as remedies of the last resort. As Ormrod LJ commented in *Ansah v Ansah*,[12] 'Committal orders are remedies of the last resort; in family cases they should be the very last.' Nevertheless, it would be wrong to extract any general principle from Ormrod LJ's dictum in *Ansah v Ansah*, and in appropriate cases it may well be right to imprison an offender.[13] Indeed, following the Court of Appeal decision in *A v N (Committal: Refusal of Contact)*,[14] in which it was held that, in considering whether to commit a mother for her persistent and flagrant breach of a contact order with the father, the child's welfare was a material but not the paramount consideration, imprisonment might be more likely than in the past.

---

9 Following *Webster v Southwark London Borough Council* [1983] QB 698, [1983] 2 WLR 217. Quaere why the opportunity was not taken to make s 14 applicable to residence orders made in the High Court and county court?

10 [1996] 1 FLR 614.

11 See *P v W (Access Order: Breach)* [1984] Fam 32 at 40 per Wood J.

12 [1977] Fam 138 at 143, [1977] 2 All ER 638, CA at 643. Note also Bennett J's comment in *Re H*, supra, that magistrates should 'take the greatest possible caution before proceeding with a hearing under s 63 – they should only proceed with the greatest possible caution to use a weapon of last resort'.

13 See eg *Jones v Jones* [1993] 2 FLR 377, CA.

14 [1997] 1 FLR 533, CA in which a mother was committed to prison for 42 days for her persistent and repeated breaches of a contact order. See also *F v F (Contact: Committal)* [1998] 2 FLR 237, CA (mother's appeal against a suspended committal for seven days was dismissed); *C v C (Access Order: Enforcement)* [1990] 1 FLR 462, CA (mother imprisoned for seven days). NB there are fewer problems in committing the non-residential parent who breaks contact conditions: see eg *G v C (Residence Order: Committal)* [1998] 1 FLR 43, CA (father imprisoned for eight months for repeated breaches of order not to threaten or abuse the mother).

7.   VARYING AND DISCHARGING ORDERS

All s 8 orders may subsequently be varied or discharged. Indeed, this is one of the important distinguishing features between these orders and adoption.[15]

All the substantive and procedural requirements for the making of a s 8 order apply to their subsequent variation or discharge.[16]

8.   APPEALS

Routes of appeal

There is a right of appeal against the making or the refusal to make any order under the Children Act, including s 8 orders. Appeals from magistrates' decisions lie to the High Court;[17] those from county courts and the High Court lie to the Court of Appeal.[18] Leave to appeal to the Court of Appeal is not required where the residence, education or welfare of the child is concerned,[19] nor where the applicant has been refused all contact[20] (which for these purposes means *physical* contact).[1]

While there is no automatic embargo against a party appealing against a consent order, it seems that leave of the court that made the order will be required.[2] Where no leave is granted, the proper procedure is to apply to the first instance court to vary the order.[3]

The position pending appeal

Under the general powers to impose directions and conditions under s 11(7) of the Children Act 1989[4] the operation of any s 8 order can be postponed pending an appeal, or other interim arrangements can be made.[5]

The powers of appellate courts

An appellate court may grant or dismiss the appeal. Alternatively, if it is satisfied that the original order was wrong but it is unsure upon the evidence what orders should be made, it can remit the case for a rehearing and in the meantime give appropriate directions as to care and control. Exceptionally, the appellate court

---

15 Adoption is discussed in Chapter 15.
16 Section 8(2), which provides that 'a section 8 order means inter alia, any order varying or discharging such an order'. For the variation and discharge of existing pre-1989 Act orders see Sch 14, para 11 and Douglas *Children Act 1989 Transitional Arrangements Guide* and the discussion at p 372 of the 8th edition of this work.
17 Children Act 1989 s 94.
18 County Courts Act 1984 s 77(1); Supreme Court Act 1981 s 16.
19 Supreme Court Act 1981 s 18(1)(h)(i).
20 RSC Ord 59 r 1B(1)(f)(iii).
 1 *Re J (A Minor) (Contact)* [1994] 1 FLR 369, per Balcombe LJ, following the pre-Children Act decision *Allette v Allette* [1986] 2 FLR 427, CA. Although leave to appeal may be granted by the first instance judge, save on difficult points of law or practice, this power should be exercised with great caution: *Re O (Family Appeals: Management)* [1998] 1 FLR 431n.
 2 See *Re R (Contact: Consent Order)* [1995] 1 FLR 123, CA.
 3 *Re F (A Minor) (Custody: Consent Order: Procedure)* [1992] 1 FLR 561, CA.
 4 Discussed ante, pp 423ff.
 5 Magistrates apparently have no powers to order a stay pending an appeal and an application needs to made to the High Court (Children Act Advisory Committee: *Handbook of Best Practice in Children Act Cases*, (1997) para 92). Stays should not normally be granted for more than 14 days: cf *Hereford and Worcester County Council v EH* [1985] FLR 975 at 977, per Wood J.

can hear fresh evidence to resolve its doubts about the original decision.[6]

In deciding what order the appellate court should make, it is established that there are no special rules governing appeals in cases involving children. The leading case is *G v G*,[7] in which the House of Lords held that an appellate court[8] cannot overturn a first instance decision merely upon the basis that it disagrees with it. An appellate court has no power simply to substitute its own view. Instead it has to be satisfied that either the judge has erred as a matter of law (ie he applied the wrong principle) or that he relied upon evidence that he should have ignored or ignored evidence that he should have taken into account or that the decision was so 'plainly wrong' that the only legitimate conclusion was that the judge had erred in the exercise of his discretion. Although this latter ground gives scope for argument in any particular case,[9] it is to be emphasised that the test is difficult to satisfy.[10]

Whether the law should be so restrictive on appeal is debatable.[11] In *G v G* the House of Lords took the view that there is desirability in putting an end to litigation, particularly as in many cases there is no obviously right answer.[12] They also endorsed the view that an appellate court should be chary of overruling a decision, particularly in cases concerning the upbringing of children where it is so important to have seen the parties and witnesses.[13]

It is desirable in all cases concerning children that appeals should be heard as speedily as possible, but it is particularly important in cases where a transfer of residence has been ordered. In *Re W (minors)*[14] it was stated that in such cases appeals should be heard within 28 days of the decision.[15]

6 Per Lord Scarman in *B v W (Wardship: Appeal)* [1979] 3 All ER 83, HL at 95–6. The admission of fresh evidence is at the court's discretion: see *A v A (Custody Appeal: Role of Appellate Court)* [1988] 1 FLR 193, CA; *M v M (Minor: Custody Appeal)* [1987] 1 WLR 404, CA; *Re C (A Minor) (Wardship Proceedings)* [1984] FLR 419, CA; and *Ladd v Marshall* [1954] 3 All ER 745. The admission of fresh evidence may justify upholding the original decision even though it has been held plainly wrong: *M v M (Minor: Custody Appeal)*, supra. Appeals concerning children do not, however, automatically call for an up-to-date welfare report: *M v M (Welfare Report)* [1989] 2 FLR 354, CA.
7 [1985] 2 All ER 225, HL. See Eekelaar (1985) 48 MLR 704 and Robinson [1985] Fam Law 330.
8 A similar rule applies both to appeals from magistrates' courts (*Re M (Section 94 Appeals)* [1995] 1 FLR 546, CA) and to appeals from a single Lord Justice to the full Court of Appeal (*Re W (minors)* (1990) Times, 22 November, CA).
9 Though it might be argued that the use of the phrase 'plainly wrong' is too inhibiting, at any rate where the trial judge is a High Court judge, since erstwhile colleagues in the Court of Appeal might be reluctant to arrive at such an apparently damning conclusion.
10 See eg *May v May* [1986] 1 FLR 325, CA. In *Re T (A Minor)* [1986] Fam Law 189, CA, it was stated that legal aid should not be granted for hopeless appeals, while in *Re G (A Minor) (Role of the Appellate Court)* [1987] 1 FLR 164, CA, it was said that where appeals which were unarguable in the light of *G v G* were brought by legally aided parties, the court might have to consider whether appropriate orders for costs ought to be made to ensure that public money was not wasted. Note also *Re O (Costs: Liability of Legal Aid Board)* [1997] 1 FLR 465, CA.
11 See the excellent critique by Eekelaar, op cit. However, in terms of the non-application of the paramountcy principle, the decision can be justified on the basis that it did not directly concern the child's upbringing and that as the normal rules of appeal do not inhibit the appellate courts from being able to safeguard the child's interests, there is no need for special rules: see Lowe 'The House of Lords and the welfare principle' in Bridge (ed) *Family Law Towards the Millennium – Essays for P M Bromley* 125 at 158.
12 See Lord Fraser [1985] 2 All ER at 228 referring to *Clarke-Hunt v Newcombe* (1982) 4 FLR 482, CA at 488, per Cumming-Bruce LJ.
13 See eg *Re F (A Minor) (Wardship: Appeal)* [1976] Fam 238, [1976] 1 All ER 417, CA.
14 [1984] 3 All ER 58n, [1984] 1 WLR 1125, CA. See also *Ridgway v Ridgway* [1986] Fam Law 363, CA, which stressed the need for legal aid to be granted quickly.
15 Failure by barristers (or solicitors) to exercise the greatest possible diligence in complying with the time limits imposed by the courts for the preparation of appeals may be regarded as professional misconduct: *Re M (A Minor)* (1989) Times, 29 December, CA.

C.   Other powers

1.   FAMILY ASSISTANCE ORDERS

Section 16 of the 1989 Act empowers the court to make a 'family assistance order'. Such an order requires either a probation officer to be made available or the local authority[16] to make an officer of the authority available 'to advise, assist and (where appropriate) befriend any person named in the order'.[17] Those who may be named are: any parent (which includes the unmarried father) or guardian of the child, any person with whom the child is living or in whose favour a contact order is in force with respect to the child, and the child himself.[18]

This power replaces the former power to make supervision orders in private law proceedings which, according to the Law Commission,[19] failed to reflect the different purposes for which supervision orders were made, ie on the one hand child protection, and on the other the provision of short-term support to the family. Family assistance orders simply have the latter function, while supervision orders (made under s 31)[20] have the former.

As the Department of Health's *Guidance and Regulations* puts it:[1]

'A supervision order is designed for the more serious cases, in which there is an element of child protection involved. By contrast, a family assistance order aims simply to provide short-term help to a family, to overcome the problems and conflicts associated with their separation or divorce. Help may well be focused more on the adult than the child.'

When orders may be made

Family assistance orders may be made in any 'family proceedings', whether or not any other order has been made.[2] The power may be exercised only by the court acting upon its own motion, though there is nothing to stop parties requesting the court to make such an order during the course of family proceedings.[3] However, the lack of the right to apply for such an order would seem to prevent parties from applying to the court *solely* for a family assistance order.

Before any order can be made, the court must be satisfied that 'the circumstances of the case are exceptional'.[4] The Act itself does not define what is meant by 'exceptional circumstances', but in general it seems clear that the order should not be made as a matter of routine. The Department of Health's *Guidance* also points out that[5] 'it will be particularly important in all orders for the court to make plain at the outset why family assistance is needed and what it is hoped to achieve by it'.

---

16 Subject to s 16(7); see below.
17 Section 16(1).
18 Section 16(2).
19 Law Com No 172, para 5.12.
20 Discussed post, pp 568ff.
1 Vol 1, *Court Orders*, para 2.50 and cited by Wall J in *Re DH (A Minor) (Child Abuse)* [1994] 1 FLR 679 at 704. See also Law Com No 172, para 5.19.
2 Section 16(1).
3 Though note *Re F (Minors) (Denial of Contact)* [1993] 2 FLR 677 in which the Court of Appeal refused to consider making a family assistance order, since the point had not been argued at first instance and, in the absence of being able to show that the original order was wrong, the court had no power to make such an order or remit the case back.
4 Section 16(3)(a).
5 Ibid at para 2.52.

As well as having to be satisfied that the circumstances are exceptional, the court must also be satisfied that the consent of every person named in the order, other than the child, has been obtained.[6] There is, therefore, no formal requirement that the child himself should consent, nor is there a statutory requirement to ascertain the child's own wishes and feelings about such an order, since the enjoinder to do so under s 1(3) does not apply to making s 16 orders.[7]

A family assistance order may not be made requiring a local authority to make one of its officers available unless the authority agrees or the child concerned lives or will live in its area.[8] It has also been held[9] that it is not a proper use of a family assistance order to require a local authority to provide someone for escort duty where no family member is prepared to take the children to visit their father in prison.

Effect and duration of order

Section 16 gives no guidance as to which officer should be appointed, but in the private law context the most appropriate appointee will usually be the welfare officer who has compiled the welfare report for the court, while in care proceedings, the obvious candidate is the social worker attached to the particular case. It is not possible to appoint a guardian ad litem (even where that person has made a report to the court) since such a person will be neither a probation officer nor an officer of the local authority and will therefore be outside the terms of s 16(1)(a) and (b).

Under s 16(4) a family assistance order may direct specified persons named in the order to keep the address of any person named in the order so that he can visit them. If a s 8 order is also in force, the officer is empowered to refer to the court the question of whether a s 8 order should be varied or discharged.[10]

A family assistance order is intended to be only a short-term remedy. Hence, s 16(5) provides that unless a shorter period is specified the order will have effect only for six months from the day on which it is made. However, there is no restriction on making any further order.[11]

Family assistance orders in practice

Before implementation of the 1989 Act it was uncertain how many family assistance orders would be made.[12] Although there are no published national

6   Section 16(3)(b).
7   See ante, pp 337–8. Nevertheless, as Clark Hall and Morrison at 1[281] argue, there is nothing to prevent the court from discovering the child's views and, indeed, in the light of *Gillick v West Norfolk and Wisbech Area Health Authority* [1986] AC 112, [1985] 3 All ER 402, HL, the court may take the view that the child's own wishes ought to be taken into account (at least where the child is mature enough to make his own decisions).
8   Section 16(7). But see *Re C (Family Assistance Order)* [1996] 1 FLR 424 where, having made an assistance order directing the local authority to make an officer available, the local authority subsequently returned to the court to say that it did not have the resources to carry the order out. Johnson J declined to take further action.
9   *S v P (Contact Application: Family Assistance Order)* [1997] 2 FLR 277, per Judge Callman.
10   Section 16(6).
11   See Department of Health's *Guidance and Regulations*, op cit, at para 2.52, and the implicit acceptance of that proposition by Booth J in *Leeds County Council v C* [1993] 1 FLR 269 at 272.
12   Some thought that, because of the requirement of 'exceptional circumstances' (criticised for being 'unduly restrictive' by Bainham *Children: The Modern Law* at p 37) coupled with the need to obtain the consent of the adults it is sought to assist, orders would be made infrequently. Others mooted whether such orders would be made relatively frequently as a 'half way house' means of making 'no orders' pursuant to s 1(5). For a discussion of the actual experience see Trinder and Stone 'Family assistance orders – professional aspiration and party frustration' (1998) 10 CFLQ 291.

statistics, few orders seem to have been made and there are few reported cases even discussing the powers, let alone making the order. One of those cases, however, is *Leeds City Council v C*,[13] in which Booth J held that the only appropriate way in which a court could make provision for supervision of contact by a local authority was by an order under s 16.

Family assistance orders have a useful role to play in providing local authority assistance to supervise contact.[14] A family assistance order was also made in *Re U (Application to Free for Adoption)*,[15] where, having rejected a local authority application to free a child for adoption and granting instead a residence order to grandparents, the Court of Appeal felt that a s 16 order was a useful way of monitoring the child's placement with them.

2. SECTION 37 DIRECTIONS

Before the Children Act 1989 courts could, in exceptional circumstances, commit children upon their own motion into local authority care or make supervision orders in private law proceedings.[16] This power, however, ran counter to the policy under the 1989 Act to have just one route into care. Accordingly, it was abolished. Under s 37, however, if in *any* family proceedings, 'it appears to the court that it may be appropriate for a care or supervision order to be made . . . the court may direct the appropriate authority to undertake an investigation of the child's circumstances'.

It may be observed that s 37 only empowers a court to direct that an investigation is undertaken. The court itself has no power to direct a local authority to bring care proceedings and a fortiori has no power itself to commit a child into care.[17]

D. Obtaining evidence

1. THE ROLE OF THE FAMILY COURT WELFARE SERVICE

Although the parties themselves will give evidence[18] and are free to call witnesses when presenting their case,[19] it is important both in contested cases and those in which the proposed arrangements are not thought to be satisfactory, that the court has an independent assessment of the facts. In private law cases this vitally

---

13 [1993] 1 FLR 269; cf *Re DH (A Minor) (Child Abuse)* [1994] 1 FLR 679 at 702, per Wall J.
14 *B v B (Child Abuse: Contact)* [1994] 2 FLR 713 at 738, ironically also per Wall J. See also *Re R (A Minor) (Residence: Religion)* [1993] 2 FLR 163, CA – a case involving a father who was a member of the Exclusive Brethren.
15 [1993] 2 FLR 992, CA.
16 See the 7th edition of this work at pp 297–8, 306 and 308.
17 The absence of any such power to direct local authorities to take steps to protect children was criticised, particularly in *Nottingham County Council v P* [1994] Fam 18, [1993] 3 All ER 815 by Sir Stephen Brown P. See also Wall 'The courts and child protection – the challenge of hybrid cases' (1997) 9 CFLQ 345 at 348–50.
18 Though note that parties do not always have a right to give oral evidence: see *Re B (Minors) (Contact)* [1994] 2 FLR 1, CA; *Re N (Contested Care Application)* [1994] 2 FLR 992.
19 But note the restrictions on the use of expert evidence connected with medical or psychiatric examinations of the child, discussed post at p 558.

important role is normally[20] played by court welfare officers.[1]

Court welfare officers are qualified probation workers. In London there is a permanent staff attached to the Supreme Court undertaking solely civil work, and in the provinces too there is increasing specialisation in family work.[2]

National standards for welfare officers' work have been issued by the Home Office in a document entitled 'National Standards for Probation Service Family Court Welfare Work'[3] (hereinafter referred to as *National Standards*). This document sets out guidance which the probation service is expected to follow. As *National Standards* explains:

> 'The primary objective of all family court welfare work undertaken by the probation service is to help the courts in their task of serving the needs of children whose parents are involved in separation or divorce, or whose families are involved in disputes in private law'.

It continues by setting out the principal tasks of the Service:

(a) meeting the parties before or during a directions appointment to make a preliminary assessment of the case and to identify areas of agreement;

(b) meeting the parties at the direction of the court to assist them to make agreed decisions about their children;

(c) carrying out enquiries and preparing a welfare report to assist the court to make decisions in the best interests of the child.

The service may also provide assistance to persons named in family assistance orders and to supervise children who are the subject of a supervision order.

Although each of these functions is important, it is upon the preparation of the welfare report that we will now concentrate.

Welfare reports

(a)   The power under s 7

Section 7(1) of the 1989 Act empowers any court, when considering *any* question with respect to a child under the 1989 Act, to ask a probation officer or a local authority to report to the court 'on such matters relating to the welfare of that child as are required to be dealt with in the report'. The power to ask for a report in relation to *any* issue under the 1989 Act means that welfare reports may be ordered in care proceedings. As we discuss in Chapter 14, this independent role is usually undertaken by guardians ad litem who, unlike welfare officers, represent the child in the proceedings. Nevertheless, on occasion it might be necessary for the court welfare officer to act in care cases to save time and resources. Indeed, in some cases such an officer may have already done so, eg in family proceedings where

---

20 But note the power (discussed below) of courts to ask local authorities to report.

1 For a general account of a welfare officer's work see James *Social Work in Divorce: Welfare, Mediation and Justice* (1995) and Hoggett, Pearl, Cooke and Bates *The Family, Law and Society* (4th edn, 1996) 551–5.

2 According to the CAAC Final Report 1997 at 55 the number of main grade court welfare officers in post at the end of December 1996 was 623 – as increase of three per cent on the previous year. For a discussion of whether welfare officers should continue to be drawn from the probation service rather than from a specialised family court service see Murch and Hooper *The Family Justice System* (1992) ch 7. The government has signalled its interest in reforming the system: see *Support Services in Family Proceedings – Future Organisation of Court Welfare Services – Consultation Paper* (1998).

3 HMSO, 1994, and brought into force January 1995.

the court decides, after hearing the evidence, that it should exercise its powers under s 37 and invite the local authority to investigate the case with a view to the authority applying for a care or supervision order.[4]

Section 7 empowers the courts in private law proceedings to ask a local authority to report rather than a court welfare officer. However, it is not intended or expected that local authorities should be asked as a matter of routine, but only in those cases where they have an obvious connection with the case.[5] If a local authority is already involved, applications can properly be made to the court hearing the private law proceedings for them to provide a report under s 7.[6] Where there are both private law proceedings and investigations being carried out by the police and social services, then s 7 can and should be used to require the local authority to report to the court on the nature, progress and outcome of the investigation. In this way the court can ensure the co-ordination of the private law proceedings with the statutory local authority child abuse investigations.[7]

Under s 7(5) it is the duty of the local authority or probation officer to comply with any court request for a welfare report. However, where the court decides to ask the local authority to report, it can ask them to arrange for this to be done either by one of their officers or 'such other person (other than a probation officer) as the authority consider appropriate'.[8] There is no power under s 7 to order a local authority to obtain further expert advice or assessment.[9] It is doubtful whether a court can appoint an independent social worker to prepare a report, at least without the other party's consent,[10] and it should not in any event do so merely because a party is dissatisfied with a welfare officer's conduct.[11] It should be appreciated that a welfare officer is an officer of the court and as such has an independent role, being neither the child's representative nor a witness for either party.

(b) When reports should be ordered

As explained by the 'Best practice note' drafted by the Children Act Advisory Committee (hereinafter referred to as *Best Practice*),[12] the ordering of a welfare officer's report is a judicial act requiring inquiry into the circumstances of the child. A report should not be ordered unless there is a live issue under the Children Act, and before a report is ordered consideration should be given to the power to refer the parties (with their consent) to mediation. Commonly these enquiries and the decision to order a report will be taken at the preliminary stages of the proceedings, though there is power to order a report at any stage. As *Best Practice* states, the attendance of the parties and their solicitors is required at this stage so as to enable the court to inquire properly into the issues to be covered by the report. Where a welfare officer is present or otherwise available, consideration can be

---

4 Discussed ante at p 455.
5 See Law Com No 172, para 6.17.
6 Per Wall J in *W v Wakefield City Council* [1995] 1 FLR 170.
7 Per Wall J in *Re A and B (Minors) (No 2)* [1995] 1 FLR 351 at 368–9.
8 Section 7(1)(b). This is intended to cover the situation where, as a result of close co-operation, the NSPCC, for example, acting on behalf of the local authority, is seen to be the key worker for the particular child: see White, Carr and Lowe *A Guide to the Children Act 1989* (1990), para 8.6.
9 *Re K (Contact: Psychiatric Report)* [1995] 2 FLR 432, CA.
10 *Cadman v Cadman* (1981) 3 FLR 275. But there is nothing to stop a party from calling a social worker to give expert evidence.
11 Where a party is dissatisfied the proper course is to invite the court to appoint another welfare officer: *Cadman v Cadman*, supra.
12 See *Handbook of Best Practice in Children Act Cases* (CAAC 1997) Appendix A.

given to inviting the parties to have a preliminary discussion with him or her. At such meetings, *National Standards* explains, the welfare officer should try to establish:

> 'exactly what issues, if any, are in dispute;
> whether there is any measure of agreement between the parties;
> whether there is any prospect of agreement being reached without the continued involvement of the court . . .'

In cases which remain unresolved the court welfare officer's findings and recommendations should be presented to the court in a way which assists it to decide how to proceed with the case. The court welfare officer should outline the issues about which there is conflict, assess the options open to the court and, if appropriate, suggest a course of action. The options may include calling for a welfare report on matters where the court will need further information or allowing the case to be referred for mediation either by the court welfare service or by an independent organisation.

Notwithstanding any recommendation, the court has an unappealable discretion to decide whether or not to ask for a report.[13] Apart from appreciating that welfare officers' time is limited and must be spent on cases where it will be most valuable,[14] it must also be acknowledged that reports can be a source of delay[15] and, mindful of the general duty under s 1(2) to be aware of the likelihood of delay prejudicing the child's welfare, the court might have to balance the advantages to be gained from a report against the disadvantage of the time it takes to obtain it.[16] Nevertheless, the expectation is that some sort of report will be required in most contested cases.[17]

If a report is ordered,[18] then, as *Best Practice* explains:

> '. . . the judge, district judge or justices' clerk should explain briefly to the parties what will be involved and should emphasise the need to co-operate with the welfare officer and specifically to keep any appointments. In particular when the principle of contact is in dispute the parties should be told that the welfare officer will probably wish to see the applicant parent alone with the child. It should also be emphasised that the report, when received, is a confidential document and must not be shown to anyone who is not a named party to the application'.

It has long been established[19] that the reporting and mediation roles are quite distinct and to some extent incompatible and that accordingly, as *Best Practice*

---

13 *Re W (Welfare Reports)* [1995] 2 FLR 142, CA.

14 As the Law Commission observed (Law Com No 172, para 6.15), the court has to be moderate when exercising its powers. Note also *Re B (Minors), B v B* (1973) 3 Fam Law 43, in which the court expressed its disapproval of ordering more than one report in any case.

15 The target set by *National Standards* is 10 weeks but, as the CAAC Final Report 1997, p 55 commented, the 1994–95 performance was poor, but with some improvement in 1995–96 where the average was between 10.5 to 11 weeks. This is nevertheless a considerable improvement on the pre-Children Act experience where delays of up to nine months were reported – see eg *Plant v Plant* (1982) 4 FLR 305, CA.

16 See eg *Re H (Minors) (Welfare Reports)* [1990] 2 FLR 172, CA.

17 Per Lord Mackay LC, 502 HL Official Report (5th series), col 1203. The number of reports ordered have steadily risen since implementation of the 1989 Act. In 1995, 35,400 were ordered – two per cent more than in 1993. The numbers were expected to rise still further in 1996 to about 36,900: CAAC Final Report 1997, p 55.

18 In the case of proceedings before magistrates a single justice can order the report: Family Proceedings Courts (Children Act 1989) Rules 1991 r 2(5)(c).

19 See *Scott v Scott* [1986] 2 FLR 320, CA, and *Re H (Conciliation: Welfare Reports)* [1986] 1 FLR 476. The Booth Committee (Report of the Matrimonial Causes Procedure Committee, 1985) at para 4.63 had already recommended that the same officer should not both conciliate and later report in the same case.

now puts it:[20] 'any court welfare officer who may have been involved in any privileged mediation proceedings[1] should not be the officer who undertakes the preparation of the welfare report'. It also expected that such appointees should carry out their investigative task and not subsequently assume a mediation role.[2]

It has been held that, once the report is ordered, the desirable practice is to ascertain when it can be expected and to fix a specific date in the light of that information.[3]

(c) The form, content and disclosure of reports

Once appointed, welfare officers are generally expected to investigate the circumstances of the child or children concerned and the important figures in their lives with a view to providing the court with factual information on which to make a decision.[4] As *National Standards* explains:

> 'The purpose of a welfare report is to provide the court with information about matters relating to the welfare of the child which will enable the court to make decisions that are in the child's best interests. Where in the course of preparing the report the court welfare officer identifies opportunities for helping the parties to reach agreement, these should be pursued in line with the general principle of promoting parental responsibility but it is not the role of the court welfare officer to set out to resolve disputes when preparing a welfare report.
>
> . . .
>
> Courts have been advised to specify the nature of the enquiries which they wish the court welfare officer to undertake. But such specification should never prevent the court welfare officer from bringing other matters to the notice of the court or from going back to the court for further directions.'

Initial contact with the parties should be made within five days of the receipt of all the relevant papers from the court. Adequate notice of the appointment should be given and the purpose of the report explained. *National Standards* contains detailed advice about the conduct of the interviews including the possibility, in appropriate cases and subject to informing the parties of their freedom to choose, of seeing the parties jointly. It emphasises that 'all children should be seen by the court welfare officer unless there are strong reasons for not doing so. If a child is not seen the reasons for this should be given in the report.'

In *Re P (A Minor) (Inadequate Welfare Report)*,[5] because the welfare officer had only seen the mother and father twice at the welfare office and the children once, she had created no opportunity of assessing the relationship between the children and either parent. As Johnson J commented:

> 'The whole point of the court welfare officer system is that, because in the nature of things the court cannot itself observe the relationship between the children and the parents, the welfare office[r] acts as the eyes and ears of the court and provides the court with an independent and objective assessment of the relationships involved. Here the report was inadequate. The welfare officer's inquiry was conducted in such a way as to make it impossible for her to form any views about the relationships involved.'

20 A similar point is also made by *National Standards*.
1 Interestingly there have been steep declines in welfare officers' involvement in privileged mediation cases: see CAAC Final Report 1997 at p 55.
2 *Scott v Scott*, supra. See also *National Standards*, set out below.
3 *B v B (Minors) (Interviews and Listing Arrangements)* [1994] 2 FLR 489.
4 Per Dillon LJ in *Scott v Scott*, supra, at 322.
5 [1996] 2 FCR 285 at 291. See also *Re W (A Minor) (Custody)* (1983) 4 FLR 492, CA at 501, per Cumming-Bruce LJ.

National Standards gives detailed guidance on the contents of a report, explaining that in addition to giving express consideration to the welfare check list under s 1(3), and a reasoned assessment of the available options, a good report will –

'be as short and focused as possible;
balance description and background with evaluation, summary and assessment;
differentiate fact from opinion;
verify significant facts and justify options;
present the information with sensitivity and in a way which does not exacerbate the relations between the parties;
be fair to the parties.'

The report may be made in writing or orally as the court requires.[6]

It is inevitable that to some extent a welfare officer will rely on hearsay evidence. Indeed, it has been said that in the nature of things such officers could not do what is required of them and comply with the hearsay rule.[7] However, although s 7(4) provides that, regardless of any rule of law which would otherwise prevent it from doing so, the court may take into account any statement contained in (or evidence given in respect of matters referred to in) the report, regard should still be had to *Thompson v Thompson.*[8] In that case it was said that on controversial issues, eg making adverse findings against a party, if an officer is constrained to pass on second-hand evidence, he should endeavour to make this explicit and indicate his source of information and his reasons, if he has any, for agreeing with such an opinion.

The welfare officer must file his report either as directed by the court or in the absence of a direction, at least 14 days before the hearing at which it will be given or considered, and as soon as practicable the court must serve a copy of the report on the parties and any guardians ad litem.[9] The report should not be disclosed to anyone other than a party, his legal representative, the guardian ad litem and the Legal Aid Board without the leave of the court.[10] In exceptional cases the court can order that the report should not be disclosed to the parties.[11] Welfare officers should give no undertaking that what they are told will be kept confidential and not disclosed in the report.[12] It is established that the divorce county court has jurisdiction to grant leave for information contained in a welfare report in a previous case to be used in the case before it.[13] The previous requirement that the welfare officer had to attend the hearing unless excused by the court has been changed. It is now provided[14] that upon the filing of a report the court *may* direct that the welfare officer attend. As *Best Practice* states, when such a direction is given, the court should 'ensure that the officer gives evidence as soon as possible after the case has opened (and in any event on the first day) and is released after the

---

6 Section 7(3). The normal expectation is that the report will be written.
7 Per O'Connor LJ in *Webb v Webb* [1986] 1 FLR 462, CA at 463.
8 [1986] 1 FLR 212n, CA at 216–17. See also *Edwards v Edwards* [1986] 1 FLR 187, and *H v H (A Minor), K v K (minors)* [1990] Fam 86, [1989] 3 All ER 740, CA.
9 Family Proceedings Rules 1991 r 4.13(1), as amended; Family Proceedings Courts (Children Act 1989) Rules 1991 r 13(1), as amended.
10 Family Proceedings Rules 1991 r 4.23(1); Family Proceedings Courts (Children Act 1989) Rules 1991 r 23(1).
11 *Re M (Minors) (Disclosure of Evidence)* [1994] 1 FLR 760, CA and *Re B (Minor) (Disclosure of Evidence)* [1993] Fam 142, [1993] 1 All ER 931, CA, but note that the appropriate test is probably now that laid down in *Re D (Minors) (Adoption Reports: Confidentiality)* [1996] AC 593, [1995] 4 All ER 385, HL, discussed post, p 663.
12 *Re G (Minors) (Welfare Report: Disclosure)* [1993] 2 FLR 293, CA.
13 *Brown v Matthews* [1990] Ch 662, [1990] 2 All ER 155, CA.
14 Family Proceedings Rules 1991 r 4.13(3), as amended; Family Proceedings Courts (Children Act 1989) Rules 1991 r 13(3), as amended.

evidence has been completed'. This change of rules and practice represents another attempt to ensure that calls on welfare officers' time are kept to a minimum. Nevertheless, these developments are not intended to prejudice the right of any party to question the welfare officer about his report.[15]

Although the major purpose of the investigation is to provide factual background information, the report normally contains recommendations by the welfare officer, or if it does not, the court will sometimes ask the officer at the hearing for his views. However, it is established practice that, save in exceptional circumstances, the judge (and a fortiori justices) should not discuss the case privately with the welfare officer in the absence of the parties.[16] Recommendations are not binding upon the court: nevertheless, the general esteem with which the welfare service is held is reflected in the requirement that if a court departs from a welfare officer's recommendation it should state the reasons for so doing.[17]

Although there are several reported examples of the court not following a recommendation,[18] in practice the welfare officer's view commands great respect and it should be appreciated that in most cases he is the most influential figure in the decision-making process.[19]

On the other hand, provided the reasons given by a judge constitute a sound basis for the exercise of his discretion and for dissenting from the court welfare officer's recommendation, the failure to state expressly his reasons for not following the latter's recommendation does not vitiate the decision.[20] Normally, clear-cut recommendations should only be rejected after hearing the welfare officer's oral evidence.[1] However, bearing in mind the principle of delay set out in s 1(2), it is within the court's power to depart from a recommendation even where the officer does not attend the hearing.[2]

2.   OBTAINING EVIDENCE FROM CHILDREN

Article 12(1) of the UN Convention on the Rights of the Child 1989 states:

'States Parties shall assure to the child who is capable of forming his or her own views the right to express those views freely in all matters affecting the child, the views of the child being given full weight in accordance with the age and maturity of the child.'

As children are not normally made parties to the proceedings,[3] the court will most commonly learn the child's view through the welfare report.[4] Indeed, it has been said that it is important that an independent welfare officer should see the child to

15 Ibid, r 4.13(3)(b) and r 13(3)(b) and see *Re I and H (Contact: Evidence)* [1998] 1 FLR 876, CA.
16 *Re C (A Minor) (Irregularity of Practice)* [1991] 2 FLR 438, CA.
17 See eg *Re V (Residence: Review)* [1995] 2 FLR 1010, CA and *Re L (Residence: Justices Reasons)* [1995] 2 FLR 445; *Re P (A Minor) (Contact)* [1994] 1 FCR 285 and *M v C (Children Orders: Reasons)* [1993] 2 FLR 584.
18 See eg *Re P (A Minor) (Inadequate Welfare Report)* [1996] 2 FCR 285; *Re W (A Minor) (Custody)* (1983) 4 FLR 492, 13 Fam Law 47, CA; *Leete v Leete and Stevens* [1984] Fam Law 21; and *H v H* [1984] Fam Law 112, CA.
19 See eg Murch *Justice and Welfare in Divorce* (1980) ch 8.
20 Per Russell LJ in *Re V (Residence: Review)*, supra at 1019.
 1 *Re CB (Access: Court Welfare Reports)* [1995] 1 FLR 622, CA. See also *Re F (Minors) (Contact: Appeal)* [1997] 1 FCR 523, CA.
 2 *Re G (Section 8 Order: Court Welfare Officer)* [1995] 1 FLR 617, CA.
 3 Though there is power to join the child as a party in the High Court and county court and to order that the child be separately represented: Family Proceedings Rules 1991 r 9.5.
 4 For the relevance of such views see post, pp 465–7.

ascertain his views.[5] In addition it is well established that the court has power to interview the child[6] in private.

Before the Children Act it had been established that the power to interview children in private resided only in the High Court and county court and not the magistrates' court[7] and, in the absence of specific rules governing the courts' powers to interview children in private,[8] it was assumed that this practice would continue to apply after the 1989 Act. However, it has since been held[9] that in exceptional circumstances magistrates can also see a child in private.

The Rules are silent as to when it is appropriate to conduct an interview in private, though the general view seems to be that it is a practice that should not readily be undertaken.[10] In any event, the decision whether or not to interview a child in private is entirely a matter for the judge (ie it is unappealable). As Ormrod LJ put it in the pre-1989 Act case, *D v D*:[11]

> 'If ever a matter was a personal matter for a judge it is the question of seeing or not seeing the children. It is a highly sensitive decision both for a judge himself and a judge, in my judgment, is fully entitled to make up his own mind . . . about whether or not to see children. It is a very delicate situation indeed in my experience and it can be extremely embarrassing to a judge when he can see already the likelihood that he will come to a decision which is adverse to the wishes of the child'.

Balcombe LJ made a similar point in the post-Children Act decision, *Re R (A Minor) (Residence: Religion)*,[12] when he said: 'a judge's decision whether or not personally to interview a child must above all be a question for the exercise of judicial discretion'.

It is established that if a judge does interview a child in private he cannot promise confidentiality and for that very reason should be cautious in agreeing to see the child in such circumstances.[13]

E.   Deciding what orders, if any, to make

1.   APPLYING THE PRINCIPLE UNDER SECTION 1(5)[14]

As we have discussed, the controlling principle in deciding whether or not to make an order under Part II of the 1989 Act is the paramountcy of the child's welfare.[15]

5　Per Dunn J in *Re A (Minors) (Wardship: Child in Care)* (1979) 1 FLR 100.
6　There is, however, no power to see the *parent* separately in private: see *C v C* (1981) 11 Fam Law 147.
7　See *Re T (An Infant)* (1974) 4 Fam Law 48; *Re T (A Minor) (Welfare Report Recommendation)* (1977) 1 FLR 59; and *Re W (Minors)* (1980) 10 Fam Law 120.
8　It is understood that the absence of rules was because there was no agreement as to what the position should be.
9　Per Booth J in *Re M (A Minor) (Justices' Discretion)* [1993] 2 FLR 706. See also *Re W (Child: Contact)* [1994] 1 FLR 843 and *Re K (A Minor) (Contact)* [1993] Fam Law 552.
10　The President of the Family Division, Sir Stephen Brown, is known to be generally against interviewing in private and has informally encouraged the judiciary to follow his lead.
11　(1979) 2 FLR 74. See also *Clarke-Hunt v Newcombe* (1982) 4 FLR 482, CA at 485, per Butler-Sloss J.
12　[1993] 2 FLR 163, CA. For a case where it was held inappropriate to see a child in private, see *Re F (Minors) (Denial of Contact)* [1993] 2 FLR 677, CA (the judge saw two boys aged 12 and nine in connection with a contact application by a transsexual father).
13　Per Wall J in *B v B (Minors) (Interviews and Listing Arrangements)* [1994] 2 FLR 489, CA at 496. See also *Elder v Elder* [1986] 1 FLR 610, CA; *Dickinson v Dickinson* (1982) 13 Fam Law 174; and *H v H (Child: Judicial Interview)* [1974] 1 All ER 1145, CA.
14　See Bainham 'Changing families and changing concepts – reforming the language of family law' (1998) 10 CFLQ 1 at 2–4.
15　As laid down by s 1(1) of the Children Act 1989, discussed ante at pp 325ff.

In applying this principle the court's first task is to decide whether to make an order at all, since under s 1(5) the court is directed not to make an order under the 1989 Act 'unless it considers that doing so would be better for the child than making no order at all'.

The substantive law

In each case the court will require to be convinced of the benefit to the particular child of any order sought. Clearly this burden will be easier to satisfy in cases of disagreement, where an order will be the only means of resolving the parties' dispute, but it does not automatically follow that no order can be granted if the parties are agreed. A good start to discussion on when it may be appropriate to make orders is the advice contained in the Department of Health's *Guidance* on the 1989 Act:[16]

> 'There are several situations where the court is likely to consider it better for the child to make an order than not. If the court has had to resolve a dispute between the parents, it is likely to be better for the child to make an order about it. Even if there is no dispute, the child's need for stability and security may be better served by making an order. There may also be specific legal advantages in doing so. One example is where abduction of the child is a possibility, since a court order is necessary for enforcement proceedings in other parts of the United Kingdom under the Family Law Act 1986, and under the European Convention and under the Hague Convention an order will be necessary if the aggrieved party is, for example, an unmarried father or a relative who would not otherwise have "rights of custody". An advantage of having a residence order is that the child may be taken out of the country for periods of less than one month without the permission of other persons with parental responsibility or the court, whereas without an order this could amount to an offence under the Child Abduction Act 1984. Also if a person has a sole residence order in his favour and appoints a [testamentary] guardian for the child, the appointment will take effect immediately on that person's death, even where there is a surviving parent. Depending on the circumstances of the case, the court might therefore be persuaded that an order would be in the child's interest.'

The *Guidance*'s reference to the need for stability and security needs to be read with caution. The problem with it is that it is all too easy to advance this argument, and it is clear that if s 1(5) is to have any meaning the court cannot, as a matter of routine, make orders for this reason. Indeed, the Children Act Advisory Committee has expressed concern[17] that applications are still being made (and presumably granted) so as to provide the parent with care with the security of an order even though there is no dispute about the child's residence or contact

Similarly, since it can be argued in *every* case that the holder of a residence order can remove the child from the United Kingdom for periods of less than one month and that any guardianship appointment comes into force on the residence holder's death, the court will surely require some especial justification for making an order on that basis.

One circumstance not mentioned in the *Guidance* but which could justify the making of a residence or contact order is where the applicant, eg an unmarried father or relative, has no parental responsibility, since it can always be argued that unless an order is made he or she will not otherwise have locus standi in relation to

---

16 Vol 1, *Court Orders*, para 2.56. Repeated verbatim in the Northern Ireland *Guidance* at para 5.48.
17 CAAC Report 1992/93, p 25.

the child.[18] Indeed, in *B v B (A Minor) (Residence Order)* [19] Johnson J was disposed to accept such an argument when he granted in what he described as 'the unusual circumstances of the case' an unopposed application for a residence order by a grandparent with whom the child had been living for over 10 years.

The application of s 1(5) to contact applications needs careful consideration. Making 'no order' is inappropriate if the court is clearly charged with the responsibility for settling a dispute. In *Re W (A Minor) (Contact)*,[20] upon a father's application for defined contact following the mother's refusal to comply with a previous order for reasonable contact and her declared intention not to obey any further order, the first instance decision to make a 'no order' was held to be an abdication of responsibility. The point has also been made that there is a clear distinction between dismissing an application and making a 'no order'. If the making of the latter is tantamount to dismissing a parent's application for contact, as opposed to holding that an order was not necessary, then, according to Wall J in *D v D (Application for Contact)*,[1] the court should at least take a proactive role and consider whether any further application should be made and, if so, when and in what circumstances.

The application of s 1(5) in practice

Before implementation of the 1989 Act there was considerable speculation as to how s 1(5) would apply in practice. It will be recalled[2] that the provision was intended to have most impact in private law proceedings and in particular in divorce and separation proceedings, the concern being that orders relating to children should cease to be seen as merely 'part of the divorce package'. How far such orders have ceased to be part of the package has yet to be fully researched.[3] The indicators, however, are that the impact of s 1(5) has not been as great as might have been expected. Overall the proportion of 'no orders' has consistently remained between nine and 10 per cent of all disposals of s 8 order private law applications. In 1996, for example, 9.75 per cent of all private law disposals were of 'no orders' with a greater concentration, 11 per cent of such orders, being made in contact applications.[4] Interestingly, the number and proportion of 'no orders' made upon residence order applications has fluctuated. Nevertheless, the point has been made[5] that while the proportion of 'no orders' has been relatively low, there was a sharp decline in the number of *applications* for residence orders as against the number of custody order applications before the Act. In other words, the impact of s 1(5) might be greater than the number of 'no orders' suggests.[6]

18 See s 10(4) and (6).
19 [1992] 2 FLR 327. Another circumstance that might justify the making of a consent order is where it can be shown that without an order the person looking after the child will not be accorded priority on a local authority housing list. Although this practice was deprecated by the Children Act Advisory Committee (see CAAC Report 1992–93, p 25), if local authorities are still operating this policy (for the position when the Act was first implemented see Yell (1992) 89 Law Soc Gaz (August Issue) p 20), it would seem to be in the child's interest that a residence order be made.
20 [1994] 2 FLR 441, CA. See also *Re S (Contact: Grandparent)* [1996] 1 FLR 158, CA.
 1 [1994] 1 FCR 694.
 2 See the discussion ante at p 340.
 3 According to one early piece of research conducted in two major divorce courts in East Anglia the number of 'no orders' was high: Bainham *Children – The Modern Law* p 130, fn 96.
 4 These figures are based on Table 5.3 of the *Judicial Statistics* Annual Report 1996.
 5 Cretney and Masson *Principles of Family Law* (6th edn) 659.
 6 In this respect it will be noted that the number of residence orders has steadily risen since the Act: 22,264 in 1993; 27,432 in 1996.

2.   APPLYING THE WELFARE PRINCIPLE

General considerations

As we have discussed,[7] pursuant to s 1(4) it is mandatory for the court, in contested applications for s 8 orders, to have regard to the statutory check list. However, before discussing the application of the check list, it is important to stress that its role is to aid the court to determine what is best for the child, not to provide *rules* for so determining. It remains the case that beyond saying that the child's welfare is the paramount consideration there are no *rules* for determining disputes over children. As Dunn LJ put it in *Pountney v Morris:*[8]

'There is only one rule; that rule is that in a consideration of the future of the child the interests and welfare of the child are the . . . paramount consideration. But within that rule, the circumstances of each individual case are so infinitely varied that it is unwise to rely upon any rule of thumb, or any formula to try to resolve the difficult problem which arises on the facts of each individual case.'

Among the most agonising cases are those where the court has to decide which of two capable, loving and caring parents should look after the child. It is in these cases where the check list that we are about to discuss comes most prominently into play. Of course, it is in the nature of a finely balanced case that some factors will weigh heavily on the side of one claimant while others will favour the other, but it is clear that in reaching its conclusion the court should consider all the circumstances of the case, and in the light of the evidence adduced, make the best decision it can. As Megarry J pointed out in *Re F (An Infant),*[9] the problem cannot be solved arithmetically or quantitatively by using some sort of 'points system'.

The statutory check list

(a)   The ascertainable wishes and feelings of the child concerned (considered in the light of his age and understanding) [10]

This enjoinder to consider the child's wishes and feelings is reflective of the international obligation under the UN Convention on the Rights of the Child 1989, Art 12(1).[11]

It will be noted that by referring to the child's 'wishes and feelings' s 1(3)(a) is wider than Art 12, which is confined to 'views'. Very young children have discernible 'feelings', even if they cannot yet express their views. In any event, the wishes and feelings need not be conveyed directly but can be obtained by third parties, commonly the court welfare officer.

Although it was only since the 1989 Act that the courts became formally obliged in private law cases other than adoption[12] to consider the child's wishes and feelings, in practice the courts had long done so. As Butler-Sloss LJ said in *Re P (A Minor) (Education),*[13] shortly before implementation of the 1989 Act:

'The courts, over the last few years, have become increasingly aware of the importance of listening to the views of older children and taking into account what children say, not

---

7 See ante, pp 337–8.
8 [1984] FLR 381, CA at 384.
9 [1969] 2 Ch 238 at 241, [1969] 2 All ER 766 at 768.
10 For the background to this provision see Law Com No 172, paras 3.22 et seq. See also Eekelaar 'The Interests of the Child and the Child's Wishes – The Role of Dynamic Self-Determinism' (1994) 8 Int Jo of Law and the Family 42.
11 See ante, p 461.
12 See s 6 of the Adoption Act 1976, discussed post, p 625.
13 [1992] 1 FLR 316, CA at 321.

necessarily agreeing with what they want nor, indeed, doing what they want, but paying proper respect to older children who are of an age and maturity to make their minds up as to what they think is best for them, bearing in mind that older children very often have an appreciation of their own situation which is worthy of consideration by, and the respect of, the adults, and particularly including the courts.'

Despite being placed first in the welfare check list, the child's view is not expressed to be determinative.[14] As Butler-Sloss LJ put it in *Re P (Minors) (Wardship: Care and Control)*:[15]

'How far the wishes of children should be the determinative factor in their future placement must of course vary on the particular facts of each case. Those views must be considered and may, but not necessarily must, carry more weight as the children grow older'.

On the other hand, it has also been said that where all other factors are evenly balanced it is appropriate to recognise the extra significance of an older child's views.[16]

Nevertheless, as Butler-Sloss LJ indicated, the court's obligation is to consider the child's wishes and feelings, not to give effect to them, but to be the better able to judge what is for his welfare. It must be remembered that the child may have been coached or brainwashed[17] by one parent and that sometimes even an older child's own wishes are so contrary to his or her long-term welfare that the court may feel justified in overriding them. A good illustrative example is *Re M (Family Proceedings: Affidavits)*,[18] in which a father applied for a residence order based largely on his 12-year-old daughter's wishes. Although the welfare officer indicated that either parent was suitable as a carer, given that the child had hitherto lived with her mother and had not had the opportunity to have any clear idea of what living with her father would really be like (the contact visits to her father had always taken place at the paternal grandparents' home), the judge upheld the welfare officer's 'instinct' that her long-term welfare would be better governed by her remaining with her mother. On appeal, the Court of Appeal rejected the argument that, given either parent was suitable, the child's views should have tipped the balance, and upheld the first instance decision. The court accepted that

---

14 *Re W (Minors) (Residence Order)* [1992] 2 FCR 461, CA; *Re W (A Minor) (Residence Order)* [1993] 2 FLR 625, CA.

15 [1992] 2 FCR 681 at 687. See also *M v M (Minor: Custody Appeal)* [1987] 1 WLR 404, CA at 411, per May LJ.

16 *Re F (Minors) (Denial of Contact)* [1993] 2 FLR 677, CA. See also *Re P (Minors) (Wardship: Care and Control)* [1992] 2 FCR 681 at 689H per Butler-Sloss LJ, cited by Cazalet J in *Re H (A Minor) (Shared Residence)* [1994] 1 FLR 717 at 724E. Note Wilson J's comment in *Re B (Change of Surname)* [1996] 1 FLR 791, CA, that it was virtually unknown to make residence or contact orders that run contrary to the wishes of normal adolescent children. However, this comment should perhaps be treated with some caution. It certainly should not be regarded as a statement of principle – see below. For pre-1989 Act cases where the child's wishes have proved decisive see eg *Marsh v Marsh* (1977) 8 Fam Law 103; *Clarke-Hunt v Newcombe* (1982) 4 FLR 482, CA; *Williamson v Williamson* [1986] 2 FLR 146, [1986] Fam Law 217, CA; and *Re P (A Minor) (Education)* supra.

17 See eg *Re R (A Minor) (Residence: Religion)* [1993] 2 FLR 163, CA, in which the wishes of a nine-year-old boy to remain with a member of the Exclusive Brethren were overridden.

18 [1995] 2 FLR 100, CA; cf *Re M (Child's Upbringing)* ('the Zulu boy case') [1996] 2 FLR 441, where the 10-year-old's wishes did seem to be ignored – see the editorial at (1996) 146 NLJ 669. See also cases such as *Re W (A Minor) (Medical Treatment: Court's Jurisdiction)* [1993] Fam 64, [1992] 4 All ER 627, CA and *Re E (an infant)* (1990) 9 BMLR 1 (discussed ante, p 315), where respectively a 16- and a 15-year-old's refusal to have medical treatment was overridden.

the judge had properly taken the child's wishes into account but was not obliged to follow them, if, as here, it was not felt to be in the child's interests to do so.

(b)   *The child's physical, emotional and educational needs*

Although some have argued that to speak of needs may be simply a way of expressing adult preferences in an apparently child-centred way,[19] it is nevertheless clear that in practice the child's needs together with the parents' capabilities are the major concern in most cases.

(I)   PHYSICAL NEEDS

Physical needs can include the need for adequate accommodation but, as Wood J said in *Stephenson v Stephenson*,[20] in most cases 'disadvantages of a material sort must be of little weight'. The court's major concern is for the child's security and happiness, not his material prospects. Any other approach would automatically put a poor parent (and mothers in particular)[1] at a disadvantage. Nevertheless, a party's financial position cannot be entirely ignored: for example, if he is so poor that he cannot even provide a home, this in itself might be sufficient to refuse him a residence order.[2] Even in a less extreme case a parent who can offer a child good accommodation must, other things being equal, have the edge over the one who cannot.[3] But again the quality of the home life that the child will have must not be measured in purely material terms: the amount of time and energy that a parent can devote to his care and upbringing is of considerable importance. This may mean that a mother who can spend the whole of her time with her children will have an advantage over a father who is out at work all day, whatever alternative arrangements he can make to have them looked after.[4] However, in *B v B (Custody of Children)*,[5] where an unemployed father was successfully looking after his child, it was held that the judge had erred in law in putting into the balance as a determining factor the man's moral duty to find work and not to rely upon the benefits provided by the welfare state.[6]

(II)   EMOTIONAL NEEDS

The child's emotional needs will often be a crucial element in the case. Chief among these needs is that of attachment perhaps to a particular parent or to a

---

19 See eg Maidment *Child Custody and Divorce*, p 149, who comments, 'when a court makes a . . . decision it may attempt to heed the child's needs but it is essentially making a decision as to which available adult . . . is to care for the child . . .'

20 [1985] FLR 1140, CA at 1148.

1 Because of women's lower wages.

2 Though note that for the purposes of the Housing Act 1996 a person caring for a child and who is unintentionally homeless has a priority need.

3 *Re F (An Infant)* [1969] 2 Ch 238, [1969] 2 All ER 766.

4 See *Re K (Minors)(Children: Care and Control)* [1977] Fam 179, [1977] 1 All ER 647, CA; *S (BD) v S (DJ)* [1977] Fam 109, [1977] 1 All ER 656, CA.

5 [1985] FLR 166, CA.

6 Nevertheless, there has in the past been some judicial suspicion about a man giving up work to look after his children: see eg *B v B (Custody of Child)* [1985] FLR 462, CA (father became unemployed after being granted custody and pending the appeal). Heilbron J commented (at 465) that this was not a case in which the father 'had deliberately given up work in order to go on social security'. See also Sir John Arnold P's comment at 466.

sibling or even to a family. It is also considered to be a fundamental emotional need of every child to have an enduring relationship with both parents.

With regard to attachment to a particular parent one influential notion, at any rate in the past, has been that young children need their mothers.[7] Indeed, Lord Donaldson MR went so far as to say in *Re W (A Minor) (Residence Order)* [8] that:

> '. . . there is a rebuttable presumption of fact that the best interests of a baby are served by being with its mother, and I stress the word "baby". When we are moving on to whatever age it may be appropriate to describe the baby as having become a child, different considerations may well apply. But, as far as babies are concerned, the starting-point is, I think, that it should be with its mother'.

Babies apart, however, it is well established[9] that there is no *principle, rule* or *presumption* that even a young child should live with his mother, nor is there a principle or presumption that an older boy should be with his father.[10] Indeed, as Butler-Sloss LJ made clear,[11] as a matter of law 'there is no presumption that one parent should be preferred to another parent at a particular age [of the child]'. However, this is not to say that a 'maternal preference' can be ignored for, notwithstanding that there seems to be no scientific basis for thinking eg that young children benefit most from a maternal upbringing,[12] or indeed that the child's well-being is affected by the sex of the parent with whom he is living,[13] it is a consideration. Over the years the courts have expressed the position in various ways,[14] but perhaps the most authoritative comment now is that of Lord Jauncey in *Brixey v Lynas*.[15] In that case, on an appeal from Scotland, the House of Lords were asked to consider what weight, if any, should be attached to the natural ability of mothers to care for very young children. At first instance, despite the fact that the 15-month-old girl was happy and well cared for by her mother, custody was granted to the father on the basis of the latter's more advantageous social background. This decision was overruled on appeal because it had overlooked the advantages both of maternal care of very young children and of maintaining the

---

7   This maternal preference was undoubtedly influenced by Bowlby's and others' theories of maternal deprivation: see the discussion in Maidment *Child Custody and Divorce* at pp 182–4. See further the discussion in the 7th edition of this work pp 323–6.

8   [1992] 2 FLR 332, CA at 336. In this case the baby was less than four weeks old.

9   See, for example, *Aldous v Aldous* (1974) 5 Fam Law 152, CA, per Megaw LJ. See also *Re A (Children: 1959 UN Declaration)* [1998] 1 FLR 354, CA in which the first instance judge, apparently relying on Principle 6 of the UN Declaration of the Rights of the Child (1959) did appear to accept it as a principle that children of tender years are better off with their mother. He was overruled on appeal and the relevance of the 1959 Declaration was doubted, especially as it was not reflected in the 1989 UN Convention on the Rights of the Child.

10 See *Re C (A) (an infant), C v C* [1970] 1 All ER 309, CA.

11 In *Re S (A Minor) (Custody)* [1991] 2 FLR 388, CA at 390.

12 See the summary of various research findings in Maidment *Child Custody and Divorce,* op cit, pp 182–6. See also King 'Maternal Love, Fact or Myth?' (1974) 4 Fam Law 61.

13 This is not to say that divorce does not affect children differently according to their age, on which see eg Wallerstein and Kelly *Surviving the Breakup* (1980); Cockett and Tripp *The Exeter Family Study* (1994); and Rodgers and Pryor *The Development of Children from Separated Families – A Review of Research from the United Kingdom* (1998).

14 See, for example, *Re W (A Minor) (Custody)* (1982) 4 FLR 492 at 504, per Cumming-Bruce LJ and *Re S (A Minor) (Custody)* [1991] 2 FLR 388, CA at 390 and *Re A (A Minor) (Custody)* [1991] 2 FLR 394, CA at 400, per Butler-Sloss LJ.

15 1996 SLT 908, [1996] 2 FLR 499, on which see Sutherland 'The unequal struggle – Fathers and children in Scots Law' (1997) 9 CFLQ 191.

status quo. In dismissing the father's further appeal the Lords rejected the argument that the court had erred in allegedly accepting the principle of maternal preference. As Lord Jauncey put it:[16]

'... the advantage to a very young child of being with its mother is a consideration which must be taken into account in deciding where lie its best interests in custody proceedings in which the mother is involved. It is neither a presumption nor a principle but rather recognition of a widely held belief based on practical experience and the workings of nature. Its importance will vary according to the age of the child and to the other circumstances of each individual case such as whether the child has been living with or apart from the mother and whether she is or is not capable of providing proper care. Circumstances may be such that it has no importance at all. Furthermore it will always yield to other competing advantages which more effectively promote the welfare of the child. However, where a very young child has been with its mother since birth and there is no criticism of her ability to care for the child only the strongest competing advantages are likely to prevail'.

Another 'emotional need' is that of sibling support. In general the courts dislike separating children. As Purchas LJ said in the leading case, *C v C (Minors: Custody)*:[17]

'It is really beyond argument that unless there are strong features indicating a contrary arrangement... brothers and sisters should wherever possible, be brought up together, so that they are an emotional support to each other in the stormy waters of the destruction of their family.'

Occasionally this consideration can be decisive. In *Adams v Adams*,[18] for example, the mother sought an order to look after her daughter but not her son, but her application failed because it was held preferable to keep the two children together. In *Clarke-Hunt v Newcombe*[19] it was held that, as it was in the younger boy's interests to be with his mother and it was inappropriate to separate the brothers, both boys should live with her, even though it was against the elder boy's wishes and possibly slightly detrimental to his interests. However influential this consideration may be, it is of course not a rule and there will be cases when separation of siblings is appropriate or unavoidable.[20]

Another aspect of emotional need is that of attachment to the family. Clearly this will come into play where the dispute is between parents and third parties. Although, as we saw from our discussion of *J v C*,[1] the paramountcy of the child's

16 At 911 and 505 respectively.
17 [1988] 2 FLR 291, CA at 302. See also *Adams v Adams* [1984] FLR 768, CA at 772, where Dunn LJ said: 'All these cases depend upon their own facts, but it is undesirable, other things being equal, that children should be split when they are close together in age and obviously fond of one another ... Children do ... support one another and give themselves mutual comfort, perhaps more than they can derive from either of their parents.' But the disapproval of splitting siblings is not new: see *Re Besant* (1879) 11 Ch D 508, CA at 512, per Jessel MR.
18 Supra.
19 (1982) 4 FLR 482, CA.
20 See, for example, *B v B (Residence Order: Restricting Applications)* [1997] 1 FLR 139, CA, in which the judge had ordered two brothers to live with their mother, but the older boy then 'voted with his feet' by going to live with his father. The judge subsequently and reluctantly concluded that the younger child should remain with the mother because she met his needs and that the older child should continue to live with the father. His decision was upheld by the Court of Appeal. See also *Re B (T) (A Minor) (Residence Order)* [1995] 2 FCR 240, CA in which it was held that, on the facts, maintaining the status quo was more important to the child than being with his siblings; and *Re O (Infants)* [1962] 2 All ER 10, CA (boy's long-term future thought to be better served by being with his father in the Sudan, whereas the girl's was with her mother in England).
1 [1970] AC 668, [1969] 1 All ER 788, HL, discussed ante, pp 307ff.

welfare principle applies equally to disputes between parents and other individuals as well as to disputes between parents, nevertheless the courts have also recognised the prima facie strength of the parents' position based on their view that children have a basic interest in being brought up by their own family. As Balcombe LJ put it in *Re W (A Minor) (Residence Order)*:[2]

'It is the welfare of the child which is the test, but of course there is a strong presumption that, other things being equal, it is in the interests of the child that it shall remain with its natural parents but that has to give way to particular needs in particular situations'.

A controversial application of the view that a child is better off being brought up in his own family is *Re M (Child's Upbringing)*.[3] In that case the Court of Appeal ordered the immediate return of a 10-year-old Zulu boy to his natural parents (who had previously been retained by the applicant whilst in South Africa as household employees) in South Africa, notwithstanding that he had been brought up for the last four years exclusively by the white applicant in England, and apparently ignoring both the child's own wishes and strong medical advice that an immediate return would be harmful. As Neill LJ put it:[4]

'Of course there will be cases where the welfare of the child requires that the child's right to be with his natural parents has to give way in his own interest to other considerations. But I am satisfied that in this case, as in other cases, one starts with the strong supposition that it is in the [child's] interests . . . that he should be brought up with his natural parents'.

Another not unrelated emotional need is that of every child to have an enduring relationship with both parents.[5] This, as we discuss shortly, has important ramifications for contact applications.

(III)   EDUCATIONAL NEEDS

Education is an important aspect of a child's upbringing and the question of which school is to be attended is a relevant factor in deciding who should look after the child. Occasionally, parental attitude to education can be significant. In *May v May*[6] care and control was granted to the father inter alia because he laid greater emphasis on academic achievements in contrast to the freer and easier attitude of the mother and her cohabitant to the time the children (aged eight and six) should be doing homework.

(IV)   OTHER NEEDS

Needs have also been held to include medical needs and hence, provided it is for the child's benefit, it is within the court's power to make an order for the taking of a blood sample to ascertain whether the child is HIV positive.[7]

---

2 [1993] 2 FLR 625 at 633 expressly approving similar comments made by Lord Donaldson MR in *Re H (A Minor) (Custody: Interim Care and Control)* [1991] 2 FLR 109, CA at 113, who in turn was explaining earlier dicta (per Fox LJ) in *Re K (a minor) (ward: care and control)* [1990] 3 All ER 795, [1990] 1 WLR 431, CA.

3 [1996] 2 FLR 441, CA. For a critique of this case see Lowe 'The House of Lords and the Welfare Principle' in Bridge (ed) *Family Law Towards the Millennium – Essays for P M Bromley* 125 at 164–5.

4 At 453. In fact, the boy later returned to England with the mother's consent to resume living with the applicant.

5 Per Wilson J in *Re M (Contact: Welfare Test)* [1995] 1 FLR 274, CA at 278.

6 [1986] 1 FLR 325, CA.

7 *Re W (A Minor) (HIV Test)* [1995] 2 FCR 184, per Kirkwood J.

(c)   The likely effect on the child of any change in his circumstances

Section 1(3)(c) is the statutory enactment of the 'status quo' or continuity factor, which in practice is particularly important in resolving private law disputes,[8] the courts being well aware of the dangers of removing a child from a well-established home.[9] As Ormrod LJ said in *D v M (A Minor: Custody Appeal)*:[10]

'. . . it is generally accepted by those who are professionally concerned with children that, particularly in the early years, continuity of care is a most important part of a child's sense of security and that disruption of established bonds is to be avoided whenever it is possible to do so.'

Good reasons will therefore have to be adduced to justify moving a child from a well established home,[11] the courts being understandably reluctant to move a child even as an interim measure in the absence of a full investigation of the facts, particularly if there is a doubt about the capability of the person with whom the child is to live.[12] Nevertheless, there will be occasions, albeit exceptional, where such a course is necessary to protect the child in the short term. An example occurred in *Re G (Minors) (Ex Parte Interim Residence order)*,[13] in which the mother admitted that she and her partner had taken drugs (though she maintained that she had now stopped and would not continue in the future) and that the children aged 10, eight, seven and five had known about it.

The status quo is, however, only a factor and the court may well think that the child's welfare in any particular case might be better served by being moved. As Ormrod LJ pointed out in *S v W*:[14]

'. . . the status quo argument depends for its strength wholly and entirely on whether the status quo is satisfactory or not. The more satisfactory the status quo, the stronger the argument for not interfering. The less satisfactory the status quo, the less one requires before deciding to change.'

Clearly, the status quo argument becomes stronger the longer the child has been with one party,[15] and is especially powerful if the other has lost contact with the child. On the other hand, if, as in *Allington v Allington*,[16] the parties have only been

---

8 Empirical evidence showed that before the Children Act 1989 the courts normally made orders confirming the situation and only rarely (in less than one per cent of the cases studied by Eekelaar, Clive, Raikes and Clarke *Custody in Divorce* (1977) paras 13.14 and 13.29) ordered that the child be moved.
9 Compare *Re Thain* [1926] Ch 676 in which the traumas of being moved were dismissed as being transitory.
10 [1983] Fam 33 at 41, [1982] 3 All ER 897, CA at 902–3.
11 See eg *Re B (Residence Order: Status Quo)* [1998] 1 FLR 368, CA in which the first instance judge was held wrongly to have placed speculative improvements in contact over and above the consideration of continuity of care. See also *Re B (T) (A Minor) (Residence Order)* [1995] 2 FCR 240, CA in which, on the facts, maintaining the status quo was thought to be more important to the child than being with her siblings, and *Re L (Residence: Justices' Reasons)* [1995] 2 FLR 445 (inadequate reasons given by magistrates for upsetting the status quo).
12 See eg *Re J (Children: Ex Parte Order)* [1997] 1 FLR 606 in which Hale J observed (at 609) that ex parte orders handing over a young child to a parent with whom she has not lived for 20 months should surely be exceptional. See also *Elder v Elder* [1986] 1 FLR 610, CA and *Re W; Re L (Minors) (Interim Custody)* [1987] Fam Law 130, CA, where the mother had a drink and anxiety problem.
13 [1993] 1 FLR 910, CA.
14 (1980) 11 Fam Law 81, CA at 82.
15 It also needs to be borne in mind that the younger the child the greater the effect of the passage of time on the child's attachment and adjustment: see Goldstein, Freud and Solnit *Beyond the Best Interests of the Child* (1973).
16 [1985] FLR 586, CA.

separated for a few weeks and the absent parent has maintained regular contact with the child, there can effectively be no status quo argument at all. In assessing what the status quo is the court should examine the whole history of the case and not simply the position immediately before the hearing. Hence, where a parent has 'snatched' a child from the other, the court may properly regard the status quo as being the position before the snatch.[17] There is however, no rule that the child should be returned in snatching cases. The only principle is that the child's welfare is the paramount consideration.[18]

(d)   *The child's age, sex, background and any characteristics of which the court considers relevant*

Consideration of the child's age is obviously linked to other matters such as the child's wishes and when combined with sex can be relevant to the choice of parents, which we have already discussed.

(I)   RELIGIOUS CONSIDERATIONS

The child's background can include his religious upbringing. In the past this was of crucial significance, but today this consideration is of much less importance.[19] It is inconceivable, for instance, that a parent would be refused a residence order on the ground of atheism.[20] In the case of a very young child (or probably any child of no fixed religious beliefs) the question of religious upbringing will have little bearing on the outcome of the case.[1] On the other hand, where religious upbringing is clearly part of the child's upbringing, the court may well consider that continuation of religious observance is vital if the evidence suggests that otherwise the child could suffer emotional disturbance.[2] Nevertheless, even in these circumstances there is no rule or legal principle that it can never be right to force a child to abandon his religious beliefs, since ultimately such beliefs are subservient to what is perceived as being overall in a child's best interests.[3] This is well illustrated in *Re R (A Minor) (Residence: Religion)*,[4] in which the court was faced with the stark choice of either granting a father a residence order in respect of his nine-and-a-half year old son, in which case the child would effectively be excluded from the Exclusive Brethren within which society he had hitherto grown up, or granting a residence order to members of the sect, in which case, because of the strict rules of the fellowship, his son would no longer even see his father. In upholding the first instance decision to grant the father a residence order, the Court of Appeal made it clear that their decision was not based on a value judgment as to the tenets of the particular religion, but rather on what was thought to be in the boy's long term interests, to continue to be brought up by his father. In reaching

---

17 As in *Edwards v Edwards* [1986] 1 FLR 187; affd [1986] 1 FLR 205, CA.
18 *Re J (A Minor) (Interim Custody: Appeal)* [1989] 2 FLR 304, CA. But see Chapter 13 for the position of international child abduction under the Hague and European Conventions.
19 For a full discussion of religious issues see Hamilton *Family, Law and Religion* (1995) chs 4 and 5 and Mumford 'The Judicial Resolution of Disputes Involving Children and Religion' (1998) 47 ICLQ 117.
20 Compare *Shelley v Westbrooke* (1817) Jac 266n in which the poet Shelley was denied custody on this ground.
 1 See *Re C (MA) (An Infant)* [1966] 1 All ER 838, CA at 856 and 864–5.
 2 This certainly influenced Willmer LJ in *Re M (Infants)* [1967] 3 All ER 1071, CA at 1074.
 3 See Balcombe LJ in *Re R (A Minor) (Residence: Religion)* [1993] 2 FLR 163, CA at 180.
 4 Ibid.

this decision the court followed *Re T (Minors) (Custody: Religious Upbringing)*,[5] in which Scarman LJ commented that:

'. . . it was not for the court to pass any judgment on the beliefs of parents where they are socially acceptable and consistent with a decent and respectable life . . .'

In other words, being a Jehovah's Witness, for example, does not ipso facto mean that that parent should not be granted a residence order,[6] but membership of an extreme sect could have this consequence. In *Re B and G (Minors) (Custody)*[7] the decisive factor in denying a father and stepmother an order to look after the children which they had been doing for five years was that they were scientologists and so held views which were found to be 'immoral and obnoxious'. In appropriate cases, eg where the care-giver has a different religion from that of the child, it would be open to the court to make a residence order on condition that the child's religious upbringing will be continued.[8] On the other hand, it could be a condition of an order that the adult does not involve a child in his religion.[9]

(II) RACIAL, CULTURAL AND LINGUISTIC BACKGROUND

Racial origin, cultural background and linguistic background[10] are issues that should be considered under this head and are likely on occasion to prove difficult in both private and public law proceedings.

The preservation of links with the child's culture and heritage are important issues that should not be overlooked. Such considerations were clearly a key motivating force in *Re M (Child's Upbringing)*,[11] in which the Court of Appeal ordered the return of a Zulu boy to his mother in South Africa, while in *Re M (Section 94 Appeals)*[12] the failure to address the question of race when denying contact of a mixed race girl (who was confused about her racial origin) to her black father, was held to justify the Court of Appeal reversing the decision.

(e) Any harm which the child has suffered or is at risk of suffering

The 'harm' referred to in s 1(3)(e) has the same meaning as it does for the purposes of care proceedings,[13] and accordingly means both ill-treatment and the

---

5 (1975) 2 FLR 239, CA.
6 Although parties are sometimes asked to undertake not to involve their children, for example, in the house-to-house visiting conducted by Jehovah's Witnesses: see eg *Re C (Minors) (Wardship: Jurisdiction)* [1978] Fam 105, [1978] 2 All ER 230, CA.
7 [1985] FLR 493, CA. The court felt that it could not rely on the father's undertaking to remove the children from 'the evil forces of scientology'.
8 In the past, however, the court has been content to accept undertakings to this effect: see eg *Re E (An Infant)* [1963] 3 All ER 874, where a Jewish couple were required to bring up a ward of court as a Roman Catholic; and *J v C* [1970] AC 668, [1969] 1 All ER 788, HL, where protestants gave a similar undertaking to bring up the child as a Roman Catholic. Contrast *Roughley v Roughley* (1973) 4 Fam Law 91, CA.
9 See eg *Re R (A Minor) (Residence: Religion)*, supra, where an aunt was granted contact upon her undertaking not to speak or communicate with the child in any way in relation to religious or spiritual matters or make any reference to the Exclusive Brethren as a religious group; cf *Re C (Minors) (Wardship: Jurisdiction)*, supra.
10 Considerations to which local authorities must have specific regard under s 22(5)(c): see post, p 530.
11 [1996] 2 FLR 441, CA, discussed ante at p 470.
12 [1995] 1 FLR 546, CA. See also *Re P (A Minor) (Transracial Placement)* [1990] 1 FLR 96, CA and *Re N (A Minor) (Adoption)* [1990] 1 FLR 58, discussed post, p 619.
13 Section 105(1) provides that 'harm' has the same meaning as in s 31(9), discussed further post, p 538.

impairment of health or development. It clearly covers both physical and psychological trauma. It also covers sexual abuse which, if proved, is obviously likely to be a significant consideration but even so may not inevitably mean that the abuser should not, for example, be allowed contact.[14]

It will be noted that, apart from actual harm, s 1(3)(e) also encompasses 'risk' of harm. Such a risk could for example, emanate from the parents' past alcoholism,[15] or sexual abuse. It is, however, established that s 1(3)(e) deals with actual harm or risk of harm and not with possibilities. As Butler-Sloss LJ said in *Re M and R (Child Abuse: Evidence)*:[16]

> 'The court must reach a conclusion based on facts, not on suspicion or mere doubts. If, as in the present case, the court concludes that the evidence is insufficient to prove sexual abuse in the past, and if the fact of sexual abuse in the past is the only basis for asserting a risk of sexual abuse in the future, then it follows that there is nothing (except suspicion or mere doubts) to show a risk of future sexual abuse'.

Re M and R also establishes that the appropriate standard of proof is the preponderance of probabilities.[17] However, the undoubted difficulties of proving primary allegations in some cases do not justify not investigating them at all.[18] The proper approach is to consider first whether the primary allegation on which the risk of harm is said to be based can be proved and then, assuming it can, to decide whether or not that is a risk of harm to satisfy s 1(3)(e).

(f)   How capable each of the child's parents, and any other person in relation to whom the court considers the question to be relevant, is of meeting his needs

A wide variety of circumstances can be brought under this heading, ranging from the parents' medical condition to their lifestyle. Although it is established that lesbianism is a factor to be taken into account, it should not be regarded as ipso facto rendering the mother unfit to look after her child.[19]

It is to be noted that as well as parents the capability of any other person in relation to whom the court considers the question to be relevant must also be examined. This will clearly include any new partner of the parent.[20]

---

14 See *H v H (Child Abuse: Access)* [1989] 1 FLR 212, CA; *L v L (Child Abuse: Access)* [1989] 2 FLR 16, CA; and *C v C (A Minor) (Child Abuse: Evidence)* [1988] 1 FLR 462; cf *Re R (A Minor) (Access)* [1988] 1 FLR 206, CA.

15 See eg *Re L (Residence: Justices' Reasons)* [1995] 2 FLR 445.

16 [1996] 2 FLR 195 at 203, applying the same test as applies to s 31 following the House of Lords' ruling in *Re H (Minors) (Sexual Abuse: Standard of Proof)* [1996] AC 563, sub nom *Re H (Minors) (Child abuse: Threshold conditions)* [1996] 1 All ER 1, HL, discussed post at pp 544ff. See also *Re P (Sexual Abuse: Standard of Proof)* [1996] 2 FLR 333, CA. See also *Re W (minors) (residence order)* [1998] 1 FCR 75, CA (judge not entitled to assume that an uninhibited attitude to nudity posed a risk of harm to the children).

17 Ibid at 203, expressly rejecting the contention that because the child's welfare was paramount the standard of proof for establishing harm should be less than the preponderance of probabilities. For a critique of *Re M and R*, see Hemingway and Williams '*Re M and R: Re H and R*' [1997] Fam Law 740.

18 See eg *Re L (Residence: Justices' Reasons)*, supra, in which magistrates were held wrong not to deal expressly with the father's contention that the mother's former alcohol problems had resumed.

19 *C v C (Custody of Child)* [1991] 1 FLR 223, CA. See also *B v B (Custody, Care and Control)* [1991] Fam Law 174. For an account of some empirical evidence on this issue see Tasker and Golombok 'Children Raised by Lesbian Mothers' [1991] Fam Law 184.

20 See eg *Scott v Scott* [1986] 2 FLR 320, CA (mother's cohabitant found to have committed acts of indecency against the child), and *M v Birmingham City Council* [1994] 2 FLR 141 at 147, per Stuart-White J.

3. CONSIDERATIONS WHEN PROHIBITING CONTACT BY PARENTS

The statutory check list is equally relevant to the issue of whether or not to make a contact order. Nevertheless, it is to be borne in mind that when considering contact the court is less concerned with a person's overall ability to look after the child and hence might more readily grant contact than a residence order.

As with all issues directly concerning the child's upbringing, the controlling principle in deciding whether or not to make a contact order is the paramountcy of the child's welfare.[1] Furthermore, the principle applies regardless of whether the child's parents are married to each other,[2] and whether it is sought to end or reintroduce contact.[3] Bearing this principle in mind, it would be wrong to say that *as a matter of law* there is a presumption that a parent should be permitted contact.[4] Nevertheless, it has been repeatedly said that the court should be slow to deny contact between a child and his or her parent. Indeed, as Butler-Sloss LJ pointed out in *Re R (A Minor) (Contact)*,[5] the principle of continuing contact is underlined by the UN Convention on the Rights of the Child 1989, Art 9(3) of which states:

> 'States Parties shall respect the right of the child who is separated from one or both parents to maintain personal relations and direct contact with both parents on a regular basis, except if it is contrary to the child's best interests'.

This provision is echoed by s 11(4) of the Family Law Act 1996, which directs the court, in divorce or separation cases, to have particular regard to –

> '. . . the general principle that, in the absence of evidence to the contrary, the welfare of the child will be best served by –
> (i) his having regular contact with those who have parental responsibility for him and with other members of his family . . .'

According to <u>Balcombe LJ in *Re H (Minors) (Access)*</u>[6] the correct test in these types of cases is to ask whether there are cogent reasons why a child should be

---

1 See generally *Re KD (A Minor) (Ward: Termination of Access)* [1988] AC 806, [1988] 1 All ER 577, HL, which expressly rejected the argument based on Art 8 of the European Convention for the Protection of Human Rights following the decision in *R v United Kingdom* (1987) 10 EHRR 74, [1988] 2 FLR 445, that what is now contact was a parental right which should only be displaced where the court was satisfied that the exercise of the right would be positively inimical to the child's interests.

2 See eg *Re M (Contact: Supervision)* [1998] 1 FLR 727, CA in which an unmarried father was granted supervised contact notwithstanding his problems concerning drug and alcohol abuse, occasional lack of control over his temper and the lack of a permanent home. Step-parents and grandparents are not in such a strong position: see respectively *Re H (A Minor) (Contact)* [1994] 2 FLR 776 and *Re A (Section 8 Order: Grandparent Application)* [1995] 2 FLR 153, CA.

3 See eg *Re R (A Minor) (Contact)* [1993] 2 FLR 762, CA, in which the court stressed the need for a five-year-old to be told who her father was and to be reintroduced to him despite not having seen him for three years. See also *A v L (Contact)* [1998] 1 FLR 361 (discussed further below) and *Re H (Minors) (Access)* [1992] 1 FLR 148, CA.

4 It is on this basis that the decision by the House of Lords on appeal from Scotland in *S v M (Access Order)* [1997] 1 FLR 980, sub nom *Sanderson v McManus* 1997 SLT 629, that technically the onus of proof is on the parent (in this case an unmarried father) to show that continued contact is for the child's welfare, could be justified. However, as Lord Clyde observed 'true questions of the burden of proof will almost invariably fade into insignificance after any inquiry'. See Sutherland 'The unequal struggle – Fathers and children in Scots Law' (1997) 9 CFLQ 191.

5 [1993] 2 FLR 762, CA at 767.

6 [1992] 1 FLR 148 at 152. In that case the court ordered visiting contact for an introductory period pending a full welfare report, notwithstanding that the father had not seen his children for over three years. See also *Re B (Minors) (Access)* [1992] 1 FLR 140, CA in which a father's eccentric and bizarre but not violent behaviour was held not to justify refusing contact.

denied contact with his parent, rather than to ask whether any positive advantages are to be gained by continuing or resuming contact.

However, although this approach has been followed on subsequent occasions,[7] arguably the more principled short-hand approach is that suggested by Wilson J in *Re M (Contact: Welfare Test)*,[8] namely that the court should consider whether the fundamental need of every child to have an enduring relationship with both parents is outweighed by the depth of harm to the particular child that might thereby be caused by the contact order. However, as an overall statement of the position one can usefully refer to *Re P (Contact: Supervision)*,[9] in which Wall J summarised the principles as follows:

'(1) Overriding all else, as provided by s 1(1) of the 1989 Act, the welfare of the child is the paramount consideration, and the court is concerned with the interests of the mother and the father only in so far as they bear on the welfare of the child.

(2) It is almost always in the interests of the child whose parents are separated that he or she should have contact with the parent with whom the child is not living.

(3) The court has powers to enforce orders for contact, which it should not hesitate to exercise where it judges that it will overall promote the welfare of the child to do so.

(4) Cases do, unhappily and infrequently but occasionally, arise, in which a court is compelled to conclude that in existing circumstances an order for immediate direct contact should not be ordered, because so to order would injure the welfare of the child . . .

(5) In cases, in which, for whatever reason, direct contact cannot for the time being be ordered, it is ordinarily highly desirable that there should be indirect contact so that the child grows up knowing of the love and interest of the absent parent with whom, in due course, direct contact should be established.'

This last point is to be noted, namely that, even where direct contact might be inappropriate, the court should still consider indirect contact as a means of preserving some kind of relationship with the absent parent. In *A v L (Contact)*,[10] for example, the father was serving a long-term prison sentence and, notwithstanding the unwillingness of any relation to facilitate any form of contact, the court thought it right to make an order for indirect contact (using the good offices of the mother's solicitors), Holman J stressing the child's fundamental right to have some knowledge of and some contact with his natural father.

Notwithstanding the predisposition to preserve contact with both parents wherever possible, there are obviously occasions when it is not in the child's interests to do so. Examples in the past have included cases where the parent had

---

7 See *Re R (A Minor) (Contact)* [1993] 2 FLR 762, CA; *Re D (A Minor) (Contact: Mother's Hostility)* [1993] 2 FLR 1, CA; and *Re H (Contact: Principles)* [1994] 2 FLR 969, CA. See also *Re W (A Minor) (Contact)* [1994] 2 FLR 441, CA in which Sir Stephen Brown P said that the starting point is always that every child has a right to be brought up in the knowledge of his non-residential parent. In that case contact with the father was granted notwithstanding the mother's opposition and the fact that the children had been brought up to believe that their stepfather was their natural father.

8 [1995] 1 FLR 274, CA at 278–9.

9 [1996] 2 FLR 314, CA at 328, relying on *Re O (Contact: Imposition of Conditions)* [1995] 2 FLR 124 at 128–30 per Sir Thomas Bingham MR.

10 [1998] 1 FLR 361. Holman J was anxious that the boy (a three-year-old) should know who his father was, and he therefore held that it was wrong for the justices to have accepted the mother's view (even though this was also accepted by the father) that the child should not be told about his parentage until he grew older. See also the similar concern and approach in *Re R (A Minor) (Contact)* [1993] 2 FLR 762, CA.

sexually abused his child[11] and where continued contact was shown to be directly harmful to the child either physically[12] or emotionally in the sense of undermining the child's security.[13] More recent examples include *Re F (Minors) (Denial of Contact)*,[14] in which contact with a transsexual father was refused primarily because of the children's (boys aged 12 and nine) own wishes; *Re T (A Minor) (Parental Responsibility: Contact)*,[15] in which an unmarried father was denied contact because of his violence towards the mother and his blatant disregard for the child's welfare; *Re C and V (Contact and Parental Responsibility)*,[16] in which the child had severe medical problems requiring constant and informed medical attention which the mother, but not the father, was able to give; and *Re D (A Minor) (Contact: Mother's Hostility)*[17] and *Re H (A Minor) (Parental Responsibility)*,[18] in which respectively the mother's and stepfather's implacable hostility towards contact with an unmarried father was held to justify prohibiting contact. Nevertheless, despite these latter two decisions, as Balcombe LJ said in *Re J (A Minor) (Contact)*,[19] judges should be very reluctant to allow one parent's implacable hostility[20] to deter them from making a contact order where they believe the child's welfare requires it. Where one parent makes contact difficult or impossible for the other, the court could transfer residence. However, this is a remedy of last resort and certainly should not be adopted to solve a relatively straightforward contact problem.[1]

11 See eg *S v S* [1988] Fam Law 128, CA and *Re R (A Minor) (Child Abuse)* [1988] Fam Law 129. Though note proof of sexual abuse does not ipso facto mean that contact should be denied: see *H v H (Child Abuse: Access)* [1989] 1 FLR 212, CA and *C v C (Child Abuse: Evidence)* [1988] 1 FLR 462.
12 As in *Geapin v Geapin* (1974) 4 Fam Law 188, CA where a boy suffered serious asthmatic attacks when in contact with his father.
13 See eg *Re C (Minors) (Access)* [1985] FLR 804, CA; *Williams v Williams* [1985] FLR 509, CA (though the children were being indoctrinated against their father); and *Wright v Wright* (1980) 2 FLR 276, CA. See also *Re C (A Minor) (Access)* [1992] 1 FLR 309, CA in which, following divorce from the stepfather, the mother resumed cohabitation with the child's natural father but then left to cohabit with another man. The child, who was still living with the mother, had discovered the identity of her natural father. It was held that, notwithstanding the long period that the child had lived with the stepfather, it was not in her interests to continue to have contact with him, given his intensity of feelings and her current situation vis-à-vis the mother's new cohabitant and her natural father.
14 [1993] 2 FLR 677, CA. See also *Re L (Contact: Transsexual Applicant)* [1995] 2 FLR 438. For pre-1989 Act cases following the children's wishes, see eg *Re N (A Minor) (Access: Penal Notices)* [1991] FCR 1000, [1992] 1 FLR 134, CA and *Churchard v Churchard* [1984] FLR 635.
15 [1993] 2 FLR 450, CA. See also *Re A (Contact)* [1998] 2 FLR 171, and *Re D (Contact: Reasons for Refusal)* [1997] 2 FLR 48, CA (mother found to be genuinely fearful for herself and her child). Other examples might include sexual abuse, or physical abuse. But note violence does not *per se* justify a refusal of contact: *Re H (Contact: Domestic Violence)* [1998] 2 FLR 42, CA. The Lord Chancellor's Advisory Board on Family Law began a consultation exercise on the issue in 1997/98: *First Annual Report: 1997/98* para 4.21. On the subject of so-called 'parental alienation' see Willbourne and Cull 'The Emerging Problem of Parental Alienation' [1997] Fam Law 807 and Maidment 'Parental Alienation Syndrome – A Judicial Response?' [1998] Fam Law 264.
16 [1998] 1 FLR 392, CA.
17 [1993] 2 FLR 1, CA.
18 [1993] 1 FLR 484. See also *Re B (Contact: Stepfather's Opposition)* [1997] 2 FLR 579, CA in which the dismissal of the father's contact application was held to be justified because of the threat of the child's stepfather to reject the child and the mother.
19 [1994] 1 FLR 729 at 736. See also *Re S (Contact: Grandparents)* [1996] 1 FLR 158 and *Re P Contact: Supervision)* [1996] 2 FLR 314, CA.
20 But note *Re D (Contact: Reasons for Refusal)*, supra, in which Hale J observed that the term 'implacable hostility' usually refers to the type of case where no good reason could be discerned for a parent's opposition to contact.
1 Per Thorpe LJ in *Re B (Residence Order: Status Quo)* [1998] 1 FLR 368, CA.

Contact may also be refused on the ground of indirect harm as, for example, where the effect on the care-giving parent is so adverse as to impair that parent's care of the child.[2] Normally this factor is only likely to justify prohibiting contact where the non-care-giving parent's conduct causes genuine and justified anxiety about the child's well-being.[3] An unusual case is *A v C*,[4] in which a man paid a woman to have his child by artificial insemination, the plan being that she would hand over the baby to the man and his wife (who could no longer have children). In the event the mother reneged on the agreement and kept the baby. The father failed both in his application to look after the child and to have contact. The latter was refused on the grounds that the father's relationship was wholly artificial and there was no sense in perpetuating it.

Although it is possible for a court, in addition to denying contact, to make a further order under s 91(14) restraining future applications without leave of the court, it is normally only appropriate to do so to prevent threatened abuse by a vexatious or oppressive party of their right of access to the courts. Furthermore, because it represents a substantial interference with the citizen's right of unrestricted access to the courts, it is a power that should be exercised with great care, with the courts having to weigh the child's interests against the fundamental freedom of access to the courts.[5]

---

2 Such an argument failed on the facts in *Re P (Contact: Supervision)* [1996] 2 FLR 314, CA.
3 See *Re BC (A Minor) (Access)* [1985] FLR 639, CA and *M v J (Illegitimate Child: Access)* (1982) 3 FLR 19. See also *Wright v Wright* (1980) 2 FLR 276, CA, where the mother feared that her husband, a Jehovah's Witness, would 'indoctrinate' her children.
4 [1985] FLR 445, CA (decided in 1978). Quaere whether this would now be decided the same way?
5 See *Re R (Residence: Contact: Restricting Applications)* [1998] 1 FLR 749, CA at 757 per Wilson J. In *B v B (Residence Order: Restricting Applications)* [1997] 1 FLR 139, CA at 147, Waite LJ said that s 91(14) had to be exercised with the paramountcy of the child's welfare in mind. It is submitted that the approach of Wilson J is to be preferred. See also *Re F (Contact: Restraint Order)* [1995] 1 FLR 956, CA, and *Re N (Section 91(14) Order)* [1996] 1 FLR 356.

Chapter 13

International parental child abduction

A. Introduction

A growing problem, particularly in the international context, is the removal from the jurisdiction of a child by one parent without the other's consent and often in breach of a court order. Such removals are harrowing for the so-called 'left at home' parent and in any event are likely to put the child's welfare at risk. The problem becomes most acute where children are taken out of the jurisdiction altogether,[1] since it then becomes much more difficult both to discover their whereabouts and to secure their return. It has been estimated that as many as four children a week are abducted and taken by their parents to another part of the United Kingdom,[2] and it is clear that in excess of 200 a year are taken abroad.[3] Until the 1980s there was little international co-operation on parental child abduction and orders made in one jurisdiction were generally neither recognised nor enforceable in another. This state of international 'anarchy' operated as an encouragement to would-be abductors who, by appropriate forum shopping, could hope to take their children from one jurisdiction to another and there obtain judgment in their favour. However, there are now two international conventions designed both to help trace abducted children and to secure their return. In addition, under the Family Law Act 1986 certain orders relating to children made in one part of the United Kingdom or the Isle of Man can be enforced in another part of the United Kingdom or the Isle of Man. As a result of these developments there are different laws dealing with abduction depending on the country to or from which the child has been taken or brought. Thus, while the chances of foiling an attempted abduction and of recovering a child wrongfully taken have improved, the resulting law is complex.

B. Preventing children from being abducted out of the United Kingdom

The best chance of recovering the child is to prevent him from leaving the jurisdiction in the first place. To this end the innocent party may invoke both the criminal and the civil law.

---

1 The court's attitude to abduction in the domestic context is discussed ante, p 472.
2 See (1986) 130 Sol Jo 325. These are likely to be conservative estimates.
3 Over 200 formal applications for the return of children were made under the Hague and European Conventions, both in 1997 and 1996: see post, p 487. These statistics, however, do not include cases where no, or only informal action was taken, nor do they include abduction of children to non-convention countries.

1.   CRIMINAL SANCTIONS

Child Abduction Act 1984[4]

Under the Child Abduction Act 1984 s 1(1)[5] it is an offence even for a married parent to take his own child (under the age of 16) out of the United Kingdom[6] without the requisite consents,[7] ie of the other parent, anyone else with parental responsibility or leave of the court.[8] The only exception to this is where a parent has a residence order in his or her favour, in which case he or she is permitted to remove the child outside the United Kingdom for a period of one month without anyone's consent, unless this is in breach of a prohibited steps order.[9] It is to be noted that where a parent has sole parental responsibility, as for example the unmarried mother where the father has not acquired parental responsibility by a court order or agreement,[10] or where the married parent is the sole living parent, then no consent for the child's removal from the jurisdiction is required.

Although the principal object of the Act is to deter parents from abducting their children out of the country, it also provides the means by which innocent parents can seek to stop the abduction. Because it is an offence to *attempt* to take a child out of the United Kingdom, the police can arrest[11] anyone they reasonably suspect of attempting to take a child out of the county contrary to the provisions of the 1984 Act.[12] Furthermore, if the police decide to act they can, through their 'All Ports Warning System', effect a port stop, or port alert as it is sometimes known.

The All Ports Warning System[13]

Under this system, details of the child at risk of abduction are circulated by way of the police national computer broadcast facility to immigration officers at ports and airports throughout the country, who will then assist the police in trying to prevent that child from leaving the country. As this is the only means of effecting a port alert,[14] any parent fearing that his child might be taken out of the country and wishing to take advantage of this facility must inform the police, who maintain a 24-hour service in this regard.[15]

---

4 See generally Lowe 'Child Abduction and Child Kidnapping – The New Laws' (1984) 134 NLJ 960 and Scot Law Memorandum No 67.

5 Discussed ante at pp 361–2. Exceptionally the common law offences of child kidnapping (see *R v D* [1984] AC 778, [1984] 2 All ER 449, HL), discussed ante, p 312, or unlawful imprisonment (see *R v Rahman* [1985] Crim LR 596) might be relevant, but these should not be prosecuted where the alleged offence is covered by the 1984 Act: *R v C (Kidnapping: Abduction)* [1991] 2 FLR 252, CA.

6 Viz England and Wales, Scotland and Northern Ireland. But *not* including the Channel Islands or the Isle of Man.

7 The consent does *not* have to be in writing.

8 Child Abduction Act 1984 s 1(3). But note that where the child is a ward of court, court leave will always be required.

9 Section 1(4) and (4A).

10 As emphasised by Hale J in *Re W; Re B (Child Abduction: Unmarried Father)* [1998] 2 FLR 146 at 151.

11 Without a warrant, since it is an arrestable offence.

12 For a successful prosecution for an attempted abduction, see *R v Griffin* [1993] Crim LR 515, CA.

13 See generally *The Child Abduction Act 1984: 'Port Stop' Procedures* Home Office Circular No 21/1986.

14 Formerly, there was a 'stop list' procedure operated by the Home Office which could only be activated if the child was a ward of court or if an injunction restraining the child's removal from the jurisdiction had been obtained.

15 *Practice Direction (Child: Removal from Jurisdiction)* [1986] 1 All ER 983.

Before instituting a port alert the police must be convinced that the complaint is bona fide and the danger of removal real and imminent.[16] Although it is not necessary to have obtained a court order beforehand,[17] the existence of an order will be good evidence of the seriousness of the request for action from the police. Parties seeking police assistance should furnish as much information as possible, and in particular furnish the following details:[18]

(a) name, sex, date of birth, description and passport number of child;
(b) name, sex, description, nationality and passport number of abductor;
(c) their relationship;
(d) whether the child will assist in the removal;
(e) name, relationship, nationality and telephone number of applicant;
(f) solicitor's name and telephone number;
(g) likely time of travel, port of embarkation and port of arrival.

If instituted, a port alert is reasonably effective if invoked in time,[19] but it is by no means fool-proof.[20] Once the alert is activated, the child's name will remain on the stop list for four weeks.[1]

2.   COURT PROHIBITIONS AGAINST REMOVAL

The need for court orders

Although, as has been said, in view of the Child Abduction Act 1984 there is no requirement to obtain a court order to obtain a port alert, there are nevertheless still advantages in having such an order:

1.   It establishes the applicant's bona fides, which may help to convince the police of the need for action.[2]
2.   A specific order prohibiting the child's removal can act as a deterrent in itself.
3.   It will enable the applicant to enlist the aid of government agencies to trace the child.[3]
4.   The High Court can specifically order publicity to trace the child.[4]

---

16 Within 24–48 hours: *Practice Direction*, supra.
17 Though note in the case of children aged 16 or 17 a court order *is* required, since the Child Abduction Act 1984 does not apply. In practice abduction of such older children would be very unusual.
18 *Practice Direction*, supra.
19 It is to be noted that as legal aid can be granted retrospectively (Civil Legal Aid (General) Regulations 1989 reg 103(6)) solicitors can act first and recover their costs and fees afterwards.
20 Presumably the system will become easier to operate once all children have to travel on their own passports. See ante, p 361.
1 Quaere whether this is long enough?
2 It may be possible that some forces have still not heard of the 1984 Act, but great efforts have been made to ensure that the police are aware both of the 1984 Act and the Port Alert system.
3 *Practice Direction (Disclosure of Addresses)* [1989] 1 All ER 765 as amended by *Practice Direction* [1995] 2 FLR 813. The agencies mentioned are the Department of Social Security, Office of Population Census and Surveys (now Office for National Statistics), National Health Service, Passport Office and the Ministry of Defence. It has been held by Ewbank J in *Re C (A Minor) (Child Support Agency: Disclosure)* [1995] 1 FLR 201 that notwithstanding that it is not mentioned by the *Direction* the court can request disclosure from the Child Support Agency. It should be noted that the assistance of telephone companies can also be useful in tracing children: see Atkinson and Nicholls 'Tracing and Recording Telephone Calls' [1995] Fam Law 104.
4 *Practice Direction* [1980] 2 All ER 806.

5. In cases where there is inadequate information as to the child's whereabouts the court can order any person who is believed to have that information to disclose it to the courts.[5]
6. Upon obtaining a prohibition against removal, steps can be taken to prevent the issue of a UK passport,[6] or, if one has already been issued, to ask the court to order its surrender.[7] To prevent the reissue of a passport the court will notify the Passport Agency in every case in which a surrender of a passport has been ordered.[8] It has been held[9] that the High Court's inherent jurisdiction extends to ordering the surrender of a *foreign* national's passport where to do so is in the child's best interests.
7. An order will be required if it becomes necessary to invoke the European Convention on International Child Abduction or to recover the child from another part of the United Kingdom or the Isle of Man.[10]
8. It will enable outstanding disputes to be resolved upon the child's return, or sanctions to be imposed if the child is not returned.[11]

Orders that may be obtained

An applicant may obtain a prohibited steps order forbidding a child's removal from the United Kingdom or any specified part of the United Kingdom under s 8 of the Children Act 1989.[12] Furthermore, as we have seen, an embargo against removal from the United Kingdom for any period in excess of one month is automatically included in any residence order.[13]

Another means by which an embargo against the child's removal from the jurisdiction can be obtained is by making the child a ward of court.[14] The unique advantage of wardship is that the embargo automatically arises immediately the child is warded,[15] and no other relief need be sought. It is this immediate effect that makes it advantageous to invoke wardship if no other proceedings are already on foot. Furthermore, unlike the automatic embargo against removal on a residence order,[16] a removal of a ward without court leave is punishable as a contempt.[17] In practice

---

5   Family Law Act 1986 s 33. For the case of wardship see FPR 1991 r 5.1(7)–(8).
6   See the guidance issued by the Passport Agency at [1994] Fam Law 651.
7   Family Law Act 1986 s 37.
8   *Practice Direction (Minor: Passport)* [1983] 2 All ER 253.
9   *Re A-K (Foreign Passport: Jurisdiction)* [1997] 2 FLR 569, CA. Note also that if a solicitor agrees to hold a foreign passport he owes a duty of care to the other parent not to let it out of his possession: *Al-Kandari v JR Brown & Co* [1988] QB 665, [1988] 1 All ER 833, CA.
10 See post, pp 506–7 and 514 respectively.
11 See post at p 483.
12 See, for example, *Re D (a minor)* [1992] 1 All ER 892, CA, according to which such orders can be applied for ex parte and, in appropriate cases, can be enforced without notice. NB, however, even if a prohibited steps or specific issue order is obtained, the port stop procedure must still be activated by the applicant.
13 Section 13(1)(b) and s 13(2) discussed ante, pp 441–3. But note the difficulties of enforcing the direction: see n 16 below.
14 Wardship is discussed in Chapter 16. NB the embargo normally prohibits the ward's removal from England and Wales without the court's leave. However, under the Family Law Act 1986 s 38, unless the court has directed otherwise, leave is not required to take the child to another part of the United Kingdom or the Isle of Man if divorce proceedings etc are continuing, or if the child is habitually resident there. See also the discussion in [1992] Fam Law 94.
15 See post, p 686.
16 *Re P (Minors) (Custody Order: Penal Notice)* [1990] 1 WLR 613, CA, discussed by Lowe 'Enforcing Orders Relating to Children' (1992) 4 Jo of Child Law 26.
17 Indeed, at common law it is a contempt to remove a ward, irrespective of the defendant's knowledge of the wardship: *Re J (An Infant)* (1913) 108 LT 554, but cf *Re F (Otherwise A) (Publication of Information)* [1977] Fam 58 at 88 per Lord Denning MR.

wardship remains the pre-eminent jurisdiction for dealing with abducted children.[18]

Whatever means are used, speed is of the essence if an attempted abduction is to be foiled, but even if all preventative measures have been taken in good time there is no guarantee that the child's removal will be stopped.

In cases where the court is prepared to give leave for the child's removal from the jurisdiction, there is power in wardship proceedings and presumably in the High Court generally to require the person given leave to enter into a bond to ensure that the child will be duly returned.[19] Subsequently, if the order is broken the court can order the bond to be forfeited and assigned to the aggrieved party. Other actions that can be taken following the breaking of a court order are fining or committing the contemnor (ie the person breaking the order) to prison[20] or, more potently in some cases, sequestering the contemnor's assets.[1] This latter remedy can be a useful lever against the abducting parent who has left property in this country, particularly as it is now established that the court has power to order the sale of sequestered assets and can direct that the money raised by the sequestrators be used to pay the costs of tracing the child and instituting proceedings abroad for the return of the child etc.[2]

C.   Dealing with children abducted to or brought from a 'non-convention country' outside the United Kingdom

1.   DEALING WITH CHILDREN ABDUCTED TO A 'NON-CONVENTION COUNTRY'

Once a child is removed outside the United Kingdom or the Isle of Man to a country that has implemented neither of the international conventions, the chances of recovering the child may be slim. Unless the abducting spouse returns voluntarily, the only legal means[3] is to institute appropriate civil proceedings in the country to which the child has been taken, if that is known, or, if the country in question has an extradition treaty with the United Kingdom, to try to have the abductor extradited for abduction and return the child.[4]

2.   DEALING WITH CHILDREN ABDUCTED FROM A 'NON-CONVENTION COUNTRY'

Children brought to England and Wales from a non-convention country remain subject to the common law. Such cases are usually litigated under the wardship

18 See Lowe and Nicholls 'Child Abduction – The Wardship Jurisdiction and the Hague Convention' [1994] Fam Law 191.
19 For details of which see Clarke Hall and Morrison on *Children* 2[4]. It is the normal practice for there to be consent to the giving of the bond and it is not appropriate to impose it on a party who was not responsible for the child's removal: see *Re H (Minors) (Wardship: Surety)* [1991] 1 FLR 40, CA.
20 For the procedure see RSC Ord 52.
1 The effect of a sequestration order is to freeze the contemnor's assets: see ante, p 448.
2 See respectively *Mir v Mir* [1992] Fam 79, [1992] 1 All ER 765, and *Richardson v Richardson* [1989] Fam 95, [1989] 3 All ER 779.
3 As opposed to re-abducting the child.
4 Apart from the length of time involved in obtaining extradition, an important drawback of the procedure is that only the 'wrongdoer' is extradited, so that there is no guarantee that the child will be returned.

484   Chapter 13   International parental child abduction

jurisdiction.[5] Provided the jurisdictional rules are satisfied,[6] a child may be made a
ward of court after he has been brought to this country even if the removal from
another jurisdiction was unauthorised.[7]

In the wardship proceedings the court will have to consider whether to hear the
full merits of the application or make a summary order for the immediate return of
the child to the place from where he was taken. In this regard it is well established
that the High Court does not regard itself as being bound by the order of a foreign
court,[8] and instead has to make its own independent judgment of the appropriate
course of action.[9] At one time, the practice of the court was to make a 'summary'
order for the child's return (ie there would be no full investigation into the merits of
the case) unless a return could be shown to be harmful to the child.[10] In this way it
was felt that the child's welfare was reasonably protected whilst the abduction was
discouraged. That approach was held to be inconsistent with the welfare principle
as applied by the House of Lords in *J v C*,[11] and it became firmly established that the
decision whether to make a summary order or to hear the full merits of the
application must be determined according to the child's welfare.[12] In *Re F (A
Minor) (Abduction: Jurisdiction)*,[13] however, the Court of Appeal emphasised that
it was normally in the child's interests not to be abducted and that any decision
about his upbringing was best decided by the court in the state in which he had
hitherto been habitually resident. Accordingly, it was held that a return should be
ordered provided the English court was satisfied that (a) the foreign court in
question would apply principles acceptable to the English court and (b) there were
no contra-indications such as those referred to in Art 13 of the Hague Convention.[14]
As will be seen, although the modern practice is to order a return, provided the
application is made quickly and the court is satisfied that the child will not be
harmed, the twin requirements mentioned in *Re F* require careful scrutiny.

Being satisfied that the foreign court will apply principles acceptable to the English court

Although it is well established that the child's summary return should only be
ordered where the court is satisfied that the foreign court in question will apply

5 Wardship is discussed in Chapter 16.
6 Viz those under ss 1–3 of the Family Law Act 1986, set out post, p 513.
7 In fact a child who has been taken from a *convention* country may also be warded, but the wardship
    is liable to be overridden by a subsequent convention application. Should the convention
    application fail, however, then any earlier wardship proceedings are revived and may be
    determined upon their merits: see *Re M (A Minor) (Abduction: Child's Objections)* [1994]
    2 FLR 126.
8 Not even (before the implementation of the Family Law Act 1986) an order made in Scotland. For
    a notorious example see *Babington v Babington* 1955 SC 115, discussed post at p 512.
9 *Re B's Settlement* [1940] Ch 54, [1951] 1 All ER 949n and *McKee v McKee* [1951] AC 352, [1951]
    1 All ER 942, PC.
10 See *Re H (Infants)* [1966] 1 All ER 886, CA, and *Re E (D) (An Infant)* [1967] Ch 287, [1967] 1 All
    ER 329, CA.
11 [1970] AC 668, [1969] 1 All ER, 788, HL, discussed ante, pp 307ff.
12 *Re L (Minors) (Wardship: Jurisdiction)* [1974] 1 All ER 913, CA (the House of Lords declined to
    hear an appeal against this ruling: see [1974] 1 WLR 266) and *Re R (Minors) (Wardship:
    Jurisdiction)* (1981) 2 FLR 416, CA.
13 [1991] Fam 25, [1990] 3 All ER 97, CA. See also *G v G (Minors) (Abduction)* [1991] 2 FLR 506,
    CA (decided in 1989) upon which the court relied in *Re F*. For a thoughtful review of this and other
    decisions, see McClean and Beevers 'International child abduction – back to common law
    principles' (1995) 7 CFLQ 128.
14 Art 13 of the Hague Convention is discussed below at pp 499ff.

principles acceptable to the English court, there is a conflict of view as to what is sufficient to so satisfy the court. On the one hand, based on the principle of comity, it was held by the Court of Appeal in *Re M (Abduction: Non-Convention Country)*,[15] in the words of Waite LJ:

'. . . it is assumed, particularly in the case of States which are fellow members of the European Union,[16] that such facilities as rights of representation, means of collecting information through independent sources and welfare reports, and opportunities of giving evidence and interrogating the other side, all of which are necessary to place the court in a position to determine the best interests of the child concerned, will be secured as well within one State's jurisdiction as within another.'

In other words, in such cases it is to be assumed, unless evidence is led to the contrary, that the foreign court will apply principles acceptable to the English court. This approach was subsequently adopted in respect of countries with which the UK has close historical ties,[17] and even more generally to courts of any State.[18]

In *Re JA (Child Abduction: Non-Convention Country)*,[19] however, the Court of Appeal held this general approach to be wrong. In Ward LJ's view, it was clearly established[20] that 'it is an abdication of the responsibility and an abnegation of the duty of this court to the ward under its protection to surrender the determination of its ward's future to a foreign court whose regime may be inimical to the child's welfare'. Accordingly, his Lordship accepted the following propositions:

'(1) The duty of this court is to determine the question [ie whether to order the child's return] by the test which makes welfare the paramount, and therefore, the dominant consideration.
(2) The court cannot be satisfied that it is in the best interests of the child to return it to the court of habitual residence in order that that court may resolve the disputed questions, unless this court is satisfied that the welfare test will apply in that court.
(3) Consequently, this court cannot abdicate its responsibility simply by assuming that welfare will apply'.

Under the '*Re JA* approach' evidence will *always* need to be led as to what principles the foreign court will apply before a return order can even be considered. In *Re JA* itself the court refused to order a child's return to the United Arab Emirates, the evidence being that that State's court powers were limited and that the child's welfare was not the test.[1]

---

15 [1995] 1 FLR 89 at 90–1, CA.
16 In *Re M* the country concerned was Italy, which at the time of the decision was the only European Union country not to have ratified either the European or the Hague Convention on International Child Abduction. Belgium has still only ratified the European Convention.
17 *Re M (Jurisdiction: Forum Conveniens)* [1995] 2 FLR 224, CA, per Waite LJ, in respect of Malta.
18 In *Re M (Minors) (Abduction: Peremptory Return Order)* [1996] 1 FLR 478, CA, also per Waite LJ, in respect of Dubai.
19 [1998] 1 FLR 231, CA.
20 Viz *Nugent v Vetzera* (1866) LR 2 Eq 704; *Di Savini v Lousada* (1870) 18 WR 425; *Re B's Settlement* [1940] Ch 54; *McKee v Mckee* [1951] AC 352, [1951] 1 All ER 942; *J v C* [1970] AC 668 at 714F, per Lord MacDermott; and *Re R (Minors) (Wardship: Jurisdiction)* (1981) 2 FLR 416 at 426, per Ormrod LJ. See also the detailed analysis of the cases relied upon by Ward LJ in Lowe and White *Wards of Court* (2nd edn, 1986) 17-50–17-56. It might also be noted, however, that apart from the '*Re M*' line of cases, the principle of comity was also emphasised by the Court of Appeal in *Re F (A Minor) (Abduction: Custody Rights)* [1991] Fam 25, [1990] 3 All ER 97, per Balcombe LJ.
1 See *Re S (Minors) (Abduction)* [1994] 1 FLR 297, CA, in which it was held that on the facts the difference of tests applied under Pakistani and English law was not such as to entitle the English court to say that the Pakistani court was not the appropriate forum in which to decide the children's future.

It remains to be seen which of these two approaches, the '*Re M* approach' or that of '*Re JA*' eventually prevails but it is submitted that the latter is preferable.

The absence of contra-indications

Under the approach advocated by the Court of Appeal in *Re F (A Minor) (Abduction: Custody Rights)*[2] it seemed that the courts were expected to apply a similar approach to that under the Hague Convention even in non-convention cases, which meant that, in the absence of contra-indications as set out by Art 13, a return order would normally be made.[3] However, the trend of subsequent cases has been to resile from this position. As Butler-Sloss LJ observed in *D v D (Child Abduction: Non-Convention Country)*,[4] it is important to remember in non-convention cases that the Articles of the Hague Convention are not to be applied literally and that, under the wardship jurisdiction in particular, the court retains the discretion to consider the wider aspects of the welfare of its wards. A similar point was made by Ward LJ in *Re P (A Minor) (Child Abduction; Non-Convention Country)*,[5] who observed that to regard Art 13 as a relevant test was contrary to the well-established principle that in such cases the welfare of the child was the only consideration that governed the courts. Accordingly, the better view is that a return order should not be made where there is evidence that the child would thereby be harmed and that in this respect Art 13 may be referred to more in the nature of an aide mémoire.

In any event, it remains of the essence in these cases that the judge should act urgently. This means, as Waite LJ observed in *Re M (Abduction: Non-Convention Country)*:[6] 'That the court has no time to go into matters of detail. The case has to be viewed from the perspective of a quick appraisal of its essential features.'

D.   Dealing with children abducted to or brought from a 'convention country'

1.   INTRODUCTION AND BACKGROUND TO THE CONVENTIONS

The United Kingdom has implemented both the Hague Convention of 1980 on Civil Aspects of International Child Abduction and the European (or Luxembourg) Convention of 1980 on Recognition and Enforcement of Decisions Concerning Custody of Children.[7] It has done this through the Child Abduction

---

2   Ibid.
3   [1991] Fam 25, [1990] 3 All ER 97, CA. See also *G v G (Minors) (Abduction)* [1991] 2 FLR 506, CA (in which case the child was ordered to be returned); *S v S (Child Abduction: Non-Convention Country)* [1994] 2 FLR 681 (in which the child was returned notwithstanding that, had it been applicable, the court would not have been *bound* by Art 12 of the Hague Convention to make a return order since there had been no breach of custody rights) and *C v C (Abduction: Jurisdiction)* [1994] 1 FCR 6 (where an immediate return was refused).
4   [1994] 1 FLR 137 at 140.
5   [1997] Fam 45 at 56, [1997] 2 WLR 233, CA. The need for the court to make its own assessment of the child's welfare was emphasised in *Re JA (Child Abduction: Non-convention Country)*, supra.
6   [1995] 1 FLR 89, CA at 90.
7   The full text together with explanation can be found in 1981 Cmnd 8155 (the European Convention) and in 1981 Cmnd 8281 (the Hague Convention). For general contemporary discussion of the Hague Convention see the Explanatory report by Pérez-Vera (1982) and Anton (1981) 30 ICLQ 357, and of the European Convention see Jones (1981) 30 ICLQ 467.

and Custody Act 1985.[8] Both conventions apply to children (under the age of 16) taken from the United Kingdom to another country that has implemented that convention (known as a 'Contracting State') and vice versa. At the time of writing over 50 countries have implemented the Hague Convention and 21 the European Convention.[9] All but two of the signatories of the latter convention have also implemented the Hague Convention.[10] Unlike the European Convention, which is necessarily confined to Europe, the signatories of the Hague Convention include countries from the Americas, parts of Africa, Asia and Australasia as well as from Europe. Indeed, apart from the UN Convention on the Rights of the Child 1989, the Hague abduction convention has the most contracting states of any international convention dealing with family law and remains the only international instrument governing family matters which the USA has ratified. The large and growing number of contracting states is testament to the general success of the Hague Convention[11] in particular in meeting the global challenge of international child abduction.

England and Wales is second only to the USA in the number of convention application made and received.[12] As can be seen from the following chart, as the number of contracting states has increased so have the numbers of cases dealt with in England and Wales.

CONVENTION APPLICATIONS MADE AND RECEIVED IN
ENGLAND AND WALES 1986–1997

Year	Applications received	Applications made
1986	5	11
1990	62	109
1996	167	208
1997	164	204

Source: Official Figures compiled by the Child Abduction Unit

The above figures do not break down the numbers according to which Convention they were made under, but in a detailed analysis of 1996 cases[13] it was found that the vast majority (93 per cent) of all applications were made under the Hague Convention.

8 For a helpful explanation of the objectives of this Act see Lord Hailsham LC in 460 HL Official Report (5th series) cols 1248 et seq, 1985. The 1985 Act contains in its Schedules the texts of the two conventions as implemented by the UK.
9 A full list of Contracting States can be found in Clarke Hall and Morrison on *Children*, Div 2 and at the back of each issue of 'Family Law' and 'International Family Law'.
10 Viz Belgium and Liechtenstein. Belgium is the only EU country not to have ratified both Conventions.
11 In 1986, for example, the Hague Convention was in force between only six countries and the European Convention between seven.
12 See the analysis of the 1996 figures by Lowe and Perry 'The Operation of the Hague and European Conventions on International Child Abduction between England and Germany, part 1' [1998] International Family Law 8.
13 By Lowe and Perry 'International Child Abduction – the English Experience' (1998) 47 ICLQ forthcoming – 95 per cent of 'outgoing' and 95 per cent of 'incoming' applications were made under the Hague Convention. For reasons why the European Convention is used so infrequently see post, p 510.

2.   THE STRATEGY AND AIMS OF THE TWO CONVENTIONS

A key difference between the two conventions is that whereas the Hague Convention is concerned with the return of children wrongfully removed in breach of rights of custody or in breach of rights of access, the European Convention is concerned with the recognition and enforcement of custody orders and decisions relating to access. In other words, whereas it is a prerequisite for applicants to have a court order in their favour to invoke the European Convention, it is not necessary to have such orders to invoke the Hague Convention. Nevertheless, although their strategy is different, both conventions have the same basic aims, namely to trace abducted children, to secure their prompt return and to organise or secure effective rights of access.

Under each convention a contracting state is bound to set up an administrative body known as the 'Central Authority' which has the duty of tracing the child and taking steps, if necessary by court proceedings, to secure the child's return or to secure access. These tasks are carried out mainly at the expense of each authority. To secure the prompt return of children and to achieve the other obligations under the conventions[14] Central Authorities are expected to co-operate with each other. In practice this administrative system has proved highly successful and, cemented by triennial reviews of the working of the Hague Convention and through meetings organised by the Council of Europe in the case of the European Convention, there has developed a close liaison and understanding between the various Central Authorities.[15]

In England and Wales the Central Authority is the Lord Chancellor.[16] In turn these functions are exercised on the Lord Chancellor's behalf by the Official Solicitor through the Child Abduction Unit. In the case of children taken from England and Wales the transmission of applications overseas will normally be handled by the Child Abduction Unit. In the case of children wrongfully brought to this country the practice is that, upon receiving an application in correct form, the Child Abduction Unit instructs a firm of solicitors on the client's behalf.[17] The firm must then immediately apply for legal aid, which will be granted regardless of the applicant's means and which will not be subject to a merits test.[18] In other words, an important advantage for a foreign citizen in using a convention rather than a domestic jurisdiction such as wardship is that they will be able to obtain free legal aid.[19] Once legal aid is granted, the solicitor has sole responsibility for the conduct of the case. On the evidence to date this system seems to work well.

A second technique used by each convention is to curb the power of the domestic courts in each contracting state to make an independent judgment of what is in the interests of a particular child, so that a return will normally be ordered. This is certainly how the conventions have been interpreted in England and Wales, where the court rarely refuses to return an 'abducted child'.[20]

---

14 Viz those set out in Art 7 of the Hague Convention and Art 5 of the European Convention.
15 See Bruch 'The Central Authority's role under the Hague Abduction conventions – A friend indeed' (1994) 28 Family Law Quarterly 34.
16 Child Abduction and Custody Act 1985 s 3 and s 14.
17 They are not instructed on the Unit's behalf.
18 Civil Legal Aid (General) Regulations 1989 reg 14.
19 Such arrangements, however, are not reciprocated in every other convention country, notably the USA.
20 Lowe and Perry 'International Child Abduction – the English Experience', op cit, found that in 1996 5 per cent of applications resulted in a judicial refusal (as opposed to 7 per cent of outgoing applications). However, practice varies from country to country. For a discussion of the German practice see Lowe and Perry 'The Operation of the Hague and European Conventions on International Child Abduction between England and Germany Parts I and II' [1998] International Family Law 8–15 and 52–6.

3.   THE HAGUE CONVENTION[1]

When the convention applies

Under Art 4 this convention applies to any child, under the age of 16 and habitually resident in one contracting state, who has wrongfully been removed or retained in another contracting state.[2] To appreciate the scope of this Article it is necessary to explore first the meaning of 'habitual residence' and then of 'wrongful removal or retention'.

(a)   Habitual residence[3]

Habitual residence is not defined either by the convention or the statute and, although it has become the standard international connecting factor, it is in truth a difficult concept to pin down.[4] According to Balcombe LJ in *Re M (Minors) (Residence Order: Jurisdiction)*[5] four basic propositions may be deduced from the authorities:

'(1) "Habitual" or "ordinary residence" refers to a person's abode in a particular place or country which he has adopted voluntarily and for settled purposes as part of the regular order of his life for the time being whether of short or of long duration . . .[6]
(2) Habitual residence is primarily a question of fact to be decided by reference to all the circumstances of any particular case . . .
(3) There is a significant difference between a person ceasing to be habitually resident in country A, and his subsequently becoming habitually resident in country B. A person may cease to be habitually resident in country A in a single day if he or she leaves it with a settled intention not to return to it but to take up long-term residence in Country B instead. Such a person cannot, however, become habitually resident in Country B in a

---

1 See generally Bruch 'Child Abduction and the English Courts' in Bainham and Pearl (eds) *Frontiers of Family Law* (1993) ch 4; Bruch 'How to Draft a Successful Family Law Convention' in Doek, van Loon and Vlaardingerbroek (eds) *Children on the Move*; Dyer 'Case-law and Co-operation as the Building blocks for Protection of International Families' in Lowe and Douglas (eds) *Families Across Frontiers* 27–40; Dyer 'the Hague Convention on the Civil Aspects of International Child Abduction towards global co-operation' (1993) 1 Int Jo of Children's Rights 273–92; Nygh 'The International Abduction Convention' in *Children on the Move* 29–45; Savolainen 'The Hague Convention on Child Abduction of 1980 and Its Implementation in Finland' (1997) 66 Nordic Jo of International Law 101; Schuz 'The Hague Child Abduction Convention' (1995) 44 ICLQ 771; and Silberman 'Hague International Child Abduction Convention: A Progress Report' (1994) 57 Law and Contemporary Problems 210.
2 But for the purposes of access it has been held sufficient for the child to be habitually resident in a Contracting state at the time of breach: *Re N (Children Abduction: Jurisdiction)* [1995] Fam 96, [1995] 2 All ER 417. In the case of a secondary abduction, the court may refuse to hear the case: *Re O (Child Abduction: Re-Abduction)* [1997] 2 FLR 712 (child abducted to Sweden and then to England).
3 See generally Clarke Hall and Morrison, 2[44]ff.
4 Ironically, one of the reasons for using it is to avoid the concept of 'domicile', which is even more difficult to apply, since it depends upon the party's intention where he or she is *permanently* to reside. It is thought less artificial than 'nationality'. For discussion of the merits of the various connecting factors see Thue 'Connecting Factors in International Law' in Lowe and Douglas (eds) *Families Across Frontiers* 53.
5 [1993] 1 FLR 495 at 499–500 and repeated by him in *Re M (Abduction: Habitual Residence)* [1996] 1 FLR 887 at 890.
6 Per Lord Scarman in *Shah v Barnet London Borough Council* [1983] 2 AC 309 at 343; *Kapur v Kapur* [1984] FLR 920 at 926. Note also *Gateshead Metropolitan Borough Council v L* [1996] 3 All ER 264 at 267, [1996] 3 WLR 426 at 429 in which Wilson J said that since *Shah* 'ordinary residence and habitual residence have been synonymous'. A similar view was expressed by Butler-Sloss LJ in *M v M (Abduction: England and Scotland)* [1997] 2 FLR 263 at 267.

single day. An appreciable period of time and a settled intention will be necessary to enable him or her to become so. During that appreciable period of time the person will have ceased to be habitually resident in country A but not yet have become habitually resident in country B . . .

(4) Where the habitual residence of a young child is in question, the element of volition will usually be that of the person or persons who has or have the parental responsibility for that child.'

It is clear that the minimum requirement is that there must be a factum of residence – a person who has never lived here cannot possibly be habitually resident here. However, it is equally true that a mere visit will not be sufficient. In considering what factors may make the factum of residence 'habitual', Waite J has helpfully observed:[7]

'Habitual residence is a term referring, when it is applied in the context of married parents living together, to their abode in a particular place or country which they have adopted voluntarily and for settled purposed as part of the regular order of their life for the time being, whether of short or of long duration.

All that the law requires for a "settled purpose" is that the parents' shared intentions in living where they do should have a sufficient degree of continuity about them to be properly described as settled.'

His Lordship added, however, that because of the summary nature of Convention proceedings, detailed enquiries into the parties' intentions are not required. As he put it:[8]

'A settled purpose is not something to be searched for under a microscope. If it is there at all it will stand out clearly as a matter of general impression.'

Evidence of the required intention can be satisfied by a relatively short period of residence. In *Re F (A Minor) (Child Abduction)*,[9] for example, the Court of Appeal approved a judicial finding that a family had acquired a fresh habitual residence only one month after arrival in a new country. In that case Butler-Sloss LJ observed[10] that a court 'should not strain to find a lack of habitual residence where, on a broad canvas, the child has settled in a particular country' since without such an habitual residence the child cannot be protected under the Convention.

In *Re V (Abduction: Habitual Residence)*[11] it was held that because the family had two established homes, one in London where they spent the winter and the other in Corfu where they spent the summer, they could be regarded as being habitually resident in both places. However, because concurrent habitual residence is not a concept that fits in with the aims of the Convention it was held that their habitual residences should be regarded as sequential, that is, whilst in London they were habitually resident in England and when in Corfu they were habitually resident in Greece.

The leading authority for the third proposition is the House of Lords' decision

7 *Re B (Minors) (Abduction) (No 2)* [1993] 1 FLR 993 at 995. See also *A v A (Child Abduction)* [1993] 2 FLR 225 in which Rattee J commented that habitual residence is not to be equated with an intention to stay in a place permanently but that it is sufficient if the intention is to take up long-term residence there.
8 Ibid at 998.
9 [1992] 1 FLR 548, CA.
10 Ibid at 555–6; cf *Re A (Abduction: Habitual Residence)* [1998] 1 FLR 497 in which a stay of three weeks of an intended six-week visit was held not to establish an habitual residence.
11 [1995] 2 FLR 992, per Douglas Brown J.

in *Re J (A Minor) (Abduction: Custody Rights).*[12] In that case an unmarried mother, a UK national, without the father's knowledge or consent left him in Western Australia and flew to England with her child, intending to live permanently in England. It was held that in these circumstances, on leaving Australia, she had abandoned her habitual residence there but had not, at the relevant date (viz in this case within the first three weeks of arrival here),[13] yet acquired an habitual residence in this country.

With regard to the fourth proposition, as Waite J put it in *Re B (Minors) (Abduction) (No 2):*[14]

> 'The habitual residence of the young children of parents who are living together is the same as the habitual residence of the parents themselves and neither parent can change it without the express or tacit consent of the other or an order of the court.'

There is no authority directly concerning an older child, but in such cases the basic position might well be different[15] in that it might be possible for a *'Gillick* competent' child to establish his or her own habitual residence.

Although it will normally be the case that while the parents are living together their young child will be regarded as having the same habitual residence as the parents, it is not an invariable rule. Indeed, in *Re M (Abduction: Habitual Residence)*[16] the Court of Appeal expressly rejected the suggestion that it was a proposition of law that a 'child's habitual residence is that of the parents unless they agree that it shall have some other habitual residence and so long as that agreement continues'. Accordingly, while parents can agree either expressly or impliedly that their child should live apart from them and thus either retain[17] or acquire[18] an habitual residence different from their own, it by no means automatically follows that upon the ending of that agreement the child's habitual residence reverts to that of the parents.[19] An agreement to send a child abroad for some temporary purpose will not be sufficient to change that child's habitual residence. For this purpose sending a child abroad to a boarding school is in itself unlikely to be regarded as being more than for the 'temporary purpose of education'.[20]

---

12 [1990] 2 AC 562 at 578, sub nom *C v S (minor: abduction: illegitimate child)* [1990] 2 All ER 961 at 965 per Lord Brandon; cf *Re B (Child Abduction: Habitual Residence)* [1994] 2 FLR 915 in which it was held that where a child had acquired an habitual residence in England it was not lost by the child returning to Canada for a short period of under four months, while his parents attempted (unsuccessfully) a reconciliation.

13 See further below at p 494.

14 [1993] 1 FLR 993 at 995. See also *Re F (A Minor) (Child Abduction)* [1992] 1 FLR 548 at 556.

15 See Hale J in *Re A (Wardship: Jurisdiction)* [1995] 1 FLR 767.

16 [1996] 1 FLR 887 at 895.

17 See the hypothetical example given in *Re M (Abduction: Habitual Residence)* ibid at 894 of a child born in India and who had spent the whole of his or her life there with grandparents, while the parents came to this country and acquired a habitual residence in England.

18 As, for example, where parents agree to send their child to live with relatives abroad, as in *Re M (Abduction: Habitual Residence).*

19 *Re M (Abduction: Habitual Residence)*, where, pursuant to parental agreement, the child was sent to and remained living with his grandparents in India and in which it was held that, upon the mother's withdrawal from that agreement, the child's habitual residence could not revert to that of his mother in England, since there was no current factum of residence there. Indeed, without finally deciding the point Sir John Balcombe commented that 'in all probability' the child was still habitually resident in India.

20 See *Re A (Wardship: Jurisdiction)*, supra, approved on this point by the Court of Appeal in *Re M (Abduction: Habitual Residence)*, supra. See also *P (GE) (An Infant)* [1965] Ch 568 at 585, per Lord Denning MR.

Of course, the foregoing problems only arise where the child is living apart from the parents. Where the child is living with both his parents it would seem hard to resist the proposition that he or she shares the same habitual residence as that of the parents. Further problems are caused where the parents separate. In such cases the child's habitual residence may change and will, in due course, follow that of the principal carer with whom he resides. However, where both parents have equal rights of custody, such a change cannot be immediately effected simply by one parent unilaterally removing the child[1] (particularly if that parent is under a duty to return the child pursuant to a court order),[2] although it could occur, for example, by order of the court or by agreement of the parties.[3] If, on the other hand, only one parent has parental responsibility, then a change can be effected unilaterally.[4] For example, in *Re M (Minors) (Residence Order: Jurisdiction)*[5] an unmarried mother unilaterally changed her children's habitual residence when she moved them from the care of the grandparents. On the other hand, where the sole holder of parental responsibility dies, the child's habitual residence cannot change simply upon his removal from the jurisdiction by a person who has his care but not parental responsibility.[6]

In *Re S (A Minor) (Custody: Habitual Residence)*[7] it was held that a child, whose Irish unmarried mother (and the sole holder of parental responsibility) was habitually resident in England before her death, remained habitually resident in England notwithstanding his removal to Ireland by his maternal grandparents. So far as the English courts are concerned it is established that it is the residence immediately before the wrongful removal or retention that is relevant.[8]

Since it is a requirement to be habitually resident in a contracting state, it follows that the Convention is not retrospective in the sense that the wrongful act must have taken place after the contracting state has implemented the Convention.[9]

(b)   'Wrongful' removal or retention

Although, as we have said, it is not necessary for the applicant to have a court order in his favour, nevertheless to invoke the Hague Convention the applicant must show[10] that the removal or retention is 'wrongful' within the meaning of

---

1   *Re S (Minors) (Abduction: Wrongful Retention)* [1994] Fam 70, [1994] 1 All ER 237.
2   *Re R (Wardship: Child Abduction) (No 2)* [1993] 1 FLR 249, CA.
3   See eg *Re F (minors)* [1992] FCR 595 (agreement); *Re O (A Minor) (Child Abduction: Habitual Residence)* [1993] 2 FLR 594 (court order).
4   But note *Re B (A Minor) (Abduction)* [1994] 2 FLR 249, CA, in which a removal was held 'wrongful' for the purpose of the Hague Convention notwithstanding that the father had neither official custodial status nor a court order in his favour but was looking for the child at the time of abduction (discussed further below at p 493).
5   [1993] 1 FLR 495, CA.
6   *Re S (A Minor) (Custody: Habitual Residence)* [1997] 4 All ER 251, [1997] 3 WLR 597, HL, per Lord Slynn.
7   Supra.
8   *Re S (A Minor) (Abduction)* [1991] 2 FLR 1, CA. See also *Re F (A Minor) (Child Abduction)* [1992] 1 FLR 548, CA.
9   *Re H (Minors) (Abduction: Custody Rights), Re S (Minors) (Abduction: Custody Rights)* [1991] 2 AC 476, [1991] 3 All ER 430, HL. The Convention has similarly been held in Scotland not to have retrospective effect: *Kilgour v Kilgour* 1987 SLT 568. For this reason the implementation dates (for which see Clarke Hall and Morrison) are important.
10   Failure to discharge this burden is fatal to the application: see *Re M (A Minor) (Abduction)* [1996] 1 FLR 315, where experts disagreed on whether under Greek law an interim custody order vested exclusive rights to determine the child's place of residence. Accordingly, the application failed.

Art 3. For these purposes the act is 'wrongful' if it is in breach of rights of custody accorded to a person or institution or other body, either jointly or alone, by the law of the contracting state in which the child is habitually resident,[11] and if at the time of removal or retention those rights were actually exercised either jointly or alone, or would have been so exercised but for the removal or retention.

As Art 5(a) states, ' "rights of custody" includes rights relating to the care of the person of the child, and, in particular the right to determine the child's place of residence'. Such rights, as Art 3 says, may arise by 'operation of law or by reason of a judicial or administrative decision, or by reason of an agreement having legal effect under the law of that State'. These rights may be vested in an individual, institution or a body, including (see below) the court.

So far as English law is concerned, 'rights of custody' should be understood in the context of the Children Act 1989, ie to refer to parental responsibility. All those vested with parental responsibility have 'rights of custody' for the purpose of the Convention, whether that responsibility is vested automatically, as in the case of married parents and unmarried mothers, or, in the case of unmarried fathers, by virtue of a parental responsibility agreement or order, or by virtue of being a guardian or having a residence order in their favour, or in the case of local authorities, having a care order.[12] It is evident, however, as *Practice Note: Hague Convention: (Application for Return Orders by Unmarried Fathers)* points out,[13] that a key concept such as 'rights of custody' which determines the scope of the Convention is not dependent for its meaning on any single legal system but instead 'draws its meaning from the definition, structure and purposes of the Convention'. As Waite LJ put it in *Re B (A Minor) (Abduction)*:[14]

'... the Convention is to be construed broadly as an international agreement according to its general tenor and purpose, without attributing to any of its terms a specialist meaning which the word or words in question may have acquired under the domestic "law of England" and that "rights of custody" is a term which, when so construed, enlarges upon, and is not necessarily synonymous with the simple connotations of "custody" when that word is used alone ...'

In his view,[15] provided the aggrieved parent was, at the time of the wrongful removal or retention, exercising functions in the requesting state of a parental or custodial nature, he could be regarded as having 'rights of custody' without the benefit of any court order or official custodial status. *Re B* was relied upon by Cazalet J in *Re O (Abduction: Custody Rights)*[16] to hold that German grandparents who had been exclusively looking after the child in question for over 12 months before the mother took the child to England had 'rights of custody' for the purposes of Art 3.

However, as Hale J observed in *Re W; Re B (Child Abduction: Unmarried Father)*,[17] the recognition of these so-called 'inchoate rights' as being within

---

11 Though the question of whether a removal or retention is 'wrongful' has to be determined by the State to which the application is made: *Re F (Minor) (Abduction: Rights of Custody Abroad)* [1995] Fam 224, [1995] 3 All ER 641, CA.

12 Child Abduction and Custody Act 1985 Sch 3.

13 [1998] 1 FLR 491, in turn relying on the Conclusion of the second meeting at the Hague of the Special Commission to discuss the operation of the Convention, 1993.

14 [1994] 2 FLR 249, CA. See also *Re F (A Minor) (Abduction; Custody Rights Abroad)* [1995] Fam 224, [1995] 3 All ER 641, CA.

15 It should be noted that Peter Gibson LJ dissented on this point, while Staughton LJ appeared to hold that the applicant's 'right of custody' arose out of an agreement made with the mother.

16 [1997] 2 FLR 702.

17 [1998] 2 FLR 146 at 155. See also *Practice Note*, supra, at 492.

Arts 3 and 5 is hard to reconcile with the House of Lords' decision in *Re J (A Minor) (Abduction: Custody Rights)*,[18] in which, notwithstanding that the child in question was living with both the unmarried parents at the time of removal, it was held that the father (who under Western Australian Law had no formal rights) had no 'rights of custody'. A distinguishing factor of *Re B* and *Re O* was that, unlike *Re J*, the applicant was exercising responsibility either alone or with someone who did not have custodial rights. However, the Central Authority takes the view that on the basis of *Re J* 'de facto joint custody is not enough'.[19]

It has, however, been held[20] that an unmarried father who had been granted interim care and control in wardship proceedings after the child's removal (but while the child still remained habitually resident in the jurisdiction from where he was taken) did have 'rights of custody' notwithstanding that they were on an interim basis and that he shared them with the High Court.

On the other hand, as Hale J observed in *S v H (Abduction: Access Rights)*,[1] the Convention draws a distinction between 'rights of custody' and 'rights of access' and the court should be reluctant to allow the latter to metamorphose into the former. In that case an unmarried mother with sole custody of her son who came lawfully to England was held not to have acted in breach of the father's 'rights of custody', since he had no parental authority and the access order in his favour did not entitle him to prevent the mother taking the child out of the jurisdiction.

Normally, a wrongful removal or retention will be in breach of someone else's rights, but it has been accepted by the English courts that a removal or retention is 'wrongful' if it is in breach of custody rights vested in a court,[2] or of the defendant's own rights.[3]

While it is clearly 'wrongful' if the removal is contrary to an express court order,[4] it is also 'wrongful' if the removal is prohibited according to the general law of the jurisdiction from where the child was taken.[5] Similarly, it is 'wrongful' to retain a child beyond the time allowed by a court or beyond the period agreed by the parties. In *Re S (Minors) (Abduction: Wrongful Retention)*[6] it was held that retention of a child *before* the expiry of the agreed period was wrongful when the mother had announced her intention never to return the child. According to Wall J in *Re S*, a retention becomes wrongful from the time the parent abandons the

---

18 Supra.
19 *Practice Note*, supra, at 492.
20 *Re S (A Minor) (Custody: Habitual Residence)* [1997] 4 All ER 251, HL.
1   [1998] Fam 49, [1997] 3 WLR 1086.
2   Such as: (1) where the child is a ward of court (see *Re J (Minor: Abduction: Ward of Court)* [1989] Fam 85, [1989] 3 All ER 590, and *Re B-M (Wardship: Jurisdiction)* [1993] 1 FLR 979), since the court has control of every aspect of the child's life (see Chapter 16); (2) where it has already embarked upon the exercise of rights of custody by adjourning the matter, giving directions as to how the matter should be dealt with and by making an interim residence order (see the analysis by the *Practice Note*, supra at 493, relying on *B v B (Child Abduction: Custody Rights)* [1993] Fam 32, [1993] 2 All ER 144, CA). NB it is not enough that proceedings are merely pending: *Re B (Abduction: Rights of Custody)* [1997] 2 FLR 594, CA.
3   *Re H (A Minor) (Abduction)* [1990] 2 FLR 439 ('wrongful' for a parent with interim custody in her favour to remove the child from the jurisdiction).
4   *Re C (A Minor) (Abduction)* [1989] 1 FLR 403, CA.
5   *C v C (Minors) (Child Abduction)* [1992] 1 FLR 163.
6   [1994] Fam 70, [1994] 1 All ER 237, per Wall J. See also *H v H (Child Abduction: Stay of Domestic Proceedings)* [1994] 1 FLR 530 in which Thorpe J held that a similar position obtained from the unilateral abandonment of an agreement to be in England for an unspecified period.

intention to honour the agreement.[7]

The Central Authority takes the view[8] that disobedience to a chasing order (ie an order requiring a child's return) made after an otherwise lawful removal can only constitute a 'wrongful retention' for the purposes of the Convention provided the child is still habitually resident in England and Wales when the chasing order was made.

It has been held[9] that the return of a government diplomat and his family in compliance with a direct order of his employing government was 'an act of a governmental nature and therefore subject to state immunity from legal process'. Accordingly, such a removal could not be considered 'wrongful' for the purposes of the Hague Convention.

As Holman J pointed out in *Re C (Abduction Consent)*,[10] it can plausibly be said that a removal or retention cannot be 'wrongful' if done with the consent of the other party. In his view, however, such an argument cannot be made under the Hague Convention, since the issue of consent is specifically dealt with under Art 13(a) (discussed below) as providing an exception to the obligation to order the child's return. In *Re O (Abduction: Consent and Acquiescence)*[11] Bennett J disagreed with Holman J insofar as he was implying that the issue of consent must always be dealt with under Art 13(a). In his view, whether consent comes within Art 3 or Art 13(a) depends on the facts. As he put it:[12]

'If the "non-removing" parent asserts or effectively has to concede that on the face of it he gave his consent, but asserts that it is vitiated by deceit or threats or some other vitiating factor, which he must raise in order to establish that his consent was no true consent, then the matter falls to be dealt with under Art 3. If, on the other hand, the very fact of consent is in issue, as it was in *Re C*, then the matter comes within Art 13(a) and the burden falls upon the person who asserts consent to prove it.'

(c)   Removal or retention

The convention refers both to wrongful *removal* and wrongful *retention*. It has been held by the House of Lords in *Re H, Re S*[13] that these are separate and mutually exclusive events, both of which occur once and for all on a specific occasion. *Removal* occurs 'when a child, which has previously been in the state of its habitual residence, is taken away across the frontier of that state, whereas *retention* occurs where a child, which has previously been for a limited period of time outside the state of its habitual residence, is not returned on the expiry of such limited period'.[14]

Alternatively, a retention can subsequently become 'wrongful' if, following the removal, the court of the child's habitual residence makes a valid order giving interim care and control to the applicant and for the return of the child which is not

---

7 Contrast the view of Sir Michael Kerr in *Re AZ (A Minor) (Abduction: Acquiescence)* [1993] 1 FLR 682 at 689D who doubted whether an uncommunicated decision to abandon an agreement could constitute a wrongful retention.

8 *Practice Note*, supra.

9 *Re P (Diplomatic Immunity: Jurisdiction)* [1998] 1 FLR 1026.

10 [1996] 1 FLR 414 at 417.

11 [1997] 1 FLR 924.

12 Ibid at 940.

13 *Re H (Minors) (Abduction: Custody Rights), Re S (Minors) (Abduction: Custody Rights)* [1991] 2 AC 476, [1991] 3 All ER 230, HL.

14 Per Lord Brandon ibid at p 500 and 240 respectively.

obeyed.[15] In *Re B (Minors) (Abduction) (No 2)*[16] Waite J held that because the Convention should be construed purposively rather than semantically, proper effect could only be given to the term 'retention' if it was construed as being wide enough to comprise not only acts of physical restraint on the part of the retaining parent, but also judicial orders obtained on his initiative. However, as Wall J has pointed out in *Re S (Minors) (Abduction: Wrongful Retention)*,[17] it is only where such applications provide clear evidence of a party's intention to break the agreement that such acts can be considered wrongful. It would not, for example, be wrongful to seek court orders solely to protect the child's presence within the jurisdiction in accordance with the agreement.

Since 'wrongful removal' is not a continuing state of affairs, it follows that a subsequent removal after a temporary return of the child to the state of habitual residence constitutes a new 'wrongful removal' within the meaning of Art 3.[18] Accordingly, the time limits under the Convention[19] run from the date of the second removal.

In each case removal or retention refers to removal or retention out of the jurisdiction of the courts of the state of the child's habitual residence. Wrongful removal or retention within the borders of the state of the child's habitual residence falls outside the scope of the Convention.[20]

Who can invoke the convention

Article 8 provides that '*any* person, institution or other body claiming that a child has been removed or retained in breach of custody rights' (emphasis added) may apply for the child's return. Hence, although commonly applicants are individuals having 'rights of custody' or 'rights of access', it would seem that *any* person (including possibly the child himself, if old enough), institution or body (eg local authorities or courts) may seek assistance provided it can be shown that the child's removal or retention is 'wrongful' within the meaning of Art 3.

To assist an application for the recovery of a child taken out of England and Wales, an application can be made to the High Court for a declaration that the removal was 'wrongful'.[1] A declaration can properly be made at the request of any person appearing to the court to have an interest in the matter and notwithstanding the pendency of other proceedings in another contracting state determining the child's habitual residence,[2] provided, at any rate, that it would serve some useful purpose and not simply delay proceedings.[3]

Seeking a child's return

(a)   The general procedure

A person claiming that a child has been taken to or detained in another contracting state, and who wishes to secure the child's return, can seek assistance from the

---

15 *Re S (A Minor) (Custody: Habitual Residence)* [1997] 4 All ER 251, [1997] 3 WLR 597, HL.
16 [1993] 1 FLR 993, [1993] Fam Law 450. See also *Re AZ (A Minor) (Abduction: Acquiescence)* [1993] 1 FLR 682 at 689 per Sir Michael Kerr.
17 [1994] Fam 70, [1994] 1 All ER 237.
18 See *Re S (child abduction)* [1998] 1 FCR 17, per Wall J. Note that Wall J left open whether mere physical presence, however transient, can form the basis of a fresh wrongful removal under Art 3.
19 Viz 12 months under Art 12: see further below.
20 See *Re V (Abduction: Habitual Residence)* [1995] 2 FLR 992.
 1 Child Abduction and Custody Act 1985 s 8.
 2 *Re P (Abduction: Declaration)* [1995] 1 FLR 831, CA.
 3 *Re P (Diplomatic Immunity: Jurisdiction)* [1998] 1 FLR 1035, CA.

Central Authority of the child's habitual residence or from the authority of the state to which the child has been taken. Direct application may be made to the judicial or administrative authorities of a contracting state. Applicants would normally be best advised to apply via their own Central Authority.

Under Art 8 applications should contain:

(a) information concerning the identity of the applicant, of the child and of the person alleged to have removed or retained the child;
(b) where available, the date of birth of the child;
(c) the grounds on which the applicant's claim for return of the child is based;
(d) all available information relating to the whereabouts of the child and the identity of the person with whom the child is presumed to be.

An application may be supplemented inter alia by an authenticated copy of any relevant decision or agreement. In the case of wardship it is helpful to supply evidence of the court's permission to apply under the Convention.

Upon receiving the relevant documents the Central Authority will transmit the application to the appropriate Central authority (Art 9) in another contracting state which must then take steps to discover the child's whereabouts and seek the child's return. The authorities must act expeditiously. If no decision has been reached within six weeks of the commencement of proceedings, the requesting Central Authority or the applicant has the right to request a statement of the reasons for delay (Art 11). The Central Authority may refuse an application where it is manifest that the requirements of the Convention are not fulfilled or that the application is not well founded (Art 27).[4]

(b) The court's role

To facilitate the child's return, application may be made to a judicial or administrative authority of the requested state. However, if the issue goes to a court, that court is forbidden by Art 16 from investigating the merits of the rights to custody until it has been determined that the child is not to be returned under the Convention or unless the application has not been lodged within a reasonable time following receipt of the notice.[5] Equally, a decision to return the child is not to be taken to be a determination on the merits of any custody issue (Art 19). So far as England and Wales is concerned all Convention applications are dealt with by the High Court.[6]

By Art 12 the court is directed, if the application is brought within one year of the removal, to 'order the return of the child forthwith'. If more than a year has elapsed, the child should still be returned 'unless it is demonstrated that the child is now settled in its new environment'. Article 12, however, is subject to Art 13, which provides for exceptional circumstances (outlined below) in which a return may be refused. The burden of establishing these exceptions lies on the defendant.

---

4 In 1996 the English Child Abduction unit refused 3 per cent of applications: see Lowe and Perry 'International Child Abduction – the English Experience', op cit.
5 Effectively this freezes any prior applications, including, in England and Wales, any residence order or wardship applications: s 9 and s 27 of the Child Abduction and Custody Act 1985.
6 Child Abduction and Custody Act 1985 s 4; by contrast, in a number of other jurisdictions (eg Germany and USA) jurisdiction is vested in courts at the lowest level. For a critique of the German system, see Lowe and Perry 'The operation of the Hague and European Conventions on International Child Abduction between England and Germany Part II' [1998] International Family Law 52.

The normal expectation is that the court will order the child's return. Accordingly it is hard to establish an exception. It has been held, for example, to be no defence that legal representation may not be available in the state to which the child is to be returned nor that such an order would mean the separation of the child and her care-giving mother.[7] Even if an exception is established, the court still has a discretion to order a return under Art 18.[8] It is conceivable that a child's return might be successfully opposed on grounds *outside* the terms of Art 12 or Art 13, but the court is likely to be reluctant to undermine the spirit of the Convention.[9]

Although there is understandably voluminous case law on the application of the exceptions, it is to be emphasised that judicial refusals are comparatively unusual. Analysis of all the 1996 cases handled by the Child Abduction Unit[10] showed that only 5 per cent of incoming and 7 per cent of outgoing cases resulted in a judicial refusal to return.

If a return is ordered,[11] then any other custody order ceases to have effect, but if a return is refused then the court can hear any other application upon its merits.[12]

It remains now to consider the application of the exceptions under Art 12 and Art 13 as interpreted by the English courts.

The application of Article 12 where the commencement of proceedings is more than 12 months after the wrongful removal or retention

As we have seen, where the commencement of proceedings is more than 12 months after the wrongful removal or retention, Art 12 provides that a return should still be ordered 'unless it is demonstrated that the child is now settled in its new environment'. If the child returns to the state of habitual residence only to be removed again then, for the purposes of Art 12, time begins to run from the date of the second removal.[13]

In *Re N (Minors) (Abduction)*[14] Bracewell J held that 'now' refers to the date of the commencement of proceedings and not the date of the hearing; that 'settled' involves both a physical element in the sense of relating to or being established in a community and an emotional constituent denoting security; and that 'new environment' encompasses place, home, school, people, friends, activities and opportunities but not, per se, the relationship with the parent. With regard to the meaning of 'settled' Thorpe J said in *Re M (A Minor) (Abduction: Acquiescence)*[15] that 'any survey of the degree of settlement of the child must give weight to emotional and psychological, as well as to physical settlement'. On the facts he considered that a four-year-old who had been brought to this country 15 months previously was now settled in his new environment.

---

7 *Re K (Abduction: Psychological Harm)* [1995] 2 FLR 550, CA.
8 See post, p 505.
9 *In Re B (Minors) (Abduction)* [1993] 1 FLR 988, for example, the court rejected an application to have proceedings stayed or dismissed because of the applicant's active participation in the respondent's English family proceedings.
10 See Lowe and Perry 'International Child Abduction – the English Experience', op cit.
11 The practice of the English courts is to return the child to the state of his habitual residence and not to the person: *B v K (Child Abduction)* [1993] 1 FCR 382, per Johnson J and *Re A (A Minor) (Abduction)* [1988] 1 FLR 365 at 373 per Nourse J.
12 Child Abduction and Custody Act 1985 s 25 and Art 16. 'Custody orders' include s 8 orders under the Children Act 1989: Child Abduction and Custody Act 1985 Sch 3.
13 *Re S (child abduction)* [1998] 1 FCR 17, where Wall J left open whether mere physical presence, however transient, can form the basis of a fresh wrongful removal.
14 [1991] 1 FLR 413.
15 [1996] 1 FLR 315 at 321.

Failure to conduct Convention proceedings with proper diligence and speed may entitle the court to strike the application out.[16]

The application of Article 13(a)

Under Art 13(a) the authority may refuse to order the child's return if it is shown that the person, institution or other body having the care of the person of the child was not actually exercising the custody rights at the time of removal or retention, or has consented to or subsequently acquiesced in the removal or retention. In practice the two most common applications of Art 13(a) are in relation to consent and acquiescence.

As with all defences the burden of proof lies on the person seeking to invoke it. With regard to consent, as Waite LJ put it in *Re B (A Minor) (Abduction):*[17]

'... the only starting-point that can be stated with reasonable certainty is that the courts of the requested State are unlikely to regard as valid a consent that has been obtained through a calculated and deliberate fraud on the part of the absconding parent'.

According to Wall J in *Re W (Abduction: Procedure),*[18] to establish consent the evidence needs to be clear and compelling, which in his Lordship's view means that the evidence normally needs to be in writing or evidenced by documentary material. Accordingly, a parent must establish the defence 'on the face of the documentation' since, if he cannot do so, 'oral evidence is unlikely to affect the issue and will not be entertained'. However, in *Re C (Abduction: Consent)*[19] Holman J, while agreeing that the evidence needs to be clear and cogent, took issue with Wall J over the need for writing. As he pointed out 'Article 13 does not use the words "in writing", and parents do not necessarily expect to reduce their agreements and understandings about their children to writing, even at the time of marital breakdown'. In his view it is sufficient that the defence is clearly established. He also disagreed with Wall J that consent had to be 'positive' if that meant 'express'. In Holman J's view it is possible in an appropriate case to infer consent from conduct. In *Re K (Abduction: Consent)*[20] Hale J, preferring Holman J's views on both counts to those of Wall J, said that while it was obvious that consent must be real, positive and unequivocal, it did not necessarily have to be in writing. She further held that once given (and acted upon) it cannot subsequently be withdrawn by the parent who gave it subsequently thinking better of it.

The leading case on the meaning of 'acquiescence' under Art 13 is *Re H (Minors) (Abduction: Acquiescence),*[1] in which the House of Lords abandoned previous attempts to distinguish between active and passive acquiescence,[2]

---

16 See eg *Re G (Abduction: Striking Out Application)* [1995] 2 FLR 410, per Connell J. Alternatively, the court can exercise its discretion not to return the child provided, at any rate, an exception under Art 13 (see below) can first be established: *Re S*, supra.

17 [1994] 2 FLR 249, CA, at 261.

18 [1995] 1 FLR 878.

19 [1996] 1 FLR 414 at 418 and 419. For another example of consent see *Re K (Abduction: Consent Forum Conveniens)* [1995] 2 FLR 211, CA and *Re D (Abduction: Acquiescence)* [1998] 2 FLR 335, CA; cf *Re R (Minors) (Abduction)* [1994] 1 FLR 190.

20 [1997] 2 FLR 212. See also Hale J in *P v P (Abduction: Acquiescence)* [1998] 1 FLR 630 at 633, not commented upon on appeal (see [1998] Fam Law 512, CA).

1 [1998] AC 72, [1997] 2 All ER 225, HL. See Bailey Harris (1997) 113 LQR 529 and McClean 'International child abduction – some recent trends' (1997) 9 CFLQ 387 at 395–8.

2 First established in *Re A (Minors) (Abduction: Custody Rights)* [1992] Fam 106, sub nom *Re A (minors) (abduction: acquiescence)* [1992] 1 All ER 929, CA and inter alia in *Re AZ (A Minor) (Abduction: Acquiescence)* [1993] 1 FLR 682, CA and *Re S (Minors) (Abduction: Acquiescence)* [1994] 1 FLR 819.

holding that instead a common approach was to be applied in all cases. That approach was summarised by Lord Browne-Wilkinson to be as follows:[3]

> '(1) For the purposes of Article 13 of the convention, the question whether the wronged parent has "acquiesced" in the removal or retention of the child depends upon his actual state of mind. As Neill LJ said in *Re S (Abduction: Acquiescence)* [1994] 1 FLR 819 at 838: ". . . the court is primarily concerned, not with the question of the other parent's perception of the applicant's conduct, but with the question whether the applicant acquiesced in fact."
>
> (2) The subjective intention of the wronged parent is a question of fact for the trial judge to determine in all the circumstances of the case, the burden of proof being on the abducting parent.
>
> (3) The trial judge, in reaching his decision on that question of fact, will no doubt be inclined to attach more weight to the contemporaneous words and actions of the wronged parent than to the bare assertions in evidence of his intention. But that is a question of the weight to be attached to evidence and is not a question of law.
>
> (4) There is only one exception. Where the words or actions of the wronged parent clearly and unequivocally show and have led the other parent to believe that the wronged parent is not asserting or going to assert his right to the summary return of the child and are inconsistent with such return, justice requires that the wronged parent be held to have acquiesced.'

In other words, unless the defendant can prove to the court's satisfaction that the applicant clearly acquiesced, the defence can succeed only if it can be brought within the 'exceptional' category.

Although *Re H* undoubtedly simplifies the law, its precise impact on existing case law has still to be established. Save in the exceptional case referred to in point (4) above, the emphasis on the subjective intention of the wronged parent supports previous decisions that delay in making an application because of erroneous legal advice can properly be taken to negative a prima facie inference of acquiescence[4] and that acquiescence is unlikely to be established if the applicant neither knows of the act nor knows that it is wrongful.[5] Similarly, the fact that the applicant has applied for custody in the state of the child's habitual residence is still likely to be regarded as a strong indication that there has been no acquiescence,[6] though there is nothing necessarily inconsistent with acquiescing in a current state of affairs and applying for the child's care and control at a later date.[7] On the other hand, absence of court action does not necessarily indicate acquiescence,[8] though delay

---

3 Ibid at 90 and 237 respectively.

4 *Re S (Minors) (Abduction: Acquiescence)*, supra; cf *Re S (Abduction: Acquiescence)* [1998] 2 FLR 115, CA at 122, in which Butler-Sloss LJ said that, while knowledge of the facts and that the act of removal or retention is wrongful will normally be necessary, to expect the applicant necessarily to have knowledge of the rights which can be enforced under the Convention is to set too high a standard. In that case, seeking contact and not a summary return of the child after being given adequate and realistic advice, but not being fully informed of his rights under the Convention, was held to amount to acquiescence.

5 *Re A (Minors) (Abduction: Custody Rights)*, supra; cf *Re D (Abduction: Acquiescence)* [1998] 2 FLR 335, CA, where the father did know of the Convention.

6 *Re A (Minors) (Abduction)* [1991] 2 FLR 241, CA.

7 *Re AZ* above.

8 *Re F (A Minor) (Child Abduction)* [1992] 1 FLR 548, CA. See also *Re R (Minors) (Abduction)* [1994] 1 FLR 190 (delay inter alia because of legal advice to await the outcome of domestic proceedings in France and because of the subsequent 'deplorable' delay in the French Central Authority's communication with the English Central Authority) and *Re S (Minors) (Abduction: Acquiescence)* [1994] 1 FLR 819, CA (delay due to erroneous legal advice).

in taking any action can be so indicative.[9] In *Re H* itself, it was held that the father, who was an Orthodox Jew, had not acquiesced in the children's removal from Israel to England merely by obeying the instruction of his local Beth Din to ignore English proceedings brought by the mother.

Although it probably remains true that merely entering an appearance in the abductor's court application in the state to which the children have been removed is not in itself acquiescence,[10] if, as in *Re D (Abduction: Acquiescence)*,[11] it is found that the applicant genuinely agreed to the making of a residence order in favour of the mother and himself intended to return permanently (in this case to Wales) to be near the children, that will be enough to establish acquiescence.

Although in principle acquiescence can be evidenced by written statements, it is well established that they must be written in clear and unambiguous terms.[12] Extracting a single and ambiguous sentence from a four page letter, for example, will not be enough to establish acquiescence.[13] Furthermore, in Lord Browne-Wilkinson's view, the clear and unequivocal conduct that brings the case within the exception is not normally to be found in passing remarks or letters written by a parent who has recently suffered the trauma of the removal of his children.

Clearly, the most difficult part of *Re H* is that which relates to the 'exception'. According to Lord Browne-Wilkinson, one example is *Re AZ (A Minor) (Abduction: Acquiescence)*,[14] in which a mother, with the father's consent, took their child from Germany (where the father was stationed with the US Air Force) to England to stay with her family. Once there the mother decided not to return. She left her son with her sister and the father asked her to look after him until he could come to England a little later. However, before his arrival the aunt applied for a residence and prohibited steps order. The father was served with the papers after his arrival in England but he indicated that he would not contest the application. However, some three months later he told the family for the first time that he intended to take the boy back to Germany, though it was not for another six weeks that he finally initiated Convention proceedings. The Court of Appeal held that the father had 'acquiesced'. In Lord Browne-Wilkinson's view[15] *Re AZ* was what he expected to be a rare example of a case falling into the exceptional category where the wronged parent's conduct is so clear as not to require proof of his subjective intention, ie it was a case 'in which the wronged parent, knowing of his rights, has so conducted himself vis-à-vis the other parent and the children that he cannot be heard to go back on what he has done and seek to persuade the judge that all along he has secretly intended to claim the summary return of the children'. Other examples falling into this exceptional category mentioned by Lord Browne-Wilkinson were[16] the signing of a formal agreement that the child is to remain in the country to which he has been abducted and the active participation in proceedings in the country to which the child has been abducted to determine the child's long-term future. On the other hand, as the Court of Appeal held in

---

9 See eg *W v W (Child Abduction: Acquiesence)* [1993] 2 FLR 211 (father's inactivity for some 10 months after learning of his wife's decision not to return held to amount to acquiescence).
10 As in *Re B (Minors) (Acquiescence)* [1993] 1 FLR 988.
11 [1998] 2 FLR 335, CA.
12 See eg *Re A (Minors) (Abduction: Custody Rights)*, supra. Indeed, such clear statements can come within Lord Browne-Wilkinson's 'exceptional category'.
13 Per Millett LJ in *Re R (Child Abduction: Acquiescence)* [1995] 1 FLR 716 at 733.
14 [1997] 1 FLR 682.
15 [1998] AC 72 at 89F, [1997] 2 All ER 225 at 236g.
16 Ibid at 89D–E and 236e.

P v P (Abduction: Acquiescence),[17] merely seeking to compromise a situation by allowing the abducting parent to remain in the country to which he or she has gone, provided that the wronged parent is satisfied as to other matters in issue between them, will not, in the absence of any concluded agreement, be regarded as falling into the 'exceptional category'.

In this case, after the mother had left the father in Cyprus and taken the child to England, the father sought through his lawyer in Cyprus to negotiate a settlement under which the child would reside with his mother in England but have extensive staying contact with him in Cyprus. When these negotiations failed, the father issued Hague Convention proceedings. It was held that in the absence of a concluded agreement the father could not be said to have 'acquiesced' within the meaning of Lord Browne-Wilkinson's 'clear and unequivocal' conduct category. Indeed Ward LJ agreed with Hale J's observation at first instance that:

'. . . it would be most unfortunate if parents were deterred from seeking to make sensible arrangements, in consequence of what is usually an acknowledged breakdown in the relationship between them, for fear that the mere fact that they are able to contemplate that the child should remain where he has been taken will count against them in these proceedings. Such negotiations are, if anything, to be encouraged'.[18]

It is established that an acquiescence cannot subsequently be withdrawn.[19]

The application of Article 13(b)

Under Art 13(b) the authority may refuse to order the child's return if it is shown that there is a grave risk that his or her return would expose the child to physical or psychological harm or otherwise place the child in an intolerable situation. The burden of establishing one of these exceptions is difficult to discharge.[20] It has been held that the risk of physical or psychological harm must be more than an ordinary one, ie weighty, substantial and not trivial.[21] In *N v N (Abduction: Article 13 Defence)*[1] an allegation of sexual abuse by the applicant was not held sufficient to justify a refusal to return. In *Re K (Abduction: Psychological harm)*[2] a mother, who contended that as she had no immigration status she would be unable to support herself and would not therefore exercise any possession rights as defined by a Texan court, failed to convince the court that the child would be placed in an intolerable position if ordered to be returned to the USA.

Nevertheless, despite the difficulty of discharging the burden there are

---

17 [1998] Fam Law 512, CA.
18 Ibid.
19 *Re A (Minors) (Abduction: Custody Rights)* [1992] Fam 106, sub nom Re A (minors) (abduction: acquiescence) [1992] 1 All ER 929, CA, not commented upon on this point by the House of Lords in *Re H*, supra, and followed in *Re S (Abduction: Acquiescence)* [1998] 2 FLR 115, CA at 122 per Butler-Sloss LJ.
20 See *Re M (Abduction: Undertakings)* [1995] 1 FLR 1021, CA; *Re F (A Minor) (Abduction: Custody Rights Abroad)* [1995] Fam 224, [1995] 3 All ER 641, CA; and *Re O (Child Abduction: Undertakings)* [1994] 2 FLR 349, per Singer J.
21 *Re A (A Minor) (Abduction)* [1988] 1 FLR 365, CA; *Re A (A Minor) (Wrongful Removal of Child)* [1988] Fam Law 383; *Re E (A Minor) (Abduction)* [1989] 1 FLR 135, [1989] Fam Law 105, CA; *C v C (minor: abduction: rights of custody abroad)* [1989] 2 All ER 465, CA; and *Re L (Child Abduction) (Psychological Harm)* [1993] 2 FLR 401. See also *Re N (Minors) (Abduction)* [1991] 1 FLR 413; *Re NB (A Minor) (Abduction)* [1993] 1 FLR 854, CA; and *Re L (Child Abduction) (Psychological Harm)* above.
1 [1995] 1 FLR 107, per Thorpe J.
2 [1995] 2 FLR 550, CA.

examples of where the defence has succeeded. In *Re F (A Minor) (Abduction: Custody Rights Abroad)*[3] a return order was refused because, accepting the defendant's uncontroverted affidavit evidence, the applicant had been shown to be violent towards the child and had been engaged in a campaign of intimidation and harassment against the mother, which had adversely affected the child. In *B v K (Child Abduction)*,[4] having held that two older siblings should not be returned because of their objections (see further below), Johnson J ruled that a return order should also be refused in respect of a third child since, if he were returned and his two siblings were not, he would be exposed to psychological harm and placed in an intolerable position within the meaning of Art 13(b). In *Re G (Abduction: Psychological Harm)*[5] a return was refused on the basis that if the mother were to return with the children, as she would have done had the order been made, there was a grave risk that the children would have been exposed to psychological harm because their mother's mental health would seriously deteriorate. This seems an extreme decision and some caution needs to be exercised when applying it. It is to be noted that the court was satisfied that the mother was not someone who was seeking to manipulate the court in order to get her own way. Ewbank J also observed that, notwithstanding the children's habitual residence was in Texas, all the parties were English. The defence might also be established if it can be shown in relation to the law of the requesting state that there is some fixed embargo on allowing the removal of children or precluding the removal of children by a parent who had once wrongly removed them, or where the length of time that the requesting state might take to decide issues concerning the children is excessive.[6]

An additional reason for the difficulty of establishing a defence under Art 13(b) is the English court practice of accepting undertakings, since they can alleviate what might otherwise be regarded as an intolerable situation.[7] As Butler-Sloss LJ explained in the leading case, *Re M (Minors) (Abduction: Undertakings)*,[8] undertakings are accepted to make the return of children easier and to provide for their necessities such as a roof over their heads and adequate maintenance. They are intended, however, to have a short life, ie until the court of the child's habitual residence becomes seized of the proceedings. Accordingly, the court should be careful not in any way to usurp or be thought to usurp the functions of the court of habitual residence. Furthermore, undertakings must not be so elaborate that their implementation might become bogged down in protracted hearings and investigations.

The child's objections

Article 13 also permits a refusal to make a return order if the judicial or administrative authority 'finds that the child objects to being returned and has attained an age and degree of maturity at which it is appropriate to take account of

---

3 [1995] Fam 224, [1995] 3 All ER 641. This was the first time the Court of Appeal has refused a return on this ground. See also *Re M (minors) (abduction: psychological harm)* [1998] 2 FCR 488, CA.
4 [1993] 1 FCR 382. Note also *Ontario Court v M and M (abduction: Children's Objections)* [1997] 1 FLR 475 (child's fears that she would have to live with her grandmother and lose her father held to amount to placing her in an 'intolerable position').
5 [1995] 1 FLR 64, per Ewbank J.
6 Per Singer J in *Re O (Child Abduction: Undertakings)*, supra, though in that case the defence was not made out.
7 Per Singer J in *Re O (Child Abduction: Undertakings)*, supra. Note also *Re K (Abduction: Child's Objections)* [1995] 1 FLR 977 (court entitled to have regard to whether any risk of harm can be reduced or extinguished by undertakings). For the practice elsewhere on undertakings see McClean 'International child abduction– some recent trends' (1997) 9 CFLQ 387 at 392–5.
8 [1995] 1 FLR 1021, CA.

its views'. In practice this is the exception most frequently relied upon.[9] To bring the case within this exception requires the judge to make findings of fact both as to whether the child objects and whether the child has attained an age and degree of maturity at which it is appropriate to take account of the child's views. These findings are sometimes referred to as the 'gateway findings'.[10] According to the leading case, *Re S (Minors) (Abduction: Custody Rights)*,[11] this part of Art 13 is independent of the rest of it. Accordingly, there is no additional requirement to establish that there is a grave risk that a return order would expose the child to psychological harm etc. *Re S* also establishes that for these purposes the return to which the child objects is that which would otherwise be ordered under Art 12. The court is not required to consider whether the child objects to returning in any circumstances, eg to see the other parent on an access visit. On the other hand, it is now established by *Re M (A Minor) (Child Abduction)*[12] that under Art 13 the court is entitled to take into account the child's objection to returning to the person and not simply the country.

In *Re S* the Court of Appeal refused to lay down general guidance to be adopted in ascertaining the child's view and degree of maturity. Instead, each issue was thought to be a question of fact 'peculiarly within the province of the trial judge'. Nevertheless, the court must always be vigilant to guard against delaying tactics and, as Waite J held in *P v P (Minors) (Child Abduction)*,[13] the court is not bound to adjourn the case to inquire into the nature of the child's objection and degree of maturity, merely because the issue has been raised. It is therefore incumbent upon the defendant to provide sufficient evidence at the outset for the court to take cognisance of the child's objections, and it is then in the court's discretion to decide by what means and to what extent such views should be investigated.[14] Nevertheless, even at the 'gateway stage' it is permissible for a child to be questioned by a suitably skilled independent person (eg a welfare officer) with a view to discovering how far the child is capable of understanding, and does actually understand, the implications of objecting to being returned.[15] In exceptional cases the child can be made a party to the proceedings.[16]

There is no chronological threshold below which a child's view will not be taken into account, though in general the younger the child the less likely that he will have the maturity to make it appropriate to take his views into account.[17] Practice varies between contracting states. So far as England and Wales is concerned the objections of children as young as a girl aged eight and a boy aged seven have been held to justify a refusal to return,[18] and there have been two

---

9 See Lowe and Perry, op cit.
10 Per Waite LJ in *Re S (Minors) (Abduction: Acquiescence)* [1994] 1 FLR 819 at 826.
11 [1993] Fam 242, sub nom *Re S (a minor) (abduction)* [1993] 2 All ER 683, CA.
12 [1994] 1 FLR 390, CA.
13 [1992] 1 FLR 155.
14 *Re M (A Minor) (Child Abduction)*, supra.
15 Per Waite LJ in *Re S (Minors) (Abduction: Acquiesence)* [1994] 1 FLR 819 at 827.
16 See *Re M (A Minor) (Abduction: Child's Objections)* [1994] 2 FLR 126, CA and *Re HB (Abduction: Children's Objections)* [1998] 1 FLR 422, CA.
17 Per Balcombe LJ in *Re R (Child Abduction)* [1995] 1 FLR 717 at 730.
18 *B v K (Child Abduction)* [1993] 1 FCR 382. See also *Re M (minors) (abduction: psychological harm)*, supra – views of brothers aged nine and eight taken into account with some hesitancy. Compare *Re K (Abduction: Child's Objections)* [1995] 1 FLR 977 in which a child aged just under eight was held on the facts not to be of an age and maturity in which it was appropriate to take account of her views. In one German case the objections of a four-year-old were relied upon – see Lowe and Perry 'The Operation of the Hague and European Conventions on International Child Abduction between England and Germany, Part II' [1998] International Family Law 52 at 55.

reported cases where the objection of nine-year-olds have been relied upon.[19] Most convention countries, however, do not apparently generally consider the views of children under the age of 10.[20]

The residual discretion to return

Even where an exception is established under Art 12 or 13, the court still has a discretion under Art 18 to order the child's return. The leading case is *Re A (Minors) (Abduction Acquiescence) (No 2)*,[1] which establishes that, while the court is entitled to take the child's interests into account, it is not bound to treat those interests as the paramount consideration, but must instead balance them against the fundamental purpose of the Convention, namely to order the child's return.

In *H v H (Abduction: Acquiescence)*[2] Waite LJ suggested that the following factors should govern the exercise of the discretion:

'(a) the comparative suitability of the forum in the competing jurisdictions to determine the child's future in the substantive proceedings;
(b) the likely outcome (in whichever forum they be heard) of the substantive proceedings;
(c) the consequences of the acquiescence, with particular reference to the extent to which a child may have become settled in the requested state;
(d) the situation which would await the absconding parent and the child if compelled to return to the requesting jurisdiction;
(e) the anticipated emotional effect upon the child of an immediate return order (a factor which is to be treated as significant but not as paramount);
(f) the extent to which the purpose and underlying philosophy of the Hague Convention would be at risk of frustration if a return order were to be refused'.

In *H v H* it was held that the first instance judge had wrongly been swayed by his sympathy for the father, and had failed to consider important issues such as which was the more appropriate forum and what was the likely outcome of the substantive proceedings. The Court of Appeal refused to return the child. In *Re S (Child Abduction Delay)*[3] Wall J held that once an exception under Art 13 had been established it was proper to take into account, in deciding whether to return the child or not, the applicant's delay in pursuing his or her Convention remedy.

Securing rights of access[4]

Applications for organising or securing the effective exercise of rights of access can be presented to a Central Authority in the same way as an application for the child's return. For the purposes of English law a decision relating to access means

---

19 Namely, *Re S (a minor) (Abduction: Custody Rights)* [1993] Fam 242, sub nom *Re S (a minor) (abduction)* [1993] 2 All ER 683, CA; and *Ontario Court v M v M (Abduction: Child's Objections)* [1997] 1 FLR 475. Other cases include *Re S (Child Abduction: Delay)* [1998] 1 FLR 651 (10-year-old); *Re R (Abduction: Hague and European Conventions)* [1997] 1 FLR 663 (10-year-old); *Re HB (Children's Objections) (No 2)* [1998] 1 FLR 564 (12-year-old); and *Re R (A Minor) (Abduction)* [1992] 1 FLR 105 (14-year-old).
20 See Lowe and Perry, op cit, at 55.
1 [1993] Fam 1, [1993] 1 All ER 272, CA.
2 [1996] 2 FLR 570, CA at 574–5 (not overruled on this point by the House of Lords).
3 [1998] 1 FLR 651.
4 See generally Lowe 'Problems Relating to Access Disputes under the Hague Convention on International Child Abduction' (1994) 8 Int Jo of Law and the Family 374.

a decision as to the contact which a child may or may not have with any person.[5] Under Art 21 the Authority is required to promote the peaceful enjoyment of access rights and to take steps to remove, as far as possible, all obstacles to their exercise, including taking proceedings to organise or protect access.

According to the leading decision, *Re G (A Minor) (Enforcement of Access Abroad)*,[6] Art 21 continues to apply even where the child is habitually resident in England and Wales at the time of the application.[7] However, this case establishes the crucial point that whilst it may impose duties upon the Central Authority, unlike Art 12 which confers a right in public law which is directly enforceable in an English court, Art 21 imposes no duties whatever upon judicial authorities. Accordingly, applicants who are seeking contact rather than a return of the child should apply for a contact order under the Children Act 1989 s 8, which will be heard on the merits. In *Re T (Minors) (Hague Convention: Access)*[8] Bracewell J held that upon receiving an application under Art 21 the Central Authority's only duty is to make appropriate arrangements for providing English solicitors to act on the applicant's behalf to institute proceedings under the Children Act 1989. It is not incumbent upon the Central Authority to issue a summons under the Child Abduction and Custody Act 1985 but for the applicant to apply for an order under the Children Act 1989. Furthermore, the advantageous provision for automatic entitlement to legal aid does not apply to applications under the Children Act nor may a legal aid certificate issued under the Convention be extended to these proceedings. Since Convention proceedings are regarded as being exhausted upon presentation to court, no stay operates against the contact proceedings under the 1989 Act.[9] In view of these restrictions, as Hoffmann LJ pointed out in *Re G*, in appropriate cases applicants might be better advised to apply to enforce access under the European Convention.[10]

4.   THE EUROPEAN CONVENTION[11]

When the Convention applies

This Convention applies to the 'improper removal' of any person of any nationality who is under the age of 16 and who does not have the right to decide his own place of residence. Under Art 1(d), 'improper removal' means:

> 'the removal of a child across an international frontier in breach of a decision relating to his custody which has been given in a Contracting State and which is enforceable in such a State; 'improper removal' also includes:
> (i)   the failure to return a child across an international frontier at the end of a period of the exercise of the right of access to this child or at the end of any other temporary stay in a territory other than that where the custody is exercised;

---

5   Child Abduction and Custody Act 1985 s 27(4).
6   [1993] Fam 216, [1993] 3 All ER 657, CA. See also *Practice Note* [1993] 1 FLR 804.
7   It is sufficient for the application of Art 21 that the child is habitually resident in *a* contracting state before any breach of a right of access: Art 4.
8   [1993] 2 FLR 617. For a shorter report of this case see *Re T (minors) (international child abduction: access)* [1993] 3 All ER 127n.
9   See Bracewell J in *Re T* [1993] 2 FLR 617 at 621.
10   Discussed below at p 510.
11   See generally Jones 'Council of Europe Convention on Recognition and Enforcement of Decisions Relating to the Custody of Children' (1981) 30 ICLQ 467 and Clark Hall and Morrison on *Children* 2[74]ff.

(ii) a removal which is subsequently declared unlawful within the meaning of Article 12.'

It is therefore a prerequisite under this Convention that an applicant has an order in his favour, although under Art 12, if there is no enforceable decision at the time of the removal, an application may subsequently be made by any interested person for a declaration that the removal is 'improper'.[12]

This power has been widely interpreted by the English courts. For example, in *Re S (A Minor) (Custody: Habitual Residence)*[13] the House of Lords held that Art 12 and s 23(2) of the 1985 Act effectively empower courts to make orders which can *subsequently* make the child's continuing retention in another country an 'improper removal' within the meaning of Art 1(d). In that case it was held that an unmarried father, habitually resident in England at the time of his child's removal, had 'an interest in the matter' for the purposes of s 23(2) notwithstanding that he did not have parental responsibility, and that following the granting of interim care and control to the father, the retention thereafter became improper, so that the court was entitled to make the declaration that the removal was unlawful.

More questionably, in *Re S (Abduction) (European Convention)*,[14] following the child's removal to Denmark by the mother, the unmarried father (who had already instituted Children Act proceedings before the removal) obtained ex parte an interim residence order and then successfully sought a declaration. Hollis J held that in these circumstances he was entitled to make the declaration notwithstanding that when the abduction took place the father had no right to determine the child's place of residence.

Under Art 1(c) 'a decision relating to custody' means a decision of a judicial or administrative authority insofar as it relates to the care of the person of the child including the right to decide on the place of his residence, or to the right of access to him. It is clear that a residence or contact order under s 8 of the Children Act 1989 will satisfy this requirement.

Unlike the Hague Convention it has been held, at any rate in England, that the European Convention has retrospective effect.[15] Hence, orders made before a state implemented the Convention can be enforced in this country.

Recognition and enforcement

Under Art 7 decisions relating to custody made and enforceable in one contracting state are recognised and enforceable in every other contracting state. But to secure that recognition and enforcement, an application has to be made for those purposes in the other contracting state. Although this scheme applies equally to custody and to access orders, the latter raises a number of separate issue which will be discussed later.

Applying for the child's return

To secure the child's return, an application may be made through a Central Authority together with the appropriate documents.[16] Upon receiving the application

---

12 In England and Wales such a declaration can be made in any custody proceedings: Child Abduction and Custody Act 1985 s 23(2).
13 [1997] 4 All ER 251, HL.
14 [1996] 1 FLR 660.
15 *Re L (A Minor) (Child Abduction)* [1992] 2 FLR 178, per Booth J.
16 Art 4(2). The requisite documents are listed in Art 13.

the Central Authority in the state addressed must, without delay, take appropriate steps, inter alia, to secure the recognition and enforcement of the custody order.[17] Recognition and enforcement are achieved by registering the court order in a court of the contracting state to which the child has been taken. In England and Wales applications to register must be made in the High Court.[18] Once the order is registered the court has the same powers of enforcement as if it had made the original order,[19] and in this way the child's return can be ordered.

Although registration and enforcement normally go hand in hand, it was established by *Re H (A Minor) (Foreign Custody Order: Enforcement)*[20] that whilst registration is a sine qua non condition of enforcement, enforcement does not automatically follow recognition, since there is a discretion to apply the exceptions (under Arts 9 and 10, discussed below) to the issue of enforcement notwithstanding a previous registration.

Refusing recognition or enforcement

Where an application has been made promptly after an improper removal, recognition and enforcement of the order and restoration of the child must normally follow but there are exceptions, namely, those provided by Arts 9 and 10 and also, in the case of England and Wales, where an application under the Hague Convention is pending.[1] The burden of proving one of the exceptions lies on the person opposing the recognition or enforcement and the court is expected to recognise and register the order unless it *expressly* finds one of the exceptions proved.[2] In no event is the court entitled to review a foreign decision as to its substance.[3]

The precise latitude for refusal depends upon whether the contracting state has implemented Art 8. If it has, then, provided the application is made within six months of the child's removal, registration is virtually mandatory, since only the narrow exceptions under Art 9 may be raised. However, most contracting states, including the United Kingdom,[4] have not implemented that Article. In these states, registration may, in all cases, be refused within the terms of Art 9 or Art 10.

As just intimated, the exceptions provided by Art 9 are narrow and may best be thought of as comprising procedural defects in the making of the order sought to be enforced. Accordingly, under this Article registration or enforcement may be refused where:

(a) through no fault of the defendant, he or she was not served with notice of the relevant proceedings in the state of origin;

(b) the court of origin lacked competence to make the order in question since it was not founded on the habitual residence of any of the parties; or

---

17 Art 5.
18 Child Abduction and Custody Act 1985 s 16. For the procedure see FPR 1991, Part VI.
19 Ibid, s 18, and Art 7.
20 [1994] Fam 105, [1994] 1 All ER 812, CA.
 1 Child Abduction and Custody Act 1985 s 16(4)(c). If, however, the Hague application is refused, it is then possible to proceed with the European Convention application: see eg *Re R (Abduction: European and Hague Conventions)* [1997] 1 FLR 663, CA.
 2 *Re A (Foreign Access Order: Enforcement)* [1996] 1 FLR 561, CA.
 3 Art 9(3).
 4 The UK did not implement Art 8 because it was felt to be too draconian and contrary to the provisions of the Hague Convention: see Lord Hailsham LC in 460 HL Official Report (5th series) col 1253, 1985.

(c) there was already a prior decision in the state addressed which became enforceable before the improper removal.

The exceptions provided by Art 10 are considerably wider, particularly that under Art 10(b),[5] which permits refusal –

> '*where it is found that by reason of a change of circumstances, including the passage of time but not including a mere change in the residence of the child after an improper removal, the effects of the original decision are manifestly no longer in accordance with the welfare of the child.*'

Before making any decision under Art 10(b) the court is required by Art 15 to ascertain the child's views 'unless this is impracticable having regard in particular to his age and understanding'. It will be noted, however, that unlike the Hague Convention a refusal is not permitted because of the child's objections per se.

In line with the spirit of the Convention, Art 10(b) has been interpreted strictly by the English courts. It has been emphasised that for the exception to operate at all there must be a change of circumstances,[6] and that there is a heavy burden to discharge to show that the original order is 'manifestly no longer in accordance with the child's welfare'. It has been held,[7] for instance, that it is not enough to show that the child has settled well and is happy. Notwithstanding this heavy burden there have been cases where registration and enforcement have been refused. For example, in *F v F (Minors) (Custody: Custody Order)*[8] it was held that a foreign order for custody should not be enforced where the children had been in England for 21 months, and 12 months had elapsed between the enforcement hearing and the making of the foreign order. Similarly, in *Re R (Abduction: European and Hague Conventions)*[9] recognition and enforcement of a Swiss order in favour of grandparents were refused on the basis that the mother had since remarried and the emotional and financial support that her new spouse provided had transformed the situation, with the child in question now thriving and happy and emphatically not wishing to return to Switzerland. The Court of Appeal upheld Hale J's conclusion that the order was manifestly no longer in accordance with the child's welfare.

As under the Hague Convention, the domestic courts' powers to hear the merits of other custody proceedings are restricted during the pendency of an application for registration.[10] Upon registration all other custody orders cease to have effect,[11] but if registration is refused other applications can be heard on their merits.[12]

---

5 Art 10(a) refers to the effect of the decision being 'manifestly incompatible with the fundamental principles' of the law in the state addressed; Art 10(c) refers to children who are nationals or habitual residents in the state addressed and who have no such connection with the state of origin; and Art 10(d) refers to the incompatibility of the decision with a decision given in the state addressed or enforceable in that state after being given in a third state. For a refusal on this ground see *Re M (Child Abduction: European Convention)* [1994] 1 FLR 551 where enforcement proceedings began after an English court had made an interim residence order and it was not thought to be in the children's welfare to be returned pending the outcome of the English decision since they had lived in England for the last 18 months.
6 Per Leggatt LJ in *Re A (Foreign Access Order: Enforcement)*, supra at 564.
7 Per Booth J in *Re G (A Minor) (Abduction: Enforcement)* [1990] 2 FLR 325. See also *Re L (Child Abduction: European Conventions)* [1992] 2 FLR 178 and *Re K (A Minor) (Abduction)* [1990] 1 FLR 387.
8 [1989] Fam 1, [1988] 3 WLR 959.
9 [1997] 1 FLR 663, CA. Enforcement was also refused in *Re H (A Minor) (Foreign Custody Order)* [1994] Fam 105, [1994] 1 All ER 812, in which a 13-year-old girl, who had been in the UK for about five years, was adamant that she did not wish to have any further contact with her father.
10 Ibid, s 20(1). For the exceptions see s 20(2).
11 Ibid, s 25(1).
12 Ibid, s 20(1).

Applying for access

Under Art 11(1) decisions on rights of access are recognised and enforceable in the same way as decisions relating to custody. Article 11(2), however, empowers the competent authority addressed to 'fix the conditions for implementation and exercise of the right of access taking into account, in particular, undertakings given by the parties on this matter'. In the words of one leading commentator on the Convention: [13]

> 'The wording of Art 11(2) represents the outcome of extensive discussion in the Committee of Experts. It reflects the difficulty frequently encountered in practice in establishing how access is to be given where the parents fail to agree on times and places. The court or other competent authority in the State where the child is living will ordinarily be in the best position to decide such details in default of agreement, since it will have better facilities than the court in the State of origin to make the necessary enquiries and a greater knowledge of local circumstances (such as, for example, when school holidays begin and end).'

In effect, Art 11(2) enables the state addressed to modify decisions of other contracting states to make them consistent with local practice. Notwithstanding this ability to modify decisions, however, the power is still subject to the embargo under Art 9(3) against reviewing orders as to their substance.[14] This extra flexibility provided for by Art 11(2) makes these provisions superior to those of the Hague Convention. Moreover, applications under the European Convention have the distinct advantage of being treated as Convention applications for the purpose of legal aid. Hence, where applicants have a choice, they would be well advised to seek to invoke the European Convention rather than the Hague in seeking to enforce access decisions.[15]

5.   EVALUATING THE USE AND EFFECT OF THE CONVENTIONS

Although both Conventions have attracted growing numbers of Contracting States, it is evident that the Hague Convention has proved far more useful than the European. In practice the European Convention is little used. In part this is because the need for a custody or access order limits its scope, but it seems its restricted use also stems from its alleged complexity.[16] In contrast there is common agreement that the Hague Convention is generally working well. Certainly, in terms of speed and the number of returns the Hague Convention can be judged an outstanding success. In this respect England and Wales stands out as a model Convention country. Applications for return are generally completed within six-and-a-half weeks (compared with 11½ weeks in outgoing cases) and the

---

13 Jones (1981) 30 ICLQ 467 at 472.
14 See *Re A (Foreign Access Order: Enforcement)* [1996] 1 FLR 561, CA, in which it was held that giving a father staying access in England rather than in France, as provided by the original French order, fell foul of Art 9(3).
15 Empirical evidence suggests that the European Convention is more commonly used for access disputes than the Hague. Lowe and Perry 'International Child Abduction – the English Experience', supra, found that in 1996, whereas only six per cent of incoming Hague applications were for access, 25 per cent of European applications were. The figures for outgoing applications were 17 per cent and 42 per cent respectively, though in each case the actual numbers were small.
16 See Lowe and Perry 'International Child Abduction – the English Experience', op cit.

proportion of judicial refusals (5 per cent) is low.[17] Of course, some contracting states perform worse than others, but even here international pressure can be brought to bear on countries which are thought to be falling below the accepted Convention standards. In this regard the periodic reviews conducted by the Permanent Bureau at the Hague are enormously helpful and influential.

There are areas where even the Hague Convention is acknowledged not to be working well, in particular in relation to access.[18] In fact, although the access provisions of the European Convention are markedly better, they are not working well under that Convention either. It is understood that the Council of Europe is currently working on drafting an entirely new instrument governing access.

Another area of concern is the lack of financial support, particularly in the USA, given to applicants. Unlike the UK, for example, the USA has no system of legal aid and applicants may have to depend on attorneys taking a case free of charge. There is a certain amount of resentment that while under the Convention US citizens can take advantage of generous legal aid schemes abroad, there is no reciprocal facility offered to foreign applicants.

There has also been discussion[19] about the appropriate level of court to deal with Convention applicants. Many countries, again notably the USA but also Germany, Spain and others, allow local courts to deal with applications. This can result in lack of expertise and experience both in the judiciary and advisers. However, notwithstanding these arguments, at the Third Review of the Hague Convention, the vesting of jurisdiction in local courts was resolutely defended.

The acid test of success is whether the Conventions deter would-be abductors. This is much harder to assess. However, there does seem to have been a discernible trend away from abductions by the non-primary carer to the prime carer.[20] In their analysis of 1996 cases handled by the Child Abduction Unit, Lowe and Perry found[1] that 70 per cent of abductions were by mothers and commonly in all cases abductors were tending to be returning to their jurisdiction of nationality (ie 'going home'). In other words, the abductions were generally not aimed, as another study[2] termed it, at 'throwing off pursuers by escaping abroad', but instead abductors were 'returning to a culturally familiar country where family and legal support may be available'.

One theory about the changing pattern of abduction is that the Conventions deter would-be abductors in the popular sense of the word, ie men (or non-primary carers) 'kidnapping' their children. On the other hand, the deterrent effect of the Convention has not been so strong among women because, it is argued, their motivation is likely to be to escape violent or abusive relationships.[3] Whether this is so has yet to be definitely established but there is undoubted concern that there is no real mechanism under the Conventions for ensuring the child's safety after being returned, nor indeed for ensuring that any steps are subsequently taken. This in turn led to the suggestion at the third review of the Hague Convention[4] that

---

17 See Lowe and Perry, supra.
18 The issue was acknowledged and extensively discussed at the Second Special Commission Meeting of the Review of the Hague Convention held in 1993.
19 At the Third Special Commission Meeting on the Hague Convention held in 1997.
20 See McClean 'International child abduction – some recent trends' (1997) 9 CFLQ 387 at 388.
  1 Op cit.
  2 Greif and Hager *When Parents Kidnap* (1993).
  3 See the discussion by Lowe and Perry, op cit.
  4 By the Australian delegation.

Central Authorities ought to be obliged to take responsibility for children returned under the Convention. Although this suggestion drew substantial support, because of the extra commitment and costs involved, no formal action has yet been taken. In practice, however, there is considerable liaison both between the judiciary and the Central Authorities, and in cases of real concern it is possible to make informal arrangements.

One further challenge is in respect of Islamic countries which have so far not acceded to the Convention. The dilemma here is that while it is desirable to have as many nations as possible within the 'Convention fold', not all nations hold to the same basic values and, in particular, they may not treat all parents equally, having different concepts of what is in children's interests.

E.   Dealing with children taken to or brought from another part of the United Kingdom and Isle of Man

1.   INTRODUCTION

Before implementation of the Family Law Act 1986, orders made in another part of the United Kingdom were treated no differently from an order made in any other part of the world: they were neither recognised nor enforceable. Moreover, as different parts of the United Kingdom had different jurisdictional rules there could be, and were, cases where competing orders were made in respect of the same child. No case illustrates this better than the infamous example of *Babington v Babington*.[5] In that case the wife, a Scottish domiciliary, left the matrimonial home in Scotland to live in England. She made her 11-year-old daughter, who attended a boarding school in England but who hitherto had spent her holidays with the parents in Scotland, a ward of court.[6] The effect of wardship was to prevent the child going to Scotland without the court's consent.[7] Meanwhile the husband, also a Scottish domiciliary, petitioned the Scottish Court of Session for what was then custody and access. Taking the view that as the court of domicile it had pre-eminent jurisdiction, it granted access to the husband. The husband then applied to the English court for leave to take the child out of the jurisdiction. The wife opposed the application and sought leave herself to take the child to Switzerland for a holiday. Notwithstanding the Scottish order the English court refused the husband's application and granted the wife's instead. As the English and Scottish Law Commissions subsequently commented:[8]

> 'The English court disregarded the order of the Scottish court and the Scottish court disregarded the fact that the child was an English ward of court. The English court's order prevailed merely because it could be enforced, although the child had stronger connections with Scotland where she was domiciled, had her home, and normally spent her holidays.'

---

5   1955 SC 115.
6   Jurisdiction being taken on the basis of the child's presence in England and Wales.
7   The full effects of wardship are discussed in Chapter 16.
8   Law Com Working Paper No 68 and Scot Law Com Memorandum No 23, *Custody of Children – Jurisdiction and Enforcement within the United Kingdom* (1976) para 3.12.

Clearly, this state of affairs was unsatisfactory,[9] and after protracted discussions[10] between the English and Scottish Law Commissions, recommendations[11] were made upon which the Family Law Act 1986 is based. This Act, which applies to England and Wales, Scotland and Northern Ireland,[12] has since been extended to apply to the Isle of Man.[13]

2. THE FAMILY LAW ACT 1986

The 1986 Act essentially does two things. First it provides for common rules of jurisdiction throughout the United Kingdom and the Isle of Man. Secondly, it provides a system for the recognition and enforcement throughout the United Kingdom and Isle of Man of orders made in any one part of the kingdom or dependent territory.

Common jurisdictional rules

The aim of the1986 Act is to ensure that only one court in the United Kingdom or Isle of Man (hereinafter simply referred to as the UK) has jurisdiction to make a 'Part 1 order' over a child, except in emergencies. 'Part 1 orders' are defined by s 1(1)(a) and (d) to mean, so far as England and Wales is concerned, s 8 orders under the Children Act 1989 (excluding variations or discharges) and orders made under the High Court's inherent jurisdiction giving care of the child to any individual or providing for contact with or the education of the child, but excluding variations or discharges of such orders.

As we have discussed the basic rules in Chapter 12,[14] it suffices here simply to outline the basic scheme, which is:[15]

(1) to vest primary jurisdiction in the UK court in which divorce, nullity or separation proceedings are continuing;
(2) where there are no such proceedings continuing, primary jurisdiction vests in the UK court in which the child is habitually resident;
(3) where the child is not habitually resident in any part of the UK, jurisdiction vests in the UK court in which the child is physically present.

In cases of emergency, ie where the court considers that the exercise of its powers is necessary for the child's protection, jurisdiction can be based on the child's physical presence, regardless of the above-mentioned rules.[16] In England and Wales this emergency jurisdiction can only be exercised by the High Court.[17]

---

9 Although *Babington* caused deep resentment in Scotland, where it was dubbed 'legal kidnapping', the Scottish courts could be equally unco-operative: see eg *Hoy v Hoy* 1968 SLT 413 discussed in Lowe and White *Wards of Court* (1st edn, 1979) at 29.

10 It took nine years to produce the final report following the working paper.

11 Viz *Custody of Children: Jurisdiction and Enforcement within the United Kingdom*, Law Com No 138 and Scot Law Com No 91, 1985. For further discussion, see Lowe and White *Wards of Court* (2nd edn, 1986) paras 17.29 to 17.31.

12 See s 42 of the 1986 Act.

13 Family Law Act 1986 (Dependent Territories) Order 1991 (SI 1991/1773), Sch 3.

14 See ante, pp 443–5.

15 Family Law Act 1986 s 2, s 2A and s 3.

16 Section 2(3)(b).

17 Section 2(3) which confines the emergency power to the court that can make s 1(1)(d) orders, ie the High Court.

With regard to point (2) above reference also needs to be made to s 41, which provides that a child under the age of 16 who has been wrongfully removed or retained outside a part of the UK in which he has been habitually resident will be deemed to continue to be habitually resident in that part for one year after the removal.[18] 'Wrongfully' is defined by s 41(2) as being a removal to or a retention in another jurisdiction either without the consent of all persons having the right to determine where the child is to reside or in contravention of a court order.[19] By s 41(3) such deemed habitual residence ceases if the child becomes 16 or habitually resident in another part of the UK with the consent[20] of all those having the right to determine where the child is to reside and not in contravention of a court order.

Section 41 is clearly designed to prevent any jurisdictional advantage being gained by abducting a child from one part of the UK to another. However, while it has the merit of clearly setting out when the child will be deemed to be habitually resident in a part of the UK despite no longer being there, it has been questioned whether the period of one year is too long for those purposes.[1]

Recognition and enforcement

Under s 25 of the 1986 Act any Part I order[2] made by a court in any part of the UK and in force in respect of a child under the age of 16 is to be recognised in any other part of the UK. This means, for example, that a prohibition against the child's removal from any part of the UK will be effective throughout the UK.[3]

Recognition does not itself mean that the order will be enforced. Instead, application must be made to the court that made the original order for it to be registered in another part of the UK. Under s 27(1) any person on whom rights have been conferred by a Part 1 order may apply for that order to be registered in another part of the UK. Such applications must be made in the prescribed manner containing the prescribed information and be accompanied by the prescribed documents.[4] Upon receiving the application the court must, unless it appears that the order is no longer in force, forward to the appropriate court (that is the Supreme Court of the relevant jurisdiction, ie the English High Court, the Northern Ireland High Court, the Scottish Court of Session or the Manx High Court):

(a)   a certified copy of the order,
(b)   prescribed particulars of any amending order, and
(c)   a copy of the application and accompanying documents.[5]

---

18 Section 41(1). For a case where this was applied, see *D v D (Custody: Jurisdiction)* [1996] 1 FLR 574.
19 But such an order must still be in force: see *Re M (Minors) (Residence Order: Jurisdiction)* [1993] 1 FLR 495, CA.
20 But it seems that it must be proved that the consent is to the child becoming 'habitually' resident, ie it is not enough to show consent to a temporary removal: see *D v D (Custody: Jurisdiction)*, supra at 580.
 1 See Lowe and White *Wards of Court* (2nd edn) at 17–59.
 2 Except those in relation to a child in local authority care. The Act does, however, apply to orders made before its implementation provided, had the Act been in force, they could properly have been made: s 32(1) and (3). It might be noted that the courts can only enforce Part I orders and not, for example, injunctions: see *Re K (Wardship: Jurisdiction: Interim Order)* [1991] 2 FLR 104, CA.
 3 Section 36.
 4 Section 27(2) and see FPR 1991, Part VI (High Court and county court) and Magistrates' Courts (Family Law Act 1986) Rules 1988 (magistrates' courts).
 5 Section 27(3).

Upon receipt of the said copies, the appropriate officer must then cause the order to be registered.[6]

It will be noted that under this system there is no scrutiny as to why it is sought to register the order, ie there is no need to show that a removal is imminent. It can therefore be invoked as an insurance, for example, where the parties come from different jurisdictions and it is felt that the one might be tempted to return home.

Once the order is registered, the registering court has the same enforcement powers as it would have had, had it made the original order which is the subject of the application for enforcement.[7] Even so, an application to enforce the order is still required.[8] At the enforcement hearing, objections may be made by any interested party, for example upon the grounds that the original order was made without jurisdiction or because of changed circumstances, that the original order should be varied. The court has power either to enforce the order or to stay or to dismiss the application.[9]

Pending the outcome of the application the court may give such interim directions as it sees fit.[10] It has been held[11] that when considering an enforcement application the English court must not purport to act as a court of appeal from the court having jurisdiction in another part of the UK. Consequently, the judge should not question the correctness of the procedures and orders of the other UK court.

It will be noted that, as under the European Convention, a prior court order is an essential prerequisite for action under the 1986 Act, but unlike that Convention there is no administrative body to help with the application. Furthermore, the costs of enforcement fall upon the parties themselves, The enforcement system itself seems elaborate. Despite these criticisms the Act is nevertheless an important step forward in dealing with abduction within the United Kingdom.

---

6 Section 27(4).
7 Section 29(1).
8 Ibid.
9 Sections 30–31. The power to order a stay may be appropriate, for example, where the original order was made without jurisdiction: see Law Com 138 and Scot Law Com No 91 at para 5.33.
10 Section 29(2).
11 Per Stephen Brown P in *Re M (Minors) (Custody: Jurisdiction)* [1992] 2 FLR 382 at 386–7; cf in Scotland *Woodcock v Woodcock* 1990 SLT 848, where the Court of Session did seem to have regard to the merits: see the criticism by Edwards 'A Domestic Muddle: Custody Orders in the United Kingdom' (1992) 41 ICLQ 444.

d local authorities

A. Introduction

There is a variety of reasons why parents cannot or should not be allowed to look after their own children. They may be prevented from doing so by illness or the child may be beyond their control. Alternatively, a parent may be unwilling or unfit to bring up his own child: he may have abandoned the child, for example, or physically or sexually abused him, or he may have neglected him. The task of handling these difficult problems is entrusted to local authorities. For this purpose local authorities are non-metropolitan counties, metropolitan districts and London Boroughs,[1] and by the Local Authority Social Services Act of 1970 they are required to set up a single social services committee responsible for all the relevant services. The day-to-day running of the authority's social services is under the control of the Director of Social Services.[2]

1. THE DEVELOPMENT OF LOCAL AUTHORITY POWERS[3]

The powers and duties of local authorities to protect and care for children now derive from the Children Act 1989. In striking contrast to the previous law, which had developed piecemeal, the 1989 Act provides a comprehensive and unified scheme for dealing with children in need.

To put the 1989 Act in its context it is worth briefly adverting to the earlier law. That law was based on two Acts, namely the Child Care Act 1980 and the Children and Young Persons Act 1969. The former Act consolidated earlier Acts, principally the Children Act 1948 and parts of the Children and Young Persons Act 1963 and the Children Act 1975. The Children Act 1948 resulted from a report of the Curtis Committee,[4] which was set up to inquire into existing methods of providing for children deprived of a normal home life and to consider what steps should be taken to ensure that they were brought up under conditions best calculated to compensate for their lack of parental care. Reflecting the concerns of the Committee the 1948 Act imposed on a local authority a duty to receive a deprived child into care in certain circumstances and then to bring him up

---

1 Children Act 1989 s 105(1).
2 Local Authority Social Services Act 1970 s 6.
3 See generally Fox Harding *Perspectives in Child Care Policy* (1997) and Parton *Governing the Family: Child Care, Child Protection and the State* (1991).
4 Cmd 6922. For a full and fascinating discussion both of the circumstances before the setting up of the Committee and of the Report itself see Cretney 'The State as a Parent: The Children Act 1948 in Retrospect' (1998) 114 LQR 419 and for a shorter version see 'The Children Act 1948 – Lessons for today?' (1997) 9 CFLQ 359.

according to his best interests. Wherever possible the authority had to secure his discharge from care to parents, relatives or friends as soon as may be.

During the 1950s there was an increasing awareness of the need to prevent families breaking up and children being received into care. Social and economic factors were seen to be important in family difficulties. Juvenile delinquency began to be attributed in many instances to 'deprivation' rather than 'depravity'. It was thought that intensive preventative work with families could help to solve the problems of offenders and non-offenders.

The Ingleby Committee,[5] set up in 1956, investigated these matters and subsequently the Children and Young Persons Act 1963 was enacted, under which all local authorities had as their first duty to give advice, guidance and assistance to diminish the need to receive children into care.

Prevention and rehabilitation became the keynote of much of the subsequent work of local authorities, and it was expected that this would lead to an improvement in the prevention of delinquency.

These principles were further emphasised in the Children and Young Persons Act 1969. Both offenders and non-offenders were to be dealt with in the same system, and the provisions were designed to discourage either coming before the courts. For both, the powers of the court were directed towards treatment. In fact the objective of reducing the relevance of criminal law by raising the age of criminal responsibility was never implemented.

In the 1970s questions were again raised about the nature and efficiency of child care services. Difficulties were experienced as a result of changes in the structure of local authorities.[6] Children's departments, previously responsible for services to children and their families, were replaced by larger social services departments with responsibilities for the old, handicapped and mentally ill, as well as for children. The creation of a profession to manage all these inevitably lowered the level of child care expertise and raised the pressure of workloads. All this in a bureaucratic structure made it impossible in many instances for local authorities to provide the personalised services for children envisaged in the 1948 Act.

Lack of constructive long-term planning caused increasing concern. In spite of the apparent emphasis on returning children to their parents, it was considered that substantial numbers of children in care were unlikely ever to go back to their families and could not benefit from waiting in vain hope.[7]

There was a rising body of opinion that it was not necessarily in a child's interest to return to his natural parents. This was given philosophical expression in the book *Beyond the Best Interests of the Child*,[8] where the importance of 'psychological' parents was emphasised. The issue came into the public eye, however, in 1973 when Maria Colwell was killed by her stepfather after she had been removed from foster parents.[9] Inevitably, there was a demand for a curtailment of parental rights, so that children could be better protected from parental rejection, and plans could be made for their long-term welfare. However, there were contrary arguments, for example, that it was often bad social work practice rather than parental failure which led to children languishing in care.

5 Cmnd 1191.
6 Under the Local Authority Social Services Act 1970.
7 See Rowe and Lambert *Children Who Wait* (1973).
8 Goldstein, Freud and Solnit (1973).
9 See the Report of the Committee of Inquiry into the Care and Supervision provided in relation to Maria Colwell (1974) HMSO.

Strengthening the powers of local authorities and third parties might serve to reinforce bad practice and lack of planning, and encourage foster parents, for example, to sabotage a parent's efforts to recover a child.

The trend towards greater recognition of children as individuals could not be ignored. The resulting legislation, the Children Act 1975, accordingly required a local authority to give first consideration to the need to safeguard and promote the welfare of the child throughout his childhood.

Still different concerns were being voiced in the 1980s. Studies had raised awareness of the damage that local authority care (however well-meaning) could do to family links,[10] but this in turn 'encouraged local authorities to operate strong gate-keeping techniques to prevent children entering the system' with the result that care was denied to those who needed it. 'Social work thus became something which was done to clients rather than a way of helping families to help themselves'.[11] Yet another concern highlighted by the 'Cleveland crisis'[12] was whether local authorities had become too powerful at the expense of family autonomy.

The Children Act 1989 attempted to take on board the lessons and experience of the past and to draw anew the balance between family autonomy and local authority powers to protect children.[13]

2.   THE CURRENT LAW: SOME KEY UNDERLYING PRINCIPLES

Non-intervention

One of the great achievements of the Children Act 1989 has been to provide a single comprehensive code governing both private and public law. As we have seen in previous chapters, one of the underlying philosophies of the Act is that of non-intervention, and this basic standpoint is one of the key changes in the public law arena. As Lord Mackay said in his Joseph Jackson Memorial Lecture:[14]

'. . . the integrity and independence of the family is the basic building block of a free and democratic society and the need to defend it should be clearly perceivable in the law. Accordingly, unless there is evidence that a child is being or is likely to be positively harmed because of a failure in the family, the state, whether in the guise of a local authority or a court, should not interfere.'

This basic non-interventionist standpoint is emphasised by the fact that compulsory measures can only be taken following a court order and that no order may be made unless the basic threshold of 'significant harm' can be proved. Moreover, the presumption under s 1(5)[15] that no order should be made at all unless it is for the child's welfare applies equally to proceedings involving local authorities. Even where an order is thought justified, the court may still not make a care order if it thinks that an alternative s 8 order would be better.

10 See eg Millham, Bullock, Hosie and Haak *Lost in Care* (1986) and *Social Work Decisions in Child Care* (1985).
11 Cretney and Masson *Principles of Family Law* (6th edn, 1997) p 775.
12 Which was concerned with the scope of removal of children because of alleged sexual abuse: see ante, p 319.
13 For the genesis of the Act, see ante, p 318.
14 (1989) 139 NLJ 505 at 507.
15 Discussed in detail ante, pp 340–3.

Working in partnership

A second key principle, allied both to the non-intervention principle and to the enduring nature of parental responsibility, is that local authorities must work in partnership with the parents. There is a strong enjoinder on authorities to make voluntary agreements with parents for the benefit of their children. As the Department of Health's *Guidance* puts it:[16]

'One of the key principles of the Children Act is that responsible authorities should work in partnership with the parents of a child who is being looked after and also with the child himself, where he is of sufficient understanding, provided that this approach will not jeopardise his welfare. A second, closely related principle is that parents and children should participate actively in the decision-making process. Partnership will only be achieved if parents are advised about and given explanations of the local authority's powers and duties and of the actions the local authority may need to take, for example, exchanges of information between relevant agencies . . . This new approach reflects the fact that parents always retain their parental responsibility. A local authority may limit parents' exercise of that responsibility when a child is looked after by a local authority as a result of a court order, but only if it is necessary to do so to safeguard and promote the child's welfare . . .

The development of a successful working partnership between the responsible authorities and the parents and the child, where he is of sufficient understanding, should enable the placement to proceed positively so that the child's welfare is safeguarded and promoted.'

The encouragement to work in partnership should not, however, be misconstrued: it does not mean that compulsory measures to remove children from their families cannot be taken until voluntary efforts have failed. If the child's welfare demands it, compulsory measures should immediately be taken.[17]

Not unrelated to the partnership ideal is the vision that the services which, under Part III of the Act, local authorities are obliged to provide should be seen as a positive response to the needs of children and not as a mark of failure by the family or the professionals.

Maintenance of links between the child and his family

In cases where it is necessary for children to live away from home either as a result of voluntary agreement or compulsory intervention, stress is repeatedly placed on the importance of children maintaining links with their family. As *The Care of Children: Principles and Practice in Regulations and Guidance* puts it:[18]

'There are unique advantages for children in experiencing normal family life in their own birth family and every effort should be made to preserve the child's home and family links.'

To this end local authorities are under a general duty when safeguarding the welfare of children in need to promote the upbringing of children by their families[19] and, if they are looking after[20] the child, to endeavour to promote contact between the child and his parents.[1] Even when in care or subject to an

16 Vol 3, *Family Placements*, paras 2.10 and 2.11.
17 See *Children Act Report 1992*, para 2.21, discussed post, p 529.
18 (HMSO, 1989) p 8.
19 Children Act 1989 s 17(1)(b).
20 For the meaning of this see post, p 529.
1 Children Act 1989 Sch 2, para 15.

emergency protection order there is a presumption that the child will have reasonable contact with his family. Local authorities wishing to restrict this must obtain the prior sanction of the court.[2]

B. Local authority support for children and families[3]

Part III of the 1989 Act contains provisions relating to the services that a local authority must or may provide for children and their families. For the first time services for children in need and disabled children are brought together under one statute. The provisions are intended to enable authorities to support family life, although they may in certain circumstances charge for the service.

It is tempting for lawyers to overlook this part of the Act, especially as it does not deal with 'court-based' law. Nevertheless, it is not without relevance to the practising lawyer since the provision of such services, both in the sense of past support to a particular family and what future support might be given, are important factors in deciding whether or not to make a care order.

1.   GENERAL DUTY TO CHILDREN IN NEED

Under s 17(1) every local authority has a general[4] duty:

'(a) to safeguard and promote the welfare of children in their area who are in need; and
(b) so far as is consistent with that duty to promote the upbringing of such children by their families,
by providing a range and level of services appropriate to those needs.'

A child[5] is defined as being 'in need' if:[6]

'(a) he is unlikely to achieve or maintain, or to have the opportunity of achieving or maintaining a reasonable standard of health or development without the provision for him of services by a local authority under this Part;
(b) his health or development is likely to be significantly impaired or further impaired, without the provision for him of such services; or
(c) he is disabled.'

For these purposes 'health' means physical or mental health and 'development' means physical, intellectual, emotional, social or behavioural development.[7]

---

2 Ibid, s 34, discussed post, pp 581ff.
3 See generally Department of Health's *Guidance and Regulations*, Vol 2, *Family Support, Day Care and Educational Provision for Young Children*. Part III is based on recommendations of the *Review of Child Care Law* (DHSS, 1985) and the government's White Paper *The Law on Child Care and Family Services* (Cm 62, 1987).
4 The inclusion of the word 'general' is intended to reverse *A-G (ex rel Tilley) v London Borough of Wandsworth* [1981] 1 All ER 1162, which had held under the former law that the welfare duty applied to individual children.
5 A person under the age of 18: Children Act 1989 s 105(1). Under normal canons of interpretation 'child' means a 'live' child: see *Elliot v Joicey* [1935] AC 209, HL and *R v Newham London Borough Council, ex p Dada* [1996] QB 507, [1995] 2 All ER 522, CA.
6 Section 17(10).
7 Section 17(11). This is the same definition as in s 31(9) in care proceedings: see post, p 538.

It will be appreciated that this definition is wide. Furthermore, as the Department of Health's *Guidance* observes:[8]

'Sometimes the needs will be found to be intrinsic to the child, at other times however it may be that parenting skills and resources are depleted or under-developed and thus threaten the child's well-being.'

In discharging this general duty towards children in need, s 17(3) states that the services may be provided for the family of a particular child in need or for any member of his family, if they are provided with a view to safeguarding or promoting the child's welfare. For these purposes, 'family' includes any person who has parental responsibility for the child and any other person with whom he had been living.[9] It is thus not limited to relatives.

As has been said, a child 'in need' also includes a disabled child, who, for the purposes of the Act, is a child who is –

'blind, deaf or dumb or suffers from mental disorder of any kind or is substantially and permanently handicapped by illness, injury or congenital deformity or such other disability as may be prescribed'.[10]

As a child in need, a disabled child is able to benefit from the same services as other children. Accordingly local authorities are obliged to provide such children with services so as to minimise the effect of their disabilities and to give them the opportunity to lead lives that are as normal as possible.[11]

The services provided under Part III may include giving assistance in kind or in exceptional circumstances in cash, unconditionally or conditionally as to repayment.[12] Authorities are required to have regard to the means of the child and each of his parents, although no person is liable for repayment at any time when he is in receipt of income support, family credit or an income-based jobseeker's allowance.[13] An authority may also contribute to the cost of looking after a child who is living with a person under a residence order, such as a relative or foster parent, except where that person is a parent or step-parent.[14]

Authorities are required to facilitate the provision of Part III services by other, in particular, voluntary organisations, and may make such arrangements as they see fit for others to provide such services (eg day care or fostering services).[15] An authority or organisation must comply with such a request if it is compatible with their own statutory or other duties and obligations and does not unduly prejudice the discharge of any of their functions.[16] It is established that a housing authority is

---

8 Vol 2, para 2.5.
9 Section 17(10).
10 Section 17(11).
11 Sch 2, para 3. See also the Department of Health's *Guidance*, Vol 2 at para 2.18. Local authorities must keep a register of children with disabilities in their area: Sch 2 para 2.
12 Section 17(6), (7).
13 Section 17(8), (9) as amended by the Jobseekers Act 1995 Sch 2, para 19(2).
14 In their study *Residence Order Allowance Survey* (1996) the Grandparents' Federation found that the practice among local authorities with regard to residence order allowances varied enormously both as to whether the allowance was paid at all and, where it was, as to its duration. Whilst acknowledging that the provision of allowances is one of the most difficult parts of a residence order policy, the Department of Health has nevertheless recommended that all authorities should have a policy addressing inter alia when they should be considered, whether they should be capped, and how the rates and periods should be set: *Children Act 1989, Residence Orders Study* (Social Services Inspectorate, 1995) 6.2.
15 Section 17(5) and see further Department of Health's *Guidance and Regulations*, Vol 2, para 2.11.
16 Children Act 1989 s 27.

Duty to consider racial groups

In making any arrangements either for the provision of day care under s 18 or to encourage persons to act as local authority foster parents, the authority shall have regard to the different racial groups to which children in need in their area belong.[16]

3.　ACCOMMODATING CHILDREN IN NEED

A key service under Part III of the 1989 Act is accommodation, under which local authorities may arrange, *without court intervention*, for the child to live away from home either with foster parents, relatives or in a community, voluntary or registered children's home.[17]

Accommodation replaced what was formerly known as 'voluntary care' but, reflecting the change of philosophy under the Act, whereas voluntary care was perceived to be a mark of failure either on the part of the family or those professionals and others working to support them, accommodation is intended to be seen, in the words of the government's White Paper.[18]

'. . . as part of the range of services a local authority can offer to parents and families in need of help with the care of their children. Such a service should, in appropriate circumstances, be seen as a positive response to the needs of families.'

A typical example of where help might be needed is where the mother falls ill and the rest of the family cannot cope.

An essential characteristic of this service is that it should be voluntary, ie it should (save where the parents are dead or have abandoned the child) be based clearly on continuing parental agreement, and operate as far as possible on a basis of partnership and co-operation between the local authority and parents.

Consistent with this philosophy, the authority do not acquire parental responsibility while they are 'accommodating children',[19] nor are there any formal restrictions on parents with parental responsibility removing their children under the age of 16 out of accommodation.[20] Another important innovation of the 1989 Act is to require written accommodation agreements (discussed below)[1] between local authorities and the parents.

The duty and discretion to accommodate

Under s 20 local authorities have both an obligation and a discretion to provide accommodation. The obligation is imposed by s 20(1) whereby local authorities must provide accommodation where a child in need appears to require it as a result of:

'(a)　there being no person who has parental responsibility for him;
(b)　his being lost or abandoned; or

16　Sch 2, para 11.
17　Section 23(2).
18　*The Law on Child Care and Family Services* (Cm 62, 1987) para 21. The government rejected the recommendation of the *Review of Child Care Law* that there should be a dual system of 'shared care' and 'respite care'.
19　But see post, p 528 for liability for the criminal acts of a child whilst being accommodated by a local authority.
20　See s 20(8), discussed below at p 526 (aliter where the child is 16 or 17: see s 20(11), discussed below at p 526).
1　At p 527.

(c) the person who has been caring for him being prevented (whether or not permanently, and for whatever reason) from providing him with suitable accommodation or care.'

The words 'for whatever reason', in s 20(1)(c) make it clear that accommodation may be provided because of the disability of the child as well as the disability of the parent.[2] Although technically this duty is owed to children under the age of 18,[3] in relation to those aged 16 or 17 the duty to accommodate only arises where the local authority considers that their welfare 'is likely to be seriously prejudiced' if they do not provide them with accommodation.[4]

How these criteria should be interpreted is largely a matter for the local authority since, being the basis of voluntary agreement, they are unlikely to come before the courts.[5] Hence, although 'abandoned' has been interpreted under the adoption legislation as 'leaving the child to its fate',[6] it is unclear whether this is how it should be interpreted in this context. It is also a matter for judgment whether in some cases the child's welfare requires a care order rather than an agreement for accommodation.

Whether accommodation is best regarded as a short-term remedy or as an appropriate means of solving long term problems has been debated in relation to orphans and those children whose parents cannot be found.[7] In this context it now seems to be accepted that, although in theory local authorities can adequately look after such children without having parental responsibility,[8] it is nevertheless preferable, where possible,[9] for local authorities to obtain a care order, since the consequential acquisition of parental responsibility will avoid any possible difficulties or delays that might ensue in authorising decisions, for example, as to the child's medical treatment.[10]

In addition to the statutory obligation to provide accommodation, s 20 vests in local authorities a *discretion* to provide accommodation in two instances. First, under s 20(4) in the case of *any* child (ie not simply a child in need) within their area, even though a person who has parental responsibility for him is able to provide him with accommodation, a local authority may provide accommodation 'if they consider that to do so would safeguard or promote the child's welfare'. It is under this provision that so-called respite care may be given. Secondly, under s 20(5) a local authority may provide accommodation for any person aged 16–21 if they consider that to do so would safeguard or promote the child's welfare.

2 See Clarke Hall and Morrison on *Children*, para 1[381].
3 Formerly the duty applied to children under the age of 17.
4 Children Act 1989 s 20(3). As Cretney and Masson, op cit, at p 783–4 say, it is not clear why such a restrictive approach was thought necessary in a duty which is in any event limited to children in need.
5 Save in the context of an action for judicial review (discussed post, p 604) on the basis that a local authority was refusing a service they were bound to provide. See further below at pp 527–8.
6 *Watson v Nikolaisen* [1955] 2 QB 286, [1955] 2 All ER 427.
7 Such situations are not so uncommon: in the year ending 31 March 1996, for example, 430 children started to be 'looked after' because they had no parents and another 950 because they were abandoned or lost: *Children Looked After by Local Authorities* Dept of Health, Personal Social Services, Local Authority Statistics A/F 96/12, Table J.
8 Since under s 3(5) a local authority may do all that is reasonable to safeguard or promote the child's welfare, while a prohibited steps or specific issue order could solve any particular dispute.
9 See *Birmingham City Council v D, Birmingham City Council v M* [1994] 2 FLR 502, discussed further, post, p 547.
10 See *Re SH (Care: Order Orphan)* [1995] 1 FLR 746 at 749 per Hollis J, and *Re M (Care Order: Parental Responsibility)* [1996] 2 FLR 84, discussed further, post, p 548.

In all cases, before providing accommodation the authority must, as far as is reasonably practicable and consistent with the child's welfare, ascertain the child's wishes regarding the provision of accommodation and give due consideration to them, having regard to his age and understanding.[11]

Limits on providing accommodation

It is of the essence of the service that it is voluntary.[12] Hence the authority cannot provide accommodation if any person with parental responsibility for the child, who is willing and able to provide or arrange for accommodation,[13] objects to the authority so doing.[14] Furthermore, any person with parental responsibility may remove the child from accommodation at any time.[15] These powers of objection and removal do not apply:

(a) where a child of 16 or over agrees to being provided with accommodation;[16] or
(b) where the person agreeing has a residence order in his favour or has the care of the child by virtue of an order made under the High Court's inherent jurisdiction.[17]

The statutory right to remove a child from accommodation without notice was one of the more controversial provisions of the 1989 Act.[18] Formerly, there had been a requirement to give 28 days' written notice of an intended removal once the child had been looked after for six months or more. Such a period of notice was, it was argued, necessary to allow the child to prepare himself for his return home and to protect the child from any rash decision on the part of the parents.[19] The government's view, however, was that any period of notice 'would blur the distinction between compulsory and voluntary' care.[20] In their view nothing should undermine the voluntary nature of the service. In line with this philosophy it was held[1] by Ward J that in the absence of a court order the local authority was powerless to prevent a mother from removing her children from accommodation. In particular the authority could not rely either on its general duty under s 22(3) to safeguard and promote the child's welfare, nor on the power under s 3(5) to do what is reasonable to promote the child's welfare. Precisely what court order Ward J had in mind may

---

11 Children Act 1989 s 20(6).
12 Parental consent is not, however, necessarily required, since accommodation may be provided where the parents are dead or where they have abandoned the child.
13 These words were added at a later stage of the Bill to prevent a person simply objecting while having no intention of looking after the child. Masson and Morris *Children Act Manual* (1992) at p 62 suggest that the words 'able and willing' could be interpreted to invalidate the objection of a homeless or inadequately housed parent.
14 Children Act 1989 s 20(7). For an example of an objection, see *Re B (A Minor) (Care Order: Criteria)* [1993] 1 FLR 815.
15 Section 20(8).
16 Section 20(11).
17 Section 20(9). The inherent jurisdiction is discussed in Chapter 16.
18 See eg HC Deb, 18 May 1989, Standing Committee B, cols 137–54.
19 See ibid at col 142 per R Sims.
20 See ibid at col 149 per D Mellor. In practice, local authorities formerly not infrequently used the period of notice to decide to take compulsory measures to keep the child, the House of Lords having ruled in *Lewisham London Borough v Lewisham Juvenile Court Justice* [1980] AC 273, [1979] 2 All ER 297, that there was no compulsion to return a child immediately upon receiving the request.
1 *Nottinghamshire County Council v J* (26 November 1993, unreported), cited by Hershman and McFarlane *Children Law and Practice* at B[195].

be speculated upon, since it is clear that the court cannot make a specific issue or prohibited steps order requiring a local authority to provide accommodation against the wishes of a parent.[2] It may, however, be possible for one parent to obtain a prohibited steps order preventing the other from objecting. Similarly, it remains a moot point as to whether s 3(5) would justify foster parents handing over a child to an inebriated parent.[3]

Notwithstanding the clear recognition of the right of removal, there has been no reported evidence of any great difficulties in this regard. In practice the period of removal is one of the matters that should be covered in any accommodation agreement, though it is to be emphasised that an agreement can be of no more than persuasive effect. In particular it cannot in itself prevent the parent exercising the right of removal.[4]

Accommodation agreements[5]

It is central to the philosophy of the Act that an authority should seek to reach agreement with the parent or other person with parental responsibility on such matters as the purpose of accommodating the child, the period for which accommodation might be provided, schooling and contact with the child.

Provision for making agreements is governed by the Arrangements for Placement of Children Regulations 1991 which, as the Department of Health's *Guidance* explains:[6]

'... place a statutory duty on responsible authorities to draw up a plan in writing for a child whom they are proposing to look after or accommodate in consultation with the child, his parents and other important individuals and agencies in the child's life (regulation 3). Planning for the child should begin prior to placement. After placement, the plan should be scrutinised and adjusted (if necessary) at the first review four weeks after the date the child was first looked after and at subsequent reviews.'

Challenging a refusal to accommodate

It seems clear that a refusal to accommodate cannot be challenged by means of a specific issue order under s 8. In *Re J (Specific Issue Order: Leave to Apply)*[7] it was held that a specific issue order could not be used to challenge a local authority decision that a particular child was not 'in need', nor therefore to require the authority to provide appropriate support under Part III (which could of course include accommodation). In Wall J's view:[8]

'the question as to whether or not a child is in need does not raise a specific question which arises in connection with any aspect of parental responsibility for the child. A s 8

2 This would seem to be the result of s 9(5)(b); and see *Re S and D (Children) (Powers of the Court)* [1995] 2 FLR 456, CA at 462, per Balcombe LJ. But note *Re G (Minors) (Interim Care Order)* [1993] 2 FLR 839, CA at 843, in which a mother's undertaking not to withdraw her agreement to the continuing accommodation of her children was accepted by the court.
3 As argued by Clarke Hall and Morrison on *Children* at 1[394], but cf *Nottinghamshire County Council v J, supra*.
4 Though, as Clarke Hall and Morrison, op cit at para 1[395], point out, breach of an agreement might provide evidence for an application for an emergency protection order or a care order.
5 See generally Department of Health's *Guidance and Regulations*, Vol 3, *Family Placements*, paras 2.13 et seq, which is repeated in Vol 4, *Residential Care*, paras 2.13 et seq.
6 See generally Department of Health's *Guidance and Regulations*, Vol 3, paras 2.17–2.74 and Vol 4, paras 2.17–2.74.
7 [1995] 1 FLR 669.
8 Ibid at 673.

order is inapplicable to the exercise of a local authority's powers and duties under Part III of the Act.'

However, Wall J did consider that such a decision was amenable to judicial review.[9] Nevertheless, notwithstanding that in principle a failure to accommodate in breach of s 20(1) is actionable ultimately[10] through judicial review, such actions are in practice difficult to win, since much of s 20(1) is itself a matter of discretion.

In *R v Royal Borough of Kingston-upon-Thames, ex p T*[11] an action for judicial review failed, inter alia, because the local authority's offer of accommodation different from that sought by the mother and the child in question (ie a project home offering support and accommodation for Vietnamese families), was held not to be perverse or unreasonable (notwithstanding that the child's elder sister was already accommodated at the project) so as to be amenable to judicial review, but to be well within the parameters of reasonableness, particularly taking into account the cost of the sought-after placement. It might be similarly difficult to challenge a local authority decision that a particular child is not a child in need.[12] This is not to say that an action can never succeed. In *Re T (Accommodation by Local Authority)*,[13] for example, the court quashed the Director of Social Services' decision not to ratify the decision of a complaints panel that the 17-year-old child should be accommodated under s 20(3), on the basis that her welfare would otherwise be seriously prejudiced. In that case the Director was held to have erred when he decided that past provision of support given to her under s 17 made it unlikely that the child's future welfare would be seriously prejudiced if she were not provided with accommodation.

The effect of being accommodated

Accommodated children are not in local authority care nor does the authority thereby acquire parental responsibility. However, this is not to say that accommodation has no legal effect. As we shall see, accommodated children are among those who are 'looked after' by the local authority, upon which certain consequential duties are imposed.[14] Furthermore, it has been held in *McL v Security of State for Social Security*[15] that because an accommodated child was in the de facto care of the local authority the mother could not claim child benefit. Equally, however, the fact of accommodation cannot be ignored when determining liability under s 55 of the Children and Young Persons Act 1933 for a child's criminal act. Accordingly, where a child is in the de facto care of the local authority and the parent has no control over the child at the time, that parent cannot be said to be responsible for the child's actions.[16]

---

9 Ibid at 673–4. Judicial review is discussed more generally post at p 604.
10 Though prima facie the first step that should be taken is to use the local authority's complaints procedure under s 26 (see post, p 597): see *R v Royal Borough of Kingston-upon-Thames, ex p T* [1994] 1 FLR 798 and *R v Birmingham City Council, ex p A* [1997] 2 FLR 841.
11 Supra.
12 See *Re J (Specific Issue Order: Leave to Apply)*, supra, in which Wall J said that such a decision could in principle be subject to judicial review.
13 [1995] 1 FLR 159.
14 See below at p 529.
15 [1996] 2 FLR 748, giving a wide definition of the words 'in the care of the local authority' contained in Sch 9 to the Social Security Contributions and Benefits Act 1992.
16 *TA v DPP* [1997] 2 FLR 887, CA, per Sir Ian Glidewell. Local authorities may be liable under s 55(5) of the 1933 Act added by the Criminal Justice Act 1991 s 57(2).

Accommodation in practice

In practice the overwhelming proportion of children 'looked after' by local authorities are those accommodated by them. According to the Department of Health's statistics *Children Looked After by Local Authorities,*[17] of 31,900 children who began to be looked after during the year ending 31 March 1996, 24,700 (77 per cent) were accommodated under s 20. For the most part the period of accommodation is short, generally less than eight weeks.[18]

Soon after the implementation of the Children Act there was some concern that local authorities were taking the view that unless or until accommodation agreements had broken down there was no scope for taking compulsory care proceedings. To counteract this apparent belief the Department of Health published new guidance[19] stressing that local authorities should not feel inhibited from taking compulsory measures and where an authority 'determines that control of the child's circumstances is necessary to promote his welfare then compulsory intervention . . . will always be the appropriate remedy'. Since then the number of care orders has steadily increased.[20]

Another problem of accommodation is how the s 20 duty relates to the duties to homeless persons under the Housing Act 1985. In general s 20 was not intended to be used to look after children where their parents are homeless, since the principal duty to house homeless families, which the 1989 Act has done nothing to abrogate, lies with the housing authority. In *R v Northavon District Council, ex p Smith*[1] the House of Lords held that the nature and scope of the functions of the housing and social services departments were not intended to change as a result of the duty to co-operate imposed under the 1989 Act.

4. LOCAL AUTHORITY DUTIES TOWARDS CHILDREN 'LOOKED AFTER' BY THEM[2]

The 1989 Act places a number of duties on the local authority in respect of children 'looked after' by them. The phrase 'looked after' refers both to children who are provided with accommodation (which is defined as accommodation for a continuous period of more than 24 hours)[3] and to those who are in care as a result of a care order.[4] Children may also be looked after by or on behalf of a voluntary organisation.[5]

In relation to such a child, the authority have the duties to:

(a) safeguard and promote his welfare and to make such use of services available for children cared for by their own parents as appears to the authority reasonable in the case of a particular child;[6]

---

17 A/F 96/12, Table K. Note, however, that as a proportion of those being looked after as on 31 March 1996, only 40 per cent were accommodated.

18 See Hoggett, Pearl, Cooke and Bates *The Family, Law and Society* (4th edn, 1996), at p 572. In fact the duration of being looked after has generally declined: see *Children Looked After by Local Authorities,* supra at p 14.

19 *Children Act Report 1992*, para 2.21.

20 See the discussion in White, Carr and Lowe *Children Act in Practice* (2nd edn, 1995) paras 8.10ff.

1 [1994] 2 AC 402, [1994] 3 All ER 313, HL.

2 See generally Department of Health's *Guidance and Regulations*, Vol 3, paras 2.17–2.74 and Vol 4, paras 2.17–2.74.

3 Children Act 1989 s 22(2).

4 Section 22(1).

5 Section 22(2). For guidance see *Looking after children* (Dept of Health, 1995).

6 Section 22(3).

(b)   ascertain as far as practicable the wishes and feelings of the child, his parents, any other person who has parental responsibility and any other person the authority consider to be relevant, before making any decision with respect to a child they look after or propose to look after;[7]
(c)   give due consideration, having regard to his age and understanding, to such wishes and feelings of the child as the authority have been able to ascertain, to his religious persuasion, racial origin and cultural and linguistic background and to the wishes and feelings of any person as mentioned in (b) above;[8]
(d)   advise, assist and befriend him with a view to promoting his welfare when he ceases to be looked after by the authority.[9]

Underscoring the general duty to consider rehabilitation with the family, s 23(6) provides that, unless to do so would not be reasonably practicable or consistent with the child's welfare, the authority should make arrangements for the child to live with his family. In any event, under s 23(7) the local authority must, so far as is reasonably practicable and consistent with the child's welfare, secure that the accommodation is near his home and that siblings are accommodated together.

Where an authority are 'looking after' a child, they must provide him with accommodation while he is in their care and must maintain him. To this end they may place the child with a family, a relative of his or any other suitable person on such terms as to payment or otherwise as the authority determines.[10] Placement may also be made in a community home, a voluntary home or a registered children's home or by such other arrangements as seem appropriate to the authority.[11]

With regard to placements with the child's own family, a distinction needs to be made between accommodated children and those in care. In the former case, as there are no formal restrictions on removal, he may simply be returned home, in which case the child ceases to be accommodated.[12] In the latter, a child may only be placed with a parent, or other person who has parental responsibility for him, or a person who had a residence order in respect of the child immediately before the care order was made, if a number of requirements, including consultation with certain prescribed persons and supervision and medical examination of the child, have been satisfied.[13]

C.   Care and supervision proceedings

1.   INTRODUCTION

As we have seen, the Children Act 1989 places considerable importance on local authorities working in partnership with families and the avoidance wherever possible of court proceedings. The expectation is[14] that voluntary arrangements through the provision of services to the child and his family should always be fully

7 Section 22(4).
8 Section 22(5).
9 Section 24(1).
10 Section 23(2)(a).
11 Section 23(2)(b)–(d).
12 Outside this circumstance, however, it is by no means clear when accommodation ceases, in particular with regard to placements with relatives or friends.
13 As laid down by the Children Act 1989 s 23(5) and Sch 2, para 13 and the Placement of Children with Parents Etc Regulations 1991.
14 See the Department of Health's *Guidance and Regulations*, Vol 1, *Court Orders*, para 3.2.

explored (though this should not be taken to mean that they must always be entered into first)[15] before compulsory powers are sought from the courts. Nevertheless, voluntary arrangements will not solve all problems and, as under the previous law, the Children Act 1989 makes provision, in the form of care and supervision orders, for compulsory measures to be taken to safeguard and promote children's welfare. Even so, as the Department of Health's *Guidance* emphasises,[16] where a care or supervision order is thought to be the appropriate remedy because control of the child's circumstances is necessary to promote his welfare, 'applications in such proceedings should be part of a carefully planned process'.[17]

As under the former law, no child may be taken into care without a court order. There is only one route into care,[18] ie as a result of a care order being made under s 31. Unlike under the former law, courts cannot make care or supervision orders on their own motion. Instead such orders can only be made upon an application by a local authority or authorised person,[19] although once proceedings have been started they can only be withdrawn with leave of the court.[20]

2. INITIATING PROCEEDINGS

Applicants

Under s 31(1) of the Children Act 1989 only a local authority or authorised person may apply for a care or supervision order. An 'authorised person' is defined by s 31(9) as the National Society for the Prevention of Cruelty to Children (NSPCC) and any of its officers or any other person authorised by the Secretary of State, of which there are none as yet. Where an authorised person proposes to make an application, he must, if it is reasonably practicable to do so and before making the application, consult the authority where the child is ordinarily resident.[1]

The police and local education authorities cannot, as formerly, apply for care or supervision orders, though the latter may apply for an education supervision order.[2] Parents or guardians have no right to initiate proceedings themselves and the 1989 Act has no procedure equivalent to that under the former law[3] which enabled parents to force a local authority to take action in relation to a child beyond their control.[4]

---

15 See the *Children Act Report 1992*, para 2.21, discussed ante at p 529.
16 Ibid at para 3.2.
17 Furthermore, an application should proceed only after the child protection conference (discussed post, pp 532–3) has concluded, having taken legal advice, that no other course is open: see ibid, paras 3.10 and 3.12.
18 Under the former law there were at least 12 different routes into compulsory care: see eg the *Review of Child Care Law*, Discussion Paper No 3, and the 7th edition of this work at pp 440 et seq. Furthermore, local authorities can no longer look to wardship as an alternative means of obtaining care orders. For a discussion of how local authorities formerly used wardship, see pp 466–8 of the 7th edition of this work.
19 The NSPCC: see below.
20 Family Proceedings Rules (FPR) 1991 r 4.5, Family Proceedings Courts (Children Act 1989) Rules (FPCA) 1991 r 5.
1 Section 31(6). Note also the restrictions under s 31(7).
2 Under s 36, discussed ante, pp 354–5.
3 Viz under the Children and Young Persons Act 1963 s 3 (as amended).
4 As Masson and Morris *Children Act Manual* say (at p 97) 'A parent who is unable to control his child can only request assistance from the local authority and make a complaint under s 26(3)(b) [discussed post, pp 597ff] if it is refused.'

The responsibility for initiating proceedings

Although the NSPCC have an important role in child protection, it is the local authority who have the prime responsibility for initiating proceedings. They alone have a statutory duty (under s 47) both to investigate (either themselves or via another agency) all cases where they have reasonable cause to suspect that a child who lives or is found in their area is suffering or is likely to suffer significant harm, and to determine whether to bring proceedings. The local authority are also obliged to investigate the child's circumstances following a court direction made under s 37 in other family proceedings,[5] or upon being notified by a local education authority that a child has persistently failed to comply with a direction given in an education supervision order.[6]

In discharging this duty local authorities do not work alone. As the Department of Health's *Guidance* puts it:[7]

'The authority cannot expect to be sole repository of knowledge and wisdom about particular cases. Full inter-agency co-operation including sharing information and participating in decision-making is essential whenever a possible care or supervision case is identified.'

Facilitating inter-agency co-operation are two important bodies: at the planning and policy level, Area Child Protection Committees and, at the local level, Child Protection Conferences.[8] The principal tasks of the former[9] include advice on, and the review of, local practice and procedure for inter-agency co-operation including training. The task of the latter is to decide what action, if any, should be taken in individual cases.

Membership of both the Area Child Protection Committees and the Child Protection Conferences comprises representatives from the various professions and agencies concerned with children, in particular from the social services, the NSPCC, the police, education, the health authority, general medical practice, the health visiting service, the probation service and appropriate voluntary organisations. In the case of the Area Child Protection Committee membership is drawn from senior representatives of each of these agencies.

As *Working Together* emphasises:[10]

'The child protection conference is central to child protection procedures. It is not a forum for a formal decision that a person has abused a child. That is a matter for the courts. It brings together the family and the professionals concerned with child protection and provides them with the opportunity to exchange information and plan together. The conference symbolises the inter-agency nature of assessment, treatment and the management of child protection.'

There are two kinds of Child Protection Conference, the initial child protection conference and the child protection review. The purpose of the former, which should only be called after investigation has been made under s 47, is first to decide whether the child should be placed on the Child Protection Register,[11] and

---

5   See ante, p 455.
6   Children Act 1989 Sch 3, para 17.
7   Vol 1, para 3.10.
8   See generally *Working Together Under the Children Act 1989* (HMSO, 1991). Area Child Protection Committees were formerly known as Area Review Committees, and Child Protection Conferences as Case Conferences: see p 450 of the 7th edition of this work.
9   See *Working Together*, para 2.12.
10   Ibid, para 6.1.
11   For a discussion of Protection Registers see *Working Together*, paras 6.36 et seq.

secondly, to recommend a future plan for the child. If it is decided to place the child on the Register, the conference must appoint a named 'key worker' whose prime task is to fulfil the statutory obligations of his agency to protect the child and to co-ordinate inter-agency co-operation.[12] The child and his family will therefore be placed under close scrutiny, but the key worker must ensure that they are fully engaged in the child protection plan.[13]

The purpose of the child protection review is generally to review the child protection plan, examine the current level of risk and ensure that the child continues to be adequately protected. The review must also consider whether inter-agency co-ordination is functioning effectively. It must also consider whether the child's name should continue to be on the Register.[14]

Although there is no right for parents to attend the Child Protection Conference,[15] *Working Together* makes it that clear their exclusion can be justified only in exceptional circumstances and that if they are excluded other means of communicating their views to the Conference are to be found.[16] According to *Working Together*,[17] children who have sufficient understanding and are able to express their wishes and feelings and to participate in the process of investigation should also be encouraged to attend conferences.

The Child Protection Conference's dual function of promoting the dissemination of information about a child among various agencies and of co-ordinating the work of these services is crucial to the management of child protection. All too often in the past tragedies have resulted in cases where vital information about a child's circumstances has not been communicated to the local authority. With properly co-ordinated services there is a better chance of spotting warning signs of abuse or neglect and of constructive action being taken before crisis points have been reached. As against this, however, there is the danger of excessive investigation which in itself may be damaging to the child and family, and of having too many children under investigation. These at any rate were two of the concerns voiced in *Messages from Research*.[18] Other concerns were that too much focus was placed on specific incidents rather than on examination of the child's needs and that in cases where the test of 'significant harm'[19] is not thought to be satisfied there tends to be a failure to provide any Part III services, regardless of the child's needs.

After publication of this research, many authorities amended their policies to reduce the number and impact of investigations, though whether this has always been a carefully thought out strategy or simply a knee-jerk reaction to the research remains to be seen. The key message is that the proper discharge of the investigative duties under s 47 requires them to be in proportion to the circumstances. Clearly, the nature of that investigation must depend on the seriousness and possible cause of any harm, whether the child (and other children) is in a safe place, and on what is already known about the family. If the child has already

12 See *Working Together*, paras 6.4 et seq.
13 Ibid, para 6.7.
14 Ibid, para 6.9.
15 See *R v Harrow London Borough Council, ex p D* [1990] Fam 133, [1990] 3 All ER 12, CA. See generally Savas 'Parental participation in case conferences' (1996) 8 CFLQ 57.
16 Ibid, para 6.9.
17 Ibid, para 6.13.
18 *Child Protection Messages from Research* (Department of Health, 1995), which makes the point that of the 160,000 annual referrals to the child protection system, 40,000 (25 per cent) are closed only after limited investigation.
19 This concept is the linchpin of s 31: see post, pp 537ff.

suffered significant harm then there will need to be an investigation of some kind so as to establish cause. If the harm is serious enough to give rise to the possibility that a criminal offence has been committed, or its cause is not adequately explained, the case ought then to be referred to a Police Child Protection Team. In fact the current practice is for there to be what is known as a 'Strategy Discussion', which may comprise a telephone discussion or meeting involving different professionals, to determine what the appropriate response ought to be.

In respect of whom applications may be made

No care or supervision orders may be made with respect to a child who has reached the age of 17 (or 16 if he is married).[20] This means, unlike the former law, that in no circumstances can compulsory measures be taken in respect of such adolescents,[1] although, as we have seen,[2] such persons may themselves approach the authority with a view to being provided with accommodation.

Originally separate application had be made for each child,[3] but the Rules have now been changed to permit one application per family. Applications must be made on a prescribed form and a copy of the application must be served on all the parties.[4]

Parties

Unlike the former law, which despite late improvements was anomalous in that parents were not automatically parties in the proceedings,[5] the current law is straightforward. The child and any person with parental responsibility are all automatically parties in care proceedings.[6] It is open to any other person to apply to be joined as a party and within the court's powers to direct that they be joined.[7]

To which court applications should be made

Although each tier of court, ie the High Court, county court and magistrates' court, has original jurisdiction in respect of care proceedings, they have normally[8] to be commenced in the magistrates' family proceedings court.[9] Subsequently, however, proceedings may be transferred either to the county court or from these to the High Court. There is also power to transfer laterally, ie from one magistrates' or county court to another.

The powers of transfer are controlled by the Children (Allocation of Proceedings) Order 1991, the scheme of which is as follows.

---

20 Children Act 1989 s 31(3). Orders can still be made if the child is under 16 and validly married according to the laws of another country: cf *Alhaji Mohamed v Knott* [1969] 1 QB 1, [1968] 2 All ER 563.
1 See *Re SW (A Minor) (Wardship: Jurisdiction)* [1986] 1 FLR 24 where the High Court acting under its inherent jurisdiction committed a 17-year-old into care (which power is specifically abolished by s 100(2)(a)). For a criticism of this position see Lowe (1989) 139 NLJ 87, but cf Eekelaar and Dingwall (1989) 138 NLJ 217 and Bainham *Children: The New Law* (1990), at para 5.7.
2 Ante, p 525 n 4.
3 FPR 1991 r 4.4; FPCA 1991 r 4. Fees are charged on all applications to the magistrates' courts: Family Proceedings Fees Order 1991. The charge for a care or supervision application is £50.
4 Ibid.
5 Discussed at pp 459–60 of the 7th edition of this work.
6 FPR 1991 r 4.7(1); FPCA 1991 r 7(1).
7 For the procedure r 4.7(2), (3) and r 7(2), (3), respectively.
8 The exception is where a higher court makes a s 37 direction, discussed ante, p 455.
9 Children (Allocation of Proceedings) Order 1991 Art 3(1). NB there is no requirement, as formerly, that the child resides in the petty sessional area.

Upon receipt of the application, the magistrates' clerk has to consider whether the proceedings should be transferred to a higher court or to another magistrates' court. With regard to transferring proceedings from one magistrates' court to another the main criteria are accelerating the determination of the proceedings and to consolidate proceedings with other pending family proceedings,[10] but another justification for a lateral transfer can be the general convenience of the parties. So far relatively little use seems to have been made of the power to transfer cases laterally.[11]

Under Art 7 cases can be transferred to a county court either upon a party's application or upon the court's own motion. The three main criteria justifying a transfer are that:

(a) the proceedings are exceptionally grave, important or complex;
(b) it is appropriate for the proceedings to be heard together with other pending family proceedings; and
(c) it would significantly accelerate the determination of the proceedings.

The first of these criteria is spelt out in more detail and refers to:

(i) the complicated or conflicting evidence about the risks involved to the child's physical or moral well-being or about other matters relating to the welfare of the child;
(ii) the number of parties;
(iii) conflict with the law of another jurisdiction;
(iv) some novel or difficult point of law; or
(v) some question of general public interest.

Although no specific mention is made of the length of proceedings, it is clear that this is a material consideration. Interestingly, however, earlier judicial pronounce-ments[12] that hearings expected to last more than two or three days should be transferred upwards have since been revised, with the Children Act Advisory Committee expressing the view that magistrates are capable of hearing straight-forward cases lasting up to four or five days.[13] This is perhaps not unconnected with the experience of greater delays in the higher courts.[14]

Such transfers are not bound to be accepted. It is within the district judge's powers to transfer the case to the High Court,[15] or to transfer the case back to the magistrates.[16] If a transfer request is refused, under Art 9 any party may apply for a transfer before the nominated district judge at the appropriate county court care centre. If he agrees to the request the district judge can transfer the case to his court, to another care centre or to the High Court.[17] Little guidance is given on whether to transfer a case to the High Court: Art 9(3) merely states that the court must consider that the proceedings 'are appropriate for determination in the High Court' and that such a determination would be in the interests of the child. There is no appeal against

10 The Children (Allocation of Proceedings) Order 1991 Art 6.
11 See White, Carr and Lowe *Children Act in Practice* (2nd edn, 1995) para 4.20.
12 *Re H (A Minor) (Care Proceedings)* [1993] 1 FLR 440, per Thorpe J and *L v Berkshire County Council* [1992] 1 FCR 481, per Sir Stephen Brown P.
13 CAAC Report 1993/94, p 50.
14 See White, Carr and Lowe, supra at para 4.20. For the issue of delay generally see Booth *Avoiding Delay in Children Act Cases* (1996), referred to ante at p 338.
15 Under Art 12. The criteria for transfer are the same as under Art 9(3), discussed below.
16 Art 11 and see FPR 1991 (as amended) r 4.6(6). An appeal may be made to a circuit judge against such a decision: the Children (Allocation of Proceedings) (Appeals) Order 1991.
17 Art 9(2), (3) of the Allocation Rules and FPR 1991 r 4.6.

the district judge's decision to allocate the case to a county court or the High Court.

It will be noted that, as magistrates' clerks cannot allocate a case to the High Court, public law cases can only be heard at that level following a second allocation decision by the district judge.

Once an application has been made, it can only be withdrawn with leave of the court,[18] which means that the court is thereafter in final control of the ultimate disposal of the application.[19] This jurisdictional scheme was new to the Children Act. Before that, care proceedings could only be brought in the magistrates' courts, although in practice more difficult cases could be brought under the High Court's wardship jurisdiction.[20] Accordingly, it is only under the 1989 Act that county courts have had any jurisdiction in respect of care proceedings. To handle this new jurisdiction, as we have seen,[1] only certain county courts are designated as care centres[2] at which only designated family judges or nominated care judges have full jurisdiction to hear public law cases. Effectively what was created was a specialist family division of the county court.

The thinking behind these jurisdictional changes is to create a flexible system under which all care proceedings can be expeditiously dealt with at an appropriate level of court. It was envisaged[3] that the majority of cases (ie the so-called straightforward applications) would be resolved at the magistrates' level, with the minority (ie the longer and more complex or difficult cases) of between 15 and 20 per cent being disposed of by the higher levels of court. Generally speaking this expectation has been borne out by experience. In 1996, for example, the Children Act Advisory Committee[4] reported that between 22 and 26 per cent of public law cases were transferred to care centres.[5] The Allocation Rules themselves seem to cause little difficulty. At any rate there is little evidence of disputes or dissatisfaction with the level of court allocated, though research suggests[6] that local authority solicitors are more likely to endorse a transfer than guardians ad litem.

3.　THE THRESHOLD CRITERIA[7]

Some preliminary observations

No care or supervision order can be made unless the conditions set out by s 31(2) have been satisfied. These conditions have come to be known as the 'threshold

---

18　Ibid, r 4.5; FPCA 1991 r 5.
19　Accordingly, a care order can be made even though a local authority no longer wishes to pursue its application. For an example, see *Re M (A Minor) (Care Order: Threshold Conditions)* [1994] 2 AC 424, [1994] 3 All 298, HL, discussed post, pp 540ff.
20　Wardship is discussed in Chapter 16.
1　Ante, p 13.
2　The current list of Care Centres, as provided by the Children (Allocation of Proceedings) Order 1991 as amended, can be found eg in Clarke Hall and Morrison at 1[8564].
3　See CAAC Report 1992/93 p 46.
4　CAAC Final Report June 1997, p 76.
5　According to Table 1A of the Final Report, however, family proceedings courts seem to have heard 83 per cent of public cases, the county court 16 per cent, and the High Court one per cent.
6　Plotnikoff and Woolfson *Timetabling of Interim Care Orders Study* (Social Services Inspectorate, 1994).
7　See generally Department of Health's *Guidance and Regulations*, Vol 1, *Court Orders*, paras 3.15 et seq; Freeman 'Care After 1991'; Cretney 'Defining the Limits of State Intervention: The Child and the Courts', both in Freestone (ed) *Children and the Law* (1990) pp 130 et seq and pp 58 at 68–71 respectively. For a collection of multi-disciplinary papers see Adcock and White (eds) *Significant Harm* (2nd edn, 1998).

criteria' to emphasise the point that they are not in themselves grounds or reasons for making a care or supervision order, but rather the minimum preconditions for obtaining such orders. As Lord Mackay LC said in his Joseph Jackson Memorial Lecture:[8]

'Those conditions are the minimum circumstances which the government considers should always be found to exist before it can ever be justified for a court even to begin to contemplate whether the State should be enabled to intervene compulsorily in family life.'

Even if the criteria are satisfied, the court must still apply the welfare principle, including consideration as to whether making any order is better for the child than making no order and whether there are no suitable alternative orders under s 8.[9] If the criteria are not satisfied then in no circumstances can a care or supervision order be made. However, this does not necessarily mean that the child will be returned to his parents, since the court could still make a s 8 order.[10]

The criteria

Section 31(2) provides that a court may only make a care or supervision order if it is satisfied:[11]

'(a) the child concerned is suffering significant harm, or is likely to suffer significant harm; and
(b) the harm or likelihood of harm is attributable to –
    (i) the care given to the child, or likely to be given to him if the order were not made, not being what it would be reasonable to expect a parent to give to him; or
    (ii) the child's being beyond parental control.'

This wording reflects the recommendations of the Child Care Review.[12] The criteria comprise two separate limbs, each of which has to be satisfied. The first focuses on present or anticipated harm. The second is that the harm or likelihood of harm is attributable to the lack of reasonable parenting of the child or to the child's being beyond parental control. It should be added that in determining whether the threshold criteria are satisfied the child's welfare is *not* the court's paramount consideration.[13]

Soon after implementation, in *Newham London Borough v AG*,[14] Sir Stephen Brown P commented:

'I very much hope that in approaching cases under the Children Act 1989 the court will not be invited to perform in every case a strict legalistic analysis of s 31. Of course, the words of the statute must be considered, but I do not believe that Parliament intended them to be unduly restrictive when the evidence clearly indicates that a certain course should be taken in order to protect the child.'

8 (1989) 139 NLJ 505 at 506.
9 Discussed post, p 550.
10 See post, p 551.
11 Because the *court* must be satisfied that the criteria exist, it is not relieved of that duty because the parties agree: see *Re G (A Minor) (Care Proceedings)* [1995] Fam 16, [1994] 2 FLR 69.
12 *Review of Child Care Law* (DHSS, 1985), paras 15.12–15.27, though during its progress through Parliament a number of changes were made to the wording: see below.
13 See *Humberside County Council v B* [1993] 1 FLR 257.
14 [1993] 1 FLR 281, CA at 289.

One can readily sympathise with the notion that legalistic arguments should not be allowed to obscure the purpose of the provisions, namely to protect the welfare of children. Nevertheless, given that s 31 is the benchmark upon which state intervention into the family is or is not justified, it seems perfectly proper that its meaning should be fully tested in court. Not surprisingly, therefore, s 31 has generated a considerable volume of case law.

Applying the criteria

(a)   Harm

The central concept of the threshold criteria is 'harm'. It is defined by s 31(9) to mean 'ill-treatment or the impairment of health or development'. It seems clear that these are to be regarded as alternatives, so that satisfaction of either is sufficient.[15]

'Ill-treatment' is defined by s 31(9) as including 'sexual abuse and forms of ill-treatment which are not physical'. The inclusion of sexual abuse gives statutory recognition to the view that such abuse is by definition ill-treatment, though the Act neither defines the term nor indicates what comes within it.[16] Physical abuse is obviously ill-treatment (though even here there is a fine line between what may be regarded as reasonable corporal punishment by a parent and ill-treatment)[17] and the inclusion of other forms of abuse which are not physical is thought to include emotional abuse[18] and, possibly, failure to obtain medical treatment.[19] The last two instances could also amount to the 'impairment of health or development'. In *Re M (A Minor) (Care Order: Threshold Conditions)*[20] Bracewell J held that the child suffered ill-treatment by being permanently deprived of the love and care of his mother when she was murdered in his presence.[1]

Section 31(9) defines development as 'physical, intellectual, emotional, social or behavioural development' and health as 'physical or mental health'. This seems, as one commentary has said,[2] 'wide enough to cover any case of neglect – poor nutrition, low standards of hygiene, poor emotional care or . . . failure to seek treatment for an illness or condition'. It has been held that truancy (formerly a

---

15 As the Department of Health's *Guidance and Regulations*, Vol 1, *Court Orders*, points out at para 3.19, this means that the child who is injured but who has made a complete recovery could be demonstrated to have suffered 'harm' for the purposes of the proceedings.

16 Whether or not certain behaviour amounts to 'sexual abuse' can sometimes be problematic: cf, for example, *Re W (Minors) (residence order)* [1998] 1 FCR 75, CA which involved an uninhibited attitude towards nudity (which in itself was not thought to be abusive) and *C v C (Child Abuse: Evidence)* [1988] 1 FLR 462, where the father was said to have indulged in 'vulgar and inappropriate horseplay' with his 14-year-old daughter by 'French kissing' her. On this whole issue see the discussion by Freeman, op cit, pp 140–2.

17 See Freeman, op cit, pp 142–6; cf the Scottish Law Commission's proposals to make all corporal punishment an offence: Scot Law Com No 135, Report on *Family Law* (1992).

18 See eg Clarke Hall and Morrison, op cit, para 1[622] and Freeman, op cit, p 140, both referring to *F v Suffolk County Council* (1981) 2 FLR 208 under the former law. Lord Mackay adverted to 'verbal abuse or unfairness' being encompassed by the definition: 503 HL Official Report col 342.

19 See Freeman, op cit, p 141.

20 See [1994] Fam 95 at 103–4, [1994] 1 All ER 424 at 431. This decision was upheld by the House of Lords [1994] 2 AC 424, [1994] 3 All ER 298, discussed below.

1 But note the criticism by Whybrow at [1994] Jo of Child Law 88 at 89 who points out that the ill-treatment was of the mother rather than the child.

2 Masson and Morris, op cit, p 99.

specific ground for a care order) can cause a child 'harm' by the consequential impairment of intellectual or social development.[3] 'Harm' would also seem wide enough to embrace 'moral danger', which was formerly a specific ground for making a care order.[4]

(b) Is the harm 'significant'?[5]

Whatever the nature of the harm, the court has to consider whether the harm caused is 'significant'. Vital though this is to the application of the section, it is not defined in the Act. A dictionary definition is that it should be 'considerable, noteworthy or important' and, reflecting the common-sense view, the Department of Health's *Guidance and Regulations* comments:[6]

'Minor shortcomings in health or minor deficits in physical, psychological or social development should not require compulsory intervention unless cumulatively they are having, or are likely to have, serious and lasting effects upon the child.'

Whether 'harm' is 'significant' is an issue of fact to be decided in each case, but it must be remembered that it is the harm that must be significant, not the incident that caused it. So, for example, while a broken leg is a serious injury, the implications of a small cigarette burn might be more significant.[7] Similarly, behaviour such as shaking that might be innocuous to an older child might be very significant for a baby. In *Re O (a minor) (care order: education: procedure)*[8] Ewbank J seemed to take the view that lack of suitable education leading to the impairment of the child's intellectual development was of itself 'significant harm'.

(c) Comparison with 'similar child'

Where the harm is due to ill-treatment, no further guidance is given, but in the case of impairment of health or development, reference must be made to s 31(10), which provides:

'Where the question of whether harm suffered by a child is significant turns on the child's health or development, his health or development shall be compared with that which could reasonably be expected of a similar child.'

Precisely what is meant by a 'similar child' in this context is hard to say: for example, is a deaf child of deaf parents a 'similar child' to a deaf child of hearing parents?[9] There is also the further question of how far one should have regard to the child's background and whether the courts should apply different standards

---

3   *Re O (a minor) (care order: education: procedure)* [1992] 4 All ER 905 per Ewbank J. See also *Re V (Care or Supervision Order)* [1996] 1 FLR 776, CA – a mother's resistance to allowing her 17-year-old son, who suffered from cerebral palsy, to attend a special school by keeping him at home instead was held likely to cause the boy 'significant harm'. Though in most cases an education supervision order under s 36 is more likely to be sought.

4   See eg Freeman op cit, pp 154–5 and 161, who, referring to a pre-Children Act decision, *Alhaji Mohamed v Knott* [1969] 1 QB 1, [1968] 2 All ER 563, involving a 13-year-old Nigerian child who was validly married under her country's law, thought that the child would now be considered to be suffering or likely to suffer significant harm by having intercourse with her husband, a man twice her age and who had venereal disease.

5   See generally Adcock and White (eds) *Significant Harm*, op cit.

6   Vol 1, *Court Orders*, para 3.2.

7   White, Carr and Lowe, op cit, at 8.20.

8   Supra.

9   This is one of a number of examples that Freeman uses (op cit, pp 147–9) to highlight the difficulties of this test.

to children from different ethnic backgrounds.[10] The Department of Health's *Guidance* comments:[11]

> 'The meaning of "similar" in this context will require judicial interpretation, but may need to take account of environmental, social and cultural characteristics of the child. The need to use a standard appropriate for the child arises because some children have characteristics or handicaps which mean that they cannot be expected to be as healthy or well-developed as others. Equally if the child needs special care or attention (because, for example, he is unusually difficult to control) then this is to be expected for him. The standard should only be that which it is reasonable to expect for the particular child, rather than the best that could possibly be achieved; applying a "best" standard could open up the risk that a child might be removed from home simply because some other arrangement could cater better for his needs than care by his parents.'

In *Re O (a minor) (care order: education: procedure)*[12] Ewbank J held that in the case of a 15-year-old truant of average intelligence:

> '... "similar child" meant a child of equivalent intellectual and social development, who has gone to school and not merely an average child who may or may not be at school.'

In other words, his Lordship was not prepared to compare the child with someone who was not properly attending school.

(d)   Is the child suffering significant harm?

The original Bill contained the words 'has suffered' rather than 'is suffering' but was changed to prevent an order being made 'on the basis of significant harm suffered several years previously and which is not likely to be repeated'.[13] Thus past harm is not in itself sufficient to satisfy the criteria, though it might be relevant to establishing future likelihood of harm. On the other hand, while the present tense implies an existing condition, it is now clear that that does not necessarily mean that the condition should exist *at the date of the hearing*. The leading decision is *Re M (A Minor) (Care Order: Threshold Conditions)*.[14] In that case, after the father had murdered the mother in the children's presence, a four-month-old baby together with his half-siblings were accommodated by the local authority. Subsequently, the siblings went to live with a cousin of the mother, but she felt unable to look after the baby as well and he was accordingly fostered. Whilst in his foster placement the boy thrived and had regular contact with the mother's cousin and his siblings. However, because he could not remain with his foster mother indefinitely, seven months later the local authority brought care proceedings. By that time the cousin had changed her mind and sought a residence order in respect of the boy. The care proceedings were heard some 16 months after the murder, at a time when the father had received a life sentence. By this time the local authority supported the cousin and were no longer actively seeking a care order. However, both the father and the guardian ad litem[15] supported the making

---

10 For cases that have raised this issue under the old law see eg *Alhaji Mohamed v Knott*, supra and *Re H (Minors) (Wardship: Cultural Background)* [1987] 2 FLR 12.

11 Vol 1, para 3.20. Note that during the debates on the Bill (see 503, HL Official Report, col 354) Lord Mackay LC suggested that comparisons should be confined to physical (and presumably intellectual) attributes rather than background.

12 Supra. For valuable comments on *Re O* see Fortin 'Significant harm revisited' (1993) 5 Jo of Child Law 151.

13 Per David Mellor MP, HC Official Report, Standing Committee B 23 May 1989, col 221.

14 [1994] 2 AC 424, [1994] 3 All ER 298, HL.

15 Guardians ad litem are discussed post at p 552.

of a care order with a view to the boy being adopted outside the birth family.

At first instance Bracewell J held that the threshold criteria were satisfied, on the basis that the child had suffered ill-treatment by being deprived of the love and care of his mother, and that this was attributable to the care given by the father in that he had deprived the child of a loving mother. In her view the relevant date for determining 'is suffering' was 'the period immediately before the process of protecting the child is first put into motion'. The Court of Appeal disagreed, holding that the threshold criteria had to be satisfied at the date of the hearing. While this was not regarded as requiring the court to be satisfied that the child is suffering significant harm at the precise moment when the court is considering the application – it being sufficient if there is a continuum in existence at that time – nevertheless, as Balcombe LJ said:

'. . . it is not enough that something happened in the past which caused the child to suffer harm of the relevant kind if before the hearing the child has ceased to suffer such harm'.

Since the boy was thriving in foster care, the Court of Appeal held that, as at the date of the hearing, he could not be said to be suffering harm. Furthermore, since the cousin was willing to look after him and his father, being in prison, could not interfere, in the court's view there was no likelihood of future harm either.[16] Accordingly, it was held that the local authority had failed to establish the threshold criteria.

The Court of Appeal decision caused considerable consternation in local authority circles. These concerns were well expressed by one commentator, who said:[17]

'It seems to follow from *Re M* that the test of present harm cannot be satisfied if the child no longer exhibits symptoms of harm, for example, because good substitute care has been provided by a foster parent. This may mean that if a child is living away from home at the time of the hearing, the placement could only continue on a voluntary basis, which may be an insecure position for the child. If a risk arose of the parents removing the child, then an application for a care or supervision order would have to be made based on the harm which was likely to occur if the child returned home. Such an application might have to be made suddenly, whereas if the local authority already had an order it would be able to exert sufficient control to prevent such an emergency arising.'

The House of Lords, however, reversed the Court of Appeal, holding that, provided it can be shown that there was significant harm at the time of the local authority intervention, and so long as protective arrangements have thereafter been continuously kept in place, the fact that the child had been removed from harm at the date of the hearing will not defeat the plea that the child 'is suffering significant harm'. As Lord Mackay LC pointed out, the problem with the Court of Appeal approach is that it substantially deprives the first limb of s 31(2)(a) of effect. Moreover, in his view:[18]

'There is nothing in s 31(2) which . . . requires that the conditions to be satisfied are disassociated from the time of the making of the application by the local authority. I would conclude that the natural construction of the conditions in s 31(2) is that where, at the time the application is to be disposed of, there are in place arrangements for the protection of the child by the local authority on an interim basis which protection has been continuously in place for some time, the relevant date with respect to which the

16 This aspect of the case will be discussed further: see p 543.
17 Whybrow '*Re M* – past, present and future significant harm' (1994) 6 Jo of Child Law 88 at 90.
18 [1994] 2 AC 424 at 433–4, [1994] 3 All ER 298 at 305.

court must be satisfied is the date at which the local authority initiated the procedure for protection under the Act from which these arrangements followed. If after a local authority had initiated protective arrangements the need for these had terminated, because the child's welfare had been satisfactorily provided for otherwise, in any subsequent proceedings, it would not be possible to found jurisdiction on the situation at the time of initiation of these arrangements.'

Lord Nolan agreeing, said: [19]

'Parliament cannot have intended that temporary measures taken to protect the child from immediate harm should prevent the court from regarding the child as one who is suffering, or who is likely to suffer significant harm within the meaning of s 31(2)(a), and should thus disqualify the court from making a more permanent order under the section. The focal point of the inquiry must be the situation which resulted in the temporary measures taken, and which has led to the application for a care or supervision order.'

Having ruled that the s 31 threshold was satisfied, the House of Lords proceeded to make the care order notwithstanding that it was accepted that the mother's cousin, with whom the boy had by now spent seven months, had perfectly satisfactorily looked after him.[20] Indeed, their Lordships made it clear that they expected the boy to continue to live with her, but held nevertheless that (in Lord Templeman's words) having regard to the history and circumstances 'it is highly desirable that the local authority shall exercise a watching brief on his behalf'.[1]

Although it is submitted that the House of Lords were right to overrule the Court of Appeal on the meaning of 'is suffering', the final disposal is more questionable and looks suspiciously like a conditional care order, which, as we shall see, is definitely not permitted under the 1989 Act.

WHAT ARE PROTECTIVE ARRANGEMENTS?

An important element in Lord Mackay LC's judgment in *Re M* is that, although the court is permitted to examine the position at the point of intervention in determining whether the child is suffering the requisite harm, it can only do so where 'there are in place arrangements for the protection of the child by the local authority on an interim basis which protection has been continuously in place for some time'. Precisely what these 'arrangements' are is open to interpretation. While there can be little doubt that they include court-sanctioned arrangements such as interim care orders and emergency protection orders, it is more arguable whether they can also embrace accommodation which, after all, can itself be in place for years. However, by expressly approving[2] *Northamptonshire County Council v S*[3] in which Ewbank J expressly stated that in judging the criterion of 'is suffering' the court –

'. . . had to consider the position immediately before an emergency protection order, if there was one, or an interim care order, if that was the initiation of protection, or *as in this case, when the child went into voluntary care* ',[4]

19 Ibid at 441 and 312 respectively.
20 This is one of the ironies of the case, since at first instance Bracewell J had hesitantly concluded that the cousin might not be able to give the boy the quality of emotional care that he was likely to require. See the comments on this by Cretney [1994] Fam Law at 503.
1 [1994] 2 AC 424 at 440, [1994] 3 All ER 298 at 311.
2 Ibid at 437 and 308 respectively.
3 [1993] Fam 136 at 140.
4 'Voluntary care' was the forerunner of what is now local authority accommodation: see ante, p 524.

Lord Mackay seemed to envisage accommodation as coming within the concept of protective arrangements. How far into the past the courts will be prepared to enquire remains to be seen, but in the *Northamptonshire* case itself the children had been in (what would now be called) accommodation for six months before the care application and 10 months before the hearing.

(e) Is the child likely to suffer significant harm?

The inclusion of the future element was an important innovation of the 1989 Act and was introduced to provide a remedy where harm had not occurred but there were considerable future risks for the child, eg where the child is in danger from birth,[5] where the parents are mentally ill or drug addicted,[6] where an abuser returns to the household, or where a previous child has died in suspicious circumstances in the household.[7]

(I) THE RELEVANCE OF POTENTIAL CARERS

Perhaps not surprisingly, given its speculative nature, the prospective test has been the subject of intense argument. In particular the words 'is likely' have been the subject of litigation before the House of Lords. However, before discussing that issue it is worth returning to *Re M*. In that case it will be recalled that the Court of Appeal rejected the plea that the child was likely to suffer significant harm on the basis that, at the time of the hearing, he was being well looked after and there was another family home available which, though not perfect, was certainly not so bad as to permit the court to find that the child was likely to suffer significant harm. In other words, according to the Court of Appeal, when considering the likelihood of harm, the court had to weigh up the situation that existed at the date of the hearing. This line of reasoning was developed further by the Court of Appeal in *Oldham Metropolitan Borough Council v E*.[8] In that case it was accepted that a 14-month-old child would suffer harm in the care of his 'inadequate' mother, and he was made the subject of interim care orders. Subsequently an aunt of the mother agreed to bring up the child, but the local authority, having assessed the aunt, took the view that the child's long term welfare would be better served by adoption. The aunt then applied for a residence order. In these circumstances the Court of Appeal refused to make a care order, holding that the threshold had not been satisfied as it could not be said that at the date of the hearing the child was likely to suffer significant harm, given that the aunt could provide adequate care. As Waite LJ put it:[9]

'... it is not enough to demonstrate that the person with parental responsibility for the child cannot provide the required degree of care and safety: if, at the hearing date, there is available some suitable carer within the family[10] willing and able to give the child

---

5 From the risks posed by inadequate mothers, for example; cf *Re B (A Minor)* (1982) 6 A & F 50, CA.
6 See *Re D (A Minor)* [1987] AC 317, [1987] 1 All ER 20, HL in which the Lords upheld the making of a care order under the former law in respect of a baby born with foetal drug syndrome derived from an addicted mother and whose parents continued to be drug dependent after the birth.
7 See *Re B (Minors) (Care proceedings: Case conduct)* (1998) Times, 14 May (discussed post, p 547), in which one of two children was injured by one parent but the court was unable to decide which parent had inflicted the injuries.
8 [1994] 1 FLR 568, CA.
9 Ibid at 572.
10 But note he left open whether a similar approach was appropriate where the carer or potential carer was not a relative: see ibid 572–3.

care to a reasonable parental standard, it is impossible to say that the criteria for a public law order are satisfied.'

He further justified this position by pointing out that it was the clear policy of the 1989 Act to preserve, wherever possible, a child's link with his birth family. What the Court of Appeal were doing in both *Re M* and *Oldham* was to consider the likely care by potential carers (at any rate, where there were family members) as part of the threshold test rather than considering that issue as part of the next stage (viz deciding what order, if any, to make), which is then subject to the welfare principle (see below).

Although the House of Lords in *Re M* reversed the Court of Appeal decision in that case and overruled *Oldham*, it is not entirely clear whether their Lordships disapproved of their approach to the prospective test as well as to their interpretation of the first limb of s 31(2)(a). It is submitted, however, that the Court of Appeal approach should be regarded as erroneous, since conflating the threshold and 'welfare' stages unnecessarily restricts the court's powers and, in any event, it is not easy to see why potential carers can be ignored when determining the first limb but not when considering the second limb of s 31(2)(a). Accordingly it is submitted that the correct approach is that stated by Ewbank J in *Northamptonshire County Council v S*:[11]

> 'The threshold test relates to the parent or other carer whose lack of care has caused the harm referred to in s 31(2)(a). The care which other carers might give to the child only becomes relevant if the threshold test is met.'

(II)   THE MEANING OF 'IS LIKELY' – *RE H*

The leading case on the meaning of 'is likely' in the second limb of s 31(2)(a) is *Re H (Minors) (Sexual Abuse: Standard of Proof)*.[12] In that case a mother had four daughters, two by her husband and two by her subsequent cohabitant. Her eldest daughter made an allegation to the police that she had been sexually abused by the cohabitant. She was subsequently accommodated by the local authority and the cohabitant was charged but acquitted of rape. Notwithstanding this acquittal the local authority proceeded with their application for care orders in respect of the three younger children. They argued that, because of the lower standard of proof in civil cases, the court could still be satisfied that the cohabitant had sexually abused the eldest daughter or at least find that there was a substantial likelihood of his having done so and from this hold that the other three girls were likely to suffer significant harm.

At first instance, the judge, though more than a little suspicious that the cohabitant had abused the eldest daughter as she alleged, nevertheless held that he could not be sure 'to the requisite high standard of proof' that the girl's allegations were true. He accordingly dismissed the care order applications. His decision was subsequently upheld by a majority in the Court of Appeal and by a bare majority in the House of Lords. The closeness of the result bears testimony to the difficulties and anxieties raised by the case.

---

11   [1993] Fam 136 at 141. See also Butterworths *Family Law Service* at E[1294], and *H v Trafford Borough Council* [1997] 3 FCR 113, per Wall J.

12   [1996] AC 563, [1996] 1 All ER 1, HL, on which see the thoughtful analyses by Hayes 'Reconciling protection of children with justice for parents in cases of alleged child abuse' [1997] 1 Legal Studies 1, and Keating 'Shifting standards in the House of Lords – *Re H and Others (Minors) (Sexual Abuse: Standard of Proof)*' (1996) 8 CFLQ 157. NB according to Charles J in *Southwark London Borough Council v B* (1998) Times, 29 July, the date at which 'likelihood' of harm is to be assessed is the same as for 'is suffering', ie at the date of the application or at the date of the intervention by the local authority where the protective arrangements have been continuously in place.

As the House of Lords saw it, the case raised the following questions: what was the meaning of 'likely' in this context; who had the burden of proof; what was the standard of proof and how was the assessment of future harm in s 31(2) to be conducted?

On the first of these issues it was unanimously held that 'likely' did not require the court to find that the harm was more likely than not: it was enough that the occurrence of such harm was a real possibility – 'a possibility that cannot sensibly be ignored.' There was similar unanimity over the burden of proof, namely that it was for the local authority as applicant to prove its case. There was broad agreement too that the standard of proof is the ordinary civil standard (the balance of probabilities).[13] In reaching this conclusion, their Lordships rejected the contention that to prove an allegation of sexual abuse required a standard between the civil and criminal standard. However, whereas Lord Nicholls (who delivered the majority judgment) accepted that, as one judge had put it:[14]

> 'The more serious the allegation the more cogent is the evidence required to overcome the unlikelihood of what is alleged and thus to prove it',[15]

Lord Lloyd (who dissented) preferred a simple balance of probabilities test. As he pointed out, the test accepted by Lord Nicholls leads to the 'bizarre' result that the more serious the anticipated injury the more difficult it becomes for the local authority to satisfy the burden of proof and 'thereby ultimately if the welfare test is satisfied, [to] secure protection for the child'.

However, it was on the fourth issue, namely upon what evidence a risk of harm can be based, that there was major disagreement. The majority view was that s 31(2)(a) obliged the court to apply a two-stage test: first, to make a finding on the primary facts giving rise to the application and secondly, based on that finding, to assess whether a risk of future harm was a real possibility. In this case, given the trial judge's finding that sexual abuse had not been proved, there was nothing from which a risk of harm could be inferred. It was certainly not enough in the majority view to base a finding of a risk of harm on mere suspicions. Were it otherwise, as Lord Nicholls said,[16] it –

> '. . . would mean that once apparently credible evidence of misconduct has been given, those against whom the allegations are made must disprove them. Otherwise it would be open to a court to hold that, although the misconduct has not been proved, it has not been disproved and there is a real possibility that the misconduct did occur. Accordingly, there is a real possibility that the child will suffer harm in the future, and, hence, the threshold criteria are met.'

His Lordship added that, although unproved allegations of maltreatment cannot form the basis of a finding by the court that either limb of s 31(2)(a) is established:[17]

> 'There will be cases where, although the alleged maltreatment itself is not proved, the evidence does establish a combination of profoundly worrying features affecting the care of the child within the family. In such cases it would be open to a court in appropriate circumstances to find that, although not satisfied the child is yet suffering significant harm, *on the basis of such facts as are proved* there is a likelihood that he will do so in the future' [emphasis added].

13 Accordingly, the first instance judge had erred on this issue.
14 Per Ungoed-Thomas J in *Re Dellow's Will Trusts, Lloyd's Bank v Institute of Cancer Research* [1964] 1 All ER 771 at 733.
15 [1996] AC 563 at 586, [1996] 1 All ER 1 at 17.
16 Ibid at 591 and 21.
17 Ibid at 591–2 and 21–2.

Lord Nicholls emphasised, however, that this was not the case in *Re H*, since the only allegation was that the cohabitant had sexually abused the eldest child and the cohabitant himself otherwise had no history of abuse. Accordingly, when the allegation could not be proved there was nothing from which it could be inferred that the younger girls were at risk of harm.

The minority view was that the two-stage approach was wrong and over-complicated. As Lord Lloyd put it: [18]

'Parliament has asked a simple question: Is the court satisfied that there is a serious risk of significant harm in the future? The question should be capable of being answered without too much over-analysis.'

Further, as Lord Browne-Wilkinson put it:

'To be satisfied of the existence of risk does not require proof of the occurrence of past historical events but proof of facts which are relevant to the making of a prognosis.' [19]

In the minority view there were sufficient worrying findings (the so-called micro facts such as the consistency of the eldest child's story, the wrongful denial of the cohabitant that he had even been alone with the child, the mother's suspicion that something had been going on and her attempt to dissuade one of the other children from speaking to social workers) to justify the finding of a likelihood of harm.

(III)   COMMENTARY

The decision in *Re H*, not surprisingly, has attracted considerable comment. As Hayes has so eloquently written, the decision raises in an acute form the question: [20]

'... how can the law and the court strike the correct balance before dispensing dispassionate justice to parents and safeguarding children from actual or likely significant harm? Parents should not be at risk of having children taken from them on the basis of false allegations of child abuse. This is unjust, it is a violation of the rights of the parents, and it is a violation of the rights and interests of children. Yet if local authorities are required to produce very powerful evidence that children are being abused, or are at risk of abuse, before courts can intervene, this may lead to some vulnerable children being subjected to horrific forms of undetected ill-treatment within the privacy of the family home. This outcome too is unjust, and it is a violation of the rights of children to be protected by the civil law. The dilemma to be resolved is how the legal framework, and the legal process, can best reconcile safeguarding children from suffering significant harm with the obligation to respect parental autonomy and family privacy'.

In Hayes's view *Re H* swings the law too heavily in favour of the rights of the parents and she wonders whether in the light of this Parliament should either lower the threshold generally or lower it for the purpose of obtaining supervision orders.

Without gainsaying some of the difficulties that undoubtedly flow from *Re H*, it is nevertheless submitted that *on the facts as found* the majority decision was right, for it does seem in principle to be wrong to justify local authority intervention into family life because of a risk of harm based on a mere suspicion. However, the propriety of the initial finding seems doubtful. Lord Lloyd was

18 Ibid at 581 and 12.
19 Ibid at 572 and 3.
20 'Reconciling protection of children with justice for parents in cases of alleged abuse' (1997) 17 Legal Studies 1 at 1–2.

surely right when he said that the first instance judge was in fact applying the now discredited higher than ordinary standard of proof and many will also agree with his Lordship's plea for a simple balance of probabilities test. Were these aspects of Lord Lloyd's judgment to be followed, then some of Hayes's fears might be allayed. Nor must it be forgotten that *Re H* was unusual in being based on a single issue on which the case stood or fell. In most cases there will be a number of issues on which a likelihood of harm could be based and certainly local authorities will be well advised to avoid wherever possible relying on just the one allegation. In an interesting decision after *Re H*, Wall J held in *Re B (minors) (Care proceedings: case conduct)* [1] that where parents had two children and there was a finding of fact that one had suffered non-accidental injury by one or both parents whilst in their care (but the court could not decide which parent was responsible) then it could properly be held that the other child was at risk of suffering significant harm, regardless of whether the parents were still living together. Nevertheless, notwithstanding *Re B*, the decision in *Re H* does mean that in certain situations the court could be powerless to intervene in profoundly worrying situations, such as where an older child had died in suspicious circumstances but non-accidental injury cannot be proved,[2] or where a child is undoubtedly harmed but both parents deny responsibility and blame a third party (eg the nanny, whom they have now dismissed) and responsibility cannot be established. Whether these dangers are the inevitable price that one pays for respecting family autonomy or whether the balance in favour of child protection should be struck anew is hard to say. In part the answer will depend on just how many cases there are in which it is felt that children cannot now be protected when they should have been.

(f) The application of the threshold criteria to orphans and abandoned children

One of Balcombe LJ's concerns in *Re M* was that if the prospective harm test could be satisfied without regard to potential carers that would mean that where a child's parents had both been killed in an accident then, even if –

'. . . there was an aunt or uncle willing to take him into his or her family and bring him up with his siblings and cousins, it would nevertheless be open to the court to say that the second threshold condition was satisfied and make a care order. This would amount to a form of social engineering which we are satisfied is wholly outside the intention of the 1989 Act.'[3]

How then in the light of the two House of Lords' decisions in *Re M* and *Re H* do the threshold criteria apply to orphans and abandoned children? There have been three decisions on this issue, though the first, *Birmingham City Council v D, Birmingham City Council v M*[4] predates both of the House of Lords' decisions. In this first case Thorpe J held that it would be a plain distortion of the threshold test to find some theoretical risk of significant harm in the case of orphans who, at the time of the application for a care order, were being accommodated by the local authority and leading well-settled lives. In his Lordship's view the local authority had adequate powers to look after and safeguard and promote the children's

1 (1998) Times, 14 May.
2 As in *Re P (A Minor) (Care: Evidence)* [1994] 2 FLR 751 (though note in that case a higher standard of proof was applied); cf *Re P (Emergency Protection Order)* [1996] 1 FLR 482 in which Johnson J was satisfied that, because medical evidence had eliminated any medical cause for the child nearly suffocating, the mother must have been responsible.
3 [1994] Fam 95 at 105, [1994] 1 All ER 424 at 432.
4 [1994] 2 FLR 502.

interests.[5] It is to be noted that in this case arguments were solely directed towards the issue of prospective harm. In contrast in the second case, *Re SH (Care Order: Orphan)*,[6] attention was focused on the first limb of s 31(2)(a) for, as Hollis J put it, the House of Lords in *Re M* had held:

> 'that the word "is" in fact means "was" in the sense that the child was suffering significant harm when the rescue operation was instigated, provided the care of the child concerned was continued until the final hearing.'

In *Re SH* the child was already being accommodated at the time of his parents' death, the father having being suspected of perpetrating, and the mother of being implicated in, the sexual abuse of the boy. Hollis J held that, as the boy had been continuously accommodated since then, he could properly be considered at the date of the initial intervention to be suffering significant harm, thereby satisfying the first limb of s 31(2)(a). In other words, the passing of the threshold was due to the alleged sexual abuse rather than the death of the parents. However, in subsequently making the care order, Hollis J, in contrast to Thorpe J,[7] held that without having parental responsibility the local authority would have difficulties in convincing whoever was concerned that they had authority to decide what to do with the boy. Accordingly, he held that it was in the child's interests for the care order to be made.

The third case, *Re M (Care Order: Parental Responsibility)*[8] involved a baby found abandoned on the steps of a health centre who was discovered to have a number of medical problems likely to require medical intervention. In Cazalet J's view, the very fact of abandonment was enough to satisfy the existing harm limb of s 31(2)(a), since it amounted to a complete dereliction of parental responsibility and as such constituted 'ill-treatment'. His Lordship further held that as a result of the abandonment the baby was also likely to suffer significant harm, thus satisfying the second limb of s 31(2)(a). Like Hollis J, Cazalet J thought that, quite apart from the baby's particular problems, it was essential that some proper person or body have parental responsibility for the baby and that in this case it was vital for the local authority to have full powers of decision-making. He therefore made a care order.

Although this latter decision is authority for saying abandonment per se satisfies the threshold test, it is not yet beyond argument whether the death of both parents ipso facto satisfies the criteria. It is submitted, however, that now it has been established[9] that the first limb of s 31(2)(a) can be satisfied as at the date of intervention, the *Birmingham* decision can no longer be relied upon and indeed that it should have been decided the other way. In other words, the death of the parents ought to be regarded as falling within the existing harm criteria if at the time of local authority intervention (be it through accommodation or emergency protection) there is no other family member able and willing to look after the child.[10] On this basis there is no need to enquire whether the prospective harm test would also be satisfied, though it may well be thought that if potential carers are

---

5   Viz under s 22(3), s 23(1) and s 24 of the 1989 Act.

6   [1995] 1 FLR 746.

7   This apparent difference of view can be explained on the basis that each judge was considering different questions: Thorpe J deciding whether the absence of responsibility ipso facto satisfied the prospective harm test – Hollis J determining whether it was in the child's interests, *the threshold test having been satisfied*, to vest parental responsibility via a care order in the local authority.

8   [1996] 2 FLR 84.

9   Viz by the House of Lords in *Re M (A Minor) (Care Order: Threshold Conditions)*, supra.

10 If, following the parents' deaths, the child is being looked after by a relative, then to justify intervention the local authority would have to prove that the child is suffering or likely to suffer significant harm notwithstanding that relative's care of the child.

ignored at this stage, then that test too might be satisfied. Satisfaction of the threshold criteria, however, does not necessarily mean that a care order should be made. That issue, which is governed by the welfare principle,[11] must depend on all the circumstances, though (unless there are other individuals in whose favour a residence order should be made) the court will, as *Re SH* and *Re M* illustrate, be predisposed to make a care order to ensure that some person or body has parental responsibility for the child. However, if subsequent to the local authority intervention another family member does emerge as able and willing to look after the child, then no doubt the courts will, mindful of the general policy under the Children Act to maintain a child's links with his birth family, generally require cogent evidence why a residence order should not be made in that person's favour.[12] In this way it is submitted that Balcombe LJ's fears about social engineering are exaggerated, though this is not to say that the preferable solution to this problem would not have been, as the government White Paper originally proposed,[13] to allow local authorities to apply to become guardians.

(g) Is the harm attributable to the care given or likely to be given?

Having satisfied itself that the harm is significant, the court has also to be satisfied that it is attributable to the care given, or likely to be given, to the child and is not what a reasonable parent would give to the child (or, as we discuss below, is attributable to the child's being beyond parental control). Harm caused solely by a third party is therefore excluded, unless the parent has unreasonably failed to prevent it. Equally clearly, harm solely attributable to disturbing the child's status quo will not satisfy the test. The Act is surprisingly silent on precisely what is meant by 'care' in this context. Although 'care' could simply be interpreted as referring to the physical day-to-day care given to the child by the person with whom the child is living, it seems clear that it means more than this, connoting in addition the emotional care and the love and affection that one would expect of reasonable parents. Hence, in a case of a child being accommodated by a local authority but living with foster parents, the threshold criteria might still be satisfied notwithstanding that the parents are now able to look after their child, if in the past they have not been visiting or keeping in touch.[14] On the other hand, if the parent has shown all the care and concern that a reasonable parent would show to a child living away from home for a time, then on either interpretation the criteria would not be satisfied. In such cases, however, the court would have to consider whether it would be preferable to make a residence order in favour of the foster parents.[15]

(h) Not being what it would be reasonable to expect a parent to give to him

This rather inelegant phrase imports an objective test. It is therefore no answer to say that the care given was to the best of the parents' limited abilities.[16] Parents

11 See below at pp 550ff.
12 Viz along the lines suggested by Balcombe LJ himself in *Re W (A Minor) (Residence Order)* [1993] 2 FLR 625 at 633, discussed ante at p 470.
13 *The Law on Child Care and Family Services* (Cm 62, 1987) at para 25.
14 Hence, in a case like *M v Wigan Metropolitan Borough Council* [1979] Fam 36, [1980] 2 All ER 958 where children were repeatedly looked after by the authority during the mother's difficult pregnancies but where the parents were repeatedly reluctant to take responsibility for them, the criteria would be satisfied.
15 See post, p 551.
16 Contrast the pre-1989 Act decision *O'Dare v South Glamorgan County Council* (1980) 3 FLR 1, CA in which, but for the availability of wardship, the argument would have succeeded under the previous legislation.

cannot argue that they have particular problems, that they are feckless, unintelligent, irresponsible, alcoholic, drug abusers, poor or otherwise disadvantaged, and are thus justified in providing a lower standard of care. It is no answer either that the care given was no different from that given by others in the same street or neighbourhood.[17] The Department of Health's *Guidance* suggests[18] that the court will wish to seek professional evidence on the standard of care which reasonable parents could be expected to provide, with support from community-wide services as appropriate, where the child's needs are complex or demanding.

The focus of attention is on the care given or likely to be given to the child in question, not to an average child. If, for example, the child has particular difficulties in relation to his behaviour or handicap, the court will have to consider what a reasonable parent would provide for him.

(i)   The child's being beyond parental control

As the Department of Health's *Guidance* states,[19] this alternative causal condition was provided for in the previous legislation but was not linked with harm to the child:

> 'It provides for cases where, whatever the standard of care available to the child, he is not benefiting from it because of lack of parental control. It is immaterial whether this is the fault of the parents or the child' [emphasis added].

In *Re O (a minor) (care order: education: procedure)*,[20] Ewbank J commented that in respect of a 15-year-old truant:

> '. . . where a child is suffering harm in not going to school and is living at home it will follow that either the child is beyond her parents' control or that they are not giving the child the care that it would be reasonable to expect a parent to give.'

According to Stuart-White J in *M v Birmingham City Council*,[1] the phrase 'being beyond parental control' imports no time element and is therefore 'plainly a substantial expression capable of describing a state of affairs in the past, in the present or in the future according to the context in which it falls to be applied'. He was also of the view that while 'parental control' refers to the parent of the child in question and not to parents, or reasonable parents, in general, regard can properly be had to the control exercised by that parent in conjunction with a partner even if that partner is not the parent of the child.

4.   THE WELFARE STAGE

Having considered the threshold criteria, it is incumbent upon the court in deciding what order, if any, to make to apply the general principles under s 1. This has now become known as the 'welfare stage'.[2] As Booth J made clear in *Humberside County Council v B*,[3] the two stages, namely the threshold and welfare stages,

---

17 These matters may, however, be relevant to the question whether an order should be made.
18 Vol 1 at para 3.23.
19 Op cit at para 3.25.
20 [1992] 2 FLR 7 at 12.
 1 [1994] 2 FLR 141 at 147.
 2 See Butler Sloss LJ in *Re M and R (Child Abuse: Evidence)* [1996] 2 FLR 195, CA at 202.
 3 [1993] 1 FLR 257 at 261. Although this analysis was subsequently accepted as being correct by the Court of Appeal in *F v Leeds City Council* [1994] 2 FLR 60, as Ward J pointed out (at 67), it is not always easy clearly to demarcate the two-stage process.

should be regarded as being quite separate, with only the latter governed by s 1.

At the welfare stage the court must, pursuant to s 1(1), regard the welfare of the child as the paramount consideration.[4] It is also *bound*[5] to have regard to the statutory check list contained in s 1(3),[6] and in particular s 1(3)(g) which directs the court to consider the range of powers available to it. This means, since Part IV proceedings rank as 'family proceedings' for the purposes of s 8,[7] that the court must consider whether it should make a s 8 order. Even if the threshold criteria are satisfied, the court may choose not to make a care order but make a s 8 order instead if that would better serve the child's welfare.[8] This power to make a s 8 order can be exercised whether or not an application has been made for it.[9] Further, as s 31(5) makes clear, supervision orders can be made upon applications for care orders and care orders upon applications for supervision orders. It is also clear that care (or supervision) orders can be made even though the local authority no longer wish to pursue that option.[10] However, as Hale J observed in *Oxfordshire County Council v L (Care or Supervision Order)*,[11] 'there must in general be urgent and strong reasons to force upon the local authority a more draconian order than that for which they have asked'. Furthermore, it has been held[12] that, if the court is minded to make an order which has not been sought, it must give the parties an opportunity to address the court on the desirability of making that order.

The court also retains its powers to make s 8 orders even if the threshold criteria have *not* been satisfied. Accordingly, even if the local authority application fails, the court is not bound to return the child to his parents.[13]

The application of the welfare principle has to be exercised in the light of s 1(5) which, as we have seen,[14] requires the court to consider whether it is better for the child to make any order than to make no order at all. To answer this question in the context of care proceedings the court will have to consider the plans which the authority is proposing for the child.

Although there is no *statutory* requirement[15] upon a local authority to submit a care plan to the court, the application form for a care or supervision order does require the applicant to state the plans for the child,[16] and this is now the well-established practice.[17] Further, as Wall J put it in *Re J (Minors) (Care: Care*

---

4 Discussed ante, pp 324ff.
5 See s 1(4)(b).
6 Discussed ante, pp 338ff.
7 Section 8(3), (4).
8 Discussed further post, p 561.
9 Viz pursuant to its powers under s 10(1)(b), discussed ante at pp 446–7.
10 See eg *Re M (A Minor) (Care Order: Threshold Conditions)* [1994] 2 AC 424, [1994] 3 All ER 298, HL, discussed ante at pp 540ff, in which a care order was made notwithstanding that the local authority wanted to withdraw their application; and *Re K (Care Order or Residence Order)* [1995] 1 FLR 675, discussed post, p 564, where a care order was made contrary to the authority's wishes.
11 [1998] 1 FLR 70 at 73.
12 *Croydon London Borough Council v A* [1992] Fam 169, [1992] 3 All ER 788.
13 Discussed post, p 562.
14 Ante at p 340.
15 Though note that under cl 87 of the proposed Adoption Bill (contained in *Adoption – A Service for Children – Adoption Bill Consultative Document* (Dept of Health and Welsh Office, 1996)) it would become a requirement.
16 Viz Form C13.
17 See eg *Manchester City Council v F* [1993] 1 FLR 419n and *Re J (Minors) (Care: Care Plan)* [1994] 1 FLR 253 in which Eastham and Wall JJ respectively said that the care plan should accord, if possible, to the format set out by the Department of Health's *Guidance and Regulations*, Vol 3, *Family Placements*, ch 2, para 2.62. Where more than one authority is involved, the care plan needs to be prepared in co-operation between them: *L v London Borough of Bexley* [1996] 2 FLR 595.

Plan),[18] the inability of the court to review the local authority's plans once a care order has been made –

'. . . requires the court carefully to scrutinise the care plan prepared by the local authority and to satisfy itself that the care plan is in the child's interests.'[19]

In carrying out this scrutiny the court should consider whether they are the best available plans for the child and, if so, why an order is necessary to implement them. Although there are limits to this scrutiny process – it does not mean, for example, that there should be an over-zealous investigation into matters that are properly within administrative discretion[20] – nevertheless, even where a care order is the inevitable eventual outcome, the court should not be deflected from using the litigation process to maximum effect.[1]

If the court is not satisfied that the plan is in the child's interests it can suggest[2] changes and, if these are not accepted, it can refuse to make an order.[3] However, as we discuss later,[4] what the court cannot do is to keep the local authority plans under review inter alia by making a conditional care order.

5.   EVIDENTIAL ISSUES

The role of guardians ad litem[5]

(a)   Background to the service

As we discussed in Chapter 12,[6] Art 12 of the UN Convention on the Rights of the Child 1989 obliges States Parties to give those children of sufficient understanding the opportunity to express their views in judicial proceedings affecting them and for the courts to give full weight to these. Unlike private law proceedings, where that obligation is in part satisfied by the court welfare service, in public law the crucial role of giving children a voice in the proceedings is provided by the guardian ad litem service.

In fact the creation of a system for the separate representation of children by guardians ad litem predates both the UN Convention and the Children Act 1989,

---

18 Ibid at 258.
19 See further below.
20 See Wall J in *Re J*, supra, at 262.
 1 Per Thorpe LJ in *Re CH (Care or Interim Care Order)* [1998] 1 FLR 402, CA – the judge was wrong to refuse to hear evidence at the behest of the guardian ad litem, having reached a consensus which was acceptable to all the parties save for the guardian. Note also *Re H (Care: Change in Care Plan)* [1998] 1 FLR 193, CA – a parent was entitled to have an order based on a flawed care plan reconsidered, even if that order remained in force.
 2 But it cannot force changes. Note also that, while the court can make non-binding observations upon what it had in mind about the order, even these can cause difficulties: see *L v London Borough of Bromley* [1998] 1 FLR 709.
 3 Though in Nourse LJ's view, at any rate, such circumstances where a refusal will be justified will be rare: *Re T (A Minor) (Care Order: Conditions)* [1994] 2 FLR 423 at 429.
 4 See post, p 567.
 5 See generally Department of Health's *Guidance and Regulations*, Vol 7, *Guardian Ad Litem and other Court Related Issues*, ch 2; Monro and Forrester *The Guardian ad Litem* (2nd edn, 1995) and Timms *Children's Representation, A Practitioner's Guide* (1995). Working guidance is provided by the *Manual of Practice Guidance for Guardians ad Litem and Reporting Officers* (HMSO 1992) and the *Manual of Management for GALRO Panel Managers* (HMSO 1992).
 6 See ante, p 461.

being first introduced in 1984.[7] This highly successful system is maintained under the Children Act 1989.

(b)   Distinguishing guardians and welfare officers – when guardians should be appointed

Unlike welfare officers, guardians ad litem represent children in the proceedings and are therefore parties to them. They also have the duty to instruct legal representation for the child.[8] There is also a much stronger direction to appoint a guardian ad litem. Indeed, under s 41 courts are required in 'specified proceedings'[9] to appoint a guardian ad litem for the child 'unless satisfied that it is not necessary to do so in order to safeguard his interests'. This enjoinder is in stronger terms than under the former law,[10] and was intended to lead to appointments being the norm in care proceedings.[11] This expectation seems to have been borne out by subsequent experience and it is now unusual, at any rate in care proceedings, for the child not to be represented by a guardian.

Notwithstanding these differences guardians ad litem and court welfare officers have many features in common. Both have a duty to report to the court and be examined on their report and both are under a duty to consider the welfare or interests of the child and thus to advise the court independently of the other parties as to what is best for the child. These similarities prompted Butler-Sloss LJ to say that one would not normally expect to have both a guardian and welfare officer appointed in the same case.[12]

(c)   Qualifications of guardians

A guardian ad litem is an individual qualified in social work. The person appointed must be selected from a panel,[13] but must not (a) be a member or officer or servant of the local authority or authorised person bringing the proceedings, or (b) have been at any time in the past an officer of the authority or voluntary organisation who has been directly concerned in that capacity in arrangements relating to the care or accommodation and welfare of the child, or (c) be a serving probation officer.[14] These provisions are designed to ensure that a guardian is independent of the parties. The independence of guardians has been held to be so important that it should not be compromised by any restriction placed directly or

---

7 The need to give the child a separate voice in care proceedings was first highlighted in 1974 by the Field-Fisher Committee of Inquiry into the death of Maria Colwell (HMSO 1974).

8 These differences were highlighted by Butler-Sloss LJ in *Re S (A Minor) (Guardian Ad Litem/Welfare Officer)* [1993] 1 FLR 110, CA at 114–15.

9 'Specified proceedings' are defined by s 41(6) and include care and supervision proceedings, cases where a s 37 direction has been made, discharge applications, applications under Part V of the Children Act and contact in care proceedings under s 34.

10 The current form of wording reflects that formerly only applied to unopposed applications for discharge.

11 During the debates on the Bill, David Mellor MP said on behalf of the government that guardians should be appointed in over 90 per cent of cases: HC Official Report, SC B, 23 May 1989, col 255.

12 In *Re S (A Minor) (Guardian Ad Litem/Welfare Officer)*, supra at 116. But for a case where this was done see *L v L (Minors) (Separate Representation)* [1994] 1 FLR 156, CA. Note also *Re T and E (Proceedings: Conflict of Interests)* [1995] 1 FLR 581 in which Wall J observed that it was not necessary to appoint more than one guardian to represent children involved in the same proceedings even if their interests conflict.

13 Panels have to be set up by each local authority pursuant to the Guardian Ad Litem and Reporting Officers (Panels) Regulations 1991.

14 FPCA 1991 r 10(7); FPR 1991 r 4.10(7).

indirectly on the carrying out of their duties. Hence in *R v Cornwall County Council, ex p Cornwall and Isles of Scilly Guardians ad Litem and Reporting Officers Panel*[15] an attempt by the local authority (which must meet the costs of guardians)[16] to lay down in advance the normal maximum time that should be spent on any particular case was quashed.

(d)   The guardians' duties

The guardian's general duty is to safeguard the interests of the child,[17] and more specifically to advise on the following:

'(a) whether the child is of sufficient understanding for any purpose including the child's refusal to submit to a medical or psychiatric examination or other assessment that the court has power to require direct or order;
(b) the wishes of the child in respect of any matter relevant to the proceedings, including his attendance at court;
(c) the appropriate forum for the proceedings;
(d) the appropriate timing of the proceedings or any part of them;
(e) the options available to the court in respect of the child and the suitability of each such option including what order should be made in determining the application;
(f) any other matter on which the court seeks his advice or about which he considers that the court should be informed.'[18]

In addition, since they should normally be appointed at an early stage of the proceedings,[19] guardians should also be able to advise the court about the discharge of an emergency protection order, the making or extending of interim care or supervision orders and about directions in interim orders.

Unless one has already been appointed, the guardian is required to appoint a solicitor to act for the child,[20] but it is for the guardian to consider how the case should be presented in court on the child's behalf and to give instructions to the solicitor, unless the latter considers the child wishes to give instructions that conflict with those of the guardian. Any solicitor so appointed must therefore work closely with the guardian ad litem. In a normal case he will take his instructions from the guardian. However, where the child wishes and is able to give instructions on his own behalf[1] which conflict with those of the guardian, the solicitor must take his instructions from the child.[2] In that event the guardian continues with his or her duties save for instructing the solicitor.[3]

(e)   Discharging the duties

To carry out his duties, a guardian must investigate all the circumstances, including interviewing such persons as he thinks appropriate or as the court

---

15 [1992] 2 All ER 471, per Sir Stephen Brown P.
16 See post, p 556.
17 Section 41(2)(b).
18 FPCA 1991 r 11(4); FPR 1991 r 4.11(4).
19 Ibid, r 10(1) and r 4.10(1) respectively. Though the court has power to make an appointment at any stage of the proceedings.
20 Ibid, r 11(2) and 4.11(2) respectively. Under s 41(3), (4) the court may appoint a solicitor for the child if there is no guardian or if the child, having sufficient understanding to instruct a solicitor, wishes to do so, or if the court thinks that it is in the child's interests to be represented. But this power is confined to 'specified proceedings': *Re W (A Minor) (Contact)* [1994] 1 FLR 843.
 1 In cases of doubt, expert opinion might be required: *Re H (A Minor) (Care Proceedings: Child's Wishes)* [1993] 1 FLR 440,.
 2 See FPCA 1991 r 12(1) and FPR 1991 r 4.12(1). See Sawyer 'The competence of children to participate in family proceedings' (1995) 7 CFLQ 180.
 3 He may, with leave, have legal representation: ibid, r 11(3) and 4.11(3) respectively.

directs, inspect local authority records (see below), and bring to the court's attention such records and documents which in his opinion may be of assistance to the case. He may also obtain such professional assistance as he thinks appropriate or which the court directs him to obtain.[4]

The guardian's investigations are confidential,[5] but it is for the court and not the guardian to waive that confidentiality.[6] Consequently, all information relevant to the enquiry should be disclosed in the report. It is not within the guardian's power to promise a child to withhold information from the court.[7] On the other hand, information revealed to the guardian in the course of the investigations should not be disclosed to third parties without prior court leave. This latter proposition is not, however, entirely straightforward, for on the basis of *Oxfordshire County Council v P*[8] and *Re G (a minor) (social worker: disclosure)*,[9] both of which involved the disclosure of parental admissions about the responsibility for non-accidental injuries to their children, it seems that while guardians should not disclose the information direct to the police without court leave, they can properly disclose the information to the social worker involved in the case and in turn that information can be revealed to the police at a subsequent child protection conference without court leave.[10]

The 1989 Act gives the guardian extensive rights to examine and take copies of any records of or held by a local authority or the NSPCC in relation to a child and compiled in connection with any function of the social services committee.[11] These include child protection conference minutes[12] and files prepared in the exercise of the authority's function as an adoption agency.[13] The guardian does not, however, have a right to see Crown Prosecution Service files, although the court may order such disclosure.[14]

At the end of these investigations the guardian produces a written report advising on the interests of the child.[15]

As with other court documents, the report is confidential and should not be disclosed to those other than the parties, their legal representatives and the Legal Aid Board without leave of the court.[16] Furthermore, it is clear that this confidentiality continues after the conclusion of the hearing. It has been held,[17] for example, that court leave was required to disclose the report to a family centre which was connected with the social services department and which offered therapeutic treatment to the children concerned.

4 See r 11(9) and r 4.11(9) respectively. But note also r 18(1) and r 4.18(1) under which no medical or psychiatric examination of the child for the purpose of adducing evidence should be carried out without leave of the court.
5 Per Ward J in *Oxfordshire County Council v P* [1995] Fam 161, [1995] 2 All ER 225 and, per Hale J in *Cleveland County Council v F* [1995] 2 All ER 236.
6 See *Re G (Minors) (Welfare Report)* [1993] 2 FLR 293, CA.
7 Compare *Re D (Minors) (Adoption Reports: Confidentiality)* [1996] AC 593, [1995] 4 All 385, HL.
8 Followed by *Cleveland County Council v F*, supra.
9 [1996] 2 All ER 65, CA.
10 See Lowe 'Guardians Ad Litem and Disclosure' [1996] Fam Law 618.
11 But not therefore of the housing or education committees.
12 Children Act 1989 s 42(1) as amended by the Courts and Legal Services Act 1990 Sch 16, para 18.
13 *Re T (A Minor) (Guardian ad Litem: Case Record)* [1994] 1 FLR 632, CA.
14 *Nottingham County Council v H* [1995] 1 FLR 115.
15 Unless the court otherwise directs, this should be filed with the court seven days before the date fixed for the hearing. Copies are served by the court on the parties as soon as practicable thereafter: FPCA 1991 r 11(7) and FPR 1991 r 4.11(7).
16 FPCA 1991 r 23(1); FPR 1991 r 4.23(1).
17 *Re C (Guardian ad Litem: Disclosure of Report)* [1996] 1 FLR 61.

Guardians are, unless specifically excused, required to attend court hearings[18] and can be questioned about their reports. However, as Ward LJ observed in *Re N (Child Abuse: Evidence)*,[19] guardians should be careful not to confuse their roles. They cannot and should not attempt to be experts in all matters about which they have to report, though as experienced social workers they may well have expertise in a particular area. Ward LJ also observed[20] that the guardians have to decide in the exercise of their duty to safeguard the child's interests, whether or not they believe what the child says. It is therefore reasonable for that belief to be stated in the report as a basis for reaching a conclusion and giving the advice advanced.

As with court welfare reports, the evidence and recommendations of guardians ad litem are not binding on the court,[1] but they are very influential and in any event the court should give its reasons for departing from them.[2]

Normally the guardian's appointment ceases at the conclusion of the proceedings and it has been held,[3] for example, that a court cannot order that a guardian should have contact with a child after a care order has been made. Nevertheless it seems that the conclusion of proceedings may not ipso facto mean that the guardian becomes functus officio. At any rate this was the view of Stuart-White J in *Oxfordshire County Council v L and F*[4] in which he held that the guardian should continue to be involved in proceedings brought after a care order had been made for the disclosure of documents of those proceedings to the police and for a variation of injunctions controlling publicity.

(f)   Commentary

It is generally thought that the guardian ad litem system works well, though there are those who ask why greater weight should be given to the guardian's opinion than to that of any other witness of similar expertise. As has been observed,[5] the guardian is likely to have more experience than the average social worker, but is working alone, with limited supervision. There is no evidence that guardians are appointed for their expertise in a particular type of case. If the local authority put forward a cogent case supported by expert evidence based on the considered opinion of experienced staff, surely the court should express with equal clarity its reasons for departing from their recommendations?

One area of disquiet, however, is whether the current arrangements provide guardians with a satisfactory level of independence and professional support. The guardians are still paid by the local authority and, if a local authority makes a complaint about the conduct of a case by a guardian, that authority is still involved in considering whether the guardian should continue to serve on the panel. If guardians are to be seen as being truly independent, it is difficult to justify these arrangements

---

18   FPCA 1991 r 11(4); FPR 1991 r 4.11(4).
19   [1996] 2 FLR 214, CA at 223 endorsing the *Manual of Practice for Guardians ad Litem and Reporting Officers*.
20   Ibid.
1   See eg *Buckinghamshire County Council v M* [1994] 2 FLR 506, CA.
2   See eg *Re W (Minor) (Secure Accommodation Order)* [1993] 1 FLR 692.
3   *Kent County Council v C* [1993] Fam 57, [1993] 1 All ER 719. For the position in cases where a s 37 direction has been made see *Re CE (Section 37 Direction)* [1995] 1 FLR 26 and *Re S (Contact: Grandparents)* [1996] 1 FLR 158, CA.
4   [1997] 1 FLR 235. But cf Butler-Sloss LJ in *Re G (Minor) (Social Worker: Disclosure)* [1996] 2 All ER 65 at 71 who commented: 'The guardian has no function outside the proceedings to which he has been appointed. *When these proceedings are completed his function is ended*' [emphasis added].
5   White, Carr and Lowe, op cit at 10.45.

and some truly independent body which can both oversee and supervise guardians seems desirable. Furthermore, whether it is sensible to have two separate systems for private and public law can surely be questioned. These systems are currently under review with a Consultation Paper, 'Support Services in Family Proceedings – Future Organisation of Court Welfare Services' being published in July 1998.

The child's direct participation in proceedings

Although the child is a party to 'specified proceedings', the Rules[6] give the court a discretion to hear the case in the child's absence if it considers it in the interests of the child, having regard to the matters to be discussed or the evidence likely to be given, and the child is represented by a guardian ad litem or solicitor. In other words, the child does not have an absolute right to attend the hearing and indeed there is a general feeling that it is commonly not in a child's interests to do so.[7]

Notwithstanding the foregoing, the child's evidence can be heard by the court if it is of the opinion that the child understands the duty to speak the truth and has sufficient understanding to justify his evidence being heard.[8] More commonly, however, the child will have been interviewed beforehand and the evidence will be presented in court on the child's behalf by the interviewer.[9]

The interviewing of children, often on video, raises a number of problems and care needs to be taken not to 'lead' the child.[10]

Other evidential issues

(a) Admission of evidence

Before the 1989 Act all evidence in care proceedings was oral: now at all court levels, including therefore in the magistrates' court, written statements of the substance of the oral evidence which the party intends to adduce have to be submitted in advance of the hearing.[11] Similarly, copies of any documents, including expert's reports, on which a party intends to rely, have to be submitted in advance.[12]

Indeed, it is within the court's power to order disclosure of reports not being relied upon because, for example, they are not favourable to the commissioning parent.[13] Whether there is a *duty* to disclose such documents to the other parties has yet to be authoritatively resolved.[14]

6 FPCA 1991 r 16(2), (7); FPR 1991 r 4.16(2).
7 See eg *Re C (A Minor) (Care: Child's Wishes)* [1993] 1 FLR 832 in which it was held that guardians ad litem should think carefully about the arrangements for children who are to be present in court.
8 Children Act 1989 s 96(2).
9 This hearsay evidence is admissible under the Children (Admissibility Hearsay Evidence) Order 1993.
10 See the discussion in Clarke Hall and Morrison on *Children* 1[834]–[837]. Police videos conducted in connection with possible criminal proceedings should be conducted in accordance with *The Memorandum of Good Practice on Video Recorded Interviews With Child Witnesses for Criminal Proceedings* (HMSO 1992) and it has been held (see *Re D (Child Abuse: Interviews)* [1998] 2 FLR 11, CA) that these guidelines should also be followed in civil proceedings. Valuable guidance can also be found in the Cleveland Report (1987, Cm 412) ch 12.
11 FPCA 1991 r 17(1)(a); FPR 1991 r 4.17(1)(a).
12 Ibid, r 17(1)(b); r 4.17(1)(b).
13 See *Re L (Minors) (Police Investigation: Privilege)* [1997] AC 16, [1996] 2 All ER 78, HL.
14 In *Essex County Council v R (Legal Professional Privilege)* [1993] 2 FLR 826, Thorpe J thought there was a duty to disclose, but in *Re B (Minors) (Disclosure of Medical Reports)* [1993] 2 FCR 241 Douglas Brown J thought that the parties could only be required to disclose reports on which they intended to rely. In *Oxfordshire County Council v M* [1994] Fam 151, [1994] 2 All ER 269, the Court of Appeal said it preferred the *Essex* decision, but see the analysis in Clarke Hall and Morrison, op cit, at 1[833]. Note that in *Re L*, supra, Lord Jauncey refrained from expressing a conclusion on this issue. See Tapper 'Evidential privilege in cases involving children' (1997) 9 CFLQ 1 at 14ff.

Further evidence or documents can only be brought in with the court's leave.[15] Subject to the court's directions, copies of the written evidence are served on the other parties, also in advance of the hearing. Magistrates are expected to have read the written evidence ahead of the hearing.[16]

The submission of written evidence does not preclude the admission of oral evidence – indeed it is normal to hear such evidence.[17] The parties, however, do not have a *right* to insist on giving oral evidence. In *Re N (Contested Care Application)*,[18] for example, in which all the experts, including the psychiatrist instructed by the parents (whose experts were before the court at the pre-trial review) recommended care orders, Thorpe J was of the view that the full trial process should not continue at public expense. It is clear, however, that this power should be exercised with caution and in such a way that, unless the child's interests make it necessary, the rules of natural justice and the rights of the parents are fully and properly observed.[19]

Under the Children (Admissibility of Hearsay Evidence) Order 1993 hearsay evidence is admissible in care and supervision proceedings before any court. This means, for example, that videos of child interviews are admissible in the magistrates' courts as well as in the higher courts.

(b)   Expert evidence [20]

Special rules govern the use of expert evidence, in that no child can be medically examined or psychiatrically examined or otherwise assessed for the purpose of the preparation of expert evidence without leave of the court.[1] It is now well established that the court should take a proactive role in the granting of leave. It should determine whether the evidence is required in the first place and, where it is, it should limit expert evidence to given categories of expertise and specify the numbers of experts to be called. It should also be proactive in laying down a timetable for the filing of the evidence, in making arrangements for the dissemination of the reports and in giving directions for experts to confer.[2]

Although expert evidence may be crucial in care proceedings, there has been some concern about its excessive or inappropriate use in care proceedings under the Children Act 1989 and the consequential delay in the conduct of proceedings.[3] The Children Act Advisory Committee[4] have advised that all experts should have

---

15 FPCA 1991 r 17(3); FPR 1991 r 4.17(3).
16 FPCA 1991 r 21(1). The Family Proceedings Rules 1991 do not make such express provision for the higher courts, since advance reading of the documents is done as a matter of course.
17 Though, given the advance submission of written evidence, there is no need for a witness to recite his statement, but he may confirm that it is true, amplifying and updating the contents where necessary and answering questions from the other parties and the court. See generally Children Act Advisory Committee Report 1993/94 p 24 and see *Practice Note: Case Management* [1995] 1 All ER 586.
18 [1994] 2 FLR 992.
19 *Re G (A Minor) (Care: Evidence)* [1994] 2 FLR 785. See also *Re I and H (Contact: Right To Give Evidence)* [1998] 1 FLR 876, CA.
20 For the use of experts generally see The Hon Mr Justice Wall (ed) *Rooted Sorrows* (1997).
 1 FPCA 1991 r 18; FPR 1991 r 4.18.
 2 *Re G (Minors) (Expert Witnesses)* [1994] 2 FLR 291. It is evident that these guidelines have not always been followed: see eg *Re CB and JB (Care Proceedings: Guidelines)* [1998] 2 FLR 211 where 13 expert witnesses submitted reports.
 3 One of the causes identified as leading to greater delay is the instruction of experts: see Plotnikoff and Woolfson *Timetabling of Interim Care Orders Study* (1994). See also Booth *Avoiding Delay in Children Act Cases* (1996).
 4 CAAC Report 1993/94, p 24.

certain basic skills which are set out in a core curriculum vitae. It is further established that:[5]

'(1) Expert evidence presented to the court should be, and should be seen to be the independent product of the expert uninfluenced as to form or content by the exigencies of litigation.

(2) An expert witness should provide independent assistance to the court by way of objective unbiased opinion in relation to matters within his expertise. An expert witness in the High Court should never assume the role of advocate.

(3) An expert witness should state the facts or assumptions on which his opinion is based. He should not omit to consider material facts which detract from his concluded opinion.

(4) An expert witness should make it clear when a particular question falls outside his expertise.

(5) If an expert's opinion is not properly researched because he considers that insufficient data is available then this must be stated with an indication that the opinion is no more than a provisional one.

(6) If, after exchange of reports, an expert witness changes his view on a material matter, such change of view should be communicated . . . to the other side without delay and when appropriate to the court.'

It is also established[6] that letters of instruction should identify relevant issues of fact, list the documents to be sent to the expert, include an agreed chronology and background history and should be disclosed to the other parties. It has been held[7] that it should be a condition of appointment of any expert that he be required to hold discussions with other experts instructed in the same field of expertise in advance of the hearing to identify areas of agreement and dispute. Such discussion should be chaired by a co-ordinator such as the guardian ad litem, if there is consent to so act. In *Re CB and JB (Care Proceedings: Guidelines)*,[8] however, Wall J held that there was no need to hold a meeting where there was agreement, and where there was disagreement a telephone conference, if properly chaired, might suffice.

As well as giving opinion as to the child's health, likely cause of injuries etc, it is now established that an expert's evidence as to witness credibility is admissible.[9]

The purpose of expert evidence is obviously to assist the judge to reach the right decision, but the judicial task is to make a decision in the light of all the evidence and the judge may therefore depart from an expert's opinion provided proper reasons are given.[10]

(c) Split hearings

So far as the conduct of proceedings is concerned, one practice that has been developed is to have so-called 'split hearings' so as first to determine contested issues of fact and then to consider what order should be made.[11] In this way

---

5 See *Re AB (Child Abuse: Expert Witnesses)* [1995] 1 FLR 181 at 194 per Wall J citing *National Justice Cia Naviera SA v Prudential Assurance Co Ltd* [1993] 2 Lloyd's Rep 68.

6 See *Re M (Minors) (Care Proceedings: Child's Wishes)* [1994] 1 FLR 749 and *Re T and E (Proceedings: Conflicting Interests)* [1995] 1 FLR 581.

7 *Re C (Expert Evidence: Disclosure: Practice)* [1995] 1 FLR 204.

8 [1998] 2 FLR 211.

9 *Re M and R (Child Abuse: Evidence)* [1996] 2 FLR 195, CA.

10 See *Re B (Care: Expert Witness)* [1996] 1 FLR 667.

11 See *Re S (Care Order: Split Hearing)* [1996] 2 FLR 773, per Bracewell J.

allegations of physical or sexual abuse can be determined at an early stage, which then enables the substantive hearing to proceed more speedily and to focus on the child's welfare with greater clarity.

(d)   Confidentiality of proceedings and the issue of disclosure

Care proceedings are not open to the public and any reports or other evidence that is adduced is confidential and should not be disclosed to third parties without court leave, even after the proceedings have concluded.[12]

It has been held[13] that statements made to a guardian ad litem during her investigation (a mother admitting her responsibility for causing non-accidental injuries to her baby) require court leave to be disclosed but, on the other hand, oral statements made to social workers have been held to attract no such protection.[14]

In deciding whether to order disclosure regard must clearly be had to the circumstances, including to whom and why disclosure is sought. Commonly, disclosure will be sought by the police to enable them to pursue their criminal investigations. In such cases it is established[15] that consideration needs to be given to the interests of the child concerned (but note those interests are *not* the court's paramount consideration), the public interest in ensuring frankness in proceedings by preserving confidentiality, and another public interest in upholding the law by providing evidence for other court proceedings.

Another consideration in deciding whether to order disclosure is the problem of self-incrimination. In *Re L (Minors) (Police Investigation: Privilege)*[16] the House of Lords said that it should not order disclosure compliance with which was likely to involve the danger of self-incrimination. In part this standpoint is supported by s 98(2) of the Children Act 1989, which provides that a statement or admission made in public law proceedings under the 1989 Act 'shall not be admissible in evidence against the person making it or his spouse in proceedings for an offence other than perjury'. The application of s 98(2) has not proved straightforward, but in an important decision, *Re EC (Disclosure of Material)*[17] the Court of Appeal held it only applies to evidence given in criminal proceedings and does not therefore prevent disclosure to the police to assist their investigations. This discussion effectively renders the protection a hollow one and is not calculated to encourage frank disclosure in care proceedings.

6.   COURT ORDERS

Introduction

At the welfare stage of care proceedings the court, guided by the welfare principle but not necessarily constrained by what the parties have themselves sought, has, if

---

12 FPCA 1991 r 23(1); FPR 1991 r 4.23(1). Note this embargo is applied strictly: see eg *Re C (Guardian ad Litem: Disclosure of Report)* [1996] 1 FLR 61 in which it was held that court leave was required to disclose a guardian's report to a family centre which was connected with the social services department and which offered therapeutic treatment to the children concerned.

13 *Oxfordshire County Council v P* [1995] Fam 161, [1995] 2 All ER 225, discussed ante at p 555.

14 *Re G (a minor) (social worker: disclosure)* [1996] 2 All ER 65, CA, discussed ante at p 555.

15 See eg *Oxfordshire County Council v L and F* [1997] 1 FLR 235, per Stuart-White J and the cases there cited.

16 [1997] AC 16, [1996] 2 All ER 78, HL.

17 [1996] 2 FLR 725, CA.

the threshold criteria have been satisfied, a wide range of powers to make no order at all, a s 8 order (with or without a supervision order), a supervision order, or a care order. Even where the threshold criteria have not been satisfied, the court still has the power to make a s 8 order. According to s 1(3)(g), a court should consider all its options before deciding which order to make, and pursuant to s 1(5) in any event only make orders where that is considered better for the child than making no order.

Even where the threshold criteria have been satisfied, as Hale J has pointed out,[18] the court should not overlook the local authorities' preventive duties to children in need under Part III of the Act[19] and 'should begin with a preference for the less interventionist rather than the more interventionist approach'.[20]

Nevertheless, the linchpin to the decision is consideration of how much public control (as exercised by the local authority) is needed to protect the child in question. Where most control is needed, a care order will be appropriate. Where least control is required, then a s 8 order might be sufficient. Supervision orders come somewhere between those two options and may be appropriate where there is a concern about the parental care but not sufficient to warrant the removal of the child and the making of a full care order.

If the court is not in a position to make a final order it can make interim orders, ie an interim care or supervision order, or an interim s 8 order. It is to be observed that at the interim stage the court retains significantly more control over the child than when it makes a final order. The philosophy of the Act is that those in whom parental responsibility is vested should be able so far as possible to exercise that responsibility without interference by the court. This is equally true whether responsibility vests in individuals or in the local authority.

It remains to consider these options in more detail.

Section 8 orders[1]

As we have said, s 8 orders can be made whether or not they have been applied for[2] and irrespective of whether the threshold criteria have been satisfied.[3]

(a) Where the threshold criteria are satisfied

Adopting Hale J's proposition[4] that the courts should begin with a preference for the less interventionist approach, in those cases where the threshold criteria have been satisfied and some order is thought necessary, consideration should first be given to the appropriateness of a s 8 order.

One example may be where it is felt that, though parental care had been inadequate in the past, given sufficient support in the future a parent could cope. A court could for instance grant a residence order to a parent on condition that she

---

18 See *Re O (Care or Supervision Order)* [1996] 2 FLR 755 at 759 and *Oxfordshire County Council v L (Care or Supervision Order)* [1998] 1 FLR 70 at 74.
19 Discussed ante at pp 520ff.
20 In *Re O*, supra, at 760.
 1 See generally Lowe 'The Application of Section 8 Orders to Care Proceedings' in Adcock, White and Holloway (eds) *Child Protection* (1992), pp 43–52.
 2 Section 10(1)(b).
 3 See ante, p 551.
 4 In *Re O*, supra, cited above.

live at a mother and baby unit for some specified time.[5] In this type of case, although it is outside the court's power to make a specific issue order forcing the local authority to provide a particular service,[6] it is a legitimate expectation that a service will be provided, since notwithstanding the residence order the child may still qualify for services as a child in need.[7]

Another example where a care order might not be thought appropriate is where abuse has been proved but the perpetrator has since left, or is prepared to leave the home.[8] In such a case a residence order might be made in favour of one parent, perhaps with a prohibited steps order forbidding the other person from contacting the child.[9]

A further example is where a parent has been proved inadequate, for example through alcohol or drug dependence, but there is a relative who is already looking after or who could look after the child. In these circumstances a residence order in favour of the relative might be thought preferable to a care order.[10]

Provided the threshold criteria have been satisfied, it is open to the court to make both a s 8 and a supervision order. The advantage of coupling a s 8 order with a supervision order is that the child's upbringing can be closely supervised, and it may be that where it is thought right to make conditional residence orders it will generally also be appropriate to make a supervision order.[11]

It is to be emphasised that it is not open to the court to make both a s 8 order and a care order. The two are inconsistent.[12]

(b)   Where the threshold criteria cannot be satisfied

If the threshold criteria under s 31 cannot be satisfied then, although the court cannot make a care or supervision order, it can still make a s 8 order.[13] One example might be where a child accommodated by a local authority has been happily fostered for some time, and the parent wishes to resume care.

5   But note that further conditions, such as having to hand over the child to the care of staff if so requested, cannot be added, as that would be inconsistent with a residence order: see *Birmingham City Council v H* [1992] 2 FLR 323, discussed ante at p 427; cf *C v Solihull Metropolitan Borough Council* [1993] 1 FLR 290 in which Ward J made a residence order conditional upon the parents undertaking a programme of assessment and co-operating with all reasonable requests by the local authority to participate in that programme.
6   See *Re J (Specific Issue Order: Leave to Apply)* [1995] 1 FLR 669.
7   Accordingly the local authority will be obliged to continue so to treat the child pursuant to the duties under s 17(1) and (10): see ante, pp 520ff.
8   For the powers to include an 'exclusion requirement' in interim care and emergency protection orders see post, pp 577 and 594 respectively. For the powers to make longer term exclusion orders under the Family Law Act 1996 Part IV see ante, pp 199ff. Note also that under Sch 2, para 5 to the Children Act 1989, the local authority may give assistance, including cash, to enable that other person to obtain alternative accommodation.
9   But it now seems that what cannot be done is to make it a condition of the residence order that the parent does not invite the other parent, or named person, back into the home: see *Re D (Residence: Imposition of Conditions)* [1996] 2 FLR 281, CA, discussed ante, p 427.
10 See eg *Re H (A Minor) (Care or Residence Order)* [1994] 2 FLR 80, but cf *Re M (A Minor) (Care Order: Threshold Conditions)* [1994] 2 AC 424, [1994] 3 All ER 298, HL (discussed ante, p 540), in which a care order was made notwithstanding that the child was happy living with his mother's cousin, and *Re K (Care Order or Residence Order)* [1995] 1 FLR 675 (discussed post, p 564), in which the grandparents did not want the responsibility of a residence order. Furthermore, it seems unlikely that a court would wish to make an order in favour of the relative without first seeing that person.
11 Compare the position on making an interim order under s 38(3) discussed post, p 572.
12 Section 9 and s 91.
13 It can also make a family assistance order under s 16, discussed ante, pp 453–5.

The ability to make a residence order in favour of third parties, even though the threshold provisions cannot be satisfied, means that under the 1989 Act children can be removed or kept away from the care of their parents simply based upon the welfare principle. However, as we have discussed, it is well established that before granting residence to a third party it must shown that the child's welfare positively demands the displacement of the parent's care.[14]

Care orders

(a) The effects of a care order

A care order places the child in the care of the designated local authority.[15] The making of a care order discharges any s 8 order,[16] supervision order, and a school attendance order. It also brings wardship to an end.[17]

As far as the designated authority is concerned, care orders have the twofold effect of:

(i) requiring them 'to receive the child into their care and to keep him in their care while the order remains in force';[18] and

(ii) vesting parental responsibility in the authority.[19]

Whilst in their care local authorities are charged with the duty of safeguarding and promoting the child's welfare.[20]

(1) PLACING THE CHILD 'IN THE CARE' OF THE DESIGNATED AUTHORITY

Although it might readily be supposed that the effect of a care order is to remove the child from his family home and to place him in institutional or foster care, in fact the phrase 'placing the child in the care of' the authority is properly understood as placing the child under the *control* of the authority. Accordingly, it is quite consistent with a care order to plan for the child to remain at home with his or her parents.[1] However, where this is the plan, the court should consider why a care order is preferable to the less draconian alternatives of a supervision order or even a residence order. As Hale J said in *Oxfordshire County Council v L (Care or Supervision Order)*,[2] there are three broad reasons why a care order might be

---

14 See *Re W (A Minor) (Residence Order)* [1993] 2 FLR 625, CA; *Re K (A Minor) (Ward: Care and Control)* [1990] 3 All ER 795, CA; and *Re K (A Minor) (Wardship: Adoption)* [1991] 1 FLR 57, CA as explained by *Re H (A Minor) (Custody) (Interim Care and Control)* [1991] 2 FLR 109, CA, discussed ante, p 470.

15 Section 31(1)(a).

16 It also discharges any *applications* for a s 8 order, which application should therefore be considered before a care order is made: *Hounslow London Borough Council v A* [1993] 1 WLR 291, [1993] 1 FLR 702.

17 Ibid, s 91(2)–(5).

18 Ibid, s 33(1).

19 Ibid, s 33(3)(a).

20 Under s 22, discussed ante, p 529.

1 As at 31 March 1996 there were 4,700 children 'looked after' who were placed with parents, representing 9 per cent of all children looked after: *Children Looked After by Local Authorities* A/F 96/12, p 13.

2 [1998] 1 FLR 70 – a care order was not made because, notwithstanding the parents' past lapses, they were not unco-operative and seemed to have the capacity to work with and learn from the local authority social worker. See also *Manchester City Council v B* [1996] 1 FLR 324; cf *Re T (A Minor) (Care or Supervision Order)* [1994] 1 FLR 103, CA, in which a care order was made, the parents' previous four children having been removed on the basis of 'massive neglect'. See also *Leicestershire County Council v G* [1994] 2 FLR 329.

preferred to a supervision order where the child is to stay at home. First, it allows the authority to remove the child in cases of emergency and to place him or her elsewhere on a long-term basis – in each case without judicial sanction. But this, in her view, would only be appropriate where the parents' behaviour merits serious criticism. Secondly, it enables the local authority to share responsibility with the parents, which is an appropriate consideration where the parents are or are likely to be unco-operative. Thirdly, it gives the local authority specific duties in relation to the child which may be thought to go beyond the general duties imposed by Part III of the 1989 Act, but this should not be used as an excuse to encourage the local authority to perform statutory duties which they already owe to a child in need under Part III.

Care orders might also be appropriate notwithstanding that the child will continue to live with relatives, though again there needs to be good reason for vesting control in the local authority. In *Re K (Care Order or Residence Order)* [3] care proceedings were brought in respect of two children aged five and six following an unexplained injury to the younger child and the accompanying disturbed and bizarre behaviour of the mother (who was subsequently found to be suffering from schizophrenia). Immediately after the incident the children went to live with their grandparents. Subsequently, both children were diagnosed as suffering from a muscle-wasting disease which would confine them to wheelchairs from about the age of 10. There was general agreement that the grandparents had responded magnificently to their grandchildren's needs and there was no question of removing them from their care. Indeed, the local authority, given the level of care by the grandparents, no longer wanted a care order. On the other hand, the grandparents considered that a care order would give them the support that they needed, not least when approaching their old age. It was held that in these unusual circumstances a care order should be made notwithstanding both that the children would continue to live with their grandparents and the local authority's opposition. It was thought right to vest parental responsibility in the authority, and to impose upon them the duty to look after the children, not least when they were older and more difficult to manage. Another consideration was the consequential financial support that would be given by the local authority if a care order was made, namely, a weekly boarding out allowance and a capital allowance to modify the current or any future home of the grandparents to accommodate the children's growing disabilities. As Stuart-White J said, while it would be wholly inappropriate to make a care order *solely* for the purpose of conferring a financial benefit on the carers, such a factor could nevertheless be properly be taken into account and weighed in the balance with other factors.

(II)   'DESIGNATED AUTHORITY'

Under s 31(8) the local authority designated in a care order (including an interim care order) is either:

(a)   the authority in whose area the child is ordinarily resident; or
(b)   where the child does not reside in the area of a local authority, the authority in whose area any circumstances arose in consequence of which the order is being made.

---

3   [1995] 1 FLR 675.

When determining ordinary residence, s 105(6) directs the court to ignore any period during which the child lives at school or while he is being accommodated by or on behalf of a local authority.[4]

Applying these provisions has proved difficult. In *Re BC (a Minor) (Care Order: Appropriate Local Authority)*[5] Bracewell J held that for these purposes a child's ordinary residence should be judged as at the time when the authority first intervened. In *Gateshead Metropolitan Borough Council v L,*[6] however, Wilson J disagreed, holding instead that, where a child was not ordinarily resident in any local authority area, he had a discretion as to which authority to designate. Although subsequent decisions have accepted Wilson J's view that s 31(8)(b) should be interpreted as referring to 'ordinary' residence,[7] there has been no unanimity of view as to whether Bracewell or Wilson JJ's view should be followed.[8]

It has been held[9] that if a care order would designate an authority other than that which applied for the order, there should be early liaison between them and a care plan prepared in co-operation between them.

(III)   VESTING PARENTAL RESPONSIBILITY IN THE DESIGNATED AUTHORITY

Notwithstanding the vesting of parental responsibility in the local authority, parents do not lose their responsibility upon the making of a care order.[10] However, important and innovative though this notion of shared responsibility is, control very much rests with the local authority, as is emphasised by s 33(3)(b) which provides that the authority has the power to determine the extent to which a parent or guardian may meet his parental responsibility insofar as it is necessary to do so to safeguard or promote the child's welfare.[11] Nevertheless, a parent or guardian who has care of the child is still entitled to do what is reasonable in all the circumstances of the case for the purpose of safeguarding or promoting the child's welfare[12] and still retains any right, duty, power, responsibility or authority in relation to the child and its property under any other enactment.[13]

(IV)   LIMITATIONS ON THE EXERCISE OF LOCAL AUTHORITY RESPONSIBILITY

The parental responsibility acquired by a local authority has some specific limitations. They are not allowed to cause the child to be brought up in any

---

4 Being placed at home under an interim care order is not regarded as being 'accommodated' under s 23 – hence s 105(6) does not apply: *Re P (Care Proceedings: Designated Authority)* [1998] 1 FLR 80.
5 [1995] 3 FCR 598.
6 [1996] 2 FLR 179.
7 It was accepted by Wall J in *Re C (Care Order: Appropriate Local Authority)* [1997] 1 FLR 544, by Sumner J in *Newham London Borough Council v I and Brent London Borough Council* [1997] 2 FCR 629 and by James Munby QC, sitting as a High Court judge, in *Re P (Care Proceedings: Designated Authority)* [1998] 1 FLR 80.
8 The 'Wilson J view' was accepted by Sumner J in the *Newham* case, supra, but queried by James Munby QC in *Re P,* supra, while Wall J declined to express a final view in *Re C* supra.
9 Per Holman J in *L v London Borough of Bexley* [1996] 2 FLR 595.
10 Ibid, s 2(6). It will be noted, however, that persons other than parents who had parental responsibility by virtue of a residence order will lose it, because a care order discharges the s 8 order.
11 According to Judge Batterbury in *Re B (A Minor) (Child in Care: Blood Test)* [1992] Fam Law 533, since it is an incident of parental responsibility to take reasonable steps to ascertain who else shares that responsibility, the local authority should pay for blood tests to determine paternity.
12 Section 33(5).
13 Section 33(9). As, for example, the right to consent to the child's marriage. See ante, p 38.

religious persuasion other than that in which he would have been brought up if no order had been made. They do not have the right to consent, or refuse to consent, to the making of an application for a freeing for adoption order, or to agree, or to refuse to agree, to an adoption order or a proposed foreign adoption order, nor to appoint a guardian.[14] Furthermore, while a care order is in force no person may cause the child to be known by a new surname without the written consent of every person with parental responsibility or by leave of the court.[15] The same consents are required before a child may be removed from the United Kingdom.[16]

If the local authority wish to arrange for a child in care to live outside England and Wales then, pursuant Sch 2 para 19(1), the court's approval is required.[17] By para 19(3) that approval may only be given if the court is satisfied that:

(a)   to live outside the jurisdiction would be in the child's best interests;
(b)   suitable arrangements have been or will be made for the child to live abroad;
(c)   the child consents (or does not have sufficient understanding to consent);[18] and
(d)   every person with parental responsibility for the child consents to the child living abroad or, if not, that consent is unreasonably being withheld.[19]

With regard to this last point it was held in *Re G (Minors) (Care: Leave to Place Outside the Jurisdiction)*[20] that the proper approach to determining whether consent was being unreasonably withheld was, applying the analogous test in adoption as established in *Re W (An Infant)*,[1] to look at the broad band within which a reasonable person might exercise a responsible choice, taking into account the sacrifice contemplated, but bearing in mind that, unlike in adoption, the parent would not lose parental responsibility. As Thorpe J observed in the subsequent decision, *Re W (Care: Leave to Place Outside Jurisdiction)*,[2] 'the more the parents are asked to concede, the more readily is their withholding likely to be recognised as reasonable. The less they are being asked to agree the more readily will their withholding be labelled unreasonable.' In that case, where the local authority sought approval for a placement in Scotland in deference to the parents' own wishes, the court had no hesitation in concluding, without a full hearing, that their subsequent withholding of consent was irrational and unreasonable.

(b)   Duration of a care order

A care order lasts until the child is 18[3] unless it is brought to an end earlier. An application to discharge the care order may be made by any person with parental responsibility, the child himself, or the designated authority.[4] A person who does not otherwise have parental responsibility can, with court leave, apply for a

---

14 Section 33(6).
15 Section 33(7). Exceptionally (eg where all contact has been lost) an order can be granted ex parte: *Re J (A Minor) (Change of Name)* [1993] 1 FLR 699.
16 Section 33(7) and (8)(a).
17 Compare the position where the child is being accommodated, when the approval of everyone with parental responsibility is required: Sch 2, para 19(2).
18 Sch 2, para 19(4).
19 Sch 2, para 19(5).
20 [1994] 2 FLR 301, per Thorpe J.
 1 [1971] AC 682, [1971] 2 All ER 49, HL, discussed post, pp 638–9.
 2 [1994] 2 FLR 1087.
 3 Section 91(12).
 4 Section 39(1), discussed post, p 579.

residence order, which, if granted, ends a care order.[5] The making of an adoption or freeing for adoption order also ends any order made under the Children Act 1989.[6]

There is no mechanism for transferring a care order from one authority to another. Accordingly, once a care order has been made, the duty to safeguard and promote the child's interest remains in the designated authority regardless of where the child is living, unless and until the order is ended.[7] This inability to transfer a care order seems an unfortunate gap in the legislation and is the reason why there has been so much litigation as to which authority should be 'designated' in the first place.

(c) Controlling the local authority after a care order

It is fundamental to the structure of the 1989 Act that, once a care order has been made, responsibility for looking after the child is vested in the authority and that therefore the court has no general power to keep the case under review. In line with this philosophy, as the Court of Appeal confirmed in *Re T (A Minor) (Care Order: Conditions)*,[8] the court cannot fetter local authority control over a child in care by imposing any conditions on a care order. As Nourse LJ put it,[9] 'it is clear beyond peradventure that the court has no power under s 31 to impose any conditions on a care order'. In so holding the Court of Appeal rejected the argument[10] that 'if the welfare principle is truly paramount, the court must have the power, when initiating the placement into care, to make an order which reflected the full scope of its perception of the child's welfare'. In the court's view[11] the scheme of the Act is clear: the welfare test applies when considering whether to make a care order, but there are no provisions which allow the court to rely on the welfare principle to superimpose conditions on the care order.

Although the court is not divested of *all* powers of control over a child in care, since it retains jurisdiction to consider issues of contact[12] and the power to decide whether or not to grant an adoption,[13] the making of a care order effectively gives the local authority control over most of the future arrangements for the child including, crucially, determining where and with whom the child is to live and

---

5 Section 91(1).

6 Adoption Act 1975 s 12(3) and s 18(5) discussed post at pp 675 and 653 respectively.

7 Note that responsibility for providing advice and assistance to young persons who have formerly been in care but who have attained their majority passes under s 24 to the authority in whose area that person is living: *R v London Borough of Lambeth, ex p Caddell* [1998] 1 FLR 253.

8 [1994] 2 FLR 423 applying *Re B (Minors) (Termination of Contact: Paramount Consideration)* [1993] Fam 301, [1993] 3 All ER 524, CA and approving *Kent County Council v C* [1993] Fam 57, [1993] 1 All ER 719 in which Ewbank J held there was no power on a care order to direct that a guardian ad litem remain involved to oversee a rehabilitation programme. See also *Re B (A Minor) (Care Order: Review)* [1993] 1 FLR 421 and *Re S (A Minor) (Care: Contact Order)* [1994] 2 FLR 222, CA, discussed post, p 584.

9 Ibid at 428–9.

10 Raised by counsel for the guardian, ibid, at 427.

11 Per Nourse LJ ibid at 429.

12 Viz under s 34, discussed post, pp 581ff. The boundary between controlling contact under s 34 and attempting to fetter the local authority powers by making a conditional care order can be difficult to draw: see eg *Kent County Council v C*, supra, but cf *Re B (A Minor) (Care Order)*, supra, and compare *Re S (A Minor) (Care: Contact Order)*, supra, with *Re E (A Minor) (Care Order: Contact)* [1994] 1 FLR 146, CA, discussed post, p 585.

13 Viz under the Adoption Act 1976, discussed in Chapter 15.

whether or not he should be rehabilitated with his family or placed for adoption. Of course, as we have discussed,[14] in deciding whether to make the care order in the first place the court will have regard to the local authority's care plan, but while it can suggest changes to the plan it cannot force the authority to alter its plan and is ultimately faced with the stark choice of whether to accept it or reject it.[15] More worryingly, once it has made the care order it has no control over whether that plan is implemented.

This lack of court control seems questionable.[16] The judges themselves clearly feel frustrated at their inability to *impose* a specific plan on a local authority, and a distinction might well be made between day-to-day issues which must remain the exclusive domain of the local authority and the more fundamental decisions over the child's future, over which it may be thought the court should retain some control.[17] Indeed, it is perhaps a matter of debate whether the restriction in effect to challenge a change of care plan is in breach of Articles 6 and/or 8 of the European Convention on Human Rights.[18] To some extent the proposed requirement in the draft Adoption Bill[19] – that court sanction would be necessary to place a child in care for adoption – would allay fears about the court's lack of control, but perhaps these proposals should be taken further so as to require court sanction to make subsequent changes to a rehabilitation plan.

Supervision orders

(a)   The nature and purpose of supervision orders [20]

A supervision order puts the child under the supervision of a designated local authority or a probation officer.[1] It does *not* vest parental responsibility in the local authority, nor does it fix them with the duty under s 22 to safeguard or promote the child's welfare.[2] The court cannot make both a care order and a supervision order, though it can make both a s 8 order and a supervision order.[3]

The person, under whose supervision the child is or is to be, is known as the supervisor,[4] and for the duration of the order it is his or her duty:

'(a) to advise, assist and befriend the supervised child;[5]
 (b) to take such steps as are reasonably necessary to give effect to the order; and

---

14 Discussed ante, p 551.
15 Though, as Nourse LJ said in *Re T*, supra, at 429, the circumstances where it is appropriate to reject the plan and refuse to make a care order should be rare.
16 See the critique in White, Carr and Lowe, op cit, at paras 8.86–8.87.
17 Such a power would be akin to that formerly enjoyed by the High Court under its wardship jurisdiction, discussed in Chapter 16.
18 See, by way of analogy, cases such as *R v United Kingdom* [1988] 2 FLR 445, E Ct HR, which held the UK to be in breach for not having a mechanism for parents to be able to challenge denials or restrictions on access to children in care. See further post, pp 609–10.
19 See cls 23 and 87 of the draft Adoption Bill attached to the Consultative Document, *Adoption – A Service for Children* (Dept of Health and Welsh Office 1996). Adoption placement orders are discussed post, p 658.
20 See generally the Department of Health's *Guidance and Regulations*, Vol 1, *Court Orders*, paras 3.87ff.
 1 Section 31(1)(b). See also Sch 3, para 9 with regard to the selection of a supervisor.
 2 Section 22 is discussed ante, p 529.
 3 See eg *Re B (Care: Expert Witness)* [1996] 1 FLR 667, CA, and *Re DH (A Minor) (Child Abuse)* [1994] 1 FLR 679.
 4 Section 105(1).
 5 Note that there is no duty owed to the parent.

(c) where –
   (i) the order is not wholly complied with; or
   (ii) the supervisor considers that the order may no longer be necessary,
to consider whether or not to apply to the court for its variation or discharge'.[6]

These basic duties are substantially expanded by Sch 3,[7] which also empowers the court to make orders inter alia for the child's psychiatric or medical examinations.[8]

Supervision orders are designed for cases where an element of child protection is involved.[9] On the other hand, they do not give local authorities the same degree of control over parents as do care orders, from which they are thus clearly distinguishable.[10]

(b)   Duration of a supervision order

A supervision order is a short-term order and initially lasts for one year,[11] though it can be made for a shorter period.[12] It can, however, be extended upon an application by the supervisor for up to a maximum of three years.[13] An application to extend the period of a supervision order is governed by the welfare principle, so that further proof of the threshold criteria is not required.[14] On the other hand, the court has no power to vary the order to a care order. Instead, if that is what is required, the local authority must make a fresh application under s 31.[15]

(c)   Requirements imposed under a supervision order

The essence of a supervision order is to subject the supervised child (regardless of whether he consents) to certain directions by the supervisor. Thus Sch 3, para 2 provides that an order may require the supervised child to comply with any directions given from time to time by the supervisor which require him to do all or any of the following:

   '(a) live at a place or places specified in the directions for a specified period or periods;
   (b) present himself to a specified person at a place and on a day specified;
   (c) participate in specified activities, such as education or training.'[16]

The precise directions are a matter for the supervisor and not the court,[17] though in no event is the supervisor empowered to give directions as to the child's medical or psychiatric treatment.[18]

As well as empowering supervisors to make directions, a supervision order may also include a requirement that, with his or her consent, a 'responsible person'[19]

---

6 Section 35(1).
7 See further below.
8 See further below.
9 Per Wall J in *Re DH (A Minor) (Child Abuse)* [1994] 1 FLR 679 at 702 relying on the Department of Health's *Guidance*, op cit, at para 2.50.
10 See further below at p 571.
11 Sch 3, para 6(1).
12 *M v Warwickshire County Council* [1994] 2 FLR 593.
13 Sch 3, para 6(3), (4).
14 *Re A (a minor) (supervision order: extension)* [1995] 3 All ER 401, [1995] 1 FLR 335, CA.
15 Consequently, the s 31 threshold will have to be re-established as at the date of the hearing: *Re A*, supra.
16 Note that the original provision that such directions may only last for 90 days under Sch 3, para 7(1) was repealed by the Courts and Legal Services Act 1990 Sch 16, para 27.
17 Sch 3, para 2(2).
18 Sch 3, paras 2(3) and 5: discussed further below.
19 Any person who has parental responsibility for the child and any other person with whom the child is living: Sch 3, para 1.

take all reasonable steps to ensure that the child complies with any direction given by the supervisor.[20]

The fact that the responsible person must consent to the requirement being imposed is crucial to the operation of a supervision order, since there are no direct means of enforcing any of the directions or requirements,[1] and it has been held that the court has no power either to make such agreement a condition of the order[2] or to accept an undertaking to agree.[3]

As we have said, the supervisor is not empowered to give directions as to the child's medical or psychiatric examination or treatment, but these can be made the subject of specific direction by the court.[4] In each case, however, the power is, in the case of a child of sufficient understanding to make an informed decision, subject to that child's consent.[5]

At one stage it looked as though Sch 3 might be interpreted as giving the courts powers to make wider directions. In *Croydon London Borough Council v A (No 3)*,[6] for example, it was held that a court could direct that the supervised child and the mother live at a rehabilitation centre, while in *C v Solihull Metropolitan Borough Council*[7] Ward J said that he could not see why an interim supervision order could not be made subject to conditions. It now seems apparent that this approach is wrong, for, as Waite LJ put it in *Re V (Care or Supervision Order)*:[8]

'The concept of a supervision order subject to conditions simply cannot be fitted into the framework of the Children Act legislation.'

As his Lordship pointed out:[9]

'Any provisions incorporated into a supervision order, either by direction of the supervisor or by requirements directly stated by the judge, are incapable of being enforced directly through any of the ordinary processes by which courts of law enforce obedience to their directions. The only sanction, when any infringement of the terms of a supervision order, or of directions given under it, occurs is a return by the supervisor to court. There the ultimate sanction will be the making of a care order under which the local authority will be given the necessary legal powers to enforce its will.'

Accordingly, Sch 3 should be narrowly construed insofar as it controls the courts' powers.

---

20 Sch 3, para 3.
1 The only sanction is for the supervisor to return to court and ultimately for the local authority to make a fresh application for a care order. See *Re V (Care or Supervision Order)* [1996] 1 FLR 776 at 785 per Waite LJ (see below).
2 *Re V*, supra.
3 *Re B (Supervision Order: Parental Undertaking)* [1996] 1 FLR 676, CA.
4 See Sch 3, paras 4 and 5. In the case of examinations the court can either require the supervised child to submit to a medical or psychiatric examination or to submit to any such examination from time to time as directed by the supervisor: Sch 3 para 4(1).
5 Sch 3, para 4(4)(a) and para 5(5)(a). This wording is stronger than the equivalent provisions in s 38(6) (interim orders), s 43(8) (child assessment orders) and s 44(7) (emergency protection orders), so that even if the decision in *South Glamorgan County Council v W and B* [1993] 1 FLR 574 (discussed post, p 576) that the High Court has inherent jurisdiction to override a child's refusal is thought right, it may nevertheless be thought inapplicable here, given the nature of the provisions.
6 [1992] 2 FLR 350, per Hollings J.
7 [1993] 1 FLR 290 at 303–4.
8 [1996] 1 FLR 776 at 785. See also *Re S (Care or Supervision Order)* [1996] 1 FLR 753, CA.
9 Ibid at 786.

(d) Supervision and care orders compared

Notwithstanding that before either order can be made the threshold conditions under s 31 have first to be satisfied, care orders and supervision orders are fundamentally different in that the former but not the latter (a) vests parental responsibility in the local authority and (b) places the local authority under an obligation, pursuant to s 22, to look after and to safeguard and promote the child's welfare. As Judge Coningsby QC put it in *Re S (J) (A Minor) (Care or Supervision Order)*:[10]

> 'We tend to look at supervision orders and care orders under the same umbrella because the threshold criteria for the coming into operation of the two is the same. But when we actually look at the content of the two orders we find they are wholly and utterly different. This is because of s 22 and because of the passing of parental responsibility. *Supervision should not in any sense be seen as a sort of watered down version of care. It is wholly different*' [emphasis added].

The effect of these differences is, as Bracewell J observed in *Re T (A Minor) (Care or Supervision Order)*,[11] that whereas the nature of a supervision order is to help and assist a child whilst leaving full responsibility with the parents, a care order places a positive duty on the local authority to promote the child's welfare and to protect him or her from inadequate parenting. As against this, however, as Hale J pointed out in *Re O (Care or Supervision Order)*,[12] whereas under a care order, contact apart, the court cedes all control over what is to happen to the children to the local authority, under a supervision order the local authority has to return to the court either for an extension, or for a care order if things do not go well. In this limited sense the court retains a greater control under a supervision order than under a care order.

(e) The use of supervision orders

Because of the differences just noted it is now well established that a supervision order should not be used to control an otherwise obdurate or inadequate parent,[13] and the temptation to regard it simply as a less invasive form of care order should be resisted.[14] However, as Hale J pointed out in *Re O (Care or Supervision Order)*,[15] given that there must be some cases in which a supervision order is in a child's best interest, and bearing in mind both the enjoinder under s 1(5) not to make orders unless to do so would be better for the child than to make no order and under s 1(3)(g) to consider the full range of powers, the court can properly begin with a preference for the less rather than the more interventionist approach. In any event, it must not be supposed that a supervision order is without effect. Indeed, one judge[16] has described it as part of a strong package, given that it provides for instant access into the home by a social worker. The ability to direct a treatment programme for the child combined with a finding that the threshold criteria are satisfied has also been described as a 'powerful tool',[17] and there seems no doubt

---

10 [1993] 2 FLR 919 at 950 and cited with approval by Dillon LJ in *Re V*, supra, at 788.
11 [1994] 1 FLR 103, CA at 106–7.
12 [1996] 2 FLR 755 at 760.
13 See eg *Re T* and *Re S*, supra. But note Hale J's point in *Re O (Care or Supervision Order)*, supra, at 761 that lack of co-operation by a parent ought not *automatically* to be regarded as removing the supervision option, since it must depend on what assessment is needed.
14 See *Re V*, supra.
15 Supra, at 759–60.
16 Judge Coningsby in *Re S (J) (A Minor) (Care or Supervision)*, supra at 947.
17 See White, Carr and Lowe, op cit at 8.138.

that, where parents are prepared to co-operate, a supervision order has a useful role to play. In *Re B (Care or Supervision Order)*[18] Holman J held that a supervision rather than a care order was more appropriate in a case where the pressing needs of the children were for them to be closely monitored within their home and to undertake work with professionals away from home to teach them how to protect themselves. A supervision rather than a care order was also made in *Oxfordshire County Council v L (Care or Supervision Order)*,[19] where, although there were concerns about the standards of parenting, the parents themselves had responded well to help in the past and there was no evidence to suggest that they would not continue to be responsive in the future.

Whether these recent decisions will encourage more supervision orders to be sought and made remains to be seen. The evidence so far, however, shows that such orders are sought and made far less frequently than care orders.[20]

Interim orders

(a)   The court's powers

Unlike under private law express provision is made, by s 38, for making both interim care and (unlike the former law) interim supervision orders. However, these are not the only options before the court, for it may also make a residence order or other s 8 orders for a limited period. As the Department of Health's *Guidance* says,[1] the two main objectives of these powers are 'to enable the child to be suitably protected while proceedings are progressing where this is required, and to see that interim measures operate only for as long as necessary.'

The combination of s 11(3) and s 11(7) allows the court to make an order for a specified period and subject to conditions, even though it is not yet in a position finally to dispose of the case. For example, the court could make a residence order until the next hearing in favour of a relative and control the child's contact with a parent for the time being through a contact order or a prohibited steps order.[2] Under s 38(3), if the court makes a residence order upon an application for care or supervision, it *must* make an interim supervision order unless it is satisfied that the child's welfare will be satisfactorily safeguarded without it. In other words, there is a rebuttable presumption that if a residence order is made, so should an interim supervision order be. In exercising its power to make s 8 orders the court must be governed by the paramountcy of the child's welfare under s 1(1) and by the enjoinder under s 1(5) not to make any order unless it considers that doing so would be better for the child than making no order.

Interim care or supervision orders may be made, either following a s 37 direction by the court to a local authority to investigate the child's circumstances, or on an adjournment in care proceedings.[3] Under s 38(2) such orders cannot be made unless the court 'is satisfied that there are reasonable grounds for believing

18   [1996] 2 FLR 693.
19   [1998] 1 FLR 70.
20   See Children Act Report 1993, paras 3.6–3.8.
1   Vol 1, *Court Orders*, para 3.35.
2   The precise order may depend against whom the order is sought to be enforced: see *Re H (Prohibited Steps Order)* [1995] 1 FLR 638, CA and the discussion ante at pp 418–19.
3   Children Act 1989 s 38(1). When considering adjourning the case the court should be mindful of the general principle that under s 1(2) delay is prima facie prejudicial to the child's welfare. Proceedings should not be adjourned because criminal proceedings are pending against the alleged abuser: *Re TB (Care Proceedings: Criminal Trial)* [1995] 2 FLR 801, CA, contradicting *Re S (Care Order: Criminal Proceedings)* [1995] 1 FLR 151, CA.

that the circumstances with respect to the child are as mentioned in section 31(2).'
In other words, the court only has to be satisfied that there are reasonable grounds
for believing that the so-called threshold conditions exist, rather than having to be
satisfied as to their existence. In *Re B (A Minor) (Care Order: Criteria)*,[4] there was
evidence before the court to satisfy the test that a girl was likely to suffer
significant harm (arising from allegations of sexual abuse), but difficulties arose
over the attribution of that harm. However, as Douglas Brown J said, it was
enough that he had reasonable grounds for believing that the s 31 threshold was
satisfied. As he put it 'I have not got to be satisfied that they exist in fact.' In that
case an assessment was crucial to attributing blame and an interim care order was
made which ensured that an investigation could properly be carried out.

(b) The nature of interim orders

It is also important to appreciate, as was emphasised by Waite LJ in *Re G (Minors)
(Interim Care Order)*,[5] that:

'The regime of interim care orders laid down by s 38 is designed to leave the court with
the ability to maintain strict control of any steps taken or proposed by a local authority in
the exercise of powers that are by their nature temporary and subject to continual
review. *The making of an interim care order is an essentially impartial step, favouring
neither one side nor the other, and affording no one, least of all the local authority in
whose favour it is made, an opportunity for tactical or adventitious advantage*'
[emphasis added].

Further, as Cazalet J observed in *Hampshire County Council v S*:[6]

'Justices should bear in mind that they are not, at an interim hearing, required to make a
final conclusion; indeed it is because they are unable to reach a final conclusion that they
are empowered to make an interim order. An interim order or decision will usually be
required so as to establish a holding position, after weighing all the relevant risks, pending
the final hearing. Nevertheless, justices must always ensure that the substantive issue is
tried and determined at the earliest possible date. Any delay in determining the question
before the court is likely to prejudice the welfare of the child [see s 1(2) of the Act].'

(c) Deciding whether to make a final or interim care order

In principle a final care order should not be made if important evidence remains
outstanding or unresolved, eg where assessments are still being made and their
outcome awaited. In *Hounslow London Borough Council v A*[7] magistrates were held
to be wrong to make a final care order at a time when the assessment of the father as
a full-time carer had not been completed. Similarly, in *C v Solihull Metropolitan
Borough Council*,[8] where children, the younger of whom had suffered serious non-
accidental injuries whilst with the parent, were placed with their grandparents who
had a residence order, Ward J held that, pending the outcome of an assessment of the
parents to see whether it was safe to return the children to them, the proper order was
an interim care order. Such an order kept control of events in the court, which in
these circumstances was preferable both to returning the children to the parents
subject to a supervision order and to making a full care order which effectively
would have abdicated the court's responsibility to the local authority.

---

4 [1993] 1 FLR 815.
5 [1993] 2 FLR 839 at 845.
6 [1993] Fam 158 at 165, [1993] 1 All ER 944 at 950–1.
7 [1993] 1 FLR 702.
8 [1993] 1 FLR 290.

However, merely because some issues remain uncertain does not necessarily mean that an interim care order has to be made. For example, in *Re L (Sexual Abuse: Standard of Proof)*[9] the judge had found that two children had been sexually abused. He also found that there was some prospect of rehabilitation with the mother but little such prospect with the father. The authority's care plan was based on removing the children from the family and placing them permanently for adoption. Although the judge expressed the hope that the local authority would be sympathetic to his views regarding rehabilitation, he nevertheless made a full care order in respect of each child based on the belief that an interim order should not be used to control what the local authority was doing. The Court of Appeal refused to interfere. After pointing out that once a care order is made, then – other than by control over contact – the court has no further part to play in the future welfare of the child, Butler-Sloss LJ commented:

> 'The Children Act provides for many of the most important decisions, including whether to place a child for adoption, to be made by the local authority and therefore there is nothing untoward in the judge leaving the ultimate decision in the hands of the local authority with whom the child is placed.'

She continued by pointing out that interim care orders should not be used to provide continuing control over the activities of the local authority and quoted with approval Wall J's earlier comments in *Re J (Minors) (Care: Care Plan)*:[10]

> '. . . there are cases (of which this is one) in which the action which requires to be taken in the interest of children necessarily involves steps into the unknown and that provided the court is satisfied that the local authority is alert to the difficulties which may arise in the execution of the care plan, the function of the court is not to seek to oversee the plan but to entrust its execution to the local authority.'

It has been said[11] that, once all the facts are known, it can seldom if ever be right for the court to continue adjourning the case, and certainly not just to enable the court to monitor the situation.

In contrast to the foregoing cases, in *Buckinghamshire County Council v M*[12] the Court of Appeal, mindful that there was no other method under the Children Act 1989 of ensuring a phased rehabilitation, made an interim order which effectively gave the court power to control the rehabilitation plan. However, this case seems to go against the accepted line and it must be doubted whether it can still be regarded as good law.

(d)   Making directions on interim applications

One of the key differences between a full and interim order is that in the latter case the court may give certain directions. This power is conferred by s 38(6), which states:

> 'Where the court makes an interim care order, or interim supervision order, it may give such direction (if any) as it considers appropriate with regard to the medical or psychiatric

---

9   [1996] 1 FLR 116. See also *Re R (Care Proceedings: Adjournment)* [1998] 2 FLR 390, CA.
10   [1994] 1 FLR 253.
11   *Re P (Minors) (Interim Care)* [1993] 2 FLR 742, CA. In overruling Hollings J's decision to make a succession of interim care orders until the placement of two young girls with their mother and her cohabitant who were proposing to move to Northern Ireland was settled, Waite LJ said: 'It can never be right for the court, in granting an interim care order at one sitting, to attempt to lay down a policy which would or might fetter the discretion of any future sitting to grant or refuse a further interim order.'
12   [1994] 2 FLR 506.

examination or other assessment of the child; but if the child is of sufficient under-standing to make an informed decision he may refuse to submit to the examination or other assessment.'

Although clearly empowering courts to make directions as to medical or psychiatric examinations of children, the precise ambit of this provision has been the subject of considerable litigation. Two 1992 decisions, *Re O (Minors) (Medical Examination)* [13] and *Berkshire County Council v C*, [14] held that a s 38(6) direction was binding upon the local authority and therefore (a) amounted to an 'order' that could be appealed under s 94, but (b) had otherwise to be obeyed, the lack of resources being no excuse. [15]

In *Re O* Rattee J upheld a magistrates' direction that medical tests be carried out on two children inter alia to determine whether they were HIV positive. [16] He dismissed the argument that the direction was made ultra vires (since the results of the tests were not relevant to the court's consideration of the threshold under s 31) on the ground that the results were bound to have a bearing on the children's long-term future, ie they were relevant to the 'welfare stage' of the care proceedings.

A s 38(6) direction that the child be assessed by a suitably qualified social worker was similarly upheld in the *Berkshire* case, where Johnson J rejected the argument that the direction was ultra vires on the ground that it imposed an obligation on the authority that could conflict with their own assessment of the priorities of competing demands upon their limited financial resources (which, they submitted, was a matter for the Director of Social Services who is account-able to the authority's elected representatives). Johnson J acknowledged that such directions could have substantial implications for the authority, but nevertheless ruled that, provided proper account was taken of the financial and resource implications, the court could properly make such a direction.

The ambit of s 38(6) was again brought into issue in relation to whether it empowered the court to direct a residential assessment. The matter was authori-tatively resolved by the House of Lords in *Re C (A Minor) (Interim Care Order: Residential Assessment)*. [17] In that case the child suffered unexplained injuries while in the care of his parents. An expert considered the injuries to be non-accidental and the local authority social workers themselves recommended (supported by the guardian ad litem and the clinical psychologist) an in-depth assessment involving both parents and the child at a residential unit. The local authority, however, resisted the recommendation inter alia because of the lack of explanation for the injuries by the parents and because of their unstable relationship. They considered that rehabilitation could expose the children to an unacceptable level of risk and accordingly were not prepared to pay the not inconsiderable sum of £18,000–£24,000 for the residential placement, which in any event, in their view, had little chance of success. Could they be ordered to carry out the assessment? The House of Lords ruled that both s 38(6) and s 38(7) (which empowers the court to direct there be no such examination or assessment)

13 [1993] 1 FLR 860.
14 [1993] 1 FLR 569.
15 See *Re JN (Care: Assessment)* [1995] 2 FLR 203 in which Thorpe J took no action against a local authority for thwarting an assessment by refusing to finance it.
16 It has since been held that applications seeking HIV tests should be heard by the High Court. *Note Re HIV Tests* [1994] 2 FLR 116, per Singer J.
17 [1997] AC 489, [1996] 4 All ER 871. See also *Re M (Residential Assessment Directions)* [1998] 2 FLR 371, in which it was held that the child's welfare was not the paramount consideration when deciding whether to make directions under s 38(6).

should be broadly construed to confer jurisdiction on the court to order or prohibit any assessment which involves the participation of the child and which is directed to providing the court with material which is necessary to enable it to reach a proper decision at the final hearing. They rejected the argument based on the ejusdem generis principle that (a) 'assessments' had to be of the same type as medical or psychiatric; and (b) the powers were confined to assessments 'of the child' and not of the parents. With regard to the latter, Lord Browne-Wilkinson pointed out that it was impossible to assess a young child divorced from his environment or his parents.[18]

The House also rejected the argument that the local authority are better qualified than the court to decide whether expenditure on such a scale is a sensible allocation of their limited resources. Lord Browne-Wilkinson pointed out that such an argument could not be made in respect of directed medical treatment under s 38(6), so why should it be for other assessments? In any event, to hold otherwise would be tantamount to allowing –

'. . . the local authority to decide what evidence is to go before the court at the final hearing – to allow the local authority by administrative decision to pre-empt the court's judicial decision.'

In his Lordship's view that cannot be the law. As he said, the 1989 Act:

'. . . should be construed purposively so as to give effect to the underlying intentions of Parliament. As I have sought to demonstrate, the dividing-line between the functions of the court on the one hand and the local authority on the other is that a child in interim care is subject to control of the local authority, the court having no power to interfere with the local authority's decisions save in specified cases. The cases where, despite that overall control the court is to have power to intervene are set out, inter alia, in s 38(6) and (7). The purpose of s 38(6) is to enable the court to obtain the information necessary for its own decision, notwithstanding the control over the child which in all other respects rests with the local authority. I therefore approach the subsection on the basis that the court is to have such powers to override the views of the local authority as are necessary to enable the court to discharge properly its function of deciding whether or not to accede to the local authority's application to take the child away from its parents by obtaining a care order.'

Notwithstanding that s 38(6) expressly says that a child of sufficient understanding to make an informed decision may refuse to submit to an examination or assessment Douglas Brown J held in *South Glamorgan County Council v W and B*[19] that he had an inherent power to override a competent child's refusal to submit to an examination. In doing so he purported to follow the Court of Appeal decision in *Re W (A Minor) (Medical Treatment)*,[20] in which the Court of Appeal overruled a 16-year-old anorexic child's refusal of treatment. However, with respect to Douglas Brown J, it is one thing to interpret a statute – in the case of *Re W*, s 8 of the Family Law Reform Act 1969, which permits 16- and 17-year-olds to give valid consent to medical treatment – restrictively, but quite another flatly to contradict it. It is suggested that the *South Glamorgan* decision is bad law and ought not to be followed.

---

18 Though note that there is apparently no power of the court to order *parents* to take part in any assessment against their wishes – see Lord Browne-Wilkinson in *Re C*.
19 [1993] 1 FLR 574.
20 [1993] Fam 64, [1992] 4 All ER 627, CA, discussed ante at p 315.

(e) Attaching an exclusion requirement to an interim care order

The Law Commission considered[1] that the courts should be able to exclude a suspected abuser from the family so as to be able to protect a child without having to remove him or her from the home. Implementing their recommendation, the Children Act 1989 was amended by the Family Law Act 1996 to empower the courts to add an exclusion requirement to an interim care order.[2] This power is conferred by s 38A.

Under s 38A(1) an exclusion requirement may only be added to an interim care order and not therefore to an interim supervision order; nor, in the former case, may it be added to an order based on the child being beyond parental control. In any event, before an exclusion requirement may be made the court must be satisfied of three conditions:[3]

(1) there is reasonable cause to believe that if a relevant person is excluded from the child's home the child will cease to suffer or cease to be likely to suffer significant harm;
(2) there is another person (whether a parent or someone else) living in the home who is able to give the child the care which it would be reasonable to expect a parent to give; and
(3) that other person consents[4] to the inclusion of the exclusion requirement.

The exclusion requirement requires[5] the relevant person to leave the dwelling house in which he is living with the child, and prohibits him from re-entering. It may also exclude him from a defined area in which the dwelling house is situated. The requirement cannot last longer than the interim order though it can be made for a shorter period.[6]

The court can attach a power of arrest to the exclusion requirement,[7] which entitles a police constable to arrest without a warrant any person whom he has reasonable cause to believe is in breach of the requirement.[8] Instead of formally making an exclusion requirement courts can accept undertakings in similar terms,[9] but in these cases no power of arrest can be attached.[10]

If, while the exclusion requirement is in force, the local authority remove the child from the dwelling house for more than 24 hours, then the requirement or undertaking ceases to have effect.[11]

(f) Duration and renewal of interim orders

The duration of interim orders is governed by s 38(4)–(5) which is surely among the most obscurely worded provisions in the whole Act. However, it was established by *Gateshead Metropolitan Borough Council v N*[12] that the court is

---

1 Law Com No 207, *Domestic Violence and the Occupation of the Family Home* (1992).
2 For a similar power to add an exclusion requirement to an emergency protection order see post at p 594. The Law Commission, op cit at para 6.17, found no support for long-term exclusion as an alternative to a care order.
3 Section 38A(2).
4 This consent must be in writing or given orally to the court: FPR 1991 r 4.24; FPCA 1991 r 25.
5 Section 38A(3).
6 Section 38A(4).
7 Section 38A(5).
8 Section 38A(8).
9 Section 38B and see Sch 2 para 5 – power to assist suspected perpetrator to obtain alternative accommodation, discussed ante, p 562 n 8.
10 Section 38B(2).
11 Section 38A(10), s 38B(2).
12 [1993] 1 FLR 811.

empowered in principle to make any number of interim orders. Under s 38(4) an initial order may last a maximum of eight weeks and any subsequent order for a maximum of four weeks. One complication is if the initial order is made for a short period, say for two weeks. In that case a second order can use up the remainder of the eight weeks, ie in the cited example, six weeks.

7.   APPEALS

Before the Children Act 1989 the law governing appeals in public law cases was complicated and anomalous. Some, but not all, parties could appeal against the making of a care or supervision order, but there was no general right of appeal against the refusal to make such orders. Where appeals did lie from magistrates' decisions, they lay before the Crown Court and were by way of a full rehearing.[13] Under the Children Act 1989 the law is straightforward: anyone who was a party in the original proceedings may appeal against the making or refusal to make a care or supervision order (including an interim order).[14] This means that, like any other party, local authorities now have full rights of appeal.

Appeals from magistrates' decisions lie to the High Court,[15] and from the county court and High Court to the Court of Appeal.[16] Although in each case the relevant rules[17] say that the appeal is by way of a rehearing, this does not mean that it is a hearing de novo. As Hollings J said in *Croydon London Borough Council v A,*[18] all that is meant by the term 'rehearing' is that the appeal court has 'a wide ranging power to consider and deal with the way in which the court below came to its decision but it is not empowered to hear evidence, except in certain exceptional circumstances.'

It is equally established[19] that these appeals are governed by the general principles laid down in *G v G,*[20] ie that before an appeal can succeed the first instance decision has to be shown to be wrong; it is not enough that the appellate court would have reached a different decision.

8.   DISCHARGE OF CARE ORDERS AND DISCHARGE AND VARIATION OF SUPERVISION ORDERS[1]

Section 39 of the Children Act 1989 makes provision for the discharge (but not a variation, since that would interfere with the general principle that management of

---

13 See generally, Bevan *Child Law* (1989) paras 14.114–14.116.
14 Including a direction made under s 38(6): see *Re O (Minors) (Medical Examination)* [1993] 1 FLR 860. Note, however, *Re S (Discharge of Care Order)* [1995] 2 FLR 639, CA, in which it was held that an application to discharge a care order should be made rather than applying for an extension to appeal out of time.
15 Children Act 1989 s 94(1) and FPR 1991 r 4.22. For the procedure see *Practice Direction* [1992] 1 All ER 864. Although this Direction directs that appeals will take place at the nearest convenient High Court Centre, it is subject to the availability of a suitable judge: cf *R v Oxfordshire County Council (Secure Accommodation Order)* [1992] Fam 150, sub nom *R(J) v Oxfordshire County Council* [1992] 3 All ER 660.
16 County Courts Act 1984 s 77(1) and Supreme Court Act 1981 s 16.
17 Viz RSC Ord 55 r 3 and Ord 59 r 3.
18 [1992] Fam 169, [1992] 3 All ER 788.
19 See eg *Croydon London Borough Council v A* supra, and *Re G (A Minor) (Care Evidence)* [1994] 2 FLR 785, CA.
20 [1985] 2 All ER 225, HL, discussed ante, p 452.
1 See generally the Department of Health's *Guidance and Regulations*, Vol 1, *Court Orders*, paras 3.54 et seq.

compulsory care is the local authority's responsibility)[2] of care orders and for the variation and discharge of supervision orders. These powers are not new but, following the recommendations of the *Review of Child Care Law*,[3] unlike the former law, parents with parental responsibility have an independent right to apply for a discharge,[4] and the paramountcy principle provides the clear basis for determining whether an order should be made.[5]

Discharge of a care order

Under s 39(1) application for discharge of a care order may be made by any person who has parental responsibility, the child himself or the local authority. The requirement to have parental responsibility means that, since the making of a care order discharges any residence order,[6] only mothers, married fathers, unmarried fathers having parental responsibility by virtue of a s 4 order or agreement,[7] and guardians can apply under s 39. Unmarried fathers without parental responsibility, relatives and foster parents cannot therefore apply under s 39, but they can seek to apply for a residence order under s 8 which, as we have seen,[8] operates to discharge a care order.[9] Unmarried fathers can apply as of right for a residence order, but others will need first to apply for leave.[10] There is nothing to prevent those with parental responsibility from applying for a residence order rather than for a discharge under s 39, though unless there is a dispute between the applicants there would be little advantage in doing so.[11]

So far as the child is concerned, it has been held[12] that s 39(1)(b) is to be interpreted as giving a right to apply, so that unlike the private law there is no requirement to obtain the leave of the court. In practice most applications for discharge of care orders are made by local authorities,[13] who are required by the Review of Children's Cases Regulations 1991[14] to consider at least at every statutory review of a case of a child in their care whether to apply for a discharge.[15] Furthermore, as part of each review the child has to be informed, inter alia, of steps he may take himself for the discharge of the order.

Rather than grant the discharge simpliciter the court is empowered to substitute a supervision order.[16] In doing this there is no requirement that the threshold provisions under s 31(2) be proved again.[17] Indeed, the controlling principle in all

---

2 Department of Health's *Guidance and Regulations*, op cit, para 3.54.
3 DHSS, 1985, ch 20.
4 Previously they applied on the child's behalf and it was open to the guardian ad litem to seek a withdrawal: *R v Wandsworth West Juvenile Court, ex p S* [1984] FLR 713.
5 The previous grounds were vague: see the 7th edition of this work at p 463.
6 Children Act 1989 s 91(2).
7 Discussed ante, pp 378ff.
8 Ante, p 430.
9 Children Act 1989 s 91(1).
10 See post, p 604 for discussion of foster parents' use of this provision.
11 See ante, p 430. Quaere whether s 40(4) operates to permit the court to substitute a supervision order and whether the automatic embargo against re-applying for six months without leave of the court under s 91(15) applies upon a s 8 application? In the latter case the court can use its powers under s 91(14) to provide that no further application may be made without leave.
12 *Re A (Care: Discharge Application by Child)* [1995] 1 FLR 599, per Thorpe J.
13 See Farmer and Parker *A Study of the Discharge of Care Orders* (1985) Table 4.
14 Sch 2, para 1.
15 Sch 1, para 5 to the 1991 Regulations.
16 Children Act 1989 s 39(4).
17 Ibid, s 39(5).

such applications is the paramountcy of the child's welfare,[18] and in reaching its decision the court is required to have regard to the statutory check list under s 1(3).[19] This means, as the Court of Appeal held in *Re S (Discharge of Care Order)*,[20] that the jurisdiction under s 39 is entirely discretionary; there is, for example, no obligation upon the applicant to satisfy the court that the threshold requirements under s 31 no longer apply. Instead, in deciding what, if any, order to make, the primary focus must be on the child's welfare as it appears to be at the date of the discharge hearing. In assessing the child's welfare, an important consideration is, as s 1(3)(e) directs the court to consider, any harm that the child has suffered or is at risk of suffering. In the vast majority of cases the court is only likely to be concerned with evidence of recent harm and appraisal of current risk. However, the Court of Appeal in *Re S* accepted that on very limited occasions the court might properly be concerned with the soundness of the original findings in the earlier care proceedings. In so ruling, however, the court emphasised that the family courts should be alert to see that this theoretical power should not be abused, by allowing issues that have already been determined to be litigated afresh. It may be added, however, that absence of a risk of harm to a child returning home may not in itself be enough to justify discharging the care order.[1] Parents (or the child) may have difficulty in establishing that a discharge is in the child's interests, especially where there has been little contact.[2]

Contrary to the recommendation of the *Review of Child Care Law*,[3] the 1989 Act makes no express provision to postpone the discharge of a care order to allow for a gradual or phased return of the child to his family. How far this can be done by other means is debatable. The best option would seem to be for the court to control rehabilitation through its powers under s 34 to make care contact orders (see further, below), though technically such orders can only be made upon express application. The power under s 40(3) to postpone the effect of a discharge order or to subject a care order to conditions, and which is suggested by some commentators[4] to provide the appropriate power, only arises where an appeal is pending. The alternative of granting a residence order to the parents coupled with conditions under s 11(7)[5] and even a supervision order is limited in the sense that essentially the child must live with the residence holder;[6] it would therefore not be possible to grant a residence order to the parents but to provide under s 11(7) that the child remains with its foster parents with increasing contact to the parents. In view of these difficulties one wonders why provision for phased returns was not made.[7]

---

18 Ibid, s 1(1).
19 Discussed ante, pp 336ff.
20 [1995] 2 FLR 639, CA.
 1 See the *Review of Child Care Law*, op cit, para 20.17 and Bainham *Children: The New Law* (1990) para 5.76.
 2 See *Re S and P (Discharge of Care Order)* [1995] 2 FLR 782 in which Singer J upheld a magistrates' decision, that having heard the mother's oral evidence, they should proceed no further with the case since it was clearly hopeless. But note FPR 1991 r 4.16(2)(b); FPCA 1991 r 16(2)(b) which require the court to give the guardian ad litem, the solicitor for the child and the child himself, if of sufficient understanding, the opportunity to make representations.
 3 Op cit, para 20.26.
 4 Masson and Morris *Children Act Manual* (1992) p 118.
 5 See eg *Re G and M (Child Orders: Restricting Applications)* [1995] 2 FLR 416, where residence orders were made on condition that the mothers did not bring their children into contact with their fathers who had been found guilty of sexual offences on young people.
 6 See *Birmingham City Council v H* [1992] 2 FLR 323, discussed ante at p 427.
 7 This was thought to be such a serious defect of the old law that in *Re J (A Minor) (Wardship: Jurisdiction)* [1984] 1 All ER 29 the Court of Appeal allowed a child to be warded as a rare exception to the so-called '*Liverpool* principle': see post, p 603 n 2.

Once an application has been disposed of, no further application without leave can be made within six months.[8]

Discharge and variation of supervision orders

Under s 39(2) applications for discharge or variation of a supervision order may be made by any person who has parental responsibility for the child, the child himself or the supervisor. In addition, under s 39(3), a person who is not entitled to apply for a discharge but is a person with whom the child is living, can apply to vary a requirement made upon him under the supervision order.[9]

As with applications for the discharge of care orders, in deciding what order to make the court must apply the principle of the paramountcy of the child's welfare. It cannot, however, make a care order unless the criteria under s 31(2) have been satisfied.[10]

No application may be made without leave of the court within six months of the disposal of a previous application.[11]

9. CONTACT WITH CHILDREN IN CARE[12]

Introduction

As we have said,[13] the Children Act 1989 places considerable importance on the active promotion by local authorities of contact between children being looked after by them and their families, even to the extent of helping with the costs incurred in the visit.[14] This duty continues after a care order has been made and is underscored by the general provision under s 34(1) that there be reasonable contact between the child and inter alia his parents, which can only be departed from by agreement or by court order.

Before the Act, although emphasis was placed on the importance of maintaining contact between the child and his family,[15] the arrangements were mainly within the exclusive control of the local authorities. Only if contact was refused or terminated (but not if restricted) was it possible for parents, guardians or custodians to challenge the decision in court.[16] Even this was an inadequate remedy, since no application could be made until well after the termination or refusal,[17] so that by the time the issue got to court, magistrates often had little

---

8 Children Act 1989 s 91(15).
9 A requirement made under Sch 3 of the 1989 Act: see ante, p 569.
10 There is no similar provision to that substituting a supervision order for a care order under s 39(5), discussed above.
11 Section 91(15).
12 See generally the Department of Health's *Guidance and Regulations*, Vol 1, *Court Orders*, paras 3.75 et seq and Vol 3, *Family Placements*, ch 6.
13 Ante, p 519.
14 Children Act 1989 Sch 2, para 16.
15 In particular by the Code of Practice: Access to Children in Care, discussed in the 7th edition of this work at pp 469–70. The Code was superseded by the 1989 Act: cf Department of Health's *Guidance and Regulations*, Vol 3, at para 6.5.
16 Child Care Act 1980 ss 12A–F, discussed in the 7th edition of this work at pp 481 et seq. It had become established that access decisions could not be 'reviewed' by the court in wardship (see post, p 602), though in cases of impropriety recourse could have been had to judicial review (discussed post, p 604).
17 This was because notice of refusal or termination had first to be served by the local authority: Child Care Act 1980 s 12B.

choice but to uphold the local authority's decision.[18] Moreover it had been held[19] that once the termination or refusal had been upheld by the court there could be no further challenges.

Implementing the recommendations of the *Review of Child Care Law*,[20] and anticipating that the continued inability to challenge restrictions would be contrary to the European Conventions on Human Rights,[1] s 34 effectively turned the previous law on its head by requiring the local authority to seek a court order *before* terminating or restricting reasonable contact. This fundamental change, arguably among the most significant changes introduced by the 1989 Act, means that parents and others have a more realistic chance of opposing local authority contact plans.

The scheme under s 34

(a)   The presumption of reasonable contact

The basic position is set out by s 34(1), namely that local authorities must normally allow the child reasonable contact with his parents (including the unmarried father regardless of whether he has parental responsibility) or guardians, a person in whose favour there was a residence order immediately before the making of the care order and a person who had the care of the child by virtue of an order under the High Court's inherent jurisdiction. The local authority, the child and any person concerned are expected, as far as possible, to agree upon reasonable arrangements before the care order is made.[2] In any event, local authorities are expected to provide details of their proposals for contact when applying for an interim or full care order.[3] Section 34(11) requires the court, before making a care order,[4] to consider any contact arrangements that the authority have made or propose to make and to invite the parties to the proceedings to comment on those arrangements. As Ewbank J observed,[5] 'reasonable contact' is not the same as contact at the discretion of the local authority: rather it implies either that which is agreed between the local authority and the parties, or, in the absence of such an agreement, contact which is objectively reasonable.

(b)   Departing from the general presumption

As an exception to the presumption of reasonable contact, s 34(6) permits a local authority in matters of urgency to refuse contact for up to seven days provided

---

18 In a study carried out by Millham, Bullock, Hosie and Little *Access Disputes in Child Care* (1989) p 53, of 309 terminations notice only nine parents (three per cent) re-established contact through legal proceedings.
19 *R v West Glamorgan County Council, ex p T* [1990] 1 FLR 339.
20 Ch 21; cf the Second Report of the House of Commons Social Services Committee 1983–1984 (the 'Short Report') HC 360, paras 73 and 324 which expressed concern that local authority power had already been eroded too far by the access provisions under the Child Care Act 1980.
1 See eg *R v United Kingdom* [1988] 2 FLR 445, E Ct HR; *O v United Kingdom* (1987) 10 EHRR 82, E Ct HR; *W v United Kingdom* (1987) 10 EHRR 29, E Ct HR; and *B v United Kingdom* (1987) 10 EHRR 87, E Ct HR.
2 See the Department of Health's *Guidance and Regulations*, Vol 1, para 3.76 and Vol 3, para 6.2.
3 Ibid, Vol 3, para 6.2.
4 Including an interim care order: see s 33(11).
5 In *Re P (Minors) (Contact with Children in Care)* [1993] 2 FLR 156 at 161; cf *L v London Borough of Bromley* [1998] 1 FLR 709 in which Wilson J held that a magistrates' order that contact be at the local authority's discretion could not be interpreted as absolving them of their duty to afford reasonable contact.

'they are satisfied that it is necessary to do so in order to safeguard or promote the child's welfare'. In such cases the local authority are required to give written notice explaining the decision to the child, if he is of sufficient understanding, and to any person with whom there is a presumption of reasonable contact.[6]

Apart from this limited power it is incumbent upon the local authority to seek a court order restricting or denying contact,[7] if they wish to depart from the general presumption.[8]

(c) The position of the child and other interested persons

A child in care has the right[9] to make an application both for defined contact to be allowed with a named person and for an order authorising the authority to refuse to allow contact with any named person.[10] No doubt in most cases the authority will take the proceedings, but where, for example, the authority are thought to be obstructive, the child may wish to take the initiative. It has been held,[11] however, that the court has no power to force the person named in the order, or, if that person was a minor, the person with whom he or she lived, to have or permit the contact provided for.

It is also open to a person to whom the Act's presumption of reasonable contact applies,[12] and any other person who has obtained leave of the court,[13] to apply for an order about contact at any time if he is dissatisfied with the arrangements made or proposed for contact between the child and himself.[14] The ability of anyone to seek leave means that relatives and former foster parents, for example, may take steps to seek orders.

In deciding whether to grant leave[15] to third parties to make an application for contact it has been held[16] that the court should take account of the criteria set out in s 10(9),[17] which means[18] that the court should have particular regard at least to –

(a) the nature of the contact being sought;
(b) the connection of the applicant to the child (the more meaningful and important the connection to the child, the greater is the weight to be given to this factor);
(c) any disruption to the child's stability or security; and
(d) the wishes of the parents and local authority, which are important but not determinative.

Additionally, in deciding whether or not to grant leave the court must be satisfied that there is a serious issue to try and that the applicant has a good arguable case. If therefore the application is frivolous or vexatious or if there only a remote prospect of the application for an order succeeding, leave should be refused.

---

6 Contact with Children Regulations 1991 reg 2.
7 As they are entitled to do respectively under s 34(2) and (4).
8 Once an order has been made it can be departed from by agreement: see further below.
9 Note, therefore, that unlike when seeking s 8 orders the child does not need leave of the court, nor, consequently, need such an application be heard in the High Court; cf *Re A (Care: Discharge: Application by Child)* [1995] 1 FLR 599, discussed ante, p 579.
10 Children Act 1989 s 34(2) and (4).
11 Per Wilson J in *Re F (Contact: Child in Care)* [1995] 1 FLR 510.
12 Viz those persons mentioned in s 34(1). See ante, p 582.
13 Section 34(3)(b).
14 Section 34(3).
15 Leave may be granted by a single justice; FPCA 1991 r 2(5).
16 *Re M (Care: Contact: Grandmother's Application For Leave)* [1995] 2 FLR 86, CA.
17 Discussed ante at pp 434–7.
18 Per Ward LJ in *Re M*, supra at 95–9.

(d)   The court's powers

The court is empowered both on making a care order and subsequently, either upon application or acting upon its own motion,[19] to make such order as it considers appropriate as to the contact to be allowed,[20] to refuse contact with a named person,[1] and in each case to impose such conditions (for example, to restrict contact to specific periods or places) as are considered appropriate.[2] The wording of these provisions is wide enough to permit the court to make interim orders, including an interim order for no contact.[3] Although not defined, it is thought that, like a s 8 contact order (from which a s 34 order must generally be distinguished),[4] 'contact' under s 34 includes visiting, staying or other contact, for example by letter or telephone.[5] Wide though the powers are, the court is not entitled to make a contact order with a direction that the matter be brought back before the judge at a later date to enable him 'to keep an eye on the case',[6] nor that a guardian ad litem should have contact with the child after the care order,[7] in each case because that was simply an attempt to keep the care order under review. It has also been said that in view of the statutory presumption of reasonable contact there should be no need to make such an order *imposing* it.[8]

In deciding what, if any, order to make the court must apply the general principles set out by s 1, ie to regard the child's welfare as the paramount consideration, to consider the statutory check list and to make an order only where it is in the child's interests to do so. The application of the welfare principle where more than one child is involved has proved problematic. In *Birmingham City Council v H*,[9] where both mother and child were in care, the mother (who was herself a 15-year-old child) sought contact with her baby. The House of Lords ruled that, as s 34(4) made it clear that the subject matter of the application is the child in care in respect of whom an order is sought, it was the baby's welfare and not the mother's that was paramount. In that case Lord Slynn also said that[10] if a child in care sought contact with a named person, then that applicant's welfare would still be paramount even if contact was being sought with another child. It seems apparent, however, from the subsequent decision in *Re F (Contact: Child in Care)*,[11] that that analysis depends on the precise nature of the action. In *Re F* a child in care sought contact with her four younger siblings who were not in care. The parents were opposed to such contact and Wilson J held that the application under s 34(2) was misplaced because it could not oblige the parents to permit the contact, since the compulsory effect only runs against the local authority. It was

---

19 Children Act 1989 s 34(5).
20 Section 34(2).
 1 Section 34(4).
 2 Section 34(7).
 3 See *West Glamorgan County Council v P* [1992] 2 FLR 369.
 4 A s 8 contact order cannot be made in respect of a child in care: s 9(1), and any such order is discharged upon making a care order: s 91(2). NB, however, a child in care can seek a s 8 contact order in respect of another child not in care: see *Re F (Contact: Child in Care)* [1995] 1 FLR 510, discussed below.
 5 See eg White, Carr and Lowe, op cit at 8.109.
 6 *Re S (A Minor) (Care: Contact Order)* [1994] 2 FLR 222, CA.
 7 *Kent County Council v C* [1993] Fam 57, [1993] 1 All ER 719.
 8 *Re S*, supra.
 9 [1994] 2 AC 212, [1994] 1 All ER 12, HL, discussed also at p 333.
10 Ibid at 222 and 18 respectively.
11 [1995] 1 FLR 510.

accepted that the appropriate action would have been to have sought a s 8 contact order which, since it concerned the children not in care, was not caught by the embargo under s 9(1).[12] In fact it emerged during the hearing before Wilson J that none of the children wanted contact, so that the s 8 application was dismissed by consent.

Notwithstanding this decision Wilson J made the following observations about the application of the welfare principle.[13] According to his Lordship, where under s 34(2) an applicant child is seeking contact with other children who are not in care and who are willing to see him, then it is the interests of the applicant child that are paramount. However, if an order is sought under s 8, then it would be the interests of the other children that would be paramount. Where the other children are also in care, some commentators,[14] following the above analysis, have taken the view that it is the children in respect of whom the order is sought whose welfare is paramount. Assuming this analysis to be correct it may be questioned whether it is right that the issue of paramountcy should be determined simply by the accident of who brought the action.[15]

As will be appreciated, these provisions give the court wide power to control the future direction of the case and, although the court must always be mindful of what the local authority considers practicable, it is not limited by what the authority thinks is reasonable. As Butler-Sloss LJ put it in *Re B (Minors) (Termination of Contact: Paramount Consideration):*[16]

'The presumption of contact, which has to be for the benefit of the child, has always to be balanced against the long-term welfare of the child and particularly, where he will live in the future. Contact must not be allowed to destabilise or endanger the arrangements for the child and in many cases the plans for the child will be decisive of the contact application . . . *The proposals of the local authority, based on their appreciation of the best interests of the child, must command the greatest respect and consideration from the court, but Parliament has given to the court, and not to the local authority, the duty to decide on contact between the child and those named in section 34(1).* Consequently, the court may have the task of requiring the local authority to justify their long term plans to the extent only that those plans exclude contact between parent and child' [emphasis added].

Agreeing with this analysis Simon Brown LJ said in the subsequent decision, *Re E (A Minor) (Care Order: Contact):*[17]

'. . . if on a s 34(4) application the judge concludes that the benefits of contact outweigh the disadvantages of disrupting any of the local authority's long term plans which are inconsistent with such contact then . . . he must give effect to it by refusing the local authority's application to terminate this contact.'

12 Section 9(1) is discussed in detail ante at pp 429–30.
13 Ibid at 513–14.
14 See White, Carr and Lowe, op cit, at 8.107 and Clarke Hall and Morrison 1[765].
15 See the criticism of the *Birmingham* decision by Douglas 'In Whose Best Interests?' (1994) 110 LQR 379, who argues that ultimately each child's welfare has to be balanced against the other's.
16 [1993] Fam 301 at 311, [1993] 3 All ER 524, CA at 532, overruling *West Glamorgan County Council v P (No 2)* [1993] 1 FLR 407.
17 [1994] 1 FLR 146, CA. See also *Berkshire County Council v B* [1997] 1 FLR 171 – since the child's welfare was paramount, contact should be ordered if it was in the child's interests, notwithstanding that the long-term plan of the local authority envisaged termination of parental contact; cf *Re D and H (Termination of Contact)* [1997] 1 FLR 841, CA where it was held on the facts to be wrong to phase out contact contrary to the local authority's recommendations.

It has been observed[18] that contact should not be refused under s 34(4) whilst there remains a realistic possibility of rehabilitation of the child with the person in question.

(e) Variation and discharge

Upon application by the local authority, child or any person named in the order, the court can vary or discharge any previous order made under s 34.[19] This means that, unlike under the former law,[20] a refusal of contact does not prevent a further application being made. However, under s 91(17) where an applicant has been refused contact he may not make another such application within six months without leave of the court.

In deciding whether or not to discharge a s 34 order it is established[1] that the child's welfare is the paramount consideration.[2] Upon such an application it is not normally appropriate to reinvestigate whether the original order was made appropriately and the court should be astute to screen out disguised appeals. Instead the court should have two main interlocking considerations in mind, namely, the extent to which circumstances have changed since the making of the order and, in the light of such changes, whether it remains in the child's interests for the original order to stay in place.

It is not always incumbent upon local authorities to seek court sanction to depart from the terms of a s 34 order, since the Contact with Children Regulations 1991[3] allow this to be done by agreement between the authority and the person in relation to whom the order is made, subject inter alia to the agreement of the child if he is of sufficient understanding.[4] The idea behind this provision is to allow for flexibility and partnership in contact arrangements and to obviate the need to go back to court when all concerned agree to this arrangement.[5] The existence of this remarkable power effectively to override a court order by consent has led one judge to say[6] that in cases where the court takes the view that there should be no contact to a child in care it would normally be better to make no order at all rather than an order authorising refusal under s 34(4). The problem, however, with making no order is that the local authority would then continue to be under an obligation to afford reasonable contact.[7]

---

18 Per Simon Brown LJ in *Re T (minors) (termination of contact: discharge of order)* [1997] 1 All ER 65, CA.

19 Section 34(9). Although the Act is not specific on the point, the making of a residence order under s 8 must discharge a s 34 order, since it is dependent upon the existence of a care order, which is itself discharged by virtue of s 91(1).

20 See *R v West Glamorgan County Council, ex p T*, supra.

1 *Re T (minors) (termination of contact: discharge of order)*, supra.

2 Aliter where an application is made under s 91(17) for leave to apply – see *Re T*, supra, at 74, per Simon Brown LJ; cf the similar stance in relation to applications for leave under s 91(14) taken by Wilson J in *Re R (Residence: Contact: Restricting Application)* [1998] 1 FLR 749, CA. See ante, p 478.

3 Reg 3.

4 It is also incumbent upon the authority to give written notification within seven days to the child's parents or guardian, a person who had a residence order before the care order was made, a person who had care under an order made under the High Court's inherent jurisdiction and any other person whose wishes and feelings the authority consider relevant.

5 See the Department of Health's *Guidance and Regulations*, Vol 3, para 6.31.

6 Ewbank J in *Kent County Council v C* [1993] Fam 57, [1993] 1 All ER 719.

7 See the comment at [1993] Fam Law 134.

D. Powers under Part V

1. INTRODUCTION

Unlike Part IV of the Children Act 1989, which is primarily concerned with the promotion of children's interests in the mid to long term, Part V of the Act is concerned with short-term need to protect children at risk. As the Department of Health's *Guidance* puts it,[8] Part V is designed:

> '. . . to ensure that effective protective action can be taken when this is necessary within a framework of proper safeguards and reasonable opportunity for parents and others connected with the child to challenge such actions before a court. The measures are short-term and time-limited, and may or may not lead to further action . . .'

Here we discuss child assessment orders, emergency protection orders and the powers of the police to take a child into police protection. However, it should also be said that pursuant to s 47 local authorities have a positive duty to investigate cases of suspected child abuse and decide what action is appropriate.[9] As the Department of Health's *Guidance* points out,[10] action under s 47 'should be seen as the usual first step when a question of child protection arises . . .' Without such investigation the local authority is unlikely to succeed in any application for a child assessment or emergency protection order.

It may be that, the matter having been investigated, the problems can be solved with the co-operation of the family. Indeed, as we have seen,[11] it is a basic tenet of the Act that the local authority work in partnership with the family and that intervention always has to be especially justified. This is no less true in so-called emergencies than at other times. Even if intervention is thought necessary, it should always be done sensitively with a view to promoting the child's interests and, so far as it is consistent to do so, without overlooking the interests of the other members of the family. So-called 'dawn raids' (ie where children are removed from their families during the night), for example, should rarely be necessary.[12] In any event, thought should always be given to whether the alleged abuser, rather than the child, should be removed from the family.[13]

2. CHILD ASSESSMENT ORDERS[14]

Described as 'a multi-disciplinary assessment in non-emergency situations',[15] a child assessment order had no parallel in the pre-1989 Act law. It was first

---

8 Vol 1, *Court Orders*, para 4.1.
9 For a detailed discussion of these duties see the Department of Health's *Guidance and Regulations*, Vol 1, op cit, paras 4.78 et seq; and see ante, pp 532ff.
10 Para at 4.78.
11 Ante, p 519.
12 Such removals, for example in Orkney's and Rochdale's satanic child abuse cases (see respectively Brett 'Orkney: aberration or symptom?' (1991) 3 Journal of Child Law 143 and *Rochdale Borough Council v A* [1991] 2 FLR 192), caused considerable public disquiet. In *Re A (Minors) (Child Abuse: Guidelines)* [1992] 1 All ER 153 it was held that such removals should only be effected when there are clear grounds for believing significant harm would otherwise be caused to the children or vital evidence is only obtainable by such means.
13 For a detailed discussion of this issue see Cobley 'Child abuse, child protection and the criminal law' (1992) 4 Journal of Child Law 78.
14 See generally Lavery 'The child assessment order – a re-assessment' (1996) 8 CFLQ 41 and Dickens 'Assessment and the Control of Social Work: An Analysis of Reasons for the Non-Use of the Child Assessment Order' [1993] JSWFL 88.
15 By David Mellor 158 HC Official Report, col 596.

proposed in the Kimberley Carlile Report,[16] but the order was only included in the 1989 Act as a late amendment in response to a demand for a power to be able to see, examine and assess a child where there is concern as to his welfare, in the face of lack of co-operation from those responsible for him.[17]

Application and criteria

As with applications for care and supervision orders,[18] only the local authority and the NSPCC (as the only authorised person)[19] may apply for a child assessment order.

Under s 43(1) the court may make an order if it is satisfied that:

'(a)   the applicant has reasonable cause to suspect that the child is suffering or is likely to suffer significant harm;

(b)   an assessment of the state of the child's health or development, or of the way in which he has been treated, is required to enable the applicant to determine whether or not the child is suffering, or is likely to suffer, significant harm; and

(c)   it is unlikely that such an assessment will be made, or be satisfactory, in the absence of a child assessment order.'

It is to be emphasised that this order is not intended to be used in an emergency, nor as a substitute for an emergency protection order. Indeed s 43(4) specifically enjoins the court *not* to make an assessment order if there are grounds for making an emergency protection order and the court thinks it ought to make such an order. The court is empowered to treat an application for an assessment order as an application for an emergency protection order.[20] The fact that applications are made on notice[1] and the hearing is inter partes further emphasises that these orders are not designed to deal with emergencies.

As the Department of Health's *Guidance* says:[2]

'The principal conditions are very specific. The order is for cases where there are suspicions, but no firm evidence, of actual or likely significant harm in circumstances which do not constitute an emergency; the applicant considers that a decisive step to obtain an assessment is needed to show whether the concern is well founded or further action is not required and that informal arrangements to have such an assessment carried out have failed.'

Accordingly, the *Guidance* suggests that such an order:

'. . . will usually be most appropriate where the harm to the child is long-term and cumulative rather than sudden and severe. The circumstances may be nagging concern about a child who appears to be failing to thrive; or the parents are ignorant or unwilling to face up to possible harm to their child because of the state of his health or development; or it appears that the child may be subject to wilful neglect or abuse but not to such an extent as to place him at serious immediate risk.'[3]

16 *A Child in Mind – The Report of an Inquiry into the Death of Kimberley Carlile* (1987).
17 The government rejected the alternative proposal for a child production notice, inter alia because it would have allowed a local authority to take control of the situation by administrative action rather than by a court order. See White, Carr and Lowe *A Guide to the Children Act 1989*, para 7.10. See also Parton *Governing the Family: Child Care, Child Protection and the State* (1991) pp 176–92.
18 But cf emergency protection orders, discussed post, p 591.
19 Children Act 1989 s 31(9) and s 43(13).
20 Children Act 1989 s 43(3).
 1 Section 43(11).
 2 Vol 1, para 4.8.
 3 Ibid at para 4.9.

Even if the court is satisfied as to the existence of the conditions, it is not bound to make the order. As with other orders under the 1989 Act, the court must, pursuant to s 1(1) and (5), have regard to the paramountcy of the child's welfare and be satisfied that making the order would be better for the child than making no order at all. However, because these proceedings do *not* rank as 'family proceedings',[4] the court *cannot* make a s 8 order.

An assessment order cannot be made either where an emergency protection or care order is made, but in principle there is no reason why it cannot be made in respect of an accommodated child, and it can co-exist with a s 8 order.

Effect, commencement and duration of the order

A child assessment order has the twofold effect of placing a duty on any person, who is in a position to do so, to produce the child to the person named in the order, to comply with such directions relating to his assessment as may be specified,[5] and of authorising any person carrying out the assessment, or any part of it, to do so in accordance with the order.[6]

The maximum period of the order is seven days, but this period runs from the date specified in the order and not from the date on which the order was made.[7]

Section 43(6) empowers the court to make directions on any matter relating to the assessment, including directions as to the kind of assessment which is to take place and with what aim, by whom and where it will be carried out, and whether it will be subject to conditions, such as that the assessment should be a joint one involving experts appointed by the child's parents or the guardian ad litem as well as by the local authority. If an intrusive examination is to take place, such as a biopsy or genital examination, specific direction should be given. The order should include a direction as to whom the result of the assessment should be given.

Directions may also be made about whether and, if so, for how long, a child may be kept away from home.[8] Indeed, since an assessment order does not confer parental responsibility, the child may only be kept away from home in accordance with court directions. If the child is to be kept away from home, the order must contain such directions as the courts thinks fit as to the contact the child is to be allowed to have with other persons.[9]

Notwithstanding any court directions, if the child is of sufficient understanding to make an informed decision he may refuse to submit to a medical or psychiatric examination or other assessment.[10]

The use of assessment orders

The expectation that child assessment orders would not be made frequently has been borne out by experience. For example, in the year ending 30 September 1992 only 105 applications were made, as opposed to 2,215 emergency protection

---

4 See s 8(3), (4), discussed ante, p 445. Nor need the check list under s 1(3) be applied: *Re R (Recovery Orders)* [1998] 2 FLR 401.
5 Section 43(6).
6 Section 43(7).
7 Section 43(5). It is thought that the period must run continuously rather than eg one day a week for seven weeks: see White, Carr and Lowe *Children Act in Practice* (2nd edn, 1995) para 7.29 and Clarke Hall and Morrison, op cit, para 1[873].
8 Section 43(9).
9 Section 43(10).
10 Section 43(8). There is a similar provision (s 44(7)) in relation to emergency protection orders, upon which note *South Glamorgan County Council v W and B* [1993] 1 FLR 574, discussed ante, p 576.

orders.[11] In the following 12 months, only 94 applications were made, of which 26 were withdrawn, and only 55 orders granted.[12] The relatively high level of withdrawals supports the supposition that in many cases the threat of the order may be sufficient to persuade parents to agree to an assessment, in which case there will be no need for an order. One reason for the lack of use of assessment orders is the seven-day time limit; indeed one researcher found[13] this to be one of the key reasons for not seeking to use the powers. Clearly, given the limited length of the order, any assessment of the child will necessarily be little more than an initial one (for this reason arrangements for the assessment need to be carefully planned). Although it has been suggested[14] that it was misconceived to apply any time limit to the order, it is important to bear in mind that the whole purpose of the order is to obtain sufficient evidence either to allay fears about the child's well-being or to justify further action. Seven days should therefore give enough time to achieve this limited purpose.

Among other reasons suggested[15] for its lack of use are the length of time before an order can be obtained and, given the requirement of an inter partes hearing combined with lack of resources, local authorities 'are not likely to spend time and money on taking proceedings to coerce unco-operative parents in marginal cases'.

In point of fact, however, the s 43 powers were never envisaged to be used frequently,[16] but they will remain of some use, particularly where parents are ignorant or resistant to thinking about the possible harm to their child because of the state of his health or development.

3.   EMERGENCY PROTECTION ORDERS[17]

Introduction and background

The purpose of an emergency protection order is to provide for the immediate removal or retention of a child in a genuine emergency.

The provisions are based on the recommendations of the *Review of Child Care Law*[18] following widespread criticism of place of safety orders which emergency protection orders replaced. For example, that they were routinely used as a method of starting care proceedings rather than in genuine emergencies;[19] that they were granted too readily, often by a single justice in his own home on an ex parte application;[20] that they lasted too long;[1] and that the grounds were not sufficiently

11 Children Act Report 1992 (HMSO).
12 Children Act Report 1993 (HMSO). As Lavery, op cit, at 42 points out, consideration of such orders is conspicuously absent from more recent Children Act Advisory Committee Reports.
13 Dickens, op cit at 97.
14 Lavery, op cit at 55.
15 White, Carr and Lowe *Children Act in Practice* (2nd edn, 1995) para 7.31.
16 As the Department of Health's *Guidance*, Vol 1, para 4.23 says 'The child assessment order should be used sparingly'.
17 See generally the Department of Health's *Guidance and Regulations*, Vol 1, *Court Orders*, paras 4.28 et seq.
18 DHSS, 1985, ch 13.
19 See eg Norris and Parton 'Administration of Place of Safety Orders' [1987] JSWL 1 at 3. Research also showed that in many cases place of safety orders did not subsequently lead to compulsory care: Packman *Who Needs Care?*
20 In Cleveland, for example, of 276 applications made between 1 January and 31 July 1987, 174 were granted by a single justice sitting at home: *Report of the Inquiry into Child Abuse in Cleveland in 1987* (Cm 412, 1988), para 10.9.
1 Viz up to 28 days – see the discussion in the *Review of Child Care Law*, paras 13.21 et seq.

focused on emergencies.[2] Furthermore, the effects of an order were unclear and often misunderstood, but were in any event inadequate in that the successful applicant had no clear responsibility for the child.[3]

The grounds for an emergency protection order

(a)   Likely to suffer harm

Section 44(1) provides the first of three grounds upon which an emergency protection order may be made, namely that on the application of any person the court is satisfied that there is reasonable cause to believe that the child is likely to suffer significant harm if he:

(i)   is not removed to accommodation provided by or on behalf of the applicant; or

(ii) does not remain in the place in which he is then being accommodated.

Although commonly the applicant will be the local authority or NSPCC, *any* person may apply under this provision, including even a parent or relative.[4] Where the applicant is not the relevant local authority, provision has been made for the authority, if they think it is in the child's best interests, to take over the order and therefore the powers and responsibilities for the child that go with it.[5] The court (and not the applicant) must be satisfied about likelihood of significant harm.[6] The ground itself is prospective, so that evidence of past or even current harm is not sufficient unless it indicates that harm is likely to recur in the future. On the other hand, this prospective test can be satisfied even though the harm to the particular child has not yet occurred, eg where a convicted sexual offender moves in with the mother.

(b)   Denial of access to the child

Under s 44(1)(b) an order can be made upon application of a local authority where they are making enquiries under s 47(1)(b) because they (ie the local authority) have reasonable cause to suspect that a child is suffering, or is likely to suffer, significant harm,[7] and 'those enquiries are being frustrated by access to the child being unreasonably refused to a person authorised to seek access and that the applicant has reasonable cause to believe that access to the child is required as a matter of urgency'. Similar provision is made[8] for an application in the same circumstances by an authorised person (ie the NSPCC).[9]

Section 44(1)(b) and (c) were intended[10] to be used in emergencies where enquiries cannot be completed because the child cannot be seen but there is

---

2   *Review of Child Care Law*, paras 13.8 et seq.
3   Ibid, paras 13.12 et seq and the Cleveland Inquiry Report, para 10–8.
4   In such cases the local authority will also have to become involved, because under s 47(1) they have a duty to investigate upon being informed of the existence of such an order. For the difficulties of individuals obtaining an extension, see post, p 594.
5   See the Emergency Protection Order (Transfer of Responsibilities) Regulations 1991, discussed by the Department of Health's *Guidance and Regulations*, op cit, paras 4.32 et seq.
6   For discussion of the meaning of 'significant harm' and 'likelihood' see ante, p 538.
7   These duties under s 47 are also discussed at pp 532ff.
8   Section 44(1)(c).
9   Children Act 1989 s 31(9).
10 The provision was introduced following a recommendation in the Kimberley Carlile inquiry (*A Child in Mind*, para 7.24). It was a late amendment to the legislation and was little debated.

enough cause to suspect the child is suffering or is likely to suffer significant harm. In cases where there is a need for further investigation of a child's health and development but he is thought to be safe from immediate danger, the proper order, if any, is a child assessment order.[11] The Department of Health's *Guidance and Regulations* puts the point well, commenting:[12]

> 'The hypothesis of the grounds at section 44(1)(b) and (c) is that this combination of factors is evidence of an emergency or the likelihood of an emergency.'

It also makes the further point:

> 'The court will have to decide whether the refusal of access to the child was unreasonable in the circumstances. It might consider a refusal unreasonable if the person refusing had had explained to him the reason for the enquiries and the request for access, the request itself was reasonable, and he had failed to respond positively in some other suitable way – by arranging for the child to be seen immediately by his GP, for example. Refusal of a request to see a sleeping child in the middle of the night may not be unreasonable,[13] but refusal to allow access at a reasonable time without good reason could well be.'

Section 44(1) provides the minimum conditions that must be satisfied before an order can be made. However, it is not intended that upon being satisfied of the condition under s 44(1) the court should automatically make an order. The court must still consider both the welfare principle and the presumption of no order, pursuant to s 1(1) and 1(5). Since these proceedings are not 'family proceedings'[14] the court cannot make a s 8 order. On the other hand, it can give directions about contact and medical or psychiatric examination or other assessment of the child.[15]

Procedure

Unless arising from a s 37 direction to investigate,[16] or there are proceedings pending in a higher court, an application for an emergency protection order must be made in the magistrates' family proceedings court and cannot be transferred to a higher court.[17] Application may, with leave of the clerk, be made ex parte,[18] though hearings can be inter partes and indeed the court has the power to direct that the application be made inter partes.[19] An order can be made by a single justice.[20] However, wherever possible applications, even those made ex parte, should be made to a court.[1] A court hearing the application may take account of any statement contained in any report made to the court in the course of or in connection with the hearing or any evidence given during the hearing, which is in the opinion of the court relevant to the application.[2] This enables the court to give

---

11 Child assessment orders are discussed ante, pp 587ff.
12 Vol 1, op cit, para 4.39.
13 Indeed, removals in the middle of the night will require special justification: cf *Re A (Minors) (Child Abuse: Guidelines)* [1992] 1 All ER 153, per Hollings J.
14 As defined by s 8(3), (4), discussed ante, p 445.
15 Children Act 1989 s 44(6), discussed below.
16 Discussed ante, p 455.
17 The Children (Allocation of Proceedings) Order 1991 arts 3 and 7(2).
18 Family Proceedings Courts (Children Act 1989) Rules 1991 r 4(4). There has been some reluctance on the part of the courts to hear ex parte applications: see *The Children Act Report 1992* (1993) Cm 2144).
19 Ibid, r 4(5).
20 Ibid, r 2(5)(a).
1 See the Department of Health's *Guidance and Regulations*, Vol 1, para 4.46 and following the recommendations of the Cleveland Inquiry Report, op cit, p 252.
2 Children Act 1989 s 45(7).

proper weight to hearsay, opinions, health visiting or social work records and to medical reports.

The effects of an order

An emergency protection order authorises either the removal to or prevention of removal from accommodation provided by or on behalf of the applicant.[3] In the former instance the order operates as a direction to any person who is in a position to do so to comply with any request to produce the child to the applicant.[4] The court may also authorise an applicant to enter specified premises and search for a child and may include another child in the order if it believes there might be another child on the premises.[5]

The order gives the applicant parental responsibility for the child,[6] but this is limited: the power to remove or to prevent removal can only be exercised to safeguard and promote the child's welfare.[7] Hence, for example, if the applicant gains access and finds that the child is neither harmed nor likely to be harmed, he may not remove the child.[8] In any event, an applicant can exercise responsibility only insofar as it is reasonably required to safeguard or promote the child's welfare, having regard in particular to the duration of the order.[9] It would not therefore be appropriate to make any changes in the child's life which would have a long-lasting effect.

The power to add directions

In the absence of a court direction the applicant must, during the subsistence of the order, allow the child reasonable contact with his parents, any other person with parental responsibility, any person with whom he was living immediately before the order, any person in whose favour there is a contact order in relation to him and any person acting on behalf of those persons.[10] The court, however, may give such directions as it considers appropriate about contact and may impose conditions.[11] Nevertheless, where the local authority is the applicant, the court will generally leave contact to the authority's discretion or at any rate order that reasonable contact be negotiated.[12] If therefore the local authority wishes to restrict contact, it should seek a court direction to that effect.

Medical evidence is likely to be of importance in any future care proceedings, so that early decisions or directions about examinations are crucial. For this reason, although the parental responsibility acquired on the making of the order would permit the applicant to consent to the child's examination or assessment, it

---

3 Ibid, s 44(4)(b).
4 Section 44(4)(a).
5 Section 48(3), (4). This does not give the power to make a forced entry. If the applicant is refused or likely to be refused entry, the court may issue a warrant authorising a constable to assist in the execution of the order using reasonable force if necessary: s 48(9).
6 Section 44(4)(c).
7 Section 44(5)(a). Removals should normally be at an agreed time following consultation with appropriate professionals. A proper explanation must be given to the child: Department of Health's *Guidance and Regulations*, Vol 1, para 4.58.
8 Similarly, if a return appears safe, the child should be returned: s 44(10). In each case this might occur where the alleged abuser vacates the home.
9 Section 44(5)(b).
10 Section 44(13). This presumption of reasonable contact is in line with the general policy of the Act: see the discussion ante, p 582.
11 Section 44(6) and (8).
12 See the Department of Health's *Guidance and Regulations*, Vol 1, at para 4.62.

might be preferable to seek directions on the issue. Section 44(6)(b) empowers the court to make directions as to a medical or psychiatric examination or other assessment of the child, and under s 44(8) the court may direct that there be no such examination or assessment. Although s 44(7) expressly provides that, notwithstanding a court order, the child can, if of sufficient understanding to make an informed decision, refuse to submit to an examination or other assessment, as we discussed in relation to the equivalent provision in relation to interim care,[13] it has been controversially held[14] that the High Court has an inherent power to override that refusal.

The power to add an exclusion requirement[15]

Following amendments introduced by the Family Law Act 1996 courts can now[16] add an exclusion requirement to any emergency protection order. Such an order requires the person named in the order to leave the child's home or defined area where the home is situated and prohibits him from re-entering the home or defined area.[17] This power, conferred by s 44A of the 1989 Act, is subject to the court being satisfied of three conditions:

(1) there is reasonable cause to believe that the child will consequently not be likely to suffer significant harm or that the enquiries will cease to be frustrated;

(2) there is someone (whether a parent or some other person) living in the home who is able and willing 'to give to the child the care which it would be reasonable to expect a parent to give to him; and

(3) that that other person consents[18] to the exclusion requirement.

The exclusion requirement may last no longer than the emergency protection order, though it can be made for a shorter period.[19] In any event, the exclusion ceases to be enforceable if the applicant removes the child for more than 24 hours.[20] A power of arrest may be attached to the requirement.[1]

Instead of making the exclusion requirement, the court is empowered to accept undertakings in similar terms.[2] However, although such undertakings are enforceable through contempt proceedings, no power of arrest can be attached.[3]

Duration of the order

In the first instance an emergency protection order may be granted for up to eight days.[4] Save where the applicant is an individual,[5] the court can, upon application,

---

13 Viz s 38(6), discussed ante, p 576.
14 Per Douglas Brown J in *South Glamorgan County Council v W and B* [1993] 1 FLR 574.
15 See generally the Law Commission report Law Com No 207, *Domestic Violence and the Occupation of the Family Home* (1992) paras 6.15ff.
16 Viz from 1 October 1997: SI 1997/1892.
17 Section 44A(3).
18 The consent must either be written or given orally to the court: FPR 1991 r 4.24; FPCA 1991 r 25.
19 Section 44A(4).
20 Section 44A(10).
 1 Section 44A(5).
 2 Section 44B.
 3 Section 44B(2).
 4 Section 45(1); cf the former place of safety orders which could be granted for up to 28 days.
 5 Section 45(4) only permits application by those entitled to apply for a care order, viz a local authority or 'authorised person'.

grant one period of extension[6] for a further seven days.[7]

There is no appeal against the making or refusal to make an emergency protection order.[8] However, an application to discharge the order may be made by the child, parent, any other person with parental responsibility or any person with whom the child was living before the order was made,[9] except where the person was given notice of and present at the original hearing.[10] No application for discharge can be heard before the expiry of 72 hours after the making of the order.[11]

The inability to appeal a *refusal*[12] to make or extend an order has been criticised on more than one occasion. A striking example was *Re P (Emergency Protection Order)*,[13] in which justices refused to extend an order notwithstanding firm medical evidence pointing to a risk of life-threatening abuse (the mother having been diagnosed as having Munchausen's syndrome by proxy). The inability to challenge that refusal prompted Johnson J to comment[14] that consideration should be given to providing a mechanism for review, though he added that such a mechanism would have to be one which could operate very quickly.

The use of emergency protection orders

Compared with the annual numbers of place of safety order made before the 1989 Act (viz about 5,000) the number of emergency protection orders since the Act has been dramatically low. Indeed, under half that number, 2,300 were made in 1993 and, although this rose to 3,100 in 1994, they had dropped back again to about 2,565 by 1996.[15] Given that the new powers were not intended to be used as a routine way of starting care proceedings, some reduction in numbers was to be expected. Furthermore, the initial reduction and subsequent rise in 1994 reflected the pattern of care orders generally, which in turn perhaps reflected initial uncertainty[16] as to how to act in an emergency and whether there was simply a higher threshold before intervention would be justified. However, given the sharp fall in the number of emergency protection orders (particularly in 1996 at a time when care orders had not similarly dropped) it is clear some other explanation needs to be sought. It has been suggested[17] that against a general background of local authorities being less interventionist, they are in fact more prepared to make alternative arrangements, and in particular to accommodate a child without prejudicing the possibility of later seeking a care order after a further investigation.

---

6 Section 45(6).
7 Section 45(5).
8 Section 45(10).
9 Section 45(8).
10 Section 45(11).
11 Section 45(9).
12 Technically it might be possible to challenge an unreasonable refusal by judicial review.
13 [1996] 1 FLR 482. See also *Essex County Council v F* [1993] 1 FLR 847, per Douglas Brown J.
14 Ibid at 484–5.
15 These at times inexact statistics can be found in the CAAC Reports of 1997, 1994/5 and 1993/4. See in particular Table 2C of the 1997 Report (note that the graph is based on a six-month period).
16 Until 1995 care orders had steadily risen and fell back less then one per cent in 1996 – see CAAC Final Report 1997 at 76.
17 White, Carr and Lowe *Children Act in Practice* 7.52–7.54.

4. POLICE PROTECTION[18]

As under the former law,[19] the police have limited but important powers to protect children. Indeed, in some areas out of hours protection is arranged through the use of police protection.[20] Section 46(1) of the 1989 Act enables a constable who has reasonable cause to believe that a child would otherwise be likely to suffer significant harm either to remove him to suitable accommodation and keep him there, or to 'take such steps as are reasonable to ensure that the child's removal from any hospital, or other place, in which he is then being accommodated, is prevented'. No child may be kept in police protection for more than 72 hours.[1]

As there is no power of search attached to this provision,[2] a child can only be taken into police protection once the officer has found the child.[3] Commonly the power has been used to hold children such as runaways or glue sniffers or those whose parents have abandoned them. It may also be used where an officer attends a domestic dispute and finds a child living in unhygienic conditions.

Section 46(4) requires a constable taking a child into police protection to inform, as soon as is reasonably practicable, relevant local authorities, the child, his parents and other specified persons about the steps that have been taken in relation to the child.

He must secure that the case is inquired into by a 'designated officer'. That officer on completing his enquiries must release the child, unless he considers that there is still reasonable cause for believing that the child would be likely to suffer significant harm if released.[4] Where the child remains at risk the designated officer may seek an emergency protection order on behalf of the local authority,[5] if necessary, without consultation.[6]

The police do not acquire parental responsibility, but must do what is reasonable in all the circumstances of the case for the purpose of safeguarding or promoting the child's welfare, having regard in particular to the length of the period during which the child will be in police protection.[7]

E.   Disputing local authority decisions

1. INTRODUCTION

Although, as the Department of Health's *Guidance* says,[8] the Children Act 1989 'envisages a high degree of co-operation between parents and authorities in

---

18 See generally the Department of Health's *Guidance and Regulations*, Vol 1, paras 4.71 et seq; Cobley *Child Abuse and The Law* (1995) pp 51ff; Cobley 'Child abuse, child protection and the criminal law' (1992) 4 Journal of Child Law 78; and Borkowski 'Police Protection and Section 46' [1995] Fam Law 204.

19 Viz the Children and Young Persons Act 1969 s 28(2).

20 See Booth *Delay in Public Children Act Cases Second Report* (1996) para 8.15.

1 Children Act 1989 s 46(6).

2 See the Department of Health's *Guidance and Regulations*, op cit, para 4.71.

3 Compare the powers to enter and search premises to save life or limb: s 17(1)(e) of the Police and Criminal Evidence Act 1984.

4 Section 46(5).

5 Section 46(7).

6 Section 46(8). It is normally expected that there will be consultation: see *Working Together*, op cit, para 4.17 and see Borkowski, op cit, at 205.

7 Section 46(9).

8 Vol 3, *Family Placements*, para 10.3.

negotiating and agreeing what form of action will best meet a child's needs and promote his welfare', nevertheless the required co-operation will not always be achieved or will break down. In any event, other members of the family may also be in dispute with the local authority: grandparents, for instance, may feel that they should be able to take over the care of the child. Disputes can also arise between foster parents and the authority. The former, for example, may wish to resist the latter's decision to remove a child from their care.

In some cases the objection may be unfounded, while in others the complaint will be of a relatively minor nature. Many such disputes can be and are resolved informally, often by patient counselling by social workers. However, not all disputes will thereby be solved and, while no doubt every effort is made to promote each child's welfare, serious mistakes are sometimes made by local authorities in their management of the child. There is little doubt too that the interests of parents, of the wider family, or of foster parents are, on occasion, unjustly ignored. The question therefore arises to what extent, and to whom, local authorities are or should be accountable for their management of children in care.

Apart from applying for a discharge of a care order under s 39 or challenging a decision about contact under s 34, which we have already discussed,[9] there are a number of other ways in which a local authority decision may be challenged. Use can be made of local authorities' formal complaints or representation procedures. Alternatively, applications may be made to the Secretary of State to use his default powers. Actions can be brought under the High Court's inherent jurisdiction or for judicial review or by seeking leave to apply for a residence order. A complaint can also be made to the 'local ombudsman'. Furthermore, it may be possible to sue the local authority for negligence. Finally, application can be made to the European Court of Human Rights.

We discuss each of these options in turn, but in the ensuing discussion it should be borne in mind that the issue of reviewing local authorities' action is not simple. Although ideally one would wish to safeguard both the child's and the parents' (or other interested adults') interests it must be remembered that ultimately priority must be given to the child's welfare. A local authority may, for example, have acted improperly, yet a court may nevertheless be forced to uphold their decision, because it has become in the child's interests to do so. On the other hand, while court scrutiny might be more effective if action had to be sanctioned by the court before it is carried out by the authority, such control might so fetter local authority action that the inevitable consequential delay would be to the general prejudice of children in care.

2.   THE COMPLAINTS PROCEDURE [10]

As has been said, it is often possible to resolve problems informally, and indeed some local authorities appoint an officer specifically to support children and their

---

9   Ante at p 579 (discharge) and p 584 (contact under s 34).

10 See generally the Department of Health's *Guidance and Regulations*, Vol 3, *Family Placements*, ch 10; Williams and Jordan 'Factors relating to publicity surrounding the complaints procedure under the Children Act 1989' (1996) 8 CFLQ 337; and Williams and Jordan *The Children Act 1989 Complaints Procedure: A Study of Six Local Authority Areas* (1996); and for the background, *Review of Child Care Law* (DHSS, 1985), paras 220 et seq and Bainham *Children, The New Law*, paras 4.62 et seq.

representatives in participation in decision-making and in voicing their concerns.[11] Under s 26(3) of the Children Act 1989, however, it is now[12] mandatory for all local authorities to have a formal representation or complaints procedure in relation to their Part III powers and functions.[13] Furthermore, to ensure that there is an independent element, s 26(4) provides that at least one person who is not a member or officer of the authority concerned must take part in the consideration of the complaint or representation and in any discussions held by the authority about the action to be taken. Equally importantly, under s 26(8) there is an obligation to publicise the complaints procedure.[14] Rules governing the scope and procedure of the complaints scheme are provided by the Representations Procedure (Children) Regulations 1991. The Department of Health and the Social Services Inspectorate have also issued practice guidance.[15]

Who can complain

Under s 26(3) complaints may be made by:

(a) a child whom the local authority are looking after or who is not being looked after but is in need. This is intended both to ensure that children are consulted on decisions taken about them and to establish the system of complaints procedures for children the authorities are looking after.[16] It may also assist a child who believes he should be accommodated where the authority are refusing to offer the service;[17]

(b) a parent;[18]

(c) any person (other than a parent) with parental responsibility;

(d) any local authority foster parent; or

(e) such other person as the authority considers has a sufficient interest in the child's welfare to warrant representations being considered by them.

In addition young people can complain if they consider that the local authority has not given them adequate preparation for leaving care or adequate after-care.[19]

Although s 26(3) permits a wide range of people, including foster parents, to use the procedure, those falling into the final category may only be heard at the

---

11 See the Department of Health's *Guidance and Regulations*, op cit at para 10.13.

12 Before the 1989 Act, although some local authorities had a complaints procedure, they were not obliged to. Failure to have a procedure or having one that fails to comply with the regulations (set out below) can be remedied by invoking the Secretary of State's default powers under s 84 (discussed post at p 601): per Auld LJ in *R v London Borough of Barnet, ex p S* [1994] 1 FLR 592 at 598.

13 Note also that local authorities have to make provision for complaints about community care: see Local Authority Social Services Act 1970 s 7B. There is also a separate complaints system in relation to the guardian ad litem service: see ante, p 556.

14 As Williams and Jordan, op cit at 33.8 observe, a complaints procedure is 'otiose, if those most in need of such a procedure are unaware of its existence and operation'. In fact they were of the view that publicity for such schemes is generally disappointing.

15 *The Right to Complain – Practice Guidance on Complaints Procedures in Social Services Departments*, HMSO 1991. Note also the Inspectorate's reports of 1993, 1994 and 1996.

16 According to the Department of Health's *Guidance and Regulations*, op cit at para 107, the responsible authority should always check with the child (subject to his understanding) that a complaint submitted on his behalf reflects his views and that he wishes the person submitting it to act on his behalf.

17 See also Ward J in *R v Royal Borough of Kingston-upon-Thames, ex p T* [1994] 1 FLR 798 at 812.

18 Including the unmarried father.

19 Children Act 1989 s 24(14), added by the Courts and Legal Services Act 1990 Sch 16, para 13.

local authority's discretion.[20] This has been criticised as being too restrictive in the case of representations being made by concerned members of the wider family,[1] and problematic in other cases.[2]

What may be complained about

As s 26(3) says, the statutory complaints procedure caters for complaints about local authority support for families and their children under Part III of the 1989 Act. This, as the Department of Health's *Guidance* says:[3]

'. . . will include complaints about day care, services to support children within their family home, accommodation of a child, after-care and decisions relating to the placement of a child or the handling of a child's case. The processes involved in decision making or the denial of a service must also be covered by the responsible authority's arrangements.'

In *R v Birmingham City Council, ex p A*[4] an attempt was made to use judicial review to challenge a local authority's apparent inability speedily to place a child with special needs with an appropriate specialist foster parent. Sir Stephen Brown P commented that, in cases such as those where neither fact nor law was in dispute but instead the ground of complaint was the way the authority was carrying out its duty, the appropriate remedy was a complaint under s 26.

Matters falling outside Part III,[5] including the placing of a child's name on the Child Protection Register and complaints by private foster parents on their own behalf, do not have to be included in the scheme. However, as the Department of Health's *Guidance* says, a responsible authority should consider what other matters might appropriately be covered by the procedures to meet the requirements of the Regulations.[6]

Procedure and outcome

Essentially the Regulations establish a two-stage process, ie a relatively informal stage and, if that does not resolve matters, a formal stage before a panel. In more detail, upon receipt of a complaint from an eligible person, the responsible authority must acknowledge it and send a leaflet describing how the procedure works and giving the name of the officer responsible for co-ordinating the handling of complaints.[7] The authority and an independent person must consider the representation and formulate a response within 28 days.[8] Their written decision must be sent to the complainant, the child (if different) and to any other person whom the authority considers has a sufficient interest in the child. The

---

20 The procedure in these cases is governed by reg 4(4) of the Representations Procedure (Children) Regulations 1991.
1 By Bainham, op cit, at p 86. Their principal form of redress will therefore be judicial review: see post, p 604.
2 For example, as to whether a teacher, who is concerned about a child, can complain: see Williams and Jordan, op cit, at 338.
3 Op cit at para 10.8.
4 [1997] 2 FLR 841.
5 Except decisions about the 'usual fostering limit' included under the Representations Procedure (Children) Regulations 1991 reg 12(2).
6 Ibid at para 10.9. In fact, as Williams and Jordan found, coverage varies considerably.
7 Department of Health's *Guidance and Regulations*, op cit, para 10.37.
8 Regulation 6 of the 1991 Regulations. The independent person can inter alia interview the child and, if different, the complainant: reg 8(1).

letter must also remind the complainant of his right to have his complaint considered by a panel. If the claimant is dissatisfied with the responsible authority's response, he has 28 days to request in writing that the complaint be heard by the panel,[9] which in turn must meet within 28 days after the receipt by the local authority of such a request.[10] The complainant and authority can each make written and oral submissions to the panel.[11] The panel must make a recommendation within 24 hours of its meeting and record it in writing,[12] and give written notification of it to the responsible authority, the complainant, the independent person (if he is not a member of the panel) and any other interested person.[13] The responsible authority must consider what action, if any, should be taken in the light of the panel's findings[14] and, within 28 days of the panel's recommendation, notify among others the complainant and the child (if of sufficient understanding) of their decision and reasons for taking that decision.[15] It is to be noted that there is no time limit for making a complaint.

Although a panel decision is not strictly binding upon the local authority,[16] as Peter Gibson LJ put it in *R v London Borough of Brent, ex p S*,[17] it would be 'an unusual case when a local authority acted otherwise than in accord with the panel's recommendations and the independent person's views'. Furthermore, simply to ignore or failing reasonably to consider the recommendations will lay the authority open to judicial review.[18]

It may also be observed that authorities are required to monitor the operation and effectiveness of the procedure. To this end records of each complaint received and the outcome must be kept and an annual report dealing with the procedure's operation must be completed and presented to the Social Services Committee.[19]

Impact of the complaints procedure

Undoubtedly one impact of the complaints procedure has been to reduce the need and indeed the ability successfully to invoke the court's powers under judicial review (discussed further below). As we have seen, the President has said[20] that where neither fact nor law is in dispute, but the way the duty was being exercised, then it is preferable to invoke the complaints procedure. But in *R v Royal Borough*

---

9 Regulation 8(2). The panel, which must include at least one independent person, is appointed by the local authority for this purpose: reg 8(2)–(3). As the Department of Health's *Guidance and Regulations*, op cit, at para 10.22 comments, this second stage of the procedure does not affect the complainant's right to complain about maladministration to the local ombudsman (discussed post, p 608), since the panel is not a decision-making body.
10 Regulation 8(4).
11 Regulation 8(5).
12 Regulation 9(1).
13 Regulation 9(2).
14 Regulation 9(3).
15 Children Act 1989 s 26(7)(b).
16 This is implicit in s 26(7) which requires the authority, having had due regard to the findings, to 'take such steps *as are reasonably practicable*' [emphasis added].
17 [1994] 1 FLR 203 at 211.
18 Per Ward J in *R v Royal Borough of Kingston-upon-Thames, ex p T* [1994] 1 FLR 798 at 814. For examples, of where judicial review was successfully invoked see *Re T (Accommodation by Local Authority)* [1995] 1 FLR 159, discussed ante at p 528, and *R v Avon County Council, ex p M* [1994] 2 FCR 259.
19 Regulation 10. Note also the Social Service Inspectorate's Reviews of the Complaints Procedure.
20 *R v Birmingham City Council, ex p A* [1997] 2 FLR 841, discussed ante, p 599.

of Kingston-upon-Thames, ex p T[1] Ward J went further, holding that it was the clear broad legislative purpose that the complaints procedure should be invoked in preference to judicial review in respect of matters within the remit of s 26. He pointed out that the remedy was quicker and more convenient and he specifically rejected both the argument that because the panel was dominated by local authority membership it was likely to be biased, and that it was ineffective. In relation to the first he was satisfied that professional integrity would ensure fairness and in relation to the second he pointed to the availability of judicial review should any recommendation simply be ignored.

The effectiveness of the system is an important issue, particularly as the existence of the complaints system was used as one of the justifications for not imposing a general duty of care in tort upon local authorities.[2] Relatively little is known about the actual use made of the procedure,[3] though there is evidence that children themselves are reluctant to complain because of fear of victimisation or retaliation.[4] Research in other contexts[5] has found that people are generally reluctant to complain, either because they are tired of battling the system or cannot see the point in doing so, the damage already having been done.

3. DEFAULT POWERS OF THE SECRETARY OF STATE

Section 84 of the Children Act 1989 enables the Secretary of State to declare a local authority in default where he is satisfied that they have, without reasonable cause, failed to comply with a duty under the Act.[6] He may then give the necessary directions to the authority to ensure their compliance with the duty within a specified period. In the event of further default, these directions may be enforced by application to the High Court for judicial review.

Although in theory this provides another option for aggrieved individuals to pursue disputes against a local authority, it was never expected that these powers would be exercised at all often,[7] still less that they will assist individuals, as it is more likely that the Secretary of State will exercise his powers, if at all, where an authority's failure to discharge its statutory duties affects a class as opposed to individual children.[8] It may be added that the existence of these default powers does not bar applications for judicial review.[9]

---

1 [1994] 1 FLR 798.
2 See *X v Bedfordshire County Council* [1995] 2 AC 633, [1995] 3 All ER 353, HL (discussed at p 607).
3 Though see Williams and Jordan *The Children Act 1989 Complaints Procedure: A Study of Six Local Authority Areas.*
4 See Williams and Jordan 'Factors relating to publicity surrounding the complaints procedure under the Children Act' (1996) 8 CFLQ 337.
5 See eg Murch, Lowe, Beckford, Borkowski and Weaver *Support Services for Families of Older Children Adopted Out of Care* (1998).
6 Compare the similar power under the Education Act 1996 s 497.
7 The default power under the Education Act is rarely used. See Logie 'Enforcing statutory duties: the courts and default powers' [1988] JSWL 185.
8 See HC Official Report S C 13 June 1989, col 492 per the Solicitor General, and Bainham, op cit, para 7.78. But note *R v London Borough of Brent, ex p S* [1994] 1 FLR 592 in which it was suggested that the default powers could be used as a remedy for an inadequate complaints system; and *R v Barnet London Borough Council, ex p B* [1994] 1 FLR 592 where the default powers were mentioned in relation to inadequate day care provision.
9 Per Peter Gibson LJ in *R v London Borough of Brent, ex p S*, supra at 214.

4.   WARDSHIP AND THE INHERENT JURISDICTION

The position before the Children Act 1989 [10]

Before the Children Act 1989, local authorities, encouraged by the courts, frequently turned to wardship as a means of committing children to their care.[11] In stark contrast, although it was accepted that the wardship jurisdiction had not been abrogated by the comprehensive statutory scheme governing local authority care,[12] the courts refused to allow their prerogative jurisdiction to be used as a means of challenging authorities' decisions over children in care. The basic rationale for what became known as the *'Liverpool* principle' was that as Parliament had vouchsafed a wide discretion to local authorities over the management of children in care, it was not for the courts to subvert that policy by allowing parents and others a right of challenge through wardship and therefore outside the statutory system. As Lord Wilberforce said in *A v Liverpool City Council*:[13]

> 'In my opinion the court has no . . . reviewing power. Parliament has by statute entrusted to the local authority the power and duty to make decisions as to the welfare of children without any reservation of a reviewing power to the court.'

In *Liverpool* itself, the House of Lords refused to interfere with a local authority's decision to restrict a mother's contact with her child in care to a monthly supervised visit limited to one hour at a day nursery.[14]

In reaching this decision the House of Lords affirmed two earlier Court of Appeal decisions[15] in which it had been held that foster parents could not use wardship as a means of challenging a local authority's decision to remove children placed with them. The *'Liverpool* principle' was again applied by the House of Lords in *Re W (A Minor) (Wardship: Jurisdiction)*,[16] in which relatives unsuccessfully sought to use wardship to challenge a local authority's decision to place a child with a stranger (with a view to adoption) rather than with them,[17] and in *Re M and H (Minors) (Local Authorities: Parental Rights)*,[18] in which an unmarried father failed in his application for custody of his child in local authority care.

These decisions successively barred the use of wardship as a means of challenge from foster parents, natural parents, relatives and unmarried fathers and there was little doubt that the *'Liverpool* principle' would equally have applied to *any* potential applicant, including a *'Gillick* competent' child. Not only was it

---

10   See generally Oliver 'Challenging local authority decisions in relation to children in care – Part I' (1988) 1 Journal of Child Law 26.
11   See post, pp 696–7.
12   See eg *Re M (An Infant)* [1961] Ch 328 at 345, [1961] 1 All ER 788, CA per Lord Evershed MR; *Re B (Infants)* [1962] Ch 201, CA at 223 per Pearson LJ; and *A v Liverpool City Council* [1982] AC 363 at 373, [1981] 2 All ER 385, HL at 388 per Lord Wilberforce.
13   Ibid at 372 and 388 respectively. See Lowe (1982) 45 MLR 96 and Freeman (1982) 145 JPN 333 and 146 JPN 188 at 202.
14   Under the law as it then stood, local authorities had complete discretion over the amount of contact with a child in care.
15   *Re M (An Infant)* [1961] Ch 328, [1961] 1 All ER 788, CA; and *Re T (AJJ) (An Infant)* [1970] Ch 688, [1970] 2 All ER 865, CA.
16   [1985] AC 791, [1985] 2 All ER 301, HL. See Bainham (1986) 49 MLR 113.
17   The birth parents had concealed from the rest of the family that they had asked the authority to take the child into care (they had agreed to an order freeing the child for adoption) and persuaded the authority, contrary to their normal practice, not to consult members of the wider family.
18   [1990] 1 AC 686, [1988] 3 All ER 5, HL. See Hayes (1989) 1 Journal of Child Law 53. See also *Re TD (A Minor) (Wardship: Jurisdiction)* [1985] FLR 1150.

established that the principle applied regardless of the applicant, but it had also been held to apply both in relation to a child in care and where the local authority were actively contemplating taking proceedings.[19]

Furthermore, in *Re W (A Minor) (Wardship: Jurisdiction)*[20] the House of Lords denied the existence of a residual category for intervention even in 'exceptional circumstances', while in *Re DM (A Minor) (Wardship: Jurisdiction)*[1] the Court of Appeal ruled that, even if a local authority could be shown to have acted improperly, the proper action was judicial review and not wardship.

Effectively,[2] therefore, by the time the Children Act 1989 was implemented wardship could not be used as a means of challenging local authority decisions unless the authority itself chose to submit to the jurisdiction.[3]

The position after the Children Act 1989

Under the Children Act 1989 wardship and local authority care are incompatible in the sense that a child cannot both be in care and a ward of court.[4] Accordingly, it is clear that individuals seeking to challenge a local authority's decision in respect of a child in care can no longer even attempt to do so by wardship and that consequently there can be no question of the local authority submitting to the jurisdiction. It is, however, possible for a challenge to be mounted under the High Court's inherent jurisdiction (which is discussed in Chapter 16). Although the point has yet to be directly tested, it is thought that the '*Liverpool* principle' will operate in this situation.[5] A fortiori the '*Liverpool* principle' will apply in cases where a wardship application can still properly be made, ie where the child is not subject to a care order. A foster parent looking after a child accommodated by a local authority can still in theory ward a child, but if it is intended to challenge the authority's decision, eg to remove the child, then the '*Liverpool* principle' will surely be applied.[6]

5. SEEKING LEAVE TO APPLY FOR A RESIDENCE ORDER

Mention has previously been made of the ability of parents and guardians to apply for a residence order as an alternative means of seeking a discharge of a care order.[7] However, it is open to any interested party to seek the court's leave to apply

---

19 See *Re E (Minors) (Wardship: Jurisdiction)* [1984] 1 All ER 21, CA; *W v Shropshire County Council* [1986] 1 FLR 359, CA; and *W v Nottingham County Council* [1986] 1 FLR 565, CA, discussed in the 7th edition of this work at p 474.

20 [1985] AC 791, see particularly Lord Scarman at 797.

1 [1986] 2 FLR 122, CA.

2 Strictly it was still open to argue that the relevant body or court had inadequate powers to deal with the particular issue, but that the court in wardship proceedings had the necessary powers which the child's welfare required to be used: see *Re J (A Minor) (Wardship: Jurisdiction)* [1984] 1 All ER 29, CA. However, this so-called 'lacuna' argument rarely succeeded because the courts generally denied that there was an unintended gap in the relevant court's or body's powers. See the discussion in the 7th edition of this work at p 475.

3 See eg *A v B and Hereford and Worcester County Council* [1986] 1 FLR 289.

4 Children Act 1989 s 100(2)(c) and s 91(4), discussed post, p 698.

5 This was Balcombe LJ's view in *Re A (Minors) (Residence Orders: Leave to Apply)* [1992] Fam 182, [1992] 3 All ER 872, CA, discussed further below.

6 As extended inter alia by *Re E (Minors) (Wardship: Jurisdiction)*, supra, and the other cases cited at n 19 above.

7 Ante, p 579.

for a residence order, pursuant to s 10 of the Children Act 1989. This possible means of challenging a local authority decision was explored in *Re A (Minors) (Residence Orders: Leave to Apply)*,[8] in which a foster mother sought to challenge a local authority's decision that she should no longer be permitted to foster four children in their care. In the course of an action for judicial review, the applicant applied for leave to apply for a residence order. In refusing leave the Court of Appeal accepted that the ability of the court, pursuant to s 9(1), to make a residence order notwithstanding that the child is in care, represents a fundamental change in the law and that to that extent the '*Liverpool* principle' had no direct application. However, that did not mean that on the application for leave the court should give no weight to the local authority's views. On the contrary, s 10(9)(d)(i) expressly provides that the court is to have particular regard to the authority's plans for the future. Furthermore, given that under s 22(3) it is the authority's duty to safeguard and promote the welfare of any child in its care, it was held that the court should approach the application on the basis that the authority's plans for the child's future were designed for his welfare and that any departure from such plans might well be harmful to the child. In other words the court should, in these circumstances, be slow to grant leave.

6.　JUDICIAL REVIEW[9]

Given that the High Court will not exercise its inherent powers, then, unless it is appropriate to seek a residence order,[10] the only means of obtaining an order to impugn a local authority's decision on the ground that they have acted improperly is by judicial review. In this context the two principal remedies sought will be certiorari, that is, that the original order be quashed, or, less commonly, mandamus, that is, that the local authority be ordered to comply with their statutory duty, for example, to provide some specific support service provided for in Part III of and Sch 2 to the 1989 Act.[11]

It is important to appreciate that judicial review is the standard administrative law remedy for correcting decisions[12] taken by inferior courts, tribunals and other bodies and as such no special rules apply in children cases.[13] The function of the court, as Scott Baker J neatly expressed it, is 'to consider in each case not whether the decision itself is right or fair but whether the manner in which the decision is made is fair'.[14]

8　Supra.
9　See generally Craig *Administrative Law* (3rd edn, 1994); De Smith, Woolf, Jowell and Le Seves *Judicial Review of Administrative Action* (5th edn, 1995); Harlow and Rawlings *Law and Administration* (2nd edn, 1997); and Wade and Forsyth *Administrative Law* (7th edn, 1994).
10　Where the applicant is seeking to have the child live with him.
11　See *R v Bolton Metropolitan Borough Council, ex p B* [1985] FLR 343 where mandamus was sought to make the local authority comply with its duty to serve notice of a refusal or termination of access.
12　There must be a reviewable 'decision': see *R v Devon County Council, ex p L* [1991] 2 FLR 541 (social worker informing applicant's cohabitant that he was suspected of sexual abuse held not to be a 'decision').
13　But this is not to say that in judging the reasonableness of a local authority's action in respect of children in their care attention should not be paid to the authority's duty to safeguard the child's interests; cf *R v Harrow London Borough Council, ex p D* [1990] Fam 133, [1990] 3 All ER 12, CA, per Butler-Sloss LJ cited post, p 606.
14　*R v Hereford and Worcester County Council, ex p D* [1992] 1 FLR 448 at 457.

The requirements for judicial review

As a safeguard against frivolous, vexatious, or merely hopeless actions, applicants must obtain leave to apply for judicial review.[15] Applications must, inter alia, specify the grounds upon which the relief is sought and be accompanied by an affidavit verifying the facts relied upon.[16] Leave is not a formality for, as Balcombe LJ said in *R v Lancashire County Council, ex p M*,[17] there must be a reasonable prospect of the court coming to the decision that the local authority's conclusion was so unreasonable that no reasonable local authority could ever have come to it. Bearing in mind that as far as individuals are concerned some information will be confidential,[18] having to establish even a prima facie case may be difficult. Yet it is only if the applicant can first negotiate this hurdle that the matter will then be heard.

To substantiate a claim for judicial review, the applicant must be able to bring himself within the so-called *Wednesbury* principle[19] as interpreted by the House of Lords in *Council of Civil Service Unions v Minister for the Civil Service*.[20] According to Lord Diplock in that case, there are three main heads under which court intervention may be justified: 'illegality' (where there was an error of law in reaching the relevant decision); 'procedural impropriety' (where the relevant rules have not been complied with); and 'irrationality' (where a decision 'is so outrageous in its defiance of logic or of accepted moral standards that no sensible person who had applied his mind to the question to be decided could have arrived at it').[21]

Circumstances in which judicial review has been sought

Actions for judicial review of local authority decisions have increased in recent years. Complainants fall mainly into two groups, parents and foster parents, though applications have also been sought by guardians ad litem.[1] Complaints have been made about a variety of decisions, including refusing to accommodate a child,[2] the placing of a child on a Child Protection Register,[3] deciding not to place the child at home on trial with the parents,[4] removing a child from foster parents,[5] removing a person from the list of approved adopters,[6] and disclosing to others allegations of child abuse by a named person.[7]

---

15 Supreme Court Act 1981 s 31 and RSC Ord 53 r 3.
16 RSC Ord 53 r 3(2). Applications should be brought promptly and normally within three months of the decisions complained of: RSC Ord 53 r 4.
17 [1992] 1 FLR 109, CA at 113.
18 Such as child protection conference records covered by the Foster Placement (Children) Regulations 1991 reg 14.
19 Following *Associated Provincial Picture Houses Ltd v Wednesday Corpn* [1948] 1 KB 223, [1947] 2 All ER 680, CA.
20 [1985] AC 374, [1984] 3 All ER 935, HL.
21 Ibid at 410 and 950, respectively.
 1 See eg *R v Cornwall County Council* [1992] 2 All ER 471, in which the authority's attempt to prescribe maximum hours a guardian could work on a particular case without express authorisation from the council was successfully challenged: see ante, p 554.
 2 See ante, p 528.
 3 *R v Norfolk County Council, ex p M* [1989] QB 619, [1989] 2 All ER 359; *R v Harrow London Borough Council, ex p D* [1990] Fam 133, [1990] 3 All ER 12, CA; and *R v East Sussex County Council, ex p R* [1991] 2 FLR 358.
 4 *R v Bedfordshire County Council, ex p C* [1987] 1 FLR 239; cf *R v Hertfordshire County Council, ex p B* [1987] 1 FLR 239 (child removed after being placed at home on trial).
 5 *R v Hereford and Worcester County Council, ex p R* [1992] 1 FLR 448 and *R v Lancashire County Council, ex p M* [1992] 1 FLR 109, CA.
 6 *R v London Borough of Wandsworth, ex p P* [1989] 1 FLR 387.
 7 *R v Devon County Council, ex p L* [1991] 2 FLR 541 and *R v Lewisham London Borough Council, ex p P* [1991] 3 All ER 529, [1991] 1 WLR 308.

By no means all of the above applications were successful, but of those that were, it was commonly because the local authority failed to give the complainant an opportunity to put his side of the case or otherwise to explain their reasons. A striking example is *R v Norfolk County Council, ex p M*,[8] which concerned a plumber working in a house where a teenage girl made allegations that she was sexually abused by him. She had twice previously been the victim of sexual abuse and a few days later made similar allegations against another man. After a case conference the plumber's name was entered on (what was then called) the Child Abuse Register as an abuser. His employers were informed and they suspended him pending a full enquiry. The first knowledge the plumber had of these allegations was the letter informing him of the decision to place his name on the register. Waite J held that, given the serious consequences of registration for the plumber, the local authority had a duty to act fairly, which they had manifestly failed to do by not giving him an opportunity to meet the allegations.

The *Norfolk* case was clearly exceptional and, as Butler-Sloss LJ said in *R v Harrow London Borough Council, ex p D*,[9] recourse to judicial review in respect of placing a name on the Child Protection Register ought to be rare. She further held that the court should not encourage applications to review case conference decisions or recommendations, because it was important for those involved in this difficult area to 'be allowed to perform their task without having to look over their shoulder all the time for the possible intervention of the court'. Furthermore, she pointed out that in 'balancing adequate protection for the child and the fairness to an adult, the interest of an adult may have to take second place to the needs of the child'.[10]

Although Butler-Sloss LJ's remarks specifically concerned case conference decisions and recommendations, her observations about the need to balance considerations have general application.[11] Indeed, it can be said that in general, given the local authority's duty to safeguard the interests of children, in the absence of procedural irregularity it is hard to impugn a local authority decision. It is certainly not enough to question the wisdom of a decision. The applicant must discharge the heavy onus of showing that no reasonable local authority could have reached the particular decision complained of. In *R v Hertfordshire County Council, ex p B*[12] a mother's action for judicial review failed. In that case a child in care was allowed home on trial with the mother, but after three months the child was removed on the ground that rehabilitation had failed. A neighbour had asserted that the mother had come home late one night and being drunk lay in the snow for some time with her child running about. In fact it was found that the

8 Supra. See also *R v Bedfordshire County Council, ex p C*, supra; *R v Hereford and Worcester City Council, ex p D*, supra; and *R v London of Wandsworth, ex p P*, supra.
9 [1990] Fam 133, [1990] 3 All ER 12, CA.
10 Ibid at pp 138 and 17 respectively. See also *R v London Borough of Wandsworth, ex p P*, supra, at 308 in which Ewbank J said: 'Foster-parents have to accept that their interests may have to be subordinated to the children they care for. Accordingly, provided the rules of fairness are complied with, the decision as to whether there is a risk or not, is one that has to be taken by the local authority. In the ordinary way, provided the rules of natural justice are complied with the foster-parents have no redress.' See also *R v Birmingham City Council, ex p A* [1997] 2 FLR 841, discussed ante, p 599.
11 See also *R v East Sussex County Council, ex p R*, supra; *R v Devon County Council, ex p L*, supra; and *R v Lewisham London Borough Council, ex p P*, supra.
12 [1987] 1 FLR 239. See also *R v East Sussex County Council, ex p R*, supra; *R v Devon County Council, ex p L*, supra; and *R v Lewisham London Borough Council, ex p P*, supra.

authority had been concerned with wider considerations, including the child's weight loss, his disruptive behaviour and hyperactivity. In dismissing the application Ewbank J observed that there were many cases where children were allowed home on trial and where the local authority had later to decide that it was not a success. Such a decision was well within the local authority's parental power and was not amenable to judicial review.

7. OTHER REMEDIES

Suing the local authority for negligence

In general, English law has set its face against superimposing a common law duty of care on local authorities in relation to performance of their duties to protect children. Accordingly, it is exceptionally difficult successfully to sue the local authority for negligence in respect of their performance of their statutory duties and powers under the Children Act 1989.

The leading case is *X (Minors) v Bedfordshire County Council*,[13] which in fact comprised five test cases, two of which concerned the way local authorities had dealt with child abuse, and three which concerned provision which local education authorities had made for children alleged to have special educational needs. In the *Bedfordshire* case, five children claimed damages for personal injury based either on breach of statutory duty or common law negligence by the local authority. The claims alleged that the local authority had failed properly to investigate reports suggesting that the children had been abused and therefore adequately to protect them. In contrast, in *M (a minor) v Newham London Borough Council*[14] a child and her mother claimed damages for personal injury against the local authority, area health authority, and a psychiatrist on the basis of the child wrongfully being taken into care following a mistaken diagnosis identifying the mother's cohabitant as the abuser.

In both instances the House of Lords held that the actions failed, since breach of a statutory duty did not, by itself, give rise to any private law cause of action. In Lord Browne-Wilkinson's view,[15] as a general principle a cause of action will only arise 'if it can be shown, as a matter of construction of the statute, that the statutory duty was imposed for the protection of a limited class of the public and that Parliament intended to confer on members of that a class a private action for breach of that duty'. His Lordship held that the careless performance of a statutory duty did not give rise to any cause of action in the absence of either a right of action for breach of a statutory duty or for breach of a common law duty of care.

As to the principles applicable to establishing a common law duty of care, Lord Brown-Wilkinson said that a distinction had to be drawn between those alleged negligent acts or decisions which involved policy matters, which were not justiciable in tort at all, and those which did not. Where policy matters were not involved, then it had to be shown that the local authority had exercised its jurisdiction so unreasonably that it had acted outside the discretion entrusted to it

---

13 [1995] 2 AC 633, [1995] 3 All ER 353, HL, on which see Cane 'Suing public authorities in tort' (1996) 112 LQR 13, Oliphant 'Tort' (1996) 49 Current Legal Problems 29 and 31 and Bailey, Harris and Harris 'The Immunity of local authorities in child protection functions – Is the door now ajar?' (1998) 10 CFLQ 227.
14 Dealt with in the same judgment.
15 Ibid at 731 and 364 respectively.

by Parliament. In this latter case the plaintiff would then have to bring him or herself within the tripartite test established by *Caparo Industries plc v Dickman*:[16]

- Was the damage to the plaintiff reasonably foreseeable?
- Was the relationship between the plaintiff and the defendant sufficiently proximate?
- Was it just and reasonable to impose a duty of care?

Although it is important to appreciate that *Bedfordshire* did not establish a blanket immunity for any action taken by a local authority in respect of children, it most certainly limited the possibilities of action. This hard line seems to have been confirmed by two subsequent decisions: *H v Norfolk County Council*[17] and *Barrett v Enfield London Borough Council*.[18] In the former the applicant, then aged 22, claimed damages in negligence against the local authority for failing properly to monitor and supervise his foster care placement (he alleged that he had been sexually and physically abused by his foster-father) and for failing to remove him from that placement.

In *Barrett* the plaintiff, then aged 24, claimed damages in negligence against the local authority for their catalogue of errors during the 17 years he had been in care as a result of which he had left care with deep-seated psychological and psychiatric problems. In both cases the actions failed on the basis of the House of Lords' decision in *Bedfordshire*.

In a subsequent case, *W v Essex County Council*,[19] however, the claim was not struck out. In that case foster parents alleged that a teenager was placed with them in breach of specific assurances by the local authority and its social worker that no adolescent known or suspected to be a sexual abuser would be fostered with them. In fact, the teenager had, as the local authority knew, been cautioned for indecent assault upon his sister. During the month of his placement he sexually abused the foster parents' four birth children, who suffered consequential psychiatric illnesses. The Court of Appeal ruled that although the foster parents' action failed, those brought on behalf of the children should not be struck out, it being ruled that in these circumstances it was arguably fair, just and reasonable to impose a duty of care on the local authority.

Whether the *Essex* ruling will lead to a general relaxation of the standpoint taken by the House of Lords in the *Bedfordshire* case remains to be seen. At the time of writing, leave to appeal to the House of Lords has been granted in the *Barrett* case,[20] while a claim under the European Convention on Human Rights has been ruled admissible by the European Commission of Human Rights in the *Bedfordshire* and *Newham* cases.[1]

Applying to the 'local government ombudsman'[2]

Another procedure for questioning local authority decisions over children is to complain to the commissioner for local administration ('the local government

---

16 [1990] 2 AC 605, HL at 616–17.
17 [1997] 1 FLR 384, CA.
18 [1998] QB 367, [1997] 3 All ER 1, CA, on which see Standley 'No duty of care to children in care *H v Norfolk County Council*, and *Barrett v Enfield London Borough Council*' (1997) 9 CFLQ 409.
19 [1998] 3 All ER 111, CA.
20 See [1998] 1 WLR 277.
 1 Sub nom, *KL v UK; TP and KM v UK*, declared admissible, 26 May 1998.
 2 See Lowe and Rawlings (1979) 42 MLR 447 and (1979) 2 Adoption and Fostering 38 and Oliver 'Challenging local authority decisions in relation to children in care – Part 2' (1989) 1 Journal of Child Law 58 at 61.

ombudsman'). Under this procedure a local commissioner may investigate written complaints of 'maladministration'. Before a complaint is made, the local authority must first be given an opportunity to address it.[3] If, however, this approach has not produced a satisfactory result, a complaint can be made. Complaints can now[4] be made directly to the commissioner or through a councillor. The commissioner cannot normally investigate complaints concerning proceedings or events that occurred more than 12 months previously.[5] To find the complaint justified the local commissioner must find that the authority has been guilty of 'maladministration'. The Court of Appeal has ruled[6] that it is not necessary for the complainant to spell out the particular maladministration which led to the injustice complained of; it is sufficient if he specifies the action alleged to be wrong. This is generally taken to refer to the procedure by which the decision is made or put into action rather than to the merits of the particular decision itself.[7] At the conclusion of his investigation the commissioner issues a report and, if he has found maladministration and injustice, he may recommend an ex gratia payment.[8] Although the local authority must consider these recommendations it is not *bound* to follow them and indeed, given the passage of time, may not be able to do so if that would be inconsistent with the child's welfare.

As a general mechanism for scrutinising administrative action, the procedure obviously has its merits, but like judicial review it is of questionable use in the context of local authority decisions in respect of children in care.[9] The main drawbacks are that the central concern is with procedural propriety and not the child's welfare; the commissioner may have no expertise in child matters; the investigation is itself a long process[10] and will probably result in delaying implementation of plans for the child's long-term future;[11] and, even if 'maladministration' is established, there is no power to interfere with the decision taken by the authority.

Applying to the European Court of Human Rights[12]

A local authority decision can occasionally be challenged as being in breach of the European Convention on Human Rights. To succeed, the applicant must show that

3 Local Government Act 1974 s 26(5).
4 Formerly they had to be initially referred to a local councillor, but this was changed by Local Government Act 1988 s 29 and Sch 3.
5 Section 26(4). A free booklet explaining the procedure is available from the Commissioner.
6 In *R v Local Comr for Administration for the North and East Area of England, ex p Bradford Metropolitan City Council* [1979] QB 287, [1979] 2 All ER 881, CA.
7 See the *Bradford* case, supra.
8 Awards of £1,000 have been recommended where a local authority failed to follow a case conference's recommendation, and of £2,000 where children were inappropriately interviewed about allegations of sexual abuse. See respectively Complaint 91/A/1176 and 90/c2717.
9 In practice very few of the complaints made relate to local authority social services' decisions about children. In 1988, for example, only 160 such complaints were made out of a total 7,055 – see Hershman and McFarlane *Children Law and Practice* B[932].
10 Though in this respect it is to be noted that in *Re A Subpoena (Adoption: Comr for Local Administration)* [1996] 2 FLR 629 it was held that the Commissioner was entitled to subpoena a local authority to produce adoption documents.
11 In the *Bradford* case, for example, where the claim of maladministration failed, the children were eventually adopted: see *Re SMH and RAH* [1990] FCR 966n (decided in 1979), though their placement was delayed pending the outcome of the Commission's investigations; cf *Re BA (Wardship and Adoption)* [1985] FLR 1008.
12 See generally Harris, O'Boyle and Warbrick *Law of European Convention on Human Rights* (1995) chs 9 and 13; Jacobs and White *The European Convention on Human Rights* (2nd edn, 1996) ch 10; Douglas 'The Family and the State under the European Convention on Human Rights' 2 Int Jo of Law and the Family 76; and O'Donnell 'Parent–child Relationships Within the European Convention' in Lowe and Douglas (eds) *Families Across Frontiers* (1996) 135.

at least one of the Articles has been broken,[13] the most relevant of which are in this context Article 8, under which there is 'the right to respect for . . . private and family life' and Article 6, under which there is a right to determine one's civil rights and obligations in a fair trial. In the past a number of applicants successfully challenged the then inability of parents to challenge local authority decisions concerning contact with children in care and an authority's refusal to give access to the case records of a child in their care.[14] Until implementation of the Human Rights Act 1998, the Convention has not been enforceable through the United Kingdom courts.[15] Instead, application has had to be made direct to the Commission in Strasbourg. This process is slow and takes years.

Although, as we have discussed elsewhere,[16] the Human Rights Act will make the European Convention internally binding (and is therefore likely to lead to more arguments based on the Convention),[17] it will not remove the option of taking a case to Strasbourg.

Notwithstanding that the rulings of the European Court are influential, and were certainly taken into account, for example, when drafting the Children Act 1989, from the individual's point of view and certainly that of the child, applications to Strasbourg are not an effective way of scrutinising individual decisions. An important drawback is that, while the UK may be forced to change the domestic law and even to compensate the individual if the application is successful,[18] the local authority cannot be forced to change its decision. In any event, by the time the case has been determined it is not very often likely to be in the child's interests to interfere with the original decision. Furthermore, the very delay can, if it impedes implementation of long-term plans, be seriously detrimental to the individual child.

13 See eg *R v United Kingdom* [1988] 2 FLR 445, E Ct HR and *O v UK* (1987) 10 EHRR 82, E Ct HR.
14 *Gaskin v United Kingdom* (1990) 12 EHRR 36, E Ct HR.
15 See generally Clements *European Human Rights – Taking A Case Under The Convention* (1994).
16 Ante, p 20.
17 Note, for example, Eekelaar's argument (in (1989) 139 NLJ 760) that the lack of a judicial procedure for adjudicating disputes over the exercise of parental responsibility by parents of children in care may contravene Article 6.
18 Pursuant to its obligations under Art 53 – see ante, p 20.

Chapter 15

Adoption

A. Introduction

1. THE NATURE OF ADOPTION, BACKGROUND TO THE LEGISLATION, AND FURTHER REFORM[1]

In English law adoption refers to the process by which a child's legal parentage is entirely and irrevocably transferred from one set of adults, usually the birth parents, and vested in other adults, namely the adoptive parents.[2] As the Houghton Committee's report[3] put it, adoption involves: 'the complete severance of the legal relationship between parents and child and the establishment of a new one between the child and the adoptive parent'. Apart from parental orders under s 30 of the Human Fertilisation and Embryology Act 1990 which, as we have seen,[4] have limited application,[5] adoption is the only child-related order under English law that lasts throughout adulthood (an adoption is truly for life) and it is the only means by which parents can lose their parental responsibility for their child whilst a minor.

Adoption can only be effected through a court process, and the jurisdiction is entirely statutory. This is because at common law parental rights and duties were held to be inalienable.[6] Hence, no change of status comparable to the adoptio or adrogatio of Roman law could be recognised. The absence of such a mechanism generated considerable dissatisfaction both from couples who were childless and anxious to bring up another's child as their own, but who hesitated to do so

---

1 For general reference see Hoggett, Pearl, Cooke and Bates *The Family, Law and Society* (4th edn, 1996) pp 663 et seq; and Clarke Hall & Morrison on *Children*, Division 3. For a detailed account of the law as it stood before the Children Act see Bevan *Child Law* (1989) ch 5.
2 In lay terms 'adoption' can have a wider meaning. For example, it is sometimes said that a person, particularly a stranger in blood, who looks after a child in the event of parental death or abandonment, has 'adopted' him. This relationship is described as foster parenthood in this book, and its legal consequences are referred to ante at p 408. For the meaning of 'adoption' for the purposes of the Immigration Rules see *R v Immigration Appeal Tribunal, ex p Tohur Ali* [1988] 2 FLR 523, CA. It should be noted that unlike French law, for example (see Arts 343–371 of the Civil Code referred to by the Inter-Departmental Review of Adoption Law, Discussion Paper No 1, *The Nature and Effect of Adoption* (1990) at para 116 and see also Pierre Verdier '"Limited Adoption" in France' (1988) 1 Adoption and Fostering pp 41–4), which makes provision for two types of adoption, ie 'full adoption' which involves the transfer of parentage, and 'simple adoption' which does not break all links with the birth family, English has but the one form.
3 Cmnd 5107, 1972, at para 14. See also *Review of Adoption Law*, Discussion Paper No 1, supra at para 2, which describes adoption as the process by which the legal relationship between a child and his or her birth parents is severed and an analogous relationship between the child and the adoptive parents is established.
4 See ante at p 267.
5 In particular, applications must be made within six months of the child's birth.
6 *Vansittart v Vansittart* (1858) 2 De G & J 249; *Walrond v Walrond* (1858) John 18; *Humphrys v Polak* [1901] 2 KB 385, CA; and *Brooks v Blount* [1923] 1 KB 257.

because of the lack of safeguards, and from those who had effected a de facto adoption but who felt vulnerable to the very real risk of the parents later turning up and taking the child back.[7]

Although there were a variety of factors[8] that contributed to the increased pressures for reform, the main catalyst was the substantial increase in the number of orphans following the First World War, which in turn led to a large increase in de facto adoptions. The resulting demand for reform led eventually to the passing of the Adoption of Children Act 1926.[9]

The 1926 Act was extensively amended in the light of subsequent experience and criticisms,[10] and all earlier legislation was repealed and consolidated by the Adoption Act 1958.[11] Further dissatisfaction with various aspects of the law and procedure led to the appointment of a Departmental Committee, the 'Houghton Committee', whose report was published in 1972.[12] Most of their recommendations (some of them in modified form) were accepted and incorporated into the Children Act 1975. However, the Act was not immediately fully implemented and, in fact, the law was consolidated by the Adoption Act 1976, which only came into force on 1 January 1988. The 1976 Act has itself since been amended by Sch 10 to the Children Act 1989.[13] Although many of the changes resulting from these amendments were consequential upon the changes of concepts, terminology and philosophy introduced by the 1989 Act, there were a number of unrelated substantive changes. These were not based on any specific report, but advantage was taken of the opportunity to make some helpful but piecemeal changes, apparently[14] to meet the needs of particular groups.

Adoption was the one area of child law not to be reviewed during the 1980s. However, after the enactment of the Children Act 1989, a full scale review of adoption law was instigated. This review, which was conducted by an Inter-Departmental Committee under the aegis of the Department of Health,[15] eventually

---

7   The Report of the Committee on Child Adoption ('The Hopkinson Report') (1921) Cmnd 1254, para 13 commented that it was not unknown for parents who had previously rejected the child to reclaim him once he had reached the age when he could work and earn wages.

8   Neatly summarised by Cretney *Principles of Family Law* (4th edn, 1984) p 420. See also the Discussion Paper No 1, op cit at para 2.

9   Passed following the 'Hopkinson Report', supra, and two Reports of the Child Adoption Committee, Cmnd 2401 and 2469 (1925).

10   Following eg the Horsburgh Committee's Report on Adoption Societies and Agencies (1937, Cmd 5499), by the Adoption of Children (Regulation) Act 1939 (discussed below at p 620) and by the Adoption of Children Act 1949 which for the first time treated the child as that of the adopters for the purpose of inheritance (see post, p 676).

11   Which was based on the Hurst Committee's Report on the Adoption of Children (1954, Cmd 9248).

12   Cmnd 5107. The original chairman of the committee was Sir William Houghton but after his death the chair was taken by Judge Stockdale.

13   See generally the Department of Health's *Guidance and Regulations on the Children Act 1989*, Vol 9, *Adoption Issues* and White, Carr and Lowe *A Guide to the Children Act 1989* ch 11.

14   As explained by David Mellor when introducing the new Schedule: HC Official Report, SC B, 6 June 1989, col 380.

15   This review produced four Discussion Papers (*The Nature and Effect of Adoption* (No 1, 1990), *Agreement and Freeing* (No 2, 1991), *The Adoption Process* (No 3, 1991) and *Intercountry Adoption* (No 4, 1992)) and three Background Papers (*International Perspectives* (No 1, 1990), *Review of Research Relating to Adoption* (No 2, 1990) and *Intercountry Adoption* (No 3, 1992)), and culminated in the publication of 'Adoption Law Review: Consultation Document' in 1992. Following this document a government White Paper 'Adoption – the Future' (Cm 2288) was published in 1993. Separate consultation papers 'Placement for Adoption' and 'The Future of Adoption Panels' were published in 1994.

led to publication in 1996 of a government White Paper 'Adoption – A Service for Children' which included a proposed Adoption Bill – A Consultative Document.[16] At the time of writing, however, there are no immediate plans to act on the proposed Bill, though there is a possibility that steps might be taken to legislate just on inter-county adoption so as to permit the UK to ratify the 1993 Hague Convention on Intercountry Adoption.[17]

2. A COMPARISON OF ADOPTION WITH OTHER LEGAL RELATIONSHIPS AND ORDERS

As we have said, an adoption order completely severs the legal relationship between the child and his natural parents and vests full parental responsibility exclusively in the adopters.[18] The result in brief is that for all legal purposes the adopters step into the shoes of the child's natural parents: by 'parents', in other words, is now meant not the child's birth parents, but his adoptive parents.[19] Such a relationship is thus distinguishable from that of a married parent and child, unmarried father and child, and guardian and ward. It resembles most closely the first, for, although there need be no blood relationship between the parties, the legal consequences are almost the same. It differs most markedly from the second, for the law does not automatically vest parental responsibility by reason of the blood relationship: adoption in fact creates virtually the converse situation. It resembles the third in that the adoptive parents, like guardians, stand in loco parentis to the child to whom they are not necessarily related in blood, but differs from it in that the relationship of guardian and ward does not make the child a member of the guardian's family, eg for the purposes of the devolution and acquisition of property.

An adoption order is distinguishable from a residence order under s 8 of the Children Act 1989 because it severs the legal ties between the child and his birth parent, whereas the latter does not. Furthermore, whereas an adoption order is permanent (ie the child remains a member of the adoptive family even after he attains his majority) and not variable,[20] the latter can subsequently be varied and, in any event, ceases to have effect once the child reaches the age of 18. Finally, as we discuss later, a different weight is placed upon the child's welfare in adoption proceedings, in that this is the *first* consideration, rather than the paramount consideration as in s 8 proceedings.

It is perhaps permanence rather than severance that is the more significant feature of an adoption order. At any rate, the psychological importance of having the security of a permanent order has been stressed by the courts[1] and, as one leading expert has put it,[2] 'Although no one can guarantee what the future will hold, a permanent placement is one that is *intended* to last and which is given the

---

16 Published by the Department of Health and Welsh Office.
17 Discussed post, pp 680ff.
18 See the Adoption Act 1976 s 12.
19 The effects of an adoption order are discussed more fully post, pp 675ff.
20 But for a limited power to set an adoption order aside, see post, pp 672–3.
1 See eg *Re F (A Minor) (Adoption: Parental Agreement)* [1982] 1 All ER 321, CA at 326, per Ormrod LJ agreeing with Bridges LJ in *Re SMH and RAH* [1990] FCR 996n (decided in 1979).
2 Adcock 'Alternatives to Adoption' (1984) Adoption and Fostering Vol 8, No 1 at 12; cf Triseliotis 'Permanency Planning' (1991) Adoption and Fostering, Vol 15, No 4.

legal security to make this possible. A permanent home provides the child with the basis for his healthy emotional development.'

3.   THE CHANGING PATTERN OF ADOPTION[3]

The adoption population

Since the 1960s there has been a dramatic reduction in the number of adoptions: from a peak of 24,831 orders made in England and Wales in 1968 there were just 5,962 orders in 1996.[4] One of the main reasons for this decline is the evident reduction in the number of babies available for adoption. In 1970, for instance, out of a total of 22,373 adoptions 8,833 (or 39 per cent) were of babies, that is of children under the age of 12 months. Figures since then show a continuous drop in the overall total of adoptions of babies, declining from eg 4,548 in 1975 and 1,115 in 1989 to just 253 (four per cent) in 1996.[5] This decline in the number of babies available for adoption was noted in 1972 by the Houghton Committee[6] and was then thought to be accounted for by the reduction in the number of unwanted babies because of the increased availability of contraception and abortion. Furthermore, more unmarried mothers tend to keep their children because of the changing attitudes to illegitimacy and the availability of state benefit and reasonable employment prospects and in some areas day care provision. Today one would add that an increasing number of children are born to unmarried couples living together in a stable union.

Although attention has perhaps understandably been focused on the dramatic reduction in the number of baby adoptions, in fact there have also been large reductions in the number of adoptions of children in most age groups.[7] A possible explanation for this overall reduction is that, as it became increasingly accepted that unmarried mothers would keep their babies, so there developed a more general culture of families being reluctant to give up their children. Eventually, however,[8] a further major reason for the decline in adoption numbers was a change in the law consequent upon the Houghton Committee's recommendation[9] aimed

---

3 See generally Lowe 'The Changing face of adoption – the gift/donation model versus the contract/services model' (1997) 9 CFLQ 371 and Cretney 'From Status to Contract?' in Rose (ed) *Consensus Ad Idem* 251.

4 Marriage, Divorce and Adoption Statistics 1995 ONS Series FM2 No 23 Table 6.1. That Table also provides statistics of adoption orders made between 1975 and 1996. NB The annual statistics contained in *Judicial Statistics* are at considerable variance with the above-mentioned statistics (for example, according to Table 5.4 of the 1996 Report only 4,936 orders were made) and are not considered to be as reliable as those published by the ONS. Unfortunately, unlike the *Judicial Statistics* the ONS Series does not differentiate figures for step-parent adoptions. A comprehensive table of statistics of orders made from 1927 to 1971 is included in Appendix B of the Houghton Report. An analysis of the adoption orders made in 1975–83 can be found in the Children Act 1975 Second Report to Parliament (HMSO 1984).

5 Marriage and Divorce Statistics, supra, Table 6.2.

6 Op cit at para 20.

7 In 1975, for example, 5,523 children aged between one and four were adopted, 7,278 between five and nine, and 3,316 between 10 and 14, whereas in 1995 the comparable figures were 1,494, 2,216 and 1,433 respectively: Table 6.2 of the Marriage and Divorce Statistics.

8 But note that the significant drop of adoptions between 1975, when there were 21,299 adoptions, 1976 when there were 17,621 and 1977 when there were 12,748, cannot be attributed to a decline of step-parent adoptions.

9 Op cit at para 115 and discussed in detail below at p 630.

at discouraging joint adoptions by natural parents and step-parents.[10] In 1971, for instance, 10,751 step-parent adoption orders were made and even in the late 1970s there were still over 7,000 a year, representing 70 per cent of all adoptions. However, by 1983 there were 2,872 such orders, which represented 31.8 per cent of the total number of orders made and, although they are now once again in the majority, in numerical terms they remain at their early 1980s level, numbering 2,737 in 1996.[11]

The obvious corollary of the decline in baby adoption is the rising *proportion* of older child adoptions. In 1970, for example, 20 per cent of the children adopted were aged between five and nine with a further 10 per cent aged 10 or over. By 1995 these proportions had risen to 37 per cent and 31 per cent respectively. These figures, however, mask another important change: in 1970, for instance, whereas most adoptions by non-relatives were of babies or toddlers, most of the adoptions of older children – in fact 90 per cent of the five to nine age group and 84 per cent of those aged 10 or over – were by step-parents. Today the profile is different. About half of all adoptions are step-parent adoption (in 1996, 55 per cent of adoption orders were made in favour of step-parents) and half by strangers. So far as the former are concerned they continue to be of older children.[12] As to the latter, a recent study by the Social Services Inspectorate[13] found that 62.9 per cent of the children placed for adoption by the agencies inspected were aged six or over and only three per cent were under the age of 12 months. A national study conducted at Cardiff[14] found that of a sample of 1,525 children placed for adoption by adoption agencies (both statutory and voluntary) in 1993–94, 42 per cent were aged five or over. In other words, so far as adoptions by non-relatives are concerned, baby adoptions have now become relatively unusual, while the adoption of older children, those aged five or over, has become quite common.

The practice of adoption

(a) Adoption of 'looked after' children

A key change in adoption practice came about when local authorities came to see adoption as a means by which they could secure the long-term welfare not just of babies but also of older children (including those who were physically or mentally disabled) in their care. This change of practice in turn sprang from the childcare policy which, in the 1970s, began in the UK to be termed permanency planning.[15] It was undoubtedly stimulated by the seminal work of Goldstein, Freud and Solnit *Beyond the Best Interests of the Child*, published in 1973, in which they challenged the then prevailing traditional mode of thought that biological and legal parenthood should take precedence over psychological parenthood. Their thesis was intended to reinforce the security of the adoptive, psychological

---

10 See post, p 630.
11 *Judicial Statistics 1996* Annual Report Table 5.4. Step-parent adoptions represented 55 per cent of all adoption orders made in 1996.
12 According to the findings of Murch, Lowe, Borkowski, Cooper and Griew *Pathways to Adoption* (HMSO, 1993) 81 per cent of step-parent adoptions were of children aged five or above.
13 *For Children's Sake II* (Department of Health, 1997).
14 By Murch, Lowe, Beckford, Borkowski, and Weaver *Support Services for Families of Older Children Adopted Out of Care*, (hereafter referred to as the 'Cardiff Study', 1998).
15 See particularly Parker *Planning for Deprived Children* (National Children's Homes, 1971). See also Ryburn 'In whose best interests? – post adoption contact with the birth family' (1998) 10 CFLQ 53 at 55–6.

parent–child relationship. Many of their – at the time revolutionary – notions subsequently came to be accepted by social work and legal practitioners working in the child care and adoption fields, and although such ideas were later questioned and qualified, a powerful residue has permeated professional thinking ever since. Certainly they strengthened the view that children from neglectful, disrupted and severely disordered families might often do much better if placed permanently with loving, secure and more stable families. This change of attitude by Social Services departments was accompanied by a more determined effort to secure adoption placements for so-called 'hard to place' children, to the extent of having extensive publicity campaigns, one of the best known being the 'Be My Parent' scheme organised by the British Agencies for Adoption and Fostering (BAAF).[16]

Further, as the House of Commons' Second Report on the Children Act 1975[17] noted, there has also been an increase in the number of adoptions in which parental agreement has been dispensed with,[18] which 'may reflect the greater willingness of agencies, acting on the welfare principle, to consider adoption in spite of parental opposition'. Evidence of this change of practice can be found in the statistics, for, at a time when the overall numbers of adoptions were falling, the number of children adopted from care rose from 1,488 in 1979 to 2,605 in 1990,[19] though it slipped back to 1,700 in 1996.[20]

(b)   Adoption and contact[1]

Traditionally, adoption had been a secretive process designed not simply to facilitate the irrevocable transfer of parentage, but to protect unmarried mothers and their children from excessive stigma and to enable childless couples to avoid the oppressive taint of infertility.[2] Hence, law and practice were designed so that the birth parents would have nothing to do with the process of selecting adopters: on the contrary they would generally have no knowledge of the adopters and of course they would have no further contact with their child. Similarly, adopters would not know the birth parents' identity. One result of this secrecy was that adopters were generally reluctant to tell their children that they were adopted. Today, however, it would be regarded as bad practice for adopters to hide the fact that their child had been adopted.[3] Indeed, studies in the 1960s and 1970s had demonstrated the deleterious effect upon adopted children of not knowing their

---

16 Under which written profiles with photographs, or video profiles of individual (but unidentified) children are widely circulated. There have also been television campaigns from time to time.
17 HMSO, 1984.
18 For a discussion on dispensing with parental agreement, see post, pp 636ff.
19 See Adoption Review, *Discussion Paper No 3*, op cit, para 9. Of children who left care in the year ending March 1985, 5.8 per cent were adopted: (1988) Adoption and Fostering, Vol 12, No 2 at 55. This proportion for the year end March 1988 rose to 7.4 per cent: see Adoption Law Review, *Discussion Paper No 1*, para 56.
20 *Children Looked After by Local Authority* A/F 96/12: see the summary at p 14 based upon Table 15. This represented five per cent of all discharges. It might be noted that as of 31 March 1996 a similar proportion, five per cent of children (amounting to some 2,300 being looked after) were placed for adoption. This compares with 2,900 in 1992, but which also amounted to five per cent of those then being looked after.
1 See generally Ryburn 'In whose best interests? – post adoption contact with the birth family' (1998) 10 CFLQ 53.
2 See Triseliotis 'Open adoption' in *Open Adoption – The Philosophy and the Practice*, p 19.
3 This is not an enforceable obligation: see eg *Re S (A Minor) (Adoption by Step-parents)* [1988] 1 FLR 418, CA. Such an attitude would, however, if known, militate against approval in the first place: see Lowe, op cit, at pp 375–6.

own identities,[4] and the law was eventually[5] changed permitting adult adopted children to obtain their original birth certificate and to pursue the possibility of establishing contact with their birth family.[6]

The change of law just adverted to only enables adopted children to consider contacting their family after they have attained adulthood, but another important change in practice has been to permit on-going contact with the birth family throughout the adoption. Commonly referred to as 'open adoption',[7] this change came about when it became realised that the automatic termination of contact between the child and his natural family was not necessarily in the child's interests.[8] In turn the courts began to accept that it is not inconsistent with adoption for the child to have continued contact with his family.[9] Although, as we shall see,[10] the courts are reluctant to *impose* a formal contact order on adopters, in practice some form of continuing contact (whether direct or indirect) is common in agency adoption. The Cardiff Study,[11] for example, found that in their questionnaire sample of 226 adopters (of children aged five or above who had formerly been looked after by local authorities) 83 per cent of the children had some form of continuing contact with some member of his birth family after the adoption.

A further stage of 'open adoption' is to involve the birth parents in the process of selecting adopters and there are some agencies that actively encourage this.

In summary, the stereotypical image of adoption being, as Sir Roger Ormrod once put it:[12] 'the process of amputating a baby from the mother and grafting it into another family, all contact with the natural mother being cut off so that a child is a child of the new family' is no longer reflective of today's practice. The reality is that adoption, whether by a step-parent or a stranger, is much more likely to be of an older child, frequently aged five or over and with that child having some form of continuing contact with his birth family.

These changes of practice pose important challenges to legislators and practitioners. Can there be a unitary concept of adoption to deal with both young and older children alike? Should adoption simply be regarded as the culmination of a process in which parentage is transferred, with the consequence that thereafter the adopters should no longer be entitled to any special claims for support?[13] These issues should be borne in mind in the ensuing discussion both of the current law and the proposals for reform.

---

4 See McWhinnie *Adopted Children: How They Grow Up* (1967) and Triseliotis *In Search of Origins* (1973).
5 In fact the Hurst Committee, op cit at para 150, had recommended in 1954 that all adopters should be required to give a formal undertaking to tell the child about his or her adoption.
6 Discussed post, pp 673–5.
7 See generally: Ryburn, op cit; A Mullender (ed) *Open Adoption – The Philosophy and the Practice* (1991); 'Openness in Adoption' (1991) Adoption and Fostering, Vol 15, No 4 at 81–115; and the Adoption Law Review, Discussion Paper No 1, op cit, Part C and paras 98–109 and the Consultative Document (1992) pp 9–14.
8 See eg Triseliotis 'Adoption with Contact' (1985) Adoption and Fostering, Vol 9, No 4 at 19 and Fratter *Family Placement and Access*.
9 See *Re C (A Minor) (Adoption Order: Conditions)* [1989] AC 1, [1988] 1 All ER 705, HL, discussed post, p 669.
10 Discussed post, pp 669–70.
11 *Support Services for Families of Older Children Adopted Out of Care*, op cit.
12 'Child Care Law: a personal perspective' (1983) Adoption and Fostering, Vol 7, No 4 at 10, 15.
13 See Lowe 'The changing face of adoption – the gift/donation model versus the contract/services model' (1997) 9 CFLQ 371 at 382–6.

(c)   Post-adoption support

The conventional view of the adoption was that it was an end in itself and that, having effected a legal transfer of the child from one family to another, the adoptive family were thereafter left to their own devices and resources to bring up the child on their own. This model, which might be conveniently labelled the 'gift/donation' model, sits uneasily with the adoption of older children and the growing practice of open adoption.[14] It has become increasingly recognised that adoption is not the end of the process but merely a part of an ongoing and often complex process of family development and that in many, if not most, cases the adoptive family will need ongoing support.

The provision of post-adoption support is becoming the subject of more attention.[15] It can take many forms, ranging from the provision of allowances, the organisation of post-adoption contact, payment for the provision of therapy for the child, ongoing counselling for the adoptive (and birth) family including the child, the provision of updating information and the organisation of support groups.[16]

So far as adoption allowances are concerned, their introduction was not without controversy. They were first recommended by the Houghton Committee[17] on the basis that more adoptive homes might be found for children in need. The issue was hotly contested in Parliament and indeed in Standing Committee it was only the chairman's casting vote that saved the provision.[18] Nevertheless, a provision permitting adoption agencies to submit a scheme for the payment of an adoption allowance for approval by the Secretary of State was introduced in 1982.[19] In fact by the 1990s virtually all statutory agencies and some voluntary agencies had successfully applied for a scheme.[20] Reflecting this development, the law was changed by the Children Act 1989[1] so as to empower *all* agencies to pay an adoption allowance, provided cash payments conform to the requirements set out by the Adoption Allowance Regulations 1991.[2] Under these Regulations agencies have a discretion whether to pay an allowance at all and, if so, how much and for how long. However, reflecting the original intention of the scheme, which was to target payments for a minority of children whose chances of being adopted needed special encouragement, the current guidance states[3] 'Adoption allowances continue to be the exception rather than the norm'.

This scheme has been criticised as penalising often especially vulnerable and frequently highly damaged children and it has been suggested there should be a national standardised system of eligibility and level of support.[4]

---

14 See Lowe, op cit.
15 Interestingly, wide though the Houghton Committee (ibid) envisaged a comprehensive adoption service should be, it made no mention of post-adoption support. For discussion about what a post-adoption service should provide see the Review of Adoption Law, Discussion Paper No 3 *The Adoption Process*, para 88, the Consultative Document 1992 (ibid) Part VII; the government White Paper *Adoption: The Future* (1993 Cm 2288) 4.25.
16 For a detailed study of those services offered during the adoption process until the year after the order see the Cardiff Study, op cit.
17 Ibid, Recommendation 17. But see the discussion by Lowe, op cit, at 379.
18 Standing Committee A (Ninth Sitting), cols 447–80.
19 Viz Children Act 1975 s 32, subsequently re-enacted by s 56(4)–(7) of the Adoption Act 1976.
20 See Lambert and Seglow *Adoption Allowances in England and Wales: The Early Years* (1988).
1   Substituting s 57A for s 56 (4)–(7) of the Adoption Act 1976.
2   S1 1991/2030.
3   *The Children Act 1989, Guidance and Regulations*, Vol 9, *Adoption Issues* at para 22.
4   This is one of the recommendations of the Cardiff Study, op cit, and see Lowe, op cit, at 383–4.

(d)   Transracial and intercountry adoptions

As the BAAF study *Focus on Adoption*[5] puts it, many of the children who had previously been considered 'unsuitable for adoption' were from minority ethnic groups. The British Adoption Project in the late 1960s pioneered permanent family placement for a number of these children, but most were placed transracially. During the 1980s in particular it began to be seriously questioned whether it was desirable to have transracial adoptions at all.[6] It was evident that many agencies were against placing ethnic minority children with white adopters, though a rigid policy to this effect is almost certainly open to judicial review.[7] Although it undoubtedly seems desirable, all things being equal, that children should be matched with those of a similar background of race, culture and religion, where this cannot be achieved, then it becomes a matter of fine judgment as to whether it is better for the child *not* to be placed permanently, rather than with potential adopters from an entirely different background.[8] In those cases that came before the courts, at any rate, where an application was to end a well-established placement, there was no predisposition towards racial matching.[9]

Recent research has shown that the number of children from ethnic minority backgrounds forms a small minority of those placed for adoption.[10] Although a number are placed transracially,[11] practice varies from agency to agency, but in general statutory agencies (especially Shire counties)[12] are more likely than voluntary agencies to do so.

Related to the issue of transracial adoptions is another matter of growing concern, namely the practice of intercountry adoption, where applicants seek to adopt children from overseas, commonly developing countries such as those in Latin America, South East Asia, or more recently from Eastern Europe, particularly Romania, Bosnia and the former Soviet Union. As the White Paper, *Adoption: The Future* comments:[13]

'The interest in adopting children from Eastern European countries was stimulated by harrowing reports of orphaned or abandoned children in institutions which emerged after the collapse of their communist regimes. The general decline in the number of babies and very young children now available for adoption in this country also helped to stimulate a general interest in adoption from overseas.'

5 *Focus on Adoption* (compiled by McCallum, 1997) 1.4.3.
6 See inter alia Gill and Jackson *Adoption and race: black, Asian and mixed race children in white families* (1983).
7 See eg *Re J K (Adoption: Transracial Placement)* [1991] 2 FLR 340; *Re P (A Minor) (Adoption)* [1990] 1 FLR 96, CA; and *Re N (Minors) (Adoption)* [1990] 1 FLR 58.
8 For most of the time this highly charged debate has been conducted in the absence of research evidence on the effects of transracial adoption. However, research by Thoburn, Norford and Rashid *Permanent Family Placement for Children of Minority Ethnic Origins* (1998) suggests that transracial adoptions are commonly successful, and the government announced in August 1998 its intention to stop adoption being blocked on these grounds.
9 See eg *Re O (Trans-racial Adoption: Contact)* [1995] 2 FLR 597 and the cases cited in note 7 above.
10 In the Cardiff Study conducted by Murch and Lowe, op cit, only 13 per cent of children placed by statutory agencies and 21 per cent by voluntary agencies were from ethnic minority backgrounds.
11 In fact almost a quarter (24 per cent) of ethnic minority children were placed transracially in the BAAF sample of local authority adoptions in 1995: *Focus on Adoption*, op cit, at 5.2.3. According to the Cardiff Study 44 per cent of statutory agencies and 31 per cent of voluntary agencies reported that they had placed children transracially, but 24 per cent of statutories and 54 per cent of voluntaries positively said that they do not place transracially: see Lowe 'Some Perspectives from National Research' in James (ed) *Post Placement Services in Adoption and Fostering* (1997) 2.8.
12 See *Focus on Adoption*, op cit, 5.2.3.
13 1993, Cm 2288, para 6.6.

There are no reliable statistics for intercountry adoption in the United Kingdom, though they were thought to number about 100–120 a year before adoption from Romania began.[14] However, in 1990 over 400 children from Romania alone were brought here for adoption,[15] although adoptions from this particular country have since been curtailed.

Intercountry adoption raises a number of fundamental issues such as the obvious dangers of exploiting vulnerable birth parents, the desirability of transracial adoptions and the difficulty of international control. Against these are the need of the adopters themselves, who are often desperate to have children but who are too old to be considered by adoption agencies, at any rate to adopt babies and, not least, the desperate plight of some of the children such as the Romanian orphans. It is by no means easy to balance these considerations, though practicality suggests that attempting to control intercountry adoption is probably better than attempting to outlaw it and, as we discuss at the end of this chapter, a bold attempt at global control is provided for by the 1993 Hague Convention on Intercountry Adoption.

4.   RESPONSIBILITY FOR PLACING CHILDREN FOR ADOPTION

Prohibition of private placements

When adoption was first introduced into England and Wales by the Adoption of Children Act 1926, it was remarkably unregulated. The 1926 Act essentially provided, as one commentator has put it, 'a process whereby, under minimal safeguards supervised by the court, a civil contract was registered and recognised'.[16] In particular, there were no provisions regulating who could arrange adoptions. Although, following the recommendations of the Horsburgh Committee, it became an offence for a body of persons other than a registered adoption society or a local authority to make any arrangements for the adoption of children,[17] until 1982 there was no restriction on individuals placing children for adoption. In fact it had been appreciated for some time just what a crucial stage the placement process is. As the Hurst Committee, reporting in 1954, put it:[18] 'Once the child is placed, much harm and unhappiness may result if a change has to be made.' It was the Committee's view that adoptions arranged by persons of special experience and training stood a much better chance of success. However, whilst it recommended that social workers employed by societies be fully trained, it stopped short of recommending the prohibition of private or third party placements. That particular bullet was bitten by the Houghton Committee. Although commonly such private arrangements were made through doctors or even solicitors, there was, as the Committee pointed out,[19] nothing to prevent a mother making a placement with a casual acquaintance she had met at the

14 See Adoption Law Review, Discussion Paper No 4, para 27. In the *Pathways Study*, op cit at para 2.7, inter-country adoption amounted to three per cent of the total sample, but six per cent of the London Sample.
15 Adoption Law Review, ibid, para 27. For a profile of inter-country adoptions in 1995, see *Focus on Adoption* (BAAF, 1997) Ch 6.
16 Cretney 'From Status to Contract?', in *Consensus Ad Idem*, op cit, at p 252.
17 Originally by the Adoption of Children (Regulation) Act 1939 s 1.
18 Op cit at para 24. See also Goodacre *Adoption Policy and Practice*, (1966), who advocated that all adoptions by strangers be handled by local authorities.
19 Op cit, at para 81.

launderette. This lack of control had obvious dangers: if the potential adopters were unsuitable (a not unlikely consequence, given the inexperience of the placers) the placement could be disastrous for the child; it could also lead to improper pressure being brought upon the mother. Following the Houghton Committee's recommendation[20] it is now unlawful for a person other than an adoption agency to place a child for adoption unless the proposed adopter is a relative of the child or he is acting pursuant to a High Court order.[1]

'Placement', for these purposes, refers to the single act of transfer rather than to a continuous state of looking after the child. Hence, because s 11 has no extra-territorial effect, a private placement abroad is no offence even if the couple then bring the child to the United Kingdom for adoption.[2] On the other hand, an offence will be committed if, as in *Re A (Adoption Placement),*[3] the child is handed over to the couple in the United Kingdom, or even if one of the couple brings the child from abroad and joins his spouse with the child in this country.[4] Prospective adopters cannot avoid the offence by using an intermediary abroad.[5] It has been held not to be an offence, however, for a third party to approach an approved adoption agency on behalf of a mentally incapable mother with a view to placing her child for adoption.[6]

It remains lawful to make private arrangements for the adoption of the child by a relative,[7] and it is not an offence to make a private placement in pursuance of a High Court order. An unlawful placement does not per se prevent an adoption order from being made, though in such cases it will be necessary to obtain *High Court* dispensation.[8] The above provisions do not prevent private *fostering* placements being made,[9] nor is there anything to prevent such foster parents from subsequently applying for adoption. However, if it is clear that the foster arrangement is a mere subterfuge and that both the placer and the recipient intended that the child should be adopted, both will be guilty of an offence.[10]

20 Op cit, at para 92.
1 Adoption Act 1976 s 11(1) and (3) as amended by the Criminal Justice Act 1982. It is an offence both to arrange private placements and to receive a child unlawfully placed. In the latter instance, however, it must be proved that the placement was unlawful and that the accused knew of the purpose of the placement: *Gatehouse v Robinson* [1986] 1 WLR 18. Those contravening these provisions are liable to a maximum of three months' imprisonment and a fine not exceeding level 5 on the standard scale.
2 As in *Re Adoption Application 8605489/99* (1988) Adoption and Fostering, Vol 12, No 2, p 58.
3 [1988] 1 WLR 229 – the child was handed over at Heathrow airport.
4 *Re An Adoption Application (Adoption of Non Patrial)* [1992] 1 WLR 596 and *Re Adoption Application (Non Patrial: Breach of Procedures)* [1993] 1 FLR 947.
5 *Re A W (Adoption Application)* [1993] 1 FLR 62, CA.
6 *Re W (Arrangements to Place For Adoption)* [1995] 1 FLR 163.
7 Adoption Act 1976 s 11(1)(a). 'Relative' is defined in the Adoption Act 1976 s 72(1) as grandparent, brother, sister, uncle and aunt whether of the full blood or half blood or by affinity and regardless of whether the child is legitimate or illegitimate. The unmarried father is specifically included in the definition. Great aunts and uncles are not 'relatives' for these purposes: see *Re S (Arrangements For Adoption)* [1985] FLR 579, CA and *Re C (Minors) (Wardship: Adoption)* [1989] 1 All ER 395, CA; nor is a 'commissioning non genetic partner' in a surrogacy arrangement: see *Re MW (Adoption: Surrogacy)* [1995] 2 FLR 759.
8 Adoption Act 1976 s 11(1)(b). NB it is now established that, although a prior illegal placement does not prevent the High Court making an adoption order, it has no power *retrospectively* to authorise the placement and hence, notwithstanding the adoption being granted, an offence will still have been committed: *Re G (Adoption: Illegal Placement)* [1995] 1 FLR 403, CA. See also Sandland 'Problems in the Criminal Law of Adoption' [1995] JSWFL 149.
9 Private foster parents are required to notify the local authority under the Children Act 1989 Sch 8, para 7.
10 *Gatehouse v Robinson*, supra.

ensure, in co-operation with voluntary societies, that a comprehensive adoption service is available throughout their area'.

By 'comprehensive' the Committee envisaged that an adoption service:[9]

'. . . should comprise a social work service to natural parents, whether married or unmarried, seeking placement for a child . . . skills and facilities for the assessment of the parents' emotional resources, and their personal and social situation; short-term placement facilities for children pending adoption placement; assessment facilities; adoption placement services; aftercare for natural parents who need it; counselling for adoptive families. In addition, it should have access to a range of specialised services, such as medical services (including genetic, psychological assessment services, arrangements for the examination of children and adoptive applications, and medical adviser) and legal advisory services.'

Although the Houghton Committee' recommendations were accepted and subsequently enacted in the Children Act 1975, because of the costs implementation was delayed and it was not until 1988 that they were brought into force by what then became s 1 of the Adoption Act 1976. Under s 1(1) of the Act:

'It is the duty of *every* local authority to establish and maintain within their area a service designed to meet the needs in relation to adoption of –
(a) children who have been or may be adopted
(b) parents and guardians of such children and
(c) persons *who have adopted* or may adopt a child and for that purpose to provide the requisite facilities, or secure that they are provided by approved adoption societies' [emphasis added].

Although the Houghton Committee made no mention of post-adoption support, it is now[10] accepted that by referring to children who '*have been adopted*' as well as those who may be adopted and to persons '*who have adopted*' as well as to persons who '*may adopt*', s 1(1) imposes an obligation to provide a post-adoption service.

It should be noted that, reflecting the Houghton recommendations, the obligation to provide a service extends to meeting the needs of children, birth parents or guardians and the adopters (both those who have adopted or who may adopt).

Section 1(2) spells out in a little more detail what the *requisite facilities* of an adoption service must minimally provide:

'(a) temporary board and lodging where needed by pregnant women, mothers or children;
(b) arrangements for assessing children and prospective adopters, and placing children for adoption;
(c) counselling for persons with problems relating to adoption.'

Section 1(3) makes it clear that such an adoption service must be provided:

'In conjunction with the local authority's other social services and with approved adoption societies in their area, *so that help may be given in a co-ordinated manner without duplication, omission or avoidable delay*'[11] [emphasis added].

---

9 See para 38.
10 One of the first to mention this were Bevan and Parry *Children Act 1975* (1979) at p 15. Post-adoption support is specifically mentioned, but only for adult adopted people, in the list of services that must be provided in Local Authority Circular LAC (87) 8 and Welsh Office Circular 35(8).
11 Bevan and Parry, ibid at p 15, argue that this falls short of the Houghton Committee's recommendations that local authorities should themselves provide such a service.

These somewhat general provisions are supplemented by the Adoption Agencies Regulations 1983,[12] under which there is an obligation (a) to provide a counselling service, (b) to explain and provide written information about the legal implications of adoption and (c) to provide approved adopters with background information about the child. Further helpful guidance as to what an adoption service should comprise is given in a Local Authority Circular. However, notwithstanding these Regulations and Guidance, there is relatively little detailed guidance as to what a general adoption service should comprise. There is, for example, as the Adoption Law Review pointed out,[13] a lack of clarity about what post-adoption services agencies are supposed to provide.

The proposed Adoption Bill would make relatively little difference to the current position, save that it would be made expressly clear that a comprehensive adoption service should include a service in relation to inter-county adoption.[14]

Ironically, given its relatively recent establishment, there are those who question[15] whether it is sensible or practical, given the other calls on their time, to impose a duty on every local authority to provide an adoption service. Indeed, given the large numbers of adoption agencies (167) and the relatively low number of adoptions, there does seem an overwhelming case for rationalisation, for there must surely be some minimum number of adoptions which the agency handles below which they cease to be viable. Whether this rationalisation should be achieved by amalgamating agencies, by removing the function from local authorities altogether and placing it solely in the voluntary sector, or creating a new national adoption service is highly contentious and is likely to be hotly debated.

6. THE WEIGHTING OF THE CHILD'S WELFARE

The current law[16]

Although the courts have always had to be satisfied that an adoption order would be for the child's benefit, until the implementation of the Children Act 1975 there was no specific guidance on the weighting to be accorded to the child's welfare during the various stages of the adoption process. The guiding principle is now provided by the Adoption Act 1976 s 6, which states:

> 'In reaching any decision relating to the adoption of a child a court or adoption agency shall have regard to all the circumstances, first consideration being given to the need to safeguard and promote the welfare of the child throughout his childhood; and shall so far as practicable ascertain the wishes and feelings of the child regarding the decision and give due consideration to them, having regard to his age and understanding.'

It will be noticed that s 6 falls short of making the child's welfare the paramount consideration as under the Children Act 1989 s 1. In *Re B (Adoption: Child's Welfare)*[17] it was argued that, since s 1(1) of the 1989 Act applies to 'any question with respect of the upbringing of a child', it effectively superseded s 6 of the 1976 Act. Wall J rejected the submission. Having pointed to the unique consequence of

---

12 Regulation 8.
13 See Discussion Paper No 3 *The Adoption Process*, para 88.
14 Clause 2(5).
15 See in particular Morgan *Adoption and the Care of Children* (1998).
16 See generally Bevan and Parry *Children Act 1975* ch 3 and Bennion 'First Consideration: A Cautionary Tale' (1976) 126 NLJ 1237.
17 [1995] 1 FLR 895 at 898. See also Bevan and Parry, op cit, para 33, for the background thinking to the legislation.

adoption in irrevocably severing the family ties, he commented 'it is in my judgment logical that a different test needs to be applied to the making of an order which extinguishes parental rights as opposed to one which regulates their operation'.

In point of fact, it is hard to state with precision what difference there is between 'first' and 'paramount'.[18] Perhaps the most authoritative guidance is that given by Lord Simon when he said:[19]

> 'In adoption proceedings the welfare of the child is not the paramount consideration (ie outweighing all others), but it is first consideration (ie outweighing any other).'

In short, while the child's welfare remains the single most important factor, it does not necessarily outweigh all other considerations. It has been held[20] that another important consideration that must be taken into account is immigration policy. Hence, sham applications or applications of convenience comparable to marriages of convenience made with the sole intention of gaining for the child a right of abode will not be permitted.

Section 6 applies to all aspects of the adoption process: it expressly applies both to adoption agencies and to the courts, and it has been held to apply to the questions of whether or not to impose a s 12(6) condition[1] and whether to grant an agency's application under s 30 for leave to remove the child from the potential adopters.[2] It is submitted that it applies[3] in relation to freeing the child for adoption.[4] It has also been held that, notwithstanding that s 6 refers to the need to safeguard and promote the child's welfare *throughout his childhood*, the courts are not thereby prevented from considering benefits that might accrue after the child's majority.[5] One complication of the current law is that while considering the adoption issue the courts are bound to treat the child's welfare as their first consideration, but when considering the s 8 alternatives they must treat the child's welfare as their paramount consideration.[6] On occasions where there are two sets of proceedings this difference in the weighting of welfare can result in the courts having to give priority to children involved in Children Act proceedings over those involved in the adoption proceedings.[7]

The proposed law

Although, given the irrevocable severance of family ties, there is some justification in not treating the child's welfare as the paramount consideration, there are powerful counter-arguments. First, even supposing it is right to protect the parents' interests, there is little justification in applying the lesser weighting to issues that do not involve the parents. Accordingly, it may be thought right to have the paramountcy principle govern all adoption issues save that of dispensing with

---

18 In *Re W (A Minor) (Adoption)* [1984] FLR 402, CA at 404, Cumming Bruce LJ described the difference as 'manifestly an extremely fine distinction'. *Re W* is an unusual example of a judge expressly but erroneously applying the paramountcy test in adoption.

19 In *Re D (An Infant) (Adoption: Parent's Consent)* [1977] AC 602 at 638, [1977] 1 All ER 145, HL. See also *Re H (Adoption: Non-Patrial)* [1996] 2 FLR 187 at 193, per Thorpe LJ and *Re J (Adoption: Non Patrial)* [1998] 1 FLR 225 at 229.

20 See in particular *Re H (A Minor) (Adoption: Non Patrial)* [1997] 1 WLR 791, CA as explained by *Re J (Adoption: Non Patrial)* [1998] 1 FLR 225, CA, discussed post, p 666.

1 *Re S (A Minor) (Blood Transfusion: Adoption Order Conditions)* [1994] 2 FLR 416, CA, discussed post, p 667.

2 *Re C (A Minor) (Adoption)* [1994] 2 FLR 513, CA, discussed post, p 664.

3 Following *Re U (Application to Free for Adoption)* [1993] 2 FLR 992, CA, discussed post, p 652.

4 Discussed post, p 650.

5 *Re D (A Minor) (Adoption Order: Validity)* [1991] Fam 137, [1991] 3 All ER 461, CA.

6 See *Re B (Adoption: Child's Welfare)*, supra.

7 See *Re T and E (Proceedings: Conflicting Interests)* [1995] 1 FLR 581.

parental consent. That indeed was the proposal made in the Consultative Document in 1992.[8] Secondly, one can argue that looked at from the child's point of view his welfare ought to be considered paramount in all cases, including adoption, where his future upbringing is directly in issue. Evidently this is the argument that ultimately prevailed with the Department of Health, for under the proposed Bill[9] both the court and adoption agency are directed 'whenever coming to a decision relating to the adoption of a child' to treat that child's welfare as the paramount consideration. At the same time, however, the court will also be directed to have regard to a statutory check list[10] modelled on that under the Children Act,[11] but with the important additional requirement to consider:[12]

> '. . . the relationship which the child has with relatives[13] and with any other person in relation to whom the court or agency considers the question to be relevant, including –
> (i) the value to the child of any such relationship continuing,
> (ii) the ability and willingness of any of the child's relatives, or of any such person, to provide the child with a secure environment in which the child can develop, and otherwise to meet the child's needs,
> (iii) the wishes and feelings of any of the child's relatives, or of any such person, about the child.'

Although much would depend on how this specific factor is interpreted, there can be little doubt that making the child's welfare paramount would represent a fundamental shift from the current position and would almost certainly make it harder for a parent to oppose the adoption, at any rate once the child had been placed. Whether the new enjoinder would lead to agencies making more adoptive placements is an interesting question.

B.   The making of adoption orders

1.   WHO MAY BE ADOPTED

An adoption order may be made only in respect of a person who is under the age of 18 and has never been married. An adopted child may be readopted.[14]

2.   WHO MAY APPLY FOR ADOPTION

Age, health, and domicile of applicant

Immediately before the Children Act 1989 the law prevented anyone under the age of 21 from applying to adopt.[15] However, the 1989 Act amended the uniform

---

8 Ibid at paras 7.1ff.
9 Clause 1(1). Note cl 1(2) expressly directs the court and agency to consider the child's welfare in childhood *and later.*
10 See cl 1(4).
11 Children Act 1989 s 1 (3), discussed ante, p 336.
12 Clause 1(4)(f).
13 Which for these purposes would include the birth parents: see cl 1(6).
14 Adoption Act 1976 s 12 (5), (7) and s 72 (1) (definition of 'child') and see *Re D (A Minor) Adoption Order: Validity)* [1991] Fam 137 at 144, [1991] 3 All ER 461, CA at 465 per Balcombe LJ. The child's domicile does not affect jurisdiction: *Re B (S) (Infant)* [1968] Ch 204, [1967] 3 All ER 629, but see post, p 666 n 5.
15 Adoption Act 1976, s 14(1) and s 15(1). Under the Adoption Act 1958, as originally enacted, a sole applicant and at least one of joint applicants had to be aged 25 unless he or she was a parent or

minimum age requirement to the limited extent of permitting a joint application by a married couple where one spouse is the mother or father of the child and aged at least 18 and the other spouse is at least 21.[16] Although there is no prescribed maximum age, it should be appreciated that in practice adoption agencies are unlikely to consider applicants over 40 (and often over 35) at any rate as potential adopters for healthy babies.[17] Obviously age, for example in the case of grandparent applicants, can be a factor that the court can take into account when deciding whether an adoption order would be for the child's benefit. Whether upper age limits should be made more explicit either in legislation or guidance was raised by the Adoption Law Review.[18]

Although there are no statutory requirements in respect of the health of adopters, as the Adoption Law Review points out,[19] adoption agencies are required in the regulations to obtain a report on the prospective adopters' health.[20]

A single applicant, or, in the case of a joint application, one of the applicants must be domiciled in a part of the United Kingdom,[1] Channel Islands or Isle of Man, unless the application is for a Convention Order,[2] or for an order permitting the applicants to adopt the child abroad.[3]

Joint or single adoptions

The Act permits both joint and single applications. In the former case, an order may not be made upon the application of more than one person unless the applicants are married to each other.[4] It has been held, however, that a joint adoption order can be made in favour of a married couple notwithstanding they have separated.[5]

---

relative of the child. The Houghton Committee (at paras 70–78) recommended the introduction of a uniform age, because there was some evidence that the minimum age of 25 was preventing some suitable couples from adopting and a minimum age of 21 would give an opportunity of testing the strength of a teenage marriage. For the present law, see Adoption Act 1976 s 14(1), (1A), (1B) and s 15(1) (as amended by the 1989 Act Sch 10 para 4).

16 Adoption Act 1976 s 14(1B) added by the Children Act 1989 Sch 10, para 4. Ironically, following this change the Adoption Law Review, Discussion Paper No 3, ibid, at para 39, asks whether there is a case for standardising the minimum age. It might be noted that Art 7 of the European Convention on the Adoption of Children 1980 (to which the UK is a Contracting Party) states that the minimum age should not be less than 21 nor more than 35 save where the applicant is a parent or there are exceptional circumstances. In fact the proposed Adoption Bill would complicate matters, since cl 45(3) would prescribe *no* minimum age limit in the case of parent seeking to adopt their own child by themselves.

17 See the discussion in the Adoption Law Review, Discussion Paper No 3, at paras 40 et seq. These conditions may be relaxed where application is made to adopt older children or those with disabilities: see para 43.

18 Ibid at para 44. But in fact no changes would be made by the proposed Adoption Bill: see cls 44 and 45.

19 Ibid at para 46.

20 Adoption Agencies Regulations 1983 reg 8(2)(c). These matters include personal and family history and the current state of health, including consumption of tobacco and alcohol. See also *R v Secretary of State for Health, ex p Luff* [1992] 1 FLR 59, where the court refused to quash a Department of Health recommendation to the Home Office that the adoptive applicants in respect of two Romanian children were unsuitable, because of the male applicant's health following a heart by-pass operation (see post, p 678).

1 England, Wales, Scotland and Northern Ireland: Interpretation Act 1978 Sch 1.

2 Adoption Act 1976 s 14(2), s 15(2). 'Convention Orders' are discussed below at p 679.

3 Adoption Act 1976 s 55.

4 Adoption Act 1976 s 14. If it later emerges that the joint applicants are not married to each other, the order is voidable and not void: *Re F (Infants) (Adoption Order: Validity)* [1977] Fam 165, [1977] 2 All ER 777, CA; cf *Re RA* (1974) 4 Fam Law 182.

5 Per Johnson J in *Re WM (Adoption: Non-Patrial)* [1997] 1 FLR 132 where a couple separated after making the adoption application, the child living with the female applicant but having regular

Confining the power to grant joint orders to married couples means that cohabiting couples (or brothers and sisters) cannot jointly adopt. Although this restriction is in line with the prohibition under Art 6(1) of the European Adoption Convention 1980 (to which the UK is a party), given the increasing incidence of children born to parents who are not married but who are living together in stable unions, the justification for this restriction may well be open to question.[6] In this regard note might be taken of *Re AB (Adoption: Joint Residence)*,[7] in which an adoption order was granted to one cohabiting applicant and a joint residence order was made in favour of both of them. In that way, both cohabitants acquired parental responsibility. Although Cazalet J expressly said that by so holding he was not intending to circumvent the provisions of the 1976 Act, many will see this decision as a back-door method for cohabiting couples to adopt a child jointly.

It has been held that the provisions governing those who can apply for adoption are widely drawn and cannot be construed as excluding as a matter of public policy a person with homosexual tendencies from applying to adopt.[8]

An order may not be made on the sole application of a married person unless his spouse cannot be found or is by reason of ill health, whether physical or mental, incapable of making an application for an adoption order[9] or, alternatively, if the spouses have separated and are living apart and the separation is likely to be permanent.[10] This is designed to avoid the highly artificial situation of a child being adopted by one of two married persons living together, the other of whom refuses to apply for an order. If the sole applicant is the mother or father[11] of the child, no order can be made unless the court is satisfied that the other natural parent is dead or cannot be found or there is some other reason justifying the other natural parent's exclusion.[12] The reason for the exclusion has to be recorded.[13] There is evidence of an increase in the numbers of single adoptions.[14]

---

contact with the male applicant. It was held to be in the child's interests for the order to be made because (a) the man would be vested with parental responsibility and (b) by thereby becoming a child of the family the child could enjoy the financial advantages under the Matrimonial Causes Act 1973 and the Inheritance (Provision for Family and Dependants) Act 1975.

6 See Adoption Law Review, op cit, at paras 51 et seq.

7 [1996] 1 FLR 27.

8 Per Singer J in *Re W (A Minor) (Adoption: Homosexual Adopter)* [1998] 2 Fam 58. See also *Re E (Adoption: Freeing Orders)* [1995] 1 FLR 382, CA. In the Cardiff Study, op cit, out of a sample 1,932 families approved for adoption, three were homosexual.

9 What does this provision contemplate? It is easy to see that a person's mental health may be such that he is incapable of making an application but difficult to see how his physical health can have this effect. Does it envisage a spouse whose health is such that no court would make an order? If so, this might in any case lead the court to conclude that the applicant's health is such that it would not be for the child's benefit to make such an order in his favour.

10 Adoption Act 1976 s 15(1)(b).

11 Notwithstanding the definition of 'parent' as including only those with parental responsibility, it is thought that this reference includes the unmarried father: cf Bevan and Parry, op cit, at para 97 and Bevan *Child Law* (1989) para 5.57.

12 The burden of proof is a heavy one: see *Re C (Minor) (Adoption by Parent)* [1986] Fam Law 360. This is in line with the Houghton Committee's recommendations, at para 98–102, on which the provision is based. The Committee was afraid that adoption was being used simply as a means of cutting out the other natural parent rather than to promote the child's welfare.

13 Adoption Act 1976 s 15(3).

14 Whereas in 1983 and 1984 there were respectively only 82 and 81 orders made in favour of single applicants and according to the *Pathways Study*, op cit, para 2.6 only two per cent of their sample of cases in 1986–88, in the Cardiff Study, conducted in the mid 90s between five per cent and eight per cent of the sample were single applicants.

Step-parent adoptions[15]

In the following discussion the expression 'step-parent adoption' refers to the case where a parent, usually the mother, and a spouse who is not the parent jointly apply to adopt the child. Commonly this occurs following divorce and remarriage (the 'post-divorce' step-parent adoption) but it also occurs following a parent's death and the surviving parent's remarriage ('post-death' step-parent adoption) or where the mother was not married in the first place ('illegitimate' step-parent adoption). Until the Children Act 1975 there were no formal restrictions on any type of step-parent adoption application. The Houghton Committee, however, was concerned[16] about the growing number of adoptions involving step-parents, which by 1970 exceeded 10,000. They were particularly concerned with 'post-divorce' step-parent adoptions which they felt were an inappropriate use of the jurisdiction and, given the consequential extinguishment of the legal links with half his family, potentially damaging to the child. The Committee felt that the preferable alternative was to extend the provisions enabling a step-parent to apply to become a guardian.

Although the reform did not exactly follow the Houghton Committee recommendations, nevertheless the courts were directed to dismiss 'post-divorce' step-parent adoption applications if they considered the matter would be better dealt with by an application to the divorce court for what was then a custody order.[17]

This direction was at first taken to be a clear expression of a policy to discourage adoptions by parents and step-parents.[18] Indeed, the appellate courts initially interpreted the provision as requiring the applicant to prove that adoption was better than a joint custody order made by the divorce court.[19] This meant, as Ormrod LJ acknowledged,[20] that, given the child would be living with the applicants regardless of the outcome of the application, they would have to rely on the intangible advantages of adoption. However, in an apparent volte face, the Court of Appeal held in *Re D (Minors) (Adoption by Step-Parent)*[1] that the section required the dismissal of the application only if it could be shown that the matter could be better dealt with by a joint custody order. This approach, as the Adoption Law Review put it, was more in accord with the actual wording of the provision, but did not reflect the original intentions of the Houghton Committee.[2]

15　For a full study of the law and practice before the Children Act 1989 see Masson, Norbury and Chatterton *Mine, Yours and Ours*, summarised in (1982) Adoption and Fostering, Vol 5, No 2 at 7; and for further analysis see Priest 'Step-parent Adoptions: What is the Law ?' [1982] JSWL 285 and Rawlings 'Law Reform with Tears' (1982) 45 MLR 637. See also the Adoption Law Review Discussion Paper No 1, paras 29–46 and 125–134 and Discussion Paper No 3, paras 26–33.

16　Op cit at paras 103–110.

17　Adoption Act 1976 s 14(3), in cases where the application was made jointly by a parent and step-parent, and s 15(4) where the application was by the step-parent alone.

18　See, for example, Local Authority Circular LAC (76) 22 at para 10(ii) which stated, inter alia, that a parent and step-parent of a child 'will not normally be able to get an adoption order if the parent has custody of the child . . . following . . . divorce proceedings'.

19　See eg *Re S (Infants) (Adoption by Parent)* [1977] Fam 173, [1977] 3 All ER 671, CA, and for a striking dismissal of an application, see *Re W v W (A Minor)* (1976) Times, 26 November. The impact of these decisions on the lower courts was by no means consistent: see the research findings of Masson et al, op cit.

20　In *Re S*, supra.

1　(1980) 2 FLR 102, CA.

2　A similar interpretation was also placed upon the tortuously worded s 37 of the Children Act 1975, which applied to 'post death' and 'illegitimate' step-parent adoptions: see *Re S (A Minor) (Adoption or Custodianship)* [1987] Fam 98, [1987] 2 All ER 99, CA.

These legislative attempts to restrict step-parent applications essentially failed and long before the Children Act 1989 they had become a dead letter. That is not to say that step-parent applications were automatically granted, for as with all applications the court had to be satisfied that adoption was in the child's interests[3] and that parental agreement had either been given or should be dispensed with.[4]

The Children Act 1989 formally repealed the provisions intended to restrict step-parent adoption applications.[5] Indeed, by specifically enacting that a parent aged at least 18 can jointly apply with a spouse aged at least 21 to adopt his or her child, the 1989 Act seemed to give tacit approval to such applications.[6] Perhaps not surprisingly, the proportion of step-parent adoptions has steadily risen since implementation of the Children Act 1989 and, at least according to the *Judicial Statistics*, are now again in the majority (55 per cent in 1996).

The whole issue of step-parent adoption was again raised during the Adoption Law Review, but although concern was expressed that some applications 'appear to be made without full consideration of the needs of the child', it was nevertheless felt inappropriate to prohibit such adoptions.[7] It was thought desirable, however, to amend the law to help discourage inappropriate applications and to provide, in those cases where a step-parent adoption was desirable, a new form of order whereby only the step-parent him- or herself actually adopted (it was felt anomalous that, as under the current law, the birth parent should adopt their own child). The Consultative Document recommended various changes aimed at discouraging step-parent adoption, including the idea that it should be revocable where the new marriage ends in divorce or death before the child is 18, and that it should be possible for step-parents to acquire parental responsibility either by agreement or a court order.[8] In the event, the proposal that a step-parent adoption could be undone was dropped and the proposed Adoption Bill makes provision for a new type of step-parent adoption order,[9] and would amend the Children Act to allow step-parents to acquire parental responsibility by agreement or order.[10]

Adoption by relatives[11]

Although there are no formal restrictions against relatives applying to adopt, the courts have long had reservations about granting adoption to such applicants fearing, inter alia, that an order would distort the natural relationship particularly in the case of adoption by grandparents.[12] It was also felt that the severance of legal

---

3 See eg *Re P (Minors) (Adoption)* [1989] 1 FLR 1, CA, where an application to adopt two out of three step-children was refused.

4 Though the Pathways Study found that in 80 per cent of their sample of step-parent applications an order was granted: *Pathways to Adoption*, op cit, Table 2.9.

5 Adoption Act 1976 s 14(3) and s 15(4) and the Children Act 1975 were repealed by the Children Act 1989 Sch 15.

6 See ante, pp 627–8.

7 Consultative Document 1992, para 19.

8 See Recommendations 19 and 20, discussed at paras 19.4 and 19.8.

9 Clause 45.

10 Clause 85.

11 See generally the Consultative Document, op cit at para 20 and Adoption Law Review, Discussion Paper No 1, paras 47–49 and 135 and Discussion Paper No 3, paras 26–33.

12 As Vaisey J said in *Re DX (An Infant)* [1949] Ch 320 at 321, 'The ostensible relationship of sisters between those who are in fact mother and child is unnatural and its creation might sow the seeds of grievous unhappiness for them both . . .' but courts now seem much less concerned about this theoretical consequence. See further below.

ties with the birth parents fits uneasily with an adoption within the family. Another concern in the case of grandparent applicants could be their age.[13] It is accepted, however, that there remain circumstances where an adoption order in such cases may be justified.[14]

The Houghton Committee reiterated concern about such adoptions, fearing the consequential dangers of hiding the real circumstances from the child.[15] They considered that an application for guardianship would normally be preferable. As a result of the Committee's recommendations a new jurisdiction, custodianship, was created, by which applicants could seek orders vesting in them parental rights and duties but which did not extinguish the legal relationship between the child and his birth parents.[16] It was hoped and expected that relatives would use this option rather than adoption,[17] but in the event the take-up was thought to be disappointing (although in fact the evidence showed that grandparents were beginning to apply for custodianship)[18] but that a custodianship order on an adoption application was rarely made.[19]

The Children Act 1989 abolished custodianship, replacing it with the much simpler scheme whereby, subject to obtaining court leave, relatives can apply for a residence order. Furthermore, since adoption proceedings rank as 'family proceedings', the court can of its own motion make any s 8 order upon an adoption application. Nevertheless, notwithstanding these alternatives it should not be assumed that adoptions by relatives have entirely disappeared. They are, however, relatively unusual.[20] It is, however, noticeable that the courts have become less concerned with the argument that an adoption order distorts the natural relationship.[1] Given that adoption has the advantage of permanence, it is likely that, even with an s 8 alternative, an adoption order will still be thought appropriate in cases where, for example, relatives have been the sole care-givers for some time, especially if the parents are virtual strangers to the child.[2] The

---

13 See eg *Re W (A Minor) (Adoption by Grandparents)* (1980) 2 FLR 161, CA.

14 See eg *Re DX supra*, *Re G (DM) (An Infant)* [1962] 2 All ER 546, and *Re B (MF) (An Infant)* [1972] 1 All ER 898, CA. In the latter case an order was granted even though continued contact between the siblings (only one of whom was adopted) was envisaged.

15 Ibid at para 111.

16 Discussed in ch 11 of the 7th edition of this work.

17 See pp 375–6 of the 7th edition of this work.

18 In their study for the Department of Health, Bullard, Malos and Parker found that more than half of custodianship applications were by grandparents: *Custodianship. Caring for other people's children* (HMSO, 1991) Tables 24–28.

19 Only two such cases were found in the *Pathways to Adoption* study, op cit, Table 2,10. See also *Re S (A Minor) (Adoption: Custodianship)* [1987] Fam 98, [1987] 2 All ER 99, CA; and *Re W (A Minor) (Adoption: Custodianship)* [1992] Fam Law 64, CA. For earlier examples of such orders see eg *Re O (A Minor) (Adoption by Grandparents)* [1985] FLR 546, where paternal grandparents had looked after the child for four years following abandonment by the mother; and *Re M (A Minor) (Adoption: Parental Agreement)* [1985] FLR 664, where the child had been with grandparents since he was 11 weeks old and had had virtually no contact with his mother.

20 In the *Pathways to Adoption* study op cit, Table 2.3, only seven per cent of the overall sample were applications by relatives.

1 See eg *Re C (A Minor) (Adoption Order: Condition)* [1989] AC 1, [1988] 1 All ER 705, HL at 713 where Lord Ackner dismissed the contention that an adoption order should be refused because the child would be devastated to learn that her natural brother would no longer be in law her brother as being 'quite unreal'. See also *Re W (A Minor) (Adoption: Custodianship)*, supra.

2 See *Re W (A Minor) (Adoption by Grandparents)* (1980) 2 FLR 161 where an adoption order was granted as the court considered that it would be in the child's interests for the grandparents to be able to appoint testamentary guardians in the event of their death.

Adoption Law Review[3] saw no reason to rule out the possibility of adoption by relatives, which they envisaged to be appropriate where the child's parents are dead, or living in another country and unlikely ever to be able to make parental decisions in respect of the child's upbringing. It did, however, consider that, as with step-parents, the legislative framework should provide adequate opportunity for applicants to explore other possibilities, particularly residence orders. It recommended[4] that, for the purpose of determining when an adoption application can be made, relatives should be treated the same as non-relatives who *wish* to adopt a child for whom they are caring. This is reflected in the proposed Adoption Bill.[5]

3. AGREEMENT TO THE MAKING OF AN ORDER

It is a fundamental requirement[6] that before an adoption order may be made each parent or guardian must either agree to the order or have had his agreement dispensed with. It is by this means that the law recognises and seeks to protect the parental interest. Indeed, so important is the right to refuse agreement, that it is not lost even if others, including a local authority, acquire parental responsibility.[7]

Whose agreement is required?

The Act requires the agreement of each parent or guardian. By 'parent' is meant a parent with parental responsibility. It does not therefore include the unmarried father,[8] unless he has parental responsibility through an order or agreement.[9] In the case of an adopted child, 'parent' refers to each adoptive parent.[10] 'Guardian' refers to any person formally appointed by an individual or by a court.

(a) The position of the unmarried father

Although his agreement is not required, an unmarried father who does not have parental responsibility is nevertheless entitled to be heard on the merits of the application if he is contributing to the child's maintenance.[11] The courts in any

3 See the Consultative Document , op cit, at para 20.4.
4 Ibid at para 20.5.
5 See cl 36 which would require that in all non-agency applications the child must have had his home with the applicants for six months: see further post, p 661.
6 Adoption Act 1976 s 16(1)(b).
7 See Children Act 1989 s 12(3) and s 33(6)(b).
8 See *Re M (An Infant)* [1955] 2 QB 479, [1955] 2 All ER 911, CA; *Re L (A Minor) (Adoption: Procedure)* [1991] 1 FLR 171, CA; and *Re C (Adoption: Parties)* [1995] 2 FLR 483, CA. Note that for the purposes of Sch 2 (which sets out matters to be covered in the guardian's report) 'each natural parent' does include a reference to the unmarried father, but even here there is a discretion as to whether to ascertain the unmarried father's wishes and feelings: *Re P (Adoption) (Natural Father's Rights)* [1994] 1 FLR 771.
9 Adoption Act 1976 s 72(1): definition of 'parent' as amended by the Children Act 1989, Sch 10, para 30(7).
10 But if the adoption order in question is a foreign order which is not recognised by the English court, then the birth parents' agreement will still be required: *Re G (Foreign Adoption: Consent)* [1995] 2 FLR 534.
11 When he must be joined as a respondent: see Adoption Rules 1984 r 15(2)(h) (applicable to High Court and county court). The rules governing magistrates' courts, the Magistrates Courts (Adoption) Rules (1984), largely follow the same wording and numbering and will not hereafter be separately cited.

event have a general discretion to add any person[12] or body as a respondent and this may include the unmarried father if he has contact or has expressed interest in attending the hearing.[13]

An entitlement to be heard on the merits of the application is not as strong a right as being able to withhold agreement, but a more effective option to oppose adoption is for the unmarried father to apply for a residence order under s 8 of the Children Act 1989.[14] In that event the issue will be whether the court should grant a residence order or make the adoption order. To arrive at a proper conclusion and enable all the parties to be heard, the court should hear both applications at the same time and not give judgment on one until it has heard the other.[15] Although overall the court is bound to resolve the problem by reference to what is best for the child, technically, when deciding the s 8 application the court is bound to treat the child's welfare as the paramount consideration, whereas it is only required to give first consideration of the child's welfare when considering the adoption application.[16]

(b)   The position of the child

As the law now stands, the child's agreement is not required.[17] However, in deciding whether an adoption order will be for the child's welfare the court and adoption agency are bound,[18] so far as practicable, to ascertain the child's wishes and feelings about the proposed adoption and 'give due regard to them, having regard to his age and understanding'.

Following the recommendations of the Consultative Document,[19] under the proposed Adoption Bill[20] it would not be possible to make an adoption order in relation to a child aged 12 or over unless the court is satisfied either that the child

---

12 *Re C (Adoption: Parties)*, supra. Note, however, that a child can only be a party in High Court proceedings: see the Adoption Rules r 4(2)(g) and r 4(3).

13 The court will learn of this through reports made to the court pursuant to the requirements under the Adoption Rules 1984 Sch 2. There is, however, no requirement to name the father in an application unless his agreement is required and a judge has no authority to order an agency to interview him: *Re L (A Minor) (Adoption: Procedure)* [1991] 1 FLR 171, CA, but see the comments at [1991] Fam Law 270. Further, there is no mandatory obligation to ascertain the father's wishes and feelings unless it is practicable to do so. In judging the practicality it is permissible to look at the end result. If the consequences of ascertaining the latter's wishes and feelings would be detrimental to the child, it is not 'practicable' to obtain them: per Ewbank J in *Re P (Adoption: Natural Father's Rights)*, supra. See also *Re Adoption Application (No 2) No 41/61* [1963] 2 All ER 1082 at 1088, per Wilberforce J.

14 But note that an application for a parental responsibility order under s 4 of the Children Act would also delay any adoption application. Under s 18(7), before making an order freeing the child for adoption (discussed post, p 651), the court must first satisfy itself that the unmarried father has no intention of applying for a s 4 order, or if he has, that it is likely to be refused.

15 *G v G (Children: Concurrent Applications)* [1993] 2 FLR 306. Ideally, therefore, both applications should be heard in the same court: see *Re Adoption Application 41/61* [1963] Ch 315, [1962] 3 All ER 553, but cf *Re Adoption Application (No 2) 41/61* [1964] Ch 48, [1963] 2 All ER 1082. It has been held that a similar position obtains if the unmarried father's application is for contact: see *Re G (A Minor) (Adoption and Access Applications)* (1979) 1 FLR 109, though apparently it is not thought to be a rigid rule: *Re G (A Minor) (Adoption and Access Applications)* [1992] 1 FLR 642, CA, where a father made an application for interim access.

16 On which see *Re B (Adoption: Child's Welfare)* [1995] 1 FLR 895, discussed ante, p 626.

17 In some other jurisdictions such as Scotland older children's agreement is required: see eg Adoption Law Review, *Background Paper No 1*, paras 116–120.

18 Adoption Act 1976 s 6.

19 Op cit at para 9.5.

20 Clause 41 (7).

consents or is incapable of giving such consent.[1] Although the importance of the child's view cannot be underestimated,[2] whether it is sensible to make it a statutory requirement that the child consent can be debated. One objection is that it would place an enormous burden on the child, since it would seem to place on him or her the responsibility for making the decision.[3] Another objection is that 12 seems a particularly young age[4] to choose and is out of line with other statutes, notably the Family Law Reform Act 1969 s 8, under which those aged 16 or over can give a valid consent to medical treatment.[5]

Form of the agreement

If the agreement is to be effective, the court must be satisfied that it was given freely and with a full understanding of what is involved.[6] Agreements must also be unconditional and may be given without knowing the applicant's identity.[7] It is no longer possible to make an agreement conditional on the child being brought up in a particular religion. Instead, when placing a child for adoption, adoption agencies are required to have regard, so far as practicable, to any wishes of the child's parent or guardian as to the religious upbringing of the child.[8]

Agreement to the making of an adoption order may be given before or at the time of the hearing; in the former event, documentary evidence of the giving of the agreement is admissible and there is no need for the parent to attend the hearing.[9] The mother cannot give an effective agreement until the child is six weeks old.[10] The agreement must be operative when the order is made and can therefore be

---

1 Quaere the meaning of this? Would it cover the child who simply says 'I do not know whether to agree or not'?
2 See *Re M (Adoption or Residence Order)* [1998] 1 FLR 570, CA, discussed post, pp 646–7, in which a residence order rather than an adoption order was made in view of the 11-year-old child's objection to being adopted.
3 Particularly if the child is required formally to sign a consent form.
4 Ironically, according to some research (see Fratter, Rowe, Sapsford and Thoburn *Permanent Family Placement: a decade of experience* (1991)), adoption placements at 12 are most likely to break down.
5 Discussed ante at p 313. Though in this respect it must be acknowledged that the courts have effectively lowered this age by accepting the validity of consent by '*Gillick* competent children' under the age of 16.
6 There is some support for saying that a parent must know all the material facts before his agreement should be regarded as having been given: cf *Re M (Minors) (Adoption)* [1991] 1 FLR 458, CA (order set aside where father agreed to adoption by mother and step-father in ignorance that his wife, who died three months later, was terminally ill), discussed further post, pp 672–3; and *Re An Adoption Application* [1992] 1 FLR 341 (mother's agreement, given in ignorance that male applicant was involved in criminal proceedings, not to be relied upon).
7 Adoption Act 1976 s 16(b)(i). Applicants can opt for anonymity, in which case they should apply, before commencing proceedings, for a serial number to be assigned to them: Adoption Rules 1984 r 14. Thereafter proceedings must be conducted so that the applicants' identity is not revealed to *any* respondent who is not already aware of it: r 23(3). According to the Adoption Law Review, Discussion Paper No 3, at para 221, the use of serial numbers may cause problems in practice outside the High Court and the suggestion has been made that the procedure be tightened by, for example, having to obtain leave to make a serial number application. The Consultative Document, op cit, at para 40.2 recommended that the court should be able to discontinue the use of the serial number if it would be in the child's interests to do so. It also recommended (at para 40.3) that birth parents should also be able to make use of a serial number.
8 Adoption Act 1976 s 7.
9 Ibid, s 61. Written agreements should be witnessed by a Reporting Officer: see Adoption Act 1976 s 65. See also the Adoption Rules 1984 r 17.
10 Adoption Act 1976 s 16(4). This condition is clearly designed to prevent the mother from being persuaded to give her agreement before she has recovered from the child's birth.

withdrawn at any time before that.[11] It should be appreciated, however, that as soon as agreement is given, 'time begins to run against the parent', as Ormrod LJ put it.[12] In other words, the longer the agreement has been effective the more likely it will be regarded as 'unreasonable' subsequently to withhold agreement.

Another important consequence of agreeing to the making of an adoption order is that thereafter that parent or guardian cannot, while the application is pending, remove the child against the will of the person with whom the child has his home, save with the court's leave.[13] Although at one time it was thought that this restriction operated only upon the formal signing of the agreement, it has been held[14] that the embargo can apply to an oral agreement, though clearly cogent evidence of such an agreement will be required.

Research evidence shows that many adoption applications proceed on the basis that they will be contested because the parent(s) has not signed the agreement, yet in many cases there is no intention actively to oppose the adoption application.[15] One of the reasons for this is that parents are reluctant to 'sign away' their children. The Consultative Document[16] attempted to address this problem by suggesting that parents should be able to attach a statement explaining why they thought it was for the child's welfare to be adopted. There is also a suggestion that consideration might be given to altering the substantive law so that parents should be required to indicate whether or not they are opposed to the adoption as distinct from requiring their positive consent.

4.   DISPENSING WITH AGREEMENT

The court's power to dispense with agreement is the means by which the law attempts to balance the parental interest with the child's welfare. It should be appreciated at the outset, however, that because agreements can only be dispensed with on certain specified grounds (outlined below), an adoption order cannot necessarily be made merely because it is for the child's welfare. This therefore distinguishes adoption from residence orders under s 8 of the Children Act 1989, the reason being that in adoption the very parent–child relationship is at stake.[17] Whether it is justifiable to subordinate a child's welfare to parental interests may be questioned and should in any event be borne in mind during the ensuing discussion of the current law.[18]

Although there are relatively few contested adoptions, they are no longer the rarity that they once were.[19] In 1978, for example, 773 orders (representing 6.3 per

11 *Re F (An Infant)* [1957] 1 All ER 819 and *Re K (An Infant)* [1953] 1 QB 117, [1952] 2 All ER 877, CA.
12 In *Re H (Infants) (Adoption: Parental Consent)* [1977] 2 All ER 339n, CA at 340, discussed post, p 641.
13 Adoption Act 1976 s 27(1). See also Adoption Law Review, Discussion Paper No 3, para 147.
14 By *Re T (A Minor) (Adoption: Parental Agreement)* [1986] Fam 160, [1986] 1 All ER 817, CA.
15 Lowe with Borkowski, Copner, Griew and Murch *Report of the Research into the use and practice of the Freeing for Adoption Provisions* (1993) at para 3.2.4. A similar finding was made in the Cardiff Study on Support Services.
16 Op cit, at paras 10.9–10.11.
17 See, for example, the discussion by Wall J in *Re B (Adoption: Child's Welfare)* [1995] 1 FLR 895 at 897–8.
18 But note under the proposed law the child's welfare would become the paramount consideration. See the discussion at pp 627 and 649–50.
19 Commenting upon the practice of the 1960s, Rowe, Hundleby, Paul and Keane (Adoption and Fostering (1981) Vol 5, No 1, 23 at 24) observed that adoption agencies seldom advised prospective adopters to resist a parent who changed her mind.

cent of all orders) were made without parental agreement, while in 1983 the figure was 956, representing 11 per cent.[20] In a sample of cases decided between 1986 and 1988 the *Pathways to Adoption* study found that 19 per cent of applications to adopt were made without the mother's agreement.[1]

Before we examine the grounds upon which agreement can be dispensed with, three preliminary points should be mentioned. First, although s 6 of the Adoption Act 1976 states that in reaching any decision relating to adoption the court should treat the child's welfare as the first consideration, it has been held by the Court of Appeal in *Re P (An Infant) (Adoption: Parental Agreement)*,[2] that the section has no application to the issue of dispensing with agreement. Although, as will be seen, this decision is not as significant as it would appear,[3] it nevertheless seems a questionable interpretation.[4] Secondly, it is now well established[5] that in cases where agreement is withheld the courts are required to apply a two-stage process, namely to determine first whether it is for the child's welfare to be adopted[6] and then, if it is, to determine whether parental agreement should be dispensed with.[7] Thirdly, although such an important issue as dispensing with agreement has understandably generated considerable case law, in fact applications are rarely refused and one research study found that statistically there was no difference in the result between those applications which were contested and those that were not.[8] Pursuant to s 16 the court may dispense with agreement in the circumstances set out below.

Cannot be found or incapable of signing agreement

If the parent or guardian cannot be found or is incapable of giving agreement, agreement may be dispensed with. Agreement will not lightly be dispensed with

---

20 See respectively Children Act 1975, First Report to Parliament, HC 266, Table D and the Second Report, HMSO 1984, Table B.
1 Op cit, Table 2.11.
2 [1977] Fam 25, [1977] 1 All ER 182, CA.
3 Because in relation to the most common dispensing ground, unreasonableness, it is well established that a reasonable parent will have the interests of his child at heart: see post at p 639.
4 As is pointed out, obiter, by Lord Simon in *Re D (An Infant) (Adoption: Parental Agreement)* [1977] AC 602, [1977] 1 All ER, 145, HL at 163. Leave to appeal to the House of Lords on this point was refused in *Re M (A Minor)* [1980] CLY 1801. The decision was thought right by Butler-Sloss LJ in *Re C (A Minor) (Adoption)* [1994] 2 FLR 513, CA at 519. See also *Re H; Re W* (1983) 4 FLR 614, CA at 624, per Purchas LJ, discussed by Waterhouse J in *Re BA (Wardship: Adoption)* [1985] FLR 1008 at 1031.
5 *Re C (A Minor) (Adoption: Parental Agreement: Contact)* [1993] 2 FLR 260, CA; *Re D (A Minor) (Adoption: Freeing Order)* [1991] 1 FLR 48, CA and *Re R (A Minor) (Adoption: Parental Agreement)* [1987] 1 FLR 391, CA. Note that in *Re C* the Court of Appeal expressly approved the first instance court deciding first to resolve the birth parents' application for a residence order before deciding their application for a contact order, and only after that determining the adoption application.
6 See further post, p 644–5.
7 Procedurally it is preferable for these two issues to be *heard* together: *Re K (A Minor) (Adoption: Procedure)* [1986] 1 FLR 295, CA. Ultimately the court retains a discretion and separate hearings could be justified in serial number cases in court where it might be difficult to maintain the applicants' anonymity: *Re LS (A Minor) (Adoption: Procedure)* [1986] 1 FLR 302, CA. Note, however, the Consultative Document's comments (op cit at para 40.5) that it should not be necessary, save in the rarest circumstance, to have split hearings to ensure anonymity. But problems continue to arise: see eg *Re E (Adopted Child: Contact: Leave)* [1995] 1 FLR 57.
8 In the *Pathways to Adoption* Study, op cit, at para 2.1, 89 per cent of applications were granted and less than one per cent refused and in the case of freeing (see Lowe et al *Freeing for Adoption Provisions*, op cit at para 3.4.11) 84 per cent of applications were granted regardless of whether or not they were contested.

on this ground. In *Re F (R) (An Infant)*,[9] for instance, it was held that before the court could be satisfied that the parent 'could not be found' it had to be shown that all reasonable and proper steps had been taken. In that case it was held that all such steps had not been taken since in their search for the birth mother the applicants had failed to get in touch with the maternal grandfather with whom the mother was still in contact. 'Incapable of giving agreement' normally refers to those who are mentally incapable,[10] but in *Re R (Adoption)*,[11] where the parents were living in a totalitarian country, it was held that their agreement could be dispensed with on the grounds that (a) they could not be found since there were no practical means of communicating with them and (b) they were incapable of giving their agreement to a proposal of which they were ignorant and could not practically be made aware.

Unreasonably withholding agreement

If the parent or guardian is withholding his agreement unreasonably, agreement may be dispensed with. This in practice is a common ground[12] for applying to the court to dispense with agreement and gives rise to the most difficulty. Whether or not agreement is unreasonably withheld is a question of fact in each case and 'reasonableness' is to be judged at the date of the hearing.[13]

(a)   Reasonableness – the Re W test

The leading case is *Re W (An Infant)*,[14] in which the House of Lords resolved an earlier conflict of opinion by unanimously rejecting the contention that as a matter of principle unreasonableness connoted culpability. The Law Lords all agreed that the test is objective: would a reasonable parent, placed in the situation of the particular parent, withhold agreement? As Lord Hailsham LC put it:[15]

'. . . the test is reasonableness and not anything else. It is not culpability. It is not indifference. It is not failure to discharge parental duties. It is reasonableness in the context of the totality of the circumstances.'

Obviously unreasonableness can include culpability; it can also include callous indifference and '(when carried to excess) sentimentality, romanticism, bigotry, wild prejudice, caprice, fatuousness or excessive lack of common sense'.[16] In many cases it will be easy to say whether, looked at objectively, the parent is acting reasonably or not, but in others one reasonable parent might withhold his agreement whilst another might not do so. In the latter type of case the court must

---

9 [1970] 1 QB 385, [1969] 3 All ER 1101, CA.

10 See eg *Re L (A Minor) (Adoption: Parental Agreement)* [1987] 1 FLR 400 where the court was unwilling to accept a mother's psychiatrist's certificate that she was incapable.

11 [1966] 3 All ER 613. Applied in *Re An Adoption Application* [1992] 1 FLR 341.

12 In the *Pathways to Adoption* Study, op cit, it was found to be the sole ground for 45 per cent of birth mothers and 63 per cent of birth fathers who refused their agreement. See also Adoption Law Review, op cit at para 37.

13 See eg *Re L (A Minor) (Adoption: Statutory Criteria)* [1990] 1 FLR 305, CA; *Re S (An Infant)* [1973] 3 All ER 88, CA; and *Re W (Adoption: Parental Agreement)* (1981) 3 FLR 75, CA; cf *Re C (Minors) (Adoption)* [1992] 1 FLR 115, in which Balcombe LJ commented, 'it does not follow that a parent who starts by reasonably refusing agreement becomes unreasonable because of the delay [in hearing the application]'.

14 [1971] AC 682, [1971] 2 All ER 49, HL.

15 Ibid at 699 and 56, respectively.

16 Per Lord Hailsham LC, ibid at 700 and 56 respectively.

respect the particular parent's decision to refuse to agree and must not substitute its own view. As Lord Hailsham said:[17]

'The question in any given case is whether a parental veto comes within the band of possible reasonable decisions and not whether it is right or mistaken. Not every reasonable exercise of judgment is right, and not every mistaken exercise of judgment is unreasonable.'

All the facts must be looked at, but obviously the reasonable parent will give the greatest weight to the child's welfare. As Lord Hailsham LC said:[18]

'But, although welfare *per se* is not the test, the fact that a reasonable parent does pay regard to the welfare of his child must enter into the question of reasonableness as a relevant factor. It is relevant in all cases if and to the extent that a reasonable parent would take it into account. It is decisive in those cases where a reasonable parent must so regard it . . .'

Although it is not necessary to show a prognosis of lasting damage if an order is not made, there must be some really serious factor justifying the use of the guillotine:[19] it was said in *Re W* that agreement may be dispensed with if the parent has ignored or disregarded some *appreciable* ill or risk or some *substantial* benefit likely to be avoided or to accrue if the child were adopted.[20] A reasonable parent must clearly take account of financial and educational prospects, but of much greater importance are the child's future happiness and stability of his home life. Although little weight should be given to the parent's vacillation under stress or to the pain that the loss of the child will inevitably cause the applicants,[1] it must be appreciated that to tear the child away from those whom he has come to regard as his parents may have disastrous consequences. This in itself may force the reasonable parent to agree to the adoption; and the longer the child has been with the applicants, the greater is the danger to be guarded against. In *Re W* itself the child had been placed with the applicants when he was a week old and had remained there for 18 months. He had settled down well. The mother, who was unmarried and who later withdrew her agreement, already had two other children by different fathers; there was a grave risk of more (which would reduce her prospects of marriage); there was no man in the household; and it was doubtful whether she had the capacity to bring up three children. In these circumstances the House of Lords held that there was ample evidence to support the finding that the mother was unreasonably withholding her agreement.

Re W marked an important shift in favour of the child's interests, though falling short (as it was bound to do) of holding that the child's welfare is of paramount importance. It is submitted that in principle the decision strikes the fairest balance between the interests of the child and those of the parents and adoptive applicants that can be achieved under the current legislation. The test, however, is not without its difficulties since, as Lord Wilberforce pointed out in *Re D (An Infant)*

---

17 Ibid at 700 and 56 respectively.
18 Ibid at 700 and 56 respectively.
19 Per Cumming-Bruce J in *Re B (Adoption By Parent)* [1975] Fam 127 at 143, [1975] 2 All ER 449 at 462, cited with approval in *Re D (An Infant) (Adoption: Parent's Consent)* [1977] AC 602 at 632 and 644, [1977] 1 All ER 145, HL at 155 and 166.
20 *Re W, supra*, per Lord Hailsham LC at 700 and 56 and Lord MacDermott at 709 and 64.
 1 Per Lord Hailsham LC, ibid at 700 and 56–7, respectively.

(Adoption: Parent's Consent),[2] it involves considering how a parent in the circumstances of the actual parent 'but (hypothetically) endowed with a mind and temperament capable of making reasonable decisions would approach a complex question involving a judgment as to the present and the future, and the probable impact of these on the child.' Of course, as the majority pointed out in *Re C (A Minor) (Adoption: Parental Agreement: Contact),*[3] such a paragon does not exist but, as they continued:

> 'Nevertheless to those who feel some embarrassment at having to consult the views of so improbable a legal fiction, we venture to observe that precisely the same question may be raised in a demythologised form by the judge asking himself whether, having regard to the evidence and applying the current values of our society, the advantages of adoption for the welfare of the child appear sufficiently strong to justify overriding the views and interest of the objecting parent or parents. The reasonable parent is only a piece of machinery invented to provide the answer to this question.'

Re D itself concerned a father who was a practising homosexual. His wife had divorced him and remarried and the child of the marriage, a boy aged seven, was living with her and her second husband who now wished to adopt him. If the father were to continue to have contact, the boy was bound to come into contact with other men of the father's predilections sooner or later. At first instance the county court judge concluded: 'A reasonable man would say "I must protect my boy even if this means parting from him for ever so that he can be free of this danger" . . . The father has nothing to offer his son at any time in the future'. In view of this finding, the House of Lords held that he had correctly concluded that the father was withholding his agreement unreasonably. It must be emphasised, however, that each case will turn upon its own facts: the parent's homosexuality will not of itself mean that his refusal to agree to the adoption will be unreasonable if this presents no dangers to the child.[4]

Clearly, the suitability of the parents to look after their child is an important factor in assessing reasonableness. If, for example, adoption is opposed on the basis that the child should be returned but the parents cannot offer a stable home, that in itself must go a long way to showing 'unreasonableness'.[5] However, even

2 [1977] AC 602 at 625, [1977] 1 All ER 145, HL at 150. In *Re W (Adoption: Parental Agreement)* (1981) 3 FLR 75, CA at 79, Ormrod LJ described it as a 'rather difficult concept – perhaps a sophisticated concept', while in *Re S (An Infant)* [1973] 3 All ER 88, CA at 91, Davies LJ pointed out that it 'is very difficult to decide what a reasonable mother would do; it is very difficult for a mother . . . where ties of blood and emotional matters are involved to be reasonable at all'. See also Balcombe LJ's similar comments in *Re L (A Minor)* [1990] 1 FLR 305 at 314. For a case where the judge erroneously applied a simple subjective test, see *Re R (A Minor) (Adoption: Parental Agreement)* [1987] 1 FLR 391, CA.
3 [1993] 2 FLR 260, CA at 272 per Steyn and Hoffmann LJJ.
4 See ibid at 629, 640, 641–2 and 153, 162, 163 and 168 respectively. Indeed, in appropriate circumstances it can be for the child's welfare to be *adopted* by a homosexual or lesbian applicant: see eg *Re E (Adoption: Freeing Order)* [1995] 1 FLR 382, CA.
5 See eg *O'Connor v A and B* [1971] 2 All ER 1230, HL, where both parents were thought to be unstable; *Re W (Adoption: Parental Agreement)* (1981) 3 FLR 75, CA, where, inter alia, the court doubted the mother's capacity to look after both the child in question and her other child in overcrowded accommodation; *Re V (Adoption: Parental Agreement)* [1985] FLR 45, CA, where young parents had no clear plans for looking after the child; and *Re M* (1988) Adoption and Fostering, Vol 12, No 3 at 49 (CA), where extensive efforts to rehabilitate children with their mother failed because of her inability to look after them and Sheldon J commented, 'Children are not guinea pigs to be used in teaching adults parenting skills, nor are they objects on which parents, however devoted , can practise indefinitely until they can achieve some acceptable standard'.

if the parent is in a position to offer a stable home (or to resume contact), that does not ipso facto make the refusal reasonable. Other considerations, notably the child's welfare and the interests of the applicants, must be taken into account. The relative importance of these considerations may well vary according to the context in which the issue arises. At any rate, it is important to distinguish the situation where the parent at first agrees to the adoption and allows the child to be placed but then withdraws that agreement, from that where the parent has never agreed to the adoption. Special considerations may also apply to adoptions within the family. Another crucial factor in all cases is the age and wishes and feelings of the child.

(b) The 'vacillating parent'

Although in *Re W* the House of Lords accepted that vacillation is not in itself unreasonable, nevertheless the fact that a parent has allowed the child to be placed for adoption cannot be ignored if agreement is subsequently withdrawn. As Lord Reid put it in *O'Connor v A and B*,[6] if it was the parent's action that first brought the adopting family in, they ought not to be displaced without good reason. The crucial factor, however, is the child's welfare. If the child has become settled with the applicants, then the longer that is allowed to continue the more unlikely it is that a parent will be considered reasonable in withholding agreement. As Ormrod LJ said in *Re H (Infants) (Adoption: Parental Consent)*:[7]

'. . . the relative importance of the welfare of the children is increasing rather than diminishing in relation to dispensing with [agreement].[8] That being so it ought to be recognised by all concerned with adoption cases that once the formal [agreement] has been given or perhaps once the child has been placed with the adopters, time begins to run against the mother and, as time goes on, it gets progressively more and more difficult for her to show that the withdrawal of [agreement] is reasonable.'

The so-called 'vacillating parent' is commonly a young mother[9] who has to make the difficult decision in traumatic circumstances of whether to relinquish her baby, yet as Ormrod LJ said:[10]

'Although it is easy to understand the difficulties of the mother as a young woman, it is equally easy to be over-indulgent in approaching her problems because, once she takes the step of initiating adoption proceedings, she starts a chain reaction which can only be stopped with great damage to some people.'

---

6 [1971] 2 All ER 1230, HL at 1232. In *Re P (Adoption: Parental Agreement)* [1985] FLR 635, CA at 637, Griffiths LJ commented, '. . . just because the mother changes her mind in the course of the agonising decision as to whether or not her child should be adopted must not be held against her as conclusive evidence that she is being unreasonable. But . . . it is a factor to be borne in mind, bearing in mind the long-term welfare of the child, because the longer the mother vacillates the more difficult it becomes for any bond to be forged with her again, and it is a factor which may show that the mother does not make the judgment of a reasonable parent, which is the test that the judge ultimately has to apply'.

7 [1977] 2 All ER 339n, CA at 340. See also his similar comments in *Re W (Adoption: Parental Agreement)* (1981) 3 FLR 75, CA at 82.

8 But note the observations of Purchas LJ in *Re H; Re W (Adoption: Parental Agreement)* (1983) 4 FLR 614, CA at 624, set out below at p 643.

9 But see *Re W (Adoption: Parental Agreement)* [1984] FLR 880, CA.

10 In *Re W (Adoption: Parental Agreement)* (1981) 3 FLR 75 at 81. See also *Re G (A Minor) (Adoption: Parental Agreement)* [1990] 2 FLR 429, CA.

If a mother changes her mind, it is imperative that she should act quickly and be in a position to offer a secure and loving home for the child if the withholding of agreement is to be regarded as reasonable.[11]

(c)   The parent who has never agreed to the adoption

As discussed earlier in this chapter,[12] mothers are now much less likely than formerly to relinquish their babies for adoption. According to a survey undertaken in 1995,[13] about 14 per cent of the total number of adoptions reported by local authorities comprised parents voluntarily approaching agencies to relinquish their child. Much more common will be the parent who has never agreed to their child being removed from them into local authority care, let alone agreed to the child's adoption.[14] A not untypical example is *Re F (A Minor) (Adoption: Parental Agreement)*,[15] in which a two-year-old child was taken into care after being ill-treated and was immediately placed with foster parents with whom the child remained for the next three years. The local authority considered that rehabilitation with the mother was not feasible and that it was in the child's interests to be adopted by the foster parents, who then applied for an order. The mother, who had not even seen her child for two years, opposed the adoption. It was held that she was unreasonably withholding her agreement because no reasonable mother could have thought that continued contact[16] with her would have been of benefit to the child. It was held that in the circumstances adoption best secured the child's home with the foster parents since, relying on Bridge LJ in *Re SMH and RAH*:[17]

'Unless the adoptive parents are put in the legal position of being in a full sense parents of [the child] they are never in the position, and never will be in the position, to give [the child] the reassurance which the sense of security required by [this child] is surely going to need.'

A more striking decision is *Re H*.[18] A six-week-old child was removed from a mother who had a history of mental illness and taken into care. At first the court

---

11 In *Re PA (An Infant)* [1971] 3 All ER 522, CA, a young mother was 'badgered' into agreeing, withdrew the agreement within three weeks, and, at the date of the hearing, had become engaged to a 'thoroughly reliable young man': her withholding of agreement was held reasonable; cf *Re V (Adoption: Parental Agreement)* [1985] FLR 45, CA and *Re J (A Minor) (Wardship: Adoption: Custodianship)* [1987] 1 FLR 455, where it was held inter alia that a West Indian mother was entitled to take into account the fact that the applicants were white and were Jehovah's Witnesses. The child, however, remained with the foster parents with access to the mother for two days each year.

12 See ante, p 614.

13 *Focus on Adoption* (BAAF, 1997) p 14; cf the *Pathways to Adoption* Study, op cit, at Table 4.3 conducted in the late 1980s which found baby adoptions accounted for eight per cent of agency placements.

14 In fact most agency adoptions are of children in care rather than accommodation (to which the parent cannot have been opposed: see ante, p 526). In the Cardiff Study, for example, out of a sample of 1,693 only 397 (23 per cent) children were previously accommodated. It is understood that in a national study of 588 children being looked after by local authorities in England with a view to adoption in 1994 19 per cent were being accommodated at the time of placement: Ivaldi *Children Adopted Out of Care* (1998).

15 [1982] 1 All ER 321, CA.

16 The evidence established beyond doubt that it was essential for the child to remain with the foster parents for the rest of his dependent life. Even future contact was regarded as a remote possibility.

17 [1990] FCR 966n (decided in 1979), cited by Ormrod LJ, ibid at p 326 and 108, respectively.

18 (1981) Adoption and Fostering, Vol 5, No 3 at 62 (CA). In *Re El-G (Minors) (Wardship and Adoption)* (1982) 4 FLR 589, CA a mother, who because of ill health had only looked after her children for a total of five weeks in four years, was held to be unreasonably withholding agreement even though her health was fully restored. See also *Re H (Adoption: Parental Agreement)* (1981) 3 FLR 386, CA.

made an order allowing the mother to see her child, but this was ended at a subsequent hearing at which the local authority received strong encouragement to place the child for adoption. Shortly afterwards, however, the mother was divorced and subsequently remarried, after which she made a miraculous recovery. She renewed her efforts to obtain contact. The authority, however, without telling the mother, placed the child for adoption. The application was not finally heard for some 18 months, in part because of the authority's delay in filing evidence. It was held that while the authority's action could be criticised,[19] the mother was nevertheless withholding her agreement unreasonably, since the child was a relative stranger to her and a complete stranger to her husband, while on the other hand the child had established a strong attachment to the adopters.

The above cases illustrate how crucial the child's welfare has become in judging reasonableness. This shift of emphasis was noted in *Re H; Re W (Adoption: Parental Agreement)*,[20] but the Court of Appeal thought that there had to be some limit to it. Purchas LJ pointed out that there was 'room for the reasonable withholding of [agreement] by the natural parent even if those responsible for the child's welfare, who are normally professionals, hold an acceptable view that the child's welfare demands adoption'. He continued:

'Where the natural parent presents himself at the time of the hearing as someone capable of caring for the child, this is a factor which even the hypothetical, reasonable parent should take into account together with the other circumstances of the case including, of course, the ultimate welfare of the child. Where there is an inherent defect likely to persist in the natural parent . . . this is clearly an important factor; but where the unsuitability of the parent can only be related to past history . . . unless the past history is likely to influence the future position . . . then it should carry little weight in the mind of the hypothetical, reasonable parent. The chance of a successful reintroduction to, or continuance of contact with, the natural parent is a critical factor in assessing the reaction of the hypothetical reasonable parent . . .'

Of the two appeals, *Re W* is the more striking. It concerned a boy who had been taken into care when he was just under two years old. The mother's marriage had broken down and she had become an alcoholic and suffered depression. Subsequently, however, her marriage was dissolved, she made a complete recovery, and following her remarriage she sought, some five years after she had last seen her son, to re-establish contact. The local authority began to make arrangements for the mother to see her son, but these were never implemented because the mother was sent to prison for fraud. At that point the authority decided to support the foster parents, with whom the child had been for the last nine years, in their adoption application. The Court of Appeal, however, upheld the decision that the mother's refusal to agree to the adoption was reasonable, based principally upon the belief that there was at least a chance of future successful contact with the child.

Re H, Re W has been criticised[1] as looking too subjectively at the parent's attitude and minimising the effect of past conduct towards the child. In *Re W* it is hard to see how contact could have been anything but speculative. Nevertheless it has to be remembered that in reaching its decision the Court of Appeal was deliberately attempting to reduce the importance of the child's welfare when

---

19 Whether a bona fide and reasonable sense of injustice might be a relevant factor in the mind of a reasonable parent is discussed below at p 646.
20 (1983) 4 FLR 614, CA.
1 By *Butterworths Family Law Service* Division E [2630].

judging reasonableness, at any rate in the context of foster parent applications.[2] Another example of a more parent-centred approach is *Re E (Minors) (Adoption: Parental Agreement)*.[3] In that case two children had been placed with long-term foster parents with a view to adoption and parental contact was terminated. The mother applied to a magistrate's court for an order that she should see the children, but this application was adjourned pending the outcome of the local authority's application to free the children for adoption.[4] In the event the freeing hearing was not heard for some months, by which time the guardian ad litem changed her mind about continuing contact with the parents, which had previously been regarded as beneficial. It was held[5] in these circumstances that the mother's withholding of agreement could not be said to be unreasonable since, notwithstanding that the evidence pointed to the children's welfare being served by adoption, the hypothetical reasonable parent was entitled to have regard to the circumstances leading to that state of affairs and to say that she had not had a proper opportunity to demonstrate that continued contact would be beneficial.[6]

Notwithstanding the decisions in *Re H, Re W* and *Re E*, there is little evidence that they have led to a consistent marked change of attitude in favour of protecting the parental interest. This is not to say, however, that there does not continue to be a tension between promoting the child's welfare and safeguarding the parents' interests and no case illustrates this better than *Re C (A Minor) (Adoption: Parental Agreement: Contact)*.[7] That case concerned a child whose care was largely left to the mother since the father worked almost all of the time. The mother, however, was of limited intelligence and had learning difficulties and there were concerns about her ability to cope with the demands of bringing up a baby. Social services were first alerted by the health visitor, who considered the child (who displayed 'frozen watchfulness') to be suffering from mental, emotional, and social deprivation. However, social services' initial involvement ceased when the father intervened, but following a second referral by a hospital doctor on the ground of suspected sexual abuse (an allegation later rejected by the judge) the child was eventually made the subject of a care order. The child, who had been placed with foster parents, was now thriving. At first the local authority plan was to rehabilitate the child with her family, but following a detailed assessment of the parents these plans were dropped because of the parents' (principally the mother's) inability to cope. The local authority sought an order to free the child for adoption. This was opposed by the parents, who brought their own action for a residence/and or a contact order.

At first instance, the judge rejected the parents' application and granted the freeing order, dispensing with the mother's agreement on the ground that it was being unreasonably withheld. Although the decision to dismiss the appeal was unanimous, the case is remarkable for their Lordships' divergent attitudes to the dispensing issue. On the one hand, Balcombe LJ had considerable reservations about the outcome. He pointed out that the whole point of the second stage of the two-stage process in deciding whether or not to grant the adoption order, namely determining whether to

---

2   (1983) 4 FLR 614, CA at 620 where Purchas LJ expressly distinguished placements with adopters with parental agreement from the conversion of an 'ordinary fostering arrangement'.
3   [1990] 2 FLR 397, CA.
4   'Freeing the child for adoption' is discussed below at p 650ff.
5   But note that Dillon LJ dissented, stressing that the test of reasonableness was to be applied at the date of the hearing.
6   In this context the mother's sense of grievance was held to be relevant. But cf *Re B (A Minor) (Adoption: Parental Agreement)* [1990] 2 FLR 383, CA, discussed below at p 646, in which it was held to be wrong to take into account the mother's sense of injustice.
7   [1993] 2 FLR 260, CA.

dispense with parental agreement, was to protect the parental interest. The child's welfare will have been considered at the first stage. In this regard, he commented:[8]

'While I accept that a reasonable parent does pay regard to the welfare of his child, in my experience a decision to dispense with the agreement of the parent to the adoption of a child who is in care usually occurs when the child is in care because of some failure on the part of the parent. In this case, once the diagnosis of sexual abuse had been rejected, the only failure on the part of the parents was their inability to give K the standard of parental care necessary for her social and emotional development, which was primarily attributable to the mother's limited intellectual capacity, and the father's inability to comprehend the effect of this or himself to provide an acceptable alternative. If normal social work intervention should prove ineffective, this could well justify K being taken into care and placed during the remainder of her childhood with long-term foster-parents, but I doubt whether Parliament intended that it should be a ground for irrevocably terminating the parents' (in this case the mother's) legal relationship with the child. It has the flavour of social engineering.'

Steyn and Hoffmann LJJ (who gave a joint judgment), on the other hand, had no doubt that the right balance had been struck in this case. In their view this was not a case of a marginal falling below an acceptable minimum level of parenting. As they pointed out, the health visitor had described the child as the most frightened child she had seen in nine years, and this bleak picture was highlighted by the child's dramatic improvement after she went to live with the foster parents. But they had a second and more fundamental objection to the argument that the judge had acted upon the 'mere inadequacy of the parent', commenting:[9]

'What is "inadequacy"? It does not appear in the statute. It is a weasel word capable of covering a very wide spectrum of cases. We think that it is illegitimate to attach a label like "mere inadequacy" to the facts and then to reason from the label rather than the facts themselves. To say that the judge should not have dispensed with the agreement on grounds of inadequacy, mere or otherwise, is to invent a principle or gloss which Parliament has not laid down and in our judgment does not exist.'

Although in one sense these divergent views encapsulate the shifts of emphasis between concern for the child's welfare and protection of the parental interest previously evident in case law, in this instance the majority view is surely to be preferred. Balcombe LJ seemed to be close to saying that unless a parent is blameworthy in some way, an adoption order should not be granted, which is inconsistent with the House of Lords' decision in *Re W (An Infant)*. This is not to say that there should be no sympathy for the parents. On the contrary, one might observe that their original application to discharge the care order was not heard for 17 months, which delay clearly did not help their case. Nevertheless, the reality of the situation faced by the court at the freeing hearing, as recognised by the majority, was that no reasonable parent could have withheld their agreement to the adoption.

As we have said,[10] the reality is that adoption applications are rarely refused and it remains the case that there are relatively few reported decisions in which a parent's refusal to agree to the adoption has been upheld by the court. One important factor, however, is the degree of contact between the child and parent at the time of the adoption application. Indeed, it was noticeable that, in the past at any rate,[11] where a refusal to agree to the adoption order was upheld, the parent had commonly, at the

8 Ibid at 269.
9 Ibid at 277.
10 See ante, p 637.
11 Though, given the increasing acceptance of open adoption in which the child continues to have contact with his birth parents (see ante, p 617), the mere fact of existing contact between parent and child ought possibly to be of diminishing importance.

time of the hearing,[12] either been seeing his child or had had contact in the recent past.[13] Indeed, in *Re C (Minors) (Adoption)*[14] Balcombe LJ commented that, where children were in local authority care and enjoying beneficial contact with their parents, it was premature for the local authority to apply to free the children for adoption.[15] On the other hand, complete absence of contact for some years will normally be a telling factor against the parent, especially if the child is well settled with the applicants and it can be shown that any change would be damaging to the child. In *Re B (A Minor) (Adoption: Parental Agreement)*,[16] following a history of neglect and inadequate parenting a brother and sister were taken into care and eventually placed with long-term foster parents. Over the next four years the mother continued to see the children and was still seeking to have them back. The local authority then decided to end contact for a trial period to see how the children would respond, but it was later restored in a compromise reached with the mother. At this stage, however, there was a marked difference in the children's attitudes. The girl, who had failed to settle with the foster parents, wanted to see her mother and eventually she went back to live with her. The boy had settled well with the foster parents and he was no longer interested in seeing his mother. Subsequently, the foster parents applied to adopt the boy. At this stage the boy was 11 years old and had lived with the applicants for seven years and was entirely integrated with that family. He wanted to be adopted. Overturning the first instance decision, the Court of Appeal dispensed with the mother's agreement and granted the adoption. In reaching this decision the appellate court, mindful that the applicants for the order would not seek to prevent future contact between the boy and his mother and sister, considered that the grant of the order offered the best chance of preserving such contact. On the other hand, they held that the judge at first instance had misdirected himself by taking into account the mother's sense of injustice stemming from the local authority's termination of contact.[17]

Another factor relates to the child's position. It is reasonable for a parent to be sensitive to the child's own wishes and needs. In *Re E (A Minor) (Adoption)*[18] it was held reasonable for a mother to take into account the benefit of contact with siblings or other new relatives and to refuse to agree to the making of a freeing order, which at that time could not also include provision for contact.[19] But the leading case in this regard is *Re M (Adoption or Residence Order)*,[20] which involved a child (M) who was placed with the adoptive applicants when she was nearly nine years old. At that stage the birth mother was addicted both to drugs and alcohol. Although, given M's age, it was made clear to the applicants at the outset that if she did not want to be adopted, the court might well make a residence order,

---

12 As in *Re H (A Minor) (Adoption)* [1985] FLR 519, CA; *Re M (A Minor) (Adoption Order: Access)* [1986] 1 FLR 51, CA; and *Re V (A Minor) (Adoption: Consent)* [1987] Fam 57, [1986] 1 All ER 752, CA.
13 As in *Re BA (Wardship and Adoption)* [1985] FLR 1008.
14 [1992] 1 FLR 115, CA.
15 Freeing for adoption is discussed below at pp 650ff.
16 [1990] 2 FLR 383, CA. See also *Re GB (Minors) (Adoption Parental Agreement)* [1985] FLR 719.
17 See *Re E (Minors) (Adoption: Parental Agreement)*, supra, discussed above at p 644, in which a sense of grievance was held to be relevant.
18 [1989] 1 FLR 126, CA.
19 Compare *Re C (A Minor) (Adoption Order: Conditions)* [1989] AC 1, [1988] 1 All ER 705, HL (discussed post at p 669), where the House of Lords dispensed with the mother's agreement and made an adoption order with a condition for access to continue with a sibling. This option was not open to the court in *Re E* as it was a freeing case (see post, p 669). Quaere whether *Re E* would now be decided the same given the new powers to make a contact order under s 8 of the Children Act 1989? See post, p 670.
20 [1998] 1 FLR 570, CA.

everyone's expectation was that M would be adopted. Unfortunately, the local authority failed to prepare for the adoption and in particular had paid no heed to M's own wishes not to be adopted. Despite M's position the placement seemed settled and nearly two years later the applicants (who had recently married so as to be able to adopt M jointly) filed their application for adoption. It was at this stage that M's own views came to the fore and the local authority then belatedly withdrew their support for the adoption. In the meantime the mother's position had dramatically improved. She was no longer dependent on drugs or alcohol and was living in a stable relationship with a new partner. She eventually sought a residence order. Understandably, the applicants had been shocked by the turn of events, and at the date of the hearing maintained the position that if they were not granted an adoption order they would not be prepared to keep M. They therefore rejected the mother's offer to withdraw her application and to consent to a residence order being made in their favour and to agree to the making of a s 91(14) direction limiting her future right to apply for a residence order.

At first instance the judge dismissed the mother's application for a residence order and, dispensing with her agreement to the adoption on the grounds that it was being unreasonably withheld, granted the adoption notwithstanding M's objections. On appeal, however, it was held by a majority[21] that the adoption application should be refused and that a residence order coupled with a s 91(14) direction should be granted instead. In reaching this conclusion the majority ruled that although the first instance judge had been wrong not to explore the alternatives when considering whether it was in the interests of the child to be adopted, nevertheless, given her need for stability and security and faced with the applicant's ultimatum that they would reject her if the adoption was not granted, it was in M's interests to be adopted. Accordingly the first stage test had been satisfied. However, in the extraordinary circumstances of the case, it could not be said that the mother's withholding of her agreement was unreasonable. She had taken and was entitled inter alia[1] to take into account her daughter's wish not to be adopted and to respect her not totally unrealistic wish to return to live with her. As Ward LJ put it:[2]

> 'The chance of M returning at some stage to her mother's home is not discounted by any of the experts. If that happens, how does a mother answer her child's angry challenge, "Why did you give me away to be adopted? Why did you not listen to what I was saying?" In my judgment, it would require fortitude bordering on indifference for a mother to shut her ears to what her child has said – for so long, with so little contact to preserve the feelings for her old family notwithstanding so much love and nurture being shown by her new family.'

She was also held entitled to take into account the wishes of her other children to maintain the family link with M and of M's own affection and need for contact with her sisters.

Although *Re M* serves as a stark reminder of the need for practitioners to listen to the child, one of the ironies of the case is that M's own reaction to the first instance decision that she would be adopted was one of muted acceptance. It also has to be said that the Court of Appeal took a huge gamble on the applicants also accepting the decision and not giving up M as they had threatened.

---

21 Ward and Judge LJJ. Simon Brown LJ dissented on the ground that the advantages of adoption for the child were sufficiently strong as to justify overriding the mother's objection.

 1 She was also entitled to take into account that the local authority did not consider the adoption to be in M's interest, that the guardian had changed her mind, and that she was entitled to differ from the opinion of an expert just as the local authority and guardian had done.

 2 Ibid at 599–600.

(d)   Adoptions within the family

A third context in which the question of unreasonable withholding of agreement arises is with respect to adoption applications from within the family.

Assuming that adoption is thought appropriate,[3] parental agreement must still be obtained or dispensed with. Given that in most cases the child will remain with applicants regardless of the outcome of the application, there is a strong analogy with the foster parent cases. However, as the Adoption Law Review has observed, there may be perceived differences in public and private law cases. Where parents separate or divorce, it is generally assumed to be for the benefit of the child to maintain links with both parents. In these cases the court is less concerned with the parent's overall ability to look after the child.[4] Hence, if there is continued contact with the child, the parent is unlikely to be held unreasonable in withholding agreement. On the other hand, if there has been little or no contact and the parent has nothing else to offer, the withholding of agreement is likely to be held unreasonable.[5]

Other grounds for dispensing with agreement

Another ground exists if the parent or guardian *has persistently failed without reasonable cause to discharge the parental duties in relation to the child.* This does not merely include the legal obligations towards the child (for example, to maintain him) but also the natural and moral duty to show affection, care and interest.[6] But the failure must be culpable and 'of such gravity, so complete, so convincingly proved that there can be no advantage to the child in keeping continuous contact with the natural parent who has so abrogated his duties that he for his part should be deprived of his own child against his wishes'.[7] In *Re D (Minors) (Adoption by Parent)*[8] the court refused to dispense with the father's agreement solely on the ground that he had failed to provide for his daughter or to see her for a year. As Baker P pointed out, when a marriage breaks down, the husband will often withdraw or drift apart from the family temporarily, particularly when, as in that case, he is living with another woman.

Other grounds are:

- If the parent or guardian has *abandoned or neglected the child.*[9]
- If he has *persistently ill-treated the child.*[10]

---

3   Though, as we have seen (ante at pp 631–3), the courts themselves have been reluctant to grant adoption to relatives and until the Children Act 1989 there had been statutory restrictions on step-parent adoption (see ante, p 630).

4   Discussion Paper No 2, op cit, para 70.

5   See eg *Re M (Adoption: Parental Agreement)* [1985] FLR 664.

6   *Re P (Infants)* [1962] 3 All ER 789; *Re B(S) (An Infant)* [1968] Ch 204, [1967] 3 All ER 629.

7   Per Baker P in *Re D (Minors) (Adoption By Parent)* [1973] Fam 209 at 214, [1973] 3 All ER 1001 at 1005. It might be noted that this draconian interpretation has meant that virtually no applications are now made on this ground.

8   Supra. See also *Re H (Minors)* (1974) Times, 26 November and *Re M (Adoption: Parental Agreement)* [1985] FLR 664, 665.

9   'Abandoned' and 'neglected' connote conduct which would render the parent or guardian liable to criminal proceedings under the Children and Young Persons Act 1933 s 1 (ante at p 366): *Watson v Nickolaisen* [1955] 2 QB 286, [1955] 2 All ER 427; *Re W* (unreported), cited in *Re P (Infants),* supra, and *Re M (Adoption: Parental Agreement),* supra.

10   'Persistent' implies a series of acts: in *Re A (A Minor) (Adoption: Dispensing with Agreement)* (1979) 2 FLR 173, CA, it was held that severe and repeated assaults over a period of three weeks sufficed.

— If he has *seriously ill-treated the child and (whether because of the ill-treatment or for some other reason) the rehabilitation of the child within the parent's or guardian's household is unlikely*. This ground was first introduced in the Children Act 1975 following the recommendations of the Houghton Committee.[11] It is intended to cover even a single act of violence. The requirement that rehabilitation is unlikely[12] provides an important limitation on the power to dispense with agreement on this ground, although it should be noted that the unlikelihood of rehabilitation does not have to stem from the ill-treatment.[13]

It will be appreciated that these last four grounds are fault-based. In practice they are relied upon only in a minority of cases.[14]

The proposed reforms[15]

The Adoption Law Review considered the present position to be 'clearly unsatisfactory'.[16] As the Consultative Paper pointed out,[17] the so-called fault-based grounds for dispensing with parental agreement are objectionable both because faults or shortcomings of parental care do not ipso facto justify adoption as a suitable option for the child nor, where adoption is thought right, should they imply that parents are necessarily at fault. Responses to the review largely favoured the removal of fault-based grounds. The Review also considered[18] the unreasonable withholding ground unsatisfactory, since it remains problematic as to how much weight a reasonable parent should place on the child's welfare; and in any event it seems wrong to fix a parent with the stigma of being an 'unreasonable parent'. With these recommendations in mind the proposed Adoption Bill provides for just two grounds upon which parental consent[19] can be dispensed with:[20]

'(a) the parent or guardian cannot be found or is incapable of giving consent, or
(b) the court is satisfied that the welfare of the child requires the consent to be dispensed with'.

The first of the grounds corresponds with the existing law and such a provision seems undoubtedly necessary. The second ground would be new and it must be considered together with the proposed general test under cl 1(2) that in adoption issues the child's welfare in childhood and later would be the paramount consideration. Whilst such a proposed test has the merit of apparent simplicity

---

11 Op cit at paras 219–20.
12 Adoption Act 1976 s 16(5).
13 Rehabilitation could be unlikely, for example, because the parent has been imprisoned for an unrelated offence or because the child is in care. It has been held that the question of rehabilitation should be interpreted in the light of s 6, ie first consideration being given to the need to promote the child's welfare: *Re PB (A Minor) (Application to Free for Adoption)* [1985] FLR 394 at 405, per Sheldon J.
14 See the discussion in Adoption Law Review, Discussion Paper No 2, op cit, at paras 34 and 37 and by the Consultative Document on Adoption Law, op cit at para 12.5.
15 See Cooke 'Dispensing with parental consent to adoption – a choice of welfare tests' (1997) 9 CFLQ 259, and Lindley and Wyld 'The Children Act and the draft Adoption Bill – diverging principles' (1996) 8 CFLQ 327.
16 Discussion Paper No 2, op cit, para 85.
17 See para 12.5.
18 See para 12.4.
19 It will be noted that the Bill reverts to the use of the term 'consent' rather than 'agreement' as under the current law. Sed quaere?
20 See Cl 46(2).

(and no one would surely lament the passing of the unreasonably withholding test, nor the ending of the fault-based grounds), effectively what the proposed Bill would do is to introduce a simple welfare test to the dispensing issue. From a theoretical perspective this proposal seems astonishing, for, as others have pointed out,[1] if a simple welfare test is considered inadequate to justify the compulsory removal of children into care, how could it be right to justify the complete and irrevocable transfer of parentage? Inevitably, such a proposal raises fear of social engineering,[2] but it can be anticipated that the courts would be very much alive to this danger,[3] though whether it is right to leave the courts with such a sweeping discretion may be questioned.

Although there are no easy answers as to how best to reconcile the child's welfare with the parents' interests, it is suggested that the earlier Consultative Paper's recommendation[4] that the 'test should require the court to be satisfied that the advantages to the child of becoming part of a new family are so significantly greater than the advantages of any alternative option as to justify overriding the wishes of a parent or guardian' comes as close as any to maintaining the right balance. Although the probability would be that the courts would work to this tenet anyway, it is submitted that such a test should be expressly written into the legislation.

If, however, the test proposed in the Adoption Bill were to be enacted, it would mean the elimination of the two-stage test, for once it is decided that adoption is in the child's interests, it must inevitably follow that parental consent should be dispensed with. This change would place great responsibility both upon adoption agencies and the courts to ensure that all the options have been carefully considered before an adoption placement is made[5] and to implement any adoptive plans expeditiously lest such an option becomes inevitable simply by effluxion of time.

5.   FREEING THE CHILD FOR ADOPTION[6]

A former weakness in the law was that there was no procedure whereby parental agreement could be made binding before the final adoption hearing. The possibility that a parent might change his mind about the adoption was an understandable source of fear to applicants and agencies alike and the attendant uncertainty was hardly conducive to the child's interest. Moreover, some felt that the law itself encouraged parental indecision.[7] To overcome such difficulties a procedure known as 'freeing the child for adoption' was introduced in 1984,[8]

---

1 See eg Cooke, ibid at 263.
2 See eg Barton 'The Adoption Bill – The Consultative Document' [1996] Fam Law 431.
3 As we have seen (see ante, p 470) the courts require cogent evidence to justify making a residence order in favour of a non-parent, at any rate in cases contested by parents.
4 Ibid, R 13.
5 See below, pp 657ff, for discussion about the proposed placement orders.
6 See generally Adoption Law Review, Discussion Paper No 2, Part 23: 'Lowe, Freeing for Adoption: The Experience of the 1980s' [1990] JSWL 220; Lowe et al *Report of the Research into the Use and Practice of the Freeing for Adoption Provisions* (1993); and the study in Scotland, Lambert, Buist, Triseliotis and Hull *Freeing Children for Adoption* summarised in (1990) Adoption and Fostering, Vol 14, No 1 at 36.
7 See the Houghton Report, op cit, at para 168.
8 See now ss 18–20 of the Adoption Act 1976. These provisions are based on, but do not exactly follow, the Houghton Committee's recommendations, op cit, paras 173–186, discussed by Lowe 'Freeing for Adoption: The Experience of the 1980s', loc cit, at pp 220–1.

under which parental agreement can be bindingly given or finally dispensed with at an earlier stage of the adoption process.

Applying for an order

Only an adoption agency can apply for a freeing order. Furthermore, following changes made by the Children Act 1989, unless at least one parent with parental responsibility,[9] or a guardian consents to the making of the freeing *application*, an agency cannot apply to free the child for adoption, unless the child is in local authority care under a care order.[10]

As with adoption, an application for a freeing order may not be made in respect of a child who is or has been married, but may be made notwithstanding that the child has previously been adopted.[11]

Agreement to the making of an order

No freeing *order* may be made unless the persons whose agreement is required to an adoption order freely and with full understanding of what is involved agree generally[12] and unconditionally to the child being adopted or their agreement is dispensed with on one of the grounds enabling the court to dispense with it when making an adoption order.[13] Furthermore, before making a freeing order, the court must be satisfied that an unmarried father who does not have parental responsibility has no intention of applying for a parental responsibility order under s 4 of the Children Act 1989 or a residence order under s 10 of that Act or, if he were to make any such application, it would be likely to be refused.[14] In cases where the father has shown a real commitment to the child it might be difficult to show that a s 4 application would fail. In *Re H (Minors) (Adoption: Putative Fathers' Rights) (No 3),*[15] for example, a s 4 order was made even though the court had no doubt that the father's agreement to the freeing order should be dispensed with on the ground that it was being unreasonably withheld. Where s 18(7) of the Adoption Act cannot be satisfied, the freeing application cannot be decided until the other issue has been settled. If a s 4 order is made or a residence order is granted, the father will then have parental responsibility[16] and his agreement to the freeing order will be required or have to be dispensed with. However, as *Re H* shows, it by no means

---

9 Not an unmarried father without parental responsibility.

10 Adoption Act 1976 s 18(2), (2A) as amended by the Children Act 1989 Sch 10, para 6. Previously no consent seemed to be required if the child was in (what would now be termed) local authority accommodation. This change is in line with the general philosophy of the Children Act 1989 that 'accommodation', being a voluntary service provided by local authorities, is not to be undermined by the possibility of parents being unable to remove their children, save where an authority can satisfy the 'threshold' requirements for a care order under s 31: ante, p 536. But note the criticism by Lowe [1990] JSWL 220 at 232, who argued that the requirement can delay the process.

11 Adoption Act 1976 s 18(2), as substituted by the Children Act 1989 Sch 10, para 6(3).

12 Unlike an adoption application the agreement is not given with a specific application in mind. The mother's agreement is ineffective if given within six weeks of the child's birth: Adoption Act 1976 s 18(4). A parent does not have to attend the hearing: Adoption Act 1976 s 66(3).

13 Adoption Act 1976 s 18(1).

14 Ibid, s 18(7), as substituted by the Children Act 1989 Sch 10, para 6(3).

15 [1991] Fam 151, [1991] 2 All ER 185, discussed ante, p 381. But note that according to *Re H (Parental Responsibility)* [1998] 1 FLR 855, CA, the so-called '*Re H* test' is but a starting point in deciding whether a s 4 order should be made. See ante, p 381.

16 Under s 12 (1) of the Children Act 1989 the court is bound upon granting the unmarried father a residence order to make a s 4 order. Fathers with parental responsibility are 'parents' under the Adoption Act 1976 s 72(1) as amended by Sch 10, para 30(7) of the 1989 Act.

follows that the granting of a s 4 order alone[17] will automatically mean that the court will not then dispense with the father's agreement to a freeing order.

Where it is sought to dispense with agreement, if the child is not already placed for adoption, the court must be satisfied that the child is likely to be so placed.[18] In practice this provision seems relatively easy to satisfy. As Sheldon J pointed out in *Re PB (A Minor)*,[19] there is no need for the local authority to have any particular candidates in mind before commencing proceedings to free for adoption since the court need only be satisfied that it is –

> '. . . likely that the child will be placed for adoption – *a likelihood which may be thought to be beyond doubt in the case of most young children*' [emphasis added].

It is submitted that, as with adoption, the court must first decide in a freeing application whether adoption is in the interests of the child before considering whether to dispense with the agreement of the parent. This was certainly the view of the Court of Appeal in *Re U (Application To Free For Adoption)*[20] when rejecting the argument that because of the mandatory terms of s 18[1] there was no scope for applying s 6. As Balcombe LJ explained:[2]

> '. . . a perfectly tenable construction of s 18 which gives full effect to both s 6 and the word "shall", is that Parliament contemplated that the court should first apply the s 6 test, and secondly, the test under s 18(1), and, if satisfied on both tests, should then make an order declaring the child free for adoption.'

Notwithstanding this unequivocal decision it has been suggested[3] that the subsequent decision both in the Court of Appeal and the House of Lords in *Re G (Adoption: Freeing Order)*[4] should be taken to have laid down the opposite conclusion. While it is true that both Butler-Sloss LJ[5] and Lord Browne-Wilkinson[6] referred to the 'mandatory' element of s 18, they were doing so to contrast it with the discretionary nature of s 20 and it seems unlikely that they were intending at the same time to imply that s 6 had no application. It is submitted that the judgments in *Re G* are perfectly consistent with Balcombe LJ's interpretation of s 18 and should be so understood.

Although the grounds for dispensing with agreement are the same as for adoption applications, it has been suggested that on the one hand it might be harder to show that a parent is being 'unreasonable' in withholding agreement if the child has not yet been placed[7] and on the other:[8]

> '. . . there is a danger that courts may contrast the readily apparent short-comings in the care offered or likely to be offered in future by a child's parents with the care likely to be offered by hypothetically perfect adoptive parents'.

17 Aliter if a residence order is granted.
18 Adoption Act 1976 s 18(3).
19 [1985] FLR 394 at 403.
20 [1993] 2 FLR 992, CA. See also *Re D (A Minor) (Adoption: Freeing Order)* [1991] 1 FLR 48, CA referred to ante, p 637 n 5.
1 Viz in s 18(1) which states that if the court is satisfied either that the parent agrees to the making of a freeing order or that his or her agreement should be dispensed with, it '*shall* make an order declaring the child free for adoption'.
2 Ibid at p 1002.
3 Richards 'Relinquishment, freeing, or abandonment – *Re G (Adoption: Freeing Order)*' (1997) 9 CFLQ 313 at 320–1.
4 [1996] 2 FLR 398, CA; revsd [1997] 2 FLR 202, HL.
5 Ibid at 404.
6 Ibid at 206.
7 See eg the 7th edition of this work at p 403.
8 Consultative Document on Adoption Law, op cit, at para 14.4

In fact case law does not provide hard evidence to support either proposition. With regard to the former there are no reported cases in which an application has been dismissed on this ground, indeed to the contrary Balcombe LJ commented in *Re E (A Minor) (Adoption)*:[9]

'. . . the hypothetical reasonable mother could also take into account – *although I doubt whether she could properly place much weight on this factor* – that the choice lay between the family unit, with all its known deficiencies, with which [the child] had never lost contact and a new and untried (although carefully vetted) placement with adopters' [emphasis added].

With regard to the latter argument, it is true that, notwithstanding that they are more likely to be contested,[10] freeing applications are rarely refused[11] (it is also unusual for any adoption application to be refused).[12] However, most of the recently reported cases in which the withholding of agreement has been held to be reasonable have in fact been freeing applications.[13]

The effect of an order

(a) Transfer of parental responsibility

The raison d'être of a freeing order is to end the parental interest in the child. To this end s 18(5) of the Adoption Act 1976,[14] provides that upon making the order 'parental responsibility for the child is given to the adoption agency' and any parental responsibility which any person had for the child before the order was made is extinguished.[15]

(b) Revocation of freeing orders

Before making a freeing order the court must be satisfied that each parent or guardian who agrees to the adoption has been given the opportunity of making, if he so wishes, a declaration that he prefers not to be involved in future questions concerning the adoption of the child. Any such declaration must be recorded by the court.[16] Notwithstanding the transfer of parental responsibility, the Act provides that unless a parent makes such a declaration, the agency must, within

---

9 [1989] 1 FLR 126 at 133. For reported instances of contested freeing applications being granted where the child had not yet been placed for adoption see eg *Re D (A Minor) (Adoption: Freeing Order)* supra; *Re C (A Minor)* (1987) Times, 16 October; and *Re L (A Minor), Re K (A Minor)* (1988) Adoption and Fostering, Vol 12, No 4 at 55.

10 See below at p 656.

11 In the *Pathways to Adoption* study only one per cent of freeing applications were refused: op cit, Table 2.9.

12 In the *Pathways* sample, ibid, no refusal was recorded but there are reported cases: see eg *Re M (Adoption or Residence Order)* [1998] 1 FLR 570, CA, discussed ante, pp 646–7.

13 See eg *Re P (Adoption: Freeing Order)* [1994] 2 FLR 1000, CA; *Re C (Minors) (Adoption)* [1992] 1 FLR 115, CA; *Re E (Minors) (Adoption: Parental Agreement)* [1990] 2 FLR 397, CA; and *Re E (A Minor) (Adoption)* [1989] 1 FLR 126, CA. The outstanding exception is *Re M (Adoption or Residence Order)*, supra.

14 As amended by Sch 10, para 6(2) to the Children Act 1989.

15 Section 18(5) of the Adoption Act 1976 applying s 12(2) to freeing orders.

16 Adoption Act 1976 s 18(6). In practice declarations are made in a minority of cases. The *Pathways* Study found they were made in 17 per cent of their sample: see Lowe et al *Report of the Research into the Use and Practice of the Freeing for Adoption Provisions*, op cit, Table 3.45. Failure to observe s 18(6) does not invalidate a freeing order: *Re C (Minors) (Adoption)* [1992] 1 FLR 115, CA at 130, per Balcombe LJ.

14 days following the date 12 months after the making of a freeing order, inform him whether the child has been adopted or placed for adoption and must thereafter give him notice whenever the child is placed or ceases to have his home with a person with whom he has been placed, until an adoption order is made.[17] Once this initial period of 12 months has elapsed, the former parent or guardian may apply for the freeing order to be revoked, provided that the child has not been adopted and does not have his home with a person with whom he has been placed for adoption.[18] Once an application for revocation is pending, the adoption agency cannot place the child for adoption without a court order.[19]

In deciding whether to revoke the order the court must have regard to all the circumstances, first consideration being given to the need to safeguard and promote the welfare of the child throughout his childhood.[20] As Lord Browne-Wilkinson emphasised in *Re G (Adoption: Freeing Order)*,[1] the power under s 20 is discretionary, so that the court is not bound to make a freeing order just because the conditions required for the making of the required order no longer obtain. The revocation of a freeing order extinguishes the parental responsibility given to the adoption agency and vests it in the parent or parents who previously had parental responsibility, or a guardian whose appointment was extinguished by the freeing order.[2] A revocation, on the other hand, does not revive a s 8 or care order previously made under the Children Act 1989, nor does it revive a duty to make payments for the child arising from a court order or agreement that has been extinguished by a freeing order.[3]

If an application to revoke is refused, the agency ceases to be under any obligation to give notice of the child's progress and the former parent or guardian making the application cannot make a further application for revocation of the order without leave of the court.[4]

On its face s 20 only permits the court to grant or refuse the application to revoke. However, the House of Lords held in *Re G (Adoption: Freeing Order)*[5] that the Adoption Act 1976 in general and s 20 in particular should not be looked at in isolation, but should instead be interpreted and applied in the context of the wider legislation regulating children, principally the Children Act 1989. Accordingly, they held that there was power to make a revocation order conditional upon the local authority obtaining a care order. In this way their Lordships overcame the alleged lacuna of the Act in dealing with a child, subject to a freeing order, who subsequently becomes unlikely to be adopted but whose parent cannot properly be permitted to resume sole and unfettered responsibility.

---

17 Adoption Act 1976 s 19. In *R v Derbyshire County Council, ex p T* [1990] Fam 164, [1990] 1 All ER 792 it was held the obligation to inform the parent arises when the agency decides to end the placement for adoption and not when the child is physically moved.
18 Adoption Act 1976 s 20.
19 Adoption Act 1976 s 20 (2).
20 Section 6 of the Adoption Act 1976 applies: see s 20(4) and Lord Browne-Wilkinson in *Re G (Adoption: Freeing Order)* [1997] 2 FLR 202 at 207. See also Bellamy 'Revocation of Freeing Orders' [1990] Fam Law 352.
1 [1997] 2 FLR at 207.
2 Adoption Act 1976 s 20(3), as substituted by Sch 10, para 8(2) to the Children Act 1989.
3 Adoption Act 1976 s 20(3A)(a), added by Sch 10, para 8(2) to the Children Act 1989. Section 20(3A)(b) makes it clear that a revocation order does not affect any person's parental responsibility insofar as it relates to the period between the making and revocation of the freeing order.
4 Adoption Act 1976 s 20(4). Leave shall not be given unless it appears to the court that, owing to a change of circumstances or for any other reason, it is proper to allow the application to be made: s 20(5).
5 [1997] 2 FLR 202 on which see Richards, op cit.

(c)   The status of the freed child

One curious effect of a freeing order is that pending the adoption the child has no human being as a parent, since the birth parents are no longer the legal parents (see further below) and there is no adoptive parent. In *Re G*[6] Lord Browne-Wilkinson described the child as becoming a 'legal orphan'. The Adoption Law Review considered[7] the status of a freed child to be 'unclear and best described as a legal limbo'. There is uncertainty, for example, as to the ensuing succession rights.[8]

Although this so-called 'limbo' status has been perhaps rendered less problematic both by the ruling in *Re G* that conditional revocations can be made and by the clarification under the Children Act 1989 that such children are formally 'looked after' children,[9] the current law does not seem to be satisfactory.[10]

(d)   The status of the former parent

It is clear that once a freeing order has been made the birth parents, or 'former' parents, as s 19 and s 20 of the 1976 refer to them, cease to have any legal status in relation to the child apart from that in relation to revocation over which they have no control. As Butler-Sloss LJ put it in *Re C (Minors) (Adoption: Residence Order)*:[11]

'The effect of a freeing order is to deprive the natural parents of parental responsibility in the same way as after an adoption order.'

One important consequence of this effect is that birth parents cease to be 'parents' for the purposes of the Children Act 1989 and hence will need leave from the court to apply for any s 8 order.[12] Furthermore, according to Thorpe J in *Re C (A Minor) (Adoption Child: Contact)*,[13] such leave ought not to be given, unless there has been 'some fundamental change of circumstances'.

The use of freeing orders

Although there is no compulsion upon agencies to apply to free children for adoption,[14] most people envisaged, and the Houghton Committee certainly intended, that it would be commonly used not least because that is what the birth

---

6   Ibid at 206.
7   Discussion Paper No 2, para 134.
8   See Discussion Paper No 2, paras 137–138. But note *Staffordshire County Council v B* [1998] 1 FLR 261, discussed post, p 677.
9   See s 22 if the Children Act 1989 as discussed by Discussion Paper No 2, para 135. The concept of being 'looked after' by a local authority is discussed ante, p 529.
10 But under the proposed placement orders the problem of status at least would be resolved: see post, pp 658–9.
11 [1994] Fam 1 at 9, sub nom *Re C (Minors) (Parent: Residence Order)* [1993] 3 All ER 313, CA at 319.
12 This ruling in *Re C* settled a point raised by Hershman and McFarlane 'The Children Act 1989: access or contact with a child freed for adoption' [1990] Fam Law 322–3, who argued that some birth parents remained 'parents' for these purposes but which had been disputed by Lowe et al *Report on the Research into the Use and Practice of Freeing for Adoption Provisions*, op cit, at p 69.
13 [1993] Fam 210, [1993] 3 All ER 259, discussed further post, p 673.
14 See Sheldon J in *Re PB (A Minor) (Application to Free for Adoption)* [1985] FLR 394 at 404 explaining Cumming-Bruce LJ's remarks which suggested otherwise in *Re M (A Minor) (Wardship:Jurisdiction)* [1985] Fam 60, CA at 71.

parents (particularly mothers) would wish.[15] In practice the frequency of use varies from agency to agency, with some not using it at all and others using it some of the time. According to the *Pathways Study* conducted in the late 1980s no agency used freeing in more than a third of their adoption placements.[16] There is some evidence of increased use of freeing since then. According to one finding,[17] in 1994 29 per cent of all children previously 'looked after' by local authorities in England before being adopted had been freed for adoption. However, it is clear that practice still varies from agency to agency[18] and that in most cases it is still used only in a minority of cases. One of the main reasons for its relatively infrequent use is that, instead of being the speedy process that it was intended to be, it has proved in practice to be a lengthy process riddled with delay.[19] The *Pathways Study* found that on average it took just over nine months from the time of application to obtain a freeing order, with a third of cases taking in excess of nine months and five per cent in excess of 18 months.[20] To overcome this problem there is anecdotal evidence that in some areas judges now regularly direct that freeing applications are to be dealt with at the final care hearing.[1]

Another problem with freeing is its relationship with openness. As Richards has observed:[2]

'Since 1991 the new culture of openness created by the Children Act 1989 has permeated adoption practice. The courts have observed[3] more than once that freeing and open adoption are uneasy bedfellows, and that contact issues are best explored in full adoption proceedings where the discussion must involve the adoptive parents.'

However, as Richards says, despite these difficulties, there is no evidence that this has reduced the incidence of freeing applications.

Although it was expected that the procedure would be useful where a parent might withhold agreement, the general assumption at the time of implementation was that freeing would be mainly a consensual process. Its principal use, however, is in contested or otherwise difficult cases, with as many as 75 per cent of applications being contested.[4] Another unintended and controversial use of the process is to free children already placed with prospective adopters.[5] The agency's motive in using the freeing process even where the child has been placed for adoption is to shield the would-be adopters from the stress of taking on the contest with the birth parents. Not everyone agrees that this is a legitimate use of the

---

15 See eg Hayes and Williams 'Adoption of Babies, Agreeing and Freeing' [1982] Fam Law 233 at 236.
16 See the Pathways Study's *Freeing Report*, sections 2.2 and 3.2.1 summarised by the Adoption Law Review, Discussion Paper No 2, paras 146 et seq.
17 Ivaldi *Children Adopted Out of Care* (1998).
18 See the BAAF study *Focus on Adoption* at 5.1.1 which found of those adopted out of care in 1995 only 18 per cent were freed for adoption, with a significantly reduced use by London boroughs.
19 The courts themselves have been critical of delay. In *Re PB* supra, for instance, where there was a delay of over a year, Sheldon J commented that with reasonable expedition it should be possible to fix a date within three months. See also *Re C (A Minor)* (1987) Times, 16 October, where 18 months elapsed between the institution of the application and the date of the judgment.
20 Tables 3.6–3.8 of the Pathways Study's *Freeing Report*.
1   See Richards, op cit, at 317.
2   Richards, ibid.
3   For discussion of the relevant case law, see post, p 670.
4   See the *Freeing Report*, op cit, Tables 3.19–3.22.
5   The *Pathways Study* found this to be the case in 21 per cent of cases, with a further nine per cent so placed during the pendency of the application: ibid, Table 3.36.

jurisdiction,[6] and in any event it is possible for the court to join the adoptive applicants as parties.[7] It is established, however, that the potential adopters are not barred from subsequently applying to adopt if the freeing application fails.[8]

The future of freeing: the proposed placement order

As the Adoption Law Review puts it, judged by the Houghton Committee's criteria, freeing has failed.[9] The question remains, should the procedure be scrapped, or retained but improved?[10]

(a)   Earlier proposals

The long-signalled view of the Adoption Law Review[11] is that the freeing provisions should be replaced by an entirely new procedure that better safeguards the interests of all parties. The problem, however, has been to devise a suitable alternative. The Consultative Document on Adoption Law[12] proposed that *all* agency placements for adoption (save those for babies) should be preceded by what was to be called a 'placement order'. Such an order could only be made where a specific placement was planned, it being envisaged that an application would be made following an introductory meeting between the child and the prospective adoptive parents. If, after an investigation by a guardian ad litem, it was found that the proposed adoption was not opposed, then a placement order would be granted by the court without a hearing. If the adoption was contested, then the agency would not be allowed to proceed with the placement (apart from continued 'introductions' between the child and prospective adopters) until the court had formally resolved the dispute.

These proposals met with considerable criticism.[13] As the subsequent White Paper *Adoption: The Future* put it:[14]

'Many acknowledge that the problem [the proposal] is intended to address does exist and needs remedy but fear the new procedure might prove cumbersome and might in some cases unnecessarily and without clear benefit add to the length and complexity of the adoption process.'

In 1994 a revised system was proposed,[15] providing for a more flexible approach which it was felt more appropriately dealt with, on the one hand, babies whose birth parents had requested adoption and, on the other, older children removed or kept from their parents against the latter's wishes. It is these later proposals that are incorporated into the proposed Adoption Bill.

6 See eg White 'Freeing or placement: the dilemma for adoption agencies' (1989) Journal of Child Law, Vol 1, No 2 at 41.
7 Adoption Rules 1984 r 4(3). Indeed, in contested cases it has been said that it is desirable that they should be made parties, per Balcombe LJ in *Re C (Minors) (Adoption)* [1992] 1 FLR 115, CA at 129.
8 The principle of res judicata does not apply: per Eastham J in *Re B* (1990) Adoption and Fostering, Vol 14, No 1 at 62.
9 Discussion Paper No 2, para 176. For a similar conclusion see the Pathways Study's *Freeing Report*, op cit at 5.4. See also the conclusion of the Scottish study, op cit.
10 Both the Pathways and the Scottish studies were in favour of its retention subject to improvements being made.
11 Adoption Law Review, Discussion Paper No 2, *Agreeing and Freeing*, (1991) para 180.
12 1992, Recommendations 16–18, discussed at para 15.1 – 15.5.
13 See eg Lowe 'Adoption placement orders – freeing by another name' (1993) 5 Jo of Child Law 62.
14 Cm 2288 (1993) para 4.9.
15 *Placement for Adoption – a consultation document* (1994).

(b)   The placement provisions under the proposed Bill[16]

Under the proposed Bill the basic position would be that an agency could only place a child for adoption with prospective adopters or leave a child already placed with persons for some other purpose (fostering) with those persons as prospective adopters, with parental consent or pursuant to a court order.[17]

Consensual placements (which in practice would be confined to mothers relinquishing their babies) would only be permitted provided (a) the child is neither in care nor the subject of pending care proceedings and (b) the agency is satisfied that each parent[18] or guardian has consented to the child being placed either with named prospective adopters or any prospective adopters chosen by the agency.[19] Furthermore, the consenting parent or guardian could make a parental responsibility agreement vesting parental responsibility in the prospective adopters while the child is with them or, in any other case, in the agency.[20] Under such an agreement, birth parents would share rather than lose their parental responsibility, though their ability to exercise it would be limited.[1]

Consenting to the child's *placement* would be separate from consenting to the adoption order (though it would be possible to consent to both at the same time),[2] but parents would only be permitted to oppose the subsequent making of an adoption order with leave of the court, which could only be given where the court is satisfied that there has been a change of circumstances since the making of the placement order.[3]

Placement orders would be required both where an agency is satisfied that the child ought to be adopted but the parent or guardian has not consented (or has withdrawn consent) to the child being placed for adoption, and where the child is the subject of a care order (or a pending application) and the local authority's care plan contains a recommendation that the child should be placed for adoption.[4] The obligation to apply for a placement order would arise either at the time of the care order application if the care plan includes a recommendation for adoption, or subsequently if the initial plan is later changed to include such a recommendation.[5] Before a placement order could be granted, the court would have to be satisfied that each parent or guardian has consented to the child being placed for adoption with any prospective adopters chosen by the agency or that such consent should be dispensed with.[6]

A placement order would automatically give parental responsibility to the prospective adopters where the child is placed, or otherwise to the agency.[7] The

---

16 See generally Lowe 'Placement of Children for Adoption under the Proposed Adoption Bill' (1996) 126 Childright 14.

17 See cl 19 of the Proposed Bill.

18 Provided they have parental responsibility – ie not the unmarried father unless he has acquired such responsibility – see cl 84(1).

19 Clause 20.

20 Clause 21.

1 See below.

2 Clause 26 – this provision is not unlike the current s 18(6) declaration, discussed ante at p 653.

3 Clause 41 (4).

4 Clause 23.

5 The Children Act 1989 would be amended to make it a *statutory* requirement to produce a care plan to the court when seeking a care order, and where that plan, and one that is subsequently modified, includes adoption, to give notice to a 'prescribed person'. See cl 87 inserting a new s 31A into the Children Act 1989.

6 Clause 23(6).

7 Clause 27.

vesting of parental responsibility would not permit a person to change the child's surname or to remove him from the UK (for more than a month) without leave of the court or the consent of each parent or guardian. Prospective adopters would not be permitted to cause the child to be brought up in any religious persuasion other than that (if any) in which the child would have been brought up by the parents.

The prospective adopters would not be *required* to allow contact (presumably they could, if they chose) save under a contact order under s 8 of the Children Act 1989. Furthermore, once a *placement order* is made, the court could not make *any* s 8 order other than for contact, nor could it make a supervision or child assessment order.[8] Like freeing orders, it would be possible to apply to revoke a placement order upon the application of a parent or guardian (with leave of the court) or by the agency authorised to place the child.[9]

When comparing freeing orders with the proposed placement orders it is important to appreciate that unlike freeing, the latter would not transfer parentage, but only operate to allocate parental responsibility either to the proposed adopters or to the agency if the child is not placed. In other words, the two orders are *conceptually* different. Furthermore, unlike freeing, agencies would *have* to obtain a placement order whenever they plan to *place* a child in care, or otherwise against the parent's wishes, for adoption, or to leave a child with persons (with whom he has previously been fostered) as prospective adopters. So far as children in care are concerned the obligation to seek a placement order arises as soon as it becomes part of the care plan. That could be as early as when the local authority are seeking a care order, in which case it resembles the former practice in wardship of seeking a committal to care 'with a view to adoption', or later if the care plan is subsequently changed to include a recommendation that the child be adopted.

There seem some clear advantages of the proposals over the current law. Having to obtain sanction either by parental agreement or by court order before a placement for adoption may be made would provide welcome certainty. In this regard it seems a much better idea to require agencies to obtain a placement order whenever adoption becomes part of the care plan in relation to a child in care rather than, as at present, allowing them to apply for a freeing order at their discretion. The proposed scheme also solves the current problems of the so-called 'legal limbo status' of the freed child and provides a clear and workable scheme for revocation and for the position following the breakdown of a placement. However, one consequential disadvantage is that because parents would retain their parental status until the final adoption order is made, an agency when placing a child even after a placement order, cannot guarantee to any potential adopter that the parents will not subsequently oppose the making of an order. On the other hand, given that in such circumstances parental opposition can only be made with court leave, which can only be given if it is satisfied that there has been a change of circumstances since the order, their chances of successfully opposing the application would be small.

The requirement that an order be sought immediately adoption becomes part of the care plan is an attempt to ensure that the court can consider the issue before the matter becomes a fait accompli. This in turn is designed to meet the argument that freeing is stacked against the birth parents. However, it is vital, if the system is to

8 Clause 28.
9 Clause 25.

work, that applications are both brought and heard promptly. The Bill does make it a duty for both court and agency to 'bear in mind that any delay in coming to the decision is likely to prejudice the child's welfare'[10] and vests both the power and the duty in the court to draw up timetables with a view to avoiding delay.[11] But it may be doubted whether this is sufficient to guarantee the end of the delays that have so bedevilled the freeing procedure. In particular one would wish to see much tighter time provisions when adoption becomes part of the care plan subsequent to the making of a care order. Unless the system can be significantly speeded up, it is likely to work no better than the current system.

Even if speed can be guaranteed, one wonders how much better off birth parents would actually be. An objection to the freeing procedure voiced by the Review of Adoption Law was that it failed to give adequate protection to the birth parents, in that the court is asked to resolve the question of parental agreement without looking at a particular (or proposed) placement, so that 'the readily apparent shortcomings in the care offered or likely to be offered in the future by a child's parents' may be unfavourably contrasted with 'the care likely to be offered by the hypothetically perfect adoptive parents'. The same objection can be levied at general placement orders. Moreover, the proposed grounds for dispensing with consent would also be significantly changed and weighted against the parents (the controlling principle being at all times the *paramountcy* of the child's welfare).[12]

C.   Procedure for the making of adoption orders

1.   THE CHILD MUST LIVE WITH THE APPLICANTS BEFORE THE MAKING OF AN ORDER

Before any adoption order may be made there has to have been a 'settling in' period so as to be able to assess whether such a placement would be in the child's interests.[13] In the case of agency placements[14] or applications by parents, step-parents or relatives, no order can be made unless the child is at least 19 weeks old and at all times during the preceding 13 weeks has had his home with the applicants or one of them. In other cases, ie where the child was originally fostered,[15] the child must be at least 12 months old and at all times during the preceding 12 months have had his home with the applicants or one of them.[16] It will be noted that these provisions prescribe the minimum period before which an

---

10 Clause 1(3).
11 Clause 82.
12 Clause 1(2) and see the discussion ante at pp 627 and 640–1.
13 Note that under s 30(1)(b) an agency may, having served due notice, end the placement by that agency. See further post, p 664.
14 Or placements made in pursuance of a High Court order.
15 It will be recalled that 'private' placements for adoption are unlawful: see ante, pp 620. A nominal fostering arrangement made with the intention that the child will be adopted is also an offence: see *Gatehouse v Robinson* [1986] 1 WLR 18, discussed ante, p 621. Note also *Re G (Adoption: Illegal Placement)* [1995] 1 FLR 403, CA at 409, in which Balcombe LJ, disagreeing with an earlier comment of Booth J in *Re ZHH (Adoption Application)* [1993] 1 FLR 83 at 85, held that s 13(2) cannot be read as empowering courts to make an adoption order notwithstanding the illegality of the placement.
16 Adoption Act 1976 s 13(1)–(2).

order may be made, but an adoption *application* may be made at any time. Under the proposed Adoption Bill, however, the probationary period, which for non-agency placements [17] (*including* for these purposes step-parents and relatives) would be reduced to six months,[18] must be satisfied before an *application* may be made.[19]

In determining with whom the child has his home, any absence at a hospital or boarding school and any other temporary absence,[20] is disregarded.[1] The possibility that the whole period could be spent away from the applicants' home is guarded against by the further provision that the agency placing him, or the local authority in non-agency placements, must have sufficient opportunities to see the child with the applicant or, in the case of a joint application, both applicants together in the home environment.[2] It has been held[3] that, though difficult to define with precision, 'home' must comprise some element of regular occupation (whether past, present, or intended for the future, even if intermittent) with some degree of permanency, based on some right of occupation whenever it is required: it is where you find the fixed comforts of a home; the fixed residence of a family or household. Though ultimately a question of fact to be decided in each case, a house that is merely visited by members of the family is unlikely to constitute a 'home' for these purposes. In all non-agency placements the 'home' must be in England or Wales,[4] though this does not mean that the applicants should be living or resident there at any particular time, provided the local authority is given sufficient opportunity to see the child in his 'home environment'.[5]

2. NOTICE TO LOCAL AUTHORITY MUST BE GIVEN IN NON-AGENCY PLACEMENTS

At one time, whenever the child was below the upper limit of compulsory school age, all applicants other than parents had to notify the local authority of their intention to apply for adoption. The purpose of such notice was to ensure the proper supervision of children placed for adoption, as it was the local authority's responsibility to visit the child and to satisfy itself as to his wellbeing. The Houghton Committee,[6] however, felt that where the placement had been made by an adoption agency the child's welfare could best be supervised by that agency.

---

17 And those made under the aegis of the High Court.
18 Clause 36(2).
19 But note that by cl 38 in the case of non-agency placements the applicants must either have the consent of the parent or guardian or have provided the child with a home for not less than three out of the preceding five years ending with the application, or have leave of the court.
20 Quaere whether this would include allowing the child to spend time with his parents: cf *Re CSC (An Infant)* [1960] 1 All ER 711 and *Re B (An Infant)* [1964] Ch 1, [1963] 3 All ER 125.
1 Adoption Act 1976 s 72(1A) added by the Children Act 1989 Sch 10, para 30(a).
2 Adoption Act 1976 s 13(3). The wording is regrettably vague. Presumably the agency or authority must have significant opportunity to see whether the proposed adoption is likely to be for the child's welfare, but cf *Re Y (Minors) (Adoption: Jurisdiction)* [1985] Fam 136, [1985] 3 All ER 33 where Sheldon J in effect refused to lay down how many visits may be necessary. Note also *Re WM (Adoption: Non Patrial)* [1997] 1 FLR 132, in which Johnson J held that s 13(3) did not prevent the making of an order in favour of applicants who had since separated.
3 *Re Y (Minors) (Adoption: Jurisdiction)*, supra.
4 In order to satisfy Adoption Act 1976 s 13(3)(b) and s 22(1).
5 See *Re Y*, supra.
6 At paras 237–239.

Following their recommendations, it is now only necessary to notify the local authority in cases where the child has not been placed for adoption by an adoption agency. In such cases the applicant must, not more than two years or less than three months before the order, give written[7] notice to the local authority within whose area the child has his home of the intention to apply for an adoption order.[8] Immediately notice is given the child becomes a 'protected child' and the local authority is under a duty to visit the child, to satisfy itself as to the child's wellbeing and to give such advice as to care and maintenance as may appear to be needed.[9]

Upon receipt of such notice the local authority must investigate the matter, in particular the suitability of the applicants, any other matter relevant to the child's long-term welfare and whether the placement was unlawful, and submit a report to the court.[10]

Although under the proposed Bill the formal status of 'protected child' would disappear, the basic scheme will continue to apply, save that in the case of local authority foster parents notice cannot be given to the local authority unless the child's home has been with them for at least three out of the preceding five years.[11] In all cases, upon notice being given the local authority must investigate the suitability of the applicants.[12]

3.   THE APPOINTMENT OF A REPORTING OFFICER OR GUARDIAN AD LITEM[13]

As soon as practicable after the making of an application, or at any subsequent stage, the court must appoint a reporting officer in cases where it appears that a parent or guardian is willing to agree to the adoption.[14] The reporting officer's duties are, inter alia:[15]

(1) to ensure that any parental agreement has been given freely and with a full understanding of what is involved;[16]

(2) to witness the parents' signature of the written agreement to the making of the order;

(3) to investigate all the circumstances relevant to that agreement; and

7 See the definition of 'notice' in the Adoption Act 1976 s 72(1).
8 Adoption Act 1976 s 22(1) and (1A) as added by the Children Act 1989 Sch 10, para 10(1). The two-year requirement was added by the 1989 Act and is in line with the amended provision under s 32(4) as to when a child ceases to be 'protected'.
9 Adoption Act 1976 s 32 and s 33. A child ceases to be 'protected' in the circumstances set out by s 32(4) (as amended by the Children Act 1989 Sch 10, para 18(4)).
10 Adoption Act 1976 s 22(2)–(3). Adoption agencies are under a similar obligation in respect of agency placements: s 23. If an agency wishes to remove a protected child, it should apply for an emergency protection order under Part V of the Children Act 1989, discussed ante, p 590.
11 Clause 39(7).
12 Clause 39(4)–(5).
13 See generally Monro and Forrester *The Guardian ad Litem* (2nd edn, 1995) ch 16.
14 Adoption Act 1976 s 65 and Adoption Rules 1984 r 5 (freeing) and r 17. Appointments are made from a panel established under the Guardians ad Litem and Reporting Officers (Panels) Regulations 1991 (issued pursuant to s 65A of the Adoption Act 1976, added by the Children Act 1989 Sch 10, para 29). They must not be employees of the agency involved in the proceedings: Adoption Act 1976 s 65(2).
15 Adoption Rules r 5(4), r 17(4).
16 This might be thought to import an obligation to inform and advise on the nature and consequences of an adoption order.

(4) in the case of freeing applications, to confirm that opportunity has been given to the parent to make a declaration that he no longer wishes to be involved in future questions about the child's adoption.

The reporting officer, must, on completion of his or her investigations, make a written report to the court drawing attention to any matters that may be of assistance. This report is confidential.

The court must appoint a guardian ad litem in cases where it appears that the parent or guardian is unwilling to agree to the adoption; it may do so if there are special reasons and it seems that the child's welfare requires it.[17] It therefore follows that if one parent agrees to the adoption but the other does not, both officers should be appointed. It also means that if a parent at first agrees but later changes his or her mind or vice versa, both officers will have to be appointed. The same person can act as a reporting officer and as a guardian.[18] Like reporting officers, guardians ad litem are generally selected from a panel, though in High Court proceedings the Official Solicitor may assume that role.[19]

The overall role of guardians is to safeguard the child's interests,[20] but more specifically, their duties are,[1] inter alia, to investigate the matters alleged in the application, any report made by the agency or local authority, any statement of facts on which the case for dispensing with agreement is based and any other matters that they consider relevant. Guardians also have to advise on whether the child should be present at the hearing and to perform such other duties as appear to them to be necessary or as the court may direct. On the completion of these duties the guardian must submit a confidential report to the court. Although the report is normally disclosed to the parties, it is within the court's discretion to withhold it. However, as the House of Lords held in *Re D (Minors) (Adoption Reports: Confidentiality)*,[2] non-disclosure should be the exception and not the rule and evidence should only be withheld from the parties where the court is satisfied that the case for it is compelling, that is:

(1) where disclosure involves a real possibility of significant harm to the child;
(2) where the child's interests point to non-disclosure, having balanced the interest in having the material properly tested against the magnitude of the risk that harm would occur and the gravity of the harm if it did occur; and
(3) the child's interests in non-disclosure are thought to be sufficient to outweigh the parties' interests in being able to look at and respond to the material.

4. THE APPLICANT'S POSITION PENDING AN APPLICATION[3]

Understandably, the 1976 Act draws a distinction between those cases where only the placement has been made and those where a formal application to adopt has

---

17 Adoption Act 1976 s 65 and Adoption Rules r 6, r 18.
18 Adoption Rules r 6(3), r 18(3).
19 He will not normally be involved in cases where the application is proceeding with the consent of the birth parents: *Practice Direction* [1986] 2 All ER 832.
20 Adoption Act 1976 s 65(1)(a).
 1 Pursuant to Adoption Rules r 6(6), r 18(6).
 2 [1996] AC 593 at 615, [1995] 4 All ER 385 at 399, per Lord Mustill. For a case where, applying the '*Re D*' test, documents were withheld from the mother see *Re K (Adoption: Disclosure of Information)* [1997] 2 FLR 74.
 3 See generally Adoption Law Review, Discussion Paper No 3, Part 8.

been made to the court. So far as agency placements are concerned, until an application to adopt has been made, the agency can end the placement by simple notice.[4] It has been held[5] that this power of removal vests a discretion in the local authority such that the court has no power to intervene and review the merits of the decision. Accordingly, the court will not normally entertain actions[6] by the would-be adopters designed to challenge the removal. This is not to say that the potential adopters are entirely remediless, for it has also been held[7] that the decision to serve a s 30 notice is amenable to judicial review, which allows the court to investigate the procedural correctness of the decision, though not its intrinsic merits.

Once an application to adopt has been made, then the adoption agency cannot, without court leave, remove the child it has placed for adoption.[8] Similarly, once a *parent* has agreed to the making of an order, he or she cannot without leave of the court remove the child against the applicants' will during the pendency of the application.[9] In the case of a freeing application, if the child is in the care of a local authority adoption agency making the application,[10] the parent is barred from removing the child even if he has not consented to the application.[11] Where leave is sought, the court is entitled to consider the merits of a removal, with first consideration being given to the need to safeguard and promote the child's welfare.[12]

Greater protection is given to applicants with whom the child has had his home for five years; in such a case no one is entitled to remove the child from the applicants' home against their will without the court's leave once an application has been made, or for three months after notice has been given to the local authority of an intention to apply.[13] This provision was designed particularly to protect foster parents by preventing parents from seeking the return of their child merely to stop the adoption.[14] Even a local authority in whose care the child is cannot remove the child once an application is pending. However, if the applicants' sole purpose is to prevent the authority from removing the child, an adoption order is unlikely to be made.[15]

---

4   Adoption Act 1976 s 30(1)(b) Under s 30(3) the child should be removed within seven days following the notice. Note that the potential adopter can also end the placement by notice: s 30(1)(a).

5   *Re C and F (Adoption: Removal Notice)* [1997] 1 FLR 190, CA.

6   Viz an application for an interim order under s 25 (discussed further below at p 670), as in *Re C and F*, supra, or wardship, as in *Re W (A Minor) (Adoption Agency: Wardship)* [1990] Fam 156, [1990] 2 All ER 463.

7   *R v Devon County Council, ex p O (Adoption)* [1997] 2 FLR 388, in which judicial review was granted because of the local authority's failure to consult the applicants prior to serving the notice and to take into account the child's own wishes and feelings.

8   Adoption Act 1976 s 30(1)(b) and (2).

9   Adoption Act 1976 s 27(1). It will be noted that the prospective adopters can agree to the child's return, but see the criticism in Bevan and Parry *Children Act 1975*, op cit, para 132.

10   Ibid, s 27(2) and s 27(2A) added by the Children Act 1989 Sch 10, para 14.

11   Adoption Act 1976 s 27(2).

12   *Re C (A Minor) (Adoption)* [1994] 2 FLR 513, CA, applying s 6 of the 1976 Act.

13   Ibid, s 28.

14   See the Houghton Report, at paras 139–47 and 161–4. The Committee abandoned their original proposal that after five years foster parents should be able to apply for adoption with the local authority's agreement (but without the parents' agreement) because this might have led foster parents to weaken links between parent and child, caused anxiety to parents, and inhibited them from placing children in care as a consequence.

15   See *Re H (A Minor) (Adoption)* [1985] FLR 519, CA, and see the comments thereon in [1985] JSWL at 364, [1985] Fam Law at 135 and (1989) Adoption and Fostering, Vol 9, No 1 at 59.

D. Jurisdiction, functions and powers of the court

1. JURISDICTION

An adoption order or an order freeing the child for adoption may be made by the High Court, a county court or magistrates' court.[16] In general applicants can choose the level of court in which they wish to proceed.[17] In practice, most orders are made by county courts.[18] Proceedings can be transferred from one county court to another and from a county court to the High Court and vice versa.[19] Applications started in a magistrates' court are heard by the family proceedings court, [20] and under the Children (Allocation of Proceedings) Order 1991[1] there is power to transfer cases to the county court.

2. FUNCTIONS OF THE COURT

The court must be satisfied about three things:[2]

- that the order, if made, will be for the child's welfare;
- that every parent or guardian of the child freely, and with full understanding of what is involved, agrees unconditionally to the making of the order (unless his agreement has been dispensed with); and
- that no unauthorised payments or reward for the adoption have been made or agreed upon.

We have already considered the second of these issues but the first and the third require further elaboration.

---

16 Adoption Act 1976 s 62. Only the High Court has jurisdiction: (i) if the child is not in Great Britain when the application is made (Adoption Act 1976 s 62(3)); (ii) if the application is for a Convention Adoption Order (ibid, s 62(4)) (discussed post, p 679); or (iii) if the placement would otherwise be unlawful (ibid, s 11(1)(b)); see also *Re G (Adoption: Illegal Placement)* [1995] 1 FLR 403, CA. It would also seem advisable to apply to the High Court in cases where illegal payments have been made: cf *Re Adoption Application (Payment for Adoption)* [1987] Fam 81, [1987] 2 All ER 826; *Re An Adoption Application* [1992] 1 FLR 341, and *Re AW (Adoption Application)* [1993] 1 FLR 62.

17 Given that Art 4 of the Children (Allocation of Proceedings) Order 1991 provides that applications for the discharge or variation of an order should be made to the court that made it, it can be argued that, in the case of children subject to a care order, applications to adopt should be made to the court that made the care order, since an adoption will end the order. Such an interpretation would mean that most agency adoption applications would have to be made in the magistrates' court, which would be both contrary to the evident practice and the statement by Sheldon J in *Re PB (A Minor) (Application to Free for Adoption)* [1985] FLR 394 at 396, that a magistrates' court might be thought to be the least suitable tribunal to hear lengthily-contested cases. It is thought that Art 4 does not apply because an adoption order terminates *any* other prior order and is not therefore to be regarded as specifically discharging a care order: cf Clarke Hall and Morrison at 3[82]. A magistrates' court must refuse to make an order if it considers the matter would be more conveniently dealt with by the High Court: Adoption Act 1976 s 63(3).

18 Under the Allocation Rules Arts 14 and 17, applications commenced at the county court start in the divorce county court and must be transferred to a family hearing centre if the application is opposed. In 1996 202 (four per cent) applications were made to the High Court, 4,482 (82 per cent) in the county court and 772 (14 per cent) in the magistrates' court: *Judicial Statistics 1996,* Table 5.4.

19 Arts 10 and 12. The High Court similarly has power to transfer cases to the county court: Art 13.

20 Children Act 1989 s 92.

1 Art 8.

2 Adoption Act 1976 s 6, s 16 and s 24(2).

With regard to the first issue it needs to be appreciated that adoption is more than just determining with whom the child is to live. As Sir Stephen Brown P put it in *Re B (Adoption Order: Nationality)*:[3]

'Adoption is a very serious matter indeed. It confers a new status on the person adopted. It takes that person into a new family'.

The principal benefit of adoption is the long-term security that it confers, thus satisfying the adopters' need to know that the child is a full member of the family and the child's need to know that he or she is fully the child of these parents and that nothing can happen to take him or her away. Accordingly the court, when investigating whether adoption is for the child's welfare, should explore other options and if it finds that a residence order would better secure the child's long-term future, as for example where the child opposes the adoption, then it should make that order instead.[4]

Although 'welfare' is a sufficiently wide term to include material benefits conferred by adoption, it is important not to confuse the purpose of adoption[5] with the benefits of rights of abode and citizenship of this country. It has long been clear that there must be a genuine intention that the applicants should stand in loco parentis to the child. An order will be refused where it is clear, for example, that the real motive for the application is to enable the child (particularly, if he has nearly attained his majority) to acquire British citizenship rather than to promote his welfare.[6] Notwithstanding that an order can only be made in respect of a 'child' and that under s 6 of the Adoption Act 1976 the court's first consideration in making an adoption order is the child's welfare *throughout his childhood*, a benefit during minority is *not* a condition precedent to the making of an order, while a benefit accruing after majority[7] is a relevant factor to be taken into account when deciding whether to make an order.[8] As we have seen,[9] under the Adoption Bill the proposed welfare principle expressly includes benefits accruing into adulthood.[10]

With regard to illegal payments, s 24(2) directs that a court shall not make an adoption order unless it is satisfied that the applicants have not committed an offence under s 57. Section 57 outlaws any payment or promise of payment for or in consideration of adoption, giving any agreement for the adoption, handing over

---

3 [1998] 1 FLR 965 at 969.

4 See eg *Re M (Adoption or Residence Order)* [1998] 1 FLR 570, CA, discussed ante, pp 646–7.

5 See eg *Re WM (Adoption: Non Patrial)* [1997] 1 FLR 132 where financial advantage to the child being adopted was taken into account. See also *Re (An Infant)* [1963] 1 All ER 531 at 534. If the child has a substantial connection with a foreign country (eg if he is domiciled there or is a foreign national), one of the matters to be taken into account in deciding whether the order will be for his benefit is whether it will be recognised in that country: *Re B (S) (An Infant)* [1968] Ch 204, [1967] 3 All ER 629.

6 *Re J (Adoption: Non Patrial)* [1998] 1 FLR 225, CA, explaining further *Re H (Adoption: Non Patrial)* [1996] 2 FLR 187, CA; *Re B (Adoption Order: Nationality)* [1998] 1 FLR 965; *Re K (A Minor) (Adoption Order Nationality)* [1995] Fam 38 [1994] 3 All ER 553, CA; *Re W (A Minor)* [1986] Fam 54, [1985] 3 All ER 449, CA. Where a UK citizen proposes to adopt a foreign child, notice should be given to the Home Office so that the Secretary of State may, if he so wishes, be added as a party: see *Re W*, supra at p 62 and p 454 respectively; and *R v Secretary of State for Health, ex p Luff* [1992] 1 FLR 59.

7 For example, the benefit of having a secure home and status, which could be particularly important if, as in *Re D*, the child is mentally handicapped.

8 *Re D (A Minor) (Adoption Order: Validity)* [1991] Fam 137, [1991] 3 All ER 461, CA.

9 See ante, p 627.

10 Clause 1(2).

the child with a view to adoption or for the making of any arrangements for the adoption. The scope of the offence is by no means clear,[11] but it means even if a prima facie offence has been committed it is within the court's powers *retrospectively* to 'authorise' the payments and to make the order.[12]

Under cl 42 of the proposed Adoption Bill, although payments will continue to be an offence, there would be no specific embargo on the court's powers to make an order.

3. THE COURT'S POWERS

The power to add terms and conditions

Under s 12(6) of the Adoption Act 1976 an adoption order (but not a freeing order)[13] 'may contain such terms and conditions as the court thinks fit'. Before the Children Act 1989 this power was the only means by which a court could make any order additional to the adoption order and as such had some importance, particularly as it was the legal vehicle by which the courts came to accept that it was consistent with adoption to provide for some regime of continuing contact between the child and his or her birth family.[14] Since the 1989 Act, however, the court may now make s 8 orders in adoption proceedings.[15] Consequently, the role of s 12(6) has become marginalised. The leading modern case is *Re S (A Minor) (Blood Transfusion: Adoption Order Condition)*,[16] which concerned the desirability of imposing a condition upon adopters,[17] who were Jehovah's Witnesses, that they would not withhold their consent to a blood transfusion being given to the child if advised that it was necessary by a medical practitioner. It was held that such a condition should not be *imposed* upon unwilling adopters, for (quite apart from the practical difficulties of enforcing it)[18] it was generally desirable for the child to become as near as possible the lawful child of the adopting parents and a condition that derogated from that should not therefore be imposed. In Staughton LJ's view, the imposition of conditions should be 'very rare'.[19]

---

11 There is uncertainty, for example, as to whether payments for home study reports or for fees for foreign lawyers constitutes an offence: see eg *Re C (a Minor) (Adoption: Legality)* (1998) Times, 4 June; *Re An Adoption Application* [1992] 1 FLR 341; and *Re WM (Adoption: Non Patrial)* [1997] 1 FLR 132, which held they were – but cf *Re Adoption Application (Non Patrial: Breach of Procedures)* [1993] 1 FLR 947 and *Re AW (Adoption Application)* [1993] 1 FLR 62, which held they were not. There is also a conflict as to whether payments abroad can constitute an offence: cf *Re An Adoption Application*, supra, which held they can – and *Re A (Adoption Placement)* [1988] 1 WLR 229; *Re AW*, supra; and *Re Adoption Application (Non Patrial: Breach of Procedures)*, supra, which held that they cannot.
12 See *Re G (Adoption: Illegal Placement)* [1995] 1 FLR 403, CA at 405 per Balcombe LJ (obiter) and *Re Adoption Application (Payment for Adoption)* [1987] Fam 81, [1987] 2 All ER 826; *Re An Adoption Application* [1992] 1 FLR 341; *Re AW*, supra; *Re MW (Adoption Surrogacy)* [1995] 2 FLR 759; and *Re WM*, supra. But cf *Re C (A Minor) (Adoption Application)* [1993] 1 FLR 87.
13 See the definition of 'adoption order' in s 72(1) of the Adoption Act 1976 and see *Re C (Minors) (Adoption)* [1992] 1 FLR 115, CA at 129 per Balcombe LJ.
14 Adoption with contact is discussed below at p 669.
15 See further pp 668ff.
16 [1994] 2 FLR 416, CA.
17 In fact, although the judge said he was imposing a condition, under the terms of the order the adopters were required to give an undertaking.
18 In theory s 12(6) conditions are enforceable through the contempt powers.
19 Ibid at 421.

Re S might also be compared with the earlier decision, *Re D (A Minor) (Adoption Order: Validity)*,[20] in which the Court of Appeal held that courts can limit or impose conditions upon the parental responsibility that would otherwise vest in the adopters,[1] but they cannot thereby impose terms that would grant to adopters more extensive rights than the natural parents would have had; and hence they could not under s 12(6) grant an injunction restraining grandparents from having further contact with the child.

It seems clear therefore that the scope for invoking s 12(6) is severely limited. Accordingly, wherever additional orders are thought desirable they should be sought under s 8 of the Children Act. Under the proposed Adoption Bill there would be no power equivalent to s 12(6).[2]

The power to make s 8 orders under the Children Act 1989

Proceedings under the Adoption Act 1976 are designated 'family proceedings' for the purposes of the Children Act 1989.[3] Consequently, courts are empowered, either upon application, or upon their own motion, to make s 8 orders.[4] It is generally accepted that s 8 orders may be made instead of or in addition to an adoption or freeing order.[5] Unlike adoption, in deciding whether to make a s 8 order courts are bound to treat the child's welfare as the paramount (not first) consideration pursuant to s 1(1) of the 1989 Act.

(a)   Adoption or residence order

Although there is no express statutory *duty* in adoption and freeing applications to consider making alternative orders under s 8 and in particular a residence order,[6] the clear implication of the Court of Appeal's decision in *Re M (Adoption or Residence Order)*[7] is that the court cannot properly determine whether adoption is in the child's interests unless it has explored the other alternatives. Under the proposed Adoption Bill[8] it would clearly be the duty of the court to consider its alternative powers.

As we have previously discussed,[9] adoption is more than simply determining with whom the child is to live. If, therefore, the change of status and permanence brought about by the adoption is not thought appropriate, perhaps because (as in *Re M*) the child objects or where the applicants are relatives or step-parents, then a residence order might be thought preferable.

20 [1991] Fam 137, [1991] 3 All ER 461, CA.
1 For example, that the child be brought up in a particular religion. Maidment 'Access and Family Adoptions' (1977) 40 MLR 293 argues that that is what the statutory provision was solely designed for.
2 See the notes to cl 40.
3 Children Act 1989 s 8(4)(d).
4 Ibid, s 10(1)(b), discussed ante, pp 446–7.
5 Section 12(3)(aa) of the Adoption Act 1976 (added by the Children Act 1989 Sch 10, para 3(3)) provides that an adoption order extinguishes 'any order under the Children Act 1989', but this presumably operates to extinguish any *previous* order: White, Carr and Lowe *A Guide to the Children Act 1989* (1990) at para 11.22 and the Adoption Law Review, Discussion Paper No 1, note 111.
6 The court cannot normally make an adoption *and* residence order, as they are mutually inconsistent. But compare *Re AB (Adoption: Joint Residence)* [1996] 1 FLR 27, discussed ante, p 629, in which an adoption order was granted to one cohabiting applicant and a joint residence order was made in favour of the couple.
7 [1998] 1 FLR 570, CA, discussed ante, pp 646–7.
8 See cl 1(5).
9 Ante at p 666.

(b) Adoption and Contact

The first reported case in which it was held that continued contact was not fundamentally inconsistent with adoption was *Re J (A Minor) (Adoption Order: Conditions)*.[10] In that case Rees J said, 'the general rule which forbids contact between an adopted child and his natural parent may be disregarded in an exceptional case where a court is satisfied that by so doing the welfare of the child may be best promoted'.[11] The access order was made to avoid lengthy litigation which would otherwise have damaged the child. This decision was authoritatively confirmed by the House of Lords in *Re C (A Minor) (Adoption Order: Conditions)*,[12] which concerned a child who was in long-term care. The mother refused to agree to her daughter's adoption on the ground that it would weaken the child's relationship with her brother. The judge held that the relationship between the siblings should be preserved and refused to make the order. The applicants appealed and sought a condition attached to the adoption that the brother should have continuing access to his sister. Overruling the Court of Appeal, the House of Lords held that the court had power to attach such a condition where it was clearly in the child's interest to do so. Lord Ackner stressed that to safeguard and promote the child's welfare it was important that the court should retain 'the maximum flexibility given to it by the Act'. However, he added:[13]

'The cases rightly stress that in normal circumstances it is desirable that there should be a complete break, but that each case has to be considered on its own particular facts. No doubt the court will not, except in exceptional cases, impose terms or conditions as to access to members of the child's natural family to which the adopting parents do not agree . . . Where no agreement is forthcoming the court will, with very rare exceptions, have to choose between making an adoption order without terms or conditions as to access, or to refuse to make such an order and seek to safeguard access through some other machinery, such as wardship. To do otherwise would be merely inviting future and almost immediate litigation.'

Lord Ackner further observed that a distinction could properly be drawn between contact with natural parents and contact with other relatives, the former being harder to justify than the latter, if an adoption order is to be made.

In theory the power to make provision for post-adoption contact can still be exercised under s 12(6), but in practice, since the Children Act, the issue is invariably considered under the court's powers to make s 8 contact orders. In fact it is only via s 8 that the court can make provision for contact as well as making a *freeing* order.[14]

Notwithstanding this change of legal regime, the courts continue to be reluctant to *impose* a contact order against the wishes of the adopters and, where they are agreed that contact should continue, it has been held[15] that there is no need for an order.[16] Although, given the general difficulty of enforcing contact orders, it is

---

10 [1973] Fam 106, [1973] 2 All ER 410.
11 Ibid at pp 115 and 418 respectively.
12 [1989] AC 1, [1988] 1 All ER 705, HL.
13 Ibid at pp 17–18 and 712–13 respectively. See also the comments of the Adoption Law Review. Discussion Paper No 1, paras 71–72.
14 Section 12(6) does not apply to freeing orders. See eg *Re A (A Minor) (Adoption: Contact Order)* [1993] 2 FLR 645, CA, which draws attention to the change of law.
15 *Re T (Adoption: Contact)* [1995] 2 FLR 251, CA.
16 Though this is not to say that orders are never made: see eg *Re O (Transracial Adoption: Contact)* [1995] 2 FLR 597.

understandable that the courts should be hesitant about imposing such orders on unwilling adopters, it is evident that the objection goes deeper than that, for, as Butler-Sloss LJ said in *Re T (Adoption: Consent)*,[17] 'the finality of adoption and the importance of letting the new family find its feet ought not to be threatened in any way by an order [for contact] in this case'. This reluctance to limit the independence of the new adoptive family is even more pronounced when considering the making of contact orders with freeing orders, since that would involve binding potential adopters to a regime with which they may not agree and that in turn could make it even more difficult for the adoption agency to place the child.[18]

It has to be said that the case law lies at odds with the increasing de facto practice of open adoption. In this respect, however, note should be taken of *Re T (Adoption Children: Contact)*,[19] in which Balcombe LJ held that adopters cannot agree to indirect contact and then simply resile from it without explanation. Where they do, the court might well be disposed to grant the former parents leave to apply for a s 8 contact order. In this case leave was given, the court being satisfied that the proposed application would not disrupt the children's lives, although all that was in issue was the adopters' promise to provide the birth parents with annual reports.[20]

Interim orders

Instead of making the order applied for, the court may, pursuant to s 25,[1] make an interim order to last for not more than two years, the effect of which is to give parental responsibility of the child to the applicant upon such terms for the maintenance of the child and otherwise as the court thinks fit. The section requires the court to be satisfied that the parents' or guardians' agreement has been given or dispensed with and, if the child was not placed by an adoption agency, three months' notice must have been given to the local authority.

As Butler-Sloss LJ said in *Re C and F (Adoption: Removal Notice)*:[2]

'Section 25 is not intended to be an order to preserve the status quo at an early stage or to define the interim position of the children and the parties. It has a different purpose. It is there to give additional powers to the court where all the necessary matters have been dealt with at a substantive hearing of the adoption application, including the requirements as to the residence and the decision about the agreement of the parent if he/she does not consent, but there is still some doubt about the wisdom of making the final and conclusive adoption order.'

---

17 [1995] 2 FLR 251 at 257.
18 See *Re P (Adoption: Freeing Order)* [1994] 2 FLR 1000, CA; and *Re H (A Minor) (Freeing Order)* [1993] 2 FLR 325, CA. A further difficulty of granting a contact order with freeing is that, unless an application for a full adoption order has been made, there is arguably no means of varying the contact order. See *Re C (Contact: Jurisdiction)* [1995] 1 FLR 777, CA. But see the comments in White, Carr and Lowe *Children Act in Practice* (2nd edn) at paras 5.41 – 5.43.
19 [1995] 2 FLR 792, CA.
20 Compare *Re E (Adopted Child: Contact: Leave)* [1995] 1 FLR 57 where leave was refused to the former parents to apply for a s 8 order to enforce a promise made at the dispensing stage of an adoption hearing that photographs and news about the child's schooling would be forwarded to them. It was held that the proper course would have been to apply to cancel the order or to appeal it on the ground that it was flawed.
1 As amended by the Children Act 1989 Sch 10, para 11. By s 25(2) the period laid down in the original order may be extended, provided that the total period is not greater than two years.
2 [1997] 1 FLR 190, CA at 195.

A good, if rare, example of its use is *Re AW (Adoption Application)*,[3] in which Bracewell J made an interim order in favour of elderly applicants who had breached both the provisions governing placements and payments, but where the welfare of the child nevertheless demanded that she should stay with them. The interim order provided for further reports pending a final hearing. It has also been used when the court was uncertain whether the child should be adopted or go to live with a parent,[4] although it must be rarely desirable for interim orders to be made in such circumstances because of the uncertainty which they produce. In *Re C and F*[5] it was held that s 25 gave no jurisdiction to grant an injunction or to stay the removal of a child on the otherwise lawful giving of notice of removal by the agency pursuant to s 30(1).[6]

Following implementation of the Children Act 1989, The Adoption Law Review[7] could see no role for interim orders, commenting that they are 'a relic' of the days when s 8 alternatives were not open to the court. There is no such power in the proposed Adoption Bill.

Refusal to make an order

Notwithstanding the court's power to do so, in practice adoption and freeing applications are rarely refused. 96 per cent of adoption applications by non-relatives sampled in the *Pathways Study* resulted in an order being made. No orders were actually refused; the remaining four per cent were withdrawn or adjourned.[8]

If the court refuses to make any order at all (or if at any stage the application is withdrawn) and the child was placed for adoption by an adoption agency, he must be returned to that agency within seven days.[9] There is no statutory obligation to return the child in other cases.[10] The reason for the difference is that in the first case the agency concerned must obviously try to find other suitable applicants, whereas in the second there may be good reasons for permitting the applicants to retain care and control even though an adoption order has not been made. This might occur, for example, if the court refuses to make the order because the child's mother withdraws her agreement; if she wishes to look after the child she will need to seek a residence order, the outcome of which is dependent upon the welfare principle.[11]

The former power to make a supervision or care order upon a refusal to make an adoption order has been repealed.[12] Instead, as in other 'family proceedings', the court may, if it thinks it appropriate, direct a local authority to investigate the

---

3 [1993] 1 FLR 62.
4 *S v Huddersfield Borough Council* [1975] Fam 113, [1974] 3 All ER 296, CA.
5 Supra.
6 Discussed ante, p 664.
7 See Adoption Law Review, Discussion Paper No 3, para 199.
8 81 per cent of step-parent applications resulted in an order and none was refused. Perhaps more strikingly, given that they are more often contested, 84 per cent of freeing applications were successful with only two applications (one per cent) being refused: *Pathways to Adoption*, op cit, 2.9. More strikingly still, it was found that it made no difference to the outcome whether the application was contested or not: see the Freeing Report, op cit, Table 3.43.
9 Adoption Act 1976 s 30(3). This also applies if an interim order expires without a full order being made. The court may extend the time for returning the child for a period not exceeding six weeks: ibid, s 30(6). This power might be exercised, eg if unsuccessful applicants wished to appeal.
10 Unless the child is in the care of a local authority and the authority demands his return: Adoption Act 1976 s 31(1).
11 See ante, p 668.
12 Adoption Act 1976 s 26, repealed by the Children Act 1989 Sch 15.

child's circumstances with a view to the authority's deciding whether or not to bring care proceedings.[13]

If the application for adoption is refused, the applicants may normally make a further application only if the court is satisfied that, because of a change of circumstances or for some other reason, this is proper.[14]

Adoption of children abroad

Persons who are not domiciled in England and Wales, Scotland or Northern Ireland (in whose favour therefore a full adoption order cannot be made),[15] but who wish to remove a child out of the country to obtain an adoption order under their lex domicilii, can apply to the High Court or county court for an order giving them parental responsibility for the child.[16] The court has jurisdiction to make such an order only if it would have had jurisdiction to make a full order had the applicant possessed the relevant domicile.[17] The order authorises the applicant to remove the child out of the country,[18] but it does not affect devolution of property or the child's citizenship. The court has no power to make an interim order or an order freeing the child for adoption.[19]

Revocation of adoption orders

Notwithstanding that adoption orders are generally irrevocable, there is one circumstance where express provision is made to revoke an order, ie in the case of a person adopted by the mother or father alone who has subsequently become legitimated by his parents' marriage. In such a case, s 52 permits 'any of the parties concerned' to apply for a revocation. Applications should be made to the court that made the original order. This power would be retained under the proposed Adoption Bill.[20]

Apart from this statutory power of revocation, there is a right of appeal both against the making and the refusal to make an adoption order.[1] In truly exceptional cases leave to appeal may be granted out of time. In *Re M (A Minor) (Adoption)*,[2] for example, a father agreed to an adoption of his children by his former wife and her new husband in ignorance of the fact that she was terminally ill. It was held in this 'very exceptional case' that in the children's interests the time for appeal would

13 Under s 37 of the Children Act 1989, discussed ante, p 455. This change is in line with the general policy of the 1989 Act that children should be committed into local authority care only if the threshold criteria laid down by the Children Act 1989 s 31 have been satisfied.
14 Adoption Act 1976 s 24(1). A court can, however, stipulate that the provision does not apply: see *Re V (A Minor) (Adoption: Consent)* [1987] Fam 57, [1986] 1 All ER 752, CA.
15 Unless they are domiciled in the Channel Islands or Isle of Man.
16 Adoption Act 1976 s 55, as amended by the Children Act 1989 Sch 10, para 22.
17 But if the applicant is a parent, a step-parent or relative, or if the child was placed by an adoption agency, the child must be 32 weeks old and have had his home with the applicants for the preceding 26 weeks: Adoption Act s 55(2).
18 Which is otherwise an offence: Adoption Act 1976 s 56. See *Re C (Minors) (Wardship: Adoption)* [1989] 1 All ER 395, CA.
19 Adoption Act 1976 s 55(2).
20 See cl 49.
1 Appeals from magistrates' courts lie to the High Court: Adoption Act 1976 s 63(2); in other cases to the Court of Appeal. An order made by a magistrates' or county court can be questioned by judicial review. As a matter of practice, when appealing against an adoption order the applicant should immediately seek a stay and expedited hearing: *Re PJ (Adoption: Practice on Appeal)* [1998] 2 FLR 252, CA.
2 [1991] 1 FLR 458, CA.

be extended and the adoption orders set aside on the ground that the father's ignorance of his wife's condition vitiated his consent. Similarly, leave to appeal out of time was granted and the adoption set aside in *Re K (Adoption and Wardship)*,[3] which was an horrific case involving a Bosnian 'orphan' who originally had been found beneath the bodies of persons thought to be her parents. The child had been allowed to come to England for medical treatment, and an English couple began to foster her after she left hospital. This couple then applied to adopt her at a time when they knew that the child's grandfather and aunt had been traced and wanted the child back and that the Bosnian Government had stopped all adoptions from that country. In the original adoption proceedings the judge had not deemed it necessary to appoint a guardian ad litem, nor was any attempt made to contact the child's guardian in Bosnia. In these extraordinary circumstances amounting to a fundamental breach of natural justice, the Court of Appeal set the order aside.[4]

Re M and *Re K* are best looked upon as truly exceptional cases and certainly not as precedents laying down a general power to set orders aside. To put these cases in context we must consider *Re B (Adoption: Jurisdiction To Set Aside)*,[5] in which the applicant, then in his thirties and whose origins were Arabic, unsuccessfully applied some 35 years after the order was made to set aside his adoption by a Jewish couple. As the Court of Appeal made clear, there is no general inherent power to set an adoption aside and, in the absence of procedural irregularities or mistakes, no power exists to revoke an order. To hold otherwise would be, in Swinton Thomas LJ's words, to 'undermine the whole basis upon which adoption orders are made, namely that they are final and for life as regards the adopters, the natural parents and the child'.

The only other way the adoption status can be changed is by a second adoption, but this is not to say that even former parents have no other remedies, since the making of an adoption order does not prevent the normal application of private and public law in relation to the adoptive family. Former parents, like anyone else, can with court leave seek to apply for s 8 orders in respect of the adopted child. However, leave will not normally be given and in any event would require, in Thorpe J's words,[6] 'some fundamental change of circumstances' before permitting the re-opening of crucial issues such as contact and a fortiori, residence. Nevertheless there is at least one reported example of a birth parent subsequently obtaining an order that the adopted child should live with her.[7]

Registration of adoption, the Adoption Contact Register and information about birth records[8]

The Registrar General is obliged to keep a separate register of adoptions.[9] Records are also kept enabling connections between entries in this register and the register

---

3 [1997] 2 FLR 221, CA.

4 In the subsequent re-hearing (see [1997] 1 FLR 230) Sir Stephen Brown P held that although the adoption application should be refused, nevertheless care and control should be granted to the foster parents together with substantial contact to the child's birth family, with the child herself remaining a ward of court.

5 [1995] Fam 239, [1995] 3 All ER 333, CA.

6 *Re C (A Minor) (Adopted Child: Contact)* [1993] Fam 210, [1993] 1 FLR 341.

7 See *Re O (A Minor) (Wardship: Adopted Child)* [1978] 2 All ER 27, CA, where the application succeeded; cf *Re C (A Minor) (Wardship: Adopted Child)* [1985] FLR 1114, CA.

8 See generally Adoption Law Review, Discussion Paper No 1, paras 73–81 and the Department of Health's *Guidance and Regulations*, Vol 9, ch 3.

9 Adoption Act 1976 s 50.

of births to be traced, but these records may be searched or information given to third parties only with the leave of the court.[10] There is a conflict of view as to the proper test to be applied when considering whether to give leave. On the one hand, in *Re H (Adoption: Disclosure of Information)*,[11] in which the applicant wanted an Agency to be able to trace her half-brother so as to inform him that she suffered from a genetically transmitted disease, Thorpe J held that the appropriate test was for the applicant to establish a case of sufficient weight and strength as to persuade the judge of the reasonableness of the order sought. On the other, in *D v Registrar General*,[12] in which the birth mother sought an order against the Registrar General to provide her with updating non-identifying information about her adopted daughter, Sir Stephen Brown P held that the appropriate test imported an exceptional element and that in any event it was necessary to show a benefit to the child.[13]

Adoptees themselves, once they are over the age of 18 may, without court leave, obtain a copy of their birth certificate, which means that they may be able to trace their birth parents.[14] There is no right of access to birth records for anyone under the age of 18, but any person under that age intending to marry in England and Wales may obtain information indicating whether or not the parties are likely to be related within the prohibited degrees.[15]

The right of access to birth records, which was introduced following the Houghton Committee's recommendations,[16] is of no assistance to those who fail to discover that they are adopted or where no records exist. It may be of little assistance to those adopted a long time ago.

Access to birth records enables some adopted persons to trace and make contact with their birth parents, but until recently it was difficult to discover whether that contact would be welcome. In this regard the newly created Adoption Contact Register is important.[17] The purpose of the register is 'to put adopted people and their birth parents or other relatives in touch with each other where this is what they both want. The register provides a safe and confidential way for birth parents and other relatives to assure an adopted person that contact would be welcome and

10 Ibid, s 50 and Sch 1. The court for this purpose means the court making the adoption order, the High Court or the Westminster County Court.
11 [1995] 1 FLR 236. Thorpe J also held that applications should *not* be made ex parte, but instead proper notice should be given to the Registrar General.
12 [1997] 1 FLR 715, CA.
13 One example might be where the child is entitled to a gift under a disposition taking effect before the adoption order but not vesting until after it had been made.
14 Ibid, s 51. By 1990 it was estimated that 33,000 adopted children had taken advantage of this provision: Adoption Law Review, Discussion Paper No 1, note 140. This, however, is not an absolute right: see *R v Registrar General, ex p Smith* [1991] 2 QB 393, [1991] 2 All ER 88, CA (where access was denied because of the danger of the birth mother being physically harmed by the applicant). Note also *Re X (A Minor) (Adoption Details: Disclosure)* [1994] Fam 174, [1994] 3 All ER 373, CA, in which it was held that the court should, under its inherent powers, order the restriction of disclosure of the details to be entered in the adoption register to prevent a violent birth mother from tracing her adopted child. See also *Re W (Adoption details: Disclosure)* [1998] 2 FLR 625.
15 Ibid, s 51(2).
16 Para 303. Controversially, this recommendation was introduced with retrospective effect. However, those adopted before 12 November 1975 are required to see a counsellor before they can be given information: ibid, s 51(7)(b), as amended by the Children Act 1989 Sch 10, para 20(2).
17 Under the Adoption Act 1976 s 51A (added by the Children Act 1989 Sch 10, para 21) the Registrar General is required to maintain such a register. In fact the register is operated on behalf of the Registrar General by the Office for National Statistics. For the operation of the register see generally Mullender and Kearn *I'm Here Waiting* (1997).

give a contact address.'[18] The register comprises two parts:[19] Part I, upon which are maintained the name and address of any adopted person who is over 18 and has a copy of his birth certificate and who wishes to contact a relative; and Part II, upon which are entered, subject to certain prescribed conditions,[20] the current address and identifying details of a relative[1] who wishes to contact an adopted person.

Surprisingly, there is no requirement for counselling, nor is there a facility for exchanging limited information, such as medical information.

E.   The legal consequences of the making of an adoption order[2]

1.   THE GENERAL EFFECT

The Adoption Act 1976 s 39 enacts in general terms:[3]

'(1) An adopted child shall be treated in law –
  (a) where the adopters are a married couple, as if he had been born as a child of the marriage (whether or not he was in fact born after the marriage was solemnised);
  (b) in any other case, as if he had been born to the adopter in wedlock (but not as a child of any actual marriage of the adopter).
(2) An adopted child shall be treated in law as if he were not the child of any other person other than the adopters or adopter.

. . .

(4) It is hereby declared that this paragraph prevents an adopted child from being illegitimate.'

It is expressly provided that adoption extinguishes any existing parental responsibility vested in a parent or guardian (other than one of the adopters) or in any other person by virtue of a court order and any duty to make payments for the child's maintenance by virtue of an order or agreement unless the agreement constitutes a trust or expressly provides to the contrary.[4] Similarly, adoption automatically discharges any order, including a care order, made under the Children Act 1989.[5]

So far as marriage is concerned, an adopted child and his adoptive parents are deemed to come within the prohibited degrees of consanguinity, so that they may not intermarry.[6] Adoption, however, does not prevent a marriage between the child and his adoptive sibling or with any other adoptive relative. Conversely, as the modern law bears some relation to genetics, the child may not marry any

---

18 Department of Health's *Guidance and Regulations*, Vol 9, para 3.2.
19 Adoption Act 1976 s 51A(2).
20 Viz upon payment of a prescribed fee, that the applicant is aged 18 or over, that the Registrar General has either a record of the applicant's birth or that the applicant is a relative: s 51A(3)–(6).
 1 Section 51A(13)(a): 'any person (other than an adoptive relative) who is related to the adopted person by blood (including half-blood) or marriage'.
 2 See generally Adoption Law Review, Discussion Paper No 1, Part A.
 3 See also *Secretary of State for Social Services v S* [1983] 3 All ER 173, CA (the mother who takes her natural son to live with her after his adoptive mother's death is not his 'parent' and is therefore entitled to a guardian's allowance).
 4 Adoption Act 1976 s 12(2)–(4) as amended by the Children Act 1989 Sch 10, para 3.
 5 Ibid, s12(3)(aa), added by the Children Act 1989 Sch 10, para 3(3).
 6 Marriage Act 1949 Sch 1. This continues to apply if a subsequent adoption order is made, and the child may not marry a former adoptive parent.

person who would have come within the prohibited degrees if no adoption had been made.[7] On the other hand, an adopted child may continue to claim a pension which was being paid to him or for his benefit at the time of the adoption as if no order had been made,[8] and adoption does not affect the descent of any peerage or dignity or title of honour.[9] Nor will adoption of an illegitimate child by a natural parent as sole adoptive parent prevent his legitimation if the adopter later marries the other parent.[10]

For the purposes of all other statutes an adopted child is to be regarded as the child of his adopter or adopters, whenever the statute was passed and the adoption took place.[11] So, for example, an adopted child may claim under the Fatal Accidents Act 1976 as a dependant of his adoptive parent or other adoptive relative, but not of his birth parent.[12] Similarly adoption bars the child's inheritance claims against the birth parents' estate under the Inheritance (Provision for Family and Dependants) Act 1975.[13]

2.   THE EFFECTS ON PROPERTY

For the purposes of the devolution of interests in property, originally under the Adoption of Children Act 1926 an adopted child was not deemed to be the child of the adopters but remained the child of his birth parents. That position was changed by the Adoption of Children Act 1949. Now as regards interests in property, the general principle is that from the date of the adoption order an adopted child is deemed to become the child of the adopter or adopters and ceases to be regarded as the child of his birth parents or, if he has been previously adopted, of his former adopters, and therefore is no longer considered as related to any other person through his birth or former adoptive parents.

Earlier legislation provided that an adopted person could claim as his adoptive parent's child only under a disposition of property made inter vivos after he was adopted or under a will or codicil of a person dying after that date.[14] Now, under the Adoption Act 1976, in the case of instruments made on or after 1 January 1976 or wills of testators dying on or after that date and, subject to any contrary indication, an adopted child may claim in such cases whether the disposition takes effect before or after the adoption. A disposition depending on the date of birth of a child of the adoptive parent or parents is to be construed as though the adopted child was born on the date of his adoption and two or more children adopted on the same day rank inter se in the order of their actual births. This provision, however, does not affect the operation of any condition depending on the child's reaching an actual age.[15] Thus, if there is a bequest in 1981 to K's eldest child at 18 and K adopts a child A and subsequently has a natural child B, A can claim when he reaches the

---

7 Adoption Act 1976 s 47(1). Nor does adoption affect the law relating to incest.
8 Adoption Act 1976 s 48. For the effect of adoption on certain policies of insurance, see ibid, s 49.
9 Ibid, s 44(1).
10 Legitimacy Act 1976 s 4. See ante, p 294.
11 Adoption Act 1976 s 39(5)–(6).
12 See *Watson v Willmot* [1991] 1 QB 140, [1991] 1 All ER 473.
13 See *Re Collins* [1990] Fam 56, [1990] 2 All ER 47. See post, p 887 n 18.
14 In this respect the legislation followed the same principle as originally applied to legitimation.
15 Adoption Act 1976 s 42. A disposition includes a power of appointment and the creation of an entailed interest: ibid, s 46(1)–(3), (5).

age of 18 whether his adoption preceded or followed the testator's death.

Section 42(4) expressly provides that an adoption 'does not prejudice any interest vested in the adopted child before the adoption, or any interest expectant (whether vested or not) upon an interest so vested'. The ambit of the provision, however, has been open to speculation. Suppose, for example, that there is a gift to X with remainder to his eldest son and that X's eldest son is S. If S has been adopted by someone other than X before the instrument creating the settlement takes effect, he can obviously claim nothing because he is no longer regarded as X's son at all. If X has died before S's adoption, so that S's interest has vested in possession, it is expressly preserved by s 42(4) notwithstanding the adoption. But what is the position if S is adopted after the disposition takes effect but before the interest vests in possession? In *Staffordshire County Council v B*[16] it was held that in such circumstances the child was still entitled to the interest notwithstanding his adoption since, properly interpreted, s 42(4) did not require the interest of the child to be vested in possession, it being sufficient that the child's contingent interest arose out of an interest vested in possession.

Notwithstanding the general rule there are various provisions designed to ensure that a child *adopted by one of his unmarried parents as the sole adoptive parent* is not thereby deprived of an interest he could otherwise have taken. In the first place, such an adoption does not affect the child's entitlement to any property depending on his relationship to the adoptive parent.[17] Secondly, if a disposition depends on the date of birth of an illegitimate child, neither his adoption by one of his parents as sole adopter nor his legitimation if he has been adopted will affect his entitlement.[18]

Unless the disposition otherwise provides, adoption does not affect the devolution of any property limited to devolve along with any peerage or dignity or title of honour (the descent of which will not be affected).[19] Trustees and personal representatives are not liable if they distribute property in ignorance of the making or revocation of an adoption order, but beneficiaries may trace property into the hands of anyone other than a purchaser.[20]

3. ACQUISITION OF CITIZENSHIP BY ADOPTION

A minor (of whatever nationality) adopted by an order made by a court in the United Kingdom will become a British citizen if one of the adopters is a British citizen.[1]

---

16 [1998] 1 FLR 261.
17 Adoption Act 1976 s 39(3).
18 Ibid, s 43; Legitimacy Act 1976 s 6(2). Similarly, the revocation of an adoption order following the marriage of a child's parents will not affect any claim he could have made to property had the order remained in force: Legitimacy Act 1976 s 4(2). If he has been adopted and dies before his parents' marriage, he is deemed to be legitimate on that date for the purpose of preserving interests to be taken by or in succession to his spouse, children and remoter issue: Legitimacy Act 1976 s 5(6). For the effect of an adoption by a woman over 55 and the operation of the presumption that she is incapable of bearing children, see Adoption Act 1976 s 42(5).
19 Adoption Act 1976 s 44.
20 Ibid, s 45.
1 British Nationality Act 1981 s 1(5). In the case of a joint adoption the child will acquire British citizenship if one of the adopters possesses it. He will retain British citizenship even if the order ceases to have effect for any reason: ibid, s1(6). But note *Re K (A Minor) (Adoption Order: Nationality)* [1995] Fam 38, [1994] 3 All ER 553, CA, in which it was held that s 1(6) does not apply to appeals: hence citizenship can be lost if an appeal against the making of an order succeeds.

4.   LEAVE TO ENTER OR REMAIN IN THE UNITED KINGDOM

As an adopted child

In addition to the usual requirements governing children's entry or remaining in the United Kingdom, where the child has been adopted abroad, it is provided that he must have been adopted in accordance with a decision taken by the competent administrative authority or court in his or her country of origin or residence; both adoptive parents must have been resident together abroad at the time of the adoption (or either or both of them were settled in the United Kingdom); the child must have the same rights and obligations as any other child of the marriage; the adoption must have been due to the inability of the original parent or current carer to care for him, and there has been a genuine transfer of parental responsibility to the adopters; the child must have lost or broken his ties with the family of origin;[2] and the adoption must not have been arranged to facilitate the child's admission or remaining in the United Kingdom.[3]

Child to be adopted here

It is more common these days for a couple settled here to seek to bring in a child from abroad, to be adopted according to English law. There are no specific rules governing entry of such a child into the United Kingdom, but the Home Office operates a policy outside the Immigration Rules in such cases.[4] The prospective adopters must apply for entry clearance for the child, after which the entry clearance officer will make enquiries as to the child's circumstances in the country of origin, especially concerning whether the child is free for adoption. After the Home Office has then been satisfied that there are no bars to the child's immigration, the application is referred to the Department of Health, which will ask the relevant local authority to undertake a 'home study' report into the suitability of the prospective adopters. Where the recommendation of the authority and Department of Health is positive,[5] the case is referred back to the Home Office, which will then determine whether, in the light of the information and recommendation, and by analogy with the rules governing entry of a child adopted abroad, clearance should be given. Not infrequently, however, the child will have been brought to this country unlawfully after an adoption abroad, and a court determining whether an adoption order should then be made may be faced with a fait accompli if there is no one in the home country to whom the child can be returned.[6] But the court may consider that, where breaches of the English adoption legislation are significant, an order other than adoption may be appropriate.[7]

---

2 Such an approach appears outdated in light of increasing recognition of the value to an adopted child of continuing links with the birth family: see ante, p 617.

3 Immigration Rules HC 395 para 310. See *R v Immigration Appeal Tribunal, ex p Tohur Ali* [1988] 2 FLR 523, CA.

4 Set out in Home Office, RON 117. For details, see Rosenblatt and Lewis *Children and Immigration* (1997) pp 22–3.

5 See *R v Secretary of State for Health, ex p Luff* [1992] 1 FLR 59 – prospective adopters of a Romanian orphan, rejected as suitable adopters because of health problems, failed in a judicial review of that decision (se ante, p 628 n 20).

6 See, for example, *Re WM (Adoption: Non-patrial)* [1997] 1 FLR 132: a child was adopted abroad, and notwithstanding concerns as to the adopters' suitability (having been rejected by an adoption agency in this country), there was no other option than an adoption order in the child's interests.

7 See *Re K (Adoption)* [1997] Fam Law 316, CA and *Re K (Adoption: No 2)* [1997] 2 FLR 221: where a Bosnian baby was brought to this country and adopted despite the adopters' knowledge of survival of members of the birth family, the adoption was set aside and the child made a ward of court (see ante, p 673).

5. ADOPTION OF A CHILD FROM ABROAD

The courts will have regard to the immigration rules when determining whether to make an adoption order in respect of a child brought to this country from abroad. In particular, they will be concerned to ignore the advantage to the child which would accrue from the acquisition of British citizenship and the ability to remain in this country. But where the adoption application is genuinely motivated by a concern for the child (and by a desire of a childless couple to create a family), the order may be made.[8]

F. Intercountry adoption

1. CONVENTION ADOPTION ORDERS[9]

Whereas the traditional basis of jurisdiction to make adoption orders in English law is the applicants' domicile, in many foreign systems it is the parties' nationality. This has caused difficulties in cases with a foreign element (eg where the applicants are British subjects domiciled abroad) and the desire to produce a uniform law of jurisdiction and recognition led to the Hague Convention on the adoption of children in 1965.[10] The terms of the Convention were embodied in the Adoption Act 1968 and so far as they relate to jurisdiction to make orders are now contained in the Adoption Act 1976 s 17. An adoption order made under s 17 is known as a Convention adoption order. A Convention country is any country outside British territory designated by the Secretary of State as a country in which the Convention is in force. To date only Austria, Switzerland and the United Kingdom are signatories.[11]

Only the High Court has power to make a Convention adoption order.[12] Orders may be granted where the appellants and the child are nationals of or habitual residents in different Convention countries.

If the child is not a United Kingdom national, no order may be made unless the provisions relating to 'consents and consultations' of the internal law of the country of which he is a national are complied with. This does not, however, apply to consents by or consultations with the applicant and members of his family (including his or her spouse). If the child is a United Kingdom national, the law relating to the consent of parents and guardians seems to be the same as it is on the other applications for adoption orders. If consent may be dispensed with under the relevant law, the body empowered to do this is the High Court in the case of any

---

8 Compare *Re H (Adoption: Non-patrial)* [1996] 2 FLR 187, CA, where an adoption order was granted to a childless couple in respect of their 15-year-old Pakistani cousin, with *Re K (A Minor) (Adoption Order: Nationality)* [1994] 2 FLR 557, CA, in which the Home Secretary's appeal was allowed against the grant of an adoption order to the aunt of a child almost 18 years old from Sierra Leone, since once the benefits of citizenship were taken out of the reckoning, the advantage to the child was minimal.

9 See generally the Adoption Law Review, Discussion Paper No 4, paras 51–52.

10 Cmnd 2613. The full effect of the Convention is described in LAC (78) 19. See also pp 453–5 of the 8th edition of this work.

11 SI 1978, No 1431.

12 Adoption Act 1976 s 62(4).

application made in England and Wales, whatever the child's nationality.[13]
In two cases the court has no power to make a Convention order at all:

(1) If the applicant or applicants are not United Kingdom nationals and the order
is prohibited by a specified provision of the internal law of the country of
which they are nationals, provided that, in the case of a joint application, they
are nationals of the same Convention country.[14] Such a prohibition might
relate, for example, to the relative ages of the child and the applicants or their
blood relationship.

(2) If the applicant or applicants and the child are all United Kingdom nationals
living in British territory.[15] The purpose here is clearly to restrict the operation
of s 17 to adoptions with a foreign element. It will be seen that there is a gap,
however, for if the above conditions are satisfied and the applicants are not
domiciled in any part of the British Isles, there is no jurisdiction to make an
order at all.

Where either the child or the adopters reside in Great Britain, the High Court may
annul an order on the ground that the adoption was prohibited by the internal law
of the country of which the adopters were nationals or that it contravened
provisions relating to consents of the internal law of the country of which the child
was a national.[16] As in the case of other orders, a Convention adoption order may
also be revoked if the child was adopted by his father or mother and has
subsequently been legitimated by their marriage.

2.   THE 1993 HAGUE CONVENTION ON INTERCOUNTRY ADOPTION[17]

As a mechanism for controlling intercountry adoption the 1965 Convention has
proved to be inappropriate, and indeed the United Kingdom intends to denounce it
when it ratifies the 1993 Convention.[18] The 1993 Convention represents a much
bolder attempt to regulate and control, on a global basis, intercountry adoption.
The 1993 Convention has three basic objects:

(1) to establish safeguards to ensure that intercountry adoptions only take place
after the best interests of the child have been properly assessed and in circumstances which protect his or her fundamental rights;

---

13   Ibid, s 17(6), (7) and s 71.
14   Ibid, s 17(4), (5), (8).
15   Ibid, s 17(3). For other difficulties, see McClean and Patchett 'English Jurisdiction in Adoption'
(1970) 19 ICLQ 1; Blom 'The Adoption Act 1968 and the Conflict of Laws' (1973) 22 ICLQ 109.
Note also the reference to this provision by Balcombe LJ in *Re K (A Minor) (Adoption Order:
Nationality)* [1995] Fam 38 at 41, [1994] 3 All ER 553 at 556.
16   Ibid, s 53(1) as amended by the Domestic Proceedings and Magistrates' Courts Act 1978 s 74(2),
and s 54(2). Section 53(1) also enables a Convention adoption order to be annulled on the ground
that it could have been impugned on any other ground under English law. The order would then
presumably be a nullity anyway.
17   The Convention on protection of children and co-operation in respect of inter-country adoption
1993. See generally The Explanatory Report by G Parra-Aranguren and by the same author 'An
Overview of the 1993 Hague Inter-Country Adoption Convention in Lowe and Douglas (eds)
Families Across Frontiers (1996) at 565; Duncan 'Conflict and Co-operation. The Approach to
Conflicts of Law in the 1993 Hague Convention on Intercountry Adoption' in *Families Across
Frontiers* at 577; and Frank 'The Recognition of Intercountry Adoption in the Light of the 1993
Hague Convention on Intercountry Adoptions' in *Families Across Frontiers* at 591.
18   See *Adoption: A Service For Children*, op cit at para 4.29.

(2) to establish a system of co-operation amongst Contracting States to ensure that these safeguards are respected; and

(3) to secure the recognition in Contracting States of adoptions made in accordance with the Convention.[19]

To achieve these broad objectives the Convention first makes a distinction between 'States of Origin' from which children are sent for adoption and 'Receiving States' in which the adopted child will live. It is the responsibility of a State of Origin, via its 'competent authorities'[20] to establish that the child is adoptable and that intercountry adoption as opposed to placement within the country of origin is in the child's best interests.[1] States of Origin are also obliged to have ensured that the requisite consents to the child's adoption (it will be noted that the Convention makes no attempt to prescribe what the internal laws on consent should be) have, after due counselling, been freely given with a full understanding of what is involved and without financial inducement.[2] Such States are similarly expected to ensure that, 'having regard to the age and maturity of the child', such a child has been counselled and duly informed about the effects of adoption and, where required, freely consented to the adoption without financial inducement.[3]

In contrast, the responsibility of Receiving States is to determine that the prospective adoptive parents are eligible and suited to adopt and to ensure that they have been counselled as may be necessary and, importantly, to have determined that the child is or will be authorised to enter and reside permanently in that State.[4]

The administrative mechanism through which the Convention operates is primarily through the tried and tested system of Central Authorities. Each contracting state is obliged to set up a Central Authority,[5] which, as the government White Paper says,[6] should normally be part of the country's central government. It is envisaged, for example, that in England that role will be discharged by the Department of Health.[7] Central Authorities are generally charged to co-operate with one another,[8] to take all appropriate measures to prevent improper financial or other gain in connection with an adoption and to deter all parties from acting contrary to the rights of the Convention.[9] Under Art 9 Central Authorities are under a duty to collate, preserve and exchange information about the situation of the child and the prospective adopters, to facilitate and expedite proceedings, to promote development of adoption counselling and post-adoption services, and to respond to requests from other Central Authorities for information about a particular adoption situation.

---

19 See Article 1 and see the explanation in the government White Paper *Adoption: The Future* (1994, Cm 2288) paras 6.19 ff.
20 See further below.
1 Article 4(a) and (b).
2 Article 4 (c).
3 Article 4(d).
4 Article 5.
5 Article 6.
6 Ibid at para 6.21.
7 And by the Welsh Office in Wales.
8 Article 7(1). Under Article 7(2) they must also provide information about the law, keep one another informed about the operation of the Convention and, as far as possible, eliminate any obstacles to its application.
9 Article 8.

These Art 9 duties may be discharged either by the Central Authority itself or by or with 'accredited bodies'. Accredited bodies should be authorised bodies capable of preparing and arranging adoptions.[10] In the United Kingdom it is envisaged that all local authorities and approved voluntary agencies would be accredited bodies.[11]

The procedure for facilitating a Convention adoption is as follows. Persons who are habitually resident in one Contracting State, who wish to apply to adopt a child habitually resident in another Contracting State, should apply to their own Central Authority.[12] If the Central Authority of the Receiving State is satisfied as to the applicants' eligibility and suitability to adopt, it should prepare and transmit the request to the Central Authority of the State of Origin.[13] There is a reciprocal duty on the State of Origin to prepare and transmit a report on the child that is considered adoptable and in that connection to ensure that the requisite consents have been given.[14]

Under Art 17 any decision in the State of Origin that a child should be entrusted to prospective adopters may only be made if the Central Authorities of *both* states agree that the adoption may proceed, the Central Authority of the State of Origin having ensured that the prospective adopters agree and the Central Authority of the Receiving State has approved such a decision, having considered the prospective adopters suitable and having determined that the child is or will be authorised to enter and reside permanently in that State.

Chapter V of the Convention deals with the important issue of the recognition and effects of a Convention adoption. The basic provision is Art 23, which provides that an adoption certified by the competent authority of the state of the adoption as having been made in accordance with the Convention shall be recognised by operation of law in the other Contracting States. Recognition may, however, be refused in a Contracting State if the adoption 'is manifestly contrary to its public policy, taking into account the best interests of the child'. Art 26(1) provides that recognition includes recognition of –

'(a) the legal parent–child relationship between the child and his or her adoptive parents;
(b) parental responsibility of the adoptive parents for the child;
(c) the termination of a pre-existing legal relationship between the child and his or her mother and father, if the adoption has that effect in the Contracting State where it was made.'

This, as one commentator has pointed out,[15] is not a comprehensive enumeration of the effects of recognition, but rather a list of the minimal consequences of recognition. Art 26(2) further provides that where the adoption has the effect of terminating a pre-existing legal parent–child relationship, the child is to enjoy in all states where the adoption is recognised as well as the Receiving State, rights equivalent to those resulting from full adoption in such states.[16]

The 1993 Convention represents a bold, if ambitious attempt to provide global control of intercountry adoption. Whether it will succeed or not depends of course

10 Articles 10 and 11.
11 See *Adoption: The Future*, op cit, para 6.22.
12 Article 14.
13 Article 15.
14 Article 16.
15 Duncan, op cit, at 586.
16 There is considerable doubt as to how this should be interpreted: see eg Frank, op cit. The *Explanatory Report*, para 439 emphasises that Article 26 was the result of compromise and that it reflects the minimum consensus that could be reached.

on how many countries ratify it in the first place. At the time of writing 17 of the 31 signatory states have ratified the Convention.[17] The United Kingdom has signed but not yet ratified it. However, the intention seems to be to ratify in due course. As the White Paper *Adoption: The Future* put it,[18] there are two very significant benefits of ratification. First, there will be mutual recognition of an adoption order: thus avoiding the applicants' need to apply in their home country for a second order (and consequential uncertainty). Secondly, immigration procedures can be brought within the adoption process.

The proposed Adoption Bill provides a scheme for full implementation of the Convention,[19] further backed up by a provision that it will be an offence for a person other than a parent or guardian to bring a child who is habitually resident outside the UK, the Channel Islands and the Isle of Man, into the UK for the purpose of adoption without satisfying prescribed requirements.[20] It has been hinted that this part of the proposed Bill might be legislated upon ahead of the rest of it.

The Convention itself provides a framework based on trust and co-operation. It is noticeably non-prescriptive, providing for the minimum safeguards and clearly avoids extensive use of traditional conflicts of laws rules.[1] Its success or failure will lie in:

(a) attracting more ratifications both by states that are likely to be mainly States of Origin and those that will mainly be Receiving States (given the huge number of children received, the position taken by the USA will be a key pointer on this);
(b) the ability of the Central Authorities to work and co-operate with one another; and
(c) whether the provisions, particularly those dealing with recognition, can stand the test of scrutiny by the courts.[2]

At this stage, however, the portent for success seem promising.

17 A full list is published monthly in *Family Law*.
18 Ibid at paras 6.24 ff.
19 See Sch 2 to the Bill and the Draft Regulation attached thereto.
20 Clause 91.
 1 See Duncan, op cit.
 2 See Dyer 'Case Law and Co-operation as the Building Blocks for Protection of International Families' in *Families Across Frontiers* op cit at 27ff.

Chapter 16

The High Court's inherent powers in respect of children

A. Introduction

No discussion of child law would be complete without having regard to the High Court's inherent powers in respect of children. It should be appreciated that the development of these powers, principally under the aegis of the wardship jurisdiction, was highly influential in the modern development of law and practice concerning children, and that the Children Act 1989 now incorporates many of its features. Even now, after the 1989 Act, the residual inherent powers remain useful, particularly when the statutory system offers no suitable remedy.

Before the Children Act, discussion of these inherent powers would have focused solely on the wardship jurisdiction which, as will be seen, is not based on any statute but is an ancient jurisdiction derived from the sovereign's obligation as parens patriae to protect the person and property of those of his subjects, such as children, who are unable to look after themselves. However, in the light of the changes made by the Children Act 1989[1] it is important to distinguish the well-established wardship jurisdiction from the separate inherent jurisdiction of the High Court referred to in the 1989 Act.

Although the existence of a parens patriae power to protect children independent of wardship had been expressly acknowledged by the court[2] before the 1989 Act, there had been little cause to develop it, given the wide-ranging nature of the wardship jurisdiction. However, in his Joseph Jackson Memorial Lecture,[3] Lord Mackay LC commented:

'... in the government's view wardship is only one use of the High Court's inherent parens patriae jurisdiction. We believe, therefore, that it is open to the High Court to make orders under its inherent jurisdiction in respect of children other than through wardship.'

The Children Act 1989 is predicated on this view. Indeed, as we shall see, if a local authority wishes to obtain a High Court order in respect of a child already in care, they must seek to invoke the inherent rather than the wardship jurisdiction.[4]

Although it has been said[5] that the High Court's inherent jurisdiction is equally

---

1 Discussed post, pp 694ff.
2 See eg *Re N (Infants)* [1967] Ch 512, [1967] 1 All ER 161, and *Re L (An Infant)* [1968] P 119, [1968] 1 All ER 20, CA, and note also the suggestion by Ewbank J in *R v North Yorkshire County Council, ex p M (No 3)* [1989] 2 FLR 82 that the High Court had an inherent power in other proceedings to make a child a ward of court.
3 (1989) 139 NLJ 505 at 507. See also the Department of Health's *Guidance and Regulations*, Vol 1, *Court Orders*, paras 3.98 et seq.
4 See post, pp 698–9 and 709–11.
5 Per Lord Donaldson MR in *Re W (A Minor) (Medical Treatment)* [1993] Fam 64, [1992] 4 All ER 627, CA; *Re M and N (Minors) (Wardship: Publication of Information)* [1990] Fam 211, [1990] 1 All ER 205, CA. See also *Re Z (A Minor) (Identification: Restrictions on Publicity)* [1997] Fam 1, sub nom *Re Z (a minor) (freedom of publication)* [1995] 4 All ER 961, CA.

exercisable whether the child is or is not a ward of court, there are important conceptual differences between the two cases. In particular, unlike wardship, the exercise of the inherent jurisdiction does not place the child under the ultimate responsibility of the court. This means that at no point will the child be subject to the rule obtaining in wardship that all important steps in the child's life have to be sanctioned by the court.[6] In other words, the inherent jurisdiction empowers the High Court to make orders dealing with particular aspects of the child's welfare, whereas wardship additionally vests in the court a continuing supervisory function over the child. Accordingly, notwithstanding the commonality of the powers and the 1989 Act's tendency to obscure the distinction by using the term 'inherent jurisdiction' to refer to both wardship and the residual jurisdiction,[7] it is probably best to regard them as separate jurisdictions.[8]

B.   Wardship[9]

1.   HISTORICAL DEVELOPMENT

Wardship has a fascinating history. Its origins[10] lie in feudal times, when it was an incident of tenure by which, upon a tenant's death, the lord became guardian of the surviving infant heir's land and body. Although there was a protective element in the guardianship in that the lord was supposed to look after his ward, maintaining and educating him according to his station, the right was a valuable one since, inter alia, the lord was entitled to keep the profits of the land until the heir reached his majority. No one benefited more than the Crown (whose rights arose upon the death of a tenant-in-chief) and in 1540 the Court of Wards was created to enforce the sovereign's rights and the execution of his duties in connection with wardship. These rights, together with the Court of Wards, were abolished in 1660.[11] The wardship jurisdiction, however, survived in the hands of the Court of Chancery.

Jurisdiction was claimed upon the basis that the sovereign, as parens patriae,

6 *Re W (A Minor) (Medical Treatment: Court's Jurisdiction)* [1993] Fam 64 at 73 F–G, [1992] 4 All ER 627 at 631d, per Lord Donaldson MR.
7 Parry 'The Children Act 1989: Local Authorities, Wardship and the Revival of the Inherent Jurisdiction' [1992] JSWFL 212 has observed, at 213: 'Section 100 has the marginal heading for guidance, "Restriction on use of wardship jurisdiction", whereas the substance of the section relates to the inherent jurisdiction as much as to wardship'. Note also that s 8(3) includes the 'inherent jurisdiction' in the definition of 'family proceedings', which is intended to cover both jurisdictions.
8 Nevertheless, note Ward LJ's comment in *Re Z (A Minor) (Identification: Restrictions on Publication)* [1997] Fam 1 at 14, sub nom *Re Z (a minor) (freedom of publication)* [1995] 4 All ER 961, CA at 968 that 'For all practical purposes the jurisdiction in wardship and the inherent jurisdiction over children is one and the same . . .'
9 For a detailed analysis of the jurisdiction before the Children Act 1989 see Lowe and White *Wards of Court* (2nd edn, 1986); Seymour ' Parens Patriae and Wardship Powers: Their Nature and Origins' (1994) 14 Oxford Journal of Legal Studies 159; and Law Com Working Paper No 101 *Wards of Court*. For valuable accounts by (then) High Court judges, see Cross 'Wards of Court', (1967) 83 LQR 200 and Balcombe 'Wardship' (1981–2) Lit 223. [1990] Fam Law 270.
10 For a more detailed historical account see Lowe and White *Wards of Court*, op cit, at paras 1.1 et seq and the references there cited. See also *Re Eve* (1986) 31 DLR (4th) 1, Canadian Supreme Court.
11 By the Tenures Abolition Act 1660.

had a duty to protect his subjects, particularly those, such as infants,[12] who were unable to protect themselves, and that this duty had been delegated to the Lord Chancellor and through him to the Court of Chancery. Although there is some doubt about the historical validity of this claim, by the end of the nineteenth century (by which time jurisdiction had become vested in the Chancery Division of the High Court), it had become the authoritatively accepted basis of the jurisdiction.[13] Furthermore, it became established that the jurisdiction was not dependent upon the existence of property belonging to the infant.[14] At about the same time it had become established that decisions had to be based on what was best for the ward.

Although by the turn of the century wardship had acquired most of the characteristics of the modern jurisdiction,[15] it did not really begin to develop until the old procedural shackles were removed in 1949.[16] Further impetus to the use of wardship was given in 1971 when the jurisdiction was transferred to the newly created Family Division of the High Court[17] and thereby became available in the provinces (through the district registries) as well as in London (in the Principal Registry).

Until 1986 wardship had been an exclusively High Court jurisdiction, but since then it has been possible, at any rate after the main issues have been resolved, to transfer cases to the county court.[18]

2.   CHARACTERISTICS OF THE WARDSHIP JURISDICTION

Control vested in the court

A unique and fundamental characteristic of the jurisdiction is that throughout the wardship legal control over both the child's person and property is vested in the court. As Lord Scarman put it,[19] once a party persuades the court that it should make the child its ward 'the court takes over ultimate responsibility for the child'. Although, in the past at any rate, wardship was quite frequently referred to as a 'parental jurisdiction', the court is not in the same position as a parent or other persons with parental responsibility in any strict sense. As Lord Donaldson MR has said, it is clear that:

'. . . the practical jurisdiction of the court is wider than that of parents. The court can, for example, forbid the publication of information about the ward or the ward's family circumstances. It is also clear that this jurisdiction is not derivative from the parents'

---

12 And, originally, lunatics. However, it is now accepted that there is no longer a parens patriae jurisdiction with regard to mentally handicapped adults: Re F (Mental Patient: Sterilisation) [1990] 2 AC 1, [1989] 2 All ER 545, HL.

13 Johnstone v Beattie (1843) 10 Cl & Fin 42 at 120 per Lord Eldon LC, and Hope v Hope (1854) 4 De GM & G 328 at 344–5 per Lord Cranworth LC.

14 See Re Spence (1847) 2 Ph 247 at 251 per Lord Cottenham LC. In point of fact, until 1949 it was common practice to begin wardship by making a nominal settlement upon the child and then commencing an action to administer the trusts of the settlement: see Re D [1943] Ch 305 at 306 and Re X's Settlement [1945] Ch 44 at 45.

15 See eg R v Gyngall [1893] 2 QB 232 at 248, CA per Kay LJ.

16 By the Law Reform (Miscellaneous Provisions) Act 1949.

17 Under the Administration of Justice Act 1970 s 1(2) and Sch 1.

18 Pursuant to s 38(2)(b) of the Matrimonial and Family Proceedings Act 1984.

19 In Re E (SA) (A Minor) [1984] 1 All ER 289, HL at 290.

rights and responsibilities, but derives from, or is, the delegated performance of the duties of the Crown to protect its subjects . . .'[20]

(a)   The effects of the court's control

Being under the court's protection does not mean that the ward is physically in the court's or judge's care, but rather that the child and those with parental responsibility or otherwise having de facto care and control are subject to the court's control. This control is both an immediate and automatic consequence of wardship.[1] As Cross J put it,[2] once the child has been made a ward 'no important step in the child's life can be taken without the court's consent'. Failure to obtain the court's consent constitutes a contempt of court, for which the ultimate sanction is imprisonment and a fine.[3]

(b)   Extent of control

Despite the potential draconian sanction it is not easy to say precisely what constitutes an 'important step'.[4] It is well established that a ward may not marry[5] nor leave the jurisdiction without the court's consent. Formerly, the latter embargo meant that leave was required before a ward could travel outside England and Wales. However, under the Family Law Act 1986 s 38 the automatic[6] embargo no longer prevents the child's removal to another part of the United Kingdom in which divorce or other matrimonial proceedings (in respect of the ward's parents) are continuing or in which the child is habitually resident.

Other 'steps' requiring prior court consent include: applying to adopt or to free a ward for adoption;[7] moving a ward to new care-givers, as for example, seeking compulsory admission to hospital of a mentally ill ward;[8] changing the ward's whereabouts;[9] making material changes in a ward's education;[10] performing major medical treatment on a ward;[11] and even conducting psychiatric or psychological examinations.[12]

---

20 In *Re R (A Minor) (Wardship: Medical Treatment)* [1992] Fam 11 at 24, [1991] 4 All ER 177, CA at 186. See also *Re W (A Minor) (Medical Treatment)* supra.

1 The control begins as soon as the originating summons has been issued and without any specific court order. It ends when the wardship ends. Whether such immediate and automatic wide-ranging protection can be justified has been questioned by the Law Commission: Law Com Working Paper No 101 paras 4.3 and 4.13.

2 In *Re S (Infants)* [1967] 1 All ER 202 at 209.

3 See Lowe and White, op cit, ch 8.

4 For a detailed discussion see Lowe and White, op cit, ch 5.

5 See now the Marriage Act 1949 s 3(6).

6 But the court can still make a specific order prohibiting the ward's removal from England and Wales.

7 See respectively *F v S (Adoption: Ward)* [1973] Fam 203, [1973] 1 All ER 722, CA; *Re F (Wardship: Adoption)* [1984] FLR 60, CA; and *Practice Direction* [1985] 2 All ER 832.

8 Mental Health Act 1983 s 33. See also *Re CB (A Minor) (Wardship: Local Authority)* [1981] 1 All ER 16, CA at 24 per Ormrod LJ. But note there is no requirement to obtain leave to apply for an emergency protection order: *Re B (Wardship: Place of Safety Order)* (1979) 2 FLR 307.

9 Family Proceedings Rules 1991 r 5.1(9). If this is a simple change of residence it is sufficient to inform the Registry.

10 See the Notice of Wardship issued with the originating summons.

11 *Re G-U (A Minor) (Wardship)* [1984] FLR 811 (abortion) and according to Lord Templeman in *Re B (A Minor) (Wardship: Sterilisation)* [1988] AC 199 at 205, [1987] 2 All ER 206 at 214, (sterilisation); cf *Re E (A Minor) (Medical Treatment)* [1991] 2 FLR 585 in which it was held the court's consent was not required to perform an operation for therapeutic purposes even though a side effect was to sterilise the child. Leave is probably required to conduct blood tests to establish paternity: see Lowe and White, op cit, at para 5-24.

12 *Practice Direction* [1985] 3 All ER 576.

It is now clear that warding a child does not *in itself* impose a complete ban on publicity about the child[13] but, because court proceedings are confidential (unless judgment is given in open court), it is a contempt to publish any information relating to those proceedings.[14] The interrelationship between wardship and the criminal law is not straightforward but in summary, while leave is not required for the police to interview a child who has been arrested merely because he happens to be a ward,[15] nor to call a ward as a witness in criminal proceedings, it is required to interview a ward on behalf of a defendant in a criminal trial[16] and for the Crown Prosecution Service to administer a caution to a ward.[17] Leave is also required to apply on a ward's behalf for compensation from the Criminal Injuries Compensation Authority.[18]

Leave to petition the European Commission on Human Rights to examine a court decision about a ward, though an important step, does *not* require court leave.[19]

The special nature of the jurisdiction

Because legal control of the child vests in the court, wardship proceedings have always been regarded as special. For example, in *Re E (SA) (A Minor) (Wardship)*[20] Lord Scarman commented that when exercising its wardship jurisdiction a court:

'... must never lose sight of a fundamental feature of the jurisdiction, namely, that it is exercising a wardship, not an adversarial jurisdiction. Its duty is not limited to the dispute between the parties: on the contrary, its duty is to act in the way best suited in its judgment to serve the true interest and welfare of the ward. In exercising wardship jurisdiction, the court is a true family court. Its paramount concern is the welfare of its ward.'

Before the Children Act the uniqueness of wardship was both especially marked and useful, since it could often be invoked to overcome other statutory jurisdictions or gaps in the law.[1] However, it is the policy of the Children Act, in the words of Butler-Sloss LJ:[2]

'... to incorporate the best of the wardship jurisdiction within the statutory framework without any of the perceived disadvantages of judicial monitoring of administrative plans.'

---

13 *Re L (A Minor: Freedom of Publication)* [1988] 1 All ER 418 and *Re W (Minors) (Wardship: Contempt)* [1989] 1 FLR 246.
14 Administration of Justice Act 1960 s 12. The embargo covers not simply the actual proceedings but also any documents, for example, the Official Solicitor's report prepared for the case: see *Re F (Otherwise A) (A Minor)* [1977] Fam 58, [1977] 1 All ER 114, CA. This embargo extends to showing papers to an independent social worker: see *Practice Direction* [1983] 1 All ER 1097, and *Re C (Wardship: Independent Social Worker)* [1985] FLR 56; to medical officers: *Practice Direction* [1987] 3 All ER 640; and to prospective adopters and their legal advisers: *Practice Direction* [1989] 1 All ER 169.
15 *Re R, Re G (Minors)* [1990] 2 All ER 633, though those having care and control should inform the wardship court at the earliest opportunity. See also *Re K (Minors) (Wardship: Criminal Proceedings)* [1988] Fam 1, [1988] 1 All ER 214.
16 *Re R (Minors) (Wardship: Criminal Proceedings)* [1991] Fam 56, [1991] 2 All ER 193, CA.
17 *Re A (A Minor) (Wardship: Police Caution)* [1989] Fam 103, sub nom *Re A (A Minor) (Wardship: Criminal Proceedings)* [1989] 3 All ER 610.
18 *Practice Direction* [1988] 1 All ER 182, and *Re G (A Minor) (Ward: Criminal Injuries Compensation)* [1990] 3 All ER 102, CA.
19 Per Johnson J in *Re M (Petition to European Commission of Human Rights)* [1997] 1 FLR 755.
20 [1984] 1 All ER 289, HL at 290. For similar comments see eg Viscount Haldane in *Scott v Scott* [1913] AC 417, HL at 437 and Cross J in *Re B (JA) (An Infant)* [1965] Ch 1112 at 1117.
1 Particularly in the context of committing children into local authority care: see post, pp 693–4 and 697–8.
2 In *Re B (Minors) (Termination of Contact : Paramount Consideration)* [1993] Fam 301 at 310, [1993] 3 All ER 524, CA at 531.

Hence, wardship now shares many of its characteristics with other child law jurisdictions. For example, in all family proceedings hearsay evidence is admissible[3] and the court can make s 8 orders whether or not they have been applied for.[4] The paramountcy principle of course applies in all proceedings concerning a child's upbringing and, fostered by the Children Act, there has been a general move away from an adversarial approach in all children cases. Nonetheless wardship remains unique in that control over the child is vested in the court. Furthermore, that control arises immediately the child becomes a ward and only ceases when the wardship itself ceases.[5]

3. WHO CAN BE WARDED[6]

Child must be a minor

Only minors, that is persons under the age of 18,[7] may be warded. There is some doubt whether a married minor can be warded.[8] Although formerly a matter of speculation[9] it is now settled that a foetus cannot be made a ward of court.[10]

The child must be subject to the jurisdiction

Any minor who can be said to owe allegiance to the Crown may be warded,[11] which in theory means any minor who is a British subject regardless of his place of birth, domicile or residence.[12] However, as the Law Commissions have pointed out,[13] there is no reported case of wardship being based on the allegiance of a child who is neither present nor resident in England and Wales. With the exception of a child who is a member of the household of a parent entitled to diplomatic immunity,[14] there is also jurisdiction to ward an alien minor who is physically

---

3 See the Children (Admissibility of Hearsay Evidence) Order 1993. In wardship hearsay evidence has always been admissible: *Re W (Minors) (Wardship: Evidence)* [1990] 1 FLR 203, CA. See now art 2 of the 1993 Order.

4 Children Act 1989 s 10(1)(b), discussed ante, pp 446–7; cf *Re E (SA)*, supra.

5 For when wardship begins and ends see post, pp 691–2.

6 See generally Lowe 'Who can be made a ward of court?' (1989) 1 Journal of Child Law 6.

7 Family Law Reform Act 1969 s 1.

8 *Re Elwes (No 2)* (1958) Times, 30 July suggests there is jurisdiction, whereas cases on guardianship, eg *Mendes v Mendes* (1747) 1 Ves Sen 89 at 91 per Lord Hardwicke LC; *R v Wilmington* (1822) 5 B & Ald 525 at 526 per Abbot CJ and *Hewer v Bryant* [1970] 1 QB 357 at 373 per Sachs LJ, suggest there is not. See Lowe and White, op cit, at paras 2.1 and 2.2.

9 See eg Phillips (1979) 95 LQR 332 and Lyon and Bennett (1979) 9 Fam Law 35 at 36 who argued that, despite an apparent ruling to the contrary in *Paton v Trustee of British Pregnancy Advisory Service* [1979] QB 276, [1978] 2 All ER 987 per Sir George Baker P, it was possible; cf Lowe (1980) 96 LQR 29 and (1980) 131 NLJ 561.

10 *Re F (In Utero)* [1988] Fam 122, [1988] 2 All ER 193, CA; Fortin 'Legal Protection of the Unborn Child' (1988) 51 MLR 54; and Grubb and Pearl (1987) 103 LQR 340. For a similar position taken in Canada, see *Winnipeg Child and Family Services (Northwest Area) v G* (1997) 152 DLR (4th) 193, Can Sup Ct.

11 See *Re P (GE) (An Infant)* [1965] Ch 568 at 587 per Pearson LJ.

12 See *Harben v Harben* [1957] 1 All ER 379 at 381 per Sachs LJ.

13 Law Com No 138, Scot Law Com No 91, 1985, at para 2.9. See further Lowe and White, op cit, at para 2.6, 7.

14 *Re C (An Infant)* [1959] Ch 363. See also *Re P (Children Act: Diplomatic Immunity)* [1998] 1 FLR 624. In *Re Mohammed Arif (An Infant), Re Nirbhai Singh (An Infant)* [1968] Ch 643, Cross J doubted whether there is jurisdiction to ward an alien minor still present in the jurisdiction but who has been refused entry by immigration officials, but on appeal the point was left open. Nevertheless, wardship cannot in practice be used to challenge immigration decisions: see post, p 707.

present in England and Wales (even aliens owe temporary allegiance whilst present in the jurisdiction)[15] and, as the House of Lords have confirmed,[16] an alien child[17] who, though not physically present, is habitually resident in England and Wales at the time of the application.

(a)   Limitations imposed by the Family Law Act 1986

Notwithstanding the width of power to make a child a ward, jurisdiction to make orders giving care of a child to any person or providing for contact with, or the education of, a child ('a s 1(1)(d) order')[18] is more limited. By s 2(3) and s 3 of the Family Law Act 1986 jurisdiction is generally confined to those cases where, at the relevant date,[19] the child is either habitually resident in England and Wales or is present here and not habitually resident in another part of the United Kingdom or Isle of Man.[20] However, jurisdiction on either of the foregoing bases is normally excluded if, at the relevant date,[1] divorce, nullity or separation proceedings are continuing[2] in another part of the United Kingdom or the Isle of Man. The latter rule does not apply where the High Court considers 'that the immediate exercise of its powers is necessary for [the child's] protection, in which case the child's physical presence will suffice'.[3] The initial burden of proof lies upon the person seeking to invoke wardship to satisfy the court that it has jurisdiction, but once this has been discharged the burden of proof shifts to the defendant to establish that the child was no longer habitually resident here at the time of application.[4]

Although enacted principally to prevent conflicts of jurisdiction arising within the United Kingdom or the Isle of Man,[5] these provisions nevertheless apply even where there is no potential conflict with another domestic court. Consequently, it is no longer possible to make a s 1(1)(d) order in respect of a British subject who is neither present nor habitually resident in the jurisdiction. There is, however, such

---

15 See *Hope v Hope* (1854) 4 De GM & G 328 at 346 per Lord Cranworth LC. For an extreme example see *Re C (An Infant)* (1956) Times, 14 December – child temporarily in England whilst en route from USA to USSR. See also *Johnstone v Beattie* (1843) 10 Cl & Fin 42 and *Re D (An Infant)* [1943] Ch 305, [1943] 2 All ER 411.
16 *Re S (a minor) (custody: habitual residence)* [1997] 4 All ER 251 at 259, [1997] 3 WLR 597, HL at 604.
17 Including a stateless child.
18 But excluding an order varying or revoking such an order: Family Law Act 1986 s 1(1)(d) as amended by the Children Act 1989, Sch 13, para 63(b).
19 That is, where an application is made for a s 1(1)(d) order, the date of the application or, where no such application has been made, the date of the order: s 3(6). This prevents the court having jurisdiction merely because the child has been warded in the past: see Law Com No 138, Scot Law Com No 91 para 4.28.
20 Section 2(3)(a) and s 3(1).
 1 See n 19, above.
 2 Proceedings are treated as 'continuing' from the issue of the petition until (unless the proceedings have been dismissed) the child reaches 18 in Northern Ireland and the Isle of Man, or 16 in Scotland: s 42(2), as amended by the Family Law Act 1986 (Dependent Territories) Order 1991 s 42(3). See, for example, *B v B (Scottish: Contact Order Jurisdiction To Vary)* [1996] 1 WLR 231.
 3 Section 2(3)(b), as amended by the Children Act 1989, Sch 13, para 64. Precisely what will trigger this 'emergency jurisdiction' is a matter of some doubt: see further Lowe and White, op cit, para 2-6.
 4 *F v S (Wardship: Jurisdiction)* [1993] 2 FLR 686, CA.
 5 To this end it should be noted that under s 41 a child under the age of 16 who is habitually resident in one part of the UK or Isle of Man, but who has been removed without the agreement of all persons having the right to determine where he should reside or in contravention of a court order, will be deemed to continue to be habitually resident in that part of the UK or the Isle of Man from where he was taken.

a residual jurisdiction to make orders not caught by s 1(1)(d). In *F v S (Wardship: Jurisdiction)*[6] Ward J held that the absence of jurisdiction under the 1986 Act did not preclude him from having jurisdiction to make an order requiring disclosure of the child's whereabouts. He refused, however, to order a parent to produce the child, since that would have enabled the court then to have taken jurisdiction under s 2(3)(b) if that was necessary for the child's protection. As he pointed out,[7] such an order would have provided 'a devious entry to the court by the back door where Parliament have so firmly shut the front door to [s 1(1)(d)] orders being made'.

(b)   Limitations imposed by the Child Abduction and Custody Act 1985

Any wardship application is frozen during the pendency of an application under the Hague or European Convention on international child abduction.[8]

The discretion to exercise jurisdiction

In cases where the court has jurisdiction, it is nevertheless not bound to exercise it. The court generally refuses to exercise jurisdiction to review the exercise of discretionary powers vested in other bodies or tribunals such as local authorities[9] or the immigration service,[10] or to interfere with the normal operation of criminal proceedings[11] or military law.[12] The court is naturally reluctant to exercise jurisdiction where the child's presence is merely a fleeting one, and in cases where the child has been abducted into this country it is established, in cases not governed by the abduction Conventions (see Chapter 13), that the court must decide whether it is in the child's best interests to be returned immediately or to have the full merits of the case heard by the English court.[13] The court has a statutory power[14] to refuse to make orders or to stay proceedings if the matter has been or is being dealt with in proceedings outside England and Wales.

4.   INVOKING WARDSHIP

Starting and ending wardship

Under the Supreme Court Act 1981 s 41(1) no minor can be made a ward of court except by an order to that effect made by the High Court.[15] Under s 41(2), however, a child (other than a child who is subject to a care order)[16] becomes a

---

6 [1991] 2 FLR 349, not commented upon in this respect by the Court of Appeal.
7 Ibid at p 356.
8 The Child Abduction and Custody Act 1985 s 9, s 20, s 27 and Sch 3 and FPR 1991 r 6.11(4). These Conventions are discussed in Chapter 13.
9 *A v Liverpool City Council* [1982] AC 363, [1981] 2 All ER 395, HL, discussed ante, p 602.
10 *Re Mohammed Arif (An Infant), Re Nirbhai Singh (An Infant)* [1968] Ch 643, [1968] 2 All ER 145, CA and *Re F (A Minor) (Immigration: Wardship)* [1990] Fam 125, [1989] 1 All ER 1115, CA. See further post, p 707.
11 *Re K (A Minor) (Wardship: Criminal Proceedings)* [1988] Fam 1, [1987] 1 All ER 214.
12 *Re JS (A Minor) (Wardship: Boy Soldier)* [1990] Fam 182, [1990] 2 All ER 861.
13 *Re F (Minor) (Abduction: Jurisdiction)* [1991] Fam 25, [1990] 3 All ER 97, CA, discussed ante, p 484.
14 Under the Family Law Act 1986 s 5.
15 Once a child has been made a ward, proceedings can be transferred to the county court: Matrimonial and Family Proceedings Act 1984 s 38(2B), but note *Practice Direction* [1992] 3 All ER 151.
16 Supreme Court Act 1981 s 41(2A), added by the Children Act 1989 Sch 13, para 45(2).

ward *immediately* an application for wardship is made (that is, as soon as the originating summons is issued),[17] but he ceases to be one unless an application for an appointment to hear the summons has been made within 21 days.[18] A child does not otherwise cease to be a ward until either the court makes a specific order to that effect[19] or a care order is made in respect of a ward,[20] or until the child attains his majority.

The parties to the proceedings

Any person having a proper interest may make a child a ward. In *Re D (A Minor) (Wardship: Sterilisation)*,[1] for example, an educational psychologist attached to a local authority warded a child to prevent her being sterilised. Children can also effectively ward themselves by issuing an originating summons, provided it is filed by a next friend.[2]

Before the Children Act 1989 these relaxed rules governing who could apply[3] meant that for many applicants wardship offered the only possible recourse to the court. Although for most an application under the Children Act would now be more appropriate, it is to be noted that unlike that Act no formal court leave is required even for those unrelated to the child, to make the child a ward. Instead applicants must[4] provide in the summons a brief description of their interest in, or relationship to, the minor, and the particulars are then sent for recording in the register of wards.[5] If it appears that the application is an abuse of process, the summons may be dismissed. It has been held,[6] perhaps questionably, that the High Court has an inherent power to make a child a ward of court of its own motion. On the other hand, it appears that the Official Solicitor cannot ward on his own initiative,[7] nor can a guardian ad litem *qua guardian*.[8] Formerly, local authorities could ward children, but their ability to do so, at any rate where there is a care order, has been ended by s 100 of the Children Act 1989.[9]

The rules are equally flexible as to who can be made defendants. Primarily, the person against whom the order is sought is made the defendant, but any other interested party can apply to be made a party.[10] Surprisingly, perhaps, the child is not automatically a party, but is made one only in cases where it is thought

---

17 An originating summons may be issued by the Principal Registry or a district registry.

18 FPR 1991 r 5.3(1)(a).

19 Discussed post, p 693.

20 Children Act 1989 s 91(4).

 1 [1976] Fam 185, [1976] 1 All ER 326. See also a case referred to in The Times on 21 May 1985 where the Brook Advisory Centre warded a child to authorise an abortion.

 2 In accordance with RSC Ord 80 r 2; cf FPR 1991 r 9.2A which permits children of sufficient understanding to apply for leave to apply for a s 8 order without a next friend.

 3 Indeed, until *Re Dunhill* (1967) 111 Sol Jo 113, in which a night club owner warded one of his striptease artists purely for publicity purposes, there were no rules at all.

 4 FPR 1991 r 5.1(6).

 5 FPR 1991 r 5.1(4).

 6 *R v North Yorkshire County Council, ex p M (No 3)* [1989] 2 FLR 82 per Ewbank J. See also the Mental Health Act 1983 s 96(1)(i).

 7 *Re D (A Minor) (Wardship: Sterilisation)*, supra, but see Lowe and White, op cit, at para 9.5.

 8 *Re T (Minors) (Wardship: Jurisdiction)* [1990] Fam 1, [1989] 1 All ER 297, CA, and *A v Berkshire County Council* [1989] 1 FLR 273, CA.

 9 Discussed post, pp 698–9.

10 In an application to restrain an undesirable relationship, discussed post, p 694, the person alleged to be undesirable should not be made a party: *Practice Direction* [1983] 2 All ER 672.

appropriate.[11] Examples of cases in which it may be appropriate to make the child a party are:[12]

(a) where a teenage ward is in dispute with his or her parents so that the Official Solicitor can express the ward's views to the court;
(b) where the ward is old enough to express a view, usually aged eight or over, where that view is likely to be of particular importance, for example, if there are allegations of 'brain-washing';
(c) where a specific task has to be carried out by an independent party, such as the psychiatric examination of a ward;
(d) where there are difficult issues on law or facts, such as international problems or questions affecting the life or death of the ward, disputed medical evidence or where there are special or exceptional points of law.

5. THE COURT'S POWERS

Confirming or discharging the wardship

At the initial hearing the judge must first decide whether or not to continue the wardship. It is at this stage that issues of jurisdiction should be taken.[13] The wardship may be discharged if the court declines to exercise its jurisdiction, for example, because it considers the application spurious, because it declines to interfere with a decision of another body or tribunal, or because it decides that wardship is of no further benefit to the child. It should be discharged where there is no significant evidence on which to exercise the jurisdiction.[14] It is now generally accepted[15] that the wardship should not be continued unless it offers advantages to the child concerned which cannot be secured by the use of the orders available under the 1989 Act or, presumably, under the residual inherent jurisdiction.

Orders that can be made

(a) The position before the Children Act 1989

Before the Children Act 1989 the unique combination of statutory and inherent powers meant that the court had jurisdiction to make a wide range of orders to protect both the person and property of its wards. Indeed, as one commentary put it,[16] 'the law knew no greater form of protection for a child than wardship'. Thus, in addition to its statutory powers[17] to commit wards into local authority care or to

---

11 See FPR 1991, r 5.1(3).
12 See *Practice Direction* [1993] 2 FLR 641, giving guidance on the appointment of the Official Solicitor in family proceedings generally.
13 Particularly where the issue is one of discretion: see eg *Re D (A Minor)* (1978) 76 LGR 653.
14 *Re F (Minors) (Wardship: Jurisdiction)* [1988] 2 FLR 123, CA. See also *Re Z (Minors) (Child Abuse: Evidence)* [1989] 2 FLR 3.
15 See *Re T (A Minor) (Wardship: Representation)* [1994] Fam 49, [1993] 4 All ER 518, sub nom *Re CT (A Minor) (Wardship: Representation)* [1993] 2 FLR 278, CA and *Re W (Wardship: Discharge: Publicity)* [1995] 2 FLR 466, CA.
16 Lowe and White, op cit at para 1.1.
17 Under the Family Law Reform Act 1969 ss 6–7. There was some authority suggesting that the court had an *inherent* jurisdiction to (a) commit wards into local authority care: see *Salford City Council v C* (1981) 3 FLR 153 and *Re S W (A Minor) (Wardship: Jurisdiction)* [1986] 1 FLR 24; and (b), more doubtfully, to make financial provision: see eg *Calderdale Borough Council v H and P* [1991] 1 FLR 461 and *W v Avon County Council* (1979) 9 Fam Law 33; but see the criticism at [1991] Fam Law 220 and by Lowe and White, op cit, para 6.45.

make supervision orders, and to make maintenance orders, it had an inherent power to make detailed orders relating to the care of wards by individuals and to resolve disputes over the ward's property. It could also resolve disputes over the ward's education and religious upbringing. Over and above this it had wide protective powers as, for example, to restrain the ward's marriage or his continued association with a named individual or group,[18] to restrain third parties from communicating, harbouring or even attempting to discover the ward's where-abouts,[19] and to make non-molestation orders both in respect of the ward and those looking after him.[20] It could also restrain the ward's removal from the jurisdiction, which power even extended to forbidding those who were not parties to assist the removal.[1] Conversely, the court could sanction the ward's temporary or permanent removal from the jurisdiction. It had been held[2] that the protective power extended to preventing a mother leaving the jurisdiction before giving a blood sample so as to be able to determine the ward's paternity. It was well established that the court had wide control over a ward's medical treatment, both to sanction or forbid it,[3] and to make specific restriction on what could be published about a ward and his family.[4]

(b)   The position after the Children Act

In accordance with the deliberate policy to reduce the need to invoke the jurisdiction[5] the 1989 Act significantly narrowed the ambit of wardship by removing all powers to commit a ward into local authority care or to make supervision orders in respect of such a child. We will discuss the impact of these changes shortly.

---

18 See eg *Re F (Otherwise A) (A Minor) (Publication of Information)* [1977] Fam 58, [1978] 3 All ER 274, CA, and *Iredell v Iredell* (1885) 1 TLR 260. Orders are usually made against the third part so as to avoid having to imprison the ward in the event of disobedience. For a case where a ward was imprisoned see *Re Crump (An Infant)* (1963) 107 Sol Jo 682.

19 See eg *Re B (JA) (An Infant)* [1965] Ch 1112, [1965] 2 All ER 168; *Re R (PM) (An Infant)* [1968] 1 All ER 691n and *Re B (A Minor) (Wardship: Child in Care)* [1975] Fam 36. In *Re JT (A Minor) (Wardship: Committal)* [1986] 2 FLR 107 the father was ordered not to attempt to remove his child from care.

20 See *Re V* (1979) 123 Sol Jo 201 and Lowe and White, op cit. There is, however, no inherent power to attach a power of arrest: see *Re G (Wardship) (Jurisdiction: Power of Arrest)* (1982) 4 FLR 538, CA.

1 In *Re Harris (An Infant)* (1960) Times, 21 May certain airlines were ordered not to carry a ward on any of their aircraft!

2 *Re J (A Minor) (Wardship)* [1988] 1 FLR 65.

3 See eg *Re B (A Minor) (Wardship: Medical Treatment)* [1990] 3 All ER 927, CA in which the court sanctioned, contrary to the parents' wishes, a life-saving treatment for a newly born child suffering from Down's Syndrome; *Re P (A Minor)* [1986] 1 FLR 272 and *Re B (Wardship: Abortion)* [1991] 2 FLR 426, where the court sanctioned an abortion in accordance respectively with a 15- and 12-year-old ward's wishes but contrary to those of the parents. See also *Re D (A Minor) (Wardship: Sterilisation)* [1976] Fam 185, [1976] 1 All ER 326 where the court restrained the sterilisation of a ward even though her mother had consented to the operation. For further discussion of these and other cases see ante, pp 358ff and post, p 710.

4 See eg *Re M and N (Minors) (Wardship: Publication of Information)* [1990] Fam 211, [1990] 1 All ER 205, CA; *A v C* [1985] FLR 445, in which the court ordered that none of the parties should disclose to the child or anyone else the bizarre circumstances about the ward's birth; and *Re C (A Minor) (Wardship: Surrogacy)* [1985] FLR 846, in which the court ordered that there should be no publicity that might identify the 'commissioning parents'. Note that according to *X County Council v A* [1985] 1 All ER 53, per Balcombe J, such orders bind the ward and not simply the parties. This power is discussed further below at p 706.

5 See Law Com No 172, *Guardianship and Custody* at para 4.35.

Another important change was brought about by the availability of s 8 orders (it may be recalled[6] that prohibited steps and specific issue orders were in fact modelled on the wardship court's inherent powers to protect children). Since wardship proceedings rank as 'family proceedings',[7] the court is empowered in those proceedings to make any s 8 order whether or not they have been applied for. Although the interrelationship between s 8 orders and the wardship jurisdiction has yet to be definitively explored, the better view would seem to be that:

(a) while it is consistent with the continuation of wardship to make a residence order, wardship should only be kept in place where there is good reason to maintain the court's continuing supervision; and

(b) while s 8 powers do not oust the court's inherent powers, whenever there is a choice, the former powers should be exercised.

With regard to (a), since a residence order only determines the person with whom the child is to live,[8] it is not inconsistent with the court's control over its ward to make such an order.[9] However, unless the court believes that there is some benefit in continuing the wardship, it should, upon making a residence order, discharge the wardship.[10] Where the wardship is ordered to continue, the parents, or anyone else who has a residence order, will still have parental responsibility but will be subject to the general need to obtain the court's consent with regard to any important steps in the child's life.[11]

With regard to (b), it has been held that, unless there is some real advantage to the child, the statutory scheme should be used in preference to the wardship or general inherent jurisdiction.[12] Accordingly, in any wardship proceedings the court's inherent powers should only be exercised where there is no statutory alternative. Hence, for example, rather than making restraining orders under their inherent powers to prevent the ward's association with or prospective marriage to a particular person, or to prevent a person associating or communicating with or harbouring the ward, the court should now make a prohibited steps order instead. Even where it is appropriate to exercise the inherent powers, consideration will still have to be given as to whether to continue the wardship. We discuss the current ambit of the inherent powers in the context of the High Court's general inherent jurisdiction.[13]

The former statutory power to make maintenance orders has been repealed,[14]

---

6 See ante, p 419.

7 Children Act 1989 s 8(3), discussed ante, p 445.

8 See ante, p 412.

9 Although it had been established before the 1989 Act that the court had power to determine a ward's place of residence (see *Re J (A Minor)* [1989] Fam 85, [1989] 3 All ER 590), it was well established that it could not make old style custody orders (see *Re CB (a minor) (wardship: local authority)* [1981] 1 All ER 16, CA) nor guardianship orders (see *Re C (minors) (wardship: adoption)* [1989] 1 All ER 395, CA) since that was inconsistent with the court's continuing control over its wards. The latter embargo still applies, but there would be nothing to prevent the court from making a guardianship appointment and de-warding the child. The court's powers to appoint guardians are governed by s 5 of the Children Act 1989, discussed ante, pp 404ff.

10 See *Re T (A Minor) (Child: Representation)* [1994] Fam 49, [1993] 4 All ER 518, CA, discussed further below at pp 699–700. Note that in *Re M (Child's Upbringing)* [1996] 2 FLR 441, CA (the 'Zulu Boy' case, discussed ante, p 470) the wardship was maintained notwithstanding the order that the boy be returned to South Africa.

11 See ante, p 687.

12 See *Re T*, supra and *Re R (A Minor) (Blood Transfusion)* [1993] 2 FLR 757.

13 See post, pp 702ff.

14 The Family Law Reform Act 1969 s 6 was repealed by the Courts and Legal Services Act 1990, Sch 20.

and insofar as the court has any power (in view of the Child Support Act 1991) to make financial provision for its ward, its jurisdiction to do so is governed by Sch 1 to the Children Act 1989, which is discussed in Chapter 17.

6.   THE PRINCIPLES ON WHICH THE COURT ACTS

From time to time statements are made which suggest that the welfare of a ward is always the paramount consideration.[15] It is clear, however, that the individual ward's interests are not always thought to be overriding.[16] The best explanation for this seems to be that the paramountcy of the ward's welfare only applies when the court is called upon to exercise what used to be termed its custodial jurisdiction, and not where it is exercising a purely protective jurisdiction. In short the ward's welfare will only be the paramount consideration when s 1(1) of the Children Act 1989 applies, namely where his upbringing or the administration of his property is directly in issue.[17]

Where the court is called upon to exercise a purely protective jurisdiction (ie where the issue falls outside the scope of s 1(1) of the 1989 Act and is not governed by other statutes), the ward's welfare is not accorded any specially weighted interest, though it will remain an important consideration. Whether the court will protect a ward will depend on how seriously and how directly the child's interests may be harmed and how important any competing interests are.[18]

7.   THE MODERN USE OF THE JURISDICTION

The position before the Children Act 1989 [19]

Before the Children Act 1989 the many and often unique characteristics of wardship proved useful to disparate applicants, although the high costs[1] and lengthy delays in obtaining a court hearing militated against an even greater use. Nevertheless, as the following table[2] (see p 697 opposite) shows, there had been, particularly during the 20 years preceding the Children Act 1989, a phenomenal rise in the number of wardships.

A key reason for this growth was the use of wardship by local authorities, who

---

15 In *Re D (A Minor) (Justices' Decision: Review)* [1977] Fam 158 at 163, Dunn J memorably referred to the 'golden thread' running through the wardship jurisdiction, namely the welfare of the child 'which is considered in this court first, last and all the time'.

16 See, for example, *Re M and N (Minors) (Wardship: Publication of Information)* [1990] Fam 211 at 223, [1990] 1 All ER 205 at 210, where Butler-Sloss LJ expressly said that in cases where restraint of publicity is sought 'the welfare of the ward is not the paramount consideration'. See further, post, pp 707–8.

17 The scope of s 1(1) is discussed ante at pp 325ff.

18 See post, pp 705ff.

19 See generally Law Com Working Paper No 101 (1987) *Wards of Court*, Part III.

1 The DHSS Child Care Review Costings Working Party (1986, para 5.21) estimated the average cost of an order confirming wardship to have been £5,960 in an uncontested case and £7,970 in a contested case.

2 The 1951, 1961 and 1971 figures can be found in Cretney *Principles of Family Law* (1st edn, 1974) p 289. The remaining statistics can be found in *Judicial Statistics* for each year.

NUMBER OF ORIGINATING SUMMONSES			
	Principal Registry	**District Registries**	**Total**
1951	74	Not applicable	74
1961	258	Not applicable	258
1971	622	Not applicable	622
1981	822	1,081	1,903
1985	965	1,850	2,815
1990	1,146	3,575	4,721
1991	1,288	3,672	4,961

for a variety of reasons found it advantageous to use the prerogative jurisdiction rather than the statutory scheme to get children into care or to keep them there.[3] Local authority use of wardship increased considerably in the latter half of the 1980s, accounting for up to 40 per cent of all applications in 1985, rising to a high of 66 per cent in 1989.[4]

Another important use of wardship was by relatives who, until 1985,[5] had no other means of initiating court proceedings either to seek to look after the child or to have contact. In 1985 24 per cent of wardships involved relatives.[6]

Parents too used to look to wardship, particularly in relation to international child abduction, where the immediacy of the prohibition against a ward's removal from the country together with the wide jurisdictional rules were an obvious advantage.[7] A more traditional use of the jurisdiction was in the so-called 'teenage wardship', where parents warded their children to prevent their marriage to or continued association with someone considered to be 'undesirable'.[8] Though occasionally useful, this declined when in 1971 the age of majority was reduced to 18. In contrast to 'teenage wardships' there was some evidence of wardship being used by children against their parents.[9]

A further important role of wardship was in respect to novel cases, where the availability of High Court expertise, as well as the jurisdiction's wide powers, was clearly an advantage. A good example of this was in relation to determining the future of Britain's first and much publicised commercially arranged surrogate child.[10]

3　See Hunt *Local Authority Wardship before the Children Act: The Baby or the Bathwater* (1993); Masson and Morton 'The Use of Wardship by Local Authorities' (1989) 52 MLR 762; and Lowe 'The Role of Wardship in Child Care Cases' [1989] Fam Law 38.

4　By 1991 this had dropped back to 55.5 per cent.

5　Until the implementation of the custodianship provisions: see the 7th edition of this work, ch 11.

6　See Law Com Working Paper No 101 (1987) *Wardship* para 3.3. Grandparents were a particularly significant user of the jurisdiction: see Law Com Working Paper No 96 (1986) *Custody* para 5.38, n 92.

7　See further Chapter 13.

8　See Cross *Wards of Court* (1967) 83 LQR 200 at 209 et seq; Turner 'Wardship and the Official Solicitor' (1977) 2 Adoption and Fostering 30 at 33; and Lowe and White, op cit, paras 12-1 et seq.

9　See the 7th edition of this work at p 434.

10　*Re C (A Minor) (Wardship: Surrogacy)* [1985] FLR 846.

The position after the Children Act 1989 [11]

(a)   Restrictions in public law cases

The major direct impact of the 1989 Act on the application of wardship is with respect to local authority use. The Act makes wardship and local authority care incompatible.[12] If a care order is made under s 31 in respect of a ward of court, the wardship ceases[13] and while a child is in care he cannot be made a ward of court.[14] Furthermore, both the former statutory and inherent powers to commit wards of court into local authority care and to make supervision orders have been respectively expressly repealed and revoked by s 100(1) and (2)(a). On the other hand, if in wardship proceedings it appears to the court that a care or supervision order might be appropriate, then, like any other court in 'family proceedings',[15] it can, pursuant to the powers under s 37,[16] direct a local authority to investigate the child's circumstances with a view to the authority making an application. In the event of such an application being made,[17] a care or supervision order can only be made provided the threshold criteria under s 31 are satisfied.

However, the restrictions imposed by the 1989 Act do *not* prevent the High Court from exercising its inherent jurisdiction to decide a specific question in relation to a child in local authority care.[18]

In view of these restrictions it is tempting to say that the use of wardship by and against local authorities, which, as we have seen, accounted for such a large proportion of pre-1989 Act cases, has effectively been ended.[19] In theory, however, wardship remains an option where the child is *not* in their care, including those being accommodated by them. Although wardship cannot be used to bring about such an arrangement,[20] unlike care, accommodation is not incompatible with wardship. However, to invoke wardship local authorities will need court leave,[1] which may only be given upon the court being satisfied that: (a) the remedy sought to be achieved cannot be achieved by the making of a s 8 order (it must be remembered that local authorities can with court leave apply to a prohibited steps or specific issue order); and (b) the child is likely to suffer significant harm if the jurisdiction is not exercised. Even if leave is given, s 100(2)(d)[2] prevents the courts from making orders the effect of which is to confer upon authorities aspects of parental responsibility that they do not already have.

Notwithstanding these restrictions, given that s 8 orders do not cover every situation, in cases where the local authority are not themselves seeking care but are

---

11 See generally White, Carr and Lowe *Children Act in Practice* (2nd edition, 1995) paras 12.5ff; Parry 'The Children Act 1989: Local Authorities, Wardship and the Revival of the Inherent Jurisdiction' [1992] JSWFL 212; and Bainham 'The Children Act 1989 – The Future of Wardship' [1990] Fam Law 270.

12 See the Department of Health's *Guidance and Regulations*, Vol 1, *Court Orders*, para 3.99.

13 Children Act 1989 s 91(4).

14 Ibid, s 100(2)(c) and the Supreme Court Act 1981 s 41(2A), added by Sch 13, para 45(2), to the 1989 Act.

15 Wardship proceedings are 'family proceedings' by reason of s 8(3)(a).

16 Discussed ante, p 455.

17 But there is no power to force the local authority to apply: see eg *Nottingham County Council v P* [1994] Fam 18, [1993] 3 All ER 815, discussed ante, p 455 and post, p 712.

18 Discussed post, p 709.

19 See Bainham, *Children: The Modern Law* p 411, who submits that wardship (as distinct from the inherent jurisdiction) is redundant in public law cases.

20 See s 100(2)(b).

1 Pursuant to s 100(3), discussed further post, p 709.

2 Discussed post, pp 703–4.

nevertheless concerned about a child's well-being, wardship might still be the right solution, at any rate, where there is thought to be a need for the court's continuing control.

In *Re R (A Minor) (Contempt)*,[3] for example, a local authority warded a 14-year-old child accommodated by them to protect her from a relationship with a 33-year-old man. A local authority has also been known to ward children to protect them from being identified in a television programme about alleged paedophiles.[4] Other possible examples are where a local authority, learning of a surrogacy arrangement, are concerned about the child's welfare[5] and where they are concerned about the refusal to authorise medical treatment for a child.[6]

(b) Private law cases

Although no express restraint is placed on the use of wardship by individuals by the 1989 Act, as the Department of Health's *Guidance and Regulations* puts it, its impact is considerable:

> 'By incorporating many of the beneficial aspects of wardship, such as the "open door" policy, and a flexible range of orders, the Act will substantially reduce the need to have recourse to the High Court.'

As a result of these changes, relatives are now generally better advised to seek, albeit with leave, s 8 orders in the lower courts. Similarly in most cases it is difficult to see what advantages parents would gain from wardship, rather than pursuing remedies under the 1989 Act.

As expected the statistics, insofar as they are available, do bear evidence of the dramatic decline in the private use of wardship. In 1991, the final year running up to implementation, 2,209 (accounting for 44.5 per cent of the record number of wardship applications made in that year) originating summonses were taken out by individuals.[7] In contrast in 1992 the total number of summonses issued was 492.[8]

(c) The ruling in Re T

Although the decline in the de facto use of wardship was predictable, it was more difficult to anticipate how the courts would react to cases where it was sought to invoke the jurisdiction. In this respect regard needs to be had to *Re T (A Minor) (Child: Representation)*[9] in which the Court of Appeal held that, given that FPR 1991 r 9.2A[10] applied to all 'family proceedings', in wardship, as in any other family proceedings, provided the child has sufficient understanding to bring or

3 [1994] 2 FLR 185, CA. Quaere whether a prohibited steps order could have been made in this case?
4 *Cornwall County Council v BBC* (1994) unreported. But see further below at p 711 n 18.
5 See *Re C (A Minor) (Wardship: Surrogacy)* [1985] FLR 846, and Local Authority Circular (85) 12.
6 See *Re B (A Minor) (Wardship: Medical Treatment)* [1981] 1 WLR 1421, CA.
7 *Judicial Statistics* for 1991 (Cm 1991), Table 5.8.
8 CAAC Report 1992/93, p 25. According to that report, 141 originating summonses for wardship were issued between January and July 1993, but we understand from the Information Management Unit of the Lord Chancellor's Department that a total of 269 summonses were issued in 1993. It is unknown how many of these summonses were issued by individuals but, given the embargo on the public law use of wardship, it is reasonable to assume that the vast majority were issued in the private law context. The 1993/94 Report gives no updating statistics for wardship and, curiously, no such information has been included in the *Judicial Statistics* since implementation of the 1989 Act.
9 [1994] Fam 49, [1993] 4 All ER 518, CA, discussed in detail in White, Carr and Lowe, op cit at paras 12.13ff.
10 Through which children of sufficient understanding can seek to apply for s 8 orders without a next friend.

defend proceedings on his or her own behalf, the court has no power to impose a guardian ad litem on such a child against his or her wishes. It was further held that, given that there were no advantages either to the child or to the defendants[11] that were not also available in ordinary family proceedings under Part II of the 1989 Act, there was nothing which, in the words of Waite LJ, would justify giving the child 'the status, an exceptional status under the modern law as it must now be applied, of a ward of court'.[12]

In concluding that the continuation of wardship was inappropriate, Waite LJ commented that while it survives as an independent jurisdiction, the:

'. . . courts' undoubted discretion to allow wardship to go forward in a suitable case is subject to their clear duty, in loyalty to the scheme and purpose of the Children Act legislation, to permit recourse to wardship only when it becomes apparent to the judge in any particular case that the question which the court is determining in regard to the minor's upbringing or property cannot be resolved under the statutory procedures in Part II of the Act in a way that secures the best interests of the child; or where the minor's person is in a state of jeopardy from which he can only be protected by giving him the status of a ward of court; or where the court's functions need to be secured from the effects potentially injurious to the child, of external influences (intrusive publicity for example) and it is decided that conferring on the child the status of a ward will prove a more efficient deterrent than the ordinary sanctions of a contempt of court which already protect all family proceedings.[13]

(d)   Some possible remaining uses of wardship

Given that no material changes have been made to the rules governing the issue of an originating summons, it is submitted that Waite LJ's comments in *Re T* ought not to be taken as restricting an individual's ability to make a child a ward of court in the first instance, though clearly the courts will require special justification to continue the wardship once the case comes before them. It remains now to consider what advantages there may be in issuing an originating summons and when the court might consider continuing the wardship.

One important remaining advantage of the wardship jurisdiction is its immediacy: as soon as the originating summons is issued, the child becomes a ward and no important step may then be taken without prior court sanction.[14] In effect the issuing of the originating summons provides a unique quasi-administrative mechanism by which the child's legal position can be immediately frozen, which is useful when dealing with emergencies, such as threatened child abduction, particularly when an international element is involved.[15] Invoking wardship can also be an effective way of halting a proposed medical operation on the child and can provide a usefully speedy means by which non-parents who would otherwise have to seek leave to apply for a s 8 order can safeguard their position, for example, by preventing parents from removing the child from their care pending a court hearing.

Although, as the above discussion shows, it may still be useful to make a child a ward of court to prevent further action without court sanction, since *Re T* it by no means follows that once invoked the court will continue the wardship. On the

---

11 Who were adoptive parents. The girl in question aged 13 was an adopted child who was seeking to live with her natural paternal aunt.
12 Ibid at 650 and 528 respectively.
13 Ibid at 60 and 524 respectively.
14 Discussed ante at pp 686ff.
15 See ante, pp 482ff.

contrary, the continuation of wardship needs special justification. In this regard the two other distinctive features of the jurisdiction, namely the width of the powers and the continued court control of a ward, need to be borne in mind. It remains the case that the court's wardship powers are wider than those under s 8 and where advantage needs to be taken of this and of the court's continued control then it would be proper both to invoke and to continue the wardship.

In *Re W (Wardship: Discharge: Publicity)*,[16] for example, a father, having been granted care and control of four sons aged between 10 and 15 in earlier wardship proceedings, had unilaterally changed their schooling and acquiesced in them talking to the press about their 'fight to stay with their Dad'. His request to discharge the wardship was refused. In the Court of Appeal's view the continuation of the wardship was justified because no comparable protection could be achieved under the Children Act 1989, since it was impossible to make a prohibited steps order which could anticipate how the father might act, and because a prohibited steps order might not be appropriate to prevent the publishing of information about the children.[17] Furthermore, the continuing nature of the wardship meant that the Official Solicitor could remain involved and act as a buffer between the parents. The case could also be reserved to the same judge.

The continuing overall control could also be thought to be advantageous, for example, in the case of an abandoned child, where no one looking after him has parental responsibility or, as in *Re C (A Baby)*,[18] in which Sir Stephen Brown P said that the courts were ready to assist with taking responsibility in cases of grave anxiety. In that case the child developed meningitis which left her brain-damaged and unable to survive without artificial ventilation and she would suffer increasing pain and distress with no hope of recovery. Sir Stephen Brown commented:

> 'It appeared appropriate that the courts should take responsibility for this child and relieve the parents in some measure of the grave responsibility which they have borne since her birth.'

The jurisdiction could also provide an effective means of protecting and managing a child's property interests in the event of the parents' death.

C.   The inherent jurisdiction[19]

1.   JURISDICTION AND PROCEDURE

The inherent jurisdiction can be invoked either upon specific application or by the High Court itself in cases where it is already seized of proceedings.[20] Since it is

---

16 [1995] 2 FLR 466.
17 But note Hobhouse LJ's dissenting judgment and the subsequent decision in *Re Z (A Minor) (Identification: Restrictions on Publication)* [1997] Fam 1, sub nom *Re Z (a minor) (freedom of publication)* [1995] 4 All ER 961, CA, discussed ante at pp 371–2.
18 [1996] 2 FLR 43.
19 See generally White, Carr and Lowe, op cit at paras 12.21ff.
20 See, for example, *Re R (A Minor) (Blood Test: Constraint)* [1988] Fam 66, [1998] 1 FLR 745 in which Hale J held there to be power under the inherent jurisdiction to order a child to provide a blood sample for the purposes of establishing paternity; and *Re X (A Minor) (Adoption Details: Disclosure)* [1994] Fam 174, in which it was held to be an appropriate use of the inherent jurisdiction by the High Court hearing an adoption application to order that during the minority of the child in question the Registrar General should not disclose to any person without leave of the court the details of the adoption entered in the Adopted Children Register.

established[1] that it is only the High Court that has inherent powers to protect children, unless proceedings relating to the exercise of the inherent jurisdiction have been transferred from the High Court to the county court pursuant to s 38(2)(b) of the Matrimonial and Family Proceedings Act 1984, it is clear that the lower courts have no comparable jurisdiction.

Applications to invoke the inherent jurisdiction must be made to the High Court.[2] Local authorities wishing to invoke the jurisdiction must first obtain leave of the court.[3] Although no specific procedure is laid down by the Family Proceedings Rules 1991,[4] in practice, like wardship, application is made by originating summons[5] with the plaintiff filing, unless otherwise directed, an affidavit in support of the application.

Jurisdiction to make orders giving the care of a child to any person or providing for contact, or the education of a child, is governed by the Family Law Act 1986 and is co-extensive with the wardship jurisdiction.[6] It seems probable that jurisdiction to make orders outside the ambit of s 1(1)(d) is the same as in wardship.[7]

2.   THE EFFECT OF INVOKING THE INHERENT JURISDICTION

Unlike wardship, the exercise of the inherent jurisdiction does not place the child under the ultimate responsibility of the court. This means that at no point will the child be subject to the rule obtaining in wardship that all important steps in the child's life have to be sanctioned by the court.[8]

3.   THE COURT'S POWERS

The general extent of the inherent powers

Proceedings under the inherent jurisdiction rank as 'family proceedings' for the purposes of the Children Act 1989,[9] so that in general terms the court is empowered either upon application or its own motion to make any s 8 order.[10]

---

1   *D v D (County Court Jurisdiction: Injunctions)* [1993] 2 FLR 802, CA, in which it was held that the county court had no inherent power to grant injunctions. See also *Devon County Council v B* [1997] 3 FCR 333, CA and *Re S and D (Children: Powers of the Court)* [1995] 1 FCR 626, [1995] 2 FLR 456, CA.

2   Supreme Court Act 1981 Sch 1, para 3(b)(ii), as amended by the Children Act 1989 Sch 13, para 45(3).

3   Children Act 1989 s 100(3), discussed post, p 709.

4   Part V specifically applies to wardship.

5   Applications are generally headed 'In the matter of the Supreme Court Act 1981'.

6   See ante, p 690.

7   See ante, p 691.

8   *Re W (A Minor) (Medical Treatment: Court's Jurisdiction)* [1993] Fam 64, [1992] 4 All ER 627 at 631d, per Lord Donaldson MR; and *Re J (A Minor) (Child in Care: Medical Treatment)* [1993] Fam 15, [1992] 4 All ER 614, CA. Note that this accords with Lord Mackay LC's comments in his Joseph Jackson Memorial lecture (1989) 139 NLJ 505 at 508 that it was not thought 'appropriate or practicable for the responsibility for a child in the care of a public authority which is statutorily charged with looking after him to be subject to the detailed directions of another public authority, namely the courts.'

9   Children Act 1989 s 8(3)(a).

10   See ante, pp 446–7.

Although these statutory powers should be used whenever possible,[11] there will be occasions when either the courts are barred from using them, as where children are already in local authority care,[12] or where what is being sought lies outside their scope. On these occasions recourse can properly be had to the court's inherent powers.

Before implementation of the 1989 Act there had been some speculation[13] as to whether these inherent powers were the same as those under the wardship jurisdiction. It had been suggested, for example, that the wardship powers might be wider because, unlike the inherent jurisdiction, ultimate responsibility for the child is vested in the court. It is now clear, however, that the powers under the general inherent jurisdiction are co-extensive with those under wardship since, properly regarded, wardship was merely the machinery by which the court traditionally exercised its parens patriae powers to protect children, but not the exclusive means by which these extensive powers could be exercised on behalf of the Crown.[14] As Lord Donaldson MR put it in *Re W (A Minor) (Medical Treatment: Court's Jurisdiction)*:[15]

'Since there seems to be some doubt about the matter, it should be made clear that the High Court's inherent jurisdiction in relation to children – the parens patriae jurisdiction – is equally exercisable whether the child is or is not a ward of court . . .'

Express limitations imposed by the Children Act 1989

The Children Act 1989 s 100(2) expressly limits the exercise of the High Court's inherent jurisdiction by preventing (a) a child being placed in the care or put under the supervision of a local authority and (b) a child from being accommodated by or on behalf of a local authority. These embargoes are in line with the general policy of the Act to prevent the courts from making care or supervision orders other than under s 31.[16] Section 100(2)(d) also prevents the High Court from exercising its inherent jurisdiction:

'. . . for the purpose of conferring on any local authority power to determine any question which has arisen, or which may arise, in connection with any aspect of parental responsibility for the child.'

The none-too-clear result of this provision would appear to be that, while the High Court may make orders under its inherent jurisdiction in respect of a child, in doing so it may not confer on the local authority any degree of parental

---

11 See *Re T (A Minor) (Child: Representation)* [1994] Fam 49, [1993] All ER 518, CA; and *Re R (A Minor) (Blood Transfusion)* [1993] 2 FLR 757.

12 See s 9(1)–(2) of the Children Act 1989, discussed ante, pp 429–32.

13 See the 8th edition of this work at 480–1.

14 A number of cases can be cited in support of this proposition, namely: *Re M and N (Wardship: Publication of Information)* [1990] Fam 211, [1990] 1 All ER 205, CA at 210, per Butler-Sloss LJ; *Re C (A Minor) (Wardship: Medical Treatment) (No 2)* [1990] Fam 39 at 46, [1989] 2 All ER 791, CA at 793, per Lord Donaldson MR; *Re N (Infants)* [1967] Ch 512, [1967] 1 All ER 161; and *Re L (An Infant)* [1968] P 119, [1967] 2 All ER 1110; cf *Re E (An Infant)* [1956] Ch 23, [1955] 3 All ER 174. A similar conclusion was reached in Canada: see *Re Eve* (1986) 31 DLR (4th) 1 at 14, per La Forest J (Canadian Supreme Court). For detailed examination of the history of the parens patriae jurisdiction see Seymour: 'Parens Patriae and Wardship Powers: Their Nature and Origins' (1994) 14 Oxford Journal of Legal Studies 159; and Lowe and White: *Wards of Court* (2nd edn), chs 1 and 7.

15 [1993] Fam 64 at 73F, [1992] 4 All ER 627 at 641c. See also Balcombe LJ at 85 and 640 respectively.

16 Discussed ante, pp 536ff.

responsibility that it does not already have.[17] This is less likely to cause problems where the child is in care, since the local authority will already be vested with parental responsibility.[18] Hence, the determination of a particular question by the court, for example, obtaining a return order against abducting parents, will not be contrary to s 100(2)(d).[19] Similarly, the court is free to determine the scope and extent of parental responsibility and can, for instance, make orders giving leave for a child in care to be interviewed by the father's solicitor to prepare a defence to criminal charges.[20] If the local authority do not have parental responsibility for the child, the High Court may not under its inherent jurisdiction make orders which in any way confer parental responsibility upon the authority. Hence, for example, while the court could sanction a named couple to look after the child (although it would probably do this by means of a residence order under s 8) it could not authorise a local authority to place the child, nor a fortiori to place the child 'with a view to adoption'. It has, however, been held wrong that s 100 be restrictively interpreted and that it is perfectly proper for a local authority to invite the court to exercise its inherent jurisdiction to protect children even if the exercise of that power would be an invasion of a person's parental responsibility, for example, by restricting a non-family member from contacting or communicating with the children in question.[1]

Other restriction on the exercise of the inherent powers[2]

Courts have traditionally declined to define the limits of their inherent powers to protect children and they have been habitually described as theoretically unlimited.[3] Nevertheless, although it is accepted that the High Court's inherent power to protect children is wider than that of a parent,[4] it is equally well established that, whatever may be the theoretical position, there are 'far-reaching limitations in principle' on the exercise of that jurisdiction.[5] As Ward LJ put it in *Re Z (A Minor) (Identification: Restrictions on Publication)*:[6]

'The wardship or inherent jurisdiction of the court to cast its cloak of protection over minors whose interests are at risk of harm is unlimited in theory though in practice the

---

17 As it is expressed by the Department of Health's *Guidance and Regulations*, Vol 1, *Court Orders*, at para 3.102.
18 See ante, p 563.
19 See *Southwark London Borough v B* [1993] 2 FLR 559 at 571 per Waite LJ.
20 Per Hale J in *Re M (Care: Leave To Interview Child)* [1995] 1 FLR 825.
 1 Per Thorpe J in *Devon County Council v S* [1994] Fam 169, [1995] 1 All ER 243, accepting the argument that the local authority were not seeking leave to apply to the court to confer any power upon themselves, but were asking the court to exercise its own powers.
 2 See generally Lowe 'The limits of the wardship jurisdiction, Part 2: The extent of the court's powers over a ward' (1989) 1 Journal of Child Law 44.
 3 See eg *Re W (A Minor) (Medical Treatment: Court's Jurisdiction)* [1993] Fam 64, [1992] 4 All ER 627 per Lord Donaldson MR and Balcombe LJ; *Re R (A Minor) (Wardship: Restrictions on Publication)* [1994] Fam 254 at 271, [1994] 3 All ER 658 at 672, per Millet LJ; and *Re B (Child Abduction: Wardship Power to Detain)* [1994] 2 FLR 479, CA at 483, per Butler-Sloss LJ and 487, per Hobhouse LJ.
 4 See *Re R (A Minor) (Wardship: Consent to Medical Treatment)* [1992] Fam 11 at 25B and 28G and *Re W (A Minor) (Medical Treatment: Court's Jurisdiction)*, supra. Note also that a similar standpoint has been taken by the Australian High Court in *Department of Health and Community Services v JWB and SMB* (1992) 66 ALJR 300.
 5 Per Balcombe LJ in *Re W*, supra, at 85 and 640 respectively, citing Sir John Pennycuick in *Re X (A Minor) (Wardship: Jurisdiction)* [1975] Fam 47, CA at 61.
 6 [1997] Fam 1 at 23, sub nom *Re Z (a minor) (freedom of publication)* [1995] 4 All ER 961 at 977.

judges who exercise the jurisdiction have created classes of cases in which the court will not exercise its powers'.

However, because of the court's tendency to approach the issue on a case-by-case basis rather then by laying down general guidance, the precise limits, even to the extent of determining whether there are, as Ward LJ suggests, necessarily de facto rather than de jure limits, are still far from clear.

(a)   The de jure limits

Notwithstanding that the established limits have developed more as a result of practice than of strict legal restraint, there are clearly some de jure as well as de facto limits to protecting the child in question. They cannot be used, for instance, to protect the parent qua parent.[7] Secondly, there is no inherent power to make orders that are prohibited by statute. As we have seen, the inherent power to commit children into local authority care or to make supervision orders has been expressly revoked by s 100(2)(a) of the Children Act.[8] As a general proposition, however, it would seem that the courts should be slow to hold that an inherent power has been abrogated or restricted by Parliament, and they should only do so where it is clear that Parliament so intended.[9]

A third possible limitation is that there is no inherent power to make orders that are purely statutory in origin, as, for example, to attach a power of arrest to a non-molestation order.[10] Whether there is a purely inherent power to make so-called ouster orders[11] is problematic. Until the House of Lords ruling in *Richards v Richards*[12] there was authority for saying that ouster orders could be made broadly on the basis of what was best for the child, and it was not unknown for such orders

7 See *Re V (A Minor) (Wardship)* (1979) 123 Sol Jo 201, where the court refused to hear a father's cross-application for an ouster order against his wife. Quaere whether this is how best to categorise *Re J S (A Minor)* [1981] Fam 22, [1980] 1 All ER 1061, CA, in which it was held that there is no inherent power to make declarations of paternity? On this point cf *T v Child Support Agency* [1997] 2 FLR 875, discussed post, p 733.
8 See ante, p 698.
9 For a scholarly treatise on the whole topic of inherent powers see Jacob 'The Inherent Jurisdiction of the Court' (1970) 23 Current Legal Problems 23. Indeed, it was for this reason that it had been held before the Children Act that, despite the then statutory scheme dealing with children in local authority care, the wardship jurisdiction had not thereby been ousted or abrogated, since the prerogative jurisdiction was neither expressly not by necessary implication so restricted: see *Re M (An Infant)* [1961] Ch 328 at 345, CA, per Lord Evershed MR and accepted by the House of Lords in *A v Liverpool City Council* [1982] AC 363, [1981] 2 All ER 385, HL. It would have to be on this basis that Douglas Brown J's ruling in *South Glamorgan County Council v W and B* [1993] 1 FLR 574 (discussed ante, p 576) that, notwithstanding s 43(8) and s 44(7) of the Children Act 1989 giving a child of sufficient understanding the right to refuse to submit to an examination or other assessment, these provisions were properly regarded as not having abrogated the inherent power to override those wishes.
10 See *Re G (Wardship) (Jurisdiction: Power of Arrest)* (1982) 4 FLR 538, discussed by Lowe, op cit, at 45–6. An alternative explanation of this case is that a distinction needs to be made between the power to make orders and the power to *enforce* them, the latter not being specially developed under the inherent jurisdiction – see also *Re B (Child Abduction: Wardship: Power To Detain)* [1994] 2 FLR 479, CA (no power to detain a person under the inherent jurisdiction in the absence of a finding of contempt). It is a nice point whether the power to make maintenance orders is a purely statutory power; cf the Report of the Committee on the Age of Majority (the Latey Committee) 1967 Cmnd 2342, para 250, which thought there was no inherent power and *Calderdale Borough Council v H and P* [1991] 1 FLR 461 and *W v Avon County Council* (1979) 9 Fam Law 33 in which it was held that there was an inherent power to make maintenance orders.
11 An ouster order excludes another person from a particular property.
12 [1984] AC 174, [1983] 2 All ER 807, HL.

to be made in wardship proceedings.[13] The decision in *Richards* seemed to put an end to such a line of reasoning, and in particular seemed to doubt the existence of an independent jurisdiction (ie outside that provided by the domestic violence legislation) to protect children by means of ouster orders.[14] Since *Richards*, however, there have been a number of Court of Appeal decisions which have complicated the position. In attempting to reconcile these post-*Richards* decisions, the Court of Appeal in *Pearson v Franklin*[15] concluded that distinctions have to be drawn according to whether the adult parties were spouses, former spouses, cohabitants or former cohabitants. Only if the adult parties were former spouses whose marriage has been dissolved by decree absolute is there an inherent power to make ouster orders.[16] Since *Pearson*, however, there have been two first instance decisions suggesting that the inherent powers may be wider. In the first, *Re S (Minors) (Inherent Jurisdiction: Ouster)*[17] Connell J granted a local authority's request under s 100 for leave to pursue an application to exclude a father from the matrimonial home, while in the second, *C v K (Inherent Powers: Exclusion Order)*[18] Wall J also concluded that there remained an inherent power to protect children by means of an ouster order. Whether the appellate courts will be disposed to uphold either decision remains to be seen, but so far as the former is concerned the need to do has been reduced by the power to include exclusion requirements in interim care orders and emergency protection orders introduced by the Family Law Act 1996.[19]

It has been argued[20] that a further limit to the jurisdiction is that there is no power to restrain the activities of those who are not in a family or personal relationship with the child in question. This argument was based on *Re X (A Minor) (Wardship: Jurisdiction)*,[1] in which the applicant sought in wardship to prevent the publication of a book containing details about the ward's dead father's alleged sexual predilections, on the basis that its publication would be grossly damaging to his 'highly strung' 14-year-old stepdaughter. The application failed, not because it was held that there was no such power, but because in this instance it was felt that freedom of speech was more important than the ward's welfare, which was in any event only indirectly at risk. The implications of reaching a contrary decision would have been enormous, since it would have meant that any activity that could be considered even indirectly harmful to a child might have been restrained by way of the wardship jurisdiction. Nevertheless, *Re X* is not authority for saying that the independent activities of others can never be restrained to protect a ward, or even that freedom of speech can never be curbed. Indeed, in *X County Council v A*[2] it was held that the press ought to be restrained from publishing details that could lead to the identity and whereabouts of the

---

13 See *Re V (a minor) (wardship)* (1979) 123 Sol Jo 201; *Rennick v Rennick* [1978] 1 All ER 817 at 819; and *Spindlow v Spindlow* [1979] Fam 52 at 58, in which Ormrod LJ assumed there was such a power. The matter was not beyond doubt, however: see to the contrary *Re D (minors)* (1982) 13 Fam Law 111.
14 See eg Lowe and White *Wards of Court* (2nd edn) pp 6–51.
15 [1994] 2 All ER 137, [1994] 1 WLR 370, discussed ante at pp 213–14.
16 Following *Webb v Webb* [1986] 1 FLR 541, and *Wilde v Wilde* [1988] 2 FLR 83, CA, each in turn applying *Quinn v Quinn* (1983) 4 FLR 394, CA.
17 [1994] 1 FLR 623.
18 [1996] 2 FLR 506.
19 Discussed ante at pp 577 and 594.
20 Everton 'High Tide in Wardship' (1975) 125 NLJ 930.
 1 [1975] Fam 47, [1975] 1 All ER 697, CA.
 2 [1985] 1 All ER 53.

ward, who was the child of a woman (Mary Bell) once convicted of manslaughter. In this latter case the restraint was on publicity directly referring to the ward and which would have been directly harmful. Subsequently restraining orders have been made, principally preventing identification of the children and their carers, and we will return to the power to restrain publicity when considering the de facto limits of the inherent powers.

Not all the cases seeking to control the activities of those unconnected with the ward have concerned publicity. In the extraordinary case of *Re C (A Minor) (Wardship: Jurisdiction)*[3] an independent day school run by a charity on orthodox Jewish principles admitted the son of Jewish parents on stringent conditions (including that the child should not live with his parents), but then indicated that the boy would be required to leave at the end of his first term. The local authority, concerned for the child's future, issued wardship proceedings seeking a mandatory injunction against the school requiring it to educate the boy. The Court of Appeal upheld the ruling that the application be refused. As Sir Stephen Brown P put it:

'If theoretically [the court] possesses such a power, I am clearly of the view that it is beyond the practical boundary of its wardship jurisdiction. This jurisdiction is not appropriate for use as an alternative to, or a cloak for, what appears, in fact, to be a claim for breach of contract by the parents against the school.'

What these cases in general, and *Re C* in particular, show is that, whilst the courts are reluctant to hold that there is no power to control the activities of those unconnected with a ward, they will only exercise that power where it is essential to do so to protect the ward from direct harm. In other words, such a limitation is de facto rather than de jure.

(b) The de facto limits

As Ward LJ said in *Re Z*,[4] the most obvious and well established of the de facto limits of the exercise of the inherent powers is where Parliament has entrusted the exercise of a competing discretion to another body or court. It has thus been long established that the court will not use its inherent powers to interfere with the exercise of discretion by local authorities over the children in their care,[5] the immigration service,[6] or by another court of competent jurisdiction.[7] By analogy it is also well established that there is no inherent power to order a doctor directly or indirectly to treat a child contrary to his or her clinical judgment.[8]

Quite apart from those limits, the courts also seem to be moving to a position of saying that the inherent jurisdiction should not be exercised so as to exempt the

3 [1991] 2 FLR 168, CA.
4 Supra, at 23 and 977 respectively.
5 See *A v Liverpool City Council*, supra, discussed ante, p 602.
6 See *Re Mohammed Arif (An Infant), Re Nirbhai Singh (An Infant)* [1968] Ch 643, [1968] 2 All ER 145, CA; *Re F (A Minor) (Immigration: Wardship)* [1990] Fam 125, [1989] 1 All ER 1155, CA; and *Re A (A Minor) (Wardship: Immigration)* [1992] 1 FLR 427, CA. However, the wardship might be continued to safeguard the children where that would not interfere with the immigration service's functions: *Re F*, supra and *Re K and S (Minors) (Wardship: Immigration)* [1992] 1 FLR 432.
7 See eg *Re A-H (Infants)* [1963] Ch 232; *Re K (KJS) (An Infant)* [1966] 3 All ER 154; and *Re PJ (An Infant)* [1968] 1 WLR 1976. Note also *Re G (A Minor) (Witness Summons)* [1988] 2 FLR 396 – no power to set aside a witness summons issued by the US authorities in connection with a Court Martial to be held in England since, under the terms of the Visiting Forces Act 1952, the court martial was a sovereign court vested with exclusive powers.
8 *Re J (A Minor) (Child In Care: Medical Treatment)* [1993] Fam 15, [1992] 4 All ER 614, CA, and *Re C (Medical Treatment)* [1998] 1 FLR 384.

child from the general law, or to obtain rights and privileges for a specific child that are not generally available to all children.[9] It is established that the inherent powers cannot be used to interfere with the normal criminal process,[10] nor with the normal operation of military law.[11] Whether the inherent powers can properly be exercised to shield a child from adverse publicity is, however, not altogether straightforward. As we have seen, while *Re X (A Minor) (Wardship: Jurisdiction)* showed that the courts were not prepared to restrain publications that were only indirectly harmful to the child, *X County Council v A* stood as authority to show that the courts might step in to prevent harmful publicity directly about the child. Furthermore, this latter power seemed to be accepted in a series of Court of Appeal decisions[12] which seemed to establish that in such cases the court had drawn a balance between the potential harm to the child and the right of others to comment on matters of public interest. This latter decision, however, was called into question in *R v Central Independent Television plc.*[13] In that case, rather as in the first *Re X* decision cited above, the publication in issue was not directly about the child but in fact a television programme about the work of the Metropolitan Police Obscene Publication Squad, which included pictures of the child's father who had been convicted of charges of indecency. In refusing an application to require the television company to obscure pictures of the father so as to avoid the possibility of identifying his children the Court of Appeal seemed to confine the inherent powers to protecting children from publicity where they were already exercising a continuing supervisory jurisdiction over the child in question. Waite LJ, for example, commented:[14]

'. . . anonymity or confidentiality for a child or its circumstances can only be enforced by injunction in cases where publicity would, or might in the view of the court threaten the effective working of the court's own jurisdiction.'

After a careful review of the authorities, Ward LJ concluded in *Re Z*[15] that, where the child was not already under the court's protective wing, then the freedom to publish material that was only indirectly, incidentally, or inferentially related to the child was 'beyond the limit of the exercise' of the inherent jurisdiction. On the other hand, the court certainly did have the power to protect children over whom it was already exercising a supervising role, to restrain publication of material that:

'. . . is directed at the child or is directed to an aspect of the child's upbringing by his parents or others who care for him in circumstances where that publicity is inimical to his welfare'.

---

9 See eg *Re R (A Minor) (Wardship: Restriction on Publication)* [1994] Fam 254 at 271, [1994] 3 All ER 658 at 672–3 per Millett LJ and *R v Central Independent Television plc* [1994] Fam 192, [1994] 3 All ER 641, CA.
10 See eg *Re K (A Minor) (Wardship: Criminal Proceedings)* [1988] Fam 1, [1988] 1 All ER 214.
11 See *Re JS (A Minor) (Wardship: Boy Soldier)* [1990] Fam 182, [1990] 2 All ER 861.
12 Notably *Re M and N (Minors) (Wardship: Publication of Information)* [1990] Fam 211, [1990] 1 All ER 205, in which a newspaper was not allowed to publish anything to identify two children (only one of whom was already a ward of court) when publishing a story after their removal from foster parents; and *Re W (a minor) (wardship: restrictions on publication)* [1992] 1 All ER 794, which again involved a publication about foster care, this time the identity of a boy with two men in a homosexual relationship in which identities were ordered not to be revealed.
13 [1994] Fam 192, [1994] 3 All ER 658. Note Hoffmann LJ in particular who at 205 and 654 respectively expressly doubted the correctness of the decision.
14 Ibid at pp 208 and 651 respectively. See also the similarly restrictive comments of particularly Millett LJ in *Re R (A Minor) (Wardship: Restrictions on Publication)* [1994] 254 at 271, [1994] 3 All ER 658 at 672–3.
15 Ibid at 23 and 978 respectively.

Equally, his Lordship considered that there was an inherent power to protect the integrity of the court's own proceedings, since by preserving the anonymity of those who come forward to assist the court, full and free disclosure would be encouraged which would ultimately inure to the benefit of the child. For this proposition he relied upon *In Re C (A Minor) (Wardship: Medical Treatment) (No 2)*,[16] in which it was held that, because publicity about the medical treatment of a terminally ill ward could affect the quality of care given to her, the court should issue an injunction prohibiting identification of the ward, the parents, the hospital at which she was being treated, and the solicitor, notwithstanding that the ward herself was incapable of being affected by any publicity. The injunction against identifying the parents was thought justified to protect the wardship jurisdiction, since parents might refuse to make a child a ward of court if they thought that they might be identified and singled out for media attention. Helpful though this analysis is, it does not entirely settle the crucial issue whether the jurisdiction can be invoked specifically to restrain publications directly about a child. As it stands there are conflicting Court of Appeal authorities on the subject.

4. LOCAL AUTHORITY USE OF THE JURISDICTION

The need to obtain leave

Although local authorities cannot look to the inherent jurisdiction as a means of putting them in charge of the child's living arrangements,[17] they can nevertheless seek to use it to resolve specific questions about the child's future. Indeed, because of the unavailability of wardship[18] and of s 8 orders (by reason of the embargoes in s 9(1) and (2)),[19] they may have to do so if the child is in their care. Nevertheless, this avenue is fettered because under s 100(3) of the 1989 Act local authorities must first obtain the court's leave to apply for any exercise of the High Court's inherent jurisdiction.[20]

Criteria for granting leave

Under s 100(4)(a) the court must be satisfied that the result being sought cannot be achieved under any statutory jurisdiction. This bar applies even where the statutory remedy is contingent upon the local authority having first to obtain leave before being able to seek an order.[1] This restriction makes it difficult for an authority to obtain leave for the exercise of the inherent jurisdiction in respect of a child not in their care, since in those circumstance they could seek to obtain a prohibited steps or specific issue order under s 8.[2]

In *Re R (A Minor) (Blood Transfusion)*[3] a local authority, wishing to obtain sanction for a blood transfusion for a child contrary to his parents' (who were

---

16 [1990] Fam 39, [1989] 2 All ER 791, CA.
17 Children Act 1989 s 100(2).
18 See ante, p 698.
19 Discussed ante, pp 429–32.
20 See *Devon County Council v B* [1997] 1 FLR 591, CA.
  1 Ibid, s 100(5)(b).
  2 See ante, p 430. But note *Nottingham County Council v P* [1994] Fam 18, [1993] 3 All ER 815, discussed ante at pp 430–2.
  3 [1993] 2 FLR 757, per Booth J. This point was apparently overlooked by Thorpe J in *Re S (A Minor) (Medical Treatment)* [1993] 1 FLR 376, [1993] Fam Law 215; cf *Re O (A Minor) (Medical Treatment)* [1993] 1 FCR 925, [1993] 2 FLR 149.

Jehovah's witnesses) wishes, were refused leave because, as the child was not in care, an appropriate remedy could have been obtained under s 8.[4] One example, however, where leave might be given is where it is sought to restrain publicity about a child, since that seems, on occasions at least, to fall outside the scope of s 8.[5]

Even if there is no alternative statutory remedy, s 100(4)(b) also requires the court to be satisfied that: 'there is reasonable cause to believe that if the court's inherent jurisdiction is not exercised with respect to the child he is likely to suffer significant harm'. Although this provision is in line with the need to establish at least a likelihood of significant harm before the court is entitled to intervene to make a care or supervision order,[6] it may be questioned whether this ground for leave should be so narrow. It has been pointed out[7] that, given that the local authority's objective cannot be the acquisition of parental responsibility, a less stringent test, such as the court having to be satisfied that the exercise of its inherent jurisdiction is necessary to secure the child's welfare, would not have upset the general philosophy of the 1989 Act and might have better served children's interests.

Circumstances in which the criteria for giving leave might be satisfied

Local authorities are not often justified in having recourse to the inherent jurisdiction. The expectation is that, since they have parental responsibility, local authorities should make decisions for themselves.[8] Nevertheless, there will be occasions when recourse to the High Court will be appropriate. Lord Mackay LC instanced[9] the exercise of the inherent power to sanction or forbid an abortion being carried out on a child in care, where there are no other statutory means of seeking a court order and the decision, if wrong, is clearly likely to cause significant harm. In *Re W (A Minor) (Medical Treatment: Court's Jurisdiction)*[10] it was thought right to invoke the inherent jurisdiction to override a refusal of a 16-year-old anorexic child in care to consent to medical treatment. Other examples of medical treatment where leave is likely to be given include sterilisation,[11] contested cases involving emergency medical treatment of a child in care,[12] or where life saving treatment is in issue.[13]

---

4 Though Booth J was doubtful about whether a specific issue order could be granted ex parte.
5 But see ante, pp 421–2.
6 Under s 31 of the 1989 Act, discussed ante at pp 536ff. It has been accepted that cases determining the meaning of 'likely to suffer significant harm' for the purpose of s 31 are also relevant to its meaning under s 100(4)(b) – per Connell J in *Essex County Council v Mirror Group Newspapers Ltd* [1996] 1 FLR 585. Leave was refused in that case.
7 By Eekelaar and Dingwall (1989) 139 NLJ 217. See also Lowe (1989) 139 NLJ 87 and Bainham *Children – The New Law* 202.
8 See the Department of Health's *Guidance and Regulations*, Vol 1, paras 3.100–3.101 and the *Guidance* to the Northern Ireland Children Order, Vol 1, ch 11.
9 (1989) 139 NLJ 505 at 507.
10 [1993] Fam 64, [1992] 4 All ER 627, CA, discussed ante at pp 315ff. See also *Re C (Detentions: Medical Treatment)* [1997] 2 FLR 180. Note also *South Glamorgan County Council v W and B* [1993] 1 FLR 574 in which Douglas Brown J, somewhat questionably (see ante, p 576) held that the High Court had an inherent power to override the statutory right conferred by s 43(8) and s 44(7) of the Children Act 1989 on a child of sufficient understanding to refuse to submit to an examination or other assessment.
11 *Practice Note: (minors and mental health patients: sterilisation)* [1993] 3 All ER 222.
12 See *Re O (A Minor) (Medical Treatment)* [1993] 2 FLR 149.
13 See eg *Re C (Medical Treatment)* [1998] 1 FLR 384, *Re T (a minor) (wardship: medical treatment)* [1997] 1 All ER 906, CA, and *Re C (A Baby)* [1996] 2 FLR 43.

The above medical problems are extreme examples of situations when High Court intervention might be justified, but circumstances do not always have to be so extraordinary. In *Southwark London Borough v B* [14] leave was granted to a local authority first to seek a return order of a child in care and then to enforce that order. In other cases, for example, where a local authority seeks an injunction to prevent a violent father from discovering his child's whereabouts, [15] or from molesting the child [16] or a social worker connected with the child, [17] or to restrain harmful publicity about the child, [18] then the inherent jurisdiction is the *only* means of obtaining the remedy and it should not be too difficult to satisfy the criteria for granting leave.

In *Devon County Council v S* [19] it was held appropriate to exercise the inherent jurisdiction to prevent a family friend (a Sch 1 offender and a paedophile) from having contact with the children and to prevent the mother from allowing the children to have contact with him, since there was no other means of obtaining such a remedy. In *Re M (Care: Leave To Interview Child)* [20] the jurisdiction was successfully invoked to permit a child in care to be interviewed by the father's solicitor with a view to preparing evidence in the father's defence in furthering criminal proceedings against him.

Although in theory the granting of leave does not automatically mean that the court must exercise its jurisdiction, given that it must be satisfied that the child is likely to suffer significant harm if the jurisdiction is not exercised [1] it would be an unusual case where leave was given and the jurisdiction not subsequently exercised. [2]

5. INDIVIDUALS' USE OF THE JURISDICTION

Although in theory it is open to individuals to invoke the inherent jurisdiction, it is unlikely to be used at all often, not least because of the continued availability of wardship. Even in the one area where wardship is unavailable to individuals, namely where children are in local authority care, as we have discussed in Chapter 14, [3] the well established embargo against using wardship to challenge local authority decisions applies equally to that use of the inherent jurisdiction.

---

14 [1993] 2 FLR 559, CA.
15 See *Re JT (A Minor) (Wardship: Committal to Care)* [1986] 2 FLR 107.
16 See *Re B (A Minor) (Wardship: Child in Care)* [1975] Fam 36, [1974] 3 All ER 915.
17 This is one example of the exercise of the inherent jurisdiction known to the authors.
18 The jurisdiction was successfully invoked by Essex County Council to prevent a newspaper revealing the identity of a boy who had a history of sexual abuse and who had been place in a foster home by the authority: see *Essex County Council v Mirror Group Newspapers Ltd* [1996] 1 FLR 585. A similar injunction was granted in wardship to prevent children being identified in a television programme about alleged paedophiles in *Cornwall v BBC* (1994) unreported.
19 [1994] Fam 169, [1995] 1 All ER 243, [1994] 1 FLR 355, per Thorpe J.
20 [1995] 1 FLR 825, per Connell J.
 1 It is submitted that this requirement distinguishes s 100 from granting leave under s 10 to apply for a s 8 order, where it is established that there is no presumption that an order be made following the granting of leave: see ante, p 435.
 2 For an example where leave was refused see *Essex County Council v Mirror Group Newspapers Ltd*, supra, in which on the facts Connell J held the potential harm had not been established.
 3 See ante, p 603.

D.   Commentary

The restriction on the use of wardship by local authorities was one of the surprises of the original Children Bill, since it had neither been recommended by the *Review of Child Care Law* nor by the Law Commission and, indeed, flew directly in the face of a recommendation to the contrary by the Cleveland Inquiry Report.[4] Admittedly, in their earlier Working Paper on *Wards of Court*[5] the Law Commission had canvassed abolishing the jurisdiction altogether, but their final report on *Guardianship and Custody Guardianship*[6] expressly postponed making any substantial recommendations for the reform of wardship. In short, what is now s 100 of the 1989 Act was introduced on the government's own initiative[7] and without the benefit of widespread consultation.

During the passage of the Bill anxieties were expressed about the wisdom of curtailing the use of wardship by local authorities.[8] In particular there was concern that it was potentially detrimental to the interests of the children:

(1)   to deprive local authorities, through the removal of the wardship option, from having direct access to the High Court;

(2)   to remove the wardship safety net underpinning the statutory scheme for obtaining care or supervision orders;

(3)   to curtail the power formerly enjoyed inter alia under the wardship jurisdiction to commit children into care on the court's own motion;

(4)   to deprive the court of being able to use its flexible powers under wardship when making care or supervision orders.

Not all the above-mentioned concerns have proved to be well-founded in practice. In particular, the lack of direct access to the High Court in care cases has not proved problematic. The Allocation Rules seem to have been working well enough and there is little or no evidence to suggest that cases that should be heard by the High Court are not in fact being heard at that level.[9] Similarly, the experience of the Act so far is that the threshold provisions under s 31 have not been found wanting,[10] though time will tell whether they will apply to all situations where it is clearly right for a care order to be made.

On the other hand, concern has been expressed about the court's inability even to direct that the local authority institute care proceedings.[11] Such concern was voiced in *Nottingham County Council v P*[12] by Sir Stephen Brown P who said:

'This court is deeply concerned at the absence of any power to direct the authority to take steps to protect the child. In the former wardship jurisdiction it might well have been

---

4   Cm 412, 1988, para 16.37.
5   Working Paper No 101, 1987.
6   Law Com No 172, 1988, para 1.4.
7   Lord Mackay LC explained in his Joseph Jackson Memorial Lecture (189) 139 NLJ at 507 that the government's decision to restrict its use was taken late in the day.
8   See inter alia Lowe (1989) 139 NLJ 87, but note the reply by Eekelaar and Dingwell at (1989) NLJ 217.
9   See ante, p 536.
10   Though no doubt some would argue that the decision in *Re H (Minors) (Sexual Abuse: Standard of Proof)* [1996] AC 563, [1996] 1 All ER 1, HL (discussed ante pp 544ff) does expose serious flaws which perhaps the old style wardship could have countered.
11   All the court can do is to made a direction under s 37 (discussed ante at p 455) that a local authority investigate the child's circumstances.
12   [1994] Fam 18 at 43, [1993] 3 All ER 815 at 828, CA.

able to do so. The operation of the Children Act 1989 is entirely dependent upon the full co-operation of all those involved. This includes the courts, local authorities, social workers, and all who have to deal with children. Unfortunately, as appears from this case, if a local authority doggedly resists taking steps which are appropriate to the case of children at risk of suffering significant harm it appears that the court is powerless'.

The former flexible powers under wardship when making care or supervision orders seem also to be missed. For example, it is established (as was clearly intended by the Act) that there is no power under the 1989 Act to make conditional care orders, yet there does seem to be an argument for sometimes being able to keep a case under review, particularly as there seems to be no simple way (if at all) under the 1989 Act to provide for a child's phased return to his or her parents. Even where it is possible to achieve a degree of flexibility under the Act, it seems considerably more complex than was formerly possible under wardship.[13]

As we have seen, the loss of the wardship jurisdiction does not deprive local authorities of all access to the High Court's inherent powers. Although more needs to be known of the de facto use of this jurisdiction,[14] case law (particularly the Court of Appeal ruling in *Re W (A Minor) (Medical Treatment: Court's Jurisdiction)*[15] that the powers under the general or residual jurisdiction are co-extensive with those under wardship, and Thorpe J's decision in *Devon County Council v S*[16] that s 100 should not be restrictively interpreted) shows that the High Court is prepared to use its inherent powers flexibly. So interpreted, the continuing availability of the wider inherent jurisdiction must go some way to allaying fears about the wisdom of restricting the ambit of the wardship jurisdiction.

Although the continued existence of both wardship and the general or residual inherent jurisdiction is undoubtedly a peculiarity of the current legal system for dealing with children and does not easily stand with a comprehensive statutory scheme, it is urged that they be retained. In the past wardship has served the interests of children well and it is evident that the High Court's inherent powers still have a useful, if small, role to play. There is no evidence that the judiciary are using their inherent powers to subvert the statutory scheme. On the contrary, they have shown restraint and only used them where no other remedy is available.

---

13 See, for example, *C v Solihull Metropolitan Borough Council* [1993] 1 FLR 290 and *Re H (A Minor) (Section 37 Direction)* [1993] 2 FLR 541.
14 No statistics are apparently maintained as to the number of applications made under s 100.
15 [1993] Fam 64, [1992] 4 All ER 627, CA, discussed ante, p 703.
16 [1994] Fam 169, [1995] 1 All ER 243, discussed ante, p 704.

Chapter 17

Financial support for members of the family

A. Introduction

A legal obligation to provide financial support for another member of the family may be seen as the most tangible recognition of the moral ties created by family relationships.[1] Where such an obligation is imposed, it also sheds light on social conceptions of the appropriate scope of those ties.[2] Different societies at different times may impose the obligation upon different degrees of relationship.[3] Under the Poor Law, there was an obligation (albeit enforceable only by the Poor Law authorities) to provide financial support for one's grandparents and grand-children.[4] Until the nineteenth century, a child born outside wedlock was not entitled to support from either parent,[5] and an unqualified liability on the father of such a child has existed only since 1987.[6] There is still no direct liability to support an unmarried partner, although, through support for the child, there may be an indirect imposition of a requirement to do so.[7]

Obligations to support may be enforced either through actions under the private law, through both legally-recognised agreements and court actions, or through social security law.[8] The last is numerically more important and a more immediate and potentially long-term source of support for families, both those which are functioning and those which have broken down. We begin with a brief résumé of the historical development of the law; then we examine those aspects of taxation and social security which relate directly to family support. We then consider mechanisms whereby family members can seek support from each other, namely under the child support scheme (the most important), private agreements and finally court orders. Recognition of the ties of affection, regardless of marriage bonds, has in some respects been more readily granted where a party has died, and the general question of how the moral support obligations of a deceased person are legally recognised is dealt with in Chapter 19.

1 Finch *Family Obligations and Social Change* (1989).
2 See Eekelaar and Maclean *The Parental Obligation* (1997) for a consideration of this issue in the context of empirical research concerning the financial ties between absent parents and their children.
3 See Millar and Warman *Family Obligations in Europe* (1996): southern European states are more likely to impose obligations upon the wider family; some northern European states impose obligations upwards from children to parents, as well as downwards; Scandinavian states are less likely to impose any support obligations at all.
4 Barton and Douglas *Law and Parenthood* (1995) p 196.
5 See post, p 717.
6 Family Law Reform Act 1987 s 17, abolishing, inter alia, the usual three year time limit on a mother applying for support from the unmarried father which had previously existed: see Affiliation Proceedings Act 1957 ss 1–2, discussed in the 6th edition of this work at p 597.
7 See post, p 724 (social security), p 734 (child support).
8 Eekelaar and Maclean, op cit, adopt a similar classification of obligations.

1. THE DUTY TO MAINTAIN A SPOUSE

At common law

The common law rules relating to spousal maintenance were the inevitable consequence of the doctrine of unity of legal personality.[9] The wife, lacking the capacity to hold property and to contract, could neither own the bare necessities of life nor enter into a binding contract to buy them. Two principles followed. First, one of the essential obligations imposed upon a married man was to provide his wife with at least necessities; and secondly, a married woman could in no circumstances be held liable to maintain her husband. The common law rule that neither spouse could sue the other precluded her from enforcing her right by action if her husband failed to fulfil his duty to maintain her: this difficulty was overcome by giving the wife a power to pledge her husband's credit for the purchase of necessities if he did not supply her with them himself.

(a) Scope of the husband's duty

The husband's common law duty to provide his wife with the necessities of life was prima facie complied with if he provided a home for her.[10] She had no right to separate maintenance in a separate home unless she could justify living apart from him. The fact of marriage raised a presumption that the husband was under a duty to maintain his wife. But her right to maintenance, generally speaking, was co-extensive with her right to her husband's consortium, and if her conduct released him from the duty to cohabit with her, he automatically ceased to be under a duty to maintain her.[11] A single act of adultery could automatically deprive her of her right, and if she deserted him her right was suspended until her desertion came to an end.[12]

(b) The agency of necessity [13]

The power to pledge the husband's credit, termed the wife's agency of necessity, extended to the purchase of necessaries both for herself and for the spouses' minor children. The term 'necessaries' in this context included not only necessary goods such as food and clothing, but also necessary services such as lodging, medical attention and education. Although the wife could divest herself of the right to be maintained by her own conduct, the husband could not revoke the authority by his unilateral act.

The agency of necessity was of great importance so long as the wife was generally incompetent to contract and own property at common law. Both these disabilities were removed by the Married Women's Property Act 1882, and by the end of the nineteenth century she could obtain maintenance from her husband not only in the High Court but also much more speedily in the magistrates' court. When it also became possible for the wife to obtain immediate assistance from what is now the Benefits Agency of the Department of Social Security and to

---

9 See ante, p 53.
10 See *Price v Price* [1951] P 413, CA at 420–1; *W v W (No 2)* [1954] P 486 at 515–16, [1954] 2 All ER 829, CA at 840.
11 *Chilton v Chilton* [1952] P 196 at 202, [1952] 1 All ER 1322 at 1325.
12 *Jones v Newtown and Llanidloes Guardians* [1920] 3 KB 381.
13 For examples of the tactical use of this power, see Stone *Broken Lives: Separation and Divorce in England 1660–1857* (1993) passim.

claim the benefits of the National Health Service and the legal aid and advice scheme, the doctrine became an anachronism and was eventually abolished by the Matrimonial Proceedings and Property Act 1970.[14]

The current position

The means by which maintenance can be claimed by a spouse are now governed by statute. Unlike the common law it is open to either spouse to claim maintenance from the other,[15] and since claims for maintenance no longer depend upon the duty to cohabit, the commission of adultery or desertion is no longer a bar. The two statutes governing maintenance between separated spouses are the Domestic Proceedings and Magistrates' Courts Act 1978 and the Matrimonial Causes Act 1973 s 27.

2. PARENTS' DUTY TO MAINTAIN CHILDREN BORN WITHIN THE MARRIAGE

At common law a father was under a duty to maintain only his legitimate minor children and to provide them with food, clothing, lodging and other necessities. But the duty was wholly unenforceable. A child has never had an agency of necessity[16] and a father was under no legal obligation to reimburse a person who has supplied his child with necessaries. Unless he constituted the child his agent, the only way in which he could be compelled to fulfil his obligation was through the wife's agency of necessity, which extended to the purchase of necessities for the children of the marriage as well as for herself.[17] With the abolition of the wife's agency of necessity, the common law position is now of purely historical interest.

As with maintaining spouses, the means by which financial provision can be claimed for children is governed by statute. Where it is sought to obtain financial provision for children alone, recourse must usually now be had to the Child Support Act 1991. Where this Act does not apply,[18] the Children Act 1989 provides an alternative (and more flexible) jurisdiction. The Domestic Proceedings and Magistrates' Courts Act 1978 or the Matrimonial Causes Act 1973 s 27 referred to above also contain powers to award maintenance for children, provided, again, that the Child Support Act is inapplicable.

3. SUPPORT OBLIGATIONS OUTSIDE MARRIAGE

Reflecting the common law position, it remains the case that even between cohabiting adults there is no duty to maintain, although, as we shall see, in

---

14 Section 41. This followed the recommendations of the Law Commission: see Law Com No 25, paras 108–109 and Appendix II, paras 41–52 and 108. Section 41 was repealed by the Matrimonial Causes Act 1973 Sch 3, and not re-enacted.

15 It is therefore difficult to see why it is apparently considered by the government that English law is incompatible with Protocol 7 Article 5 to the European Convention on Human Rights, which guarantees equal rights to spouses during marriage: Hansard, HL, Written Answers col 197, 21 April 1998 (Lord Williams of Mostyn).

16 *Mortimore v Wright* (1840) 6 M & W 482.

17 *Bazeley v Forder* (1868) LR 3 QB 559.

18 See post, p 746.

assessing the level of maintenance to be paid by an unmarried parent for any child, an element to cover the costs of the carer may be included.[19]

With regard to children born outside marriage, at common law neither the father nor the mother was liable for maintenance.[20] Although the Poor Law legislation cast upon the mother the obligation of maintaining her illegitimate child, she could still not recover the expenses of maintenance from the father in the absence of any contract to that effect between them.[1] A statute of 1576 empowered justices to make an order against the unmarried father for the maintenance of an illegitimate child charged on the parish,[2] but it was not until the Poor Law Amendment Act 1844 that the mother was given the power to apply for an order for maintenance to be paid to herself. The law was amended and consolidated in the Bastardy Laws Amendment Act 1872 and again in the Affiliation Proceedings Act 1957. Under this legislation the right of unmarried mothers to claim from alleged fathers was circumscribed. For example, applications could only be made to magistrates' courts, applicants had to be 'single' mothers, claims had to be brought within three years of the child's birth,[3] and the mother's evidence had to be corroborated. These limitations were removed by the Family Law Reform Act 1987, now embodied in the Children Act 1989, and, as we shall discuss, the Child Support Act 1991 has gone still further in equalising the law governing the support of children born inside and outside marriage.

4. ENFORCEMENT OF THE DUTY TO MAINTAIN

Maintenance agreements

Once it was accepted that separation agreements were not contrary to public policy,[4] it became possible for a husband to enter into an enforceable contract to pay maintenance for his wife and his children. Now either spouse may covenant to pay maintenance to the other, and either parent (whether married or not to each other) can covenant to pay maintenance for their children. Their rights are basically governed by the general principles of contract law but, as we shall see, some special rules apply to maintenance agreements.[5]

State support

Broadly speaking, anyone over the age of 18 whose income falls below the relevant sum laid down by the Social Security Contributions and Benefits Act 1992 is entitled to apply to the Benefits Agency for income support or job-seeker's allowance.[6] A spouse or unmarried partner without support will frequently turn to

---

19 See post, p 734.
20 *Ruttinger v Temple* (1863) 4 B & S 491. In *Hesketh v Gowing* (1804) 5 Esp 131 the father was held liable if he 'adopted' the child as his own, but today it would probably be necessary to establish an authority to incur expenses on the child's behalf by the person seeking reimbursement.
1 As to agreements to pay maintenance, see post, pp 753 et seq.
2 18 Eliz 1 c 3.
3 Unless the father was voluntarily paying money for the child.
4 See eg *Merritt v Merritt* [1970] 2 All ER 760, CA; *Re Windle* [1975] 3 All ER 987.
5 See post, p 750.
6 Determination of which benefit is appropriate in different circumstances, and at what level of payment, is dependent upon the relevant legislation, discussed fully in Mesher and Wood *Income-Related Benefits: The Legislation* (1997). The text below deals only with the position concerning families.

the Agency before taking any other action. If support is given to a married person, it is recoverable from that person's spouse, and if support is given to any child under the age of 16, it is recoverable from either or both parents.[7]

Obtaining maintenance from the courts

Until 1878 only the ecclesiastical courts or their successors, the Divorce Court and the High Court, could make orders for maintenance. The Matrimonial Causes Act 1878 enabled a criminal court, before which a married man had been convicted of an aggravated assault upon his wife, to make an order that she should no longer be bound to cohabit with him if it felt that her future safety was in peril.[8] The court could also order a husband to pay maintenance to a wife in whose favour such a separation order was made, and vest in her the legal custody of any children of the marriage under the age of 10. The powers of the magistrates' courts were gradually extended, although limits on the amount of maintenance which could be ordered to be paid each week remained until 1968 (£7.50 for a spouse and £3.50 for a child). After the divorce law was reformed in 1971, removing the emphasis upon marital misconduct and extending the court's powers to deal with the spouses' finances and property, the jurisdiction to order maintenance was also reformed to bring it into line with that approach.[9]

The separate limits for spouse and child illustrate the earlier lack of recognition that their needs cannot be divorced from one another.[10] The current matrimonial jurisdiction, however, has learnt this lesson, in providing that in deciding what orders to make for a *spouse*, magistrates must treat the welfare of any child of the family as the first consideration.[11]

The Child Support Scheme

So far as maintenance for children is concerned, dissatisfaction with the effectiveness of the court system to collect amounts of maintenance which would be sufficient to provide realistic levels of support for them, and concern at the dramatic increase in the number of single-parent families dependent upon state benefits,[12] led to the introduction of the Child Support Act 1991, which came into effect in April 1993. This set up an entirely new system of assessing and collecting maintenance for children, through the medium of a government agency, the Child Support Agency. The Act deprives the courts of jurisdiction to order maintenance for children in many instances, and permits the Agency to pursue absent parents for child support, often regardless of any prior settlements made on a divorce. No distinction is drawn between children whose parents were married to each other and those whose were not, but the basis of liability under the

---

7 See post, p 724.
8 See Hammerton *Cruelty and Companionship: Conflict in Nineteenth-Century Married Life* (1992) pp 52–67.
9 See Law Com No 77, *Report on Matrimonial Proceedings in Magistrates' Courts* and the Domestic Proceedings and Magistrates' Courts Act 1978.
10 See also the discussion by Eekelaar and Maclean *Maintenance After Divorce* (1986) pp 21–8.
11 Domestic Proceedings and Magistrates' Courts Act 1978 s 3(1); the corresponding power of the county court or High Court under s 27 of the Matrimonial Causes Act 1973 imposes that duty only where an order is sought for the *child*: s 27(3A). The Child Support Act 1991, however, represents a retrograde step in seeking once again to attempt to deal with one aspect of family finances – child maintenance – in isolation from the rest. See post, p 727.
12 White Paper *Children Come First* Cm 1264 (1990) Vol 2, p i.

Act is parenthood,[13] so that the maintenance of step-children remains a matter for the courts and private law.

B.   State support

1.   INTRODUCTION

The state may provide financial support to individuals and families through two main mechanisms. On the one hand, it may provide tax allowances (or 'credits') so that the beneficiary pays less tax than would otherwise be the case, and hence retains more of his income for expenditure on his own and his family's wants.[14] Entitlement to the tax credit depends upon earning, or having, an income of a size at which tax is payable and upon meeting the particular criteria (such as marital or parental status) laid down. On the other hand, the state may establish a social security system, whereby 'benefits' are paid to eligible applicants as a cash sum to meet their particular needs. Entitlement to such benefits may depend upon past contributions (the 'national insurance' approach), or simply upon fulfilment of criteria based on the particular needs to be met, such as disability or poverty.

Tax credits have the psychological and political advantages of presenting state support of those in need as if it were a mechanism which costs the state nothing (because all that is done is to leave the recipient with more take-home pay by reducing his tax bill) rather than as a direct expense for the state (because, although the amount of benefit paid to the recipient may be calculated according to his wages, it comes directly from the state). In reality, the state 'pays' under either system, since, under the tax allowance/credit system it forgoes tax revenue it would otherwise have received, while under the social security system the money is received in taxes but then paid out again as benefits. However, tax credits carry less stigma to recipients and to 'reinforce the distinction between the rewards of work and remaining on welfare'.[15]

The present social security system derives in part from the Beveridge reforms enacted in the National Assistance Act 1948 which abolished the old Poor Law. Since then, however, there have been substantial changes. The present structure of the benefits of particular relevance to families was established by the Social Security Act 1986, and revised and consolidated by the Social Security Contributions and Benefits Act 1992 and Social Security Administration Act 1992. The election of a Labour Government in 1997 led to a further review of the social security system and the development of a strategy intended to encourage more people into work and out of dependence upon state benefits.[16] One of the key elements in this strategy was to provide tax credits, rather than social security payments, as the bridge between total dependence upon benefits and take-up of full-time employment.[17]

---

13 Child Support Act 1991 s 54.
14 For a discussion of the use of the tax system to meet welfare needs, see Kvist and Sinfield 'Comparing Tax Welfare States' in May, Brunsdon and Craig (eds) *Social Policy Review 9* (1997).
15 HM Treasury, *Work Incentives* (1998) para 3.19.
16 Department of Social Security, *New ambitions for our country: A New Contract for Welfare* Cm 3805 (1998).
17 *Work Incentives* (supra) ch 3.

2. SUPPORT THROUGH THE TAX SYSTEM

Tax allowances

The assumption, at one time well-founded, that a married man would be expected to meet the bulk, if not all, of the financial needs of his wife and family out of his own income, was reflected by the grant, in 1918, of a married man's tax allowance enabling him to start to pay tax at a higher threshold than a single person. In 1990, in a belated acknowledgement of women's financial contributions to the living standards of their families, all married women became separately taxed from their husbands, and the allowance became a 'married couple's' allowance, payable to either spouse (although it continues to be paid to the husband unless the couple request its transfer to the wife, or apportionment between both of them).[18] Recognition of changing family structures had already led to the allowance of a sum, equal in value to the married couple's allowance, to lone parents and unmarried couples with children, effectively creating a parents' tax allowance in lieu.[19] However, the value of the allowance has been steadily eroded, and in 1998/99 was payable at only 10 per cent although the standard rate of income tax was 25 per cent.

Working Families Tax Credit

In 1998, the government, influenced by the 'Earned Income Tax Credit' in the United States tax system,[20] proposed introducing a 'Working Families Tax Credit' (WFTC) to replace the main in-work benefit to lower income families ('Family Credit') from October 1999.[1] The aim is to encourage the jobless to take employment, even at low wages, by providing, in effect, a government subsidy or wage supplement through the tax collection system. The tax credit is also assumed to carry less stigma than receiving a separately paid social security benefit. It will be administered through the Inland Revenue and payable through the wage packet, rather than paid as a separate benefit. It is proposed that parents may opt as to which should receive the credit, in order to allay fears that otherwise the credit might simply make the wage earner personally better off, with no consequential benefit to the family.[2] As with Family Credit, assessment and payment will be for a six-month period.

The credit will be allowed to low-income families with children under the age of 18, where the main earner works more than 16 hours per week. Such a family will receive a basic tax credit, plus additional credits, of varying amounts depending upon age, for each child. Where the family's net income exceeds £90 per week, the credit will be progressively withdrawn at a rate of 55 per cent for each additional pound of net earnings. Where the main earner works more than 30

---

18 Finance Act 1988, which came into effect on 6 April 1990. See Wylie *Taxation of the Family* (1993, 3rd edn) ch 1.

19 Income and Corporation Taxes Act 1988 s 259. An additional personal allowance was granted to single parents in 1960 and its value equalised with the married man's allowance in 1975, following a recommendation by the Finer Committee; *Report on One-Parent Families* Cmnd 5629. Note that the parent of a child born out of wedlock must be maintaining that child to qualify for the allowance: Wylie, op cit, p 143.

20 *Work Incentives* (supra) ch 3.

1 HM Treasury, *The Modernisation of Britain's Tax and Benefit System: Number 3 The Working Families Tax Credit and work incentives* (1998). Family Credit is discussed post, p 725.

2 Ibid, para 2.12; *Work Incentives* (1998) para 3.25. Clearly, if only one parent is earning, the other cannot opt to receive the credit, and the risk of detriment to the family remains.

hours per week, he or she will receive an additional credit as an incentive to work longer hours. Since the proposal has yet to be implemented, its effects on family incomes cannot be assessed, but the government were confident that its introduction would improve work incentives and prove more generous to families than the existing Family Credit.[3]

Childcare tax credit

Where a family is receiving working families tax credit, it will also be eligible for a childcare tax credit, worth 70 per cent of eligible child care costs, subject to an overall limit on these costs of £100 per week for one child and £150 for two or more.[4] The aim of providing such an allowance is to recognise the need of working women to provide child care for their children while they are at work, so as to act as an incentive to them to take employment. The value of the credit is significantly higher than the child care allowance provided in Family Credit, as explained below.[5]

3. SOCIAL SECURITY BENEFITS[6]

Introduction

Social security benefits comprise: (a) contributory benefits dependent upon the National Insurance contributions paid by the beneficiary,[7] such as contribution-based Jobseeker's Allowance and retirement pension; (b) non-contributory income-related benefits dependent upon a means test, such as income support; and (c) non-contributory, non income-related benefits – 'universal' benefits to which all who fit within the category are entitled, most notably child benefit.

Contributory benefits are not discussed in detail here, since they do not relate directly to support for families.[8] However, it should be noted that the requirement to have made contributions to be eligible for the benefit (or for the full benefit) means that those unable to build up contributions, in particular women who give up work to have children,[9] may be disadvantaged. They may be ineligible for a full retirement pension based on their own contributions, and be dependent upon their husband's contribution record, in which case a reduced pension is payable to them. Women's career breaks, lower average earnings and concentration in lower status employment all combine to mean that they are also less likely to have access to valuable occupational or personal pensions.[10] If their marriages are terminated by divorce, they were, until 1995, unable to take advantage of the former husband's pension unless nominated by him as a beneficiary.[11] They will accordingly be more likely to have recourse to the non-contributory income-related benefits, to which we now turn.

---

3 Ibid, para 1.04.
4 Ibid, para 3.05.
5 Post, p 725.
6 See Ogus, Barendt and Wikeley *The Law of Social Security* (4th edn, 1995).
7 The benefits may also be payable to a spouse or dependant of the contributor.
8 For a detailed account, see Ogus, Barendt and Wikeley, op cit.
9 Interrupted contributions may be supplemented by counting years of 'home responsibility': see Social Security Contributions and Benefits Act 1992 s 60.
10 See Maclean *Surviving Divorce* (1991).
11 See now Pensions Act 1995 s 166 and s 167 and Family Law Act 1996 s 16, inserting and amending ss 25B–D into the Matrimonial Causes Act 1973, discussed post, p 795.

Income-related (or means-tested) benefits are intended to provide a safety net through which no person should fall into destitution. There are two main types of such benefits relevant to families: Income Support and Jobseekers' Allowance (JSA), for those not in work, and Family Credit (to be replaced from 1999 by Working Families Tax Credit – 'WFTC') for a person who is working over 16 hours per week.[12] JSA is the benefit paid to those who are required to be available for employment as a condition of receiving benefit.[13] In two-parent families where neither adult is working, JSA will be the main benefit relied upon. At present, the partner of a recipient of benefits such as JSA does not need to register for work, but the government is considering changing this.[14] Lone parents are not required to be available for employment and hence do not receive JSA, but may instead be eligible for Income Support.[15] JSA is not discussed in detail here, since it applies to all those who are unemployed and required to seek work.[16]

Income support is frequently the first line of support for a parent who is on her own with a child and unable to work full-time when her partner has left her. If she is later able to obtain a job, but one which is low-paid, she may be eligible for Family Credit (or, in future, WFTC) to boost her income. The government aims to reduce dependence upon JSA and Income Support by encouraging the take-up of paid work. Such a strategy is said to reflect what single parents themselves want, and to teach a more positive attitude to work and independence among children.[17]

Income support[18]

(a)   Eligibility

Section 124 of the Social Security Contributions and Benefits Act 1992 together with the Income Support (General) Regulations 1987 r 21(3) provide that, to be eligible for Income Support and other income-related benefits, a claimant must be present in Great Britain and habitually resident in the United Kingdom,[19] and at least 16 years old. The claimant claims not just for himself or herself but for the family unit, including the spouse or partner living with the claimant, and dependent children under 19 living at home for whom the claimant is responsible. The claimant must:

(a)   have no income, or an income below the 'applicable amount';
(b)   have no capital, or capital below a prescribed amount;
(c)   not be engaged in remunerative work;
(d)   not be entitled to a Jobseeker's Allowance; and
(e)   not be receiving relevant education.

The applicable amount is set by regulations, and comprises (a) the 'personal allowance' for which the claimant would be eligible (for example, allowance for a

---

12 Ante, p 720.
13 Jobseekers Act 1995 s 1.
14 *Work Incentives* (1998) ch 4.
15 Income Support (General) Regulations 1987 reg 4ZA and Sch 1B, para 1.
16 For detailed consideration, see Mesher and Wood, op cit passim.
17 White Paper, *Children Come First*, Vol 1, Cm 1264, para 6.1. Department of Social Security, *New ambitions for our country: A New Contract for Welfare* Cm 3805 ch 3, para 13.
18 See Ogus, Barendt and Wikeley, ch 11.
19 Or the Republic of Ireland, Channel Islands or the Isle of Man; the habitual residence requirement was added by reg 21(3) as amended by SI 1994 No 1807.

single adult, or married couple, allowance for each child in the family, dependent upon age); (b) appropriate 'premiums' (for example, an extra sum for a family including a child or young person, the amount dependent upon whether the claimant is a lone parent and whether she was in receipt of benefit before April 1998),[20] and (c) assessable housing costs made up of mortgage interest repayments, so long as these are not regarded as 'excessive'.[1]

If the claimant's income is below the applicable amount, the benefit received is the difference between the two sums. Apart from the claimant's home and certain other assets, capital will be taken into account in assessing eligibility. Capital above £8,000 renders the claimant ineligible for Income Support,[2] while that between £3,000 and £8,000 will be treated as generating income, which will then reduce the amount of benefit payable.[3]

Since the claim is for the family unit, the income and capital of the whole unit (except any capital belonging to the children) are 'aggregated'.[4] Spouses no longer living together may claim separately, as they live in separate units. In contrast, a man and woman living together as husband and wife will be treated as a couple and their resources aggregated. The investigation of whether a claimant is living with another adult *as husband and wife* is a controversial and complicated exercise, involving, as it may, investigation of intimate relationships and sexual conduct.[5] The income to be taken into account includes net earnings (with the first £15 per week disregarded for those who are lone parents)[6] and all other gross income. Maintenance payments (even those intended to be made for the benefit of a child and not the parent)[7] are fully taken into account and reduce Income Support entitlement pound for pound.[8]

Claimants must not be engaged in remunerative work, which for these purposes means 'work in which a person is engaged . . . for not less than 16 hours a week being work for which payment is made . . .'[9] Limited part-time work can therefore be undertaken, although earnings received will affect the amount of Income Support payable.[10]

20 The Income Support (General) Regulations 1987 Sch 2, para 3, as amended by the Social Security Amendment (Lone Parents) Regulations 1998 reg 12.
1 Capital payments are not included. The maximum loan which may be covered is £100,000. Where a new claimant takes out a mortgage after 2 October 1995, no payments on it will be made by the DSS for the first 39 weeks of income support. If the new claimant took out the mortgage before that date, or is a lone parent and claims income support because her spouse or partner has left her, no payments will be made on it for the first eight weeks, and payments will be limited to half the interest instalments for the next 18 weeks. Interest is paid at a standard rate rather than that which may actually be charged by the mortgagee: Income Support (General) Regulations 1987 Sch 3, paras 1, 8 and 11.
2 A higher limit applies to those living in residential care or nursing homes: Income Support (General) Regulations 1987 reg 45.
3 Income Support (General) Regulations 1987 reg 53.
4 Social Security Contributions and Benefits Act 1992 s 136.
5 See Ogus, Barendt and Wikeley, op cit pp 389–93, and see *Re J (Income Support: Cohabitation)* [1995] 1 FLR 660. The latter decision by the Social Security Commissioner makes clear that such probing may be necessary in some cases.
6 Income Support (General) Regulations 1987 Sch 8, para 5.
7 *Supplementary Benefits Commission v Jull, Y v Supplementary Benefits Commission* [1981] AC 1025, [1980] 3 All ER 65, HL.
8 Income Support (General) Regulations 1987 reg 55.
9 Income Support (General) Regulations 1987 reg 5(1).
10 Interestingly, and reinforcing stereotyped images of women's work, childminding in the claimant's own home is not treated as remunerative work, and only one-third of the net earnings from childminding are taken into account in assessing the claimant's income: ibid, reg 6(b) and reg 38(9).

(b) 'Liable relatives'

Under s 78(6) and s 105(3) of the Social Security Administration Act 1992:

'(a) a man shall be liable to maintain his wife and any children of whom he is the father; and

(b) a woman shall be liable to maintain her husband and any children of whom she is the mother.'

Although liability to support a *spouse* terminates on divorce, liability to support children continues, and may not be excluded by a consent order.[11] From April 1993, the Child Support Act 1991[12] in practice superseded this provision where children are concerned. Liability under both the Social Security Administration Act and under the Child Support Act exists only in relation to a person's own children; there is no concept of 'child of the family' as in family proceedings.[13]

The Social Security Administration Act remains relevant in respect of spouses. A 'liable relative' may be traced by the Benefits Agency, and asked to meet the obligation to maintain. In deciding how much to expect the liable relative to contribute to the claimant's support, the Agency applies a non-statutory formula, whereby the relative will be allowed to keep an amount equal to the Income Support payable for him or herself and any partner or children living with him, rent or mortgage costs, *and* 15 per cent[14] of net earnings. If the relative has extra commitments, the Agency may negotiate a lower sum, and the exercise of this discretion in different offices, not surprisingly, apparently results in considerable variations in practice.[15]

Failure to make a contribution may result in proceedings being taken against the liable person in the magistrates' court under s 105 or s 106 of the 1992 Act. The latter is a civil proceeding which results in an order to pay a sum, weekly or otherwise, to the Secretary of State to meet the Income Support being claimed. The former is a criminal prosecution whereby a person who persistently refuses or neglects to maintain himself, or anyone he is liable to maintain, is guilty of an offence. Proceedings are rarely taken.[16]

11 *Hulley v Thompson* [1981] 1 All ER 1128. Such an order ought not to be made, given the courts' recognition of the continuing parental obligation to maintain, eg in *Minton v Minton* [1979] AC 593, [1979] 1 All ER 79, HL. The Child Support Act 1991 s 9(4) provides that any provision in an agreement which purports to restrict the right of a person to apply for a maintenance assessment under that Act shall be void.

12 Discussed post, p 727.

13 See p 288.

14 Mesher and Wood, op cit, p 1106. This appears to be less generous than before the Child Support Act was implemented, since it was previously understood that 25 per cent of net earnings would be retained: see Street *Money and Family Breakdown* (2nd edn, 1994) ch 14. This position may be contrasted with the much more rigid operation of the formula under the Child Support Act, discussed post.

15 Street, op cit.

16 To improve the recovery of maintenance from absent parents, s 107 provides that, where a parent is claiming income support for herself and her children, the Department of Social Security may seek recovery from the other parent of an amount to meet the claimant's income support personal allowance, *even though the parents are not married to each other so that there is no liability to support the claimant herself.* If the claimant ceases to claim benefit, the order may be transferred to her under s 107(3), but the element covering her allowance will not be included. This provision therefore enables the Department to recover more of the actual costs of supporting the lone parent. Furthermore, s 108 enables it to enforce a *private* maintenance order obtained by the claimant, even without her consent to such action being taken. There is usually little incentive for a benefits recipient to take or enforce private proceedings (as the maintenance recovered simply reduced the benefit she would receive), but s 108 sidesteps this difficulty, by enabling the Department to pursue the absent parent of its own volition. It is unclear how much use is made of these provisions in the wake of the Child Support Act.

(c) The 'diversion procedure'

Where the amount of maintenance ordered by a court is less than the amount of benefit due, the Benefits Agency may sometimes agree to the payee authorising the court to pay the maintenance received direct to the Agency, which continues to pay her the full amount of benefit due, whether or not the maintenance is paid, or paid in full. Under this procedure, any shortfall in maintenance is borne by the Agency, rather than the claimant. Without the procedure, a claimant would have to make a fresh claim for extra benefit each time the payment was late or inadequate.

The Social Fund [17]

Income Support is intended to meet the weekly needs of those with no, or very low income. The 'applicable amounts' do not take into account the need for larger purchases, such as for furniture, or even substantial items of clothing such as a winter coat. Before the social security reforms in the mid-1980s, help to purchase such items could be obtained by seeking a 'single payment', eligibility for which was subject to highly complex rules. Refusals led to numerous appeals to social security appeal tribunals. The cost of meeting single payments grew rapidly and was 'demand-led'. The Social Fund operates quite differently. It has two parts. One is non-discretionary, based on regulations, and provides maternity, funeral and cold weather payments to those on Income Support or Family Credit.[18] Such payments are in the form of grants. The other is a discretionary fund available to Income Support recipients, who may be granted repayable *loans* for 'important intermittent expenses' (for example, essential furniture, bedclothes, reconnection charges) or for expenses caused by an emergency or a disaster (in which case, the recipient need not have been in receipt of Income Support), or to meet short-term needs or living expenses for a period not exceeding 14 days.[19] There is no right of appeal to an independent tribunal against decisions taken by Social Fund Officers in relation to the discretionary fund.[20]

Family Credit

Unlike Income Support, which requires a claimant not to be working full-time, Family Credit is designed as an alternative benefit for low-income families where the claimant or partner is working. The claimant must be present and ordinarily resident in Great Britain and, in the case of a couple seeking the benefit, must usually be the woman.[1] She, or her partner, must be 'normally engaged in remunerative work' defined as 16 hours-a-week,[2] and responsible for a child member of the same household. To attract *maximum* Family Credit, the net income of the family (excluding any earnings of the children, Child Benefit and the first £15 of any maintenance payments, and making allowance for expenditure of up to £60 per week in child care costs for a child under 11)[3] must be below the

---

17 See Buck *The Social Fund: Law and Practice* (1996); Ogus, Barendt and Wikeley, op cit, ch 15.
18 Or Disability Working Allowance.
19 Community care *grants* are also available, on a discretionary basis, to those leaving institutional or residential care.
20 Although independent Social Fund Inspectors, answerable to the Social Fund Commissioner, can review decisions of Social Fund Officers: see *Annual Reports of the Social Fund Commissioner.*
1 Social Security (Claims and Payments) Regulations 1987 reg 4(2).
2 The Family Credit (General) Regulations 1987 reg 4 (as amended). An extra £10 bonus is paid if the claimant is working at least 30 hours per week.
3 The Family Credit (General) Regulations 1987 Sch 1, para 2; Sch 2, paras 15, 47; regs 13, 13A.

'applicable amount' set by regulations. Where net income exceeds this amount, credit is reduced by 70 per cent of the amount of excess.[4] A family is ineligible if they have capital over £8,000, and capital between £3,000 and £8,000 is treated in the same way as for Income Support.[5] Once assessed, the amount is payable for 26 weeks, even if the recipient's circumstances change.[6]

Only around 70 per cent of those eligible to claim Family Credit apparently do so.[7] Potential recipients may be deterred by the lack of provision to pay mortgage interest instalments.[8] The proposed working families tax credit, which will replace Family Credit, is intended to achieve a higher take-up.

4.   CHILD BENEFIT[9]

Direct financial aid to assist families bringing up children was proposed as long ago as 1796 by William Pitt. However, it was not until the Family Allowance Act 1945 that such a scheme was put into practice. Under that Act family allowance was paid to the mother, but only to families with at least two children. The amount hardly changed in 20 years. Tax allowances for all children were also available to set against income tax. Since married women were less likely to be in paid employment than is now the case, such allowances generally enhanced the take-home pay of the father, and it was argued that the children did not always receive the benefit of them. Integration and reform of the two schemes were called for in the late 1960s, and finally achieved under the Child Benefit Act 1975, after which child tax allowances were phased out.[10]

The basic scheme is that Child Benefit is paid as a flat-rate benefit regardless of need for each child (although a higher amount is paid for the first),[11] usually to the mother.

Section 141 of the Social Security Contributions and Benefits Act 1992 provides:

'A person who is responsible for one or more children in any week shall be entitled . . . to a benefit . . . for that week in respect of the child or each of the children for whom he is responsible.'

A child is defined by s 142 as a person under the age of 16; or under the age of 18 and not receiving full-time education, in respect of whom prescribed conditions are satisfied;[12] or under the age of 19 and receiving full-time non-advanced (ie non-degree, or Higher National Diploma) education. Child Benefit is not payable in respect of children on youth training schemes.[13]

---

4 The Family Credit (General) Regulations 1987 regs 46–48.
5 Social Security Contributions and Benefits Act 1992 s 134(1) and the Family Credit (General) Regulations 1987 reg 28.
6 Social Security Contributions and Benefits Act 1992 s 128.
7 HM Treasury, *The Modernisation of Britain's Tax and Benefit System: Number 3 The Working Families Tax Credit and work incentives* (1998) para 2.09.
8 Ogus, Barendt and Wikeley, op cit, p 522.
9 See Ogus et al, op cit, ch 10.
10 Compare concern that the new WFTC may also enhance the wage-earner's standard of living at the cost of his children's, and the government's proposal to allow couples to choose who should receive the credit: ante, p 720.
11 Thus reversing the old family allowance rule excluding the first child altogether: Child Benefit and Social Security (Fixing and Adjustment of Rates) Regulations 1976 (as amended) reg 2(1).
12 The Child Benefit (General) Regulations 1976 (as amended).
13 Ibid, regs 7A, 7B.

Under s 143 a person is treated as responsible for a child if he has the child living with him or is contributing to the cost of providing for the child at a weekly rate not less than the Child Benefit payable for that child. Where care of a child is split between parents, for example where there is a shared residence order, or extensive staying contact, they may agree between themselves who is to receive the benefit, or, in default of agreement, the Secretary of State may decide.[14] The recipient need not be a parent of the child, or even a relative, and there may be many cases where there are competing claims. Schedule 10 sets out an order of priority, so that a person having the child living with him or her has priority over a person contributing to the cost of providing for the child; a wife has priority over her husband where they are residing together; a parent takes priority over a non-parent; and a mother takes priority over an unmarried father where they are residing together.

Until 1998, an additional amount was payable in respect of the first child of a claimant who: (a) was receiving child benefit; (b) had no spouse or was not residing with his or her spouse; and (c) was not living with any other person as his or her spouse.[15] This was said to be in recognition of the extra financial burden on lone parents, but the last Conservative Government proposed phasing it out, so as not to advantage lone parents over two-parent families, and the Labour Government adopted this proposal.[16]

Child Benefit is not currently taxable (but it is expected that higher-rate taxpayers will pay tax on it in future),[17] and is not taken into account when assessing eligibility for Family Credit. It is, however, included as income for the purposes of calculating Income Support.

C.   Maintenance under the Child Support Act 1991 [18]

1.   BACKGROUND

During the 1980s increasing attention was paid to the question of whether the existing provision for the assessment and collection of child maintenance through private law mechanisms was satisfactory. The law was amended in 1984 to require that, in deciding what orders for financial provision should be made on divorce or matrimonial breakdown, the court should give first consideration to the welfare whilst a minor of any child of the family,[19] and attempts were made to increase the awareness of the courts as to the real costs of raising children, by circulating them with information on current Income Support rates, and the National Foster Care

---

14 Social Security Contributions and Benefits Act 1992 Sch 10, para 5.
15 The Child Benefit and Social Security (Fixing and Adjustment of Rates) Regulations 1976 reg 2(1), as amended by the Child Benefit, Child Support and Social Security (Miscellaneous Amendments) Regulations 1996 reg 5.
16 'We believe that additional support should be provided for children in poorer families on the basis of the identifiable needs of children, not on whether there happens to be one parent or two. So there is no case for a one-parent benefit, and the Government will not return to that approach' (*New ambitions for our country: A New Contract for Welfare* Cm 3805, p 57).
17 Cm 3805 at p 58.
18 See Jacobs and Douglas *Child Support: The Legislation* (3rd edn, 1997); Knights and Cox *Child Support Handbook* (5th edn, 1997); Street *Money and Family Breakdown* (2nd edn, 1994).
19 See post, p 818.

Association's recommended rate for paying foster-parents. Notwithstanding the availability of such information, the government found that the 'going rate' for maintenance for one child, of any age up to 18, was £18 per week in 1990,[1] at a time when the National Foster Care Association was recommending a payment of £34.02 per week for a child under the age of five. Such disparity is hardly surprising, given the finding by Eekelaar that, in his survey of 38 registrars (now district judges) handling financial provision, 14 rejected the National Foster Care Association rates as irrelevant because they were regarded as unrealistically high.[2] The government found that maintenance awards represented only about 11 per cent of total net incomes of absent parents on above average incomes.[3] It further found wide variations in the amounts of maintenance being awarded, one example being of two fathers, each earning £150 per week net. One was required to pay £5 per week in maintenance, and the other £50 per week.[4]

Not only was there concern that the amounts of maintenance awarded might be too low, but also that awards were neither being complied with nor adequately enforced.[5] Where maintenance awards are low, there is little incentive to seek their enforcement, especially where the recipient is in any event dependent upon social security benefits. Yet even where the Department of Social Security had the power to seek enforcement against liable relatives, in only 23 per cent of cases was the full amount of arrears of maintenance recovered.[6]

While low levels of maintenance and high proportions of orders in arrears were not particularly new, a further element which led to a determination to alter the law was the impact of these factors on the social security budget. The government found that about 770,000 single parents, or around two-thirds of the total number, were dependent upon Income Support in 1989, up from 330,000 such families in 1980.[7] Fewer than one-quarter of these were receiving any maintenance, while the cost to the Treasury of their benefits was £3.2 billion in 1988/89. The cost of supporting lone parent families appeared incompatible with the renewed emphasis upon asserting and strengthening parental responsibility for children under the Children Act 1989.

The desire to do something more fundamental about parental obligations to support children was translated into the government's White Paper, *Children Come First*, published in 1990, and followed by the Child Support Act 1991.[8] The scheme set up by the Act draws, to some extent, upon similar initiatives in both the United States of America and Australia.[9] Its introduction was highly controversial, and its initial workings lived down to the expectations of those who criticised it as a futile attempt to re-impose 'traditional family values' on a society which has

---

1 White Paper, *Children Come First*, Cm 1264, Vol 1, para 1.5.
2 Eekelaar *Regulating Divorce* (1991) p 95.
3 *Children Come First*, loc cit.
4 Ibid.
5 Edwards, Gould and Halpern 'The Continuing Saga of Maintaining the Family after Divorce' [1990] Fam Law 31.
6 White Paper Vol 2, para 5.1.2, and see Gibson 'The Future for Maintenance' [1991] CJQ 330.
7 White Paper Vol 2 p i.
8 See Eekelaar 'A Child Support Scheme for the United Kingdom' [1991] Fam Law 15; Maclean 'The Making of the Child Support Act 1991: Policy Making at the Intersection of Law and Social Policy' (1994) 21 Journal of Law and Society 505.
9 See Weitzman and Maclean (eds) *Economic Consequences of Divorce: The International Perspective* Part Four; Parker 'Child Support in Australia: Children's Rights or Public Interest?' (1991) 5 International Journal of Law and the Family 24.

moved increasingly away from the normative typical family of married parents living with their dependent children. Reception of the new ideology promoted by the legislation was not helped by unacceptably high levels of error and inefficiency in the Child Support Agency.[10] Organisations concerned with child poverty commissioned research in the first year of the Act's operation and found that 'it was very difficult to find evidence of any benefits – either financial or emotional – to the children' who were meant to be supported.[11] Many parents 'with care' found that they saw none of the maintenance collected, as it is offset against Income Support paid to the carer,[12] and were concerned that the activity of the Child Support Agency had disrupted their relationship with the absent parent. Children too seem to have suffered from the deterioration in the parents' relations.[13] But what finally forced the government to respond to criticism was the probably unprecedented level of anger expressed by those, mainly fathers, who were required to meet their obligations under the new scheme.[14] Less than two years after the legislation came into force, the government was forced to make numerous changes both to the detailed regulations underpinning it, and to the primary legislation, through the enactment of the Child Support Act 1995.[15]

2. THE SCHEME OF THE ACT

The two key characteristics of the child support scheme are first, that it lays down a *formula* to be applied to calculate the amount of maintenance needed by the child and to be met by the absent parent. The aim of the formula is to ensure that adequate amounts of maintenance are awarded, and to achieve consistency, so that families in similar circumstances will be assessed for similar amounts of maintenance.[16] Secondly, the assessment, collection and enforcement of maintenance are carried out, not by the courts, but by the Child Support Agency, which comes under the wing of the DSS. The courts have only a residual role to play in relation to child maintenance, with significant implications for the way they now deal with spousal support and property adjustment on divorce.

---

10 See *The Performance and Operation of the Child Support Agency* 2nd report of the House of Commons Social Security Committee, Session 1995–96; *Investigation of complaints against the Child Support Agency 3rd Report – session 1995–1996 of the Parliamentary Commissioner for Administration*, March 1996. The R*eport of the Chief Child Support Officer 1996/97* found that 22 per cent of assessments monitored were incorrect in cash terms, and in a further 15 per cent accuracy was impossible to determine, and the Select Committee on Public Accounts found that, on the Agency's own projected accuracy targets, one in six assessments is likely to be incorrect: *21st Report: Child Support Agency, Client Funds Account 1996/97* (1998) para 19.
11 Clarke, Glendinning and Craig *Losing Support: Children and the Child Support Act*, p 112. The study was updated, and the findings replicated by the researchers, in *Small Change: The Impact of the Child Support Act on Lone Mothers and Children*. For similar findings, see Abbott 'The Child Support Act 1991: the lives of parents with care living in Liverpool' (1996) 18(1) JSWFL 21.
12 Nearly 80 per cent of applicants were receiving Income Support, with a further 12 per cent on Family Credit, in a statistical survey carried out by the Child Support Agency in November 1995: *Quarterly Summary of Statistics* May 1996.
13 Gillespie 'Child Support – The Hand that Rocks the Cradle' [1996] Fam Law 162.
14 See Collier 'The Campaign against the Child Support Act: "errant fathers" and "family men"' [1994] Fam Law 384; Willbank 'The Campaign for Change of the Child Support Act 1991: Reconstructing the "Absent Father"' (1997) 6 Social & Legal Studies 191.
15 See White Paper *Improving Child Support* and Jacobs and Douglas, op cit, pp 1–4.
16 However, changes introduced by the 1995 Act undermine this approach: see post, p 737.

The Child Support Agency

The term 'Child Support Agency' does not in fact appear in the legislation, which instead refers only to child support officers and the Secretary of State, whose actions and decisions, of course, must be carried out in practice by officers in the Agency.[17]

Where the exercise of any discretionary power[18] conferred by the Act is to be considered, the Secretary of State or child support officer shall, under s 2, 'have regard to the welfare of any child likely to be affected by his decision'. This requirement is both narrower and wider than similar conditions in other legislation. Since welfare is not made the first consideration, still less the paramount consideration, s 2 is narrower than s 25(1) of the Matrimonial Causes Act 1973, or s 1 of the Children Act 1989. On the other hand, the duty to consider welfare lies in respect of *any* child who may be affected by the decision, and not just the child directly in issue. The Act gives no guidance on how welfare is to be taken into account, nor on how a balance should be struck between different children who may be affected. The provision has been characterised by one judge as 'hollow indeed'.[19]

The relevant parties

(a)   Qualifying child

Section 1(1) provides that 'each parent of a qualifying child is responsible for maintaining him'. A child is defined in s 55 as a person under the age of 16, or under the age of 19 and receiving full-time non-advanced[20] education, who has not been married. Such a child is a 'qualifying child' within s 3(1) if:

'(a)   one of his parents is, in relation to him, an absent parent; or
(b)   both of his parents are, in relation to him, absent parents.'

(b)   Absent parent

A parent is an 'absent parent'[1] under s 3(2) if:

'(a)   that parent is not living in the same household with the child; and
(b)   the child has his home with a person who is, in relation to him, a person with care.'

A parent is defined in s 54 as 'any person who is in law the mother or father of the child'. This definition covers birth parents, parents by virtue of adoption, and parents by virtue of the Human Fertilisation and Embryology Act 1990. There is no concept of 'child of the family' which underpins private support obligations.[2] The approach of the Act is, like the Social Security Administration Act 1992, to attach liability only to those with the legal status of parents.

---

17 Child Support Act 1991 s 13. There is also a Chief Child Support Officer. The functions of 'child support officers' will be transferred to the 'Secretary of State' when the Social Security Act 1998 s 1 comes into force.
18 This excludes the calculation of the assessment under the formula, since this is not discretionary.
19 Per Thorpe J in *R v Secretary of State for Social Security ex p Biggin* [1995] 1 FLR 851 at 855E–F.
20 Effectively, education up to A level: Child Support (Maintenance Assessment Procedure) Regulations 1992 Sch 1, para 2.
1 This terminology has been criticised by the House of Commons Social Security Committee as offensive and in need of change: *The Performance and Operation of the Child Support Agency* 2nd report of the House of Commons Social Security Committee, Session 1995–96, para 54.
2 See ante, p 288.

(c)   Person with care

A 'person with care' is defined as a person:

'(a)   with whom the child has his home;
(b)   who usually provides day to day care for the child (whether exclusively or in conjunction with any other person); and
(c)   who does not fall within a prescribed category of person.'[3]

More than one person may be a person with care in relation to the child under s 3(5).

(d)   Application for a maintenance assessment under s 4

The person with care or an absent parent may apply to the Child Support Agency, under s 4(1), for a 'maintenance assessment' to be made with respect to the qualifying child.[4] The applicant completes a 'maintenance application form' (MAF). Application may also be made for the Agency to arrange for the collection and enforcement of the 'child support maintenance' so assessed.

(e)   Application for a maintenance assessment under s 6

If, however, the person with care is the child's parent, and she is claiming Income Support, Family Credit or any other benefit of a prescribed kind, she *must* usually authorise the Agency, when asked by it to do so, to take action under the Act to recover child support maintenance from the absent parent.[5] Only some 8 per cent of persons with care are s 4 'volunteer' applicants,[6] an extra-ordinarily low proportion reinforcing the view that the child support scheme is basically a device designed to recoup social security spending.

Providing information to make the assessment

(a)   Parents with care

A person applying under s 4, or under a duty to authorise action under s 6, must, so far as she reasonably can, supply information to the Agency to enable the absent parent to be traced (if necessary), and for the child support officer to make the maintenance assessment. To accommodate the concern that a parent dependent upon benefits (and therefore obliged to authorise action under s 6), might not wish to reveal the identity of the absent parent to the Agency, because she fears violence from him, or wishes to put an unhappy relationship behind her, s 6(2) and s 46(3) provide that the requirements to give authorisation, or provide information, can be waived by the Agency where they consider that there are reasonable grounds for believing that compliance would lead to a risk of the claimant, or any child living with her, suffering harm or undue distress as a result. In deciding this, the requirement to consider the child's welfare under s 2 will be relevant.[7]

3   The Secretary of State shall not so prescribe parents, guardians, persons with a residence order in their favour, under s 8 of the Children Act 1989.
4   No such application may be made where there is in force a written maintenance agreement made before 5 April 1993 or maintenance order in respect of the child: Child Support Act 1991 s 4(10) inserted by s 18(1) of the Child Support Act 1995.
5   The Agency determines when to ask for such authorisation, giving priority to new benefit claimants: *Improving Child Support* paras 6.2, 6.3.
6   *Quarterly Summary of Statistics* May 1996.
7   But there is no obligation to consult the absent parent on whether he considers there would be a risk to the child's welfare if an assessment were required to be authorised: *R v Secretary of State for Social Security ex p Lloyd* [1995] 1 FLR 856.

REDUCED BENEFIT DIRECTION

However, as a deterrent to claimants who might prefer to withhold information, s 46(5) provides that, where the child support officer considers that there are no reasonable grounds for non-compliance, he may give a 'reduced benefit direction', whereby the amount of benefit otherwise payable will be reduced. If the parent co-operates by providing the relevant information, the direction is lifted. In 1996, the Child Support Agency found that increasing numbers of parents with care were apparently willing to accept the reduction in order to avoid compliance.[8] The House of Commons Social Security Committee were concerned that this might reflect either an increasing resort to violent threats against a parent with care in order to evade liability, in which case they recommended that the Agency should inform the police,[9] or that many parents are colluding to evade the Agency's grasp by agreeing that, in return for her refusal to give the Agency the information needed, the absent parent will compensate the parent with care by making up her loss of benefit and perhaps paying her a little extra, but still an amount which is less than would be owed by him under an assessment.[10] As a consequence, the government increased the penalty to be incurred for failure to co-operate. Originally, there was a deduction of 20 per cent of the Income Support adult personal allowance for the first six months, followed by 10 per cent for a further 12 months, after which the penalty was exhausted. In 1996, the deduction was raised to 40 per cent of the allowance, to last for three years, the penalty to be renewed if the parent with care is still on benefit and refusing to co-operate.[11]

(b)   Absent parents

Information will also be needed from the absent parent in order to discover his means and liabilities. Absent parents and their current or recent employers are required to provide information. The Agency may also obtain information from the Inland Revenue, and local authorities administering housing benefit, as to the income or housing costs of an absent parent or person with care.[12] Inspectors may be appointed to exercise powers of entry and enquiry with a view to obtaining information required under the Act,[13] although there is no evidence that in practice use has been made of this power. On the contrary, the Agency has been described as a 'toothless dragon' which is ill-equipped, and reluctant, to challenge assertions by absent parents about their financial circumstances, especially when they are self-employed, and hence is incapable of determining the true situation from which a reliable and fair assessment could be made.[14]

---

8 *Child Support: Good Cause and the Benefit Penalty*, House of Commons Social Security Committee Fourth Report, Session 1995–96, June 1996, para 6. Only 16 per cent of claims of 'good cause' are accepted; *Child Support Agency Annual Report and Accounts 1996/97* (1997).
9 House of Commons Social Security Committee Second Report, Session 1995–96, para 51. The government rejected this suggestion, fearing that the risk of violence might be increased by such action: *Child Support: Reply by the Government to the Second Report from the Select Committee on Social Security Session 1995–1996* (1996) Cm 3191.
10 House of Commons Social Security Committee Second Report, Session 1995–96, para 50.
11 Child Support (Maintenance Assessment Procedure) Regulations 1992 reg 36 as amended.
12 Child Support Act 1991 s 14.
13 Section 15.
14 Davis, Wikeley and Young (with Barron and Bedward) *Child Support in Action* (1998).

INTERIM MAINTENANCE ASSESSMENT

Under s 12 the child support officer may make an interim maintenance assessment where it appears to him that he does not have sufficient information to form a final judgment. The intention is that, by making a higher assessment than might otherwise have been expected, he will be able to prompt the provision of additional information so that the final assessment can be reduced.[15]

Disputes about parentage

A question may arise whether the absent parent is in fact the father (or mother) of the qualifying child. Under s 26, if the alleged parent denies parentage, the child support officer shall not make a maintenance assessment unless the case falls within one of a number of categories. These are:

Case A: the parent has adopted the child;[16]
Case B: the parent has a parental order under s 30 of the Human Fertilisation and Embryology Act 1990;[17]
Case C: a declaration that the alleged parent is the parent is in force under s 56 of the Family Law Act 1986[18] and the child has not subsequently been adopted;
Case D: a declaration is in force under s 27 of the Act[19] and the child has not subsequently been adopted;
Case F:[20]   the alleged parent has been found or adjudged to be the father of the child in relevant proceedings[1] in England and Wales or in affiliation proceedings in the United Kingdom, the finding still subsists and the child has not subsequently been adopted.

Where the alleged parent denies parentage and falls outside these categories, then under s 27 the Agency or the person with care may apply to the court[2] for a declaration that he is, or is not, a parent of the child.[3] The court may direct that blood tests take place to establish parentage.[4] The declaration has effect only for

---

15 Child Support (Maintenance Assessment Procedure) Regulations 1992 Part III, as amended. There is an exception for self-employed absent parents who require a reasonable period of time before they are able to produce accounts etc to enable the Agency to assess their income: such parents pay £30 per week or less at the officer's discretion: reg 8A(6). The average interim maintenance assessment is around £89 per week: *Quarterly Summary of Statistics* (covering period to February 1997).
16 See ante, Chapter 15.
17 See ante, p 267.
18 See ante, p 295.
19 See below.
20 Case E applies to Scotland only.
 1 Within s 12 of the Civil Evidence Act 1968, as amended.
 2 Children (Allocation of Proceedings) Order 1991, Art 3(5), added by the Children (Allocation of Proceedings) Amendment Order 1993, provides that proceedings commence in the family proceedings court but may be transferred up to the county court or Family Division of the High Court.
 3 There is no appeal from a declaration made under this section: *T v Child Support Agency* [1997] 2 FLR 875, where a man was found to be the father of the child, after he had been notified of, but failed to attend, the hearing before the magistrates. Subsequent DNA testing established he was not the father. A declaration was granted under RSC Ord 15 r 16 to the effect that he was not the father of the child, but the court drew attention to the lack of any statutory right of appeal against such a finding.
 4 Compare Family Law Reform Act 1969 s 23, discussed ante, p 281: *Re E (A Minor)(Child Support: Blood Test)* [1994] 2 FLR 548. Where such tests are carried out other than by direction, and show that the alleged parent cannot be excluded from being one of the child's parents, the Agency can recover the costs of the test from the absent parent if he accepts parentage or has been declared a parent: s 27A of the Child Support Act 1991.

the purposes of the Child Support Act, or where maintenance is sought from the courts by virtue of s 8(6)–(8) of the Act.[5]

Calculating the assessment

The formula for calculating the amount of child support maintenance which the absent parent must pay for the qualifying child is set out in Sch 1 to the Act. It is expressed in algebraic terms, with the amounts or percentages of income which these represent left to delegated legislation.

(a)   The maintenance requirement

The starting point is to calculate the child's maintenance requirement, defined[6] as 'the minimum amount necessary for the maintenance of the qualifying child, or, where there is more than one qualifying child, all of them'. The formula used is:

$$MR = AG - CB$$

MR means the maintenance requirement. AG means the aggregate of the amount of income support which would be payable for each qualifying child, the adult income support allowance for a person over 25 for the child's carer if the child is aged under 16, graduated downwards depending upon the age of the youngest qualifying child,[7] and the appropriate level of family premium, depending upon whether the carer has a partner. CB is the child benefit payable for the child. So the maintenance requirement is the amount of income support the carer would receive for herself and the child or children, less child benefit. Housing costs are not included since, according to *Children Come First*,[8] the courts will determine what is to happen to the home when the parties' relationship breaks down. For unmarried parties who have not lived together, the only jurisdiction which could be used to determine that a parent should assist in housing costs for the parent with care is provided by Sch 1 to the Children Act 1989. The power to order periodical payments under that Act is excluded where the Child Support Act is applicable, except in certain situations detailed below.[9] Yet such a parent might have to live in more expensive accommodation because of having to take care of the child. It is unclear why, if this is the case, the absent parent should not be expected to contribute to the extra expense through the assessment.

(b)   Assessable income

The next step is to calculate the contribution to this figure to be met by the absent parent. This is done by working out his 'assessable income' and that of the person with care. By para 5(1):

$$A = N - E$$

---

5 Section 27(3). The Lord Chancellor's Department has issued a Consultation Paper, *1. Court Procedures for the Determination of Paternity, 2. The Law on Parental Responsibility for Unmarried Fathers* (1998) to canvass opinion inter alia on the possibility of making such a declaration valid for all proceedings (para 25): see ante, p 296.
6 By Sch 1, para 1.
7 Allowed in full where the child is under 11; 75% if under 14 and 50% if under 16.
8 Cm 1264, para 3.7.
9 Section 8(3). See post, p 746.

where A means the absent parent's assessable income, N is the amount of that parent's net income, calculated by taking his gross income and deducting income tax, national insurance contributions and half of pension contributions and E means the absent parent's exempt income.

EXEMPT INCOME

Exempt income represents a parent's own essential expenses which must be met before maintenance is paid. It is set as the sum of the income support personal allowance which would be payable to him (but not including an allowance for a new partner), income support allowances for any of the absent parent's own children living with him in his new home (but not step-children) and any income support premiums payable for such children, and *reasonable* housing costs. In 1995, in response to criticism that the formula was too strict, two further allowances were added. First, an allowance of 10p per mile is permitted to employees in respect of travel to work costs where the straight-line distance[10] travelled between the home and the work place exceeds 150 miles per week.[11] Secondly, for those parents who, before the Act came into force, gave up property or capital in a divorce settlement and in return had expected a reduced liability to pay maintenance for the child, a 'broad brush' allowance is made proportionate to the value of the transfer, as follows:[12]

Transfer under £5,000	= nil
£5,000–£9,999	= £20 per week
£10,000–£24,999	= £40 per week
£25,000 and over	= £60 per week.[13]

For low-paid absent parents, the exempt income could well exceed net income and their assessable income hence be nil.

A similar calculation is then carried out, if the person with care is the child's other parent, to ascertain her assessable income, referred to as 'C'.[14] A non-parent with care of the child is deemed to have no assessable income.[15]

(c)   The maintenance assessment

Having calculated the child's maintenance requirement and the parents' assessable incomes, the child support officer must then calculate:

$$(A + C) \times P$$

In other words, the two assessable incomes are added together, and multiplied by P, which is 0.5 or 50 per cent. If the result of this calculation is a sum equal to, or less than the child's maintenance requirement, then the absent parent must pay an amount equal to A × P, ie half his assessable income.

Where the child's maintenance requirement can be met without exhausting the absent parent's assessable income, he is required to pay something over and above

10 The shortest distance between the two points, regardless of the distance actually to be travelled by road or other transport links.
11 Child Support (Maintenance Assessments and Special Cases) Regulations 1992 Sch 3B.
12 Ibid, Sch 3A, para 10.
13 Compare the allowance for capital and property transfers made under the departure directions scheme: post, p 739.
14 A parent with care receiving Income Support or Family Credit is deemed to have nil assessable income: Child Support Act 1991 Sch 1, para 5(4), as amended.
15 Child Support Act 1991 Sch 1, para 2(1).

that amount, so that his children may share in his higher standard of living. The question of how much of his excess assessable income should be diverted to his children is not straightforward. In Australia, a ceiling of two and a half times average earnings is imposed.[16] It was felt to be unreasonable to expect a millionaire, for example, to contribute 25 per cent of the vast bulk of his income which exceeds the child's maintenance requirement, to that child's support. Initially, the Child Support Act set a 'deduction rate' of 25 per cent of the excess, with an absolute ceiling set at the sum of the child's maintenance requirement and three times the child's income support allowance and family premium. This was regarded as too high and so was reduced in 1994 to 15 per cent of the excess where there is one qualifying child, 20 per cent where there are two, and 25 per cent only where there are three or more.[17] The ceiling was reduced in 1995 to the sum of the maintenance requirement and 1.5 times the income support allowance and family premium.[18]

Where an absent parent is receiving jobseeker's allowance or income support, his or her assessable income is deemed to be nil.[19] However, the government envisaged that an absent parent receiving benefit should still make some contribution to his child's maintenance. Accordingly, unless the parent is exempt, for example because he is sick or disabled and unable to work, or has other children living with him, 10 per cent[20] of his personal Income Support adult allowance should be deducted in order to stress the importance of his responsibility to the children of his first family.

(d)   'Protected income'

To prevent payment of child support maintenance leaving the absent parent with a disposable income equivalent to, or below, what he would be entitled to if claiming JSA or Income Support,[1] Sch 1 para 6 to the Act states that the amount of the assessment shall be adjusted:

'with a view to securing so far as is reasonably practicable that payment by the absent parent of the amount . . . so assessed will not reduce his disposable income below his protected income level'.

The 'protected income level' is the amount of Income Support which would be payable to the absent parent to cover his own needs, those of his children living with him and any other dependants such as a new partner and step-children, his housing costs, council tax and an earnings disregard of £30 per week. A further 15 per cent of the amount by which his disposable income exceeds this sum is allowed as an added incentive to work. In this way the true financial obligations of the absent parent are taken into account, having been partially disregarded when assessing his exempt income earlier. The aim is to ensure that the absent parent is left with at least 70 per cent of his net income after paying the

16 See Parker 'The Australian Child Support Scheme' [1990] Fam Law 210.
17 Child Support (Maintenance Assessments and Special Cases) Regulations 1992 reg 6.
18 Ibid, reg 6(2).
19 Child Support Act 1991 Sch 1, para 5(4).
20 Child Support Act 1991 s 43; Child Support (Maintenance Assessments and Special Cases) Regulations 1992 reg 13. Raised from 5 per cent by the Child Support (Maintenance Assessments and Special Cases) and Social Security (Claims and Payments) Amendment Regulations 1996.
1 For as *Children Come First* comments (at Vol 1, para 3.23): 'There is no point in alleviating one family's possible dependence on Income Support at the expense of creating such dependence for another family.'

maintenance assessment, and adjustment to protected income will be made if this would otherwise not be the case. Nonetheless, where the absent parent is not receiving benefit, but his assessable income is calculated as a negative amount and is therefore to be nil under para 5(3), he may be required to pay the minimum amount, just as he could if in receipt of JSA or Income Support. In 1997, almost 40 per cent of absent parents had a nil liability, and a further 15 per cent were assessed to pay the minimum amount.[2] The average full assessment in February 1997 for absent parents in employment was £39 per week, falling to £23.72 for self-employed absent parents.[3] Given that a maintenance assessment is an amount set for all the qualifying children in the family, rather than for each child, this does not seem to be significantly higher than the average amount previously ordered by the courts, which, as we have noted, was criticised as too low by the government.[4]

Departure directions

Despite the various attempts made to respond to criticism that the formula was too rigid and harsh,[5] such as the introduction of extra allowances in exempt income, and reductions in the maximum amounts of child support which can be deducted from the absent parent's disposable income, both noted above, the child support scheme continued to be the object of strong criticism. The sheer weight of opposition and effective lobbying of Members of Parliament forced the government to enact further primary legislation, the Child Support Act 1995. This fundamentally struck at the objective of ensuring consistency through a formulaic approach to the calculation of maintenance, by introducing an element of discretion into the process. Again, the legislation drew on the Australian model. However, whereas in Australia, it is for the courts to determine whether to give a 'departure order' diverting from the formula, in the United Kingdom, the discretion is vested in the Child Support Agency.[6] Under ss 28A–I of the 1991 Act, where a maintenance assessment is in force, the person with care or the absent parent, may apply for a 'departure direction', the effect of which is to direct the child support officer to make a fresh maintenance assessment which departs from the formula amount on the basis of specifications in the direction.

A direction may be given where the Secretary of State is satisfied that the case falls within one or more of the cases set out in Sch 4B to the Act, or the regulations thereto, and it is his opinion that it would be just and equitable to give a direction.[7] There are three classes of case. First, special expenses which ought to be added to the applicant's exempt income; secondly, certain property or capital transfers which occurred before 5 April 1993; and thirdly, additional cases which basically relate to the lifestyle of the absent parent.

---

2 Knights 'Child Support Update' [1997] Fam Law 559.
3 Ibid.
4 See ante, p 728.
5 For American perspectives on the strengths and weaknesses of employing a formula, see Takas 'Improving Child Support Guidelines: Can Simple Formulas Address Complex Families?' (1992) 26(3) Fam Law Q 171; Bergmann and Wetchler 'Child Support Awards: State Guidelines vs. Public Opinion' (1995) 29(3) Fam Law Q 483.
6 There is provision for an application to be referred direct to to an Appeal Tribunal (see post, p 744) where it is particularly novel or contentious: s 28D(1)(b).
7 Section 28F.

(a)   Special expenses

Many complaints about the formula related to the narrow range of items allowed to the absent parent as part of his exempt or protected income. Both these categories ignore many financial commitments which are a part of everyday life and which people are required, or certainly encouraged, to take on. On the other hand, the fundamental philosophy of the legislation is to require parents to meet their obligations to their children before incurring further expenditure and to prevent them from claiming that, because of such expenditure, they are less able to support their children. Thus, the government sought to extend, but only to a limited degree, the types of expenditure which absent parents would be able to claim as having a higher priority on their resources than the cost of maintaining their first family.

The items which may be claimed as special expenses[8] and additional allowances in exempt and protected income under the regulations are as follows: costs incurred in travel to work not otherwise or adequately taken into account in the exempt income formula; costs of travel for contact with qualifying children (many absent parents having complained that it was nonsensical to require them to pay so much maintenance that they could no longer actually afford to see their children);[9] and costs arising from the long-term illness or disability of the applicant or of a dependant of his, which are essential to meet and which are not covered by social security benefits.

The items so far listed may usually have arisen after the breakdown of the relationship. The next group of items relates to financial obligations incurred before the breakdown which continue to have to be met. Thus, an application can be made for allowance to be given for certain debts incurred while the parents were married or cohabiting, and which were incurred for the parties' joint benefit or for the benefit of the parent with care or a child of both, or either of the parties. The applicant must remain wholly responsible for the repayment of the debt. Many types of debt are excluded from consideration, such as credit card debts, legal costs of the separation or divorce, and debts taken over as part of a financial settlement of the divorce or separation. The types of expenditure which would be covered include the purchase by credit agreement or hire purchase of furniture, home improvements, private medical or dental treatment, or taking out a loan to help an older child through university. Also eligible for consideration are other financial commitments, incurred before 5 April 1993, from which it is impossible or unreasonable to expect the applicant to withdraw. The argument for allowing such items is that the commitment was entered into before the applicant could have known the effect of the child support scheme and therefore he should not be penalised for it. The items which might be covered include life assurance policies, paying private school fees for a step-child or child of the second family, or paying residential home fees for an aged relative. Where an absent parent has formed a new relationship and has step-children, it is, of course, highly likely that he is paying for, or at least towards, their support. Although the government initially claimed that sufficient recognition is given to this through the protected income

8 For several of these, the expenses must be over £15 per week to qualify for a departure: Child Support Departure Direction and Consequential Amendments Regulations 1996 reg 19(2).
9 For example, *B v M (Child Support: Revocation of Order)* [1994] 1 FLR 342. The Secretary of State may decide to allow a sum lower than the cost claimed if he regards this as unreasonably high, but he cannot set a figure so low as to make it impossible, in his opinion, for contact to be maintained at the frequency specified in any court order: reg 14(3).

safety net, they succumbed to pressure by permitting the support of step-children to be claimed as a special expense, *provided that the costs were first incurred before the Child Support Act came into force*. The ability of the applicant's partner to support her own children will be taken into account before deciding whether to grant a departure.[10]

(b) Property or capital transfers made before 5 April 1993

The strongest criticism of the formula was probably its lack of any recognition of the effect of divorce settlements on the parties' expectations of their continuing financial obligations to each other and to their children. The trend in the past 20 years has been towards a clean break on divorce,[11] whereby the wife – who is usually the children's carer – forgoes any maintenance for herself in return for a share, or larger share, in the capital and, most often, the transfer to her of the former matrimonial home. Implicit, at least in part, in such an arrangement, is the idea that the home will provide a continuing secure base for the couple's children. Accordingly, despite the view of the courts that parents cannot divest themselves of the obligation to maintain their children,[12] couples may well have agreed that the father would pay little or no maintenance for the children. Since the enactment of the Child Support Act, it has been argued that such a transfer of property represents, at least in part, capitalised maintenance for the children, and should therefore reduce the father's child support liability. The courts were unable to respond to this argument. In *Crozier v Crozier*,[13] a father applied to the court to have his divorce settlement set aside, on the basis that, when he had transferred his share in the former matrimonial home to the wife, he had done so in the light of a child maintenance liability of £4 per week. Under the child support assessment, he was expecting to pay some £29 per week. Booth J refused his application, holding that the fact that Parliament had changed the system for the assessment of maintenance liability for children did not fundamentally undermine the assumptions of the parties' original clean break agreement. She pointed out that it had been held long before the Act that the state, through the social security system, may pursue a liable relative to support his children, regardless of what might have been agreed or ordered under matrimonial law.[14] With the courts unable or unwilling to do the government's business for it and reverse the unfairness of the situation, ultimately legislative change became inevitable.

We have seen[15] that a rough and ready partial recognition of the absent parents' argument was introduced by the 'broad brush' provision in exempt income. Where that inadequately reflects what the parties had agreed or the court had imposed, either may now seek a departure from the formula.[16] It may be noted that the person with care may seek a departure on the basis that, in fact, the transfer was intended only to compensate the other spouse, and not to provide a form of maintenance for the children,[17] but it is much more likely that the provisions will be relied upon by absent parents seeking to argue the opposite. Again, only

---

10 Regulation 18(2)(c).
11 See post, p 820.
12 *Minton v Minton* [1979] AC 593, [1979] 1 All ER 79.
13 [1994] Fam 114, [1994] 2 All ER 362.
14 *Hulley v Thompson* [1981] 1 All ER 1128.
15 Ante, p 735.
16 Child Support Act 1991 Sch 4B.
17 In which case, the broad brush allowance will be removed from the exempt income figure.

transfers which occurred before 5 April 1993 may be considered; couples divorcing since the child support scheme have had ample opportunity to arrange their financial and property affairs in the light of their child support liabilities.[18]

(c)   Additional cases

Although clamour for reform has come mainly from absent parents seeking reductions in their child support liability, concern has also been expressed at the limited efforts apparently made by the Child Support Agency to establish the true financial situation of many absent parents who are self-employed or who appear to have complicated business affairs. Since one of the original motives for introducing the scheme was to tackle the all too common situation of lone parents and their children living on subsistence benefits while the absent parent enjoys a much more affluent standard of living,[19] it is hardly surprising if many parents with care might resent the apparent disparity in lifestyle and seek to argue that the absent parent can afford to pay far more than he ostensibly appears to do. Such claims may already be made, and the Agency does have power to treat a parent as having income where satisfied that he has intentionally forgone remuneration or deprived himself of capital.[20] Nevertheless, it was felt that a broader category of 'extravagant lifestyle' cases ought to be created. Accordingly, there is provision to base a departure application on a range of claims of this kind, such as, for example: the absent parent having assets capable of producing income and failing to utilise them accordingly; diverting income to others (eg paying a new partner a company director's salary in his own business and drawing a small salary himself); having a lifestyle which is substantially inconsistent with declared income;[1] having unreasonably high housing costs which ought not to be allowed despite his coming within a category for exemption from the reasonableness limit;[2] having unreasonably high travel costs. There is also another category which one would expect to be frequently asserted by parents with care. This provides that it may be reasonable to expect the absent parent's *partner* to contribute to his housing costs and that therefore these should not be allowed in his exempt income in full. Under the original formula, housing costs were apportioned between the absent parent and his partner, and he could not claim them in full. This was abolished when it was accepted that apportionment, which reduced the absent parent's exempt income and therefore left more income available for child support, indirectly forced his partner to contribute to the support of the absent parent's children and ignored the reality that the absent parent might be having to pay all the housing costs for his step-children. These thoughts led the government to leave open the possibility of effectively reintroducing apportionment, perhaps where the absent parent moves into property already owned by the partner.

---

18 But the possible effects of the child support scheme on the pattern of divorce settlements are not yet clearly documented by research.
19 Weitzman's famous study of divorce in America has been broadly reflected in this country by Eekelaar and Maclean *Maintenance after Divorce* (1986) ch 5, although they thought the absent parent's enhanced position was likely to be short-lived, given he might well start a second family.
20 Child Support (Maintenance Assessments and Special Cases) Regulations 1992 Sch 1 Part V.
 1 See *Phillips v Peace* [1996] 2 FLR 230, where an absent parent lived in a house worth £2.6 million and owned cars worth £190,000, but was assessed by the Child Support Agency as having no income from his share-dealing business and was given a nil assessment.
 2 See ante, p 735.

(d) Determining what is just and equitable

Once the application is found to come within one or more of the cases in Sch 4B, the Secretary of State must then determine whether it would be just and equitable[3] to give a departure direction. Section 28E and s 28F provide guidance on how this is to be determined. Section 28E sets out two 'general principles':

'(a) parents should be responsible for maintaining their children whenever they can afford to do so;
(b) where a parent has more than one child, his obligation to maintain any one of them should be no less of an obligation than his obligation to maintain any other of them.'

These provisions were apparently intended to remind parents of their obligation and also to reassert that, contrary to what has become the judicial view,[4] duties to the first family should not be superseded by those taken on towards the second. But they can equally be read the other way – that the children of the second family should not be subordinated to those of the first. On this basis, the needs of all of a parent's children ought to be ranked and met equally.

The Secretary of State is not to have regard to the fact that the person with care might be receiving benefits so that any child support maintenance goes to offset entitlement. This is to forestall the argument that children rarely see any of the maintenance money, since it goes to reduce the social security budget instead.

Section 28F[5] sets out further matters to which the Secretary of State either is, or is not, to have regard. Clearly, the financial circumstances of the parties are relevant and it is valid to consider the disparity in their standards of living, and also how far the applicant could meet the extra expenses he is claiming, without a departure being given. However, the officer is to consider whether giving the direction is likely to result in the other party's ceasing paid employment. For example, if a departure were given on the basis of the extravagant lifestyle of the absent parent, would he simply become dependent upon benefits, thus wiping out most of his liability to pay child support anyway? It will also be relevant, although not expressly stated in the regulations, to consider whether the *refusal* to give a direction would equally provide an incentive to give up work. The officer must also consider, where the applicant is an absent parent, the extent of any liability to pay maintenance under a prior court order or agreement. Although there have been phasing-in arrangements to soften the blow of a large increase,[6] the increase in maintenance liability consequent upon the Act has been one of the greatest complaints of absent parents who had previously been used to paying smaller amounts. Persons with care, however, may be justifiably annoyed to find that, while the absent parent applicant may point to a low liability under the former law as part of his case for justifying a departure, the fact that he had not actually kept up the payments is not to be taken into account![7] Other facts to be ignored include

3 It is hard to see what is added to the word 'just' by the word 'equitable'. The phrase appears to have been borrowed from the Australian legislation: Child Support (Assessment) Act 1989 s 98C(1)(b)(ii) and s 117(1)(b)(ii).
4 See post, p 836.
5 And reg 30 of the Departure Direction Regulations.
6 The Child Support (Miscellaneous Amendments and Transitional Provisions) Regulations 1994 Part III (as amended) provide that, where maintenance was previously being paid under a court order or agreement, the amount of child support due under an assessment may be reduced for a transitional period, and gradually increased over time until the full amount is payable.
7 Regulation 30(2)(e). A failure to pay under a child support assessment is also to be ignored in considering what is just and equitable: ibid.

that the child's conception was unplanned; that a party may have been responsible for the breakdown in the relationship; that a new relationship has been formed; and that contact arrangements have, or have not, been made and are, or are not, being adhered to.[8] In reaching a decision, the officer will have regard to the representations of the parties, but may not consider representations by anyone else. The welfare of any child likely to be affected must also be considered, but, as with the general requirement to have regard to welfare under s 2 of the Act, it is unlikely that this will have much impact.

(e)   The effects of a direction [9]

A departure direction requires the child support officer to carry out a fresh assessment. The extent of the difference in the calculated figure will depend upon the type of case. Where special expenses are claimed, these are included in the applicant's exempt income and (except where they relate to the support of step-children) protected income.[10] Where a direction is given based on a property or capital transfer, the broad brush allowance in exempt income is deleted, and the quantified weekly value of the transfer is subtracted from the maintenance assessment.[11] Where the direction is given on the basis of lifestyle, the quantified amount of extra income is added to net and disposable income; unreasonably high housing costs are reduced to the limit allowed in the regulations; and apportioned housing or excessive travel costs are reduced in exempt and protected income.[12]

Termination of assessments

Under Sch 1 para 16 the assessment ceases to have effect on the death of the absent parent or person with care; on there no longer being a qualifying child with respect to whom it would have effect; on the absent parent ceasing to be the child's parent (that is, if the child is adopted or made the subject of a parental order); and where the absent parent and person with care have been living together for a continuous period of six months. Additionally, an assessment must be cancelled at the request of a person who applied for it under s 4, or who was an applicant under s 6 and is no longer dependent upon benefits.[13] Under para 6, where the absent parent and person with care both ask for the assessment to be cancelled, the child support officer *may* do so, if satisfied they are living together.[14] The officer may himself cancel an assessment where satisfied that the applicant for the assessment is no longer the person with care, or where a review is being conducted and the person with care has failed to provide sufficient information to enable the officer to complete it.[15]

---

8 Regulation 30(2).
9 A departure direction will not be given where the amount by which the assessment would be adjusted is below £1 per week; the amount of the adjusted assessment may not exceed the maximum amount under the formula, nor fall below the minimum amount unless the absent parent is exempt from paying this: regs 31; 41.
10 Regulations 37 and 38. Where travel to work costs have been included in the basic formula, these are replaced by the amount allowed by the departure officer.
11 Regulation 39 and Schedule.
12 Regulation 40.
13 Sch 1, para 16(2), (3).
14 Quaere the application of this provision, given the mandatory nature of paras 2 and 3?
15 Para 4(A).

Reviews of assessments

(a)   Periodic reviews

To remedy the problem of maintenance awards failing to keep pace with inflation or to be uprated to meet changed circumstances, s 16 provides that the Secretary of State shall make arrangements for the maintenance assessment to be reviewed by a child support officer as soon as is reasonably practicable after the end of a prescribed period. The period was at first one year, so that assessments could be adjusted in line with the annual adjustment of benefit rates and the fact that employees generally receive annual pay rises. However, the Child Support Agency was unable to cope with its workload, and in 1995 the periodical review was therefore reduced to once every two years.[16] Even this has proved too much for the Agency to deal with.[17]

(b)   Reviews on change of circumstances

Under s 17 the absent parent or the person with care may himself seek a review of a maintenance assessment upon the ground that, by reason of a change of circumstances since the original assessment was made, the amount of child support maintenance payable would be significantly different if it were to be re-assessed, for example, where the absent parent becomes unemployed, or has another child with a new partner and therefore seeks a downward revision of his maintenance assessment. Equally, the person with care might seek an increased assessment if the absent parent was known to have obtained a higher paid employment, or acquired some other gain.

Under either s 16 or s 17, where a review is completed, the Agency must then make a fresh maintenance assessment, unless satisfied that the original assessment has ceased to have effect or should be brought to an end. In the case of a s 17 review, however, this need not be done if the difference in amounts between the original assessment and that of the review is less than a prescribed amount.[18] The problem of keeping up to date with the numerous changes of circumstance in people's lives has proved particularly difficult for the Child Support Agency. It would not be unusual for an absent parent to move house a couple of times in the course of a year, perhaps first into rented and then into mortgaged accommodation, to be joined by a new partner and her children, to become a father of a child of his new relationship, to change jobs or become unemployed, to cease earning overtime or to gain a profit-related bonus of pay. The parent with care could experience just as many changes. Each could be the subject of an application for a review.

To enable mistakes in assessment to be corrected, and to obviate the need for a person with care or absent parent to seek a review, s 19 enables the child support officer himself to make a fresh maintenance assessment where he is satisfied that the one currently in force is defective by reason of having been made in ignorance of a material fact, based on a mistake as to a material fact, or being wrong in law;

---

16 Child Support (Maintenance Assessment Procedure) Regulations 1992 reg 17 (as amended).

17 The Select Committee on Public Accounts found over 60,000 such reviews were outstanding at 31 March 1997: *21st Report: Child Support Agency, Client Funds Account 1996/97* (1998) para 28.

18 Child Support (Maintenance Assessment Procedure) Regulations 1992 reg 20: the prescribed amount is currently £10 per week.

or that it would be appropriate to make a fresh assessment if application to do so were made under s 17 or s 18. This is a necessary power, given the level of error which has dogged the Agency's work.[19]

Challenging the Child Support Agency's decisions

Under s 18 a person who is aggrieved by a decision may seek a review by another officer who was not involved in the original decision. A review may be sought against a refusal to grant an application for a maintenance assessment under s 4 or to carry out a review under s 17, or to challenge a maintenance assessment presently in force, or against a cancellation or refusal of cancellation of such an assessment. The officer need not carry out the review if satisfied that there are no reasonable grounds for supposing that the decision was made in ignorance of a material fact, was based on a mistake as to a material fact, or was wrong in law. If, as a result of the review, the officer is satisfied that a maintenance assessment, or fresh assessment, should be made, then he shall make it.[20]

Appeals against an officer's review or his refusal to carry one out, or against a refusal to make a departure direction, lie to an appeal tribunal.[1] If the appeal succeeds, the tribunal must remit the case to be dealt with by the Agency, and may give such directions as it considers appropriate. Further appeals on questions of law may be made to a Commissioner,[2] and then to the Court of Appeal.[3]

Collection and enforcement of assessments

One of the main objectives of the Act is to improve the collection and enforcement of maintenance. The Agency may carry out the collection and enforcement of assessments where this is requested by those applying for assessment under s 4, and in respect of all s 6 assessments.[4] Section 30 gives the Secretary of State power to make regulations to collect and enforce other types of maintenance, such as periodical payments,[5] and the original intention was that ultimately all forms of periodical payments would be so collected, at least where the recipient is claiming benefits or has a child.

Section 31 empowers the Secretary of State to make a 'deduction from earnings' order, akin to an attachment of earnings order, directed to the liable person's employer, instructing him to make deductions from earnings and pay them to the Secretary of State. However, the order is made by the Secretary of State (or, in practice, the Agency) and not by a court, although there is provision for an appeal to be made to a magistrates' court by a liable person who is aggrieved by the making

---

19 See Select Committee on Public Accounts *21st Report: Child Support Agency, Client Funds Account 1996/97* (1998), which found that 39% of payments being made by absent parents were for wrong amounts and 85% of debt balances contained errors: para 10. The Agency's own accuracy target is 85%; its performance was castigated by the Committee as wholly unacceptable: para 19.
20 Section 18(9).
 1 Section 20. The tribunal is set up under s 21. Appeals concerning issues of disputed parentage lie to the family proceedings court: s 45 and the Child Support Appeals (Jurisdiction of Courts) Order 1993.
 2 Office created by s 22.
 3 Section 24 and s 25.
 4 Section 29.
 5 Child Support (Collection and Enforcement of Other Forms of Maintenance) Regulations 1992. The Child Support Act 1991 (Consequential Amendments) Order 1993 provides that, from 1994, magistrates (but not other courts) may order that qualifying maintenance orders be collected by the Child Support Agency where it is already collecting child support maintenance.

of the order, or by its terms.[6] Like attachment of earnings orders, the order can be made before any arrears of payments have accrued.[7] Such an order is only suitable for those in regular employment.

Where a payment has been missed, the Secretary of State may apply to a magistrates' court for a liability order against the liable person under s 33. This enables the Secretary of State either to levy 'the appropriate amount' (the amount of maintenance unpaid together with charges connected with the distress) through seizure of goods,[8] or to apply to the county court for a garnishee or charging order as if the amount unpaid were payable under a county court order.[9] The ultimate sanction for non-payment is committal to prison for a maximum period of six weeks by a magistrates' court, but only if the court is of the opinion that there has been wilful refusal or culpable neglect on the part of the liable person.[10] Enforcement by means of either deduction from earnings or liability orders is much more likely to be taken against employed absent parents than against the self-employed, a matter of major concern to the House of Commons Social Security Committee.[11]

This array of powers would suggest that, once an absent parent has been tracked down and assessed, there should be little scope for avoiding compliance, but this has not proved to be the case. As at 31 March 1997, £1,127 million was owed by absent parents, with some £869 million regarded as uncollectable (much of this based on interim maintenance assessments).[12] These figures suggest that one of the main aims of the scheme, to improve the collection and enforcement of maintenance, has not yet been realised.

---

6 Section 32(5) and the Child Support (Collection and Enforcement) Regulations 1992 reg 22. The magistrates may not question the validity of the assessment in respect of which the order is made. The absent parent's remedy is to seek a review of the assessment: *Secretary of State for Social Security v Shotton* [1996] 2 FLR 241. Similarly, an alleged failure to consider the welfare of a child affected by the assessment is not a ground for granting an appeal against a deduction from earnings order: *R v Secretary of State for Social Security, ex p Biggin* [1995] 1 FLR 851.

7 Arrears of child support maintenance usually begin to accrue eight weeks from the date the maintenance enquiry form (MEF) is sent to the absent parent, provided he returns the form within four weeks of that date with his name, address, and confirmation that he is the parent of the qualifying child; otherwise they run from the date the MEF was sent, unless a court order has been in effect, in which case liability commences two days after the full assessment is made: Child Support (Maintenance Assessment Procedure) Regulations 1992 reg 30 and Child Support (Maintenance Arrangements and Jurisdiction) Regulations 1992 reg 3.

8 Section 35.

9 Section 36. The duty to pay a maintenance assessment is not expressed as a civil debt and cannot be directly enforced by action in any civil court or by any means other than as provided in the Act: *Department of Social Security v Butler* [1996] 1 FLR 65. The Child Support legislation, according to the Court of Appeal, provides a complete code for the collection of payments due under maintenance assessments and the enforcement of liability orders made on the application of the Secretary of State. (If, however, a liability order has already been made under s 33, then the county court has jurisdiction to grant a *Mareva* injunction under the County Court Remedies Regulations 1991 reg 3(3)(a), (c).)

10 Section 40(3).

11 926 liability orders were taken against the self-employed in the first eight months of the financial year 1995–96 compared with 65,730 deduction from earnings orders against employees from April 1994 to November 1995: *The Performance and Operation of the Child Support Agency* 2nd report of the House of Commons Social Security Committee, Session 1995–96, para 35. The failure to engage fully with the task of collection and enforcement is described in detail by Davis et al *Child Support in Action* (1998) passim.

12 Select Committee on Public Accounts 21st Report: *Child Support Agency, Client Funds Account 1996/97* (1998) para 40.

3.   THE RESIDUAL ROLE OF THE COURTS

Where there is no jurisdiction under the Child Support Act

Section 8(1) and (3) of the Child Support Act provides that:

> '. . . in any case where [the Agency] would have jurisdiction to make a maintenance assessment with respect to a qualifying child and an absent parent of his on an application duly made by a person entitled to apply for such an assessment with respect to that child . . . no court shall exercise any power which it would otherwise have to make, vary or revive any maintenance order in relation to the child and absent parent concerned.'[13]

Under s 44 the Child Support Agency only has jurisdiction if the person with care, the absent parent and the qualifying child are habitually resident in the United Kingdom. Where any of these is not so resident, the jurisdiction of the Agency is therefore excluded and the court may make an order. Secondly, a child support assessment may only be made against an absent parent who is the parent of the qualifying child. Where maintenance is sought for a step-child, the jurisdiction of the courts, which is based on the concept of the 'child of the family',[14] will be the only applicable jurisdiction and the Act will not apply. Thirdly, where a child is over the age of 16, or is not a qualifying child within s 3(1), the court may still have jurisdiction (for example, if the child is not in full-time non-advanced education but still needs financial support).[15]

Orders instead of or in addition to child support assessments

In some situations, notwithstanding the fact that a maintenance assessment may be carried out, it will remain possible to utilise the courts' jurisdiction. First, the court may still make a maintenance order in favour of a child, *by consent*.[16] Secondly, where there is a maintenance assessment in force, which was set at the ceiling fixed by Sch 1, and 'the court is satisfied that the circumstances of the case make it appropriate for the absent parent to make or secure the making of periodical payments under a maintenance order in addition to the child support maintenance' the court may continue to exercise its powers to award maintenance.[17] In the case

---

13   Under transitional arrangements regarding the Act's implementation, where there is in force a written maintenance agreement made before 5 April 1993, or a maintenance order (where made under legislation prescribed by the Act or Regulations: s 8(11)) in respect of the qualifying child, or benefit is being paid to the parent with care, no application may be brought under s 4 for a maintenance assessment: s 4(10) (but see *AMS v Child Support Officer* [1998] 1 FLR 955, CA – the Act originally omitted Guardianship of Minors Acts as prescribed legislation: hence, until the lacuna was corrected by Regulations in 1995, there was no bar on applications under s 4 where an order had been made under those Acts); and the court's jurisdiction to *vary* the order or agreement, is not excluded by s 8(3): s 8(3A). Courts dealing with applications to vary should be provided with information as to the amount of any child support assessment which would be payable if the Agency had jurisdiction: *E v C (Calculation of Child Maintenance)* [1996] 1 FLR 472. Section 8(4) permits the court to revoke a maintenance order, but it has been held that it is not appropriate to do so simply to bring the applicant within the jurisdiction of the child support scheme when she would otherwise be caught by the transitional provisions: *B v M (Child Support: Revocation of Order)* [1994] 1 FLR 342.
14   See ante, p 288.
15   Since the scheme of the Act imposes liability to pay child support maintenance only on an absent parent, where maintenance is sought from the person with care instead, the courts may continue to be used: s 8(10).
16   Section 8(5). Quaere if variation must also be by consent? See s 8(11), read with s 8(5).
17   Section 8(6).

of a very wealthy absent parent it will therefore still be possible to increase the amount of maintenance to be paid by recourse to the court. The court, however, can only 'top up' the assessment: it cannot carry out a whole maintenance assessment exercise itself. Similar powers exist in s 8(7) and (8) to enable the court to make a maintenance order where this is solely to meet costs incurred in receiving education or training, or to cover expenses attributable to the child's disability. School fees, support for a student, and special expenses connected with a child's disability may therefore be met through the court system.[18]

The 1991 Act defines a maintenance order as 'an order which requires the making or securing of periodical payments' and so does not affect the court's powers to make an order for the payment of a lump sum or property adjustment.[19] Although traditionally the courts have not approved of such orders as being appropriate for children, the jurisdiction to make them is unaffected by the Act, and, as discussed below, there may be situations where they will be suitable.

4. REFORM OF THE CHILD SUPPORT SCHEME

Notwithstanding the attempts to reform the system detailed above, continued criticism of the Child Support scheme led the Labour Government to undertake a more thorough review of its working. As the Prime Minister stated in his Foreword to the ensuing Consultation Paper, 'The Child Support Agency has lost the confidence of the public . . . the system . . . is a mess [and] needs urgent reform.'[20]

A new formula

The government proposed that the formula be radically simplified so that parents could predict for themselves the amount of child support they would be required to pay, and so that the Child Support Agency could devote the bulk of its time to collecting, rather than assessing, maintenance. This simplification would be achieved by abolishing the present rules and replacing the formula with a simple requirement that the non-resident parent[1] pay a fixed percentage of his net income, depending upon the number of children in the family. Thus, 15 per cent of that income would be paid in respect of one child, 20 per cent where there are two children, and 25 per cent where there are three or more.[2] Where the non-resident parent has a second family, his net income would be proportionately reduced before determining how much he would pay to his first family.[3] However, the government did not indicate whether this would apply in respect of step-children

---

18 In *C v F (Disabled Child: Maintenance Order)* [1998] 2 FLR 1, the Court of Appeal held that the court may require that such an order continue in effect after the child reaches the age of 19, since its jurisdiction to do so derives inter alia from the Children Act and not from the Child Support Act, and Sch 1, para 3(2) permits an order to extend beyond the child's 19th birthday.
19 Section 8(11).
20 Department of Social Security, *Children First: a new approach to child support* Cm 3992 (1998) p iii.
1 A term to be used in place of the allegedly derogatory 'absent parent'.
2 *Children First* at p 24. These proportions match those currently used in the additional formula, and may be compared with the 'safety net' of 30 per cent of net income which triggers the protected income calculation.
3 At p 48. Alternatively, an equal proportion of the parent's net income would be allocated for all the children.

in the second family. It will be recalled that the present system makes no allowance, other than in protected income, or through a departure direction, for the cost of supporting step-children. Other costs, such as those for housing, debts, care of elderly relatives etc, would not be taken into account, because the child support assessment would be taking a lower proportion of the person's income anyway.[4] Nonetheless, it is doubtful that this will satisfy those who currently seek departure directions because of their living costs, and this is accepted by the retention of the possibility of an appeal to a tribunal in respect of special expenses.[5] No account would be taken of the income of the parent with care, on the basis that since the child shares that parent's standard of living anyway, the contribution of that parent to the child's support is already taken into account.[6] The Consultation Paper includes tables showing how much a person could expect to pay, according to his net income, similar to tables illustrating a person's national insurance and tax deductions under PAYE. Parents on low incomes would pay a fixed amount of child support, as now, as would those on benefits. 'Virtually all' the exemptions from paying the minimum amount would be removed, to reinforce the symbolic importance of paying for one's children.[7] Where the child has staying contact with the non-resident parent, or there is shared residence, a deduction in child support would operate on the basis of 52, rather than the present 104, nights in a year.[8]

Checking income

The government proposed that information about the non-resident parent's net income could be provided by him simply by a phone call to the Agency, or by checking with other government departments (presumably the Inland Revenue in particular). Proof of earnings would then be sent to the Agency to confirm the figures. For the self-employed, tax returns to the Inland Revenue would be used. Such an approach appears simplistic in the extreme. There are clearly ample opportunities for the non-resident parent to distort his earnings by forgoing overtime, and tax returns may bear little relation to the true standard of living. It was for these reasons, after all, that the possibility of seeking a departure direction on the basis of a person's lifestyle was introduced in the first place.

Review and challenge

Seeking to curtail the opportunity to have the assessment reviewed every time a person's circumstances change, the government proposed a biennial periodic review, as now, and the requirement to show a 'substantial change in circumstances' for a further review.[9] How 'substantial' should be defined was not explained.

Dissatisfaction, by either parent, with the amount assessed would be dealt with by an internal review, or recourse to a tribunal. For a parent with care who considers, for example, that the non-resident parent has extra income, the position would be as now. She could appeal, but would have to provide proof to support her case – a difficult undertaking and one unlikely to be fruitful.

As noted above, it would still be possible for a non-resident parent to claim

4 At p 27.
5 See post, p 749.
6 Ibid, p 31.
7 At p 26.
8 At p 27.
9 At p 26.

special expenses justifying a departure from the formula. Additionally, recognition would be given to other forms of support for the children, such as the provision of accommodation through the meeting, say, of the mortgage payments on the former family home. It was presumably envisaged that a divorce settlement involving a transfer of the non-resident parent's share to the former spouse, so that she and the children can remain in the home, would also be included. If so, this would clearly redress the very strong sense of grievance felt by those who have given up property and capital in the form of capitalised maintenance and have hitherto had only limited recognition for this.

Incentives to co-operate

Given the apparently increasing resistance to co-operating with the Child Support Agency, the government proposed enabling parents with care in receipt of income support to retain up to £10 per week of child support maintenance (as a 'premium') without any deduction from their benefit.[10] In consequence, the complicated child maintenance bonus would be abolished. The assumption is that this will prove sufficient incentive to such parents to help the Agency trace the non-resident parent. In turn, that parent's co-operation is expected to be forthcoming because of the lower level of child support he can expect to pay under the revised system.

Collection and enforcement

Although the government were concerned that only 10 per cent of the Agency's time is spent on collecting child support, their proposals for improving collection of maintenance appear merely to restate what is already possible under the existing legislation. While it was stated that, in cases of non-compliance, 'it will be possible to find out who [the non-resident parent's] employer is, assess his child support liability . . . and deduct it from his wages' and that 'he will face a penalty' if he does not pay,[11] the details of how this is to be done were not elaborated. It is unlikely that, simply because the system might be quicker and easier to follow, there will not continue to be successful attempts at evasion.

Evaluation

The Consultation Paper provided a devastating critique of the current system, and also placed child support in the much broader context of changes in family structure and general family policy than has hitherto been the case. The simplified system, and its comparative generosity to non-resident parents – 70 per cent of whom are expected to be paying less – may prove, if not popular, at least more acceptable. The government estimated that 75 per cent of parents with care will be better off too – but this will clearly come mainly from the £10 child maintenance premium they will be permitted to keep before their benefits are reduced. The effect should be to increase the burden on the tax payer – but, given the low rate of compliance with existing assessments, there may in fact be a gain in that more money will actually be collected.

However, although the Consultation Paper is much more straightforward than that which first proposed a child support scheme,[12] there will still, inevitably, be

10 At p 16.
11 At p 30.
12 *Children Come First* Cm 1264 (1990).

complexity. Assessing the true level of earnings, determining when liability first arises, and collecting arrears, will remain difficult. Scope for disagreement between parents, and resulting conflict, may continue to prove detrimental to their relationship with their children. There is still little real attempt to combine the private law, with its emphasis upon settlement and mediation, with what will remain an adjunct of the social security system.

D.   Private agreements

1.   BETWEEN SPOUSES

It will be recalled that the courts have traditionally been reluctant to enforce agreements between cohabiting spouses on the ground that it is presumed that they had no intention to enter into legal relations.[13] Pre-nuptial agreements seeking to determine what divorce settlement should be made in the event of the marriage breaking down have been regarded as either contrary to public policy or irrelevant to the considerations which a court must take into account under Part II of the Matrimonial Causes Act 1973.[14] But no such arguments apply once the couple have separated[15] and, indeed, the general trend in the law and practice relating to financial provision after the breakdown of a marriage has been to encourage the making of fair agreements so as to obviate the need to resort to litigation.[16] To be legally enforceable, an agreement, traditionally called a main-tenance agreement, must constitute a contract between the parties. Consequently, if it is not by deed,[17] the party seeking to enforce a promise to pay maintenance must show that she (or he) has furnished consideration. This will normally not be difficult because the undertaking will be embodied in a separation agreement in which each party gives consideration by releasing the other from the duty to cohabit, or will be part of a much more complicated financial transaction involving the division of property and the compromising of other claims. If there is no consideration at all, however, a promise not made by deed will be unenforceable. Basically the parties' rights and duties are determined by the general law of contract,[18] but the law imposes certain extra requirements in the case of spouses, as a protection to them and the state.

---

13   *Balfour v Balfour* [1919] 2 KB 571; *Gould v Gould* [1970] 1 QB 275; *Re Windle* [1975] 3 All ER 987. See the discussion above at p 63.

14   See Chapter 18. But compare *F v F (Ancillary Relief: Substantial Assets)* [1995] 2 FLR 45, where Thorpe LJ regarded the agreement as basically irrelevant to his determination of what orders to make under the 1973 Act, with *N v N (Foreign Divorce: Financial Relief)* [1997] 1 FLR 900 and *S v S (Divorce: Staying Proceedings)* [1997] 2 FLR 100 which both concerned determining the appropriate venue to settle the divorce involving foreign parties, and where the existence of a pre-nuptial agreement which would be applied in the foreign venue was regarded as a highly relevant circumstance.

15   *Merritt v Merritt* [1970] 2 All ER 760, CA.

16   See Davis, Cretney and Collins *Simple Quarrels* (1994) chs 9–11; Family Law Act 1996 s 9(2) discussed below; Cretney 'From Status to Contract?' in Rose (ed) *Consensus ad Idem* (1996).

17   For the meaning of which see the Law of Property (Miscellaneous Provisions) Act 1989 s 1.

18   It may therefore be set aside on the basis of frustration or mistake etc; cf *Amey v Amey* [1992] 2 FLR 89, where the wife died before an agreement could be put before the divorce court to be made into a consent order. Since terms of the agreement were based on the parties' past contributions and not their future health, the agreement stood.

Negotiated agreements

For the purpose of obtaining a divorce or separation order,[19] the parties will be required, under s 9(2) of the Family Law Act 1996, to produce to the court evidence that they have made arrangements for their and their children's futures, and this may be done by producing 'a negotiated agreement as to their financial arrangements'. This is defined, by Sch 1 para 7, as:

'a written agreement between the parties as to future arrangements –
(a) which has been reached as the result of mediation or any other form of negotiation involving a third party; and
(b) which satisfies such requirements as may be imposed by rules of court.'

The requirements of this provision will be noted. The agreement must be in writing; it must have been reached with the assistance of a third party – preferably, it would seem, a mediator, but solicitors will of course still have an important role to play. Where the parties prefer to arrive at arrangements without anyone else's assistance, they will be required to produce a declaration in prescribed form that they have made their own arrangements.[20]

Maintenance agreements

Secondly, where marital proceedings for a divorce or separation order are not on foot, but the parties have separated and wish to sort out their financial liabilities, or where such proceedings are under way but there is a need to settle some of their finances in the meantime, or they do not wish to make use of a court order for the purpose of settling their financial affairs, the agreement they reach may be a 'maintenance agreement' for the purpose of s 34 of the Matrimonial Causes Act 1973. In such a case, two particular rules apply: certain provisions may be void by statute, and in certain circumstances either party may apply to have the agreement altered. The result is that in many cases the wife (who will usually be the party to whom payments are to be made) will have the best of both worlds, because she can hold her husband to his covenant and also take other proceedings to obtain maintenance.[1] For this reason, and also because parties who have separated will probably in due course divorce and seek a final resolution of their financial and property relationship through the courts, maintenance agreements per se have become relatively uncommon in recent years.[2] However, the greater length of time which parties will have to wait for their divorce under the Family Law Act 1996, and the requirement to complete the details for a settlement before the divorce order may be granted, may well encourage them to negotiate arrangements to cover the period during as well as post-divorce, and so private maintenance

---

19 See ante, Chapter 7.
20 Section 9(2)(c) and Sch 1, para 8.
 1 A similar situation exists in relation to liability under the Child Support Act 1991: see p 755.
 2 The public policy of encouraging agreement rather than litigation is achieved through the device of having the court embody the agreement in a 'consent order' which settles the rights and duties of the parties at the time of the divorce etc; such orders are very common: see post, p 801. The order cannot usually take effect until the divorce is granted, but the court can give approval prospectively: *Pounds v Pounds* [1994] 1 FLR 775 (cf *Wicks v Wicks* [1998] 1 FLR 470, CA). The Family Law Act 1996 Sch 2 inserts s 22B and s 23B into the Matrimonial Causes Act 1973 preventing a financial provision or property adjustment order taking effect before the making of a divorce or separation order unless the court is satisfied that the circumstances are exceptional and it would be just and reasonable for the order to be made. See post, p 782.

agreements may enjoy something of a renaissance.

To come within s 34 of the Matrimonial Causes Act 1973, an agreement must be *in writing* and made between spouses or former spouses. It must also be:

'(a)   an agreement containing financial arrangements, whether made during the continu-
       ance or after the dissolution or annulment of the marriage; or
 (b)   a separation agreement which contains no financial arrangements in a case where
       no other agreement in writing between the same parties contains such arrange-
       ments.'

From this it will be seen that an agreement entered into after a divorce order or decree absolute of nullity can come within the statute only if it contains financial arrangements. An agreement containing no such arrangements can come within the statute only if it is a separation agreement made whilst the parties are still married to each other.

Financial arrangements are defined as:

'. . . provisions governing the rights and liabilities towards one another when living
separately of the parties to a marriage (including a marriage which has been dissolved or
annulled) in respect of the making or securing of payments or the disposition or use of
any property, including such rights and liabilities with respect to the maintenance or
education of any child, whether or not a child of the family.'[3]

Void provisions in maintenance agreements

It was at one time fairly common in separation agreements for the husband to covenant to make periodical payments to the wife in exchange for her giving an undertaking not to take any other steps to obtain maintenance from him. An application for maintenance in other matrimonial proceedings might also be compromised by the wife's promising to withdraw it in consideration of the husband's paying her maintenance or transferring property to her. In *Hyman v Hyman*,[4] however, the House of Lords held that no arrangement of this sort can preclude her from applying for financial relief in divorce proceedings. The reason for this decision is that the court's power to order the husband to maintain his former wife after divorce is intended to protect not only her but also any person dealing with her and, indirectly, the state, in view of the possibility of her having to apply for social security benefits. Consequently, it would be contrary to public policy to permit the parties to oust the court's jurisdiction by agreement.[5] This does not mean that the court will ignore the agreement in subsequent proceedings, and the wife may well be held to it.[6] The uncertainty of not knowing whether the court will, or will not, uphold the terms of an agreement has been criticised. In *Pounds v Pounds*[7] Hoffmann LJ characterised the position as the worst of all worlds and noted that counsel for one of the spouses in that case had told the Court

---

3   Matrimonial Causes Act 1973 s 34(2). It has been held that this does not include the making of a
    lump sum payment: *Furneaux v Furneaux* (1973) 118 Sol Jo 204. Sed quaere? A lump sum is a
    'payment'. The point was left open in *Pace v Doe* [1977] Fam 18 at 23, [1977] 1 All ER 176 at 181,
    but the decision in *Furneaux* is consistent with the approach taken to the court's powers on variation
    of a court order under s 31 of the Act: *Boylan v Boylan* [1988] 1 FLR 282.
4   [1929] AC 601, HL.
5   Ibid, at 608 and 629. For a more recent example of application of this principle in the context of
    determining whether a disposition to a wife was void for the purposes of bankruptcy proceedings,
    see *Re Kumar (a bankrupt), ex p Lewis v Kumar* [1993] 2 All ER 700.
6   See *Edgar v Edgar* [1980] 3 All ER 887, post, p 804.
7   [1994] 1 FLR 775.

that in Northampton an agreement had an 80 per cent chance of being upheld but that attitudes varied from district judge to district judge.

'In our attempt to achieve finely ground justice by attributing weight but not too much weight to the agreement of the parties, we have created uncertainty and, in this case and no doubt others, added to the cost and pain of litigation.'[8]

It must also be stressed that, unless the wife's undertaking not to claim financial provision is the sole or main consideration, it does not make the whole agreement illegal, so that she may still elect to sue the husband on his covenant rather than to apply for maintenance.[9]

Section 34 of the Matrimonial Causes Act 1973 provides that any term in a 'maintenance agreement' purporting to restrict any right to apply to a court for an order containing financial agreements shall be void. It also provides that any other financial arrangements in the agreement shall not *thereby* be rendered void or unenforceable but shall be binding on the parties unless void or unenforceable for any other reason. The precise effect of this section is uncertain. Clearly the inclusion of the offensive term does not make the whole agreement illegal: consequently, even if the wife's undertaking not to apply for an order is the sole consideration, the husband can be sued if his covenant to pay her maintenance is made by deed. If it is not made by deed, however, it seems that the husband's promise is still not actionable if the sole consideration is the wife's undertaking not to institute other proceedings for the further reason that, as her promise is void, his promise is supported by no valuable consideration at all.[10]

Alteration of maintenance agreements

Although any sum agreed on by the parties by way of maintenance might well have been reasonable at the time the agreement was made, it is obvious that in some cases an adherence to this in the light of subsequent events could work serious hardship. The husband's earning capacity may be reduced, which will make reasonable a reduction in the sum he has undertaken to pay the wife; alternatively, the wife's illness or increases in the cost of living may well make the sum absurdly small, particularly if it was agreed on some years ago. To overcome difficulties such as these, s 35 and s 36 of the Matrimonial Causes Act 1973 empower the court to alter any agreement which is a maintenance agreement for the purpose of s 34.[11]

2. BETWEEN PARENTS

Validity

As we have seen from the foregoing discussion, binding agreements made between spouses can include making provision for their children, but spouses can

8 At p 791G.
9 *Goodinson v Goodinson* [1954] 2 QB 118, [1954] 2 All ER 255, CA. But if this is the sole or main consideration for the husband's promise to pay her maintenance, the whole agreement is illegal and unenforceable even if it is by deed: *Bennett v Bennett* [1952] 1 KB 249, [1952] 1 All ER 413, CA.
10 *Sutton v Sutton* [1984] Ch 184, [1984] 1 All ER 168, where an oral agreement was held void, since there was no other consideration.
11 Compare the *automatic* reviews of child support maintenance provided by s 16 of the Child Support Act 1991, discussed ante, p 743.

also make binding agreements solely for the benefit of their children. It is equally established that binding agreements can be made between unmarried parents for the benefit of their children. Indeed, as early as 1842 it was recognised that an agreement between the mother and father of an illegitimate child that the latter should pay the former maintenance for the child was actionable.[12] The consideration for the father's promise has been variously stated: it is usually recognised as a counter-promise on the mother's part either to maintain the child herself (notwithstanding her liability to do so under what is now the Social Security Administration Act 1992)[13] or to refrain from taking proceedings.[14] If there is no agreement as to the time for which the father is to remain bound, it would seem that either side may terminate the contract by giving the other reasonable notice.[15] The father's liability will automatically terminate on the mother's death unless the parties otherwise agree, for her personal representatives cannot claim the benefit of the agreement without at the same time accepting the burden of maintaining the child – an obligation which will not normally have been contemplated.[16] On the other hand, since the father's obligation is not personal but can be met out of his estate, there seems to be no reason why his personal representatives should not be bound.[17]

Section 9(2) of the Child Support Act 1991 provides that maintenance agreements to or for the benefit of a child are not restricted by the Act. However, s 9(3) and (4) state that the existence of such an agreement cannot prevent a party, or any other person, from seeking a maintenance assessment under the Act, and any clause in the agreement purporting to restrict the right of any person to seek an assessment shall be void. In *Smith v McInerney*,[18] it was held that, where, as part of a separation agreement, the husband had transferred his share in the matrimonial home to the wife in return for release from any future obligation to maintain her or the children, and the wife could not guarantee that he would not in the future be pursued for maintenance for their children under the Child Support Act 1991 s 6,[19] he was entitled to an indemnity from her in respect of any substantial periodical payments the Agency might extract from him. With respect, it is arguable that this approach conflicts with the spirit of s 9(4), since inevitably it imposes a deterrent upon the wife from seeking the child support to which her children are entitled.

Alteration of agreements

Powers to alter agreements made between fathers and mothers (regardless of whether they are married to each other) first introduced by the Family Law Reform Act 1987,[20] are now contained in Sch 1 paras 10 and 11 to the Children Act 1989. As with court orders, agreements may be altered only where the Child

12 *Jennings v Brown* (1842) 9 M & W 496; cf *Tanner v Tanner* [1975] 3 All ER 776, CA.
13 *Ward v Byham* [1956] 2 All ER 318, CA.
14 *Jennings v Brown* (supra); *Linnegar v Hodd* (1848) 5 CB 437.
15 *Knowlman v Bluett* (1873) LR 9 Exch 1, Ex; ibid, 307, Ex Ch.
16 *James v Morgan* [1909] 1 KB 564.
17 This was apparently accepted in *Jennings v Brown* (supra). In each case, of course, it will be a question of the construction of the particular contract.
18 [1994] 2 FLR 1077.
19 See ante, p 731.
20 Section 15 and s 16, introduced following the recommendations of the Law Commission, Law Com No 118, paras 6.42–6.46.

Support Act 1991 does not restrict this;[1] only written agreements[2] may be altered; and only where the court is satisfied either:[3]

'(a) that, by reason of a change in the circumstances in the light of which any financial arrangements contained in the agreement were made (including a change foreseen by the parties when making the agreement) the agreement should be altered so as to make different financial arrangements; or

(b) that the agreement does not contain proper financial arrangements with respect to the child.'

Provided it is satisfied, the court may vary or revoke any financial arrangements when it may appear just to do so.[4]

E.   The courts' jurisdiction to make orders for financial support[5]

1.   ORDERS FOR SPOUSES

Introduction

There are two statutes providing powers to the courts to order financial support outside of divorce in respect of spouses: the Domestic Proceedings and Magistrates' Courts Act 1978, which applies only to the magistrates, and the Matrimonial Causes Act 1973 s 27 which applies to the county or High Court. The courts' jurisdiction to make such orders has declined in popularity. The total number of applications for maintenance (including orders for children) dealt with by *magistrates* declined from 18,590 in 1987 to 3,600 in 1992.[6] This is probably due to four main reasons. First, the availability of social security means that women who are unable to work due to child care responsibilities may be supported by the state and need not seek maintenance from their husbands when the marriage breaks down. In many ways the Benefits Office has become the 'marital casualty clearing station' which the Law Commission had considered the function of the magistrates' courts when reviewing their jurisdiction in 1976.[7] Indeed, it was this preference for state support, with the consequent drain on public resources, which,

1 Section 9(5).
2 Defined by Sch 1, para 19(b) as those containing: 'provision with respect to the making or securing of payments or the disposition or use of any property, for the maintenance or education of the child . . .'
3 Sch 1, para 10(3).
4 Any altered periodical payment provision should not in the first instance extend beyond the child's seventeenth birthday, save where the child is or will be receiving instruction at an educational establishment or undergoing training for a trade or profession, or where there are special circumstances: Sch 1, para 10(5).
5 We deal here only with domestic jurisdiction. Courts may also have jurisdiction to enforce orders made in other parts of the United Kingdom or abroad, or to make orders against a person resident abroad, to be enforced in the other country. For details, see the 8th edition to this work, pp 701–7.
6 Home Office Statistical Bulletin *Domestic Proceedings England and Wales 1992* Table 2. These figures are the most recent available. The statistics do not distinguish between orders for spouses and orders for children, but the commentary to them does explain that the vast decline reflects the implementation of the Children Act 1989 Sch 1 (see post, p 767).There will have been further decline with the introduction of the Child Support Act in 1993. The figures demonstrate that the bulk of orders sought have been for children rather than spouses. There are no figures recorded for the number of applications for maintenance *outside of divorce*, in the county or High Court.
7 Law Com No 77, *Report on Matrimonial Proceedings in Magistrates' Courts* para 2.4.

as we have seen lay, in part, behind the enactment of the Child Support Act.[8] Secondly, with the liberalisation of divorce by the Divorce Reform Act 1969, couples found that their marriages could be dissolved relatively quickly and easily,[9] and there was a less pressing need to seek a maintenance order in the meantime. Where such maintenance was required, it could be sought, once a petition had been filed for a divorce,[10] via provision under the Matrimonial Causes Act 1973[11] or by agreement. Thirdly, as more women have remained in or returned to the work place notwithstanding marriage and having children, they have become more likely to favour a clean break from their husbands, involving no on-going financial support for themselves and, provided that their children's needs are met, they may be reluctant to seek orders for their own benefit. Finally, a further reason for reluctance to resort to law may have been the unpopularity of the *magistrates' court* as a forum for hearing matrimonial disputes because of its association with criminal matters.

Orders under the Domestic Proceedings and Magistrates' Courts Act 1978[12]

(a)   Jurisdiction

A magistrates' court may make an order under the Domestic Proceedings and Magistrates' Courts Act 1978 if, at the date of the making of the application, either the applicant or the respondent ordinarily resides within the commission area for which the court is appointed.[13]

(b)   Orders for financial provision

Application for financial provision may be made in one of three different sets of circumstances. First, there is what one might term the 'normal' application, when the applicant must establish the ground set out in s 1 of the Act.[14] Secondly, if the spouses have agreed what financial provision should be made, either may apply to have the terms of the agreement embodied in a court order. Thirdly, the court may make an order if the spouses are living apart[15] and the respondent has been making periodical payments to the applicant.

---

8 Ante, p 728.

9 But see Davis et al *Simple Quarrels* (1994) who demonstrate that this speed and ease are only relative; negotiations concerning divorce settlements can still take a number of years to conclude. See Chapter 18.

10 See ante, p 228.

11 Matrimonial Causes Act 1973 s 22, to be replaced by s 22A and s 22B, inserted by the Family Law Act 1996. See post, p 786.

12 For the background to the legislation see generally McGregor, Blom-Cooper and Gibson *Separated Spouses; Report of the Committee on One-Parent Families*, Cmnd 5629, passim; Law Com No 77, *Matrimonial Proceedings in Magistrates' Courts*, Pt II.

13 Section 30(1). See Law Com No 77, paras 4.77–4.90. As the jurisdiction is statutory, it cannot be enlarged by agreement or submission: *Forsyth v Forsyth* [1948] P 125 at 132, [1947] 2 All ER 623, CA at 624.

14 Section 1 as originally enacted contained three grounds: that the respondent has failed to provide reasonable maintenance; that the respondent has behaved in such a way that the applicant cannot reasonably be expected to live with him; and that the respondent has deserted the applicant. The last two were repealed by the Family Law Act 1996 s 18 and will cease to have effect when that section is brought into force. For discussion of these grounds, see the 8th edition of this work at pp 671–2.

15 Until the Family Law Act 1996 s 18(2) comes into force, this provision requires that neither spouse be in desertion: see post, p 758 n 12.

(I) APPLICATIONS UNDER S 1

Either party to a marriage may apply to a magistrates' court[16] for an order on the ground that the respondent spouse has failed to provide reasonable maintenance for the applicant.[17] The ground must exist when the application[18] is made and also at the time of adjudication.

(II) FAILURE TO PROVIDE REASONABLE MAINTENANCE

Whether the respondent has provided reasonable maintenance for the applicant or any child of the family is clearly a question of fact. To answer it the bench must ask itself a hypothetical question: assuming that a ground for applying for an order existed, what order should we make? If the provision in fact being made by the respondent is lower – or at least significantly lower – than this, then he must be failing to provide reasonable maintenance. The word 'failure' implies culpability only insofar as it suggests that the respondent has the means to make the provision; and as his resources must be taken into account in deciding what sum to order, the court must ex hypothesi be satisfied that he has the capacity to make the payments.

(III) RECONCILIATION

When hearing an application under s 1, the court is required to consider whether there is any possibility of a reconciliation between the parties and if, either then or later, it appears that there is a reasonable possibility, it may adjourn the proceedings and, if it sees fit, request a probation officer or other person to attempt to effect one.[19] In the past courts have claimed to have achieved a measure of success in this regard but, as in the case of divorce, it may be more practicable in most cases to concentrate on mediation rather than reconciliation.[20]

(IV) ORDERS THAT MAY BE MADE

The court may order the respondent to do one or more of the following:

(a) to make periodical payments to the applicant;[1]
(b) to pay a lump sum not exceeding £1,000 for the applicant.[2]

It may allow the respondent to pay a lump sum or may order him to pay it by instalments.[3] All orders for periodical payments may run from the date of the

---

16 The magistrates may refuse to deal with an application if they consider that it would be more conveniently dealt with by the High Court: Domestic Proceedings and Magistrates' Court Act 1978 s 27.
17 There is also a ground relating to failure to provide reasonable maintenance for any child of the family: s 1(b). See further post, pp 764 et seq.
18 For procedure, see the Family Proceedings Courts (Matrimonial Proceedings Etc) Rules 1991.
19 Domestic Proceedings and Magistrates' Courts Act 1978 s 26.
20 See ante, pp 232 et seq.
 1 Such orders may subsequently be varied or revoked on the application of either spouse: s 20(5), (12)(a).
 2 Domestic Proceedings and Magistrates' Courts Act 1978 s 2. A lump sum order may not be varied, although if it is payable by instalments, the amount of these, and the dates of their payment, may be varied: s 22. For orders for children of the family, see post, p 764.
 3 Magistrates' Courts Act 1980 s 75.

application and may be made for a limited period of time.[4] This may be useful where a wife is likely to need money for a comparatively short period whilst she adjusts to living alone, because the husband will not have to go back to the court at a later date to seek a variation or discharge. Similarly, magistrates may deliberately use this device as a means of encouraging the wife to obtain paid employment, if they consider this to be the proper course (though before doing this justices should be confident that the wife can reasonably obtain employment).[5] If she will continue to need maintenance after the end of the period stipulated, she should take care to have the order varied before it runs out, because otherwise it will automatically lapse and she will have to start fresh proceedings. The court may also order that the payments should begin from a future date, and it may wish to use this power if, for example, the husband is unemployed but is to start work in a short time. The order will terminate on the remarriage (but not divorce),[6] or death of the recipient spouse or on the death of the person liable to make the payments.[7]

(V)   CONSENT ORDERS

Magistrates are able to make a consent order without the applicant having to establish any ground. Under s 6, upon either party's application and provided the court is satisfied that either the applicant or the respondent has agreed to make the financial provision[8] specified in the application, it may make an order giving effect to the agreement.[9] The order may contain precisely the same terms as an order made following an application under s 1 except that, as the respondent has agreed to it, a lump sum may be for *any amount* and is not limited to £1,000. The court may not make the order proposed if it considers that it would be contrary to the interests of justice to do so.[10] This seems most likely to occur if the amount specified in the application looks too low, or if it appears that undue pressure has been put on either party. In such cases, however, it is open to the parties to come forward with a fresh agreement. Alternatively, the court itself might take the initiative and suggest what order would be appropriate: if the parties both agree, this may be embodied in an order.[11]

(VI)   ORDERS FOLLOWING SEPARATION

In cases where the parties have separated and the husband is actually providing the wife with reasonable maintenance, she may be concerned that, without the security of an order, he may choose to stop at any time. To secure her position, she may apply to the court under s 7. The parties must have lived apart for a continuous period exceeding three months,[12] and the respondent must have been

---

4 Domestic Proceedings and Magistrates' Courts Act 1978 s 2(1)(a) and (c), s 4(1) and s 5(2). Interim orders may also be made pending a final order or dismissal of the application: s 19.
5 As in proceedings for a separation order (see ante, p 257 and post, p 820 n 18), the 'self-sufficiency' principle does not apply.
6 Section 4(2). This is so even if the second marriage is void or voidable: s 4(2) and s 88(3).
7 Section 4(1). An order ceases to have effect if the parties continue, or resume, living together for a continuous period exceeding six months: s 25(1), s 88(2).
8 Periodical payments or lump sum payments: s 6(2).
9 If proceedings are begun under s 1 and the respondent then agrees to the order, the applicant may apply for an order under s 6: s 6(4).
10 Section 6(1)(b).
11 Section 6(5).
12 Until the Family Law Act 1996 s 18(2) comes into force, it must also be shown that neither is in desertion.

making periodical payments for the benefit of the applicant.[13] 'Living apart' is not defined, but it presumably bears the same meaning as under the former law of divorce.[14]

If these conditions are satisfied, the court may make an order for periodical payments for the benefit of the applicant for such term as may be specified.[15] The purpose of s 7 is to enable legal effect to be given to the de facto situation. Consequently, no lump sum order may be made and the court may not require the respondent to make payments which exceed in aggregate during any period of three months the amount actually paid by him for the benefit of the applicant during the three months immediately preceding the making of the application. If this is greater than the sum which the court would have ordered on an application under s 1, the respondent is protected by the further provision that the order must not be for more than this smaller sum.[16] Conversely, if the court considers that the sums paid fail to provide reasonable maintenance for the applicant, this ground under s 1 must necessarily be made out; the court may therefore treat the application as though made under that section and will then have full powers to make such orders for periodical payments and lump sum payments as it thinks fit.[17] Perhaps unsurprisingly, given its convoluted nature, very few orders appear to have been made under this section.[18]

(VII) PAYMENT OF MAINTENANCE

Upon the making of a periodical payments order, magistrates' courts are required to specify the method of payment,[19] which must be one of the following: payments made directly by the debtor to the creditor; payments made to the clerk of the court or to the clerk of any other magistrates' court; payment by standing order or direct debit; payments made to the Secretary of State under the collection provisions of the Child Support Act;[20] and payments by way of an attachment of earnings order.[1]

The power to order payment by standing order (or some similar method) was introduced by the Maintenance Enforcement Act 1991[2] and is intended to ensure prompt payments without the parties having to come face to face. The more traditional method of providing for this is for payment to be made to the clerk of the magistrates' court on behalf of the recipient.

13 Section 7(1). The payments need not have been made to the applicant. Hence, for example, the payment of rent could amount to periodical payments for this purpose.
14 Under which it was established that spouses living under the same roof might be regarded as living apart provided that they are living in two separate households: *Mouncer v Mouncer* [1972] 1 All ER 289.
15 If the spouses resume living together, the order ceases to have effect immediately: s 25(3); cf orders made under s 1 or s 6, which may continue in force for up to six months: ante, n 7.
16 Section 7(3).
17 Section 7(4).
18 Only 20 in 1992: Home Office Statistical Bulletin *Domestic Proceedings England and Wales 1992* Table 2.
19 Magistrates' Courts Act 1980 s 59(1). This requirement is contingent upon the 'debtor' (ie the person against whom the order is made) being ordinarily resident in England and Wales at the time that the order was made: ibid, s 59(2).
20 Added by the Child Support Act 1991 (Consequential Amendments) Order 1993. It is doubtful if the Agency has the capability to handle the collection of spousal maintenance, given its difficulties in enforcing child support, discussed ante, p 744.
1 Ibid, s 59(3), (6). Attachment of earnings orders are discussed post, p 774.
2 Where payment is so ordered, the court can require the debtor to open an account: ibid s 59(4).

(c)   Assessment

The Domestic Proceedings and Magistrates' Court Act sets out a check list of the matters which a magistrates' court is to take into account when making an order. The court must 'have regard to all the circumstances of the case, first consideration being given to the welfare while a minor of any child of the family who has not attained the age of 18'.[3] In addition, in determining whether the respondent is to be required to make periodical payments or to pay a lump sum to the applicant and, if so, how much he is to pay, the court is directed 'in particular' to have regard to:[4]

'(a)   the income, earning capacity, property and other financial resources which each of the parties to the marriage has or is likely to have in the foreseeable future, including in the case of earning capacity any increase in that capacity which it would in the opinion of the court be reasonable to expect a party to the marriage to take steps to acquire;

(b)   the financial needs, obligations and responsibilities which each of the parties to the marriage has or is likely to have in the foreseeable future;

(c)   the standard of living enjoyed by the parties to the marriage before the occurrence of the conduct which is alleged as the ground of the application;

(d)   the age of each party to the marriage and the duration of the marriage;

(e)   any physical or mental disability of either of the parties to the marriage;

(f)   the contributions which each of the parties has made or is likely in the foreseeable future to make to the welfare of the family, including any contribution by looking after the home or caring for the family;

(g)   the conduct of each of the parties, if that conduct is such that it would in the opinion of the court be inequitable to disregard it.'

Comparison with the matters which the court must take into account in making an order for financial relief after divorce shows that, with minor exceptions,[5] the guidelines are identical. As the law has been much more fully worked out in connection with divorce, detailed examination of these matters will be deferred until Chapter 18, but some general principles and certain points of dissimilarity should be mentioned here.

(I)   ABSENCE OF POWER TO ADJUST PROPERTY RIGHTS

The main difference between the powers of the magistrates' courts and those of divorce courts is that magistrates cannot make property adjustment orders. This is because the making of property adjustment orders is inconsistent with the principle that magistrates should regulate the parties' financial position during a period of marital breakdown which is not necessarily permanent or irretrievable.[6] It is to be assumed that whichever spouse is in the matrimonial home will stay there for the time being: if either of them wishes to bring about a change, he or she must invoke the jurisdiction of the courts in some other way.[7]

---

3 Section 3(1).

4 Section 3(2). In the case of applications made under s 7, para (c) is amended to read: 'the standard of living enjoyed by the parties to the marriage before they lived apart' (s 7(5)).

5 Para (c) of s 25(1) of the Matrimonial Causes Act 1973 refers to 'the standard of living enjoyed by the family before the breakdown of the marriage' and (g) (as amended by the Family Law Act 1996 Sch 8, para 9(3)(b)) refers to the conduct of each of the parties 'whatever the nature of the conduct and whether it occurred during the marriage or after the separation of the parties or (as the case may be) dissolution or annulment of the marriage'. The divorce court is additionally required to consider the loss, inter alia, of pension rights. See post, p 795.

6 See ante, Chapter 7.

7 See Chapter 6.

(II) NO REQUIREMENT TO CONSIDER 'SELF-SUFFICIENCY'

Another important difference between magistrates' powers and those of the divorce court is that the former are not directed to consider whether the parties could become self-sufficient. Magistrates have no powers to make a 'clean break' order settling financial liability in a once-and-for-all order. On the other hand, they are directed to have regard to whether it is reasonable to expect a party to take steps to increase his earning capacity. This could justify, for example, making a periodical payments order to last for a limited time in a case where the applicant could reasonably be expected to start work or to obtain higher paid work. Even if such a limited term order were to be made, the applicant could still return to the court to seek an extension to the order,[8] or, if the order had already expired, could bring fresh proceedings to seek a new order.

(III) FIRST CONSIDERATION TO BE GIVEN TO THE WELFARE OF A CHILD UNDER THE AGE OF 18

This requirement is the same as on divorce and we discuss it more fully in that context.[9] Suffice to say here that (a) children's welfare is a consideration, even where the application is for *spousal* support; (b) priority is only given to children of the spouses' family;[10] and (c) the court is only required to give first and not paramount consideration to the child's welfare.[11] This means that other considerations should be taken into account and in some circumstances could be overriding. The enjoinder means, for instance, that the husband's moral obligations towards his second family should not be ignored.[12]

(IV) THE PARTIES' NEEDS

According to Dunn LJ in *Vasey v Vasey*,[13] the proper approach for magistrates, when considering an application for financial provision, is to make findings seriatim upon each of the matters set out in what is now s 3(2) and to balance the factors against one another to arrive at an order which is just and reasonable. But, as Dunn LJ also pointed out, the most important function of magistrates is to balance the needs and responsibilities against the financial resources.

Only the family's reasonable needs should be taken into account. The parties require shelter and food, but over and above this there can be no hard and fast rules, since what amounts to 'reasonable' must inevitably be judged against the available resources.[14] Commonly in cases before magistrates, the parties' means will be so slight that all the court can do is to concentrate on their needs. The need to support

---

8   There being no equivalent of s 28(1A) of the Matrimonial Causes Act 1973, which enables the court to direct that the party not be entitled to seek an extension of the term specified in the order (see post, p 823).

9   See post, p 818.

10   Not those of the parent's second family.

11   On which, see *Suter v Suter and Jones* [1987] Fam 111, [1987] 2 All ER 336, CA.

12   See *Blower v Blower* [1986] 1 FLR 292. The balancing of needs and responsibilities to first and second families is also attempted under the Child Support Act, although there the approach is strongly to favour the first family: ante at p 730.

13   [1985] FLR 596, CA at 603.

14   One problem is the need for a car. Whether this is a reasonable need depends in part upon whether it is genuinely needed to get to work: cf *Clarke v Clarke* (1979) 9 Fam Law 15, where a car was not thought to be needed, and *Slater v Slater* (1982) 3 FLR 364, where it was. In *Girvan v Girvan* (1983) 13 Fam Law 213, where a husband had just been made redundant, it was thought that a television was a reasonable need, but not a video.

two families will often mean that the husband will not be able to keep both above subsistence level; in that case any order made must not reduce his resources to such an extent that, were he unemployed, he would be entitled to jobseeker's allowance. Given that he can be ordered to pay something, however, magistrates should make a full assessment of the sum, notwithstanding that it will be so small that the wife will still have to look to the Benefits Agency to make up the balance.[15] To this extent the court must know what the benefits payable to both parties would be.[16]

Where the payer is himself dependent upon social security, the courts at one time considered that he should still be required to pay something, to remind him of his obligations.[17] However, in *E v C (Child Maintenance)*[18] it was held that, where a father would have been exempt from paying the minimum amount of child maintenance under the Child Support Act, magistrates hearing his application to reduce the maintenance he paid under a court order should have discovered what his child support liability would have been, and should have appreciated that where a person 'is on, by way of government benefits, fair subsistence, any order which deducts from that is an order which puts him into difficulties.'[19] A nominal order of £1 per annum for each child was substituted. Since obligations to one's children appear to carry more weight with the courts than obligations to a spouse, the same approach to the ability of the husband to pay should apply a fortiori where a wife is seeking maintenance from her husband.

(V)   THE PARTIES' CONDUCT

In some cases the parties' conduct, or the short duration of the marriage, may be significant. Both these facts are relevant on divorce and will be discussed in detail in Chapter 18. Suffice it here to say that the generally held view is that conduct will rarely be relevant. As Dunn LJ said, in *Vasey v Vasey*,[20] conduct should only be taken into account in exceptional cases, because 'experience has shown that it is dangerous to make judgments about the cause of breakdown of a marriage without full inquiry, since the conduct of one spouse can only be measured against the conduct of the other, and marriages seldom break down without faults on both sides'.[1] Even if conduct is thought to be relevant, magistrates should still balance that fact against all the others laid down by statute, and in particular against each party's needs.[2]

In cases where the marriage has been short-lived, reduced orders may be justified.[3]

---

15 *Ashley v Ashley* [1968] P 582, [1965] 3 All ER 554; *Barnes v Barnes* [1972] 3 All ER 872, CA. Contrast the situation where the couple are divorced, where the courts are readier to end the parties' financial ties even though this means one of them will be totally dependent upon state benefits: *Delaney v Delaney* [1990] 2 FLR 457, CA.

16 *Williams v Williams* [1974] Fam 55, [1974] 3 All ER 377.

17 *Freeman v Swatridge* [1984] FLR 762, CA. The Child Support Act similarly seeks to do this by exacting the minimum amount of maintenance except where the absent parent is exempt: see ante, p 736.

18 [1996] 1 FLR 472.

19 Per Douglas Brown J at 476E–F.

20 [1985] FLR 596, CA at 603.

1 But note that divorce law under the Family Law Act 1996 provides no means for holding an inquiry into the cause of the breakdown of the marriage, although conduct is a relevant factor in assessing the financial arrangements for the spouses: Matrimonial Causes Act 1973 s 25(2)(g), as amended.

2 Ibid. The wife actually conceded that a reduced order should be made, since she had deserted her husband after only nine months of marriage.

3 See eg *Khan v Khan* [1980] 1 All ER 497; *Graves v Graves* (1973) 4 Fam Law 124; *Brady v Brady* (1973) 3 Fam Law 78.

(VI) REMARRIAGE AND COHABITATION

The payer's remarriage will not normally be relevant in magistrates' proceedings, but it may become so if the order continues in force after a later divorce. In this case it may be proper to reduce the order because of the payer's increased financial responsibilities; the same result will follow if he lives with another woman, particularly if they have children whom he has to support.[4] Likewise, the wife's living with another man may lead the court make a reduced order, or none at all, not because she is committing adultery, but because the man will be, or may be expected to be, supporting her.

(VII) LUMP SUM PAYMENTS

The power conferred on magistrates to order lump sum payments was introduced by the 1978 Act. Although such a power, of course, is of no practical value unless the respondent has the necessary capital (or, possibly, income),[5] there are a number of situations in which relatively small orders may be made. The Act itself provides that a lump sum may be ordered to meet any liability or expenses already incurred in maintaining the applicant or any child of the family:[6] in other words, in appropriate cases it will be an alternative to backdating the order. It might also be used to enable a wife to take a course of training, or even to help provide the capital to set her up in business. If the spouses have low incomes but the respondent has some savings, a just solution might be to order part of the savings to be paid to the applicant.

Orders for financial provision under s 27 of the Matrimonial Causes Act 1973

Section 27 of the Matrimonial Causes Act 1973 (as amended)[7] provides that either party to a marriage may apply to a divorce court for an order on the ground that the other has failed to provide reasonable maintenance for the applicant. The court has jurisdiction if either party is domiciled in England and Wales, if the applicant has been habitually resident here for one year, or if the respondent is resident here.[8] The proceedings must be commenced in a divorce county court,[9] but the court has the power, either upon its own motion or upon application by a party, to order the transfer of the whole or any part of the proceedings to the High Court.[10]

The ground upon which an application may be made is the same as that on which a spouse may apply to a magistrates' court for an order under the Domestic Proceedings and Magistrates' Courts Act 1978 s 1, ie that the respondent has failed to provide reasonable maintenance for the applicant. However, in determining whether this ground is made out and, if so, what order to make, the court is also required to take into account the matters set out in s 25(2) of the

---

4 See *Delaney v Delaney* [1990] 2 FLR 457, CA.
5 See *Burridge v Burridge* [1983] Fam 9, [1982] 3 All ER 80, where the court ordered an unemployed husband to pay a lump sum by instalments, expecting him to obtain employment within six weeks.
6 Section 2(2).
7 By the Family Law Act 1996 Sch 8, para 13.
8 Section 27(2).
9 Matrimonial and Family Proceedings Act 1984 s 34(1)(a).
10 Ibid, s 39. *Practice Direction* [1992] 3 All ER 151.

Matrimonial Causes Act 1973.[11] The welfare of a child of the family is to be regarded as the court's first consideration only where an application is made in respect of such a child, and not where spousal maintenance alone is sought, but it is doubtful whether this change of emphasis makes any difference in practice.

The court may make an interim order for periodical payments or a lump sum or sums to the applicant if it appears that the latter is in immediate need of financial assistance.[12] If the ground is made out, the court may make one or more financial provision orders[13] against the respondent.

The question of assessment of orders is essentially the same as that of orders made in magistrates' courts, except that periodical payments may be secured and there is an unlimited power to order lump sum payments. Both these matters will be dealt with more fully when we consider financial provision after divorce;[14] in the case of lump sum payments, however, it should be borne in mind that the court has no power to make property adjustment orders under s 27, and consequently a lump sum order should not be used as a means of circumventing this restriction. Section 27(7) specifically provides that a lump sum may be ordered to enable the applicant to meet any liabilities or expenses already incurred in maintaining herself (or himself); in addition, it may properly be ordered (as on divorce) whenever a capital sum is more valuable to the applicant than periodical payments.[15] Orders are payable and enforceable in the same way as orders for periodical payments on divorce.[16]

It would seem that few applications are made for orders under s 27. Statistics are not now recorded separately for proceedings under this section. Most spouses would probably prefer to take the cheaper and speedier proceedings available in magistrates' courts unless they are also seeking a divorce, in which case the court has powers to deal with their financial needs anyway.[17]

2.   OBTAINING FINANCIAL RELIEF FOR CHILDREN

Matrimonial jurisdictions

Where the Child Support Act does not apply,[18] it will be possible to utilise either of the jurisdictions discussed above to obtain an order for a child, as orders under the Domestic Proceedings and Magistrates' Courts Act 1978 and the Matrimonial Causes Act 1973 may be made payable both to the applicant and to, or for the

---

11 Section 27(3). See post, pp 829–44. These matters, which apply also in relation to divorce, are to be read as if they referred to a failure to provide reasonable maintenance instead of the breakdown of the marriage: s 27(3B).

12 Section 27(5) as amended by the Family Law Act 1996 Sch 8, para 13(2).

13 Section 27(6) as amended by the Family Law Act 1996 Sch 8, para 13(3). Financial provision orders are orders for periodical payments (secured or unsecured) or for lump sums: Matrimonial Causes Act 1973 s 21(1) as amended by the Family Law Act 1996 Sch 2, para 2. A lump sum may be made payable in instalments and the instalments may be secured: s 27(7)(b). Orders for periodical payments may be varied, but in the case of a lump sum payable by instalments, while the provisions relating to the instalments may be varied, the total sum payable may not: s 31. See further post, p 850.

14 See post, p 789 (secured payments) and p 791 (lump sum payments).

15 See post, p 792.

16 See post, p 859.

17 See post, p 833.

18 See ante, p 746.

benefit of, any 'child of the family'. The court may make an order for financial provision for a child whether or not it makes any other order relating to the child.

(a) Factors to be considered

In deciding what, if any, orders should be made in addition to those considerations applicable to orders for spouses, discussed above, the court must also have regard to: [19]

(a) the financial needs of the child;
(b) the income, earning capacity (if any), property and other financial resources of the child;
(c) any physical or mental disability of the child;
(d) the standard of living enjoyed by the family before the occurrence of the conduct which is alleged as the ground of the application (or before the parties to the marriage lived apart); and
(e) the manner in which the child was being and in which the parties to the marriage expected him to be educated or trained.[20]

We have already considered the meaning of 'child of the family',[1] but it should be emphasised that just because a child is found to be a child of the family does not ipso facto mean that the respondent will be ordered to make financial provision for him.[2] When deciding whether to make an order against a party to the marriage in favour of a child who is not his natural or adopted child and, if so, how much to award, the court must further have regard:[3]

(a) to whether he has assumed any responsibility for the child's maintenance and, if he did, to the extent to which, and the basis on which, he assumed that responsibility and to the length of time during which he disregarded that responsibility
(b) to whether in assuming and discharging that responsibility he did so knowing that the child was not his own child; and
(c) to the liability of any other person to maintain the child.

Whether a spouse assumed responsibility for a child must be judged objectively, and, in the absence of a clear contrary indication, the payment of the expenses of a family unit including the child implies an assumption of responsibility, even though other resources may be available for his maintenance.[4] In para (a) the word 'extent' refers to the amount of the spouse's contribution in contradistinction to the length of time during which he made it.[5] The reference in para (c) to the liability of any other person to maintain the child covers any liability enforceable at law, and thus embraces the potential liability of a parent or of a party to another marriage who has treated the child as a child of the family.[6] It will be seen that the need to take all these

19 Domestic Proceedings and Magistrates' Courts Act 1978 s 3(4), s 7(5).
20 A court hearing an application under s 27 of the Matrimonial Causes Act must consider a similar list of factors: s 27(3A) and s 25(3).
1 Ante, p 288.
2 Compare liability under the Child Support Act 1991 (discussed ante, pp 727–50), which depends upon legal parenthood.
3 Domestic Proceedings and Magistrates' Courts Act 1978 s 3(4), s 7(5); Matrimonial Causes Act 1973 s 27(3A) and s 25(4).
4 *Snow v Snow* [1972] Fam 74 at 111–12, [1971] 3 All ER 833, CA at 863.
5 *Roberts v Roberts* [1962] P 212, [1962] 2 All ER 967.
6 *Snow v Snow* (supra) at 112 and 863 respectively.

matters into account means that the court might well conclude, for example, that no order should be made against a husband who had married the wife in the mistaken belief that he was the father of her child, or who had made it clear at the time of the marriage that he was undertaking no financial responsibility for her children by a previous marriage if their own father was quite capable of providing for them.[7]

In determining what is reasonable maintenance for a child, as Bagnall J said in a comment approved by the Court of Appeal in *Lilford v Glynn*:[8]

'In the vast majority of cases the financial position of a child of a subsisting marriage is simply to be afforded shelter, food and education, according to the means of his parents.'

As we have seen, courts are encouraged to have regard to the level of support which would be assessed under the Child Support Act in deciding on an appropriate amount of maintenance for the child, including a nil amount.[9] Lump sum orders may be useful to meet particular expenses for a child, for example, to buy a uniform or other clothes for a new school, or to pay for fees and other incidental expenses on starting a course of training.

(b)   Duration of orders

Since some children will start earning when they reach the upper limit of the compulsory school age, no order for periodical payments is to extend in the first instance beyond the date of the child's birthday next following his attaining 16, unless the court thinks it right to specify a later date (as it obviously must if he is already over that age). No order may be made at all, however, if the child is over the age of 18, and an existing order may not continue after his eighteenth birthday. To both limbs of this rule there are two exceptions: there is no age limit on the making or continuation of orders so long as the child is (or, if an order were made, would be) receiving instruction at an educational establishment or undergoing training for a trade, profession or vocation (whether or not he is also gainfully employed) or, in any event, if there are special circumstances justifying this.[10] Periodical payments could therefore continue indefinitely, if, for example, the child were incapable of earning his own living owing to some physical or mental handicap. The order terminates on the death of the child or of the person liable to make the payments.[11]

(c)   Variation on the child's application

The child himself may apply for a variation if he has attained the age of 16. He may also, once he has attained the age of 16 but before he reaches 18, apply for an order to be revived.[12] He may well wish to take advantage of this provision if he

---

7 See *Bowlas v Bowlas* [1965] P 450, [1965] 3 All ER 40, CA. In the case of an application under s 7 of the Domestic Proceedings and Magistrates' Courts Act 1978 the court shall not require the respondent to make payments for the benefit of a child of the family who is not his child if it would not have made an order in the child's favour in proceedings brought under s 1: s 7(3)(c).
8 [1979] 1 All ER 441 at 447. See also *Kiely v Kiely* [1988] 1 FLR 248.
9 *E v C (Child Maintenance)* [1996] 1 FLR 472, discussed ante at p 762.
10 Domestic Proceedings and Magistrates' Courts Act 1978 s 5(1)–(3), s 6(7) and s 7(7); Matrimonial Causes Act 1973 s 29; *G v G (Periodical Payment: Jurisdiction)* [1997] 1 FLR 368, CA; *B v B (Adult Student: Liability to Support)* [1998] 1 FLR 373, CA.
11 Domestic Proceedings and Magistrates' Courts Act 1978 s 5(4), s 6(7) and s 7(7); Matrimonial Causes Act 1973 s 29(4). Under the former Act, where payments are ordered to be made *to the child himself*, neither the continuation nor the resumption of cohabitation by the spouses will have any effect on the order unless the court otherwise directs: s 25(2).
12 Domestic Proceedings and Magistrates' Courts Act 1978 s 20(12)(b); Matrimonial Causes Act 1973 s 27(6B).

decides to undergo further education or training at some stage after leaving school and beginning to earn his own living.

Proceedings under Sch 1 to the Children Act 1989

Courts are also empowered by the Children Act 1989 s 15 and Sch 1 to make financial provision solely for the benefit of children in circumstances where the Child Support Act does not apply. The 1989 Act also permits children over the age of 18 to seek financial orders against their parents in certain circumstances. We shall discuss these proceedings in turn.

(a)   When orders may be made

The court may make financial provision for children either upon application [13] or upon its own motion when making, varying or discharging a residence order. [14] Unless the child is a ward of court, [15] the court cannot make a Sch 1 order upon its own motion if it has not made a residence order.

(b)   Who can apply

Applications may be made by parents, guardians and any person in whose favour a residence order is in force. [16] For these purposes 'parents' includes both married and unmarried parents (including the unmarried father) [17] and 'any party to a marriage (whether or not subsisting) in relation to whom the child concerned is a child of the family', eg a step-parent. [18]

Although guardians are entitled to apply, they are unlikely to do so very often, since they can only take office during the lifetime of the surviving spouse when the deceased appointing parent had a residence order in his favour at the time of death. [19]

(c)   Against whom orders can be made

Orders may be made against either or both parents [20] of the child. As with applicants, 'parents' for these purposes includes unmarried fathers [1] and step-parents of 'children of the family'. However, only those who have been married to

---

13 Children Act 1989 Sch 1, para 1(1).
14 Sch 1, para 1(6). Note also the powers under para 8 when making a residence order to vary or revoke any existing financial relief order made under any enactment other than the Children Act 1989. A court is required, when minded to make an order which has not been asked for or canvassed during the hearing, to give the parties an opportunity to make representations and to reopen the evidence: *Re C (Financial Provision: Lump Sum Order)* [1995] 1 FLR 925.
15 Sch 1, para 1(7).
16 Sch 1, para 1(1). Although a residence order must be in force before a financial order may be made in favour of a person other than a parent, an *application* may be made together with an application for a residence order: cf Family Proceedings Rules 1991 r 4.3(4).
17 Section 2(3).
18 Sch 1, para 16(2). And see *Re A (Child of the Family)* [1998] 1 FLR 347 (grandfather who had brought up grandchild as part of his own family).
19 See ante, p 403.
20 For a rare example of using this provision to seek an order post-divorce (and hence where the parent, who had since remarried, could no longer seek an order under the Matrimonial Causes Act 1973), see *B v B (Transfer of Tenancy)* [1994] Fam Law 250.
1 Before the implementation of the Children Act, it had been held in *Hager v Osborne* [1992] 2 All ER 494, in respect of unmarried fathers, that equivalent provisions under the Guardianship of Minors Act 1971 were retrospective in the sense that they applied to children born before they came into force, and that the dismissal of a previous application following inconclusive blood tests did not preclude a fresh application being made so that advantage could be taken of DNA testing.

a parent of the child are within the definition of step-parent in Sch 1 para 16(2).[2]

Although there is power to order step-parents of 'children of the family' to make financial provision, the Law Commission envisaged that applications are more likely to be made by them.[3] No orders may be made against a guardian. This is in line with the general policy of not making such persons liable to make financial provision or property transfers in the same way as a parent.[4] Similarly, no orders can be made against those, other than parents, who have residence orders in their favour.[5]

(d)   Powers

The High Court, county courts and magistrates' courts all have jurisdiction to make Sch 1 orders, though magistrates' powers are more restricted than those of the higher courts.

All courts may order the making of unsecured periodical payments either to the applicant for the benefit of the child or to the child himself, or partly to both, for such term as may be specified in the order.[6] Similarly, they can order lump sum payments,[7] although in the case of magistrates' orders there is a prescribed maximum limit of £1,000 or such larger amount as the Secretary of State shall fix.[8] Lump sum orders may provide for payment to be made by instalments.[9] An order for periodical payments or lump sums may be made, notwithstanding that the child is living outside England and Wales, provided it is sought against a parent living in England and Wales.[10]

The High Court and county court may additionally order the making of secured periodical payments, settlements of property and property transfers.[11] The £2,500 exemption from the statutory legal aid charge and the postponement of the charge over orders for money, where it is to be used to purchase a new home, apply to orders made under Sch 1.[12]

In *K v K (Minors: Property Transfer)*[13] it was held that the words 'the benefit of

2   The term 'parent' includes 'any party to a marriage (whether or not subsisting) in relation to whom the child concerned is a child of the family . . .' Hence, a non-married step-parent cannot apply for, or be required to meet, an order under the Schedule: *J v J (A Minor: Property Transfer)* [1993] 2 FLR 56.
3   Law Com No 172, para 4.63.
4   Ibid, para 2.25.
5   See *S v X and X (Interveners)* [1990] 2 FLR 187 (third party interveners who had been granted custody were held not liable to maintain the child). Sch 1, para 15 provides that a local authority may make contributions to a person (other than a parent or step-parent of the child) with a residence order, towards the cost of the accommodation and maintenance of the child, but it is unclear how this could be enforced: see *Re K and A (Local Authority: Child Maintenance)* [1995] 1 FLR 688.
6   Sch 1, para 1(1)(a), (b) and 1(2)(a); *G v G (Periodical Payments: Jurisdiction)* [1997] 1 FLR 368, CA.
7   Sch 1, para 1(1)(a), (b) and 1(2)(c). A lump sum order may be made notwithstanding the respondent's bankruptcy: *Re G (Children Act 1989: Sch 1)* [1996] 2 FLR 171.
8   Sch 1, para 5(2).
9   Sch 1, para 5(5).
10 Sch 1, para 14.
11 Sch 1, paras 1(1)(a) and respectively 1(2)(b), (d) and (e). See Cooke 'Property adjustment orders for children' (1994) 6 Journal of Child Law 156.
12 Civil Legal Aid (General)(Amendment)(No 2) Regulations 1991 regs 15 and 16. The legal aid charge is discussed post, p 807.
13 [1992] 2 All ER 727, CA. This case was brought under the Guardianship of Minors Act 1971, but it was accepted (at 733 per Nourse LJ) that the provisions of the Children Act 1989 were not materially different in this respect.

the child' are not confined to *financial* benefit for the child, so that powers to order a transfer are not restricted to orders giving the child a beneficial interest in the property. Accordingly, it was held that there was power to order an unmarried father to transfer to the mother for the benefit of the children his interest in the family home, namely a joint council tenancy.

In recommending the power to order transfers of property, the Law Commission thought[14] that the provisions could be useful to enable the court to make a once-and-for-all settlement in cases where the father did not intend to have anything to do with the child. They noted that few commentators thought it a valid objection that a transfer was tantamount to giving the unmarried mother a right to support for her own benefit.[15] However, they did not envisage the power being used at all frequently, relying on the practice of the divorce courts to lean against making such orders.[16] That practice has indeed been followed by courts when considering their powers under this jurisdiction; they appear to prefer to make a limited transfer (not dissimilar to *Mesher* orders in the divorce context)[17] until the child has grown up.[18]

Although it is perhaps an arguable point, applications for financial relief under the 1989 Act would appear to rank as 'family proceedings' for the purposes of s 8.[19] Accordingly, the court has power to make any s 8 order upon its own motion as well as being able to exercise its powers under s 37 to direct the local authority to undertake an investigation into the child's circumstances. If this is so, it ensures that this jurisdiction is in line with that under the Domestic Proceedings and Magistrates' Courts Act 1978 and Matrimonial Causes Act 1973.

(e)   Exercising the powers

In assessing what, if any, order to make and what amount will be appropriate, the court is directed[20] to have regard to all the circumstances of the case including the following matters:

(a)   The income, earning capacity, property and other financial resources which [any parent, the applicant and any other person in whose favour the court proposes to make the order][1] has or is likely to have in the foreseeable future.

(b)   The financial needs, obligations and responsibilities which [any parent, the applicant and any other person in whose favour the court proposes to make the order] has or is likely to have in the foreseeable future.

(c)   The financial needs of the child.

---

14 Law Com No 118, para 6.6.
15 Ibid, para 6.7. However, where the aim of the transfer is as much to benefit the mother as the children, it may be preferable to utilise Sch 7 to the Family Law Act 1996, where tenancies are concerned: see ante, p 179.
16 See *Chamberlain v Chamberlain* [1974] 1 All ER 33, CA at 38 per Scarman LJ and *Draskovic v Draskovic* (1980) 11 Fam Law 87.
17 See post, p 847.
18 See *T v S (Financial Provision for Children)* [1994] 2 FLR 883, *A v A (A Minor: Financial Provision)* [1994] 1 FLR 657, discussed post, p 770; but cf *Pearson v Franklin (Parental Home: Ouster)* [1994] 1 FLR 246 at 250B–C per Nourse LJ.
19 The argument centres on whether technically applications are made under s 15, which is within Part II of the Act and clearly 'family proceedings', or under Sch 1, which falls outside the definition of 'family proceedings' in s 8(3), (4).
20 Sch 1, para 4(1).
1 Sch 1, para 4(4).

(d) The income, earning capacity (if any), property and other financial resources of the child.
(e) Any physical or mental disability of the child.
(f) The manner in which the child was being, or was expected to be educated or trained.

These guidelines are the same as under the Matrimonial Causes Act 1973 s 27 and the Domestic Proceedings and Magistrates' Courts Act 1978 save that the court is not specifically enjoined to have regard to the family's standard of living, and no weighting of the child's welfare is specified.[2] It has also been held that courts should have information as to the level of any child support assessment that might otherwise be made, so that they can take this into account when exercising their discretion.[3]

The absence of an express direction concerning standard of living leaves open the question of whose standard of living an order should judge. This is likely to be a particularly difficult issue where an unmarried couple have never lived together. Where, for example, the mother is a woman who is never likely to enjoy a high income and the father earns a high salary, it is tempting to say that the child (for whose benefit the order is being made) ought not to be prejudiced by his mother's position, and this is the view of the courts.[4] In *A v A (A Minor: Financial Provision)*[5] the court ordered a wealthy father to make (inter alia) periodical payments of £20,000 per annum to his 10-year-old daughter, notwithstanding that part of these might be used to benefit her half-siblings. Ward J commented:[6]

> 'Were [the daughter] to live her life treating her sisters as Cinderella, then she would live her life most unhappily. If, on the other hand, she generously says that this is her income to spend as she wishes and she wishes to share some of it with her sisters, then she will prove to be a daughter of whom father can justly be proud.'

However, as noted above, the courts regard their function under Sch 1 as being to seek to secure the child's financial position during dependency, and capital windfalls in adulthood are not to be made. For example, in *T v S (Financial Provision for Children)*,[7] it was ordered at first instance that a property be bought from the father's resources, to be held on trust with sale postponed until the youngest of the five children of the parents reached the age of 21 or all had ceased full-time education, the equity then to pass to the children in equal shares. On appeal, Johnson J held that the property should revert to the father.[8] Similarly, in *A v A*, discussed above,[9] a house was settled upon trust for A for a term expiring six months after she reached the age of 18 or ceased full-time education.

---

2 The child's welfare is not the paramount consideration, because s 105(1) expressly excludes maintenance from the definition of upbringing, and unlike the 1973 or 1978 Acts there is no direction in Sch 1 to treat the child's welfare as the first consideration. See also *K v H (Child Maintenance)* [1993] 2 FLR 61 at 64G.
3 *E v C (Child Maintenance)* [1996] 1 FLR 472.
4 See, for example, *H v P (Illegitimate Child: Capital Provision)* [1993] Fam Law 515.
5 [1994] 1 FLR 657 – *Haroutunian v Jennings* (1977) 1 FLR 62, followed.
6 At 667F–G. See, in similar terms, *H v P (Illegitimate Child: Capital Provision)* [1993] Fam Law 515, and *J v C (child: financial provision)* [1998] 3 FCR 79, where the father won a fortune on the National Lottery, and the mother sought a home, car and money for furnishings. The home was to be held on trust, to revert to the father when the child reached adulthood.
7 [1994] 2 FLR 883.
8 At 888–9.
9 At n 5.

Since, in most circumstances, the Child Support Act has removed the juris-diction to order periodical payments for a child, it has been held that it is not right to award a lump sum to the child instead, as a form of capitalised maintenance. The purpose of a lump sum, according to Johnson J, should be to meet the child's need with respect to a particular item of capital expenditure, such as to provide a home or, for instance, to modify a home for a child with disabilities. He accordingly ordered an apparently very wealthy father, who yet had been able to persuade the Child Support Agency that he had nil assessable income and therefore should not be required to pay *any* maintenance for his child, to pay sums of around £90,000 to purchase a home for the child and mother to live in, and a further £24,500 for furniture, equipment and clothing for the child.[10]

Lump sum orders may also be made to enable the applicant to meet any liabilities or expenses incurred in connection with the birth of the child or in maintaining the child or reasonably incurred before the making of the order.[11]

Where an order against a step-parent of a child of the family is contemplated, then, as under the matrimonial jurisdictions, the court is directed[12] to have regard to:

'(a) Whether that person had assumed responsibility for the maintenance of the child and, if so, the extent to which and the basis on which he assumed that responsibility and the length of the period during which he met that responsibility.
 (b) Whether he did so knowing that the child was not his child.
 (c) The liability of any other person to maintain the child.'

If the court makes an order against a person who is not the father of the child, it must record in the order that it is made on that basis.[13]

(f) Duration, variation and enforcement

Orders for periodical payments may begin with the date of the making of the application and shall not in the first instance extend beyond the child's seventeenth birthday, and in any event shall not extend beyond his eighteenth birthday, save where the child is receiving instruction at an educational institution or undergoing training for a trade, profession or vocation 'whether or not he also is, will be or would be in gainful employment' or where there are other special circumstances.[14] Such circumstances will usually relate to the child, rather than, for example, the unwillingness of the respondent to provide full details of his present and future finances.[15]

Periodical payment orders may be made notwithstanding that the parents are living together but, as under the 1978 Act, cease to have effect if they continue to live together or subsequently resume living together for a continuous period of more than six months.[16] Unsecured orders cease upon the death of the payer.[17]

There is a general power to vary, suspend, revive and revoke orders for periodical

---

10 *Phillips v Peace* [1996] 2 FLR 230.
11 Sch 1, para 5.
12 Sch 1, para 4(2).
13 Sch 1, para 4(3).
14 Sch 1, para 3(1), (2). The jurisdiction exists even though the Child Support Act 1991 provides that a child support assessment (which may also be in force in respect of the same child) cannot continue after the child's nineteenth birthday: *C v F (Disabled Child: Maintenance Order)* [1998] 2 FLR 1, CA.
15 *T v S (Financial Provision for Children)* [1994] 2 FLR 883 at 889C.
16 Sch 1, para 3(4).
17 Sch 1, para 3(3).

payments, and the court may order the payment of a lump sum on an application for a variation. The power of a child over the age of 16 to apply for a variation or to revive an order is similar to that under the matrimonial jurisdictions.[18]

Independent right of a child over 18 to seek financial relief from his parents

Sch 1 para 2 to the Children Act 1989 preserves the independent right, first introduced by the Family Law Reform Act 1987, of a person who has attained 18 years of age to apply for an order requiring either or both of his parents to make periodical and/or lump sum payments to him. Applications may be made in the magistrates' court as well as the county court or the High Court. Before any order may be made, the court must be satisfied that the applicant is or will be (or would be if an order were made) receiving instruction at an educational institution, or undergoing training for a trade, profession or vocation, or that[19] there are other exceptional circumstances justifying an order. An order may not be made if, immediately before the applicant reached the age of 16, a periodical payments order was in force,[20] nor may an order be made if the applicant's parents are living together in the same household.[1] In deciding what order to make, the court is to have regard to the same circumstances as it would have in the case of other applications for financial orders under the Children Act 1989.[2]

Both the child and the parent (or parents) ordered to pay may subsequently seek a variation or discharge of a periodical payments order.[3] There is no power to vary a lump sum payments order save, where the sum has been ordered to be paid in instalments, to vary the number or amount or date of those instalments.[4]

3.   ENFORCEMENT OF ORDERS[5]

Registration of orders in other courts

Orders made by a magistrates' court may be registered in the High Court, and orders made by the High Court or a divorce court under s 27 of the Matrimonial Causes Act may be registered in a magistrates' court. The order must then be paid and can be enforced as though it has been made by the court in which it is registered. The purpose and details of this procedure will be considered further in Chapter 18.[6]

Methods of enforcement

Money due under magistrates' courts maintenance orders may be enforced by distress or committal to prison.[7] Orders may also be enforced by the attachment of

---

18 Sch 1, para 6(4).
19 Children Act 1989 Sch 1, para 2(1).
20 Sch 1, para 2(3). As with the matrimonial jurisdictions (ante, p 766), if such an order is in force, the child, once he has attained 16, may himself apply for a variation or, if the order has ceased to have effect, can apply for a revival of the order: para 6(4), (5).
1 Sch 1, para 2(4).
2 Sch 1, para 4.
3 Sch 1, para 2(5).
4 Sch 1, para 6(6).
5 See *Children Come First* Vol 2 (1990, Cm 1264) ch 5; Edwards, Gould and Halpern 'The Continuing Saga of Maintaining the Family after Divorce' [1990] Fam Law 31.
6 See post, p 864.
7 Magistrates' Courts Act 1980 s 76.

earnings procedure.[8] In addition, the defaulting payer (the debtor) may be fined up to £1,000 for his default to make periodical payments.[9] While the number of applications for orders has been in decline, the number of applications to enforce orders already made appears to have remained high, although most of these are probably orders made on divorce and registered in the magistrates' court precisely to take advantage of the enforcement mechanisms.[10]

Procedure and general considerations for recovering arrears

The procedure for enforcement of orders made by the magistrates is laid down by the Magistrates' Courts Act 1980. If payments are being made to a magistrates' clerk, or by standing order (or its equivalent), the clerk himself may take proceedings, provided that he has the written consent of the person to whom the money is to be paid.[11] No order for enforcement may be made except by an order on complaint.[12] On hearing such complaint the court must first decide whether to enforce the arrears in toto or to remit the whole or any part of them; the answer to this question must obviously depend upon the spouses' financial position, their conduct and all the circumstances of the case. Arrears over one year old are not generally enforced unless there are special circumstances, and the court's approach must be to decide how to exercise its discretion to enforce the arrears, rather than how it should exercise its discretion to remit them.[13] Where the court is minded to remit arrears, it must give notice to the complainant, so that she has the opportunity to argue against this.[14] Appeals against decisions on enforcement are by case stated to the High Court.[15]

The court may issue a warrant of distress, a warrant committing the payer to prison, or make an attachment of earnings order.[16]

(a) Distress

The warrant directs the police to distrain on the husband's goods and to sell them to raise the sum adjudged to be paid.[17]

---

8 Attachment of Earnings Act 1971 ss 1–2.
9 Magistrates' Courts Act 1980 s 59B.
10 In 1992, 93,270 applications to enforce maintenance were made to magistrates' courts, compared with 84,890 in 1987: *Home Office Statistical Bulletin: Domestic Proceedings England and Wales, 1992* Table 5.
11 Magistrates' Courts Act 1980 s 59A(3).
12 Magistrates' Courts Act 1980 s 93(1)–(2).
13 *B v C (Enforcement: Arrears)* [1995] 1 FLR 467. For an example of a case where special circumstances were present, see *C v S (Maintenance Order: Enforcement)* [1997] 1 FLR 298. Appeal against a refusal to remit lies to the Divisional Court of the Family Division under s 29 of the 1978 Act and r 8.2 of the Family Proceedings Rules 1991: *P v P (Periodical Payments: Appeals)* [1995] 1 FLR 563; *E v C (Child Maintenance)* [1996] 1 FLR 472; following *Berry v Berry* [1987] Fam 1, [1986] 2 All ER 948, CA. Because arrears can be remitted, they are not provable in the husband's bankruptcy, but continue to be enforceable in the same way as before: *James v James* [1964] P 303, [1963] 2 All ER 465. Compare the tougher line taken on arrears by the Child Support scheme, unless they have accumulated due to the default of the Agency: Child Support (Arrears, Interest and Adjustment of Maintenance Assessments) Regulations 1992 regs 3 and 4.
14 *R v Bristol Magistrates' Court, ex p Hodge* [1997] 1 FLR 88.
15 Magistrates' Courts Act 1980 s 111; *Berry v Berry* [1987] 1 FLR 105; *R v Bristol Magistrates' Court, ex p Hodge* [1997] 1 FLR 88.
16 Magistrates' Courts Act 1980 s 76(1); Attachment of Earnings Act 1971 s 1(3)(a).
17 Magistrates' Courts Rules 1981 r 54. Clothing, bedding and tools of the husband's trade up to the value of £150 are exempt. The court may order the husband to be searched and any money belonging to him and found on him to be applied towards the arrears: Magistrates' Courts Act 1980 s 80.

(b)   Committal

A warrant of committal (which may also be issued if payment is insufficient to satisfy the debt) commits the husband to prison for a period varying from five days to six weeks, the maximum period being graduated according to the sum owed.[18] But since committal proceedings are in effect designed to punish the husband for failing to carry out the order, he may be imprisoned only if the default was due to his wilful refusal or culpable neglect and the court feels that it is inappropriate to make an attachment of earnings order.[19]

Two further powers that the court possesses are those of ordering the payment of arrears by instalments and of postponing the issue of a warrant of committal upon conditions.[20] Used together, these powers constitute a valuable weapon, particularly when it is financially impossible for the husband to pay off all the arrears at once. For example, suppose that £200 is due under the order: the court may order the husband to be imprisoned for 14 days, but the issue of the warrant of committal to be postponed on condition, say, that he pays off the arrears at the rate of £10 per week.

If the husband pays the arrears, the order of committal immediately ceases to have effect and, if he pays a part of the sum due, the period of imprisonment is proportionately reduced.[1] But serving the sentence does not wipe off the arrears,[2] although no further arrears accrue whilst the husband is in custody unless the court orders otherwise.[3]

(c)   Attachment of earnings

The Attachment of Earnings Act 1971 allows the enforcement of any judgment debt by attaching the debtor's earnings. Payment of any order for maintenance may be secured in this way.[4] Until the implementation of the Maintenance Enforcement Act 1991, attachment of earnings orders could only be made when

---

18 Magistrates' Courts Act 1980 s 76(2), s 93(7), s 132 and Sch 4.
19 Magistrates' Courts Act 1980 s 93(6). No order for committal may be made unless the husband has appeared in court; he may be arrested if he fails to answer the summons. The debtor's conduct must amount to deliberate defiance or reckless disregard: improvidence or dilatoriness are insufficient: *R v Luton Magistrates' Court, ex p Sullivan* [1992] 2 FLR 196. Magistrates who consider that the debtor has wilfully refused or culpably neglected to pay must record that they have considered his ability and means to pay the current arrears, and have considered the most suitable method by which he should do so before committing him to prison: *SN v ST (Maintenance Order: Enforcement)* [1995] 1 FLR 868. They must also ensure that the debtor has been given a full opportunity to respond to argument that he should be imprisoned, if necessary ensuring that he is legally represented: *R v Slough Magistrates' Court, ex p Lindsay* [1997] 1 FLR 695.
20 Magistrates' Courts Act 1980 s 75 and s 77; Maintenance Orders Act 1958 s 18.
1 Magistrates' Courts Act 1980 s 79.
2 Ibid, s 93(8). But the debtor cannot be imprisoned more than once for failure to pay the same sum: Maintenance Orders Act 1958 s 17.
3 Magistrates' Courts Act 1980 s 94, for the committal will probably deprive the debtor of the power of earning his living in the meantime.
4 Attachment of Earnings Act 1971 Sch 1, para 4. Such orders may also be made by the High Court and a county court: ibid, s 1. There are no up-to-date figures for the number of attachment orders made by magistrates in respect of maintenance. In 1992, 5,420 such orders were made: *Home Office Statistical Bulletin: Domestic Proceedings England and Wales* Table 6. In 1996, *county courts* made 1,948 attachment orders: *Judicial Statistics 1996* Table 5.8. These figures may be compared with the 65,730 deduction from earnings orders made in respect of child support assessments in 1994/95, discussed ante, p 744. It would be expected that the number of attachment orders would decrease once the child support scheme came into effect with its own methods of enforcement, and this appears to have been the case.

an existing maintenance order was in arrears, but now such orders can be made by the court itself when making a maintenance order in the first place.[5]

In cases where it is sought to recover arrears, application may be made by the person to whom payments are due under the maintenance order, by a magistrates' clerk if an order is in force directing payments to be made through him, or by the debtor himself.[6]

If an attachment of earnings order is made, it is directed to the debtor's employer, not to the debtor himself. It orders the employer to make periodical deductions from the debtor's earnings and to remit the amount deducted to the collecting officer of the court.[7] The officer must then pay the money received to the person to whom the money is due under the order.[8]

The order must specify two rates: the *normal deduction rate*, which is the amount which the court thinks is reasonable to secure the payment of sums falling due under the order in the future together with the arrears already accrued; and the *protected earnings rate*, that is, the rate below which the husband's earnings shall not in any event be reduced by payments deducted under the order.[9] The purpose of the latter is to keep the husband's remaining income above subsistence level; consequently, only in exceptional circumstances would it be reasonable to fix it below the figure which, if it represented the husband's total resources, would entitle him to apply for income-related benefits.[10]

Once an attachment of earnings order has been made, no committal order may be made as a consequence of proceedings begun beforehand; similarly, if a committal order is made or a warrant is issued after an attachment of earnings order has been made, the latter will automatically be discharged.[11] A court before which proceedings for committal or distress are brought may always make an attachment of earnings order instead if it thinks that that would be a more efficacious means of securing payment.[12]

If the debtor ceases to be employed by the person to whom the order has been directed, it lapses until the court directs it to a fresh employer.[13]

As with deduction from earnings orders under the child support legislation, in many cases it may be questioned whether the value of an order to the wife is worth the administrative trouble that it causes. The procedure will be most effective when the husband is in steady employment, but when he is in casual employment, he may be able to escape the order by the simple expedient of changing jobs frequently, if they are available to him.

---

5 Magistrates' Courts Act 1980 s 59(4) as amended.
6 Attachment of Earnings Act 1971 s 3(1).
7 The clerk of that or another magistrates' court: Attachment of Earnings Act 1971 s 6(7).
8 Ibid, s 13(1).
9 Ibid, s 6(5)–(6).
10 *Billington v Billington* [1974] Fam 24, [1974] 1 All ER 546; cf the protected income level in the child support formula: ante, p 736.
11 Attachment of Earnings Act 1971 s 8(1), (3).
12 Ibid, s 3(4).
13 Ibid, s 9(4).

Chapter 18

Financial relief for family members on divorce, nullity and in relation to separation orders

A. Introduction[1]

The growth of divorce in the post-war period, and especially since the 1970s, has inevitably led to much greater significance being attached to the financial consequences of marriage breakdown, both for the parties and their children, and for the state. Research studies in this country, the United States and Australia, all confirm that, for mothers with children to care for, divorce is likely to have a major detrimental effect on their standard of living, while divorced men are likely to see no major decline in theirs.[2] The reason for the differential is primarily that the earning capacity of divorced women is less than that of men – they are more likely to have interrupted their careers to have children and hence earn lower amounts than men, and they are less likely to be able to resume (or remain in) full-time employment to make up the shortfall when their marriage breaks down. Even after their children have grown up, they are likely to remain less well off because they are unable to build up sufficient funds for a decent pension for when they retire. The policy dilemma for government is to decide whether, and to what extent, it should attempt to meet the resulting shortfall by either making the former husband maintain, or compensate, the wife, or by taking on the burden through the social security system. As we saw in the previous chapter, attempting to make absent *parents* support their children and thus relieve public expenditure, at least in part, has been a consistent policy objective, though with limited success. As regards the termination of marriage (most usually by divorce), the law again seeks to regard the financial consequences as a matter to be dealt with as far as possible by adjusting the spouses' assets and earnings between them, with state support providing a safety net. But while there is a legal logic to attaching liability to a parent, or a spouse, in recognition of a *continuing* legal relationship between payer and recipient, the argument is more complicated once the legal tie between husband and wife has been ended.

In this chapter, for convenience, we discuss the law in the context of a divorce (but refer to nullity and separation where relevant), and we refer to the husband as the payer and the wife as recipient, unless otherwise specified. However, it should be noted that the obligations of the spouses are equal and reciprocal.

---

1 See generally Jackson's *Matrimonial Finance and Taxation* (6th edn, 1996) by Hayward Smith and Newton. For empirical studies, see Eekelaar and Maclean *Maintenance After Divorce* (1986) and the more recent Davis, Cretney and Collins *Simple Quarrels: Negotiating Money and Property Disputes on Divorce* (1994). Weitzman and Maclean *Economic Consequences of Divorce* (1992) is a particularly interesting collection of essays, whose contributors are drawn from a wide variety of different disciplines and countries.

2 For England and Wales, see Eekelaar and Maclean op cit; Maclean and Eekelaar *The Parental Obligation* (1997) ch 7; Jarvis and Jenkins *Marital Splits and Income Changes: Evidence from Britain* (1997); for Australia, McDonald *Settling Up: Property and Income Distribution on Divorce in Australia* (1986); for the United States, see Weitzman *The Divorce Revolution* (1985).

1. DEVELOPMENT OF THE COURT'S POWERS

The ecclesiastical courts were able to give financial protection to a wife by ordering the husband to pay her alimony[3] pending suit and permanent alimony after granting a decree of divorce a mensa et thoro.[4] After 1857 this power was vested in the Divorce Court, which was also empowered on granting a decree of divorce to order the husband to secure maintenance for the wife's life.[5] If the husband had no capital on which the payments of maintenance could be secured, hardship was likely to be caused to the wife; this was cured in 1866, when the court was given the power to order the husband to pay unsecured maintenance to the wife. As this would have to come out of his income, however, the maximum term for which it could be ordered was the spouses' joint lives.[6] After 1937 a wife petitioning for divorce or judicial separation on the ground of her husband's insanity could be ordered to pay him alimony pending suit and, if the decree was granted, maintenance (secured or unsecured) or permanent alimony.[7] In 1963 the courts were given a power, long overdue, to order the payment of a lump sum in addition to or instead of maintenance or alimony on divorce, nullity and judicial separation.[8] Ancillary orders could also be made by a court granting a decree of restitution of conjugal rights to a wife.[9]

Except when the husband was incurably of unsound mind, orders for alimony and maintenance could not be made against a wife. This reflected the fact that in the middle of the nineteenth century it was very unlikely that a wife would have an income. She might have property settled to her own use, however, and as early as 1857 the court was empowered to order this to be settled for the benefit of the husband or children if he obtained a divorce or judicial separation on the ground of her adultery. This power was later extended to the property of wives who were divorced for cruelty or desertion or whose husbands obtained a decree of restitution of conjugal rights.[10] On divorce or nullity, either party could benefit from the exercise of the court's jurisdiction, going back to 1859,[11] to vary ante-nuptial and post-nuptial settlements.

The Matrimonial Causes Act 1973

Piecemeal modifications of the law spread over more than a century produced confusing anomalies, and pressure for wholesale reform increased after the passing of the Divorce Reform Act 1969, when the fear was expressed that many innocent wives, divorced against their will, would be left with inadequate provision. The result was the passing of the Matrimonial Proceedings and Property Act 1970, which was based upon the recommendations of the Law

---

3 Periodical maintenance.
4 See ante, p 225 n 3.
5 Matrimonial Causes Act 1857 s 32.
6 Matrimonial Causes Act 1866 s 1.
7 Matrimonial Causes Act 1937 s 10(2).
8 Matrimonial Causes Act 1963 s 5.
9 Alimony pending suit, alimony on making the decree on the wife's application, and periodical payments (which could be secured) if the husband failed to comply with the decree: Matrimonial Causes Act 1857 s 17; Matrimonial Causes Act 1884 s 2.
10 Matrimonial Causes Act 1857 s 45; Matrimonial Causes Act 1884 s 3; Matrimonial Causes Act 1937 s 10(3).
11 Matrimonial Causes Act 1859 s 5.

Commission.[12] Most of its provisions were repealed and re-enacted in Part II of the Matrimonial Causes Act 1973, which, in its amended form,[13] governs the award of financial relief in the High Court and divorce county courts. The Act abolished the confusing variations in types of order for maintenance, and described all as 'financial provision', which may take the form of periodical payments or a lump sum payment. The court was given equal powers to order either spouse to make financial provision for the other, regardless of who is seeking the divorce. The Act also widened the court's powers in two important respects. First, the court's redistributive powers extend to all the assets that either or both the spouses own, irrespective of when and from whom they acquired them. Secondly, in making orders in respect of the spouses' property, the court is not bound to enforce existing rights and can, for instance, order the transfer of ownership from one spouse to another. This latter power was vested in the court partly in response to the decisions in *Pettitt v Pettitt*[14] and *Gissing v Gissing*,[15] which, as we have seen,[16] established that the powers under the Married Women's Property Act 1882 s 17 are declaratory only and that therefore the courts had no power to transfer ownership of property between spouses. These wider redistributive powers represent one of the key remaining distinctions between the ending of a marriage by divorce or nullity and the ending of cohabitation.

Subsequent legislative change

The 1973 Act was amended by the Matrimonial Homes and Property Act 1981, which gave the divorce courts the express statutory power to order the sale of any of the spouses' property.[17] More importantly, the Matrimonial and Family Proceedings Act 1984[18] both extended the court's powers by enabling it to *impose a clean break* (ie a once-and-for-all settlement between the spouses with no continuing financial ties) upon a spouse,[19] and altered the way that the powers are to be exercised. Two of the most important changes were: (1) to require the court, when deciding what orders should be made, to give first consideration to the welfare, whilst a minor, of any child of the family under 18;[20] and (2) to impose a duty upon the court to consider whether it is appropriate so to exercise its powers that the financial obligations of each party terminate immediately or as soon as

---

12 Law Com No 25, *Report on Financial Provision in Matrimonial Proceedings* (1969); see Cretney 'The Maintenance Quagmire' (1970) 33 MLR 662.
13 Principally by the Matrimonial Homes and Property Act 1981, the Matrimonial and Family Proceedings Act 1984, the Pensions Act 1995 and the Family Law Act 1996.
14 [1970] AC 777, [1969] 2 All ER 385, HL.
15 [1971] AC 886, [1970] 2 All ER 780, HL. See also Law Com No 25, paras 64–75.
16 Ante, p 136.
17 By s 7 which added s 24A to the 1973 Act. See also Law Com No 99 (*Orders for the Sale of Property under the Matrimonial Causes Act 1973*).
18 This Act is based on the Law Commission's recommendations: see Law Com No 112 (*The Financial Consequences of Divorce*). See also their earlier paper, Law Com No 103 (*The Financial Consequences of Divorce: The Basic Policy*). For an interesting account of the background and reasons for the Law Commission recommending changes, see Cretney 'Money After Divorce – The Mistakes We Have Made?' in Freeman (ed) *Essays in Family Law* 1985 pp 34 et seq, particularly at pp 36–42.
19 Under the Matrimonial Causes Act 1973 s 25A(3), which was originally added by s 3(4) of the Matrimonial and Family Proceedings Act 1984, and now amended by the Family Law Act 1996 Sch 8, para 10.
20 Section 25(1) as substituted by s 3 of the 1984 Act and amended by the Family Law Act 1996 Sch 8, para 9. For 'child of the family', see ante, p 288.

possible.[1] The 1984 Act also ended the obligation of the court to attempt to place the parties in the position that they would have been had the marriage not broken down. Subsequently, the Pensions Act 1995[2] extended the court's powers to enable it to make orders directing that all or part of any lump sum or pension arising on a spouse's retirement be paid to the other spouse. The Matrimonial Causes Act 1973 was further amended by the Family Law Act 1996, principally[3] to reflect the changes to the substantive law of divorce, and the new policy that the parties' financial and other arrangements for the future are to be settled before a marriage is brought to an end, rather than afterwards.[4]

2. POWERS OF THE COURT

The court has statutory power[5] to make an order against *either spouse* with respect to any one or more of the following matters:[6]

(1) Unsecured periodical payments to the other spouse.
(2) Secured periodical payments to the other spouse.
(3) Lump sum payments to the other spouse.
(4) Unsecured periodical payments for any child of the family.
(5) Secured periodical payments for any child of the family.
(6) A lump sum payment for any child of the family.
(7) Transfer of property to the other spouse or for the benefit of any child of the family.
(8) Settlement of property for the benefit of the other spouse or any child of the family.
(9) Variation of any marriage settlement.

Orders coming within (1)–(6) are collectively known as financial provision orders and those coming within (7)–(9) as property adjustment orders.[7]

Where a court makes a secured periodical payments order, a lump sum order or a property transfer order, it can further order a sale of property belonging to either or both spouses.[8]

In proceedings commenced after 1 July 1996 the court has power to make financial provision orders (periodical payments and lump sums) directing that a share of a spouse's pension be 'earmarked' and paid to the other on retirement.[9]

---

1 Section 25A(1), (2) as substituted by s 3(4) of the 1984 Act and amended by the Family Law Act 1996 Sch 8, para 10.
2 Pensions Act 1995 s 166(1) which inserts ss 25B–25D into the Matrimonial Causes Act 1973.
3 Family Law Act 1996 s 15. Schs 2 and 8 of the 1996 Act, while not intended to make changes to the general principles of the legislation, do make a number of amendments which, although described as 'minor and consequential', are significant in their effect. These changes are considered in the following text.
4 See ante, p 239. The following text assumes that the 1996 Act is in force, but indicates the amendments introduced by that Act in the relevant notes.
5 But the court can accept a party's undertaking to accept other obligations: see post, p 807.
6 Under the Matrimonial Causes Act 1973 s 21, s 22A and s 23A to be substituted respectively by the Family Law Act 1996 Sch 2, paras 2, 3 and 5.
7 Ibid.
8 Matrimonial Causes Act 1973 s 24A as originally added by the Matrimonial Homes and Property Act 1981 s 7 and amended by the Family Law Act 1996 Sch 8, para 8. Orders for the sale of property are neither classified as financial provision nor property adjustment: see *Omielan v Omielan* [1996] 2 FLR 306, CA; *Harper v O'Reilly and Harper* [1997] 2 FLR 816.
9 Under the Matrimonial Causes Act 1973, ss 25B–25D as inserted by the Pensions Act 1995 s 166(1).

The Family Law Act 1996[10] gives the court a new power, presently only in principle but which when fully implemented, would enable it to 'split' or share pensions, that is, to re-allocate part or all of a spouse's accrued pension rights to the other on divorce.[11]

Although, as we shall see, there are statutory guidelines on the matters to be taken into account when exercising these powers, it should be appreciated at the outset that considerable discretion is left to the judge in deciding what order should be made in any individual case.[12] This discretion applies equally to determining what order should be made with regard to the spouses' property and with regard to their income. This vesting of wide discretion in the courts is in contrast to the position taken even in some other common law jurisdictions.[13] In New Zealand, for instance, the matrimonial home and family chattels must generally be divided equally,[14] while in Scotland there is a statutory presumption

---

10 Family Law Act 1996 s 16 amending Matrimonial Causes Act 1973 ss 25B, 25D.

11 See Department of Social Security *Pension sharing on divorce: reforming pensions for a fairer future* Cm 3345 (1998), discussed further post, p 795.

12 For judicial acknowledgement of this discretion and that it should be exercised with restraint, see Waite J in *Thomas v Thomas* [1995] 2 FLR 668, CA at 670: '. . . The discretionary powers conferred on the court by the amended ss 23–25 of the Matrimonial Causes Act 1973 to redistribute the assets of the spouses are almost limitless. That represents an acknowledgment by Parliament that if justice is to be achieved between spouses at divorce the court must be equipped in a society where the forms of wealth-holding are diverse and often sophisticated, to penetrate outer forms and get to the heart of ownership. For their part, the judges who administer the jurisdiction have traditionally accepted the Shakespearean principle that "it is excellent to have a giant's strength but tyrannous to use it like a giant" [*Measure for Measure*, II, ii, 107]. The precise boundaries of that judicial self-restraint have never been rigidly defined – nor could they be if the jurisdiction is to retain its flexibility.' See also *White v White* [1998] 2 FLR 310, CA. For criticism of the operation of the discretionary approach see Davis, Cretney and Collins *Simple Quarrels: Negotiating Money and Property Disputes on Divorce* (1994) especially at ch 11. Of their empirical survey, the authors say (at p 270) 'One possible conclusion to draw from our research is that a discretionary system is not geared to mass proceedings such as we have in divorce these days. The proposal that outcomes may be determined by the application of a formula, and usually by an administrative authority can certainly by supported in relation to the relatively straightforward cases which comprised the bulk of our sample.'

13 In most continental legal systems there is some form of community of property which severely restricts or even precludes the court from being able to redistribute the parties' property or even income. For an account of various community of property regimes, see Law Com Working Paper No 42, Part 5 and Appendix C. In most States of the USA there is a principle of equal division of property between the spouses. For research into the effects of this, see eg Weitzman op cit, summarised by her in 'The Divorce Revolution and Illusion of Equality: A View from the United States' in Freeman (ed) *Essays in Family Law 1985* at 91 and by the same author 'Marital Property: Its Transformation and Division in the United States' in Weitzman and Maclean (eds) *Economic Consequences of Divorce–The International Perspective* at 85. Such a divergence of approach between different jurisdictions towards the division of matrimonial assets undoubtedly leads to 'forum shopping', especially amongst the very wealthy. In *Dart v Dart* [1996] 2 FLR 286, CA the parties were American, and the wife's counsel asserted she could have expected an award of £100 million, and possibly even £200 million from the husband's fortune (conservatively estimated at £400 million) from a Michigan court. Thorpe LJ observed at 288 'It is plain that Mrs Dart decided she would do better in Michigan whilst Mr Dart thought he would do better in London'. The wife's application for a stay of the husband's English proceedings was dismissed, and the Court of Appeal upheld an award of (just) £10 million in her favour. For another example, see *W v W (Financial Relief: Appropriate Forum)* [1997] 1 FLR 257.

14 Under the Family Property Act 1976, save in certain defined circumstances, eg where the marriage has been of short duration. There is also a more restricted power than in England to award income support for a spouse. In Australia the courts, under the Family Law Act 1975, enjoyed a wide discretion to redistribute property (though it seems established that equal division should be the starting point). Recent legislative changes have sought to curb judicial discretion, however, with the intention of reducing uncertainty of outcome, and facilitating settlements: see Bailey-Harris 'Family Law Reform – Changes Down Under' [1996] Fam Law 214.

in favour of equal division unless special circumstances exist which justify a departure from this principle.[15] Consideration is being given to the question whether the position in England and Wales should be assimilated to that in Scotland.[16]

3. THE COURT'S JURISDICTION TO MAKE ORDERS

Before the Family Law Act 1996, except for maintenance pending suit and orders with respect to children, no order could be made unless a decree nisi of divorce or nullity or a decree of judicial separation was granted and, in the case of divorce or nullity, the order could not take effect until the decree was made absolute.[17] As we have seen,[18] it is an important objective of the 1996 Act that the parties should have settled their financial and other arrangements during the period for reflection and consideration; before a divorce order is granted the court must, in effect, be satisfied that this is so.[19] This reversal of the pre-1996 Act position is implemented by a number of significant amendments to the Matrimonial Causes Act 1973. The 1973 Act will provide that the court may make any order at 'the appropriate time', which is defined[20] as any time:

(a) after a statement of marital breakdown has been received by the court and before any application for a divorce order or for a separation order is made to the court by reference to that statement;
(b) when an application for a divorce order or a separation order has been made under s 3 of the 1996 Act and has not been withdrawn;
(c) when an application for a divorce order has been made under s 4 of the 1996 Act and has not been withdrawn;
(d) after a divorce order has been made;
(e) when a separation order is in force.

The effect of these provisions is that the court retains a flexible jurisdiction to make orders at any time after the statement of marital breakdown is filed (provided, that is, it is not withdrawn), whether or not a divorce or separation order has been granted.[1] However, the 1973 Act places a number of time restrictions

---

15 Family Law (Scotland) Act 1985 s 9(1) and s 10(1). For a recent case, where the husband failed to establish that special circumstances justified an unequal division, see *Lightbody (or Jacques) v Jacques* [1997] 1 FLR 748 (HLS).
16 The Lord Chancellor asked his Ancillary Relief Advisory Group in 1998 to examine the question: see [1998] Fam Law 381 and post, p 866.
17 Matrimonial Causes Act 1973 ss 23, 24 as originally enacted. As regards nullity proceedings this rule has been preserved by the 1996 reforms: see Family Law Act 1996 Sch 2, paras 4 and 6. For a case where the practical operation of the rule caused some difficulties, see *Pounds v Pounds* [1994] 1 FLR 775, CA. Here, the judge's order approving the parties' financial settlement (as a result of a clerical mix up) pre-dated the pronouncement of the decree nisi. The Court of Appeal held that the judge's approval had been a continuing one, and the order validly made; its date could be corrected under the slip rule. See also *Board (Board Intervening) v Checkland* [1987] 2 FLR 257, CA.
18 Ante, p 239.
19 See Family Law Act 1996 s 9.
20 Matrimonial Causes Act 1973 s 22A as inserted by Family Law Act 1996 Sch 2, para 3.
1 It would seem that prior to the filing of the statement the only application for a financial order which a spouse may make is under the Matrimonial Causes Act 1973 s 27 as amended by the Family Law Act 1996 Sch 8, para 13 (failure to provide reasonable maintenance): see ante, p 763.

upon the exercise of the court's jurisdiction. Except for interim orders,[2] the court may not make an order after the parties have jointly notified it that they are attempting a reconciliation, thus stopping the period for reflection and consideration.[3] The court may also not make an order where an application for a divorce or separation order has ceased to be possible by lapse of time after the making of the statement of marital breakdown.[4] Most importantly, an application for a financial provision or property adjustment order must be made before the divorce or separation order itself has been made, failing which leave of the court is required.[5]

Having spelt out when an application for orders may be made, it was necessary for the new legislation to establish when the court's orders would take effect. While the underlying policy is to encourage the resolution of a couple's financial disputes before divorce, to allow an irrevocable court order to take effect at too early a stage could jeopardise the parties' attempts at reconciliation. Equally, too long a delay between the making of an order and its taking effect could be artificial and damaging. By way of compromise, it is now provided[6] that, with the exception of interim orders, no order for financial provision or property adjustment will take effect before a divorce or separation order is made unless the court is satisfied that (a) the circumstances of the case are exceptional and (b) it would be just and reasonable for the order to be made. It remains to be seen what criteria the court will apply in justifying a departure from the general rule, and at least one commentator has suggested this provision may give rise to much matrimonial litigation.[7]

By s 22A(3) of the Matrimonial Causes Act 1973,[8] the court is empowered to make various combinations of financial provision order in favour of the parties and their children, although this is subject to the prohibition that no more than one periodical payment order or lump sum order may be made in favour of the same party.[9] The clear legislative intention is that, after the court has made a financial provision order, it may be altered only in subsequent variation proceedings.[10] Slightly different restrictions, albeit of similar effect, govern the making of property adjustment orders. While, at 'the appropriate time'[11] the court is expressly empowered to make one or more property adjustment orders, it may only make a single order of each type, ie one property transfer order, one

---

2 See post, p 786.
3 Matrimonial Causes Act 1973 s 22B(2) (financial provision orders) and s 23B(2) (property adjustment orders) as inserted by Family Law Act 1996 Sch 2, paras 3 and 5.
4 Matrimonial Causes Act 1973 s 22B(3) (financial provision orders) and s 23B(2) (property adjustment orders) as inserted by Family Law Act 1996 Sch 2, paras 3 and 5. As we have seen (ante, p 246), after the expiry of a specified period from the date of filing of the settlement of marital breakdown, the proceedings effectively lapse and the time expired statement cannot be used as the basis of applying for a divorce order – see Family Law Act 1996 s 5(3) and s 7(9).
5 Matrimonial Causes Act 1973 s 22B(4) (financial provision orders) and s 23B(4) (property adjustment orders) as inserted (respectively) by Family Law Act 1996 Sch 2, paras 3 and 5.
6 Matrimonial Causes Act 1973 s 22B(1) (financial provision orders) and s 23B(1) (property adjustment orders) as inserted (respectively) by Family Law Act 1996 Sch 2, paras 3 and 5.
7 See Burrows *Family Law Act 1996* (1996), p 43.
8 As inserted by Family Law Act 1996 Sch 2, para 3. The section provides that the court may make the following: (a) a combined order against the parties on one occasion; (b) separate orders on different occasions; (c) different orders in favour of different children; (d) different orders from time to time in favour of the same child.
9 Matrimonial Causes Act 1973 s 22A(3).
10 Under the Matrimonial Causes Act 1973 s 31 as amended. The court's jurisdiction to vary lump sums is confined to cases where lump sum payments are to be made by instalments: see post, p 851.
11 See above n 20.

settlement of property order, one variation of settlement order and one order extinguishing or reducing a party's interest under a marriage settlement.[12] In addition, the court is directed, wherever practicable, to exercise its powers to make property adjustment orders on the same occasion.[13] Again, the clear legislative policy is to promote finality in the resolution of the parties' financial disputes, and encourage the court to make one or more property adjustment orders *at the same time*, embracing all the capital assets of the parties.

Two further restrictions should be noted. It is a general principle of the Matrimonial Causes Act 1973 that, if the former spouse remarries, she (or he) must look to the new partner for financial provision for herself, and not to the old one. Consequently, a party who has remarried cannot apply for an order at all, except for a child of the family,[14] although an application already made can be entertained notwithstanding the remarriage.[15] This rule applies even though the second marriage is void or voidable:[16] the party's remedy lies in seeking financial provision in nullity proceedings. Furthermore, an application for financial relief is not a cause of action which survives against the other party's estate, so that no order can be made after the death of either of them.[17] The effect of this is mitigated by the extensive powers given to the court by the Inheritance (Provision for Family and Dependants) Act 1975.[18]

4. ASPECTS OF PROCEDURE: DISCOVERY AND HEARING

Underlying the whole basis of the exercise of the court's discretion in financial proceedings is the duty of the parties to provide the court with information about all the circumstances of their case; the court is exercising not merely a paternal, but also, in appropriate instances, an inquisitorial jurisdiction.[19] Both spouses are

12 Matrimonial Causes Act 1973 s 23A(2) as inserted by Family Law Act 1996 Sch 2, para 5.

13 Matrimonial Causes Act 1973 s 23A(3) as inserted by Family Law Act 1996 Sch 2, para 5.

14 Matrimonial Causes Act 1973 s 28(3), as amended by the Matrimonial and Family Proceedings Act 1984 s 5(3) and Family Law Act 1996 Sch 8, para 14. The Law Commission, who assumed that this proposal would be highly controversial, found that it received almost unanimous support: Law Com No 25, para 14. It may, however, act as a trap and what is no more than a pleading slip may prevent a property adjustment order from being made when this would be proper: see generally *Hargood v Jenkins* [1978] Fam 148, [1978] 3 All ER 1001. See also *Nixon v Fox* [1978] Fam 173, [1978] 3 All ER 995. If the embargo applies and the former spouse wishes to dispute ownership of any matrimonial property, he or she can, within three years after the divorce, seek a declaration under the Married Women's Property Act 1882 s 17, in which case ownership will be determined upon strict property principles: *Bothe v Amos* [1976] Fam 46, [1975] 2 All ER 321, CA. The amendment makes it clear that the embargo applies whenever the applicant remarried, even if the marriage took place before the implementation of the Matrimonial Causes Act 1973, thereby reversing *Bonning v Dodsley* [1982] 1 All ER 612, CA.

15 *Jackson v Jackson* [1973] Fam 99, [1973] 2 All ER 395. This does not apply to an application for periodical payments for the spouse which will in any case cease on remarriage: see post, p 788.

16 Matrimonial Causes Act 1973 s 52(3). This means that, if the second husband is a person of no substance, the taxpayer may have to support the wife even though the first husband is capable of doing so.

17 *Dipple v Dipple* [1942] P 65, [1942] 1 All ER 234. It should be noted that the court has jurisdiction to make lump sum or property adjustment orders after a spouse's bankruptcy, although the court should have a clear picture of the bankrupt's assets and liability, and the expenses of the bankruptcy, and should consider the effect of the bankruptcy on the debtor spouse's ability to pay – see *Woodley v Woodley (No 2)* [1993] 2 FLR 477, CA. *Hellyer v Hellyer* [1996] 2 FLR 579, CA.

18 See post, pp 884–902.

19 *Hildebrand v Hildebrand* [1992] 1 FLR 244 at 247 (per Thorpe J).

under a duty to make full, frank and up-to-date disclosure of their assets.[20] Unless the parties are agreed on the terms of the order to be made, each is required to file an affidavit setting out full particulars of the property and income,[1] but in practice it is notorious that some spouses, particularly wealthy men, may seek to conceal the full extent of their property and means.[2] Those who attempt to deceive the court by failing to make full disclosure will forfeit its sympathy,[3] and it is open to the court to draw the adverse inference that beneath a false presentation there are undisclosed assets.[4] The court may, in its discretion, penalise a reluctance or refusal to make proper disclosure in its order for costs.[5] The court possesses extensive powers to enable one party to obtain additional information from the other,[6] and may, and often does, make orders for discovery where financial and other documents and records are required to be produced.[7] While resort to such

20 *Livesey (formerly Jenkins) v Jenkins* [1985] AC 424, [1985] 1 All ER 106, HL.
1 Family Proceedings Rules 1991 r 2.58–2.61 and see Rae 'Affidavits of Means – Past their Sell-by Date' [1995] Fam Law 186. See further below for reform of the rules of procedure.
2 One legitimate concealment tactic is the so-called 'millionaire's defence', where the respondent, contending his wealth is more than sufficient to support any order that the court might make, will not be ordered to make full disclosure. See *Thyssen-Bornemisza v Thyssen-Bornemisza (No 2)* [1985] FLR 1069, CA; *S v S* [1986] Fam 189; *B v B (Discovery: Financial Provision)* [1990] 2 FLR 180; *Primavera v Primavera* [1992] 1 FLR 16, CA. However, even the super-rich must provide the court with a minimum of information so it can properly exercise its jurisdiction under Matrimonial Causes Act 1973 s 25: see *Van G v Van G (Financial Provision: Millionaire's Defence)* [1995] 1 FLR 328. See also Wilson J 'Conduct of the Big Money Case' [1994] Fam Law 504: 'The millionaire who invokes the millionaire's defence must be obliged to state very broadly ie perhaps to the nearest million an actual figure for total wealth and how that figure is calculated'. For other recent 'big money' cases see eg *F v F (Ancillary Relief: Substantial Assets)* [1995] 2 FLR 45; *Dart v Dart* [1996] 2 FLR 286, CA and *Conran v Conran* [1997] 2 FLR 615.
3 See *C v C (Financial Relief: Short Marriage)* [1997] 2 FLR 26, CA.
4 *Baker v Baker* [1995] 2 FLR 829, CA.
5 Although not formally enshrined in the Rules of Court, the divorce courts have adopted the principle (which applies generally in litigation) that, at least where there are sufficient assets, 'costs follow the event', ie the loser pays the winner's costs as well as his own: *Gojkovic v Gojkovic (No 2)* [1992] Fam 40, CA. For examples of cases where a spouse's failure to make full disclosure was reflected in the costs award made by the court see eg *P v P (Financial Relief: Non Disclosure)* [1994] 2 FLR 381 and *S v S (Financial Provision) (Post Divorce Cohabitation)* [1994] 2 FLR 228 (the latter where costs were awarded on a full indemnity basis).
6 This includes the use of detailed questionnaires which the recipient is required to complete and which these days are 'a routine feature of financial cases': *Hildebrand v Hildebrand* [1992] 1 FLR 244 at 247 (per Waite J).
7 See eg *B v B (Financial Provision)* [1989] 1 FLR 119; *P v P* [1989] 2 FLR 241; *Newton v Newton* [1990] 1 FLR 33, CA; *Re T (Divorce: Interim Maintenance: Discovery)* [1990] 1 FLR 1. A useful power available to the court is the production appointment, whereby a person is ordered to produce documents which he could be required to produce at the hearing – see Mostyn and Moor 'The Production Appointment' [1991] Fam Law 506 and Burrows 'Production Appointments and Khanna Hearings' [1995] Fam Law 199. This is an effective means of obtaining advance disclosure, particularly from a reluctant witness. The application for an appointment should normally be made inter partes: *B v B (Production Appointment: Procedure)* [1995] 1 FLR 913. In appropriate cases an order may be made against third parties: compare *Frary v Frary* [1993] 2 FLR 696 with *D v D (Production Appointment: Procedure)* [1995] 2 FLR 497. In the latter case it was said that, where there was manifest evidence of non-disclosure, the court's discretion as to the bounds of disclosure should be broad rather than narrow. However, the production appointment can only be used to bring forward the time when disclosure occurs – it does not extend the court's powers as to the scope of disclosure which may be ordered: see *Frary v Frary* (above). The court may also make *Anton Piller* and *Mareva* injunctions, although such orders are draconian, and even where a spouse is devious and deceitful and has shown no respect for other court orders, such orders will only be granted in exceptional circumstances: *Araghchinchi v Araghchinchi* [1997] 2 FLR 142, CA. See also *Burgess v Burgess* [1996] 2 FLR 34.

powers may be necessary in appropriate cases, there has been judicial criticism of excessive and unnecessary enquiries into the means of the parties, which can be time-consuming, acrimonious and above all expensive, with enormous legal and professional costs swallowing up the value of the family's assets available for distribution.[8] In *Evans v Evans*,[9] Booth J, with the concurrence of the President of the Family Division, issued a series of guidelines designed to be followed by practitioners in the preparation of substantial ancillary relief cases. In *F v F (Ancillary Relief: Substantial Assets)*[10] Thorpe J considered the parties' professional costs, which together amounted to almost £1.5 million, to be unacceptable. Advocating that the co-operative process, prevalent in the preparation of Children Act cases, should spread into the field of ancillary relief, he concluded:[11]

'It seems to me that as a society it is incumbent upon us to develop systems for the determination of financial disputes at a much more realistic cost.'

In October 1996, the Lord Chancellor's Department established a pilot scheme, to run in certain selected courts, to evaluate a number of substantial changes in ancillary relief procedures.[12] The new procedures are intended, as their stated objective, to reduce delay, facilitate settlement, limit costs and give the court closer control of the conduct of proceedings. Central to new procedures is that a case's progress, prior to trial, is controlled by a fixed timetable, which can be varied only by judicial order. In all but exceptional cases there will also be a financial dispute resolution appointment ('FDR'), a privileged meeting at which the district judge (who will not hear the case if it fails to settle) assists the parties, and their legal advisers, in exploring common ground and narrowing the issues in dispute with a view to reaching agreement. Despite these radical changes (and further reform of the procedural rules is likely),[13] a practitioner's task remains far from easy.[14] On the one hand, he must avoid making excessive enquiries and incurring heavy professional costs,[15] while, on the other hand, he can only properly advise his client on the basis of information which is complete and accurate. In this latter context, it has been held that a solicitor's failure properly to investigate a husband's financial and property resources before advising a wife to settle her claim for ancillary relief

---

8 See eg *Newton v Newton* [1990] 1 FLR 33, CA; *Re T (Divorce Interim Maintenance: Discovery)* [1990] 1 FLR 1; and *H v H (Financial Relief: Costs)* [1997] 2 FLR 57.

9 [1990] 2 All ER 147. These guidelines were later embodied in a *Practice Note*: see [1990] 1 WLR 575. Subsequently Booth J advocated tighter court control of ancillary relief proceedings – see her address to the Solicitors' Family Law Association annual conference 1992, entitled 'Life after *Evans*', reprinted at [1992] Fam Law 178.

10 [1995] 2 FLR 45.

11 Ibid, at p 69. See also his remarks in *White v White* [1998] 2 FLR 310, CA.

12 For the background to the establishment of the pilot scheme see Thorpe J 'Procedural Reform in Ancillary Relief' [1996] Fam Law 356. The scheme was formally incorporated into the Family Proceedings Rules by the Family Proceedings (Amendment No 2) Rules 1997 (SI 1997/1056). See also the *Practice Direction Ancillary Relief Procedure: Pilot Scheme* [1997] 2 FLR 304. For further commentary, see Coleridge, Simpson, Mostyn and Rae 'FDR – The Pilot Scheme' [1996] Fam Law 746; Burrows *Ancillary Relief Pilot Scheme* (1997).

13 It is likely that further changes to the procedural rules will be required when the Family Law Act 1996 (and its changes to the substantive law of divorce) is brought into force.

14 For the views of two family practitioners, see Collis and Kleanthous 'Should *Evans* be Ignored? A No-Win Situation'[1991] Fam Law 466.

15 A solicitor who embarks on excessive enquiries may be made the subject of a wasted costs order and held personally liable for costs: *Re A Solicitor (Wasted Costs Order)* [1993] 2 FLR 959, CA.

may constitute negligence, for which substantial damages may be awarded.[16]

The hearing will normally be before a district judge who may, however, refer the application to a judge.[17] Cases are normally heard in the divorce county court, but there is power to transfer proceedings to the High Court in cases of complexity, difficulty or gravity.[18]

B.   Orders that may be made

1.   INTERIM ORDERS

The power to order the husband to pay maintenance pending suit (or alimony pendente lite, as it was formerly called) goes back to the ecclesiastical courts. It was based on the idea that a wife was entitled to be maintained by her husband so long as the marriage remained in existence; the purpose of interim orders was to ensure that she and any children of the marriage living with her obtained a sufficient allowance until the outcome of the proceedings.

As originally enacted, the Matrimonial Causes Act 1973 gave the courts power, on a petition for divorce, nullity or judicial separation, to order either spouse to make such periodical payments to the other pending suit as it thought reasonable.[19] The court could also order the payment of unsecured or secured periodical payments or a lump sum in favour of a child of the family.[20] No guidelines were laid down governing the exercise of the court's discretion,[1] although, so far as possible, all the circumstances were to be taken into account, with the most attention being paid to the spouses' immediate financial position and the needs of the children of the family.[2] In *F v F (Ancillary Relief: Substantial Assets)*[3] Thorpe J said that even in 'big money' cases disputes about the amount of interim awards were 'almost unknown'. His Lordship added that in an application for maintenance pending suit it would be superfluous to conduct an extensive investigation into the parties' reasonable needs; nor was the level of an interim award significant in terms of the final outcome. If necessary any underprovision or overprovision at the interim stage could be corrected at the final hearing.

Under the 1973 Act the court was given little statutory power to deal with the

16 *Dickinson v Jones Alexander & Co* [1993] 2 FLR 521 (decided in 1989); *Griffiths v Dawson & Co* [1993] 2 FLR 315; *Duffield v Gilbert H Stephens & Sons* [1988] Fam Law 473. In *B v Miller & Co* [1996] 2 FLR 23, the wife issued proceedings alleging her former solicitors had acted negligently in advising her on the terms of a consent order, which was approved by the court. The court rejected the solicitor's argument that the wife's claim should be struck out as a collateral attack on a final court order (see further post, p 803). See also *Young v Purdy* [1996] 2 FLR 795.
17 Family Proceedings Rules 1991 r 2.65.
18 Including where there are substantial allegations of fraud, deception, non-disclosure, or conduct. See Matrimonial and Family Proceedings Act 1984 s 39; *Practice Direction* [1992] 3 All ER 151.
19 Matrimonial Causes Act 1973 s 22.
20 Ibid. s 23(1)(d)–(f).
 1 The guidelines laid down under Matrimonial Causes Act 1973 s 25 did not apply to orders made under s 22.
 2 See eg *Peacock v Peacock* [1984] 1 All ER 1069. In *Re T (Divorce: Interim Maintenance: Discovery)* [1990] 1 FLR 1, the court ordered a wealthy husband to pay his wife £25,000 per annum by way of maintenance pending suit. The fact that the parties had previously agreed this figure was considered to be compelling evidence of the sum which it was reasonable to award. The old practice (long discontinued) had been to bring the wife's income (if any) up to one-fifth of the spouses' joint income.
 3 [1995] 2 FLR 45.

parties' *capital assets* by way of interim order. In *Wicks v Wicks*,[4] after the marriage broke down, the wife claimed income support but was told that she would have to sell the matrimonial home, which had been put into her name by the husband who was being pressed by creditors. When the husband refused to give possession of the property, the wife sought, and was granted, within the ancillary relief proceedings, an order that the property be sold and part of the proceeds paid to her to be used to purchase a new home for herself and the children. The Court of Appeal held, overruling earlier authority,[5] that there was no power to make such orders, although a sale of the home could have been ordered under s 17 of the Married Women's Property Act 1882.[6]

This problem is ameliorated, but not solved, as a consequence of amendments to the 1973 Act introduced by the Family Law Act 1996. The term 'maintenance pending suit' disappears from the legislation, and applications for interim orders are placed generally on the same footing as other financial provision orders. As we have seen,[7] financial provision orders may effectively be made at any time after the filing of the statement of marital breakdown. If after the statement is filed the court is not in a position to make a final order, s 22A(4) of the Matrimonial Causes Act 1973[8] now provides that the court may make an interim periodical payments order, an interim lump sum order or series of orders in favour of a spouse or child. This statutory power to award an interim lump sum or sums is new and may prove useful. It may be used, for example, to enable the recipient to pay the fees of her lawyers or other expert witnesses,[9] to purchase a new home, or otherwise meet unexpected expenses and needs. The 1996 reforms do not give the courts the power to make interim property adjustment orders: it remains the legislative policy that these are better made as part of the court's final order.[10]

In exercising its discretion to make interim orders, the court is now to have regard to the same statutory guidelines which it must consider in making other orders.[11] In addition (and clearly appropriate in the context of interim orders where the immediate needs of the parties and their children may be an issue) the court is expressly required, in carrying out its duties to consider relevant issues, not to act in such a way as would cause inappropriate delay having regard:

(a) to any immediate need for an interim order;
(b) to the matters in relation to which it is practicable for the court to inquire

---

4 [1998] 1 FLR 470, CA.
5 *Barry v Barry* [1992] 2 FLR 233; *Green v Green* [1993] 1 FLR 326 where it was held that the court had power in divorce proceedings, even at the interim stage, to order the sale of land pursuant to RSC Ord 31 r 1 (as applied to ancillary relief application by Family Proceedings Rules 1991 r 2.64).
6 See ante, p 115. But the court would then have had no power to adjust the parties' respective beneficial interests. See Brasse 'Interim Lump Sums' [1998] Fam Law 415.
7 Ante, pp 781.
8 As inserted by Family Law Act 1996 Sch 2, para 3. The court enjoys a similar power on the filing of a nullity petition: see Matrimonial Causes Act 1973 s 26(1) and s 23(1) as inserted (respectively) by Family Law Act 1996 Sch 8, para 4 and Sch 2, para 4.
9 This was suggested in *F v F (Ancillary Relief: Substantial Assets)* [1995] 2 FLR 45 – see Thorpe J's comments at 50. See also Wilson J in *Sears Tooth (A firm) v Payne Hicks Beach (A firm)* [1997] 2 FLR 116 at 133: 'The Lord Chancellor has indicated informally that he regards the power [to award an interim lump sum] as exercisable in making provision for the wife's costs of substantive litigation . . . I expect that, in some cases, particularly where the husband admits substantial ready capital, the provision will prove to be some answer to the problem . . .'
10 Though, as we have seen, it will be possible to make a *final* property adjustment order which takes effect before the divorce order is made, if the court is satisfied that the circumstances of the case are exceptional and it would be just and reasonable to do so: s 23B(1).
11 Matrimonial Causes Act 1973 s 25(1) as amended by Family Law Act 1996 Sch 8, para 9.

before making an interim order; and

(c) to the ability of the court to have regard to any matter and to make appropriate adjustments when subsequently making a financial provision order which is not interim.[12]

2.   PERIODICAL PAYMENTS

Orders in favour of spouses

(a)   *Unsecured payments*

The court may order either spouse to make unsecured periodical payments to the other or to secure periodical payments to the other.[13] Any order for periodical payments may be backdated, depending upon the circumstances in which the court has made the order.[14] The general rule is that an order may be backdated to the date on which the application for the order was first made.[15]

As periodical payments are intended for the payee's maintenance, they must in any event terminate on her (or his) death. Unsecured periodical payments will normally come out of the payer's income, which will presumably come to an end on his death; consequently an order for their payment cannot extend beyond the payer's death.[16] There is, however, no reason why *secured* payments should not continue after the payer's death, as the capital will always have been charged; consequently in this case the order can last for the payee's life. Furthermore, (whether the payments are secured or not) the order must also provide for their termination on the payee's marriage.[17] She (or he) must thereafter look to the new spouse for support.

Formerly, it seemed doubtful whether a claim for periodical payments could be dismissed without the applicant's consent, so as to preclude the latter from making further application.[18] This meant that the courts had no power to impose a 'clean break' order upon the parties, ie a once-and-for-all order whereby the husband (in practice), usually in return for transferring a share (or larger share) of the capital assets to the wife, would not be required to make any periodical payments to her. However, in line with the policy introduced by the Matrimonial and Family Proceedings Act 1984 of directing the courts to consider whether the parties could become self-sufficient either immediately after the divorce or nullity or within a reasonable time thereafter,[19] there is now express statutory power to impose a 'clean break'. Under s 25A(3) of the Matrimonial Causes Act 1973,[20] if the court considers that no continuing obligation should be imposed on a party to a marriage, it may direct that the other party shall not be entitled to make any further application for periodical payments. The court is also under a duty to consider making a 'deferred

---

12 Matrimonial Causes Act 1973 s 25(5) as inserted by Family Law Act 1996 Sch 8, para 9.
13 Matrimonial Causes Act 1973 s 21(1)(a), (b) as inserted by Family Law Act 1996 Sch 2, para 2.
14 Matrimonial Causes Act 1973 s 28(1)(a) as inserted by Family Law Act 1996 Sch 2, para 7.
15 Ibid, s 28(1)(a)(iv).
16 Matrimonial Causes Act 1973 s 28(1)(b)(i) as inserted by Family Law Act 1996 Sch 2, para 7.
17 Matrimonial Causes Act 1973 s 28(1)(b)(ii) as substituted by Family Law Act 1996 Sch 2, para 7. It is immaterial that the second marriage is void or voidable: ibid s 52(3).
18 Following the decision in *Dipper v Dipper* [1981] Fam 31, [1980] 2 All ER 722, CA.
19 Discussed post, p 820.
20 As substituted by Family Law Act 1996 Sch 8, para 10.

clean break order' where periodical payments continue for a fixed period only, during which time the recipient will be able to adjust 'without undue hardship' to the termination of financial dependence on his or her former spouse.[1]

(b) Secured payments

The very fact of security obviously makes secured payments more attractive to the payee, for there is no problem of enforcement. By tying up the payer's capital, it also prevents him from trying to frustrate the order by disposing of his assets, and the payee will be protected even though the payer becomes bankrupt. We have also seen that the payee can continue to benefit from a secured order after the other's death; moreover, although the survivor cannot *apply* for an order after the other party's death, an order made before his death may be implemented by his personal representatives, who may therefore be called upon to carry it out.[2] Because of these advantages, the court may order a smaller sum to be secured than it would have ordered by way of unsecured provision.[3]

Payments may be secured by ordering the spouse against whom the order is made to transfer specified assets to trustees. They hold them on trust to pay the sum ordered to the payee and the balance to the payer or, alternatively, to pay the income to the payer so long as he complies with the order but to use the income and, if necessary, the capital, if he defaults. The court may alternatively order specific property to be charged with the payment of the sum in question. When the order comes to an end, the capital must be returned to the payer (or his estate, if he has already died) and any charge must be cancelled.

If a party is not in need of immediate provision but may require it in the future, a nominal order may be made secured on assets yielding a substantial income. She (or he) can then apply for a suitable variation if necessary; in the meantime the income can be paid over to the other party.[4]

The court is naturally anxious to give the maximum protection, particularly to a wife whom the husband has maltreated and is likely to leave penniless.[5] Whether periodical payments can be secured, however, must depend on the capital or secured income which the other has available, and the number of spouses against whom such an order can be made is obviously small. Thorpe LJ has commented that secured orders 'have been virtually relegated to the legal history books',[6] being replaced in practice by a commuted capital payment.[7]

Orders in favour of children of the family

As well as having power to make orders in favour of a spouse the court may, in proceedings for divorce, nullity and separation, provided that the provisions of the Child Support Act 1991 are inapplicable,[8] make periodical payment orders (which may be secured or unsecured) in favour of a 'child of the family'.[9] The court's power

---

1 Matrimonial Causes Act 1973 s 25A(2) and s 28(1A).
2 *Hyde v Hyde* [1948] P 198, [1948] 1 All ER 362; *Mosey v Mosey* [1956] P 26, [1955] 2 All ER 391.
3 *Chichester v Chichester* [1936] P 129, [1936] 1 All ER 271.
4 *Foard v Foard* [1967] 2 All ER 660.
5 See *Aggett v Aggett* [1962] 1 All ER 190, CA.
6 *AMS v Child Support Officer* [1998] 1 FLR 955 at 964A.
7 Discussed post, p 792.
8 See ante, pp 727–50.
9 See ante, p 288.

to make an order for a child over the age of 18 and the term for which periodical payments may be ordered are the same as under the Domestic Proceedings and Magistrates' Courts Act 1978.[10] Normally the sums will be payable by one spouse (or former spouse) to the other, but either (or presumably both)[11] of them may be ordered to make payments to a third person, if the child is living with that person, or to the child himself.[12] As will be seen, orders payable to the child no longer have tax advantages. However, unlike orders in favour of spouses there is no power to dismiss an application for periodical payments to or in favour of the child.

Income tax[13]

Before the Finance Act 1988, a binding obligation[14] upon one spouse or former spouse to pay the other maintenance attracted tax relief at both basic and higher rates for the payer. Such payments correspondingly counted as the recipient's taxable income. Furthermore, payments made direct to a child, pursuant to a court order to do so,[15] also attracted tax relief for the payer, while the receipt of such monies ranked as the child's income for tax purposes. Under the 1988 Act, however, only payments to a spouse or former spouse now attract limited tax relief,[16] while payments to children attract no tax relief at all. For maintenance orders and maintenance agreements made on or after 15 March 1988,[17] payments are made gross (ie without deduction of tax) and are not taxable in the hands of the recipient.[18] The payer will only qualify for tax relief (at basic and higher rates) for 'qualifying maintenance payments' to a divorced or separated spouse up to a limit equal to the difference between the married person's relief and the single person's relief (which is the equivalent to the amount of the married couple's allowance) until the recipient re-marries.[19]

As we have said, the payer cannot claim tax relief for payments direct to children.[20] However, where the order or agreement expressly provides for payments to be made to a divorced or separated spouse for the benefit of a child of the family, the payments do attract relief.[1] Hence, if no order would otherwise be

---

10 Section 29; see *B v B (Adult Student: Liability to Support)* [1998] 1 FLR 373, CA. For the 1978 Act, see ante, p 764.
11 The court had power under previous legislation to make an order against both spouses: *Freckleton v Freckleton* [1966] CLY 3938.
12 An application for an order may be made by a parent, guardian, any person in whose favour a residence order has been made with respect to the child or any other person who is entitled to apply for a residence order with respect to the child, a local authority, the Official Solicitor as guardian ad litem, or the child himself, if given leave: Family Proceedings Rules 1991 r 2.54.
13 See generally Jackson's *Matrimonial Finance and Taxation* (6th edn, 1996) ch 6 and Wylie *Taxation of The Family* (3rd edn, 1993).
14 Whether under a binding maintenance agreement, a court order or (see *Gandolfo v Gandolfo* [1981] QB 359, [1980] 1 All ER 833, CA) pursuant to an undertaking formally given to the court.
15 Even one made against the parent looking after the child: see *Sherdley v Sherdley* [1988] AC 213, [1987] 2 All ER 54, HL.
16 Under the Finance Act 1992 binding maintenance payments under European Community court orders or agreements attract tax relief.
17 Obligations arising before that (but including cases where an order was made before 1 July 1988 for which an application had been made before 15 March 1988) continue to be governed by the old law.
18 Income and Corporation Taxes Act 1988 s 347A(1)(b).
19 Ibid, s 347B.
20 Ibid.
1 If the order or agreement is not in these terms, and provides for payments to be made to a child, the fact that the payer makes the payments to his former wife for the child's benefit will not enable him to claim the relief: *Billingham (Inspector of Taxes) v John* [1998] 1 FLR 677.

made in the spouse's favour, or if any such order amounted to less than the difference between the single and married person's allowance, then there would be tax advantages in making an order for the benefit of the child.

3. LUMP SUM PAYMENTS

The court may order either party to pay a lump sum or lump sums to the other.[2] It can also order a lump sum to be paid to a specified person for the benefit of any child of the family or to the child himself.[3] In practice, lump sum orders in favour of children, and in particular children whose parents are of limited means, are rare.[4]

The power to order the payment of a lump sum was first given to the courts in 1963 and was initially little used.[5] The reason is perhaps to be found in a dictum of Willmer LJ in the Court of Appeal in *Davis v Davis*,[6] where he said that it was likely to be used only in relatively rare cases where the party had sufficient assets to justify it. The Law Commission's hope[7] that following the passing of the Matrimonial Proceedings and Property Act 1970 wider use might be made of lump sums in favour of spouses does seem now to have been fulfilled.[8]

It is provided by the Matrimonial Causes Act 1973 that a lump sum may be ordered to enable the payee to meet any liabilities or expenses already incurred in maintaining herself or himself or any child of the family before an application is made.[9]

However, the most important use of this statutory power is to adjust the parties' capital assets. If, for example, the husband owns shares, the court may wish the benefit of a proportion of these to be given to the wife. It may do this directly by

---

2 Matrimonial Causes Act 1973 s 21(1)(c) as substituted by Family Law Act 1996 Sch 2, para 2.
3 Ibid, s 21(3)(b) as substituted by Family Law Act 1996 Sch 2, para 2. The court may *in the same order* direct the payment of more than one lump sum. These may be payable at different dates (eg one payable immediately to enable a wife to put down a deposit on a home and another payable when the husband sells the matrimonial home); one may be payable by instalments and the other not. Where a lump sum is payable by instalments, the court has power to vary the amount of, or even suspend or discharge future instalments which are due: *Tilley v Tilley* (1979) 10 Fam Law 89. This jurisdiction, however, is to be exercised with caution: *Penrose v Penrose* [1994] 2 FLR 621, CA at 634 (per Balcombe LJ). The court also has power to extend the time for payment of a lump sum, at least where the payer is not at fault for the delay, the payee is not prejudiced by it, and time for payment is not of the essence of the payment: *Masefield v Alexander* [1995] 1 FLR 100, CA. There is no power to make a second or subsequent order for a lump sum in favour of a spouse: *Coleman v Coleman* [1973] Fam 10 and, when the 1996 Act is in force, s 22A(3). In *Hill v Hill* [1998] 1 FLR 198, CA (a case of remarkable facts), the parties agreed an order at the time of their divorce in 1969, whereby (inter alia) the wife received a lump sum of £75. After the divorce the parties cohabited for 25 years. In 1995 they separated and the wife sought a lump sum order. The Court of Appeal held that the 1969 settlement was not a comprehensive one. The lump sum in 1969 ('extremely rare at the time') would have been regarded as settlement of the wife's claim under s 17 of the Married Woman's Property Act 1882. There had been no proper adjudication and disposal of the wife's claim for a lump sum, and the court still had jurisdiction to deal with it.
4 Per Booth J in *Kiely v Kiely* [1988] 1 FLR 248, CA at 251.
5 See eg *Hill v Hill* [1998] 1 FLR 198, CA above.
6 [1967] P 185 at 192, [1967] 1 All ER 123, CA at 126.
7 Law Com No 25, para 9.
8 See Eekelaar and Maclean *Maintenance after Divorce* Tables 5.6 and 5.7 and pp 74–9 who found that in their sample nearly half of owner-occupied homes were sold principally to give the wife a lump sum. If the home was not sold, husbands not uncommonly bought out the wife's share. Note that in their 1997 study fewer homes were sold, perhaps because of the decline in the housing market: Maclean and Eekelaar *The Parental Obligation* (1997) p 112.
9 Matrimonial Causes Act 1973 s 23(4) as inserted by Family Law Act 1996 Sch 2, para 4.

ordering them to be transferred to her, but it may alternatively order him to make a lump sum payment to her. This makes no financial difference to the wife and it will leave the husband free to sell some of his shares or to raise the money in some other way if he prefers to do so.[10] When the matrimonial home is the only capital asset and it is sold or the wife leaves and the husband remains,[11] the court will commonly make an order for the payment of a lump sum representing the value of that part of the assets of which the other party is to be given the benefit.[12]

The award of a lump sum is not confined to these two situations, however. It is, of course, true that an order will not be made if the consequence would be to deprive the payer of his livelihood, eg if a partner would have to realise his share of the partnership.[13] Nor is a lump sum order appropriate where the payer's wealth is locked up in assets which cannot readily be sold to raise capital, eg in a shareholding in a private family company.[14] But given these restrictions a lump sum will be ordered whenever it is more valuable to the payee than periodical payments, and it is impossible to lay down any hard and fast rules.[15]

Normally a lump sum payment should not be regarded as the capitalisation of periodical payments, but rather as a separate provision on its own.[16] In computing

---

10 But the tax implications should not be ignored. If the husband has to sell property to raise the money to satisfy a lump sum order, he will have to pay capital gains tax on the disposal of the property. The Law Commission are of the view that, if the court orders the transfer of property, it is 'reallocating the property so as to give effect to the existing equitable rights of the marital unit' and consequently no capital gains tax will be payable: Law Com No 25, para 76. Sed quaere? The wife is acquiring something to which she was formerly not entitled and consequently there appears to be a disposal for the purpose of the Taxation of Chargeable Gains Act 1992. There will normally be no chargeable gain on the transfer of the matrimonial home by one spouse to another: ibid, ss 222–226, and the Inland Revenue Concession No D6 (reprinted in 117 Sol Jo 800). But a tax liability may sometimes arise. In *M v M (Sale of Property)* [1988] 1 FLR 389, CA the judge ordered the wife to transfer her interest in the home to the husband in return for a lump sum of £50,000 which, he assumed, would be free of capital gains tax. On an examination of the facts, the Court of Appeal doubted the availability of the 'principal private residence' tax exemption. It ordered the property to be sold, with a lump sum of £60,000 being paid to the wife from the net sale proceeds.

11 See Lord Denning MR in *Wachtel v Wachtel* [1973] Fam 72 at 96, [1973] 1 All ER 829, CA at 840–1.

12 In making such orders the court must, however, be aware of the Law Society's charge, discussed post, p 807.

13 *P v P* [1978] 3 All ER 70, CA; *B v B (Financial Provision)* [1989] 1 FLR 119 (aliter if the partnership is breaking up: cf *Davies v Davies* [1986] 1 FLR 497, CA). An order should not be made if there is no prospect that the party will be able to comply with it: *Martin v Martin* [1976] Fam 335, [1976] 3 All ER 625, CA; *W v W (Periodical Payments: Pensions)* [1996] 2 FLR 480.

14 *P v P* [1989] 2 FLR 241. Even if there is a liquidity problem, however, a lump sum may be ordered if the payer does not produce evidence that he cannot raise the necessary capital by borrowing upon the security of his assets rather than by selling them: *Newton v Newton* [1990] 1 FLR 33, CA; cf *H v H (Financial Provision: Lump Sum)* [1994] 2 FLR 304 where, although the husband's income was high, and he was willing to borrow to achieve a clean break, the court considered it would be 'wrong' to impose too great a borrowing requirement on him.

15 Per Davies LJ in *Jones v Jones* [1971] 3 All ER 1201, CA at 1206.

16 *Trippas v Trippas* [1973] Fam 134, CA at 139 per Lord Denning MR. But cf Thorpe LJ in *AMS v Child Support Officer* [1998] 1 FLR 955, CA, who noted (at 964B) that capitalised maintenance has taken the place of secured periodical payments. And compare *Van Den Boogaard v Laumen*, a decision of the European Court of Justice reported at [1997] 2 FLR 399. The Court held that a lump sum order in English ancillary relief proceedings was 'maintenance', and thus enforceable in the Netherlands under the terms of the Brussels Convention on Jurisdiction and the Enforcement of Judgments in Civil and Commercial Matters. In reaching its decision, the court concluded that the crucial question was not the form which the order took, but its aim. As this was to enable the recipient spouse to provide for herself, after a consideration of her needs and resources, the award

the sum regard is to be had to the paying spouse's means and the reasonable needs of the other spouse and child. In the case of lengthy marriages the view may commonly be taken that the recipient spouse has earned a share in the matrimonial property and that therefore the contingency of remarriage should normally be irrelevant.[17]

Lump sums will be commonly ordered where one party has substantial means, but such an order might also be the best solution if the husband has a little capital (for example, the proceeds of sale of the matrimonial home) but little or no income: the capital may be of real value to the wife, because it will give her some financial base, whilst the husband will be relieved of the obligation of finding continuing support for her out of meagre earnings.[18] A lump sum payment with consequent reduction in periodical payments may also be ordered if the wife (or husband) has particular need of capital, eg to enable her to purchase a house, furniture,[19] or the goodwill of a business,[20] or to clear off a mortgage with which she is buying a new house so that she can make a fresh start.[1] A further use is to protect the payee against probable default on the other's part, eg if it appears that the party against whom financial provision is being sought is likely to remove his assets from the jurisdiction,[2] or to enable the payee to take bankruptcy proceedings against a contumacious party.[3] Further advantages of a lump sum are that, as the

---

was 'concerned with maintenance'. It should be noted that even where a lump sum is intended to provide a regular and secure income to provide for a spouse's future reasonable needs, this does not mean that the capital must remain untouched: '. . . As a matter of principle, capital sums provided post divorce are not intended to be inflation proof and are, in part at least, specifically intended to be drawn down to sustain the beneficiary during the period of survivorship' (*H v H (Financial Provision)* [1993] 2 FLR 35 at 45 (per Thorpe J)).

17 See eg *Duxbury v Duxbury* (1987) [1992] Fam 62n, [1990] 2 All ER 77; cf periodical payments which automatically cease upon the recipient spouse's marriage. Occasionally a party's remarriage will be a relevant factor (provided there are very real prospects: see *H v H (Financial Provision: Remarriage)* [1975] Fam 9, [1975] 1 All ER 367). For example, if the party's financial resources are limited and a decision to give the wife capital (eg the matrimonial home) rather than periodical payments is regarded as the most satisfactory way of meeting her needs, it will be material to know if those needs will change as a result of remarriage.

18 Their total income will also be increased if the wife can claim welfare benefits; cf *Hunter v Hunter* [1973] 3 All ER 362, CA. For the calculation of the period during which a lump sum is to be regarded as income, thus disentitling the recipient to supplementary benefit, see *Bolstridge v Chief Adjudication Officer* [1993] 2 FLR 657. See also *Chamberlain v Chamberlain* [1974] 1 All ER 33, CA, and *Hector v Hector* [1973] 3 All ER 1070, CA, in each of which the husband's interest in the proceeds of sale of the matrimonial home was reduced to compensate the wife for loss of other financial provision.

19 *S v S* [1977] Fam 127, [1977] 1 All ER 56, CA.

20 *Von Mehren v Von Mehren* [1970] 1 All ER 153, CA (husband ordered to pay £4,000 to his former wife to enable her to purchase a house which she intended to run as a boarding house). *Gojkovic v Gojkovic* [1992] Fam 40 (lump sum order of £1 million to wife to buy hotel).

1 *Harnett v Harnett* [1974] 1 All ER 764, CA; cf *Calderbank v Calderbank* [1976] Fam 93, [1975] 3 All ER 333, CA (husband given lump sum to enable him to buy house in which to live and see children to whom he had been granted contact).

2 *Brett v Brett* [1969] 1 All ER 1007, CA.

3 *Curtis v Curtis* [1969] 2 All ER 207, CA (husband who had considerable means and was practising delaying tactics, ordered to pay wife £33,600, capitalising an annual sum of £2,400); cf *Bryant v Bryant* (1976) 120 Sol Jo 165, CA. It will also be the only effective order that can be made if the husband has disappeared so that there is no hope of obtaining periodical payments from him: *Ally v Ally* (1971) Times, 24 August. A lump sum order is not provable in bankruptcy proceedings, although the order will survive the bankruptcy's discharge – r 12(3) of the Insolvency Rules 1986 (SI 1986/1925); and see *Woodley v Woodley (No 2)* [1993] 2 FLR 477, CA where Balcombe LJ called for a change in the rules so that lump sum orders would be both provable and not released on

payment is final, there are no continuing problems of enforcement, which may be of particular importance if the parties' relationship is unusually bitter.[4]

Lump sum applications should ordinarily be disposed of once and for all, but there is jurisdiction to adjourn the application where there is a *real* possibility of capital from a specific source becoming available in the near future.[5]

The court can order the sum to be paid in instalments and may also require the payment of instalments to be secured[6] and to carry interest.[7] Such an approach differs from an order for periodical payments because the total sum will be fixed and cannot be varied, and the balance will still be payable even if one of the parties dies before the whole sum has been paid.

Unlike a periodical payments order,[8] the rights under a lump sum payment have all the incidents of outright ownership; they cannot be varied or discharged,[9] and so may be validly assigned.[10] It follows that a wife, who is ineligible for legal aid, may assign part of her entitlement to a future lump sum order to her solicitors to pay off her legal fees in relation to ancillary relief proceedings. Such an assignment may enable a 'significant constituency of wives'[11] to secure proper legal advice and representation to assert their rights against their husbands, who are economically more powerful, and may be seeking to exploit their position in their conduct of the proceedings.[12]

---

discharge. The court may make a lump sum order notwithstanding the payer spouse's bankruptcy, provided the court considers the effect of the bankruptcy on the payer's ability to pay, and has a clear picture of his assets and liabilities: see *Woodley v Woodley* [1992] 2 FLR 417; *Hellyer v Hellyer* [1996] 2 FLR 579. If a husband obtains a bankruptcy order on his own petition and, because of his failure to disclose his financial position the order is an abuse of the process of the court, the order may be set aside and the court may order a lump sum: *F v F (Divorce Insolvency: Annulment of Bankruptcy Order)* [1994] 1 FLR 359.

4 See *Griffiths v Griffiths* [1974] 1 All ER 932, CA at 942.
5 *Davies v Davies* [1986] 1 FLR 497, CA, where the break-up of the husband's business partnership seemed imminent and upon its dissolution the husband's capital would be unlocked; cf *Burgess v Burgess* [1996] 2 FLR 34, CA, where the husband's prospects of obtaining substantial assets from his business were not taken into account, since there was no real likelihood of a sale. In *Michael v Michael* [1986] 2 FLR 389, CA, *K v K (financial provision: conduct)* [1990] 2 FLR 225 and *H v H (Financial Provision: Capital Assets)* [1993] 2 FLR 335, a spouse's inheritance expectancy was held too remote, while in *MT v MT (Financial Provision: Lump Sum)* [1992] 1 FLR 362 the wife's application was adjourned until the death of her 83-year-old German father-in-law. Under German law the husband would automatically inherit one-eighth of his father's estate.
6 Matrimonial Causes Act 1973 s 22A(5)(b) as substituted by Family Law Act 1996 Sch 2, para 3.
7 Ibid s 22A(7)(b). The subsection enables the court, when making orders that a lump sum be paid by instalments or be deferred (in whole or part), at the time of making the order *or at any time afterwards*, to carry the payment of interest. This alters the pre-1996 Act position, when the court had power to make an order for payment of interest only on the making of a lump sum order, but not afterwards: *L v L (Lump Sum: Interest)* [1994] 2 FLR 324.
8 For which see ante, p 788.
9 Under the Matrimonial Causes Act 1973 s 31 as amended (see post, p 850).
10 *Sears Tooth (a firm) v Payne Hicks Beach (a firm)* [1997] 2 FLR 116. Wilson J acknowledged that lump sum orders which are payable by instalments may be varied and, as such, may, like periodical payments, be incapable of assignment. He added (at 126) that lump sums payable by instalments 'might need to be revisited in another case'.
11 Ibid at 133 (per Wilson J).
12 In providing a way for a spouse of modest means to fund the legal and other professional costs of ancillary relief proceedings *Sears Tooth* may prove of considerable significance. Wilson J suggested two requirements which are necessary for the assignment to be valid: the spouse concerned should be independently legally advised before entering into the deed of assignment, and the deed itself should be disclosed to the court. (In appropriate cases it may well be of tactical advantage for the existence of the deed to be disclosed to the opposing side.) Note also that one possible use of an interim lump sum order is to pay the recipient's legal and other professional costs in relation to ongoing ancillary relief proceedings (see ante, p 787).

4. FINANCIAL PROVISION ORDERS IN RELATION TO PENSIONS[13]

Pension earmarking

As we have seen, the Pensions Act 1995 amends the Matrimonial Causes Act 1973 to introduce new provisions giving the court powers to re-allocate the pension rights of the spouses.[14] By s 25B(1) of the Matrimonial Causes Act 1973 the court is placed under a duty to have regard to the spouses' pension entitlements, being:

(a) any benefits under a pension scheme which a party to the marriage has or is likely to have; and

(b) any benefits under a pension scheme which, by reason of dissolution or annulment of marriage, a party will lose the chance of acquiring.

For this purpose, a pension scheme is defined as an occupational pension scheme or personal pension scheme, and includes a retirement annuity.[15] The court has powers to order the trustees or managers of a pension scheme to make payments (including lump sums) for the benefit of a pensioner's spouse as and when such payments fall due on retirement.[16] The court may only order payments of an amount which does not exceed those which are due to the pensioner.[17] If a pensioner enjoys the appropriate rights under the terms of a pension scheme, the court may also order him to commute the whole or any part of his pension,[18] or to nominate his spouse as the beneficiary of any lump sum payment which he may receive.[19] These provisions enable a court to 'earmark' some or all of a spouse's future pension rights on retirement in favour of the other.[20] It has been held,[1] however, that their enactment does not *require* the court to compensate a spouse for actual or potential loss of pension benefits. All that they do is to provide a further option available to the court, as a form of financial provision order under s 23, to deal with the parties' assets in a way best suited to the circumstances of the case.

Pension sharing

The Family Law Act 1996[2] has introduced further provisions which in principle at least seek to give the court power to 'split' or 'share' pensions on divorce, re-adjusting the spouses' pension entitlements and enabling each party to make future pension arrangements independently of the other. The advantage of this approach over that of earmarking is that, by allocating the pension *rights* at the time of the divorce, the intended recipient knows that she can take the benefit of those rights regardless of whether the other spouse dies before retirement.

---

13 See generally Ellison and Rae *Family breakdown and pensions* (1997), Dries *The Division of Marital Assets following Divorce with Particular Reference to Pensions*, Lord Chancellor's Department Research Series 7/97.

14 Pensions Act 1995 s 166 which inserts new ss 25B–D into the Matrimonial Causes Act 1973. These powers are available in relation to divorces where proceedings were commenced after 1 July 1996: Pensions Act (Commencement) (No 5) Order 1996 (SI 1996 No 1675).

15 Matrimonial Causes Act 1973 s 25D(4).

16 Ibid, s 25B(4) and s 25C(2)(a).

17 Ibid, s 25B(5).

18 Ibid, s 25B(7).

19 Ibid,s 25C(2)(b).

20 For a cautious approach to the provisions, and a decision ultimately not to make an earmarking order, see *T v T (Financial Relief: Pensions)* [1998] 1 FLR 1072, discussed further post, p 843.

1 In *T v T (Financial Relief: Pensions)* [1998] 1 FLR 1072.

2 Family Law Act 1996 s 16 amending Matrimonial Causes Act 1973 s 25B and s 25D.

However, the complexity of achieving these results is such that the government must enact further legislation to provide the necessary statutory framework and detailed rules. It announced its proposals for a 'Pension Sharing Bill' in June 1998.[3] Pension sharing will be open to couples where rights exist under an occupational or personal pension scheme, or under the State Earnings Related Pension Scheme (SERPS), but not in respect of the basic state retirement pension, which already enables a divorced spouse to substitute the contribution record of their former spouse for their own.

To settle pension rights, the couple will have to obtain a valuation of these from any pension scheme to which either or both belongs or has belonged in the past. The valuation will be based on a cash equivalent transfer value (CETV) of the accrued rights and, in the case of SERPS, on a notional capitalisation. Depending upon the type of pension scheme in question, recipients of a pension sharing order will be able to become members of the scheme, or transfer the accrued rights to another. The pension scheme will be notified by the court of the order which it has made, and will have four months to implement it. The order will be in the form of a percentage share of the member's rights, and the scheme will recover, from the parties, the reasonable administrative costs involved, either in cash, or by deduction from the pension rights. The recipient of the order will acquire 'pension credit rights' in the original pension scheme or that to which the rights are transferred. Her eventual pension will depend on the rules of that scheme and her own circumstances when the pension becomes due, and not those of the former spouse from whom the rights have been transferred.

5.   TRANSFER AND SETTLEMENT OF PROPERTY

The court may order either party to the marriage to transfer such property as may be specified to the other party or to or for the benefit of a child of the family. The court may also order either of them to settle any property for the benefit of the other party or any child of the family.[4] The court's power to transfer (but not to settle) property on a child over the age of 18 is limited to where the child is receiving instruction at an educational establishment or is undergoing training for a trade, profession or vocation, or where there are other special circumstances (eg the child is suffering from some physical or mental disability).[5]

The transfer power is currently of particular importance to enable the court to make appropriate orders with respect to the matrimonial home and similar assets (eg furniture or the family car), but it may also be ordered as an alternative to the payment of a lump sum when it is more sensible to order one spouse to transfer investments than to compel him to sell them to raise the necessary capital, or to supplement or replace periodical payments when the party in question has a limited interest (eg a life interest under a family settlement) which can conveniently be used for this purpose.

---

3 Department of Social Security, *Pension sharing on divorce: reforming pensions for a fairer future* Cm 3345 (1998).

4 Matrimonial Causes Act 1973 s 21(2)(a), s 21(2)(b) as substituted by Family Law Act 1996 Sch 2, para 2. For an example of settlement of property on children, see *H v H (Financial Provision: Conduct)* [1998] 1 FLR 971 (lump sum settled on trusts for husband to enable him to buy suitable home in which children could have contact with him; reversion to the children).

5 Section 29(1), (3) as amended by Family Law Act 1996 Sch 8, para 15.

Property that may be the subject of an order

The Act empowers the court to make an order with respect to any property to which the spouse in question is entitled either in possession or in reversion.[6] This form of words follows that of earlier Acts dealing with settlements of the wife's property, under which it was held that 'property' included income as well as capital,[7] and 'reversionary interests' embraced those to which the wife was contingently entitled as well as those already vested in interest.[8] The established view is that there is no power to order a transfer or settlement that the party could not make voluntarily: eg of a protected life interest (which is determinable on the occurrence of any event which will deprive the beneficiary of the right to receive any part of the income), or of a lease containing a covenant against assignment.[9] The latter limitation may be of particular importance when the court is dealing with rights in the matrimonial home. Similarly it was accepted that the party must be able to claim the property *as of right*; hence, if he is a beneficiary under a discretionary trust, the court apparently has no power to order the settlement of any income which the trustees *may* in their discretion pay him,[10] nor presumably could it order the settlement of any property which *might* come to him as the result of the exercise of a power of appointment vested in another. More recently, however, the Court of Appeal[11] has suggested that the court should look at the reality of the situation; it ought not to disregard the potential availability of wealth from sources owned or administered by others. In appropriate circumstances a judge may frame his order to afford 'judicious encouragement' to third parties to provide a spouse with the means to comply with the court's view of the justice of the case.

No transfer or settlement will be ordered if the property is outside the jurisdiction and effective control of the court.[12] But the fact that the property is situated abroad will not prevent the order from being made provided that it can be effectively enforced; and so the court might order the settlement of income receivable in this country from capital invested elsewhere. But if such an order might prove to be difficult to enforce, the court will prefer to make an order with respect to property in England.[13]

---

6 For an illustration of the breadth of the courts' powers in this regard see *Harwood v Harwood* [1991] 2 FLR 274, CA (husband ordered to transfer to wife his interest in assets of a dissolved partnership).

7 See *Savary v Savary* (1898) 79 LT 607, CA at 610; *Style v Style* [1954] P 209, [1954] 1 All ER 442, CA.

8 *Stedall v Stedall* (1902) 86 LT 124; *Savary v Savary* (supra).

9 See *Hale v Hale* [1975] 2 All ER 1090, CA. The question was left open by Lord Penzance in *Milne v Milne* (1871) LR 2 P & D 295, but cf *Loraine v Loraine* [1912] P 222, CA.

10 *Milne v Milne* (1871) LR 2 P & D 295. Nevertheless, the existence of the interest can be taken into account: cf *Browne v Browne* [1989] 1 FLR 291, CA.

11 *Thomas v Thomas* [1995] 2 FLR 668, CA where the court applied the principles to a private family company (rather than a discretionary trust) where the shareholders were the husband, his brother, his mother and a family trust. See also *T v T and others (Joinder of Third Parties)* [1996] 2 FLR 357 where the husband had transferred in excess of £25 million to a Jersey Trust, in respect of which he claimed he had no overall control. Wilson J said 'I have to get to the bottom of the reality behind the trust' adding 'Are these funds . . . which, in effect, if not in form, are able to be deployed by the husband?' The judge felt, in answering this question, that he would need to join the trustees as parties to the proceedings and upheld the appropriate order.

12 *Hamlin v Hamlin* [1986] Fam 11, [1985] 2 All ER 1037, CA.

13 See *Style v Style* (supra).

Orders that can be made

The court can apparently order an absolute transfer of the whole of the party's interest in the property specified or any part of it. It has equally wide powers when ordering a settlement and may either divest the spouse of his whole interest[14] or grant a limited interest to the other spouse or children, leaving the beneficial owner with the reversion.[15] Although the factors which the court should take into account when deciding what order (if any) to make will be considered later,[16] it might be said here that the courts rarely make substantial capital orders in favour of children.[17]

6.   VARIATION OF MARRIAGE SETTLEMENTS

The court may make an order varying any marriage settlement for the benefit of the parties to a marriage and the children of the family or either or any of them.[18] The court may also make an order extinguishing or reducing the interest of either of the parties under any marriage settlement.[19] For this purpose, a marriage settlement means an ante-nuptial or post-nuptial settlement made on the parties, including one made by will.[20]

These powers are complementary to those already discussed and are used less in view of the wider powers to order transfer and settlements of property. But there are still cases where the only power that can be exercised is that of varying a settlement, eg if one party has an interest that cannot be transferred (such as a protected life interest) or if it is desired to vary or destroy limitations in favour of children or other beneficiaries.

The parties cannot oust the court's jurisdiction by agreement, nor apparently is this jurisdiction in any way fettered by express provisions in the settlement as to how the property is to be held if the marriage is terminated.[1]

The terms 'ante-nuptial and post-nuptial settlements' are used in a sense much wider than that usually given to them by conveyancers, the essential condition being that the benefit must be conferred on either or both of the spouses *in the character of spouse or spouses*.[2] It is immaterial whether the benefit comes from

---

14 As in *Compton v Compton* [1960] P 201, [1960] 2 All ER 70, where property was settled on children for life with remainder to grandchildren. Quaere whether the remainder to the grandchildren was not ultra vires, as this does not benefit *children of the family*.

15 *Style v Style* [1954] P 209, [1954] 1 All ER 422, CA (settlement on husband for life).

16 See post, pp 816ff.

17 See *Kiely v Kiely* [1988] 1 FLR 248, CA; *Chamberlain v Chamberlain* [1974] 1 All ER 33, CA; *Lilford v Glynn* [1979] 1 All ER 441, CA; and *Draskovic v Draskovic* (1980) 11 Fam Law 87. But cf *H v H (Financial Provision: Conduct)* (supra) and *Tavoulareas v Tavoulareas* [1998] 2 FLR 418, CA.

18 Matrimonial Causes Act 1973 s 21(2)(c), as substituted by Family Law Act 1996 Sch 2 and Sch 4.

19 Ibid, s 21(2)(d).

20 Ibid, s 21(6).

1 See *Prinsep v Prinsep* [1930] P 35, CA at 49; *Woodcock v Woodcock* (1914) 111 LT 924, CA; Denning LJ in *Egerton v Egerton* [1949] 2 All ER 238, CA at 242. The decision to the contrary in the early case of *Stone v Stone* (1864) 3 Sw & Tr 608 cannot now be regarded as good law. In nullity proceedings a settlement may be varied even though the marriage is void: *Radziej v Radziej* [1967] 1 All ER 944; affirmed [1968] 3 All ER 624, CA but if it is not to take effect until the celebration of the marriage, it would appear not yet to be in existence and therefore to be incapable of variation.

2 Per Hill J in *Prinsep v Prinsep* [1929] P 225 at 232. See also *Bosworthick v Bosworthick* [1927] P 64, CA at 69; *Worsley v Worsley* (1869) LR 1 P & D 648 at 651.

one of the spouses or from a third person, provided that this condition is satisfied.[3] It is possible that a transaction may be a settlement for this purpose if it confers a benefit upon the children of the marriage, even though it confers none upon either spouse, provided that the beneficiaries take *in the character of children of the family*.[4] Conversely, a transaction which would otherwise be a settlement will not cease to be one merely because it makes provision for any future spouse of either of the parties or the children of such a marriage.[5]

Provided that the condition stated above is fulfilled, it is immaterial that one or both of the spouses are merely the objects of a discretionary trust and can therefore claim nothing as of right.[6] A separation agreement comes within the section even if it is not in writing.[7] Similarly a bond by which a wife undertakes to pay an annuity to her husband,[8] and a policy of life assurance taken out by a husband for the benefit of his wife[9] have been held to be post-nuptial settlements. But there cannot be a settlement for this purpose if there has been an absolute and unqualified transfer of property unless payments of some sort still have to be made at the time that the court has to enquire into the existence of the settlement.[10]

The court may vary a settlement only if it was made on the footing that the marriage *which is the subject of the divorce* should continue.[11] Thus, if a husband marries successively W1 and W2, a settlement made by him on the eve of his marriage to W1 cannot be varied in divorce proceedings brought by W2.[12] Conversely, if an agreement was ostensibly entered into on the footing that the marriage would be dissolved, it cannot be a post-nuptial settlement.[13]

3 *Prinsep v Prinsep* (supra).
4 Apparently so held in *Compton v Compton* [1960] P 201, [1960] 2 All ER 70 (where, however, the wife was trustee and had a power of appointment in favour of children); cf Greer LJ in *Melvill v Melvill* [1930] P 159, at 176, 177. But it is difficult to see how this could be in 'settlement made on the parties to the marriage'.
5 As in *Prinsep v Prinsep* (supra).
6 *E v E (Financial Provision)* [1990] 2 FLR 233 (post-nuptial settlement constituted where, during the subsistence of a marriage, property purchased by the husband's father was settled on a discretionary trust whose beneficiaries were the husband, the wife, the husband's children and remoter issue by any subsequent wife). See also *Janion v Janion* [1929] P 237n and *T v T (Joinder of Third Parties)* [1996] 2 FLR 357. A protected life interest can also be varied without producing a forfeiture: *General Accident, Fire and Life Assurance Corpn Ltd v IRC* [1963] 3 All ER 259, CA. In *Howard v Howard* [1945] P 1, [1945] 1 All ER 91, CA, MacKinnon LJ left open the question whether a discretionary trust can be a post-nuptial settlement merely because one of the spouses comes within the class of possible beneficiaries. The court may vary such a settlement even though it is in a foreign form because the parties were domiciled elsewhere at the time of the marriage: *Forsyth v Forsyth* [1891] P 363.
7 *Tomkins v Tomkins* [1948] P 170, [1948] 1 All ER 237, CA; *Jeffrey v Jeffrey (No 2)* [1952] P 122, [1952] 1 All ER 790, CA. If it were in writing it could also be varied under s 35 of the Matrimonial Causes Act (ante, p 753).
8 *Bosworthick v Bosworthick* [1927] P 64, CA; cf *Parrington v Parrington* [1951] 2 All ER 916.
9 *Gunner v Gunner* [1949] P 77, [1948] 2 All ER 771, followed in *Brown v Brown* [1949] P 91, [1948] 2 All ER 778.
10 *Prescott v Fellowes* [1958] P 260, [1958] 3 All ER 55, CA. In *Brooks v Brooks* [1996] AC 375, [1995] 3 All ER 257, HL, Lord Nicholls considered (at 391–2 and 263) that in the case of gifts the appropriate order would be a property transfer or property settlement order.
11 *Young v Young* [1962] P 27, [1961] 3 All ER 695, CA.
12 *Burnett v Burnett* [1936] P 1. See also *Hargreaves v Hargreaves* [1926] P 42.
13 *Young v Young* (supra). Surrounding circumstances may be taken into consideration if they do not contradict the written agreement, although the settlor's motive is *per se* immaterial: *Joss v Joss* [1943] P 18, [1943] 1 All ER 102; *Parrington v Parrington* [1951] 2 All ER 916 at 919; *Prinsep v Prinsep* [1929] P 225 at 236.

In *Brooks v Brooks* [14] the power of the court to vary marriage settlements was given a new and contemporary application. The parties had married in 1977 when the husband, who owned a successful building company, was 47 and the wife 38. Some eleven years later divorce proceedings began when the husband left the matrimonial home. The husband had a number of pension arrangements, including a scheme set up by his company and established in 1980 under a policy with a life assurance company. Under the rules of the scheme the husband was the beneficiary, but he could surrender a portion of his pension entitlement upon retirement to his spouse and/or dependants. The House of Lords, unanimously upholding the decision of the courts below, [15] held that the husband was to be taken to have entered into the scheme to provide a highly tax-efficient means to provide for himself and his wife on retirement. As such, the scheme fell within the wide meaning of 'ante-nuptial settlement' given by the Matrimonial Causes Act 1973, and so could be varied for the benefit of the wife. [16] The implications of the decision ought not to be overstated. On the facts, the scheme had just one member, the wife had earnings of her own from the same employer to provide for her immediate needs, and the variation was likely to obtain Inland Revenue approval. As Waite LJ acknowledged in the Court of Appeal, [17] '. . . the present case . . . appears to me to pass safely through a narrow mesh in a broad net . . .' In the more usual case of a multi-member scheme, it would not be right to vary a member's rights to prejudice those of others, particularly if Inland Revenue approval was not first obtained. As Lord Nicholls put it: [18] 'This decision should not be seen as an overall solution for the pension problem.' [19]

7.   ORDERS FOR THE SALE OF PROPERTY

As originally enacted, the Matrimonial Causes Act 1973 conferred no *express* power to order a sale of spouses' property. However, following the Law Commission's recommendation, [20] it is now expressly provided by s 24A [1] that where the court makes

---

14   [1996] AC 375, [1995] 3 All ER 257, HL. And see Plumstead and Salter 'Pensions after *Brooks*: Part II' [1995] Fam Law 490.

15   [1993] 2 FLR 491 (Ewbank J) and [1994] 2 FLR 10, CA. It was Ewbank J who, in *Griffiths v Dawson & Co* [1993] 2 FLR 315, first suggested that an 'adventurous solicitor', when advising a middle-aged wife faced with a husband in pensionable employment, might consider the use of the court's powers under Matrimonial Causes Act 1973 s 24 to vary pension entitlements.

16   It should be noted that the House of Lords held the court's power only extended to property which formed part of the marriage settlement. This comprised only the money in the scheme required to fund the husband's pension (apart from his other pension arrangements). The surplus belonged to the husband's company.

17   [1994] 2 FLR 10, CA at 23. For a case where the court followed *Brooks v Brooks*, see *W v W (Periodical Payments: Pensions)* [1996] 2 FLR 480. Here, however, the court's power of variation, in relation to the husband's managed pension fund, took effect 'by doing what the husband could do for himself' under the rules of the pension scheme, effectively 'earmarking' future benefits. The court ordered the wife be nominated as dependant for all purposes during her lifetime or until remarriage. See also *K v K (Financial Relief: Widow's Pension)* [1997] 1 FLR 35 for what the judge described as a 'graphic illustration' of the inadequacy of the court's powers in relation to pensions in the context of marriage breakdown.

18   [1996] AC 375 at 396, [1995] 3 All ER 257 at 267, HL.

19   See ante at p 795 for the legislative reforms to deal with pensions made subsequent to *Brooks v Brooks*.

20   Law Com No 99, *Orders for Sale of Property under the Matrimonial Causes Act 1973*.

1   Added by the Matrimonial Homes and Property Act 1981 s 7 and amended by the Family Law Act 1996 Sch 8, para 8.

a secured periodical payments order, a lump sum order, or a property adjustment order, then it may make:

'. . . a further order for the sale of such property as may be specified in the order, being property in which or in the proceeds of sale of which either or both of the parties to the marriage has or have a beneficial interest, either in possession or reversion.'

The power to order a sale is a consequential or ancillary power and not an independent one. In other words, it can only be made where an order relating to the parties' capital has already been made under s 23 and s 24; it does not confer a jurisdiction to order a sale 'in the air'. That s 24A does not extend the court's powers has been emphasised in *Omielan v Omielan*,[2] where it was held that the section was inserted into the Act to clarify or expand the court's power of enforcement, implementation and procedure, ancillary to the substantive orders which it can make.

In the case of property belonging to one spouse and a third party the court is directed that, before it decides whether to order a sale, the third party must be given the opportunity to make representations, and any such representations are then to be included in the circumstances to which the court must have regard under s 25 of the 1973 Act.[3]

8. CONSENT ORDERS

Encouraging agreement

There is nothing to prevent the parties themselves from agreeing to the terms of the financial provision and property adjustment orders to be made: indeed, the whole trend in recent years has been to encourage them to do so:

'Agreements are not just "flavour of the month". Agreement is now the name of the game. Practitioners are getting this message from every quarter and every litigation process is being geared towards expeditious dispute resolution . . .'[4]

We have already noted the emphasis placed by the Family Law Act 1996 on mediation, as a process by which the parties might reach agreement on financial and other disputes arising on marriage breakdown.[5] The Lord Chancellor's Ancillary Relief Pilot Scheme,[6] designed to introduce and monitor changes in the rules of ancillary relief procedure, has as one of its avowed aims the promotion of settlements. An integral part of the new procedures is the holding of an early financial dispute resolution appointment ('FDR') where the parties, in the presence of a district judge, will be encouraged to address the outstanding issues between them with a view to reaching agreement. Negotiated settlements may

---

2 [1996] 2 FLR 306, CA. See also *Harper v O'Reilly and Harper* [1997] 2 FLR 816; *Burton v Burton* [1986] 2 FLR 419; *Thompson v Thompson* [1986] Fam 38, [1985] 2 All ER 243, CA.
3 Matrimonial Causes Act 1973 s 24A(6), added by the Matrimonial and Family Proceedings Act 1984 Sch 1, para 11.
4 Salter and Bruce *Matrimonial Consent Orders and Agreements* (3rd edn, 1996) p ix. The development of the so-called 'settlement culture' is not without its critics: see generally Davis, Cretney and Collins *Simple Quarrels: Negotiating Money and Property Disputes on Divorce*, and especially at pp 260–3.
5 See ante, p 255.
6 See Family Proceedings (Amendment No 2) Rules 1997, SI 1997/1056; *Practice Direction: Ancillary Relief Procedure: Pilot Scheme* [1997] 2 FLR 304; and ante, p 233.

work to reduce hostility and acrimony between the parties;[7] furthermore, it makes obvious sense for the parties to reach agreement to save the costs of a full court hearing, which can be extremely heavy.[8] The court has used its discretion in awarding costs as a means of promoting settlements, notably in the development of the '*Calderbank* offer'.[9] This bears a resemblance to a payment into court,[10] where one party makes an offer to the other 'without prejudice as to costs'. If the offer is rejected, no reference is made to it until after the court has made its order. If the order is more favourable to the offeree than the terms of the *Calderbank* offer, the court will usually award the offeree his or her costs; if not, the court may order the offeree to pay the costs of both sides from the date on which the *Calderbank* offer was made.[11] In *H v H (Financial Relief: Costs)*,[12] however, Holman J criticised the tactical 'poker' of *Calderbank* exchanges, and suggested that the time was fast approaching when it should be removed altogether. His Lordship noted[13] that the rules contained in the Ancillary Relief Procedure Pilot Scheme[14] force the parties into making 'open' proposals at an early stage, so that, in those cases which do not settle, the judge at final hearing has all the information necessary for him to do overall justice between the parties, instead of having to divide the available assets on two separate occasions, first substantively, and then in relation to costs.

The information before the court

When the parties have come to terms, it is commonly sought to have their agreement incorporated into a court order. The court may make an order on the

---

7 See eg Lord Scarman in *Minton v Minton* [1979] AC 593 at 608, HL: 'The law now encourages spouses to avoid bitterness after family breakdown and to settle their money and property problems'.

8 See eg *F v F (Ancillary Relief: Substantial Assets)* [1995] 2 FLR 45, where the parties' total costs approached £1.5 million. See also *H v H (Financial Relief: Costs)* [1997] 2 FLR 57, where the husband was 'horrified' to find costs spiralling up to £175,000. At the third day of the hearing, the gap between the parties had narrowed to just £30,000 on the substantive issues. As Holman J remarked (at 58): 'If costs had not been incurred, a fair resolution of this case would have been easy. As it is, it has become impossible because the burden of costs is likely to be penurious to one or other or both of them'. The husband was ordered to pay the wife's costs, even though the sum involved virtually wiped out his liquid assets and it was by no means certain he would be able to raise the additional sums required by borrowings.

9 *Calderbank v Calderbank* [1976] Fam 93, CA. See also *Gojkovic v Gojkovic (No 2)* [1991] 2 FLR 233, CA, where the Court of Appeal endorsed 'this useful practice' (per Butler-Sloss LJ at 237).

10 *Gojkovic v Gojkovic (No 2)* (supra) at 237 (per Butler-Sloss LJ at 239).

11 Although not enshrined in the procedural rules, the general principle in ancillary relief proceedings is that, in the absence of special factors, costs follow the event; the winner is entitled to his or her costs: *Gojkovic v Gojkovic (No 2)* (supra). For a case where the court's order 'beat' the husband's '*Calderbank* offer' so the wife received her costs see *Thompson v Thompson* [1993] 2 FLR 464, CA. See also *A v A (Costs Appeal)* [1996] 1 FLR 14: 'A spouse who does not respond constructively to a *Calderbank offer* stymies whatever chance there is of settlement. Such a spouse cannot with impunity expect immunity from responsibility [for costs]' (per Singer J at 25). It should be remembered that the court still retains the broadest discretion in deciding issues of costs. In *P v P (Financial Relief: Non Disclosure)* [1994] 2 FLR 381, although the court's order 'beat' the terms of the husband's *Calderbank* offer, the court declined to make a costs order in the wife's favour to reflect the wife's serious misconduct, and culpability within the litigation.

12 [1997] 2 FLR 57.

13 Ibid at 59.

14 See ante, p 801. The rules of the Pilot Scheme require both parties to lodge all offers and proposals and responses (ie all *Calderbank* correspondence) with the court: Family Proceedings (Amendment No 2) Rules 1997 (SI 1997/1056) r 2.75, while r 2.77 requires that prior to the final hearing both parties shall file and serve open statements setting out their proposals.

agreed terms only on the basis of prescribed information furnished with the application.[15] The court retains the power, and indeed the duty, to scrutinise the proposed arrangements: in particular it must still have regard to the considerations set out in s 25 of the 1973 Act.[16] The realities of life in the Principal Registry and the divorce county courts, however, mean that district judges have only limited time to examine the terms of proposed consent orders put up to them and '. . . whilst the court is no rubber stamp nor is it some kind of forensic ferret'.[17] The paternal function of the court when approving financial consent orders is confined to a broad appraisal of the parties' financial circumstances, without descent into the valley of detail.[18] The fact that the parties have arrived at a settlement will itself be prima facie evidence that its terms are reasonable, at least if they were at arms length and were both legally advised:

> 'The statutory duty [ie to consider the proposed arrangements in the context of s 25 of the 1973 Act] cannot be ducked, but the court is entitled to assume that parties who are sui juris and who are represented by solicitors know what they want.'[19]

Consequently, the court will normally approve the terms of the agreement which is proposed by the parties, provided it is not contrary to public policy, and will incorporate it in an order.[20]

In *Livesey (formerly Jenkins) v Jenkins*[1] the House of Lords held that, because the court cannot properly discharge its function under s 25 without complete and up-to-date information, the parties owe a duty to the court to make full and frank disclosure of material facts to each other, not simply up to the time of the agreement, but right up until the time of the court order. Failure to make such disclosure can lead to the order being set aside. In *Livesey v Jenkins* the wife agreed to relinquish all claims for maintenance in return for the husband's agreeing to transfer to her his half-share in the matrimonial home. After the agreement had been reached, but before it had been embodied in a court order, the wife became engaged to be married, but this was not disclosed to the husband or the court. It was held that this failure to disclose was so important[2] that the order should be set aside. Lord Brandon, however, emphasised[3] that not every failure of disclosure would justify setting a consent order aside. On the contrary, to justify setting an order aside the absence of disclosure must have led the court to make a substantially different order from that which it would have made had there been

---

15 Matrimonial Causes Act 1973 s 33A added by the Matrimonial and Family Proceedings Act 1984 s 7 as amended by Family Law Act 1996 Sch 8, para 19. For the prescribed information, see the Family Proceedings Rules 1991 r 2.61. For further detail on the procedure, see *Pounds v Pounds* [1994] 1 FLR 775, CA.

16 Discussed post, pp 816–50.

17 *Harris v Manahan* [1997] 1 FLR 205, CA at 213, per Ward LJ.

18 *Pounds v Pounds* [1994] 1 FLR 775, CA at 779, per Waite LJ.

19 *Harris v Manahan* (supra) per Ward LJ at 213.

20 *Dean v Dean* [1978] Fam 161, [1978] 3 All ER 758, following *Brockwell v Brockwell* (1975) 6 Fam Law 46, CA. See also *B v Miller & Co* [1996] 2 FLR 23 where experienced counsel for one of the parties suggested that, if both parties were legally represented, the judge would be unlikely to examine the terms of the settlement very closely and it was virtually 'unknown' for the court to refuse to approve agreed terms.

1 [1985] AC 424, [1985] 1 All ER 106, HL approving *de Lasala v de Lasala* [1980] AC 546, [1979] 2 All ER 1146, PC and disapproving on this point *Wales v Wadham* [1977] 2 All ER 125.

2 It will be appreciated that once the wife had remarried she would no longer be entitled to receive periodical payments, so she was not relinquishing very much.

3 Ibid at 445 and 119 respectively.

full disclosure.[4] This test has been strictly applied, no doubt to prevent a flood of applications to set aside on the basis of material non-disclosure.[5] For the same reason the Court of Appeal has sought to restrict the development of an earlier judicial suggestion[6] that the poor quality of legal advice which a spouse receives prior to entering into an agreement may enable him (or her) subsequently to resile from it. This approach had been adopted in *B v B (Consent Order: Variation)*,[7] where the judge held that the 'manifestly bad legal advice' which a wife received in agreeing to a fixed term periodical payment order, when she needed the security of lifetime support, justified the court in re-opening the order and extending the duration of the periodical payments. In *Harris v Manahan*,[8] however, the Court of Appeal recognised that, while bad legal advice did have a part to play in deciding whether a spouse should be held to a bargain, the need for finality in litigation requires that '. . . only in the most exceptional case of cruellest injustice' should bad legal advice be a ground for the court interfering with a consent order. The remedy for a badly advised spouse lies in an action in negligence against his (or her) solicitors in the appropriate case.[9]

The weight attached to the parties' agreement

A further problem arises if one of the parties wishes to go back on an agreement before the court approves it and embodies it in an order. We have already seen that the agreement cannot preclude an application to the court[10] but, as the Court of Appeal held in *Edgar v Edgar*,[11] considerable attention will be paid to it if it was

---

4 A similar rule applies to contested orders and to justify appealing out of time: see post, p 855. On the procedure for setting aside a consent order, see *B-T v B-T (Divorce Procedure)* [1990] 2 FLR 1; *Harris v Manahan* [1997] 1 FLR 205, CA; and Bennett 'Challenging Ancillary Relief Orders' [1993] Fam Law 84.

5 See eg *Cook v Cook* [1988] 1 FLR 521, CA, where the court refused to set aside a consent order because, it was alleged, the wife had not disclosed the depth of her relationship with a third party. It was held that any change in the quality of the wife's relationship would not have substantially affected the terms of the original order. Compare *Vicary v Vicary* [1992] 2 FLR 271, CA, in which the court set aside a consent order where the husband had not disclosed that negotiations were taking place for the sale of his company (which took place shortly after the order was made), significantly increasing the husband's asset worth. See also *T v T (Consent Order: Procedure to Set Aside)* [1996] 2 FLR 640 where the husband had 'dishonestly and fraudulently' concealed the true value of his business until it was taken over shortly after the making of the consent order, which was therefore set aside.

6 *Camm v Camm* (1982) 4 FLR 577, CA at 580 per Ormrod LJ (referring to his earlier judgment: *Edgar v Edgar* [1980] 3 All ER 887, CA). His Lordship made it clear that it was not necessarily negligent legal advice which was required.

7 [1995] 1 FLR 9; cf the views of Hoffmann LJ in *Pounds v Pounds* [1994] 1 FLR 775, CA who said (at 791) of the principle of examining the quality of legal advice given to a spouse: 'It is . . . understandably a matter of surprise and resentment on the part of the other party that one should be able to repudiate an agreement on account of the inadequacy of one's own legal advisers, over whom the other party had control, and of whose advice he had no knowledge. We have created uncertainty and . . . added to the cost and pain of litigation'.

8 [1997] 1 FLR 205, CA. While recognising that on the facts the wife had suffered injustice, Ward LJ accepted, with regret, that '. . . a wronged individual is to be sacrificed on the high altar of policy'. He added (at 224): 'To deny justice to the wife is hard – and to that extent justice is imperfect; but justice must be done to the husband; to do justice to children is paramount; to do justice to the system into which these disputes are fed is essential'.

9 But no action for negligence will apparently lie where the settlement was made at the door of the court: *Kelley v Corston* [1998] 1 FLR 986, CA, discussed post, p807 n 9.

10 Ante, p 752.

11 [1980] 3 All ER 887, CA.

entered into with full knowledge of all the relevant facts and on legal advice. Obviously a party will not be bound if the agreement was made under duress or undue influence, but the fact that one of the parties was in a superior bargaining position will not justify the other in going back on it unless the former took an unfair advantage by exploiting the position. In *Edgar v Edgar* a multi-millionaire and his wife entered into a separation deed in which the husband made capital provision for her amounting to some £100,000 and undertook to make periodical payments to her of £16,000 a year together with periodical payments for the children. In return she covenanted not to seek financial relief in any divorce proceedings that might take place in the future. She executed the deed after being warned by her legal advisers that she would probably obtain a much better order from the court. When divorce proceedings were launched, she attempted to resile from the agreement and claimed a lump sum payment. Dismissing her application, the Court of Appeal held that, although the husband's financial position put him in a much stronger bargaining position, there was no evidence that he had exploited it, and consequently the wife must be held to her agreement. The court might be justified in ignoring an agreement if the wife found it impossible to maintain herself owing to unforeseen circumstances[12] or, possibly, if injustice would be done for some other reason, but the facts of *Edgar v Edgar* make it clear that a large disparity between the sum that a wife stipulated for and that which the court might have awarded her will not itself be a ground for releasing her from the contract she made.[13]

In *Pounds v Pounds*[14] the Court of Appeal considered the decision in *Edgar v Edgar*, and the law relating to the setting aside of out-of-court agreements to be 'extremely problematical'[15] and 'unsatisfactory'.[16] Hoffmann LJ canvassed a number of new approaches. The parties' agreement could be binding on them subject to the normal contractual remedies, fraud, misrepresentation, undue influence etc.[17] Alternatively, until the court had embodied the agreement in a consent order nothing the parties had negotiated or agreed would be legally binding or even admissible. Whilst giving both of the parties the opportunity to back out up to the last moment, at least both parties would know where they stood. His Lordship described the decision in *Edgar v Edgar* as 'the worst of both worlds' since '. . . the agreement may be held to be binding, but whether it will be can be determined only after litigation'.[18]

Pre-nuptial agreements

The approach of the court in upholding out of court financial agreements between spouses on the dissolution of their marriage stands contrasted to that in relation to 'pre-nuptial agreements' where the established view, as succinctly expressed by Thorpe J in *F v F (Ancillary Relief: Substantial Assets)*[19] is that 'In this jurisdiction

---

12 *Wright v Wright* [1970] 3 All ER 209, CA at 214.
13 For a case where a total change in the parties' financial circumstances justified the court in departing from the terms of a separation agreement, see *Beach v Beach* [1995] 2 FLR 160.
14 [1994] 1 FLR 775, CA.
15 Ibid at 790 (per Waite LJ).
16 [1994] 1 FLR 775, CA at 791 (per Hoffmann LJ).
17 His Lordship accepted that this would not be possible under the present policy of the law as expressed in *Hyman v Hyman* [1929] AC 601.
18 [1994] 1 FLR 775 at 791.
19 [1995] 2 FLR 45 at 66.

they must be of very limited significance'. Two subsequent cases, however, suggest that the court will be prepared to consider a pre-nuptial agreement as of evidential value, and a relevant circumstance, in resolving an application for ancillary relief. In *N v N (Foreign Divorce: Financial Relief)* [20] the parties were Swedish nationals, and Cazalet J considered that, while their pre-nuptial agreement would not be conclusive in England (as it was in Sweden), it was nonetheless a material consideration, to which the court should have regard in applying the criteria in s 25 of the 1973 Act. In *S v S (Divorce: Staying Proceedings)* [1] Wilson J said that there was a danger that the words of Thorpe J in *F v F* might be taken out of context. Looking to the future, his Lordship added:

> 'There will come a case . . . where the circumstances surrounding the pre-nuptial agreement and the provision therein contained might, when viewed in the context of other circumstances of the case prove influential or even crucial . . . I can find nothing in s 25 to compel a conclusion . . . at odds with personal freedoms to make agreements for ourselves . . . carefully struck by informed adults. It all depends.'

The advantages and disadvantages of encouraging couples to make pre-nuptial agreements and giving effect to them in ancillary relief proceedings are under consideration by the government. [2]

The effects of a consent order

It should be appreciated that, once the parties' agreement is incorporated into a court order, it derives its authority from the order and not from the agreement. [3] This has two important consequences. First, the court is no more entitled to make orders outside the terms of the 1973 Act than it is in respect of contested orders. [4] Secondly, the rules against reopening 'clean break' orders [5] and varying property adjustment orders [6] apply equally to consent orders as they do to a contested order. [7] The courts have on more than one occasion warned of the need for legal representatives to be especially careful in drafting the terms of proposed consent orders and to advise their clients on precisely what impact their agreement will have. [8] The failure by a solicitor to protect his client's interests in respect of a

---

20 [1997] 1 FLR 900.
1 [1997] 2 FLR 100 at 102. See further, Harcus 'Pre-Nuptial Agreements' [1997] Fam Law 669.
2 The issue was referred to the Lord Chancellor's Ancillary Relief Advisory Group in 1998: see [1998] Fam Law 381 and Barton 'Pre-marital Contracts and Equal Shares on Divorce' [1998] Fam Law 423. See further post, p 866.
3 *de Lasala v de Lasala* [1980] AC 546, [1979] 2 All ER 1146; *Thwaite v Thwaite* (1981) 2 FLR 280, CA; *Masefield v Alexander* [1995] 1 FLR 100, CA.
4 See Lord Brandon in *Livesey v Jenkins* [1985] AC 424 at 444, [1985] 1 All ER 106 at 118, and see *Belcher v Belcher* [1995] 1 FLR 916.
5 Discussed post, pp 820–3. The most common form of consent order provides for a clean break.
6 See post, pp 852 et seq.
7 See *Minton v Minton* [1979] AC 593, [1979] 1 All ER 79, HL. For a good example of the harsh realities of the binding nature of a consent order see *Dinch v Dinch* [1987] 1 All ER 818, HL, in which it was held that there was no power to interfere with an agreement to a delayed sale of the matrimonial home, even though the husband by accepting voluntary redundancy had been unable to meet his maintenance commitments under the agreement.
8 See eg *Dinch v Dinch*, supra, at 820 per Lord Oliver; *Sandford v Sandford* [1986] 1 FLR 412 at 425 per Oliver LJ; and *Pounds v Pounds* [1994] 1 FLR 775 at 790 per Waite LJ. See also Cleary 'Icebergs and Elephant Traps' [1987] Fam Law 43 and 'Icebergs and Elephant Traps Revisited' [1990] Fam Law 102. See also Salter and Bruce *Matrimonial Consent Orders and Agreements* (3rd edn, 1996).

consent order may constitute professional negligence, for which substantial damages are awarded.[9]

It will not infrequently be the case that the parties will have reached an agreement which is perfectly proper in itself but which is outside the terms of the Matrimonial Causes Act 1973, as in *Livesey v Jenkins*, where, after the transfer of the husband's share in the matrimonial home, the wife agreed to be solely responsible for the mortgage and all other outgoings on the house and to be solely responsible for certain specific bank overdrafts. As we have said, the court has no power to incorporate such agreements in a consent order. However, it is possible to make such agreements binding by, for example, including them in an undertaking to the court,[10] or the court could dismiss the application conditionally upon the parties' entering into the agreement in question.[11]

9. THE LEGAL AID BOARD'S STATUTORY CHARGE

In cases where either or both parties have been granted legal aid, an important factor to be borne in mind in deciding what orders should be made or agreed to is the Legal Aid Board's charge.[12] Under the Legal Aid Act 1988 s 16(6), in return for the responsibility for all the legally aided party's appropriately taxed legal costs, the Legal Aid Board has a charge, to the extent of those costs, over property

---

9 *Dickinson v Jones Alexander & Co* [1993] 2 FLR 521 (decided in 1989) (£330,238 damages awarded to a wife for being deprived, through her solicitor's negligence, of proper and reasonable financial provision). On the approach to be adopted in assessing whether a solicitor has shown a proper standard of professional competence, see *Dutfield v Gilbert H Stephens & Sons* [1988] Fam Law 473. In *Kelly v Corston* [1998] 1 FLR 986, CA, it was held that a barrister had immunity from suit by a client complaining about allegedly negligent advice given in relation to a door of the court settlement, inter alia because the court has to exercise an independent judgment in scrutinising the terms of the agreement under s 33A of the 1973 Act. However, in *Frazer Harris v Schofield Roberts & Hill (A Firm)* [1998] Fam Law 524, Toulson J distinguished the case where the alleged negligence arose prior to the hearing and, because of non-disclosure by the other spouse, the court had been unable adequately to consider the terms of the agreement.

10 Per Lord Brandon in *Jenkins v Livesey*, ibid at 444 and 119 respectively. But an undertaking given neither by deed nor for valuable consideration (and therefore not a contract) creates an obligation only towards the court. Consequently it can be enforced, eg by committal but not by an action for arrears by the payee: *Re Hudson* [1966] Ch 209, [1966] 1 All ER 110. This may leave the payee completely unprotected on the other party's death, as in *Re Hudson*. The extent to which undertakings are enforceable by judgment summons is not free from doubt or controversy – compare Bird 'Problems in Ancillary Relief Orders' [1990] Fam Law 420 with Mostyn and Moor 'Enforcing Financial Undertakings by Judgment Summons' [1992] Fam Law 233; and see Burrows '"Undertakings" and Consent Orders' [1998] Fam Law 158. Certain financial undertakings have been held to be enforceable by judgment summons – see *Symmons v Symmons* [1993] 1 FLR 317 (to pay school fees and a monthly maintenance supplement) and *M v M (Enforcement: Judgment Summons)* [1993] Fam Law 469 (undertaking to pay capital gains tax in respect of shares transferred by one spouse to another pursuant to consent order).

11 This is known as a 'Tomlin order'. Whether the court would be prepared to accept an undertaking in respect of a provision which it *is* empowered to order has yet to be determined. If it would, then subject to the consent of the party giving the undertaking, it may be that a court could subsequently vary eg a property transfer order, which under the Matrimonial Causes Act 1973 is not variable: see the comment at [1985] Fam Law 227 and Burrows '"Undertakings" and Consent Orders' [1998] Fam Law 158.

12 See Shute 'The Effect of the Statutory Charge on Legally Aided Matrimonial Litigation' (1993) 109 LQR 636 and 'Avoiding the Charge: Legally Aided Matrimonial Disputes' [1992] Fam Law 392.

'recovered or preserved'.[13] Periodical payments are expressly exempted from this charge, as is the first £2,500 of any lump sum or property adjustment order.[14] In effect, therefore, the Legal Aid Board is entitled to recover its costs out of lump sums, property adjustment orders or proceeds of sale insofar as in the first two instances they exceed £2,500 and in any event can be regarded as property 'recovered or preserved'. Given the high costs of proceedings, this charge can be substantial. In *Hanlon v Hanlon*,[15] for example, where the matrimonial home with an equity worth £10,000 was transferred to the wife, the wife's legal aid costs amounted to £8,025. The courts have, on more than one occasion, warned advisers to explain to their clients the folly of protracted argument and litigation.[16]

In cases where the matrimonial home is transferred to the legally aided party, the charge arises and vests in the Legal Aid Board and may be enforced as a charging order.[17] The Civil Legal Aid (General) Regulations 1989, Part XI,[18] provide that enforcement may be deferred on condition that, from the date of registration of the charge, simple interest at 10.5 per cent per annum will accrue for the benefit of the Legal Aid Board[19] where:

(1) in the case of *money* recovered or preserved the order or agreement made provides for its use by the assisted person for the purpose of purchasing a home for himself or his dependants;[20] or

(2) in the case of *property* recovered or preserved the order or agreement provides that it is to be used as a home for the assisted person or his dependants.[1]

---

13 See *Parkes v Legal Aid Board* [1997] 1 FLR 77, CA where the Court of Appeal held the Legal Aid Board's charge applied to property co-owned by two unmarried parents. A compromise was reached whereby the female cohabitant would remain in the house with her child until certain events occurred, whereupon it would be sold and the proceeds divided between the parties. The Court of Appeal upheld the decision of the lower court that the obtaining, by the female cohabitant, of an exclusive right of occupation against her former cohabitant amounted to a 'recovery', so that the charge attached to her interest in the property.

14 Civil Legal Aid (General) Regulations 1989 reg 94(c)(d)(i). Note that, in relation to the court's power to 'earmark' pensions under the Pensions Act 1995 s 166, 'deferred' maintenance orders will (like periodical payments orders) be exempt from the operation of the statutory charge. Subject to the £2,500 exemption, the charge will operate in relation to lump sums unless the particular pension involved is not capable of being assigned or charged. Note, too, that the Legal Aid Act 1988 s 13c (as inserted by the Family Law Act 1988 s 28) sets out provisions to enable regulations to be made for the imposition of the statutory charge in relation to any property recovered or preserved as a result of mediation.

15 [1978] 2 All ER 889, CA. See also *Stewart v Law Society* [1987] 1 FLR 223, where costs amounted to £4,600 in a case where a wife was awarded £7,000 in full and final settlement of her rights to receive and claim periodical payments. As was pointed out in a commentary on that case (at [1987] Fam Law 53), the wife lost £1,820 annually (the value of the original periodical payments order) for a single payment of £2,400.

16 For example in *Anthony v Anthony* [1986] 2 FLR 353, CA at 355 per Parker LJ, and *Mason v Mason* [1986] 2 FLR 212 at 223–4 per Purchas LJ. For the statement of the duty of practitioners to advise their clients on the impact of costs and the incidence of the Legal Aid Board's charge, see *Evans v Evans* [1990] 1 FLR 319, sub nom *Practice Note* [1990] 1 WLR 575n.

17 Civil Legal Aid (General) Regulations 1989 reg 95.

18 First introduced as the Legal Aid (General) (Amendment) (No 2) Regulations 1988.

19 Civil Legal Aid (General) Regulations 1989 reg 96(3)(b) and reg 97(4). The rate of interest payable on postponement of the charge was reduced, with effect from 1 January 1992, from 12 per cent per annum to 10.5 per cent by the Civil Legal Aid (General) (Amendment) (No 3) Regulations 1991 reg 4.

20 Ibid, reg 96 – thereby reversing the effect of the decisions referred to in n 15 above.

1 Ibid, reg 97.

If money recovered or preserved has not been used within one year of the date of the order or agreement, the assisted person's solicitor must pay it to the Legal Aid Board.[2] The substitution of another property, in place of that originally charged, is permissible, provided that the assisted person agrees to comply with certain conditions, including the execution of a registered charge in respect of the substituted property in favour of the Legal Aid Board, and the payment of interest.[3] In *Scallon v Scallon*[4] it was held that a court may assume that the Legal Aid Board will exercise its statutory discretion to defer enforcement of the charge, so as not to frustrate the purpose of the court order.

The ambit of the Legal Aid Board's statutory charge is both wide and at times bizarre. It has been held to apply, for example, to a lump sum payment in commutation and in full and final settlement of a spouse's rights to claim and receive periodical payments,[5] and to the obtaining of possession of an amount representing the share of the matrimonial home, even though title had not been in issue and the final order was a consent order.[6] In another case,[7] where both parties were legally aided and an order was made dividing the proceeds of the matrimonial home equally, the charge only attached to the husband's share because he had successfully resisted his wife's claim for a larger share, whereas it did not attach to the wife's share since the husband had made no claim to it.

Although it is clear that the existence of the charge can materially alter the effect or even destroy the intention of orders, it seems established that the court is not allowed to compensate for this (even where the higher costs are attributable to one side's intransigence) by making a larger award than would be the case had the parties' needs been considered without reference to the charge.[8] On the other hand, it would seem proper to make a different *type* of order if that would be a more efficient use of the parties' resources, such as a property transfer order rather than a lump sum order.[9]

---

2 Ibid, reg 96(6).
3 Ibid, reg 98.
4 [1990] 1 FLR 194, CA. It will be appreciated that the regulations require that the agreement or court order must *expressly provide* that the money or property be used for a *specific purpose*, namely the purchase or use of a home for the assisted person or his dependants. A court order in these terms was approved, without judicial comment, by the Court of Appeal in *Scallon v Scallon*, although there appears to be no express authority for making such an order in Part II of the Matrimonial Causes Act 1973.
5 *Stewart v Law Society* [1987] 1 FLR 223; *Watkinson v Legal Aid Board* [1991] 2 All ER 953, CA.
6 *Curling v Law Society* [1985] 1 All ER 705, CA.
7 *Parry v Parry* [1986] 2 FLR 96, CA.
8 *Parry v Parry* (supra) and *Collins v Collins* [1987] 1 FLR 226, CA. Sed quaere whether the potential liability could be regarded as a potential liability within the meaning of s 25(2)(b) of the Matrimonial Causes Act 1973 (discussed post, p 833): see the comment at [1987] Fam Law 53. The decision in *Collins v Collins* appears to have been overlooked by Anthony Lincoln J in *B v B (Real Property: Assessment of Interest)* [1988] 2 FLR 490, where he expressly enlarged the award of a lump sum to a wife 'to allow for the legal aid charge'.
9 Or a periodical payments order instead of a lump sum order – see eg *Anthony v Anthony* [1986] 2 FLR 353, CA. Lawyers must not try and manipulate the destination of money payable to an assisted person so as to avoid the statutory charge: *Manley v Law Society* [1981] 1 All ER 401; *Clark v Clark* [1989] 1 FLR 174. A solicitor owes a duty of care to the Legal Aid Fund, and the court has an inherent jurisdiction to order a solicitor personally to pay costs to the Legal Aid Fund where it has suffered loss as a result of the solicitor's serious dereliction of duty: *Clark v Clark (No 2)* [1991] 1 FLR 179, CA.

10.   THE LIMITS OF THE COURT'S POWER

Although the powers to redistribute spouses' property upon divorce etc are extremely wide, they are not unlimited. One obvious limitation is that the court has no power over property that does not belong to either of the spouses. It cannot order the sale of the matrimonial home which is owned by someone else as, for example, where the parties live in tied accommodation.[10] Similarly, there is no power to order the transfer of a spouse's interest under a discretionary trust,[11] though the existence of the interest can be taken into account in determining that spouse's needs.[12] The court must, however, look at the reality of the situation. If a spouse enjoys access to wealth through eg a discretionary trust or a family company, the court may make an order which will offer judicious encouragement to the third party to put the spouse in a financial position to satisfy its terms.[13] But the court must not place any improper pressure upon the trustees to exercise their discretion in such a way as they would not otherwise have thought right.[14]

The court also has no power to make an order against a third party, so no order should be made which will effectively have to be paid out of a spouse's new partner's capital or income, though that partner's assets are relevant to the extent that they relieve the spouse's needs.[15] A further consequence of this is that the court will not make an order against a limited company in which one or both of the spouses hold shares,[16] although this will not be the case where the company may be regarded as the spouse's 'alter ego', where he owns or controls all its shares, or a majority of them in circumstances where minority shareholdings may be disregarded.[17]

A further limitation of the court's powers is that the relief granted must come within the terms of the Matrimonial Causes Act 1973. In *Milne v Milne*,[18] for instance, it was held that there was no power to order a husband to take out an insurance policy to make capital provision for his wife because the Act only empowers payments to be made to a spouse or child of the family and not to a third party. It has been similarly held that there is no power to order one party to pay out

---

10 Exceptionally, where one or both of the spouses own property together with a third party, the court will have to determine the parties' respective beneficial entitlements before it can exercise its adjustive powers: see *Harwood v Harwood* [1991] 2 FLR 274, CA. Compare *Lloyds Bank plc v Semmakie* [1993] 1 FLR 34, CA, where the question of the extent of a spouse's beneficial interest arose *after* ancillary relief proceedings. In ancillary relief proceedings, the court held the wife had a half-share beneficial interest in the former matrimonial home. The husband's bank later commenced possession proceedings and the Court of Appeal held the wife was not subsequently estopped from claiming more than a one-half share: there was no privity between the wife and the bank in terms of the earlier matrimonial proceedings.
11 See ante, pp 797.
12 *Browne v Browne* [1989] 1 FLR 291, CA.
13 *Thomas v Thomas* [1995] 2 FLR 668, CA.
14 *Howard v Howard* [1945] P 1; see also *J v J (C Intervening)* [1989] Fam 29.
15 *Macey v Macey* (1981) 3 FLR 7, and *Brown v Brown* (1981) 3 FLR 161. See further post, p 833.
16 *Crittenden v Crittenden* [1990] 2 FLR 361, CA (no statutory power to order a company, whose issued shares were held by the spouses, to sell its assets and goodwill, or to require the husband to enter into a covenant not to compete with a proposed purchaser).
17 *Green v Green* [1993] 1 FLR 326 following *Nicholas v Nicholas* [1984] FLR 285, CA.
18 (1981) 2 FLR 286, CA. See also *Standley v Stewkesbury* [1998] Fam Law 397, CA where a consent order included provision for H to buy W a new car every three years; H claimed the agreement should have included an additional clause terminating this obligation in the event of W's remarriage or cohabitation. Held: agreement to be rectified accordingly, but quaere whether the consent order should have included such a clause at all?

of the proceeds of sale of the matrimonial home the debts of either party which were unconnected to the interest in the property.[19]

At first sight these latter limitations may seem an unfortunate gap in the court's powers, particularly as in some cases, in order to do justice between the parties, a complete restructuring of their financial affairs may be required.[20] However, as we have seen,[1] in practice this type of restructuring can be achieved by the parties giving binding undertakings to the court or on a Tomlin order.[2]

C. Financial relief after foreign divorce, annulment or legal separation[3]

1. BACKGROUND TO THE LEGISLATION

Formerly, the court could only make financial provision or property adjustment orders under the Matrimonial Causes Act 1973 in the course of divorce, nullity or judicial separation proceedings instituted in England and Wales. This meant that spouses who had been divorced, or whose marriage had been annulled, abroad could not seek such relief from the English divorce courts.[4] Though logical, this rule could nevertheless cause hardship, particularly to those who were habitually resident in England and Wales and who, having been divorced abroad, sometimes without their knowledge,[5] had no other means of redress.[6] Responding to pleas for reform,[7] the Law Commission[8] recommended widening the jurisdiction of the

---

19 *Burton v Burton* [1986] 2 FLR 419, and *Mullard v Mullard* (1981) 3 FLR 330. See also *Livesey (formerly Jenkins) v Jenkins* [1985] AC 424, [1985] 1 All ER 106, HL (wife agreeing to be solely responsible for discharging a bank overdraft and for mortgage repayments – held to be outside the court's powers to order: see ante, p 807). There appears to be no power to order a spouse to use money or property for a *designated purpose*. However, as was noted earlier (at p 809), such an order appears to be *required* under the regulations relating to the postponement of the statutory charge, and an order in those terms was approved, sub silentio, by the Court of Appeal in *Scallon v Scallon* [1990] 1 FLR 194, CA. Similarly, there is no express statutory power to require a spouse to execute a charge over the former matrimonial home, although such orders appear to be frequently made in practice. See eg *Barber v Barber* [1993] 1 FLR 476, CA and *M v M (Property Adjustment: Impaired Life Expectancy)* [1993] 2 FLR 723, CA. See further Bird 'Problems in Ancillary Relief Orders' [1990] Fam Law 421 and the discussion post at p 848.

20 See the comment at [1986] Fam Law 331.

1 Ante, p 807.

2 For a common use of an undertaking, whereby one spouse indemnifies the other against mortgage payments due on the former matrimonial home, see Roberts 'Property Adjustment Orders and Negative Equity' [1993] Fam Law 351.

3 See generally Canton 'The Matrimonial and Family Proceedings Act 1984: Financial Relief After Foreign Divorce' [1985] Fam Law 13 and Gordon 'Part III of the MFPA 1984: A Panacea for Foreign Divorcees?' [1986] JSWL 329.

4 Similarly, since they were no longer married, they could not seek maintenance under the Matrimonial Causes Act 1973 s 27, or under the Domestic Proceedings and Magistrates' Courts Act 1978.

5 As could happen, for example, where divorce by talaq is permitted. See also *Lamagni v Lamagni* [1995] 2 FLR 452, CA where an English wife obtained a divorce decree in England without knowledge that her Italian husband had earlier obtained a divorce in proceedings in Belgium.

6 See eg *Torok v Torok* [1973] 3 All ER 101 and *Quazi v Quazi* [1980] AC 744, [1979] 3 All ER 897, HL.

7 Not least by the Law Lords in *Quazi v Quazi*, supra.

8 Law Com No 117 *Financial Relief after Foreign Divorce* (1982).

divorce courts to give redress to such applicants. These recommendations were enacted in the Matrimonial and Family Proceedings Act 1984, Part III, which came into force in 1985.[9] Jurisdiction is vested in the Family Division of the High Court and any county court designated by the Lord Chancellor.[10]

2.   WHEN RELIEF MAY BE SOUGHT

Under s 12(1) of the 1984 Act, where a marriage has been dissolved or annulled, or the parties to the marriage are legally separated, by means of judicial or other proceedings in an overseas country, and the divorce, annulment or legal separation is entitled to be recognised as valid in England and Wales,[11] then either party may apply to the court for financial relief. It will be noted that under this provision:

(1)   The divorce etc must have been granted in an 'overseas country', which means a country or territory outside the British Islands.[12] Hence, for example, a spouse who has been divorced in Scotland cannot, under these provisions, subsequently seek financial relief in the English court.

(2)   The divorce etc must have been by means of 'judicial or other proceedings'. The phrase 'other proceedings' is intended to cover cases where the marriage has been terminated extra-judicially, for example by talaq.[13] This view would seem to be in line with the House of Lords' interpretation in *Quazi v Quazi*[14] of the similarly worded provision in the Recognition of Divorces and Legal Separations Act 1971 s 2(a).[15]

(3)   It is established that Part III is retrospective and that therefore applicants whose marriage was dissolved etc before Part III came into force may apply for relief.[16]

(4)   Provided the above criteria are satisfied, *either* party may apply for relief.

(5)   A party who has been legally separated abroad can apply for relief even though he may be able to petition for divorce etc in an English court.

(6)   A party who remarries (but not the other party) loses the right to apply for relief.[17]

3.   APPLICANTS ARE REQUIRED TO OBTAIN LEAVE

Procedure

Before any substantive claim may be made, applicants must first obtain the court's leave to make an application for a financial order. The court cannot grant

---

9   The 1984 Act is amended by Family Law Act 1996 Sch 8, paras 32 and 52, essentially to reflect the amendments made to the Matrimonial Causes Act 1973 by the 1996 Act.

10   Section 27, s 33(4) and s 34(1)(b) of the 1984 Act.

11   For a discussion of the rules of recognition see eg Cheshire and North *Private International Law* (12th edn, 1992 by North and Fawcett).

12   Matrimonial and Family Proceedings Act 1984 s 27. British Islands means England and Wales, Scotland, Northern Ireland, the Isle of Man and the Channel Islands: Interpretation Act 1978 Sch 1.

13   See Law Com, op cit, at p 21 in their explanatory notes on clause 1 of their draft Bill.

14   [1980] AC 744, [1979] 3 All ER 897, HL.

15   But cf the arguments of Gordon, op cit, at pp 336–8.

16   *Chebaro v Chebaro* [1987] Fam 127, [1987] 1 All ER 999, CA.

17   Matrimonial and Family Proceedings Act 1984 s 12(2). The right is lost even if the subsequent marriage is void or voidable: s 12(3).

leave unless it considers that there is a substantial ground for making the application and that there is jurisdiction to make the order.[18] In *Holmes v Holmes*,[19] the Court of Appeal held that this requirement means that a court, in considering whether to grant leave, must take into account the statutory criteria contained in s 16 (discussed below) which apply in relation to the determination of the substantive application. If it is clear that, if leave were given, the application must founder 'at the first hurdle of s 16(1)' then it would be wrong to grant leave. Applications for leave are made ex parte and should be accompanied by an affidavit stating the facts relied upon and the grounds upon which it is alleged the court has jurisdiction.[20] Leave may be granted notwithstanding that an order has been made by a court outside England and Wales requiring the respondent to make financial provision for, or to transfer property to, the applicant or a child of the family.[1]

In *Hewitson v Hewitson*[2] the Court of Appeal held that the mischief the 1984 Act was designed to redress was a narrow one: to give the English courts power to entertain applications for financial provision where no, or no sufficient, relief had been awarded abroad. The Act is not intended to provide an applicant with 'two bites at the one cherry',[3] or to invite the English courts to act as a court of appeal from the courts of other countries. On the facts, the Court of Appeal found the parties' claims to ancillary relief had been settled by a final clean break order in California. The Court refused leave, even though the wife argued that after the divorce the parties had resumed cohabitation as a result of which she was left in a parlous financial position. In *Lamagni v Lamagni*[4] leave was granted when the wife had not received any financial order at all in any court, even though there was a delay of 13 years since the divorce, and much of the delay was caused by her lawyers' inability to get her case off the ground. Where the court grants leave, it may impose such conditions as it thinks fit.[5]

The requirement to obtain leave is intended to filter applications whilst at the same time providing maximum protection for all those concerned. The idea of the ex parte procedure is to save the potential respondent the time and expense of being involved in the case before the bona fides of the application have been tested. Given the one-sided nature of the application, there are those that doubt

---

18 Ibid, s 13(1) and s 15.
19 [1989] Fam 47, [1989] 3 All ER 786, CA. See also *M v M (Financial Provision after Foreign Divorce)* [1994] 1 FLR 399. The burden of showing that there are substantial grounds for granting leave falls on the applicant: *Z v Z (Financial Provision: Overseas Divorce)* [1992] 2 FLR 291. However, if leave is granted ex parte, it does not follow that the onus is then transferred to the other party to establish that leave should not have been granted or continued: *N v N (Foreign Divorce: Financial Relief)* [1997] 1 FLR 900.
20 Family Proceedings Rules 1991 r 3.18. It seems that the court has a discretion to allow the potential respondent to be heard, at any rate, where objection is taken to jurisdiction: *Chebaro v Chebaro* [1986] Fam 71 at 72, [1986] 2 All ER 897 at 898 per Sheldon J at first instance. The affidavit should pay particular reference to the matters set out in s 16(1) of the 1984 Act: see below.
1 1984 Act s 13(2), though this is a factor to be taken into account in deciding whether to make an order: s 16(2), discussed below. The reference to a court outside England and Wales means that there is jurisdiction even if a court in another part of the United Kingdom has made an order. This could happen, for example, where the divorce takes place abroad, the applicant is domiciled in Scotland and the matrimonial home is in England.
2 [1995] 1 FLR 241, CA.
3 *Lamagni v Lamagni* [1995] 2 FLR 452, CA at 454 (per Butler-Sloss LJ).
4 Ibid.
5 1984 Act s 13(3).

whether the potential respondent is well protected by this procedure.[6] It is, however, essential for a judge hearing the ex parte application to have all the material facts before him to consider whether a substantial ground exists for the making of the order and in order to estimate the applicant's prospects of success. If the applicant fails to make a full and frank disclosure of all relevant facts, then the leave granted ex parte will be set aside.[7]

Jurisdiction

Before leave may be granted, the court must be satisfied that there is jurisdiction to make the order.[8] Subject to the provisions of the Civil Jurisdiction and Judgments Act 1982 (discussed below) the court has jurisdiction if:

(a) either party to the marriage was domiciled in England and Wales on the date of the application for leave or when the divorce, nullity or legal separation took effect; or

(b) either party was habitually resident there throughout the period of one year ending on the date of the application for leave or when the divorce etc took effect; or

(c) either or both parties had at the date of the application for leave a beneficial interest in possession[9] in a dwelling house[10] situated in England and Wales which was at some time during the marriage a matrimonial home of the parties to the marriage.[11]

If jurisdiction is taken on the last basis, the court's powers are more limited.[12]

In cases where Part I of the Civil Jurisdiction and Judgments Act 1982 (by which the United Kingdom has implemented the Brussels Convention on the enforcement of civil and commercial judgments) applies,[13] jurisdiction is determined by the rules of that Act rather than the 1984 Act. Effectively this increases jurisdiction, since under the Convention in matters relating to maintenance[14] a person who is domiciled in one Contracting State may be sued in the court of the place where the maintenance creditor is domiciled or habitually resident or, in the case of ancillary proceedings, in the court of the State which by its own law has jurisdiction to hear the divorce etc.[15]

---

6 See eg Scot Law Com No 72, para 2.13. Quaere whether the procedure would be improved by allowing potential respondents to be heard if they so desired; cf *Chebaro v Chebaro*, supra. See also *Hewitson v Hewitson* (supra) where, at 245, Butler-Sloss LJ considered '. . . the procedure for leave under s 13 might be usefully reviewed'.
7 *W v W (Financial Provision)* [1989] 1 FLR 22.
8 Pursuant to s 15(1) of the 1984 Act.
9 This includes the receipt of or the right to receive rent or profits: s 27.
10 This includes any building or part thereof which is occupied as a dwelling, and any yard, garden, garage or outhouse belonging to the dwelling-house and occupied therewith: s 27.
11 This latter requirement implies that the married parties must have lived together in the property in question.
12 Under s 20: see below.
13 Part I of the 1982 Act came into force in January 1987.
14 This expression is not without its difficulties (see Law Com, op cit, para 2.11), but it may include lump sum orders: see *Van Den Boogaard v Laumen*, a decision of the European Court of Justice reported at [1997] 2 FLR 399, and discussed ante at p 792 n 16.
15 This explanation is taken from that of the Law Commission, op cit, para 2.11. For a detailed account of the Brussels Convention see eg Cheshire and North, op cit.

Interim orders

Once leave has been granted, then, save where jurisdiction has been taken solely upon the matrimonial home basis, and provided that it appears to the court that the applicant or any child of the family is in need of immediate financial assistance, the court may make an interim order for maintenance.[16]

4. APPLYING FOR AN ORDER

Once leave has been granted, application may be made for financial relief.[17] It should be stressed that the granting of leave does not ipso facto mean that an order will be made. Indeed, before an order will be made the court must consider whether in all the circumstances it is appropriate for an English court to do so.[18] In deciding that issue the court is directed[19] to have regard to a number of matters:

- the connection the parties have with England and Wales;
- the connection the parties have with the country in which the marriage was dissolved etc and any other country outside England and Wales;
- any financial benefit which the applicant or any child of the family has received or is likely to receive in consequence of any agreement or operation of law of a country outside England and Wales;
- if any overseas order has been made, the extent to which it has been or is likely to be complied with;
- what rights the applicant has to apply for financial relief in a country outside England and Wales and, if an application was not pursued, the reasons why;
- the availability of property in England and Wales;
- the extent to which an order made here is likely to be enforceable, and the length of time since the divorce etc has been granted.

It can be seen that these considerations are designed to test whether the parties have any real connection with England and Wales; whether adequate relief has been or could be obtained elsewhere, and whether in any event it would be worthwhile making an order here.[20] Purchas LJ said in *Holmes v Holmes*[1] that the requirements in s 16 reflect the fundamental rule of comity as between competent courts dealing with matters of this kind. The Court of Appeal stressed that an English court must always be slow to interfere with the competent court seized of the matter, which has made orders which are clearly enforceable, and which has dealt with the matter on a reasonably careful assessment of all its features.[2]

---

16 Section 14 of the 1984 Act. Under this provision the court may order the respondent to make periodical payments to the applicant or any child of the family for such term as the court thinks fit but beginning no earlier than the date of the grant of leave and ending with the date of the determination of the application for the order.

17 For the procedure, see the Family Proceedings Rules 1991 r 3.18.

18 Section 16(1) of the 1984 Act.

19 By s 16(2).

20 See *N v N (Foreign Divorce: Financial Relief)* [1997] 1 FLR 900 where Cazalet J, in setting aside an ex parte leave obtained by the husband, considered that the parties, who were both Swedish nationals and had been divorced in Sweden, had their main connection with that country which '... would outweigh the other considerations arising under s 16 such that the court would not regard it as appropriate for an order to be made [in England]'.

1 [1989] Fam 47 at 53, [1989] 3 All ER 786, CA at 791.

2 Which reflects the decisions in relation to the grant of leave referred to earlier (see ante, p 813).

5.   ORDERS THAT MAY BE MADE

Provided it is satisfied that it should make an order, the court has the same powers (save where jurisdiction is taken on the matrimonial home basis) as under the Matrimonial Causes Act 1973, Part II, viz: it can make periodical payments or lump sum orders, property transfer orders and orders for the sale of property.[3] In deciding what orders to make the court must have regard to the same considerations as it would when dealing with a domestic application,[4] though in addition it must consider the extent to which any overseas order has been or is likely to be complied with.[5]

Where jurisdiction is assumed on the matrimonial home basis, the court's powers are confined to making orders concerning that property or to making lump sum orders not exceeding the paying party's interest in it.[6]

There are also similar provisions to domestic proceedings for dealing with consent orders[7] and for variation and discharge.[8]

In addition to the above powers, the court may, provided leave has been given, make such orders as it thinks fit restraining any disposition about to be made with the intention of defeating the claim for financial relief or setting aside any such disposition already made.[9] This power can be exercised even where the jurisdictional requirements are not satisfied, provided the court is satisfied that the marriage has been dissolved etc abroad and that the applicant intends to apply for leave for financial relief as soon as he has been habitually resident in England and Wales for one year.[10]

D.   Assessment of financial provision

1.   GENERAL PRINCIPLES

Following the reform of the law in 1971, the general principles to be applied when the court is making an order for financial provision or the adjustment of property rights on divorce, nullity or judicial separation were contained in s 5 of the Matrimonial Proceedings and Property Act 1970 and re-enacted in s 25 of the Matrimonial Causes Act 1973. As the Act of 1970 was a reforming statute which had introduced a new code, cases decided before 1971 were to be applied only insofar as they laid down common-sense principles.[11]

Section 25 remained unamended for over a decade, though by no means

---

3 Section 17 as substituted by Family Law Act 1996 Sch 8, para 32.
4 Section 18(1)–(5).
5 Section 18(6).
6 Section 20.
7 Orders can be made in the terms agreed on the basis only of prescribed information furnished with the application: s 19.
8 Section 21 as amended by Family Law Act 1996 Sch 8, para 32.
9 Section 23. Where jurisdiction is taken upon the matrimonial home basis, the court's powers are confined to restraining or setting aside dispositions of the property: s 23(4). See also s 37 of the 1973 Act, discussed post, pp 861–4.
10 Section 24.
11 *Wachtel v Wachtel* [1973] Fam 72 at 91, [1973] 1 All ER 829, CA at 836; cf *Trippas v Trippas* [1973] Fam 134 at 144, [1973] 2 All ER 1, CA at 7.

everyone was happy with its principles or underlying assumption.[12] In 1980, however, much wider discussion was stimulated when the Law Commission published a discussion paper questioning the basic policy of the then law.[13] In the following year the Law Commission published their final report,[14] in which they concluded that on the material available to them[15] radical change in the law could not be justified.[16] Instead they recommended that there should be changes in emphasis in the way in which the court's discretionary powers should be exercised, such changes being 'evolutionary rather than revolutionary'.[17]

Following the Law Commission's recommendations, the Matrimonial and Family Proceedings Act 1984 introduced three changes in the ways that courts are directed to exercise their powers and these changes remain substantially unaffected by the Family Law Act 1996. They can be summarised as being:

(1) the removal of the status quo ideal or minimal loss principle;
(2) giving priority to the welfare of any child of the family; and
(3) placing greater emphasis on the parties becoming self-sufficient.

The removal of the status quo ideal or minimal loss principle

Under s 25, as originally enacted, the court was directed, as its overall object, to have regard to all the circumstances of the case and so to exercise its powers 'as to place the parties, so far as it is practicable and, having regard to their conduct, just to do so, in the financial position in which they would have been if the marriage had not broken down and each had properly discharged his or her financial obligations and responsibilities towards the other'. In most cases this objective or target (variously referred to as the status quo ideal or the minimal loss principle)[18] was impossible to achieve, since few, if any, can afford to support two households at the same standard as the former one. One judge[19] described it as 'an elusive concept based on a difficult hypothesis', while one commentator[20] criticised it as being 'the mandate of restitution . . . misconceived [and] . . . almost always incapable of fulfilment'.

---

12 See in particular the discussion by Gray *Reallocation of Property on Divorce* (1977). See also Eekelaar *Family Law and Social Policy* (2nd edn, 1984) ch 6; Deech 'The Principles of Maintenance' (1977) Fam Law 229 (in turn criticised by O'Donovan 'The Principles of Maintenance; An Alternative View' (1978) Fam Law 180).

13 Law Com No 103 (*The Financial Consequences of Divorce: the Basic Policy*).

14 Law Com No 112 (*The Financial Consequences of Divorce, The Response to the Discussion Paper*). For an interesting account of the Law Commission's role in promoting reform, see Cretney 'Money After Divorce – The Mistakes We Have Made?' in Freeman (ed) *Essays In Family Law* (1985) pp 34–42. For a commentary on the two Law Commission papers see Deech 'Financial Relief: the Retreat from Precedent and Principle' (1982) 98 LQR 621 at 639–52; Eekelaar and O'Donovan 'Law Commission Reports on the Financial Consequences of Divorce' (1982) 45 MLR at 420 and 424 respectively.

15 The Law Commission were concerned at the general absence of empirical information about the working of divorce law and recommended (Law Com No 112 at para 46) that provision be made for monitoring any amending legislation. This recommendation was not implemented. For empirical research on the financial consequences of divorce, see Eekelaar and Maclean *Maintenance after Divorce* (1986); Maclean and Eekelaar *The Parental Obligation* (1997) ch 7.

16 Law Com No 112, para 11, but see the criticisms of Symes 'Indissolubility and the Clean Break' (1985) 48 MLR 44.

17 Law Com No 112, para 23.

18 See eg Eekelaar *Family Law and Social Policy* (2nd edn, 1984) p 109.

19 Bagnall J in *Harnett v Harnett* [1973] Fam 156 at 161, [1973] 2 All ER 593 at 598.

20 Gray, op cit, at p 319.

It was implicit in the status quo principle that a spouse had a right to life-long support from the other spouse even after divorce, but in their Discussion Paper the Law Commission questioned whether such a principle could any longer be justified, given, inter alia, the change to irretrievable breakdown as the basis of divorce, the impossibility in most cases of attaining the objective, and the changed economic role of women. The responses received by the Law Commission were overwhelmingly of the view that the status quo directive was no longer appropriate. Accordingly, in their final report, the Commission felt able to recommend its removal.

Although at first sight it seems odd not to have statutory guidance on the basic objective for the redistribution of resources after divorce,[1] it may be pointed out that even before the removal of the basic objective, the courts regarded themselves as being vested with very flexible and wide-ranging powers and that therefore even Court of Appeal decisions should be regarded as guidelines rather than precedents.[2]

Another possible effect of the removal of the status quo objective is that it must in theory be harder for a spouse to claim a share in the other's future income or capital, at any rate where there is an unexpected increase in wealth after the divorce. Whereas under the former law it could simply have been argued that had the marriage not broken down the spouse would have had a share in that newly acquired wealth,[3] under the current law any claim will have to be based upon the claimant's reasonable needs. This is not to say that future income or capital is irrelevant. On the contrary, as will be seen, it is a factor that the courts are expressly enjoined to take into account, since it will obviously be relevant to determining the future needs of the parties and of their ability to meet those needs.

Treating the welfare of any child of the family as the first consideration

As we have said, with the removal of the status quo objective the court no longer has an overall statutory target. Instead, under s 25(1) of the Matrimonial Causes Act 1973[4] the court is directed, when considering whether to exercise its powers and, if so, in what manner:

'... to have regard to all the circumstances of the case, first consideration being given to the welfare while a minor of any child of the family who has not attained the age of eighteen.'

It will be observed that the court is required to give first and not paramount consideration to the welfare of any child of the family. This means, as was emphasised in *Suter v Suter and Jones*,[5] that the child's welfare is not the

---

1 Contrast the approach of the Scottish Law Commission: Scot Law Com No 67 (*Report on Aliment and Financial Relief*) para 3.37. The government's Ancillary Relief Advisory Group is considering whether the Scottish principles of fair (ie equal) shares of matrimonial assets should be introduced into English law: [1998] Fam Law 381, discussed further post, p 866.
2 See *Chamberlain v Chamberlain* [1974] 1 All ER 33, CA at 38, per Scarman LJ; *Sharpe v Sharpe* (1981) Times, 17 February, CA, per Ormrod LJ; and *White v White* [1998] 2 FLR 310, CA.
3 Compare *Trippas v Trippas* [1973] Fam 134, [1973] 2 All ER 1, CA, where after the divorce the husband sold his business and thereby freed his capital and was ordered to pay his wife a lump sum, inter alia because, had they remained married, the wife would have had a 'good chance of receiving financial benefit on the sale of the business.'
4 As amended by the Matrimonial and Family Proceedings Act 1984 s 3 and further by the Family Law Act 1996 Sch 8, para 9.
5 [1987] Fam 111, [1987] 2 All ER 336, CA; cf *Anthony v Anthony* [1986] 2 FLR 353, CA, where not all the children's interests were necessarily identical.

overriding consideration, though of course it is an important one.[6]

It should also be noted that priority is only accorded to children of the family[7] and not, for example, to any children of the spouses' second families, though a spouse's obligation to the second family is a relevant consideration in deciding what order to make.[8] It might be added that not even all children of the family are necessarily accorded priority. Where, for example, the child is not that of the husband, then even if he has 'treated' the child as one of the family he is not ipso facto liable to maintain him. In determining this the court is directed by s 25(4) of the Matrimonial Causes Act[9] to have regard:

'(a) to whether that party assumed any responsibility for the child's maintenance, and, if so, to the extent to which, and the basis upon which, that party assumed such responsibility and to the length of time for which that party discharged such responsibility;
(b) to whether in assuming and discharging such responsibility that party did so knowing that the child was not his or her own;
(c) to the liability of any other person to maintain the child.'

If the court decides that the husband is not liable[10] to maintain the child at all, then of course that child's welfare ceases to be of any relevance in that case.

It will be noted that priority is only to be given to the child's welfare during his minority. This reflects the previously well established principle that orders for children should be related to their dependency and should not, in the absence of special needs such as mental or physical handicap, provide for continuing support during adulthood.[11] In fact recent cases do show that the court is prepared to take a broader view, and (if not necessarily according priority) at least recognise that a child's needs, and the period of his dependency, do not necessarily come to an end on his eighteenth birthday, but may continue, for example, until he completes his university education or professional training. In *Richardson v Richardson (No 2)*[12] the Court of Appeal upheld the decision of Thorpe J,[13] who had set aside a consent order, and extended a periodical payment order in favour of the wife, so she could complete her responsibility for bringing up her two daughters whilst they were at college. As Thorpe J added:[14]

'In my judgment, the fact the children of the family are no longer minors is not decisive. What is decisive is that they are still dependent.'[15]

6 The statutory weighting is the same as, for instance, in the adoption legislation: see ante, p 625.
7 For a detailed discussion of the meaning of 'child of the family', see ante, pp 288–90.
8 See eg *Fisher v Fisher* [1989] 1 FLR 423, CA where the wife's responsibility to a child born after the marriage was dissolved was taken into account to increase a periodical payments order.
9 As amended by the Family Law Act 1996 Sch 8, para 9.
10 As in *W v W (Child of the Family)* [1984] FLR 796, CA, and *Leadbeater v Leadbeater* [1985] FLR 789.
11 See eg *Lilford v Glynn* [1979] 1 All ER 441, CA. It is on this basis that capital orders for children are not common: see *Kiely v Kiely* [1988] 1 FLR 248, CA; *Chamberlain v Chamberlain* [1974] 1 All ER 33, CA; cf *Griffiths v Griffiths* [1984] Fam 70, [1984] 2 All ER 626, CA; *A v A (A Minor: Financial Provision)* [1994] 1 FLR 657.
12 [1996] 2 FLR 617, CA.
13 [1994] 2 FLR 1051.
14 Ibid at 1054.
15 See also eg *Barber v Barber* [1993] 1 FLR 476, CA, where the Court of Appeal rejected the husband's submission that the court should only have regard to the children's' welfare whilst they were minors, and *B v B (Adult Student: Liability to Support)* [1998] 1 FLR 373, CA, where the father's argument that he should not be expected to support his daughter since she was receiving a full student maintenance grant was rejected in the light of the clear statutory recognition that support could be ordered under s 29 (and see ante, p 790).

Placing greater emphasis on the parties becoming self-sufficient

Inextricably bound up with the idea that it is no longer appropriate to have a right to life-long support from a former spouse is that of expecting the former spouses to become financially independent of each other wherever, and as soon as, possible after the divorce. The Law Commission found that there was widespread support for the view that the courts should be more clearly directed to the desirability of 'promoting the severance of financial obligations between the parties at the time of divorce' and to give greater weight to the view that periodical payments in favour of one spouse 'should be primarily directed to secure wherever possible a smooth transition from marriage to the status of independence'.[16]

Following the Commission's recommendations, the courts are now, pursuant to s 25A(1) of the Matrimonial Causes Act 1973,[17] under a *duty* in all cases (other than in relation to interim orders) to consider:

> '. . . whether it would be appropriate so to exercise those powers that the financial obligations of each party towards the other will be terminated as soon after the grant of a divorce order or decree of nullity as the court considers just and reasonable.'[18]

If a periodical payments order is thought appropriate, the court is directed by s 25A(2) to consider:

> '. . . whether it would be appropriate to require those payments to be made or secured only for such term as would in the opinion of the court be sufficient to enable the party in whose favour the order is made to adjust without undue hardship to the termination of his or her financial dependence on the other party.'

In effect, under s 25A(1) the court is directed to consider whether it can make an immediate 'clean break' order, ie an order which will settle once and for all the parties' financial liability to each other. If this is not thought possible, then under s 25A(2) the court is directed to consider whether it can nevertheless make a periodical payments order for a limited term rather than for an indefinite period. In order to achieve these objectives the court has been given the power under s 25A(3)[19] to impose a clean break order upon the parties, by which it is empowered to direct that one party may not apply for the making of a periodical payments order against the other or, if such an application is pending, to dismiss it without the applicant's consent.[20] Further, under s 28(1A)[1] the court may make a 'deferred clean break order' by directing that a party is not entitled to apply for an

---

16 Law Com No 112, para 30. The House of Lords had endorsed this view in *Minton v Minton* [1979] AC 593, [1979] 1 All ER 79.

17 Added by the Matrimonial and Family Proceedings Act 1984 s 3, as further amended by Family Law Act 1996 Sch 8, para 10.

18 It will be noted that the statutory duty does not apply to separation orders, since the marriage is not terminated.

19 As substituted by Family Law Act 1996 Sch 8, para 10 which changes the wording of s 25A(3) but with the same effect. The wording of the subsection as originally enacted provided that, if the court considered that no continuing obligation should be imposed *on either party* to make periodical payments in favour of the other, the court could dismiss the application with the direction that the applicant should not be entitled to make further application. Despite the ambiguity of the language, it was held that the court did have power to dismiss the claims of one party for periodical payments, while leaving those of the other alive: *Thompson v Thompson* [1988] 2 FLR 170.

20 It should be noted that there is no comparable power to dismiss an application for periodical payments to or for the benefit of any child of the family. There is no provision for a 'clean break' between parent and child: see *Crozier v Crozier* [1994] 1 FLR 126, discussed ante at p 739.

1 As amended by Family Law Act 1996 Sch 8, para 14.

extension of a fixed term periodical payments order.[2] In its most extended form, either type of clean break order will incorporate a declaration that neither party may make any further application for a lump sum or property adjustment order,[3] nor be entitled to apply for financial provision out of the other's estate under the Inheritance (Provision for Family and Dependants) Act 1975.[4]

(a)   Imposing an immediate clean break

Although the courts had previously been able to make clean break orders, until 1984 they could not do so against a spouse's will. It was not expected, however, that the new power would lead to a sudden increase in the number of clean break orders. For example, in his evidence to the Special Standing Committee on the 1984 Bill,[5] the President of the Family Division said that an immediate clean break would be:

'. . . entirely inappropriate in cases in which the wife has a continuing charge of young children, or where the marriage has been long and the wife has not worked during it or during the larger part of it and is middle aged at the time of the divorce.'

He added:

'. . . it would be equally inappropriate where the evidence suggests an impossibility in obtaining employment however well equipped for this purpose the spouse may be.'

Since the enactment of s 25A there have been a number of general judicial statements made about its effect. In *Harman v Glencross*,[6] for example, Balcombe LJ commented that the modern practice is to 'favour the clean break wherever possible'. In *B v B (Financial Provision)*[7] Ward J said that the primary object of the new law is to strive to make the parties self-sufficient. However, while emphasising the importance of s 25A, the higher courts have declined to offer any definitive guidance on how the statutory power is to be exercised. Indeed, in one of the few reported cases where a clean break was imposed against a spouse's will, namely *Seaton v Seaton*,[8] the Court of Appeal refused to lay down any general guidelines, in part because the facts of the case were so unusual. In that case the wife had borne the financial burden of the marriage after the husband lost his job and because of a drink problem could not subsequently obtain another. Eventually she left him and some time after the separation the husband suffered a stroke which left him with permanent disabilities. At the time of the divorce the husband

---

2 See also s 25(2)(a), discussed post, p 829 et seq, under which the court is directed to consider whether there is any increase in earning capacity which it is reasonable to expect a party to take steps to acquire.

3 The court may make such a declaration despite the absence of express statutory authority: *H v H (Financial Provision)* [1988] 2 FLR 114.

4 Inheritance (Provision for Family and Dependants) Act 1975 s 15 as amended by Matrimonial and Family Proceedings Act 1984 and the Family Law Act 1996 Sch 8, para 27, discussed post at p 901. The court will only make this order if it considers it just to do so. It must therefore have evidence as to the likely size of the spouse's estate and an indication of those who are likely to have claims upon it: *Whiting v Whiting* [1988] 2 All ER 275, CA. Note also *Cameron v Treasury Solicitor* [1997] 2 FLR 716, CA where it was suggested (in the context of a consent order) that a clean break order which did not bar claims under the 1975 Act would be so irregular as to suggest a fundamental drafting error.

5 HC Official Report, col 78, 22 March 1984.

6 [1986] 1 All ER 545, CA at 557.

7 [1990] 1 FLR 20 at 26.

8 [1986] 2 FLR 398, CA.

was living with his parents and because of his limited capacity to enjoy life his income, derived from his disability pension, was sufficient to meet his needs. It was held that in the circumstances it would be wrong to impose upon the wife a continuing obligation to support her husband and accordingly the husband's application for periodical payments was dismissed under s 25A(3).

A more significant decision, however, is *Suter v Suter and Jones*.[9] Earlier cases[10] seemed to have established that where there were children for whom the parties shared a continuing obligation there was, in the absence of capital resources, little or no scope for the parents to have a clean break from each other. According to *Suter*, however, these cases must be read subject to the enjoinder in s 25A. Hence, it was held to be wrong in that case for the judge not to consider the issue of the possible financial independence of the wife simply because there were dependent children. On the facts, it was held that the husband should pay periodical payments to his wife, albeit at the nominal rate of one pound a year.[11] The significance of a nominal order, as distinct from the court ordering a dismissal under s 25A(3) or making a direction under s 28(1A),[12] is that the recipient may apply subsequently for an upward variation if circumstances change. For the payee it provides a 'last backstop' against unforeseen contingencies or disasters in the future; but the payer is subject to the continuing risk that his financial liabilities may be increased in a later variation application.

In *Whiting v Whiting*[13] the judge at first instance accepted the 'last backstop' argument, and dismissed the husband's application to discharge a nominal periodical payment order in favour of the wife. The wife, after the divorce, had completed teacher training and at the time of the hearing was earning over £10,500 per annum. The husband had remarried, but had been made redundant and received less than £4,500 per annum as a self-employed consultant. The Court of Appeal unanimously indicated they would have reached a different decision, on the merits, from the judge. However, only Balcombe LJ (to whom the making of a nominal order 'negated entirely' the clean break principle) was prepared to allow the husband's appeal. The majority refused to overturn the judge's decision, on the basis that it was not 'clearly wrong'.[14] Slade LJ nonetheless stressed that the court's duty to consider imposing a clean break was real and substantial: the easy course of declining a clean break order would not always be the right one.[15]

In *Barrett v Barrett*[16] the Court of Appeal held that, although consideration of s 25A was mandatory, this does not mean the section should necessarily be given priority. The requirements of s 25A must be brought into balance with the specific factors in s 25,[17] and an immediate clean break imposed only if appropriate in the

---

9 [1987] Fam 111, [1987] 2 All ER 336, CA.
10 Viz *Pearce v Pearce* (1979) 1 FLR 261, CA, and *Moore v Moore* (1981) 11 Fam Law 108, CA.
11 Compare *Mortimer v Mortimer-Griffin* [1986] 2 FLR 315, CA, where a clean break order was made even though there were dependent children, but the fact that there were dependent children was not even commented upon in the Court of Appeal.
12 See post, p 823.
13 [1988] 2 All ER 275, CA at 287.
14 Applying *G v G (Minors: Custody Appeal)* [1985] 2 All ER 225, HL, in which it was held that an appellate court is only to interfere with the first instance judge's decision if satisfied that the judge has exceeded the generous ambit within which judicial disagreement was reasonably possible, or was otherwise 'plainly wrong'.
15 [1988] 2 All ER 275, CA at 287.
16 [1988] 2 FLR 516, CA.
17 Post, pp 829ff.

circumstances of a given case. This approach, which gives the court extended scope to exercise its broad statutory discretion, has been expressly approved in at least one later case,[18] and followed in several others.[19] In general, and despite one or two apparent inconsistencies in individual cases,[20] it remains true to say that the most obvious cases for imposing an immediate clean break are short childless marriages and those where there are adequate resources to cater for each spouse's reasonable needs.[1] In the latter case, particularly where there is evidence of bitterness between the parties, an immediate clean break may remove the tension which can be incidental to enduring financial dependence.[2] Even in cases which seem appropriate for the imposition of an immediate clean break, however, the individual merits need to be examined. For example, in *M v M (Property Adjustment: Impaired Life Expectancy)*,[3] a middle-aged wife had been diagnosed with a tumour and had a life expectancy of ten years which would restrict her earning capacity. It was held by the Court of Appeal that notwithstanding the parties' substantial assets, this could never be a clean break case.

(b) Making limited term orders or deferred clean break orders

Even before 1984 the courts had the power to order a limited term periodical payments order, but the *requirement* to consider whether such an order should be made was introduced in that year. Similarly, the power under s 28(1A) to make a deferred clean break order by adding the direction that no application can be made to extend the term provided for in an original periodical payments order was also introduced in 1984. It should be understood, however, that unless the court expressly adds a s 28(1A) direction, there is nothing to stop a spouse from returning to the court prior to the expiry of the term to ask that the term be extended.[4]

In considering whether to make a limited term order, the court is directed under s 25A(2) to consider whether the party in whose favour an order is made can adjust *without undue hardship* to the termination of financial dependence on the other

---

18 *Fisher v Fisher* [1989] 1 FLR 423, CA.
19 Such as *Hepburn v Hepburn* [1989] 1 FLR 373, CA; *B v B (Financial Provision)* [1990] 1 FLR 20.
20 See Wright 'Financial Provision, the Clean Break and the Search for Consistency' [1991] Fam Law 76.
1 'I have to say in my judgment that for a young or young middle aged wife in possession of substantial capital the idea of periodical payments for life is largely obsolescent': *C v C (Financial Provision)* [1989] 1 FLR 11 at 20 (per Ewbank J) and see *Attar v Attar (No 2)* [1985] FLR 653, *Preston v Preston* [1982] Fam 17, [1982] 1 All ER 41, CA; *Gojkovic v Gojkovic* [1992] Fam 40, [1990] 2 All ER 84, CA; *F v F (Duxbury Calculation: Rate of Return)* [1996] 1 FLR 833.
2 *CB v CB* [1988] Fam Law 471.
3 [1993] 2 FLR 723, CA.
4 In *Richardson v Richardson* [1994] 1 FLR 286 a consent order was made whereby the husband was to make periodical payments to the wife for three years. Although it was intended that the wife would not have the right to extend this term, the order did not expressly contain any direction under s 28(1A). Shortly before the three-year term expired the wife applied for an extension and it was held that the court could entertain the application. Compare *G v G (Periodical Payments: Jurisdiction)* [1997] 1 FLR 368, CA where the original order in favour of the wife limited the term of periodical payments to the date on which the youngest child attained 18, but did not include a s 28(1A) direction. The wife applied for an extension one month after the child's eighteenth birthday. The Court of Appeal, approving *T v T (Financial Provision)* [1988] 1 FLR 480, held it had no jurisdiction to extend the term. Ward LJ suggested that to avoid this situation in the future, one possibility would be to make a substantial periodical payments order for a term, followed by a nominal order which would 'give a peg on which to hang any later variation application'.

party. As was stressed in *Morris v Morris*,[5] this is a mandatory requirement needing specific evidence. It is unclear precisely what is meant by 'undue hardship' (though it is implicit that a party can expect some hardship), but it is evident that a limited term order and, a fortiori, a s 28(1A) direction should not be made upon some vague expectation that the dependent spouse will be able to obtain a job, nor should that spouse's potential earning capacity be unrealistically viewed. As was recognised eg in *M v M (Financial Provision)*,[6] the prospects of a middle-aged woman returning to the job market after several years' absence are far from good. As Ward LJ said in *Flavell v Flavell*:[7]

> 'There is, in my judgment, often a tendency for these [ie finite term] orders to be made more in hope than in serious expectation. Especially in judging the case of ladies in their middle years, the judicial looking into the crystal ball rarely finds enough of substance to justify a finding that adjustment can be made without undue hardship. All too often, these orders are made without evidence to support them.'

In the same way, if a wife has a young child, it may be appropriate to make a limited term order in her favour whilst she devotes herself to child care responsibilities rather than paid employment.[8] But even here, as the Court of Appeal has held,[9] the question is: *can* she adjust, not *should* she adjust? In answering this question, the court will assess the effect the marriage and its breakdown and the need to care for any minor children have had and will continue to have. The wife may have difficulties in re-entering the labour market, resuming a fractured career and making up lost ground. Facts, supported by evidence, must justify a reasonable expectation that the wife can and will become self-sufficient within the fixed term which the court may direct.[10]

Ultimately, the facts of each case must be scrutinised carefully, bearing in mind that there is no presumption that periodical payments should be terminated as soon as possible unless the payee can show some good reason why they should not be.[11]

---

5 [1985] FLR 1176, CA.
6 [1987] 2 FLR 1. See also the discussion of s 25(2)(a) post, p 829.
7 [1997] 1 FLR 353, CA at 358.
8 *Waterman v Waterman* [1989] 1 FLR 380, CA. In *Mawson v Mawson* [1994] 2 FLR 985 the young couple, both of whom had careers, separated after a three-year marriage; there was a six-year-old child. On the basis that the husband continued to pay the child support assessment in respect of the child, Thorpe J ordered a periodical payment order of nine months which would enable the wife 'to stand on her own feet and bring to an end her financial dependency'. Compare *Fisher v Fisher* [1989] 1 FLR 423, CA where the court increased the periodical payments in favour of a wife and child and refused to impose a time limit on the order, notwithstanding the child was born after the divorce, and was not the husband's. It was 'quite insupportable' for the husband to argue that by becoming pregnant, the wife had released the husband from his obligation to support her. Nor could the court ignore the wife's responsibility for the child because it was not a 'child of the family'.
9 *C v C (Financial Relief: Short Marriage)* [1997] 2 FLR 26, CA.
10 Compare *N v N (Consent order: Variation)* [1993] 2 FLR 868, CA, where the parties, who had a son, divorced after a seven-year marriage. An agreement was reached whereby (against legal advice) the wife accepted periodical payments for a five-year term, and entered into a 'side letter' whereby she agreed not to apply for an extension except 'for the protection of the child in a case of quite unforeseen circumstances of serious illness or disability'. The wife realised that she would not be successful as an opera singer, and decided to train as a barrister. She applied for an extension of the specified term. The Court of Appeal rejected her application. While questioning the appropriateness of a side letter in child cases, and whilst itself unenforceable, it was nonetheless 'highly relevant'. On the principles of *Edgar v Edgar* [1980] 3 All ER 887, CA, the court considered it should uphold agreements freely entered into on legal advice.
11 *Barrett v Barrett* [1988] 2 FLR 516, CA.

Of course, if there are substantial assets available, then any potential hardship can be offset by ordering payment of the appropriate sums.[12]

Judging the overall fairness of orders[13]

(a) Satisfying the needs of the members of the family

As we have said, the courts no longer have an overall statutory objective and although, as will be seen, there are guidelines setting out the considerations to which the court must have regard, ultimately they do not provide guidance on what may be regarded as a fair and just order overall. It is obvious, however, that the court's primary concern must be for the needs of all the members of the family with priority having to be given to the needs of any child of the family. Clearly, the most important need is for adequate accommodation and support. In cases where there are dependent children these needs will frequently determine what is to be done with the matrimonial home, for it will usually be desirable to permit the spouse with day-to-day responsibility for the children to remain in the home to provide a roof over their heads.[14] Even if there are no children, the matrimonial home may be preserved as a home for one of the spouses. We consider this matter further at the end of this section.

Satisfying the parties' needs, though an important objective, does not, however, provide an overall guideline in all cases. In any event, a party's reasonable needs depend in large measure upon the standard of living that he is used to. Furthermore, there will be cases where a spouse can adequately cater for his own needs, yet there ought to be a redistribution of the capital assets to reflect each party's past contributions. What yardstick of fairness might be appropriate in these cases?

(b) The one-third rule[15]

One guideline, which has had a chequered history in the courts, is the so-called one-third rule. After its surprising reintroduction in the divorce courts by *Ackerman v Ackerman*[16] and its subsequent endorsement in *Wachtel v Wachtel*,[17] the one-third approach was, for a time, widely used by the courts as a convenient starting point in respect of the parties' income and their capital. Insofar as it applied to income, the approach was to order the husband to pay such sums as would bring the wife's income (if any) up to one-third of the spouses' joint income. The reason for starting with a third rather than, say, a half was defended by Lord Denning MR in *Wachtel v Wachtel*[18] on the ground that the husband was likely to have greater expenses than the wife (for example, in having to maintain

---

12 In *Attar v Attar (No 2)* [1985] FLR 653, after a marriage lasting six months, a millionaire husband was ordered to pay £30,000 lump sum to his wife who, during the marriage, had given up her job as an air hostess, to enable her to adjust over a period of two years. In *S v S* [1986] Fam 189, [1985] 3 All ER 566 it was thought that £400,000 was the appropriate figure to compensate the divorced wife of a millionaire pop star for the loss of periodic payments estimated at £70,000 a year.

13 See *Page v Page* (1981) 2 FLR 198 and *White v White* [1998] 2 FLR 310, CA.

14 See Eekelaar and Maclean *Maintenance after Divorce* (1986) Table 5.7 and their later study, Maclean and Eekelaar *The Parental Obligation* (1997) p 112, which showed an increased tendency for the carer and children to remain in the former matrimonial home.

15 See generally Deech 'Financial Relief: The Retreat from Precedent and Principle' (1982) 98 LQR 621 at 623–30.

16 [1972] Fam 225 at 234, [1972] 2 All ER 420, CA at 426.

17 [1973] Fam 72, [1973] 1 All ER 829, CA. See also *O'D v O'D* [1976] Fam 83, sub nom *O'Donnell v O'Donnell* [1975] 2 All ER 993, CA.

18 [1973] Fam 72 at 94, [1973] 1 All ER 829, CA at 839.

the children and to pay a housekeeper) and that both might remarry (thus increasing the husband's liabilities and the wife's financial resources). This argument is frankly unconvincing: the reference to paying a housekeeper is unrealistic in most cases and, if it is relevant, the wife should be allowed the value of her services in kind; the husband could apply for a variation in the order if he later remarried, and the wife's marriage would automatically terminate it.

Although in *Wachtel v Wachtel* the Court of Appeal applied the rule to capital assets, Lord Denning MR [19] pointed out that, if it were possible to close the account between the spouses completely, it would be fair to divide their capital equally between them, but the husband must be given some compensation for the fact that he will usually have to continue to make periodical payments for the wife and children. It follows that, if a lump sum represents not only a division of capital assets but also the capitalisation of income (so that no periodical payments are ordered), the court may award a sum which will equalise the parties' financial position rather than apply the one-third rule. [20]

The one-third approach was never regarded as a rigid rule, but merely a starting point against which the needs and resources of the particular parties could then be tested and the resulting sum adjusted upwards or downwards. It became recognised, however, that even as a starting point the one-third approach was not very useful in respect of very low incomes, [1] nor was it thought appropriate in the cases involving large capital assets. [2] As Sir John Arnold P put it in *Slater v Slater*, [3] the guideline was useful provided the cases did not involve great wealth or unusual poverty. It may still have a place in determining what orders are appropriate, [4] but it should not be regarded as a rigid rule, nor should it be divorced from the other considerations to which the court is bound to have regard under s 25(2). It would seem to have no application in cases where the parties are either poor or very rich, [5] or in cases involving short childless marriages, [6] and it is possible that the approach will have less relevance in cases involving children of the family, given the injunction to consider their interests first, and also the impact of child maintenance assessments under the Child Support Act 1991.

(c)   Other approaches

As Anthony Lincoln J said in *Dew v Dew*, [7] the one-third approach is but one approach that a court can properly apply in arriving at a fair order in the appropriate case. Another (perhaps more currently favoured) is the so-called 'net effect'

---

19 Ibid at 95 and 839–40 respectively.
20 And see *White v White* supra, n 13, where the spouses were business partners and the wife was an equal working partner throughout the marriage it was held the starting point should be equal shares.
1 See eg *Cann v Cann* [1977] 3 All ER 957.
2 See eg *Preston v Preston* [1982] Fam 17, [1982] 1 All ER 41, CA.
3 (1982) 3 FLR 364, CA at 370.
4 Even in relation to capital: see eg *Dew v Dew* [1986] 2 FLR 341.
5 See eg *Dart v Dart* [1996] 2 FLR 286, CA, where the Court of Appeal rejected the wife's arguments that she should receive a fractional share – perhaps one-third or one-half – of the husband's wealth, conservatively estimated at £400m. Thorpe LJ suggested (at 294) that the *Wachtel v Wachtel* approach produced a manifestly fair result in the 'essentially middle class family, that has prospered through a long marriage in an inflationary era'. However, he added, '. . . the reality [is] it has been consistently rejected as an authority of general application'. Compare *F v F (Duxbury Calculation: Rate of Return)* [1996] 1 FLR 833 where the lump sum order made to the wife (after a long marriage) amounted to £1.1 million out of total assets 'in a bracket of £3m to £4m'.
6 See *B v B (Real Property: Assessment of Interests)* [1988] 2 FLR 490.
7 Supra n 4, at 344.

approach. This involves working out the position of the respective parties on the assumption that a hypothetical order is made and taking into account, inter alia, their respective tax liability. The resulting figures are then compared and related to the parties' respective needs.

In the case of very low incomes, where the parties' resources are insufficient to keep both households above subsistence level,[8] even the net effect method may be inappropriate. In these cases two principles have been established.[9] First, the fact that the wife is receiving (or could claim) income support should prima facie be ignored in assessing the amount the husband should pay her: otherwise he would be able to shift his duty to provide for her onto the community as a whole. This will apply even though the maximum sum that could possibly be ordered will be less than the benefit she is receiving, so that there will be no personal advantage to her at all.[10] Secondly, since the husband, if he is in full-time employment, will not be able to claim income support, the courts should not normally[11] make an order which depresses him below subsistence level. In assessing what order should be made, it seems that the proper approach[12] is to calculate the husband's net available income, consider the effect of the proposed order on his living expenses and compare the sum that he would receive, if in receipt of income support (or job-seekers' allowance), to ensure that he is not left with a sum below that amount. It seems that it is appropriate to allow the husband a margin above subsistence level (to meet his particular requirements and provide some incentive to remain in employment) though this is a matter for the court's discretion.[13]

Two later decisions, however, marked a significant departure from the approach outlined above. In both cases, the court imposed a clean break, even though its direct effect was to enable the less impoverished spouse to throw onto the state the financial burden of supporting his dependants. In *Ashley v Blackman*[14] Waite J dismissed a husband's liability for maintenance where a wife, aged 48, was a long-term schizophrenic in receipt of state benefits. The husband, aged 55, had remarried, and had two young children but an income of just £7,000 per annum. The judge drew a distinction between the 'devious and feckless' husband and the 'genuine struggler'. The latter was to be allowed to see 'light at the end of the tunnel' by being spared the obligation to pay to his ex-wife, with no commensurate financial benefit to her, the few pounds which separated him from penury.[15] In the second case, *Delaney v Delaney*,[16] the husband purchased a home

---

8 That is the level by reference to the current income support rates.
9 *Barnes v Barnes* [1972] 3 All ER 872, CA, approving *Ashley v Ashley* [1968] P 582, [1965] 3 All ER 554; *Shallow v Shallow* [1979] Fam 1, [1978] 2 All ER 483, CA.
10 As in eg *Peacock v Peacock* [1984] 1 All ER 1069.
11 But cf *Billington v Billington* [1974] Fam 24, [1974] 1 All ER 546.
12 See *Allen v Allen* [1986] 2 FLR 265, CA and *Peacock v Peacock*, supra.
13 Compare the margin allowed in protected income in the child support formula, discussed ante at p 736.
14 [1988] Fam 85, [1988] 3 WLR 222.
15 For a similar approach see *C v C (Financial Provision: Personal Damages)* [1995] 2 FLR 171 where the husband had sustained 'catastrophic' injuries in a motor car accident, and received a 'structured settlement' damages award of about £950,000 which would increase should he achieve his estimated life expectancy. The husband had returned to his home country, Cyprus, where he was cared for by his family. The wife's claims for financial provision were dismissed; she received income support and related 'passported' benefits – eg free school meals, prescriptions. Any periodical payments order would have made a negligible difference to the wife's income, but would have had a severe impact on the husband's.
16 [1990] 2 FLR 457, CA.

with his cohabitant but, after paying the mortgage, was left with insufficient income to support his former wife and children. The Court of Appeal held that the needs of the wife and children had to be balanced with the husband's ability to pay, and the availability of social security benefits (including income support) should be considered. It discharged the wife's periodical payments order and made nominal orders for the children. Ward J stated that a former husband was entitled so to order his life as to fulfil his aspirations for the future: there is, after all, 'life after divorce'.[17]

If these cases indicate the court's willingness to recognise the underlying financial realities, the potential for making clean break orders in similar situations is restricted by social security legislation[18] and the Child Support Act.[19] Statutory provisions[20] entitle the Department of Social Security effectively to side-step a clean break order by proceeding in the magistrates' court against a husband, as a liable relative, should a former wife become dependent upon income support for her children and her own needs. In the same way, once a parent with care receives family credit or income support, she will usually be required to authorise the Child Support Agency to recover child maintenance from the absent parent.[1]

Financial relief after a decree of nullity

The Family Law Act 1996 extensively amends the Matrimonial Causes Act 1973 to put the court's powers to make financial provision and property adjustment orders in nullity proceedings on the same footing as those available in relation to divorce and separation orders.[2] This includes giving the court powers to make interim periodical payment orders and orders for interim lump sums.[3] Unlike in relation to divorce, however, where financial orders will not usually take effect until the divorce order is made,[4] in nullity proceedings the pre-1996 position is preserved. Although the court may make a financial provision or property adjustment order on or after granting a decree of nullity, it is expressly provided that such orders will not take effect until the decree is made absolute.[5]

There is clearly power to order financial relief after a decree of nullity, even though the marriage is void.[6] In *Whiston v Whiston*[7] the Court of Appeal held that a person who, knowingly being married, has gone through a ceremony of marriage to another cannot pursue a claim for ancillary relief against the innocent party under the Matrimonial Causes Act 1973; as a matter of policy, the court will not assist a person who must found a claim on the serious criminal offence of bigamy. However, a majority of the Court of Appeal held in *J v S-T (Formerly J)*

17 Ibid at 461.
18 See Wood 'The Social Security Act 1990 – the Clean Break Rejoined' [1991] Fam Law 31.
19 See ante, pp 727ff.
20 Social Security Administration Act 1992 ss 107–108. See also ante, p 724.
1 Child Support Act 1991 s 6, discussed ante, p 731.
2 Family Law Act 1996 s 15(2); Matrimonial Causes Act 1973 s 23 as substituted by Family Law Act 1996 Sch 2, para 4 (financial provision orders); Matrimonial Causes Act 1973 s 24 as substituted by Family Law Act 1996 Sch 2, para 6 (property adjustment orders).
3 Matrimonial Causes Act 1973 s 23(2) (as amended).
4 See ante, p 781.
5 Matrimonial Causes Act 1973 s 23(10) (as amended) in relation to financial provision orders; Matrimonial Causes Act 1973 s 24(4) (as amended) in relation to property adjustment orders.
6 A fortiori there is power to order financial relief if the marriage is voidable: see *Johnston v Johnston* (1976) 6 Fam Law 17, CA.
7 [1995] Fam 198, [1995] 2 FLR 268, CA.

(Transsexual: Ancillary Relief) [8] that the rule in *Whiston* may be limited to cases of bigamy, where the marriage itself is a crime. Here, after a seventeen-year marriage, the plaintiff was granted a decree of nullity on the basis that the parties were not respectively male and female. The defendant, a female, who had undergone sexual reassignment surgery, applied for financial provision. The judge had found that the defendant had committed perjury in declaring, at the marriage ceremony, that there was no lawful hindrance to it taking place. Potter LJ and Sir Brian Neill [9] declined to follow *Whiston* and held that the defendant's claim was not barred in limine on public policy grounds. However, as a matter of the court's discretion, and taking into account the factors in s 25 of the Matrimonial Causes Act 1973 including the defendant's conduct, the application was dismissed.

2. FACTORS TO BE TAKEN INTO ACCOUNT WHEN ASSESSING WHAT ORDERS SHOULD BE MADE FOR A SPOUSE

Reference has already been made to the fact that, whilst the court must have regard to all the circumstances of the case, it must also take into account certain specific factors. Some of these are relevant to calculating the parties' resources and needs; others will lead the court to make a greater or smaller award than it otherwise would have done. Although the list is not intended to be exhaustive, it covers almost all the matters to which the court had always had regard in the past. It is proposed to consider the facts in the order in which they are set out in s 25(2) of the Matrimonial Causes Act. [10]

'the income, earning capacity, property and other financial resources which each of the parties to the marriage has or is likely to have in the foreseeable future, including in the case of earning capacity any increase in that capacity which it would in the opinion of the court be reasonable to expect a party to the marriage to take steps to acquire'

The court must have regard to all the income and capital belonging to the spouses. So far as capital is concerned, provided it belongs to one of the spouses, it must be taken into account and it is irrelevant how the spouse came to own it. Hence, inherited property is included and even damages recovered for loss of earnings or damage to property forms part of the recipient's assets. Insofar as damages for personal injuries represent compensation for pain and suffering and loss of amenity, the position was formerly not so clear. Earlier decisions indicated that they should be left out of account, [11] but after a detailed consideration of the authorities the Court of Appeal concluded in *Daubney v Daubney* [12] that the views expressed in those cases had not been necessary to the decisions and that such damages were assets which should be brought into account. However, Scarman LJ was careful to point out that it would not be a correct exercise of the court's discretion to make an order which would in effect deprive the spouse of all benefit

---

8 [1997] 1 FLR 402, CA.
9 Ward LJ followed *Whiston* in holding that the application failed in limine; the defendant had attempted to gain a benefit from wrongdoing, and such a claim was against public policy.
10 As amended by the Matrimonial and Family Proceedings Act 1984 and the Family Law Act 1996.
11 For example, *Jones v Jones* [1976] Fam 8, [1975] 2 All ER 12, CA.
12 [1976] Fam 267, [1976] 2 All ER 453, CA.

of the compensation:[13] the court apparently must decide in each case what would be a fair sum to bring into account. In *Wagstaff v Wagstaff*[14] the Court of Appeal held that the fact that substantial damages had been received by a husband as compensation for pain and suffering and loss of amenity did not *necessarily* make that sum unavailable to a wife. The fact that an injured spouse may have special needs, or an impaired future earning capacity would, of course, be considered by the court in the exercise of its discretion.[15] But, subject to this, damages for personal injury are properly to be regarded as part of the financial resources available to the parties.[16]

In appropriate cases regard must be had to the husband's ability to earn higher wages by working overtime,[17] to raise money by overdrafts,[18] or loans secured on his property[19] or, if he is unemployed, to obtain work if he wishes.[20] Increases in either spouse's income or capital after their separation must also be considered, as these are properly to be regarded as part of their resources.[1] In the case of a very rich man, who may well live largely on capital and capital profits, his capital assets will be of particular importance,[2] and such a person's standard of living may be the best guide to the level of his real income.[3]

The court must have regard not only to the resources which each party has at the time of the hearing,[4] but also to those which they are likely to have in the foreseeable future.[5] If the benefit is one to which a party may be contingently entitled in the future, the court may take it into account by ordering him to pay an appropriate lump sum if and when he acquires the interest.[6] On the other hand, if

---

13 At 277 and 459, respectively.
14 [1992] 1 All ER 275, CA.
15 See *C v C (Financial Provision: Personal Damages)* [1995] 2 FLR 171, in which the husband received a structured settlement damages award after a car accident of about £950,000, but potentially worth up to £5m if he achieved his estimated life expectancy. The court declined to award the wife a lump sum which would frustrate the husband's reasonable expectation of obtaining a suitable house and long-term care.
16 This seems also to include compensation payments made by the Criminal Injuries Compensation Board (now Authority): see *A v A (Financial Provision: Conduct)* [1995] 1 FLR 345.
17 *Klucinski v Klucinski* [1953] 1 All ER 683. It is not unknown for husbands deliberately to refuse overtime before the hearing so as to give a false picture of their normal earnings.
18 *J-PC v J-AF* [1955] P 215, [1955] 2 All ER 617, CA.
19 *Newton v Newton* [1990] 1 FLR 33, CA.
20 *McEwan v McEwan* [1972] 2 All ER 708; cf *Bromilow v Bromilow* (1976) 7 Fam Law 16. If the husband is in receipt of income support (or job seekers' allowance) and the payments made to him have not been reduced or stopped, this indicates that the Benefits Agency's officers are satisfied after extensive enquiries that he is genuinely unable to find work and, whilst this does not bind any court, is a valuable piece of evidence which should be taken into account: *Williams v Williams* [1974] Fam 55, [1974] 3 All ER 377.
1 *Schuller v Schuller* [1990] 2 FLR 193 (the wife's property inheritance after a decree absolute was taken into account to reduce her lump sum).
2 *Brett v Brett* [1969] 1 All ER 1007, CA.
3 See *W v W (No 3)* [1962] P 124.
4 If a party's income is liable to fluctuate, it is customary to take an average to assess future earnings: *Sherwood v Sherwood* [1929] P 120, CA; and the fact that these fluctuations make it precarious may be a reason for reducing the amount of periodical payments ordered: *Dean v Dean* [1923] P 172. On the question of allowances of men serving in the armed forces, see *Powell v Powell* [1951] P 257, CA; *Collins v Collins* [1943] P 106, [1943] 2 All ER 474; *Buttle v Buttle* [1953] 2 All ER 646.
5 See Daniel 'Considering Future Capital Assets' [1993] Fam Law 265.
6 *Calder v Calder* (1975) 6 Fam Law 242, CA (interest contingent on husband's surviving his mother); cf *MT v MT (Financial Provision)* [1992] 1 FLR 362 (wife's application adjourned pending the death of her 83-year-old German father-in-law: under German law, husband entitled to

the contingency is too uncertain or remote, it may be left out of account altogether.[7]

The specific requirement to consider whether a spouse could increase his or her earning capacity results from an amendment introduced by the Matrimonial and Family Proceedings Act 1984 s 3. In his evidence to the Special Standing Committee[8] the President of the Family Division instanced what he described as the 'obvious case' of a husband who had reached the point in his career at which he had the right or an opportunity to take some examination which would lead to a higher grade or a better remunerated appointment. While this is an example of how the provision could be relevant, it is much more likely that attention will be directed to the wife's potential earning capacity. The provision is clearly related to the general requirement to consider whether the spouses can become self-sufficient.[9]

It is to be noted that the court should only pay regard to any increase in earning capacity that it is 'reasonable' to expect the spouse to take steps to acquire. Obviously, in deciding this, the court must take into account all the circumstances of the case, but particularly relevant will be any commitments to look after any children;[10] the age, health and qualifications of the spouse; and the time since the spouse last worked. The courts seem acutely aware of the difficulties that older

---

a fixed portion of his father's substantial estate). In *Priest v Priest* (1978) 1 FLR 189, CA, a husband was ordered to pay one-third of the gratuity payable on the completion of his service in the Royal Marines some five years later. It was later held that because of the terms of the Army Act 1955 s 203 the court had no power to order payments to be made *specifically* out of an army terminal gratuity or resettlement grant: see *Walker v Walker* [1983] Fam 68, [1983] 2 All ER 909, CA, and *Roberts v Roberts* [1986] 2 All ER 483. Nor would the court make an order which indirectly had this effect, eg by making a lump sum payment order equivalent to a percentage of a terminal grant: see *Ranson v Ranson* [1988] 1 WLR 183, CA (a case involving an RAF serviceman where the legislation, Air Force Act 1955 s 203, is in similar terms to the Army Act). The position in relation to the Royal Navy was different: see *Cotgrave v Cotgrave* [1992] Fam 33, [1991] 4 All ER 537, CA, although legislation in 1991 put seamen on the same footing as other servicemen (Naval Discipline Act 1957 s 128G, as inserted by the Armed Forces Act 1991 s 16, replacing the Naval and Marine Pay and Pensions Act 1865 ss 4, 5). In *Legrove v Legrove* [1994] 2 FLR 119, CA it was held that the 1991 legislation was not retrospective in effect so as to render void a 1982 court order that a serving sailor pay a lump sum of one-third of the retirement sum he received on his leaving the Royal Navy. Despite this special legislation affecting servicemen's gratuities the court could still take such entitlements into account when considering the parties' resources – perhaps (say) by making a larger lump sum order in favour of a wife (if other capital is available) on the basis that a husband's needs would be met by a terminal grant upon his discharge. Once a terminal grant had been *received* by an ex-serviceman, the Army Act 1955 did not prevent the court from making an order in respect of what had become free and available capital: see *Happé v Happé* [1991] 4 All ER 527, CA. The Pensions Act 1995 s 166(4), (5) now provides that nothing in the restrictions in the legislation relating to servicemen (discussed above) or in the Pensions Act 1995 or in '. . . any corresponding provision in any other Act [or] restriction in any pension scheme corresponding to [such] statutory restrictions' is to prevent the court from exercising its powers to make financial provision orders in respect of pension scheme benefits which a spouse has or is likely to have in the foreseeable future.

7 See eg *Michael v Michael* [1986] 2 FLR 389 where, because of the uncertainty whether and when the wife would receive an interest under her mother's will, it was left out of account. This was followed in *K v K* [1990] 2 FLR 225 and *H v H (Financial Provision: Capital Assets)* [1993] 2 FLR 335. See also *Priest v Priest*, supra, where a gratuity that could arise 15 years after the hearing was thought to be too far in the future to be taken into account.

8 HC Official Report, col 77, 22 March 1984.

9 See in particular ante at p 820.

10 This may include, it seems, a child who is *not* the husband's, and who was born after the breakdown of the marriage: see *Fisher v Fisher* [1989] 1 FLR 423, CA.

women may experience in obtaining suitable employment. In *Leadbeater v Leadbeater*,[11] for example, it was held to be unreasonable to expect a 47-year-old woman with no particular skills (she was, at the time of the marriage, the secretary to her former husband) to adapt to new methods used in offices, namely word processors and so on. However, it was thought that she could increase the number of hours that she was currently working as a receptionist. Hence, her earnings were assessed at £2,500 per year as against her actual earnings of £1,680.[12] On the other hand, in *Mitchell v Mitchell*[13] it was held that a wife who was an experienced secretary but who had taken a part-time job in a canteen could, when the children had left school (the younger child was 13), reasonably be expected to increase her earning capacity, and the resulting lump sum awarded her reflected this.

Another issue is the presence of a new partner.[14] The fact that the wife has remarried or is about to remarry or is living with another man who is supporting her clearly affects her financial position. Remarriage automatically terminates periodical payments[15] and although, for this purpose, cohabitation is not necessarily to be equated with remarriage,[16] it may nonetheless lead the court to conclude that the wife no longer needs the husband's support;[17] but leaving aside the question of the matrimonial home, all these facts should generally be disregarded in dividing capital assets unless a lump sum award represents the capitalisation of periodical payments.[18] The wife is withdrawing her part of the capital from the former family partnership, and the amount she receives should not depend on what she proposes to do with it.[19] The mere chance that the wife may remarry at some time in the future should be ignored when dividing capital assets.[20]

So far as the husband's second wife's means are concerned, it is established that they are relevant (though there can be difficulties in discovering those means),[1] but only to the extent that they diminish the needs of the husband, thereby extending his resources to support his first family. An order cannot be made which has the effect of making the new partner pay out of her income or capital.[2]

---

11 [1985] FLR 789.
12 See also *M v M (Financial Provision)* [1987] 2 FLR 1 in which the difficulties of another 47-year-old wife were discussed. See also *Boylan v Boylan* [1988] 1 FLR 282; *Barrett v Barrett* [1988] 2 FLR 516, CA; and *C v C (Financial Relief: Short Marriage)* [1997] 2 FLR 26, CA.
13 [1984] FLR 387, CA.
14 See Hodson 'The New Partner After Divorce' [1990] Fam Law 77, CA.
15 See ante, p 788.
16 *Atkinson v Atkinson* [1987] 3 All ER 849, CA.
17 See *Atkinson v Atkinson* [1995] 2 FLR 356 where the court reduced the periodical payments made by a wealthy man to his former wife from £30,000 to £10,000 per year. The wife cohabited with a younger man, and had provided a comfortable home enabling the latter to develop a successful business consistently and industriously. The wife's new partner's worth was relevant insofar as it impacted on an assessment of the wife's financial needs. The husband's subsequent application for leave to appeal against the order made was dismissed by the Court of Appeal: *Atkinson v Atkinson (No 2)* [1996] 1 FLR 51, CA.
18 See eg *Duxbury v Duxbury* [1992] Fam 62n, [1990] 2 All ER 77, CA.
19 Ibid (it was irrelevant that the wife would spend part of a lump sum award to benefit her cohabitant); *Gojkovic v Gojkovic* [1992] Fam 40, [1990] 2 All ER 84, CA (the wife had earned her share of the family wealth and was entitled to use the lump sum to purchase a hotel to run as a business).
20 *S v S* [1976] Fam 18n at 23, [1975] 2 All ER 19n at 22.
 1 See *Wynne v Wynne and Jeffers* [1980] 3 All ER 659, CA; *W v W* (1981) 2 FLR 291. One method is the so called 'production appointment' which may, in appropriate cases, be ordered against a third party – compare *Frary v Frary* [1993] 2 FLR 696 with *D v D (Production Appointment: Procedure)* [1995] 2 FLR 497.
 2 *Macey v Macey* (1981) 3 FLR 7, and *Brown v Brown* (1981) 3 FLR 161.

'The financial needs, obligations and responsibilities which each of the parties to the marriage has or is likely to have in the foreseeable future'

The most obvious examples of factors to be considered under this head are the parties' need to maintain themselves and their responsibility to provide for their dependants. The maintenance of children must come first; in addition one must take into account the needs of a second spouse,[3] infirm parents, brothers and sisters unable to work, and any other person whom it is reasonable to expect either party to look after in the circumstances. It will be seen that not all these obligations are legally enforceable: in this context a moral obligation and the voluntary assumption of a responsibility (provided that it is reasonable) may be as relevant as a legal obligation. For example, a father's moral duty to make voluntary payments for the upkeep of his stepchild is indistinguishable for this purpose from his legal liability to comply with a court order.[4] But if the liability has been assumed in a purely voluntary way, the court can obviously take it into account only if it is reasonable. Thus repayments of a mortgage entered into after the parties separated in order to enable one of them to buy an expensive house may be disregarded if their financial position does not justify the purchase.[5]

As in the case of the parties' resources, the court must have regard to the needs, obligations and liabilities that they are likely to have in the foreseeable future as well as those already incurred at the time of the order.

In all cases the spouses are entitled to have only their *reasonable* needs taken into account but, of course, what is 'reasonable' very much depends upon the circumstances of each case. At the poverty end of the spectrum, for example, it has been held that a video recorder is not a reasonable need,[6] and running a car can only be a justified expense if it is needed to get to work.[7] Even if there are ample resources the claims must still be reasonable. In *Leadbeater v Leadbeater*,[8] for example, where the husband's assets amounted to some £250,000, it was held that while the wife could reasonably justify the purchase of a two bedroom house, given that she would live in it by herself, she could not justify the need for a three bedroom property.

At the very wealthiest end of the spectrum it has been said that it is impossible to lay down guidelines to help calculate the appropriate levels of lump sum payments,[9] though in *Preston v Preston*[10] Ormrod LJ considered that the word 'needs' in s 25(2)(b) of the Matrimonial Causes Act 1973 is equivalent to 'reasonable requirements', and seemed to hint there might be some ceiling to awards that might

---

3 *Barnes v Barnes* [1972] 3 All ER 872, CA. But this does not justify postponing the interests of the first family (and a fortiori any child of the family) to those of the second family: *Roberts v Roberts* [1970] P 1, [1968] 3 All ER 479.
4 *Blower v Blower* [1986] 1 FLR 292; *Roberts v Roberts*, supra. See also *Williams v Williams* [1965] P 125, [1964] 3 All ER 526, CA, and *P (JR) v P (GL)* [1966] 1 All ER 439 (concerning liability to educate children of a previous marriage); cf *Fisher v Fisher* [1989] 1 FLR 423, CA, for a mother's responsibility towards a child born outside the marriage. Note also *Vicary v Vicary* [1992] 2 FLR 271, CA where the Court of Appeal held, at least where there were plentiful resources, that the financial provision made for a wife may include prospective payments which she might make to adult daughters and grandchildren, if such payments had been made during the marriage, and the husband had contributed to them or, at least, had not objected to the payments having been made.
5 See *G v P* [1978] 1 All ER 1099, CA.
6 *Girvan v Girvan* (1983) 13 Fam Law 213.
7 See eg *Clarke v Clarke* (1979) 9 Fam Law 15; *Delaney v Delaney* [1990] 2 FLR 457, CA; cf *Slater v Slater* (1981) 3 FLR 58.
8 [1985] FLR 789.
9 *Gojkovic v Gojkovic* [1992] Fam 40 at 50, [1990] 2 All ER 84 at 90, per Russell LJ.
10 [1982] Fam 17.

be made where the parties' available resources are very large. On the facts, the husband, who had capital assets estimated at £2.3 million, was ordered to pay a lump sum of £600,000 to produce an annual income of £20,000 after tax. In a number of later 'big money' cases the 'reasonable requirements' approach has been adopted and followed.[11] In *Dart v Dart*[12] (where it was said the husband's fortune was conservatively estimated at over £400 million) Thorpe LJ explained:[13]

> 'As a matter of ordinary language what a person requires is likely to be greater than what a person needs. So the check on what the applicant subjectively requires is the word "reasonable". There must be an objective appraisal of what the applicant subjectively requires to ensure it is not unreasonable.'

His Lordship added that the court's objective appraisal must embrace other criteria – 'obviously' including resources, standard of living, age and health, and 'less obviously' the duration of the marriage, contributions and pension rights.

One consequence of an approach based primarily on an assessment of 'reasonable requirements' is that the courts are necessarily drawn into a close scrutiny of a claimant wife's estimated budgeted expenditure;[14] another is that, particularly where it is used to award a lump sum calculated by reference to a wife's projected future income requirements, awards may be lower than might otherwise be the case. In *Dart v Dart*,[15] where the wife had made no direct contribution to the husband's family wealth, she was awarded approximately £10 million, despite claiming £122 million. Butler-Sloss LJ acknowledged that the courts may have given too great weight to an assessment of a spouse's 'reasonable requirements' over and above the other criteria set out in s 25 of the Matrimonial Causes Act 1973, with the result, in 'big money' cases, that awards may have been 'over-modest'. Any change, however, should be a matter for the legislature.

One common feature of 'big-money' cases first made its appearance in *Duxbury v Duxbury*,[16] where the *Preston* decision was followed to the extent that a capital sum was ordered which would produce an annual income of £28,000 (a figure calculated on the basis of *Preston* suitably adjusted to take account of inflation) which was thought to be a reasonable sum to preserve a luxurious standard of

---

11 See eg *H v H (Financial Provision: Lump Sum)* [1994] 2 FLR 309; *R v R (Financial Provision: Reasonable Need)* [1994] 2 FLR 1044; *W v W (Judicial Separation: Ancillary Relief)* [1995] 2 FLR 259. But compare *C v C (Financial Relief: Short Marriage)* [1997] 2 FLR 26, where the Court of Appeal rejected an approach based on needs, saying it was only one factor to be considered under s 25; in addition to the wife's personal requirements, the court also had to consider the needs of the child of the marriage, whose welfare should be considered first under Matrimonial Causes Act 1973 s 25(1).

12 [1996] 2 FLR 286, CA.

13 Ibid at 296. See *A v A (Financial Provision)* [1998] 2 FLR 180 for an example of the court's assessment of the wife's reasonable needs, bearing in mind a lifestyle compatible with the husband's extensive wealth even though the spouses had lived relatively frugally during the marriage.

14 See eg *F v F (Ancillary Relief: Substantial Assets)* [1995] 2 FLR 45 where Thorpe J scrutinised the details of the wife's suggested budget which had been produced acknowledging '. . . there is every incentive to put the figures as high as they can reasonably be put and perhaps some temptation to gild the lily'. Among the items his Lordship found 'unjustifiable even in a super-rich case' were £5,000 for knick-knacks for the home, £12,000 for telephone bills and £4,000 to keep a Labrador. In *C v C (Financial Relief: Short Marriage)* [1997] 2 FLR 26, CA Ward LJ suggested the court should adopt a 'broad brush' approach in the determination of at least certain items of budgeted expenditure which a claimant spouse produces. See further: George 'In All the Circumstances – Section 25' [1997] Fam Law 729.

15 [1996] 2 FLR 286, CA.

16 [1992] Fam 62n, [1990] 2 All ER 77, CA; cf *S v S* [1986] Fam 189, [1986] 3 All ER 566, where an annual income of £70,000 was thought appropriate.

living. The firm of accountants who acted for the wife devised a sophisticated computer program, designed to take account of a number of financial and other variables, including life expectancy, inflation, tax, investment return and capital growth to produce an estimate of the lump sum required to meet the recipient's needs for life.[17] This so-called '*Duxbury* calculation' has been used by the courts as a helpful guide to the assessment of the reasonable requirements of a wife whose husband is wealthy.[18] However, as Butler-Sloss LJ explained in *Gojkovic v Gojkovic*,[19] it ought not to be elevated to a rigid arithmetical calculation; each case must be decided upon its own facts, and in accordance with the principles set out in s 25 of the Matrimonial Causes Act.

Where a wife has made a significant contribution to the creation of the family wealth, a '*Duxbury* calculation' and, indeed, the adoption of the 'reasonable requirements,' approach may be inappropriate and restrictive. In *Gojkovic v Gojkovic*[20] the husband and wife had, by dint of their efforts, built up a hotel and property business worth over £4 million. The Court of Appeal rejected contentions that (a) there was, in principle, a ceiling for lump sum awards and (b) that *Duxbury v Duxbury* laid down any binding authority as to the reasonable requirements of every millionaire's former wife. Quite apart from her reasonable needs, the wife's substantial contribution to the development of the family business should be recognised. The Court of Appeal upheld the award of a lump sum of £1 million to the wife, which she intended to use to acquire and run her own hotel. In the later case of *Conran v Conran*,[1] Wilson J described as 'in every sense outstanding' the wife's contributions over 30 years in helping to develop the husband's 'Habitat' furniture stores and restaurants, her work and reputation as a nationally recognised cookery writer and journalist and her other family contributions. The judge considered the correct approach would be to assess the wife's reasonable requirements without reference to her contributions, and then to bring the latter into the balance. From the husband's total wealth of some £85 million, the wife was awarded £8.4 million for her 'reasonable requirements' and a further £2.1 million for her 'contributions'.[2]

17 For a further explanation by the program's inventor, see Lawrence '*Duxbury* Disclosure and Other Matters' [1990] Fam Law 12.
18 See eg *S v S (Financial Provision) (Post Divorce Cohabitation)* [1994] 2 FLR 228; *H v H (Financial Relief: Costs)* [1997] 2 FLR 57. A simplified version of the *Duxbury* tables is published in a booklet produced by the Family Law Bar Association entitled 'At a Glance'. In *F v F (Duxbury Calculation: Rate of Return)* [1996] 1 FLR 833, the court rejected the husband's argument that the assumed real rate of return on capital invested (which should be used for the purpose of a *Duxbury* calculation) should be 5 per cent. Holman J suggested in his experience the 'industry standard' should be settled at around 4.25 per cent. For a response from the program's author, and others, see Lawrence, Mainz and Collinson '*Duxbury* – Is there a Right Rate of Return?' [1996] Fam Law 560. Contrast *Wells v Wells* [1998] 3 All ER 481, HL: lump sum compensation for injured plaintiffs should be calculated on assumption of investment in index-linked government securities, at that time returning only 3%.
19 [1992] Fam 40, CA at 48. A similar approach was taken by Ward J in *B v B (Financial Provision)* [1990] 1 FLR 20 who discusses the limitations and restrictions of the '*Duxbury* calculation' and the dangers of its 'unblinkered application'. See also *Newton v Newton* [1990] 1 FLR 33, CA.
20 Supra. See also *White v White* [1998] 2 FLR 310, CA.
1 [1997] 2 FLR 615.
2 These cases do seem to confirm the views of one commentator who suggests (critically) '... it would appear that, certainly at higher levels, effective contribution by way of money or money's worth is more valuable than any contribution to the welfare of the family': Gerlis 'Ancillary Relief – Need v Equality' [1995] Fam Law 632. For further criticism see Willbourne 'Reasonable Requirements and the Millionaire's Defence' [1997] Fam Law 337 who argues that since Parliament enacted s 25(2)(f) of the Matrimonial Causes Act 1973 (see post, p 839) it should be taken to have intended that a wife's contribution to the welfare and development of the family should be regarded as being of equal weight to her contribution to the generation of the family's wealth.

Two matters require special comment. It may be possible to meet the needs of a wife who is unable to work (either because of her own physical condition or the necessity of looking after a child or other dependant who requires constant care) only by transferring the former matrimonial home to her so that she has at least the security of a roof over her head.[3] Secondly, in its anxiety to protect the wife and children, the court should not lose sight of the difficulties likely to be faced by the husband, particularly if he has remarried. He should never be left in a position where the effect of the order will have a crippling effect on him. In *Backhouse v Backhouse*,[4] for example, Balcombe J said that it would be repugnant to the court's sense of justice to make an order which would have necessitated the husband's selling the former matrimonial home in which he was living with his second wife and two children, and he limited the husband's liability to paying a lump sum which he could reasonably be expected to raise by a mortgage.

'The standard of living enjoyed by the family before the breakdown of the marriage'

This is particularly important when substantial assets are available and one of the spouses has been living at a much higher level than he or she did before the marriage.[5] In *Calderbank v Calderbank*[6] the wife, a relatively rich woman, was ordered to pay a lump sum of £10,000 to the husband (who had no capital and had remarried) so that he might buy a house suitable to the former spouses' ways of life in which he might see his children. But neither party's standard of living should be raised above what it otherwise would have been, for this would in effect mean that the order was being used as a means of punishing the other.[7]

'The age of each party and the duration of the marriage'

This must be looked at in conjunction with the contribution made by each of them to the welfare of the family (considered below). Even before 1971 it was clear that

---

3 *Jones v Jones* [1976] Fam 8, [1975] 2 All ER 12, CA; *S v S* [1976] Fam 18n, [1975] 2 All ER 19n. But compare *M v M (Property Adjustment: Impaired Life Expectancy)* [1993] 2 FLR 723, CA, a case involving a middle income couple, where the wife was diagnosed as suffering from a brain tumour which significantly reduced her life expectancy and present and likely future earning capacity. The Court of Appeal rejected the wife's arguments that the matrimonial home be preserved for herself and the children. It upheld an order for the sale of the house after a year, with the proceeds being divided 75 per cent to the wife, and 25 per cent to the husband, who was given a charge over the wife's share, realisable on her death.

4 [1978] 1 All ER 1158. See also *Wachtel v Wachtel* [1973] Fam 72 at 96, [1973] 1 All ER 829, CA at 841; *H v H* [1975] Fam 9 at 14 [1975] 1 All ER 367 at 371.

5 An assessment of the former spouses' standard of living has featured largely in a number of 'big money' cases: see eg *Dart v Dart* [1996] 2 FLR 286 and *F v F (Ancillary Relief: Substantial Assets)* [1995] 2 FLR 45 where Thorpe J noted (at 63) that the standard of living enjoyed by the parties before the marriage breakdown 'is the yardstick against which the wife's needs must be measured'. See also *R v R (Financial Provision: Reasonable Needs)* [1994] 2 FLR 1044.

6 [1976] Fam 93, [1975] 3 All ER 333, CA. See also *H v H (Financial Provision: Conduct)* [1998] 1 FLR 971, in which the children's welfare required that the husband – the family's 'poor relation' – should have a home they could regard as belonging to him.

7 See *Attwood v Attwood* [1968] P 591 at 595, [1968] 3 All ER 385 at 388. Compare *H v H (Clean Break: Non Disclosure: Costs)* [1994] 2 FLR 309 where the wife lived frugally during the early years of the marriage with a view to long-term security. The judge held that while it would be wrong to penalise the wife for her frugality, nonetheless the standard of living during the marriage had to be taken into account. He assessed the wife's income requirements at £35,000 per annum, rather than the £46,000 for which the wife had argued. But cf *A v A (Financial Provision)* [1998] 2 FLR 180, where the family's past relatively simple lifestyle was not regarded as determining entirely the wife's future standard of living, which should reflect the reality of the husband's substantial wealth.

a young wife, whose marriage has lasted for only a short time, would generally get much less favourable terms that one who had been deserted after years of married life. Today the courts are not likely to make more than a nominal order if the marriage is childless and has lasted only a matter of months and the wife has made virtually no contribution to the home and is young, fit and capable of earning her own living.[8] They are, however, more sympathetic to such a wife if the breakdown has caused her financial loss or other hardship, in which case she can expect a substantial order in her favour.[9] In *C v C (Financial Relief: Short Marriage)* [10] the Court of Appeal upheld an award 'at the very top of the bracket' where a marriage had broken down after just nine months, but there was a small child and the wife's fragile health had been seriously impaired by the marriage breakdown, and her prospects of successful medical treatment and her future earning capacity were uncertain. In the case of an older woman who may find it difficult to return to work, it was said in *S v S* [11] that the court should concentrate on the parties' needs and try at least to restore them to the position they were in before the marriage. In that case both parties were over 50 when they married and the marriage lasted only two years. The court ordered the husband to settle on the wife a sum which would enable her to buy a house similar to that which she had sold on her marriage and which would revert to the husband or his estate on her death; to pay her a lump sum to enable her to furnish it; and to make periodical payments (which would bring her income up to something less than a fifth of their joint incomes) to compensate her for loss of pension rights and the comfortable old age she could have looked forward to had the marriage continued.

In *Leadbeater v Leadbeater* [12] it was held that 25 per cent should be discounted from the sum that was thought appropriate to meet the wife's reasonable needs since the marriage had been short, lasting only four years. It is tempting to say that what is important is the length of cohabitation rather than the length of the marriage.[13] In *Krystman v Krystman* [14] no order was made at all when the parties had cohabited for only a fortnight at the beginning of a marriage which had taken place 26 years earlier.

A more difficult problem arises if the parties cohabited before the marriage. Obviously this cannot be taken into account under this heading, but it may be relevant under the general requirement that the court should have regard to all the circumstances of the case. Two different situations have to be considered. If the spouses lived together from choice simply because they could not be bothered 'to get round to the paper work' of going through a ceremony of marriage, their cohabitation will generally be disregarded in determining financial provision. Marital rights and duties do not begin before the celebration and it would cheapen

---

8 See *Khan v Khan* [1980] 1 All ER 497; *Taylor v Taylor* (1974) 119 Sol Jo 30; *Warder v Warder* (1978) 122 Sol Jo 713; *West v West* [1978] Fam 1, [1977] 2 All ER 705, CA. In *Browne v Pritchard* [1975] 3 All ER 721, CA, the wife's half-share in the matrimonial home (to the purchase of which she had contributed nothing) was reduced to a third after a marriage which lasted only three years.
9 *Whyte-Smith v Whyte-Smith* (1974) 5 Fam Law 20 (separation after three months; breakdown caused wife illness and loss of job); *Abdureman v Abdureman* (1978) 122 Sol Jo 663 (separation after 12 weeks; wife had given up job and lost pension on marriage).
10 [1997] 2 FLR 26, CA.
11 [1977] Fam 127, [1977] 1 All ER 56, CA.
12 [1985] FLR 789.
13 See generally Deech 'Financial Relief: The Retreat from Precedent and Principle' (1982) 98 LQR 621 at 630–2.
14 [1973] 3 All ER 247, CA.

marriage to permit such a wife to take advantage of the earlier relationship.[15]

This must be distinguished from the case where the parties could not get married because one of them was unable to obtain a divorce, particularly if they lived together for a long time before the marriage and there were children of the union. This occurred in *Kokosinski v Kokosinski*.[16] The husband was a Polish refugee who had lived in this country since the Second World War. He started to live with the petitioner in 1947 and a son was born in 1950. He could not marry her until his first wife (who was still living in Poland) divorced him, which she did not do until 1969. In the meantime the petitioner had been loving, faithful and hardworking, had brought up their child and had played a substantial part in building up the husband's business. The parties married in 1971 but separated in the following year. Wood J was of the opinion that in these circumstances it would offend a reasonable person's sense of justice to ignore this long period of cohabitation and took it into account in deciding what order to make.

A rather different problem arose in *Chaterjee v Chaterjee*,[17] where the parties lived together for 12 or 13 years *after* being divorced. Following their final separation the wife pursued a claim for financial relief. It was held that this cohabitation was akin to marriage for this purpose and consequently that the court could deal with property acquired since the divorce. The same approach was adopted in *S v S (Financial Provision) (Post Divorce Cohabitation)*[18] and, while doubted in *Hewitson v Hewitson*,[19] in *Hill v Hill*[20] the Court of Appeal allowed a 'wife' to seek further financial relief, over twenty-five years after the parties had divorced, and during which period they had cohabited. Just as the court could take pre-marital cohabitation into account in the appropriate circumstances, so too could it consider a period of post-divorce cohabitation in arriving at a reasonable and just solution. It must be emphasised, however, that it is only in the somewhat unusual circumstances of cases like these that cohabitation outside marriage (whether before or after) is likely to affect the order made.

'any physical or mental disability of either of the parties to the marriage'

In practice, these issues are subsumed under the other heads in s 25, especially, of course, that referring to the parties' needs. As noted above, eg in *C v C (Financial Provision: Personal Damages)*,[1] a husband who was rendered paraplegic in a car accident was deemed to need all of the damages awarded to him in a structured

---

15 *Campbell v Campbell* [1976] Fam 347, [1977] 1 All ER 1; cf *Gojkovic v Gojkovic* [1992] Fam 40, [1990] 2 All ER 84, where the substantial award to the wife was in large part based upon her outstanding contribution to the family business and much of her effort was made during pre-marital cohabitation.

16 [1980] Fam 72, [1980] 1 All ER 1106. The facts are not dissimilar from those which would entitle a cohabitant to an order under the Inheritance (Provision for Family and Dependants) Act 1975 after the man's death. See post, p 895.

17 [1976] Fam 199, [1976] 1 All ER 719, CA.

18 [1994] 2 FLR 228, where the parties had divorced in 1977, when a consent order was made, and had resumed cohabitation until 1993. The court set aside the consent order on the basis that the resumption of cohabitation had destroyed the fundamental assumption upon which it had been made.

19 [1995] 1 FLR 241, CA.

20 [1998] 1 FLR 198, CA, reversing the decision of Holman J reported at [1997] 1 FLR 730. While noting 'as a matter of policy' that a cohabitant should not have the equivalent rights of a wife, or former wife, the court pointed to another policy issue – that of encouraging reconciliation – which (in this case) meant that the parties' children had been brought up by them both, in a settled home.

1 [1995] 2 FLR 171. See ante, p 830 n 15.

settlement, and thus his wife and child received nothing, notwithstanding their dependence upon social security benefits.

'the contributions which each of the parties has made or is likely in the foreseeable future to make to the welfare of the family, including any contribution by looking after the home or caring for the family'

It is expressly provided that this is to include any contribution made by looking after the home or caring for the family,[2] but it could no doubt include a financial contribution as well.[3] Although this principle enables the court to recognise the exceptional contribution of a spouse to the family business,[4] it was primarily introduced to give the wife credit for her contribution in kind as housekeeper, wife and mother.[5] There seem to be few cases where the court has expressly given the wife a larger award because of her contribution to the welfare of the family[6] (indeed, as we have seen,[7] in recent 'big money' cases the court appears to be making larger awards in recognition of a wife's contribution, in money or money's worth, to the creation of the family's wealth). Conversely, in *H v H*[8] a wife who had left her husband for another man after 15 years of married life and bringing up four children was given a smaller award on the ground that she had 'left the job unfinished'. The enjoinder to consider what contributions each party is likely to make in the foreseeable future was introduced as a result of the amendment by the Matrimonial and Family Proceedings Act 1984 s 3. It is intended to emphasise in particular the continuing role a parent (usually the mother) may have in looking after any children of the family. As such, it may be a useful counterweight to any contention that there should be a 'clean break' order.

'the conduct of each of the parties, whatever the nature of the conduct and whether it occurred during the marriage or after the separation of the parties or (as the case may be) dissolution or annulment of the marriage if that conduct is such that it would in the opinion of the court be inequitable to disregard it'

The extent to which the court should take a spouse's conduct during the marriage into account when assessing what order should be made, is understandably an emotionally charged issue. Yet even before 1971, when the substantive law was based upon the concept of matrimonial fault, there had been a tendency by the courts, when hearing undefended cases, to place much less stress on the technical

---

2 In *Kokosinski v Kokosinski* (supra), Wood J was of the opinion (at 1115) that the subsection refers only to contributions made after the marriage has taken place. The point is of little importance, as any pre-marital contribution will be taken into account (if at all) under the heading of 'all the circumstances of the case': see supra.

3 So held by Ormrod LJ in *P v P* [1978] 3 All ER 70, CA at 74. Normally this would form part of the parties' property, but this would not be the case if for some reason the capital had disappeared.

4 *Gojkovic v Gojkovic* [1992] Fam 40, [1990] 2 All ER 84, CA.

5 See eg *Duxbury v Duxbury* [1992] Fam 62n, [1990] 2 All ER 77, CA (a wife who had done 'everything expected of her as a wife and mother' was entitled to have her reasonable requirements recognised by the court). See also *Vicary v Vicary* [1992] 2 FLR 271, CA, where the wife's lump sum was assessed by reference to her acting as an 'unimpeachable wife and mother', enabling the husband to concentrate on his business activities.

6 But see *Brisdion v Brisdion* (1974) 5 Fam Law 92, CA; *White v White* [1998] 2 FLR 310, CA: W's contribution as wife and mother over a long marriage justified award of additional £184,500 on top of her share as equal business partner in the family firm, worth £1.5 million.

7 See ante, p 835. See also Thorpe LJ in *Dart v Dart* [1996] 2 FLR 286, CA at 296: '. . . in a big money case where the wife has played an equal part in creating the family fortune it would not be unreasonable for her to require what might even be an equal share'.

8 [1975] Fam 9, [1975] 1 All ER 367; cf *West v West* [1978] Fam 1, [1977] 2 All ER 705, CA.

finding of innocence or guilt. When irretrievable breakdown became the sole ground for divorce in 1971, conduct arguably became of much less significance. The law has been subject to further changes, in 1984 and in 1996, and each stage in this process of reform will be considered in turn.

(a)   The law before the 1984 reform

Under s 25 as originally enacted, the court was directed, inter alia, to exercise its powers so:

'. . . to place the parties, so far as it is practicable and, *having regard to their conduct just to do so*, in the financial position in which they would have been if the marriage had not broken down and each had properly discharged his or her financial obligation and responsibilities towards the other.'[9]

It soon became apparent that 'conduct' should not often be taken into account. The basic principle was established in the leading case of *Wachtel v Wachtel*,[10] in which Lord Denning MR, delivering the judgment of the court, said:[11]

'It has been suggested that there should be a "discount" or "reduction" in what the wife is to receive because of her supposed misconduct, guilt or blame (whatever word is used). We cannot accept this argument. In the vast majority of cases it is repugnant to the principles underlying the new legislation . . . There will be many cases in which a wife (though once considered guilty or blameworthy) will have cared for the home and looked after the family for many years. Is she to be deprived of the benefit otherwise to be accorded to her by s 25(1)(f) because she may share responsibility for the breakdown with her husband? There will no doubt be a residue of cases where the conduct of one of the parties is . . . "both obvious and gross", so much so that to order one party to support another whose conduct falls into this category is repugnant to anyone's sense of justice. In such a case the court remains free to decline to afford financial support or to reduce the support which it would otherwise have ordered. But, short of cases falling into this category, the court should not reduce its order for financial provision merely because of what was formerly regarded as guilt or blame. To do so would be to impose a fine for supposed misbehaviour in the course of an unhappy married life . . . In the financial adjustments consequent upon the dissolution of a marriage which has irretrievably broken down, the imposition of financial penalties ought seldom to find a place.'

In brief, conduct would not affect the order made unless it would be offensive to one's sense of justice to ignore it.[12]

In view of the above, it is hardly surprising that conduct was rarely taken into account. Matrimonial misconduct such as adultery was usually ignored,[13] as were 'brief periods of callous unkindness or brutality'.[14] But of course there were some cases where conduct was held to be relevant. Amongst reported cases, the wife's share was reduced where she had accepted a half-share of the matrimonial home whilst carrying on an adulterous affair,[15] where she had fired a shotgun at her husband,[16] and where she had twice wounded her husband and damaged his career

9 Emphasis added.
10 [1973] Fam 72, [1973] 1 All ER 829, CA.
11 At 90 and 835–6 respectively.
12 Per Orr LJ in *Jones v Jones* [1976] Fam 8 at 15, [1975] 2 All ER 12, CA at 17.
13 See eg *Trippas v Trippas* [1973] Fam 134, [1973] 2 All ER 1, CA, and *Harnett v Harnett* [1974] 1 All ER 764, CA.
14 *Griffiths v Griffiths* [1974] 1 All ER 932.
15 *Cuzner v Underdown* [1974] 2 All ER 351, CA (wife ordered to transfer the half-share to husband).
16 *Armstrong v Armstrong* (1974) 4 Fam Law 156, CA (wife's share reduced to a quarter). A comparison of this case with the last suggests that the courts look more leniently on a wife who intends to inflict serious injury on a husband than on one who is unfaithful!

by her behaviour.[17] In general, however, conduct seemed rarely to have been taken into account.[18]

(b) The law after the 1984 reform

In 1984, with the removal of the status quo ideal or minimal loss principle,[19] conduct was reintroduced as a new s 25(2)(g) of the Matrimonial Causes Act 1973, as a result of an amendment made under the Matrimonial and Family Proceedings Act 1984 s 3. The court was directed to have regard to 'the conduct of each of the parties, if that conduct is such that it would in the opinion of the court be inequitable to disregard it'.

In his evidence to the Special Standing Committee, the President of the Family Division said of the new provision: [20]

> 'In case some attempt were made to argue that the new provision enlarged the extent to which conduct should be taken into account I do not anticipate that this would be likely to be the subject of more than one appeal in the judgment of which I would expect it to be firmly rejected.'

Others[1] felt that the new provision represented a change in emphasis and that it was likely to be seen as a signal to the courts to pay a much greater regard to matrimonial conduct. They shared the view of Lord Denning[2] that the courts would have to inquire into the conduct of the parties before it could be said whether or not it was inequitable to disregard it.

It could also have been said that, since conduct stood as a separate circumstance to which the court had 'in particular' to have regard, not only did it have a higher profile (though that was the necessary drafting consequence of the removal of the 'tail piece' of the original s 25) but it had been given greater statutory emphasis. In the event, however, there seemed to have been no change in practice. In one reported case, *Anthony v Anthony*,[3] where the trial judge took conduct into account because, in his view, the wife 'broke up the marriage', the Court of Appeal held that there was nothing in her conduct of such a serious nature as to justify any reliance upon it. In *Leadbeater v Leadbeater*,[4] conduct was again dismissed as an

---

17 *Bateman v Bateman* [1979] Fam 25, [1979] 2 WLR 377.
18 Though there were those (eg Levin [1984] LAG 101–3) who believed that there had been a shift of emphasis. See also *Kokosinski v Kokosinski* [1980] Fam 72, [1980] 1 All ER 1106 where 'good' conduct was taken into account, as it was in *R v R (Financial Provision)* [1993] Fam Law 282 (wife's payment for a wedding in short childless marriage); cf *E v E (Financial Provision)* [1990] 2 FLR 233 where the wife's adultery and disengagement from family life amounted to a 'negative contribution' which was taken into account.
19 See ante, p 817.
20 HC Official Report, cols 77–78, 22 March 1984. See also Cretney's submission at cols 68–69.
1 Notably the Law Society: see their evidence to the Special Standing Committee at cols 206–207.
2 445 HL Official Report, col 967, 1983–4.
3 [1986] 2 FLR 353, CA.
4 [1985] FLR 789; cf *Suter v Suter and Jones* [1987] Fam 111, [1987] 2 All ER 336, CA, where there is some suggestion that introducing a lover into the former matrimonial home could be taken into account under s 25(2)(g); but contrast *Duxbury v Duxbury* [1992] Fam 62n, [1990] 2 All ER 77, CA where Ackner LJ said that applying s 25 is essentially a 'financial not a moral exercise'. In *Atkinson v Atkinson* [1988] Fam 93, [1987] 3 All ER 849, CA it was said that, in general, a former spouse's cohabitation with a third party after divorce is to be disregarded, since the court ought not to impose an unjustifiable fetter on the freedom of the former spouses to live their lives as they chose. On the other hand, the court did suggest that there may be cases where the conduct of a former spouse in the context of cohabitation, such as financial or sexual or other conduct, may mean that it cannot be ignored.

issue, in part because each spouse's conduct cancelled the other's out, but mainly because the judge did not think it inequitable to ignore it.

Perhaps the leading authority was *Kyte v Kyte*,[5] where the husband suffered from manic depression, which caused the wife suffering and unhappiness. On several occasions the husband tried, unsuccessfully, to commit suicide. The registrar found that on one of these occasions the wife (who knew she stood to inherit on the husband's death) did nothing to stop him. On another she provided drugs and alcohol to facilitate the attempt. The wife had also formed 'a deceitful relationship' with another man. In the Court of Appeal, Purchas LJ (giving the judgment of the court) said[6] that the court must look at the whole picture, including conduct during the marriage and after the marriage which might or might not have contributed to the breakdown. Although the parties may not each have been blameless, a spouse should only be penalised where the imbalance of conduct, one way or the other, would make it inequitable to ignore the comparative conduct of the parties. On this basis, the wife's behaviour (even when considered in the context of the husband's) was gross and obvious and so her lump sum award was reduced from £14,000 to just £5,000. In the later case of *Evans v Evans*[7] (where conduct would surely have been relevant whatever approach was adopted) the Court of Appeal upheld the discharge of a periodical payments order in favour of a wife when she was convicted of inciting others to kill her husband. The test propounded in *Kyte v Kyte*, in terms of the 'comparability' of the spouses' behaviour, was applied in *K v K (Financial Provision)*.[8] Here the wife had made great efforts to improve herself, in contrast to the husband, who had failed to make adequate efforts to find employment and had a serious drink problem which resulted in disagreeable behaviour and his neglect of the matrimonial home. The lump sum payable to the husband was reduced. It should be noted that the conduct to which the court could have regard was not restricted to that in relation to the breakdown of the marriage: it also embraced conduct in the context of the ancillary relief proceedings themselves. Whilst misconduct in the proceedings was usually reflected in the court's order for costs, on occasion it influenced the amount of the award the court made. For example, in *B v B (Real Property: Assessment of Interests)*[9] a wife's deceitful behaviour in relation to discovery was held to be conduct inequitable to ignore.

(c)   The Family Law Act 1996

On numerous occasions in the debates on the Family Law Bill the concern was expressed that the courts were reluctant to take into account conduct in relation to the making of financial and property orders. Although initially the Lord Chancellor expressed satisfaction with the existing law,[10] the government

---

5 [1988] Fam 145, [1987] 3 All ER 1041, CA.
6 At 155 and 1048 respectively.
7 [1989] 1 FLR 351, CA. See also *H v H (Financial Provision: Conduct)* [1994] 2 FLR 801 (husband's conduct in brutally assaulting wife taken into account) and *A v A (Financial Provision: Conduct)* [1995] 1 FLR 345 (husband's assault upon wife was conduct which was taken into account but not so as to deprive the husband of all his capital).
8 [1990] 2 FLR 225.
9 [1998] 2 FLR 490. See also *Beach v Beach* [1995] 2 FLR 160 and *H v H (Financial Relief: Conduct)* [1998] 1 FLR 971 – husband's misuse of family funds taken into account.
10 Official Report (HL) 4 March 1996, vol 570, no 54, col 131.

subsequently accepted the need for change, the Parliamentary Secretary in the Lord Chancellor's Department explaining:

> '. . . there is a perception that conduct is not, in practice, taken into account by the courts. Anecdotal evidence suggests that if conduct is taken into account only conduct of a financial nature is considered.'[11]

The statutory amendment, which was brought forward, inserts the additional wording '. . . whatever the nature of the conduct and whether it occurred during the marriage or after the separation of the parties or (as the case may be) dissolution or annulment of the marriage' into s 25(2)(g) of the 1973 Act. Its intention is '. . . to emphasise that conduct of the parties of whatever nature, should it be inequitable for the court to disregard it, has to be considered and that it is not only conduct in the course of ancillary relief proceedings that is to be considered.'[12] It is difficult to assess what effect this change of statutory language will have. It sits uneasily with the greater emphasis in the Act on irretrievable breakdown as the sole criterion of the failure of the marriage, and on mediated settlements and compromise. Although the Lord Chancellor denied that the role of conduct in ancillary relief proceedings would be likely to change or '. . . of conduct being introduced through the back door',[13] the statutory amendment must be taken to be intended to have some effect. If there is likely to be a greater emphasis on conduct than in the past, then those thinking of alleging it should still carefully consider whether it is in their interests to do so, since such allegations are likely to be contested and in consequence, of course, the costs of the proceedings will be higher.

'the value to each of the parties to the marriage of any benefit (for example a pension) which, by reason of the dissolution or annulment of the marriage, that party will lose the chance of acquiring'

The obvious example of such a benefit (which the Act specifies) is a pension. As we have seen, the court's power to make financial provision orders in relation to pensions has recently been the subject of legislative changes, although the working in practice of these changes cannot yet be clearly assessed. In *T v T (Financial Relief: Pensions)*[14] Singer J declined to use the earmarking power in s 25B to order deferred periodical payments to a wife, where the spouses were still in their forties and there were too many uncertainties in seeking to predict their situation by the time the husband reached retirement age. She should, however, be secured against the termination of ongoing periodical payments by the husband's death prior to retirement, through a direction to the pension trustees to pay her a lump sum out of any death benefits arising under the scheme.

One additional right that a divorced wife loses is that of claiming social security benefits by virtue of her husband's contributions; another is the loss of an entitlement on the husband's intestacy. A further example of a lost benefit is to be seen in *Trippas v Trippas*.[15] After the parties had separated, the husband received a

---

11 Standing Committee E, Official Report, 16 May 1996, col 370.
12 Ibid.
13 Official Report (HL) 27 June 1996, no 1672, col 1113.
14 [1998] 1 FLR 1072.
15 [1973] Fam 134, [1973] 2 All ER 1, CA but was not the loss to the wife caused by the breakdown of the marriage, rather than by its dissolution? See also *Kokosinski v Kokosinski* [1980] Fam 72, [1980] 1 All ER 1106.

considerable sum from the sale of a family business. The court awarded the wife a lump sum of £10,000 on the ground that, had the marriage still been on foot, she would have received such a benefit either directly in cash or indirectly in kind; furthermore, the husband could have been expected to leave her a large sum if he had predeceased her, so that she had lost something analogous to a pension.

3.   THE MATRIMONIAL HOME [16]

We have already noticed that the matrimonial home presents particular problems. In many cases (perhaps apart from accrued pension rights) it will be the only asset of any value owned by either spouse. It may be the only means of giving one of the spouses (whom, for the sake of argument, we shall assume to be the wife) the security of a home with the children in the future. Consequently the parties' interests will often be in direct conflict: the wife will wish to be given the right to occupy the house, whilst the husband will want an immediate sale so as to realise his capital, without which he may be unable to buy another home for his second family. Faced with this, the court's first concern must be to ensure that the children (and therefore the spouse with whom the children are living) have a home.[17] It should certainly do its utmost to avoid ordering a sale of the matrimonial home if this will merely result in having to re-house the party in occupation.[18]

Once the children's accommodation has been secured, the court must try to make an order which will give the other spouse a home as well. In *M v B (Ancillary Proceedings: Lump Sum)* [19] the Court of Appeal considered that in any case where, by stretch and risk-taking, there is the possibility of a division which will enable both parties to rehouse themselves, this is an exceptionally important consideration and one which, almost invariably, will have a decisive impact on the outcome. This is so particularly where young children are involved; while the primary carer needs to make the main home for the children, it is also important (albeit to a lesser extent) that the other parent has a home where the children can enjoy contact. Very often, however, it will be impossible to rehouse both spouses, since if the former matrimonial home is sold, the division of the proceeds of sale will be insufficient to enable the spouses to buy anything else.

A temporary solution is to defer the sale of the house until the children have left home so that the parent with whom they have been living can reasonably be expected to move into smaller accommodation. By that time, of course, she (or he) may find it difficult to raise a mortgage, and if it is impossible to find a way of giving them both a home, either immediately or in the future, the court will have no alternative to leaving one of them in occupation indefinitely. This occurred in *Martin v Martin*.[20] The husband had gone to live with another woman in a council

---

16 See generally Jackson's *Matrimonial Finance and Taxation* (6th edn, 1996, by Hayward Smith and Newton) ch 9; and Hayes and Battersby 'Property Adjustment: Order or Disorder in the Former Matrimonial Home?' [1985] Fam Law 213; Hayes and Battersby 'Property Adjustment: Further Thoughts on Charge Orders' [1986] Fam Law 142; and Hayes 'Cohabitation Clauses: Financial and Property Adjustment Orders – Law Policy and Justice' (1994) 110 LQR 124.

17 *Browne v Pritchard* [1975] 3 All ER 721, CA at 724; *Scott v Scott* [1978] 3 All ER 65, CA.

18 See eg *Ross v Ross* [1989] 2 FLR 257, CA.

19 [1998] 1 FLR 53, CA. See also *H v H (Financial Provision: Conduct)* [1998] 1 FLR 971.

20 [1978] Fam 12, [1977] 3 All ER 762, CA; cf *Eshak v Nowojewski* (1980) 11 Fam Law 115, CA (sale deferred until death of husband who had custody of children and was unable to work; wife had remarried and her second husband was catering for her needs).

house of which the latter was the tenant and which would apparently be transferred to them both jointly. The wife was left alone in the former matrimonial home which belonged to both spouses beneficially in equal shares. The Court of Appeal affirmed the judge's order that the house should be held on trust for the wife during her life, or until her remarriage or such earlier date as she should cease to live there and thereafter on trust for them both in equal shares. The husband was already provided with another home and consequently had no need of the capital; the wife, on the other hand, would have been unable to purchase alternative accommodation with her half-share of the capital and so an immediate sale would have deprived her of the modest comfortable home that she had before the marriage broke down.[1]

We must now consider the various ways in which the court may use the wide range of powers that it has at its disposal.

Buying out the other spouse's share

The court may force the wife to buy out the husband's interest by ordering him to transfer his share to her and ordering her to pay him a lump sum equal to its value. This is the ideal solution because she retains a roof over her head and he gets the immediate use of his money. Obviously, however, such an order can be made only if the wife has sufficient capital or, alternatively, a large enough income to pay the sum in instalments, or to raise it by borrowing (perhaps secured by mortgage on the property) and consequently it is not likely to be met often in practice. If, however, the husband does not need the capital immediately, the payment can be deferred until the house is sold.

Outright transfer of share to other spouse with no compensation

The court can order the husband to transfer his share of the home to the wife without any compensating payment on her part. There are a number of quite dissimilar situations in which this may offer the best solution. If the house forms only part of the capital assets which have to be apportioned, it may be transferred to the wife in part or complete extinction of her claim for a lump sum or other capital settlement. Again, if the husband is a rich man, the wife might take the house as representing the capitalisation of part, or all of her claim for periodical payments which will be proportionately reduced or, in a suitable case, discharged altogether, thereby achieving an 'immediate' clean break. It might also be felt desirable to capitalise periodical payments if the husband's past behaviour indicated that any other order might prove to be ineffective.[2] At the other end of the economic scale, if the husband's earnings are so small that it will be impossible for him to make an adequate contribution towards the support of the wife and children of the family, the only possible solution might be to transfer the matrimonial home to her unconditionally and make no order, or only a minimal order, against him for periodical payments. This occurred, for example, in *S v S*,[3] where the husband was ordered to pay a total of £4 a week for

---

1 The implications for legally aided parties of the Legal Aid Board's statutory charge (discussed ante, p 807) must not be overlooked.
2 As in *Bryant v Bryant* (1976) 6 Fam Law 108, CA.
3 [1976] Fam 18n, [1975] 2 All ER 19n.

his wife and daughter and to transfer his half-share in the matrimonial home to the former. This may prove to be much more valuable to the wife than a relatively greater order for periodical payments if she can claim income support, because the value of the house will not be taken into account in assessing the benefit payable. Even if the parties are not at either extreme of the economic spectrum, the particular circumstances may make it necessary to order a transfer of the matrimonial home without payment, but with a compensating reduction in periodical payments, as the only way of ensuring that either of them has a home. In *Hanlon v Hanlon*[4] the husband was a police officer who, since separating from his wife, was living rent-free in a police house. On his retirement he could expect a lump sum payment of up to £7,000. The wife was living in the matrimonial home with the two sons of the marriage (then both apprentices over the age of 18) and the two daughters, who were still at school. The most that the parties could expect from the sale of the house was £10,000[5] which, if divided equally, would give neither of them enough to buy any other accommodation. In these circumstances the Court of Appeal ordered that the husband's half-share should be transferred to the wife, in return for which she was prepared to forgo any further periodical payments for the two girls. It will be appreciated, of course, that the effect of the Child Support Act 1991[6] means that such orders do not enable the absent parent to avoid his continuing maintenance liability towards the children, and hence the incentive for agreeing to such a settlement has been reduced.

A transfer of the husband's interests without compensation might also be appropriate if his conduct justified the extinction of his share.[7] In conjunction with other factors such an order has also been made when the wife's earning capacity has been so seriously impaired that she is in greater need of security than usual: in *Jones v Jones*[8] this was the result of the husband's conduct in inflicting an injury on her, and in *S v S*[9] of having to nurse a young daughter suffering from kidney trouble.

Two further points should be borne in mind which may be of particular importance when dealing with the property of less affluent spouses. In the first place, the court may make an order transferring a protected statutory, secure or assured tenancy from one spouse to the other.[10] Secondly, like any other lease, a council tenancy is 'property' for the purpose of s 24 of the Matrimonial Causes Act and the court may therefore make an order in relation to it.[11] In exercising its powers, the court is entitled to have regard to the local authority's housing policy, and its likely impact on the parties, and their separate prospects of re-housing.[12]

---

4 [1978] 2 All ER 889, CA.
5 In point of fact, because of (what was then) the Law Society's legal aid charge for costs (see ante, p 808), this expectation was considerably reduced: see the later case of *Hanlon v Law Society* [1981] AC 124, [1980] 2 All ER 199, HL.
6 See ante, pp 727–50.
7 See *Bryant v Bryant* (supra); *S v S* (infra); *H v H (Financial Provision: Conduct)* [1994] 2 FLR 801.
8 [1976] Fam 8, [1975] 2 All ER 12, CA. See Ellis 'The Discretion to Adjust Property Rights after Divorce' (1976) 39 MLR 97.
9 [1976] Fam 18n, [1975] 2 All ER 19n followed in *Jones v Jones* (supra).
10 Family Law Act 1996 Sch 7, discussed ante, p 179.
11 *Thompson v Thompson* [1976] Fam 25, [1975] 2 All ER 208, CA; cf *Hale v Hale* [1975] 2 All ER 1090, CA. See also *Newlon Housing Trust v Al-Sulaimen* [1998] 3 WLR 451, HL.
12 *Jones v Jones* [1997] 1 FLR 27, CA, reversing dicta in *Thompson v Thompson* (supra) on the basis of changes in the relationship of council tenant and council in what is now Housing Act 1985.

Postponing sale of the home until a specified event

(a) Mesher orders

The order may provide that both spouses shall keep or acquire an interest in the house as equitable tenants in common, which will involve settling it on them on trust (if it is not already so held), and that sale of the home should be deferred until some specified time in the future. In the meantime the wife will be given exclusive possession. Such an order enables both spouses to keep their interest in the capital, but also resolves the immediate problem of accommodation for the wife and the children. For some years perhaps the commonest type of order made was referred to as a *Mesher* order.[13] Here, it was normal to order that the sale of the property should not take place until the youngest child reached a specified age (often 17) or, perhaps, until all the children completed their education, or until the wife died, or until further order.[14]

Although frequently made in practice, *Mesher* orders have a number of defects and have been heavily criticised by the courts.[15] In the first place, the husband and wife will have to act together to effect the sale, perhaps many years after the divorce, and this may cause difficulties, particularly if their relationship is bitter.[16] Secondly, children often do not leave home until long after they have completed their education and may therefore still need the house as their home. Thirdly, being 'property transfer orders' they are not variable even if, for example, the husband reneges on his obligation to make periodical payments.[17] Finally, and perhaps most significantly, a *Mesher* order may lead to a wife being thrown on the housing market in middle age, after her children have left home, without the capital or income to secure adequate alternative accommodation for herself. In short, as Parker LJ said in *Mortimer v Mortimer-Griffin*,[18] such orders are likely to produce harsh and unsatisfactory results. There may be exceptional cases where the *Mesher* order continues to produce the best solution,[19] but where there is doubt as to a wife's ability to re-house herself, then a *Mesher* order should not be made.[20]

(b) Martin orders

A rather different order, in effect, if not in form, is the *Martin* order named after the case discussed earlier.[1] As with the *Mesher* order, the matrimonial home is

---

13 From the name of the case in which such an order was made, *Mesher v Mesher and Hall* (1973) reported [1980] 1 All ER 126n, CA.
14 It is important that the court should retain the option of ordering an earlier sale in case the wife remarries or some unforeseen event occurs. See further post, p 852.
15 See eg *Hanlon v Hanlon* [1978] 2 All ER 889, CA at 892–3, per Ormrod LJ; *Carson v Carson* [1983] 1 All ER 478, CA at 482–3, per Ormrod LJ; and *Harman v Glencross* [1986] Fam 81, [1986] 1 All ER 545, CA at 556 per Balcombe LJ.
16 For problems relating to the need for repairs to the house: see *Harvey v Harvey* [1987] 1 FLR 67. But see *Teschner v Teschner* [1985] FLR 627, CA.
17 As in *Carson v Carson*, supra. See also *Dinch v Dinch* [1987] 1 All ER 818, HL.
18 [1986] 2 FLR 315, CA at 319.
19 See eg *Rushton v Rushton* (1978) 1 FLR 195, CA, where Ormrod LJ said that the right order 'for once' seemed to be a *Mesher* order.
20 *Clutton v Clutton* [1991] 1 All ER 340, CA at 346 (per Lloyd LJ). A similar approach can be seen, by way of analogy, in *Greenham v Greenham* [1989] 1 FLR 105, CA where it was said to be 'wrong' to order a husband to sell his home, and pay a lump sum to the wife, on his attaining the age of 70. The Court of Appeal varied the order to provide for a lump sum to be payable on the husband's death or on the earlier sale of the property.
1 [1978] Fam 12, [1977] 3 All ER 762, CA; see ante, p 845.

settled upon the spouses on trust for themselves as beneficial tenants in common. However, the contingent events specified in the order as triggering a sale are designed to ensure that the wife remains in occupation of the house for as long as she needs a roof over her head. In *Harvey v Harvey*,[2] for example, the court ordered the sale to be postponed until the wife's death or remarriage, or until she voluntarily left home or became dependent upon another man. In *Clutton v Clutton*[3] the Court of Appeal gave its approval to a *Martin* order in a slightly different form. The sale was to take place on the death, remarriage or cohabitation of the wife whereupon the proceeds were to be divided, two-thirds to the wife and one-third to the husband. The Court held that a *Martin* order in these terms did not suffer from the same disadvantages as a *Mesher* order as far as the occupying spouse was concerned. Nor did it offend against the clean break principle which ought not to mean that one of the spouses was to be deprived of any share in an asset acquired by the joint efforts of both. The wife had argued that the effect of the order would be to make her subject to 'perpetual supervision' by the husband, who would be anxious to establish cohabitation and trigger a sale. While accepting the force of this argument, Lloyd LJ[4] suggested that the bitterness the wife might feel on being 'spied on' was far outweighed by the bitterness the husband would feel if the wife, despite her present assertions, soon remarried or cohabited and continued to occupy the former matrimonial home.[5]

Transfer with charge on the home

The court may order the husband to transfer his interest to the wife and give him a charge on the house equal to the value of his share.[6] The charge should not be realised until the wife no longer needs to live in the house and it can be sold. This solution is to be preferred because the husband will not have to concur in the sale and the spouses can make a clean break.[7] His charge should represent a given fraction of the value of the house at the time of the sale;[8] if it is fixed by reference to its present value, the sum which the husband will eventually receive will not have increased to take account of inflation.[9]

---

2 [1982] Fam 83, [1982] 1 All ER 693, CA. See also *Brown v Brown* (1981) 3 FLR 161, CA.
3 [1991] 1 All ER 340, CA.
4 Ibid at 344 and 345.
5 For criticism of the *Clutton* Order, see Hayes 'Cohabitation Clauses in Financial Provision and Property Adjustment Orders – Law, Policy and Justice' (1994) 110 LQR 124.
6 Although such orders appear to be frequently made in practice there is no express statutory power in the Matrimonial Causes Act 1973, Pt II to *order* a spouse to execute a charge over the former matrimonial home, or *impose* a charge on property ordered to be transferred from one spouse to another. However, it appears such orders can be effected by imposing conditions on the exercise of the express powers in ss 21–24A (eg H can be ordered to *transfer* Whiteacre to W *upon condition* W executes a charge in favour of H) or, alternatively, they can be incorporated into consent orders formulated as undertakings given to the court following *Livesey (formerly Jenkins) v Jenkins* [1985] AC 424, [1985] 1 All ER 106, HL. See further Bird 'Problems in Ancillary Relief Orders' [1990] Fam Law 420.
7 See *Schuller v Schuller* [1990] 2 FLR 193, CA where, on the facts, the court refused to order a deferred charge which was to be enforceable on the death of the elderly husband or on earlier sale of the property. Butler-Sloss LJ said (at 199) that such an order would 'fly in the face of the duty upon the court to try, wherever possible, to create a clean break'.
8 As in *Browne v Pritchard* [1975] 3 All ER 721, CA. See also *H v H* [1975] Fam 9, [1975] 1 All ER 367.
9 Such an order was made in *Hector v Hector* [1973] 3 All ER 1070, CA but was regarded as out of line by Latey J in *S v S* [1976] Fam 18n at 21, [1975] 2 All ER 19n at 21.

Settlement on spouse and children

The possibility of settling the house for the benefit of the wife and children[10] appears to be little used in practice. It would usually involve giving the wife a life interest with remainder to children and consequently will rarely provide the best solution, because neither spouse will ever have the use of the capital and, save in exceptional circumstances, the court does not make an order providing for children after they have completed their education or training.[11]

Occupation only

The court could leave the whole beneficial interest in the house with the husband and give the wife exclusive occupation until she no longer needs the security of the house to bring up the children (for example, until all the children have completed their full-time education) or until further order. This will of course in the end leave her homeless and consequently should be used only if she will be able to make provision for her own accommodation when her right to occupation comes to an end, or if the circumstances are such that she should be given no part of the capital value. It may also be necessary to make such an order if the husband has no power to assign the matrimonial home so that the court cannot order it to be transferred or settled.[12] There is apparently no power to make an order relating to occupation alone under the Matrimonial Causes Act 1973, and a wife seeking such an order would have to apply for it under s 17 of the Married Women's Property Act 1882 or ask the court to continue her matrimonial home rights under s 30 of the Family Law Act 1996 after the dissolution or annulment of the marriage.[13]

Immediate sale and division of proceeds

The court could order the house to be sold[14] and the proceeds to be divided in such proportions as it thinks fit. This might be the best way of dealing with the situation if there were no children living at home and the house was too big for either spouse to live in alone. The money should be sufficient to give at least one of them (and preferably both) enough to put down as a deposit on the purchase of a new house or flat. This solution is not appropriate if its effect would be to deprive both of them of a home.

If there is any danger that the husband will try to dispose of the home before an order is made, the wife's simplest remedy before the divorce takes effect is to register her matrimonial home rights as a Class F land charge under the Land Charges Act 1972 or, in the case of registered land, by notice under the Land Registration Act 1925; alternatively she could apply to have the husband restrained

---

10 See *Wachtel v Wachtel* [1973] Fam 72 at 96, [1973] 1 All ER 829, CA, where Lord Denning MR referred to settling a lump sum.
11 *Chamberlain v Chamberlain* [1974] 1 All ER 33, CA, allowing an appeal against such an order, and *Kiely v Kiely* [1988] 1 FLR 248, CA. But cf *H v H (Financial Provision: Conduct)* [1998] 1 FLR 971 where a lump sum to enable the husband to buy a house was settled on trust for him with reversion to the children.
12 See ante, p 797.
13 See ante, p 115 (Married Women's Property Act) and p 68 (Family Law Act). An application for the former may be made for three years after dissolution or annulment but an order under the latter must be made before decree absolute. Neither remedy is available if the marriage is void.
14 Under s 24A of the Matrimonial Causes Act 1973.

from selling it on the ground that the disposition would defeat her claim for financial relief.[15] A further problem arises if the house is subject to a mortgage (as will frequently be the case). If the husband is to continue to pay the instalments, in theory any periodical payments should be reduced by the amount of interest repaid (which can be regarded as equivalent to rent) whilst he ought to be given an enlarged share of the proceeds of sale representing the capital repaid. This would involve highly complex calculations and constant variations of periodical payments as a progressively larger fraction of the instalments represented the repayment of capital; in practice, therefore, the husband will be compensated by being ordered to make smaller periodical payments or given a larger share of the capital on sale.

E.   Variation, discharge, suspension and revival of orders

1.   ORDERS THAT MAY BE VARIED

The court has power to vary, discharge or suspend any of the following orders and to revive any term suspended:[16]

- interim maintenance orders;
- periodical payments (secured and unsecured);
- an order relating to instalments in the case of lump sum payments;
- a deferred order made in relation to pensions;
- an order for the settlement (but not the transfer) of property made on or after the making of a separation order;
- an order for the variation of a marriage settlement made on or after the making of a separation order;
- any order for the sale of property.

Periodical payments are normally variable because they are intended as maintenance for the payee and, if either party's needs or resources change, justice may demand a corresponding change in the amount payable. Accordingly, unless the fixed term for which the court may have ordered periodical payments to continue has expired,[17] an application may be made to vary an order. The principal exception is where the court has expressly added a s 28(1A) direction, ie that the period fixed

---

15 See ante, p 69 (matrimonial home rights) and post, p 861 (restraining dispositions). But registration of a Class F land charge will be set aside as an abuse of process if the wife has no intention of occupying the house: *Barnett v Hassett* [1982] 1 All ER 80.

16 Matrimonial Causes Act 1973 s 31(1), (2), as amended by the Family Law Act 1996 Sch 8, para 16. The court may also order any instrument to be varied etc: s 31(3).

17 In *T v T (Financial Provision)* [1988] 1 FLR 480 a periodical payments order in favour of a wife was expressed to take effect until the wife remarried, or the husband retired or until further order. It was held that the wife could not apply for a variation after the husband retired. The words 'or further order' could be relied on for an earlier variation, ie before the happening of the specified event, but not afterwards. The same approach was adopted in *Richardson v Richardson* [1994] 1 FLR 286 and approved by the Court of Appeal in *G v G (Periodical Payments: Jurisdiction)* [1997] 1 FLR 368, CA. Here Ward LJ suggested that one way around the problem would be for a court to make a substantial periodical payments order for a fixed term followed by a nominal order. This, at least, would 'give a peg on which to hang a late variation application'. See further Harcus 'Periodical Payments Order – End of Term?' [1997] Fam Law 340.

for the order cannot be extended. As we have seen,[18] such orders are intended to provide for a 'deferred clean break' between the parties where it is thought that the parties can become financially independent of one another. On the other hand, once a lump sum has been paid, it cannot be discharged or varied; it would therefore be unfair to the payee if her right to a sum not yet paid could be prejudiced on the ground that the court had softened the blow to the payer by providing that he could pay the sum in question over a period of time. The same objection cannot be raised, however, to a change in the period or manner in which the instalments are paid, and consequently these can be varied by an alteration of their size or frequency. In *Tilley v Tilley*[19] the Court of Appeal held that this power enables the court to suspend or to remit future instalments entirely: a decision endorsed in *Penrose v Penrose*,[20] where Balcombe LJ considered such power should be exercised 'with caution'. The reason that, generally speaking, orders relating to property cannot be varied is that they are designed to make a final adjustment of the spouses' rights, so that any subsequent change in their needs and resources is irrelevant. Settlements of property and variations of marriage settlements made on the making of separation orders will come into a different category, however, because a further adjustment may have to be made if the marriage is later dissolved, and the spouses themselves may wish to have the order varied if they become reconciled. Consequently, variations of these orders will be made only in proceedings on an application for a divorce order in relation to the marriage.[21]

Section 31(7)(a) of the 1973 Act 1973[1] places the court's duty to consider making a 'clean break' on a variation application on the same footing as in relation to original orders. On applications to vary periodical payments (secured or unsecured) made in divorce or nullity proceedings, the court shall consider:

'. . . whether it would be appropriate to vary the order so that payments under the order are required to be made or secured only for such further period as will in the opinion of the court be sufficient . . . to enable the party in whose favour the order was made to adjust without undue hardship to the termination of those payments.'

The court has power[2] to direct that an order for variation or discharge of a periodical payments order shall not take effect until the expiry of a specified period, thus enabling the payee to adjust, in the interim, to a termination of the payments in her favour or a reduction in their amount. Where, on a variation application, the court imposes a 'clean break' (by either discharging a periodical payments order or directing it continues only for a fixed period), it will have power[3] to order a 'compensating' lump sum[4] or property adjustment order.[5] The court may also order that the payee under the original periodical payments order shall not be entitled to apply for a further order, or for an extension of its term.[6] This power to order a

---

18 Ante, p 823. There is no power to vary an order dismissing an application for periodical payments made under s 25A(3).
19 (1979) 10 Fam Law 89, CA.
20 [1994] 2 FLR 621, CA.
21 Matrimonial Causes Act 1973 s 31(4) as amended by Family Law Act 1996 Sch 8, para 16.
1 As amended by Family Law Act 1996 Sch 8, para 16.
2 Matrimonial Causes Act 1973 s 31(10).
3 Ibid, s 31(7A) and (7B) as inserted by Family Law Act 1996 Sch 8, para 16.
4 Where a lump sum is ordered in these circumstances, it may be ordered to be paid by instalments, which may be secured: Matrimonial Causes Act 1973 s 31(7c).
5 Where the court makes more than one property adjustment order in favour of the same party, it may only make a single order of each type: Matrimonial Causes Act 1973 s 31(7E).
6 Matrimonial Causes Act 1973 s 31(7B)(c).

spouse to make capital provision in substitution of future periodical payments was introduced following the recommendation of the Law Commission.[7] It remains to be seen how often the power will be used. The court is not given any statutory guidance on calculating a fair level of capital commutation, although, no doubt, in an appropriate case of substantial figures, the application of a *Duxbury*-type calculation[8] may be of assistance.

A *Mesher* order, being a property adjustment order, cannot be varied.[9] In *Norman v Norman*[10] a husband attempted to invoke the court's powers of sale under s 24A to accelerate a sale following a *Mesher* order, but the court rejected this on the ground that such an order would in reality be a variation of the *Mesher* order. It was held that the proper procedure was to apply for a sale under what was then the Law of Property Act 1925 s 30.[11] In *Thompson v Thompson*,[12] however, it was held that, provided the sale was deferred inter alia 'until further order',[13] there was power to order an earlier sale under s 24A, at any rate on the application of the party in occupation, since in the court's view this would be to work out the terms of the original order rather than to amount to a substantive variation of its terms.[14] On the other hand, in *Taylor v Taylor*,[15] in which the matrimonial home was made subject to a charge in favour of the wife who retained exclusive right of occupation, the husband applied under s 24A for an earlier sale and the Court of Appeal seemed to take the view that this was a matter which went to the court's discretion rather than jurisdiction. In other words, there was power to order the sale under s 24A, but the question remained whether, on the merits, that power should be exercised.

In *Omielan v Omielan*,[16] the question raised was whether a sale could be ordered to be deferred on a subsequent variation application. A consent order had been made whereby the parties agreed to divide the proceeds of sale of the former matrimonial home, 75 per cent to the children, 25 per cent to the wife. The sale was to be postponed until the wife remarried, died or cohabited with another man for longer than six months. When it became known that the wife had been living with another man for six months, the husband applied for an order for sale; the wife applied for a variation, asking that the sale be postponed until the youngest child attained 18. The Court of Appeal held it had no jurisdiction to entertain the wife's application. The original order constituted a variation of settlement to which an ancillary order for sale was attached. The court's powers to vary orders for sale are limited to subsidiary matters of implementation, enforcement or procedure; they do not give jurisdiction to re-open primary property adjustment orders.[17]

---

7   Law Com No 192, paragraphs 6.8–6.10. Until the entry into force of the Family Law Act 1996, there is no such power, although in *S v S* [1986] Fam 189 Waite J held that as a matter of law it was open to the court to terminate a wife's periodical payments on the basis of a suitable capital offer from the husband. See also *Boylan v Boylan* [1988] 1 FLR 282; *Peacock v Peacock* [1991] 1 FLR 324.
8   See the discussion ante at p 835.
9   *Carson v Carson* [1983] 1 All ER 478. See the views of the Law Commission: Law Com 192 paragraph 6.3.
10   [1983] 1 All ER 486.
11   Now Trusts of Land and Appointment of Trustees Act 1996 s 14.
12   [1986] Fam 38, [1985] 2 All ER 243, CA.
13   Or words to similar effect. Express authority can be given to allow the parties to come back to the court to ask for an earlier sale: see eg *Anthony v Anthony* [1986] 2 FLR 353, CA at 359.
14   Aliter if it was sought to *delay* the sale or if the party not in occupation sought the sale.
15   [1987] 1 FLR 142, CA.
16   [1996] 2 FLR 306, CA. See also *Harper v O'Reilly and Harper* [1997] 2 FLR 816.
17   For the position concerning redemption of a charge over the matrimonial home, see *Popat v Popat* [1991] 2 FLR 163 and *Knibb v Knibb* [1987] 2 FLR 396.

As we have seen,[18] the legislative approach is to encourage the parties to reach early agreement on their financial arrangements for the future; financial provision or property adjustment orders may be made before divorce, although they will not generally take effect until the divorce order is made. The courts will have special powers of variation to deal with the situation where future orders turn out to have been made prematurely, and, in particular, where the parties subsequently become reconciled.[19]

2. FACTORS TO BE TAKEN INTO CONSIDERATION

The Act provides that, on hearing an application for variation, the court shall have regard to all the circumstances of the case, first consideration being given to the welfare while a minor of any child of the family who has not attained the age of 18, and the circumstances of the case shall include any change in the matters to which it was required to have regard when making the order in the first place.[20] If the application is made after the death of the party against whom the order was originally made, the court must also take into account the changed circumstances resulting from the death.[1] It should be noted that while it is important not to allow variation applications to be used as a disguised appeal against the terms of the original order, the court's discretion is completely unfettered.[2] In *Flavell v Flavell*[3] the Court of Appeal held that jurisdiction to vary an order does not depend upon an exceptional or material change of circumstance, although the absence of such change may affect the exercise of the court's discretion. The court is not required to proceed from the starting point of the original order, but will consider the matter de novo.

Two judicial limitations have been placed on the court's power, however. First, the parties are still estopped per rem judicatem from raising matters inconsistent with a previous decree or order, and neither party may adduce evidence which could have been put before the court when the original order was made.[4] Secondly, a party who has led the other to act to his or her detriment on the assumption that he will continue to honour the order may not later apply to have it reduced or discharged. In *B (MAL) v B (NE)*[5] the husband and the wife had entered into a separation agreement before the wife petitioned for divorce, with the result that she did not immediately seek financial provision. Some years later the husband was adjudicated bankrupt and the wife agreed to consent to his discharge on his undertaking not to oppose an application by her for leave to apply to the court for maintenance. In the maintenance proceedings the husband

18 See ante, p 801.
19 See Matrimonial Causes Act 1973 s 31A, as inserted by Family Law Act 1996 Sch 2, para 8. Note also the court's powers to vary orders made during the period for reflection and consideration – see Matrimonial Causes Act 1973 s 31(4A) and (4B) as inserted by Family Law Act 1996 Sch 8, para 16.
20 Matrimonial Causes Act 1973 s 31(7)(a).
1 Ibid s 31(7)(b). See *Jones v Jones* [1971] 3 All ER 1201 at 1206 and 1207.
2 *Lewis v Lewis* [1977] 3 All ER 992, CA; *Garner v Garner* [1992] 1 FLR 573, CA (a case concerning child maintenance); *Cornick v Cornick (No 2)* [1995] 2 FLR 490, CA.
3 [1997] 1 FLR 353, CA.
4 *Hall v Hall* (1914) 111 LT 403, CA.
5 [1968] 1 WLR 1109.

alleged that the wife had been guilty of adultery, but in the event he did not pursue these allegations and submitted to a consent order for periodical payments against himself. He later established that the wife's youngest child was illegitimate and then sought to have the maintenance order discharged on the ground that the wife had obtained it by fraud. It was held that he must fail for two reasons. Having raised the matter of the wife's adultery at a time when he had evidence to prove it and then submitted to judgment by consent, he was estopped from opening the question again: it certainly did not lie in his mouth to say that she had misled the court. Furthermore, having induced the wife to consent to his discharge in bankruptcy by undertaking to maintain her, he could not now argue that he was under no liability to do so.

If the change of circumstances on which the application is based is not likely to be permanent (eg the husband's temporary unemployment), the order should be suspended rather than discharged, so that it can be revived later if necessary.[6]

3.   VARIATION OF CONSENT ORDERS

The fact that a party has consented to an order being made against him cannot act as an estoppel or give the other party a contractual right to have the order kept in force indefinitely, and a consent order may generally be varied in the same circumstances as any other order.[7] This is so even though the order provides that the parties shall not apply for a variation: it is doubtful whether such a provision is valid[8] and, even if it is, it may itself be suspended along with the other provisions of the order.[9] Usually, however, the court should be slower to accede to an application to vary consent orders, because otherwise parties and their solicitors might be deterred from negotiating them altogether. Hence a variation sought on the ground that the applicant's consent was given as a result of a mistake (eg about the other party's income) should be made only if justice demands it and a substantially different order would be made.[10] The court might also exercise its power if the applicant had not been independently and competently advised[11] (although the Court of Appeal subsequently held[12] that only in the most exceptional case will bad legal advice be a ground for interfering with a consent order) or if, for whatever reason, the order

---

6 See *Mills v Mills* [1940] P 124, [1940] 2 All ER 254, CA.
7 *B (GC) v B (BA)* [1970] 1 All ER 913.
8 See *N v N (Consent Order: Variation)* [1993] 2 FLR 868, CA where a consent order was made providing periodical payments to the wife for five years. Separate from the order, the wife entered into a 'side letter', agreeing not to apply for the extension of the term except '. . . for the protection of [the child] in circumstances of serious illness or disability'. When the wife decided to retrain for a new career, she applied for a three-year extension of maintenance. Although the Court of Appeal held the side letter void, it was nonetheless highly relevant and could not be disregarded. On the principles of *Edgar v Edgar* [1980] 3 All ER 887, CA (ante, p 804) the court declined to allow the wife's variation application. The court doubted the suitability of a side letter of this sort in a 'child case' and suggested, in any event, such side letters should be shown to the judge.
9 *Jessel v Jessel* [1979] 3 All ER 645, CA. See Douglas 'The Not so Clean Break' (1980) 96 LQR 196.
10 *B (GC) v B (BA)* (supra).
11 Per Baker P in *Wilkins v Wilkins* [1969] 2 All ER 463; cf *Peacock v Peacock* [1991] 1 FLR 324 where Thorpe J said (at 328) that he would not hold the parties to any agreement that they may have concluded, since the area of negotiation was complicated, neither spouse had had the benefit of legal advice, and both were 'way out of their depth'.
12 *Harris v Manahan* [1997] 1 FLR 205, CA.

was grossly unjust.[13] In any case, it is doubtful whether the court can vary or discharge an order which it has no power to make in the first place, eg an order for unsecured periodical payments for the payee's life.[14]

4. APPEALING OUT OF TIME

All the orders that we have been discussing are appealable. In exceptional circumstances it is possible to obtain leave to appeal out of time. This may be the only option in cases where, whether upon a consent order or a contested one, a clean break order has been made. Of course, the whole point of a clean break order or a property adjustment order is that there should be a final settlement between the parties. Nevertheless, circumstances may subsequently occur that so fundamentally change the position that in all justice the order should be reopened. It seems established, however, that, in the absence of fraud, misrepresentation or material non-disclosure, or a fundamental mistake common to both parties, events occurring after the making of an order only give grounds for appeal in exceptional circumstances. The leading case is *Barder v Caluori*.[15] Here, in a full and final settlement made in a consent order the husband agreed to transfer to his wife his half-interest in the matrimonial home subject to her undertaking responsibility for two outstanding mortgages. The order specified that the transfer should take place within 28 days. Neither party gave notice of appeal, but before the order was executed the wife killed both the children and committed suicide. It was held by the House of Lords that because the fundamental assumption on which the order had been made, namely that the wife and children would require a suitable home for a substantial period, had been totally invalidated within so short a time of the original order being made, leave to appeal should be granted. It was further held that the original order should be set aside.

The House of Lords laid down four conditions which must be satisfied if leave to appeal out of time is to be granted from an order for financial provision or property adjustment (whether or not made by consent):

(1) new events must have occurred since the making of the order which have invalidated the basis or assumption upon which the order was made so that the appeal would be certain, or very likely, to succeed;
(2) the new events should have occurred within a relatively short time of the order being made;
(3) the application for leave should be made reasonably promptly;
(4) the grant of leave should not prejudice third parties who have acquired interests in good faith and for value in the property which is the subject of the order.

In Lord Brandon's view, these conditions sought to reconcile two conflicting principles: on the one hand, that there should be finality in litigation and, on the other, that justice requires that cases be decided on their true facts rather than on

---

13 As in *Smethurst v Smethurst* [1978] Fam 52, [1977] 3 All ER 1110 where, for reasons which were not apparent, the sum originally ordered was about twice that which the husband could reasonably afford to pay. See Miller (1980) 10 Fam Law 196, 252.
14 See *Mills v Mills* (supra) and *Hinde v Hinde* [1953] 1 All ER 171, CA. But they probably can be varied etc by consent, and an undertaking given to the court may be discharged: *Russell v Russell* [1956] P 283, [1956] 1 All ER 466, CA.
15 [1988] AC 20, [1987] 2 All ER 440, HL.

assumptions or estimates which turn out to be erroneous.[16]

Perhaps not surprisingly, there has since been a number of cases on the application of the *Barder* criteria, which may perhaps be categorised into several broad groups. In the first, as in *Barder v Caluori* itself, the supervening event has been the unexpected death of one of the spouses. In *Smith v Smith (Smith Intervening)*,[17] for example, the wife committed suicide six months after the making of a 'clean break' consent order, and the Court of Appeal set the original order aside. In contrast, in *Amey v Amey*,[18] the court refused to set aside a 'clean break' agreement under which the husband paid a £120,000 lump sum to the wife, and, just two months later, before the agreement could be approved by the court, the wife died of a heart attack. Scott Baker J held that, since the wife had died, it was no longer open to the court to affirm or vary the agreement under the Matrimonial Causes Act 1973. Nor was the agreement vitiated at common law by common mistake or frustration: the parties had divided their capital entitlements without making any assumption as to the wife's future health, so her unexpected death did not entitle the court to intervene.[19]

In the second category there are two cases where a spouse has sought leave to appeal out of time where, subsequent to the making of the original order, the other spouse has remarried and vacated the former matrimonial home. In *Wells v Wells*,[20] just six months after the husband had been ordered to make a property transfer to provide a home for the wife and children, the wife remarried and began living with her second husband. The Court of Appeal held that these new events had invalidated the basis of the original order, and substituted an order for the sale of the property and the division of the proceeds of sale. In *Chaudhuri v Chaudhuri*[1] the husband's application was dismissed where the wife had remarried and moved out of the former matrimonial home 15 months after the making of the property transfer order in her favour. The original order had expressly contemplated the possibility of the wife's remarriage,[2] and the change of circumstances was said to be much less drastic than that in *Wells v Wells*.

In a third group of cases, the unforeseen event has been the reconciliation of the spouses after their divorce, and their subsequent cohabitation. In *S v S (Financial Provision) (Post Divorce Cohabitation)*[3] a consent order was set aside, some 15

---

16 Ibid at 41 and 451 respectively.
17 [1992] Fam 69, [1991] 2 All ER 306, CA. See also *Passmore v Gill and Gill* [1987] 1 FLR 441, CA and *Barber v Barber* [1993] 1 FLR 476, CA where the order was set aside when the wife died intestate three months after the order.
18 [1992] 2 FLR 89.
19 See also *Benson v Benson* [1996] 1 FLR 692 where the court held that the wife's death 15 months after the making of the order was an event entitling the court to intervene but nonetheless dismissed the husband's application. The husband had delayed his application for over a year, and so had not proceeded with reasonable promptness. In deciding whether application for leave to appeal has been made reasonably promptly, account should be taken of the situation in which the individual finds himself; there should be no unreasonably inflexible rule of thumb: *Heard v Heard* [1995] 1 FLR 970, CA and see *S v S (Financial Provision) (Post-Divorce Cohabitation)* [1994] 2 FLR 228 and *Hill v Hill* [1998] 1 FLR 198, CA. In any event, in assessing if an individual has proceeded reasonably promptly, time will be taken to run from the date of the order, rather than from the date on which the order is implemented: *B v B (Financial Provision: Leave to Appeal)* [1994] 1 FLR 219.
20 [1992] 2 FLR 66, CA (decided in 1980).
1 [1992] 2 FLR 73, CA.
2 The original order provided for the transfer of the property to the wife subject to a charge in favour of the husband enforceable upon the happening of the following events: the children ceasing full-time education, the death or remarriage of the wife, or her permanent cohabitation with another man.
3 [1994] 2 FLR 228.

years after it was made, where the divorced couple had cohabited in the meanwhile. The judge considered that, in the highly unusual circumstances of the case, the wife had satisfied the *Barder* criteria, since she had applied to set aside the order with reasonable promptness when she realised the relationship had finally broken down. In *Hewitson v Hewitson*,[4] the Court of Appeal later doubted whether post-divorce cohabitation could amount to relevant circumstances entitling the court to set aside an order: 'There has to be finality and an end to litigation . . . the umbrella of the dissolved marriage which covers the post-divorce period cannot remain open for ever.'[5] However, subsequently the Court of Appeal in *Hill v Hill*[6] adopted a rather different approach. The parties had cohabited for a 25-year period following a divorce, and a consent order which had been made in 1969. At first instance, Holman J dismissed the wife's application to set aside the 1969 order, which she had made after the parties had separated in 1995. The wife's appeal was successful. While not setting aside the 1969 order on *Barder* principles, the Court of Appeal, on reviewing its terms, considered it had not constituted a comprehensive financial settlement of the wife's capital and property claims. The court therefore had jurisdiction to entertain the wife's application for further relief.

In *Crozier v Crozier*[7] Booth J effectively closed off a fourth basis upon which it had been argued that the *Barder* criteria applied to justify the setting aside of an earlier order. Here, a consent order had been made whereby the husband had transferred his interest in the former matrimonial home to the wife who, in return, had accepted nominal maintenance payments for herself and her child. Following the implementation of the Child Support Act 1991, the husband's maintenance payments for the child, as an absent parent, were substantially increased. Booth J rejected the husband's argument that the 1991 Act, and its new administrative machinery for the assessment and collection of child maintenance, constituted a 'new event' which invalidated the fundamental basis upon which the earlier consent order and capital settlement had been made. The 1991 Act did not alter the position which had existed previously – that parents could not, by agreement or otherwise, throw off their continuing legal liability to support their children.[8]

In the largest group of cases, it has been argued that a property valuation, which was used by the court in making its original order, has turned out to be inaccurate and unreliable, thus invalidating the basis upon which the order was made. In *Hope-Smith v Hope-Smith*[9] the husband was ordered to pay to the wife £32,000 out of the proceeds of sale of the former matrimonial home, then valued at £116,000. As a result of the husband's 'wilful conduct and dilatory tactics' the house remained unsold some two years later when it was worth over £200,000. The Court of Appeal held that the *Barder* conditions were satisfied through no fault of the wife.[10] It substituted an order that the wife was to receive 40 per cent of the ultimate net sale

---

4 [1995] 1 FLR 241, CA.
5 Ibid at 244 (per Butler-Sloss LJ).
6 [1998] 1 FLR 198, CA.
7 [1994] 1 FLR 126.
8 The position of spouses who made pre-1993 capital settlements has been to some extent ameliorated, principally by the introduction of a system of departure directions: see ante, pp 737–42 and further Priest 'Capital Settlements and the CSA Part I' [1997] Fam Law 115 and 'Part II' [1997] Fam Law 170.
9 [1989] 2 FLR 56, CA.
10 The case demonstrates the flexibility of the court in applying the second of the *Barder* criteria. The property remained unsold two years after the making of the original order. In *Barder v Caluori* Lord Brandon had suggested ([1988] AC 20 at 43) that although the length of time within which the change of circumstances or the new event must occur could not be laid down precisely, he regarded

proceeds, which would be sufficient to enable her to re-house herself.[11] In contrast, in *Rooker v Rooker*,[12] on broadly similar facts, the court dismissed the wife's appeal because, although the husband had delayed the sale, the wife had not taken proper steps to enforce the original order. In *Edmonds v Edmonds*[13] the Court of Appeal refused to reopen a case where a house, valued by the judge at £70,000 and which the wife had claimed she intended to keep as her home, was sold by her for £110,000 six months later. Although the husband had asserted throughout his belief that the valuation should be higher, he had failed to produce any corroborative expert evidence to support his view. It was held that, since the husband had not taken the opportunity to challenge the false assumption upon which the judge had proceeded, he could not subsequently be heard to say that the new events had invalidated the judge's decision.[14] In a later decision, *Thompson v Thompson*,[15] the Court of Appeal granted leave to appeal out of time against a clean break order where the husband's business had been valued at £20,000, and just one week later was sold for £45,000. The circuit judge dismissed the wife's application for leave because she had agreed the valuation of £20,000 despite having previously received a valuation report of the business at £45,000. On appeal, however, Mustill LJ drew a distinction between the situation where a valuation was unsound when made and that where a reasonable estimate had been falsified by new events. In the first situation, the court must inquire whether the applicant was in some way responsible for the error. If she was, then, as in *Edmonds v Edmonds*, she may not succeed. The mere fact that a valuation report had been agreed, however, cannot be conclusive against an order being reopened, but deliberate fault on the part of the applicant would prevent leave being granted. The second situation is clearly a new event regardless of how the valuation came into existence. Provided that the other criteria in *Barder v Caluori* were satisfied, leave to appeal out of time would be given.

Mustill LJ, concerned lest his decision be seen as opening the floodgates and encouraging applicants to seek leave to appeal out of time, emphasised the severity of the requirements laid down in *Barder v Caluori*, adding:[16]

'... advisers must be alert, and the circuit judge will be alert if they are not, to make sure that the courts are not swamped with meritless applications for leave to appeal out of time.'

---

it as 'extremely unlikely' that it could be as much as a year and that 'in most cases it will be no more than a few months'. Compare *Worlock v Worlock* [1994] 2 FLR 689, CA, where the new event – a large increase in the value of the husband's construction company and a transfer of shares to the husband – occurred two years after the original order. The Court of Appeal held that it was 'far too late' to re-open the order.

11 See also *Heard v Heard* [1995] 1 FLR 970, CA, where an order was made that the wife receive £16,000 from the proceeds of the former matrimonial home, with the husband receiving the balance. The valuation before the judge suggested the house was worth £67,000. In the event no offer was received above £33,000. The Court of Appeal set aside the order, which had been invalidated by an unsound valuation: the judge had clearly intended that the husband was to be left with enough money to re-house himself. Contrast *B v B (Financial Provision: Leave to Appeal)* [1994] 1 FLR 219 where a fall in the value of a house from £340,000 to £250,000 was held not to justify re-opening an order.

12 [1988] 1 FLR 219, CA.

13 [1990] 2 FLR 202, CA.

14 Compare *Warren v Warren* [1982] 4 FLR 529, CA where there was a 'gross error' through no-one's fault of almost 100 per cent in the agreed valuation. Since neither party had had the opportunity to correct the false assumption on which the order was made, it was held to be unfair to hold them to it, so the order was set aside.

15 [1991] 2 FLR 530, CA.

16 [1991] 2 FLR 530, CA at 539.

In subsequent cases the courts have adopted a restrictive approach, particularly where the substance of an application is based on little more than that property has turned out to be worth more, or less, than at the date of the court's order. In *Rundle v Rundle*,[17] for example, the Court of Appeal rejected the wife's application for leave to appeal where she argued that the value of the former matrimonial home had fallen by nearly 15 per cent after the court order, but before its sale. Purchas LJ considered that fluctuations in the value of assets, and particularly real property, are inevitable; to allow them on their own to form the basis of an appeal would deny the maxim that there should be finality in litigation. In *Cornick v Cornick*[18] there was a dramatic increase in the value of the husband's shareholdings, the effect of which was to reduce the wife's share of the family wealth from some 51 per cent, at the date of the court order, to just 20 per cent 18 months later. Hale J reviewed earlier authorities, and considered that for the *Barder* principles to apply, something unforeseen and unforeseeable must have happened which dramatically affected the value of assets so as to bring about a substantial change in the balance of assets effected by the court order. This was not such a case, and the sharp increase in the value of the husband's shares was not a 'new event' within the scope of the *Barder* principles. The husband's shares had been properly valued at the date of the hearing and the case law showed that the property price fluctuations, however dramatic, did not of themselves entitle the court to intervene.

Where the court does grant leave to appeal out of time, it should reassess the order for financial provision or property adjustment afresh, and consider the criteria in s 25(2) of the Matrimonial Causes Act 1973 having regard to all the facts as they are known at the time of the appeal hearing.[19]

F.   Enforcement of orders

1.   METHODS OF ENFORCEMENT

Periodical payments

If periodical payments are secured, there is of course no question of enforcement. When arrears[20] of unsecured periodical payments accrue, the payee has a number of means of enforcing the order at his or her disposal. But her position is basically different from that of a successful plaintiff in an action for damages for tort or breach of contract, for the order is not a final judgment and she does not have the

17 [1992] 2 FLR 80, CA.
18 [1994] 2 FLR 530. In *Worlock v Worlock* [1994] 2 FLR 689, CA the husband's wealth was greatly increased some two years after a consent order, where his family company's land gained the benefit of planning permission, and he took a transfer of shares from his mother. The Court of Appeal held this was not a *Barder* situation. The relevant circumstances (the husband's expectation to acquire the mother's shares and the landholding) were known at the time of the original order. It was only the scale of events, and their timing, which were different from originally envisaged. Contrast *Penrose v Penrose* [1994] 2 FLR 621, CA where the Court of Appeal accepted the husband's argument that an unexpectedly large tax liability could be a 'new event' under *Barder* principles. The Court, however, declined to set the order aside; the husband could have established his likely tax liability if he had made due and proper inquiry before the hearing.
19 *Smith v Smith (Smith Intervening)* [1992] Fam 69, [1991] 2 All ER 306, CA; *Garner v Garner* [1992] 1 FLR 573, CA.
20 The court also has power to order the recovery of overpayments: see Matrimonial Causes Act 1973 s 33 and s 38.

full rights of a judgment creditor.

In the first place, if the party in default applies to have the order varied or discharged, the court in effect has a discretion to remit the arrears in part or even entirely by making a retrospective order.[1] In order to prevent large sums from mounting up, arrears which have been due for twelve months or more may not be enforced without the leave of the court: this gives some protection to a party who has stopped paying the full sum ordered and has been mistakenly led to believe by the other's acquiescence that he will not enforce the rest.[2] The court can also give the debtor time to pay and, in particular, may order payment by instalments. Because of this discretion, the arrears do not constitute a legal debt and cannot be sued for as such,[3] nor may the payee institute bankruptcy proceedings as a means of execution or prove in the other party's bankruptcy for arrears.[4] But with these important exceptions he has available all the usual means of execution open to a judgment creditor in the High Court or a county court, as the case may be.[5]

One of the most useful ways of enforcing the payment of arrears is by issuing a judgment summons under the Debtors Act 1869, when the court can make an order for the payment by instalments and commit the payer for contempt if he wilfully fails to pay them.[6] Alternatively, the payee may apply for an attachment of earnings order. The detailed provisions are mutatis mutandis the same as those relating to attachment orders made in a magistrates' court.[7] The Maintenance Enforcement Act 1991 extended the enforcement powers of the High Court and county courts as regards maintenance orders (which include orders for periodical payments). These powers apply when the court makes a maintenance order, or in subsequent proceedings for its revocation or variation. The first is to order payment by standing order, or by other similar method.[8] A debtor who has unreasonably refused to open a bank account can be ordered to do so for this purpose.[9] The second is an unrestricted power to make an attachment of earnings order.[10] Previously, the latter could only be made if the debtor consented, or if he was guilty of wilful neglect or culpable default in failing to meet the order.[11]

Other orders

An order for the payment of a lump sum is more in the nature of a judgment for damages and generally may be enforced in the same way. However, a lump sum is

---

1 *MacDonald v MacDonald* [1964] P 1, [1963] 2 All ER 857, CA.
2 Matrimonial Causes Act 1973 s 32, as amended by the Family Law Act 1996 Sch 8, para 17. See further Law Com No 25, para 92.
3 *Bailey v Bailey* (1884) 13 QBD 855, CA; *Robins v Robins* [1907] 2 KB 13.
4 Consequently the arrears are not affected by bankruptcy and may be enforced by other methods: *Linton v Linton* (1885) 15 QBD 239; *Re Henderson* (1888) 20 QBD 509, CA. For bankruptcy proceedings as a means of enforcing payment of a lump sum, see below.
5 An undertaking to make payments given to the court may be enforced in the same way as an order (at least if the court would have had jurisdiction to make a similar order): *Gandolfo v Gandolfo* [1981] QB 359, [1980] 1 All ER 833, CA. An order made by a divorce county court may be transferred to the High Court if it cannot be conveniently enforced in the county court. It is then enforceable as though it had been made by the High Court: Family Proceedings Rules 1991 r 7.3.
6 For the procedure, see the Family Proceedings Rules 1991 r 7.2, r 7.4–7.6.
7 See ante, p 774. If the order is a High Court order, the collecting officer is the proper officer of the High Court or the appropriate officer of the county court specified in the order: Attachment of Earnings Act 1971 s 6 (7).
8 Maintenance Enforcement Act 1991 s 1(5).
9 Ibid, s 1(6).
10 Ibid, s 1(4)(b).
11 Attachment of Earnings Act 1971 s 3(5), repealed by Maintenance Enforcement Act 1991 Sch 3.

not provable on the bankruptcy of the payer spouse.[12] The payee may issue a judgment summons or apply for an attachment of earnings order.[13] As in the case of periodical payments, a lump sum payment (or any part payable by instalment) cannot be enforced more than twelve months after it falls due without the leave of the court.[14]

Failure to comply with an order to transfer or settle property may be enforced in the same way as any other similar order in the High Court or a county court.

2. ATTEMPTS TO DEFEAT CLAIMS FOR FINANCIAL RELIEF

A spouse might well try to defeat an application for financial relief by disposing of his property or transferring it out of the jurisdiction. He might do this beforehand in anticipation of an application or order or, alternatively, after an order has been made in order to reduce the property available to meet it. To prevent fraudulent dispositions of this kind, a measure of protection is given by the Matrimonial Causes Act 1973 s 37.[15] This applies to any interim order, financial provision or property adjustment order, any order made under s 27 of the Act on the ground of failure to provide reasonable maintenance, the variation of any of these orders during the payer's lifetime, and the alteration of a maintenance agreement during the parties' joint lives. For the sake of convenience, it will be assumed throughout the following discussion that the wife (or former wife) is applying for or has obtained an order against the husband; it must be appreciated, however, that exactly the same principles apply if the husband is seeking financial provision from the wife or if anyone is seeking it for the children of the family.

If the court is satisfied that the husband is about to make any disposition or to transfer out of the jurisdiction or otherwise deal with any property with the intention of defeating the wife's claim, it may make such an order as it thinks fit to restrain him from doing so and to protect the claim.[16] In *Crittenden v Crittenden*[17] the Court of Appeal held that, for the purpose of s 37, 'property' means property in which either or both spouses has or had a beneficial interest, in possession or reversion, while 'dealing with' refers to some *positive* dealing with property, and

12 Insolvency Rules 1986 (SI 1986/1925) r 12.3 and see *Woodley v Woodley (No 2)* [1993] 2 FLR 477, CA, where Balcombe LJ suggested the rules be changed to allow a lump sum order to be provable on a payer's bankruptcy and yet not to be released on his discharge. Note that the court has power to make a lump sum order against a bankrupt spouse, although it should have a clear picture of the assets and liabilities of the bankrupt and consider the effect the bankruptcy has on the debtor spouse's ability to pay: *Woodley v Woodley* [1992] 2 FLR 417, CA and *Hellyer v Hellyer* [1996] 2 FLR 579, CA. In *Russell v Russell* [1998] 1 FLR 936 it was held that a bankruptcy order could properly be made to enforce a lump sum even though the sum was not provable in the bankruptcy where the debtor had failed to comply with other orders of the court.

13 See the definition of 'maintenance order' in the Administration of Justice Act 1970 s 28 and Sch 8, and the Attachment of Earnings Act 1971 Sch 1, para 3, as amended in each case by the Matrimonial Causes Act 1973 Sch 2, and the Domestic Proceedings and Magistrates' Courts Act 1978 Sch 2.

14 Matrimonial Causes Act 1973 s 32 as amended by the Family Law Act 1996 Sch 8, para 17.

15 As amended by the Family Law Act 1996 Sch 8, para 21. The power was originally given by the Matrimonial Causes (Property and Maintenance) Act 1958 s 2.

16 It has been held that this power extends to restraining dispositions of property already situated abroad: *Hamlin v Hamlin* [1986] Fam 11, [1985] 2 All ER 1037, CA. However, the court will only make an order if it can be enforced.

17 [1990] 2 FLR 361, CA.

not to anything which is purely negative, such as failing to deal with property.[18] It followed that the court had no power, under s 37, to make orders relating to assets owned by a *company* in which the husband held the issued shares. Nor could the court make an order under s 37 requiring the husband to enter into a covenant not to compete with a proposed purchaser of the company's assets. *Crittenden v Crittenden* was not followed in *Green v Green* [19] (where Connell J preferred the earlier authority of *Nicholas v Nicholas*)[20] to the extent that the court held it may make an order against a limited company which may be regarded as a spouse's 'alter ego', ie where he owns or controls all its shares, or a majority of them in circumstances where minority shareholdings could be disregarded.

If the court is satisfied that the husband has already made a disposition with the intention of defeating the wife's claim, it may make an order setting the disposition aside. In this case, however, a wife who has not yet obtained an order for financial relief must also show that, if the disposition were set aside, the court would make a different order from that which it would otherwise make. Defeating the wife's claim may take the form of preventing her from obtaining an order at all, reducing the amount that might be ordered, or impeding or frustrating the enforcement of any order that might be made or has been made. It seems, despite an earlier judicial suggestion to the contrary,[1] that where a husband declares himself bankrupt to avoid a claim for ancillary relief, the bankruptcy itself is not a reviewable disposition entitling the court to intervene under s 37. The correct procedure is for application to be made under s 282(1)(a) of the Insolvency Act 1986 to annul the bankruptcy order on the basis it ought not to have been made.[2]

In many cases it may be difficult to establish what the husband's intention was when he made a disposition. Consequently the Act has introduced a compromise designed to protect in part the interests of the wife, the husband and the transferee. If the husband made the disposition three years or more before the application to set it aside, the wife must prove affirmatively that he had the intention to defeat her claim. If he made it less than three years before or is about to make it, this intention will be presumed if the effect of the transaction would be to defeat her claim or, where the disposition has already taken place and an order is in force, if it has had this effect: the burden then shifts on to him to prove that this was not his intention. In *Kemmis v Kemmis (Welland Intervening)* [3] it was held that the husband's intention to defeat the wife's claim has to be a subjective intention, but does not have to be the husband's sole or even dominant intention. It suffices if it plays a

---

18 On the other hand, 'dealing with' in s 37 does *not* require there to be a disposition in favour of the third party: *Shipman v Shipman* [1991] 1 FLR 250, where Anthony Lincoln J held that a husband's use of his funds as a deposit on the purchase of a house, to maintain himself and to pay off existing debts was caught by s 37. The judge also held, following *Roche v Roche* (1981) 11 Fam Law 243, CA, that the court has an inherent jurisdiction to grant injunctions freezing assets which might otherwise be put beyond reach of an applicant, notwithstanding the enhancement of s 37. See the comment by Cretney [1991] Fam Law 146. Note also *Newlon Housing Trust v Al-Sulaimen* [1998] 3 WLR 451, HL where the House of Lords held that a concession by counsel that the service of a notice to quit by one of the spouses, who were joint tenants of a council tenancy (the effect of the notice being to terminate the tenancy), was a 'disposition' of property reviewable under s 37, had been wrongly made, following its earlier opinion in *Harrow London Borough Council v Johnstone* [1997] 1 All ER 929, HL at 940a (Lord Mustill) and 940h (Lord Hoffmann).
19 [1993] 1 FLR 326.
20 [1984] FLR 285, CA.
 1 *Woodley v Woodley* [1992] 2 FLR 417 at 423F (per Ewbank J).
 2 *F v F (Divorce: Insolvency: Annulment of Bankruptcy Order)* [1994] 1 FLR 359.
 3 [1988] 1 WLR 1307, CA.

substantial part in the husband's intention as a whole.

Certain transactions may not be upset at all. No order may be made after the husband's death with respect to any disposition made by him by will or codicil. A disposition inter vivos *already* made may not be set aside if it was made for valuable consideration (other than marriage) to a third party acting in good faith and without notice of the husband's intention to defeat the wife's claim.[4] Where a third party had *actual* knowledge of the husband's intention, it is difficult to see how he could claim to act in good faith, and so the transaction will be set aside. However, in *Kemmis v Kemmis (Welland Intervening)*[5] the Court of Appeal held the defence is not available to a third party who has *constructive* notice of the husband's intentions. Here, the position is rather more complex, but the test was laid down by Purchas LJ, who cited[6] with approval a passage from the judgment of Farwell J in *Hunt v Luck*:[7]

'Constructive notice is the knowledge which the courts impute to a person upon presumption so strong of the existence of knowledge that it cannot be allowed to be rebutted either from his knowing something which ought to have put him to further inquiry or from his wilfully abstaining from inquiry to avoid notice.'

Purchas LJ continued:[8]

'The basic concepts are "knowing something" which ought to have stimulated inquiry, or "wilfully abstaining from inquiry to avoid notice". Both import that inquiry, if made, would necessarily have revealed the knowledge, constructive notice of which is to be imported.'

The application of these criteria can be seen in the later case of *Sherry v Sherry*,[9] where the wife obtained injunctions under s 37, restraining the husband from selling or disposing of certain properties, and subsequently registered inhibitions against the properties at HM Land Registry. Later, by consent, the injunctions were discharged. The husband then entered into contracts for sale and mortgage of the properties with a purchaser, whose solicitor's searches revealed the existence of the inhibitions whose registration had not been cancelled. On being shown the order discharging the injunctions, the solicitor advised the purchaser to proceed and the transactions were completed. The Court of Appeal adopted the test in *Kemmis v Kemmis*, and set the transactions aside on the basis that the purchaser had constructive notice of the husband's intentions. The purchaser knew of the acrimonious dispute between the spouses, and his discovery that injunctions had been made, and the inhibitions registered, should have caused him to make simple enquiries as regards the properties. His failure to do so meant he was bound by constructive notice, and the transactions were reviewable under s 37.

A wife's application for a property adjustment order relating to a *specific* piece of land (eg the matrimonial home) is registrable as a pending land action.[10] Once registered, the wife's claims will take priority over subsequent purchasers or

4 A purchaser acts in good faith provided that he acts honestly: *Central Estates (Belgravia) Ltd v Woolgar* [1972] 1 QB 48, [1971] 3 All ER 647, CA. No order may be made if the disposition took place before 1 January 1968, as there was an absolute limitation of three years before the Matrimonial Proceedings and Property Act 1970 came into force: Matrimonial Causes Act 1973 s 37(7).
5 Supra. See Fortin (1989) 53 Conv 24.
6 [1988] 1 WLR 1307, CA at 1317.
7 [1901] 1 Ch 45 at 52.
8 [1988] 1 WLR 1307, CA at 1317.
9 [1991] 1 FLR 307, CA.
10 Under the Land Charges Act 1972 s 5(7). If the land is *registered*, a pending action is protected by lodging a caution: Land Registration Act 1925 s 59.

mortgagees, regardless of whether they make the appropriate land charges or land registry search, or whether they have notice of the husband's intentions to defeat the wife's claims.[11] If a wife *fails* to register, then the Court of Appeal has held in *Whittingham v Whittingham*[12] that she cannot attack any subsequent transfer to any person taking any interest in the land, or any charge on it for valuable consideration, unless he had actual notice that she had made an application for a property transfer. In *Kemmis v Kemmis*,[13] however, both Purchas LJ and Lloyd LJ expressed doubts about the decision in *Whittingham v Whittingham*.

The disposition is voidable and not void, and consequently, even if it is set aside, this cannot affect any subsequent dealings with the property in good faith. Hence, if the husband's immediate transferee is not protected but disposes of the property to a bona fide purchaser for value without notice, the latter's title cannot be upset by the order. In *National Provincial Bank Ltd v Hastings Car Mart Ltd (No 3)*[14] the husband, who had deserted the wife, conveyed the matrimonial home to the defendant company, who immediately charged it to the plaintiff bank. Although the conveyance to the defendants was set aside on the ground that it was made with the intention of defeating the wife's claim to maintenance, it was held by the Court of Appeal that this did not extinguish the plaintiff's mortgage, which remained a valid charge.

3.   REGISTRATION OF ORDERS IN OTHER COURTS

It will readily be seen that if the spouse ordered to pay money duly fulfils his or her obligations, orders made in magistrates' courts have the advantage that payment may be made through the clerk of the court; conversely, if he fails to fulfil them, a spouse who has an order made in the High Court or a county court has superior means of enforcing it at his or her disposal. Consequently the Maintenance Orders Act of 1958 introduced the means of registering in one court a 'maintenance order'[15] made by another. Under this Act a person entitled to payments under a maintenance order made by the High Court or a county court may apply to the court that made the order to have it registered in a magistrates' court; whether or not the application is granted lies completely in the discretion of the court.[16] In the same way a person entitled to payments under a maintenance order made by the magistrates' court may apply to that court to have it registered in the High Court; again, the court has a discretion[17] whether or not to grant the application.

If the application is granted, no proceedings may be begun or continued to

11   *Perez-Adamson v Perez-Rivas* [1987] Fam 89, [1987] 3 All ER 20, CA where it was held sufficient for a wife to particularise the property to be charged at the time of *registering* the land charge entry. The wife's application for a property adjustment order had not specified any particular property.
12   [1979] Fam 9, [1978] 3 All ER 805, CA.
13   [1988] 1 WLR 1307 at 1320, CA.
14   [1964] Ch 665, [1964] 3 All ER 93n, CA. See further the same case in the House of Lords (*National Provincial Bank Ltd v Ainsworth*) ante, p 65. There was no appeal on the point discussed here. Presumably in circumstances such as these the immediate transferee may be ordered to pay over the value of the property.
15   As defined by the Maintenance Orders Act 1958 s 1(1A) added by the Administration of Justice Act 1970 s 27(3) and Sch 8 as subsequently amended. The statutory definition includes (inter alia) orders for periodical or other payments made, or having effect if made, under the Matrimonial Causes Act 1973 Pt III, the Domestic Proceedings and Magistrates' Courts Act 1978 and the Children Act 1989.
16   Section 1(1)(a), s 2(1).
17   Section 1(1)(b), s 2(3).

enforce the order in the original court and any attachment of earnings order already in force ceases to have effect.[18] Once the order has been registered, it may be enforced only as though it had been made by the court in which it is registered.[19]

An order may be varied, revoked, suspended and revived only by the original court, except that, in the case of orders made by the High Court or a county court and registered in a magistrates' court, variation of rates of payment (as distinct from a variation of other provisions and complete revocation, suspension and revival of the order) may be made only by the magistrates' court in which it is registered[20] if both parties are in England or Wales.[1]

The party entitled to payments under a registered order may give notice to have the registration cancelled. This has a similar effect to an application to have the order registered in the sense that no proceedings may be begun or continued to enforce the order in the court of registration[2] and any attachment of earnings order is automatically discharged. The court in which the order is registered must then cancel the registration, provided that no process for the enforcement of the order is in force and, in the case of an order registered in a magistrates' court, no proceedings for variation are pending in that court. If the court that originally made an order registered in a magistrates' court varies or discharges it, it may itself direct that the registration be cancelled; if a magistrates' court discharges an order registered in the High Court, it must direct that the registration be cancelled (if there are no arrears remaining to be recovered).[3]

G. Reform

The legislation, case law and practice which we have discussed in this chapter is so immensely complex and important that, inevitably, it remains the subject of continuing proposals for reform. The high level of divorce in England and Wales means that substantial numbers of couples are caught up in the web of negotiation, settlement and litigation over finance and property post-divorce each year. The costs, for the parties themselves and the state through the Legal Aid Board and the Court Service, are high and, although the encouragement of mediation by the Family Law Act 1996 may have some effect in lowering them, it might be argued that greater certainty of outcome would reduce disputes and hence cut costs

---

18 Section 2(2), (4); Attachment of Earnings Act 1971 s 11(1)(a), (2). But a warrant of committal remains in force if the defendant is *already* detained under it: s 2(4)(b).

19 Section 3. This includes the power to remit the whole or any part of arrears due. In the case of an order made under the Domestic Proceedings and Magistrates' Court Act and registered in the High Court, the leave of that court must be obtained to enforce arrears which have been due for more than twelve months: see the Domestic Proceedings and Magistrates' Courts Act 1978 s 32(4)–(6).

20 Or any other magistrates' court having jurisdiction in the place where the complainant is for the time being: Magistrates' Court (Maintenance Orders Act 1958) Rules 1959 r 9.

1 Section 4, as amended by the Administration of Justice Act 1970 Sch 11. Hence an order for maintenance pending suit and an interim order made under s 27 of the Matrimonial Causes Act 1973 should normally not be registered in a magistrates' court because this removes control from the divorce court: *Armsby v Armsby* (1973) 118 Sol Jo 183; cf *Practice Direction* [1980] 1 All ER 1007. The magistrates' court has a discretion to remit the application to the original court and the original court may vary the order of payment in proceedings to vary other provisions of the order.

2 Save that a warrant of committal remains in force if the defendant is *already* detained under it.

3 Section 5; Attachment of Earnings Act 1971 s 11(1)(b).

further.[4] We have noted judicial concern at the high cost of litigation in ancillary relief.[5] Indeed, Thorpe LJ has gone so far as to suggest that the courts should not make orders unless there is a manifest need to do so, with the parties relying instead upon negotiation and mediation to settle their affairs.[6]

It is not surprising, therefore, that the government established an Ancillary Relief Advisory Group, composed of legal practitioners, the judiciary, and academics, to advise the Lord Chancellor on all aspects of ancillary relief, and to consider ways of reforming the law. In particular, the Group has been invited to consider whether the Scottish system (which applies a presumption of equal sharing of family assets) might be applied in England and Wales and whether pre-nuptial agreements should be given greater weight.[7]

One of the many difficulties in producing reform proposals will be in reconciling competing interests and competing objectives. For example, we have seen that the current law requires the welfare of children of the family to be given first consideration. Should their welfare become the *paramount* concern? This would no doubt lead to greater emphasis on preserving the matrimonial home as a home for the children and their primary carer, but this will in turn leave the absent parent potentially worse off, and the problems associated with the *Mesher* order[8] show that no easy solution is available. When, if at all, should spouses – in practice only wives – receive continuing and indefinite maintenance from a person to whom they no longer have any legal ties? Should there be, as in Scotland, a presumption that periodical payments will last for no longer than three years?[9] It might be difficult to reconcile such a stance with any government policy seeking to limit expenditure by the state on the consequences of marriage breakdown through the social security system. A presumption of equal sharing of assets[10] might do justice to wives who have contributed to their family's welfare in non-financial ways and may reflect public expectations, but might lead to disputes over what should constitute 'family assets'. Finally, encouragement of pre-nuptial agreements might have limited impact if, as seems to have been assumed in the government's reference to its Advisory Group, they would *not* be binding where children have subsequently been born, since over half of divorces do involve couples with children. The scope for unequal bargaining and the imposition of unfair terms might be considerable – and in any event, it might be doubted whether couples would very often be sufficiently concerned to make an individualised agreement rather than rely upon the presumption of half-shares. No doubt, valuable lessons will be learned by considering the experience in both Scotland and other jurisdictions, such as France, where such approaches are already part of the law. Whatever reforms are finally decided upon, it is to be hoped that they will be implemented slowly, after adequate consultation, and without retrospective effect, in order to avoid the worst features of the child support experiment.

4　See Davis et al *Simple Quarrels: Negotiating Money and Property Disputes on Divorce* (1994) p 270.
5　See ante, p 808.
6　*White v White* [1998] 2 FLR 310, CA, reiterating his view in *H v H (Financial Provision: Capital Allowance)* [1993] 2 FLR 335 at 347.
7　[1998] Fam Law 381.
8　See ante, p 847.
9　Family Law (Scotland) Act 1985 s 9(1)(d).
10　As under s 10(1) of the Scottish Act.

Chapter 19

The legal consequences of a death in the family

When a person dies, there are various legal consequences, the most important of which will concern the status of his spouse, if the deceased was married, and the distribution of any property the deceased owned. In this chapter we consider first the rare situation where a person's death must be legally presumed so that his spouse can regard herself as free to remarry, and his relatives can deal with his estate. We then consider the law concerning succession and inheritance. Finally, we discuss the position where death is caused by a fatal accident and family members seek compensation.

A. Presumption of death

The death of either party ipso facto brings a marriage to an end. Before 1938, if a spouse disappeared in circumstances which led to the reasonable inference that he or she was dead, but the death could not be proved, the other could remarry without committing the crime of bigamy and the second marriage would be *presumptively* valid. But if it were later proved that the spouse was in fact alive when the other remarried, then the second marriage would be *conclusively* void, with all the legal consequences that this entailed. To deal with this problem, the Matrimonial Causes Act 1973 s 19[1] permits the court to make a decree[2] of presumption of death and of dissolution of the marriage if it is satisfied that there are reasonable grounds for supposing that the petitioner's spouse is dead. The general common law presumption of death which may be raised by seven years' absence[3] is specifically applied to these proceedings by s 19(3), which provides:

> '. . . the fact that for a period of seven years or more the other party to the marriage has been continually absent from the petitioner and the petitioner has no reason to believe that the other party has been living within that time shall be evidence that the other party is dead until the contrary is proved.'

The petitioner is not bound to rely on this period of absence. The court may accept any satisfactory evidence from which it may be presumed that the spouse is dead:[4]

---

1 As amended by Family Law Act 1996 s 66(1), Sch 8 paras 4 and 7. The power was originally given by the Matrimonial Causes Act 1937. Proceedings must be commenced in a divorce county court but should normally be transferred to the High Court: Matrimonial and Family Proceedings Act 1984 s 33(3); *Practice Direction (Family Division: Distribution of Business)* [1992] 3 All ER 151.
2 Note that, as with nullity but not divorce, once the Family Law Act is in force, a decree nisi and decree absolute are granted.
3 *Chard v Chard* [1956] P 259, [1955] 3 All ER 721. See Treitel 'Presumption of Death' (1954) 17 MLR 530; *Tweney v Tweney* [1946] P 180, [1946] 1 All ER 564; *Re Watkins* [1953] 2 All ER 1113; *Bullock v Bullock* [1960] 2 All ER 307.
4 Such as the otherwise inexplicable disappearance of an explorer or round-the-world yachtsman.

the inference to be drawn from the seven years' absence is of particular importance when there is no evidence at all of what has happened since.

The statutory presumption is different from that which arises at common law after seven years' absence. What is important under the statute is the petitioner's belief. In *Thompson v Thompson*[5] Sachs J held that nothing must have happened during the period of seven years from which the petitioner, as a reasonable person, would conclude that the other spouse was still alive. Although the point was left open, the court is hardly likely to accept that the belief is reasonably held unless the petitioner has made all appropriate enquiries. The jurisdiction is discretionary; consequently, even if the petitioner can claim the benefit of the presumption, the court will not pronounce a decree, contrary to the justice of the case, where there is a possibility that the other party is still alive.

A decree nisi must be rescinded if the other spouse is found to be still alive.[6] Once it has been made absolute, however, it dissolves the marriage irrevocably even though the other subsequently reappears.[7]

As in the case of divorce, the court has jurisdiction if the petitioner is domiciled in England and Wales when the proceedings are begun, or has been habitually resident here throughout the period of one year ending with that date.[8]

B.   Succession[9]

We discuss the rules governing the disposition of property in four different contexts. First, we examine the position where the deceased dies leaving a will. Secondly, we discuss the intestacy rules applying where no will (or valid will) has been made. Thirdly, we note the rules governing the statutory succession to tenancies. Finally, we consider the opportunities to challenge the disposition of property where a person considers that they have not been adequately provided for under either the will which was made, or under the intestacy rules. In all of these contexts, it will be seen that the rules make assumptions about what constitute family relationships and the appropriateness of recognising these through devolution on death.

1.   TESTATE SUCCESSION[10]

The law relating to wills and testate succession generally presents few problems peculiar to family law. Until the beginning of this century the most important question was the testamentary capacity of a married woman. At common law she

---

5 [1956] P 414, [1956] 1 All ER 603. A pure speculation is insufficient. The petitioner must give evidence: *Parkinson v Parkinson* [1939] P 346, [1939] 3 All ER 108. For the common law presumption, see the 8th edition of this work, pp 68–70.

6 *Manser v Manser* [1940] P 224, [1940] 4 All ER 238.

7 But in that case the court has power to make orders for financial relief: *Deacock v Deacock* [1958] P 230, [1958] 2 All ER 633, CA.

8 Domicile and Matrimonial Proceedings Act 1973 s 5(4).

9 See Borkowski *Textbook on Succession* (1997) for a concise and entertaining account of the law. For an empirical study of family wills, see Finch et al *Wills, Inheritance and Families* (1996).

10 See Sherrin, Barlow and Wallington *Williams on Wills* (7th edn, 1995).

had virtually no power to make a will,[11] although she could always devise and bequeath property held to her separate use in equity even if it were subject to a restraint upon anticipation. When the equitable concept of separate property was extended to legal separate property by the Married Women's Property Act 1882, her power to dispose of it by will was likewise extended, so that her testamentary incapacity remained only with respect to property acquired by her before 1883. Under the Law Reform (Married Women and Tortfeasors) Act 1935 she was given full power to dispose of all her property as if she were a feme sole.

There are, however, still certain matters of particular importance to spouses and children which we must note.

Revocation of wills by marriage

By s 18 of the Wills Act 1837 every will made by a man or woman is revoked by his or her marriage.[12] The section does not apply if the marriage is void,[13] but does in the case of voidable marriages.[14]

There are, however, a number of exceptions to the general rule. First, a will is not to be revoked by marriage, insofar as it is made in exercise of a power of appointment, if the property thereby appointed would not pass in default of appointment to the testator's personal representatives.[15] The reason for this exception is obvious: the marriage cannot possibly affect the devolution of the property involved.

The other exceptions are designed to fulfil the intention of a testator who makes his will on the eve of his wedding. If it appears from a will that at the time it was made the testator was expecting to be married to a particular person and that he intended that the will should not be revoked by the marriage, the marriage to that person is not to revoke it. The same rule applies if it appears that the testator intended that a particular disposition should not be revoked by the marriage: in that case the disposition is to take effect, as are all other dispositions in the will, unless it appears that the testator intended that a particular disposition was to be revoked.[16]

The exceptions relating to wills made in contemplation of marriage replace an exception (couched in significantly different terms) contained in s 177 of the Law

---

11 She had no power at all to dispose of realty and leaseholds, although she could exercise a power of appointment by will. With the consent of her husband copyholds could be surrendered to the use of her will. Although all her choses in possession vested in her husband, she could bequeath personalty if there were an ante-nuptial contract to that effect or if her husband assented to the bequest and did not revoke his consent before probate was granted. For further details, reference must be made to the editions of standard works on property, wills and married women published in the late nineteenth and early twentieth centuries.
12 As substituted by s 18 of the Administration of Justice Act 1982, implementing the recommendations of the 22nd Report of the Law Reform Committee (The Making and Revocation of Wills) 1980 (Cmnd 7902). The changes made by the Administration of Justice Act do not apply to wills *made* before 1 January 1983: s 73(3).
13 *Mette v Mette* (1859) 1 Sw & Tr 416.
14 *Re Roberts* [1978] 3 All ER 225, CA.
15 Section 18(2). Hence the will may be revoked in part but not insofar as the power is exercised: *In the Goods of Russell* (1890) 15 PD 111. See also *In the Goods of Gilligan* [1950] P 32, [1949] 2 All ER 401; Mitchell 'The Revocation of Testamentary Appointments on Marriage' (1951) 67 LQR 351.
16 Section 18(3), (4). This provision does not apply to wills made before 1 January 1983 (Administration of Justice Act 1982 s 73(7) and s 76(11)) which will still be governed by s 177 of the Law of Property Act 1925.

of Property Act 1925. This section was liberally construed. Thus in *In the Estate of Langston* [17] a will by which the testator left his whole estate to 'my fiancee MEB' was held not to have been revoked by his marriage to her two months later. Similarly, a will would now be saved if the testator made a bequest 'to my fiancee ABC' but gave the residue of his estate to others. [18] Difficulty arises because it is frequently impossible to tell whether, by making a gift to his fiancee, a testator was intending to provide for his future wife or was merely making a temporary arrangement in case he should die before the proposed marriage took place. It would appear that in many cases this problem is resolved by s 21 of the Administration of Justice Act 1982, which permits extrinsic evidence to be admitted to resolve ambiguities in the wording of a will. [19]

Revocation of wills by divorce and nullity

Whereas the contracting of marriage automatically revokes a will (unless one of the exceptions just considered applies), its dissolution used not to do so. Consequently, if the testator did not make another will, his estate might pass to a former wife from whom he had long been divorced and who might have remarried. To overcome this difficulty, s 18A of the Wills Act [20] was added to provide that, if a testator's marriage was dissolved or annulled, any will previously made by him (or her) should take effect as if any appointment of the former spouse as executor (or executor and trustee) were omitted and any devise or bequest to the former spouse should lapse unless (in either case) a contrary intention appeared in the will.

In *Re Sinclair* [1] the Court of Appeal held that the word 'lapse' must be given its ordinary meaning of 'fail' and that the former spouse was not to be deemed to have predeceased the testator. [2] His property therefore had to pass on intestacy, even though he had intended it to pass to charity. The Law Commission reviewed the decision, [3] and recommended that it should be replaced to provide that, in the event of a divorce or annulment, property should pass as if the former spouse had

---

17 [1953] P 100, [1953] 1 All ER 928. See also *Pilot v Gainfort* [1931] P 103, where the testator made a will by which he bequeathed his personalty to 'DFP my wife'. Although he was living with her at the time, he did not marry her until 18 months later. It was held that the will was not revoked by the marriage. Sed quaere? On the face of the will it appeared that the testator was *already* married. Contrast *In the Estate of Gray* (1963) 107 Sol Jo 156.
18 Thus reversing *Re Coleman* [1976] Ch 1, [1975] 1 All ER 675.
19 In any case, the surviving spouse now needs less protection because of the substantial sums that she (or he) takes on intestacy and the court's wide powers to make financial provision for a dependant under the Inheritance (Provision for Family and Dependants) Act 1975 (see post, pp 875–81 and 884–902 et seq). But other beneficiaries, with no alternative claim, may be deprived of their gifts by revocation. See Tiley 'Wills and Revocation – Marriage and Contemplation' (1975) 34 CLJ 205.
20 Added by the Administration of Justice Act 1982 s 18(2). The question was considered by the Law Reform Committee who were unable to agree: 22nd Report (Cmnd 7902), paras 3.26–3.38. The section does not apply to testators dying before 1983 (Administration of Justice Act 1982 s 73(6)(b)) but it will apply even though the decree was obtained before that year.
1 [1985] Ch 446, [1985] 1 All ER 1066. See Prime 'Making the Worst of Divorce' (1986) 49 MLR 108. The same principle was applied in *Re Jones (Deceased): Jones v Midland Bank Trust Co Ltd* [1998] 1 FLR 246, CA. There, a son killed his mother. Her will had left her estate to him, or, should he predecease her, to her nephews. It was held that the estate would devolve as if she had died intestate, since the son (who could not succeed to the estate as of right because of the operation of the forfeiture rule) could not be deemed to have predeceased the mother.
2 Overruling *Re Cherrington* [1984] 2 All ER 285.
3 Law Com No 217, *Family Law, The Effect of Divorce on Wills* (1993); see Kerridge 'The Effect of Divorce on Wills' (1995) 59 Conv 12.

predeceased the testator.[4] The Law Reform (Succession) Act 1995 s 3[5] accordingly amended the Wills Act by inserting a new s 18A(1), which provides:

'(a) provisions of the will appointing executors or trustees or conferring a power of appointment, if they appoint or confer the power on the former spouse, shall take effect as if the former spouse had died on the date on which the marriage is dissolved or annulled, and

(b) any property which, or an interest in which, is devised or bequeathed to the former spouse shall pass as if the former spouse had died on that date,

except in so far as a contrary intention appears by the will.'[6]

The section will operate if the marriage was dissolved or annulled by a court of civil jurisdiction in England and Wales or by a divorce or annulment obtained elsewhere and entitled to recognition in this country by virtue of Part II of the Family Law Act 1986.[7] It will not operate, however, if no proceedings are taken for the annulment of a void marriage.

The 1995 Act also amended the law to provide that, where the spouse of the testator is appointed in his will as a guardian, the appointment is revoked if the marriage is subsequently dissolved or annulled.[8]

Mutual wills

Although mutual wills are rare, they are still made occasionally, and they are of particular interest in family law as mutual testators are usually (although not invariably) husband and wife. The essence of mutual wills is that the parties agree to make wills in similar terms and to be bound to dispose of their estate in a specified manner. It is not sufficient that the testators agreed to make identical wills: it must also be established that there is a contract enforceable at law to the effect that each party will give effect to the agreement between them and will not exercise his testamentary freedom to make a will with different provisions.[10] Although English law knows of no such thing as an irrevocable will, equity takes the view that it would be inequitable to permit the survivor to take the benefits under the other's will[9] without giving effect to the agreement himself and it protects the other beneficiaries by attaching a trust to the property on the first testator's death.

Let us suppose that a husband, H, and wife, W, agree to make mutual wills in the following form: 'I devise and bequeath the whole of my estate to trustees on trust for my wife W (or my husband H) for life and then on trust for my son S

---

4 Ibid paras 3.7–3.8.
5 See Barton and Wells 'A Matter of Life and Death – the Law Reform (Succession) Act 1995' [1996] Fam Law 172; Miller 'Intestacy, divorce and wills' (1995) 145 NLJ 1693.
6 This formulation applies where the testator dies on or after 1 January 1996, regardless of the date of the will or of the divorce or annulment.
7 Family Law Act 1986 s 53. For recognition of divorces and annulments see North and Fawcett *Cheshire and North's Private International Law* (12th edn, 1992) pp 655–90. In certain circumstances an overseas divorce or annulment will be recognised even though it was not obtained by means of any formal proceedings (eg a Muslim talaq).
8 Children Act 1989 s 6(3A) inserted by s 4 of the 1995 Act. See further, p 402 ante.
9 But note that in *Re Dale* [1994] Ch 31, [1993] 4 All ER 129 it was held that the mutual wills doctrine applied to parents who had made wills in favour of their children, even though they had left no property to each other. As Borkowski (op cit, p 45) points out, there is therefore no need for mutual wills to confer reciprocal benefits upon their makers.
10 *Re Cleaver* [1981] 2 All ER 1018; *Re Oldham* [1925] Ch 75; *Gray v Perpetual Trustee Co Ltd* [1928] AC 391, PC; *Re Goodchild (Deceased)* [1997] 2 FLR 644, CA.

absolutely' or alternatively ' – to W (or H) provided that she (or he) survives me, and if she (or he) does not, to S'. The following illustrations will show how the equitable principle operates.

(1) H and W agree that they will no longer be bound by their agreement. Both are free to revoke their wills and no trust is created on the death of either.
(2) H revokes his will and tells W that he has done so. W is free to revoke her will and no trust is created.[11]
(3) H revokes his will without telling W. H dies first and W discovers the revocation. As she is still free to make other testamentary dispositions, she may do so and no trust is created.[12]
(4) W dies first without having revoked her will. As it would be unconscionable to permit H to take the interest given by W's will without adhering to the agreement which effectively gave it to him, equity imposes an obligation on him to observe it and regards him as holding both estates on trust to carry out its terms. Consequently, if he later revokes his will[13] (or revoked it before W's death without informing her), his personal representatives are bound to give effect to the agreement and take his estate with a trust impressed on it for the benefit of S.[14] There are conflicting dicta on whether H would still be bound by the agreement if he repudiated it by disclaiming the gift to himself, but since the trust arises from the prior agreement, the better view is that it is automatically impressed on the property on the first party's death and the survivor's accepting the gift is therefore immaterial.[15]

If these conditions are satisfied, the trust takes effect from the moment the first testator dies.[16] Consequently the remaindermen have a vested interest from this time, and the gifts to them will not lapse if they die after this date but before the surviving testator.[17] But it is still not settled whether any property acquired by the survivor after the first party's death is also subject to the trust or whether this will attach only to the property which he has at that time.[18] Whatever the answer, there

---

11 *Birmingham v Renfrew* (1936) 57 CLR 666 at 682 (Aust) cited with approval in *Re Cleaver* (supra) at 1023.
12 *Stone v Hoskins* [1905] P 194; the same applies if H alters his will without telling her: *Re Hobley, deceased* (1997) Times, 16 June.
13 Quaere if the will is revoked by operation of law if H remarries. In *Re Marsland* [1939] Ch 820, CA, it was held that this did not amount to a breach of an express covenant not to revoke a will. It is submitted that this principle should not be applied to mutual wills, because the trusts attach on the death of the first testator and, if it were applied, they would frequently fail; and see *Re Goodchild (Deceased)* [1996] 1 FLR 591 (upheld on appeal, [1997] 2 FLR 644, CA) where it was held (obiter) that effect should be given to the original intention, and that it was immaterial that revocation was by operation of law. See Grattan 'Mutual wills and remarriage' (1997) 61 Conv 153.
14 *Dufour v Pereira* (1769) 1 Dick 419, 2 Hargrave Juridical Arguments 304.
15 See the different interpretations placed on Lord Camden's judgment in *Dufour v Pereira* (supra) by Lord Hailsham LC in *Gray v Perpetual Trustee Co Ltd* (supra) at 399, and by Clauson J in *Re Hagger* [1930] 2 Ch 190 at 195. If this were not so and the survivor were the widow or widower of the other, he or she might disclaim the legacy and take the estate on intestacy, thus obtaining the benefit whilst going back on the agreement: Mitchell 'Some Aspects of Mutual Wills' (1951) 14 MLR 136. See also Burgess 'A Fresh Look at Mutual Wills' (1970) 34 Conv 230 at 240. *Re Dale* (supra) supports this view: since neither testator was to benefit under the other's will, the trust could not be conditional upon acceptance of the gift.
16 *Re Hagger* (supra); *Re Green* [1951] Ch 148, [1950] 2 All ER 913; *Re Goodchild* (supra).
17 *Re Hagger* (supra).
18 See Mitchell, loc cit, for a fuller discussion of this and other difficulties.

are considerable problems. For example, may the survivor deal with his property as he wishes, including disposing of or dissipating it, or is he, as a trustee, bound to convert it into authorised investments?[19] If the wills appear to give an absolute interest to the survivor, the following practical solution was propounded by Dixon J in *Birmingham v Renfrew*:[20]

'The object of the transaction is to put the survivor in a position to enjoy for his own benefit the full ownership so that, for instance, he may convert [the property passing under the will of the party first dying] and expend the proceeds if he choose – No doubt gifts and settlements, inter vivos, if calculated to defeat the intention of the compact, could not be made by the survivor and his right of disposition, inter vivos, is, therefore, not unqualified. But, substantially, the purpose of the arrangement will often be to allow full enjoyment for the survivor's own benefit and advantage upon condition that at his death the residue shall pass as arranged.'

Not the least of the practical difficulties facing beneficiaries is in determining what property is subject to the trust.

Gifts to the testator's wife or husband

Provided it was obviously the testator's intention, a gift to the testator's 'wife' (or 'husband') will take effect in favour of a woman (or man) with whom he (or she) is living as husband and wife, even though they are not legally married.[1] Such a gift will even be valid if it is directed to be held on trust during widowhood: in this case it will be construed as being determinable upon the other's contracting a valid marriage after the testator's death.[2]

In a home-made will it is not uncommon for a testator to make a bequest in the form: 'I give my whole estate to my wife, W, and after her death to my children'. His probable intention was that she should have full power to dispose of capital and income but that anything that was left at her death should go to the children.[3] The effect, however, was to give her only a life interest, because an absolute interest would be incompatible with the gift over. To remedy this, Administration of Justice Act 1982 s 22[4] provides that, if a testator makes a gift to his or her spouse in terms which in themselves would confer an absolute interest and by the same instrument gives an interest in the same property to his or her issue, the gift to the spouse takes effect absolutely unless a contrary intention is shown. The section is not well drafted. The absolute gift to the spouse presumably destroys the gift to the issue: if, therefore, the wife predeceases the testator, the gift will fall into residue and may not pass to the issue, which will again defeat the testator's intention. It will also be observed that the section does not apply to a gift to an unmarried cohabitant or if the gift over is to someone other than the testator's issue (as might be the case if he were childless).

---

19 See Borkowski, op cit, pp 48–9.
20 (1936) 57 CLR 666 at 689.
1 *Re Brown* (1910) 26 TLR 257. A fortiori if he names her (eg 'to my wife EAS'): *Re Smalley* [1929] 2 Ch 112, CA.
2 Even though the 'wife' is already married to another man: *Re Wagstaff* [1908] 1 Ch 162, CA; *Re Hammond* [1911] 2 Ch 342; cf *Re Lynch* [1943] 1 All ER 168. The decision to the contrary in *Re Gale* [1941] Ch 209, [1941] 1 All ER 329 cannot be reconciled with these decisions and must be wrong.
3 See the 19th Report of the Law Reform Committee (*Interpretation of Wills*) 1973 (Cmnd 5301), para 60.
4 Implementing the recommendations of the Law Reform Committee: ibid, para 62.

Unlike the position on intestacy,[5] the surviving spouse cannot demand that the matrimonial home or personal chattels should be appropriated as part of a gift (eg a residuary bequest). If they have not been specifically disposed of by the will, the only thing a widow or widower wishing to retain such property can do is to ask the personal representatives to exercise their power of appropriation in this way.[6]

Gifts to children

The common law presumption that the term 'children' in a will applied only to legitimate children was reversed by the Family Law Reform Act 1969 s 15.[7] The Legitimacy Act 1926, which enabled legitimated children to take under a disposition after their legitimation, was extended by the Children Act 1975 to wills taking effect after 1 January 1976, even where they came into operation before the parents' marriage.[8]

Testamentary gift to a deceased child

In the normal way, if a devisee or legatee predeceases the testator, the gift lapses and either it drops into residue or the testator is deemed to die intestate with respect to it. The application of this rule to a testamentary gift to a child, however, might well defeat the intention of a testator who had failed to foresee the possibility of the child's predeceasing him. If, for example, a father left a substantial legacy to a daughter with a residual gift to a charity, it is probable that he would wish the daughter's legacy to go to her children rather than to the charity in the event of her untimely death. If he himself dies before changing his will, his wishes will be defeated. Consequently the Wills Act 1837 s 33[9] provides that a devise or bequest to a child or remoter descendant who predeceases the testator and leaves issue shall take effect as a gift to the intended beneficiary's issue living at the testator's death. A similar rule operates if there is a gift to a class consisting of the testator's children or remoter descendants: in such a case the deceased member's issue take the share to which he or she would have been entitled.

A testator may prevent the operation of this section by stating a contrary intention in his will. Such an intention could also be implied: the issue of a deceased child could claim nothing, for example, if the gift were to the testator's *surviving* children or conferred a life interest on the intended beneficiary.

The rule against double portions

This rule is a direct application of the equitable presumption that a father or other person in loco parentis intends to favour none of his children at the expense of the others and in particular intends to divide his estate or fortune amongst them all equally. They may obviously take a share of this in two ways: by payments made to the child by the parent during the latter's lifetime, and by a gift to the child in the parent's will. Consequently, in certain circumstances, unless the presumption that

5 See post, p 876.
6 For the personal representatives' powers of appropriation, see the Administration of Estates Act 1925 s 41.
7 In respect of any disposition made on or after 1 January 1970.
8 Schedule 1, Pt III, re-enacted in Legitimacy Act 1976 s 5(3). For the position of adopted children, see ante, p 676.
9 As substituted by s 19 of the Administration of Justice Act 1982. For the section as originally enacted, which applies to the wills of testators dying before 1983, see the 6th edition of this book, pp 608–9.

all the children were to share alike can be rebutted, they must bring into account what they have received during the testator's lifetime before they can take the gift under the will. Hence equity is said 'to lean against double portions'. A similar rule used to apply in respect of intestacy, but has now been abolished.[10]

2.   INTESTATE SUCCESSION[11]

Intestate succession before 1926

Before the Administration of Estates Act 1925 came into force, there was a considerable difference between the descent of realty and the descent of personalty. All inheritable estates of freehold descended to the heir at law subject to the husband's curtesy and the wife's dower.[12] The husband took all his wife's personalty (including her separate estate if she had not disposed of it by will). On the death of a married man his widow took one-third of his personalty if he left issue and one-half if he did not; the remainder of his estate was divided among his issue or, in default of issue, among his next-of-kin as defined by the Statutes of Distribution of 1670 and 1685. Under the Intestates' Estates Act 1890, which was passed to give a widow a larger provision if the estate was small and the intestate left no issue, she took the whole of the real and personal estate if the total value did not exceed £500; if it exceeded this sum, the estate was to stand charged with the payment to her of £500.

Administration of Estates Act 1925

This Act radically overhauled the law relating to intestate succession in two respects. First, the law relating to realty and personalty was put on the same footing; and secondly the distribution of estates was completely changed. The principal effect of this Act, and subsequent amendments, was to give the surviving widow a much greater interest than she had before 1926 and to give the surviving widower the same rights as the surviving widow.

In 1989, the Law Commission recommended that the surviving spouse should receive the whole estate as the best means of ensuring her or him adequate provision. Furthermore, it would greatly simplify the rules. It also appeared to be in line with public opinion.[13] However, their view has been criticised as failing adequately to consider the needs of the deceased's minor children, and of unduly benefiting second or subsequent spouses,[14] and the government rejected it when enacting other reforms to the intestacy rules in the Law Reform (Succession) Act 1995. The Law Commission also considered, but rejected, the view that a surviving unmarried cohabitant should be treated like a surviving spouse, on the grounds that this would increase the complexity and cost of administration, and

---

10 See post, p 879.
11 See Sherrin and Bonehill *The Law and Practice of Intestate Succession* (2nd edn, 1994); Law Commission Working Paper No 108 (1988), and Report No 186 (1989) *Distribution on Intestacy*.
12 See ante, p 107. See works on real property for a fuller discussion.
13 Law Com No 187 *Distribution on Intestacy* paras 25, 29.
14 Cretney 'Reform of Intestacy: The Best We Can Do?' (1995) 111 LQR 77; Kerridge 'Distribution on Intestacy: The Law Commission's Report' (1990) 54 Conv 358. Finch et al (supra, p 868 n 9) found that the intestacy rules favouring close kin, especially the surviving spouse and children, are reflected in English wills, although there is also significant evidence of a concern to bequeath property to a wider range of relationships based on affection, friendship etc: see op cit ch 7.

special rules would be needed to deal with the situation where both a spouse and a cohabitant survived. They considered that any hardship done to a cohabitant, or to a relative or dependant of the deceased by the intestacy rules is adequately remedied by a claim under the Inheritance (Provision for Family and Dependants) Act 1975,[15] and they proposed strengthening the claim of a cohabitant under that Act. It is also always open to all the beneficiaries under a will or an intestacy, if of full age and capacity, to agree to distribute the estate in any way they wish.[16]

The rights of the surviving spouse

The spouse must survive the intestate by 28 days.[17] This requirement is to prevent 'the assets of both spouses going to the parents or relatives of the second to die, in cases of not quite simultaneous death, usually in accidents'[18] and echoes survivorship clauses usually inserted into wills. Where it is uncertain which spouse died first, the younger of the two is usually deemed to have survived the other,[19] but on intestacy the estate is to be distributed as though the intestate had survived.[20]

The surviving widow or widower takes the following interests.[1]

(a)   Personal chattels

The surviving spouse is always entitled to the personal chattels (provided that the estate is solvent), and personal representatives may not sell them unless this is necessary to pay debts and expenses.[2] Personal chattels are defined as:[3]

> 'Carriages, horses, stable furniture and effects (not used for business purposes), motor cars and accessories (not used for business purposes), garden effects, domestic animals, plate, plated articles, linen, china, glass, books, pictures, prints, furniture, jewellery,[4] articles of household or personal use or ornament, musical and scientific instruments and apparatus, wines, liquors and consumable stores, but [they] do not include any chattels used at the death of the intestate for business purposes[5] nor money or securities for money.'

(b)   Residuary interests[6]

The interest which the surviving spouse takes over and above the personal chattels depends upon what other relatives the intestate leaves surviving.

If he leaves any children or remoter issue, the spouse takes what is usually

---

15 See post, pp 884–902.
16 Known as the rule in *Saunders v Vautier* (1841) Cr & Ph 240.
17 Where the death occurs on or after 1 January 1996: Administration of Estates Act 1925 s 46(2A), inserted by Law Reform (Succession) Act 1995 s 1(1).
18 Law Com No 187 para 57.
19 Law of Property Act 1925 s 184.
20 Administration of Estates Act 1925 s 46(3) as amended.
 1 Administration of Estates Act 1925 s 46 as amended; Family Provision (Intestate Succession) Order, SI 2906/1993.
 2 Administration of Estates Act 1925 s 33(1).
 3 Ibid, s 55(1)(x). This section has been widely construed and has been held to include a 60-foot motor yacht (*Re Chaplin* [1950] Ch 507, [1950] 2 All ER 155) and a collection of clocks and watches (*Re Crispin's Will Trusts* [1975] Ch 245, [1974] 3 All ER 772, CA). The mere fact that the property might be regarded as an investment does not prevent it from being a personal chattel too: *Re Reynold's Will Trusts* [1965] 3 All ER 686 (valuable stamp collection, which was deceased's principal hobby, held to be an article of personal use).
 4 Including cut but unmounted jewels: *Re Whitby* [1944] Ch 210, [1944] 1 All ER 299, CA.
 5 See *Re Ogilby* [1942] Ch 288, [1942] 1 All ER 524.
 6 Administration of Estates Act 1925 s 46.

termed a 'statutory legacy' of £125,000 with interest at six per cent per annum until it is paid and a *life* interest in half the residue.

If he leaves no issue but a parent or a brother or sister of the whole blood or issue of such a brother or sister, the surviving spouse takes a statutory legacy of £200,000 with interest at six per cent per annum until it is paid and an *absolute* interest in half the residue.

If he leaves neither issue nor any of the above relations, the surviving spouse takes the whole of the residue absolutely.

(c) Redemption of life interest

The spouse may, if he wishes to do so, insist on the personal representatives' redeeming his life interest by paying the capital value to him.[7] He must elect to do so within 12 months after representation is taken out, but the court may extend this period if it considers that the limit will operate unfairly because a previous will was revoked or invalid, or because the interest of some person in the estate had not been determined when representation was taken out, or because of any other circumstances affecting the administration or distribution of the estate.[8]

(d) Rights with respect to the matrimonial home

The Intestates' Estates Act 1952 gives the surviving spouse a right within certain limits to retain the matrimonial home.[9] Where the intestate's estate comprises an interest in a dwelling-house in which the surviving spouse was resident at the time of the intestate's death, the survivor may require the personal representatives to appropriate the house in or towards satisfaction of any absolute interest that the survivor has in the estate,[10] and if the value of the house exceeds the value of the survivor's interest, he may exercise this option if he pays the excess value to the representatives.[11] He must exercise this option within 12 months of representation being taken out, but this period may be extended by the court, as in the case of an application to have a life interest redeemed.[12] Consequently the personal representatives are forbidden to sell the house within this period without the written consent of the surviving spouse unless this is necessary for the payment of expenses or debts.[13]

There are two limitations upon this power. First, these provisions normally do not apply if the house is held upon a lease which had less than two years to run from the date of the intestate's death or which could be determined by the landlord within this period.[14] This means that many houses (eg those held on periodic

---

7 Administration of Estates Act 1925 s 47A.

8 Ibid s 47A(5).

9 Sch 2.

10 Ibid, para 1(1). 'Dwelling-house' includes part of a building occupied as a separate dwelling and an absolute interest includes a redeemed life interest: ibid, para 1(4)–(5).

11 Ibid, para 5(2); *Re Phelps* [1980] Ch 275, [1979] 3 All ER 373, CA. The value is to be assessed at the date of appropriation: *Robinson v Collins* [1975] 1 All ER 321.

12 Ibid, para 3. It cannot be exercised after the surviving spouse's death by his or her personal representatives: ibid, para 3(1)(b).

13 Ibid, para 4. But if they fail to observe this provision, the spouse has no right to claim the house from the purchaser: ibid, para 4(5).

14 Ibid, para 1(2). But the personal representatives have a discretionary power to appropriate the lease under s 41 of the Administration of Estates Act 1925: ibid, para 5(2). For exceptional cases (where the surviving spouse would be entitled to acquire the freehold or an extended lease), see the Leasehold Reform Act 1967 s 7(8).

tenancies) fall outside these provisions, but to offset this it must be remembered that there will usually be a statutory transmission to the surviving spouse.[15] Secondly, the spouse cannot require the personal representatives to appropriate the house in the following cases except on an order of the court, which must be satisfied that the appropriation is not likely to diminish the value of assets in the residuary estate (other than the interest in the house) or make these assets more difficult to dispose of.[16] This is where:

'(a) the dwelling-house forms part of a building and an interest in the whole of the building is comprised in the residuary estate;[17] or
(b) the dwelling-house is held with agricultural land and an interest in the agricultural land is comprised in the residuary estate; or
(c) the whole or part of the dwelling-house was at the time of the intestate's death used as a hotel or lodging house; or
(d) a part of the dwelling-house was at the time of the intestate's death used for purposes other than domestic purposes.'

(e)   Separation order

By s 21 of the Family Law Act 1996, if either spouse dies intestate as respects any real or personal property whilst a separation order is in force and the parties remain separated, his or her property is to devolve as though the other were dead. The reason for this provision is that the rules of intestate succession are intended to reflect the testamentary dispositions the deceased might reasonably be expected to have made, and as separation almost always marks the de facto end of the marriage, it is highly unlikely that either would have left anything to the other.[18]

Interests taken by the intestate's children and remoter issue

If the intestate leaves a surviving spouse, the personal representatives must hold one-half of the residue (after taking out the personal chattels and the spouse's £125,000) on the statutory trusts for the intestate's issue and the other half on the same trusts subject to the surviving spouse's life interest. If the intestate leaves no surviving spouse, the personal representatives must hold the whole of the residue on the statutory trusts for the issue.[19]

(a)   The statutory trusts

The property is to be held on trust for all the children alive at the intestate's death who reach the age of 18 or marry under that age in equal shares. But if any of his children has predeceased him, that child's share is held upon the same trusts for his own children or remoter issue.[20]

Thus, suppose that the intestate had four children, A, B, C and D. The first three are alive at their parent's death but D is already dead. D had two children, K and L, of whom K is still alive but L is also dead, leaving two children, X and Y. By applying the above rules, we see that A, B and C each take one-quarter; K takes

---

15 See post, pp 881–4.
16 Intestates' Estates Act 1952 Sch 2 para 2.
17 If the house is attached to a shop and the owner would normally live in it, for example.
18 Until the 1996 Act comes into force, the equivalent provision is s 18(2) of the Matrimonial Causes Act 1973, which relates to decrees of judicial separation.
19 Administration of Estates Act 1925 s 46(1).
20 Ibid, s 47(1)(i) (as amended); Family Law Reform Act 1969 s 3(2).

half of D's share (ie one-eighth) and the other half of D's share goes to X and Y, who get one-sixteenth each. If the share of any of the above fails to vest because he dies a minor and unmarried, his share will go over to the others as if he had predeceased the testator.[1] So, if A were to die in such circumstances, B and C would each take one-third of his share, K would take a sixth, and X and Y would each take a twelfth. If K were to die, his share would pass to X and Y equally; and if X were to die, his share would go to Y.

Until a beneficiary obtains a vested interest by attaining his majority or marrying, the trustees may use the whole of the income of the part to which he is contingently entitled for his maintenance, education or benefit, and they may use one half of the capital to which he is contingently entitled for his advancement.[2] Subject to this they must accumulate the income at compound interest.[3] They may also at their discretion permit him to have the use of any personal chattels.[4]

(b) Hotchpot

The Administration of Estates Act expressly applied the rule against double portions[5] to intestacies. However, this was abolished in respect of persons dying intestate after 1 January 1996 by s 1(2) of the Law Reform (Succession) Act 1995.[6]

Children of unmarried parents

Originally, in accordance with the general rule at common law, only legitimate persons and those claiming a relationship through legitimate persons, could participate in intestate succession. Those who had been legitimated could claim after the passing of the Legitimacy Act 1926,[7] and the Family Law Reform Act 1969 permitted illegitimate children and their parents to succeed to each other.[8] In pursuance of the policy of removing the disadvantages flowing from birth outside marriage, the Family Law Reform Act 1987 s 18 now provides that, for the purposes of the distribution of the estate of an intestate, any relationship shall be construed without regard to whether the parents of the deceased, the claimant or any person through whom the claimant is related to the deceased were married to each other.[9] But because of the difficulty in tracing some fathers, whose identity

1 *Re Young* [1951] Ch 185, [1950] 2 All ER 1040.
2 Administration of Estates Act 1925 s 47(1)(ii); Trustee Act 1925 s 31(1), s 32(1).
3 Trustee Act 1925 s 31(2).
4 Administration of Estates Act 1925 s 47(1)(iv).
5 See ante, p 874.
6 See Borkowski, op cit, pp 22–5 for detailed discussion.
7 Now see the Legitimacy Act 1976 s 5. This also applied to the issue of a person who would have been legitimated had he not died before his parents' marriage. If the intestate died before 1976, the claimant could succeed only if he was legitimated before the death and, if an entailed interest was created before 1976, he can still claim by descent only if it was created after his legitimation: Legitimacy Act 1926 s 3(1)(a), (c).
8 Section 14. Except that the legitimate issue of a deceased illegitimate person could succeed on the death intestate of that person's parent, succession was limited to these two cases. Hence an illegitimate person could claim nothing on the intestacy of a grandparent or collateral relative and the latter could claim nothing on his intestacy. This provision implemented the recommendations of the majority of the Committee on the Law of Succession in Relation to Illegitimate Persons 1966, Cmnd 3051, and applied to deaths occurring on or after 1 January 1970.
9 Applying s 1 of the 1987 Act. The section applies if the intestate died on or after 4 April 1988. Any reference to statutory next of kin in an instrument taking effect on or after this date is to be construed likewise: s 18(3).

might not be known, a person whose parents were not married to each other is to be presumed not to have been survived by his father or by anyone related to him through his father unless the contrary is shown.[10]

Adopted children

An adopted child is treated as though he were the child of his adopters and of no other person.[11] If he was adopted by two spouses jointly, he will be in the position of a brother (or sister) of the whole blood of any other child or adopted child of both the adopters and a brother of the half blood of any child or adopted child of one of them; if he was adopted by one person only, he will be in the position of a brother of the half blood of any child or adopted child of his adopter. He has no claims on the death of his natural parents or anyone related to them.[12]

Interests taken by other members of the family

If the intestate dies leaving a surviving spouse but no issue, the other half of the residue (after taking out the personal chattels, the £200,000 and the half-interest which has gone to the surviving spouse) is to be held on trust for the intestate's parents in equal shares (or for one parent absolutely if only one parent survives the intestate), and if neither of his parents survives him, on the statutory trusts for his brothers and sisters of the whole blood and their issue.

If the intestate leaves neither a spouse nor issue surviving, his whole estate must be held on trust for the persons coming into the first of the following classes that can be satisfied:

(1) For the intestate's parents (if they are both alive) in equal shares, or, if one only is still alive, for that parent absolutely.
(2) On the statutory trusts for the brothers and sisters of the whole blood of the intestate and their issue.
(3) On the statutory trusts for the brothers and sisters of the half blood of the intestate and their issue.
(4) For the surviving grandparents of the intestate in equal shares.
(5) On the statutory trusts for the uncles and aunts of the intestate (being brothers or sisters of the whole blood of one of his parents) and their issue.
(6) On the statutory trusts for the uncles and aunts of the intestate (being brothers or sisters of the half blood of one of his parents) and their issue.

If none of these classes is filled, the whole estate will go to the Crown as bona vacantia.[13]

The statutory trusts are exactly the same in the above cases as the statutory trusts for the intestate's children and issue. All the interests are contingent upon

10 Family Law Reform Act 1987 s 18(2). See Miller 'The Family Law Reform Act 1987 and the Law of Succession' (1988) 52 Conv 410.
11 Adoption Act 1976 ss 39, 42 and 46(4). Hence a child adopted by one of his natural parents cannot claim on the death of the other.
12 But cf *Staffordshire County Council v B* [1998] 1 FLR 261, where it was held that, by virtue of s 42(2) of the Adoption Act 1976, a child whose birth mother had a life interest in her grandmother's estate would keep his entitlement to a share of the remainder because he had a contingent interest vested in possession. The decision has been criticised by Cretney, at [1998] Fam Law 8, because it depends upon the existence of a fortuitous prior life interest.
13 Administration of Estates Act 1925 s 46.

the beneficiary's attaining his majority or marrying, and if no member of any class takes a vested interest, the members of the next class will take.[14]

Partial intestacy

These rules apply equally to a partial intestacy.[15] But in this case, if the deceased devises or bequeaths property to the surviving spouse (other than personal chattels or under the exercise of a special power of appointment), the spouse must take this in partial or total satisfaction of the statutory legacy to which he or she is entitled under the intestacy.

C.   The statutory transmission of tenancies

1.   THE PRIVATE SECTOR

We have already seen that the Rent Act 1977 and Housing Act 1988 provide some protection to tenants from arbitrary eviction by the landlord.[16] The protection extends to members of the tenant's family so long as they are living with him, but this would be completely defeated if the landlord could evict them immediately the tenancy was ended by the tenant's death. It is open to the landlord to grant a fresh contractual tenancy to the person remaining in possession, but where this is not done, there may be a right to remain in the property by virtue of the statutory transmission of the tenancy. As with other aspects of housing law, the extent to which the tenant's family can benefit from these rules has been greatly reduced as part of the policy of freeing landlords from restrictive controls, and the protection will eventually wither away.

2.   REGULATED TENANCIES UNDER THE RENT ACT 1977

Surviving spouse or cohabitant

On the tenant's death, a statutory tenancy automatically vests in his surviving spouse, or the person who was living with the tenant as his wife, provided in each case that the survivor was residing in the dwelling-house immediately before the death.[17] The residence qualification prevents the spouse or cohabitant from claiming the benefit of the Act if the parties had separated and the survivor left the premises before the

---

14   Administration of Estates Act 1925 s 46(4), (5). If all the members of a particular class (excepting (1) and (4)) are dead, but one or more have left issue, the issue will take in preference to the members of a more remote class: *Re Lockwood* [1958] Ch 231, [1957] 3 All ER 520. For example, issue of a brother or sister of the whole blood will take before a brother and sister of the half blood.
15   Administration of Estates Act 1925 s 49.
16   See ante, pp 171–7.
17   Of course, the legislation includes widowers and male surviving cohabitants as well. The extension of this provision to a surviving cohabitant was introduced by the Housing Act 1988, which gave statutory effect to the decision of the Court of Appeal in *Dyson Holdings Ltd v Fox* [1976] QB 503, [1975] 3 All ER 1030 in which the Court declined to follow its previous decision in *Gammans v Ekins* [1950] 2 KB 328, [1950] 2 All ER 140 and held that, whatever the position had been 25 years earlier, in 1975 a cohabitant could properly be regarded as a member of the deceased tenant's family. An attempt to extend the meaning of living together as husband and wife to include homosexual couples failed in *Fitzpatrick v Sterling Housing Association Ltd* [1998] Ch 304, [1997] 4 All ER 991, CA (Ward LJ dissenting): see further post, p 882.

tenant's death. The successor remains a statutory tenant so long as she occupies the dwelling-house as her residence, even though she subsequently remarries.[18]

Member of the deceased's family

If the tenant leaves neither a surviving spouse nor cohabitant who can succeed to the tenancy, then a member of his family may stay in the property, provided that this person resided in the dwelling-house immediately before the tenant's death and for a minimum period of two years immediately before then.[19] However, he will obtain, not a statutory tenancy under the Rent Act, but an assured periodic tenancy under the Housing Act.[20]

It is not sufficient that the claimant and the deceased were members of the same family; the claimant must show that he was a member of the *deceased*'s family.[1] This expression is not a term of art and must be construed in its ordinary and popular sense.[2] However, it has been held that it does not (yet) extend to two homosexuals who have lived together. In *Fitzpatrick v Sterling Housing Association Ltd*[3] the applicant had lived with his male partner for 18 years in a flat of which the partner was a protected tenant. When the partner died, the applicant sought a declaration that he was entitled to succeed to the tenancy. A majority of the Court of Appeal upheld the trial judge's dismissal of the application, although with regret. Waite and Roche LJJ considered that if 'endurance, stability, interdependence and devotion were the sole hallmarks of family membership, there could be no doubt'[4] that the applicant and his partner constituted a family. However, the law is 'firmly rooted in the concept of the family as an entity bound together by ties of kinship (including adoptive status) or marriage.'[5] While Parliament had been prepared in the past to make a concession to this test by including cohabiting heterosexual couples within the legislation, and although the law was arbitrary and discriminatory, only Parliament could remedy the situation. By contrast, Ward LJ, dissenting, was prepared to hold, by adopting a functionalist approach to defining the family, both that the couple had lived together as husband and wife, and that their relationship was familial. He argued that a family –

'. . . is a social organisation which functions through its linking its members closely together. The functions may be procreative, sexual, sociable, economic, emotional . . . Save for the ability to procreate, these functions were present in the relationship between the deceased and the applicant.'[6]

Even where the parties *were* blood relations, it does not follow that the claimant will necessarily be regarded as a member of the tenant's family. The parties' conduct must be taken into account as well, and the more remote the relationship,

---

18 Rent Act 1977 Sch 1, paras 1 and 2, as amended by the Housing Act 1980 s 76 and the Housing Act 1988 Sch 4, paras 1 and 2.

19 Rent Act 1977 Sch 1, para 3. For deaths after 15 January 1989 the residence must be in the same house as the tenant, but it need not be shown that it was as part of the tenant's household (cf *Swanbrae Ltd v Elliott* (1986) 19 HLR 86,CA where a tenant's daughter continued to sleep at her own house three or four nights a week, her son still lived there, her post was sent there and she gave it as her usual address, it was held she was not residing with her mother).

20 Housing Act 1988 s 39(5)–(6).

1 *Langdon v Horton* [1951] 1 KB 666 at 669, 671; [1951] 1 All ER 60, CA at 60, 61.

2 *Carega Properties SA v Sharratt* [1979] 2 All ER 1084, HL at 1086, 1088.

3 [1997] 4 All ER 991, CA.

4 Ibid per Waite LJ at 1003j.

5 Ibid at 1004b.

6 At 1023d.

the more important this may become. In *Langdon v Horton*,[7] for example, the Court of Appeal held that two sisters, who had gone to live with their widowed cousin and stayed with her until she died 29 years later, were no more members of her family than would be two friends sharing a flat. In *Jones v Whitehill*,[8] on the other hand, it was held that a niece who had gone to look after her elderly aunt and uncle in their declining years was a member of their family as she had assumed 'out of love and natural affection the duties and offices peculiarly attributable to members of a family'.[9]

As Wikeley has pointed out,[10] judicial interpretation of the term 'family' has generally failed to take notice of the social policy objective of the Rent Act legislation. However, this objective has now changed from a primary concern to secure the tenant and his family in their home towards encouraging the flexible provision of rented sector accommodation by enabling landlords to regain possession of their property. Ironically, just as some judges, as evidenced in *Fitzpatrick*, may be prepared to show greater willingness to adopt an extended view of family relationships, the legislature has curtailed the opportunity to rely on these in this context.

Death of the first successor

Where the first successor obtained a statutory tenancy on the tenant's death (ie as his surviving spouse or cohabitant), then a person who was a member of the family, both of the original tenant and of the first successor, may succeed – but to an assured periodic tenancy only – provided that he resided in the dwelling-house with the first successor at the time of, and for the period of two years immediately before, the first successor's death.

No further successions are possible.

3. ASSURED TENANCIES

The surviving spouse or cohabitant of a tenant holding an assured periodic (but not fixed-term) tenancy, may succeed to the tenancy provided that he or she occupied the dwelling-house as his or her only or principal home.[11] No right of succession is given to any other members of the tenant's family.

No succession at all is offered in the case of assured shortholds (now the primary form of private sector tenancy).

4. SECURE TENANCIES

A member of a secure tenant's family may succeed to a secure fixed-term, or periodic, tenancy provided that he is a *qualified successor*.[12] Section 113(1) defines a member of the tenant's family as follows:

'(a) he is the spouse of that person, or he and that person live together as husband and wife, or

7 *Langdon v Horton* [1951] 1 KB 666, [1951] 1 All ER 60, CA.
8 [1950] 2 KB 204, [1950] 1 All ER 71, CA.
9 At 207 and 72, respectively.
10 '*Fitzpatrick v Sterling Housing Association Ltd*: Same-sex partners and succession to Rent Act tenancies' (1998) 10 CFLQ 191 at 196.
11 Housing Act 1988 s 17.
12 Housing Act 1985 ss 89, 90.

(b) he is that person's parent, grandparent, child, grandchild, brother, sister, uncle, aunt, nephew or niece.'

And s 113(2) continues, for the purposes of subsection (1)(b):

'(a) a relationship by marriage shall be treated as a relationship by blood,
(b) a relationship of the half-blood shall be treated as a relationship of the whole blood,
(c) the stepchild of a person shall be treated as his child, and
(d) an illegitimate child shall be treated as the legitimate child of his mother and reputed father.'

It will be seen that cohabitants are included within the definition but, as is the case with regulated tenancies, homosexual partners are not.[13] Although the precise wording of the section avoids the mass of litigation to which the term has given rise under the Rent Act, it is not free from ambiguity. For example, does the term 'stepchild' include a child of the secure tenant's cohabitant?

If there is more than one person qualified to succeed, the surviving spouse is preferred to any other member of the family; if there is no surviving spouse and two or more persons are qualified, they must agree amongst themselves which of them is to succeed and, if they cannot agree, the landlord may select one of them.[14]

To be a qualified successor, the claimant must have occupied the dwelling-house as his only or principal home at the time of the tenant's death. In addition, if he is a member of the tenant's family other than a spouse, he must have resided with the tenant throughout the period of 12 months ending with the tenant's death. Temporary absences will not necessarily break the chain of continuity of residence; thus, where the tenant's grandson was absent from her flat for some three months while 'house sitting' for friends, but retained his postal address at the tenancy and left his possessions there, the Court of Appeal held that continuity was not broken, even though he had hoped to avoid returning to the grandmother's flat by finding alternative permanent accommodation for himself and his wife.[15]

No further succession is possible after the first.

D.   Provision for members of the family and other dependants[16]

By permitting a husband to extinguish his wife's right to dower, the Dower Act 1833 abolished the last vestige of family provision in English law.[17] After that there was nothing to stop a man (or a woman with respect to her separate property) from devising and bequeathing his whole estate to a charity or a complete stranger and leaving his widow and children penniless. To prevent this evil, the Inheritance (Family Provision) Act 1938 was passed. This did not cast upon a testator any

---

13 *Harrogate Borough Council v Simpson* [1986] 2 FLR 91, CA.
14 Section 89(2).
15 *Camden London Borough Council v Goldenberg* [1997] 1 FLR 556, CA; cf *Swanbrae Ltd v Elliott* (supra) where a similar test resulted in the claimant failing to establish residence with her mother, because she had retained links with another property of which she was tenant.
16 See Oughton *Tyler's Family Provision* (3rd edn, 1997).
17 See ante, p 107; Unger 'The Inheritance Act and the Family' (1943) 6 MLR 215.

positive duty to make reasonable provision for his dependants – indeed, it would have been impossible to do so – but enacted that, if he failed to do so, the court might order such reasonable provision as it thought fit to be made out of his estate for the benefit of the surviving spouse and certain classes of children. In 1952 the principle underlying this Act was applied to cases of intestacy.[18] It is easy to see that the law of intestate succession might leave a child without adequate support: the whole estate might go to a widow who refused to make any provision for the children of a previous marriage or might be divided between a daughter married to a rich man and a minor son whose education was incomplete. In 1958 a similar power to apply for provision was given to a former spouse, that is, one whose marriage to the deceased had been dissolved or annulled and who had not remarried.[19] This, of course, was of particular value to a divorced wife who had obtained an order for unsecured periodical payments which would cease on her former husband's death.

Notwithstanding these extensions, there were still many gaps and deficiencies in the law. The term 'dependant' was so narrowly defined that it excluded many who had been supported by another during his lifetime and who had a moral, if not a legal, claim on his estate. No application could be made, for example, by a parent, brother or sister, another's children who had been treated as members of the deceased's family, or a person with whom he had been cohabiting outside marriage. Provision could be ordered only out of property which the deceased had power to dispose of by will, so that he could defeat the operation of the Act altogether by settling his property during his lifetime or by contracting to leave it to a third person after his death.[20] Furthermore, the court was limited to ordering reasonable provision for the dependant's maintenance and had no power to divide capital assets: the result was that a surviving wife could be in a worse position than a divorced wife who obtained a property adjustment order. When the Law Commission examined the whole question of family property law, they rejected the proposal that a surviving spouse should have a right to inherit a fixed proportion of the deceased's estate in favour of the more flexible approach of family provision. They added, however, that this would need strengthening, and in particular 'the surviving partner of a marriage should have a claim upon the family assets at least equivalent to that of a divorced person'.[1] Their detailed recommendations were published in 1974,[2] and led to the enactment of the Inheritance (Provision for Family and Dependants) Act 1975, which replaced the existing relevant legislation with a new code. This, in turn, was further amended in the light of the Law Commission's recommendation that cohabitants should be given additional rights to claim family provision.[3]

The Act applies only if the person against whose estate the claim is being made died domiciled in England and Wales.[4]

18 Intestates' Estates Act 1952.
19 Matrimonial Causes (Property and Maintenance) Act 1958, subsequently re-enacted in the Matrimonial Causes Act 1965 ss 26–28.
20 *Schaefer v Schuhmann* [1972] AC 572, [1972] 1 All ER 621, PC. But the disposition might possibly have been set aside had it been fraudulent: see post, p 897.
1 Law Com No 52, *First Report on Family Property: a New Approach* (1973) paras 31–45.
2 Law Com No 61, *Second Report on Family Property: Family Provision on Death* (1974).
3 Law Com No 187, *Distribution on Intestacy* (1989) paras 58–60. The recommendation was enacted by s 2 of the Law Reform (Succession) Act 1995, discussed further post, p 887.
4 Section 1(1).

1.   WHO MAY APPLY FOR AN ORDER

Application for provision may be made only by the following persons.[5]

Deceased's wife or husband

This category includes a person who had in good faith entered into a void marriage with the deceased. The reason is that such a person is de facto in the position of a surviving spouse and may not discover that the marriage is void until after the other party's death, when it will be too late to apply for financial relief in nullity proceedings. Consequently, the survivor may not make an application under this head if during the deceased's lifetime the marriage has been dissolved or annulled by a decree recognised in England or he has entered into a later marriage and thus in effect treated the first marriage as at an end.[6]

A party to a polygamous marriage is a spouse for the purposes of the Act.[7]

A former spouse of the deceased, who has not remarried

A former wife or husband of the deceased, whose marriage with the deceased was dissolved or annulled during his lifetime under the law of any part of the British Isles or recognised as valid in England and Wales and who, in either case, has not remarried, may apply.[8] This enables the court to make or continue financial provision for those to whom it could award financial relief under the Matrimonial Causes Act 1973. An application by a former spouse will, as the Court of Appeal pointed out in *Re Fullard*,[9] rarely be successful. In that case it refused to make an order in favour of the plaintiff who had accepted a half-share of the matrimonial home (the parties' only asset) only a few months before her former husband's death. Normally, the court said, it would be appropriate to make an award in such circumstances only if the sole order made in previous proceedings had been for periodical payments, which had been running for a long time, and the deceased's estate could support their continuation,[10] or if the death had released a substantial capital sum, such as the payment of an insurance policy, of which the deceased was aware and which therefore should be taken into account in deciding whether he had made reasonable provision for the applicant.[11]

---

5 An application may not be made more than six months after the date on which representation is first taken out without the permission of the court: ss 4 and 23. The personal representatives will not be personally liable for distribution after this time if no application is then pending, but property may be recovered from the beneficiaries to whom it has been transferred if it is needed to make provision for a dependant to whom the court gives leave to make a late application: s 20(1). For examples of permission being granted, see *Stock v Brown* [1994] 1 FLR 840 (applicant was elderly widow in financial difficulties – leave was given six years after grant of probate); *Re C (Deceased) (Leave to Apply for Provision)* [1995] 2 FLR 24 (applicant was eight-year-old illegitimate child of the deceased: leave given two-and-a-half years after the death).

6 Section 25(4). A later marriage includes a void or voidable marriage (because the person in question would have a claim against the other party to it): s 25(5).

7 *Re Sehota* [1978] 3 All ER 385.

8 Section 25(1), as amended by the Matrimonial and Family Proceedings Act 1984 s 8 and Family Law Act 1996 s 66(1), Sch 8, para 27(1)(8). Remarriage includes a void or voidable marriage: s 25(5).

9 [1982] Fam 42, [1981] 2 All ER 796, CA.

10 As in *Re Crawford* (1982) 4 FLR 273.

11 But not other accretions of wealth since the divorce: *Re Fullard* (supra) at 52 and 804 respectively.

A person who was cohabiting with the deceased when he or she died[12]

The Law Reform (Succession) Act 1995 s 2 added to the list of applicants a person who has lived as husband and wife with the deceased in the same household, for the whole of the period of two years ending immediately before the date of his death.[13] The definition of cohabitation is the same as that required for a claim under the Fatal Accidents Act 1976.[14] The aim of this reform, recommended by the Law Commission,[15] was to give greater recognition to the position of cohabitants who, previously, had to show dependence upon the deceased if they were to succeed in a claim.[16] However, a cohabitant may only receive provision based on his or her need for 'maintenance';[17] there is no entitlement to seek a capital share of the deceased's estate as there is for a surviving spouse.

A child of the deceased

This includes a child whose parents were not married to each other, an adopted child, and a child en ventre sa mère at the time of the death.[18] The age and marital status of the child are irrelevant.[19]

Any other person whom the deceased treated as a child of the family

This corresponds to the court's power to award financial relief to a child of the family under the Matrimonial Causes Act. Obviously anyone who is a child of the family for the purpose of that Act[20] will qualify as an applicant under the Inheritance Act. However, the category of persons able to apply for provision after death is wider, for only the deceased (and not his or her spouse) need have treated the applicant as a child of the family, and children placed as foster children are not automatically excluded. The decision of the Court of Appeal in *Re Leach*[1] shows how wide the category can be. The applicant was a spinster aged 53 on her stepmother's death. She frequently visited her father after his remarriage and had a room in his bungalow. After his death she continued to visit her stepmother, who regarded her as a daughter rather than as a stepdaughter. The Court of Appeal held that it is not necessary for the applicant to have been treated as a child of the family by the deceased during the latter's marriage: as Slade LJ pointed out, a young child, who had lived with others during his father's second marriage and came to live with his stepmother after his father's death, would properly be regarded as a member of her family in relation to that marriage.[2] A display of affection, kindness or hospitality is not of itself sufficient to constitute treatment for this purpose: the question is whether 'the deceased has, *as wife or husband* (or widow or widower) under the relevant marriage, expressly or impliedly, assumed the position of a

---

12 See Harrap 'Provision for Cohabitants on Death' [1997] Fam Law 422.
13 Applies to deaths on or after 1 January 1996.
14 See post, pp 902–5.
15 Law Com No 187, paras 58–61.
16 See further post, p 888.
17 See post, p 891.
18 Section 25(1); Adoption Act 1976 s 39. Conversely, if the deceased's natural child is adopted after the deceased's death, he cannot subsequently apply for an order under the Act as the deceased's child: *Re Collins (decd)* [1990] Fam 56, [1990] 2 All ER 47.
19 *Re Callaghan* [1985] Fam 1, [1984] 3 All ER 790.
20 See ante, p 288.
 1 [1986] Ch 226, [1985] 2 All ER 754, CA.
 2 At 234 and 760 respectively.

parent towards the applicant, with the attendant *responsibilities and privileges* of that relationship'.[3] The deceased's privileges might well increase and his or her responsibilities diminish with age, and it follows from this approach that the applicant can qualify even though he was treated as a child of the family only when he was an adult[4] and the treatment ceased before the death. Applying this test, the court concluded that the applicant in this case had clearly been treated as a child of the family.

Any other person who was being maintained, either wholly or in part, by the deceased immediately before his death

This provision, which was controversial when first introduced, gives an applicant a legal claim after the deceased's death whereas she (or he) may have had no claim at all during his lifetime. However anomalous this may be, it can be justified on the ground that the deceased would presumably have continued to provide for the applicant had he survived. In many cases there will be a clear moral claim, and the deceased's failure to provide for her after his death may be due to oversight or accident, eg the failure to make a will in time or the revocation of an earlier will by marriage.[5] Although in some cases the applicant and the deceased will have been members of the same family – eg two sisters who lived together – it is not necessary to establish such a relationship. What is essential is a de facto dependence, and the commonest example is still, notwithstanding the amendment made by the 1995 Act, likely to be that of a cohabitant.

(a)   'Maintained'

For the purpose of this provision, the applicant will be regarded as having been maintained by the deceased only if the latter had been making a substantial contribution in money or money's worth towards his or her reasonable needs otherwise than for full valuable consideration.[6] Two classes of possible claimant are immediately seen to be outside this definition. The first are those who have not been in receipt of a *substantial* contribution. This means that the deceased's mistress may have a claim if he set her up in her own home and paid all her domestic bills,[7] but not if he did no more than make her casual payments and gifts. Secondly, the requirement that the contribution must have been made otherwise than for full valuable consideration clearly excludes claims by, for example, a housekeeper or companion who worked for an economic salary. It is not essential, however, that the consideration should have been provided under a contract between the applicant and the deceased.[8] According to Stephenson LJ in *Jelley v Iliffe*:[9]

> 'The court has to balance what [the deceased] was contributing against what [the applicant] was contributing, and if there is any doubt about the balance tipping in favour

3 At 237 and 762 respectively.
4 See also *Re Callaghan* supra.
5 See Law Com No 61, paras 85–94.
6 Section 1(3); *Jelley v Iliffe* [1981] Fam 128, [1981] 2 All ER 29, CA; *Bishop v Plumley* [1991] 1 All ER 236, CA; *Graham v Murphy* [1997] 1 FLR 860 (male cohabitant living in deceased's house at her expense); *Rees v Newbery and the Institute of Cancer Research* [1998] 1 FLR 1041 (applicant living in flat owned by the deceased at substantially below the market rent).
7 As in *Malone v Harrison* [1979] 1 WLR 1353.
8 *Jelley v Iliffe* (supra) at 136, 141, and 35, 38 respectively.
9 At 138 and 36 respectively.

of [the deceased's] being the greater contribution, the matter must go to trial. If, however, the balance is bound to come down in favour of [the applicant's] being the greater contribution, or if the contributions are clearly equal, there is no dependency.'

Provided one is dealing with tangible matters such as the provision of accommodation or board and lodging, this is a relatively simple matter of assessment and accounting. Difficulty arises because Stephenson LJ added that the court must put a financial value on imponderables like companionship and weigh these against contributions of money and accommodation.[10] Bearing in mind that the Act speaks of contributions *in money or money's worth*, it is submitted that companionship and the like should be brought into account only insofar as they involve services which can and should be evaluated. The court would be put in an impossible position if it had to place a price on the emotional and other support which the two gave each other, and one would be forced to the absurd conclusion that, the more the applicant had offered the deceased, the less chance he would have of succeeding.[11]

If a claim is made by a relative or friend who lived with the deceased and performed domestic services for him in exchange for free board and lodging, the obvious approach is to assess what the latter would have had to pay for the benefit he received. But this would produce an unacceptable result in the case of a cohabitant. As Griffiths LJ stressed in *Jelley v Iliffe*,[12] it is essential to use common sense and ask whether the applicant could fairly be called a dependant: it would not be right to deprive a woman, with whom a man had been living as his wife, of a claim by arguing that she had been performing the duties of a housekeeper whom it would have cost more to employ.

(b) 'Immediately before the death of the deceased'

The applicant must also prove that the deceased was maintaining him (or her) immediately before his death. This requirement was subject to a detailed examination by the Court of Appeal in *Jelley v Iliffe*.[13] As Stephenson LJ said:[14]

'In considering whether a person is being maintained "immediately before the death of the deceased" it is the settled basis or general arrangement between the parties as regards maintenance during the lifetime of the deceased which has to be looked at, not the actual, perhaps fluctuating, variation of it which exists immediately before his or her death. It is, I think, not disputed that a relationship of dependence which has persisted for years will not be defeated by its termination during a few weeks of mortal sickness.'

On the other hand, if the deceased had clearly abandoned responsibility for the applicant's maintenance before his death, the latter will have no claim.[15] Nor will the applicant have one if he was being maintained on a purely temporary basis or by chance at the time of the death, eg if he was a friend whom the deceased had taken in for a few days whilst he recovered from an illness.

---

10 Following *Re Wilkinson* [1978] Fam 22, [1978] 1 All ER 221.
11 *Bishop v Plumley* (supra) at 242.
12 At 141 and 38 respectively. Applied in *Bishop v Plumley* (supra).
13 [1981] Fam 128, [1981] 2 All ER 29, CA.
14 At 136 and 34–5 respectively, following *Re Beaumont* [1980] Ch 444 at 456, [1980] 1 All ER 266 at 272. Griffiths LJ expressed the same view at 141 and 38 respectively. Cumming-Bruce LJ agreed with both judgments.
15 *Kourkgy v Lusher* (1981) 4 FLR 65 (claimant unsuccessful when deceased had stopped cohabiting with her and returned to his wife three weeks before his death).

Death of applicant

As the claim is essential for a dependant's provision, an application automatically abates if the applicant dies before an order is made.[16]

2.   REASONABLE PROVISION

The applicant must also show that the provisions of the deceased's will or the law relating to intestacy (or the combination of both if there is a partial intestacy) are not such as to make reasonable financial provision for him.[17] This, of course, is a question of fact, but if the applicant cannot discharge the burden of proof, he has no claim at all. It is not the purpose of the Act merely to enable the court to provide legacies or rewards for meritorious conduct.[18]

For a surviving spouse[19]

In defining reasonable provision, the Act draws a significant distinction between surviving spouses and all other applicants. If the application is made by a surviving husband or wife (except where a separation order was in force and the separation continuing at the deceased's death),[20] reasonable financial provision means such financial provision as it would be reasonable in all the circumstances of the case for a husband or wife to receive, *whether or not that provision is required for his or her maintenance.*[1]

The reason for this is that a surviving widow or widower would normally expect to receive a share of the deceased spouse's estate and it would be anomalous if the court could give her (or him) less after the other spouse's death than it could on divorce.[2] In other words, the Act has two distinct objects: to provide appropriate support for a dependant (including a surviving spouse) and to make a fair division of assets between the spouses, although it is apparent that the courts do not always keep these two objects distinct.[3]

---

16 *Whytte v Ticehurst* [1986] Fam 64, [1986] 2 All ER 158; *Re Bramwell* [1988] 2 FLR 263; see also applications for financial provision under the Matrimonial Causes Act 1973 (ante, p 783). Presumably an order (eg for a lump sum), once made, can be enforced after the applicant's death, although the death should be a ground for giving personal representatives leave to appeal out of time: cf *Barder v Caluori* [1988] AC 20, [1987] 2 All ER 440, HL (ante, p 855).
17 Section 1(1) and s 2(1).
18 *Re Coventry* [1980] Ch 461 at 486 and 495, [1979] 3 All ER 815, CA at 821 and 828; *Re Abram (Deceased)* [1996] 2 FLR 379 at 388H; cf *Re Christie* [1979] Ch 168, [1979] 1 All ER 546, doubted in *Re Coventry* at 490 and 824.
19 See Miller 'Provision for a Surviving Spouse' (1997) 61 Conv 442.
20 Section 1(2)(a) as amended by the Family Law Act 1996 s 66(1) and Sch 8, para 27. Until the 1996 Act comes into force, the provision refers to a decree of judicial separation.
1 Section 1(2).
2 This accounts for the exception where a separation order is in force, because the survivor will already have had an opportunity of applying to the court for a lump sum or property adjustment order. Hence, if the deceased's marriage had been dissolved or annulled and he died within 12 months of this (or if he died within 12 months of a separation order) and no application for financial relief has been made or, if it has and the proceedings have not been determined, the court may consider an application for an order under the Inheritance Act as though no order (or decree) had been made: s 14. Otherwise the applicant would lose the benefit of both statutes.
3 See Miller 'Provision for a Surviving Spouse' (1986) 102 LQR 445.

Maintenance for any other applicant

In all other cases, the financial provision to be considered is that which it would be reasonable in all the circumstances of the case for the applicant to receive *for his maintenance*. When considering the provision of maintenance, the court is not limited to assessing the amount needed for bare necessities, nor must it take into account everything which the applicant might regard as reasonably desirable for his benefit or welfare. One must ask whether he will be able to maintain himself in a manner suitable to the circumstances.[4]

'Maintenance' means –

'. . . payments which, directly or indirectly, enable the applicant in the future to discharge the cost of his daily living . . . The provision that is to be made is to meet recurring expenses, being expenses of living of an income nature.'[5]

Such payments may embrace the payment of debts, provided that these will enable the applicant to carry on his business or profession,[6] but not where they will simply be used to reduce liabilities in bankruptcy or an individual voluntary arrangement under the Insolvency Act 1986.[7] A payment intended to relieve someone of income expenditure, eg to buy a house without taking on a mortgage, may be appropriate.[8]

3.   FACTORS TO BE TAKEN INTO ACCOUNT

The Act specifically requires the court to have regard to the following matters when determining whether reasonable financial provision has been made for the applicant, and, if not, what orders it should make.[9]

Factors relevant to all applications

'(a) the financial resources and financial needs which the applicant has or is likely to have in the foreseeable future;

(b) the financial resources and financial needs which any other applicant for an order . . . has or is likely to have in the foreseeable future;

(c) the financial resources and financial needs which any beneficiary of the estate of the deceased has or is likely to have in the foreseeable future;

(d) any obligations and responsibilities which the deceased had towards any applicant for an order . . . or towards any beneficiary of the estate of the deceased;

(e) the size and nature of the net estate of the deceased;

(f) any physical or mental disability of any applicant . . . or any beneficiary of the estate of the deceased;

---

4 *Re Coventry* [1980] Ch 461, [1979] 3 All ER 815, CA, at 485 and 819–20 (per Goff LJ), and 494 and 827 (per Buckley LJ) respectively. As it was put per Roach JA in *Re Duranceau* [1952] 3 DLR 714 (Canada) at 720, is 'the provision sufficient to enable the dependant to live neither luxuriously nor miserably but decently and comfortably according to his or her station in life?' cited by Goff LJ in *Re Coventry* (supra) at 485 and 819 respectively, and Slade LJ in *Re Leach* [1986] Ch 226 at 240, [1985] 2 All ER 754, CA at 764.
5 Per Browne-Wilkinson J in *Re Dennis (Deceased)* [1981] 2 All ER 140 at 145–6.
6 Given as an example by Browne-Wilkinson J in *Re Dennis* (supra).
7 *Re Abram (Deceased)* [1996] 2 FLR 379.
8 *Re Callaghan* [1985] Fam 1, [1984] 3 All ER 790.
9 Section 3.

(g) any other matter, including the conduct of the applicant or any other person, which in the circumstances of the case the court may consider relevant.' [10]

(a)   *Financial resources and financial needs*

The financial resources and needs [11] of the applicant, any other applicant for an order, and any beneficiary of the estate, [12] and any physical or mental disability from which any of them suffers, must be considered.

In this connection the court must take into account the individual's earning capacity, any resources and needs which he is likely to have in the foreseeable future, and his financial obligations and responsibilities. [13] It is, of course, necessary to consider the position of other applicants and beneficiaries, because any order made will limit the property available for them; consequently an applicant is more likely to succeed if an order in his favour can be made at the expense of a beneficiary towards whom the deceased had no obligations. [14] Generally speaking, the court must pay regard to similar matters when considering the question of financial relief on divorce, and they have already been considered more fully in the discussion of that problem, [15] but in one or two respects the court's approach must be different. The standard at which the applicant lived whilst the deceased was alive is clearly relevant but cannot be conclusive in the changed circumstances brought about by the death. For example, [16] money will no longer be needed to maintain the deceased, and it will usually be more reasonable to expect a woman to make provision for her widower, particularly if his earning capacity is reduced, than to support her divorced husband. [17] In the case of a small estate it is particularly important to consider the extent to which an applicant can claim social security benefits or may be expected to make use of the NHS or community care provision. If an order for financial provision would be so small that it would merely reduce the amount payable to him out of public funds without giving him any advantage, it may be eminently reasonable to use the whole estate to give a benefit to another applicant or beneficiary. [18] Conversely, if the estate is large and the applicant is in later middle age or elderly, consideration should be given to his or her provision in later life or possible infirmity, [19] but this need not require the provision of an absolute interest in property where a life interest will suffice. [20]

---

10 Section 3(1).
11 That is, reasonable requirements: *Harrington v Gill* (1983) 4 FLR 265, CA.
12 Beneficiary includes not only a person claiming under the deceased's will or on his intestacy, but also anyone nominated by him to receive money or property after his death and any recipient of a donatio mortis causa, because all this property forms part of the net estate: s 25(1).
13 Including his debts: *Re Goodchild (Deceased)* [1996] 1 All ER 670.
14 As in *Re Besterman* (supra), *Re Bunning* (supra), *Rees v Newbery and the Institute of Cancer Research* [1998] 1 FLR 1041. In each of these cases the residuary legatees were charities.
15 Ante, pp 829–44.
16 See post, p 895.
17 See *Re Clayton* [1966] 2 All ER 370 (widower crippled and earning only £10 a week); *Re Wilson* (1969) 113 Sol Jo 794 (widower aged 92).
18 See *Re E, E v E* [1966] 2 All ER 44; *Re Clayton* (supra); *Re Watkins* [1949] 1 All ER 695. Contrast *Re Collins (decd)* [1990] Fam 56, [1990] 2 All ER 47 (lump sum ordered for applicant on income support). (It should be noted, however, that Hollings J seems to have misstated Stamp LJ's conclusions in *Re E, E v E* (at 62 and 52 respectively).)
19 *Re Besterman* (supra).
20 *Davis v Davis* [1993] 1 FLR 54, CA.

(b)   Obligations and responsibilities of the deceased

Both legal and moral obligations are included in this provision, but they must have been in existence immediately before the deceased's death. Thus, a failure to support a child after the deceased's marriage broke down did not justify an award to the now adult child.[1] Since such an applicant, as distinct from a surviving spouse, may only receive an award constituting *maintenance*, this approach[2] is consistent with the general view of the courts that adult children should not generally expect to receive financial support from their parents.[3]

The cases on this issue seemed to establish that an adult child would have to show either that the deceased owed him a moral obligation, going beyond the mere fact of a blood relationship, to make provision for him out of his estate, or some other reason why, in the circumstances, it was unreasonable that no, or no more, provision had been made. In *Re Coventry*, for example, the plaintiff, who at the time of the application was aged 48 and divorced, had left the Royal Navy and lived with his father for the last 19 years of the latter's life. Shortly after he returned home, his mother left because of the way in which her husband and son treated her. The plaintiff ran the house and looked after his father, and sought an order under the Act on the latter's death intestate. His disposable income was about £40 a week; his mother (who was the only other person interested in the estate, which was worth about £7,000) lived entirely on social security benefits. The Court of Appeal considered that it would be rare for a relatively young and able-bodied man in employment to succeed in a claim under the Act,[4] and upheld Oliver J's decision to dismiss his claim. In *Williams v Johns*[5] a judge dismissed an adult adoptive daughter's claim because the deceased had made a written statement, filed with her will, that she felt no obligation towards her daughter, who had caused her much distress. The judge specifically stated that the plaintiff had to establish a moral obligation on the part of the deceased to make provision for her.

However, in *Re Hancock (Deceased)*[6] the Court of Appeal held that this approach was wrong. The adult daughter, now in her seventies, had lived in precarious financial circumstances for many years. After her father's death, the land occupied by his family business (now run by several of her siblings), which had been valued at the time of probate at £100,000, was sold for some £650,000 for redevelopment. The Court of Appeal upheld the first instance decision to award her £3,000 per annum maintenance, and held that the Act imposes no express requirement to establish a moral obligation or special circumstances. Rather, *in the absence* of such factors, it may be difficult to make out a claim where the claimant is in employment, possibly in affluent circumstances, and with an earning capacity in the foreseeable future. By contrast, since the daughter was in modest financial circumstances, facing a future where she would not be

1 *Re Jennings (Deceased)* [1994] Ch 256, [1994] 3 All ER 27 CA.
2 Which has been criticised as regrettable by Chatterton 'Inheritance Act Claims by Children' [1994] Fam Law 330; Borkowski, op cit, p 276.
3 See ante p 849. See also Miller 'Provision for Adult Children under the Inheritance (Provision for Family and Dependants) Act 1975' (1995) 59 Conv 22.
4 Prima facie it is not unreasonable for the deceased not to make financial provision for any adult (other than his or her spouse) capable of maintaining himself: *Re Dennis* [1981] 2 All ER 140 at 145; *Williams v Johns* [1988] 2 FLR 475.
5 [1988] 2 FLR 475.
6 [1998] 2 FLR 346, CA, followed in *Re Pearce (Deceased)* [1998] 2 FLR 705, CA.

working and thus could not improve her condition in life, and since the evidence showed that the father had recognised that some provision ought, if possible, to be made for her after his widow's death, her claim could be supported. Similarly, where the claimant has health problems,[7] or has worked in the family business at a very low wage in the expectation that he will inherit,[8] or where the deceased previously made a will in favour of the applicant as part of a mutual understanding with his spouse,[9] then provision may be made.

(c)   The size and nature of the estate[10]

If, for example, the deceased had a large income but little capital, it might be reasonable for him to leave the whole of his estate to his widow to the total exclusion of others whom he had supported during his lifetime. Likewise the source of the deceased's capital may be relevant; for example, if it came largely from a former spouse, the children of that spouse may have a stronger claim than the deceased's spouse or relations.[11] If the estate is small, the courts discourage applications altogether because of the danger that it will be entirely swallowed up by the costs of the action.[12]

(d)   Any other relevant matter, including the conduct of the applicant or any other person[13]

In the case of a former spouse the test should be the same whether the application is made on divorce or after the other party's death.[14] It is submitted that this should be applied if the applicant is a widow or widower, because he should be in no worse position than he would have been if the marriage had been dissolved.[15] It is accepted that the court should take into account the fact that a child has given up work to look after a parent,[16] but, on the other hand, it is not easy to see what weight should be given to a child's hurtful conduct. It is submitted that the test should be this: bearing in mind the deceased's treatment of the applicant, was the latter's conduct towards him such that a reasonable parent would have considered that he had forfeited any further claim to financial provision?[17]

Factors relevant to applications by spouses or former spouses

If the applicant is a surviving or former spouse, the court must also have regard to the duration of the marriage, the applicant's age, and the contribution he or she made to the welfare of the deceased's family, including any contribution by

7   *Millward v Shenton* [1972] 2 All ER 1025, CA; *Re Debenham* [1986] 1 FLR 404.
8   *Re Abram (Deceased)* [1996] 2 FLR 379.
9   *Re Goodchild (Deceased)* [1997] 2 FLR 644, CA.
10 Including property forming part of an unsevered joint tenancy or a transaction or contract intended to defeat an application under the Act which may be made available for financial provision (see post, p 897): *Kourkgy v Lusher* (1981) 4 FLR 65 at 81.
11 *Re Callaghan* [1985] Fam 1, [1984] 3 All ER 790.
12 See *Re Coventry* (supra), at 486 and 820–1 (per Goff LJ); *Re Fullard* [1982] Fam 42 at 46, [1981] 2 All ER 796, CA at 799 (per Ormrod LJ).
13 But this does not include undertakings given by other beneficiaries not to claim their rights under the will, because the question is whether *the will* (or the law of intestacy) makes reasonable financial provision for the applicant: *Rajabally v Rajabally* [1987] 2 FLR 390, CA.
14 *Re Snoek* (1983) 13 Fam Law 18.
15 See ante, p 890.
16 See *Re Coventry* [1980] Ch 461 at 489–90, [1979] 3 All ER 815 at 823.
17 See *Williams v Johns* [1988] 2 FLR 475, discussed ante, p 893.

looking after the home or caring for the family.[18] If the spouses have been living apart, the length of their separation will also be relevant.[19] Again, the similarity with the law of divorce will be seen. In the case of a surviving spouse (except when a separation order[20] was in force and the separation was continuing at the deceased's death), the court must also consider what provision the applicant might reasonably have expected to receive had the marriage been terminated by divorce instead of death,[1] on the ground that it would be anomalous if the latter could expect less on death than she would have got on divorce. However, it does not follow that it is incumbent upon the court to produce an outcome for the surviving spouse which mirrors what would have been awarded on divorce. After a death, there is only one spouse to consider (apart from any other beneficiaries, of course) while a divorce settlement must cater for both spouses' needs.[2] The survivor may therefore be left with rather more of the deceased's estate under the 1975 Act than he or she could expect to receive after a divorce.[3]

Factors relevant to applications by cohabitants

In such cases, the court must additionally have regard to the age of the applicant, the length of the period of cohabitation, and the contribution made by the applicant to the welfare of the family or of the deceased, including any contribution made by looking after the home or caring for the family.[4]

Factors relevant to applications by a child, or child of the family, of the deceased

If the applicant is a child of the deceased or a person whom he treated as a child of the family, the court must also have regard to the manner in which he was being or might expect to be educated or trained. If he is a child of the family but not the deceased's own child, the court must also consider the same matters as it has to take into account when deciding whether to make an order in favour of such a child on divorce.[5]

Factors relevant to applications by dependants

If the applicant is relying on a de facto dependence during the deceased's lifetime, the court must specifically have regard to the extent to which the deceased had assumed responsibility for his maintenance, the basis upon which he had done so, and the length of time for which he had discharged it.[6] These are three of the

---

18 Section 3(2).
19 *Re Rowlands* [1984] FLR 813, CA.
20 Or, until implementation of the Family Law Act 1996, a decree of judicial separation.
1 Section 3(2). See *Re Besterman* (supra); *Re Bunning* (supra); *Jessop v Jessop* [1992] 1 FLR 591, CA at 597.
2 *Re Krubert* [1997] Ch 97, CA.
3 See *Moody v Stevenson* [1992] 2 All ER 524, CA where it was considered that provision should correspond as closely as possible to the spouse's prospective entitlement under matrimonial law (per Waite J at 533). In *Re Krubert* the court preferred the approach outlined above which had been applied in two earlier decisions, *Re Besterman* [1984] Ch 458, [1984] 2 All ER 656, CA and *Re Bunning* [1984] Ch 480, [1984] 3 All ER 1.
4 Section 3(2A).
5 Section 3(3). For the matters to be taken into account, see the Matrimonial Causes Act 1973 s 25(4) (ante, p 765).
6 Section 3(4); *Graham v Murphy* [1997] 1 FLR 860 ; *Rees v Newbery and the Institute of Cancer Research* [1998] 1 FLR 1041.

matters which the court has to take into account when considering applications from persons who have been treated as children of the family, and the similarity of their position is obvious. The assumption of responsibility may be inferred from the fact of the deceased having maintained the applicant.[7]

Objective test

In *Re Coventry* Goff LJ said:[8]

'The question is not whether it might have been reasonable for the deceased to assist . . . the plaintiff, but whether in all the circumstances, looked at objectively, it is unreasonable that the effective provisions governing the estate did not do so.'

Accordingly, the Act provides that the court shall take into account the facts as known at the hearing.[9] The injustice that could otherwise be worked can be seen by examining the facts of *Re Goodwin*.[10] A testator provided for his children by making specific bequests in their favour and for his widow, their stepmother, by a legacy and the bequest of the residue of his estate. He expected the residue to be worth over £8,000 whereas it turned out to be worth about £1,500. Megarry J concluded that in the event the provision for the widow was not reasonable and made an order in her favour. Similarly, in *Re Hancock (Deceased)*[11] the value of the deceased's estate had increased six-fold between probate and the date of the hearing some ten years later. Since the delay was not the fault of the claimant, it was held that it was right to take the full value into account in assessing whether reasonable provision had been made for her.

4.   PROPERTY AVAILABLE FOR FINANCIAL PROVISION

Except for the power to order the variation of an ante-nuptial or post-nuptial settlement (which will be considered later), the court can only make orders for the payment of money out of the deceased's net estate or affecting property comprised in that estate.[12] Basically, this means such property as the deceased had power to dispose of by will (otherwise than by virtue of a special power of appointment), less the amount of funeral, testamentary and administration expenses and any liabilities.[13] Five other types of property are also comprised within the definition. First, property in respect of which the deceased had a general power of appointment not exercisable by will is included if the power was never exercised, for he could have exercised the power in his own favour and thus brought it within his estate.[14] Secondly, some statutes enable a person to nominate another to take the benefit of a fund after his death. This is equivalent to a testamentary disposition, and such property is therefore part of his estate for this purpose notwithstanding any

---

7 *Jelley v Iliffe* [1981] Fam 128, [1981] 2 All ER 29, CA overruling *Re Beaumont* [1980] Ch 444, [1980] 1 All ER 266 on this point.
8 [1980] Ch 461 at 488–9, [1979] 3 All ER 815 at 822f.
9 Section 3(5).
10 [1969] 1 Ch 283, [1968] 3 All ER 12.
11 Discussed ante, p 893.
12 Sections 2(1), 8(1). For net estate generally, see Law Com No 61, paras 127–143.
13 Section 25(1), (2).
14 Section 25(1).

nomination.[15] Thirdly, for a similar reason donationes mortis causa made by the deceased are included.[16] Fourthly, the court may order the severance of a joint tenancy or joint interest (eg in a bank account) or any part of a joint tenancy or interest to which the deceased was entitled immediately before his death and which would therefore otherwise pass to the other joint tenants, for the same reason that he could have effected a severance himself and thus brought the property into his estate.[17] The undivided share will then form part of the net estate. Finally, the estate includes any money or property ordered to be restored or provided if a disposition or contract is set aside under the provisions now to be considered.

Transactions intended to defeat applications

One of the weaknesses of earlier legislation was that the deceased could defeat an application by settling or disposing of his property during his lifetime so that it never formed part of his estate at all or, alternatively, could contract to leave it to a third person after his death.[18] The 1975 Act contains provisions designed to frustrate such transactions.

Dispositions

Under s 10 the court has a power to set aside a disposition made with the intention of defeating an application for financial provision under the Act which is similar to, but not identical with, the power to set aside transactions made with the intention of defeating an application for financial relief under the Matrimonial Causes Act.[19] There is no presumption of such an intention and the applicant must prove that the deceased intended to prevent an order being made under the Act or to reduce the amount of provision which might otherwise be granted, but this does not have to be his sole intention or, apparently, his principal intention.[20] Because of the difficulty of establishing intention at a remote time in the past, the court has no power to set aside a disposition made more than six years before the deceased's death. Nor, whatever his intention was, can any disposition be set aside if the transferee gave full valuable consideration.[1]

---

15 But not if the power arises purely under a contract or trust deed: *Re Cairnes* (1982) 4 FLR 225 (death benefits payable under occupational pension scheme). It might be possible to have such a nomination set aside as a transaction intended to defeat an application under the Act: see infra.
16 Section 8(2). In this case and the last, any person giving effect to the nomination or gift is protected.
17 Section 9. See *Jessop v Jessop* [1992] 1 FLR 591, CA. This power can be exercised only if an application for an order for financial provision was made within six months from the date on which representation was first taken out. Any person dealing with the property before an order for severance is protected.
18 If the transaction was effected fraudulently with intent to defeat the dependant's claim, it is arguable that it could be set aside under the court's general power to upset fraudulent transactions, or perhaps under s 423 of the Insolvency Act 1986: see *Cadogan v Cadogan* [1977] 3 All ER 831, CA. This might still be relevant eg if the transaction was made more than six years before the deceased's death.
19 See ante, p 862. See further generally Law Com No 61, Part V.
20 Section 10(2)(a) and s 12(1). The court must be satisfied on the balance of probabilities that this was the deceased's intention.
1 Section 10(2)(a), (b). Valuable consideration does not include marriage or a promise of marriage: s 25(1). A disposition does not include any testamentary gift, nomination or donatio mortis causa (all of which form part of the net estate) or any appointment made under a special power, but subject to these exceptions it includes any payment of money (including the payment of a premium under a policy of insurance) and any conveyance, assurance, appointment or gift of property: s 10(7). See also *Clifford v Tanner* [1987] CLY 3881, CA (deceased transferred home to daughter in return for her covenant to allow him and his wife to live there for life. He later released her from the covenant. Held: the release was a disposition within s 10).

If the court is satisfied that the exercise of the above powers would facilitate the making of financial provision for the applicant, it may order the donee of the property in question to provide such sum of money or other property as it shall direct. It is immaterial that the latter no longer holds any interest in the original property, but he may not be ordered to pay or transfer more than the amount paid to him by the deceased (if the disposition took the form of the payment of money) or the value at the date of the deceased's death of any property transferred.[2] Some measure of protection is given to the donee by the further provision that, before exercising its powers, the court must have regard to all the circumstances of the case, including particularly the circumstances in which the disposition to him was made, any valuable consideration given for it, the relationship (if any) of the donee to the deceased, and the donee's conduct and financial resources.[3]

Contracts

Section 11 deals with contracts by which the deceased agreed that a sum of money or other property would be left by his will or paid or transferred out of his estate. If such a contract were unimpeachable, it would obviously be more valuable than an actual disposition inter vivos which could be set aside. Consequently, if it was made with the intention of defeating an application for financial provision under the Act and full valuable consideration was not given or promised for it, the court may direct the personal representatives not to pay or transfer the whole or any part of the money or property involved. If any payment or transfer has already been made to any person (who, for convenience, is also referred to as the donee), the court may order him to provide such sum of money or other property as may be specified.[4] There is, however, one important qualification to the court's powers under s 11: it may restrain the personal representatives and order restitution only to the extent that the amount of the sum or the value of the property in question exceeds the value of the consideration given or promised under the contract.[5] As in the case of a disposition already made, the deceased's intention to prevent the making of an order or to reduce the amount available need not have been his sole intention, but there is an important difference between contracts and dispositions in that, if no valuable consideration was given or promised for the contract, it will be presumed that he had this intention unless the contrary is shown.[6] A contract may be attacked, however long before the deceased's death it was entered into, except that there is no power at all to upset a contract made before the Act came into force (1 April 1976).[7] In other respects the provisions relating to the two types of transaction are similar.

5.   ORDERS THAT MAY BE MADE

Interim orders

If a dependant is in immediate need of financial assistance, and property forming part of the net estate can be made available to meet his needs but it is not yet

---

2 Section 10(2)–(4); *Re Dawkins* [1986] 2 FLR 360 (donee ordered to provide £10,000 for deceased's widow out of proceeds of sale of property of £27,000). The value of any inheritance tax borne by the donee must also be deducted. If the donee has himself disposed of the property, he may not be required to restore more than its value when he disposed of it.
3 Section 10(6).
4 Section 11(2). The personal representatives may themselves postpone performance for six months without an order: s 20(3).
5 Section 11(3). Valuable consideration does not include marriage or a promise of marriage: s 25(1).
6 Section 12(1), (2).
7 Section 11(6).

possible to make a final order, the court may make an interim order. This may take the form of one payment or of periodical payments, and the court may later direct that any sum paid under an interim order shall be treated as having been paid on account of the final order. As far as possible, the same matters should be taken into account in making an interim order as in making a final order.[8]

Final orders

If the court is satisfied that reasonable financial provision has not been made for the applicant, it may make a final order containing one or more of the provisions set out below.[9] In determining what order (if any) to make, the court must have regard to the same matters as it has when deciding whether reasonable provision has been made.[10]

(a) *Periodical payments*

This may be for a specified amount or for an amount equal to the whole or any part of the income of the net estate or of such part of the estate as the court directs to be set aside or appropriated for this purpose, or it may be determined in any other way the court thinks fit.[11] The order may last for such term and be subject to such conditions as the court directs. Remarriage of the deceased's widow or widower will not automatically discharge the order (although it may be a ground for an application to have it discharged by the court). It would be anomalous, however, to give former and separated spouses greater rights on the deceased's death than they had when the divorce or separation order was made, and consequently an order for periodical payments made in their favour will terminate automatically on remarriage.[12] In other cases it would normally be reasonable to direct that payment to a child should terminate on his ceasing to receive education or training, or that payment to a parent who is temporarily unable to work owing to illness should terminate on his ceasing to be under a disability.

An order may be varied, suspended or discharged on the application of anyone who has already applied for an order or would be entitled to apply if he were not time-barred.[13] The variation can only be made in respect of property being used for the making of such payments and, if in favour of another person, only at the expense of the recipient. The variation can take the form of a lump sum or the transfer of the property, as well as the provision of further periodical payments.

(b) *Lump sum*

Such an order would be particularly valuable if the estate is so small that any periodical payments would be valueless. It could also enable, say, a widow to purchase the goodwill of a business: indeed, if the estate is large enough, it is submitted that this will normally be the proper order to make in favour of a surviving spouse. If the order is made at the expense of beneficiaries towards whom the deceased had no obligations, a spouse will probably obtain more under the

8 Section 5. For the protection of personal representatives, see s 20(2).
9 Section 2(1). See generally Law Com No 61, paras 109–126.
10 Section 3(1). See ante, pp 891–6.
11 Section 2(2), (3).
12 Section 19(2). This applies to separated spouses only if the order (or, pending implementation of the Family Law Act 1996, decree) was in force and the separation continuing at the time of the deceased's death.
13 Section 6.

Inheritance Act than she (or he) would have obtained in divorce proceedings, because the estate is no longer needed for the deceased's support and it may be reasonable to give the applicant a cushion to provide against future contingencies.[14]

A lump sum in favour of a non-family dependant may be valuable if relationships in a family are so bitter that a clean break is desirable,[15] or to avoid embarrassment, or to achieve finality in the interests of the other beneficiaries.[16] The disadvantage of such an order is that it cannot be varied to take account of unforeseen changes in the circumstances of the applicant or a beneficiary and, if it represents the capitalisation of periodical payments, events may prove the estimate to have been wildly inaccurate. Consequently, the courts have been reluctant to order the payment of a lump sum to an applicant who is elderly or in poor health, because premature death would often result in the deceased's assets being vested in someone outside the family.[17]

As on divorce, the court may order that a lump sum be paid by instalments.[18]

(c)   The transfer or settlement of property comprised in the net estate

The court might well order that the former matrimonial home be transferred or settled for the benefit of a surviving spouse or unmarried cohabitant who has been living with the deceased,[19] particularly if he or she has to bring up young children. In other cases it may be more convenient, as on divorce, to order the transfer of property than the payment of a lump sum.

(d)   The transfer or settlement of property to be acquired out of the estate

This has no counterpart in the Matrimonial Causes Act and is designed particularly to enable a home to be bought for the applicant.[20]

(e)   The variation of any ante-nuptial or post-nuptial settlement

This is strictly equivalent to the court's powers on divorce and the variation may be made only for the benefit of the surviving party to the marriage or a child of the family in relation to that marriage.[1]

---

14 See *Re Besterman* [1984] Ch 458, [1984] 2 All ER 656, CA; *Re Bunning* [1984] Ch 480, [1984] 3 All ER 1; Miller 'Provision for a Surviving Spouse' (1986) 102 LQR 445; Prime 'Family Provision – The Spouse's Application' [1986] Fam Law 95.

15 See *Re Collins (decd)* [1990] Fam 56, [1990] 2 All ER 47 (need to achieve finality where defendant was violent man and applicant, his daughter, had been fostered).

16 *Graham v Murphy* [1997] 1 FLR 860; *Rees v Newbery and the Institute of Cancer Research* [1998] 1 FLR 1041.

17 See *Re Debenham* [1986] 1 FLR 404 (daughter aged 58, epileptic, given small lump sum and annuity). In *Stead v Stead* [1985] FLR 16, CA, the lump sum awarded to a widow, aged 82, was limited to the amount needed to cover certain eventualities, apparently on the ground that, if she were given more, she would merely save it. But this is not an invariable rule and a lump sum may be ordered in other circumstances: *Kusminow v Barclays Bank Trust Co Ltd* [1989] Fam Law 66, *Re Pearce (Deceased)* [1998] 2 FLR 705, CA.

18 Section 7. The court may subsequently vary the number and amount of instalments and the dates on which they are to be paid, but not the total sum payable. A lump sum or the transfer of property could also be of particular benefit to an applicant in receipt of income support, because it would have a limited effect on his income and might enable him to make a capital purchase which he might not otherwise be able to afford (eg a television set): *Millward v Shenton* [1972] 2 All ER 1025, CA.

19 As in *Harrington v Gill* (1983) 4 FLR 265, CA.

20 See Law Com No 61, para 116.

1 For the variation of such settlements, see ante pp 798–800.

6. RELATIONSHIP TO EXISTING AGREEMENTS AND MATRIMONIAL ORDERS

It must not be forgotten that other liabilities to support a dependant may survive the deceased's death. An order for secured periodical payments may have been made in his favour during previous matrimonial proceedings or he may be a party to a maintenance agreement under which payments continue. Not only will the existence of the continuing right affect any order that may be made if he applies for financial relief under the Act but also, in the changed circumstances brought about by the death, it may make unfairly generous provision for him compared with the amount left for other applicants. To prevent the unnecessary duplication of proceedings, the court may vary existing orders and agreements in proceedings under the 1975 Act.[2]

If the applicant for financial relief under the Inheritance Act continues to be entitled to secured periodical payments on an order made under the Matrimonial Causes Act 1973, the court may vary or discharge the order or revive the operation of any provision which has been previously suspended.[3] Similarly, if the applicant is still entitled to payments under a maintenance agreement, the court may vary or revoke the agreement.[4] The definition of a maintenance agreement is the same as that contained in s 34 of the Matrimonial Causes Act except, importantly, that it need not be in writing.[5] The court has no power to reduce the sums payable if, in proceedings brought by another applicant under the Act, it comes to the conclusion that they are too large. This can be done only if the personal representatives themselves take proceedings to have the order or agreement varied under the Matrimonial Causes Act, which they may be unwilling to do.

Conversely, if the personal representatives, the recipient of secured periodical payments or a party to a maintenance agreement applies for a variation of the order or agreement under the Matrimonial Causes Act,[6] the court may deem the application to have been accompanied by an application for an order under the Inheritance Act and exercise all the powers it has under that Act.[7] This may be of particular importance to a party to an agreement, because it will be recalled that under the Matrimonial Causes Act there is no power to set aside a disposition intended to defeat an application for a variation of a maintenance agreement after the payer's death. By invoking this jurisdiction, the court can exercise its jurisdiction to set aside dispositions and contracts under s 10 and s 11.

Whether as part of an agreed financial settlement, or in pursuance of the principle that a clean break should be made wherever possible, the court dealing with financial provision on divorce, nullity or separation may wish to exclude the possibility of a future application under the Inheritance Act. Accordingly it may make an order having this effect on the application of either party to the marriage if it is satisfied that it is just to do so.[8] However, the fact that such a clause has not

---

2 See further Law Com No 61, Part VII.
3 Section 16. The court must have regard to all the circumstances, including any change in the matters to which it was required to have regard when making the order for secured periodical payments.
4 Section 17. The court must have regard to all the circumstances, including any change in the circumstances in the light of which the agreement was made.
5 Section 17(4). For the definition of a maintenance agreement under s 34 of the Matrimonial Causes Act, see ante, p 752.
6 See ante, pp 753, 850. In such a case, the agreement must be a maintenance agreement within s 34 of the 1973 Act.
7 Section 18 of the Inheritance (Provision for Family and Dependants) Act 1975.
8 Section 15(1) as amended by the Family Law Act 1996 s 66, Sch 8 para 27.

been included does not, of itself, strengthen a claim.[9] The order will take effect only when a decree of nullity is made absolute or the divorce order is made or, in the case of a separation order, if the order is in force and the separation is continuing on the death of one of the parties.[10] The court has the same power if it makes an order for financial relief following a foreign dissolution, annulment or legal separation granted in an overseas country and recognised here.[11]

By analogy with applications for financial relief in matrimonial proceedings, a party presumably cannot contract out of his or her power to apply under the Inheritance Act except by way of a consent order.[12]

E.   Compensation under the Fatal Accidents Act[13]

1.   BACKGROUND

It was a firm rule of tort that 'the death of a human being could not be complained of as an injury'.[14] Consequently the dependants of a person killed as the result of another's negligence could not claim damages from him. With the advent of heavy industry in the nineteenth century, the problem became more serious, and the Fatal Accidents Act 1846 (known as Lord Campbell's Act) was enacted to deal with it. The Act permitted certain dependants to recover the financial loss suffered as a result of a person's death caused by the defendant's wrongful act, neglect or default. The legislation was extensively amended, and is now contained in the Fatal Accidents Act 1976, which itself was amended by the Administration of Justice Act 1982 s 3.

2.   WHO MAY CLAIM

A claimant[15] must come within one of the categories laid down by the Act as follows:

(a)   The deceased's wife or husband, or former wife or husband of the deceased, ie a person whose marriage to the deceased has been dissolved, annulled or declared void.

(b)   Anyone who was living with the deceased in the same household immediately

---

9 *Cameron v Treasury Solicitor* [1996] 2 FLR 716, CA (but note that there the divorce had taken place at a time when such a clause could only be added by consent and was not routine); cf *T v T (Financial Relief: Pensions)* [1998] 1 FLR 1072 where Singer J thought that such an application might be fairer than attempting to earmark the husband's pension many years before he might be expected to die.

10 Section 15 as prospectively amended by the Family Law Act 1996 s 66, Sch 8 para 27.

11 Section 15A, inserted by the Matrimonial and Family Proceedings Act 1984 s 25(3). In this case, however, an order following a legal separation will have effect provided that the separation is in force on the party's death, whether or not the separation is continuing de facto.

12 See *Re M (Deceased)* [1968] P 174, [1967] 3 All ER 412.

13 See Duncan and Marsh *Fatal Accident Claims* (1993); Law Commission Consultation Paper No 148, *Claims for Wrongful Death* (1997).

14 *Baker v Bolton* (1808) 1 Camp 493 per Lord Ellenborough CJ. The principle was affirmed by the House of Lords in *Admiralty Comrs v SS Amerika (owners)* [1917] AC 38, [1916–17] All ER Rep 177.

15 The action must be brought by the personal representatives of the deceased on behalf of all the claimants, within six months of the death or, thereafter, by a claimant himself (again on behalf of all claimants): s 2.

before the latter's death and had been so living for not less than two years as her husband or his wife.[16]

(c) A parent or other ascendant of the deceased.

(d) Anyone whom the deceased had treated as his parent.

(e) A child or other descendant of the deceased.[17]

(f) Anyone who was treated by the deceased as a child of the family[18] in relation to any marriage to which the deceased was a party.

(g) The deceased's brother, sister, uncle or aunt, or the issue of any of these.[19]

It will be seen that those coming within classes (a), (e) and (f) may all have had a claim or potential claim for maintenance against the deceased had he survived. With respect to cohabitants, it may be assumed that, if the survivor had been financially dependent on the deceased, that dependency would have continued. All the other cases consist of comparatively close relations who in certain circumstances might have received financial support from the deceased. The range of possible claimants is wider than under the intestacy rules, but is narrower than under the Inheritance (Provision for Family and Dependants) Act 1975 for, in contrast to that Act, if a person cannot bring himself within the categories listed, he has no claim even though he was financially dependent upon the deceased.

The claimant must establish a pecuniary loss as a result of the death,[20] unless the claim relates to damages for bereavement suffered by the spouse of the deceased, or, where the deceased was a minor who never married, by his parents (if he was legitimate), and by his mother (if he was not).[1] Thus, a former spouse, for example, whose claims for financial relief in the divorce suit have been dealt with by a clean break settlement, could not apply. But even though the deceased had made no contribution to the claimant's support before his death, an action will lie provided that the latter had a reasonable expectation of pecuniary advantage in the future if the other had survived.[2] This is particularly important in the case of a child who could have looked to the deceased to pay for her education or, conversely, of a parent who had reasonable hopes of being supported by his child in his old age.[3] In any case, the financial benefit that the claimant has lost as a result of the death must derive from the relationship and must not be a mere business loss.[4]

---

16 Brief absences by the deceased from the claimant do not prevent a claim being brought: *Pounder v London Underground Ltd* [1995] PIQR P217.

17 Including an unborn child conceived before the death, if born alive: *The George and Richard* (1871) LR 3 A & E 466.

18 See ante, p 288.

19 Fatal Accidents Act 1976 s 1(3) as amended by the Administration of Justice Act 1982 s 3(1). In deducing any of these relationships, '(a) any relationship by affinity shall be treated as a relationship by consanguinity, any relationship of the half blood as a relationship of the whole blood, and the stepchild of a person as his child, and (b) an illegitimate person shall be treated as the legitimate child of his mother and reputed father': s 1(5).

20 *Duckworth v Johnson* (1859) 4 H & N 653.

1 Section 1A.

2 There must be more than a 'mere speculative possibility of a benefit' per McCardie J in *Barnett v Cohen* [1921] 2 KB 461 at 471.

3 *Taff Vale Rly Co v Jenkins* [1913] AC 1, HL; *Kandalla v British Airways Board* [1981] QB 158, [1980] 1 All ER 341.

4 *Burgess v Florence Nightingale Hospital for Gentlewomen* [1955] 1 QB 349, [1955] 1 All ER 511 (no claim for loss of income due to death of plaintiff's wife who had been his professional dancing partner). Contrast *Malyon v Plummer* [1964] 1 QB 330, [1963] 2 All ER 344, CA – wife could recover for loss of value of directorship in company in which she and her deceased husband had been co-directors because her appointment was due to the relationship of husband and wife – applied in *Hack v Personal Representatives of Gangaram (deceased)* (21 February 1996, unreported), QBD.

3. AGAINST WHOM THE ACTION MAY BE BROUGHT

The action will lie against any person whom the deceased could himself have sued in respect of the fatal injury had he not died.[5]

4. ASSESSMENT OF DAMAGES

Damages are to be measured by reference to the material loss which the claimant has suffered as a result of the death.[6] Funeral expenses may also be recovered.[7] Where an action is brought on behalf of a cohabitant, the court is required to take into account the fact that the claimant had no enforceable right to be maintained by the deceased.[8] Difficult problems can arise in attempting to assess loss based on a quantification of the value of services provided by the deceased, rather than income brought into the household or paid to the claimant. For example, if a mother is killed in an accident, cash amounts can be attributed to her child-care, housekeeping, cooking etc, by comparing these with rates payable for a nanny or housekeeper, but commercial rates may distort the true measure of loss actually suffered, and consideration also needs to be given to the age of the children left behind and their diminishing need for care as they grow up. The courts therefore prefer to adopt a discretionary approach, and may reduce an award if the evidence establishes that the mother was unreliable.[9]

Bizarrely, a widow's remarriage, or her prospects of remarriage, may not be taken into account when assessing her damages,[10] but the likelihood of her and the deceased having divorced if he had survived is to be considered.[11] This is anomalous, especially since the likelihood of remarriage *is* taken into account when assessing compensation for a widower or cohabitant. Even more illogically, a *widow's* prospect of remarrying will be a relevant factor when assessing her *child's* damages for loss of the child's father.

5. REFORM OF THE LEGISLATION

The Law Commission reviewed the working of the Fatal Accidents Act in a Consultation Paper issued in 1997.[12] They considered the list of possible claimants

---

5 Hence no action will lie if the deceased had already sued for his own injuries, and if he had received full compensation in his lifetime: *Read v Great Eastern Rly Co* (1868) LR 3 QB 555; or usually if his own claim was statute-barred: Limitation Act 1980 s 12(1) and s 33.

6 Except in respect of bereavement damages, where a fixed sum of £7,500 is awarded: s 1A(3); Damages for Bereavement (Variation of Sum) (England and Wales) Order 1990, SI 1990/2575.

7 Section 3(5).

8 Section 3(4). Thus, in *Drew v Abassi and Packer* (24 May 1995, unreported) CA, cited by Law Commission op cit para 2.16 n 50), notwithstanding the finding by the trial judge that the relationship between the plaintiff and the deceased was one which 'would have survived as well as any marriage', he was held entitled to have discounted the appropriate multiplier by two years. Compare Family Law Act 1996 s 41, which requires the court, in determining whether to make an occupation order in favour of a cohabitant who has no property rights in the home, to have regard to the fact that the parties 'have not given each other the commitment involved in marriage' (discussed ante, p 205).

9 *Stanley v Saddique* [1992] QB 1, [1991] 1 All ER 529, CA.

10 Section 3(3).

11 *Owen v Martin* [1992] PIQR Q151.

12 Op cit, supra, n 8.

too restrictive, drawing attention to the unfairness of excluding, for example, the survivor of a couple who have lived together for less than two years, or who have been lovers but have not cohabited, or of children who have been treated as part of the deceased's family, but who fall outside the statutory definition of a 'child of the family' since this is restricted to relationships within a marital context.[13] The Commission's provisional recommendation was to replace the list with a general right of recovery by anyone who had a reasonable expectation of a non-business benefit had the deceased survived, or alternatively who, but for the death, would have been wholly or partly dependent upon the deceased.[14] The latter option has the benefit of bringing this area of the law more closely (though not completely) into line with the Inheritance (Provision for Family and Dependants) Act 1975.

The Law Commission also criticised the inconsistent approach required under the current law to the question whether a claimant's future life prospects can be taken into account. They noted that the bar on considering a widow's chances of remarriage was introduced only in 1971, in response to criticisms that widows were being subjected to distressing and embarrassing questioning and assessment by lawyers and judges in court, and even to investigation by private detectives in attempts to determine whether they were likely to form new attachments.[15] But the Law Commission criticised the rule as illogical and inconsistent and doubted whether the original criticism was based on firm evidence. However, they were undecided as to how the position should be altered, and in particular were uncertain whether some calculation based on the statistical probabilities of remarriage might be appropriate. Assuming that such an approach found favour, they further questioned whether it might be equally relevant to apply it to a person's prospects of divorce had the deceased survived.[16]

The Law Commission's considerations on these matters, and the Parliamentary and judicial recognition of a broad range of 'family relationships' as deserving of legal significance, as discussed throughout this chapter, reflect the extent to which families are undergoing profound and rapid changes. The certainties of definition which could be applied a century ago by a society confident of its values have given way to a more questioning attitude as to which relationships in what circumstances should be given legal recognition, and what forms that recognition should take. Family law will continue to be shaped by the efforts of policy makers and legal practitioners to keep abreast of the social revolution which has so profoundly transformed family life. As Ward LJ noted in *Fitzpatrick v Sterling Housing Association Ltd*,[17] the key issue for family lawyers both now and in the future is likely to be to determine what the family does, in terms of its procreative, sexual, sociable, economic and emotional functions, rather than how it is formally constituted.

13 Para 3.18 et seq.
14 Para 3.36.
15 See Law Com op cit paras 2.38–2.39 and 3.56–3.68.
16 At paras 3.70–3.72.
17 [1997] 4 All ER 991, CA at 1023–4.

Index

5